# Domestic Violence

# Domestic Violence

*Law, Policy, and Practice*

SECOND EDITION

## Diane Kiesel

Acting Justice, New York Supreme Court and
Adjunct Professor, New York Law School

CAROLINA ACADEMIC PRESS
Durham, North Carolina

Copyright © 2017
Diane Kiesel
All Rights Reserved

LCCN: 2017947249
ISBN: 978-1-63281-558-3
eISBN: 978-1-63281-559-0

Carolina Academic Press, LLC
700 Kent Street
Durham, North Carolina 27701
Telephone (919) 489-7486
Fax (919) 493-5668
www.cap-press.com

Printed in the United States of America

*For the late Judge Judith Kaye,
chief judge of the state of New York (1993–2008), and
retired Acting Justice Judy Harris Kluger, director of policy and
planning for the New York State Courts (2009–2013),
with my gratitude for giving me the opportunity to do
this important work in the court system.*

# Contents

| | |
|---|---|
| Table of Cases | xix |
| Acknowledgments | xxix |
| Preface | xxxvii |
| **Chapter 1 · Introduction** | 3 |
|   I. In Harm's Way — The Dynamic of Domestic Violence | 9 |
|     Mary Ann Dutton, Symposium on Domestic Violence: | |
|       *Understanding Women's Responses to Domestic Violence:* | |
|       *A Redefinition of Battered Woman Syndrome* | 10 |
|     Kathleen Waits, *The Criminal Justice System's* | |
|       *Response to Battering: Understanding the Problem,* | |
|       *Forging the Solutions* | 12 |
|     Jane K. Stoever, *Transforming Domestic Violence Representation* | 16 |
|     Sarah M. Buel, *Fifty Obstacles to Leaving, A.K.A.,* | |
|       *Why Abuse Victims Stay* | 19 |
|   II. A Man's Home Is His Castle | 25 |
|     A. Slow Change | 26 |
|       *Bradley v. State* | 27 |
|   III. Modern Times | 29 |
|   IV. Domestic Violence as a Crime | 31 |
|     *Bruno v. Codd* | 31 |
|     Notes and Questions | 37 |
| **Chapter 2 · Race, Culture, Religion and Sexual Orientation &** | |
|     **Domestic Violence** | 41 |
|   I. Introduction | 41 |
|   II. African American Women | 42 |
|     Linda L. Ammons, *Mules, Madonnas, Babies, Bathwater,* | |
|       *Racial Imagery and Stereotypes: The African-American* | |
|       *Woman and the Battered Woman Syndrome* | 43 |
|   III. Latinas | 45 |
|     Jenny Rivera, *Intimate Partner Violence Strategies:* | |
|       *Models for Community Participation* | 45 |

| | |
|---|---|
| IV. Socioeconomic Status | 47 |
|     Jody Raphael, *Battering Through the Lens of Class* | 47 |
| V. Muslim Societies | 49 |
|     Lisa Hajjar, *Religion, State Power, and Domestic Violence in Muslim Societies: A Framework for Comparative Analysis* | 49 |
|     Kenneth Lasson, *Bloodstains on a "Code of Honor": The Murderous Marginalization of Women in the Islamic World* | 52 |
| VI. Jewish Communities | 59 |
|     Lydia M. Belzer, *Toward True Shalom Bayit: Acknowledging Domestic Abuse in the Jewish Community and What to Do About It* | 59 |
| VII. Native American Women | 63 |
|     Kathryn A. Ritcheske, Note: *Liability of Non-Indian Batterers in Indian Country: A Jurisdictional Analysis* | 63 |
|     *United States v. Bryant* | 66 |
|     Commission on the Status of Women, Sixtieth session, 2016 Violence Against Indigenous Women and Girls, *Statement submitted by Indian Law Resource Center, National Congress of American Indians, and Native American Rights Fund, and other non-governmental organizations in consultative status with the Economic and Social Council* | 72 |
| VIII. Women With Disabilities | 75 |
|     Karen Nutter, Note: *Domestic Violence in the Lives of Women With Disabilities: No (Accessible) Shelter From the Storm* | 75 |
| IX. Cultural Defenses | 78 |
|     *State v. Vue* | 78 |
| X. Law Enforcement/Military "Culture" | 83 |
|     Simeon Stamm, Note: *Intimate Partner Violence in the Military: Securing Our Country, Starting with the Home* | 85 |
|     Diane Wetendorf, *Representing Victims of Police-Perpetrated Domestic Violence* | 94 |
| XI. Lesbians, Gay Men and the Transgendered Community | 100 |
|     Sharon Stapel & Virginia M. Goggin, *Lesbian, Gay, Bisexual, Transgender and Queer Victims of Intimate Partner Violence* | 101 |
|     Leigh Goodmark, *Transgender People, Intimate Partner Abuse, and the Legal System* | 104 |
|     Notes and Questions | 117 |
| **Chapter 3 · The Criminal Law of Domestic Violence** | **121** |
|     Linda McGuire, *Criminal Prosecution of Domestic Violence* (1994), written for The Battered Women's Justice Project | 121 |
| I. Crimes of Domestic Violence | 124 |
|     A. Homicide | 124 |
|         Minn. Stat. 609.185 (2015) | 124 |

|   |   |
|---|---|
| *State v. Barnes* | 125 |
| B. Fatality Reviews/Danger Assessments | 128 |
| Jacqueline C. Campbell, et al., *Assessing Risk Factors for Intimate Partner Homicides* | 131 |
| *Pettingill v. Pettingill* | 134 |
| *Petriciolet v. Texas* | 138 |
| C. Domestic Violence as a Specific Crime | 143 |
| California Penal Code 273.5 (2016) | 144 |
| *People v. Abrego* | 145 |
| D. Witness Tampering | 147 |
| *People v. Yascavage* | 147 |
| E. Criminal Contempt — Violation of Protective Orders | 151 |
| *People v. Wood* | 151 |
| *State v. Grayhurst* | 154 |
| *State v. Lucas* | 157 |
| F. Marital Rape | 161 |
| *People v. Liberta* | 161 |
| S.C. Code Ann. 16-3-615 (2014) | 166 |
| G. Strangulation | 166 |
| 11 Del. C. § 607 (2016) | 167 |
| NY Penal Law § 121.12 (2015) | 167 |
| H. Stalking | 167 |
| Paul E. Mullen & Michele Pathe, *Stalking* | 168 |
| Cal Pen Code 646.9 (2016) | 172 |
| *People v. Zavala* | 173 |
| II. Domestic Violence in the New Technology Era | 177 |
| *Elonis v. United States* | 177 |
| Mary Graw Leary, Symposium: *Emerging Issues in Crime Victims' Rights: The Third Dimension of Victimization* | 182 |
| III. Fighting Back | 188 |
| Fla. Stat. § 776.013 (2016) | 189 |
| Fla. Stat. § 776.032 | 190 |
| *Bartlett v. State* | 190 |
| IV. Consequences of the Criminalization of Domestic Violence | 193 |
| Lois A. Ventura & Gabrielle Davis, *Domestic Violence: Court Case Conviction and Recidivism* | 194 |
| A. Bail Considerations | 196 |
| 18 USCS § 3142 (2015) | 197 |
| *United States v. Rogers* | 197 |
| NY Criminal Procedure Law § 510.30 (2016) | 201 |
| 18 Pennsylvania Consolidated Statutes § 2711 (2016) | 202 |
| Suraji R. Wagage, *When the Consequences Are Life and Death: Pretrial Detention for Domestic Violence Offenders* | 203 |
| Notes and Questions | 213 |

**Chapter 4 · Evidentiary Issues in Domestic Violence Cases** ... 217
   I. *Crawford* and the Fate of Victimless Prosecutions ... 218
      *Crawford v. Washington* ... 218
      *Davis v. Washington* ... 223
      *Giles v. California* ... 229
      Sarah M. Buel, *Putting Forfeiture to Work* ... 232
   II. Evidence of Prior Acts of Domestic Violence in Homicide and Other Domestic Violence Cases ... 256
      *People v. Bierenbaum* ... 256
      *People v. Dorm* ... 268
      *Rufo v. Simpson* ... 269
      *Peters-Riemers v. Riemers* ... 276
   III. Evidentiary Tools Unique to Domestic Violence Cases ... 279
      A. Propensity for Intimate Partner Abuse ... 279
         Andrew King-Ries, *Responding: Two New Solutions: True to Character: Honoring the Intellectual Foundations of the Character Evidence Rule in Domestic Violence Prosecutions* ... 279
         Minn. Stat. 634.20 (2015) ... 282
         C.R.S. (Colorado) 18-6-801.5 (2015) ... 282
      B. Medical Record Evidence in Domestic Violence Cases ... 283
         *People v. Benston* ... 283
         Nancy E. Isaac & V. Pualani Enos, *Documenting Domestic Violence: How Health Care Providers Can Help Victims* ... 287
   IV. Special Evidentiary Considerations with Child Witnesses in Family Violence or Sexual Abuse Cases ... 288
      A. The Ability to Testify Under Oath ... 289
         Fla. Stat. 90.605 (2015) ... 289
      B. Accomodations for Child Witnesses ... 290
         N.J. Stat. Sec. 2A:84A-16.1 (2016) ... 290
         42 Pa. C.S. Sec. 5987 (2016) ... 290
         A.C.A. Sec. 16-44-203 (Arkansas 2015) ... 290
         *Maryland v. Craig* ... 291
         *Ohio v. Clark* ... 300
   V. Courthouse Dogs ... 306
      Casey Holder, Comment: *All Dogs Go to Court: The Impact of Court Facility Dogs as Comfort for Child Witnesses on a Defendant's Right to a Fair Trial* ... 307
      *State v. Dye* ... 311
   VI. Evidentiary Privileges in Domestic Violence Cases ... 317
      A. The Marital Privilege ... 317
         Utah R. Evid. Rule 502 (2016) ... 317
      B. Domestic Violence Counselor/Social Worker ... 318
         *People v. Turner* ... 318
         Notes and Questions ... 322

## Chapter 5 · Expert Testimony & Syndrome Evidence ... 323

Introduction ... 323
I. Use of Syndrome Evidence by Defendants in Self-Defense Cases ... 324
    *State v. Kelly* ... 325
    *State v. Hanks* ... 331
II. Use of Expert Testimony by Prosecutors ... 335
    *State v. Grecinger* ... 335
III. Other Uses of Syndrome Evidence by Defendants ... 340
    A. Duress ... 340
        Model Penal Code § 2.09. Duress. ... 340
        *State v. B.H.* ... 341
    B. Competency ... 346
        *Commonwealth v. Conaghan* ... 346
IV. Syndrome Evidence in Cases Involving Children ... 349
    A. Battered Child Syndrome ... 349
        Nancy Wright, *Voice for the Voiceless: The Case for Adopting the "Domestic Abuse Syndrome" for Self-Defense Purposes for All Victims of Domestic Violence Who Kill Their Abusers* ... 350
        *State v. Janes* ... 359
    B. Child Sexual Abuse Accommodation Syndrome ... 365
        *State v. Chauvin* ... 365
V. Jurors as Experts ... 369
    *People v. Arnold* ... 369
    Notes and Questions ... 373

## Chapter 6 · The Violence Against Women Act — Fighting Domestic Violence on a Federal Level ... 377

I. Setting the Stage for VAWA ... 378
II. Violence Against Women Act Becomes Law ... 379
    A. The *Morrison* Decision ... 380
        *United States v. Morrison* ... 380
    B. After *Morrison* — What Remains ... 387
        *United States v. Larsen* ... 388
III. Federal Firearms Restrictions ... 393
    Darren Mitchell & Susan B. Carbon, *Firearms and Domestic Violence: A Primer for Judges* ... 393
    *United States v. Hayes* ... 397
    *United States v. Castleman* ... 401
    *Voisine v. United States* ... 406
    *Fraternal Order of Police v. United States* ... 410
    Tom Lininger, *An Ethical Duty to Charge Batterers Appropriately* ... 413
    Notes and Questions ... 430

## Chapter 7 · Children, the Elderly and Domestic Violence — 435

- I. The History of Abuse Against Children and the Emergence of Child Welfare Groups — 436
  - A. Ten Centuries of Child Abuse — 436
    - Martin Ventrell, *Evolution of the Dependency Component of Juvenile Court* — 436
  - B. Emergence of Modern Child Protective Measures — 439
- II. The Modern Fight Against Child Abuse — 442
  - A. Mandated Reporters — 443
    - Maryland Family Law Code Ann. § 5-704 (2016) — 443
    - N.J. Stat. § 9:6-8.10. (2016) — 444
    - *B.H. v. County of San Bernardino* — 444
    - *L.A. and L.A. v. D.Y.F.S.* — 452
    - *Brown v. Pound* — 457
    - *Wilson v. Darr* — 459
    - *State v. Wilson* — 461
  - B. Scope and Limit of Duties to Protect Children — 466
    - Col. Rev. Stats. § 18-6-401 (2015) — 466
    - *People v. Steinberg* — 466
  - C. Shaken Baby Syndrome — 470
    - Deborah Tuerkheimer, *The Next Innocence Project: Shaken Baby Syndrome and the Criminal Courts* — 470
    - *State v. Edmunds* — 477
- III. Teen Dating Violence — 481
  - Andrew Sta. Ana & Stephanie Nilva, *Teen Victims of Intimate Partner Violence* — 481
- IV. Family Violence as a Form of Child Abuse — 485
  - *People v. Johnson* — 485
- V. Family Violence and Child Custody — 488
  - A. Should Batterers Be Custodial Parents? — 488
    - Ala. Code § 30-3-131 (2015) — 488
    - Ind. Code Ann. § 31-17-2-8 (2016) — 488
    - Nancy Ver Steegh, *Differentiating Types of Domestic Violence: Implications for Child Custody* — 489
  - B. Failure to Protect Children from Witnessing Violence — 499
- VI. Domestic Violence and Interjurisdictional Custody Disputes — 501
  - A. The Uniform Child Custody and Jurisdiction Enforcement Act — 501
    - Joan Zorza, *The UCCJEA: What Is It and How Does It Affect Battered Women in Child-Custody Disputes?* — 501
  - B. International Child Abduction — 513
    - *Souratgar v. Fair* — 513
- VII. Domestic Violence and the Elderly — 520
  - David France, *And Then He Hit Me* — 521
  - Tex. Penal Code § 22.04 (2016) — 522

| | |
|---|---|
| Cal. Pen. Code § 368 (2016) | 523 |
| N.Y. Penal Law § 260.32 (2015) | 525 |
| Lisa Fischel-Wolovick, *Police Response: Mandatory Arrest & Primary Physical Aggressor* | 526 |
| Notes and Questions | 527 |

## Chapter 8 · Divorce and Domestic Violence — 533

| | |
|---|---|
| I. Domestic Violence as a Ground for Divorce | 535 |
|     *Echevarria v. Echevarria* | 536 |
|     *Brady v. Brady* | 537 |
|     Louisiana R.S. 9:307 (2016) | 539 |
| II. Domestic Violence, Economic Issues and the Distribution of Marital Assets | 540 |
|   A. California's Divorce Law | 540 |
|     Cal. Fam. Code § 4320 (2016) | 541 |
|     Cal. Fam. Code § 4325 (2016) | 542 |
|     Cal. Fam. Code § 2603.5 (2016) | 542 |
|     *In re Marriage of Cauley* | 543 |
|   B. The Consideration of Domestic Violence in the Awarding of Marital Assets in Other Jurisdictions | 546 |
|     *Havell v. Islam* | 547 |
|     *Wheeler v. Upton-Wheeler* | 551 |
|   C. Economic Issues for Domestic Violence Survivors | 554 |
| III. Divorce Mediation and Domestic Violence | 555 |
|     Connie J.A. Beck & Bruce D. Sales, Family Mediation: Facts, Myths and Future Prospects | 555 |
|     Nancy Ver Steegh, *Yes, No, and Maybe: Informed Decision Making About Divorce Mediation in the Presence of Domestic Violence* | 557 |
|     Dafna Lavi, *Divorce Involving Domestic Violence: Is Med-Arb Likely to be the Solution?* | 559 |
|     Alaska Stat. 25.24.060 (2015) | 580 |
|     Notes and Questions | 581 |

## Chapter 9 · Civil Actions and Domestic Violence — 583

| | |
|---|---|
| I. Interspousal Tort Immunity | 584 |
|     *Thompson v. Thompson* | 584 |
|     *Brown v. Brown* | 588 |
|     *Townsend v. Townsend* | 591 |
|     Ill. Comp. Stat. Ann (2016) 750 ILCS 65/1 | 593 |
| II. Statutes of Limitations | 593 |
|     Lisa Napoli, *Tolling the Statute of Limitations for Survivors of Domestic Violence Who Wish to Recover Civil Damages Against Their Abusers* | 594 |
|     *Nussbaum v. Steinberg* | 597 |
|     *Nussbaum v. Steinberg* | 600 |

III. Expanding Tort Liability for Domestic Violence ... 601
    A. Battered Women's Syndrome ... 601
        *Cusseaux v. Pickett* ... 601
    B. The Tort of Domestic Violence ... 603
        California Civil Code § 1708.6 (2016) ... 603
        California Penal Code § 13700 (2016) ... 603
        California Code of Civil Procedure § 340.15 (2016) ... 604
    C. Infliction of Emotional Distress ... 604
        *Feltmeier v. Feltmeier* ... 604
        *Kloepfel v. Bokor* ... 609
IV. Tort Actions in Divorce ... 614
    *Chen v. Fischer* ... 614
    *Lord v. Shaw* ... 617
V. Insurance Issues in Domestic Violence Tort Litigation ... 619
    A. Lack of Coverage for Acts of Domestic Violence ... 620
        Jennifer Wriggins, *Interspousal Tort Immunity and Insurance
          "Family Member Exclusions": Shared Assumptions, Relational
          and Liberal Feminist Challenges* ... 620
    B. The Patient Protection and Affordable Care Act and
       Domestic Violence ... 622
        Maggie Jo Buchanan, *Fighting Domestic Violence Through
          Insurance: What the Affordable Care Act Does and Can
          Do for Survivors* ... 623
VI. Tort Actions Against Police and Public Agencies ... 629
    *DeShaney v. Winnebago County Department of Social Services* ... 629
    *Town of Castle Rock v. Gonzales* ... 633
VII. Domestic Violence Torts at the Workplace ... 639
    John E. Matejkovic, *Which Suit Would You Like? The Employer's
       Dilemma in Dealing With Domestic Violence* ... 639
    *Carroll v. Shoney's, Inc.* ... 644
    Georgia Code. Ann. § 34-1-7 (2016) ... 645
    *Green v. Bryant* ... 646
    NYC Administrative Code 8-107.1 ... 648
    R.I. Gen. Laws § 12-28-10 (2016) ... 648
VIII. False Arrest Claims ... 649
    *Wildoner v. Borough of Ramsey* ... 649
    Notes and Questions ... 655

**Chapter 10 · Domestic Violence and Family Law** ... 659
    Catherine F. Klein & Leslie E. Orloff, *Protective Orders and
      Other Injunctive Relief: Civil Protection Orders* ... 660
I. Who Is Part of the Family? ... 663
    N.Y. Family Ct. Act § 812 (2016) ... 663
II. The Legality of *Ex Parte* Orders of Protection ... 664

| | |
|---|---|
| *Shah v. Shah* | 664 |
| Official Code of Georgia Annotated § 19-13-2 (2016) | 670 |
| *Anderson v. Deas* | 670 |
| III. Relief Provided Under Protective Orders | 672 |
| *Maldonado v. Maldonado* | 672 |
| *V.C. v. H.C.* | 676 |
| *Stuckey v. Stuckey* | 682 |
| IV. Assessing the Effectiveness of Protective Orders | 685 |
| Susan L. Keilitz, Paula L. Hannaford & Hillery S. Efkeman, *Civil Protective Orders: The Benefits and Limitations for Victims of Domestic Violence* | 685 |
| V. Sanctions for Violations | 689 |
| *United States v. Dixon* | 689 |
| *Walker v. Walker* | 695 |
| Notes and Questions | 698 |
| Tex. Prop. Code § 92.016 (2016) | 700 |

## Chapter 11 · Immigration and Domestic Violence — 703

| | |
|---|---|
| I. The History of Women and Immigration Law | 704 |
| Leslye E. Orloff & Janice V. Kaguyutan, *Offering a Helping Hand: Legal Protections for Battered Immigrant Women: A History of Legislative Responses* | 704 |
| II. The Violence Against Women Act and Immigration Reform | 708 |
| Sarah M. Wood, Note: *Queer Theory, Feminism, and the Law: VAWA's Unfinished Business: The Immigrant Women Who Fall Through the Cracks* | 708 |
| III. Further VAWA Improvements | 710 |
| IV. Immigration Law in Context | 711 |
| *Johnson v. Attorney General* | 711 |
| *Hernandez v. Ashcroft* | 715 |
| *Rosario v. Holder* | 723 |
| V. The U VISA | 728 |
| *Hyoun Kyung Lee v. Holder* | 728 |
| VI. The Impact of Criminal Conviction on Removal | 730 |
| *Padilla v. Kentucky* | 731 |
| *Singh v. Ashcroft* | 735 |
| VII. Domestic Violence as Torture, a Violation of International Human Rights or the Basis for Asylum | 738 |
| Lori A. Nessel, *"Willful Blindness" to Gender-Based Violence Abroad: United States' Implementation of Article Three of the United Nations Convention Against Torture* | 738 |
| *In re R—A—* | 749 |
| Asylum and Withholding Definitions Proposed Rules | 758 |
| Notes and Questions | 766 |

| | |
|---|---|
| **Chapter 12 · Domestic Violence and the Justice System** | **769** |
| I. Problem-Solving Courts | 770 |
|     A. Judicial Attitude and Demeanor in Domestic Violence Cases | 770 |
|     B. The Debate About Specialized Domestic Violence Courts | 774 |
|         Bruce Winick, *Applying the Law Therapeutically in Domestic Violence Cases* | 774 |
|         Hon. Janice Rosa (ret.), *The Judge as Community First Responder: Because ACE's High is a Losing Hand* | 778 |
| II. Representing Clients in a Domestic Violence Court | 780 |
|     A. Victims | 780 |
|         B.J. Cling & Dorchen A. Leidholdt, *Interviewing and Assisting Domestic Violence Survivors* | 780 |
|     B. Perpetrators | 781 |
|         Lisa Angel & Lee Rosen, *Zealous and Ethical Representation of Batterers* | 781 |
| III. Sentencing — Jail, Probation, Batterers' Programs, Judicial Monitoring or Circles of Peace | 783 |
|         Cheryl Hanna, *The Paradox of Hope: The Crime and Punishment of Domestic Violence* | 785 |
|     A. Jail Sentences for Federal Crimes of Domestic Violence | 801 |
|         18 U.S.C. § 2262 | 801 |
|         *United States v. Robinson* | 802 |
|         *United States v. Fiume* | 806 |
|     B. Sentences in State Courts | 808 |
|         S.C. Code Ann. § 16-25-20 (2016) | 808 |
|         N.Y. C.L.S. Penal § 60.12 (2015) | 812 |
|     C. Electronic Monitoring and Batterers' Programs | 813 |
|         Rev. Code Wash. § 26.50.150 (2016) | 817 |
|     D. Alternative Solutions | 818 |
|         C. Quince Hopkins, Mary P. Koss & Karen J. Bachar, *Responding: Two New Solutions: Applying Restorative Justice to Ongoing Intimate Violence: Problems and Possibilities* | 819 |
| IV. Ethical Considerations in Domestic Violence Cases | 826 |
|     A. The Role of the Judge: Neutral Umpire or Societal Problem Solver? | 826 |
|     B. The Domestic Violence Judge in the Courtroom | 830 |
|         *In re Greene* | 830 |
|     C. The Lawyer as Advocate in the Domestic Violence Case | 833 |
|         1. Defense Dilemma: Where to Draw the Line | 833 |
|         District of Columbia Bar Ethics Opinion 321 | 834 |
|         2. Ethical Problems of the Prosecutor | 835 |
| V. When Domestic Violence Hits Close to Home | 835 |
|     *In re Nevill* | 836 |
|     *In the Matter of Magid* | 841 |

|  |  |
|---|---|
| *In The Matter of Fawn Balliro* | 844 |
| *In the Matter of Williams* | 852 |
| Notes and Questions | 858 |
| **Index** | 861 |

# Table of Cases

**A**

Abbott, State v., 329
Abrego, People v., 145
Acosta, Matter of, 755
Alabama v. Shelton, 70
Alberton v. State Bar, 839
Alejo v. City of Alhambra, 448, 449
Alice C. v. Joseph C., Matter of, 679
Allery, State v., 363
Aly v. Aden, 518
A-M-E- & J-G-U-, Matter of, 765
Anderson v. Deas, 670
Anderson v. Deas, 670
Anderson v. Johnson, 138
Andreiu v. Ashcroft, 719
Angel, People v., 268
Anonymous, People v., 285
Arakawa, State v., 251
Arceneaux v. K-Mart Corp., 643
Archie v. Racine, 631
Argersinger v. Hamlin, 68
Argueta v. Holder, 725
Armstrong v. United States, 407
Armstrong, State v., 479
Armstrong, United States v., 407
Arnold, People v., 369
Avdel Corp. v. Mecure, 667

**B**

B.H. v. County of San Bernardino, 444
B.H., State v., 341
Bailey, Estate of, by Oare v. County of York, 631
Bailey, Matter of, 850
Bailey, United States v., 391
Baker v. McCollan, 632
Balint, United States v., 181
Barber v. Thomas, 406
Barco-Sandoval v. Gonzales, 725, 726
Barnes, State v., 125
Barnes, United States v., 399, 401
Barnhart v. Thomas, 400
Barnier v. Barnier, 536
Barry v. Barry, 538
Barry, United States v., 412
Barshaw v. State, 143
Bartelho, United States v., 654
Bartlett v. State, 190
Bauer, State v., 82
Beaugez, People v., 464
Begay v. United States, 404
Belless, United States v., 402
Belleville Toyota, Inc. v., 608
Benoy v. Simons, 611
Benston, People v., 283
Berger v. Sonneland, 611
Bergerson, People v., 486
Bess, State v., 326, 329
Bierenbaum v. Graham, 322
Bierenbaum, People v., 256
Bifulco v. United States, 401
Birchler v. Castello Land Co., 613
Blakey v. Cont'l Airlines, Inc., 667, 668
Bleakley, People v., 469
Bledsoe, People v., 373
Blickstein v. Blickstein, 549, 616
Blockburger v. United States, 152, 155, 691
Bloom v. Illinois, 691, 692, 693
Blyden, People v., 371
Board of Regents of State Colleges v. Roth, 637
Bock, In re, 842

Boerne, City of, v. Flores, 385
Bolling v. Sharpe, 411
Bolton, United States v., 412
Bonello, State v., 297
Booker, United States v., 801, 803, 804
Borja v. INS, 760
Borse v. Piece Goods Shop, Inc., 647
Boudreau, State v., 155
Bracey, People v., 469
Bradley v. State, 27
Brady v. Brady, 537
Brady v. Maryland, 835
Brancoveanu v. Brancoveanu, 550
Brauer, Matter of, 845
Brawner v. Brawner, 592
Brennan v. Orban, 616, 655
Brooks, People v., 487
Brower v. Ackerley, 611
Brown v. Brown, 588
Brown v. Ohio, 153, 691, 808
Brown v. Pound, 457
Brown v. United States, 328
Brown, People v., 165
Brown, United States v., 348
Browne v. New York State Bd. of Parole, Matter of, 697
Bruno v. Codd, 31, 32, 34, 35
Bryant, People v., 152
Bryant, United States v., 66
Brzonkala v. Virginia Polytechnic and State Univ., 380, 382
Budnitz, Matter of, 850
Burbano, Matter of, 750
Burden, State v., 219
Burgett v. Texas, 69, 71
Burns, People v., 146
Butler v. Bonner & Barnewall, Inc., 666

## C

C-A-, Matter of, 765
Caccese, People v., 285
Cagle v. Burns & Roe, Inc., 613
California v. Cabazon Band of Mission Indians, 67
California v. Green, 293, 294, 295
Callender, Commonwealth v., 209
Cameron, People v., 146
Caminetti v. United States, 391, 392
Camps Newfound/Owatonna, Inc. v. Town of Harrison, Me., 392
Carfagno v. Carfagno, 653
Carlson, State v., 127
Carmille A. v. David A., 696
Carmody v. Trianon Co., 613
Carr, People v., 487
Carroll v. Shoney's, Inc., 644
Carron, People v., 176
Castle Rock, Town of. v. Gonzales, 633, 634, 635, 636, 637, 639
Castleman, United States v., 66, 401, 406, 407, 408, 409
Catena v. Seidl, 669
Cauley, In re Marriage of, 543
Cavallo, State v., 330
Cavanaugh, United States v., 70
Ceron-Sanchez, United States v., 737
Cesare v. Cesare, 653, 655
Chapman, In re, 692
Chauvin, State v., 365
Chen v. Fischer, 614
Chevron, U.S.A., Inc. v. Natural Resources Defense Council, Inc., 722
Chiaradio, United States v., 807
Chiarello, State v., 329
Chretien, Commonwealth v., 165
Cintron, People v., 264
Ciskie, State v., 335
Cisneros, United States v., 198
City of, See Name of City
Civil Rights Cases, 380, 381, 384, 385
Clark v. Modern Group, Ltd., 647
Clay v. Commonwealth, 136
Cleveland v. United States, 391, 392
Coble v. State, 142, 143
Coe & Payne Co. v. Wood-Mosaic Corp., 671
Coker v. Georgia, 163
Colas v. Watermain, In re, 643
Committee on Professional Ethics and Conduct of the Iowa State Bar Association v. Patterson, 843
Commonwealth v., See Name of Defendant
Conaghan, Commonwealth v., 346
Conaghan, Commonwealth v., 346
Concemi, Matter of, 850
Contes, People v., 468

Conti, State v., 156
Coy v. Iowa, 219, 292, 293, 294, 295, 296, 297
Crandon v. United States, 406
Crawford v. Washington, 218, 226, 228, 229, 301, 302, 303, 305
Crawford, Commonwealth v., 348
Cressey, State v., 368
Crow Dog, Ex parte, 67
Cruz-Foster v. Foster, 673, 674
Culhane, People v., 370
Cunefare, People v., 638
Cusseaux v. Pickett, 601

## D

D.O.H. v. T.L.H, 499
Daniels v. Williams, 631, 632, 633
Darby, United States v., 383
Daubert v. Merrell Dow Pharmaceuticals, 324
Davidson v. Cannon, 631
Davidson, State v., 297
Davis People v., 486
Davis v. Munie, 608
Davis v. State, 142
Davis v. Tacoma Ry. & Power Co., 612
Davis v. Washington, 223, 224, 225, 302
De Angelis v. De Angelis, 164
De Stefano, People v., 165
Debs, In re, 692
Delahunty v. Massachusetts Mut. Life Ins. Co., 616
Delaware v. Fensterer, 294, 320, 321
Descamps v. United States, 409
DeShaney v. Winnebago County Department of Social Services, 629, 636
Dhinsa, United States v., 249
Dielmann v. INS, 730
DiGuilio, State v., 190
Dillard, United States v., 198, 199, 200
Dinius v. Dinius, 530
DiProspero v. Penn, 455
Discipline of an Attorney, Matter of, 850
District of Columbia v. Heller, 397
Dixon, United States v., 152, 689
Donaldson v. Seattle, 637
Dorm, People v., 268
Douglas E. Rowe, A Suspended Attorney, In re, 858

Dowdell v. United States, 293
Driscoll, Matter of, 849
Duarte, United States v., 808
Dunning, State v., 364
Duro v. Reina, 64, 67
Dusky v. United States, 346, 348, 349
Dutton v. Evans, 220, 266
Dye, State v., 311, 313, 316

## E

E-A-G-, Matter of, 765
Eames v. Eames, Matter of, 681
Ebel v. Ferguson, 592
Echevarria v. Echevarria, 536
Edmunds, State v., 477
Edwards, Commonwealth v., 228
Elonis v. United States, 177, 178, 179
English v. English, 29
Ennis v. Truhitte, 592
Ewoldt, People v., 272
Ex parte, See Name of Party
Eyrich for Eyrich v. Dam, 602
Eyrich v. Dam, 602

## F

Fader, State v., 338
Fair, State v., 329
Farmer v. Brennan, 408
Fawn Balliro, Matter of, 844
FCC v. Beach Communications, Inc., 411
FCC v. Pacifica Foundation, 296
Felix, United States v., 694
Feltmeier v. Feltmeier, 604
Ferraro v. Chadwick, 448
Finn, Matter of, 850
Fisch v. Bellshot, 455
Fisher, State v., 463, 464
Fiume, United States v., 806
Flayhart, People v., 468
Flores v. Ashcroft, 403
Florida Prepaid Postsecondary Ed. Expense Bd. v. College Savings Bank, 385
Fogerty, Commonwealth v., 163
Foley v. Foley, 656
Fong Haw Tan v. Phelan, 732
Fong Yue Ting v. United States, 732
Forcucci v. Forcucci, 538, 539
Foster, State v., 315

Fraternal Order of Police v. United States, 410, 411
Frye v. United States, 323
Fulgham v. State, 28

## G

G.S. v. Department of Human Services, 454
Gadbury v. Bleitz, 612
Gardner v. State, 253
Garlow v. State Bar, 838
Gateward, United States v., 412
Gavieres v. United States, 691, 694
Gebardi v. United States, 158
Gideon v. Wainwright, 68
Giglio v. United States, 835
Giles v. California, 229, 303, 305
Ginsberg v. New York, 296
Globe Newspaper Co. v. Superior Court of Norfolk County, 296
Gluzman, United States v., 391
Goldberg, In re, 842
Gomez v. INS, 762
Gomez v. State, 314
Grady v. Corbin, 691, 692, 694
Grayhurst, State v., 154
Grecinger, State v., 333, 335
Green v. Bryant, 646
Green v. United States, 669
Greene, In re, 830
Greenlee, People v., 285
Grella, Matter of, 852
Grimsby v. Samson, 610, 613
Guaragno v. Guaragno, 518
Gust v. Flint, 671
Gutierrez, People v., 146, 147
Guzman v. C.R. Epperson Construction, Inc., 609

## H

H-A-, Matter of, 730
Haggard, United States v., 720
Hail v. Regency Terrace Owners Ass'n, 645
Hakimi, State v., 314
Hall, State v., 368
Halvey v. Halvey, 501
Hamilton v. Ali, 698
Hamilton v. Fulkerson, 592
Hammon v. Indiana, 226, 302
Handa v. Handa, 679
Hanks, State v., 331
Hardy, United States v., 805
Harrington v. State, 468
Harris v. City of Montgomery, 458
Harris v. Oklahoma, 692
Harris, United States v., 380, 384
Harrison, United States v., 674
Hart, State v., 277
Hartfield v. State, 244
Haskell's Inc. v. Sopsic, 128
Haubry v. Snow, 611
Havell v. Islam, 547, 548
Havrish, People v., 432
Hayes v. Mercer County, 652
Hayes, United States v., 397, 401, 403, 404, 405, 406, 409
Heacock v. Heacock, 617
Heart of Atlanta Motel, Inc. v. United States, 387, 392
Heckman, State v., 192
Hegel v. McMahon, 611
Heller v. Doe, 412
Hennum, State v., 333, 338, 339
Henriksen v. Cameron, 606, 607, 617
Henson, People v., 468
Hernandez v. Ashcroft, 713, 714, 715
Hessen v. Hessen, 536, 538
Higbie, In re, 839
Hiibel v. Sixth Judicial Dist. Court of Nev., Humboldt Cty., 227
Hill v. Lockhart, 734
Hipplewith, State v., 328, 329
Hodel v. Virginia Surface Mining & Reclamation Assn., Inc., 384
Hofbauer, Matter of, 468
Holmes v. United States, 314
Howlett, Commonwealth v., 137
Huddleston v. United States, 401
Hudson v. United States, 152, 156
Huesers v. Huesers, 278
Hughes, State v., 364
Hunsley v. Giard, 610, 612
Huntington v. Attrill, 638
Hyoun Kyung Lee v. Holder, 728

## I

Idaho v. Wright, 266
In re, See Name of Party

In re Marriage of, See Name of Spouse
In the Matter of, See Name of Party
Ingber, People v., 697
Ingraham v. Wright, 631
Innie, United States v., 736, 737
Innovative Clinical & Consulting Svcs. v. First Nat. Bank, 670
INS v. Abudu, 766
INS v. Aguirre-Aguirre, 766
INS v. Cardoza-Fonseca, 753
INS v. Elias-Zacarias, 760
INS v. Lopez-Mendoza, 732
INS v. St. Cyr, 724
International Shoe Co. v. Washington, 667

## J

J.D.C., In re, 674
Jackson v. State Bar, 838
Jackson, City of, United States v., 675
Jacobs v. Walt Disney World, Co., 667
James W. v. Superior Court, 449
James, People v., 266, 267
Janes, State v., 359, 362
Jayson, State v., 329
Jeffries, United States v., 181
Jensen v. Conrad, 631
Jian Hui Shao v. BIA, 766
John, United States v., 67
Johnson v. Attorney General, 711
Johnson v. Drummond, Woodsum, Plimpton & MacMahon, P.A., 643
Johnson v. Johnson, 536, 537
Johnson v. United States, (1979), 673
Johnson v. United States (2010), 402, 403, 404
Johnson, People v. (Cal. 2000), 322
Johnson, People v. (N.Y.), 370, 485
Johnson, State v., 610
Jones, State v., 209
Jurney v. MacCracken, 692

## K

Kalaw v. INS, 719
Katzenbach v. McClung, 387
Keifer v. Keifer, 138
Keller, State v., 737
Kelly, State v., 325, 856, 602, 654
Kennedy v. Kennedy, 538
Kentucky Dep't of Corrections v. Thompson, 636
Kerlinsky, Matter of, 850
Khouzam v. Ashcroft, 746, 748
Kilmer v. Kilmer, 679, 680
King v. Brasier, 305
King v. State, 143
Kinney, State v., 374
Kirby v. United States, 293
Kirby, State v., 463
Kirkman, State v., 316, 317
Kloepfel v. Bokor, 609, 611
Knight, In re, 843
Koskela, State v., 80
Kuhn v. Kuhn, 380
Kumho Tire Co. v. Carmichael, 324
Kurzke v. Nissan Motor Corp., 664
Kushner, In re, 842
Kyllo v. United States, 228

## L

L.A. and L.A. v. D.Y.F.S., 452
L.A. ex rel. S.A. v. N.J. Div. of Youth & Family Servs., 453
Lane, United States v., 199
Lankford, United States v., 391
Lara, United States v., 65
Larsen, United States v., 388
Lawson v. Boeing Co., 611
Lear v. Township of Piscataway, 652
Lebel v. Everglades Marina, Inc., 668
Lee, State v., 82
Leffingwell v. Leffingwell, Matter of, 679
Leocal v. Ashcroft, 405
Lewis, People v., 267
Lewis, United States v., 412
Liberta, People v., 161
Libretti v. United States, 734
Lilly v. Virginia, 227
Lilly, United States v., 807
Linkenauger, People v., 272, 275
Lionetti, State v., 328
Littlefield, In re Marriage of, 313, 315, 316
Litwin, In re, 842
Logan v. United States, 693
Lopez, United States v., 380, 382, 383, 384, 385, 391
Lord v. Shaw, 617

Lucas, State v., 157
Lucio-Lucio, United States v., 200
Ludwig, Commonwealth v., 297
Lunetta, In re, 842

## M

M.D.Z., In re, 668
Mack, Commonwealth v., 464
MacLennan, State v., 334, 351
Magid, Matter of, 841
Maldonado v. Maldonado, 672
Malette, State v., 209
Malone, People v., 487
Manley, State v., 128
Mannion, State v., 297
Manufacturers Mut. Ins. Co. v. Sullivan, 639
Maragh, People v., 371, 372, 373
Mark Len, State v., 328
Marri v. Stamford Street R. Co., 589
Martinez v. California, 632
Martinez v. State, 193
Mary L. v. Dep't of Social Services, Matter of, 527
Maryland v. Craig, 291, 315
Mathewson v. Mathewson, 588, 589
Matter of, See Name of Party
Mattox v. United States, 221, 293, 294, 295
Maurer, People ex. Rel., v. Jackson, 697
May v. Anderson, 502
McAfee, Commonwealth v., 28
McAllister, United States v., 412
McBride v. County of Westchester, 598
McCann v. McCann, 549, 550
McCarty, United States v., 807
McClure v. Campbell, 612
McCray, People v., 272
McDonald v. City of Chicago, 397
McGrath v. Fahey, 606
McLaughlin, In re, 844
McMahan v. McMahan, 549
McMann v. Richardson, 732
McMaugh v. State, 348, 349
McRae's of Alabama, Inc., Ex parte, 645
Meade, United States v., 398
Meagan R., In re, (1996), 158, 159
Melendez-Diaz v. Massachusetts, 301
Meli, People v., 163
Mellillo, State v., 328

Mellum v. Mellum, 277
Mendez v. Holder, 726
Mendez-Moranchel v. Ashcroft, 712
Merenoff v. Merenoff, 606
Merola v. Merola, 679
Merrill Lynch, Pierce, Fenner & Smith Inc. v. Dabit, 400
Michigan v. Bryant, 302, 303, 305, 306
Milliken v. Meyer, 667
Mischlich, In re, 842
Moghararrabi, Matter of, 755
Molineux, People v., 256, 267
Montero-Martinez v. Ashcroft, 719
Moore v. Cnty. of Delaware, 518
Moore v. Jones, 675
Morissette v. United States, 181, 409
Morris v. Snappy Car Rental, 697
Morrison, United States v., 380, 391, 392, 393
Morrissey v. Brewer, 632
Moses, People v., 469
Motherwell, State v., 460
Mount, State v., 328
Mulder, State v., 363
Mullally v. Langenberg Bros. Grain Co., 591
Murphy v. Workers' Comp. Appeals Bd., 642
Myers, State v. (N.J. 1990), 602
Myers, State v. (Minn. 1984), 81

## N

Nason, United States v., 402
Natale v. Ridgefield, 638
National Cable & Telecomms. Ass'n v. Brand X Internet Servs., 766
Nemeth, State v., 352
Nenno v. State, 142
Nevill, In re, 836, 843
New Jersey v. Townsend, 373
New Orleans v. Steamship Co., 691, 693
New York v. Ferber, 296
New York v. Havrish, 432
Nguyen, United States v., 412
Nichols v. United States, 69, 70
Nicholson v. Scoppetta, 500
Nord v. Shoreline Sav. Ass'n, 613
Nordgren v. Lawrence, 612
North Carolina v. Pearce, 691

Nudd v. Matsoukas, 656
Nussbaum v. Steinberg, 600
Nystrom, State v., 81

## O

O'Brien v. City of Syracuse, 615
O'Brien v. O'Brien, 549, 616
O'Connell v. Corcoran, 615
Obergefell v. Hodges, 104, 663
Ohio v. Clark, 300
Ohio v. Roberts, 218, 219, 221, 222, 231, 294, 295, 301
Ohio v. Schneider, 472
Olano, United States v., 808
Olguin v. State Bar, 838
Oliphant v. Suquamish Indian Tribe, 64
Oliver, State v., 26, 27
Order of Railroad Telegraphers v. Railway Express, 593
Ortiz, People v., 275
Osborne v. Ohio, 296
Ozaltin v. Ozaltin, 517

## P

Padilla v. Kentucky, 731
Page, United States v., 391
Palabay, State v., 314
Palmer, Matter of, 850
Palsgraf v. Long Island R.R., 612
Panpat v. Owens-Brockway Glass Container, Inc., 643
Parker v. United States, 693
Parr, People v., 487
Parrt v. Taylor, 632
Paul v. Davis, 632
Payne v. Tennessee, 695
Peavler v. Mitchell & Scott Mach. Co., 643
Pennsylvania v. Ritchie, 293, 321
People v., See Name of Defendant
Perales-Cumpean v. Gonzales, 713
Perez v. United States, 382, 383, 391
Perovich, State v., 314
Peters-Riemers v. Riemers, 276
Petriciolet v. Texas, 138
Pettingill v. Pettingill, 134
Petty, In re, 840
Pike, Commonwealth v., 348, 848
Plains Commerce Bank v. Long Family Land & Cattle Co., 66, 68
Planned Parenthood v. Danforth, 164

Pointer v. Texas, 219
Ponzi v. Fessenden, 697
Possino, In re, 838, 840
Precision Instrument Mfg. Co. v. Auto. Maint. Mach. Co., 518
Prescott, People v., 152
Price, State v., 156
Prince v. Massachusetts, 296
Principato, In re, 842, 843
Profitt, State v., 80
Public Finance Corp. v. Davis, 606

## Q

Quintana v. Quintana, Matter of, 679, 681

## R

R-A-, 749, 764, 765
Rainbow v. Swisher, 615
Rawls, United States v., 412
Reid v. Pierce County, 610
Resek, People v., 269
Reyes, State v., 666
Reynolds v. United States, 230, 231
Rice v. Janovich, 610
Rider, State v., 165
Rios v. Rios, 536
Ritt, State v., 82
Rivera-Maldonado, United States v., 807
Robbins, Commonwealth v., 348, 349
Robel v. Roundup Corp., 611
Robinson, United States v., 802
Rochin v. California, 632
Rodgers v. State, 142
Rodriguez v. Gonzales, 725, 726
Rodriguez, State v., 155
Roe v. Flores-Ortega, 734
Rogers v. Rogers, 591
Rogers v. United States, 181
Rogers, United States v., 197
Rohan, In re, 840
Rosario v. Holder, 723
Rosen, In re, 842
Ross v. Ross, Matter of, 679
Rothrock, In re, 838
Roy v. Roy, Matter of, 680
Rufo v. Simpson, 269
Runyon, In re, 843
Russeau v. State, 142
Russell, United States v., 733
Rydder v. Rydder, 520

## S

Salerno, United States v., 209
Sanchez, People v., 338
Sandbeck v. Rockwell, 278
Sandin v. Conner, 638
Sangha v. INS, 760
Santa Clara Pueblo v. Martinez, 68
Santiago, People v., 235
Schaefer v. Souris River Telecom., 277
Scott v. Illinois, 66, 68
Scott, United States v., 228
S-E-G-, Matter of, 765
Sepulveda v. Gonzales, 725, 726
Shabani, United States v., 401
Shah v. Shah, 664
Shah v. Shah, 665, 668
Shavanaux, United States v., 70, 71
Shaw, Matter of, 850
Shepard v. United States, 404
Silverman v. Silverman, 518
Simmons, People v., 486
Singh v. Ashcroft, 735
Singleton, United States v., 198, 199
Sleeper, Matter of, 851
Smiley v. Citibank (South Dakota), N.A., 766
Smith v. Allwright, 695
Smith v. Russell Sage College, 616
Smith, People v., 469
Smith, State v. (Tex. 2011), 142
Smith, State v. (Fla.), 165
Smith, State v. (N.J), 164, 165
Smith, United States v., 412
Snyder v. Massachusetts, 293
Solorio v. United States, 694
Sorrentino, United States v., 412
Souratgar v. Fair, 513, 514, 515, 516, 517, 519, 520
Southern R. Co. v. United States, 383
Soutiere v. Soutiere, 374, 375
Spence, People v., 313, 314
Spurrell v. Block, 611
Stanley v. Illinois, 488
State v., See Name of Defendant
Steinberg, People v., 466
Stepanovic v. Filip, 713, 714
Stewart, People v., 146
Stillman v. Moore, 245
Stoker v. Stoker, Utah, 618, 619

Strickland v. Washington, 732, 733, 734, 735
Stuckey v. Stuckey, 682
Suarez, People v., 487
Sullivan v. State Bar, 839
Sundance Homes, Inc. v. County of Du Page, 608
Swinger, People v., 285

## T

Tampa Maid Seafood Prods. v. Porter, 642
Tarasoff v. Regents of Univ. of California, 265
Tarver v. State Bar, 839
Taylor v. United States, 404, 736
Taylor, People v., 374
Tevis v. Tevis, 616
Theroff, State v., 364
Thomas, People v., 146
Thompson v. Thompson, 584
Thompson, In re, 693
Thompson, State v., 210
Thurman v. City of Torrington, 629
Tierney v. Davidson, 654
Till, People v., 269
T-M-B-, Matter of, 760
Toennis, State v., 363
Tohom, People v., 313, 314
Tokatly v. Ashcroft, 736
Toll v. State Bar, 839
Tom Olesker's Exciting World of Fashion, Inc. v. Dun & Bradstreet, Inc., 609
Torpey, People v., 371
Town of, See Name of Town
Townsend v. Townsend, 591
Trammel v. United States, 164
Turner, People v., 318
Turner, United States v., 412
Tuso, In re, 842

## U

United States v., See Name of Defendant

## V

V.C. v. H.C., 676
Van Dyke, State v., 344
Vana v. Elkins, 619
Vance v. Chandler, 607
Vang v. Toyed, 82
Vela v. State, 142

Voisine v. United States, 406
Voisine, United States v., 407
Vue, State v., 78

## W
Wahlberg, State v., 127
Walker v. Walker, 695
Walker, In re (Cal. 2007), 374
Walker, In re (Ind. 1992), 843, 844
Walker, State v., 462
Wallace, In re, 843
Wallace, United States v., 807
Warguleski v. Warguleski, 538
Watson, People v., 177
Weber, In re, 840
Weir v. State Bar, 838
Weishaupt v. Commonwealth, 165
Weiss v. City of Milwaukee, 642
Wells, United States v., 412
Wenzel v. Wenzel, 549
West, People v., 487
Westgate v. Westgate, 552
Whallon v. Lynn, 517, 518, 519
Wheeler v. United States, 289
Wheeler v. Upton-Wheeler, 551
White River Estates v. Hiltbruner, 613
White, United States v., 249
Wildermuth v. State, 296, 297, 298
Wildoner v. Borough of Ramsey, 649
Wilhite, State v., 297
Williams v. Alexander, 285
Williams, In the Matter of, 852
Williams, People v., 371, 372
Willott v. Willott, 591
Wilmore v. Gonzales, 713, 714
Wilson v. Darr, 459
Wilson, State v., 461
Windauer v. O'Connor, 619
Windsor, United States v., 104
Wisconsin v. Larsen, 389, 390
Wood, People v., 151
Woodward, Commonwealth v., 470, 473
Wright v. Beardsley, 612
Wright, People v., 146

## X
X-Citement Video, Inc., United States v., 181
Xiao Ji Chen v. Gonzales, 724, 725, 726

## Y
Yascavage, People v., 147
Youngberg v. Romeo, 632

## Z
Zack, People v., 275
Zamora-Mallari v. Mukasey, 714
Zapata, United States v., 807
Zavala, People v., 173
Zessman v. State, 468
Zheng v. Ashcroft, 746

# Acknowledgments

I want to thank Justice Rosalyn Richter of the New York State Supreme Court, Appellate Division, author of two chapters for the first edition of this text, who generously allowed me to include and update them in this one. She was my first supervising judge when I was appointed to the bench in 1999, and assigned me to the Bronx County Misdemeanor Domestic Violence Court. In addition, she and I developed a course in Domestic Violence and the Law at New York Law School, which I still teach.

I also must thank LexisNexis/Matthew Bender & Co. for publishing the first edition of this book more than a decade ago, recognizing the importance of this subject to the law school curriculum. I thank LexisNexis/Matthew Bender Academic Editor Cristina Gegenschatz who did long distance brain-storming, hand-holding, advising, and editing for the duration of the first edition and who assisted in the early stages of this latest edition until the project was taken over by its new publisher, Carolina Academic Press (CAP). I also thank Sean Caldwell, former Director of Market Planning for LexisNexis who stayed on at CAP and whose insights helped make this second edition shorter, tighter and more relevant to the students and professors who will be using it.

I also want to thank my new editorial team at CAP: Senior Editor Linda Lacy, Managing Editor Ryland Bowman, Editor Keith Moore, and Grace Pledger, Head of Production, all of whom worked hard to move this book to completion. I thank Georges G. Lederman, Esq., for just being there when wanted and needed, which is always, and my family, Helen and June Kiesel.

Thank you to Catherine Christian, chief of the New York County District Attorney's Elder Abuse Unit; Susan Zirinsky, senior executive producer of *48 Hours* and Dr. Ludy Green, founder of *Second Chance Employment Services*, for consenting to be interviewed for this book. Finally, I want to thank the professors around the country who have had the confidence in me to use this book as a teaching tool for their students. I appreciate it.

Diane Kiesel
New York, NY

I additionally thank the authors and publishers for permission to reprint portions of the following copyrighted material:

Ammons, Linda L., *Mules, Madonnas, Babies, Bathwater, Racial Imagery and Stereotypes: The African-American Woman and the Battered Woman Syndrome*, 1995 WIS. L. REV. 1003. Copyright © 1995 by The Board of Regents of the University of Wisconsin System. Reprinted by permission of the Wisconsin Law Review.

Angel, Lisa and Lee Rosen, *Zealous and Ethical Representation of Batterers*, in MARGARET B. DREW ET AL., THE IMPACT OF DOMESTIC VIOLENCE ON YOUR LEGAL PRACTICE 83 (ABA Comm'n on Domestic Violence, 2d ed. 2004). Copyright © 2004 by the American Bar Association. Reprinted with permission.

Beck, Connie J.A. and Bruce D. Sales, FAMILY MEDIATION: FACTS, MYTHS, AND FUTURE PROSPECTS (2001). Copyright © 2001 by the American Psychological Association. Reprinted with permission of the authors and the American Psychological Association.

Belzer, Lydia M., *Toward True Shalom Bayit: Acknowledging Domestic Abuse in the Jewish Community and What To Do About It*, 11 CARDOZO WOMEN'S L.J. 241 (Winter 2005). Copyright © 2005 Cardozo Women's Law Journal. Reprinted with permission.

Berman, Greg, Derek Denckla and John Feinblatt, *Judicial Innovation at the Crossroads: The Future of Problem-Solving Courts*, 13 THE COURT MANAGER 28 (2000). Copyright © 2000. Reprinted by permission of The New Press.

Berman, Greg and John Feinblatt, GOOD COURTS: THE CASE FOR PROBLEM SOLVING JUSTICE (2005). Reprinted by permission.

Boat, Barbara W., *Abuse of Children and Abuse of Animals: Using the Links to Inform Child Assessment and Protection*, in CHILD ABUSE, DOMESTIC VIOLENCE, AND ANIMAL ABUSE: LINKING THE CIRCLES OF COMPASSION FOR PREVENTION AND INTERVENTION 83 (Frank R. Ascione & Phil Arkow eds., 1999). Copyright © 1999 Purdue University Press. Reprinted by permission.

Brummer, Bennett H., *Criminal Law Symposium: Independent, Professional Judgment: The Essence of Freedom*, 10 ST. THOMAS L. REV. 607 (1998). Copyright © 1998. Reprinted by permission of St. Thomas Law Review.

Buchanan, Maggie Jo, *Fighting Domestic Violence Through Insurance: What the Affordable Care Act Does and Can Do For Survivors*, 23 TEX. J. WOMEN & L. 77 (Fall 2013). Copyright © 2013. Reprinted by permission.

Buel, Sarah M., *Fifty Obstacles to Leaving, a.k.a., Why Abuse Victims Stay*, 28 COLO. LAW. 19 (1999). Reproduced by permission of the Colorado Bar Association from *The Colorado Lawyer*, Oct. 1999, 19 © Colorado Bar Association, and the author. All rights reserved.

Buel, Sarah M., *Putting Forfeiture to Work*, 43 U.C. DAVIS L. REV. 1295 (April 2010). Copyright © 2010. Reprinted by permission.

Campbell, Jacqueline C. et al., *Assessing Risk Factors for Intimate Partner Homicides*, NIJ Journal 15 (Issue No. 250) (Nov. 2003). Reprinted by permission of the U.S. Department of Justice, National Institute of Justice.

———, *Assessing Dangerousness* (Newbury Park: Sage 1995). J.C. Campbell, D. Webster, J. Koziol-McLain, C.R. Block, D.W. Campbell, M.A. Curry, F. Gary, C.J. Sachs, P.W. Sharps, Y. Ulrich, S. Wilt, J. Manganello, J. Schollenberger, S. Su, and V. Frye. Risk Factors in Abusive Relationships: Results From a Multi-State Case Control Study, *Am. J. Public Health*, in press.

Cling, B.J. and Dorchen A. Leidholdt, *Interviewing and Assisting Domestic Violence Survivors in* LAWYER'S MANUAL ON DOMESTIC VIOLENCE: REPRESENTING THE VICTIM, 6TH ED. (Mary Rothwell Davis, Dorchen A. Leidholdt and Charlotte A. Watson, eds. 2015). Copyright © 2015. Reprinted by permission.

Conference of State Court Administrators, POSITION PAPER ON SAFETY AND ACCOUNTABILITY: STATE COURTS AND DOMESTIC VIOLENCE 3 (Nov. 2004). Copyright © 2004. Reprinted by permission of the National Center for State Courts, Conference of State Court Administrators.

Dutton, Mary Ann, *Understanding Women's Responses to Domestic Violence: A Redefinition of Battered Women Syndrome*, 21 HOFSTRA L. REV. 1191 (1993). Copyright © 1993. Reprinted with permission of the Hofstra Law Review Association.

Ferrato, Donna, *Elisabeth & Bengt in the bathroom the first night she was hit*, photograph in LIVING WITH THE ENEMY. Copyright © 1991 by Donna Ferrato. Reprinted by permission.

Fischel-Wolovick, Lisa, *Police Response: Mandatory Arrest & Primary Physical Aggressor, in* LAWYER'S MANUAL ON DOMESTIC VIOLENCE: REPRESENTING THE VICTIM, 6TH ED. 52 (Mary Rothwell Davis, Dorchen A. Leidholdt and Charlotte A. Watson, eds. 2015). Copyright © 2015. Reprinted by permission.

France, David, *And Then He Hit Me*, AARP MAGAZINE 73 (Jan.–Feb. 2006). Copyright © 2006. Reprinted with permission of the author.

Goodmark, Leigh, *Transgender People, Intimate Partner Abuse, and the Legal System*, 48 HARV. C.R.— C.L.L. REV. 51 (Winter 2013). Copyright © 2013. Reprinted with permission.

Hajjar, Lisa, *Religion, State Power and Domestic Violence in Muslim Societies: A Framework for Comparative Analysis*, 29 LAW & SOC. INQUIRY 1 (Winter 2004). Copyright © 2004. Reprinted with permission of Blackwell Publishing Ltd.

Hanna, Cheryl, *The Paradox of Hope: The Crime and Punishment of Domestic Violence*, 39 WM. & MARY L. REV. 1505 (1998). Copyright © 1998 by the William and Mary Law Review. Reprinted by permission.

Holder, Casey, Comment: *All Dogs Go to Court: The Impact of Court Facility Dogs as Comfort for Child Witnesses on a Defendant's Right to a Fair Trial*, 50 HOUS. L. REV. 1155 (Symposium 2013). Copyright © 2013. Reprinted by permission.

Hopkins, C. Quince, Mary P. Koss & Karen J. Bachar, *Responding: Two New Solutions: Applying Restorative Justice to Ongoing Intimate Violence: Problems and Possibilities*, 23 St. Louis U. Pub. L. Rev. 289 (2004). Reprinted with permission of the St. Louis University Public Law Review. © 2004 St. Louis University School of Law, St. Louis, Missouri.

Indian Law Resource Center, et al., *Statement to the Commission on the Status of Women, Sixtieth Session, 2016 Violence Against Indigenous Women and Girls*. Copyright ©2016 United Nations. Reprinted by permission of the United Nations.

Isaac, Nancy E. and V. Pualini Enos, *Documenting Domestic Violence: How Health Care Providers Can Help Victims* (Nat'l Inst. of Justice, U.S. Dep't of Justice, September 2001). Reprinted by permission.

Juhler, Jennifer and Justice Mark Cady, *Morality, Decision-making, and Judicial Ethics*, available at www.abanet.org. Reprinted with permission.

Keilitz, Susan L., Paula L. Hannaford and Hillery S. Efkeman, *Civil Protective Orders: The Benefits and Limitations for Victims of Domestic Violence*, National Center for State Courts Research Report *vii* (1997). Copyright © 1997. Reprinted by permission of the National Center for State Courts.

King-Ries, Andrew, *Responding: Two New Solutions: True to Character: Honoring the Intellectual Foundations of the Character Evidence Rule in Domestic Violence Prosecutions*, 23 St. Louis U. Pub. L. Rev. 313 (2004). Reprinted with permission of the St. Louis University Public Law Review. © 2004 St. Louis University School of Law, St. Louis, Missouri.

Klein, Catherine F. and Leslie E. Orloff, *Protective Orders and Other Injunctive Relief: Civil Protection Orders*, in Margaret B. Drew et al., The Impact of Domestic Violence on Your Legal Practice 200 (ABA Comm'n on Domestic Violence, 2d ed. 2004). Copyright © 2004 by the American Bar Association. Reprinted with permission.

Knauer, Nancy, *Same-Sex Domestic Violence: Claiming a Domestic Sphere While Risking Negative Stereotypes*, 8 Temp. Pol. & Civ. Rts. L. Rev. 325 (1999). Copyright © 1999. Reprinted by permission of the author.

Kutner, Jenny, *Domestic Violence Victims Can Be Evicted for Calling Police. Here's Why*, connections.mic.com/articles/148484/domestic-violence-victims-can-be-evicted-for-calling-police-here-s-why#zQRqkpyY1. July 14, 2016. Reprinted by permission.

Lasson, Kenneth, *Bloodstains on a 'Code of Honor:' The Murderous Marginalization of Women in the Islamic World*, 30 Women's Rights L. Rep. 407 (Spring/Summer 2009). Copyright © 2009. Reprinted by permission.

Lavi, Dafna, *Divorce Involving Domestic Violence: Is Med-Arb Likely to be the Solution?* 14 Pepp. Disp. Resol. L. J. 91 (2014). Copyright © 2014. Reprinted by permission.

Leary, Mary Graw, *Symposium: Emerging Issues in Crime Victims' Rights: The Third Dimension of Victimization,* 13 Ohio St. J. Crim. L. 139 (Fall 2015). Copyright © 2015. Reprinted by permission.

Lininger, Tom, *A Duty to Charge Batterers Appropriately,* 22 Duke J. Gender L. & Pol'y 173 (Spring 2015). Copyright © 2015. Reprinted by permission.

Library of Congress, "Contrasted husbands" illustration by Richard Newton (1795), *available at* Library of Congress Online Catalogue, http://catalog.loc.gov/.

Library of Congress, "Judge Thumb, or—patent sticks for family correction: warranted lawful!" illustration by James Gillray (1782), *available at* Library of Congress Online Catalogue, http://catalog.loc.gov/.

Library of Congress, "Sensible Roosevelt—A whipping-post for wife-beaters" illustration by Thomas Worth (1883), *available at* Library of Congress Online Catalogue, http://catalog.loc.gov/.

Lippman, Hon. Jonathan, *Foreword to* Lawyer's Manual on Domestic Violence: Representing the Victim, 6th Ed. 52 (Mary Rothwell Davis, Dorchen A. Leidholdt and Charlotte A. Watson, eds. 2015). Copyright © 2015. Reprinted by permission.

Matejkovic, John E., *Which Suit Would You Like? The Employer's Dilemma in Dealing With Domestic Violence,* 33 Cap. U. L. Rev. 309 (2004). Copyright © 2004. Reprinted by permission of the Capital University Law Review.

McGuire, Linda, *Criminal Prosecution of Domestic Violence* (1994), written for The Battered Women's Justice Project, *available at* http://data.ipharos.com/ bwjp/website/ (under topic: Prosecution). Reprinted by permission of the author and The Battered Women's Justice Project.

Meier, Joan S., *Domestic Violence, Child Custody, and Child Protection: Understanding Judicial Resistance and Imagining the Solutions,* 11 Am. U. J. Gender Soc. Pol'y & L. 657 (2003). Copyright © 2003. Reprinted by permission of the American University Journal of Gender, Social Policy & the Law.

Minnesota Program Development, Inc., The Duluth Model, Domestic Abuse Intervention Project, Power and Control Wheel. Reprinted with permission.

Mitchell, Darren and Susan B. Carbon, *Firearms and Domestic Violence: A Primer for Judges,* 39(2) Ct. Rev.: J. Am. Judges Ass'n (2002). Reprinted by permission of the American Judges Association.

Mullen, Paul E. and Michele Pathe, *Stalking,* 29 Crime & Justice 273 (2002). Copyright © 2002 University of Chicago Press. Reprinted by permission of the University of Chicago Press.

Napoli, Lisa, *Tolling the Statute of Limitations for Survivors of Domestic Violence Who Wish to Recover Civil Damages Against Their Abusers,* 5 Circles BU. W. J. L. & Soc. Pol'y 53 (1997). Copyright ©1997. Reprinted by permission.

New York City Mayor's Office to Combat Domestic Violence, Anti-domestic violence poster, Fall 2013. Reprinted by permission of the Mayor's Office of Legal Counsel.

Nessel, Lori A., *"Willful Blindness" to Gender-Based Violence Abroad: United States' Implementation of Article Three of the United Nations Convention Against Torture*, 89 MINN. L. REV. 71 (2004). Copyright © 2004 Minnesota Law Review. All rights reserved. Reprinted by permission.

New York Society for the Prevention of Cruelty to Children, The George Sim Johnson Archives, Photograph of Mary Ellen (taken upon her rescue, April 1874). Reprinted with permission of the New York Society for the Prevention of Cruelty to Children.

Nutter, Karen, Note: *Domestic Violence in the Lives of Women With Disabilities: No (Accessible) Shelter From the Storm*, 13 S. CAL. REV. L. & WOMEN'S STUD. 329 (2004). Reprinted with permission of the author.

Orloff, Leslye E. and Janice V. Kaguyutan, *Offering a Helping Hand: Legal Protections for Battered Immigrant Women: A History of Legislative Responses*, 10 AM. U.J. GENDER SOC. POL'Y & L. 95 (2001). Copyright © 2001 American University Journal of Gender, Social Policy and Law. Reprinted with permission.

Ptacek, James, BATTERED WOMEN IN THE COURTROOM: THE POWER OF JUDICIAL RESPONSES 50 (1999). (Boston: Northeastern University Press, 1999) Copyright © 1999 by James Ptacek. Reprinted by permission of University Press of New England.

———, "Judicial Responses That Empower Battered Women" Wheel, from BATTERED WOMEN IN THE COURTROOM: THE POWER OF JUDICIAL RESPONSES 176 (1999). Copyright © 1999 by James Ptacek. Reprinted by permission of University Press of New England.

Raphael, Jody, *Battering Through the Lens of Class*, 11 AM. U.J. GENDER SOC. POL'Y & L. 367 (2003). Copyright © 2003 American University Journal of Gender, Social Policy and Law. Reprinted with permission.

Rosa, Janice, *The Judge as Community First Responder: Because ACE's High is a Losing Hand*, (19)(2) SYNERGY 16 (Spring 2016) Copyright © 2016, National Council of Juvenile and Family Court Judges. Reprinted by permission.

Ritcheske, Kathryn A., Note: *Liability of Non-Indian Batterers in Indian Country: A Jurisdictional Analysis*, 14 TEX. J. WOMEN & L. 201 (2005). Copyright © 2005 Texas Journal of Women and the Law. Reprinted with permission.

Rivera, Jenny, *Intimate Partner Violence Strategies: Models for Community Participation*, 50 ME. L. REV. 283 (1998). Copyright © 1998 Maine Law Review. Reprinted with permission.

Sta. Ana, Andrew and Stephanie Nilva, *Teen Victims of Intimate Partner Violence*, in LAWYER'S MANUAL ON DOMESTIC VIOLENCE: REPRESENTING THE VICTIM, 6TH ED. 254 (Mary Rothwell Davis, Dorchen A. Leidholdt and Charlotte A. Watson, eds. 2015). Copyright © 2015. Reprinted by permission.

Stamm, Simeon, Note: *Intimate Partner Violence in the Military: Securing our Country, Starting with the Home*, 47 Fam. Ct. Rev. 321 (April 2009). Copyright © 2009. Reprinted by permission.

Stapel, Sharon and Virginia H. Goggin, *Lesbian, Gay, Bisexual, Transgender and Queer Victims of Intimate Partner Violence* in Lawyer's Manual on Domestic Violence: Representing the Victim, 6th Ed. 241 (Mary Rothwell Davis, Dorchen A. Leidholdt and Charlotte A. Watson, eds. 2015) Copyright © 2015. Reprinted by permission.

Stoever, Jane K., *Transforming Domestic Violence Representation*, 101 Ky. L. J. 483 (2012). Copyright © 2012. Reprinted by permission of the Kentucky Law Journal and the author.

Trost, Caroline T., Note: *Chilling Child Abuse Reporting: Rethinking the CAPTA Amendments*, 51 Vand. L. Rev. 183 (1998). Copyright © 1998. Reprinted with permission of the Vanderbilt Law Review.

Tuerkheimer, Deborah, *The Next Innocence Project: Shaken Baby Syndrome and the Criminal Courts*, 87 Wash. U. L. Rev. 1 (2009). Copyright © 2009. Reprinted by permission.

Ventrell, Martin, *Evolution of the Dependency Component of Juvenile Court*, 4 Juvenile & Fam. Ct. J. (1998). Copyright © 1998. Reprinted by permission of the National Council of Juvenile and Family Court Judges.

Ventura, Lois A. and Gabrielle Davis, *Domestic Violence: Court Case Conviction and Recidivism*, 11(2) Violence Against Women 255 (2005). Copyright © 2005 by Sage Publications, Inc. Reprinted by permission of Sage Publications, Inc.

Ver Steegh, Nancy, *Differentiating Types of Domestic Violence: Implications for Child Custody*, 65 La. L. Rev. 1379 (2005). Copyright © 2005 Louisiana Law Review. Reprinted by permission.

———, *Yes, No, and Maybe: Informed Decision Making About Divorce Mediation in the Presence of Domestic Violence*, 9 Wm. & Mary J. Women & L. 145 (2003). Copyright © 2003 by the William and Mary Journal of Women and the Law. Reprinted by permission.

Wagage, Suraji R., *When Consequences Are Life and Death: Pretrial Dentention for Domestic Violence Offenders*, 7 Drexel L. Rev. 195 (Fall 2014) Copyright © 2014. Reprinted by permission.

Waits, Kathleen, *The Criminal Justice System's Response to Battering: Understanding the Problem, Forging the Solutions*, 60 Wash. L. Rev. 267 (1985). Copyright © 1985. Reprinted with permission.

Wetendorf, Diane, *Representing Victims of Police-Perpetrated Domestic Violence*, 16(2) Family Law Forum (Fall 2007). Copyright © 2007, New Mexico State Bar, Family Law Section. Reprinted by permission.

Winick, Bruce, *Applying the Law Therapeutically in Domestic Violence Cases*, 69 UMKC L. Rev. 33 (2000). Copyright © 2000. Reprinted by permission of the UMKC Law Review.

Wood, Sarah M., Note: *Queer Theory, Feminism, and the Law: VAWA's Unfinished Business: The Immigrant Women Who Fall Through the Cracks*, 11 Duke J. Gender L. & Pol'y 141 (2004). Copyright © 2004. Reprinted by permission of Duke University School of Law.

Woodhouse, Barbara Bennett, *Sex, Lies and Dissipation: The Discourse of Fault in a No-Fault Era*, 82 Geo. L.J. 2525 (1994). Reprinted with permission of the publisher, Georgetown Law Journal © 1994.

Wriggins, Jennifer, *Interspousal Tort Immunity and Insurance "Family Member Exclusions": Shared Assumptions, Relational and Liberal Feminist Challenges*, 17 Wis. Women's L.J. 251 (2002). Copyright © 2002 by The Board of Regents of the University of Wisconsin System. Reprinted by permission of the Wisconsin Women's Law Journal.

Wright, Nancy, *Voice for the Voiceless: The Case for Adopting the 'Domestic Abuse Syndrome' for Self Defense Purposes for All Victims of Domestic Violence Who Kill Their Abusers*, 4 Crim. L. Brief 76 (Spring 2009). Copyright © 2009. Reprinted by permission.

Zorza, Joan, *The UCCJEA: What Is It and How Does It Affect Battered Women in Child-Custody Disputes?*, 27 Fordham Urb. L.J. 909 (2000). Copyright © 2000. Reprinted by permission of the Fordham Urban Law Journal.

# Preface

In the 10 years since the first edition of *Domestic Violence: Law, Policy and Practice* was published, much has changed in the legal community. The subject is firmly entrenched in the upper-level law school curriculum around the country. The Violence Against Women Act has been reauthorized and strengthened repeatedly and through it money has been awarded for legal and judicial training, victim services and police programs. Despite the fact the United States Supreme Court has determined that the Second Amendment permits an individual the right to bear arms, sound, reasonable restrictions on the rights of convicted batterers to keep guns have been upheld—again and again. There has been improved understanding of the impact of domestic violence on minority communities. It has become easier to divorce an abusive spouse with the nationwide implementation of no-fault divorce statutes, New York being the last to change. The definition of "intimate partner" has been expanded and gays now have a constitutional right to marry—everywhere in the country. As a result, more victims of domestic violence are able to seek protection from abusive partners in courts. All of this portends well for the fight to end the scourge of domestic violence.

But domestic violence continues to be an international problem of seemingly insurmountable proportions. It is a major public safety issue; a legal and human rights issue; a criminal justice problem and a dark stain on society; all of it to the detriment of women, who continue to be the vast majority of its victims.

This topic remains a highly emotional one, and I have attempted as best I can, as I attempted in the first edition, to present it in as neutral a manner as possible. In each of the more than 15 years that I have taught this topic to upper-level students at New York Law School, I have struggled in choosing the right words to convey what I mean. My concern for neutrality carries over from my professional role as a judge, where for nearly 20 years I presided in a specialized domestic violence court in New York state, where I had multiple duties. I was charged with protecting the safety of victims, upholding the constitutional rights of the accused and requiring accountability from those convicted of domestic violence crimes. It was a place where victory was measured in small increments. I could not wave a magic wand and end the violence; but I could give women the chance to escape a terrible cycle of physical, emotional and economic oppression while signaling to those convicted of the violence that society would no longer accept what was once the norm.

To be sure, to present the topic of domestic violence in a *neutral* way does not mean I condone it, nor does it mean that I do not feel compassion and concern for those who suffer from it. Neutrality does not mean I think both victim and perpetrator share "blame" for the occurrence. Domestic violence is criminal conduct. It is the result of a conscious choice made by one party to an intimate relationship to engage in dangerous, hurtful and highly inappropriate conduct against the other to gain or maintain power and control. My neutrality reflects the recognition that we live in a society which enjoys a healthy and vigorous legal system, of which I am a part, and reflects my effort to approach the topic as an academic, not an advocate, to encourage critical thinking about how our society addresses domestic violence.

This book is written in the traditional casebook style, although I have drastically cut the contents from the first edition. The cases, law review excerpts, government studies and statutory examples are shorter and more succinctly on point. We now live in an era of Internet messages and Twitter feeds. Attention spans are shorter and information delivery faster and those of us in academia must bow to that reality. In an effort to show the intersection between domestic violence and other areas of study I have included articles about the subject from journals of medicine, social science, psychology and even economics. There are notes and questions at the end of each chapter that will encourage lively (hopefully) class discussion. Faculty adapters are urged to supplement the materials with cases, newspaper articles and information unique to the local community. The topics have been expanded in this edition to include more about stalking, particularly on the Internet and with the use of new technologies such as GPS. It also contains sections on domestic violence in the international community, as well among those in law enforcement and the military. There is a new focus on domestic violence among the transgendered and among the elderly. The United States Supreme Court has issued a number of opinions in recent years about the constitutionality of keeping guns out of the hands of convicted batterers. The late Justice Scalia's original-intent judicial philosophy has altered the evidentiary landscape and new cases about testimonial-versus-non-testimonial statements have been issued by the high court. These cases seem to come up often in domestic violence situations, as its victims are sometimes unwilling to cooperate with law enforcement in convicting their abusers, thus forcing prosecutors to introduce other proof at trial. Judges have begun allowing service dogs in the courtroom to calm litigants at trial in domestic violence cases. These topics are also included. At the beginning of each chapter is a small box outlining what students should glean from it.

Students taking this course and using this book may follow one of many career paths. In my experience, many students want to become advocates for battered women. Often, they are the most attentive and outspoken, rightfully eager to demand that the law be more receptive and creative in protecting women from intimate partner abuse. Future prosecutors populate the course. There has been much discourse of late as to whether concepts like "mandatory arrest," and "victimless prosecution," are of value in fighting domestic violence, or whether they improperly wrest control from the victim who needs to be empowered in order to move on with her life. This topic has made for interesting classroom discussion in recent years. Those who intend to join District Attorneys' offices need to understand the limitations of the criminal law in ending family violence and how far they can legally and ethically "push the envelope" in prosecuting it. Students who hope to become defense lawyers tend to be greatly outnumbered in these classes by future victims' advocates and young D.A.'s. Yet their concern that the pendulum has swung too far, and that a mere allegation of domestic violence is tantamount to guilt, is a valid one. Due process is a precious right that must be protected, even for a man facing domestic violence charges. For students hoping to enter family or matrimonial law, this book provides a basic entry point on how these topics intersect with domestic violence.

One look at the text demonstrates that domestic violence permeates every legal discipline; thus there are chapters on criminal law, federal law, family law, civil law and matrimonial law. There is a chapter on child and elder abuse and another on how the justice system addresses intimate partner violence. There is an immigration chapter and another on domestic violence among various societal groups.

Finally, there is the issue of terminology. It has become acceptable to refer to those who have suffered domestic violence as "survivors" rather than "victims." The survivor label signifies strength and resilience and self-empowerment, and certainly those who have endured domestic violence have all of those traits. Nonetheless, one can survive an accident, an illness or bad luck. Something bad *happens* to a survivor who makes it through to the other side. Domestic violence does not just "happen." A perpetrator chooses to engage in it, thus victimizing another. And tragically, as homicide figures demonstrate every day, some victims do not survive.

Diane Kiesel<br>
New York, New York<br>
July 2017

# Domestic Violence

# Chapter 1

# Introduction

---

> **CONSIDER AS YOU READ THE INTRODUCTION**
> 1. The 1,000-year history of domestic violence
> 2. How domestic violence has been addressed in law, literature, religion, social science and the press
> 3. The prevalence of domestic violence in modern society
> 4. The evolution of domestic violence from social and cultural acceptance to a criminal act

*You cannot have a conversation about human rights and human dignity without talking about the right of every woman on this planet to be free from violence and free from fear.*

—Vice President Joseph R. Biden, author of the Violence Against Women Act, April 2, 2013[1]

On the peaceful, bucolic west shore of Michigan's Lake St. Claire lies a burial site dating back to 800 A.D. In 1936, an archeological team from the University of Michigan unearthed a cemetery with the human remains of 370 individuals from 145 burials. Among the dead were 15 females of reproductive age and four young males with multiple head wounds in various stages of healing. The injuries ranged from small circular depressions on the faces and skulls of the deceased to large, and ultimately fatal, fractures.[2]

Archeologists re-examined the old remains in the 1990s and made a new and startling observation as to the cause of death of the young victims: domestic violence. The hypothesis was supported by the four-to-one ratio of female-to-male head injuries; a number with "statistical significance."[3] Researchers noted that the "high frequency of injured females in the 21–25 year age group presents an exception to the general

---

1. Office of the Vice President of the United States, *1 is 2 Many: Twenty Years Fighting Violence Against Women and Girls* 2 (September 2014).
2. Richard G. Wilkinson & Karen M. Van Wagenen, *Violence Against Women: Prehistoric Skeletal Evidence From Michigan*, 18(2) Midcontinental J. Archeology 190–91 (Fall 1993).
3. *Id.* at 193.

relationship between age and injury . . . and may provide evidence for a peak period of violence directed at women . . . ."[4]

One disturbing description involved the skeletal remains of a female who died when she would have been about 20. Researchers observed the woman had a "displaced maxilla and nasal septum and a series of bony ridges or wrinkles in the maxillae and superior lacrimals, immediately lateral to the nasal bones on each side."[5] This forensic evidence strongly suggests that in life, the young woman suffered one or more blows to the face.

The archeologists considered, but rejected, other causes of death. "Female fracture victims are relatively uncommon in the literature dealing with prehistoric populations," they wrote. They discounted the possibility of death by warfare because: (1) too few of the male skeletons exhibited injuries; (2) there were no signs of weaponry imbedded in the bones, and (3) no scalps appeared to have been taken. Moreover, death by raids or warfare would not have resulted in so many *healed* head wounds.[6]

Twelve centuries later, the tragedy of domestic violence played out on the front pages of newspapers around the world as disabled Olympic running hero Oscar Pistorius was charged with the shooting death of his girlfriend, Reeva Steenkamp. On Valentine's Day 2013, in his gated, guarded home in South Africa, Pistorius fired four shots with a 9mm pistol into his bathroom door, claiming he feared a burglar was hiding inside. Instead, it was his girlfriend. After a seven-month trial, he was convicted of negligent homicide, which in South Africa may be appealed by the prosecution, which had sought a murder conviction. Pistorius initially was sentenced to five years in prison. Had he been convicted of pre-meditated murder, he faced a minimum of 25 years behind bars.[7] On appeal, the South African Supreme Court of Appeal ruled his actions constituted murder. Prosecutors sought a minimum 15-year sentence, but the 29-year-old fallen hero was sentenced to six years.[8]

The Pistorius love story had everything. He was a handsome double-amputee runner who overcame unimaginable adversity to compete in the Olympic and Paralympic Games, running on blades instead of legs. His blonde girlfriend was smart and stunning; a model, reality television star and law school graduate.[9] The headlines said it all: "A Nation Reels as a Star Runner is Charged in Girlfriend's Death." It harkened back to the story that riveted Americans a generation ago when

---

4. *Id.* at 194.
5. *Id.* at 195.
6. *Id.* at 197, 199–200.
7. Gerald Imray, *Oscar Pistorius' Lawyers Fight Back, Challenge Judge's Decision to Allow Prosecution to Appeal,* Associated Press, February 24, 2015, http://www.usnews.com/news/world/articles/2015/02/24/pistorius-lawyers-to-challenge-appeal-ruling, accessed March 4, 2015.
8. Norimitsu Onishi, *Pistorius Sentenced to Six Years in Girlfriend's 2013 Murder,* N.Y. Times, July 7, 2016.
9. BBC News, Africa: *Oscar Pistorius Given Five Years for Reeva Steenkamp Death,* October 24, 2014, http://www.bbc.com/news/world-africa-29700457, accessed March 4, 2015.

handsome football hero turned Hollywood star O.J. Simpson stood trial for the murder of his beautiful wife, Nicole Brown Simpson, and her friend, Ronald Goldman.[10]

Pistorius and Steenkamp were the "it" couple on the South African celebrity circuit, just as O.J. and his wife had been in their day in Southern California. Their televised trials were watched by millions around the world and provided windows into a domestic life where all was not what it seemed. Pistorius tearfully testified at his bail hearing that he heard an intruder in his home. He said he thought Steenkamp was in bed. He claimed he grabbed his gun, screamed out to the burglar and ordered Steenkamp to call the police. Hearing movement in the bathroom he fired into the closed door, accidentally killing his girlfriend.[11] Prosecutors dismissed the story as absurd. They asserted Pistorius was jealous of a former boyfriend with whom Steenkamp remained close, and the couple violently fought over it.[12]

Domestic violence is neither rare, nor limited to the rich and famous, although it is *their* stories that end up on the front pages. In fact, three women a day are murdered by their husbands or boyfriends. In 2014, the *Huffington Post* reported that close to 2,000 women a year were killed by male partners during the prior decade. Women were far more likely than men to be killed by a lover of the opposite sex — 34 percent for women as compared to just 2.5 percent for men.[13] Women are also disproportionately the victims of intimate partner murder-suicides; in 96 percent of the cases, the murder victims are females. The weapon of choice is almost always a firearm; in 92 percent of these killings a gun is involved.[14] Between 2003 and 2012 there were 656 domestic violence homicides in New York; 30.5 percent of those victims were killed with guns.[15]

---

10. Lydia Polgreen, *A Nation Reels as a Star Runner is Charged in Girlfriend's Death,* N.Y. TIMES, February 15, 2013.

11. Lydia Polgreen, *In Affidavit at Bail Hearing, Track Star Denies He Intended to Kill Girlfriend,* N.Y. TIMES, February 20, 2013.

12. Julian Rademeyer & Corky Siemaszko, *Judge Tells Oscar Pistorius to Maintain Composure as he Weeps While Statement on Mistaking Reeva Steenkamp with Burglar in Bathroom is Read,* DAILY NEWS (New York), February 20, 2013, www.nydailynews.com/news/world/blade-runner-speaks-article-1.1267882, accessed July 19, 2016.

13. Melissa Jeltsen & Alissa Scheller, *At Least a Third of All Women Murdered in the U.S. are Killed by Male Partners,* HUFFINGTON POST, October 9, 2014, http://www.huffingtonpost.com/2014/10/09/men-killing-women-domestic_n_5927140.html, accessed May 3, 2015.

14. *American Roulette: Murder-Suicide in the United States,* May 2006, Violence Policy Center, Washington, DC, www.vpc.org, accessed May 3, 2015.

15. U.S. Department of Justice, Federal Bureau of Investigation, Supplemental Homicide Data, 2003–2012.

There were 158 women killed by their intimate partners in Texas in 2015.[16] Between July 2014 and June 2015, there were 42 domestic violence fatalities in Maryland.[17] In Ohio in 2013 there were 38 domestic violence fatalities.[18]

The National Center for Victims of Crime reports that 1.4 million people are stalked each year, slightly more than one million of them women and 370,000 of them men. The vast majority of victims of stalking—83 percent—never report the crime to law enforcement.[19]

Domestic violence extracts a tremendous financial toll on the United States' economy. Collectively, victims of domestic violence lose eight million days of paid work each year, costing $4.1 billion for health care and another $1.8 billion due to lost productivity or wages.[20]

Domestic violence is present everywhere. Around the globe, 35 percent of all women have suffered domestic violence.[21] Nor is it just a heterosexual problem; 21 percent of homosexual men and 35 percent of lesbian women have experienced domestic violence, as have 35 percent of transgendered persons.[22] It strikes in big cities and in the hinterlands; 51 percent of the homicides in North Dakota between 1992 and 2012 involved domestic violence.[23] Domestic violence is a problem on Indian reservations in the United States. A 2008 study by the Center for Disease Control found that 39 percent of Native American women were victims of intimate partner violence.[24]

As former New York Chief Judge Jonathan Lippman has said:

> For most of human history, acts of domestic violence have been minimized, denied, swept under the carpet, and hidden behind closed doors. It is only in the last few decades that our criminal justice system and our

---

16. Honoring Texas Victims; Family Violence Fatalities in 2015, 3. Tcfv.org/resource-center/honoring-texas/victims, accessed March 4, 2017.

17. Maryland Network Against Domestic Violence Annual Report: 2015-2016, mnadv.org/_mnadvweb/wp-content/uploads/2011/07/final-report.pdf, accessed March 4, 2017.

18. NCADV: Domestic Violence in Ohio, http://www.ncadv.org/files/Ohio.pdf, accessed March 4, 2017.

19. Women and Gender Advocacy Center, *Stalking Statistics*, Colorado State University, http://www.wgac.colostate.edu/stalking-statistics, accessed May 4, 2015.

20. Family Violence Prevention Fund, *Domestic, Sexual & Other Violence; Domestic Violence is a Serious, Widespread Social Problem in America: The Facts,* Tarrant.tex.networkofcare.org/dv/library/article.aspx?id=1048, accessed July 18, 2016.

21. Violence Against Women: Fact Sheet No. 239, November, 2014, World Health Organization, http://www.who.int/mediacentre/factsheets/fs239/en/, accessed May 5, 2015.

22. J.D. Glass, *Two Studies Refute Myth That Intimate-Partner Violence is not an LGBT Crisis,* advocate.com, http://www.advocate.com/crime/2014/09/04/2-studies-prove-domestic-violence-lgbt-issue, accessed May 5, 2015.

23. *2013 Report of the North Dakota DV Fatality Review Commission,* December 31, 2013, http://attorneygeneral.nd.gov/sites/ag/files/documents/DVFR-Report-2013.pdf, accessed May 4, 2015.

24. Futures Without Violence, *The Facts on Violence Against American Indian/Alaskan Native Women,* https://www.futureswithoutviolence.org/userfiles/file/violence%20against%20AI%20An%20women%20Fact%20sheet.pdf, accessed May 5, 2015.

culture have recognized domestic violence for the insidious and destructive crime that it is.[25]

References to domestic violence go back to Greek mythology where Zeus, the King of the Gods, struck his Queen, Hera, to keep her in line.[26] Fifteenth century theologian, Friar Cherubino, taught in his *Rules of Marriage* that a husband should not only scold his wife but "bully and terrify her. And if this still doesn't work, take up a stick and beat her soundly."[27]

William Shakespeare treated domestic violence as fodder for comedy in *The Taming of the Shrew,* where Petruchio's treatment of Katharina, his strong-willed wife, included his promise to change her "from a wild Kate to a Kate conformable as other household Kates."[28] He accomplishes this by knocking down a priest at their wedding; beating a family servant in front of her; throwing the dinner and the dishes around the kitchen (because the meat was burned) and refusing to allow her to eat or sleep. He tells her he will not buy her any new clothes until her disposition improves and he attempts to drive her crazy by insisting the moon is out when the sun is shining. Ultimately, his pattern of physical and psychological abuse succeeds in breaking her spirit as witnessed by her speech:

> Thy husband is thy lord, thy life, thy keeper,
> Thy head, thy sovereign; one that cares for thee,
> . . . .
> And craves no other tribute at thy hands
> But love, fair looks and true obedience. . . .[29]

One of the world's most famous operas, Georges Bizet's *Carmen,* first performed in 1875, involves dating violence. When the opera's namesake rejects her security-guard boyfriend for a handsome bullfighter, the boyfriend stabs her to death.[30] The musical play, *Carousel,* by Rodgers and Hammerstein charmed mid-20th century

---

25. Foreword by Hon. Jonathan Lippman, *xxv* in Mary Rothwell Davis, Dorchen A. Leidholdt and Charlotte Watson, eds., LAWYER'S MANUAL ON DOMESTIC VIOLENCE; REPRESENTING THE VICTIM (6th ed. New York Appellate Division, First Dept., 2015).

26. In *The Iliad,* Homer's epic tale of the Trojan War, the goddess Thetis, mother of the warrior, Achilles, travels to Olympus to beg Zeus, king of the gods, to grant victory to the Trojans until the Greeks properly honor her son. Thetis strokes Zeus' knee as they talk. Zeus tells her to cut it out because his jealous wife, Hera [who happens to be a supporter of the Greeks], is watching. When Hera confronts Zeus about what she has seen, he shows himself to be a batterer. He tells her to sit down and be quiet, or else none of the Gods in Olympus would be able to save her from his wrath.

Meanwhile, Hera's own son, Hephaistos, chimes in, aligning himself with his father. "Better make up to Father or he'll start thundering and shake our feast to bits. Dear mother, patience, hold your tongue, no matter how upset you are. I would not see you battered dearest." THE ILIAD 27–30 (Robert Fitzgerald trans., 1974).

27. DONNA FERRATO, LIVING WITH THE ENEMY 17 (1991).

28. WILLIAM SHAKESPEARE, THE TAMING OF THE SHREW, Act II, scene I, 228 THE COMPLETE WORKS OF WILLIAM SHAKESPEARE (1936).

29. *Id.* Act V, Scene ii.

30. Carmen, Opera by Bizet, https://www.britannica.com/topic/carmen-opera-by-Bizet, accessed March 4, 2017.

audiences with its romantic love story and inspirational songs. But the underlying book told a dark tale of domestic violence. The hero, Billy Bigelow, is an angry, failed carnival barker who strikes, berates and bullies his wife, Julie. He suffers a violent death in a robbery gone wrong, leaving Julie a pregnant widow. He is given a chance to redeem himself in the afterlife. He returns to Earth and tries to give a gift of a star to the child he never met and when she refuses it, he slaps her.[31] While it may be easy to dismiss Shakespeare as ancient theater, or Rogers and Hammerstein as Broadway fantasy, their creations reflected attitudes about the rights of men to control their wives that have permeated popular culture, legislation and law.

Meanwhile, domestic violence has remained a staple of popular fiction. In his novel that became an Oscar-winning Hollywood movie, *L.A. Confidential,* writer James Ellroy's main character, Police Officer Wendell White, was cuffed to a bed as a child by his sadistic father who beat his mother to death with a tire iron while the boy watched. "He screamed his throat raw; he stayed cuffed in the room with the body: a week, no water, delirious—he watched his mother rot. A truant officer found him...." The father is convicted of manslaughter, does his prison time, and disappears. White vows to kill him. His efforts to find his paroled father prove futile, however, so he avenges his mother's death by roughing up wife beaters on the way to the station house.[32]

In Alfred Hitchcock's 1963 horror movie, *The Birds,* actor Rod Taylor plays a San Francisco lawyer whose client was acquitted of shooting his wife six times. When asked by a family member why the man shot her, Taylor's character responds: "He was watching a ball game, she changed the channel."[33]

Violence to women shows up throughout literature. Fictional detective Sherlock Holmes picked up its scent in Sir Arthur Conan Doyle's short story, "The Adventure of the Cardboard Box." In it, Holmes investigates a package delivered to an elderly woman that contains two severed human ears, one from a man, the other from a woman. The ears belong to the old lady's sister and her lover, both murdered by the cheating sister's husband. As Holmes reads the husband's confession to his ever-present sidekick, Dr. Watson, he asks: "What is the meaning of it, Watson? ... What object is served by this circle of misery and violence and fear? ... There is the great standing perennial problem to which human reason is as far from an answer as ever."[34]

The question asked by the fictional Holmes would be asked by women's advocates in the 1970s who, after taking on the nation's rape crisis, turned their attention to domestic violence. They demanded that police officers protect battered wives and that lawmakers change statutes to protect battered women.

---

31. Rodgers & Hammerstein, Our Shows, *Carousel,* www.rnh.com/show/20, accessed May 17, 2015.
32. James Ellroy, L.A. Confidential 27 (1990).
33. Alfred J. Hitchcock, *The Birds* (Alfred J. Hitchcock Productions, 1963).
34. *See* Lisa Surridge, Bleak Houses: Marital Violence in Victorian Fiction 216–17 (2005).

## I. In Harm's Way — The Dynamic of Domestic Violence

In 1979, Rutgers University faculty member and psychologist Lenore E. Walker published her seminal work, *The Battered Woman,* which revolutionized the way we look at domestic violence. Through her research and writing she changed the once-accepted view that women contributed to their own victimization and then masochistically remained in abusive relationships.

Her trail-blazing work provided a definition of the battered woman and a framework for future studies that emphasized to legislators, policy makers and law enforcement officials what the emerging advocacy community already knew: domestic violence was dangerous, deadly and pervasive. And women were its primary victims. Dr. Walker defined a battered woman as one in an intimate relationship with a man who controls her through physical or psychological abuse. Dr. Walker's theorized that to qualify as a true battering relationship, a victim had to suffer through abuse more than once. "If it occurs a second time, and she remains in the situation, she is defined as a battered woman."[35]

Dr. Walker coined the phrase "learned helplessness," to explain why a woman would remain with an intimate partner who abused her. It was the fact women remained with abusers that confounded judges, police and policy makers, and caused them not to take complaints of domestic violence seriously.

Extrapolating from experiments done on animals, which showed if caged dogs were repeatedly subjected to electric shocks without reason or a means of escape, they became incapable of saving themselves, even if the opportunity became available, Professor Walker developed her theory about battered women. This so-called "learned helplessness," renders a woman, like the animals in the experiments, unable to see a way out of their abuse, rendering them submissive and helpless.[36]

Dr. Walker determined that women acquired their "learned helplessness" through a three-phase cycle of domestic violence. The first phase is the tension-building phase during which minor battering incidents occur and the victim accepts the "blame" for the abuse. Perhaps she really *did* burn the toast. By accepting responsibility, Walker writes, the victim maintains some level of control. It allows her to believe that if her behavior improved, or outside tensions faced by the abuser diminished, then the abuser would stop hurting her.[37]

As the incidents intensify, the second phase of the cycle begins, which is the acute battering incident. The batterer's brutality increases, his possessiveness and jealousy

---

35. Lenore E. Walker, The Battered Woman xv (1979). Over time, domestic violence has been documented in gay and lesbian relationships as well, which is discussed in the following chapter.
36. *Id.* at 47–50.
37. *Id.* at 56–57.

crescendo, and the victim suffers a severe beating. Walker found the victim sometimes provoked this second-phase incident to get the inevitable over with. This is when the police are often called—although Walker found that only 10 percent of the victims had sought police intervention.[38]

The final phase is the "honeymoon phase," in which the batterer professes profound sorrow for his abusive acts, promises to change and showers his victim with presents, attention and what appears to be love. And then, of course, the cycle begins anew.[39]

In the years since Walker published her ground-breaking work, some professionals posited theories indicating women were not passively helpless but engaged in a variety of coping strategies.

## Mary Ann Dutton, Symposium on Domestic Violence: *Understanding Women's Responses to Domestic Violence: A Redefinition of Battered Woman Syndrome*
21 Hofstra L. Rev. 1191, 1225–1231 (1993)

. . . .

All women exposed to violence and abuse in their intimate relationships do not respond similarly, contradicting the mistaken assumption that there exists a singular "battered woman profile." Like other trauma victims, battered women differ in the type and severity of their psychological reactions to violence and abuse, as well as in their strategies for responding to violence and abuse.

. . . .

Battered women utilize an impressive array of strategies for attempting to stop the violence, strategies which include efforts to escape, avoid, and protect themselves and others from the violence and abuse of their intimate partners. These strategies have been categorized as personal, informal, and formal.

Personal strategies include complying with the batterer's demands (or anticipated demands) in order to "keep the peace," attempting to talk with the batterer about stopping the violence, temporarily escaping from the batterer's presence, hiding or disguising one's appearance, physically resisting the batterer's violence or abuse, defending oneself against the batterer's violence, and using the children. Informal strategies include soliciting help from neighbors, family, and friends in efforts to escape or hide from the batterer, or asking others to intervene in an attempt to get the batterer to stop his violence and abuse. Formal strategies may include efforts that involve the legal system, such as calling the police, seeking protective orders, initiating contact with a state attorney's office and/or participating in criminal prosecution against the batterer, or seeking help from a divorce lawyer. Formal strategies may also include

---

38. *Id.* at 59-62, 64. Walker writes: "In Kansas City in 1976, a study found that over 80 percent of all women murdered by their men had called for police help one to five times prior to being killed." *Id.* at 64.

39. *Id.* at 65–70.

efforts that involve shelters for battered women, or specialized domestic violence programs offered by women's support groups, health and mental health professionals, or members of the clergy.

No single strategy has been identified as clearly and consistently the most effective means to end battering. In one study, the most common strategy employed by those surveyed, talking with friends, was cited as being most effective by only 14% of the study sample. When determining the consequences of using a specific strategy, one needs to consider not only the strategy's effectiveness in ending violence, but also its propensity for increasing violence and the concomitant levels of danger in both the short and long run. . . .

Among strategies cited, perhaps those most commonly expected of the battered woman by the layperson include calling the police and leaving the home. However, empirical studies have shown that most battered women do not call police for help with domestic violence. When battered women do call the police, the consequences may not always be positive. In one study, only 39% of battered women who called the police reported the outcome to be fairly effective, and almost 20% indicated that calling the police resulted in increased violence by the batterer, a rate higher than any other formal help-seeking strategy. In a study of sheltered battered women who had previously called the police, an arrest was made only 28% of the time, even though 60% of the women reported having asked to have their partners arrested.

Most battered women do not use battered women's shelters. One study reported 74% of battered women had never used a shelter, although it should be understood that many battered women's shelters must turn away women due to lack of space. Another study found that among women who eventually sought shelter support, 70% delayed doing so for more than a year, in spite of their experience of severe or life-threatening abuse. When battered women do seek shelter support, they often return to the abusive relationship following their stay. Overall, studies of shelter residents have found that approximately half of all women return to their relationship upon leaving the shelter, although that number appears to decrease the longer the shelter stay. . . . Another consideration to interpreting the data regarding the decision to return to an abusive partner is the number of prior occasions on which the woman has attempted to leave, since women who eventually leave an abusive partner often report numerous prior efforts to do so. . . .

———

The National Coalition Against Domestic Violence defines battering as:

> [T]he willful intimidation, physical assault, battery, sexual assault, and/or other abusive behavior as part of systematic pattern of power and control perpetrated by one intimate partner against another.[40]

---

40. National Coalition Against Domestic Violence, *What is Domestic Violence?* www.ncadv.org/need-help/what-is-domestic-violence, accessed March 4, 2017.

In their book, CHANGING VIOLENT MEN 4 (2000), Professors Rebecca Emerson Dobash and Russell P. Dobash insist that "an exchange of slaps or minor blows at some time," while hardly acceptable, does not constitute the type of systemic cycle of violence described by Lenore Walker and considered by most authorities to be part of a pattern of using violence to dominate and control. It is the ever-escalating and continuing violence in an intimate relationship that requires the intervention of law enforcement, the courts and child protective services to stop the violence and protect the abused family members.

Another article, although written long ago, is still relevant in its explanation for what motivates a batterer.

## Kathleen Waits, *The Criminal Justice System's Response to Battering: Understanding the Problem, Forging the Solutions*
### 60 WASH. L. REV. 267 (1985)

... At first blush, the batterer's actions seem as inexplicable as the victim's. Like hers, his behavior springs from a complex web of personal and social factors. Indeed, the batterer is in many ways a tragic mirror image of his wife. He, too, is a strong traditionalist when it comes to sex roles. He believes that a man should be "the master" of the house, and that it is the woman's job to satisfy all his needs and wants. Additionally, he often believes that he has the right to use violence against her in order to enforce his will. While the abuser has a tremendous need to dominate and control his wife, and may project a macho exterior, inside he is filled with doubt and insecurity. He may resort to battering because physical intimidation is the only way he is confident of getting his way with her. His low self-esteem manifests itself in other ways as well. He is usually emotionally isolated from everyone except his wife, and he is therefore extremely dependent on her. His dependence and fears of inadequacy typically translate into pathological jealousy. He must have sole possession of her, and not only to the exclusion of other men. He also tries to drive away her relatives and friends, and is even jealous of their own children. Unfortunately, the battered woman usually yields to his demands and isolates herself from all outsiders, because she perceives his possessiveness as a sign of love rather than insecurity or just because she wants to keep the peace.

The batterer's jealousy is but one symptom of his infantile personality. Like a child, he is both impulsive and easily frustrated. This combination of traits makes him dangerous: when he feels frustrated, he impulsively responds by lashing out at his wife. In dealing with her, he has not learned to separate his emotions from his actions.

Although the abuser may give some signs of his impulsiveness and low frustration threshold in other aspects of his life, he is rarely violent in other relationships. In fact, with people outside the family, he is generally charming. He is violent at home because he has a bully's "sure winner" mentality. He beats his wife because he can win a physical battle with her, and because he can get away with it, as long as society does not intervene. In contrast, he doesn't beat his boss or his male acquaintances not because he is never angry at them, but because the price of such behavior is too great.

Even with this information about the batterer's psyche, his conduct may still mystify us. If he loves his wife—and he will loudly proclaim that he does—how can he justify his brutality toward her? Even if he believes that "slapping her around" is all right, how can he possibly rationalize beating her senseless or threatening her with a weapon? The answer consists of two related elements. First, battering is learned behavior which, for all his remorse, does "work" for the batterer. Second, the batterer is able to delude himself about his abuse and thereby avoid taking responsibility for it.

One piece of evidence pointing to battering as a learned response is that most batterers were themselves beaten as children or saw their fathers beat their mothers, or both. Batterers learn from their violent homes that hurting loved ones is normal, and that strong family members, be they parents or husbands, have the right to use force against weak ones. Once they become adults and start beating their wives, batterers learn (although usually not consciously) that battering "helps" them deal with their problems. Their childhood experiences leave abusers with a bottomless rage, and battering temporarily dissipates their anger. By using physical violence rather than other methods, the abuser may also succeed in getting what he wants from his wife, whether it is having her stay with him and cutting herself off from other people, or handing over her earnings to him, or preparing dinner the way he likes it.

For all the "rewards" that their violence brings, batterers could not live with themselves and maintain their patterns without a variety of self-deceptive psychological tricks. Denial and minimization are crucial defense mechanisms for the batterer, because they allow him to evade accountability for his actions.

By refusing to believe that any problem exists, he thus feels no need to change. Even when confronted with undeniable evidence of his violence, he will minimize its severity. Batterers are also quite remarkable in their ability to externalize and rationalize their acts. The most obvious and frequent target of blame is, of course, his victim. Naturally, his blame feeds right into her guilt. Consequently, they *both* blame *her* for the battering. Even when the batterer does not blame his wife, he attributes his behavior to other forces. He will say that he cannot control his temper, even though his actions belie this excuse.

Perhaps the most common excuse, and one worthy of special mention, is alcohol. Many batterers have serious problems with alcohol and/or drug abuse. Both the couple and outsiders often think that the husband's alcoholism creates the violence. This explanation is unconvincing: beatings typically occur not only when the alcoholic batterer is drunk but also when he is sober. His drinking may well facilitate his battering, but it is *not* its cause.

The false link between alcoholism and battering is only one example of the tendency to confuse the triggers for battering with its underlying causes. In the violent household, the events that arouse the abuser's anger and "lead to" a beating are almost always trivial. A batterer has learned how to set himself off. Once he has reached the point in the battering cycle when he is ready to abuse the woman severely, the victim's behavior becomes largely irrelevant. He attributes negative motives to her behavior and reacts violently to whatever she does.

So far, we have painted a monstrous picture of the abusive man. Does this mean that batterers are all hopelessly ill individuals who can never change? The experts say no; they believe that many batterers can be helped. Most batterers are not antisocial personalities who feel no remorse for their violence. Ironically, it is the very depth of their guilt that causes them to search so vigorously for external explanations for their behavior. In his own way, an abuser usually does love his wife and children, and it may ultimately be possible to use this love to effectuate changes in his actions.

Such changes will not occur, however, until the wife beater takes responsibility for the battering *and* is punished for his behavior. Unhappily, third parties often encourage his continued denial of responsibility. Every time someone takes the attitude that "she brought it on herself," or "I know it's the alcohol which made you do it," or "I'll let you off this time if you promise never to do it again," that person only succeeds in making it easier for the batterer to persist in his behavior.

. . . .

---

Karla DiGirolomo, former director of Unity House, a Troy, New York, battered woman's shelter, put it succinctly to a group of judges at a family violence training program: "Domestic violence is tremendously beneficial behavior for the abuser."[41] Sociologist Richard Gelles who has researched and written about family violence for decades has said: "A man beats up his wife because he can."[42]

To facilitate understanding of the nature and dynamic of domestic violence, battered women who were abused by their male partners and were receiving services at the Duluth, Minnesota Domestic Abuse Intervention Project devised the "Power and Control Wheel," depicting the methods batterers use to achieve their ends.

As described by the wheel's creators: "The Power and Control Wheel represents the lived experience of women who live with a man who beats them. It does not attempt to give a broad understanding of all violence in the home or community but instead offers a more precise explanation of the tactics men use to batter women. Battering is one form of domestic or intimate partner violence. It is characterized by the pattern of actions that an individual uses to intentionally control or dominate his intimate

---

41. Speech by Karla DiGirolomo at the New York State Judicial Institute, White Plains, N.Y. (May 3, 2005). DiGirolamo is the former executive director of the New York State Governor's Commission on Domestic Violence and was herself a battered woman. She once told a reporter her first husband broke her nose while she was pregnant but she told everyone she had fallen. "I felt worthless, totally to blame, responsible for my husband's actions. I kept thinking, 'If I had done something different, things would improve.'" Jane O'Reilly, *Wife Beating: The Silent Crime*, Time Magazine, Sept. 5, 1983, at 23, 24.

42. *Wife Beating: The Silent Crime*, Time Magazine, at 26.

partner. That is why the words 'power and control' are in the center of the wheel. A batterer systematically uses threats, intimidation, and coercion to instill fear in his partner. These behaviors are the spokes of the wheel."

Although domestic violence cuts across all socio-economic, ethnic, racial and cultural lines, one study suggests it is more prevalent when economic stress is present. In September 2004, the National Institute of Justice reported: "Women in couples with low incomes, high debt, and male job instability are more likely to be victimized by

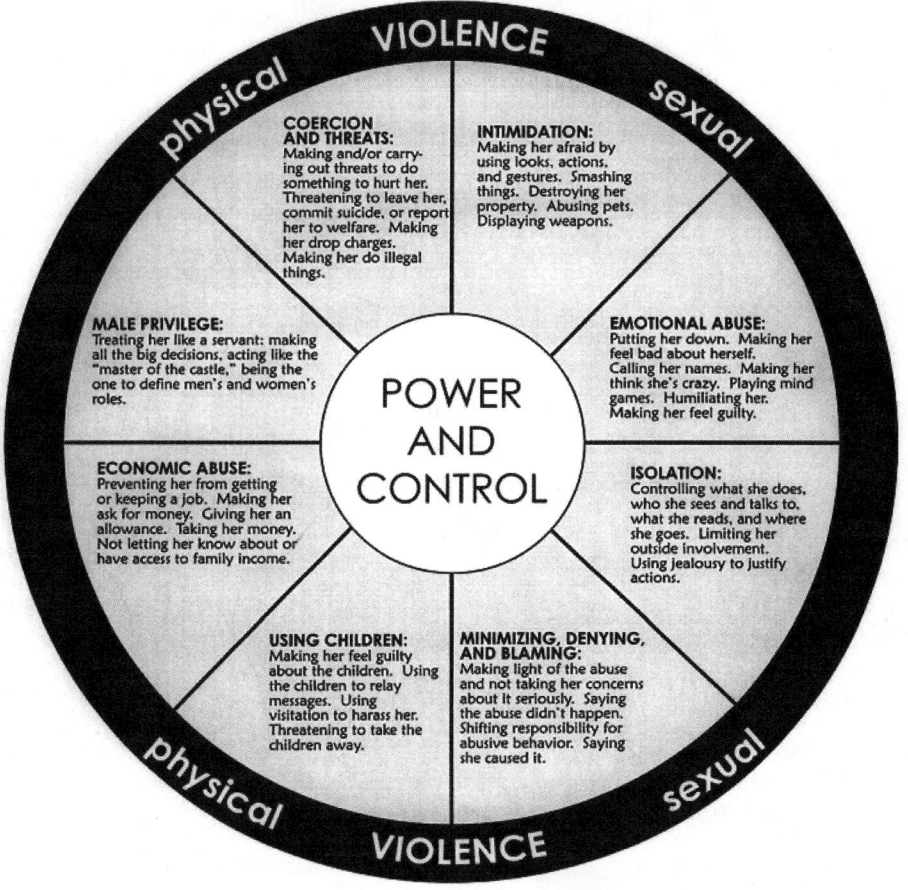

their intimate partner than women in couples that are more financially well off, and the seriousness of their victimizations are likely to be greater as well."[43]

Some scholars suggest there is a need for updated models for the dynamic of domestic violence. Professor Jane Stoever of the law school at the University of California at Irvine suggests there is more to the battering dynamic than Dr. Walker's Cycle of Violence theory or the Duluth Power and Control Wheel.

## Jane K. Stoever, *Transforming Domestic Violence Representation*
101 Ky. L.J. 483 (2012)

. . . .

1. Battered Woman Syndrome and the Cycle of Violence.

An early model for understanding domestic violence-and the source of the Cycle of Violence model-was Lenore Walker's theory of Battered Woman Syndrome, introduced in her 1979 book, The Battered Woman, and further developed in her 1984 book, The Battered Woman Syndrome.

. . . .

Walker's theory of Battered Woman Syndrome predominated during the 1980s and 1990s and continues to be employed in criminal cases. Abused women who have killed their abusers use this theory as a self-defense argument in showing that they, the victim-defendants, were in imminent danger. The theory has also been used by prosecutors to explain witness recantation, inconsistencies in a victim's testimony, or loyalty to an abusive partner.

Contrary to Walker's early theories, research now shows that women who experience abuse are typically active survivors who are vigorously engaged in seeking help as well as terminating and ultimately surviving violence. . . . A survivor's apparent helplessness may instead reflect the reality of insufficient resources, such as the inadequacy of police responsiveness and protection, limited childcare

---

43. Michael L. Benson & Greer L. Fox, "*Economic Stress, Community Context and Intimate Violence: An Application and Extension of Social Disorganization Theory, Final Report*" www.ncjrs.org/pdffiles1/nij/grants/193434.pdf, accessed July 18, 2016. To reach their conclusions, the authors compiled data from the National Survey of Families and Households, which is a representative sample of American households, which was later merged with data from the 1990 U.S. Census. A first series of interviews were conducted with 13,007 adult respondents who represented 9,637 households. Face-to-face interviews were conducted with a randomly-selected primary respondent from each home. Questionnaires were given to the primary respondent's spouse or cohabiting partner. Those interviews were completed in 1988. The process was repeated in 1994 with the survivors of the first survey.

Far less scientific methods of seeking answers to questions about domestic violence have been undertaken. In one magazine interview, rock star and reality television personality Ozzy Osbourne described his battering behavior during his first marriage: "I was a raving drug addict and an alcoholic and about as much good as an ashtray on a motor bike. My father was abusive to my mom, and I would slap my first wife around because I thought that's what men have to do." Ross Johnson, interviewing Osbourne in, *What I've Learned*, Esquire, Jan. 2005, at 64.

options, or scarce financial and legal support. There is also high risk to one's safety in leaving, and behaviors that could be interpreted as helplessness may actually be the result of a survivor's common-sense evaluation of the potential for violent response.

. . . .

2. The Power and Control Wheel.

. . . .

Currently, the Power and Control Wheel is the most prevalent model used for teaching about domestic violence. It is featured prominently in Domestic Violence Law textbooks for law students. Professors teaching domestic violence clinics also routinely use the Power and Control Wheel when teaching about the dynamics of relationships with domestic violence. It is employed in training judges, law enforcement personnel, attorneys, social workers, advocates, and other professionals about domestic violence. Advocates, counselors, and social workers use the Wheel as part of their counseling of battered women and when conducting community outreach. Some lawyers use the Wheel with their clients to explain that abuse extends beyond physical violence, and lawyers may ask their clients to identify the opposing party's behavior on the Wheel. The Wheel is also used in batterer treatment programs as a way for abusive individuals to recognize their own use of power and control in intimate partner relationships. . . .

However, for all the benefits of the Power and Control Wheel, it provides only a partial education. After decades of legal reform and action in the courts, the question "Why doesn't she leave?" and variations of this question-including "Why does she stay?" and "Why don't they just get up and leave?" and why does the petitioner "not leave if the abuse is so bad"—are still being asked, and the Wheel does not provide ready answers. . . . The Wheel does not tell us what the survivor does in response to the violence; therefore, it lacks a robust sense of the survivor as agent.

. . . .

B. The Stages of Change Model

The Stages of Change Model, which is also referred to as the Transtheoretical Model of Behavior Change, addresses many of the issues that the traditional models leave unanswered. . . . In describing the process of how domestic violence survivors seek an end to relationship violence, the Stages of Change Model includes five distinct stages that emerged from researchers' interviews with women who were abused by intimate partners: (1) pre-contemplation, (2) contemplation, (3) preparation, (4) action, and (5) maintenance. The Model posits that progress through the stages occurs in a cyclical and dynamic sequence rather than in a linear fashion, and it is expected that people experiencing domestic violence will revisit earlier stages as they move toward "maintenance." . . .

In pre-contemplation, someone who is experiencing abuse is not aware of the extent of the problem, minimizes or denies the abuse, and has no intention of making any changes. At this point, the abused individual accepts both the abuser's definition of the situation and the blame for the violence and may respond defensively to any suggestion that there is a problem or need for change.... To move from pre-contemplation to contemplation, an abuse survivor will need to come to his or her own definition of the situation and recognize that he or she is not responsible for the abusive partner's violence.

In the second stage, contemplation, the violence has typically escalated and become more severe, and the survivor begins to name the violence against him or her. The survivor thinks about the possibility of making changes, begins to build social, emotional, and financial support, and may make an initial attempt to leave the relationship. However, the survivor also experiences ambivalence and vacillates between feeling troubled and unconcerned as he or she considers whether the relationship can continue unchanged. The survivor considers the advantages and disadvantages of taking action, such as leaving or seeking a court order, in the face of obstacles and externalities, but may be overwhelmed by the consideration of emotional and economic factors.

In the preparation stage, the survivor seeks out others to re-conceptualize the problem and to determine possible actions. The survivor has heightened awareness of the abuse and attempts to determine the best course of action for his or her situation and a plan to carry it out. In the preparation or "determination" stage, survivors may set aside money, call an abuse hotline, investigate safe housing options, gather information about legal and advocacy help, and reconnect with people from whom they have been isolated.

In the fourth stage, action, the survivor is motivated to change the environment and carries out strategies to protect herself or himself and children from future violence, such as going into a shelter, seeking a protection order, or having relatives, friends, or the police intervene to keep the abusive partner at bay.

Finally, the maintenance stage involves a continuation of actions by the survivor that are necessary to sustain the desired change. There are substantial obstacles to remaining in this stage, including an overwhelming fear of impending danger and separation assault; symptoms of post-traumatic stress disorder, including hypervigilance and flashbacks; and mourning the loss of positive aspects of the relationship, including the emotional connection and financial security. Despite these challenges, many abuse survivors do succeed in carrying out strategies through the action and maintenance stages to successfully end relationship violence.

. . . .

Any model regarding domestic violence can be critiqued as being an overly simplistic, reductive construct to apply to a complex situation.... Rather than limiting how we think about domestic violence, ideally the Stages of Change Model can spark new realizations and surface aspects of ending violence that have heretofore been unrecognized by attorneys. In particular, the Stages of Change Model engages the survivor, reflects the survivor's assessment of his or her situation and process of surviving abuse, and prioritizes the survivor's voice, while the dominant models of the Power and Control Wheel and Cycle of Violence fail to offer such insights.

. . . .

---

Change never comes easily. To those still asking the question: "Why Does She Stay?" Professor Sarah Buel, an attorney and one-time battered wife, has at least 50 answers. She is a clinical professor of law at the Sandra Day O'Connor College of Law, Arizona State University.

## Sarah M. Buel, *Fifty Obstacles to Leaving, A.K.A., Why Abuse Victims Stay*

28 Colo. Law. 19 (October 1999)

*It is when my head makes contact with the wall that I freeze, though his fist is coming toward me again. I have not yet taken behavior psychology and do not know that some animals flee when attacked. It would take me yet another year of planning, forgiving, calling, reaching for help, before I could leave. The Legal Aid Office told me there was a three-year wait, even for a divorce when you were getting hit. All the private attorneys wanted at least $10,000 for a retainer since he threatened to contest custody. The judge told me I needed to help keep the family together. The priest told me to diversify the menu and stop cooking so much Italian food. Only the older, male marriage counselor told me that it was dangerous for me to stay. So, now I'm a single Mom, without child support and trying to go to night school and keep my job. But with minimum wage, I can't seem to pay both day care and the rent, so sometimes I think about going back, just to make sure my son has enough to eat. It hurts more to watch him eat macaroni with ketchup for the third night, than it ever did to get beaten.*[44]

That abuse victims make many courageous efforts to flee the violence is too often overlooked in the process of judging them for *now* being with the batterer. Regardless of whether I am providing training to legal, law enforcement, medical, mental health, or social service professionals, when people find out I also have been a victim of abuse, some inevitably ask, "How is it you could get a full scholarship to Harvard Law School, but you stayed with a violent husband for three years?" This question has been fueled by those who believe that remaining with a batterer indicates stupidity, masochism, or codependence. Far from being accurate, such labels prove dangerous to victims because they tend to absolve batterers of responsibility for their crimes.

Domestic violence represents serious violent crime: this is *not* codependence, for there is nothing the victim can do to stop the violence, nor is there anything she does to deserve the abuse. Domestic violence victims stay for many valid reasons that must be understood by lawyers, judges, and the legal community if they are to stem the tide of homicides, assaults, and other abusive behavior. The following represents a

---

44. [n1] From the author's personal journal, 1977.

much-abbreviated, alphabetical list of some reasons I have either witnessed among the thousands of victims with whom I have worked over the past twenty-two years — or that reflect my own experiences.

**1. Advocate:** When the victim lacks a tenacious advocate, she often feels intimated, discouraged, and, ultimately, hopeless about being able to navigate the complex legal and social service systems needed to escape the batterer. Some well-intentioned advocates engage in dangerous victim-blaming with the assumption that there is *something* about the victim's behavior or past that precipitates the violence. . . .

**2. Batterer:** If the batterer is wealthy, a politician, famous, a popular athlete, or otherwise a powerful player in his community, he can generally afford to hire private counsel and pressure the decision makers to view his case with leniency. Some wealthy abusers not only hire private detectives to stalk, terrorize, and frivolously sue their partners, but the advocates who assist them as well.

**3. Believes Threats:** The victim believes the batterer's threats to kill her and the children if she attempts to leave. It is estimated that a battered woman is 75 percent more likely to be murdered when she tries to flee or had fled, than when she stays. . . .

**4. Children's Best Interest:** Some victims believe it is in the children's best interest to have both parents in the home, particularly if the abuser does not physically assault the children. The victims — as well as their counsel and the judge — may be unaware of the deleterious impact on children witnessing domestic violence, *whether or not they have been beaten by the abuser.*

**5. Children's Pressure:** Children's pressure on the abused parent can be quite compelling, especially with those batterers capable of manipulating the children into begging the victim to "just let Daddy come home!" Children are often torn, for they want the violence to stop, but they also want the family to stay together.

**6. Cultural and Racial Defenses:** Cultural defenses may be cited by offenders, victims and other community members who may not be cognizant that, while domestic violence occurs among all races, no excuse, save self-defense, ever justifies the abuse. Some believe stereotypes about their own or other cultures, but the bottom line is that domestic violence is against the law, regardless of what behavior is permitted in the "home" country or what is tolerated here in various communities. . . .

**7. Denial:** Some victims are in denial about the danger, instead believing that if they could be better partners, the abuse would stop. . . .

**8. Disabled:** Victims who are disabled or physically challenged face great obstacles, not only in gaining access to the court and social services, but because they also are more likely to be isolated from basic information about existing resources.

**9. Elderly:** Elderly domestic violence victims tend to hold traditional beliefs about marriage. They believe they must stay, even in the face of physical abuse. Others are dependent on the batterer for care, and are more afraid of being placed in a nursing home than of remaining with a perpetrator whose abusive patterns they can more readily predict.

**10. Excuses:** The victim may believe the abuser's excuses to justify the violence, often blaming job stress or substance abuse, in part because she sees no one holding the offender responsible for his crimes. Domestic violence is *not caused by* stress or substance abuse, although they can exacerbate the problem....

**11. Family Pressure:** Family pressure is exerted by those who either believe that there is no excuse for leaving a marriage or have been duped into denial by the batterer's charismatic behavior.

**12. Fear of Retaliation:** Victims cite fear of retaliation as a key obstacle to leaving. The acute trauma to which battered women are exposed induces a terror justified by the abuser's behavior....

**13. Fear of Losing Child Custody:** Fear of losing child custody can immobilize even the most determined abuse victim. Since batterers know that nothing will devastate the victim more than seeing her children endangered, they frequently use the threat of obtaining custody to exact agreements to their liking....

**14. Financial Abuse:** Financial abuse is a common tactic of abusers, although it may take many different forms, depending on the couple's socioeconomic status. The batterer may control estate planning and access to all financial records, as well as make all money decisions. Victims report being forced to sign false tax returns or take part in other unlawful financial transactions. Victims also may be convinced that they are incapable of managing their finances or that they will face prison terms for their part in perpetrating a fraud if they tell someone.

**15. Financial Despair:** Financial despair quickly takes hold when the victim realizes that she cannot provide for her children without the batterer's assistance....

**16. Gratitude:** The victim may feel gratitude toward the batterer because he has helped support and raise her children from a previous relationship. Additionally, a victim who is overweight or has mental health, medical, or other serious problems often appreciates that the abuser professes his love, despite the victim's many perceived faults. Many batterers tell a victim, "You are so lucky I put up with you; certainly nobody else would," fueling the victim's low self-esteem and reinforcing her belief that she deserves no better than an abusive partner.

**17. Guilt:** Guilt is common among victims whose batterers have convinced them that, but for the victims' incompetent and faulty behavior, the violence would not occur....

**18. Homelessness:** Homeless abuse victims face increased danger, as they must find ways of meeting basic survival needs of shelter, food, and clothing while attempting to elude their batterers. . . .

**19. Hope for the Violence to Cease:** A victim's hope for the violence to cease is typically fueled by the batterer's promises of change; pleas from the children; clergy members' admonishments to pray more; the family's advice to save the relationship; and other well-intentioned, but dangerously misguided counsel. . . .

**20. Isolation:** Victim isolation is typical, although the process of cutting the victim off from family, friends, and colleagues usually happens gradually, as the batterer uses manipulation to assure compliance. Isolating the victim increases the likelihood that she will stay, for without safety plans and reality checks, it will be more difficult for her to assess her level of danger.

**21. Keeping the Family Together:** Wanting to keep the family together motivates many abuse victims to stay, believing that it is in their children's best interest to have their father or male role model in the family. . . .

**22. Illiterate Victims:** Illiterate victims may be forced to rely on the literate batterer for everyday survival . . . Without the ability to read job applications, notices regarding rights, and other important correspondence, illiterate victims are more likely to remain unaware of resources.

**23. Incarcerated or Newly Released Abuse Victims:** Such victims often have few, if any, support systems to assist them with re-entry to the community. Parole officers may require that they return home if that appears to be a stable environment without determining whether a batterer is present. . . .

**24. Law Enforcement Officer:** If the perpetrator is a law enforcement officer, the victim may fear, or may have had past experiences of, other officers refusing to assist her. . . .

**25. Lesbian and Gay Victims:** Such victims may feel silenced if disclosing their sexual orientation (to qualify for the protective order) could result in their losing job, family, and home. . . .

**26. Low Self-Esteem:** Victims with low self-esteem may believe they deserve no better than the abuse they receive, especially if they have grown up in families with domestic violence. . . .

**27. Love:** A victim may say she still loves the perpetrator, although she definitely wants the violence to stop . . .

**28. Mediation:** Mediation, required in some jurisdictions even with evidence of domestic violence, puts the victim in the dangerous position of incurring the batterer's wrath for simply disclosing the extent of the violence. Given the power imbalance, it is puzzling that anyone could assume an equitable resolution would result. . . .

**29. Medical Problems:** Medical problems, including being HIV- or AIDS-positive, may mean that the victim must remain with the batterer to obtain medical services. If the abuser's insurance covers the family or he is the victim's primary caretaker, the victim knows that without adequate care, her *life* is also imperiled....

**30. Mentally Ill Victims:** Such victims face negative societal stereotypes in addition to the batterer's taunts that the victim is crazy and nobody will believe anything she says....

**31. Mentally Retarded or Developmentally Delayed Victims:** These victims are particularly vulnerable to the batterer's manipulation and are likely to be dependent on him for basic survival....

**32. Military:** If the victim or the perpetrator is in the military, an effective intervention is largely dependent on the commander's response regardless of the Uniform Code of Military Justice ("UCMJ"), its provisions for a military protective order, and the availability of assistance from the Family Advocacy Programs. Many commanders believe that it is more important to salvage the soldier's military career than to ensure the victim's safety....

**33. No Place to Go:** Victims with no place to go understand the bleak reality that affordable housing is at a premium in virtually every community in this country, including our Tribal Nations. Often, there is *no shelter space,* particularly for victims with children, or the shelter policy dictates that victims must quit their jobs to be admitted....

**34. No Job Skills:** Victims with no job skills usually have no choice but to work for employers paying minimum wage, with few, if any, medical and other benefits. Thus, any medical emergency or need for prolonged care ... often forces the victim to return to welfare to obtain Medicaid coverage—or to return to the batterer.

**35. No Knowledge of Options:** Victims with no knowledge of options and resources logically assume that none exist....

**36. Past Criminal Records:** Victims with a past criminal record are often still on probation or parole, making them vulnerable to the batterer's threats to comply with all of his demands or be sent back to prison....

**37. Previously Abused Victims:** Sometimes previously abused victims believe the batterer's accusation. "See, this is what you drive your men to do!" If the victim truly believes this, she will find it easier to blame herself for the abuse.

**38. Prior Negative Court Experience:** Those victims with prior negative experiences with the court system may have no reason to believe that they will be accorded the respect and safety considerations so desperately needed.

**39. Promises of Change:** The batterer's promises of change may be easy to believe because he sounds so sincere, swearing that he will never drink or hit the victim again. In part because she wants to desperately to give credence to such assertions, the victim may give him another chance, even if such promises have been made repeatedly in the past. . . .

**40. Religious Beliefs and Misguided Teachings:** Such beliefs may lead victims to think they have to tolerate the abuse to show their adherence to the faith. Particularly if the batterer is a priest, rabbi, minister, or other high-level member of the faith community, the victim can feel intimidated by the status of the batterer and the likelihood that the congregation will support the perpetrator.

**41. Rural Victims:** Such victims may be more isolated and simply unable to access services due to lack of transportation, or the needed programs are distant and unable to provide outreach. . . .

**42. Safer to Stay:** Assessing that it is safer to stay may be accurate when the victim can keep an eye on the batterer, sensing when he is about to become violent and, to the extent possible, taking action to protect herself and her children. . . .

**43. Students:** Students in junior or senior high school, college, or graduate university studies may fear that not only may their requests for help be stymied by untrained administrators, but worse, that their student records would reflect their involvement with unsavory criminals. . . .

**44. Shame and Embarrassment:** Shame and embarrassment about the abuse may prevent the victim from disclosing it or may cause her to deny that any problem exists when questioned by well-intentioned friends, family, co-workers, or professionals.

**45. Stockholm Syndrome:** The victim may experience the Stockholm Syndrome[45] and bond with the abuser, making her more sympathetic to the batterer's claims of needing her to help him.

**46. Substance Abuse or Alcohol:** Either the victim's or offender's substance abuse or alcoholism may inhibit seeking help, often for fear that the children will be removed, in spite of efforts to get treatment. . . .

**47. Teens:** Teens, especially those pregnant and who are already parents, are at greater risk for abuse in their relationships than any other age group, yet are the least likely to either report or seek adult intervention . . .

**48. Transportation:** For many victims, a lack of transportation condemns them to a choice between welfare and returning to their abusers. Without a car to access child care and a job, such victims may express hopelessness about avoiding further harm or dire poverty. . . .

---

45. [n41] . . . The Stockholm Syndrome refers to the phenomenon that occurred when a Stockholm bank was robbed and several hostages were taken. After several days in captivity with the robbers, all of the hostages—both men and women—had bonded with their captors, sympathizing with their cause and fully excusing their crimes.

**49. Unaware that Abuse is a Criminal Offense:** The victim may be unaware that the abuse constitutes a criminal offense, often because family, friends, and community professionals minimize the crimes. They apply the double standard of downplaying domestic violence offenses, while taking seriously the same crimes committed against strangers.

**50. Undocumented Victims:** Undocumented victims facing complex immigration problems if they leave are often forced to stay with the batterers who may control their Immigration and Naturalization Service ("INS") status. . . .

Conclusion

As attorneys and judges, we should be celebrating that domestic violence victims are increasingly turning to the courts for protection from abuse, for they offer us the opportunity to use the law to save lives. We must acknowledge that many obstacles exist for the victims fleeing such terror. Additionally, we can interrupt the intergenerational cycle of learned abuse by teaching our children that the community will not tolerate the violence. "We have a choice," a Virginia juvenile and family court judge says. "Will our children have homes they can run to or homes they must run away from?"

. . . .

## II. A Man's Home Is His Castle

Historically, women have been at the mercy of men. In the Bible, men were ordained the dominant sex. Thus, God instructed Eve, ". . . thy desire *shall be* to thy husband, and he shall rule over thee."[46] Harsh physical punishment was meted out for wives who got out of line. In the Old Testament, if a man suspected his wife of adultery, he was required to bring her to God's tent where a priest would make her drink bitter water.[47] Adulterous wives could also be stoned and impaled by swords.[48]

Women fared no better under early Roman civil law, despite the reputation of the Roman Empire for advanced government. Under Roman law wives could be beaten or killed for marital infractions.[49] Constantine I, the first Christian emperor of Rome, killed his wife, Fausta, by boiling her in a pot of water over a slow flame.[50] Martin Luther, father of the Protestant Reformation in 1517, professed he was happily married to his wife, Katherine, a former nun. Yet his method for maintaining that marital

---

46. Genesis 3:16.
47. Numbers 5:11–27.
48. Ezekiel 16:38–40.
49. Virginia H. Murray, *A Comparative Survey of the Historic Civil, Common, and American Indian Tribal Responses to Domestic Violence*, 23 Okla. City U. L. Rev. 433, 441 (1998).
50. Terry Davidson, *Wife Beating: A Recurring Phenomenon Throughout History*, in Battered Women: A Psychosociological Study of Domestic Violence 11 (Maria Roy ed. 1977).

bliss could have been hardly pleasant from her perspective: "when Katie gets saucy, she gets nothing but a box on the ear."[51]

Long before the remark "a man's home is his castle," was uttered by the Earl of Chatham, during the reign of King George III of England, men have ruled not only their own homes, and by implication what took place in privacy there, but have also been the dominant gender in the business, professional, political and religious worlds. As a result, the manner in which they have dealt with the women in their lives has been unassailable.

Whether allegorical or not, the expression "the rule of thumb," survives to this day. What it means is that at some point in our jurisprudence, a man was free to whip his wife, provided the instrument he used was "no larger than his thumb." Regardless of its origin, it was the phrase used by the court in *State v. Oliver,* 70 N.C. 44, 60 (1874).

## A. Slow Change

By 1775, in England, the practice of "moderate correction," by a husband of his wife through physical force was beginning to be frowned upon.[52] Nonetheless, William Blackstone wrote: "the lower rank of people, who were always fond of the old common law, still claim and exert their ancient privilege: and the courts of law will still permit a husband to restrain a wife of her liberty, in case of any gross misbehavior."[53]

In practice, Blackstone's description of the level of legal tolerance for domestic violence was accurate. In *People v. Winters,* 2 Parker Cr. Rep. 10 (1823), Circuit Judge Walworth determined that while a husband could not beat his wife for just any reason, he could do so to defend himself, and to protect others against her. In *Winters,* as a husband attempted to beat his child, his wife jumped in to protect her offspring "and made such a noise as to alarm the neighborhood." As a result, the husband struck her in the head and severely injured her. A jury rendered a verdict of "not guilty," which was upheld by the circuit court.

In the early case of *State v. Oliver,* 70 N.C. 44 (1874), a husband, unhappy over the quality of his breakfast, "threw the coffee cup and pot into the corner of the room and went out; while out he cut two switches, brought them in, and, throwing them on the floor, told his wife ... that he was going to whip her, for she and her d—d mother had aggravated him near to death." *Id.* at 45.

Thus, he struck her "as hard as he could" four times, at which point witnesses intervened. The wife was left bruised for two weeks; the husband was arrested, tried,

---

51. *Id.* at 13–14.
52. *Id.* at 14–15.
53. WILLIAM BLACKSTONE, COMMENTARIES ON THE LAWS OF ENGLAND 444–45 (7th ed. 1775). Blackstone explained that the "old law" allowing for "moderate correction" of a wife by a husband existed because he was answerable for her foibles. But, under the law, the husband was only allowed to do it to the extent he could correct "his apprentices or children." *Id.* at 444.

found guilty and fined $10. In upholding the conviction on appeal, the Court was not so much offended by the beating, as by the intensity of it. "[I]n order to preserve the sanctity of the domestic circle, the Courts will not listen to trivial complaints. If no permanent injury has been inflicted, nor malice, cruelty nor dangerous violence shown by the husband, it is better to draw the curtain, shut out the public gaze and leave the parties to forget and forgive." *Id.* As far as the law was concerned, the curtain would remain drawn another 100 years. Meanwhile, in the United States, the Supreme Court of Mississippi continued to accept the right of a husband to moderately chastise his wife, as described below.

## Bradley v. State
Supreme Court of Mississippi
1 Miss. 156 (1824)

Hon. Powhattan Ellis

. . . .

The only question submitted for the consideration of the court, is, whether a husband can commit an assault and battery upon the body of his wife. . . . I am fully persuaded, from the examination I have made, an unlimited licence of this kind cannot be sanctioned, either upon principles of law or humanity. It is true, according to the old law, the husband might give his wife moderate correction, because he is answerable for her misbehaviour; hence it was thought reasonable, to intrust him, with a power, necessary to restrain the indiscretions of one, for whose conduct he was to be made responsible. Strange, 478, 875; 1 H.P.C. 130. Sir William Blackstone says, during the reign of Charles the first, this power was much doubted.—Notwithstanding the lower orders of people still claimed and exercised it as an inherent privilege, which could not be abandoned, without entrenching upon their rightful authority, known and acknowledged from the earliest periods of the common law, down to the present day. I believe it was in a case before Mr. Justice Raymond, when the same doctrine was recognised, with proper limitations and restrictions, well suited to the condition and feelings of those, who might think proper to use a whip or rattan, no bigger than my thumb, in order to enforce the salutary restraints of domestic discipline. I think his lordship might have narrowed down the rule in such a manner, as to restrain the exercise of the right, within the compass of great moderation, without producing a destruction of the principle itself. If the defendant now before us, could shew from the record in this case, he confined himself within reasonable bounds, when he thought proper to chastise his wife, we would deliberate long before an affirmance of the judgment.

The indictment charges the defendant with having made an assault upon one Lydia Bradley, and then and there did beat, bruise, &c.—and the jury have found the defendant guilty, which never could have taken place, if the evidence supported either the second or third pleas of the accused. . . . However abhorrent to the feelings of every member of the bench, must be the exercise of this remnant of feudal authority, to inflict pain and suffering, when all the finer feelings of the heart should be warmed into devotion, by our most affectionate regards, yet every principle of public policy and expediency, in reference to the domestic relations, would seem to require, the establishment of the rule we have laid down, in order to prevent the deplorable spectacle of the exhibition of similar cases in our courts of justice.—Family broils and dissentions cannot be investigated before the tribunals of the country, without casting a shade over the character of those who are unfortunately engaged in the controversy. To screen from public reproach those who may be thus unhappily situated, let the husband be permitted to exercise the right of moderate chastisement, in cases of great emergency, and use salutary restraints in every case of misbehaviour, without being subjected to vexatious prosecutions, resulting in the mutual discredit and shame of all parties concerned. Judgment affirmed.

---

In the United States, wife beating was sanctioned well into the 19th century. It was not until 1871 in the case of *Fulgham v. State,* 46 Ala. 143, that the court ruled:

> [A] rod which may be drawn through the wedding ring is not now deemed necessary to teach the wife her duty and subjection to the husband. The husband is therefore not justified or allowed by law to use such a weapon, or any other, for her moderate correction. The wife is not to be considered as the husband's slave. And the privilege, ancient though it be, to beat her with a stick, to pull her hair, choke her, spit in her face or kick her about the floor, or to inflict upon her like indignities, is not now acknowledged by our law.... [54]

In New England, by the late 19th century, courts began to look unfavorably on wife beating as well. In *Commonwealth v. McAfee,* 108 Mass. 458 (1871), a Boston man was convicted of manslaughter for beating his drunken wife to death. The conviction was upheld on appeal. The Court reasoned: "Beating or striking a wife violently with the open hand is not one of the rights conferred on a husband by marriage, even if the wife be drunk or indolent. The blows being illegal, the defendant was at least guilty of manslaughter." *Id.* at 461.

Some of the impetus for a change in American attitudes towards the treatment of wives by their husbands was influenced by enlightenment philosopher John Stuart Mill (1806–1873), a staunch supporter of women's rights. His famous essay, "The Subjection of Women," was the first to focus on the sorry state of battered wives. He wrote: "Men are not required as a preliminary in marriage to prove that they are fit to be trusted with absolute power over another human being.... The vilest malefactor has some wretched woman tied to him, against whom he can commit any atrocity except killing her—and even that he can do without too much danger of legal

---

54. 46 Ala. at 146.

penalty."[55] Although Mill's essay generated debate, it failed to inspire Parliament to enact laws addressing the miserable plight of abused wives.[56]

By the late 19th century, there was a surge in divorce petitions on the ground of marital cruelty, brought mostly by battered wives. "[A]lmost a quarter of a million husbands found themselves successfully accused of matrimonial cruelty between 1867 and 1906."[57]

But because courts were dominated by men, judges often fell for the same remorseful promises of change by abusive husbands that women a century later would be criticized for believing. In the case of *English v. English,* 27 N.J. Eq. 579, 582 (1876), the wife sought to legally separate from her husband because he insisted on nightly sexual intercourse, using force if necessary, although his wife had a physical condition rendering sexual activity extremely painful. The wife's separation petition was granted in the lower court. But the New Jersey Court of Errors and Appeals, in a nine-to-five decision reversed, citing the repentant husband's many demonstrations he had changed; by writing remorseful letters, "entreaties to ministers, Christmas presents for the children, [and] promises of self-denial and forebearance." *Id.* at 734.

It was with the birth of the women's movement that the private hell of abused wives was thrust into public view. At Seneca Falls, New York, the first women's rights convention in history took place in 1848. It was organized by abolitionists Elizabeth Cady Stanton and Lucretia Mott, and signaled the beginning of the women's movement in the United States.[58] It would slowly but inexorably lead to women's suffrage, federal laws to prevent discrimination against women, abortion rights, the widespread acceptance of women into the professions, and the criminalization of domestic violence.

At Seneca Falls, a Declaration of Rights and Sentiments was written. In part, it stated: "In the covenant of marriage, she is compelled to promise obedience to her husband, he becoming, to all intents and purposes, her master — the law giving him power to deprive her of her liberty and to administer chastisement . . . ."[63]

## III. Modern Times

The anti-Vietnam War movement of the late 1960s spawned a consciousness-raising effort about the roles of women. As young people questioned the war and the male-dominated military-industrial complex that fostered it, women began to look at their societal roles.

---

55. JOHN STUART MILL, THE SUBJECTION OF WOMEN 40 (1861) (Prometheus 1986).
56. Terry Davidson, *supra,* at 16–17.
57. Robert L. Griswold, *Law, Sex, Cruelty and Divorce in Victorian America, 1840–1900,* 38(5) AM. Q. 721, 722–23 (1986).
58. SISTERHOOD IS POWERFUL: AN ANTHOLOGY OF WRITINGS FROM THE WOMEN'S LIBERATION MOVEMENT 15 (Robin Morgan ed., 1970).
63. *Id.* at 15–16.

*Behind Closed Doors* © Donna Ferrato

The 1970s harkened the birth of the modern women's movement—known then as "Women's Liberation." Early feminists coalesced around issues of violence against women, particularly rape. As late as the mid-1970s, the criminal law of rape in the United States defined it as "forcible penetration of an act of sexual intercourse on the body of a woman *not one's wife.*"[59] In addition, many states had laws requiring that women use so-called "earnest resistance" against their rapist and that an accusation of rape be corroborated by independent evidence.[60]

In 1971, the women's movement politicized rape and demanded that laws requiring corroboration be eliminated.[61] Organized events such as the January 24, 1971, New York Radical Feminists Speak Out on Rape quickly expanded to include positions in favor of working to combat all violence against women.[62]

Nonetheless, as late as 1976, the perception still existed that "wife beating is a serious and widespread problem which is ignored by society."[63] Marjory Fields, an attorney who went on to become a battered women's advocate and New York family court judge, blamed police unwillingness to arrest perpetrators of domestic violence and the

---

59. Susan Brownmiller, Against Our Will: Men, Women and Rape 380 (1975).
60. Linda A. Fairstein, Sexual Violence: Our War Against Rape 15–16, 110 (1993).
61. Brownmiller *supra*, at 390.
62. *Id.* at 405. The New York Radical Women's Manifesto included a description of the battered woman: "Her lot, her suffering and abuse is the threat that men use against all of us to keep us in line." *Id.* at 520.
63. Marjory D. Fields, *Forum for the Young Lawyer: Wife Beating: The Hidden Offense*, N.Y.L.J., April 29, 1976, at 1.

women's lack of safe shelter as the major obstacles to addressing the problem.[64] It was not until that year that the first domestic violence shelter opened in New York City.[65]

## IV. Domestic Violence as a Crime

In every neighborhood in America in the 1950s and 60s, there would be a home from which the sounds of slapping and banging, followed by a woman screaming could be heard. If the police were called, often they would go inside and take out the man of the house, who was often angry and drunk, walk him around the block, give him a stern lecture, and send him home. In many jurisdictions, a battered wife could not even file a criminal complaint against her husband for assault because domestic violence was a matter solely for the family courts.

Sick and tired of having the police and the legal system treat domestic violence as a family spat rather than as the crime it was, battered wives sued the New York Police Department for refusing to arrest assaultive husbands. They also sued petition clerks in the family court and city probation officials for impeding their access to a judicial hearing following an assault. *Bruno v. Codd,* 90 Misc. 2d 1047 (Sup. Ct. N.Y. Co. 1977). After two years of litigation, a settlement was reached that was a turning point in making public officials realize — and react — to the reality that domestic violence was a serious crime. In *Bruno,* the trial court denied the defendants' motions to dismiss. They appealed, and the Appellate Division reversed. 64 A.D.2d 582 (1st Dep't 1978). Prior to the reversal, however, the police department settled with the plaintiffs. In addition, the police department agreed to change its policies to require that officers remain with the victims at the crime scene as long as necessary to protect them from further spousal violence. The lawsuit against the court clerks and the probation department continued and was ultimately heard in the New York Court of Appeals.

### Bruno v. Codd
New York Court of Appeals

47 N.Y.2d 582 (1979)

This appeal brings before us so much of an action for declaratory and injunctive relief as was brought by 12 "battered wives" against clerks of the Family Court in New York City and officials of the New York City Department of Probation, each individually and as a defendant class representative. In a nutshell, the gravamen of their complaint is that probation and Family Court nonjudicial personnel, with the knowledge and either the tacit consent or express approval of their supervisors, engage in a pattern of conduct calculated (1) to deter battered wives from filing petitions for orders of protection against their offending husbands, (2) to block them from meaningful access

---

64. *Id.* at 4.
65. N.Y. Office for the Prevention of Domestic Violence, New York State's Response to Domestic Violence: Systems and Services Making a Difference 6 (2006).

to Family Court Judges empowered to issue temporary orders of protection, and (3) by failing to advise the wives that the defendants' proffer of counseling is voluntary, to dissuade complainants from pursuing their legal remedies.

. . . .

Special Term denied defendants' motions "to dismiss or, in the alternative, for summary judgment" (90 Misc 2d 1047). The Appellate Division reversed and dismissed the complaint, holding the dispute nonjusticiable because its resolution would inevitably entail an impermissible "invasion of executive authority" (64 AD2d 582, 583).

. . . .

In essence, the concern that plaintiffs would have us confront is simply the threshold obligation of functionaries of the entity, here the Family Court, to apprise a woman of her options with respect to mediation and to afford her prompt access to a Family Court Judge.

Also, in this connection, the fact that the overwhelming majority of documented instances of alleged departure from statutory and regulatory provisions to which plaintiffs point were at the hands of the probation personnel, formally employees of a city executive agency rather than a judicial one, does not take away from the justiciability of the controversy. For the probation service, in participating in the processing of family offense matters, does not act on its own. Rather it carries out a specified statutory obligation "to assist" the Family Court (Family Ct Act, § 252, subd [d]). Thus, court and probation employees work as a team in the implementation of the Family Court's intake procedure. Indeed, it is the rules of the court itself that spell out authorization for such details of the probation service activity as obtaining the initial description of the problem that brings a wife to court, delving into social data and other background information relevant to the family offense and informing the interviewee that she may either avail herself of the probation department's mediation and conciliation procedures or proceed at once via the petition route (see Committee Comments, McKinney's Cons Laws of NY, Book 29A, Part 1, Family Ct Act, § 823, p 710; Besharov, Practice Commentaries, McKinney's Cons Laws of NY, Book 29A, Part 1, Family Ct Act, § 252, pp 182–183; Family Ct Rules, 22 NYCRR 2508.1-2508.3). Thus, while the probation department technically may not be part of the judicial establishment, the intertwining of its activities with those of the clerks of the Family Court entails responsibilities which basically are under court control.

. . . .

These caveats in mind, we are less than convinced that any sufficiently useful purpose would be served by a plenary trial.

Among the factors that lead us to this conclusion is the disposition already arrived at in the police branch of this litigation. A primary concern voiced in plaintiffs' complaint is frequent failure of officers of the New York City Police Department to respond to requests for safeguarding made by or on behalf of a battered or threatened wife, presumably because of reluctance on the part of the police to intervene in what they reflexively characterized as "domestic disputes" rather than criminal offenses. And because 40% of all police night calls in New York City are said to involve such cases (Wife Beating: The Hidden Offense, NYLJ, April 29, 1976, p 1, col 1), this lack of police cooperation in guarding the offended wives makes Family Court processing delays critical and renders orders issued by the Family Court largely ineffective.

Negotiated with the police even before the Appellate Division handed down its decision, the consent judgment afforded the plaintiffs substantially all the relief they reasonably could expect. By its terms the police have agreed hereafter to respond swiftly to every request for protection and, as in an ordinary criminal case, to arrest the husband whenever there is reasonable cause to believe that a felony has been committed against the wife or that an order of protection or temporary order of protection has been violated. Moreover, officers are to remain at the scene of the alleged crime or violation in order to terminate or prevent the commission of further offenses and to provide the wife with other assistance. To assure that these undertakings are fulfilled, supervisory police officers are to make all necessary revisions in their disciplinary and other regulations.

It is also not without moment that an affidavit filed by Administrative Judge Joseph B. Williams of the Family Court makes it clear that his administration is dedicated to enforcing the statutes and rules in a manner consistent with the declarations sought by plaintiffs, particularly with regard to informing petitioners of the voluntariness of the conciliation option and to making Family Court Judges readily accessible to mistreated wives.

Significantly, in not a single instance did any plaintiff or affiant complain to Judge Williams, his executive officer or his chief clerk so that investigation or discipline of any offending employee could be initiated. Thus, there is no indication that, until commencement of this suit, the alleged derelictions had been brought home to those responsible for the administration of this branch of our courts.

The record also indicates that the Director of the New York City Probation Department has conceded that its employees assigned to the Family Court have to advise women who appear for intake interviews in family offense cases of their right to reject offers of mediation and to proceed directly by petition. Within three months after this suit was instituted, and perhaps in response to it, the director issued General Order 5-77 promulgating a disciplinary procedure for the processing of oral and written complaints against probation employees who fail to adhere to these mandates. In addition, to limit the incidence of misunderstanding in communicating the alternatives open to wives who receive intake interviews, the probation people now are also required to routinely provide each prospective petitioner with a printed notice advising of the availability of professional counseling services and the right to reject them and go directly to court. To reach New York City residents who are Spanish-speaking, the notice is bilingual.

Nor has there been a lack of legislative and administrative response. Since the commencement of this suit section 812 of the Family Court Act was amended to prohibit officials from discouraging or preventing any person who wishes to file a petition from having access to the court for that purpose (L 1977, ch 449, § 1; see, also, Family Ct Rules, 22 NYCRR 2508.1[c][3][4], [d], 2508.3[c][1]).

Of course, we are conscious of plaintiffs' argument that the court practices of which they complain are unallayed despite the suit. But support for that position rests solely on nonrecord references (made for the first time in their brief to us) to a limited number of incidents occurring early in 1977. Even if taken at face value, these episodes transpired soon after plaintiffs' action had been commenced and before the practical steps described above could have had any effect in a court which then was trying to cope with 20,000 pending family offense cases and was to face an intake of 9,540 new ones in 1977 (see Twenty-Third Ann Report of NY Judicial Conference, 1978, p 102). Realistically, we must also recognize that any system administered by human beings will unavoidably encounter occasions on which employees will err or be misunderstood, all the more so midst the stress and excitement that usually propels the *pro se* litigant into the legal arena.

Finally, we observe that societal concern with the underlying problem exemplified by brutality to women at the hands of their husbands must be carefully distinguished from the far narrower task committed to the Family Court—to deal with the local manifestations of this social malaise that are brought to its official attention. Except insofar as an awareness of general conditions helps put the matters at hand in perspective, only the latter can be within the scope of the suit before us.

So confined, the welcome efforts of plaintiff's counsel and the *amici* in this case have no doubt alerted, even sensitized, our courts to the full measure of their responsibilities. With no real disagreement among the parties as to the goals toward which they must now aim, with constructive monitoring of Family Court staff performance by organizations such as the *amici*, and with an appreciation of the *raison d'etre* for this suit by all courts that have been exposed to it, it could be fruitless, if not self-defeating, to go through a long and tortuous trial to no other end than the airing of what already has been made clear.

For all these reasons, and though our rationale, as indicated, in some respects differs from that of the Appellate Division, we find no reason to disturb the result it reached and therefore affirm its order, but without costs.

. . . .

---

The lawsuit galvanized the emerging women's rights movement and paved the way for the decades of activism against domestic violence. Friends of the Court briefs on behalf of the battered wives were filed by, *inter alia,* the Association of the Bar of the City of New York, Women's Survival Space, Shelter Our Sisters, The Coalition for Abused Women, New York Women Against Rape, NOW Legal Defense and Education Fund, the New York Chapter of The National Lawyers Guild and the National Conference of Black Lawyers.[66]

---

66. 47 N.Y.2d at 592 n.9.

Domestic violence became national news. In her keynote address to the first National Women's Conference in Houston in 1977, congresswoman Bella Abzug, with her familiar big hat and uncompromising defense of women, urged that the plight of battered wives be placed on the public and government agenda.[67] President Jimmy Carter convened a National Advisory Committee for Women[68] and the United States Commission on Civil Rights began a series of public hearings around the country about domestic violence. The hearing officials listened to police and policy makers, medical experts, welfare agencies and operators of shelters for battered women. They heard testimony from battered women, some of who testified anonymously out of fear of reprisals from their brutal husbands.[69]

Experts cite the 1984 Minneapolis Domestic Violence Experiment as "perhaps the most widely cited and influential criminal justice experiment in recent criminological and policy literature."[70] As part of the experiment, police officers were randomly assigned to handle misdemeanor domestic violence offenders in one of three ways: (1) arrest the suspect; (2) order one of the parties out of the residence; or (3) advise the couple. When a suspect was arrested, the recidivism rate for domestic violence offenses fell by 50 percent.[71] The results were reported in more than 300 newspapers, editorials were written about it, and all the major television networks broadcast prime-time programs or documentaries, heavily influencing public officials. Consequently, the attorney general's Task Force on Domestic Violence endorsed the study's findings and recommended that state and local police departments adopt an arrest policy for domestic abusers.[72]

In 1983, reporting that there is "no place so violent as home," *Time Magazine* published its first cover story on the subject.[73] Since then, there has been an explosion of federal law, new funding sources, women's shelters, police and judicial sensitivity, and public awareness of domestic violence as a serious social welfare concern. Much of this grew out of the first Violence Against Women Act of 1994, which authorized millions of dollars to combat crimes against women, including domestic violence, and which has been reauthorized repeatedly.

---

67. INDEPENDENT LENS: SISTERS OF '77 (PBS Broadcast documentary of the 1977 National Women's Conference in Houston, Texas, Mar. 1, 2005).

68. Alessandra Stanley, *A Trip Back in Time, to 1977, in Search of Feminism's Glory Days*, N.Y. TIMES, Mar. 1, 2005. President Carter later fired Abzug as co-chairwoman because she was "so combative and outspoken." *Id.*

69. John Rose, Jr., *Letter of Transmittal, in* BATTERED WOMEN IN HARTFORD, CT. iii (Conn. Advisory Comm. to the U.S. Comm. on Civil Rights, Apr. 1979).

70. Jeffrey Fagan, *The Criminalization of Domestic Violence: Promises and Limits* 12 (U.S. Dep't of Justice, Office of Justice Programs, Nat'l Institute of Justice, Jan. 1996) *available at* http://www.ncjrs.org/pdffiles/crimdom.pdf.

71. *Id.*

72. *Id.* at 13.

73. Kurt Anderson, *Private Violence; The Unspeakable Crimes Are Being Yanked Out of the Shadows* 18; Ed Magnuson, *Child Abuse: The Ultimate Betrayal* 20; Jane O'Reilly, *Wife Beating: The Silent Crime* 23; Maureen Dowd, *Rape: The Sexual Weapon* 27, *all in* TIME MAGAZINE, Sept. 5, 1983.

State laws have changed drastically as well, some following the 1995 acquittal of former football star O.J. Simpson, who had been charged with the slashing death of his wife, Nicole Brown Simpson, following a history of domestic violence. In California, lawmakers amended the state's evidence statute to allow courts to admit evidence of prior acts of domestic violence to show the defendant is a batterer. Other states enacted special bail statutes specifically to address those arrested for crimes of domestic violence. A specific crime "domestic violence," with designated penalties, has been created in some states. Registries of orders of protection issued in domestic violence cases are now maintained on government computers. As the police have upgraded their response to domestic violence, so have prosecutors and the courts. Most big city prosecutors' offices have specialized domestic violence units that aggressively pursue batterers. Court systems in many states have recognized that domestic violence cases should be handled by specially-trained judges in an atmosphere that does not discourage victims from seeking help.

Although domestic violence is universally condemned today, periodically a new incident comes to the public's attention—usually involving a famous person—giving us a stark reminder that work remains to be done. This was the situation in the summer of 2014 after hotel surveillance camera footage of Baltimore Ravens running back Ray Rice knocking his girlfriend unconscious went viral. Rice initially was arrested for assault, his girlfriend (whom he later married) refused to testify against him and charges were dropped. The National Football League slapped him on the wrist by suspending him for two games. But after the popular website TMZ released the video—which showed Rice knocking his future wife to the floor of a hotel elevator and dragging her motionless body—the public was outraged at the mild sanction. Suddenly, NFL Commissioner Roger Goodell was on the hot seat, along with Rice.[74]

Goodell claimed he had not seen the offensive video when he imposed the mild punishment on Rice. But as one newspaper columnist noted, "When a man or a woman pushes a spouse down a flight of stairs . . . do we really need to see video evidence to realize that the act was wrong and cruel, or to adequately punish the offender?"[75]

Ray Rice was valuable to his team and to the NFL; in 2012 he signed a five-year contract for $35 million and was known as a community activist in Baltimore.[76] The NFL hired former FBI director Robert Mueller to investigate how Goodell and the League handled the situation.[77] Judy Harris Kluger, a retired New York judge and the executive director of Sanctuary for Families, an anti-domestic violence group,

---

74. Ken Belson, *After Punch is Seen, Rice is Out*, New York Times, September 9, 2014.

75. Juliet Macur, *Sports of the Times: Forget Video; the Facts Are Shocking Enough*, N.Y. Times, September 9, 2014.

76. Steve Fishman, *"Man, They Just Don't Know Who I Am," Ray Rice's Redemption Campaign*, New York Magazine, April 6-19, 2015, 38, 40.

77. Kevin Clark, *A New Twist in the NFL's Ray Rice Probe: Goodell Didn't Investigate Vigorously Out of Respect for Rice's Wife, Says Owner*, Wall Street Journal, September 14, 2014.

called on the NFL to adopt a zero-tolerance policy on domestic abuse.[78] The League got the message; the Ravens fired Rice, and Goodell ordered that he be indefinitely suspended from the NFL.[79] But that was hardly the end of it; Rice challenged his harsher punishment and won—an arbitrator determined Rice's indefinite suspension from the League, after having already been suspended for two games, amounted to the administrative equivalent of double jeopardy—a second sanction for the same behavior. She called it an "abuse of discretion."[80] Although Rice was eligible to play football following the arbitrator's decision, as of the summer of 2016, no team would touch him.[81]

In the aftermath of the Rice/NFL contretemps, Congress held hearings on domestic violence. NFL owners announced a get-tough policy on players who committed acts of family violence; first-time domestic abusers would face a six-game suspension and second offenders would be banned from the League for life.[82]

## *Notes and Questions*

- **48 HOURS — DV ON TV**

The award-winning weekly CBS news show *48 Hours*, which first aired in 1988, has evolved in the last 20 years to a program often depicting true-crime accounts of domestic violence homicides. Each week, an average of 5.5 million viewers tune in to episodes with names like "The Accidental Husband," "Death of an Olympian," and "The Soldier's Wife," in which (usually) husbands shoot, strangle or push their wives over the edges of cliffs. During the 2015–16 season, *48 Hours* aired 19 episodes featuring domestic violence themes. The popular program has won multiple prestigious journalism awards, including 20 Emmys and three Peabodys. Susan Zirinsky, the senior executive producer, says the program aims to give a voice to the survivors of domestic violence and to the families of the victims who are murdered by intimate partners. In a recent interview, Zirinsky observed: "People must be snapping. The arrogance of the belief that you are smarter than the system; nobody gets away with it." From time to time, viewers who have suffered domestic abuse contact the network offices in New York seeking help. In those instances, the staff has attempted to connect the caller with services. "We can have an impact," Zirinsky said. But in contemplating the many shows she has produced over the years and in considering what they say about the state of domestic relations, Zirinsky can only shake her head. "I can't believe divorce was not an option." Susan Zirinsky, interview with the author, April 27, 2016.

---

78. *Executive Director Judy H. Kluger Speaks Out About Rice, #Why I Stayed*, www.sanctuaryforfamilies.org/index.php?option=content&task=view&id=813, accessed June 15, 2015.

79. Fishman, *"Man, They Just Don't Know Who I Am," supra* at 40.

80. Charles Walker & Aaron Wilson, *Ray Rice Wins Appeal of Suspension, But Future Uncertain*, Baltimore Sun, November 28, 2014, www.baltimoresun.com/sports/bs-ray-rice-appeal-decision-20141128-story.html, accessed March 4, 2017.

81. Rotoworld, *Ray Rice, Running Back; Latest News*, www.rotoworld.com/recent/nfl/4645/ray-rice, accessed July 18, 2016.

82. Annie Linsky, *NFL's Lead Blocker: Hogan Calms Domestic Violence Furor*, N.Y. Post, January 31, 2015.

- **DOMESTIC VIOLENCE AMONG THE RICH AND FAMOUS**

F. Scott Fitzgerald, author of the classic of modern literature, *The Great Gatsby*, asked in December 1926: "Is there any man present who can honestly say he has never hit his wife in anger?" SARAH CHURCHWELL, CARELESS PEOPLE: MURDER, MAYHEM AND THE INVENTION OF THE GREAT GATSBY 335 (London: Virago Press, 2013). Former New York Yankees manager Joe Torre grew up in Brooklyn in the 1940s where his father, a New York City detective, routinely beat his mother. When Torre's father learned his mother was pregnant with him, he tossed her down a flight of stairs. After years of witnessing his abuse, the Torre children demanded their father leave the house. In 2003, Torre and his wife formed the Joe Torre Safe at Home Foundation to help children in families where domestic violence is present. Jean Sheff, *Joe Torre: Stepping Up to the Plate for Kids Affected by Domestic Violence,* NEW YORK FAMILY 18 (June 2005). Former President Bill Clinton wrote of family violence he experienced when his mother was married to his stepfather, Roger Clinton. One night, his mother and stepfather fought because he would not allow her to go to the hospital to see her dying grandmother. Roger Clinton pulled a gun and shot at her, but missed. Young Bill Clinton and his mother ran to a neighbor's house to call the police. His stepfather was led away in handcuffs. BILL CLINTON, MY LIFE 20 (2000). On another occasion, his stepfather hit his mother behind their closed bedroom door. Clinton heard his mother scream and found her on the floor with his stepfather standing over her, beating her. Clinton threatened him with a golf club and his stepfather stopped. *Id.* at 45. As was typical of the times, the local police chief drove Clinton's father around in the patrol car until he calmed down. *Id.* at 48–49. Arrest and prosecution was out of the question. After these incidents, his mother would leave, his stepfather would stalk her and promise to change, and his mother would take him back. *Id.* at 52.

In 1960, during a drunken spat at a party at the home of late author Norman Mailer and his second wife, Adele Morales, Mailer stabbed Morales in the heart with a penknife. As one writer aptly put it: Mailer "got off lightly, with the law and his peers." Evan Hughes, *Norman Mailer Runs for Mayor, Stabs Wife; Manly Men Like Swords,* NEW YORK MAGAZINE, April 1, 2012, http://www.nymag.com/features/scandals/norman-mailer-2012-4/, accessed July 16, 2014. Initially, Mrs. Mailer told authorities she fell on shattered glass, but at the hospital, she told the truth. Later, she refused to cooperate in the prosecution of her husband, although the district attorney indicted Mailer anyway. In his biography of Mailer, author J. Michael Lennon wrote "family and friends rallied around him," blaming Morales for what they referred to as "The Trouble." See J. MICHAEL LENNON, NORMAN MAILER: A DOUBLE LIFE, 283-290 (New York: Simon & Schuster, 2013). It apparently was not the first time Mailer was violent with his wife. He struck her earlier at a New Year's Eve party and she told her sister-in-law she was afraid of him. *Id.* at 282.

In a case that gripped tabloid newspaper readers in 1959, married New York lawyer Burton N. Pugach hired three thugs to throw lye in the face of his beautiful, young lover because she ended their affair. Linda Riss was blinded and disfigured in the attack, and Pugach spent 14 years in prison for it. In 1974, the couple's sensational story hit the newspapers again—this time because Riss married her abuser. The marriage lasted 38 years until her death from heart failure in 2013. It was strange union; in 1997 Pugach was again arrested and charged with sexually abusing another woman and threatening to kill her. He was convicted of harassment and sentenced to 15 days in jail. The couple was the subject of a 2007 documentary film directed by Dan Klores, *Crazy Love*. The film was described by the *New York Times* as "part cautionary tale, part psychological study, part riveting disaster narrative." Margalit Fox, *Linda Riss Pugach, 1937–2013: Life Ripped From the Headlines*, NEW YORK TIMES, January 24, 2013.

Defensive end Ray McDonald of the San Francisco 49ers was held accountable by his employers for alleged domestic violence in the wake of the Ray Rice debacle. In August 2014, he was charged with felony domestic violence in California and released on bail. *49ers' McDonald is Arrested on Felony Domestic Violence Charges*, NEW YORK TIMES, September 1, 2014. At the end of the season he was axed by the team and hired as a defensive tackle by the Chicago Bears. But after a subsequent arrest for domestic violence, he was fired. Conor Orr, *Around the NFL: Bears Release McDonald After Domestic Violence Arrest*, May 26, 2015, www.nfl.com/news/story/0ap3000000494037/article/bears-release-mcdonald-after-domestic-violence-arrest, accessed June 16, 2015. Then there is the seemingly endless saga of singer Rihanna and her former boyfriend, R&B singer Chris Brown. Six years after he was convicted of assaulting her and sentenced to five-years probation, he was still feeling the repercussions. In the fall of 2015, Brown was denied a visa to perform in Australia. The country's minister for women told the press Brown was "not of the character we expect in Australia." *Visa Issues Prompt Chris Brown to Cancel Concerts*, N.Y. TIMES, December 3, 2015.

Consider the pros and cons of so much media attention on famous couples caught in the cycle of domestic violence. Is there something to be gained for victims not-so-famous by what may seem like an inordinate amount of media attention on the subject? What about the impact this attention has on the accused? Are there other issues surrounding the scourge of domestic violence that should be brought to public attention but are ignored by the media?

- **WAYS TO HELP**

The American Bar Association has for years been urging lawyers to fulfill their *pro bono* obligations by working on domestic violence issues. "A lawyer's skilled assistance is critical to help a survivor heal, regain stability and move forward with life," wrote then-ABA President William C. Hubbard in the bar journal in 2014. He noted that federal funds for civil assistance for domestic violence victims were insufficient to handle the problem and suggested that lawyers take on cases with local anti-violence groups. William C. Hubbard, *Justice and Healing: Domestic Violence Survivors Need Your Pro Bono Legal Help and Other Support*, ABA JOURNAL 8 (December 2014).

- **THE STORY BEHIND THE PICTURE**

Donna Ferrato's picture, *Behind Closed Doors*, reprinted in this chapter, was named by *Time Magazine* as one of the 100 most influential images of all time. It was taken in 1982 and launched Ferrato's career as an activist artist who has used her talent to open the world's eyes to the ugliness of domestic violence. Ferrato obtained the picture while shadowing a couple to illustrate a story on wealthy swingers. Perhaps because they had grown so comfortable in her presence, the husband had no qualms about beating his wife while Ferrato snapped away with her camera. "I was unprepared for his violence — it shattered the belief I'd been raised with that home is a refuge from the chaos of life," Ferrato says on her website, www.iamunbeatable.com. She launched the site in 2006 after nearly 30 years focusing her camera on the abuse women have suffered at the hands of their so-called "loved ones." Ferrato learned quickly that the popular myth that women are passive victims who masochistically keep returning for more abuse is wrong. Instead, she came to learn they were unbeatable survivors. "Unbeatable is a word used over and over again for everything from football teams to dishwashing soap," she said in a recent interview. But she thinks the adjective really belongs to the brave women who leave abusive relationships — often without a place to live, financial support for their children, or assistance from the legal system. In her experience, the majority of women who have experienced domestic violence eventually leave their batterers. After beginning her professional life as a legal secretary, Ferrato took up photography at the Art Institute of San Francisco and traveled the country taking pictures. She considers her work an "intervention" to help women who have not yet had the courage to leave abusive relationships gather the strength to do so.

Ferrato's work, besides being honored in *Time*, has been recognized elsewhere. Her first book, *Living With the Enemy*, published in 1991 by Aperture, has sold 40,000 copies and been through four printings. Her photographs have been included in 1,000 gallery exhibits over the last 35 years, and she has been the recipient of numerous prestigious awards. In 1987, she was awarded the Robert F. Kennedy Award for Humanistic Photography; in 1996, she was given the International Women in Media, Courage in Journalism Award and was named Artist of the Year at the 2008 Tribeca (NY) Film Festival. On October 30, 2008, Ferrato's New York City home celebrated "Donna Ferrato Appreciation Day."

# Chapter 2

# Race, Culture, Religion and Sexual Orientation & Domestic Violence[1]

---

> **CONSIDER AS YOU READ ABOUT RACE AND CULTURE**
> 1. How different ethnic, racial, religious and cultural groups define and address domestic violence
> 2. The impact group membership has on how other groups, i.e., lawyers, courts, police, fight domestic violence
> 3. The challenges of addressing domestic violence in the LGBTQ community
> 4. The existence of "cultures" we choose
> 5. The similarities of domestic violence among the young and the elderly

## I. Introduction

Understanding the dynamic of domestic violence requires consideration of issues of race, ethnicity, culture, religion and class. An African American woman's reluctance to cooperate with the prosecution of her batterer may by affected by her concern about the alarming number of men in her community in prison; just as the decision of the police to arrest the alleged abuser, or to arrest both parties, may be affected by their own racial bias or perception that a particular neighborhood is a "high-crime" area. Another victim's decision to stay with her abuser might be based on the difficulty of obtaining a divorce within her religious community. The abuser's actions and his perception of what may be appropriate behavior for his wife also may be affected by issues of race and class and by the ethnic traditions in which he was raised.

Ethnic, religious, cultural and language barriers may prevent women of color and immigrant women from reporting crimes, leaving abusive relationships or accessing social services. Keep in mind there is not a single set of behaviors exhibited by all women of color or within a particular racial or ethnic group. Issues of geographic

---

[1]. This chapter was authored in the original text by the Hon. Rosalyn Richter. She generously has consented to allowing it to be reprinted and updated.

difference, class, urban versus rural backgrounds, the woman's country of origin, age, sexual orientation and her religion impact how she, and her family and friends, respond to domestic violence.

Government data on the extent of domestic violence and race differ, depending on the relationship involved. Between 2003 and 2012, domestic violence victimization rates per 1,000 were higher for blacks than for whites or Latinos if the relationship involved intimate partners. In that group, the rate for whites was 3.9, for blacks it was 4.7 and for Latinos 2.8. But when parents, children and siblings are the subjects of the violence, the rate per 1,000 victims changes to .6 per 1,000 for Latinos, .7 for blacks and for 1.2 for whites. Looking at all the violence considered by the government to constitute "domestic violence" which includes all of those previously mentioned interpersonal connections, the rate for blacks jumps to 6.7 per 1,000, for whites, 5.7, for Latinos, 4 and for groups labeled "other," constituting American Indians, Alaska natives, Hawaiian Asian and Pacific Islanders, 3.7.[2]

It is dangerous to be a woman in her own home anywhere in the world. The World Heath Organization reported in 2013 that 40 percent of the women murdered around the globe were killed by an intimate partner and that being assaulted by a significant other was the most common form of violence committed against a woman.[3]

## II. African American Women

Discussions of race and domestic violence requires opening up the door to talks about the sensitive question of race in the criminal justice system. The National Association for the Advancement of Colored People reports that African Americans are incarcerated at six times the rate of whites; African Americans and Hispanics made up 50 percent of the nation's prisoners in 2008 but only a quarter of the nation's population.[4] The following article focuses on this as well as the stereotypes that exist about intimate partner relationships in the black community.

---

2. Jennifer L. Truman and Rachel E. Morgan, "Nonfatal Domestic Violence, 2003–2012," United States Department of Justice, Office of Justice Programs, Bureau of Justice Statistics, April 2014, www.bjs.gov/content/pub/pdf/ndv0312.pdf, accessed July 19, 2015.
3. Maria Cheng, *WHO: A Third of Women Have Suffered Violence*, Palm Beach Post, June 21, 2013.
4. NAACP, "Criminal Justice Fact Sheet," www.naacp.org/pages/criminal-justice-fact-sheet, accessed January 18, 2016.

## Linda L. Ammons, *Mules, Madonnas, Babies, Bathwater, Racial Imagery and Stereotypes: The African-American Woman and the Battered Woman Syndrome*

1995 Wis. L. Rev. 1003

. . . .

A. The Plight of Battered Black Women

Women in America are violated by their current or former partners at such an alarming rate that domestic violence is considered epidemic. Annually, women, as compared to men, experience over ten times as many incidents of violence by an intimate. According to the National Institute of Health, in the mid-1980s homicide was the leading cause of death among African-Americans. Some studies indicate that black women rank second in the frequency of arrests for murder. The typical victim of a black female who kills is a black male with whom she had a relationship.

Until recently, the public, criminal justice agencies, and the courts have ignored the plight of the battered woman. Battered women are not believed either because society has historically been in denial about the terrorism that occurs in the home, or because abused women who do not leave their partners are thought to be lying about the seriousness of the abuse they suffered. Black women face similar hurdles, but additionally they must overcome the presumption that their race predisposes them to engage in and enjoy violence. "Police trainees are frequently told that physical violence is an acceptable part of life among 'ghetto residents.'" In other words, blacks are "normal primitives," or violence-prone. African-American women who are battered face unique challenges in getting relief and support. For example, when black women are treated for domestic violence related injuries in inner-city hospitals, protocols for wife beating are "rarely introduced or followed." Trusting health-care providers with their stories of abuse is difficult because black women have often felt that systems do not have their best interests at heart. However, when the provider is sensitive to their needs they will reveal their stories of abuse. Julie Blackman, a psychologist, illustrated how the mental health system deals with black and white women in abusive relationships by contrasting the Hedda Nussbaum-Joel Steinberg case with that of Frances and Herman McMillian. Nussbaum was the battered lover of Steinberg. Lisa, Steinberg's daughter, was also abused. When Lisa was killed in a battering episode, Nussbaum turned state's evidence against her lover. Steinberg was convicted of manslaughter in the first degree, and sentenced to a maximum term of eight and one-third to twenty-five years. Nussbaum was never charged and was given the psychiatric and social services support she needed.

On the other hand, Frances McMillian, a poor black woman who was arrested for endangering the welfare of her children, was denied treatment by the same facilities. McMillian and her nine children lived in a two-room apartment in the Bronx with an abusive husband and father, Herman McMillian. The family was discovered because of a fire. When Blackman attempted to get Mrs. McMillian admitted to the treatment facilities that had treated Nussbaum, they would not accept her. . . .

The district attorney took nine misdemeanor counts to a grand jury even though he was "sympathetic to her condition." McMillian was indicted. Battered African-American women are also particularly vulnerable because of the lack or the underutilization of resources. For example, African-American women hesitate to seek help from shelters because they believe that shelters are for white women. Because the shelters are associated with the women's movement, and many black women are estranged from women's politics, they may feel that only white women's interests are served in the shelters. African-American women are not totally mistaken in this assumption. A study of the shelter movement in America led a researcher to conclude that black women are ignored in the policymaking, planning and implementation of shelter services. The lack of community outreach in black neighborhoods by the shelters also contributes to the perception that the safe havens are not for women of color. Finally, black women have found the shelter environment inhospitable to their cultural differences.

When leaving shelters, black women are more likely to need health care, material goods and help with their children. A National Institute of Health funded study of sixty battered African-American women over an eight month period found that black women remained in shelters for a significantly longer time than their white counterparts before they could get the necessary resources to start over. Racism also affected the ability of some black women to leave. For example, African-American women would be quoted an apartment rental price over the phone, only to have that price raised when the landlord met the women. White social service personnel would sometimes patronize, ignore or exhibit hostility toward black women.

African-American women depend on informal networks and seek support through prayer, personal spirituality, and the clergy. The African-American church is a traditional source of strength. Pastors (typically male), are a central authority figure in many black communities. However, misinformed ministers may overemphasize the value placed on suffering as a test from God. Further, some clergy have misconstrued biblical principles of love, forgiveness and submission to reinforce sexism and subordination which can be used to justify abuse. Black female parishioners are often told from the pulpit to protect the black male because he is an endangered species.

The inconsistency of police intervention and the lack of other community resources, including hospitals, contribute to the acuteness of violence in African-American neighborhoods. Black women may have to resort to more extreme violence to resolve a battering situation because the police are not interested. African-American women have no historical basis for believing that the world is just and fair and therefore traditional institutions are viewed with great skepticism. . . .

Cooperating with authorities in prosecuting her abuser could result in community abandonment or scorn because of the perception that black men are selectively penalized. Further, black battered women may connect the physical abuse with racism. Some feel that they become the object of their partner's rage triggered by the persistent maltreatment of black males by the greater society, and therefore the abuser is less culpable.

. . . .

The justice system has not rushed to protect black women who have been beaten. Analogies to rape and other gender discriminatory practices illustrate how black female victimization has been and remains unimportant. White men have had carte blanche access to all women. Heinous crimes have been committed in the name of protecting white womanhood. Interracial sexual or physical assault (e.g., minority male/white female) still produces outrage that is not comparable to any other kind of inter-or intraracial adult abuse.

. . . .

The "looking glass" experience of black women is one of being trapped between sub- and super-human imagery and expectations. In addition to the negative stereotypes African-American women encounter, attributes that in their truest sense should be considered positive, when applied to black women, can be detrimental. For example, as previously discussed, African-American women have been characterized as strong and independent. They are blamed for the breakup of their families. Often the strength of black women to survive and progress despite the almost insurmountable obstacles and odds is labeled as pathological at one extreme and disloyal at the other. Sociologist Calvin Herton attributes the black women's drive (a character flaw) to the historical treatment of African-American women. If these stereotypes can affect public policy, routine transactions, and normal discourse, to what extent is the African-American female defendant at a disadvantage when she is brought to trial for a violence crime—even if she claims that she acted in self-defense because she was being battered?

. . . .

## III. Latinas

Although nearly 20 years old, the following excerpt from an article by former law professor Jenny Rivera, now a judge on the New York Court of Appeals, still has relevance as it reminds us that Latinas, like members of any other ethnic group, do not speak in one voice on the subject of domestic violence.

### Jenny Rivera, *Intimate Partner Violence Strategies: Models for Community Participation*
50 Me. L. Rev. 283 (1998)

. . . .

The Latina community efforts at eliminating intimate partner violence demonstrate the Herculean challenge facing underrepresented communities in attempting to develop and realize legislative and policy initiatives that address their specific concerns.

. . . .

Communities and groups of women speak with numerous voices and represent a variety of positions concerning appropriate antiviolence strategies. They are not univocal. These multivocal realities are illustrated in the reactions to criminalization of intimate partner violence. While some members of discrete communities are supportive of expansive and far-reaching criminal penalties, others question the success and long-term benefits of such strategies. For example, mandatory arrest policies and laws, pursuant to which police must arrest under certain circumstances, regardless of the requests of the parties, or of the officer's bias against criminalization or arrest, are controversial. Amongst women of different ethnic and racial groups, there is no single position on mandatory arrest. Similarly, arguments favoring state and federal civil penalties for intimate partner violence have faced counterarguments that such remedies are ineffective and promote excessive government involvement in women's lives.

Nevertheless, there are threads of commonality which bind groups and easily create identifiable and cohesive strategy foundations. Consider this proposition: Not all Latinos need to be poor for there to be agreement that poverty is detrimental to the lives of individual Latinos and to the survival of the Latino community. Applying this same analytic formula to intimate partner violence leads to the following proposition: Latinos can agree that intimate partner violence is injurious to individuals and communities, but they need not agree on any single response because the impact of strategies affects the entire community, not just women. The community may express various strategies for addressing such violence, which take into account the impact on the community as a whole, as well as the impact on individual male and female members. The existence of multiple voices is not equivalent to being voice-less—or having "no voice"—it simply reflects voice, tone, and pitch.

. . . .

---

In their article *Characteristics of Help-Seeking Behaviors, Resources and Service Needs of Battered Immigrant Latinas: Legal and Policy Implications*, 7 Geo. J. On Poverty L. & Pol'y 245 (2000), Mary Ann Dutton, Leslye E. Orloff and Giselle Aguilar note that battered Latinas, when compared to other immigrant groups, tend to underutilize both the informal support network provided by relatives and family members as well as more formal strategies such as contacting law enforcement and social services. Their article, which is based on a study conducted by Ayuda Inc., a non-profit agency in Washington, D.C. that offers services to battered immigrant women and children, notes that language problems were a concern because the Latina immigrant women either spoke little or no English and others were not literate in Spanish. Of particular note, the article indicated the battered immigrant Latinas surveyed were isolated from legal and social services and even when the women consulted with immigration attorneys, one of the few services accessed by them, they did not discuss their domestic violence issues. The article underscores the need for culturally sensitive, community based, multi-lingual services exists in every community, especially those serving diverse immigrant populations.

# IV. Socioeconomic Status

## Jody Raphael, *Battering Through the Lens of Class*
11 Am. U.J. Gender Soc. Pol'y & L. 367 (2003)

. . . .

National studies have documented the fact that, although domestic violence is indeed prevalent throughout all economic classes, household income does predict the probability of family violence: the lower the household income, the higher the rates of violence. For example, The National Crime Victimization Survey finds that households with less than $7,000 in annual income suffer five times the amount of domestic violence as do households with income above $50,000. Those with incomes between $7,500 and $25,000 experience nearly three times the amount of domestic violence as those with incomes above $50,000. Within the past six years, researchers have demonstrated extremely high levels of domestic violence within Temporary Assistance to Needy Families ("TANF") caseloads, and how that violence serves as a welfare-to-work barrier.

. . . .

Women receiving TANF are current victims of domestic violence at rates about ten times higher than women in the general population. Twenty percent of 753 women in a longitudinal study of welfare recipients in Michigan ("Michigan Women's Employment Study") interviewed in 1997 and annually since then, were victims of physical domestic violence within the previous twelve months. When a broader definition of domestic violence that included emotional abuse and coercion was used in a study in California, 35% of recipients in Kern County and 49% in Stanislaus County were found to be current victims.

Research has thoroughly demonstrated the many ways the partners of these women on welfare sabotage their efforts at education, training, and work by using violence and threats of violence. Quantitative research has corroborated qualitative reports from welfare-to-work and job training providers, showing that abusers directly interfere with women's attempts to work by destroying homework assignments, keeping women up all night with arguments before key tests or job interviews, turning off alarm clocks, destroying clothing, inflicting visible facial injuries before job interviews, disabling the family car, threatening to kidnap the children from child care centers, and harassing women on the job. Threatened by the victim's potential economic independence, the abusers use violence to keep their partners at home and out of the labor market. Keeping a woman on welfare not only separates her from economic resources, but it also relegates her to a highly stigmatized position in society, subject to control and abuse from governmental bureaucracies that contribute to her further disempowerment.

With its mandatory work requirements, welfare reform has somewhat disrupted abusers' ability to use the welfare program to dominate their partners. However, recent research is demonstrating that many women are unable to comply with work requirements because of the violence, which makes them even more economically dependent and places them at greater risk of abuse from their partners....

Abusers also sabotage birth control arrangements in order to keep their partners out of the labor market and to make them unattractive and or unmarriageable due to large numbers of children, among other motives. A recent study from Harvard University of over 2000 ninth to twelfth grade students in randomly selected classrooms in high schools throughout Massachusetts found a strong connection between domestic violence and sexual risk behavior, which is defined as first intercourse before the age of fifteen, not using a condom at last intercourse, pregnancy, and substance abuse. The authors concluded that "the implicit coercion involved in both sexual and physical partner abuse is likely to have implications for pregnancy prevention." Other research has demonstrated abusers' sabotage of birth control arrangements as well as verbal coercion to force women to bear their children. In a sample of 474 teen mothers on TANF in 1998, teens who were victims of domestic violence endured almost twice the amount of birth control sabotage, measured by a six-item scale, than did the teens who were not abused. The greater the severity of the domestic violence, the more aggravated was the birth control sabotage.

Studies have indicated that the incidence of intimate partner violence among drug-involved women is higher than among non-drug involved women.

In recent research involving 204 women in a methadone maintenance program, 50% of the women had suffered physical assaults from intimate partners within the past year, and almost 31% were victims of severe abuse. Within the sample, those women in more extreme poverty were more likely to be battered. The researchers found that those women who did not have adequate food and who suffered other severe economic hardships were more likely to be seriously abused. They hypothesized that women without any money at all are forced to rely upon their partners to financially support them, and thus are less able to either leave the relationship, or resist sexual coercion and domestic violence. In other settings, researchers have documented how abusers encourage substance abuse and sabotage detox or drug treatment opportunities to keep the victims at a disadvantage and dependent upon the abusers.... Anecdotal evidence demonstrates that many women in public housing are magnets for homeless men, who will control the women through violence in order to maintain their own access to this affordable housing.

Research also demonstrates that many women involved in prostitution are the victims of violence, not only from customers or police, but also from intimate partners who are dependent on their earnings and control the women through violence. This violence makes escape from the life of prostitution difficult and dangerous. In recent research conducted at the Cook County Jail in Chicago, with a volunteer sample representing about 21% of the jail's population that day, 67% of the women reported domestic violence within the last year. Among those women who disclosed they had been regularly involved in prostitution, the figure rose to 82%.

These examples demonstrate how violence and threats of violence are used purposefully by the poor women's partners to subordinate the women, especially through sabotage of efforts that are key to their economic self-sufficiency. Freedom to pursue employment and freedom from violence are essential ingredients of women's liberation, but only rarely have feminists analyzed how the two intersect to keep women from being subordinated. Thus, rather than eschew the class analysis of domestic violence in the name of feminism, we can develop solid evidence of how that violence is deliberately used to disempower women and subordinate them economically to their partners if we demonstrate the effects of that domestic violence while considering the issue of class.

. . . .

# V. Muslim Societies

## Lisa Hajjar, *Religion, State Power, and Domestic Violence in Muslim Societies: A Framework for Comparative Analysis*
29 Law & Soc. Inquiry 1 (Winter 2004)

### 1. INTRODUCTION

. . . .

[T]he problem of domestic violence in Muslim societies in many ways resembles its counterpart elsewhere and so too do the difficulties in combating it, given the gender biases operative in all societies. However, the use of shari'a as the legal framework for administering Muslims' family relations (marriage, divorce, custody and inheritance) constitutes an important consideration. Shari'a functions both as specific legal rules and as a general religio-cultural framework for Islamic norms and values. Therefore, efforts to implement law reforms to enhance the rights and protection of women within the family are bound up in contestations over the role and the jurisprudence of religious law, and social acceptance of reforms is contingent on their perceived compatibility with religious beliefs.

Although shari'a[5] is critically important for understanding family relations in Muslim societies, it does not constitute an explanatory device for the problem of domestic violence. Rather, explanations must be sought by analyzing the relationship between religious law and state power as it bears on the permissibility or prohibition of violence within the family and the rights of women.

---

5. [n1] Shari'a encompasses the ordinances derived from the Qur'an (which believers accept as the literal word of God), hadith (sayings by and stories about the Prophet Muhammad), and any other laws that are deduced from these two sources by methods considered valid in Islamic jurisprudence (fiqh). . . . [Footnote moved from original location.—Eds.]

## 2. FRAMEWORK FOR COMPARATIVE ANALYSIS

. . . .

While shari'a contributes to some commonalities in gender and family relations in Muslim societies, there are marked variations in the uses and interpretations of shari'a that evince a lack of consensus among Muslims and should deter overgeneralizing about Islam. Many factors contribute to these variations, including different schools of Islamic jurisprudence, and the histories and politics of religious institutions, conversions, reforms, and education. However, the most important variable is the state, and my analysis builds toward a state-centered comparative framework. The history and politics of the state—that is, the specific experiences and legacies of colonial rule and the trajectories of national independence, integration, and development—inform state projects and agendas in regard to gender and family relations and women's rights.

While the focus of this article is Islam, it is worth noting that the history and politics of all states are affected and influenced in some way(s) by religion, and no society could be described accurately as "post-religious." In the Middle East, Africa, and Asia, the relationship between religion and the state can be framed and compared using three general categories. In some countries, notably where the population is religiously diverse, the state communalizes religion by according religious authorities and institutions semi-autonomy from the national legal regime, the latter under the direct control of the state. In countries where Muslims constitute a majority and Islam is recognized as the official religion, the state nationalizes religion by incorporating shari'a principles into the national legal regime. And in a few countries, the state theocratizes religion by declaring itself Islamic and basing the national legal regime on shari'a.

. . . .

In the 1970s, women's rights activists in many Western societies began pursuing an agenda (generally successfully) of bringing criminal law to bear on intrafamily violence. . . . One outcome was to open up the private sphere to increased state intervention, at least in principle, by establishing prohibitions and punishments for violence between family members. Criminalization undermines the ability of perpetrators to claim that what they do at home is private. The model of criminalizing domestic violence has become a popular goal in other parts of the world as well.

Advocates of the criminal justice approach point to the symbolic power of the law and argue that arrest, prosecution and conviction, with punishment, is a process that carries the clear condemnation of society for the conduct of the abuser and acknowledges his personal responsibility for the activity. . . .

The challenges to promoting women's rights in societies where family relations are governed by religious law are daunting. As I elaborate below, in most Muslim societies, shari'a is interpreted to allow or tolerate some forms and degrees of intrafamily violence. This raises questions—and stimulates debates—about what religion "says" (or is believed to say) about the rights of women. It also raises questions about the willingness or ability of the state to prevent and punish violence within families, especially when prevailing views or powerful constituencies regard any curbs on male authority and prerogatives as a contravention of shari'a.

Dominant interpretations of shari'a accord men the status as heads of their families with guardianship over and responsibility for women. The complement to this is the expectation that women have a duty to obey their guardians. This hierarchical and highly patriarchal relationship is based on the Qur'anic principles of qawwama (authority, guardianship) and ta'a (obedience), from which gender-differentiated rights and duties are derived. The primary source of the Qur'anic principles of qawwama and ta'a is Sura 4, Verse 34. This same verse contains the most commonly cited reference used to assert men's right or option to beat disobedient women.

. . . .

Other Qur'anic verses and hadith condemn violence between spouses. For example, Sura 30, Verse 21, describes marital relations as tranquil, merciful, and affectionate, and the relationship itself as based on companionship, not service or tyranny.

The notion that beating constitutes a right available to men certainly contradicts the Qur'anic ideal of marital relations as companionable and mutually supportive. It also runs contrary to the Qur'anic right of both men and women to dissolve a failed marriage, which would seemingly override the notion that women have a duty or obligation to submit to violence. Yet because there is a mention of beating in the Qur'an, Islamic jurists and scholars have grappled with the question of whether hitting constitutes a de jure right under shari'a or a de facto option. . . .

Marital rape is another form of domestic violence for which justification on the basis of shari'a can be found. Although rape is a punishable crime in every Muslim society, nowhere is the criminal sanction extended to rape within marriage, because sexual access is deemed elemental to the marriage contract. Under shari'a, there is no harm—and thus no crime—in acts of sex between people who are married. Thus, marital rape is literally "uncriminalizable" under dominant interpretations of shari'a. For example, Sura 2, Verse 223, provides a Qur'anic basis for men's unabridged sexual access to their wives. This verse stipulates that "your wives are ploughing fields for you; go to your field when and as you like." . . . Indeed, a wife's refusal to have sex with her husband can be construed as "disobedience," thereby triggering legalistic justification for beating.

Forced marriage is a form of psychological and emotional violence. Although the Qur'an does not expressly sanction this practice, the principles of male authority and female obedience create conditions that enable men to impose their will on matters of marriage. While the Qur'an recognizes "mature" (postpubescent) women's right to enter freely into marriage, their status as legal minors often undermines their ability to assert this right in the face of male opposition.

. . . .

## 5. CULTURES OF RESISTANCE, OR SAYING "NO" TO UNIVERSALISM

In many societies, official and popular aversion to enforcing international standards for domestic relationships is far more powerful and influential than the forces promoting them. Indeed, the issues associated with women's rights in the context of family relations constitute the quintessential challenge to the "universality" of human rights. In many developing countries, critics of international human rights have seized upon the emphasis on individuals as rights-bearing subjects, charging that these are inherently Western values, and thus alien to societies that prioritize collective relations and mutual duties rather than competitive individualized rights claims.

Resistance to international human rights cannot be understood as a regressive reaction to change. Rather, it must be understood as a relational response to globalization, one aspect of which is the articulation of increasingly detailed standards and norms of government that apply, at least in principle, to all states. Since rights are, by definition, legal, the internationalization of rights establishes expectations and obligations (e.g., through UN commission reporting mechanisms) to reform national legal regimes in conformity with international legal standards. The greater the expected changes, the more foreign and alien they can appear, and the more they provoke or exacerbate anxieties about cultural imperialism.

. . . .

## Kenneth Lasson, *Bloodstains on a "Code of Honor": The Murderous Marginalization of Women in the Islamic World*
30 WOMEN'S RIGHTS L. REP. 407 (Spring/Summer 2009)

[Although honor killing has been increasingly condemned by several international instruments as a serious violation of fundamental human rights, the practice continues to occur throughout the world. The best estimate is up to 5,000 per year, most of them in Middle Eastern countries, but they happen frequently elsewhere as well—1,000 each year in both India and Pakistan, but also in civilized multi-cultural democracies like the United States (some two dozen per year) and Great Britain (around 12). According to the Honour Based Violence Awareness Network, these figures are severe underestimates.

The practice appears to be getting worse, although it's unclear whether the higher numbers reflect better reporting or greater frequency. The Internet appears to play an important role, both in disseminating more information about the violence and in creating a greater opportunities for families to monitor what they consider to be inappropriate behavior by relatives. The introduction of liberal Western values into ancient cultures, either through immigration or popular media, appears to be a contributing factor as well.] *Kenneth Lasson, update, written December 21, 2016, for this book.*

In early February of 2009, the decapitated body of Aasiya Zubair Hassan was found in Orchard Park, New York, an upstate suburb of Buffalo. The dead woman had recently filed for divorce from her husband, Muzzammil Hassan—whom police promptly arrested and charged with murder. There was widespread speculation that the gruesome death was an "honor killing" based on Islamic religious or cultural beliefs.

As unfathomable as it is to Western minds, "honor killings" occur frequently. A vestige of traditional patriarchy, its condonation can be traced largely to ancient tribal practices. Justifications for it can be found in the codes of Hammurabi and in the family law of the Roman Empire. In the real world of the twenty-first century, deep biases against women are prevalent in much of Muslim society. Although there is no explicit approval of honor killing in Islamic law (Sharia), it remains part of the fundamentally patriarchal culture.

In that tradition, "[a] man's honor consists of two main components: his reputation is determined by his own actions in the community . . . and the chastity or virtue of the female members of his family." When the latter is threatened because of the perceived sexual misconduct of a female member of the family, many believe its honor can be regained only by murdering the miscreant. Family elders usually sanction the decision to kill. A relative of the woman who "sullied" the family does the deed—a husband, brother, uncle, father, or son.

For some the practice of honor killing represents a kind of social umbrella that allows for a wide range of other often violent acts against women and girls, including torture and female infanticide. It should go without saying that such behavior violates virtually all established norms of legal and civilized society. But the phenomenon of honor killing is not rare, nor is it exclusive to the predominantly Islamic countries. It also occurs in Western nations, including Britain, Canada, Germany, Italy, and the United States. As waves of people from the Middle East have emigrated to Europe and America over the past generation, honor killings have increased exponentially.

. . . .

[T] he rights of women—while generally progressing in America and some other Western nations—appear to be regressing among many countries that are predominantly Islamic. In the past, for example, women in Iraq were relatively free of traditional restraints: they could choose whom they married, obtain a divorce, attend school, and work. Over the past five years, though, women in many Islamic nations, including parts of Iraq, have lived in constant fear both for their safety and lives and for that of their families. The primary cause of this backlash is the absence of strong central governments in whose stead are a growing roster of countries controlled by tribal leaders and warlords.

In 2008, religious clerics and tribal chieftains controlled a number of Islamic nations. There is virtually no separation of church and state. Grossly discriminatory religious and tribal views are imposed upon women, regardless of whether they share in the beliefs and practices of the religion.

Although many Islamic women become victims of gender-based violence simply for having been born female, they are marginalized and discriminated against in a variety of other ways as well. Strict standards are set for how they shall dress and act, including to whom they may speak and whom they must marry. They are often forced into arranged marriages, some at as young an age as nine years old. They are raped, physically abused, and mutilated. . . .

As different Islamic countries evolved over time, the law relating to crimes against women took different forms. In Iran, the secular government established by Reza

Shah Pahlavi in the early twentieth century and ceded to his son, Mohammed Reza, during World War II, was denounced by Ayatollah Khomeini in 1979. This was the beginning of the Iranian Revolution (1978–79), when ascendant religious clerics rejected the Shah's adoption of western culture, which they claimed "robbed Iranians of their own identity."

If the revolutionaries were to succeed in overthrowing the Shah, the popular support of Iranian women was vital to their success. While many women were opposed to the creation of a theocracy, others believed it would provide women with greater opportunities. In fact, though, after the revolution, the government's policies towards women became more repressive. Secular women holding positions in government were forced to leave these positions. Female judges, who tended to be secular, were forced to resign and were effectively confined to their homes. When in public, they were required to conform to a state-enforced dress code, covering their hair, and avoiding makeup or adornment. Iranian women who committed adultery were subjected to death by stoning.

. . . The clerical regime reinstated strict Sharia law, which further subjugated women, especially relating to marriage. The minimum age requirement for girls to marry was reduced to nine; many young girls were forced into early marriage by their parents. In order to engage in sexual relations with women besides their wives, Iranian men can arrange a temporary marriage (sigheh), which terminates upon completion of the sex act. After the revolution, Special Civil Courts authorized the registration of these arrangements.

. . . .

The founder of Pakistan (Mohammad Ali Jinnah) held a more moderate view of Islamic law, and his sister (Fatima) played a large role in the development of the nation. After his death in 1977, General Muhammad Zia-ul-Haq, a fundamentalist, came into power and instituted more restrictive measures.

In the 1970s, the President of Pakistan implemented ordinances "to bring the laws of Pakistan into 'conformity with the injunctions of Islam.'" Thus a 1979 law criminalizes extramarital sexual relations (zina). A man and woman are said to commit zina "'if they willfully have sexual intercourse without being validly married to each other.'"

. . . .

Punishment for zina is harsh. Stove burning is a common occurrence in Pakistan. In the typical scenario, the victim is doused with kerosene and set afire from the stove.

. . . .

In Jordan, the Ottoman Empire ruled from the Fourteenth century to shortly after World War I. When the Ottomans lost power in the region, Jordanian law retained a number of Islamic principles. The current Jordanian Penal Code reflects those of Turkey, France, Lebanon, and Syria.

It suggests a "defense of honor" in certain crimes, under which those convicted are treated leniently. Thus one who catches his wife or another female relative committing adultery and injures or kills either of them is exempt from any penalty....

The Turkish Empire, evolved from the Ottomans, began in 1923. Although it adopted the Swiss Civil Code in 1926, the Turks maintained elements of Islamic law that oppressed women....

In early Egypt marriage required an offer and acceptance, and the husband was obligated to pay a dowry. Once the wife received the dowry, she then moved to her husband's home; in exchange, she agreed to provide "conjugal society." The wife was entitled to daily support from her husband, but she would lose that entitlement if she were "disobedient"—which included "leaving the house without his permission or without good reason, or denying him sexual access."

The jurisprudence in modern-day Egypt originates from an Islamic legal system known as the Taqlid, which was adopted in 1948. Under that system both parties to a marriage retain the rights to property they owned before marriage. The husband could easily obtain a divorce, often simply by "uttering a legally accepted formula." The divorced wife would then spend a waiting period in her husband's residence, during which time the husband could cancel the divorce without the wife's permission....

## II. Honor Killings in the Modern World

. . . .

Unfortunately, honor killings in the twenty-first century are not isolated incidents, nor can they be regarded as mere relics of a primitive past. Instead they are part and parcel of an ancient culture with strong roots and an ever-increasing population—a tribal custom where family honor is determined largely by its women's compliance with accepted standards of propriety. Their pre-marital virginity is considered to be the property of their male relatives, who are duty-bound to guard it. Even suspicions of infidelity—whether consensual or coerced—may be punished by beatings, torture, or execution. Usually the punishment is meted out by a male member of the family who, like the alleged paramour, seldom faces recrimination.

. . . .

### A. A Country-by-Country Examination of Honor Killings Reveals Both Their Ubiquity and Differences

In Jordan, although there is some evidence that courts are working to stem the tide of honor killings—which currently result in the death of around twenty Jordanian women per year, each killed by their own family members—until very recently, honor crimes were punishable by as little as six months in prison. Courts frequently invoke Article 98 of the Penal Code to such crimes because it provides discretionary sentencing for crimes committed in a "state of great fury." In addition, Jordanian courts allow the victim's family to waive the complaint against the murderer.

. . . .

In Pakistan, the incidence of honor killing annually has reached epidemic proportions. Killings under the guise of honor also occur when a daughter seeks a divorce from her husband. . . .

It is unknown how many women are maimed or disfigured for life in attacks that fall short of murder. Punishment for such crimes is rare. In another case in Pakistan, a man, with the help of his mother-in-law, set his pregnant sixteen year old wife on fire for disobeying him. A brother set his seventeen year old sister on fire after tying her to a bedpost. A religious figure at a local mosque bound his wife to the bed and thrust a red-hot iron bar inside her.

Honor killings occur for more trivial reasons as well, such as when a wife is slow to serve a meal or when her husband dreams that she has betrayed him. In Pakistan, where only men decide upon matters of religion and culture, such crimes are likewise seldom punished.

Moreover and to the contrary, women who pursue their claims in court frequently lose because of the inherently male-biased judicial system in Pakistan. Victims of domestic violence are frequently told they will bring dishonor to their families by reporting such crimes and are discouraged from contacting the police. Worse, victims who have reported the crimes are often subjected to further abuse at the hands of the very people who are supposed to protect them; sexual assault by the police is a frequent occurrence. Women do not report these crimes because, if they cannot prove rape, they are viewed as willing participants and, therefore, are promiscuous and liable for adultery. In these cases, a woman must prove rape "beyond a reasonable doubt." Unable to substantiate such a charge against the police, a large number of rape victims are charged with adultery.

Somewhat ironically, "Pakistan is one of the few [countries]" to maintain and publish substantial data on honor killings. According to the Human Rights Commission of Pakistan, over "1,500 cases of honor killings were reported there between 2000 and 2005":

> Of the victims: 97 percent were female, 63 percent were married, 37 percent were single, 26 percent were minors, and 2 percent were male. Of those accused of committing the crime: 35 percent were the victims' brothers, 26 percent their husbands, 24 percent were in-laws, relatives, neighbors, or employees, 9 percent were their fathers, 5 percent were their sons, 52 percent were reported to police, and 17 percent were held or arrested.

. . . .

B. Perhaps Less Understandable are Honor Killings in Countries with Western Alliances, Where One Might Expect Human-Rights Sensitivities to be Exercised More Firmly

. . . .

One might expect to hear at least some discussion of the Saudi Arabian practice of wife beating, which (as in other Islamic nations) is both culturally accepted and often even encouraged. In 2007, for example, when "a prominent Saudi cleric" appeared on television to teach "Muslim men how to properly beat their wives" he made certain to instruct them never to beat the face: "[That] is forbidden . . . even if you want your camel or donkey to start walking, you are not allowed to beat in the face. If this is true for animals, it is all the more true when it comes to humans."

. . . .

Abuse of and discrimination against Muslim women occurs in virtually all democracies with growing Muslim populations, including the United States. Although there are currently "no solid statistics on the rate of domestic violence within the Muslim-American community, and it is difficult to determine whether Muslim women are victimized" at a different rate "than women in the general population," some cases present compelling evidence of heightened abuse of Muslim women. For example, a young Pakistani immigrant in Dallas, Texas, was forced into an arranged marriage with a violent husband; she was routinely beaten and forbidden from going out into the public without her husband. In 2006, she escaped after being physically abused by her husband, who threatened to kill her for not cleaning the kitchen. . . .

### III. Moral Imperatives and Reasoned Responses

. . . .

Countries with large Islamic communities—such as, Australia, Britain, Canada, Germany, Italy, and the United States—are often constrained by domestic considerations. For example, a recent wave of honor killings in Germany, accompanied by extremist preaching in German mosques, has led government officials to speak out against various multi-cultural initiatives, and there have been moves in the Legislature to expel Islamic extremists who condone such activity. However, the high concentration of Islamic migrant workers, combined with their poor economic conditions, make the situation tense and fluid. . . .

In the United States, the National Organization for Women ("NOW") has posted articles about honor killing and other forms of serious violence against women in the Islamic world. However, NOW's primary focus remains on domestic issues, not international relations and United States foreign policy.

Perhaps the most vociferous Internet analyses and condemnations have come from individual American commentators. Of them, Phyllis Chesler is among the most prominent. She is an academic, author, and psychotherapist and she includes on her website a section on Islamic Gender and Religious Apartheid, which includes several dozen articles that explore the problem—many of which strongly criticize the failure of Western feminism in this regard.

In a recent book review, Chesler chided what she views as feminist hypocrisy, asserting that mainstream feminism appears to be more concerned with Israel's alleged "occupation" of Palestine, or the United States' incursions into Afghanistan and Iraq, than with the Islamist persecution of women. "Incredibly, those same Western feminists who condemn Western patriarchal institutions of marriage, biological motherhood, heterosexuality, and religion now view Islamic veiling, the hijab (head scarf), purdah, arranged marriage, and polygamy as sacred religious rights."

. . . .

Cinnamon Stillwell is a San Francisco blogger who has focused on honor killings among Islamic immigrants in Western countries. She laments the "Islamophobia" label that inevitably comes from the political left, the unwitting complicity of multiculturalists who ignore the problem or seem to excuse it, and the inadequacy of feminist groups like the National Organization for Women ("NOW"). . . .

Although a great deal of information could be generated via the Internet, reporting in the mainstream media on honor killings has been relatively sparse. In the mid-1990's, the Jordan Times published an investigative report on such violence against women, which until then was a taboo subject rarely addressed by the Arab media. Although the report provoked severe criticism from conservative elements, it triggered a campaign to fight the killings. The royal family threw its weight behind the effort, and the religious establishment issued fatwas prohibiting the killing of women by male members of their families for alleged acts of dishonor. But the Jordanian parliament, still essentially traditional, aborted a government initiative to amend laws that were lenient to the perpetrators of these crimes. . . .

Perhaps the most direct and salutary response to honor killings is the establishment of hotlines and shelters. In the United Kingdom, in response to the high volume of calls (about fifty a month) to the authorities in Stoke-on-Trent, North Staffordshire, a hotline was set up for women being forced into unwanted marriages. Entitled Karma Nirvana, the service assists distressed women in finding new jobs and homes, getting legal advice, gaining access to healthcare, planning security, and claiming benefits.

In April of 2008 Karma Nirvana launched the Honour Network (based in Derby, U.K.), which acts as a surrogate family and lends emotional and practical support to abused women. In the fall of 2008, the Forced Marriage (Civil Protection) Act was enacted, enabling courts to prevent coerced marriages and adequately protect victims. Partially funded by the government, the Honour Network currently handles nearly 400 cases a year.

Women who call the hotlines often express fear for their own safety, as well as apprehension that reporting their "abuse will shame their families." Many do not comprehend that they are crime victims, "because in their home country," physical punishment and murder of a woman by her husband or father for dishonoring the family is often legal and accepted custom.

In the United States, many domestic-violence shelters have opened for Muslim women, mainly in large cities, advocating the fundamental human-rights principle that acts of domestic violence are unacceptable. Community support is often difficult to come by, especially since some religious leaders adhere to the cultural traditions instilled by their homeland and refuse clearly to reject violent acts against women.

Various advocacy centers around the country offer support for victims. Rafia Zakaria, a professor at Indiana University whose work is focused on "educating Muslims about spousal abuse . . . has launched a legal defense fund." The Tahirih Justice Center in northern Virginia offers shelter for battered Muslim women; the Baitul Salaam shelter in Atlanta does the same. DAYA ("compassion" in Sanskrit) provides legal and financial assistance to abused families. In the last five years, it has reported an "increase in distress calls" about twenty times greater than when it began in 2003.

. . . .

In February 2008, the United Nations launched a multi-year campaign designed to intensify action that would end violence against women and girls worldwide. Secretary-General Ban Ki-moon cited many statistics, including the fact that

> "at least one out of every three women is likely to be beaten, coerced into sex, or otherwise abused in her lifetime" . . . . Through the practice of pre-natal sex selection, countless other females are even denied the right to exist. Others suffer from trafficking, sexual harassment, female genital mutilation, dowry murder, honor killings, and female infanticide.

Noting that in over 100 countries there are "no specific legal provisions against domestic violence," Mr. Ban called on all nations "to review their current laws and to enact new ones, if needed, to ensure that violence against women would be treated as a criminal offense." . . .

## VI. Jewish Communities

### Lydia M. Belzer, *Toward True Shalom Bayit: Acknowledging Domestic Abuse in the Jewish Community and What to Do About It*

11 Cardozo Women's L.J. 241 (Winter 2005)

#### I. Introduction

Like many other religious and cultural communities, Judaism places a heavy emphasis on the importance of family. Holidays and rituals are designed to encourage family gatherings, interaction between family members, and education of younger generations. Religious laws instruct children to honor and respect their parents, and parents to nurture and pass on traditions to their children. The family, after all, is where learning begins, and the vehicle for the survival of the religion. One particular concept in Judaism that demonstrates the high priority of the family is that of "shalom bayit," or "peace in the home."

. . . .

Unfortunately, shalom bayit is an idea that is absent from some Jewish households. Not a single religion, socioeconomic class, or culture escapes the tragedy of domestic abuse, and Judaism is no exception. Ironically, ideas such as shalom bayit might even unwittingly encourage women to remain in abusive marriages, in an effort to preserve their home and family, perhaps under the misguided belief that if they only avoid behaviors that provoke their significant other, the abuse will stop. This is not to say that all abused Jewish women, or even a majority of them, would consider shalom bayit as their main reason for staying. A variety of Jewish traditions and beliefs, in combination with non-religious reasons, may play a part in the decision to stay. Regrettably, these same traditions and beliefs hide the problem of domestic abuse within the Jewish community.

. . . .

Traditional halachic sources varied on the issue of whether wife-beating was ever permissible. Some scholars opined that wife-beating constituted grounds for compelling a husband to divorce his wife, even if the woman had initially "accepted the situation." A particularly strong condemnation comes from the eleventh-century scholar Rabbi Simhah ben Shmuel of Vitri, who suggested excommunication, corporal punishment, compelled divorce, and in extreme cases, cutting off the hand of the abusive husband. Other rabbis echoed these sentiments, including Rabbi Meir (the Maharam) of Rothenburg.

Other scholars, including one of the greatest Jewish commentators, Maimonides, accepted limited beatings, generally in circumstances where the wife was considered to have merited punishment for a particular wrong.

. . . .

Regardless of the opinions of scholars from the Middle Ages, or more recent ones for that matter, the Rabbinical Council of America (RCA) passed an anti-domestic violence resolution in June 1994, stating a "zero-tolerance" policy and petitioning Orthodox rabbis to "do everything in their power to protect victims." While it may seem shocking that this resolution was not passed until 1994, it is likely that the pervasive attitude of denial-which is a large part of what this paper seeks to demonstrate- might explain the delay: passing such an ordinance admits that the problem exists and requires attention.

4. Jewish Divorce: Getting a Get

. . . .

Initially, a husband had the right to unilaterally divorce his wife, with or without consent. Further, conventional practice held that a husband could divorce his wife for any reason. During the eleventh-century, in an attempt to protect women against forced divorce, a rabbinic edict came into effect "which forbade divorcing a woman against her consent." Currently, although either a man or woman may technically sue for a get, "divorce laws maintain women in a position of weakness." A woman's ability to request a divorce does not entail her right to ensure it: he must grant her the get. If he chooses not to, then she remains technically married, although in reality single. The Hebrew term to refer to a woman in this state is agunah, which literally means "a chained woman."

. . . .

1. The Sanctity of the Jewish Home

The home and family are the central points of Jewish life. . . .

In other words, shalom bayit is the ideal to strive for, and this is ingrained, especially in girls, throughout their lives. Unfortunately, while shalom bayit should be the goal of both spouses, more pressure is usually put on the wife to uphold the responsibility for shalom bayit, and to keep the family—seen as the foundation—"together at all costs."

Further compounding the pressure is the "endangered-species imagery" that has been prevalent in the post-Holocaust era. This mentality manages to influence many modern women, and results in their feeling pressured to marry Jewish, produce and raise Jewish children who are aware of their heritage, and generally preserve the community. Motherhood takes on an additional dimension of necessity beyond one's own maternal tendencies (if any), and integrates the concept of childbearing into a woman's religious identity.

How do these attitudes affect women who are abused by their spouse? While the issue remained largely unacknowledged, one common response was self-blame: women faulted themselves for failing to be good Jewish wives and mothers as was expected of them. . . .

Additionally, Orthodox communities are often tightly-knit, acting as a large extended family. Within the value system of the community, the wife-mother role serves as an identity by which women "give coherence and sanctity to daily living." When someone advises an Orthodox woman to publicly admit being abused or to leave her batterer, her decision is more complex than simply deciding to leave her husband: "We ask [these women] to forfeit their place in an extended family rooted in social stability in exchange for secular chaos, moral uncertainty, and economic insecurity." . . .

3. Fear of Shame/Shonda

Other relevant concepts in Judaism are the ideas of kiddush HaShem and chilul HaShem—the bringing of positive and negative attention, respectively, to the Jewish community. Bringing negative attention to the Jewish community is considered a shonda, a shame. Especially given the history of anti-Semitism throughout the world, many Jews resist coming forward publicly about faults within the community, lest they reinforce negative images. Not surprisingly, such concepts can be harmful to a battered woman, who may hesitate to seek advice from an outside source, call the police, or turn to the courts. She also might not be quick to risk damaging her husband's reputation, or losing her own network of community-based support. Such fears result in one of two opposite responses, possibly depending on the type of community the woman is in: first, she might turn to someone completely disconnected from her Jewish world, or second, she might turn completely inward, relying on the support network that she has within her own community. Workers in the field of Jewish domestic violence understand that these interpretations of chilul HaShem, and further, what constitutes a shonda, are barriers to encouraging abused women to come forward. . . .

### 4. The Difficulties of Divorce & Fear of Becoming an Agunah

Aside from any difficulties she has in securing a get, an abused Jewish woman may find that her civil divorce is not much easier. Perhaps she never called the police when her husband abused her, and so she has no record to prove the abuse ever happened. This can be especially problematic in states that have mandatory arrest laws; in other words, if police arrive at the scene of a domestic violence incident, they must arrest somebody. She can still of course obtain her civil divorce, but to whatever extent her settlement would be affected by her proving herself an abused spouse, she could lose.

Should her husband refuse to grant her the get, thus making her an agunah, she is unable to move on, find a new mate, or produce more children, without violating Jewish law. This provides the husband with a powerful "bargaining chip" and leaves a wife considering leaving in a precarious position. If she decides to attempt to get a Jewish divorce, she will have to face a beth din in addition to a civil court, and she may not be familiar with the processes involved or aware of any protections that might be available to her. If she goes through a secular proceeding, her attorney may not understand this other (and to the woman often primary) process of get. Neither the woman nor the attorney may be aware of the protections available (such as her ability to select her own beth din) or the potential dangers (such as the possibility that the beth din insist upon the wife's dropping her protective order to be granted a get). Having to go through not one, but two unfamiliar court processes can be daunting for an abused woman, especially where there are so many other obstacles to her ability to leave.

. . . .

### D. How Jewish Concepts Repudiate Domestic Abuse

It is important to note that in spite of some people's view that Jewish religious principles encourage women to remain in abusive relationships, Jewish philosophy clearly rejects such a notion. Shalom bayit is widely misunderstood as a reason for enduring abuse or unhappiness; in fact, it is a concept designed to promote happiness and genuine tranquility. And while shonda remains a very real barrier to encouraging abuse victims to come forward, it seems that the greater chilul HaShem is to ignore these problems and feign ignorance of their existence, rather than to address them and work toward a solution. An abused person is not obligated to automatically grant forgiveness to a batterer who attempts teshuvah. Valid teshuvah requires five elements: the wrongdoer must acknowledge that the behavior was sinful; feel remorse; cease to commit the sin; provide restitution (when possible); and confess the behavior. In most abusive relationships, the batterer would fail to meet these obligations, and the abused partner is thus absolved from the responsibility to grant forgiveness.

On a much more basic level, the Jewish marriage contract, ketubah, includes a duty for the husband to honor his wife. Also, any Jew may break almost any Jewish rule for the sake of pikuach nefesh, saving a life, which means that all other concerns are secondary to that of helping any person in danger. Finally, Jewish belief compels a concept known as tikkun olam, which literally means "heal the world." . . .

## VII. Native American Women

The number of Native Americans in the United States is small—4.1 million or about 1.5 percent of the population—but the domestic violence problem in these communities is huge.[6] Native American women suffer domestic violence at a far greater rate than other women. In 2008, the federal Centers for Disease Control and Prevention (CDC) reported that 39 percent of native women identified themselves as victims of domestic violence.[7] In May 2016, the National Institute of Justice released a report, *Violence Against American Indian and Alaska Native Women and Men, 2010 Findings from the National Intimate Partner and Sexual Violence Survey* indicating violence against women in this community was worse than previously thought. In fact, more than 4 out of 5 American Indian and Alaskan Native women, or 84.3 percent, have been victims of violence over their lifetimes. Ninety-seven percent of these victims have been attacked by non-Native perpetrators over whom tribes have lacked jurisdiction to hold accountable. This intolerable situation has improved with the federal Violence Against Women Reauthorization Act of 2013, as will be discussed more fully below. The article excerpt and the recent Supreme Court case of *United States v. Bryant,* which follow, shed light on the challenges involved in holding perpetrators responsible for the domestic violence they commit in Indian country. The Ritcheske article, although now dated, provides background about how domestic violence was addressed on tribal land in the past and sets the stage for understanding how it might be combatted in the future.

### Kathryn A. Ritcheske, Note: *Liability of Non-Indian Batterers in Indian Country: A Jurisdictional Analysis*
14 Tex. J. Women & L. 201 (2005)

#### I. Introduction

Indian tribes are not recognized as juridical entities in the international law context, but neither are they arms of the federal government or of any state government—they possess an inherent sovereignty that is subject only to the overriding power of the federal government. However, a tribe's sovereignty—unlike that of states—is not based on the boundaries of its reservation. Rather, whether a tribe has jurisdiction depends on the status of the actors involved and the nature of the offense committed. . . . Tribes have no criminal misdemeanor jurisdiction over non-Indian people, even if they reside

---

6. National Congress of American Indians, *An Introduction to Indian Nations in the United States,* 15, www.ncai.org/about-tribes_indians_101.pdf, accessed October 1, 2016.
7. Futures Without Violence: The Facts on Violence Against American Indian/Alaskan Native Women, https://www.futureswithoutviolence.org/userfiles/file/Violence%20Against%20AI%AN%20Women%20Fact%20Sheet.pdf, accessed September 28, 2016.

on the reservation. While tribes can exercise civil jurisdiction, the remedies available often do not effectively serve as a deterrent to future violence....

A. Jurisdiction over Member Indians

If an Indian defendant is charged with one of the offenses listed in the federal Major Crimes Act and the crime was committed in Indian Country, the federal government has jurisdiction. If either the victim or the defendant is an Indian and the crime is not listed in the Major Crimes Act, federal courts have jurisdiction under the General Crimes Act....

Tribes also presumably have concurrent subject matter jurisdiction over major crimes. However, the Indian Civil Rights Act (ICRA) limits the sentences tribes can impose in criminal cases: for conviction of any one offense, the maximum penalty is one year in prison and a $5000 fine. As a result of these limitations and the lack of correctional system infrastructures on some reservations, tribes rarely initiate prosecution for felonies.

B. Jurisdiction Over Non-Indians

....

1. Criminal

In *Oliphant v. Suquamish Indian Tribe*,[8] the U.S. Supreme Court held that tribes do not have criminal misdemeanor jurisdiction over non-Indians.... The Court expressed concerns that non-Indian defendants would not be given the same due process protections in tribal court as they would in federal or state court. These specific due process concerns were only a part of the Court's deep distrust of tribal court systems. To support its conclusion that tribes did not have criminal misdemeanor jurisdiction over non-Indians, the Court cited the legislative history and text of bills never enacted, Attorney General's opinions from 1834, and an Arkansas district court case from 1878. The Court also concluded that "upon incorporation into the territory of the United States," Indian tribes implicitly lost much of their inherent sovereignty....

C. Jurisdiction Over Non-member Indians

1. *Duro v. Reina*

In *Duro v. Reina*,[9] the U.S. Supreme Court held that tribes did not have criminal jurisdiction over non-member Indians. In that case, Albert Duro was charged with committing murder within the boundaries of the Salt River Indian Reservation.... The Supreme Court noted that, as a non-member resident of the reservation, Duro was not entitled to vote in Pima-Maricopa elections, hold tribal office, or serve as a juror for the tribal court. The Court held that Indian tribes, because of their "dependent" status, did not possess full territorial sovereignty that extended to non-members.

---

8. [Oliphant v. Suquamish Indian Tribe, 435 U.S. 191 (1978).—Eds.]
9. [Duro v. Reina, 495 U.S. 676 (1990).—Eds.]

## 2. Amendment of ICRA

The Supreme Court's decision in *Duro* threatened the security of tribal communities because many reservations have high numbers of non-member Indian residents and because, at the time of the decision, neither the states nor the federal government had jurisdiction over Indians who committed crimes not covered by the Major Crimes Act.... In 1991, Congress responded to *Duro v. Reina* by adding to the Defense Appropriations Act a rider that amended the definition sections of ICRA. Section 8077(b) amended the definition of "powers of self-government" to mean "the inherent power of Indian tribes, hereby recognized and affirmed, to exercise criminal jurisdiction over all Indians." Section 8077(c) added a definition of "Indian": "any person who would be subject to the jurisdiction of the United States as an Indian under section 1153, Title 18, if that person were to commit an offense listed in that section in Indian country to which that section applies." Congress's power to lift restrictions on tribal jurisdiction over non-member Indians was ... upheld by the Supreme Court in *United States v. Lara*.[10]

. . . .

## D. Congressional Intent to Assist Tribes in Enforcing Domestic Violence Laws

As a result of the jurisdictional intricacies discussed above, victims of domestic violence in Indian Country often do not seek help or receive protection from state or tribal government agencies....

Congress has also legislated with respect to the federal government's obligation to help with the general enforcement of laws in Indian Country and to join tribes in efforts to curb domestic violence in Indian communities. The Indian Law Enforcement and Reform Act of 1990 made the Secretary of the Interior, through the Bureau of Indian Affairs, responsible for "providing, or for assisting in the provision of, law enforcement services in Indian Country" and established the Division of Law Enforcement Services. Unfortunately, many Indian communities have woefully understaffed law enforcement agencies. The federal government could help to remedy this problem by providing more funding and personnel support through the Bureau of Indian Affairs (BIA) and the Federal Bureau of Investigation (FBI). The BIA and the FBI are also authorized to submit a report to the tribal government if the federal bureau "declines to initiate an investigation of a reported violation of Federal law in Indian country, or terminates such an investigation without referral for prosecution...." Congress has also recognized the need to create a stronger infrastructure for services to victims of domestic violence. However, after *Oliphant*, the policing of "minor" crimes (such as domestic violence) committed by non-Indians in Indian Country declined — the states were uninterested in enforcing these laws or unwilling to spend the money necessary to effectively police the crimes, and federal prosecutors' distance from Indian Country and priorities for allocating resources resulted in their inaction as well. Under VAWA, protection orders issued by a tribal court are to be given full

---

10. [n50] 124 S. Ct. 1628, 1632 (2004)....

faith and credit by state courts and by other tribal courts. While this section of VAWA refers to a civil remedy and not to a criminal prosecution, it indicates the federal government's acknowledgement that domestic violence is a serious problem in Indian Country and elsewhere.

. . . .

## United States v. Bryant
Supreme Court of the United States
136 S. Ct. 1954 (2016)

JUSTICE GINSBURG delivered the opinion of the Court.

In response to the high incidence of domestic violence against Native American women, Congress, in 2005, enacted 18 U.S.C. § 117(a), which targets serial offenders. Section 117(a) makes it a federal crime for any person to "commi[t] a domestic assault within ... Indian country" if the person has at least two prior final convictions for domestic violence rendered "in Federal, State, or Indian tribal court proceedings." See Violence Against Women and Department of Justice Reauthorization Act of 2005 (VAWA Reauthorization Act), Pub. L. 109-162, §§ 901, 909, 119 Stat. 3077, 3084.[11] Respondent Michael Bryant, Jr., has multiple tribal-court convictions for domestic assault. For most of those convictions, he was sentenced to terms of imprisonment, none of them exceeding one year's duration. His tribal-court convictions do not count for § 117(a) purposes, Bryant maintains, because he was uncounseled in those proceedings.

The Sixth Amendment guarantees indigent defendants, in state and federal criminal proceedings, appointed counsel in any case in which a term of imprisonment is imposed. *Scott v. Illinois*, 440 U.S. 367, 373-374, 99 S. Ct. 1158, 59 L. Ed. 2d 383 (1979). But the Sixth Amendment does not apply to tribal-court proceedings. See *Plains Commerce Bank v. Long Family Land & Cattle Co.*, 554 U.S. 316, 337, 128 S. Ct. 2709, 171 L. Ed. 2d 457 (2008). The Indian Civil Rights Act of 1968 (ICRA), Pub. L. 90-284, 82 Stat. 77, 25 U.S.C. § 1301 *et seq.*, which governs criminal proceedings in tribal courts, requires appointed counsel only when a sentence of more than one year's imprisonment is imposed. § 1302(c)(2). Bryant's tribal-court convictions, it is undisputed, were valid when entered. . . .

I

A

As this Court has noted, domestic abusers exhibit high rates of recidivism, and their violence "often escalates in severity over time." *United States v. Castleman*, 572 U.S. ___, ___, 134 S. Ct. 1405, 188 L. Ed. 2d 426, 432 (2014) ). . . .

---

11. [n1] "Indian country" is defined in 18 U.S.C. § 1151 to encompass all land within any Indian reservation under federal jurisdiction, all dependent Indian communities, and all Indian allotments, the Indian titles to which have not been extinguished.

The "complex patchwork of federal, state, and tribal law" governing Indian country, *Duro v. Reina*, 495 U.S. 676, 680, n. 1, 110 S. Ct. 2053, 109 L. Ed. 2d 693 (1990), has made it difficult to stem the tide of domestic violence experienced by Native American women. Although tribal courts may enforce the tribe's criminal laws against Indian defendants, Congress has curbed tribal courts' sentencing authority. At the time of § 117(a)'s passage, ICRA limited sentences in tribal court to a maximum of one year's imprisonment. 25 U.S.C. § 1302(a)(7) (2006 ed.). Congress has since expanded tribal courts' sentencing authority, allowing them to impose up to three years' imprisonment, contingent on adoption of additional procedural safeguards. 124 Stat. 2279-2280 (codified at 25 U.S.C. § 1302(a)(7)(C), (c)). To date, however, few tribes have employed this enhanced sentencing authority....

States are unable or unwilling to fill the enforcement gap. Most States lack jurisdiction over crimes committed in Indian country against Indian victims. See *United States v. John*, 437 U.S. 634, 651, 98 S. Ct. 2541, 57 L. Ed. 2d 489 (1978). In 1953, Congress increased the potential for state action by giving six States "jurisdiction over specified areas of Indian country within the States and provid[ing] for the [voluntary] assumption of jurisdiction by other States." *California v. Cabazon Band of Mission Indians*, 480 U.S. 202, 207, 107 S. Ct. 1083, 94 L. Ed. 2d 244 (1987) (footnote omitted). See Act of Aug. 15, 1953, Pub. L. 280, 67 Stat. 588 (codified, as amended, at 18 U.S.C. § 1162 and 25 U.S.C. §§ 1321-1328, 1360). States so empowered may apply their own criminal laws to "offenses committed by or against Indians within all Indian country within the State." *Cabazon Band of Mission Indians*, 480 U.S., at 207, 107 S. Ct. 1083, 94 L. Ed. 2d 244; see 18 U.S.C. § 1162(a). Even when capable of exercising jurisdiction, however, States have not devoted their limited criminal justice resources to crimes committed in Indian country....

That leaves the Federal Government. Although federal law generally governs in Indian country, Congress has long excluded from federal-court jurisdiction crimes committed by an Indian against another Indian. 18 U.S.C. § 1152; see *Ex parte Crow Dog*, 109 U.S. 556, 572, 3 S. Ct. 396, 27 L. Ed. 1030 (1883) (requiring "a clear expression of the intention of Congress" to confer federal jurisdiction over crimes committed by an Indian against another Indian). In the Major Crimes Act, Congress authorized federal jurisdiction over enumerated grave criminal offenses when the perpetrator is an Indian and the victim is "another Indian or other person," including murder, manslaughter, and felony assault. § 1153.... In short, when § 117(a) was before Congress, Indian perpetrators of domestic violence "escape[d] felony charges until they seriously injure[d] or kill[ed] someone." 151 Cong. Rec. 9062 (2005) (remarks of Sen. McCain).

As a result of the limitations on tribal, state, and federal jurisdiction in Indian country, serial domestic violence offenders, prior to the enactment of § 117(a), faced at most a year's imprisonment per offense—a sentence insufficient to deter repeated and escalating abuse. To ratchet up the punishment of serial offenders, Congress created the federal felony offense of domestic assault in Indian country by a habitual offender. § 117(a) (2012 ed.).... The section provides in pertinent part:

"Any person who commits a domestic assault within ... Indian country and who has a final conviction on at least 2 separate prior occasions in Federal, State, or Indian tribal court proceedings for offenses that would be, if subject to Federal jurisdiction any assault, sexual abuse, or serious violent felony against a spouse or intimate partner ... shall be fined ..., imprisoned for a term of not more than 5 years, or both ...." § 117(a)(1)....

B

This case requires us to determine whether § 117(a)'s inclusion of tribal-court convictions is compatible with the Sixth Amendment's right to counsel. The Sixth Amendment to the U.S. Constitution guarantees a criminal defendant in state or federal court "the Assistance of Counsel for his defence." See *Gideon v. Wainwright*, 372 U.S. 335, 339, 83 S. Ct. 792, 9 L. Ed. 2d 799 (1963). This right, we have held, requires appointment of counsel for indigent defendants whenever a sentence of imprisonment is imposed. *Argersinger v. Hamlin*, 407 U.S. 25, 37, 92 S. Ct. 2006, 32 L. Ed. 2d 530 (1972). But an indigent defendant has no constitutional right to appointed counsel if his conviction results in a fine or other noncustodial punishment. *Scott*, 440 U.S., at 373-374, 99 S. Ct. 1158, 59 L. Ed. 2d 383.

"As separate sovereigns pre-existing the Constitution, tribes have historically been regarded as unconstrained by those constitutional provisions framed specifically as limitations on federal or state authority." *Santa Clara Pueblo v. Martinez*, 436 U.S. 49, 56, 98 S. Ct. 1670, 56 L. Ed. 2d 106 (1978). The Bill of Rights, including the Sixth Amendment right to counsel, therefore, does not apply in tribal-court proceedings. See *Plains Commerce Bank*, 554 U.S., at 337, 128 S. Ct. 2709, 171 L. Ed. 2d 457.

In ICRA, however, Congress accorded a range of procedural safeguards to tribal-court defendants "similar, but not identical, to those contained in the Bill of Rights and the Fourteenth Amendment." *Martinez*, 436 U.S., at 57, 98 S. Ct. 1670, 56 L. Ed. 2d 106; see *id.*, at 62-63, 98 S. Ct. 1670, 56 L. Ed. 2d 106 (ICRA "modified the safeguards of the Bill of Rights to fit the unique political, cultural, and economic needs of tribal governments"). In addition to other enumerated protections, ICRA guarantees "due process of law," 25 U.S.C. § 1302(a)(8), and allows tribal-court defendants to seek habeas corpus review in federal court to test the legality of their imprisonment, § 1303.

The right to counsel under ICRA is not coextensive with the Sixth Amendment right. If a tribal court imposes a sentence in excess of one year, ICRA requires the court to accord the defendant "the right to effective assistance of counsel at least equal to that guaranteed by the United States Constitution," including appointment of counsel for an indigent defendant at the tribe's expense. § 1302(c)(1), (2). If the sentence imposed is no greater than one year, however, the tribal court must allow a defendant only the opportunity to obtain counsel "at his own expense." § 1302(a)(6)....

It is undisputed that a conviction obtained in violation of a defendant's Sixth Amendment right to counsel cannot be used in a subsequent proceeding "either to support guilt or enhance punishment for another offense." *Burge*tt v. *Texas*, 389 U.S. 109, 115, 88 S. Ct. 258, 19 L. Ed. 2d 319 (1967)....

In *Nichols* v. *United States*, 511 U.S. 738, 114 S. Ct. 1921, 128 L. Ed. 2d 745 (1994), we stated an important limitation on the principle recognized in *Burgett*. In the case under review, Nichols pleaded guilty to a federal felony drug offense. 511 U.S., at 740, 114 S. Ct. 1921, 128 L. Ed. 2d 745. Several years earlier, unrepresented by counsel, he had been convicted of driving under the influence (DUI), a state-law misdemeanor, and fined $250 but not imprisoned. *Ibid*. Nichols' DUI conviction, under the then-mandatory Sentencing Guidelines, effectively elevated by about two years the sentencing range for Nichols' federal drug offense. *Ibid*. We rejected Nichols' contention that, as his later sentence for the federal drug offense involved imprisonment, use of his uncounseled DUI conviction to elevate that sentence violated the Sixth Amendment. *Id.,* at 746-747, 114 S. Ct. 1921, 128 L. Ed. 2d 745....

### C

Respondent Bryant's conduct is illustrative of the domestic violence problem existing in Indian country. During the period relevant to this case, Bryant, an enrolled member of the Northern Cheyenne Tribe, lived on that Tribe's reservation in Montana. He has a record of over 100 tribal-court convictions, including several misdemeanor convictions for domestic assault. Specifically, between 1997 and 2007, Bryant pleaded guilty on at least five occasions in Northern Cheyenne Tribal Court to committing domestic abuse in violation of the Northern Cheyenne Tribal Code. On one occasion, Bryant hit his live-in girlfriend on the head with a beer bottle and attempted to strangle her. On another, Bryant beat a different girlfriend, kneeing her in the face, breaking her nose, and leaving her bruised and bloodied.

For most of Bryant's repeated brutal acts of domestic violence, the Tribal Court sentenced him to terms of imprisonment, never exceeding one year. When convicted of these offenses, Bryant was indigent and was not appointed counsel. Because of his short prison terms, Bryant acknowledges, the prior tribal-court proceedings complied with ICRA, and his convictions were therefore valid when entered. Bryant has never challenged his tribal-court convictions in federal court under ICRA's habeas corpus provision.

In 2011, Bryant was arrested yet again for assaulting women. In February of that year, Bryant attacked his then girlfriend, dragging her off the bed, pulling her hair, and repeatedly punching and kicking her. During an interview with law enforcement officers, Bryant admitted that he had physically assaulted this woman five or six times. Three months later, he assaulted another woman with whom he was then living, waking her by yelling that he could not find his truck keys and then choking her until she almost lost consciousness. Bryant later stated that he had assaulted this victim on three separate occasions during the two months they dated.

Based on the 2011 assaults, a federal grand jury in Montana indicted Bryant on two counts of domestic assault by a habitual offender, in violation of § 117(a). Bryant was represented in federal court by appointed counsel. Contending that the Sixth Amendment precluded use of his prior, uncounseled, tribal-court misdemeanor convictions to satisfy § 117(a)'s predicate-offense element, Bryant moved to dismiss the indictment. The District Court denied the motion, App. to Pet. for Cert. 32a, and Bryant entered a conditional guilty plea, reserving the right to appeal that decision. Bryant was sentenced to concurrent terms of 46 months' imprisonment on each count, to be followed by three years of supervised release.

The Court of Appeals for the Ninth Circuit reversed the conviction and directed dismissal of the indictment. 769 F.3d 671 (2014). Bryant's tribal-court convictions were not themselves constitutionally infirm, the Ninth Circuit comprehended, because "the Sixth Amendment right to appointed counsel does not apply in tribal court proceedings." *Id.*, at 675. But, the court continued, had the convictions been obtained in state or federal court, they would have violated the Sixth Amendment because Bryant had received sentences of imprisonment although he lacked the aid of appointed counsel....

In disallowing the use of an uncounseled tribal-court conviction to establish a prior domestic violence conviction within § 117(a)'s compass, the Ninth Circuit created a Circuit split. The Eighth and Tenth Circuits have both held that tribal-court "convictions, valid at their inception, and not alleged to be otherwise unreliable, may be used to prove the elements of § 117." *United States v. Cavanaugh*, 643 F. 3d 592, 594 (CA8 2011); see *United States v. Shavanaux*, 647 F.3d 993, 1000 (CA10 2011). To resolve this disagreement, we granted certiorari, 577 U.S. ___, 136 S. Ct. 690, 193 L. Ed. 2d 518 (2016), and now reverse.

## II

. . . .

*Nichols*' reasoning steers the result here. Bryant's 46-month sentence for violating § 117(a) punishes his most recent acts of domestic assault, not his prior crimes prosecuted in tribal court. Bryant was denied no right to counsel in tribal court, and his Sixth Amendment right was honored in federal court, when he was "adjudicated guilty of the felony offense for which he was imprisoned." *Alabama v. Shelton*, 535 U.S. 654, 664, 122 S. Ct. 1764, 152 L. Ed. 2d 888 (2002). It would be "odd to say that a conviction untainted by a violation of the Sixth Amendment triggers a violation of that same amendment when it's used in a subsequent case where the defendant's right to appointed counsel is fully respected." 769 F.3d, at 679 (Watford, J., concurring)....

In keeping with *Nichols*, we resist creating a "hybrid" category of tribal-court convictions, "good for the punishment actually imposed but not available for sentence enhancement in a later prosecution." 511 U.S., at 744, 114 S. Ct. 1921, 128 L. Ed. 2d 745. . . .

Our decision in *Burgett*, which prohibited the subsequent use of a conviction obtained in violation of the right to counsel, does not aid Bryant. Reliance on an invalid conviction, *Burgett* reasoned, would cause the accused to "suffe[r] anew from the deprivation of [his] Sixth Amendment right." 389 U.S., at 115, 88 S. Ct. 258, 19 L. Ed. 2d 319. Because a defendant convicted in tribal court suffers no Sixth Amendment violation in the first instance, "[u]se of tribal convictions in a subsequent prosecution cannot violate [the Sixth Amendment] 'anew.'" *Shavanaux*, 647 F.3d, at 998.

. . . .

Because Bryant's tribal-court convictions occurred in proceedings that complied with ICRA and were therefore valid when entered, use of those convictions as predicate offenses in a § 117(a) prosecution does not violate the Constitution. We accordingly reverse the judgment of the Court of Appeals for the Ninth Circuit and remand the case for further proceedings consistent with this opinion.

It is so ordered.

———

A 2010 government report noted that United States Attorneys were reluctant to prosecute what they considered minor domestic violence offenses in federal court, which has been problematic for addressing domestic violence on tribal lands in that most D.V. offenses are misdemeanors. Between 2005 and 2009, federal government lawyers declined to prosecute 46 percent of the assault cases referred to them from Indian reservations.[12]

On March 7, 2013, President Obama signed the Violence Against Women Reauthorization Act of 2013 into law. Section 904 of the Act affirms the inherent authority of tribes to exercise criminal jurisdiction over certain non-Indians who commit acts of domestic violence in Indian country. Specifically, this latest version of VAWA allows tribal prosecution of a non-Native perpetrator if (1) the crime involves intimate partners, (2) the victim is Native and (3) the perpetrator has significant ties to the reservation such as living or working on tribal land or having a relationship with a tribe member. The defendant's legal rights must be protected as set out in the Tribal Law and Order Act of 2010, which includes a right to counsel, trained tribal judges who are attorneys, recorded trial proceedings and a jury that includes a cross-section of the reservation community and does not systematically exclude non-Indians.[13]

An inconsistency in the law still leaves Alaskan women with less protection than that given to American Indian women. The Indian Law Resource Center, the National Congress of American Indians and the Native American Rights Fund

---

12. Lorelei Laird, *Reclaiming Sovereignty*, ABA Journal, April 2015, 48.
13. *Tribal Implementation of VAWA: Resource Center for Implementing Tribal Provisions of the Violence Against Women Act (VAWA)*, http://www.ncai.org/tribal-vawa, accessed January 5, 2016.

brought the issue to the attention of the United Nations Human Rights Council, in a statement submitted for the 60th Session of the Commission on the Status of Women between March 14 and 24, 2016. An excerpt of the group's official presentation follows.

## Commission on the Status of Women, Sixtieth session, 2016 Violence Against Indigenous Women and Girls, *Statement submitted by Indian Law Resource Center, National Congress of American Indians, and Native American Rights Fund, and other non-governmental organizations in consultative status with the Economic and Social Council*[14]

American Indian and Alaska Native women and girls are 2.5 times more likely to be sexually assaulted or raped than other women in the United States. One in three will be raped in her lifetime; three in five will be physically assaulted. Native women and youth are particularly vulnerable to human trafficking and to impacts from the extractive industry. On some reservations, the murder rate is ten times the national average. The Indian Law and Order Commission's 2013 Report to the President and Congress of the United States found the situation even more severe for Alaska Native women in rural villages, noting that these "[w]omen have reported rates of domestic violence up to 10 times higher than in the rest of the United States and physical assault victimization rates up to 12 times higher."

This extreme level of violence against indigenous women and girls is not unique to the United States. It is a global scourge, an epidemic, and it demands immediate, sustained actions from states and the United Nations to restore safety to indigenous women and girls and to prevent and respond to such egregious human rights violations.

This Commission, in its 2013 Agreed Conclusions noted that "violence against women and girls persists in every country" and is "a form of discrimination that seriously violates and impairs or nullifies the enjoyment by women and girls of all human rights and fundamental freedoms." (E/2013/27- E/CN.6/2013/11 Para. 10). This Commission specifically recognized that "indigenous women often suffer multiple forms of discrimination and poverty which increase their vulnerability to all forms of violence" (Para. 27). It recommended that states "ensure women's and girls' unimpeded access to justice" and "just and effective remedies" and urged states to "end impunity by ensuring accountability and punishing perpetrators of the most serious crimes against women and girls." (Recommendations f and n).

The disproportionately high rates of violence against American Indian and Alaska Native women are largely due to an unworkable, discriminatory legal system that severely limits the authority of Indian and Alaska nations to protect indigenous

---

14. UN Document E/CN.6/2016/NGO/125.

women and girls from violence, and persistently fails to respond adequately to acts of violence against Native women and children. Together, these factors create a situation where American Indian and Alaska Native women are denied access to justice and to meaningful remedies, and are less protected from violence than other women because they are indigenous and are assaulted on tribal lands or within Alaska Native villages.

Indian tribes, Native woman, and their advocates have successfully worked for important reforms in United States law in recent years. These reforms promote the collective rights of self-determination and self-government recognized in the United Nations Declaration on the Rights of Indigenous Peoples. The United States has improved its laws by enacting legislation such as the Tribal Law and Order Act of 2010 to enhance tribal sentencing authority, and tribal provisions in the Violence Against Women Reauthorization Act of 2013 that restore limited criminal authority over certain non-Indians that commit domestic violence, dating violence, or violate protection orders within the tribe's jurisdiction.

But many significant barriers remain. Indian nations must meet stringent requirements to use the new laws and this, coupled with the lack of sufficient funding for implementation, may delay, deter, or even prevent tribes from proceeding at all. Even where tribes do exercise the new jurisdiction, it is limited. Tribes are generally still unable to prosecute many non-Indians who rape, murder, stalk, or traffic American Indian and Alaska Native women. Strangers may also still enter reservations and commit violent crimes against Indian women with impunity.

Among the most egregious legal barriers still existing in the United States is the one impacting Alaska Native tribes and Alaska Native women. All but one of the 229 tribes in Alaska are prevented from exercising the restored criminal jurisdiction over non-Indians available to nearly all other tribes simply because of the way the United States classifies their land. Through this exclusion, United States law denies Alaska Native women equal protection under the law and treats them differently than other women, including other indigenous women.

Combating violence by implementing decisions of the World Conference on Indigenous Peoples.

The Declaration on the Rights of Indigenous Peoples calls on states, in conjunction with indigenous peoples, to take measures to protect indigenous women and children against all forms of violence and discrimination. Restoring safety to indigenous women is inextricably tied to upholding all the rights affirmed in the Declaration, including the rights to self-determination and self-government. This work will require the sustained efforts of the United Nations, of states, and of indigenous nations, women, and communities.

The Outcome Document of the 2014 World Conference on Indigenous Peoples reaffirms United Nations Member states' commitment to promote and advance the rights of indigenous peoples and uphold the principles of the Declaration (A/Res/69/2).

To achieve this objective and further implementation of the Declaration, states committed in the Outcome Document to intensify their efforts to end violence against indigenous women and girls and they called on the Human Rights Council and the Commission to act as well.

. . . .

The Outcome Document calls on the Commission on the Status of Women to consider the issue of the empowerment of indigenous women at a future session, and both the Permanent Forum on Indigenous Issues and the Special Rapporteur on the rights of indigenous peoples support such consideration in the immediate future. When this Commission does so, we urge full and effective participation of indigenous women and indigenous governments in these discussions, and the development of concrete recommendations or agreed conclusions to address existing legal barriers, empower indigenous women, build the capacity of indigenous juridical systems, and provide reliable access to justice and meaningful remedies within their local indigenous governments.

On June 24, 2014, 35 states made a joint-statement to the Human Rights Council observing that "indigenous peoples themselves may well be in the best position to combat violence against indigenous women and girls . . . . They are closer and better able to address the issue when provided with tools and the legal capability to stop the violence." The Special Rapporteur on the rights of indigenous peoples recently recommended that states "ensure clarity with regard to the relationship between indigenous, national and local jurisdictions in relation to violence against women; and ensure that the justice process is accessible and sensitive to the needs of indigenous women." (Para. 79(e)).

Too often violence against indigenous women goes unprosecuted, offenders go unpunished, and victims' human rights are violated with impunity due to legal and other barriers and unfair restrictions on indigenous self-government.

We respectfully urge the Commission to consider the issue of the empowerment of indigenous women on an accelerated basis. As recognized by many international experts, violence against indigenous women is a serious human rights violation — a violation so significant that it precludes their realization of all other human rights. Violence against indigenous women and girls is a worldwide crisis that cannot wait to be addressed. The time for serious consideration and treatment of the issue by the Commission and other bodies of the United Nations is now.

*This statement is supported by the Alaska Native Women's Resource Center, Alliance of Tribal Coalitions to End Violence, Anvik Village Council, Clan Star, Inc., National Indigenous Women's Resource Center, Native Women's Coalition, Sacred Hoop Coalition, Southwest Indigenous Women's Coalition, Strong Hearted Native Women's Coalition, and Women Spirit Coalition.*

# VIII. Women With Disabilities

## Karen Nutter, Note: *Domestic Violence in the Lives of Women With Disabilities: No (Accessible) Shelter From the Storm*
13 S. Cal. Rev. L. & Women's Stud. 329 (2004)

. . . .

A. What is a Disability?

The word "disability" may bring to mind obvious physical impairments, such as blindness, deafness, and paraplegia. However, as defined by Title III of the Americans with Disabilities Act, which covers public accommodations and commercial facilities, "disability" means much more, describing any physical or mental impairment that does limit or has substantially limited one or more major life activities. It also protects persons who are regarded as having such an impairment.

. . . .

B. Domestic Violence: The Experience of Women With Disabilities

In addition to the "traditional" types of domestic violence, women with disabilities face additional types of abuse. A batterer may take away or dismantle a wheelchair or other assistive device, disconnect the telephone or otherwise put it out of her reach, withhold food, or, if the woman has a visual impairment, put something dangerous in her path. He may withhold her medication, give her too much or too little medication, refuse to help her dress, leave her unclothed, refuse to turn her if she is at risk of pressure sores, refuse to help her use the toilet, or leave her in the bathtub for several days.

. . . .

Regardless of the percentage of women with disabilities who experience domestic violence, there are many reasons why they may find it more difficult to leave their batterers than do women without disabilities. In the first place, a woman, particularly if she has a developmental disability, may not know that what she is experiencing is abuse. If her batterer has kept her isolated from peers who enjoy loving relationships, she may accept the abuse as an inevitable part of the life of a person with a disability. This is especially true in situations in which the woman has been given few opportunities in the past to make decisions about how she lives her life.

Even a woman who recognizes the abuse may feel that she can do little to escape. Obviously, women with mobility or visual impairments may not be able to physically flee from their abusers, and women who cannot drive may depend on transportation services that require them to call in advance for a ride. In addition, women who, due to disabilities, grew up in protected atmospheres or were otherwise isolated from general activities may not feel that they can make decisions on their own. Further, women who have lived under the supervision of health practitioners or institutional personnel may be inclined to passively accept the dictates of authority figures, making them particularly attractive to men who seek vulnerable women to control.

Moreover, general social prejudice against women with disabilities, including the notion that they are "asexual," may make the women feel that they should appreciate any kind of intimate attention, even if it is abusive. A woman may then be prone to believing her batterer when he calls her names or tells her that without his care, she would be in an institution, that no other man would want her.

Indeed, another large hurdle is the fact that for women with disabilities, their batterers are often their caretakers. Even if a woman has access to a telephone, her batterer's isolation of her may mean that he is her only link to society, and she may not have a back-up caretaker to call. In addition, she may not think that domestic violence shelters will be able to accommodate her needs and, even if they will, she will need to face the difficult task of finding accessible housing after she leaves the shelter. Reporting her batterer and facing the real possibility of a fatal reprisal, might then lead her only to institutional care and further loss of autonomy. Therefore, in contrast to women without disabilities, whose escape signals the beginning of safety and independence, women with disabilities may face further abuse and dependence if they leave their batterers. Women who have children also face the threat of having no one to care for the children or having the children taken from them if they leave. Threats to take children away are common in abusive relationships involving women with disabilities, and courts may be inclined to award batterers custody because they think that being able-bodied makes the batterers more fit as parents.

Financial considerations also play a role in a woman's ability to leave. Employer discrimination, the constraints of her disability, and/or her batterer's possessive control may have made it difficult for her to find or keep a job, leaving her financially dependent on her batterer. Alternatively, her batterer may be dependent on her social security checks or his "caretaker" payment from the government for his livelihood, making him particularly resistant to ending the relationship.

C. The Failure of Protective Orders and Domestic Violence Shelters to Adequately Provide Refuge for Women With Disabilities

1. Protective Orders

. . . .

Even if she is able to secure an EPO, a woman must then properly fill out myriad forms and declarations to begin the process of securing a restraining order. Without someone to help them complete and file these forms, women with developmental or vision impairments may find it impossible to go through this process. Compounding the problem is the fact that many courthouses themselves are not accessible. Despite a state rule of court that provides for modifications in policies, practices, and procedures; alteration of existing facilities; and the use of auxiliary aids and services to qualified persons with disabilities, women with disabilities may still find themselves in buildings with insufficient ramping, elevators that cannot take them to the necessary floors without security guard assistance, accessible restrooms on different floors, and filing counters that are too high for wheelchair users.

Women who are able to file their requests for protective orders must then go through the arduous task of appearing in court. In addition to the architectural barriers they must face, women with speech difficulties or developmental disabilities may find it difficult to relate a story that the court will understand. In addition, women who have been conditioned to submit to authority figures may want to "please" rather than "complain," leaving them at the mercy of a cross-examining attorney. In addition, undercutting the entire proceeding may be the myths that no one would abuse a person with disabilities and that caretakers should be awarded sympathy for and leeway in their work, rather than being condemned for it.

2. Domestic Violence Shelters

Seeking refuge in a domestic violence shelter is a difficult decision for any woman to make; as one shelter staff member admitted, going into a shelter means a woman needs to "drop her job, share a room with another family and leave the stability [she knows]." What's more, the woman may have a "pretty grim" idea of what shelters are like; visions of cots set up in cavernous rooms may lead many women to avoid shelters, even at the cost of staying with their batterers. But for many women with disabilities, apprehension of what they will find at a shelter is compounded by the fear that they will not even be admitted.

Domestic violence shelters are covered under Title III of the Americans with Disabilities Act, which prohibits discrimination in public accommodations and commercial facilities. The Technical Assistance Manual for Title III, issued by the federal government to "assist individuals and entities in understanding their rights and duties under the Act," includes "places of lodging" and "social service center establishments" in its nonexhaustive list of covered entities and explains how a homeless shelter that provides both short-term stays and services such as meals and counseling could be covered under the Act as either a place of lodging or a social service center establishment. As domestic violence shelters also provide lodging and services, they are also covered under the Act.

. . . .

However, despite being Title III entities, domestic violence shelters generally are not equipped to serve the needs of women with disabilities. A main reason is lack of funds; many shelters are located in older buildings, such as former private homes, and may be able to remodel their spaces to include such accommodations as ramps, wide doorways and passageways, low sinks and counters, and single-floor layouts only with "significant difficulty and expense." Small budgets also keep staff sizes small, and staff may not be available to provide extra assistance, from help with tasks to rides to doctor's appointments, to women who need it. These budgets also restrain shelters from providing auxiliary aids, such as sign language interpreters, which means that women who have hearing impairments but who are physically capable of meeting the limits of the shelter may need to spend their time there communicating via note. In addition, shelters may not have TDD lines, which enable hearing-impaired women to call them, and those that do may not have time to adequately train staff on their use.

Shelter rules may also work against women with disabilities. Rules against visitors may make it difficult or impossible for a woman to get help from a personal assistant, friend, or visiting nurse. Rules prohibiting women from keeping appointments that their batterers know about may make it difficult for them to attend regularly scheduled doctor's visits. Rules against pets may make service animals, if not prohibited, at least unwelcome. In addition, women with some disabilities may not be able to perform certain mandated chores. However, changing these rules to accommodate the needs of a woman with a disability may either constitute a "fundamental alteration" in its services or compromise the safety of its clients.

. . . .

### VI. CONCLUSION

Contrary to myth, women with disabilities do have relationships and enjoy intimacy. Unfortunately, just like women without disabilities, they may be abused by their partners and may in fact face an even greater threat of domestic violence. Certainly, they face more barriers when they attempt to escape their batterers. While myriad factors exist to keep these barriers in place, some changes to the ways in which legal protections are afforded to women with disabilities, as well as to the ways in which shelters serve them, may help to make escape easier.

---

A report published for the 20th anniversary of the Violence Against Women Act by the office of Vice President Joseph Biden, *1 is 2 Many,* noted that studies suggested that disabled women were some 40 percent more likely to experience both physical and sexual violence. Moreover, the violence they suffer may be more severe than that which is experienced by women who are not disabled. It should also come as no surprise that the report acknowledges disabled women have greater challenges utilizing services designed to help victims of domestic violence. Following the reauthorization of VAWA in 2000, federal funding has been available for grants to help state and local governments meet the special needs of this particularly vulnerable population.[15]

## IX. Cultural Defenses

### State v. Vue
Minnesota Court of Appeals
606 N.W.2d 719 (2000)

RANDALL, JUDGE

Appellant and M.V. are Hmong immigrants who came to the United States from Laos in the late 1970's. They were never legally married, but lived as husband and wife

---

15. *1 is 2 Many: Twenty Years of Fighting Violence Against Women and Girls*, 24–25.

from 1980 through the mid-to-late 1990's, when their relationship deteriorated. In February 1998, M.V. obtained an order for protection against appellant.

On June 5, 1998, M.V. reported appellant to the police, claiming he had raped her four times in four separate incidents occurring between February and May 1998. Appellant was arrested and charged with four counts of criminal sexual conduct, four counts of violating an order for protection, and one count of pattern of harassing conduct.

Before jury selection, the court and counsel had a preliminary discussion on the state's plan to introduce expert testimony on Hmong culture. The prosecutor noted that the jury pool's responses to questionnaires showed a poor understanding of Hmong culture. The prosecutor sought to introduce expert testimony to provide context for the jury's determinations of witness credibility, but said the expert would not comment on the case itself. The prosecutor described the scope of the proposed testimony and added that it could help explain M.V.'s delay in coming forward and rebut the defense theory that the allegations were rooted in M.V.'s jealousy of appellant's second wife. The defense objected to the proposed testimony, and the court took the matter under advisement.

At trial, M.V. testified about the clan structure of Hmong society, the hierarchy of leadership within the clan, and the role of Hmong women in choosing a husband. She said it was inappropriate in Hmong culture for individuals with family or clan-related problems to seek help from outside the clan and that she was being treated as an outcast for having reported her husband to the police. She claimed appellant had been threatening and abusive to her throughout their marriage and had forced her to have sex with him hundreds of times. She said she did not report the rapes earlier because of Hmong social pressure and because appellant said he would kill her if she did.

During a break in the state's case-in-chief, the court held a voir dire examination of the proposed expert witness, a white Minneapolis Park Police officer, and a hearing on the defense motion to exclude his testimony. On direct and cross-examination, the officer described his interest in and personal and professional exposure to Hmong culture.

The prosecutor said the officer would testify to the following: a general history of the Hmong in America; the clan system and the hierarchy within the clans; assimilation issues facing the Hmong in America; Hmong-Americans' attitudes toward the American criminal justice system; the traditional system for resolving family and clan-related problems; issues with going outside the clan for help; the role and position of women in Hmong culture; and male-female relations in traditional marriages.

In allowing the testimony, the court compared it to expert testimony on battered woman syndrome, noted it was being offered to promote a complete understanding of the evidence, and found it would be helpful to the jury.

As an example of a conflict between Hmong culture and the American legal system, the officer described a traditional marriage practice in which men "kidnap" young girls. Among other generalized statements, the state's expert testified that Southeast Asian victims are generally reluctant to report crimes. Speaking of Hmong culture, he testified in part:

> Well, as I indicated it is a male-dominated culture, very clearly. It's not the only culture that's male dominated, I might add, but it's very clear in Hmong culture. Women are to be obedient, to be silent, to suffer rather than to tell. Domestic abuse is a very private situation. I'm not even so sure if the abuse is shared with other women. I think it's kept very much internal.

On cross-examination, the officer stated that "male-dominance" was "fairly universal in the Hmong culture." In addition, the defense counsel asked and the expert responded as follows:

> Q: Are you suggesting that what male dominance really means is abuse?
>
> A: I have seen evidence—secondhand, I might add, maybe third-hand, not firsthand or I would have to act as a police officer—of male aggression within the Hmong community to keep the female in her place.
>
> Q: Are you saying that that is a general trait or are you saying that all Hmong traditional males are abusive?
>
> A: I've been around long enough to know that you can never make a statement that says all of anything will happen all of the time. I think there are patterns that can be identified over time and that that pattern is disturbing in the Hmong culture. . . .

## ANALYSIS

Appellant argues the expert testimony was inadmissible cultural stereotyping calculated to appeal to cultural and racial prejudice. He claims it (1) lacked foundation, (2) was irrelevant and unduly prejudicial, and (3) violated public policy and his state and federal constitutional rights to a fair trial, the presumption of innocence, due process, and equal protection. We agree.

Generally, admission of expert testimony rests within the district court's discretion and will not be reversed absent clear error. *State v. Koskela*, 536 N.W.2d 625, 629 (Minn. 1995). Even where a defendant alleges a constitutional violation, we review evidentiary questions for abuse of discretion. *State v. Profitt*, 591 N.W.2d 451, 463 (Minn. 1999), *cert. denied*, 145 L. Ed. 2d 130, 120 S. Ct. 153 (1999).

Minn. R. Evid. 702 sets the basic standard for admission of expert testimony:

> If scientific, technical, or other specialized knowledge will assist the trier of fact to understand the evidence or to determine a fact in issue, a witness qualified as an expert by knowledge, skill, experience, training, or education, may testify thereto in the form of an opinion or otherwise.

But, along with the bare bones provisions of Minn. R. Evid. 702, a district court may consider the offered expert testimony under a balancing test embodied in Minn. R. Evid. 403:

> Although relevant, evidence may be excluded if its probative value is substantially outweighed by the danger of unfair prejudice, confusion of the issues, or misleading the jury, or by considerations of undue delay, waste of time, or needless presentation of cumulative evidence.

*See State v. Nystrom*, 596 N.W.2d 256, 259 (Minn. 1999) (holding district court must scrutinize proffered expert testimony and exclude it if it is irrelevant, confusing, or not helpful).

. . . . In this case, the primary issue at trial was whether M.V. consented to the sexual contact with appellant. Both sides addressed her delay in bringing the allegations. The prosecutor offered the testimony of a park policeman to bolster M.V.'s story by "explaining" why a Hmong immigrant who had been raped by her husband would be reluctant to go to the police. There is little in this record suggesting cultural testimony was necessary. The complainant was a grown woman; she was bilingual and educated; and she had been in the United States for many years. A lay jury would not have had trouble understanding or believing her testimony simply because she was Hmong. It is patronizing to suggest otherwise. *See State v. Myers*, 359 N.W.2d 604, 610 (Minn. 1984). . . . The expert testimony itself confirmed the lack of relevancy to this case and to this victim. The transcription shows the following questions and answers:

> Q: Are you saying then—and this is what I'm leading up to, Lieutenant—that all of the Hmong people in Minnesota are following the same cultural trends?
>
> A: I would not say that all Hmong follow the same cultural trends, but I would say that the Hmong culture that I've observed is slower to change than other cultures that I've observed.
>
> Q: Would you say that language is one reason why, at least in your observations, there has been a slower cultural change?
>
> A: I would strongly agree that, *particularly among older Hmong citizens where English is nonexistent or very difficult at best*. I would say that the isolation that comes from not being able to go to a mall and shop and exchange normal conversation with shopkeepers or other people in society has kept Hmong women, in particular older Hmong women, prisoners in their homes.

(Emphasis added.) Thus, the "expert's" cultural testimony emphasized the barriers on reporting "among older Hmong citizens where English is nonexistent or very difficult at best." This is not our case.

Further, the credentials of this Minneapolis Park Police officer to give expert opinions on Hmong culture are suspect. The record shows that the officer's contact with Hmong culture arose primarily from personal experience with family friends, that his exposure to Hmong culture as a police officer was limited, and that he had little or no academic training involving Hmong culture.

While we acknowledge there is no formal requirement to qualifying as an expert under Minn. R. Evid. 702, the informal nature of this officer's familiarity with Hmong culture brings his qualifications to be an expert into doubt. *See Vang v. Toyed,* 944 F.2d 476, 480–81 (9th Cir. 1991) (holding district court properly allowed *epidemiologist* to testify as expert on Hmong culture in *civil action* related to rapes of Hmong victims); *State v. Lee,* 494 N.W.2d 475, 480 (Minn. 1992) (stating in dictum that university professor's testimony on Hmong culture was helpful to jury in rape trial involving Hmong victims).

We note that here, unlike *Lee,* the defense did not open the door to the testimony by attacking the complainant's credibility with its own expert. *See Lee,* 494 N.W.2d at 480–81 (finding no reversible error in allowing state's expert to testify about unrelated rape of Hmong woman to rebut testimony by defense expert, a Hmong elder, attacking victims' credibility).

The "expert" testimony was inherently prejudicial. It went far beyond describing Hmong cultural practices that would help explain the alleged victim's behavior, *if* such testimony was needed. The testimony included generic statements about "male-dominance" in Hmong culture and directly implied a generalized perceived pattern of abuse of Hmong females by Hmong males.

While some of these statements could conceivably be relevant to a complainant's reluctance to come forward, their probative value, if any, is based on generalizations that appellant is part of a "guilty class" of spouse-abusers, and the victim is part of a "victim class" of abused women. By asserting that Hmong men tend to abuse their wives, the expert testimony directly implied to the jury that because defendant was Hmong, he was more likely to have assaulted his wife. It is self-evident that this is highly prejudicial. It is impermissible to link a defendant's ethnicity to the likelihood of his guilt. . . .

Reversal is not required when an erroneous admission of objected-to evidence is harmless beyond a reasonable doubt. *State v. Bauer,* 598 N.W.2d 352, 367 (Minn. 1999) (citation omitted). . . .

Admitting expert testimony always risks that the expert's opinions will inordinately influence the jury. *See, e.g., State v. Ritt,* 599 N.W.2d 802, 811 (Minn. 1999) (citing *Myers,* 359 N.W.2d at 609–10), *cert. denied,* U.S., 120 S. Ct. 1183, 145 L. Ed. 2d 1090 (Feb. 22, 2000). The record shows appellant's conviction was based on disputed testimonial evidence. The outcome of the trial depended on whom the jury believed. By implying appellant's Hmong descent made him a probable spouse-abuser, the improper testimony clearly implied a conviction should be forthcoming. In view of the severe risk of prejudice it posed, we cannot escape the conclusion that the improper testimony strongly influenced the jury's decision to convict.

We conclude that the state failed to meet its burden of proving harmless error. We reverse and remand for a new trial.

# X. Law Enforcement/Military "Culture"

Cultures are not only those groups into which we are born, but also include groups that we choose to join or in which circumstances place us. In our post-9/11 world, the role of the military in our society is stronger than ever. We have great respect for the men and women who don uniforms and sacrifice their lives for our safety. Similarly, in a world that feels increasingly dangerous, we appreciate the police officers who work to keep communities safe. How do we address the fact that some of our military and law enforcement "heroes" in the world turn out to be abusers at home? How do we reconcile the good they do for strangers with the fear they unleash on their loved ones? Is there a reluctance to hold these public servants accountable?

When a police officer is accused of a particularly violent act of domestic violence, the press and public take notice. In the spring of 2011, the body of 40-year-old Tina Adovasio was discovered in a woodsy area of suburban Westchester County outside New York City. Almost immediately, the prime suspect was her husband, a former New York City police officer who had faced previous allegations of domestic violence.[16] The officer, Eddy Coello, had been forced off the NYPD after having abused a prior girlfriend.[17]

Coello had been arrested three times for acts of domestic violence against the wife he eventually killed. Shortly before she was murdered, she had filed for divorce. Coello was convicted of strangling his wife and sentenced to the maximum sentence allowed under New York law — 25 years to life in prison.[18]

In 2009, Drew Peterson, a former police officer in suburban Chicago, was charged with the 2004 murder of his third wife—whose bathtub drowning death was originally ruled an accident—while under suspicion for the killing of his fourth, who disappeared three years later. Both marriages were troubled.[19] Although he was convicted and sentenced to 38 years in jail for the killing of his third wife, his legal woes are not over yet—while the investigation into the demise of his fourth wife continued, Peterson attempted to hire a hit man from jail to kill what he viewed as an overzealous prosecutor. He was convicted of the attempt on the prosecutor in 2016.[20]

---

16. Karen Zraick, *Man is Person of Interest in Wife's Death*, N.Y. Times, March 18, 2011.
17. Andrew Strickler, *Ex-cop accused of strangling wife and dumping her body off rejects plea deal*, N.Y. Post, September 27, 2012.
18. *Former NYPD Cop Gests 25 Years to Live for Murder of Wife Whose Body Was Found in Yorktown*, Yorktown-SomersPatch, http://yorktown-somers.patch.com/articles/former-nypd-cop-get-25-years-to-life-for-murder/html, accessed February 1, 2016.
19. Steven Yaccino, *Murder Trial Tests Leeway for Giving Dead a Say*, N.Y. Times, July 31, 2012.
20. Matthew Walberg, *Drew Peterson Found Guilty of Trying to Have Prosecutor Killed*, Chicago Tribune, June 1, 2016, www.chicagotribune.com/news/ct-drew-peterson-trial-closings-met-20160531-story.html, accessed October 1, 2016.

In Canton, Ohio, former police officer Bobby Lee Cutts, Jr., was sentenced to 57-years-to-life for murdering his pregnant girlfriend in the presence of their two-and-a-half-year-old toddler in a case that attracted national attention.[21]

The military and the police are alike in many ways; armed organizations created to maintain safety and order and structured in a manner that values obedience based on rank. And, until recent years, both institutions were largely male-populated and male-oriented. Both organizations have trouble with domestic violence, although gauging actual numbers is difficult. A 2012 study conducted by a pair of Ohio State University professors, Philip M. Stinson and John Liederbach, looked at cases involving 281 police officers arrested for domestic violence. Almost all of the cases involved male street-level patrol officers (86.7). In 40 percent of the cases, the charge involved physical assault. Of those cases where the researchers were able to determine the outcomes (233), one-third of the accused lost their jobs through resignations or firings while the rest of those charged received only temporary suspensions.[22] The International Association of Chiefs of Police, headquartered in Alexandria, Virginia, has had a zero-tolerance policy on domestic violence by officers for more than a decade. "It is imperative to the integrity of the profession of policing and the sense of trust communities have in their local law enforcement agencies that leaders, through the adoption of clear policies, make a definitive statement that domestic violence will not be tolerated."[23]

Domestic violence in the military is said to be on the rise. As early as 1999, Congress established a task force within the U.S. Department of Defense because the incidence of violence in military families had grown from 18.6 incidents per 1,000 soldiers in 1990 to 25.6 per 1,000 soldiers in 1996.[24] In a 2011 article in *Stars and Stripes*, writer Nancy Montgomery reported that in 2010, the rate of spousal abuse was 11.2 per 1,000 couples, which had been up from 10.1 the year before and 9.4 per thousand in 2008. There were also 16 domestic violence homicides in 2010; in 81 percent of the cases the alleged assailant was an active-duty soldier. Child abuse cases were also up in 2010, from 4.8 per 1,000 children in 2008 to 5.7 per 1,000 in 2010. The reason was hard to determine. Whether it was due to "more people reporting who had kept silent in the past, better record-keeping or more people in the

---

21. Mallory Simon & Ann O'Neill, *Killer Ex-Cop Gets 57 to Life After Jury Spares Him,* CNN, February 27, 2008, www.cnn.com/2008/CRIME/02/27/cutts.sentence/index.html?iref=nextin, accessed October 11, 2016.

22. Philip M. Stinson and John Liederbach, *Research in Brief: Officer-Involved Domestic Violence,* (79)(9) Police Chief: The Professional Voice of Law Enforcement, September 2012, http:www.policechiefmagazine.org/magazine/index.cfm?fuseaction=print_display&article_id=2752&issue_id=92012, accessed February 2, 2016.

23. International Association of Chiefs of Police, *Domestic Violence by Police Officers: A Policy of the IACP Police Response to Violence Against Women Project,* July 2003.

24. Fox Butterfield, *Wife Killings at Fort Reflect Growing Problem in Military,* N.Y. Times, July 29, 2002.

military abusing their spouses and children—is unknown."[25] The following article puts the problem of domestic violence in the military into perspective.

## Simeon Stamm, Note: *Intimate Partner Violence in the Military: Securing Our Country, Starting with the Home*
47 Fam. Ct. Rev. 321 (April 2009)

*"Domestic violence is a pervasive problem that transcends all ethnic, racial, gender and socioeconomic boundaries, and it will not be tolerated in the Department of Defense. Domestic violence destroys individuals, ruins families and weakens our communities."*

—Defense Secretary Donald Rumsfeld

### I. INTRODUCTION

Donna was twenty years old when she married her college sweetheart, James, who was an officer serving in the U.S. Army. Prior to his deployment overseas, James occasionally yelled at Donna about her supposed excessive spending and her lack of house-cleaning skills. He also called her names and threatened to use violence, one time even shoving her to the floor. Despite the verbal and physical abuse, Donna never called the police, nor did she ever file a report of abuse due to fear of what would happen to her, her husband, and her family.

Shortly after his return from overseas, the military transferred James, Donna, and their two children, Ted (thirteen) and Marshall (seven), from their on-base home in New Jersey to an off-base residence in Colorado. Donna believed that moving to a new location would bring a fresh new start. However, the verbal and physical abuse resumed once the family settled into their new home.

While living in Colorado, James continually limited the amount of money Donna was allowed to spend. On one particular evening, Donna approached James to have a discussion about this money-spending issue. Their conversation started out civil and calm. In a matter of seconds, though, James became loud and argumentative. The verbal exchange then came to an abrupt end when James knocked down Donna, dragged her through their home, and strangled her with his bare hands until she lost consciousness. As a result, Donna sustained bruising on her back, chest, and neck.

Following the violent incident, Ted, who witnessed the whole thing, called local law enforcement to their off-post residence. When the sheriff's deputies arrived, James, dressed in his uniform, warmly greeted them and invited them into the home. First, the deputies interviewed James in the entry hall of the home. The deputies then discussed with James the medals, awards, and commendations hanging on the walls of their home. They discussed James' life in the military and praised him for his valuable service to the United States. The deputies left the home without conducting an

---

25. Nancy Montgomery, *Reports of Family Violence, Abuse Within Military Rise*, Stars and Stripes, July 10, 2011.

interview of the victim, Donna, and without taking any further actions to alleviate the violent situation that had been reported.

The following day, Donna sought medical treatment at the military hospital. There, the nursing staff notified the military police of a domestic disturbance that occurred off base at an unknown time. The hospital staff tried to gain information from Donna about what had happened. The nurses noted Donna's reluctance to give any information regarding the incident, which they believed was mainly due to fear that revealing such details would harm her husband's career. Donna was treated and released back home that same day. Eventually, James was processed by the military police, read his rights, but declined to provide a statement concerning the incident. His commander issued a military protective order (MPO) that required James to stay away from Donna, which included not going to the family home, until a more thorough investigation could be undertaken. However, as soon as Donna returned home from the hospital, James violated the order when he returned to their home.

The Case Review Committee, which is a multidisciplinary team that assesses reports of substantiated spousal abuse, determined that, because Donna did not need to spend the night in the hospital, the abuse ranked at a mild level on the Incident Severity Index for Spouse Abuse. They recommended a treatment plan that included stress and anger management classes. The treatment recommendations of the Family Advocacy Program and CRC were not supported by the Command, due to the Command believing that the severity of the incident was mild and therefore it being something that both Donna and James could work out by themselves. The commander did not order James to attend either of the two classes, nor did he monitor James' progress or attendance. The commander did not take any disciplinary action with regards to James' violation of the military protective order. Two months later, James killed Donna after another "conversation" over money-spending issues got out of hand.

Although this was a fictional example of violence, such instances are certainly present in the U.S. Military. Domestic violence in the U.S. Military is a growing concern. Research shows that the rates of domestic violence in the U.S. Military are two to five times higher than among the civilian population. In the past, the U.S. Army has demonstrated the highest rates of domestic violence out of any other military sector. Although the Department of Defense has attempted to find ways to minimize the recurring problem of domestic violence in the military, they have not been able to solve all of them.

In cases of domestic abuse in the military, the Incident Severity Index for Spouse Abuse is used by the CRC to determine the severity of abuse. The CRC uses this index when determining the treatment and punishment options for the perpetrator of domestic violence. However, this index is extremely inconsistent with the current views and emerging research of domestic violence. Currently, the Index only has three levels of abuse: "mild," "moderate," and "severe." . . .

## II. THE PREVALENCE OF DOMESTIC VIOLENCE IN THE MILITARY

. . . .

### B. DOMESTIC VIOLENCE AND THE MILITARY

The prevalence of domestic violence in the military is higher than in the civilian population. The typical victim of military domestic violence is a female, civilian spouse of an active duty military soldier. On average, the victim is under the age of twenty-five years old. Most victims are also parents and more than half of the victims have been married two years or less. In most cases, when domestic violence involving members of the military has been substantiated, the perpetrator is predominantly a male serving on active duty.

### C. RISK FACTORS

. . . .

In addition to the general risk factors associated with domestic violence, statistics show that military families are substantially more vulnerable to domestic violence than others. A high percentage of military personnel have prior experiences of domestic violence. For example, among Navy recruits, 54% of women and 40% of men witnessed parental violence prior to enlistment. Moreover, 30% of active duty military women report lifetime intimate partner physical or sexual assault, and 22% report some form of intimate partner sexual assault during their time of military service. Furthermore, the age groups most likely to commit domestic violence are those between the ages of twenty and forty, and 66% of active duty military personnel are between ages of seventeen and thirty-four.

The constant relocation of military families may also make them more vulnerable to domestic violence than others. Military families frequently move from place to place, sometimes to locations with unfamiliar cultures and values. This can lead to isolation for the victims by cutting them off from family and other familiar support systems. Deployments and military personnel returning to the family also create unique stresses on military families. When a soldier is deployed, the partner who is left at home (usually the wife) needs to assume new roles, such as running the household and becoming more independent. There may be issues related to this role reversal upon the soldiers return home. For example, when the husband is deployed, the wife will bear the brunt of the economic decision-making responsibilities. Upon the husband's return, there may be a power struggle in the family. Furthermore, long separations can also foster distrust between the couple, and uncertainty about their future.

### D. BARRIERS TO REPORTING

Military domestic violence victims experience the same barriers to reporting domestic violence that their civilian counterparts experience. Common to both are feelings of shame, isolation, fear of retaliation from the abusive partner and economic concerns are just a handful of them. However, there are issues unique to the military that make military victims even less likely to report an incident of intimate partner violence. Underreporting in the military may be due to the limited confidentially of domestic violence reports in military cases, as the confidentially of disclosed information cannot be guaranteed. Currently, new policies allow for restricted reports to be made by victims to a Health Care Provider or Victim Advocate. Though this policy is only a year old and as such, it is too early to measure its impact on increased reporting.

Another possible reason that reporting is low is that victims fear what will happen to the abuser's career. "Many survivors fear reporting domestic violence because they believe the report will affect their husbands' chance for promotions and pay increases or will result in their husbands' discharge." This can have a significant impact on the family. For instance, if the husband losses his job, then there will be a loss of money coming into the family, which can be the cause of even more violence. Furthermore, for many military members, being in the military is more than just a career; it is their identity. The loss of this identity can lead to higher risks of violence, because the abuser may feel like he has nothing left to lose now that he has lost his identity and career.

Similarly, victims who are military members show low rates of reporting domestic violence for fear of career consequences. Many women in the military are fearful that if they report their abuse, their fellow soldiers will no longer trust them and will no longer want them in their company. According to the Department of Defense's *Final Report of the Study of Spousal Abuse in the Armed Forces,* domestic violence victims currently serving in the military "fear they will be perceived as 'weak' and be proven unsuitable for career advancement." . . .

## IV. HOW THE MILITARY PROCESSES DOMESTIC VIOLENCE INCIDENTS TODAY

. . . .

### A. PHASE 1

In phase 1, a victim of domestic violence makes a report of the incident. A domestic violence report can originate through military or civilian law enforcement, medical personnel on military bases, the Family Advocacy Program, the victim or the offender, command or others such as coworkers, neighbors, or friends. Suspected cases of abuse should be reported to either the Provost's Marshal's Office (PMO), also known as the military police, the Family Advocacy Program, or to the soldier's Command. The military police will investigate the report if they were the first agency to be contacted about the alleged abuse, or if there is reason to believe that a crime was committed involving a military family. If the couple lives on the military base, the military police will be sent to the couple's home to talk to them about the allegation of domestic violence. If the couple has children, the military police will also talk to the children in an effort to make sure that they are safe as well.

However, studies show that 70% of military families reside off-base; therefore, a high percentage of domestic violence crimes committed by military personnel will come to the attention of civilian authorities. In the past, there were many problems because of the lack of collaboration between the civilian authorities and the military police.... However, through the creation of Memoranda of Understanding (MOU), this problem has been greatly improved. These Memoranda of Understanding allow the civilian law enforcement agencies and the military to work together to exchange information relating to charges and/or arrest of military personnel that occur off the installation.

B. PHASE II

During phase II, the FAP takes over the case. The FAP, like the one established under Army Regulation 608-18, is one of the most significant elements of the military's response to domestic violence. It was set up to establish the military's policy on the prevention, identification, reporting, investigation, and treatment of spousal and child abuse.

The FAP is responsible for ensuring the victim's safety and access to support and advocacy services, as well as ensuring that abusers receive appropriate intervention services. It handles a case from the initial report of abuse all the way to case closure. The FAP provides many valuable services, which may vary among the different services and among the different installations. These services can include outreach, victim advocacy, stress and anger management classes, support groups, and batterer's intervention programs to name a few. The communications of the FAP are not privileged, unless reported under the new restricted policy, and so, the allegations of intimate partner violence and the FAP response will be reflected in the service member's FAP case records. An FAP social worker will schedule an appointment with the alleged victim and another appointment with the offender to obtain information about the incident and history of abuse in the relationship. The social worker will also gather relevant law enforcement, medical and other reports, and conduct a clinical spouse abuse assessment of both the victim and the abuser. Finally, the FAP social worker will present the case to the Case Review Committee ("CRC"), a team created under the umbrella of the FAP, for case determination.

The Case Review Committee is a "multidisciplinary team appointed by an order from the installation commander and supervised by the Medical Treatment Facility (MTF) commander." The CRC typically consists of both Active Duty military personnel and civilian providers. Members of the CRC include a chairperson, usually a senior social worker, a representative from the Army Substance Abuse Program, the installation chaplain, the case manager, a physician, a law enforcement representative, and a legal representative. The purpose of the CRC is "to coordinate medical, legal, law enforcement, and social work assessment, identification, command intervention, and investigation and treatment functions from the initial report of spouse or child abuse to case closure." Furthermore, the CRC will determine whether a report of abuse is "substantiated" or "unsubstantial" after the FAP social worker has presented a report and other participants have offered their input.... If the case is "unsubstantiated," it is closed, though services are still usually offered. If it is substantiated, the CRC will then classify it according to the Incident Severity Index for Spouse Abuse, under Army Regulation 608-18.

The Incident Severity Index for Spouse Abuse is a regulation created by the Department of Defense to help the CRC determine the level of severity of an incident of domestic violence. Since it is only a regulation, it does not carry any penalties under the Uniform Code of Military Justice, and the CRC will only base treatment recommendations off of it. However, a commander will factor the level of severity into his decision making process when determining the proper action to take for a perpetrator of domestic violence. The higher the severity of abuse, the more likely there will be significant action from the Command.

The Incident Severity Index is broken down into three different levels of severity for domestic violence. The categories of abuse are "mild," "moderate," and "severe." . . .

An incident of domestic abuse may be considered "moderate" when it is "an incident or ongoing pattern of incidents that does not meet the criteria of mild or severe." An example of moderate would be if one spouse pushed, grabbed, kicked, shoved or bit the other spouse. Moderately severe abuse is usually deliberate, resulting in either minor or major physical abuse. There may even be short term medical treatment involved.

Finally, "severe" incidents of abuse are those where "an incident or ongoing pattern of incidents that resulted in serious injury, chronic interference with personal liberty, serious impairment, or death." An example of severe abuse would be if one spouse severely beats another spouse, threatens the spouse with a weapon or kills the other spouse. Major physical injury or long term medical treatment is associated with severe abuse.

Based on whether a case is "substantiated" or not, and on the level of severity, the CRC will make treatment recommendations to the commander for both the abuser and the victim. Treatment can range from life skills training, anger management classes, stress management, communication workshops and financial workshops. Other forms of treatment include family and marriage counseling, mental health evaluations and alcohol and drug programs.

### C. PHASE III

Finally, during phase III, the commander decides what disciplinary action to take on the allegation of abuse. Military base commanders have broad discretion when it comes to dealing with incidents that take place on the base, and the courts have been unwilling to interfere in decisions made in the exercise of that discretion. . . . . Moreover, the commander has broad discretion in regard to what disciplinary action the abuser will get. There are numerous options that a commander has at his disposal. These actions can range anywhere from administrative sanctions (i.e. docking of pay, increased duty, etc.) all the way to the possibility of a court martial and prosecution under the Uniform Code of Military Justice (UCMJ).

## V. CURRENT PROBLEMS OF DOMESTIC VIOLENCE IN THE MILITARY

. . . .

### A. INCONSISTENT LEVELS OF SEVERITY

... [A]ccording to the National Coalition Against Domestic Violence, "The Department of Defense severity definitions are inconsistent with commonly held 'characterizations of domestic violence.' As a result, 69% of intimate partner violence cases reported in 1999 were mild, and only 6% were classified as severe."

. . . .

As seen in the Donna and James hypothetical, the CRC categorized the incident of abuse as mild. However, in the civilian population, especially due to the fact that there was strangulation involved, the level of abuse would have easily been categorized as moderate, if not even severe. Therefore, these three categories are simply not working and they need to be replaced with updated, more precise categories of severity.

### B. CATEGORIES PLACE A HEAVY FOCUS ON PHYSICAL ABUSE

The second problem is that the categories place a heavy focus on physical abuse and take a very limited view of emotional abuse. Domestic violence is not just a problem of physical abuse, but also of emotional abuse. Emotional abuse is used to control, degrade, humiliate and punish a spouse and it includes verbal abuse such as yelling, name-calling, blaming, and shaming. Isolation, intimidation, and controlling behavior are also examples of emotional abuse. Furthermore, abusers who use emotional or psychological abuse add threats of physical violence as another way to control their victims. ...

## VI. RESTRUCTURED INCIDENT SEVERITY INDEX FOR INTIMATE PARTNER VIOLENCE

... The CRC should focus on three specific factors to determine the level of severity: physical and emotional abuse and the impact of the violence on the victim. By combining these factors, the CRC will make a proper determination for the appropriate level of severity. The new incident severity index will be broken down into five clearly defined categories. Violent incidents will be ranked between 1 (representing the lowest severity) and 5 (representing the greatest severity).

### A. LEVEL 1

A level one incident represents what is known as Situational Couple Violence. In terms of behavior, this encompasses non-accidental abuse such as shouting, spitting and blocking an exit. Emotional abuse is determined by looking at whether there is a pattern of ongoing attempts by the abuser to control his or her partner through coercion or intimidation. Here, the impact on the victim is having either no or an inconsequential fear of recurring abuse, no visible or internal physical injury and either no or an inconsequential degree of psychological distress as a result of the incident.

The intent of intervention at this level is to provide the family with services in the hopes of working through any problems and getting the family back to a healthy and safe state. The commander should have some informal meetings with the abuser in an attempt to stop the abuse before it starts. The commander should recommend any programs to the abuser or the victim that might benefit them at this early stage of abuse. Further, the commander should also consider punishing the abuser by confining the abuser to the military barracks, in an attempt to give the abuser a chance to calm down.

B. LEVEL 2

While level 2 also deals with Situational Couple Violence, the violence involved often escalates to non-accidental physical abuse such as light pushing, shoving, slapping, biting, grabbing, scratching and twisting. The emotional abuse also escalates To Whom It May Concern: to encompass an emerging pattern of power and control through the use of verbal intimidation, isolation and economic restrictions, and emotional or psychological put-downs. Here, the impact on the victim is found when there is an injury not lasting more than 24 hours, a low-level fear of recurring abuse, or a low-level of psychological distress resulting from the abuse.

The intent of punishment at this level is to stop any emerging patterns of violence or control before they harden into primary patterns of interaction. The commander's response in this level should be similar to the commander's response at level 1. However, when this level of severity has been determined, the commander should have an increased awareness of safety for the victim and increased monitoring of the abuser. The commander should conduct supportive counseling sessions with the abuser. The commander may also want to consider non-judicial administrative sanctions, such as providing the abuser with a warning notice, giving the abuser a reprimand or docking the abuser in pay. Additionally, the commander should consider issuing a MPO to ensure the safety of the victim.

C. LEVEL 3

Level 3 deals with intentional physical abuse such as punching, kicking, slapping with a closed hand, choking, locking up or confining, interfering with the victim's eating or sleeping habits and/or physically assaulting a pregnant spouse. Further, it includes instances of emotional abuse such as placing the victim in fear for his/her own safety, frequent use of put-downs, insults or criticism and threats or use of reprisals for reporting or seeking help. Additionally, another form of emotional abuse that would be included occurs with the presence of a pattern of isolation, emotionally abusing or economically controlling the victim. . . .

Here, victim impact would be assessed by looking at any physical injury lasting more than 24 hours. Other types of victim impact would be the victim's expression of fear of recurrent abuse or the beginning signs of psychological distress. This level is also the first to deal with sexual abuse. The sexual abuse in this category would deal with pressured unwanted sexual activity through threats or intimidation.

At this level, the purpose of punishment should be to monitor and reduce the risk of recurring violence and to hold the abuser accountable for his or her actions. The commander could accomplish this by monitoring the abuser's progress on a regular basis and ensure that the victim has been offered the services of a Victim Advocate. Moreover, the commander should take appropriate action to keep the victim and the abuser separated and away from each other, such as by ordering the abuser to live in the barracks or by issuing an MPO. Further, the commander should make an entry into the service member's record documenting the abuse. Furthermore, the commander should consider appropriate administrative or disciplinary action such as a termination of classification authority, suspension without pay or forfeiture of pay.

D. LEVEL 4

Level 4 represents a high level of severity and deals with a significant use of non-accidental physical force such as hard punching, hard kicking, burning, strangling without the victim losing consciousness, physically assaulting a pregnant spouse, or the use of a weapon. The emotional abuse is comprised by a significant pattern of power and control by the abuser over the victim. . . .

Victim impact is assessed by looking at any physical injury lasting more than 24 hours which would indicate medical attention regardless of whether the victim actually received medical care. Another way to assess the impact on the victim is by looking at psychological distress evident by symptoms of a stressful reaction, depression, anxiety related to the abuse, behavior changes to avoid future violence, learned helplessness, hopelessness and suicide. A third way of determining the impact on the victim is to determine whether the victim has a persistent fear of recurring abuse to the victim, the victim's family or the victim's friends.

The CRC will also focus on sexual abuse in this level. They will look to see if the abusive spouse coerced the victim to participate in unwanted sexual activity through threats, intimidation, or the use of force.

At this level, the objective of taking disciplinary action is to deter any further abuse and consider whether the abuser has further potential for usefulness in the military. The commander should monitor the offender's progress and ensure that the victim has been offered the services of a Victim Advocate. The commander should issue a MPO until risk assessment and safety planning has been accomplished. The commander should consider appropriate disciplinary action such as removal or discharge from service, regardless of office or level of employment.

E. LEVEL 5

Finally, level 5 represents the highest level of severity, dealing with severe life-threatening use of intentional psychical force such as strangling or beating the victim to unconsciousness and the use of a weapon in the incident. Emotional abuse is represented by an extreme use of power and control by the abuser. Some examples may include placing the victim in imminent fear for his or her own physical safety, danger for the loss of life, an unrelenting use of put-downs, insults or criticism and the use of severe punishment for seeking help. Other examples of this degree of emotional abuse include the abuser's extreme use of isolation tactics and the victim's complete denial of access to a telephone, transportation, base services, medical care, family, or money. Other forms of emotional abuse include prolonged stalking, serious threats of murder, and the killing, maiming, or seriously harming of the victim's pets.

The impact on the victim is established by major or life threatening injury warranting medical attention. This includes life threatening injury to a pregnant spouse and/or fetus, imminent fear of recurring violence or loss of life to the victim, the victim's family, the victim's friends, or the victim's pets. Finally, victim impact can be determined by the presence of psychological distress evident in symptoms of a stressful reaction, depression, anxiety related to the abuse, behavior changes to avoid future violence, learned helplessness, post trauma reaction or suicidal behavior. Rape and forcible sodomy are examples of sexual abuse that can be found in this category.

The aim of punishment here is to deter further abuse and prosecute abusers in accordance with the Uniform Code of Military Justice (UCMJ) and State law. The commander should issue a MPO and ensure Victim Advocacy services are offered to the victim and family. The commander should consider pretrial detention and involve the civilian court system when appropriate. . . .

## Diane Wetendorf, *Representing Victims of Police-Perpetrated Domestic Violence*

16(2) Family Law Forum (Fall 2007)
(NM State Bar Association Family Law Section)

. . . .

Police tactics

The abusive officer's entitlement to authority in society bolsters and reinforces his sense of entitlement within his personal relationships. His very presence is a symbol of authority. Officers learn to use gestures, body language, tone and volume of voice to exert their authority. The officer who batters demands respect and unquestioning obedience and deference from his intimate partner. He is likely to interpret any conflict or disagreement as a direct threat to his dominant position. An abusive officer is capable of terrorizing his victim without using physical force; he simply employs the verbal and psychological techniques that he uses on the job to manipulate and coerce his victim to comply with his demands. The victim understands that if she resists his psychological and emotional coercion and continues to resist his control, he is capable of resorting to physical violence. He may escalate his behavior along the continuum of violence, using only the degree of force necessary to gain and maintain control. He may later defend his actions by stating that the victim was attacking him, was hysterical, or that he had to restrain her from hurting herself. He may remind her of his professional power by threatening to have her arrested, jailed or committed to a psychiatric facility. This non-physical coercion, of course, leaves no tangible evidence.

Even if the officer has used physical violence, it is unlikely that the victim ever reported it to the police or to her physician. Her perception of the possible consequences of the system's intervention are often more frightening than her abuser's violence. The officer may have told her that if she called the police, they would not believe her word against his, that he would invoke the "code of silence" or that he would instruct them to arrest her. All too often, he is able to carry out these threats and the victim receives little or no assistance from responding officers. He may have warned her that if she called the police, he would lose his job, and they would lose their income, health insurance, and other benefits, including his pension. The victim knows he would hold her responsible for these losses and for destroying his career. . . .

Standard strategies often inadequate

The professional status, training and worldview of a police officer who batters differentiate this population of batterers from batterers in the civilian population. Officers' professional credibility allows them to explain, defend and summon institutional support and assistance from the very systems to which victims are theoretically supposed to turn to for protection. Civilians who batter do not automatically receive that credibility or deference. The attorney who understands how police use police authority, police training, and police cultural ethos to reinforce their power and control over their victim is better prepared to serve his/her client.

Many attorneys have come to realize that the remedies and legal strategies they normally use in civilian domestic violence cases are sorely inadequate or ineffective in cases involving police officers. They experience the power and impact of police, prosecutorial and judicial discretion as the authorities refuse to enforce laws and policies against a member of law enforcement. They are frustrated as they watch the batterer demonstrate his ability to repeatedly violate the law and court orders with impunity. Many attorneys end up admitting that they have "never seen anything like it before."

It may be unwise to focus on safety measures that rely on the police or the courts for enforcement. This reliance draws the police victim further into the abuser's personal and professional arena of power. In this arena, the abuser knows how things work, has personal and professional influence, and has access to restricted information. The victim and her attorney must carefully consider the possibility of the abuser's immediate reaction and possible retaliation, as well as the long-term implications of each step they take. The abuser's advantages require that attorneys rethink, reevaluate, adjust, or possibly avoid altogether the standard legal strategies and safety measures that they routinely employ in "civilian" cases, such as the victim obtaining an order of protection, reporting to the police, or going to a domestic violence shelter.

Officers' preemptive strategies

Officers who batter are becoming savvy in ways to circumvent the gun laws and police department domestic violence policies. More and more, we see batterers using preemptive strategies that shift the focus and blame to the victim. If the officer has any suspicion that the victim is going to seek help or pursue a legal action, he may block the victim's access to divorce lawyers by being the first to contact them for information. If the victim subsequently calls the attorneys the batterer has already contacted, they will not be able to speak to her due to conflict of interest.

He may call the local domestic violence agency (where he may even be friends with the advocates and staff attorneys) claiming to be the victim and seeking to access services. This may prevent the agency from providing services to the real victim.

The abuser may meet (formally or informally) with his department's supervisor and confide that he and his intimate partner are having "trouble at home." He may warn the department that she may come in with "some sort of allegation" against him, inferring that she is lying, mentally or emotionally unstable, and/or trying to threaten his employment.

He may call 911 during an incident and claim to be the victim of assault or battery. When the police respond, he may insist that fellow officers arrest her. He may petition the court for an Order of Protection. He may be able to elicit the sympathy of the judge regarding his vulnerable professional position, and may obtain not only an Order of Protection, but also possession of the marital home and temporary custody of the children. All of these strategies work to protect his status as a police officer.

Orders of protection

The attorney must listen to the client's reasons for wanting or not wanting a protective order, and respect that she is in the best position to predict how the officer will respond. If she believes that he is likely to view a court order as a sign of aggression or declaration of war, prioritizing her safety may require *not* obtaining a protective order. If she feels that an order is necessary because of child custody or some other consideration, the attorney should obtain information from the abuser's employer regarding the department's policy on protective orders against their officers. Though federal law allows an "official use" exemption for police officers, the abuser's department may have a policy requiring confiscation of an officer's service weapon while a protective order is in effect. Even if the department does not have a formal policy, the attorney should inquire as to possible ramifications the order may have on the abuser's employment status.

The attorney needs to consider whether the judge is likely to issue a permanent order upon the expiration of the emergency order; if not, it may be better not to obtain an emergency order. Whether or not the order poses a real threat to the officer's employment, the officer is likely to fight to vacate the emergency order and/or prevent the issuance of a permanent order. The officer is likely to deny the alleged abuse and attempt to destroy the victim's credibility. If the judge determines there are no grounds for a permanent order, this decision reinforces the abuser's sense of power to control the victim.

In the case where the abuser's attorney argues against a permanent order and is willing to "compromise" with a "mutual order," the victim's attorney must be aware that a mutual order implies mutual responsibility for the alleged abuse. The abuser can use the mutual order as a tool with which to further intimidate the victim by threatening to charge her with violations of the order (for example, during the exchange of the children for visitation). Such a mutual order could have even graver ramifications in a custody dispute. Whereas an order entered against the officer would give the victim an advantage in the custody dispute, a mutual order could be viewed more negatively against the victim than the abuser. Although one would think a mutual order would have equal consequences for both parents, realistically mothers tend to be held to a higher standard.

Of course, any order of protection has little practical value without the cooperation of law enforcement to serve and enforce it. Instead of, or in addition to a court order, the attorney might explore the willingness of the abuser's employing department to issue an Administrative Order of Protection. This is a direct order from a supervisor to the officer stating that he is to refrain from particular conduct toward the victim.

Regardless of the type of order, it is critical for attorneys to realize that such documents are, in the end, only pieces of paper. Without enforcement, and without the battering officer's respect for the order, reliance on its value may prove deadly for the victim.

Department notification

If the victim is considering talking to the officer's supervisor or chief, the attorney can educate the victim about the officer's right to due process and explain what that entails. Victims sometimes incorrectly believe that they will be able to have a confidential discussion with the officer's supervisor, which is neither a realistic nor an accurate expectation. The department's responsibility for the officer dictates that it informs the abuser that the victim has contacted the department and the exact nature of her allegations, and that the department will then conduct an investigation. The victim should anticipate that the department will extend the officer a great deal of credibility and classify conflicting versions of events as "he said, she said" incidents. On the other hand, should the department find her complaint credible, the department is likely to confiscate the officer's department-issued weapons and strip him of his police powers pending further investigation. These actions serve to protect the police department from liability, but may also place the victim in grave danger from the abuser's retaliation.

Prosecution

Prosecutors rely on the cooperation of the police to investigate all crimes and apprehend suspects. Without an adequate investigation and proper handling of evidence the prosecutor's ability to competently perform his/her job would be decimated, making the prosecutor reluctant to damage the working relationship between the prosecutor's office and the police department. The conviction of a police officer for a qualifying domestic violence misdemeanor results in his inability to carry a weapon (18 U.S.C. §922(g)). If the prosecutor does pursue charges, he/she typically reduces the charge to disturbing the peace, criminal destruction of property, or reckless conduct to avoid triggering the gun law.

Prosecutors may anticipate a show of solidarity by the accused's fellow officers that may intimidate the victim and send a message to the prosecutor, witnesses, judge and jury. Prosecutors may also anticipate terrified and "uncooperative" witnesses in the case who are likely to change their testimony or recant their statements. Many times prosecutors do not pursue cases they believe they cannot win.

Flight from the abuser

Domestic violence victims are at serious risk of physical harm after they have left their abusers. The abusive police officer will view the fleeing of the victim as the ultimate defiance of his professional and personal authority and control over her. Police officers are trained to pursue suspects who flee from them, and advocates and other professionals must always consider this professional mind-set when they discuss the victim's plans to leave the relationship. Officers are trained in investigation techniques, have access to official channels of information, and pride themselves on being able to find anyone anywhere. They tend to go to great lengths to hunt down their victims. Frequently, officers use their professional network to help them find their victims by convincing them that the woman has disappeared with his children, is a danger to herself or others, or has committed a crime.

Divorce and custody battles

The batterer may perceive the victim's filing for divorce as the ultimate betrayal, and a lengthy legal battle over *his* property, money, and the children may ensue. He may be determined to have the last word and be obsessed with winning. Victims' attorneys complain that departments stonewall the court's orders for their employees' financial information and provide loopholes that allow officers to misrepresent the amount of their income. Many officers are creative in hiding property and other assets and accounts. . . .

Many states encourage judges to grant joint custody, grant sole custody to the "friendly parent" (the parent who is willing to foster a relationship with the non-custodial parent), yet require judges to consider domestic violence in determining custody. Unfortunately, these three factors often conflict and according to many experts, "domestic violence is often the first to fall by the wayside." Allegations of domestic violence are particularly problematic in custody disputes involving police officers because of the secrecy, denial and cover-up by abusive officers and the lack of documentation of abuse. Many abusive officers demand liberal visitation that accommodates their erratic schedules, causing hardship to the victim and the children. If supervised visitation is ordered, it is extraordinarily difficult to determine a safe place to exchange the children, as the victim may not feel safe doing the exchange at the local police department.

Most of society, including victims, believes the myth that mothers do not lose custody unless they are "unfit" or mentally unstable. This erroneous belief leads them to seriously overestimate the benevolence of the court and seriously underestimate the danger of losing custody. They are not aware that the "American Psychological Association reported that abusive fathers were at least twice as likely to dispute custody as nonabusive men" and that "approximately 70% of contested custody cases [in the

United States] that involve a history of domestic violence result in an award of sole or joint custody to the abuser."

Fathers' rights groups instruct fathers' attorneys on how to charge the mother with the scientifically debunked "Parental Alienation Syndrome." Despite some state legislatures banning the use of this false syndrome, many courts still accept it as a valid scientific theory and use it to base their award of custody to battering fathers. Some courts also still believe that many mothers raise false allegations of child or domestic abuse in a custody battle. Victims' attorneys should impress upon their clients the seriousness of making allegations of child abuse against the father, particularly allegations of child sexual abuse. Battered women's attorneys must warn their clients that alleging abuse, even when true, may actually result in the court giving the abuser custody. Police officers understand how the system works and know that allegations of physical and sexual child abuse are very difficult to prove, especially against a member of law enforcement.

Fathers' rights groups also coach fathers on how to produce evidence that they have been the "primary caretaker" of the children. They recommend that fathers obtain affidavits from teachers, coaches, friends, neighbors and family members testifying that he is a good father. A police officer can include testimony from the chief of police, the mayor and other prestigious and respected members of the community. He may use his professional standing and relationships to garner the support of the GAL, mediator, custody evaluators, psychologist and child protective service workers who may find it difficult to believe that a police officer can be a batterer. Some of these professionals may share the abuser's worldview and values, some think that domestic violence is a myth, and others simply believe that women typically make false allegations of abuse. When proof of the abuse is right before their eyes they may ignore, dismiss, minimize or rationalize the behavior—often by holding the woman responsible for the abuser's behavior. As a result, women and children are left without legal protection as the courts refuse to give them protective orders and grant abuser's liberal visitation privileges and/or custody.

Abusive officers have been known to access official police channels of information to run background checks on anyone with whom the victim associates. Should the background check reveal that someone the mother associates with or is dating has a criminal record, the batterer can use this against her in a custody dispute. He might say that the mother's new partner or a friend is a danger to his children. Officers can also harass the victim by manipulating fellow officers to conduct "wellness checks" on the children and their mother, issue citations for interference with visitation, and/or make reports of suspected child abuse/neglect to child protective services.

Safety concerns

Many victim advocates and other professionals, who have worked with victims of domestic violence, know that professionals who represent or assist victims of domestic violence can also be targets of the perpetrator. It is not uncommon for the officer who batters to intimidate and threaten the GAL, the victim's and his own attorney, the custody evaluator, therapists and anyone else involved in the case. In recognition of this, the ABA Commission on Domestic Violence states "... if their safety is at risk while you are representing them, your safety may be at risk as well." A police officer may represent himself in the case, forcing the victim's attorney and staff to negotiate with him. This gives the officer ample opportunity to intimidate opposing counsel, flaunt his personal and professional connections to judges, clerks, bailiffs and other attorneys. Few attorneys consider that an officer who batters has a range of intimidation tactics available, ranging from something as subtle as a sudden flurry of traffic tickets to the extreme of a false arrest. . . .

Conclusion

The International Association of Chiefs of Police (IACP) acknowledges victims of police officers are "especially vulnerable" because of their abusers' status within law enforcement circles and because "an abusive officer may escalate behavior to extreme acts of violence such as abducting the victim, taking hostages, and committing homicide and/or suicide" when he feels his power is threatened. IACP also acknowledges that these victims may feel powerless because of the "formidable obstacles" they may encounter when seeking police assistance. Police agencies and judges may misuse their power of discretion to avoid implementing policies or enforcing the law against one of their own. When they do implement policies or enforce the law, they may place the victim in greater danger than before the system intervened.

In the end, victims typically report that the abuser "did everything he said he'd do" and "it all went the way he said it would go." Their attorneys are typically as amazed as their clients are at the twists and turns these cases take because of the batterer's ability to manipulate the system. The attorneys are stunned by the outcomes and their inability to predict or prevent the systemic abuse. Police officers who batter will continue to enjoy the protection of the legal system as long as attorneys, judges and other professionals involved in criminal and family court cases refuse to believe that some police officers do batter their intimate partners and their children. Attorneys who represent victims of domestic violence at the hands of police officers owe it to their clients to educate themselves on the dynamics of this insidious problem.

# XI. Lesbians, Gay Men and the Transgendered Community

It is a myth that domestic violence is something that only occurs between heterosexual couples in which men abuse women. It exists in the lesbian, gay and transgender communities as well. As Nancy Knauer notes in *Same-Sex Domestic Violence: Claiming a Domestic Sphere While Risking Negative Stereotypes*, 8 TEMP. POL. & CIV. RTS. L. REV. 325 (1999), "same-sex domestic violence does not fit the existing gendered model of domestic violence where a male batterer seeks to control and dominate a female victim with the support of patriarchal institutions and constructs such as the family and privacy." She argues that a more realistic view of same-sex relationships would "uncouple their concepts of power and dominance from the frame of gender difference and consider the role of other identifications such as race, age, sexual orientation and disability, in the deployment of power and violence."

## Sharon Stapel & Virginia M. Goggin, *Lesbian, Gay, Bisexual, Transgender and Queer Victims of Intimate Partner Violence*
in Lawyer's Manual on Domestic Violence: Representing the Victim, 241-253 (6th Ed.)

. . . .

Understanding 'LGBTQ'

The lesbian, gay, bisexual, transgender and queer communities are not interchangeable. For practitioners new to the issues of the LGBTQ communities, some of the language used to describe LGBTQ people and their partners or their identifiers can be confusing. Gender identity is often confused with sexual orientation. *Sexual orientation* is commonly defined as the culturally-defined set of meanings through which people describe their sexual attractions, or their preference for sexual partners—either same, opposite-sex, gender non-conforming partners or a combination thereof. Lesbians generally identify themselves as female-identified people who partner with other female-identified people. Bisexual people often identify themselves as people who partner with more than one gender. Queer, both an umbrella term and a specific sexual orientation, often indicates a desire to be more fluid in identifying either one's own gender or the gender of their partner and/or the general concept of binary gender in defining sexual relationships. *Gender identity*, on the other hand, is commonly defined as a sense of ourselves as masculine, feminine or at some other point along that spectrum. Transgender people may define themselves as male or female and gender non-conforming people or genderqueer people may define their gender in a non-binary way (or as a lack of gender). Many transgender people define their sexual orientation as straight or heterosexual, but the two should not be conflated as gender identity and sexual orientation are two different types of identities.

LBGTQ Intimate Partner Violence

As in heterosexual communities, intimate partner violence in the LGBTQ communities is defined as a pattern of behavior where one partner coerces, dominates, or isolates the other partner. It is the exertion of power to maintain control in a relationship. LGBTQ abusive partners employ the same forms of abuse as heterosexual batterers, including physical, emotional, psychological, sexual or economic abuse.

Some weapons of abuse, however, are unique to the LGBTQ communities. . . . Abusers may threaten to "out," or disclose, a partner's sexual orientation or gender identity to family, friends, employers, landlords or other community members. Those faced with custody battles may still worry that sexual orientation will negatively impact their case and decide to stay with an abuser rather than risk losing custody or visitation rights. Abusers may tell transgender partners that no one will understand or love them because of their gender identity or transition process, or they may threaten to throw out their transgender partner, leaving the survivor homeless and facing dangers in the streets, the homeless shelters and the job market. A victim may be reluctant to access services that are not perceived as LGBTQ-friendly. The batterer may be the first person to accept their sexual orientation or gender identity, and batterers may use this knowledge to keep a survivor isolated.

Intimate partner violence occurs within the lesbian, gay and bisexual communities at the same, or higher rates, as within non-LGB communities. The Centers for Disease Control found that nearly 44% of lesbians and 26% of gay men have been the victim of rape, physical violence, and/or stalking by an intimate partner in their lifetime. Occurrence of sexual violence is especially high; 46% of lesbians, 75% of bisexuals, 40% of gay men, and 47% of bisexual men reported being the victim of sexual assault. In 2011 the National Coalition of Anti-Violence Programs (NCAVP), received the highest number of homicides ever recorded (19, including two in NYC), up 300% from 2010, and in 2012 and 2013 recorded 21 IPV-related homicides, the highest number ever recorded for two years in a row. In 2013, NCAVP reported that transgender and gender non-conforming people were 1.9 times more likely to experience physical violence. Transgender and gender non-conforming people of color were 4.3 [times] as likely to experience police violence when reporting intimate partner violence to the police.

Barriers to Service for LGBTQ Survivors

Social service models based on heterosexual cisgender relationships can be alienating and even unavailable to LGBTQ survivors.[26] Survivors who disclose their orientation to service providers may be afraid that they will be treated disrespectfully or be denied services. LGBTQ survivors may not have the energy to educate advocates unfamiliar with LGBTQ communities about their experiences and cultural norms. LGBTQ survivors also face ever-changing and often restricted access to civil legal remedies, and may not seek services because of doubts that the law will afford protection.

These barriers prevent LGBTQ survivors from accessing support. NCAVP reports that in 2013, 5.5% of all survivors sought access to domestic violence shelters, an increase from 3.7% in 2012. Of those seeking shelter, 20.3% were turned away. That same year 22.4% of all survivors reported information about interacting with the police, an increase from 2012 (16.5%), and while only 17.0% of total survivors applied for orders of protection, that number represents a large increase from 2012 (4.9%).

---

26. The term "cisgender" refers to persons who consider themselves the gender with which they were born. [Eds. Note]

Through education and social and legal issues specific to the LGBTQ communities, many barriers can be easily eliminated.... Literature that advertises LGBTQ-specific services, support groups and legal service providers can be displayed in a waiting room or office. Most critically, practitioners should form meaningful collaborations with other service providers who have worked with LGBTQ intimate partner violence issues....

Identifying the Victim or the Abuser

When it is unclear to a practitioner which party is the aggressor, assumptions can have devastating effects. Assuming that the more "butch" or masculine-acting (or identifying) partner is an abuser, or assuming that the more effeminate-acting (or identifying) partner is the victim, creates not only a barrier to talking with clients, but also potentially erroneous analysis of who is the victim and who is the perpetrator in the relationship. The process of identifying perpetrators in an LGBTQ relationship can be complex, but is a critically important process to assuring a victim's safety and preventing a batterer from entering a support system meant for victims.

Instead of relying on gender stereotypes, practitioners must look to factors that indicate typical behaviors of an abuser or a victim. For example, victims are more likely to blame themselves, to minimize violent attacks, to excuse the behavior of their abuser, or to hesitate to take action against the abuser. Abusers are more likely to blame the victim, to use aggressive and hostile language in describing incidents, and they may exhibit a sense of entitlement in punishing their partner. Sometimes clients who are victims also indicate that they are seeking "justice" or want their abuser "to pay." This can be a normal reaction and may not indicate that the client is an abuser. According to the New York City Anti-Violence Project, batterers may request services pretending to be the victim, both to prevent the victim from accessing services and to keep track of the victim's options in reaching out for assistance. None of these factors is determinative. There is no way to assess which partner is statistically more likely to be the batterer based on gender in LGBTQ relationships. Therefore, practitioners must be vigilant both in welcoming LGBTQ and in engaging in a victim/aggressor analysis of the relationship....

Conclusion

As LGBTQ communities and allies continue to press for full legal recognition and protections for themselves, their partners, and their children, laws and regulations are constantly changing and evolving. LGBTQ communities are confronting intimate partner violence and have the right to access and the legal and social services that are available. Anti-violence service providers must be aware of, and educated about, issues specific to the LGBTQ communities, and they must be willing to work in coalition with LGBTQ organizations to address LGBTQ intimate partner violence.

When the first edition of this book was published in 2007, the legal landscape for same-sex couples was vastly different. In 2013, the U.S. Supreme Court in *United States v. Windsor,* 570 U.S. 12, held the federal government had to recognize valid same-sex marriages and that the federal Defense of Marriage Act, which declared that marriage was limited to heterosexual couples, was unconstitutional. Two years later, on June 26, 2015, in a 5-4 decision, the Supreme Court issued the landmark ruling that gay couples had the same fundamental right to marry as straight couples. *Obergefell v. Hodges,* 135 S. Ct. 2071. As will be discussed in the section on family law, because every state allows spouses to seek restraining orders to protect against domestic violence, the right of gay married couples to seek them is now assured. But, like heterosexual couples, all homosexual and lesbian relationships do not lead to marriage which requires that states interpret intimate partnership broadly.

The difficulties outlined in the previous article become particularly profound when it comes to addressing intimate partner violence in the transgendered community as this next article demonstrates.

## Leigh Goodmark, *Transgender People, Intimate Partner Abuse, and the Legal System*
48 Harv. C.R.-C.L. L. Rev. 51 (Winter 2013)

### Introduction

On August 28, 2009, Paulina Ibarra, a twenty-four-year-old transgender woman, was stabbed to death in her apartment in Hollywood. Although her death was originally investigated as a hate crime, police later dismissed that theory because the victim knew her attacker, according to Lieutenant Wes Buhrmester of the Los Angeles Police Department. Neighbors heard fighting and a woman screaming; police arrived seven minutes after a resident called 911 and found Ibarra lying on the floor. Jesus Catalan was arrested in July 2010, and in April 2011, he pled guilty to involuntary manslaughter in Ibarra's death. According to Buhrmester, prosecutors likely took the plea instead of trying Catalan for murder because "Catalan had apparently been injured during a struggle with Ibarra ... Ibarra and Catalan knew each other and she was not killed during the course of a felony (like robbery)." Catalan was sentenced to twelve years' imprisonment and is eligible for parole in 2021.

On March 30, 2010, Amanda Gonzalez-Andujar, a twenty-nine-year-old transgender woman, was found strangled to death and soaked with bleach in her apartment in New York City. Gonzalez-Andujar was lying naked on her bed; her apartment had been ransacked, her belongings destroyed, and her laptop missing. Detectives quickly came to suspect that Gonzalez-Andujar had been killed by a man she had been dating, and sources said that the damage in the apartment was likely attributable to a struggle between Gonzalez-Andujar and her killer. Security videos from the apartment building showed Gonzalez-Andujar's alleged killer, Rasheen Everett, entering the building at approximately 9:00 a.m. on March 27. Shortly thereafter, neighbors heard screaming and loud noises coming from Gonzalez-Andujar's apartment. Everett left the building seventeen hours later, carrying two bags. Gonzalez-Andujar and Everett may have met in an Internet chat room; sources speculated that Everett stole Gonzalez-Andujar's laptop to prevent police from finding email correspondence between them. Everett has been charged with murder, burglary, tampering with physical evidence, and possession of stolen property. If convicted, Everett could be sentenced to twenty-five years imprisonment.[27]

Paulina Ibarra was killed by a man she knew. Amanda Gonzalez-Andujar may have been killed by a man she was dating. Yet articles about their deaths do not mention the possibility that what Ibarra and Gonzalez-Andujar experienced was intimate partner abuse. . . . Had these not been transgender women, however, the stories would certainly have been different; when women are killed, intimate partner abuse is often immediately considered by the police. Did the gender identities of Ibarra and Gonzalez-Andujar preclude the media and the police from seeing their deaths as possibly resulting from intimate partner abuse?

If so, that oversight would not be terribly surprising. There is little information about intimate partner abuse in the transgender community in either the legal or social science literature. Where information about violence against transgender individuals does exist, that violence is often characterized as generalized violence or as a hate crime rather than as intimate partner abuse. . . .

### I. The Challenges of Writing About Intimate Partner Abuse in the Transgender Community

A. Writing as a Cisgender Person[28]

. . . .

B. Writing About Transgender Issues

A major challenge of writing this Article was that of language. We do not yet have a common language accepted by all interested parties for talking about the experiences of transgender people. . . . Transgender is often defined as an "umbrella term used to refer to all individuals who live outside of normative sex/gender relations— that is, individuals whose gendered self-presentation (evidenced through dress, mannerisms, and even physiology) does not correspond to the behaviors habitually associated with the members of their biological sex." Two dangers of using the term "transgender" in this broad way are the possibilities of including those who do not

---

27. Everett was convicted and sentenced to 29 years in prison. At sentencing, his lawyer urged the judge to go easy on his client because, in his view, the deceased was not "in the higher end of the community." The judge disagreed, telling the defense lawyer, "This court believes every human life is sacred. It is not easy living as a transgender . . . ." Christina Carrega-Woodby, *Hey, She Was Just a Ho: Sick Bid by Killer's Lawyer*, N.Y. Post, December 6, 2013, http://nypost.com/2013/12/06/hey-she-was-just-a-ho-sick-bid-by-killers-lawyer/ accessed October 3, 2016. [Eds. Note.]

28. [n28] The term "cisgender" refers to people whose gender identity is consistent with their birth-assigned sex. *See* Dean Spade, *Be Professional!*, 33 Harv. J.L. & Gender 71, 76 n.6 (2010) (explaining that "cisgender" is a term "commonly used in trans and allied communities and in trans scholarship for people who are not transgender").

themselves identify as transgender and of elevating a single commonality over other differences in identity—race, class, disability, sexual orientation—that shape an individual transgender person's experiences.

. . . .

Other language choices raise similar issues. While some use the term "cisgender" to refer to people whose gender identity is consistent with their birth-assigned sex, others have not adopted the term. Similarly, the thoughtful use of pronouns is essential in discussing the lives of transgender people. While some transgender people have adopted the terms "hir" and "ze" as generic pronouns for both genders, others choose not to use those terms because they identify solely and strongly as a particular gender—as him or her rather than hir, she or he rather than ze. . . .

The decision about whether to use the term "passing"—a term that is quite contested among transgender people—was equally difficult. "Passing" is frequently used as shorthand to describe the experience of having one's gender identity accepted unquestioningly by those around hir. . . . Passing is a complicated concept; it can be a derogatory term to the extent that it signifies deception by the transgender person or represents images imposed upon transgender people by a society with expectations about how men and women should look and act. I have chosen to use the term sparingly and largely limited to the context of discussing the desire to be perceived by others as one's authentic gender. I recognize, however, that even with this limited use, the presence of that term in this Article may be perceived as offensive.

C. Writing About Transgender People and Intimate Partner Abuse

. . . .

A final challenge involves teasing out intimate partner abuse from the other forms of violence that transgender people regularly confront. As is clear from the stories of Paulina Ibarra and Amanda Gonzalez-Andujar, it is often difficult to determine whether the violence transgender people experience should be characterized as hate crimes, bullying, intimate partner abuse, random acts of violence, or ordinary assaults. Regardless of the label attached to such actions, however, violence against transgender people is disturbingly common. Surveys of transgender people document the disproportionately high rates of violence they experience. One survey featuring data collected from 1996 to 1997 found that over their lifetimes, almost 60% of transgender people experienced either violence or harassment: over half experienced verbal abuse, 23% were stalked or followed, almost 20% were assaulted without a weapon, 10% were assaulted with a weapon, and almost 14% experienced rape or sexual abuse. Other surveys have found similarly high rates of violence against transgender people. In its 2010 survey of hate violence in the lesbian, gay, bisexual, transgender, queer, and HIV-affected communities in the United States, the NCAVP found that transgender people were twice as likely to be assaulted or discriminated against and 1.5 times more likely to experience intimidation than cisgender white individuals.[29] In 2011, NCAVP found that transgender people of color were 1.85 times more likely to experience discrimination, 1.28 times more likely to experience physical violence, and 2.38 times more likely to experience police violence than other survey respondents. The survey also found that transgender people were more likely than other survey respondents to experience severe violence, and less likely to receive law enforcement assistance.

Transgender women are particularly likely to be marked for violence. The 2011 NCAVP survey found that transgender women made up 40% of murder victims in the survey, but constituted only 10% of the overall sample; the 2010 survey reported similar findings. Surveys of the transgender community have found that 98% of violence in the transgender community was targeted at transgender women, and that transgender women of color accounted for 70% of all murders of transgender people reported internationally in 2003.

A. The Transgender Experience of Intimate Partner Abuse

. . . .

Transgender advocacy groups have identified forms of abuse unique to relationships involving transgender people. Physical abuse tactics include "assault, mutilation or denigration of body parts such as chest, genitals, and hair that signify specific cultural notions of gender." Other forms of physical abuse may entail touching one's body in ways or places one has asked not to be touched, or insisting that rough sex is the way that "real" men or women enjoy intercourse. Transgender-specific forms of emotional abuse include calling someone by the wrong pronoun or referring to hir as "it," threatening to reveal the transgender person's gender identity or birth-assigned sex to employers, landlords, immigration officials, friends, or family members, and making threats related to the transgender person's custody of or relationship with hir children. Some transgender people experience low self-esteem and anxiety around body issues. Abusers play on these emotions by telling the transgender person that ze isn't a "real" man or woman, ridiculing hir body, and dictating how hir gender identity is expressed (through selection of clothes, hairstyles, and such). Abusers also destroy or hide clothing, wigs, binders, and other accessories used to reinforce the transgender person's authentic gender identity.

The medical needs of transgender people also provide opportunities for abuse. Abusers deny access to transgender people's medical treatments or hormones, destroy needed medical supplies, and coerce their partners into refraining from pursuit of medical treatment. Abusers may also withdraw or withhold support for transgender-specific medical care or services (surgery, hormones, or electrolysis, for example). Economic abuse may include exploitation of the transgender person's financial dependence by demanding that ze reimburse hir partner for any financial assistance provided—even requiring hir partner to work illegally to pay hir back. . . .

---

29. The NCAVP stands for the National Coalition of Anti-Violence Programs. [Eds. Note.]

B. Barriers to Seeking Assistance

. . . .

1. Social and Economic Support.

The relationship a transgender person has with hir abusive partner may be that person's only source of support, in any number of ways. Transgender people receive less emotional support from their families than cisgender people, which may make them more reliant upon their partners for love and stability. The support needed to acknowledge publicly one's abuse may be hard to find in the broader transgender community. The same type of "gag order" that keeps some members of marginalized communities from reporting abuse, due to fear of bringing unwanted negative scrutiny to their communities, operates within the transgender community as well. . . .

2. Access to Shelter.

Access to safe shelter is particularly problematic for transgender people. Housing insecurity is a tremendous issue for transgender people, who are often homeless or at risk of homelessness and who may only find temporary shelter by moving from friend to friend. The 2011 National Transgender Discrimination Survey found that of those transgender people surveyed who sought shelter, 55% were harassed by shelter staff, 29% were turned away because of their gender presentation, and "22% were sexually assaulted by residents or staff." . . .

Those shelters that refuse to admit transgender women do so largely because they do not see transgender women as women; instead, transgender women are usually defined "as men, regardless of how the individual battered [transgender] person identifies him-or herself or lives his or her life . . . ." These shelters often admit residents based on their sex at birth rather than their gender identity, and in some cases without regard to whether the individual has undergone sex reassignment surgery. Underlying the refusal to admit transgender women to shelters is fear; transgender women are seen as "invaders" if they attempt to access gender-segregated services.

Other shelters and domestic violence services providers open their doors to transgender women on the condition that they look to others like women—that they "pass." . . .

Such shelters often make case-by-case decisions about whether transgender women are eligible for their services. This process can entail ad hoc decisions regarding whether the transgender woman is "appropriate" as a client, requirements that the client be undergoing or have completed sex reassignment surgery, or requirements conditioning the provision of services on whether the transgender woman promises not to "exhibit any crossgendered expression or disclose information relating to being [transgender]." In addition to "passing," the transgender woman may also have to conform to other stereotypes of women subjected to abuse, like passivity or powerlessness, in order to qualify for services. . . .

Transgender women who are denied access to domestic violence services, particularly shelters, are left with few options when they decide to seek separation from their partners. Transgender women subjected to abuse are frequently sent to men's homeless shelters, where they are vulnerable to attack. Once in men's shelters, transgender women "are told that they cannot wear any feminine clothing and have to present as men, which obviously is not only disrespectful but personally painful as well."

In some areas, particularly in major cities, shelters are required by statute or policy to admit residents based on gender identity rather than birth-assigned sex. Such requirements exist in both New York City and the District of Columbia. In New York, explains attorney Pooja Gehi, transgender advocates worked for a very long time to get shelters to agree to house residents based on their gender identity rather than their birth sex. Prior to that change, transgender women subjected to abuse rarely accessed the shelter system because if they could not go to a women's shelter, they were not willing to go to a shelter at all. Despite the changes, transgender women subjected to abuse are still afraid to access shelters. . . .

C. Transgender Abuse and the Legal System

. . . .

1. Police.

Negative interactions with and perceptions of the police, both generally and in the specific context of cases involving intimate partner abuse, keep transgender people subjected to abuse from asking for help from the police. For transgender people, "dealing with the police is usually humiliating at best and dangerous at worst.". . . . Reports of harassment and abuse of transgender people by police are common; studies routinely find high percentages of police among the perpetrators of abuse and harassment against transgender people. Given that context, it is not surprising that the 2010 NCAVP study found that transgender people were less likely than lesbian, gay, or bisexual respondents to report incidents of abuse or violence to police.

Historically, the police have been responsible for enforcement of laws explicitly created to ensure conformity with gender norms; such laws included statutes requiring that individuals wear three articles of clothing that conformed to their birth-assigned sex. More recently, however, policing of gender norms has taken the form of refusals to recognize transgender people's authentic gender identities, as well as harassment and profiling based on gender nonconformity. Transgender women report police using their male names and male pronouns to describe them, even when they have changed their identification documents. . . .

Police perpetration of violence against transgender people is depressingly common. In 2011, the National Transgender Discrimination Survey found that 22% of transgender respondents had been harassed by police (the numbers were higher for people of color); 6% had been physically assaulted, and 2% had been sexually assaulted. Twenty percent reported denials of equal service by police and 46% of those surveyed said they were uncomfortable seeking police assistance. A 2012 study of Latina transgender women in Los Angeles found that 66% had been verbally abused by law enforcement, 21% physically assaulted, and 24% sexually assaulted. . . .

Finally, the police ignore the violence done to transgender people by others by refusing to take reports, failing to classify crimes against transgender people as hate-motivated crimes, or failing to respond at all. In one particularly disturbing incident, Los Angeles police refused to respond to "a violent assault on an undocumented Latina transgender" woman; the police were reported to have said, "If they kill her, call us."

. . . .

Not all transgender people experience skepticism or violence at the hands of police. Sixty-eight percent of respondents to the 2011 National Transgender Discrimination Survey reported that officers generally treated them with respect. Some advocates report mixed experiences with police intervention, depending on the responses of the individual officers involved. Kristin Tucker notes that although very few of her clients choose to call the police, those who have interacted with Seattle police have had moderately positive experiences. Her clients felt validated by those interactions, believing that the police saw them as having been subjected to abuse, rather than dismissing their experiences.

. . . .

2. The Court System.

Transgender people subjected to abuse may also be skeptical of their chances of finding protection from abuse within the court system. Transgender people are disproportionately involved in the court system, particularly the criminal justice system. A 2011 survey found that 17% of transgender people had been incarcerated at some point in their lives; 21% of transgender women and 10% of transgender men reported being incarcerated. Transgender people of color have been especially affected by the ever-increasing trend toward incarceration in the United States. On the civil side, transgender people may find themselves forced to ask courts to determine their legal gender, with a myriad of rights and claims dependent upon that determination. . . . .

(a.) Individuals within the Court System.

Transgender people subjected to abuse hesitate to engage the court system as a result of the discrimination and insensitivity they face at the hands of the judiciary. Judges profile transgender people in many of the same ways that police do. . . .

That undercurrent of distrust and fear colors the way that judges treat individual litigants. A transgender advocate reported judges referring to transgender people as "it" in open court, and advocates confirm that some judges seem flustered or uneasy in the presence of transgender people. Some advocates believe that the criminal histories and illegal employment of some transgender people subjected to abuse are to blame for courts' skepticism of their claims. The prevalence of sex work among transgender people is particularly damaging to their credibility in two ways. First, sex workers are viewed as less credible (or fear that they will be viewed as less credible) because they are engaged in criminal activity. Second, past engagement in sex work causes courts to view claims of abuse more skeptically; abuse may be seen as a byproduct of sex work, even when that abuse happens within noncommercial intimate relationships. These credibility challenges are particularly acute for more marginalized transgender people — poor people, people of color, and HIV-positive people. As Gehi notes, the same stereotypes that operate in other parts of the legal system are present in the domestic violence system; there is a reason that successful transgender litigants are typically wealthy and white.

Transgender people's interactions with other legal system actors can be similarly problematic. At worst, court staff ridicule transgender people seeking assistance, referring to them using demeaning terms like "he/she." Court staff sometimes seem uncomfortable working with transgender litigants, particularly if the client does not "pass" easily in hir authentic gender; staff relieve this tension by avoiding transgender people, interacting with attorneys rather than communicating directly with transgender litigants. Court staff may also require transgender people to use names that appear on their state-issued identification, even if that documentation no longer matches the person's gender presentation. . . .

Transgender people may also be denied effective, competent legal services as a result of overtly discriminatory or dismissive behavior by lawyers. Even well-meaning lawyers serve clients poorly when they fail to understand the realities of their transgender clients' lives. Some lawyers simply refuse to serve transgender people, telling them to access services elsewhere. Lawyers may also utilize harmful stereotypes of transgender people as deceptive and deviant in their efforts to persuade finders of fact. . . .

Transgender people suffer gravely in jails and prisons, where they are usually housed according to their birth-assigned sex rather than their authentic gender. Transgender people, especially transgender women, face heightened risk of sexual abuse in prison at the hands of both other prisoners and correctional officers. Transgender women suffer from . . . sexual degradation and harassment from penal officials who routinely subject them to excessive, abusive, and invasive searches, groping their breasts, buttocks, or genitalia, repeatedly leering at them while they shower, disrobe, or use the bathroom, and generally, in the words of Human Rights Watch . . . creating an environment that is "highly sexualized and excessively hostile."

Some transgender women report being strip-searched or frisked four to five times daily while incarcerated. Some systems segregate transgender inmates from the general population, requiring inmates to self-identify as transgender, but allowing staff to make the final determination as to whether an inmate will be categorized as transgender. Corrections officials routinely refuse to recognize the chosen names and gender identities of transgender inmates and deny transgender people medical care relating to their gender—this can include restricting access to hormone treatments and gender reassignment surgery. Knowing both that the possibility of arrest and incarceration are very real if an abuse claim is made, and of the negative experiences of transgender people who become defendants, transgender people subjected to abuse may be understandably wary of engaging the criminal system.

(b.) The Family Court System.

Transgender people subjected to abuse might seek protective orders through the family court system, but those courts have also been hostile to the claims of some transgender litigants. Transgender people subjected to abuse may be wary of relying on the family court system for protection given its insensitivity to other claims by transgender litigants. For instance, several courts have found that, for the purposes of adjudicating the validity of a marriage, a transsexual's birth-assigned sex is determinative, notwithstanding any surgical transition a person may have undergone. Although a transsexual may have official documents recognizing hir gender identity, courts have refused to recognize those documents as dispositive in the context of challenges to marriages. As a result, transsexuals who have married individuals whose anatomical sex matches their birth-assigned sex have found their marriages invalidated in states that do not recognize same-sex marriage.

Defending transgender parents' relationships with their children poses similar challenges. "Transgender parents face tremendous discrimination and bias, particularly in custody and visitation cases." Court decisions on the validity of marriages involving transsexuals operate particularly harshly on transsexual parents, who may lose legal and/or physical custody of their children if their marriages are invalidated or if they choose to undergo gender reassignment surgery. Indeed, the reported cases all involve transsexuals who have undertaken some level of surgical gender reassignment. For transgender people who eschew surgery altogether, who have not been diagnosed with gender identity disorder, or who do not have medical experts willing to testify for them, courts may be even less tolerant.

The perils of dealing with family court are magnified for low-income transgender people. The cost of retaining lawyers and experts in family law matters is prohibitive even for those with means, and especially so for "[transgender] persons who are multiply marginalized, including many [transgender] persons of color, as well as those who are immigrants, sex workers, poor, or homeless." ...

(d.) Seeking State Protection from Abuse.

. . . .

The court process is a public process. In many states, court records of criminal and civil cases are open to the general public; in an increasing number of states, those records are available online, making it far easier to find information about people using the domestic violence legal system. Courtrooms themselves are open to the public; petitioners seeking relief from abuse or testifying in criminal cases frequently tell their stories in front of a gallery of onlookers. Engaging the legal system may mean "coming out"—publicly identifying oneself as transgender, possibly for the first time. Such exposure can lead to negative reactions from family and friends, discrimination by landlords, employers, and others, and potentially, greater violence. The public nature of the process also puts transgender people on display and opens their lives to scrutiny before both system actors and courtroom observers. ...

The legal system may also require transgender people seeking protection from abuse to deny their authentic gender in order to qualify for the court's assistance. Attorney Morgan Lynn notes that transgender people are pressured to complete forms that require designation of an individual's sex, checking boxes that are listed on court documents, even if those boxes do not accurately reflect how the transgender person sees hirself. Courts usually require transgender people to use their legal names and legal genders in petitions for protection; courts want to know if they are talking to a "mister" or a "miss." But transgender people may not use these terms to describe themselves or might fear being accused of fraud for checking the "wrong" gender box. . . .

Confronted with the possibility that the legal system will refuse to recognize hir authentic gender and require the transgender litigant to acknowledge publicly and respond to an identity that ze does not recognize as authentic, the transgender person subjected to abuse may simply opt out of that system altogether.

3. Gender Stereotypes and the Transgender Litigant.

Abuse narratives that succeed in the legal system share key features: a meek, passive, powerless victim; physical violence; and a monstrous, controlling abuser. Gender sits at the core of these narratives. Victims are weak women; abusers are strong men. Securing a criminal conviction or order of protection requires that victims tell abuse stories that resonate with how judges, prosecutors, police, and juries understand domestic violence.

. . . .

Advocates do, in fact, deploy stereotypical gendered domestic violence narratives on behalf of transgender clients—when those narratives fit the facts of a case. These narratives might seem to be particularly effective in cases involving transgender women—especially transgender women who easily pass—and heterosexual men. But even when armed with stories that conform to what judges expect to hear in domestic violence cases, advocates encounter judicial resistance to the abuse narratives of transgender litigants. Some judges are skeptical of gender-based claims of violence made by transgender litigants, insisting that because a transgender woman is not "biologically female" in the traditional sense, the abuse must instead be mutual violence within a same-sex relationship. Others have suggested that a claim of abuse is not credible because, by virtue of hir gender, the petitioner should have been able to protect hirself.

. . . .

B. Enforcing Gender Roles

Intimate partner abuse of transgender people may also serve as a form of policing binary gender norms. In such relationships, abuse is deployed to punish the transgender partner for that person's failure to conform to traditional gender categories or presentations. . . . The cisgender abuser's need to engage in gender policing may grow from the doubt, confusion, and anxiety some cisgender people experience when confronted with the transgression of gender roles. . . .

Gender policing in the context of intimate partner relationships poses an odd dichotomy. Those involved in intimate relationships with transgender individuals often know that their partners are living outside of societal gender norms. Nonetheless, abusers may use the transgender person's "transgressive" status to punish them. . . .

Intimate partner abuse against transgender people, then, works on multiple levels. Violence serves both to maintain control within individual relationships, and to reinforce societal gender norms; abuse is the ultimate assertion of control in a relationship that may prompt deep and unsettling feelings of insecurity or discomfort in the cisgender partner, who sees not just hir partner, but hirself as transgressing gender norms by engaging in the relationship. Such abuse may be particularly painful for the transgender partner who does not view hirself as transgressing gender norms, but rather as conforming to hir authentic gender identity. While abuse born of gender policing may not look like the type of policing typically associated with the battering of heterosexual women, it serves nonetheless as a desperate assertion of control within an intimate context.

C. Abuse as Reinforcing Gender Identity

Being recognized as one's authentic gender is of central importance to many transgender people, and passing can serve as one indicia of that recognition. Passing allows transgender people to live openly and comfortably in their authentic gender and decreases the transgender person's exposure to violence and discrimination. . . .

Intimate partner abuse often serves to reinforce gender norms. Many individuals subjected to abuse—cisgender and transgender—are transgressive in some way: women who fight back against their abusers, women who are economically better off than their partners, or women who assert their power and independence, for instance. Transgender people in particular challenge gender norms in ways that their partners may find disconcerting or frightening—even for those who seek transgender people out as partners.

IV. Rethinking the Response to Abuse of Transgender People

. . . .

A. Within the Legal System

The vast majority of transgender people subjected to abuse never come into contact with the legal system, purposefully avoiding a system that they believe will not help them. But some of the very few transgender people subjected to abuse who actually choose to use the legal system are, according to advocates, achieving positive outcomes. Notwithstanding the many hurdles transgender people subjected to abuse confront when turning to the legal system, then, there is some hope that the legal system could be a viable option for responding to abuse. . . . .

Building such a system may require rejecting the primacy of the criminal justice system in domestic violence law and policy. The continued involvement of transgender people in unlawful work, the long history of police involvement in gender role enforcement, the frequency and severity of police abuse of transgender people, the horrendous conditions of confinement that transgender people endure in the criminal system, and the inability of police to tell abusers from the abused all militate against characterizing the criminal justice system as a safe haven for transgender people subjected to abuse. Particularly for transgender people of color and undocumented transgender immigrants, the stakes of turning to an oppressive state system for relief from abuse may always be too high.

A responsive system would require fundamental changes to both the law itself and to those who enforce it. Civil protection order statutes should clearly and unequivocally provide protection for transgender people subjected to abuse. Although gender neutral statutes might seem to promise the same result as specific provisions authorizing transgender people to seek state protection, in practice, "the lack of explicit inclusion has given those in the system a way out" of assisting transgender people. Moreover, if targeted language is not included, transgender people may not believe that they are eligible to seek the protection of courts. Additionally, the law should permit transgender people to seek protection consistent with their authentic gender identity—using the names, pronouns, and genders in which they live on a day-to-day basis. Finally, the legal system should provide transgender people with the full range of remedies and resources that it provides cisgender people subjected to abuse.

Changing the culture of the legal system is as important as substantively changing the law. Courts should be a space where transgender people subjected to abuse feel safe and welcome. Courts should affirm and validate the stories of transgender people subjected to abuse. Judges and other court officers should respect and value the personhood of transgender litigants. Clearly, a fundamental shift in society's treatment of transgender people is required; the judiciary could help to start that movement....

Finally, building a more responsive legal system will require expansion of our understanding of abuse beyond the current binary conception of men as abusers and women as victims. The stereotypical narrative of intimate partner abuse fits some cases, but is inapposite in many others. Transgender women subjected to abuse, like other marginalized women, may be more likely to fight back against their abusers. So long as abusers continue to be coded male and victims coded female, transgender people subjected to abuse will remain in limbo. Transgender people may be subjected to abuse both as a function of their expressed gender identity and as a result of their failure to conform to their birth-assigned sex. Understanding abuse as an exercise of power and control that is affected by gender, but not necessarily one that is inherently gendered, will be essential if transgender people are to secure the protection they need.....

B. The Extralegal Response

. . . .

LGBTQ organizations are in the beginning stages of developing community accountability models to address intimate partner abuse. NCAVP has convened a Transformative Justice Study Group to consider ways of addressing violence without resorting to the criminal justice system. Community United Against Violence (CUAV) in San Francisco, California, uses peer counseling, education and outreach, and grassroots organizing to address intimate partner violence in the LGBTQ community. The organization opposes the increasing use of the criminal justice system in cases of intimate partner violence, but acknowledges that it has not yet developed a workable model of community accountability that engages both those who abuse and those who are abused. These advocates could build on efforts like The Audre Lorde Project's Safe OUTside the System (SOS) Collective, which challenges hate and police violence in New York City by using community-based strategies to stop violence without involving law enforcement.

Asking the community to take responsibility for responding to abuse is a complicated matter. Communities may not be able or willing to protect transgender people subjected to abuse: "Often the very families, neighborhoods, and networks we rely on to address violence internalize and reflect the very systems of oppression that drive the criminal legal system." Some people subjected to abuse report that the worst abuse they encountered came not from their partners but from the community-based organizations that purported to serve them. Nonetheless, advocates like Kristin Tucker and others increasingly look to the development of community-based interventions that provide support and healing to transgender people subjected to abuse, and that pursue transformation of the conditions that support violence as the best alternative to a system that transgender people rightfully approach with deep suspicion and skepticism.

## Conclusion

The choice to vest the legal system with primary responsibility for addressing domestic violence assumes that the legal system can adequately meet the myriad of needs of people subjected to abuse. That system, however, has been inadequate even for those it was designed to serve — white, straight women who represent the stereotypical victims of domestic violence. For marginalized populations, the system as it currently exists is even less responsive; for transgender people, the prospect of using the legal system is so fraught that very, very few even consider it a viable option, and those that do turn to the system have decidedly mixed results.

. . . . It is certainly possible that transgender people could find justice within the justice system (albeit a significantly altered justice system). It is equally possible that better solutions might lie beyond the reach of the state. But the experiences of transgender people and other marginalized communities with the legal system suggest that those concerned with the needs of people subjected to abuse should reconsider the decision to make the legal system the primary societal response to intimate partner abuse. Rather than assuming that we already know which interventions would be most useful to people subjected to abuse, we should ask what systems, supports, and services would be most beneficial to them. Learning more about how marginalized communities experience domestic violence, from the people experiencing it, would be a good place to start in rebuilding our systemic response to intimate partner abuse.

## *Notes and Questions*

- **FAMILY JUSTICE CENTERS**

Some of the concerns about the futility that non-white and non-English speaking women may feel about seeking help for domestic violence may be alleviated by so-called "family justice centers" in urban areas around the county. These centers tout themselves as "one-stop shopping" for victims of domestic violence, elder abuse and sexual assault. Rather than having to report domestic violence in a police precinct, then to a local prosecutor's office to pursue a criminal court case, and then meet with a social worker elsewhere and travel to yet another location for help with housing, these centers have staffers from multiple municipal and non-profit agencies working under one roof to make it easier and more welcoming for victims of domestic violence to receive all the help necessary. In New York City, for example, family justice centers have sprouted up as places for victims to meet with assistant district attorneys, civil lawyers, and social workers. Thirty languages are spoken in these centers with the capability of obtaining interpreters for more if necessary. *See* New York City Mayor's Office to Combat Domestic Violence, *Family Justice Centers*, http://www1.nyc.gov/site/ocdv/programs/family-justice-centers.page, accessed January 18, 2016.

In New Orleans, the family justice center has operated for seven years offering multiple services at a single location, including help with the immigration concerns of victims of battering. *New Orleans Family Justice Center*, www.nofjc.org, accessed January 18, 2016. It is a trend gaining traction; a family justice center opened in the fall of 2015 in Van Nuys, California in Los Angeles County. Dana Bartholomew, *One-Stop Van Nuys Center Opens to Help Victims of Sexual Assault*, Los Angeles Daily News, October 15, 2015, www.dailynews.com/social-affairs/20151015/one-stop-van-nuys-center-opens-to-help-victims-of-sexual-assault, accessed January 18, 2016.

- **NATIVE AMERICANS AND DOMESTIC VIOLENCE**

Violence on Indian land was first brought to the attention of some of white America by a novel, *The Round House,* by Louise Erdrich, which won the National Book Award in 2012. The book is about a teenage boy's investigation into his mother's sexual assault on their North Dakota Indian reservation. In accepting the award in her Native American language, Ms. Erdrich said: "This is a book about a huge case of injustice ongoing on reservations. Thank you for giving it a wider audience." Leslie Kaufman, *Novel About Racial Injustice Wins National Book Award*, N.Y. Times, November 15, 2012.

- **INTERNATIONAL VIOLENCE AGAINST WOMEN**

An International Violence Against Women Act, modeled on VAWA, has been introduced in Congress for the last several years, but has failed to gain traction. The latest version, HR 1340, was introduced in the 114th Congress by Illinois Rep. Janice Schakowsky on March 6, 2015, and referred to the House Committee on Foreign Affairs. The bill would direct the Secretary of State to establish an Office of Global Women's Issues run by a senior coordinator for gender equality and women's empowerment to direct programs to aid women. https://www.congress.gov/bill/114th-congress/house-bill/1340. The effort is supported by Amnesty International and the Family Violence Fund and would earmark funds for educational programs, healthcare for international victims of sexual assault and better training of U.S. and foreign soldiers to protect women against violence. www.unifemusa.org/support-i-vawa. Does this legislation run the risk of imposing Western values on Third World cultures? What about violence against women in other First World cultures, such as those in Western Europe? In France, a national domestic abuse helpline receives 90,000 calls a year with 84 percent of the callers complaining of psychological abuse. In 2010, the French Parliament approved a bill that made "psychological violence" a crime. Ten percent of all French women between the ages of 18 and 60 are said to be impacted by domestic violence. Steven Erlanger, *France Makes 'Psychological Violence' a Crime,* N.Y. TIMES, June 30, 2010. Italy strengthened its laws against domestic violence in 2013. Approximately 75 percent of the 2,200 women murdered between 2000 and 2012, were killed by intimate partners. In numbers far higher than those cited in France, violence against women in Italy is said to affect nearly 32 percent of women between 16 and 70, and a shocking 90 percent of all rape or abuse victims do not report it to the police. Victims' advocates link the high levels of abuse of women to the Italian culture, where until 1981, honor killings of women were legal. Other factors may include the prolonged Italian recession, making it financially difficult for women to escape bad relationships and the country's notoriously slow legal system. In 2013 Italy toughened penalties for batterers, although women's advocates said victims of domestic violence needed more government services to assist them in leaving abusive relationships. Elisabetta Povoledo, *A Call for Aid, Not Laws, to Help Women in Italy: Critics Say Government Measures Miss the Mark,* N.Y. TIMES, August 19, 2013.

Early in 2017, Russian legislators (members of what is called the State Duma) passed an amendment to the country's criminal code that would decriminalize some low-level domestic violence acts by first offenders. Supporters said it would keep the government out of family life, and opponents argued it would sanction violent behavior by domestic abusers. Svetlana G. Aivazova, described as a "Russian specialist in gender studies," in an article in the N.Y. TIMES, called the Duma members supporting the change as "archaic." She maintains that statistics show in 2013 more than 9,000 women were killed and 11,000 seriously injured in domestic attacks. That is a shocking statistic when compared with the United States, which has twice the population of Russia, where about 1,000 women are killed by intimate partners each year. The article put some of the blame for the weakening of domestic violence laws on the Russian Orthodox Church, which has become increasingly powerful in that country, as well as on conservative lawmakers. The church accepts physical punishment within families as part of the "Russian tradition." Ivan Nechepurenko, *Russia Moves to Soften Domestic Violence Law,* N.Y. TIMES, January 26, 2017. The new law makes domestic violence offenses that do not cause "serious bodily harm" punishable by what is known as "mandatory work" or a fine up of to 30,000 rubles, which is the equivalent of $500. Laura Mills, *Russia: Bill Decriminalizes Domestic Violence,* WALL

Street Journal, January 28–29, 2017. Would you attribute all of the increased numbers of women killed by their husbands or boyfriends to the influence of the church? What other factors might be at play that would cause such levels of violence? Is this sanction that much different from the community service, conditional discharges and suspended sentences now often handed down in courts around the United States for low-level domestic violence offenses?

As if they have not been through enough, women from Afghanistan also face unacceptable levels of family violence. A group called Women for Afghan Women in Queens, N.Y., an advocacy center that helps resettle Afghan immigrants in New York City, has seen an increase in the number of women battered by spouses and their husband's families. As of 2011, 35 women overcame strong cultural biases against reporting abuse to seek help from the organization. Naheed Bahram, the organization's case manager, suspected the number of abused women was probably closer to 300 but theorized they were too frightened to report it. Language barriers, dependency on husbands for support and ignorance of the laws against family violence are all reasons Afghan women do not reach out for help. *See* Kirk Semple, *Domestic Abuse Follows Afghans to New York: As a Culture of Violence Persists, Advocates for Women Discover That the Problem is Extensive*, N.Y. Times, February 28, 2011.

Chapter 3

# The Criminal Law of Domestic Violence

---

> **CONSIDER AS YOU READ ABOUT CRIMINAL LAW**
> 1. What crimes constitute crimes of domestic violence
> 2. How new technology impacts the fight against domestic violence
> 3. What happens when victims of domestic violence fight back
> 4. Bail considerations in domestic violence cases

Battered women's advocates fought hard for strong criminal laws against domestic violence. The numbers showed that the law enforcement response to intimate partner violence was dismal, at best. For example, in Washington, D.C. as late as 1986, there were 19,000 emergency telephone calls to police from victims complaining of domestic violence; yet that same year there were less than 40 arrests.[1]

What follows is an excerpt of an article by an advocate for stronger criminal prosecution of batterers.

## Linda McGuire, *Criminal Prosecution of Domestic Violence* (1994), written for The Battered Women's Justice Project

*available at* http://data.ipharos.com/bwjp/website/ (under topic: Prosecution)

. . . .

1. Domestic violence is a crime and prosecutors can take effective steps to end it.

The criminal behavior at the heart of most abusive relationships is not unlike the criminal behavior which generates most of a prosecutor's case load. . . . For example, when the batterer uses physical force or threatens to use such force, and it is clear that he can carry out the threats, the abuse is an assault. On the other hand, the emotional

---

[1]. Testimony of Sandra Sands, *citing, Report on District of Columbia Police Response to Domestic Violence, 1992,* Dist. of Columbia Coalition Against Domestic Violence at *Hearing on Violence Against Women,* HOUSE SUB. ON CRIME AND CRIMINAL JUST. H. COMM. ON THE JUD., HOUSE OF REP. 102D CONG., 2D SESS. 98 (1992).

or financial abuse frequent in most battering relationships will not be prosecuted because it usually does not rise to the level of an otherwise defined crime. By focusing on assaultive behavior—the most dangerous type of abuse—prosecutors can create a safer community for women and save women's lives. It is not possible to guarantee the safety of any one victim, because it may still be necessary for her to maintain contact with her abuser during (and after) the prosecution. But the proper prosecution strategy can have a measurable effect on the community as a whole. Sophisticated approaches by prosecutors and law enforcement have reduced homicide rates in their communities. For example, the domestic homicide rate in San Diego was reduced by 59% from 1991 to 1993....

2. Prosecutors take public sentiment into account when they set priorities.

Prosecutors are either elected or appointed to office. As public officials, many are responsive to the increasing public awareness of domestic violence and its terrible effects on its victims, including children....

### Principles or goals for prosecuting woman battering

A pro-active prosecution policy can make an important contribution to a community's efforts to end domestic violence. Aggressive and consistent prosecution of domestic violence:

1. shifts the burden of ending the violence from the victims to the community. It can serve to protect individual battered women and children who are the victims in specific cases.

2. makes batterers accountable to the community for their actions, not just to their partners or families. Requiring batterers to face consequences for their criminal acts forces them to be accountable. If the consequence is prosecution, the abuser is more likely to perceive the act as a crime against the community than as a "family matter." Batterers must learn that their efforts to pressure or force their victims to drop charges or testify in their favor are useless. This message is communicated only when all parts of the criminal justice system communicate it consistently and persistently.

3. can help restore the power and respect that the victim lost as a result of the battering. Because battered women face different problems from those of other victims of violence crimes, prosecutors must develop a certain sophistication in dealing with these cases. An effective approach ensures early contact with the victim, avoids blaming her for the violence, gives her information about the criminal court process and her role as a witness, and involves her in case decision-making. These actions break the isolation the victim feels and communicate to her that prosecution can help to end the violence in her life. In sharp contrast, some prosecutor's actions can re-victimize the battered woman. One example is a blanket policy to hold battered women in contempt of court for failing to obey subpoenas to testify against their abusers. A battered woman's non-compliance with a subpoena is likely the product of her judgment that it is better not to aggravate the batterer by testifying. When she is

punished for protecting herself, criminal prosecution of the batterer is not a future option for her.

4. sends a clear message to all members of the community that intimate violence is unacceptable. By taking an active interest in the response to these cases, and furthering that concern by allocating resources, the public acknowledges that this is no longer a private family problem.

While the goals achieved by aggressive prosecution are having positive results in many communities, it is equally important to recognize the limitations of this approach. Sometimes, creating this community ethic against domestic violence puts an individual battered woman in more danger despite the system's best efforts to protect her. This typically occurs because the batterer blames her for the prosecution. Therefore, prosecutors must maintain a balance between creating an intolerance for domestic violence in the community and doing what best protects an individual battered woman. . . .

Laws, policies or practices for domestic violence cases

Special laws and policies have been developed throughout the country in an attempt to effectively respond to criminal domestic violence assaults, including:

<u>Prosecution.</u> Victim/witness support and information services, whether provided by an outside agency or within the prosecutor's office or police department: "no drop" policies; prosecution by an experienced and specialized staff who handles a case from beginning to end; training for police on how to investigate cases so they can be proven without the victim's testimony. . . .

<u>Police.</u> Mandatory or pro-arrest laws or policies; a protocol which requires that police call an outreach worker from a battered women's program, or make some other referral to services for the victim immediately after arrest; investigative and report-writing protocols which streamline evidence collection and make convictions more probable even when the victim is unavailable to testify. . . .

<u>Judges.</u> Use of sentencing options which include educational programming for batterers; probation with conditions, including alcohol treatment, no further violence, or other protective conditions; enhanced penalties for repeat domestic violence offenses; and, jail time.

However, there are concerns about enhanced penalties and jail time. While appropriate in some cases, "more punishment equals more justice" is not necessarily true, either. Some battered women's advocates believe that laws which mandate jail time are problematic because batterers are less likely to plead guilty and because some battered women do not want their abusers to go to jail and are less likely to participate in the prosecution if a conviction means the batterer must go to jail.

<u>Probation.</u> Post-arrest interviews with the victim and others in order to gather information which the judge can use to issue no-contact orders or otherwise protect the victim during pendency of the case; various forms of diversion programs; whereby a

batterer can avoid conviction if he successfully completes a batterers program and complies with conditions for the woman's safety, such as no further threats or violence.

However, some advocates oppose any form of diversion, and most advocates and prosecutors believe that diverting batterers before they enter guilty pleas is not advisable. Some are willing to consider post-plea diversion where the batterer's progress while on probation is closely monitored, and where the plea alone is sufficient to convict and sentence the batterer if he does not follow the conditions of the diversion program....

# I. Crimes of Domestic Violence

## A. Homicide

Placed into context, the extent of the senseless slaughter of women in their own homes by their supposed "loved ones," is shocking. Between 2001 and 2012 the United States has participated in wars in Afghanistan and Iraq during which 6,488 American soldiers were killed. But during that same period, 11,766 American women were killed in domestic violence homicides. Each day, three women are killed in the United States by an intimate male partner. In 2011, 1,509 women were killed by men they knew.[2] In most jurisdictions, a perpetrator of a domestic violence homicide is charged with the same crime as any other murderer. But in Minnesota, domestic violence homicide is a special category of murder with harsher penalties for defendants with a history of engaging in domestic abuse.

### Minn. Stat. (2015)

**609.185 Murder in the first degree**

(a) Whoever does any of the following is guilty of murder in the first degree and shall be sentenced to imprisonment for life:

. . . .

(6) causes the death of a human being while committing domestic abuse, when the perpetrator has engaged in a past pattern of domestic abuse upon the victim or upon another family or household member and the death occurs under circumstances manifesting an extreme indifference to human life. . . .

---

2. Alanna Vagianos, *30 Shocking Domestic Violence Statistics That Remind Us It's an Epidemic*, HUFFPOST WOMEN, October 23, 2014 and updated February 13, 2015, www.huffingtonpost.com /2014/10/23/domestic-violence-statistics_n_5959776.html, accessed January 23, 2016.

## State v. Barnes
Minnesota Supreme Court
713 N.W.2d 325 (2006)

Appellant Charles Ray Barnes appeals from his conviction of first-degree domestic abuse murder, Minn. Stat. §609.185(a)(6) (2004).[3] He argues that domestic abuse murder violates the Equal Protection Clause of the Minnesota Constitution because the elements of the crime overlap with those of third-degree depraved mind murder, Minn. Stat. §609.195(a) (2004), but domestic abuse murder provides for significantly greater penalties. . . . We affirm.

Minutes before midnight on July 13, 2004, Barnes called 911 from his Burnsville apartment reporting that he had just arrived home and found his ex-wife, Erin Rooney, unconscious and not breathing. He told the dispatcher that he thought she had overdosed on drugs or alcohol. He said he dragged her from the living room to the bathroom to try to wake her up with water because he thought she had just passed out. Barnes performed some chest compressions at the dispatcher's direction.

Two police officers attempted CPR by administering chest compressions and tilting Rooney's head to open her airway. The paramedics arrived shortly thereafter and learned that Rooney had been in this state for 20 to 30 minutes before Barnes called 911. The officers stopped resuscitation efforts a few minutes later when paramedics pronounced her dead.

One officer observed a syringe with a small amount of liquid inside and a rolled-up dollar bill on a table in the living room. When the officer asked Barnes about it, he said it belonged to Rooney and that she was a heroin addict. Rooney had a puncture mark on her inner right arm that appeared to be from a needle. An officer then briefly interviewed Barnes and his version of what happened changed slightly from what he had told the dispatcher. He said he and Rooney ate dinner together and that he went to bed around 9:00. He said he woke up a few hours later and found Rooney unconscious. The officers acknowledged that there was no sign of a struggle in the apartment and that they initially treated the case as a death investigation, not a homicide. Although they took some photographs, they did not change the locks on the apartment or otherwise secure it, they allowed Barnes to leave with his relatives, and they collected no evidence. . . .

The next day the medical examiner, Dr. Lindsey Thomas, performed an autopsy on Rooney's body and documented numerous injuries: (1) several bruises and abrasions; (2) defensive injuries on her hands; (3) hemorrhaging in her neck; (4) a broken hyoid bone (in her neck); (5) petechiae (ruptured blood vessels) in her eyes; (6) swelling and congestion in her face; (7) injuries to her lips and tongue; and (8) a contusion under her chin. At trial Dr. Thomas conceded that until she discovered the

---

3. Although the case refers to 2004 statute, the language is the same as the 2015 version printed above. [Eds. Note.]

neck injuries, the numerous other injuries on Rooney's body were consistent with a drug overdose. It was not until Dr. Thomas found the broken hyoid bone and hemorrhage in Rooney's neck that the police began treating the investigation as a homicide.

Barnes was arrested that evening at his mother's house. The only injury officers found on Barnes was a scratch on his back. Police executed a search warrant on the apartment but found nothing else of significance. At trial, the state introduced medical evidence through the medical examiner who performed the autopsy, Dr. Thomas, and a forensic pathologist who reviewed Dr. Thomas' conclusions, Dr. Dean Hawley. The state's theory was that Barnes strangled Rooney during the course of a domestic assault, and then injected her with heroin to create the appearance of a drug overdose. Dr. Hawley gave his opinion that each of Rooney's injuries occurred while she was still alive and that she died from asphyxiation due to manual strangulation.

Barnes' theory was that Rooney died from an overdose of heroin and alcohol. On cross-examination of the state's witnesses, he tried to show that all of Rooney's injuries could be explained by other causes. He argued that the drugs and alcohol she consumed caused her to fall down and bump into things, which caused all of her bruises and abrasions. He also suggested that the hyoid bone either broke when Rooney fell and hit some furniture, or when the coroner's investigator mishandled Rooney's body. Finally, he suggested that the neck hemorrhages were the result of an improper autopsy procedure.

. . . .

Barnes was found guilty of first-degree domestic abuse murder, Minn. Stat. § 609.185(a)(6); second-degree unintentional felony murder, Minn. Stat. § 609.19, subd. 2(1) (2004); and first-degree felony assault, Minn. Stat. § 609.221, subd. 1 (2004), but not guilty of second-degree intentional murder, Minn. Stat. § 609.19, subd. 1(1) (2004). He was sentenced to life in prison based on the first-degree domestic abuse murder conviction. This appeal followed.

I.

. . . .

Barnes makes two equal protection arguments. First, he claims that first-degree domestic abuse murder impermissibly overlaps with third-degree depraved mind murder. Second, he argues that first-degree domestic abuse murder singles out domestic abusers for harsher punishment without a rational basis.

A. *Overlapping Statutes*

Section 609.185(a)(6), the domestic abuse murder statute, makes it first-degree murder to cause "the death of a human being while committing domestic abuse, when the perpetrator has engaged in a past pattern of domestic abuse upon the victim * * * and the death occurs under circumstances manifesting an extreme indifference to human life." Section 609.195(a), the depraved mind murder statute, makes it third-degree murder to, without intent to effect the death of any person, cause "the death of another by perpetrating an act eminently dangerous to others and evincing a depraved mind, without regard to human life." The penalty for first-degree domestic abuse murder is life imprisonment and the penalty for third-degree depraved mind murder is a maximum of 25 years in prison, with a presumptive sentence under the sentencing guidelines of 150 months in this case. Barnes argues that "there is no significant difference in the culpable mental state required by these statutes" and that "the lack of a meaningful variance between the two does not justify the huge disparity in the two sentences under the equal protection provisions of the Minnesota Constitution."

. . . .

First, domestic abuse murder focuses on a specific type of actus reus — death while committing domestic abuse — while depraved mind murder is much more broad — death while "perpetrating an act eminently dangerous to others." . . .

Second, domestic abuse murder is more specific because it only applies to (1) a specific group of defendants who cause the death of (2) a specific group of victims. Domestic abuse murder only applies to defendants who have "engaged in a past pattern of domestic abuse upon the victim." Minn. Stat. §609.185(a)(6). Depraved mind murder applies to any defendant. Minn. Stat. §609.195(a). Domestic abuse murder only applies with a victim who had a domestic relationship with the defendant. Minn. Stat. §609.185(c)(2); *see* Minn. Stat. §518B.01, subd. 2(b) (2004). Depraved mind murder, on the other hand, can apply with "any person" as the victim. Minn. Stat. §609.195(a).

The statutes can also be distinguished because the mens rea elements have a different focus. Domestic abuse murder requires that the extreme indifference be directed at the specific person. Depraved mind murder, on the other hand, cannot occur where the defendant's actions were focused on a specific person. . . . *State v. Wahlberg*, 296 N.W. 2d 408, 417 (Minn. 1980). . . .

There is a further basis to distinguish the mens rea elements of the two statutes. We have interpreted the "depraved mind" standard from depraved mind murder to be equivalent to a reckless standard. *See State v. Carlson*, 328 N.W.2d 690, 694 (Minn. 1982). Domestic abuse murder requires proof of at least one of the underlying domestic abuse crimes, each of which has an intent element. *See* Minn. Stat. §609.185(c) (requiring that the state also prove one of the enumerated underlying "domestic abuse" crimes).

Because the two statutes do not punish identical conduct, their coexistence does not present an equal protection concern.

### B. Disparate Treatment

Barnes suggests that domestic abuse murder violates equal protection because, without a rational basis, it singles out domestic abusers for harsher punishment than those who commit depraved mind murder. He focuses on the "past pattern of domestic abuse" element of domestic abuse murder. . . .

The obvious purpose of the domestic abuse murder statute is to combat domestic violence. This is certainly a legitimate legislative goal. And providing harsher punishment for those who have a past pattern of domestic abuse serves that goal. Barnes focuses only on the first prong, arguing that the "past pattern of domestic abuse" element creates an arbitrary classification because it is both overinclusive and underinclusive.

As for overinclusiveness, Barnes argues that because domestic abuse murder only requires prior allegations of domestic abuse, and not prior convictions, some defendants may be wrongfully convicted of domestic abuse murder based on unproven allegations. But we have repeatedly upheld this portion of the statute against similar arguments made in the context of due process challenges. *State v. Manley*, 664 N.W.2d 275, 283 (Minn. 2003). . . .

As to underinclusiveness, Barnes argues that because "domestic abuse is an underreported crime," some defendants who actually have a past pattern of domestic abuse are not charged with first-degree domestic abuse murder because the past incidents were unreported. But the authority he cites refers to domestic assault being unreported to law enforcement. The past pattern requirement can be proven by incidents that were not reported to law enforcement. *See Manley*, 664 N.W.2d at 280. Further, substantial deference is given to the legislature where an underinclusiveness challenge is made on rational basis review. *See Haskell's Inc. v. Sopsic*, 306 N.W.2d 555, 559 (Minn. 1981).

We hold that the domestic abuse murder statute does not violate the Equal Protection Clause of the Minnesota Constitution.

---

Domestic violence homicides once were considered justified, particularly when a wife was found to be unfaithful. As noted in the 1988 book, *Homicide*, by Martin Daly and Margo Wilson, many legal systems supported a cuckolded husband's right to kill his wife or her lover. In fact, until 1974 in Texas it was considered justifiable homicide if a husband killed his wife while catching her in the act of adultery. And many juries still acquit husbands for this same behavior.[4]

## B. Fatality Reviews/Danger Assessments

On January 15, 1990 outside an elementary school in San Francisco, Joseph Charan shot to death his estranged wife as she was bringing their son to school. He then killed himself. The couple had been separated. For 15 months before he killed her, Joseph Charan had been tormenting his wife through acts of domestic violence, and she repeatedly had contacted police.

Shortly before he shot her, Joseph Charan had been arrested for felony wife beating and malicious mischief. He was convicted and received a 12-month suspended jail sentence with probation requiring he attend domestic violence counseling; have no further contact with his wife; and serve four days in jail with the remainder on work release.

---

4. Martin Daly & Margo Wilson, Homicide, 193–95, 205 (1988).

Following Mrs. Charan's death, the City and County of San Francisco, Commission on the Status of Women, conducted a year-long "fatality review," which included an in-depth examination of the case files. Public hearings were conducted with the goal of trying to prevent future tragedies like the Charan murder.

The panel concluded there was inadequate domestic violence training for police, court personnel and judges; there was an insufficient exchange of information among agencies charged with preventing domestic violence; and there were barriers to access to these agencies such as cultural insensitivity and lack of translation services. Thereafter, the California Legislature passed a law establishing county-level domestic violence fatality review teams to coordinate government efforts to address domestic violence-related deaths and work toward preventing them.[5] Fatality review boards "examine domestic violence related deaths including the events leading up to [them] ... to determine what led to the homicide(s). The goal ... is to uncover holes or gaps in the various government systems' responses to domestic violence."[6]

As of early 2016, 41 states had established domestic violence fatality review procedures; the majority by statute, and the rest—Kansas, New Hampshire, New Jersey, New York and Wyoming—by executive order.[7]

In New York City, Local Law 61 established a citywide fatality review committee in 2005. From 2002 through 2013, there were 851 domestic violence homicides in the city. Although a stunningly high number, it nonetheless signals an 18 percent decline for the period; there were 76 family related homicides (including child abuse and sibling murder cases as well as intimate partner homicides) in 2002 compared to 62 in 2013. And, as in other studies, the NYC fatality review committee determined that domestic violence disproportionately impacts the city's African American population and the poor. Blacks made up 23 percent of the NYC population but nearly half of its DV fatalities; 415 of the 851. Four in 10 victims of domestic violence homicides came from poor neighborhoods. These statistics were the basis for the committee's recommendations that expanded services be offered at the city's family justice centers; that city employees offering services to the poor be trained to recognize the signs of DV and be prepared to offer services for victims.[8] A city-provided poster, reprinted below, hangs in storefronts in the Bronx, a county with significant poverty.

---

5. Details of the Charan fatality review from Neil Websdale, Maureen Sheeran & Byron Johnson, *Reviewing Domestic Violence Fatalities: Summarizing National Developments,* www.vaw.umn.edu/documents/fatality/fatality.html at 5–6. *See also* LA Chung, SF *Revamps Aid for Battered Women: Murder Reveals Poor Agency Coordination,* S.F. CHRONICLE, Oct. 19, 1991.

6. The Advocates for Human Rights, *Stop Violence Against Women, Domestic Violence Fatality Review Boards,* November 1, 2006, www.stopvaw.org/domestic_fatality_review_boards, accessed March 4, 2017.

7. *National Domestic Violence Fatality Review Initiative,* www.ndvfri.org/documents.php, accessed January 23, 2016.

8. *New York City Domestic Violence Fatality Review Committee: 2014 Annual Report,* www.nyc.gov/html/ocdv/downloads/pdf/statistics_9th_Annual_Report_Fatality_Review_Committee_2014.pdf, accessed January 23, 2016.

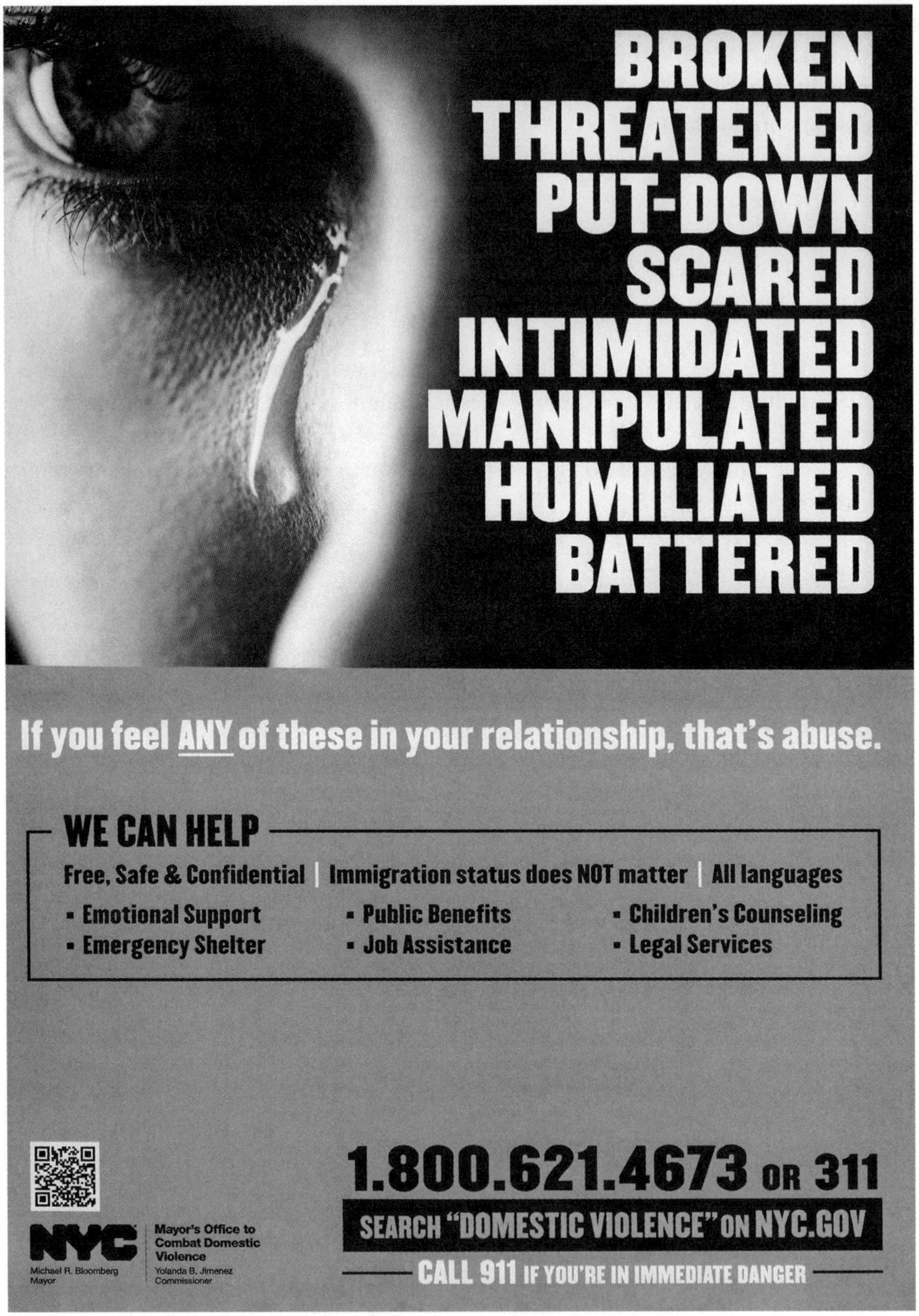

Courtesy: New York City Mayor's Office to Combat Domestic Violence

In Texas, there were 111 domestic violence homicides in 2009, 29 of which took place that year in Harris County, where Houston is located. The local fatality review committee reviewed 57 cases and learned that in 27 of them, a firearm was used, in 13 a knife was the weapon of choice, two murderers used their bare hands and one relied on a hammer.[9]

While fatality reviews are one more tool designed to help save the lives of future victims of domestic violence, the question arises whether there is any method of reliably predicting whether domestic abuse will escalate to murder. Dr. Jacqueline C. Campbell, a registered nurse and professor at Johns Hopkins University, in Baltimore, Md., is a nationally recognized expert on domestic violence. In 1985, she developed the "danger assessment," which is a series of questions designed to help law enforcement officers, health care workers and domestic violence advocates evaluate and determine the level of risk facing a particular victim. It is available online and reprinted below.[10]

## Jacqueline C. Campbell, et al., *Assessing Risk Factors for Intimate Partner Homicides*
NIJ JOURNAL 15-19 (Issue No. 250) (Nov. 2003)

Why does domestic violence turn to murder? Can we measure the risk of death for a battered woman? Which women in abusive relationships are most likely to be killed? One helpful tool for finding answers to these questions is called the Danger Assessment. The series of 15 questions on the Danger Assessment is designed to measure a woman's risk in an abusive relationship.

A team of researchers studied the Danger Assessment and found that despite certain limitations, the tool can with some reliability identify women who may be at risk of being killed by their intimate partners. The study found that women who score 8 or higher on the Danger Assessment are at very grave risk (the average score for women who were murdered was just under 8). Women who score 4 or higher are at great risk (the average score for abused women was just over 3). The findings indicate that the Danger Assessment tool can assist in assessing battered women who may be at risk of being killed as well as those who are not.

The study also found that almost half the murdered women studied did not recognize the high level of their risk. Thus, a tool like the Danger Assessment — or any other risk assessment process — may assist women (and the professionals who help them) to better understand the potential for danger and the level of risk.

Limitations and Caveats

Eighty-three percent of the women who were killed had scores of 4 or higher, but so did almost 40 percent of the women who were *not* killed. This finding indicates

---

9. *Harris County Death Review Team Annual Report: 2010*, www.ndvfri.org/reports/texas/Texas_Harris_AnnualReport_2010.pdf, accessed January 23, 2016.

10. Jacquelyn C. Campbell, *Danger Assessment*, https://www.dangerassessment.org/DA.aspx, accessed October 9, 2016.

# DANGER ASSESSMENT

*Jacquelyn C. Campbell, Ph.D., R.N.*
Copyright, 2003; www.dangerassessment.com

Several risk factors have been associated with increased risk of homicides (murders) of women and men in violent relationships. We cannot predict what will happen in your case, but we would like you to be aware of the danger of homicide in situations of abuse and for you to see how many of the risk factors apply to your situation.

Using the calendar, please mark the approximate dates during the past year when you were abused by your partner or ex partner. Write on that date how bad the incident was according to the following scale:

1. Slapping, pushing; no injuries and/or lasting pain
2. Punching, kicking; bruises, cuts, and/or continuing pain
3. "Beating up"; severe contusions, burns, broken bones
4. Threat to use weapon; head injury, internal injury, permanent injury
5. Use of weapon; wounds from weapon

(If **any** of the descriptions for the higher number apply, use the higher number.)

Mark **Yes** or **No** for each of the following. ("He" refers to your husband, partner, ex-husband, ex-partner, or whoever is currently physically hurting you.)

\_\_\_ 1. Has the physical violence increased in severity or frequency over the past year?
\_\_\_ 2. Does he own a gun?
\_\_\_ 3. Have you left him after living together during the past year?
   3a. (If have *never* lived with him, check here\_\_\_)
\_\_\_ 4. Is he unemployed?
\_\_\_ 5. Has he ever used a weapon against you or threatened you with a lethal weapon?
   (If yes, was the weapon a gun?\_\_\_)
\_\_\_ 6. Does he threaten to kill you?
\_\_\_ 7. Has he avoided being arrested for domestic violence?
\_\_\_ 8. Do you have a child that is not his?
\_\_\_ 9. Has he ever forced you to have sex when you did not wish to do so?
\_\_\_ 10. Does he ever try to choke you?
\_\_\_ 11. Does he use illegal drugs? By drugs, I mean "uppers" or amphetamines, "meth", speed, angel dust, cocaine, "crack", street drugs or mixtures.
\_\_\_ 12. Is he an alcoholic or problem drinker?
\_\_\_ 13. Does he control most or all of your daily activities? For instance: does he tell you who you can be friends with, when you can see your family, how much money you can use, or when you can take the car? (If he tries, but you do not let him, check here: \_\_\_)
\_\_\_ 14. Is he violently and constantly jealous of you? (For instance, does he say "If I can't have you, no one can.")
\_\_\_ 15. Have you ever been beaten by him while you were pregnant? (If you have never been pregnant by him, check here: \_\_\_)
\_\_\_ 16. Has he ever threatened or tried to commit suicide?
\_\_\_ 17. Does he threaten to harm your children?
\_\_\_ 18. Do you believe he is capable of killing you?
\_\_\_ 19. Does he follow or spy on you, leave threatening notes or messages, destroy your property, or call you when you don't want him to?
\_\_\_ 20. Have you ever threatened or tried to commit suicide?
\_\_\_ Total "Yes" Answers

**Thank you. Please talk to your nurse, advocate or counselor about what the Danger Assessment means in terms of your situation.**

that practitioners can use the Danger Assessment (like all intimate partner violence risk assessment tools) as a guide in the process rather than as a precise actuarial tool. . . .

High Correlations: Guns and Threats to Kill

Previous studies have looked at the relationship of gun ownership or possession to intimate partner homicide, particularly when the partners live apart. The Danger Assessment study found that women who were threatened or assaulted with a gun or other weapon were 20 times more likely than other women to be murdered. Women whose partners threatened them with murder were 15 times more likely than other women to be killed. When a gun was in the house, an abused woman was 6 times more likely than other abused women to be killed. . . .

Low Correlation: Threatened or Attempted Suicide

Threatened or attempted suicide by either males or females in the study were not found to be predictors of intimate partner homicide. However, there is an increased risk of homicide when the man is suicidal and there has not been any physical abuse. Approximately one-third of the murders studied were homicide-suicides. Further analysis is needed to learn how a man's potential for suicide increases his partner's risk of becoming a homicide-suicide victim. . . .

The Safety Plan

In safety planning, an abuser's threats with a weapon or threats to kill should be rated as particularly serious, as should a possible murderer's access to a gun. Thus, the researchers suggest that legal prohibition against gun ownership for those convicted of domestic violence is especially important to enforce, and any protection order should include firearms search-and-seizure provisions.

However, criminal justice practitioners making decisions about an alleged batterer's bail or sentencing should keep in mind that more than a third of women who had a score of 4 or higher were not murdered. The research showed only that a score of 8 or 9 reliably identified those women who were killed. Thus, while the current cut-off score of 4 suggests the need for great caution and for protective action, it does not reliably identify a woman's risk of death.

---

There are few reported decisions discussing the admissibility of lethality assessments in court. There is concern about the prejudicial impact of relying on a social worker's assessment—as opposed to the factual evidence—to determining whether a defendant committed a particular crime. In the following case, the prosecution introduced testimony about a lethality assessment during the penalty phase of a criminal trial in Texas. Although the appellate court found the trial judge committed error by allowing the testimony, it refused to overturn the conviction.

## Pettingill v. Pettingill

Supreme Court of Kentucky

480 S.W.3d 920 (2015)

Opinion of the Court by Justice Keller

AFFIRMING

The Jefferson Circuit Court, Family Division, entered a domestic violence order (DVO) against Jeffrey Pettingill. The Court of Appeals affirmed, and we granted discretionary review. On appeal to this Court, Jeffrey argues that he was deprived of a full appellate review and that the family court erroneously relied on "lethality factors" when entering the DVO. For the reasons stated herein, we affirm the opinion of the Court of Appeals.

### I. BACKGROUND.

On July 2, 2013, Sara Pettingill filed a domestic violence petition against her husband, Jeffrey. In her petition, Sara alleged that Jeffrey's violent, controlling, and unstable behavior made her fear for her own safety as well as the wellbeing of their minor daughter. She was particularly afraid because she had recently separated from Jeffrey and was seeking a divorce. Specifically, Sara described an incident when Jeffrey became angry and abused the family pet in front of their daughter. Sara also recounted numerous examples of Jeffrey's controlling behavior, including: setting up surveillance cameras inside their home; locking her out of bank accounts; accessing her private email and social media accounts; and breaking her cell phone. Furthermore, Sara indicated that Jeffrey had become mentally unstable and alleged that he: boasted about keeping a firearm in their home even though he was a convicted felon; threatened the life of his ex-wife who had filed domestic violence charges against him in Tennessee; and claimed to be an ex-CIA agent.

Based on Sara's petition, the Jefferson family court entered an emergency protective order (EPO). The Sheriff was originally unable to serve Jeffrey, noting on the summons, "is avoiding, someone told him about paperwork." Nonetheless, Jeffrey did eventually receive notice of the EPO and summons and appeared, represented by counsel, at the scheduled domestic violence hearing on July 11, 2013.

Following that hearing, the family court entered a DVO against Jeffrey on Administrative Office of the Courts (AOC) Form 275.3. In so doing, the court found by a preponderance of the evidence that acts of domestic violence or abuse had occurred and may occur again. For support, the family court noted further findings of fact on its docket sheet:

[Jeffrey] avoided service, served 7/10/13

The Court finds: 9 out of 12 top lethality factors in intimate partner

   1) [Jeffrey] has abused the family pet;

   2) Cyber stalking [Sara];

3) Threatened the life of his ex-wife in the presence of [Sara];

4) Shown possessive—jealous behavior by monitoring [Sara]'s cell phone;

5) Damaged property ([Sara]'s cell phone) throwing it against the wall;

6) Engaged in rulemaking behaviors including not allowing [Sara] to drive her own car;

7) Has prior felony conviction;

8) Recently purchased a firearm (3/29/13);

9) Recent separation—of the parties

Places [Sara] at extreme risk of physical harm.

Jeffrey appealed the DVO to the Court of Appeals. Jeffrey argued, *inter alia*, that the family court erred when it took judicial notice of, and based its decision on, the domestic violence lethality factors rather than the standard set forth in Kentucky Revised Statute (KRS) 403.720 and 403.750.

The Court of Appeals disagreed and affirmed the family court's DVO. However, as an initial matter, the Court noted that its review was "severely hampered" by the lack of a complete record, stating that it had not received the video record of the hearing. The Court concluded, however, that it was Jeffrey's duty, as appellant, to ensure the record on appeal was sufficient and that because it could not review the testimony, it must assume the omitted record supported the decision of the family court.

Notwithstanding the incomplete record, the Court of Appeals found that the family court applied the appropriate standard based on the fact that it properly completed the AOC 275.3 standard form. The Court reasoned that the additional findings noted on the docket sheet could not be seen to indicate the family court's disregard of the correct standard nor did the reference to lethality factors render the decision infirm. Furthermore, the Court found no inference by the family court that it was taking judicial notice of any fact and that comparing its findings to the lethality factors did not change the nature or character of the adjudicated facts adduced during the hearing.

The Court of Appeals denied Jeffrey's petition for rehearing, in which he argued that his constitutional right to judicial review had been violated by the Court's failure to obtain and review the complete record. This Court granted discretionary review, and for the following reasons, we affirm the decision of the Court of Appeals. We set forth additional facts as necessary below.

## II. ANALYSIS.

On appeal to this Court, Jeffrey makes three assignments of error: (1) that he was denied his constitutional right to an appellate review; (2) that the family court erred when it took judicial notice of the lethality factors; and (3) that the court erred when it used the lethality factors as the standard to enter a DVO. We address each argument in turn.

A. Appellate Review.

Jeffrey argues that the circuit court clerk failed to certify the video record of the domestic violence hearing on appeal, and, as a result, the Court of Appeals did not receive a copy and could not render a full constitutional appellate review. Jeffrey contends that Kentucky Rule of Civil Procedure (CR) 98(2) requires a circuit court clerk to automatically transmit a copy of the video record of a domestic violence hearing to a reviewing court. Thus, he contends, an appellant has no duty to take action whatsoever to ensure the video record is transmitted. We do not need to reach the merits of this argument . . . .

B. Judicial Notice.

As he did before the Court of Appeals, Jeffrey continues to argue that the family court impermissibly took judicial notice of the lethality factors for intimate partner violence. He alleges the factors are not the kind of facts that are the proper subject of judicial notice and that the court did not follow proper procedure set forth in Kentucky Rule of Evidence (KRE) 201 when adopting them. The Court of Appeals found that this argument was without merit, and we agree.

A trial court may take judicial notice of adjudicative facts that are not subject to reasonable dispute. KRE 201. In other words, KRE 201 allows judicial notice to be taken of facts which can be determined from "unimpeachable sources" such as "encyclopedias, calendars, maps, medical and historical treatises, almanacs, and public records." Robert G. Lawson, *The Kentucky Evidence Law Handbook* § 1.00(2)(c), at 7 (5th ed. 2013); *see also Clay v. Commonwealth*, 291 S.W.3d 210, 219 (Ky. 2008). Classic examples of facts taken by judicial notice include the definition of words, the phases of the—moon, and reliability of some scientific tests.

Lethality factors or "lethality predictors" for intimate partner violence are not facts but risk factors used by courts, law enforcement, counselors, and social scientists to evaluate the threat of domestic violence between partners. Louise E. Graham and James E. Keller, 15 *Kentucky Practice: Domestic Relations Law* § 5:13 (West 2014); Symposium, *Death by Intimacy: Risk Factors for Domestic Violence*, 20 Pace L. Rev. 263 (2000). Common factors include: threats of homicide or suicide, or suicide attempts; history of domestic violence and violent criminal conduct; stalking; depression or other mental illness; obsessive attachment to victim; separation of parties; drug or alcohol involvement; possession or access to weapons; abuse of pets; destruction of victim's property; and access to victim and victim's family and other supporters. *Id.* at n. 89.

We agree with Jeffrey that these factors are not the type of facts that are normally taken by judicial notice, but we also agree with the Court of Appeals that these factors were not taken by judicial notice. The family court's reorganization of facts elicited during the hearing was not done according to judicial notice; all the adjudicative facts were proven through testimony. The list of lethality factors—presumably contained in the court's mind—was judicial knowledge rather than judicial notice. This Court has previously held that judicial knowledge and notice are inherently different and that "[w]hile a resident judge's background knowledge of an area may 'inform the judge's assessment of the historical facts,' the judge may not actually testify in the proceeding or interject facts (excluding facts for which proper judicial notice is taken)." *Commonwealth v. Howlett*, 328 S.W.3d 191, 193 (Ky. 2010) (quoting *U.S. v. Berber-Tinoco*, 510 F.3d 1083, 1091 (9th Cir.2007)). The family court had permissible judicial knowledge of the lethality factors. In other words, the court employed its background knowledge of domestic violence risk factors to inform its judgment as to whether the facts of this case indicated that domestic violence may occur again.

Because no adjudicative facts were taken according to judicial notice, there was no violation of KRE 201.

C. DVO Standard.

Jeffrey also maintains his argument below that the family court erroneously relied on the lethality factors as the standard for issuing the DVO. Jeffrey asserts that KRS 403.750 and 403.720 make up the proper standard.

A court may issue a DVO if, "[f]ollowing the hearing provided for under KRS 403.740 and 403.745, [it] finds from a preponderance of the evidence that an act or acts of domestic violence and abuse [has] occurred and may again occur...." KRS 403.750. "'Domestic violence and abuse' means physical injury, serious physical injury, sexual abuse, assault, or the infliction of fear of imminent physical injury, serious physical injury, sexual abuse, or assault between family members or members of an unmarried couple." KRS 403.720. Thus, in this case, the family court was required to determine whether, by a preponderance of the evidence, Jeffrey inflicted fear of imminent physical injury, serious physical injury, sexual abuse, or assault and whether fear, injury, abuse, or assault might occur in the future. The court properly made this finding.

Following the hearing, the family court found that Sara had met the burden above and entered a DVO against Jeffrey. To document this order, the court completely and accurately filled out AOC Form 275.3 and, under the "Additional Findings" header, checked the box corresponding to "for [Sara] against [Jeffrey] in that it was established, by a preponderance of the evidence, that an act(s) of domestic violence or abuse occurred and may again occur." To supplement this finding, the family court made further factual findings on its docket sheet, which are recounted above.

We agree with the Court of Appeals that the family court adhered to the proper standard and that its reference to lethality factors does not indicate otherwise. The finding made on AOC Form 275.3 clearly tracks the language of KRS 403.750 and applies the proper standard. Additionally, the reference to lethality factors on the docket sheet does not negate the court's previous finding. The court merely used its judicial knowledge of common risk factors to evaluate whether domestic abuse may occur in the future, as required by the statutory standard. The predictive nature of the standard requires the family court to consider the totality of the circumstances and weigh the risk of future violence against issuing a protective order. In hindsight, perhaps the family court should not have employed social science terminology in describing its analysis; nonetheless, the substance of the court's reasoning was not erroneous.

Finally, Jeffrey argues that the family court did not specify sufficient findings of fact to support its DVO because the AOC Form 275.3 is deficient. We disagree.

CR 52.01 provides that "[i]n all actions tried upon the facts without a jury or with an advisory jury, the court shall find the facts specifically and state separately its conclusions of law thereon and render an appropriate judgment . . . ." We are also guided by this Court's holding in *Anderson v. Johnson*, 350 S.W.3d 453, 458 (Ky. 2011) ("CR 52.01 requires that the judge engage in at least a good faith effort at fact-finding and that the found facts be included in a written order") as well as *Keifer v. Keifer*'s admonishment to trial courts to include written findings in all orders affecting child custody. 354 S.W.3d 123, 125 (Ky. 2011).

The family court's written findings of fact were more than sufficient to satisfy CR 52.01. In addition to clearly finding that an act or acts of domestic violence had occurred and may occur again on the form, the court also listed on its docket sheet nine specific findings to support its order. Jeffrey does not contend that these findings are not accurate or that they had not been proven during the hearing; therefore, we need not weigh their substantive value. This effort more than satisfies the court's good faith duty to record fact-finding.

We need not consider Jeffrey's argument that AOC Form 275.3 is deficient because, as we held above, the family court made more than sufficient findings of fact. Therefore, regardless of the alleged deficiencies in AOC Form 275.3, proper findings were made and recorded in the case at bar.

### III. CONCLUSION.

For the reasons stated above, we affirm the opinion of the Court of Appeals.

. . . .

## Petriciolet v. Texas

### Court of Appeals of Texas, First District, Houston

### 442 S.W. 3d 643 (2014)

A jury found appellant, Arturo Petriciolet, guilty of the offense of aggravated assault of a family member and assessed his punishment at confinement for fifty years. The trial court further found that he used a deadly weapon, namely, a firearm, in the commission of the offense. In his sole issue, appellant contends that the trial court erred in admitting expert testimony during the punishment phase of trial.

We affirm.

### Background

During the guilt phase of trial, the complainant, Leticia Gracia, testified that she is appellant's former girlfriend and the mother of his youngest child. Their relationship had been "off and on" during the five-year period preceding the incident at issue, and they had lived together for a portion of that time. Once their relationship ended, the complainant maintained an amicable relationship with appellant, and he frequently visited his daughter and the complainant's older daughter at the complainant's house.

The complainant explained that on the evening of July 28, 2010, appellant came over to her house for dinner, to plan a birthday party for one of the children, and to watch television. She noted that appellant, who usually carried a semi-automatic firearm, placed the firearm on a living room table upon his arrival at her home. At the end of the evening, appellant and the complainant went upstairs for him to say goodnight to the children. The complainant then followed appellant down the stairs, into the dark living room, where he, without warning, "picked up his gun" and shot her "in the face." . . .

After the jury found appellant guilty, the complainant, during the punishment phase of trial, testified that, during the course of their relationship, appellant had been "very controlling" of her and would often wait for her in the parking garage where she worked. He did not allow her to wear make-up or brush her hair, see her mother or her friends, or receive telephone calls outside of work. The complainant explained that appellant is an alcoholic, had a history of violent behavior towards her, including slapping her on at least two occasions, and had threatened to "beat [her] up" if she tried to have a romantic relationship with anyone else.

The complainant further testified that she and her children "live in constant fear." Although she has been paying the mortgage on her house for the past two years, she it is too "scared" to go home. Thus, the complainant and her daughters live together in a single bedroom at her parents' home. They sleep with the lights on and do not attend school functions or otherwise leave the house unless required. As a result of the shooting, the complainant lost vision in her left eye, has had five facial operations, and will require future reconstructive surgeries. Her teeth have fallen out and she cannot open her mouth. The complainant's food must be prepared in a blender, and she drinks it through a straw.

. . . .

The State presented as an expert witness, J. Varela, Director of Family Violence Services at the Harris County District Attorney's Office. She testified that she has a master's degree in social work, is a licensed clinical social worker, has received professional training in dealing with domestic violence, has taught a class at the graduate level, and speaks at professional conferences. Varela's duties at the District Attorney's office include overseeing twelve staff members in providing crisis intervention counseling to approximately 3,500 people per year. She has previously testified "[a]t least 150 [times] as an expert witness" in civil and criminal cases.

. . . .

Appellant objected to Varela's testimony and requested a hearing to determine whether it "[met] the threshold of scientific evidence." At a hearing outside the jury's presence, Varela testified that she has "been a social worker for 17 years"; has been the Director of Family Violence Services for twelve years; has a master's degree in social work, concentrating in the area of "[p]olitical social work"; and has trained "probably—hundreds of police officers on domestic violence issues." She explained that she has "seen thousands of people" and has evaluated "a lot of cases," but has never done any field work related to domestic violence.

Varela further testified that she met with the complainant for "[o]nly a couple of hours" on August 3, 2010 and performed "a typical assessment," which involved asking the complainant about "the course of the relationship" with appellant and the "first, worst and last incidents of violence." . . . .

[State]: Can you explain to us what is a [lethality] assessment?

[Varela]: A [lethality] assessment[] is an instrument that can be used to assess the level of risk in a domestic violence situation. It's important to realize risk is not predictive. You know, you cannot say because they have a high risk factor, it's research [sic] based on a whole big group of people that say it's more likely to happen or not more likely to happen.

[State]: Is the [lethality] assessment[] that you just told us based on a lot of something that's commonly used in your field?

[Varela]: Yes. And this one was published by the National Institute of Justice. . . .

[State]: Is [it] something that other experts like yourself rely upon across the country in testifying in these types of cases?

[Varela]: Yes.

[State]: Have you testified as an expert in other courts regarding a [lethality] assessment?

[Varela]: Yes.

[State]: Has your testimony been accepted in those other courts regarding this assessment?

[Varela]: Yes.

[State]: Did you perform this same [type] of assessment and use these same questions or procedures in this case?

[Varela]: Yes.

[State]: And do you have an opinion in this case?

. . . .

[Varela]: Yes.

Varela noted that although she was not sure if the use of lethality assessments had been tested, she was aware that they have a "pretty high" rate of error—"[i]t's like 30 or 40 percent."

. . . .

Varela opined that, based on the lethality assessment that she performed in this case, appellant "scores high on the risk assessment," noting that the use of a weapon alone is "the highest risk factor." She further noted that her testimony had been excluded in other courts on the basis of a lack of relevance.

Appellant objected that Varela's testimony was unnecessary for the jury to make a determination regarding whether his use of a firearm created a high-risk situation. Varela agreed, stating, "The number one thing is the fact that he's used a weapon in the past and he's actually shot her and I think like the average man on the street, I don't even know if we need research to tell us that. . . . I should hope that . . . most of us would have enough common sense to realize that." The trial court decided to admit Varela's testimony.

After the jury returned, the trial court stated that it would allow Varela "to testify as an expert in domestic violence, social work[,] and to testify concerning an assessment instrument that's used in her field and her conclusion as a basis of that assessment instrument." It then instructed the jury as follows:

> [I]n coming to her conclusion using that assessment instrument, [Varela] has to rely on information given to her from other people; and she uses that information to reach her assessment. She cannot tell you whether or not the information that's given is true or not true. All right; but we do know that is the information that she has to reach her assessment. In other words, those things are not offered for the truth of the matter, just so that you know what she used to reach her assessment.

Varela told the jury that although she had not interviewed appellant, she had interviewed the complainant, her daughters, and appellant's ex-wife. She noted that she had formed an opinion in this case based on her investigation and the testimony at trial. . . .

### Expert Testimony

In his sole issue, appellant argues that the trial court erred in allowing Varela to testify, during the punishment phase of trial, as an expert on "lethality assessment" because she was not qualified to testify on the issue and her testimony was not reliable.

"If scientific, technical, or other specialized knowledge will assist the trier of fact to understand the evidence or to determine a fact in issue, a witness qualified as an expert by knowledge, skill, experience, training, or education may testify thereto in the form of an opinion or otherwise." TEX. R. EVID. 702. Before admitting expert testimony, a trial court must determine that (1) the witness qualifies as an expert by reason of his knowledge, skill, experience, training, or education; (2) the subject matter of the testimony is an appropriate one for expert testimony; and (3) admitting the expert testimony will actually assist the fact-finder in deciding the case. *Rodgers v. State*, 205 S.W.3d 525, 527 (Tex. Crim. App. 2006). Thus, the trial court must determine that the expert is qualified to testify and the proffered testimony is reliable and relevant. *Vela v. State*, 209 S.W.3d 128, 131 (Tex. Crim. App. 2006).

*Reliability*

"'[R]eliability depends upon whether the evidence has its basis in sound scientific methodology,'" which "'demands a certain technical showing.'" *Id.* at 133 (quoting *Jordan v. State*, 928 S.W.2d 550, 555 (Tex. Crim. App. 1996)). . . .

In *Nenno v. State*, the court of criminal appeals held that when assessing the reliability of expert testimony concerning the so-called "soft sciences," those that are based on experience or training as opposed to scientific method, "[the] requirement of reliability applies but with less rigor than to the hard sciences." 970 S.W.2d 549, 561 (Tex. Crim. App. 1998), *overruled on other grounds, State v. Terrazas*, 4 S.W.3d 720, 727 (Tex. Crim. App. 1999). The appropriate considerations are (1) whether the field of expertise is a legitimate one, (2) whether the subject matter of the expert's testimony is within the scope of that field, and (3) whether the expert's testimony properly relies upon or utilizes the principles involved in that field. *Id.* . . .

As the proponent of Varela's expert testimony, the State had the burden to show by clear and convincing evidence that Varela's testimony was reliable. *State v. Smith*, 335 S.W.3d 706, 712 (Tex. App.—Houston [14th Dist.] 2011, pet. ref'd). The State does not direct us to any cases in which "lethality assessment" has been deemed a legitimate area of expertise. *See Nenno*, 970 S.W.2d at 561. In support of its assertion that "the admissibility of expert testimony assessing risk is not a new concept and has been evaluated by courts of appeals," the State relies on two "future dangerousness" cases: *Davis v. State*, 313 S.W.3d 317 (Tex. Crim. App. 2010), and *Russeau v. State*, 171 S.W.3d 871 (Tex. Crim. App. 2005). In capital-murder cases, a "future-dangerousness" special issue ensures that no defendant is sentenced to death unless the jury first finds that he poses a threat of future violence. *Coble v. State*, 330 S.W.3d 253, 268 (Tex. Crim. App. 2010). . . .

Here, Varela testified that she is a licensed social worker and that "lethality assessment" is "commonly" used in her field. However, she did not offer any specifics to support her assertion, and she did not cite any books, articles, studies, journals, or other clinical social workers who practice in this area. Rather, she relied solely on a single "journal article" that she did not identify and the State did not tender to the trial court. . . . Varela did not testify regarding any specific methodology used to conduct a lethality assessment. She explained that "[t]here's an instrument that we *can use* that has the questions on it; *but what we've done—we sort of put that into our own data base* so we can collect statistics on it." (Emphasis added.) She further explained that her assessment involved asking questions of the victim, but not the defendant. And although she "thinks" lethality assessment "has been tested," she was not sure and would need "to look at the [journal]," which she did not do before completing her testimony at trial. However, she did concede that lethality assessments have a "pretty high" rate of error—that "[i]t's like 30 or 40 percent."

. . . .

Here, the State presented no evidence to validate Varela's methodology and conclusions. Thus, it did not show by clear and convincing evidence that "lethality assessment" is a legitimate field of expertise. . . .

*Harm*

Having concluded that the trial court erred in admitting Varela's testimony, we next determine whether appellant was harmed. Non-constitutional error requires reversal only if it affects the substantial rights of the accused. *See* TEX. R. APP. P. 44.2(b); *Barshaw v. State*, 342 S.W.3d 91, 93 (Tex. Crim. App. 2011). A substantial right is affected when the error had a substantial and injurious effect or influence in determining the jury's verdict. *King v. State*, 953 S.W.2d 266, 271 (Tex. Crim. App. 1997). We will not overturn a criminal conviction for non-constitutional error if, after examining the record as a whole, we have fair assurance that the error did not influence the jury, or had but a slight effect. *Barshaw*, 342 S.W.3d at 93.

. . . .

Varela's testimony was quite weak. *See Coble*, 330 S.W.3d at 286-88. She equivocated, emphasized that her assessment was not predictive of anything, and asserted that expert testimony was not even necessary for the jury to determine whether appellant, having shot the complainant in the face, posed a "high risk" for future domestic violence.

Moreover, the trial court instructed the jury not to consider the truth of the information underlying Varela's conclusions. . . .

And we emphasize that the State did not mention Varela's testimony in its closing punishment argument to the jury.

Finally, we note that the evidence of appellant's guilt, which was overwhelming, showed that he committed a particularly brutal act—shooting the complainant in her face shortly after putting their children to bed. The long-term effects of his brutal act upon the complainant are severe and will last the remainder of her life. Thus, there is ample evidence to support the jury's assessment of punishment of confinement for fifty years.

Accordingly, we cannot conclude that the erroneous admission of Varela's testimony had a substantial and injurious effect on the jury's decision on punishment. . . .

We affirm the judgment of the trial court.

## C. Domestic Violence as a Specific Crime

Unless otherwise provided for by statute, crimes of domestic violence involve the same offenses and standards of proof as any other crime. But domestic violence often consists of pushing, shoving, slapping, spitting and other hurtful, vile conduct that may not necessarily rise to the level of a provable crime. In response to that reality, some states have created specific crimes of domestic violence, which do not require proof of the level of injury necessary for a misdemeanor or felony assault conviction. The California legislature, for example, has created the crime of "domestic assault" in which even a minor injury causing a "traumatic condition" may be the basis of a conviction.

## California Penal Code 273.5 (2016) Infliction of injury on present or former spouse, present or former cohabitant, present or former fiance/fiancee, present or former dating partner, or parent of child . . .

(a) Any person who willfully inflicts corporal injury resulting in a traumatic condition upon a victim described in subdivision (b) is guilty of a felony, and upon conviction thereof shall be punished by imprisonment in the state prison for two, three, or four years, or in a county jail for not more than one year, or by a fine of up to six thousand dollars ($6,000), or by both that fine and imprisonment.

(b) Subdivision (a) shall apply if the victim is or was one or more of the following:

(1) The offender's spouse or former spouse.

(2) The offender's cohabitant or former cohabitant.

(3) The offender's fiance or fiancee, or someone with whom the offender has, or previously had, an engagement or dating relationship . . . .

(4) The mother or father of the offender's child.

(c) Holding oneself out to be the husband or wife of the person with whom one is cohabiting is not necessary to constitute cohabitation as the term is used in this section.

(d) As used in this section, "traumatic condition" means a condition of the body, such as a wound, or external or internal injury, including, but not limited to, injury as a result of strangulation or suffocation, whether of a minor or serious nature, caused by a physical force. For purposes of this section, "strangulation" and "suffocation" include impeding the normal breathing or circulation of the blood of a person by applying pressure on the throat or neck. . . .

---

The following California mid-level appellate court decision addresses what constitutes "traumatic injury" under the statute. Although the reference is to an earlier version of the statute, the applicable language has not changed.

## People v. Abrego
### Court of Appeal of California
### 21 Cal. App. 4th 133 (1993)

Dabney, Acting P. J.

. . . .

On September 25, 1991, Ester Abrego (Ester) was married to Abrego, but had been living separately from him for several months. In the early morning of that day, Ester was at home sleeping after a party. Leonardo Gonzalez and two other men were also sleeping at her house. Abrego knocked at the door, and Ester let him in. He appeared angry and started swearing at Ester and called her a bitch and a whore. He slapped or punched her five times in the face and head. Ester went to the living room to awaken Gonzales.

Abrego followed Ester while continuing to shout obscenities at her. Gonzales told Abrego to leave Ester alone, and Abrego responded that he had the right to tell her what to do because he was her husband. Ester testified that Abrego kicked Gonzales in the hip and pulled the telephone cord out of the wall. Abrego left the house and threw a rock through the living room window.

Ester testified she had not been injured or bruised when Abrego slapped her, and she did not seek medical treatment. She testified she had not felt any pain from the blows. However, she had told an investigating officer that she felt pain and tenderness where she had been struck, although the officer did not observe any injuries.

Ester had also told an investigating officer she had seen Abrego make a swinging or stabbing motion toward Gonzales. Gonzales required medical treatment for a two-inch deep puncture wound to his thigh.

Later the same day, Abrego called Ester and asked if she had called the police. He said he was going to come over and finish what he had started earlier.

. . . .

*SUFFICIENCY OF EVIDENCE OF INJURY CAUSING A TRAUMATIC CONDITION.*

Abrego was convicted in count 1 of spousal abuse under section 273.5, subdivision (a). That section states, "Any person who willfully inflicts upon his or her spouse, . . . corporal injury resulting in a traumatic condition, is guilty of a felony . . . ."

Subdivision (c) of section 273.5 defines a traumatic condition as "a condition of the body, such as a wound or external or internal injury, whether of a minor or serious nature, caused by a physical force." (§ 273.5, subd. (c).) Abrego contends that his slapping Ester did not cause any "corporal injury resulting in a traumatic condition" within the meaning of section 273.5, subdivision (a).

When reviewing a claim of insufficiency of the evidence to support a conviction, we view the entire record in the light most favorable to the judgment and presume the existence of every fact the trier of fact could reasonably deduce from the evidence in support of the judgment. (*People v. Wright* (1985) 39 Cal.3d 576, 592 [217 Cal.Rptr. 212, 703 P.2d 1106].)

Ester testified that when Abrego struck her she was drunk, and she did not feel any pain. She further testified she had not been injured or bruised, and she did not seek medical treatment. However, she had told a police officer who responded to the scene that her face and head were sore and tender where Abrego had struck her. The officer did not notice any injuries.

A traumatic condition is a condition of the body such as a wound or internal or external injury, whether minor or serious, caused by physical force. (§ 273.5, subd. (c); *People v. Gutierrez* (1985) 171 Cal.App.3d 944 [217 Cal.Rptr. 616].) The court in *Gutierrez* traced the use of the words "traumatic condition" in statutes and case law:

> "The *Burns* [*People v. Burns* (1948) 88 Cal.App.2d 867 (200 P.2d 134)] court set out definitions of 'trauma' and 'traumatic' found in various dictionaries, treatises, and cases from other jurisdictions. Later courts then used some of the definitions. For example, 'traumatic condition' was defined in *People v. Stewart* (1961) 188 Cal.App.2d 88, 91 . . . , as 'a wound or other abnormal bodily condition resulting from the application of some external force.' *People v. Cameron* [1975], 53 Cal.App.3d [786] at p. 797 [126 Cal.Rptr. 44], used the definition '" . . . an abnormal condition of the living body produced by violence."' *People v. Thomas* (1976) 65 Cal.App.3d 854 at page 857 . . . used the *Stewart* definition.
>
> "Webster's Third New International Dictionary (1981), page 2432, defines 'trauma' as: 'an injury or wound to a living body caused by the application of external force or violence (injuries . . . such as sprains, bruises, fractures, dislocation, concussion—indeed *traumata* of all kinds . . . ).' It is inherent in the definition that both serious and *minor* injury is embraced—'*traumata* of *all* kinds.' (Second italics added.)
>
> "It is *injury* resulting in a traumatic condition that differentiates this crime from lesser offenses. Both simple assault [citation] and misdemeanor battery [citation] are included in a prosecution of section 273.5. . . .
>
> "Some other offenses do require higher degrees of harm to be inflicted before the crime denounced by them is committed: felony battery, section 243, subdivision (d), requires 'serious bodily injury'; and, felony assault, section 245, subdivision (a), requires 'force likely to produce great bodily injury.' But, the Legislature has clothed persons of the opposite sex in intimate relationships with greater protection by requiring less harm to be inflicted before the offense is committed. Those special relationships form a rational distinction

which has a substantial relation to the purpose of the statute. [Citations.]" (*Gutierrez, supra*, 171 Cal.App.3d at p. 952.)

The People argue that the soreness and tenderness Ester experienced were sufficient to constitute a traumatic condition within the meaning of section 273.5. However, as the *Gutierrez* court explained, the statute requires *injury* from a traumatic condition, even though the injury may be minor. The record discloses no evidence of even a minor injury sufficient to satisfy the statutory definition.

We note that in other penal statutes the Legislature has differentiated infliction of pain from infliction of injury. In section 273a, the Legislature has made it a crime to willfully cause or inflict unjustifiable physical pain on a child. In section 273d, the Legislature has made it a crime to "willfully inflict[] upon any child any cruel or inhuman corporal punishment or injury resulting in a traumatic condition...." If the Legislature intended pain to constitute an injury resulting in a traumatic condition, section 273a would be superfluous. We conclude that the evidence is insufficient to establish Abrego's guilt of spousal abuse.

The People also suggest that Ester's emotional upset after the incident was sufficient to elevate the crime from simple battery to a violation of section 273.5. However, the statute requires a "corporal injury" rather than solely emotional harm. We conclude that the evidence does not support a finding that Ester suffered "corporal injury resulting in a traumatic condition" within the meaning of section 273.5.

We shall therefore modify the judgment under section 1260 to reflect a conviction for the lesser included offense of battery. (§ 242.)....

---

## D. Witness Tampering

Victims of domestic violence sometimes fail to appear in court to testify against their abusers. Proving the accused has played any role in securing their absence is difficult.

### People v. Yascavage
Colorado Supreme Court
101 P.3d 1090 (2004)

I. Facts and Procedural History

Larriane Collier and Daniel P. Yascavage met in May of 1999. After several months of an "on-again-off-again" relationship, Collier sought to terminate the relationship and obtained a restraining order against Yascavage in April, 2000. Yascavage continued contacting Collier until he was arrested on charges of harassment and domestic violence in May, 2000.

While Yascavage was in custody awaiting trial he telephoned a friend and said the charges against him might be dropped if someone "got to" Collier and she failed to show up for court. The Adams County Sheriff's office recorded this telephone conversation. Yascavage was charged with criminal solicitation to tamper with a witness or victim. See § 18-2-301, C.R.S. (2004); § 18-8-707, C.R.S. (2004).

Jury trial commenced on March 12, 2001 on three counts of harassment by stalking, three counts of violation of a restraining order, and criminal solicitation to tamper with a victim or witness. Collier testified against the defendant at trial but there is no evidence that she was under subpoena at the time....

On March 14, 2001, the jury returned guilty verdicts on one count of harassment by stalking, two counts of violation of a restraining order, and criminal solicitation to commit tampering with a witness or victim. Yascavage was sentenced to two years imprisonment on the tampering count, to be served consecutively to the sentences imposed on the other counts.

Yascavage appealed each of his convictions. With respect to his tampering conviction, the defendant argued that the evidence was insufficient to sustain the conviction because the prosecution presented no evidence to the jury that Collier had been "legally summoned" as required by section 18-8-707.

In a published opinion, the court of appeals agreed, vacating the tampering conviction and holding that neither the mere presence of the victim at trial nor the information listing Collier as a potential witness would permit the jury to conclude that she was legally summoned.

We granted certiorari to decide whether the tampering statute requires proof that the witness or victim was legally summoned to an official proceeding and whether the general assembly intended "legally summoned" in the context of the tampering statute, to mean "subject to legal process." We now hold that section 18-8-707 does require that the victim or witness be legally summoned when the defendant is prosecuted under section 18-8-707(1)(b) and that the general assembly intended "legally summoned" in that subsection to mean that the witness have some obligation to the court to appear.

II. Analysis

. . . .

C. The Language of the Statute

. . . .

Section 18-8-707 identifies the class of persons the legislature intended to protect, when such persons would be protected, and from what actions these persons would be protected. The introductory provision of the tampering statute provides:

> A person commits tampering with a witness or victim if he intentionally attempts without bribery or threats to induce a witness or victim or a person he believes is to be called to testify as a witness or victim in any official proceeding or who may be called to testify as a witness to or victim of any crime to [do one of the following].

... § 18-8-707(1), C.R.S. (2004). The Model Penal Code section 241.6 referenced "witnesses" and "informants" only. Colorado chose to refer to "witnesses" and "victims" and adopted an expansive definition of "witness" encompassing a much broader class than proposed by the Model Penal Code.

"Witness" means any natural person:

(a) Having knowledge of the existence or nonexistence of facts relating to any crime;

(b) Whose declaration under oath is received or has been received as evidence for any purpose;

(c) Who has reported any crime to any peace officer, correctional officer, or judicial officer;

(d) Who has been served with a subpoena issued under the authority of any court in this state, of any other state, or of the United States; or

(e) *Who would be believed by any reasonable person to be an individual described in paragraph (a), (b), (c), or (d) of this subsection (2).*

§ 18-8-702(2), C.R.S. (2004) (emphasis added). The general assembly has also explicitly defined "victim." In the context of the tampering statute, a victim is any person against whom any crime has been perpetrated or attempted. § 18-8-702(1)....

The nexus, however, is that the defendant must believe the person is or will be a participant in any official proceeding. Section 18-8-501, C.R.S. (2004) defines official proceeding as "a proceeding heard before any legislative, judicial, administrative, or other government agency, or official authorized to hear evidence under oath, including any magistrate, hearing examiner, commissioner, notary, or other person taking testimony or depositions in any such proceedings."

In the context of section 18-8-707, tampering thus occurs when a defendant intentionally attempts to interfere with someone he believes is to be called, or who may be called, to testify in any proceeding covered by section 18-8-501. The purpose of the "official proceeding" language is to tie the defendant's conduct to the ultimate harm to be avoided: namely, obstruction of justice....

As a whole, the introductory provision of section 18-8-707 offers far-ranging protection to a broad class of persons. However, the subsections of the statute are clear in the conduct they prohibit. An individual may not induce or attempt to induce a victim or witness to: (a) testify falsely or unlawfully withhold testimony; (b) absent himself from a proceeding to which he has been legally summoned; or (c) avoid legal process. Each subsection of 18-8-707 presents an independent objective prohibited under the tampering statute. Therefore, to sustain a conviction under section 18-8-707 the subject of the defendant's influence must be a person encompassed by the introductory provision and the defendant's objective must be prohibited in subsection (1)(a),(b), or (c) of section 18-8-707....

Although a "summons" most often refers to a court order notifying the defendant of a civil case against him, "summons" generally includes a legal notice requiring a person to appear in court. Black's law dictionary defines summons as a writ directing a sheriff to summon a defendant to appear in court or a writ or process commencing the plaintiff's action and requiring a person to appear in court as a juror or witness. Black's Law Dictionary 1477 (8th ed. 2004). Summons has often been interpreted to be synonymous with "process." . . .

We are guided by the expansive definition of witness or victim in the introductory portion of the statute, and by the overall legislative intent. However, we must also give effect to each subsection. In interpreting "legally summoned," we do not read it strictly to mean that a subpoena is the only acceptable form of process. Were the legislature to have intended that outcome, it would presumably have used the word subpoena. On the other hand, we do assign some meaning to the use of the term "legally summoned" and therefore conclude that it means some action taken by the official tribunal that obligates a witness to appear at an official proceeding.

Again, we stress that neither subsection (1)(a) nor subsection (1)(c) require such legal process in order to trigger the crime. Only subsection (1)(b) requires that element.

### III. Application

Yascavage was charged with criminal solicitation to tamper with a witness. The evidence shows that while Yascavage was in jail awaiting trial on charges of harassment by stalking and violation of a restraining order, he contacted a friend and asked him to "get to" the victim so the charges would be "thrown out" when she failed to appear. The defendant was aware Collier was a potential witness against him. Thus, there was evidence that Yascavage attempted to stop the victim from attending an official proceeding.

However, the jury was instructed as to the elements of section 18-8-707(1)(b) only. Thus, to find defendant guilty of tampering with a witness, the jury would have been required to conclude that he attempted to cause the victim to absent herself from an official proceeding to which she had been legally summoned.

We have concluded that "legally summoned" means that the witness must be under some obligation to the court to appear. Here, the only potential evidence was that Collier's name appeared on the charging document as a potential witness. Even that evidence was not presented to the jury in support of the charges. Because there was no evidence that Collier was under any legal obligation to appear at the proceeding, there was a failure of proof on one element of the charge. . . .

We affirm the court of appeals' decision to vacate the tampering by criminal solicitation conviction.

## E. Criminal Contempt — Violation of Protective Orders

To protect a victim while a case is pending, or as a sanction against a convicted batterer and a tool for keeping victims safe for a substantial period after a defendant has been successfully prosecuted, courts will issue what are variously called orders of protection, restraining orders or stay-away orders.

In 1997, the National Center for State Courts in Williamsburg, Virginia, reported the results of a three-year study which found two-thirds of all civil orders of protection were never violated. The study focused on 285 women who had sought orders of protection in three communities—Denver, Colorado; Wilmington, Delaware; and Washington, D.C. As reported by Joan Zorza and Nancy K.D. Lemon in their article, *Two-thirds of Civil Protection Orders Are Never Violated; Better Court and Community Services Increase Success Rates,* DOMESTIC VIOLENCE REPORT 51–52 (April/May 1997), the authors wrote that within the first month, 72 percent of the victims reported their protective orders had not been violated. After six months, the number decreased to 65 percent.

Another study conducted between October 1997 and December 1998, of 448 adult female residents of Seattle, Washington who had obtained civil orders of protection, found that obtaining the orders were associated with lowered risks of future partner abuse.[11]

Orders of protection and sanctions for violating them raise numerous issues in the context of criminal law. First, there is the question of whether it is appropriate to impose criminal sanctions for violations of civil orders. If sanctions, including jail time, are appropriate, the double jeopardy implications inherent in imposing incarceration must be considered.

### People v. Wood
New York Court of Appeals
95 N.Y.2d 509 (2000)

WESLEY, J.

Defendant Timothy Wood's ex-wife obtained two separate orders of protection—one issued pursuant to CPL 530.12 by Rochester City Court on February 9, 1996, and the other issued under Family Court Act article 8 by Monroe County Family Court on December 11, 1996. Both orders directed defendant to have "no contact whatsoever" with his former wife.

During the early morning hours of December 25, 1996, defendant's ex-wife received 11 prank phone calls. Each time she answered the telephone, the caller simply hung up. Five of the calls were traced to defendant's residence. Defendant's ex-wife then

---

11. Victoria L. Holt, Mary A. Kernic, Marsha E. Wolf & Frederick P. Rivara, *Do Protection Orders Affect the Likelihood of Future Partner Violence and Injury?* 24 AM. JOUR. OF PREVENTIVE MEDICINE 16–21 (2003).

commenced a contempt proceeding in Family Court for defendant's violation of the Family Court order. After trial, Family Court found defendant guilty of willfully violating the order of protection and sentenced him to six months incarceration.

Thereafter, defendant was indicted for five counts of criminal contempt in the first degree, five counts of aggravated harassment in the second degree and one count of harassment in the first degree. The criminal contempt and aggravated harassment charges were based on defendant's violation of the City Court order of protection as a result of the same five phone calls. Opposing defendant's motion to dismiss on double jeopardy grounds, the People argued that the Family Court contempt proceeding was based upon the violation of a different order of protection than that which served as a basis for the criminal contempt charge. Supreme Court denied the motion. After a jury trial, defendant was found guilty of each of the five counts of first degree criminal contempt and second degree aggravated harassment. . . .

We note at the outset that the problematic double jeopardy situation presented by this case has its genesis in the parallel family offense jurisdiction of Family Court and our criminal courts. This overlap is the key to our resolution of the issue at hand.

Recognizing that domestic violence should be regarded as criminal behavior warranting strong intervention, the Legislature in 1994 amended the Family Court Act and the Criminal Procedure Law to provide criminal courts and Family Court with concurrent jurisdiction for certain enumerated criminal offenses when committed by one family member against another (*see*, Family Ct Act § 115[e]; § 812[1]; Criminal Procedure Law §§ 100.07, 530.11[1]). Although a family member may choose to address the family offense in Family Court, a parallel criminal proceeding is also available (*see*, Family Ct Act § 813[3]). . . .

The Double Jeopardy Clause "protects only against the imposition of multiple criminal punishments for the same offense" (*Hudson v. United States*, 522 US 93, 99). The "applicable rule is that, where the same act or transaction constitutes a violation of two distinct statutory provisions, the test to be applied to determine whether there are two offenses or only one is whether each provision requires proof of an additional fact which the other does not" (*Blockburger v. United States*, 284 US 299, 304). If each of the offenses contains an element which the other does not, they are not the "same offense" under the rule enunciated by *Blockburger* and any claim of constitutional double jeopardy necessarily fails (*People v. Bryant*, 92 NY2d 216, 229, n 3). The test focuses on "the proof necessary to prove the statutory elements of each offense charged against the defendant, not on the actual evidence to be presented at trial" (*People v. Prescott*, 66 NY2d 216, 221; *see also, United States v. Dixon*, 509 US 688, 714–716 [Rehnquist, Ch. J., concurring in part and dissenting in part]).

The application of the *Blockburger* test in this case is unusual in that two successive contempt prosecutions are involved, rather than prosecutions for contempt and an underlying substantive offense (*see, United States v. Dixon*, 509 US 688, *supra*).

A comparison of the two statutes in this case similarly reveals that *each* provision does not contain an additional element which the other does not. First degree criminal contempt contains the additional element of proof of a defendant's prior contempt conviction and can be based on violation of an order of protection from one of several enumerated courts, including a Family Court order issued under article 8.[12] The Family Court contempt provision contains no other element different from Penal Law § 215.51(c), but must be based on an order issued by Family Court.[13] As enumerated, the statutory elements of the Family Court provisions are subsumed by those of Penal Law § 215.51(c).

Because the same acts violated both orders, it would be impossible for defendant to be guilty of first degree criminal contempt for violating the City Court order of protection without concomitantly being guilty of contempt for violating the Family Court order of protection....

Moreover, under *Blockburger,* a lesser included offense is the "same" as a greater offense and, thus, the successive prosecution and cumulative punishment for a greater offense after conviction for a lesser included offense is barred by the Double Jeopardy Clause (*see, Brown v. Ohio,* 432 US 161, 166–167). Comparing the elements, we conclude that the contempt provision of the Family Court Act article 8 is clearly a lesser included offense of criminal contempt in the first degree. That the People sought to prove a violation of a City Court order and not a Family Court order does not, under these circumstances, alter the double jeopardy analysis under *Blockburger*.

We conclude that defendant's prosecution for criminal contempt in the first degree under Penal Law § 215.51(c) is barred because he was previously prosecuted for contempt under Family Court Act article 8....

Accordingly, the order of the Appellate Division should be affirmed.

---

Orders of protection cover conduct from life-threatening assaults to batterer apologies. To understand why the latter might be considered frightening conduct, one must

---

12. [n4] Under Penal Law § 215.51(c), a person is guilty of criminal contempt in the first degree when he or she: "commits the crime of criminal contempt in the second degree ... by violating that part of a duly served order of protection, or such order of which the defendant has actual knowledge because he or she was present in court when such order was issued, under [domestic relations law §§ 240 and 252], articles four, five, six and eight of the family court act and section 530.12 of the criminal procedure law, or an order of protection issued by a [foreign] court of competent jurisdiction ... and where the defendant has been previously convicted of the crime of criminal contempt in the second degree by violating an order of protection ... within the preceding five years." In relevant part, a person is guilty of criminal contempt in the second degree by "[i]ntentional disobedience or resistance to the lawful process or other mandate of a court." (Penal Law § 215.50[3].)

13. [n5] Family Court Act § 846-a requires proof that a "lawful order [was] issued under [article 8]" and that defendant "willfully failed to obey [it]."

consider the conduct in the context of a long-term abusive relationship and the recognized pattern of domestic violence behavior.

## State v. Grayhurst

Rhode Island Supreme Court

852 A.2d 491 (2004)

WILLIAMS, CHIEF JUSTICE.

The defendant, Michael R. Grayhurst (defendant), appeals from his convictions on twenty-five criminal counts after a jury trial in the Superior Court. The defendant contends that his convictions should be overturned for various reasons, which are enumerated below. For the reasons indicated hence, we affirm the judgment of the Superior Court.

### Facts and Travel

A therapist once commented on the problem of "Women Who Love Too Much."[14] The defendant is a man who by his own admission loves too much; he is, in fact, a man who claims to "love the s*** out of" his ex-wife, Jane Grayhurst (Ms. Grayhurst). Ms. Grayhurst filed for divorce in 1994. In 1996, Ms. Grayhurst sought and was granted a no-contact order from the District Court enjoining defendant from harassing or threatening her. The divorce was finalized in 1997. In 1998, after defendant had violated the no-contact order numerous times, Ms. Grayhurst obtained a second no-contact order from the District Court. Despite the no-contact orders, defendant, who was incarcerated at the Adult Correctional Institutions (ACI), began sending Ms. Grayhurst mail. The correspondence consisted of greeting cards, letters, pamphlets and newspaper clippings on topics such as domestic violence and alcoholism. The correspondence additionally included threats against Ms. Grayhurst and various public officials, including judges. Ms. Grayhurst eventually decided to contact authorities about the correspondence, and in November 1997 contacted the office of the Special Assistant Attorney General Bethany Macktaz and Detective John A'Vant (Det. A'Vant) of the Rhode Island State Police. A mail monitor subsequently was placed on all outgoing mail that defendant sent to Ms. Grayhurst.

Additionally, in 1997, as he was leaving the courtroom after a hearing before General Magistrate John O'Brien of the Family Court relating to the sale of the Grayhursts' marital domicile, defendant yelled at General Magistrate O'Brien, "stick it up your ass, you son of a bitch." Upon hearing this, General Magistrate O'Brien ordered that defendant be brought back into the courtroom. The defendant resisted being brought back into court, and, during the struggle, kicked Deputy Sheriff Richard Ploude (Sheriff Ploude), who suffered serious injuries and who testified that he has been unable to return to work since the 1997 Family Court incident. As a result of the incident, General Magistrate O'Brien found defendant in contempt of court.

---

14. [n2] Robin Norwood, Women Who Love Too Much (1985).

Based on defendant's continued violation of the no-contact orders, as well as a complaint that General Magistrate O'Brien lodged with the Rhode Island State Police, Det. A'Vant decided to charge defendant with violating a no-contact order and with threatening a public official.... The defendant eventually was charged with nine counts of threats to public officials, ten counts of violating a no-contact order, three counts of extortion and blackmail, one count of stalking, one count of assault on a uniformed sheriff/officer and one count of obstructing a police officer.

The Attorney General filed three informations, charging defendant with the above-mentioned criminal counts, against defendant: information No. P2/00-1114A, which was filed on March 22, 2000; information No. P2/97-3209A, which was filed on September 23, 1997; and information No. P2/00-1052A, which was filed on March 16, 2000. After a jury trial in the Superior Court, defendant was convicted on twenty-five counts and sentenced to a total of thirty five years to serve....

## II
### Double Jeopardy

The defendant argues that (1) his conviction on count 1 of information No. P2/97-3209A for assaulting Sheriff Ploude was based on the same acts for which General Magistrate O'Brien found defendant to be in contempt of court; therefore, the assault charge should be barred on double jeopardy grounds; (2) his conviction on count 1 of information No. P2/00-1052A for extortion and blackmail should merge with count 21 of the same information for violation of a no-contact order because a letter defendant sent to Ms. Grayhurst formed the basis for both of these charges; and (3) his conviction on count 10 of information No. P2/00-1052A for stalking should merge with counts 12, 17, 18, 21, 23 and 26 of the same information for violations of a no-contact order because defendant's repeated contacts with Ms. Grayhurst, by the correspondence defendant sent her, formed the basis of both charges of stalking and the violations of a no-contact order. Merger is essentially a double jeopardy argument. *State v. Boudreau*, 113 R.I. 497, 502, 322 A.2d 626, 629 (1974)....

The prohibition against double jeopardy contained in the Fifth Amendment to the United States Constitution is echoed in Article 1, section 7, of the Rhode Island Constitution, which provides "no person shall be subject for the same offense to be twice put in jeopardy." The Double Jeopardy Clause "protects against a second prosecution for the same offense after acquittal" or conviction. *State v. Rodriguez*, 822 A.2d 894, 905 n.13 (R.I. 2003) (quoting *United States v. Abreu*, 952 F.2d 1458, 1464 (1st Cir. 1992)). It also protects against "multiple punishments for the same offense." *Id.* (quoting *Abreu*, 952 F.2d at 1464). In determining whether an accused is in danger of being punished more than once for the same offense, "the applicable rule is that where the same act or transaction constitutes a violation of two distinct statutory provisions, the test to be applied to determine whether there are two offenses or only one, is whether each provision requires proof of a fact which the other does not." *Id.* at 905 (quoting *Blockburger v. United States*, 284 U.S. 299, 304, 76 L. Ed. 306, 52 S. Ct. 180 (1932)).

We initially note that defendant never was charged with contempt, and therefore, we assume that it was civil contempt. Double jeopardy does not preclude criminal punishment after a civil sanction has been imposed. *See Hudson v. United States*, 522 U.S. 93, 99, 139 L. Ed. 2d 450, 118 S. Ct. 488 (1997) (stating that the double jeopardy clause "protects only against the imposition of multiple criminal punishments for the same offense"). Even if this were treated as criminal contempt, however, there would be no double jeopardy violation. In this case, the crimes of criminal contempt and assault of a police officer constitute separate crimes with different elements for each....

The defendant's argument that his conviction for extortion and blackmail should merge with one of his convictions for violating a no-contact order on count 21 of information No. P2/00-1052A also fails. Pursuant to G.L. 1956 § 11-42-2, "this Court has consistently stated that the crime of extortion [and blackmail] consists of two basic elements: (1) an oral or a written threat to harm a person or property, (2) accompanied by the intent to compel someone to do something against his or her will." *State v. Price*, 706 A.2d 929, 933 (R.I. 1998). The crime of violating a no-contact order consists of intentionally contacting a victim in contravention of such an order. *See State v. Conti*, 672 A.2d 885, 886 (R.I. 1996) (per curiam) (stating that the defendant's conduct, which consisted of greeting the victim at the post office and while driving, did not violate a no-contact order because the meetings were coincidental, and implying, therefore, that a defendant's contact with a victim must be intentional for it to violate a no contact order). Conviction for extortion and blackmail, however, requires proof of both a threat and of intent to force someone to act against his or her will. Section 11-42-2. In addition, unique to a conviction for violating a no-contact order is the requirement that a no-contact order be in place. Thus, the two crimes require proof of separate and additional facts that the other does not.

The defendant makes a final double jeopardy argument relating to his convictions for stalking and for certain violations of no-contact orders (P2/00-1052 counts 10, 12, 13, 17, 18, 21, 23 and 26). According to defendant, the stalking count merged with the counts alleging violation of a no-contact order. We disagree.

General Laws 1956 § 11-59-2 provides: "(a) Any person who: (1) harasses another person; or (2) willfully, maliciously, and repeatedly follows another person with the intent to place that person in reasonable fear of bodily injury, is guilty of the crime of stalking."...

Accordingly, conviction for stalking requires proof of harassment over a period of time. As stated above, a conviction for violating a no-contact order also requires that a no-contact order be in place. Thus, stalking and violating a no-contact order each require proof of separate and additional facts that the other does not.

....

---

Victims may continue to have contact with their batterers who must stay away from them pursuant to orders of protection. Is it unfair to punish a man who returns to his former home following a frantic telephone call from his wife who claims their child is sick, or from a girlfriend who promises a romantic meal and says all is forgiven? The Hon. John Leventhal of New York, who presided over the nation's first felony domestic violence court from 1996 until he was promoted to the appellate court in 2008, had a standard warning to the offenders against whom he issued orders of protection. He said: "This is my order, not hers. The name of the case is People of the State of New York against you, Mr. Smith. Not Mrs. Smith versus you. If she invites you over to dinner and you go, it will be the most expensive dinner you will ever eat. The next night, you will be eating in jail. If I wake up in the middle of the night and I dream that you are doing something in violation of my order, I will bring you back to court the very next day." Justice Leventhal said he made the speech because he wanted to ensure the defendant was responsible to the Court, "even if he cannot be responsible to his girlfriend or spouse."[15] Conversely, some judges have questioned whether a victim who invites her abuser back into the home is really fearful of him or is just manipulative. Victims' advocates argue the order of protection is aimed at the perpetrator's behavior and not the victim's. The case below drew considerable attention as it was working its way through the Ohio appellate courts.

### State v. Lucas
Ohio Supreme Court
100 Ohio St. 3d 1 (2003)

On May 23, 2001, defendant-appellant, Betty S. Lucas, was charged with one count of domestic violence and one count of complicity to violate a protection order. She had been granted a protection order against Joseph Lucas, her ex-husband, on October 4, 2000. The charges against appellant arose from an incident at her home on May 10, 2001. On that day, appellant had invited her ex-husband into her home for the birthday celebration of one of their children. Appellant and Joseph Lucas consumed alcohol together there, and later had an argument that led to a physical altercation. Joseph Lucas sustained a fractured and dislocated elbow and head injuries and was treated at a hospital. Appellant suffered a bruised nose. Police charged Joseph Lucas with a violation of the protection order. Appellant was charged with complicity to violate a protection order, as well as with domestic violence.

On June 12, 2001, appellant filed a motion to dismiss the complicity charge. The trial court denied the motion. On August 8, 2001, appellant entered a plea of no contest to the complicity charge and a plea of guilty to the domestic violence charge. The trial court found her guilty of both offenses and sentenced her to 90 days in jail on each charge, but suspended the time and placed her on probation for two years.

Appellant appealed from the conviction on the complicity charge. Appellant argued that a person sheltered by a protection order is the victim of any violation of that order and that as a victim, she is a member of a protected class. Therefore, she maintained,

---

15. E-mail from John Leventhal, Sept. 6, 2006, on file with the author.

prosecuting the victim runs counter to the intent of the General Assembly. The court of appeals rejected appellant's arguments and affirmed the trial court. The appellate court eschewed public-policy analysis and found that appellant's behavior went beyond what R.C. 2923.03(A)(2), the complicity statute, requires to show that someone aided or abetted another in the commission of a crime. . . .

## Law and Analysis

R.C. 2919.27(A)(1) states, "No person shall recklessly violate the terms of * * * [a] protection order issued or consent agreement approved pursuant to section 2919.26 or 3113.31 of the Revised Code." The protection order against Joseph Lucas was issued by the court pursuant to R.C. 3113.31.

The inclusion of the mental state of "recklessly" in R.C. 2919.27(A)(1) ensures that if there is a chance meeting between the subjects of a protection order, the result is not a crime. There is a crime, however, if, in visiting a certain place, the restrainee "perversely disregards a known risk." R.C. 2901.22(C).

R.C. 2923.03, Ohio's complicity statute, states:

> "(A) No person, acting with the kind of culpability required for the commission of an offense, shall do any of the following:
>
> * * * "(2) Aid or abet another in committing the offense."

The issue before us is whether a protected subject of a protection order can be complicit in the violation of a protection order.

The United States Supreme Court was faced with an analogous question in construing the Mann Act in *Gebardi v. United States* (1932), 287 U.S. 112, 53 S. Ct. 35, 77 L. Ed. 206. Under the Mann Act, it was a felony for any person to "transport or cause to be transported, or aid or assist in obtaining transportation for, or in transporting, in interstate or foreign commerce, * * * any woman or girl for the purpose of prostitution or debauchery * * *." *Id.* at 118, 53 S. Ct. 35, 77 L. Ed. 206, quoting Section 398, Title 18, U.S.Code. In *Gebardi*, the court addressed the issue of whether a female willingly transported across state lines could be convicted of conspiracy to violate the Mann Act.

The court recognized that "the statute is drawn to include those cases in which the woman consents to her own transportation" and first looked at whether the Mann Act itself punished acquiescing women. *Id.* at 119, 53 S. Ct. 35, 77 L. Ed. 206. The court found that punishment of transported women was not a focus of the statute. . . .

The *Gebardi* court reasoned that, had Congress intended to punish the behavior of the women transported in violation of the Mann Act, it would have done so within the Act. The court found that Congress had "set out * * * to deal with cases which frequently, if not normally, involve consent and agreement on the part of the woman to the forbidden transportation." *Id.* at 121, 53 S. Ct. 35, 77 L. Ed. 206.

. . . .

In a more recent case, the court in *In re Meagan R.* (1996), 42 Cal.App.4th 17, 49 Cal.Rptr.2d 325, considered the issue of whether a victim of statutory rape can be charged with aiding and abetting that crime. The court held that "where the Legislature has dealt with crimes which necessarily involve the joint action of two or more persons, and where no punishment at all is provided for the conduct, or misconduct, of one of the participants, the party whose participation is not denounced by statute cannot be charged with criminal conduct on either a conspiracy or aiding and abetting theory." 42 Cal.App.4th at 24, 49 Cal.Rptr.2d 325....

In the language of R.C. 3113.31, the General Assembly evinces its recognition that in some instances of violations of protection orders, the protected party invites the violation. R.C. 3113.31(E)(7)(a) provides:

> "If a protection order issued * * * under this section includes a requirement that the respondent * * * refrain from entering the residence, school, business, or place of employment of the petitioner or a family or household member, the order or agreement shall state clearly that *the order or agreement cannot be waived or nullified by an invitation to the respondent from the petitioner* or other family or household member to enter the residence, school, business, or place of employment or by the respondent's entry into one of those places otherwise upon the consent of the petitioner or other family or household member." (Emphasis added.)

The General Assembly both recognizes and addresses the potential problem of a protected party's acquiescence in the violation of a protection order. The General Assembly demonstrates its cognizance of the volatile and mercurial nature of certain interpersonal relationships and insulates protection orders from the heat and chill of shifting emotions. It removes the excuse of an invitation, a perceived invitation, or a concocted invitation from affecting the power of a protection order. The General Assembly has made the issue of an invitation entirely irrelevant as to the culpability of a respondent's violation of a protection order....

The General Assembly further demonstrates that complainants are not to be held criminally liable for violations of protection orders by statutorily restricting the issuance of mutual protection orders. Mutual protection orders require both complainants and restrainees to refrain from activities identified in a protection order. R.C. 3113.31(E)(4) prohibits mutual protection orders—"[a] court may not issue a protection order that requires a petitioner to do or to refrain from doing an act that the court may require a respondent to do or to refrain from doing under * * * this section"—unless certain factors apply. For a petitioner to be held to the terms of the protection order, the respondent must file a separate petition for a protection order. R.C. 3113.31(E)(4)(a). Then, the court must determine (1) that the petitioner has committed an act of domestic violence or violated a temporary protection order issued pursuant to section 2919.26 of the Revised Code, (2) that both parties acted primarily as aggressors, and (3) that neither party acted primarily in self-defense. R.C. 3113.31(E)(4)(d).

The General Assembly has set forth a specific process, with a specific burden, by which a protection order's protected party may be subject to the terms of a protection order. Prosecuting a protected party under a protection order for aiding and abetting the violation of her own protection order is tantamount to issuing and enforcing a mutual protection order against the victim without going through the mandated process for making the protected party subject to the requirements of the protection order.

This court, in its Rules of Superintendence, also notes the difference between the treatment of a petitioner and a respondent when a protection order is violated. Pursuant to Sup.R. 10.01(D) and 10.02(C), all civil and criminal domestic violence protection orders issued by the courts of the state of Ohio contain two sets of warnings—one for the petitioner and one for the respondent—that must be substantially similar to Sup.R. Form 10.01-G. The Sup.R. Form 10.01-G warning to petitioners reads as follows:

> "You **cannot** change the terms of this order by your words or actions. Only the Court can allow the Respondent/Defendant to contact you or return to your residence. If you and the Respondent/Defendant want to resume your relationship, you **must** ask the Court to modify or dismiss this Protection Order." (Emphasis sic.)

For the respondent, the threat of criminal charges on Sup.R. Form 10.01-G is front and center:

> "Only the Court can change this order. The Petitioner/Alleged Victim cannot give you legal permission to change this order. If you go near the Petitioner/ Alleged Victim, even with the Petitioner's/Alleged Victim's consent, you may be arrested. If you and the Petitioner/ Alleged Victim want to resume your relationship you must ask the Court to modify or dismiss this Protection Order. You act at your own risk if you disregard this WARNING." (Emphasis sic.)

The sharp distinction between how the Rules of Superintendence address petitioners and respondents reflects the General Assembly's intention that only one party—the respondent—can be criminally responsible for the violation of a protection order....

The practical application of Ohio's protection-order statutes demands this result. If petitioners for protection orders were liable for criminal prosecution, a violator of a protection order could create a real chill on the reporting of the violation by simply threatening to claim that an illegal visit was the result of an illegal invitation.

Finally, this case is different from most. Had Betty Lucas not gotten the better of her husband, this case would probably not be here. In most instances of an invited violation of a protection order, police are not called until the violence starts. In those cases, the protected party receives the brunt of the injuries. If we were to find against appellant in this case, we would also be finding against those other protected parties. We would be, in effect, allowing abused women to be charged with complicity. That is a prospect neither intended by the General Assembly nor acceptable as a matter of public policy.

The General Assembly has made an invitation by the petitioner for the respondent to violate the terms of a protection order irrelevant to a respondent's guilt. Protection orders are about the behavior of the respondent and nothing else. How or why a respondent finds himself at the petitioner's doorstep is irrelevant. To find appellant guilty of complicity would be to criminalize an irrelevancy.

Accordingly, we hold that an individual who is the protected subject of a temporary protection order may not be prosecuted for aiding and abetting the restrainee under the protection order in violating said order. We therefore reverse the judgment of the court of appeals.

Judgment reversed.

## F. Marital Rape

Marital rape is another form of domestic violence. But once upon a time, it was not a crime. In 1978, John Rideout of Salem, Oregon made international news by being the first man in the United States to be tried for raping his wife, Greta, while the two were married and living together, under a 1977 Oregon statute making it a crime. He was acquitted, but the case attracted extensive media attention and inspired women to continue their fight to reform marital rape laws.[16] Throughout the next decade, states changed their statutes. In New York, the landmark case of *People v. Liberta* abolished the marital rape exemption in that state.

### People v. Liberta
New York Court of Appeals
64 N.Y.2d 152 (1984)

... Defendant Mario Liberta and Denise Liberta were married in 1978. Shortly after the birth of their son, in October of that year, Mario began to beat Denise. In early 1980 Denise brought a proceeding in the Family Court in Erie County seeking protection from the defendant. On April 30, 1980 a temporary order of protection was issued to her by the Family Court. Under this order, the defendant was to move out and remain away from the family home, and stay away from Denise. The order provided that the defendant could visit with his son once each weekend.

On the weekend of March 21, 1981, Mario, who was then living in a motel, did not visit his son. On Tuesday, March 24, 1981 he called Denise to ask if he could visit his son on that day. Denise would not allow the defendant to come to her house, but she did agree to allow him to pick up their son and her and take them both back to his motel after being assured that a friend of his would be with them at all times. The defendant and his friend picked up Denise and their son and the four of them drove to defendant's motel.

---

16. *See* Les Ledbetter, *Oregon Man Found Not Guilty on a Charge of Raping His Wife*, N.Y. Times, Dec. 28, 1978.

When they arrived at the motel the friend left. As soon as only Mario, Denise, and their son were alone in the motel room, Mario attacked Denise, threatened to kill her, and forced her to perform fellatio on him and to engage in sexual intercourse with him. The son was in the room during the entire episode, and the defendant forced Denise to tell their son to watch what the defendant was doing to her.

The defendant allowed Denise and their son to leave shortly after the incident. Denise, after going to her parents' home, went to a hospital to be treated for scratches on her neck and bruises on her head and back, all inflicted by her husband. She also went to the police station, and on the next day she swore out a felony complaint against the defendant. On July 15, 1981 the defendant was indicted for rape in the first degree and sodomy in the first degree.

## II

Section 130.35 of the Penal Law provides in relevant part that "A male is guilty of rape in the first degree when he engages in sexual intercourse with a female * * * by forcible compulsion". "Female", for purposes of the rape statute, is defined as "any female person who is not married to the actor" (Penal Law, § 130.00, subd 4). Section 130.50 of the Penal Law provides in relevant part that "a person is guilty of sodomy in the first degree when he engages in deviate sexual intercourse with another person * * * by forcible compulsion". "Deviate sexual intercourse" is defined as "sexual conduct between persons not married to each other consisting of contact between the penis and the anus, the mouth and penis, or the mouth and the vulva" (Penal Law, § 130.00, subd 2). Thus, due to the "not married" language in the definitions of "female" and "deviate sexual intercourse", there is a "marital exemption" for both forcible rape and forcible sodomy. The marital exemption itself, however, has certain exceptions. For purposes of the rape and sodomy statutes, a husband and wife are considered to be "not married" if at the time of the sexual assault they "are living apart * * * pursuant to a valid and effective: (i) order issued by a court of competent jurisdiction which by its terms or in its effect requires such living apart, or (ii) decree or judgment of separation, or (iii) written agreement of separation" (Penal Law, § 130.00, subd 4).

. . . .

## III

. . . Until 1978, the marital exemption applied as long as the marriage still legally existed. In 1978, the Legislature expanded the definition of "not married" to include those cases where the husband and wife were living apart pursuant to either a court order "which by its terms or in its effect requires such living apart" or a decree, judgment, or written agreement of separation (L 1978, ch 735; see Penal Law, § 130.00, subd 4). We agree with the Appellate Division that the order of protection in the present case falls squarely within the first of these situations.

. . . .

## IV

The defendant's constitutional challenges to the rape and sodomy statutes are premised on his being considered "not married" to Denise and are the same challenges as could be made by any unmarried male convicted under these statutes. The defendant's claim is that both statutes violate equal protection because they are underinclusive classifications which burden him, but not others similarly situated (see Tribe, American Constitutional Law, p 997)....

### A. THE MARITAL EXEMPTION

As noted above, under the Penal Law a married man ordinarily cannot be convicted of forcibly raping or sodomizing his wife. This is the so-called marital exemption for rape (see 1881 Penal Code, tit X, ch II, § 278). Although a marital exemption was not explicit in earlier rape statutes (see 1863 Rev. Stats, part 4, ch I, tit 2, art 2, § 22), an 1852 treatise stated that a man could not be guilty of raping his wife (Barbour, Criminal Law of State of New York [2d ed], p 69). The assumption, even before the marital exemption was codified, that a man could not be guilty of raping his wife, is traceable to a statement made by the 17th century English jurist Lord Hale, who wrote: "[The] husband cannot be guilty of a rape committed by himself upon his lawful wife, for by their mutual matrimonial consent and contract the wife hath given up herself in this kind unto her husband, which she cannot retract" (1 Hale, History of Pleas of the Crown, p 629)....

The first American case to recognize the marital exemption was decided in 1857 by the Supreme Judicial Court of Massachusetts, which stated in dictum that it would always be a defense to rape to show marriage to the victim (*Commonwealth v. Fogerty*, 74 Mass 489). Decisions to the same effect by other courts followed, usually with no rationale or authority cited other than Hale's implied consent view. In New York, a 1922 decision noted the marital exemption in the Penal Law and stated that it existed "on account of the matrimonial consent which [the wife] has given, and which she cannot retract" (*People v. Meli*, 193 NYS 365, 366 [Sup Ct])....

We find that there is no rational basis for distinguishing between marital rape and nonmarital rape. The various rationales which have been asserted in defense of the exemption are either based upon archaic notions about the consent and property rights incident to marriage or are simply unable to withstand even the slightest scrutiny. We therefore declare the marital exemption for rape in the New York statute to be unconstitutional.

Lord Hale's notion of an irrevocable implied consent by a married woman to sexual intercourse has been cited most frequently in support of the marital exemption ("Equal Protection Considerations", *supra*, n 6, 16 N Eng L Rev, at p 21). Any argument based on a supposed consent, however, is untenable. Rape is not simply a sexual act to which one party does not consent. Rather, it is a degrading, violent act which violates the bodily integrity of the victim and frequently causes severe, long-lasting physical and psychic harm (see *Coker v. Georgia*, 433 U.S. 584, 597–598; Note, Rape Reform and a Statutory Consent Defense, 74 J of Crim L & Criminology 1518, 1519,

1527–1528). To ever imply consent to such an act is irrational and absurd. Other than in the context of rape statutes, marriage has never been viewed as giving a husband the right to coerced intercourse on demand (see *De Angelis v. De Angelis*, 54 AD2d 1088; "Abolishing The Marital Exemption", *supra*, at n 4, 1983 U of Ill L Rev, at p 207; "Marital Rape Exemption", *supra*, at n 5, 52 NYU L Rev, at pp 311–312). Certainly, then, a marriage license should not be viewed as a license for a husband to forcibly rape his wife with impunity. A married woman has the same right to control her own body as does an unmarried woman ("Equal Protection Considerations", *supra*, n 6, 16 N Eng L Rev, at pp 19–20; cf. *Planned Parenthood v. Danforth*, 428 U.S. 52). If a husband feels "aggrieved" by his wife's refusal to engage in sexual intercourse, he should seek relief in the courts governing domestic relations, not in "violent or forceful self-help" (*State v. Smith*, 85 NJ 193, 206).

The other traditional justifications for the marital exemption were the common-law doctrines that a woman was the property of her husband and that the legal existence of the woman was "incorporated and consolidated into that of the husband" (1 Blackstone's Commentaries [1966 ed], p 430; see *State v. Smith, supra*, at pp 204–205; "Marital Rape Exemption", *supra*, n 5, 52 NYU L Rev, at pp 309–310). Both these doctrines, of course, have long been rejected in this State. . . .

Because the traditional justifications for the marital exemption no longer have any validity, other arguments have been advanced in its defense. The first of these recent rationales, which is stressed by the People in this case, is that the marital exemption protects against governmental intrusion into marital privacy and promotes reconciliation of the spouses, and thus that elimination of the exemption would be disruptive to marriages. While protecting marital privacy and encouraging reconciliation are legitimate State interests, there is no rational relation between allowing a husband to forcibly rape his wife and these interests. . . .

Similarly, it is not tenable to argue that elimination of the marital exemption would disrupt marriages because it would discourage reconciliation. Clearly, it is the violent act of rape and not the subsequent attempt of the wife to seek protection through the criminal justice system which "disrupts" a marriage (*Weishaupt v. Commonwealth*, 227 Va 389, 315 SE2d 847, at p 855). Moreover, if the marriage has already reached the point where intercourse is accomplished by violent assault it is doubtful that there is anything left to reconcile (see *Trammel v. United States*, 445 U.S. 40, 52, *supra*; "Marital Rape Exemption", *supra*, n 5, 52 NYU L Rev, at p 315). This, of course, is particularly true if the wife is willing to bring criminal charges against her husband which could result in a lengthy jail sentence.

Another rationale sometimes advanced in support of the marital exemption is that marital rape would be a difficult crime to prove. A related argument is that allowing such prosecutions could lead to fabricated complaints by "vindictive" wives. The difficulty of proof argument is based on the problem of showing lack of consent. Proving lack of consent, however, is often the most difficult part of any rape prosecution, particularly where the rapist and the victim had a prior relationship (see "Spousal Exemption to Rape", *supra*, at n 4, 65 Marq. L. Rev., at p 125; "Marital Rape Exemption", *supra*, n 5, 52 NYU L Rev, at p 314). Similarly, the possibility that married women will fabricate complaints would seem to be no greater than the possibility of unmarried women doing so ("Marital Rape Exemption", *supra*, n 5, 52 NYU L Rev, at p 314; "Equal Protection Considerations", *supra*, n 6, 16 N Eng L Rev, at p 24). The criminal justice system, with all of its built-in safeguards, is presumed to be capable of handling any false complaints. Indeed, if the possibility of fabricated complaints were a basis for not criminalizing behavior which would otherwise be sanctioned, virtually all crimes other than homicides would go unpunished.

The final argument in defense of the marital exemption is that marital rape is not as serious an offense as other rape and is thus adequately dealt with by the possibility of prosecution under criminal statutes, such as assault statutes, which provide for less severe punishment. The fact that rape statutes exist, however, is a recognition that the harm caused by a forcible rape is different, and more severe, than the harm caused by an ordinary assault (see "Marital Rape Exemption", *supra*, n 5, 52 NYU L Rev, at p 316; "Abolishing the Marital Exemption", *supra*, n 4, 1983 U of Ill L Rev, at p 208). "Short of homicide, [rape] is the 'ultimate violation of self'" (*Coker v. Georgia*, 433 U.S. 584, 597 [citation omitted], *supra*). Under the Penal Law, assault is generally a misdemeanor unless either the victim suffers "serious physical injury" or a deadly weapon or dangerous instrument is used (Penal Law, §§ 120.00, 120.05, 120.10). Thus, if the defendant had been living with Denise at the time he forcibly raped and sodomized her he probably could not have been charged with a felony, let alone a felony with punishment equal to that for rape in the first degree.

Moreover, there is no evidence to support the argument that marital rape has less severe consequences than other rape. On the contrary, numerous studies have shown that marital rape is frequently quite violent and generally has *more* severe, traumatic effects on the victim than other rape (see, generally, Russell, Rape In Marriage, pp 190–199; "Rape Prosecution", *supra*, at n 6, Vt. L. Rev., at pp 45–46; "Abolishing the Marital Exemption", *supra*, n 4, 1983 U of Ill L Rev, at p 209).

Among the recent decisions in this country addressing the marital exemption, only one court has concluded that there is a rational basis for it (see *People v. Brown*, 632 P2d 1025 [Col]). We agree with the other courts which have analyzed the exemption, which have been unable to find any present justification for it (see *People v. De Stefano*, 121 Misc 2d 113; *Commonwealth v. Chretien*, 383 Mass 123; *State v. Smith*, 85 NJ 193, *supra*; *Weishaupt v. Commonwealth*, 227 Va 389, *supra*; *State v. Rider*, 449 So 2d 903 [Fla App]; *State v. Smith*, 401 So 2d 1126 [Fla App]). Justice Holmes wrote: "It is revolting to have no better reason for a rule of law than that so it was laid down in the time of Henry IV. It is still more revolting if the grounds upon which it was laid down have vanished long since, and the rule simply persists from blind imitation of the past" (Holmes, The Path of the Law, 10 Harv. L. Rev. 457, 469). This statement is an apt characterization of the marital exemption; it lacks a rational basis, and therefore violates the equal protection clauses of both the Federal and State Constitutions (US Const, 14th Amdt, § 1; NY Const, art I, § 11).

. . . .

---

Marital rape statutes have continued to fall, but several states have retained vestiges of them. By way of example, the law of South Carolina will permit prosecution for marital rape, but only if the victim reports the attack within 30 days.

### S.C. Code Ann. 16-3-615 (2014) Spousal sexual battery.

(A) Sexual battery, as defined in Section 16-3-651(h), when accomplished through use of aggravated force, defined as the use or the threat of use of a weapon or the use or threat of use of physical force or physical violence of a high and aggravated nature, by one spouse against the other spouse if they are living together, constitutes the felony of spousal sexual battery and, upon conviction, a person must be imprisoned not more than ten years.

(B) The offending spouse's conduct must be reported to appropriate law enforcement authorities within thirty days in order for that spouse to be prosecuted for this offense.

. . . .

## G. Strangulation

Strangulation is among the most dangerous of domestic violence offenses. Within seconds, strangulation can cause unconsciousness and within minutes, death. Until rather recently, however, it was often treated as a misdemeanor assault. In 2011, the Training Institute on Strangulation Prevention was created to enhance knowledge about this severe form of abuse within law enforcement and the domestic violence advocacy communities. The organization was formed with assistance from a federal grant from the Department of Justice and trains some 5,000 people each year.[17]

The Training Institute describes strangulation as "the ultimate form of *power and control,* where the batterer can demonstrate control over the victim's next breath; it may have devastating psychological effects or a potentially fatal outcome."[18]

Although strangulation—provided it causes sufficient injury—would constitute an assault in all jurisdictions, very few states have stand-alone statutes naming strangulation as a crime. As of 2014, only Connecticut, Indiana, Nebraska, New York, Oregon, Virginia and Wisconsin had strangulation statutes.[19] Two examples follow.

---

17. www.strangulationtraininginstitute.com/about-us, accessed October 9, 2016.
18. www.strangulationtraininginstitute.com, accessed March 5, 2017.
19. www.ndaa.org/pdf/strangulation_statutory_compilation_11_7_2014.pdf, accessed October 10, 2016.

### 11 Del. C. § 607 (2016) Strangulation; penalty; affirmative defense

(a) (1) A person commits the offense of strangulation if the person knowingly or intentionally impedes the breathing or circulation of the blood of another person by applying pressure on the throat or neck of the other person.

(2) Except as provided in paragraph (a)(3) of this section, strangulation is a class E felony.

(3) Strangulation is a class D felony if:

a. The person used or attempted to use a dangerous instrument or a deadly weapon while committing the offense; or

b. The person caused serious physical injury to the other person while committing the offense; or

c. The person has been previously convicted of strangulation.

### NY Penal Law § 121.12 (2015) Strangulation in the second degree

A person is guilty of strangulation in the second degree when he or she commits the crime of criminal obstruction of breathing or blood circulation, as defined in section 121.11 of this article, and thereby causes stupor, loss of consciousness for any period of time, or any other physical injury or impairment.

Strangulation in the second degree is a class D felony.

## H. Stalking

Laws against stalking exist in all 50 states, the District of Columbia and in federal statues. It is defined as "a course of conduct directed at a specific person that involves repeated visual or physical proximity, non-consensual communication, or verbal, written or implied threats or a combination thereof, that would cause a reasonable person to fear."[20]

Stalking first came to the public's attention in the late 1980s with the tragic shooting death of a young television actress named Rebecca Shaeffer by an obsessed admirer who believed the two had a relationship, even though they had never met. Consequently, in California, where the killing had occurred, the legislature enacted the country's first criminal law against stalking. Although stalking receives considerable media attention when celebrities are involved, it is an all-too common form of frightening violence against many women — and some men — by their intimate partners.

---

20. Patricia Tjaden & Nancy Thoennes, *Stalking in America: Findings From the National Violence Against Women Survey*, U.S. Dep't of Justice, Nat'l Inst. of Justice, Washington, D.C. (1998).

In a report issued by the federal government in 2012, it was revealed that 3.3 million adults were stalked each year. Nearly 7 in 10 of those victims knew their stalker. Most shocking is the extent to which stalking is perpetrated against women; the adult female population in the United States is approximately 114 million, of which 2.2 percent or 2.5 million women have been stalked. By comparison, of an adult male population of 107 million, 85,600 men report having been stalked. While most stalking victims indicate the behavior lasted six months or less, a startling 11 percent of the victims have been subjected to stalking for five years or more.[21] The following article puts the behavior into context.

## Paul E. Mullen & Michele Pathe, *Stalking*
### 29 Crime & Justice 273 (2002)

Stalking has emerged as a significant social problem. Antistalking legislation has been introduced in most Western nations. The nature, prevalence, and impact of stalking are only now being systematically studied. There are debates on how best to conceptualize stalking and how to understand what drives stalkers persistently to pursue and harass the targets of their unwanted attentions. The prevalence of being victimized by stalkers is relatively high, with those subjected to extended periods of harassment often suffering both significant psychological damage and being at risk of physical and sometimes sexual assault. A variety of strategies have been developed to curb and prevent stalking and to relieve the distress of victims.

The word "stalk" has long had the meaning of both following and walking stealthily. In the late 1980s the media appropriated "stalking" and "stalker" to describe a group of individuals who persistently followed and intruded on others. Initially those so described were pursuers and pesterers of the famous. From the outset the media linked stalking to violence. . . .

Star stalkers could be either men or women and were portrayed as people inappropriately obsessed with someone famous, and, by implication, stalkers were likely to be mentally disordered. These were rare and exotic creatures found only in the ecological niches inhabited by the famous. When the use of the word "stalking" broadened to incorporate the harassers of ex-partners, it was initially reframed as "a woman's issue, a widespread precursor of serious violence . . . a common problem . . . a form of domestic violence against women." . . . This newer construction was typified by an angry and vengeful male pursuing a terrified female. In the process, a social problem that had initially been confined to the famous was transformed into an experience open to all women. . . .

Stalking progressed rapidly from being a media neologism to becoming an established social problem and a specific form of criminal offending. The murder of Rebecca Shaeffer was the impetus for the introduction of antistalking legislation in California.

---

21. Shannan Catalano, *Stalking Victims in the United States*, U.S. Dep't of Justice, Office of Justice Programs, Bureau of Justice Statistics, Washington, D.C. (September 2012), 1–4.

Her death became virtually synonymous with the public outcry and media pressure for new laws to control such harassment. The public pressure culminated in the passage of the world's first antistalking statute in California, which came into effect on January 1, 1991.

. . . .

Other American states followed California. States either adopted the California approach, requiring the perpetrator to engage in a course of conduct, or specified in legislation those activities that constitute stalking. Since 1992 every U.S. state has introduced antistalking legislation. . . .

Stalking is all too often a lengthy and intense harassment continuing for months or years. The effects on victims of such chronic stress have started to be studied systematically. Prior to stalking emerging as an area of legitimate interest for mental health professionals, most work on the impact of psychological trauma had been concerned with the effects of overwhelming acute stresses produced by life-threatening situations or by the horrors of such events such as rape. The possible impact of ongoing fear and apprehension experienced over months or years had received little attention. For this reason the initial stalking studies . . . focused on the description of the impact of such chronic fear-inducing behaviors. . . . Increased anxiety, sleep disturbance, significant depression, and suicidal ruminations were common, with the majority of victims having symptoms of a post-traumatic stress disorder. Major lifestyle changes—including reducing or ceasing work, curtailing social activities, and moving home—were common. . . .

Stalking has been classified as an integral part of violence against women . . . [and] is often a strategy of intimidation and control used by men to force their female partners to remain in a relationship. This emphasis on stalking as an extension of domestic violence creates view of stalking that focuses on women as victims and men as perpetrators.

. . . .

The context in which the stalking arises is also of relevance given its relationship to the stalker's likely aims and manner of advancing those aims. . . . The rejected are responding to an unwelcome end to a close relationship by actions intended to lead to reconciliation or to extract reparation, or both. Their stalking is reinforced by the continuance of a semblance of the relationship, however conflicted. . . . The rejected group used the widest range of stalking behaviors including following, repeatedly approaching, telephoning, letter writing, and leaving notes. . . . The duration of the stalking was by far the longest in the rejected. . . .

Prior intimates. This is the largest category, the most common victim profile being a woman who has previously shared an intimate relationship with her (usually) male stalker. We include only cases in which the relationship has been explicitly terminated, because in these cases the behavior is unequivocally unwanted, although approximately half the victims in this category will have been subjected to harassment while still in the relationship. This most often involves following, surveillance and damage to personal property....

Victims in this category are exposed to the widest range of harassment methods, repeated phone calls, persistent following, and threats being more commonly experienced by this group. They are also more likely to be subject to violence, particularly if the perpetrator has prior criminal convictions. Victims of ex-intimate stalkers can also expect the pursuit to be more persistent, though legal sanctions may persuade their former partners to refrain from further harassment. This is obviously more complicated if victim and stalker share children; the stalker may have legitimate visitation rights (though these are often exceeded) or may embark on a custody battled fueled by a strong sense of entitlement, vengeance, or determination to maintain contact with the rejecting party. "Date" stalkers—with whom the victim may have had only a brief romantic liaison—are less likely to be violent than are ex-partners, whose emotional investment in the victim is considerably greater. The victim of a date stalker often gives a history of feeling uneasy early in the relationship. They are, however, reluctant to hurt their (most commonly) boyfriend's feelings, and they may accept further dates beyond the point at which they perceive any future in the relationship. When they do make an assertive attempt to leave, their partner typically reacts badly, often in a pathetic, childlike manner that exploits the victim's guilt and sympathy.

The guilt frequently experienced by victims of ex-intimates can be reinforced by the propensity of others to judge their predicament. Family and friends may express disapproval of the victim's relationship choices, and helping agencies may convey their suspicions that the victim in some way encouraged the stalking. This is particularly likely when there has been a previous intimate relationship but also in situations where the victim may have failed to respond assertively to the stalker's advances, usually as a consequence of naivete or reluctance to upset or anger the stalker. These victims are more likely than those in other categories to seek police help and legal advice, where they may encounter similar attitudes.... The response of the judicial system does not always live up to the victim's expectations, as victims are confronted by lawyers, magistrates, and judges who are ignorant of stalking issues and who trivialize the stalker's actions. This has led to calls for comprehensive training for those who work in these areas in the special needs of the victims of prior intimate stalking.

. . . .

Management strategies with stalkers must also specifically target the stalking behaviors. Stalking is a time-consuming, resource-expending, emotionally draining, and ultimately futile activity. Even stalkers caught up in a delusional system generally have some realization, however remote, of the costs and self-defeating nature of their pursuit. Changing those behaviors is in part about helping them focus on the negative consequences of continuing to stalk. Strategies aimed at encouraging victim empathy, even in the deluded, should also be included. Most stalkers deceive themselves into believing their activities will further the aims of either attracting or reconciling with the object of their unwanted attentions, and even those pursuing agendas of revenge or vindication rarely admit to themselves the extent to which they are damaging their victims. Providing information about the impact of stalking in general and of their behavior in particular may be useful, together with other elements of victim empathy training borrowed from sex offender training programs.

Stalking is sustained, in no small part, because the behavior is gratifying in and of itself. Despite this, few stalkers admit that they find the stalking rewarding. They explain their actions to themselves as being necessary to attain their goal (be that goal a relationship, retribution or whatever).... [T]he rejected can sometimes be helped to understand that they have substituted the stalking for the lost relationship. As a result they can neither reestablish a connection to nor free themselves from their ex-partner.

. . . .

Working with Victims

Central to the amelioration of suffering in stalking victims is the provision of sound guidelines aimed at combating the stalking and ensuring the victim's personal safety. To date, it has been difficult for many victims of stalking to gain access to responsive, coordinated services, but a growing awareness of the magnitude of this problem has seen the establishment of stalking victim support organizations and specialized services within the helping professions....

Victims are well advised to inform trusted individuals that they are being stalked, report their concerns to the police, and involve helping agencies such as victim support organizations or, where applicable, domestic violence programs. They should document all suspicious incidents and retain any evidence, such as taped answering machine messages, letters, or other unsolicited material, and police reports of any illegal acts that occur during the course of the stalking. These can be invaluable in the event of legal proceedings against the stalker. Victims should inform their pursuer firmly, unambiguously, and at the earliest opportunity that they do not want any further contact. Any subsequent contact with their stalker, including attempts to reiterate or renegotiate this message, must be strictly and consistently avoided. It is important for stalking victims to understand that any contact with the perpetrator, however intermittent, will reinforce the unwanted behavior. Unfortunately, the victim's resolve may occasionally be overridden by other forces, an example being the victim who is forced to appear before his or her stalker in the courtroom to answer spurious charges concocted by the stalker. The "no contact" edict may also prove difficult in situations of neighbor or workplace stalking, or when the offender is an estranged husband awarded regular access visits to his children.

The use of restraining or nonmolestation orders is a contentious issue. When restraining orders are contemplated, it is preferable to initiate the application early in the course of harassment. For stalkers who fail to appreciate that their behavior is a nuisance and source of distress, the issuance of a restraining order may succeed in conveying this message. Restraining orders taken out a relatively early stage are likely to be more effective than those obtained after months or even years of stalking, when the stalker's emotional investment in the relationship has intensified and the stalker may well be left to wonder, "Why now?"... Prosecution under antistalking laws offers greater flexibility in sentencing and more serious penalties than do civil approaches. Legal sanctions raise the stakes sufficiently high for a substantial number of stalkers to abandon their quest.

. . . .

---

The personal impact of stalking was recounted in a terrifying memoir written under a pseudonym by a survivor. In 2008, *In His Sights,* a book by "Kate Brennan" and published by HarperCollins under its Harper Perennial imprint, told of the torture of 14 years of harassment by a former lover against the author. Her stalker knew no bounds. He moved to her neighborhood after their breakup, tampered with her computer, broke into her apartment, made telephone threats and encouraged third parties to relay ominous messages. The stalker's actions destroyed "Brennan's" quality of life, causing her to live a nomadic existence. Remaining in one place or building new relationships became impossible.

The California anti-stalking statute served as the inspiration for others. Stalking is now a crime in all 50 states and the District of Columbia. Under certain circumstances, it is a crime under federal law as well. The California stalking statute is reprinted below.

## Cal Pen Code 646.9 (2016) Stalking

(a) Any person who willfully, maliciously, and repeatedly follows or willfully and maliciously harasses another person and who makes a credible threat with the intent to place that person in reasonable fear for his or her safety, or the safety of his or her immediate family is guilty of the crime of stalking, punishable by imprisonment in a county jail for not more than one year, or by a fine of not more than one thousand dollars ($1,000), or by both that fine and imprisonment, or by imprisonment in the state prison.

(b) Any person who violates subdivision (a) when there is a temporary restraining order, injunction, or any other court order in effect prohibiting the behavior described in subdivision (a) against the same party, shall be punished by imprisonment in the state prison for two, three, or four years.

(c)

(1) Every person who, after having been convicted of a felony under Section 273.5, 273.6, or 422, commits a violation of subdivision (a) shall be punished by imprisonment in a county jail for not more than one year, or by a fine of not more than one thousand dollars ($1,000), or by both that fine and imprisonment, or by imprisonment in the state prison for two, three, or five years.

(2) Every person who, after having been convicted of a felony under subdivision (a), commits a violation of this section shall be punished by imprisonment in the state prison for two, three, or five years.

(d) In addition to the penalties provided in this section, the sentencing court may order a person convicted of a felony under this section to register as a sex offender pursuant to Section 290.006.

. . . .

(h) For purposes of this section, the term "electronic communication device" includes, but is not limited to, telephones, cellular phones, computers, video recorders, fax machines, or pagers. . . .

(1) The sentencing court also shall consider issuing an order restraining the defendant from any contact with the victim, that may be valid for up to 10 years, as determined by the court. It is the intent of the Legislature that the length of any restraining order be based upon the seriousness of the facts before the court, the probability of future violations, and the safety of the victim and his or her immediate family. . . .

## People v. Zavala
### California Court of Appeal
### 130 Cal. App. 4th 758 (2005)

McDonald, J.

. . . .

### I. FACTUAL BACKGROUND

Zavala and Wife were married in 1989. However, they separated in 1991 after a domestic violence incident prompted Wife to obtain a temporary restraining order against him, and they were divorced in 1992. At the time of their divorce, they had one daughter (Daughter). Zavala and Wife subsequently reconciled and they resumed living together without remarrying, and had a second child together. In the first part of 2003, the family lived together at 1262 Waxwing Lane in Chula Vista (the home).

. . . .

On June 20, 2003, Wife obtained a temporary restraining order and an order for Zavala's removal from the home.

*The Stalking Offense*

On July 11, at approximately 4:00 a.m., Wife was at home when she was awakened by the sound of Zavala's car engine. She looked outside and saw Zavala's car, a white Porsche, parked in the yard. She called police because she did not know what he was going to do. However, after sitting in the car for a while, Zavala left.

On the morning of August 2 Wife received more than 20 telephone calls. In many of the calls, no one spoke but Wife heard noise in the background. In several other calls, Zavala spoke to Wife, stating words to the effect of "you stupid bitch, you fucked up, you fucked up again." Wife again contacted police.

On August 3, Wife was packing her car with supplies for a planned trip to the beach to celebrate her son's birthday. Zavala unexpectedly drove up and stopped at the driveway of the home. Wife told Daughter to run inside and call the police. Wife stood in the doorway to block Zavala's entry and told him to leave. Zavala said, "Fuck you, bitch," and pushed past Wife and entered the home. Once inside, he politely wished his son happy birthday, and began yelling Daughter's name. Daughter, who had already telephoned police, told Zavala he should leave. Zavala responded that he was not going to leave, and he could not believe Daughter was "backstabbing" him. Daughter began to cry, and Zavala finally left. When police arrived, Wife (who was shaky and scared) and Daughter told police what had happened and that they feared Zavala.

The following evening at approximately 8:00 p.m., Zavala drove past the home while Wife was outside. They made eye contact, and Wife went inside and locked the doors. A short time later, Wife and the children were inside when she saw Zavala walking up the driveway. Daughter immediately went to call the police. Zavala confronted Daughter before leaving. Wife feared Zavala would return and was afraid for her safety.

The following morning, August 5, Zavala telephoned Wife around 9:00 a.m. and stated, "You fucked up, bitch. You had everything, you had everything and you fucked up." He then hung up. Wife was afraid and called her divorce attorney, but she declined her attorney's recommendation to call police because it was just a telephone call. However, around 11:00 a.m., as Wife drove away from her home with her son, she saw Zavala parked on a street near her home. Zavala followed her to a shopping center, and Wife called police on her cellular telephone during the drive, but Zavala broke off contact before police arrived. At 11:00 p.m. that night, Wife was inside the home when she heard Zavala's car engine; she looked out and saw him next to his car in the driveway of the home. After a few minutes, he drove away. She telephoned police and told them she was scared of what he might do to her.

At approximately 5:00 p.m. the following day, Wife and the children were at Wife's parents' home, having spent the previous night there because of the incident the previous evening. Daughter came inside, crying, "He's here, he's here, he's doing it again," and Wife looked outside and saw Zavala sitting in his car. Wife called 911. An officer monitoring traffic a block from the parents' house saw a white Porsche drive past him shortly after he heard the radio broadcast of the restraining order violation.

The next day, August 7, Wife was still at her parents' home. Zavala called her cellular telephone multiple times, telling her she was a "stupid bitch." He also told her, "I'm going to kill you, just watch," and told her the children would be better off with a foster parent than with her. He concluded, "The next time they see me I'll be behind a glass wall." Wife reported these calls to police, and police responded. While police were at the house, her cellular telephone rang, and Wife gave it to a deputy, who heard a male voice on the other end of the line. When the deputy said "Hi Mario," the person said, "Stop calling me" and hung up. About 20 minutes later, the telephone again rang, and Wife answered, heard Zavala's voice, and again gave the telephone to the deputy, who again said, "Hi Mario." The voice replied, "Yeah," and the deputy told Zavala this was the second time Zavala had called and that Zavala was violating the restraining order. Zavala again replied, "Stop calling me" and hung up.

After a few days of respite, Zavala on August 13 again made multiple calls to Wife, leaving voice messages laced with vulgarities and calling Wife a "bitch" and threatening to kill her. During this time, Wife was taking precautions for her safety, including staying at her parents' house, keeping her windows closed at night, and going around the block to make sure Zavala was not in a position to intercept her before she could get inside the home.

On the morning of August 15, Wife returned home (after again having slept at her parents' house) and found the security alarm beeping. She discovered wire cutters had been taken from a tool chest and were on a worktable. The power to the residence was off, the wires to the garage door opener had been cut, an off-road vehicle was missing from the garage, and Wife's motor home (parked in the back) had been vandalized. Later that evening, Wife was waiting near the home with her sister and children when they saw Zavala (accompanied by his father) arrive at the home in the father's pickup truck. Zavala jogged to the front door, while Zavala's father backed the truck up to the garage. However, when Zavala's father saw Wife, he yelled to Zavala, who quickly returned to and got inside the truck. As the truck passed by Wife, Zavala waved and smiled at Wife and the children. Wife was afraid and reported the incident to police.

On August 29, Wife went to the Chula Vista Police Department to meet with a detective about the case against Zavala, and signed the visitors log at approximately 1:10 p.m. The detective later found that Zavala's name appeared in the visitors log with a time of 3:00 p.m. next to it. . . .

## II. THE STALKING CONVICTION

### A. *Sufficient Evidence Supports the Verdict*

Zavala contends the evidence was insufficient to support a conviction of stalking under section 646.9. He argues (1) the prosecution did not satisfy the harassment element of stalking because there was no evidence Wife suffered substantial emotional distress and (2) there was insufficient evidence Zavala made a credible threat of death or great bodily injury to Wife. . . .

*Analysis*

. . . .

The record shows that, notwithstanding the restraining order, Zavala repeatedly contacted Wife in person and by telephone, followed her on at least three occasions, and made various express or implied threats against her. Zavala argues there was no evidence Wife was "seriously" alarmed or terrorized by his conduct, because she merely testified she feared he might harm her. Wife's direct testimony of her fear of Zavala, coupled with spending nights at her parents' house because of her fear of Zavala, circling the home to make sure Zavala was not present to prevent her from entering the home safely, and locking the windows on hot summer nights to protect against his intrusion, provides evidentiary support for the finding Zavala's conduct seriously alarmed, annoyed, tormented, or terrorized her.

Zavala also asserts there was no credible threat that caused Wife to reasonably fear for her safety (§ 646.9, subd. (g)) because there was no evidence Zavala threatened Wife with death or great bodily injury, as required by *People v. Carron* (1995) 37 Cal. App. 4th 1230, 1235–1237 [44 Cal. Rptr. 2d 328]. However, *Carron* interpreted a prior version of the statutory definition for "credible threat" (*id*. at pp. 1236–1237), and subsequent statutory amendments have modified the "credible threat" element to require that the target of the threat need only fear for the target's safety or that of his or her family while deleting any requirement that the threat be "against the life of, or [threaten] great bodily injury to" the target. (See Stats. 1994, ch. 931, § 1, p. 5398.) Moreover, there was substantial evidence Zavala threatened to kill Wife, which would satisfy the requirements even under the prior statute.

Zavala finally argues there was no evidence he had the "apparent ability" to carry out the threat because he presented character witnesses vouching for his peaceful nature, and Wife told an officer she did not believe Zavala would kill her. However, Zavala's violent character *toward Wife* was demonstrated by the Easter 2002 assault on Wife, as well as the June 17, 2003 choking incident, and her belief that he might not be capable of *murder* did not exclude a reasonable belief that he was capable of violently assaulting her. . . .

C. *The Trial Court Correctly Rejected Zavala's Proffered Instruction*

The trial court rejected Zavala's proposed special instruction, submitted in connection with the stalking count, which read: "In order to be found guilty of the crime of [stalking], the prosecution must prove beyond a reasonable doubt that the victim must have actually *feared death or great bodily injury* as a result of the threat and that fear must be reasonable." (Italics added.)

Zavala argues the court erroneously rejected this instruction. It is not error to reject a legally incorrect instruction. . . . The statutory amendments have eliminated the former requirement that the threat be "against the life of, or [threaten] great bodily injury to" the target (See Stats. 1994, ch. 931, § 1, p. 5398), and the statute now requires that the target fear only for the target's (or his or her family's) safety. The italicized language made the proffered instruction legally incorrect and it was properly rejected by the trial court.

. . . .

*The Instructional Issue*

Zavala argues the trial court erred when it instructed the jury on the use of the prior violent acts evidence. Zavala notes that Evidence Code section 1109 is a limited exception to the general ban (under Evid. Code, § 1101) against using prior acts to infer the defendant's disposition to commit the charged acts, and permits such evidence as the basis for such inference if the defendant is accused of a crime involving domestic violence within the meaning of section 13700. (See Evid. Code, § 1109, subd. (d).) Zavala asserts that, to the extent the stalking offense does *not* require that the threat induced the victim to fear great bodily injury or death, stalking is concomitantly *not* a crime of domestic violence (as defined by section 13700) and therefore the prior violent acts evidence may not be used by the jury to infer Zavala had a disposition the type of which made it likely he committed the stalking offense.

We agree it was error to give the instruction as to the count charging Zavala with stalking. However, we are also convinced it is not reasonably probable Zavala would have obtained a more favorable result absent the instruction, and therefore the error was harmless under *People v. Watson* (1956) 46 Cal.2d 818, 836 [299 P.2d 243].... First, the jury's acquittal of Zavala on count two shows it carefully weighed and considered the evidence of his guilt independent of the inference permitted by the instruction. More importantly, the evidence of Zavala's *acts* (e.g. repeatedly contacting her in person and by telephone between July 11 and August 29, 2003, notwithstanding the restraining order) was corroborated by numerous witnesses, including Daughter and investigating police officers. Thus, it appears (as to the stalking offense) the only issue in substantial dispute was whether Wife actually feared for her safety, or was instead exaggerating or lying about her alleged fear to obtain a conviction that would provide her an advantage in the looming child custody battle. Although the erroneous instruction had tangential relevance to the issue of what *acts* Zavala may have committed, it was almost entirely irrelevant to the central disputed issue—Wife's state of mind—and therefore it is not reasonably likely Zavala would have obtained a more favorable result absent the instruction.

.... The judgment is affirmed.

## II. Domestic Violence in the New Technology Era

New satellite technologies have enabled better and faster communications between loved ones and have assisted families, health care providers and law enforcement in times of emergencies. Social media bring people closer together and GPS devices protect the directionally challenged from getting lost. But these 21st century technologies may be used as threatening and, in particular, stalking devices. The prevalence of Facebook accounts—some one billion people are on Facebook worldwide[22]—provides a quasi-public forum for a batterer to control his victim. But it will not be easy for law enforcement to fight this phenomenon. The United States Supreme Court has held the government must prove intent to convict a defendant of using that medium to make threats.

### Elonis v. United States
Supreme Court of the United States
135 S. Ct. 2001 (2015)

CHIEF JUSTICE ROBERTS delivered the opinion of the Court.

....

---

22. *Company Info/Facebook Newsroom*, www.newsroom.fb/company-info/ accessed January 26, 2016.

Anthony Douglas Elonis was an active user of the social networking Web site Facebook. Users of that Web site may post items on their Facebook page that are accessible to other users, including Facebook "friends" who are notified when new content is posted. In May 2010, Elonis's wife of nearly seven years left him, taking with her their two young children. Elonis began "listening to more violent music" and posting self-styled "rap" lyrics inspired by the music. App. 204, 226. Eventually, Elonis changed the user name on his Facebook page from his actual name to a rap-style nom de plume, "Tone Dougie," to distinguish himself from his "on-line persona." *Id.*, at 249, 265. The lyrics Elonis posted as "Tone Dougie" included graphically violent language and imagery. This material was often interspersed with disclaimers that the lyrics were "fictitious," with no intentional "resemblance to real persons." *Id.*, at 331, 329. Elonis posted an explanation to another Facebook user that "I'm doing this for me. My writing is therapeutic." *Id.*, at 329; see also *id.*, at 205 (testifying that it "helps me to deal with the pain").

Elonis's co-workers and friends viewed the posts in a different light. Around Halloween of 2010, Elonis posted a photograph of himself and a co-worker at a "Halloween Haunt" event at the amusement park where they worked. In the photograph, Elonis was holding a toy knife against his co-worker's neck, and in the caption Elonis wrote, "I wish." *Id.*, at 340. Elonis was not Facebook friends with the co-worker and did not "tag" her, a Facebook feature that would have alerted her to the posting. *Id.*, at 175. . . .

Elonis's posts frequently included crude, degrading, and violent material about his soon-to-be ex-wife. Shortly after he was fired, Elonis posted an adaptation of a satirical sketch that he and his wife had watched together. *Id.*, at 164-165, 207. In the actual sketch, called "It's Illegal to Say . . . ," a comedian explains that it is illegal for a person to say he wishes to kill the President, but not illegal to explain that it is illegal for him to say that. When Elonis posted the script of the sketch, however, he substituted his wife for the President. The posting was part of the basis for Count Two of the indictment, threatening his wife:

> "Hi, I'm Tone Elonis.
>
> Did you know that it's illegal for me to say I want to kill my wife? . . .
>
> It's one of the only sentences that I'm not allowed to say. . . .
>
> Now it was okay for me to say it right then because I was just telling you that it's illegal for me to say I want to kill my wife. . . .
>
> Um, but what's interesting is that it's very illegal to say I really, really think someone out there should kill my wife. . . .
>
> But not illegal to say with a mortar launcher.
>
> Because that's its own sentence. . . .
>
> I also found out that it's incredibly illegal, extremely illegal to go on Facebook and say something like the best place to fire a mortar launcher at her house would be from the cornfield behind it because of easy access

to a getaway road and you'd have a clear line of sight through the sun room. . . .

Yet even more illegal to show an illustrated diagram.

[diagram of the house]. . . ." *Id.,* at 333.

The details about the home were accurate. *Id.,* at 154. At the bottom of the post, Elonis included a link to the video of the original skit, and wrote, "Art is about pushing limits. I'm willing to go to jail for my Constitutional rights. Are you?" *Id.,* at 333.

After viewing some of Elonis's posts, his wife felt "extremely afraid for [her] life." *Id.,* at 156. A state court granted her a three-year protection-from-abuse order against Elonis (essentially, a restraining order). *Id.,* at 148-150. Elonis referred to the order in another post on his "Tone Dougie" page, also included in Count Two of the indictment:

"Fold up your [protection-from-abuse order] and put it in your pocket

Is it thick enough to stop a bullet?

Try to enforce an Order

that was improperly granted in the first place

Me thinks the Judge needs an education

on true threat jurisprudence

And prison time'll add zeros to my settlement . . .

And if worse comes to worse

I've got enough explosives

to take care of the State Police and the Sheriff's Department." *Id.,* at 334.

At the bottom of this post was a link to the Wikipedia article on "Freedom of speech." *Ibid.* Elonis's reference to the police was the basis for Count Three of his indictment, threatening law enforcement officers. . . .

B

A grand jury indicted Elonis for making threats to injure patrons and employees of the park, his estranged wife, police officers, a kindergarten class, and an FBI agent, all in violation of 18 U.S.C. § 875(c). App. 14-17. In the District Court, Elonis moved to dismiss the indictment for failing to allege that he had intended to threaten anyone. The District Court denied the motion, holding that Third Circuit precedent required only that Elonis "intentionally made the communication, not that he intended to make a threat." App. to Pet. for Cert. 51a. At trial, Elonis testified that his posts emulated the rap lyrics of the well-known performer Eminem, some of which involve fantasies about killing his ex-wife. App. 225. In Elonis's view, he had posted "nothing . . . that hasn't been said already." *Id.,* at 205. The Government presented as witnesses Elonis's wife and co-workers, all of whom said they felt afraid and viewed Elonis's posts as serious threats. See, *e.g., id.,* at 153, 158.

Elonis requested a jury instruction that "the government must prove that he intended to communicate a true threat." *Id.*, at 21. See also *id.*, at 267-269, 303. The District Court denied that request....

The Government's closing argument emphasized that it was irrelevant whether Elonis intended the postings to be threats—"it doesn't matter what he thinks." *Id.*, at 286. A jury convicted Elonis on four of the five counts against him, acquitting only on the charge of threatening park patrons and employees. *Id.*, at 309. Elonis was sentenced to three years, eight months' imprisonment and three years' supervised release.

Elonis renewed his challenge to the jury instructions in the Court of Appeals, contending that the jury should have been required to find that he intended his posts to be threats. The Court of Appeals disagreed, holding that the intent required by Section 875(c) is only the intent to communicate words that the defendant understands, and that a reasonable person would view as a threat. 730 F.3d 321, 332 (CA3 2013).

We granted certiorari....

## II

### A

An individual who "transmits in interstate or foreign commerce any communication containing any threat to kidnap any person or any threat to injure the person of another" is guilty of a felony and faces up to five years' imprisonment. 18 U.S.C. § 875(c). This statute requires that a communication be transmitted and that the communication contain a threat. It does not specify that the defendant must have any mental state with respect to these elements. In particular, it does not indicate whether the defendant must intend that his communication contain a threat....

For its part, the Government argues that Section 875(c) should be read in light of its neighboring provisions, Sections 875(b) and 875(d). Those provisions also prohibit certain types of threats, but expressly include a mental state requirement of an "intent to extort." See 18 U.S.C. § 875(b) (proscribing threats to injure or kidnap made "with intent to extort"); § 875(d) (proscribing threats to property or reputation made "with intent to extort"). According to the Government, the express "intent to extort" requirements in Sections 875(b) and (d) should preclude courts from implying an unexpressed "intent to threaten" requirement in Section 875(c)....

The Government takes this *expressio unius est exclusio alterius* canon too far. The fact that Congress excluded the requirement of an "intent to extort" from Section 875(c) is strong evidence that Congress did not mean to confine Section 875(c) to crimes of extortion. But that does not suggest that Congress, at the same time, also meant to exclude a requirement that a defendant act with a certain mental state in communicating a threat. The most we can conclude from the language of Section 875(c) and its neighboring provisions is that Congress meant to proscribe a broad class of threats in Section 875(c), but did not identify what mental state, if any, a defendant must have to be convicted....

## B

The fact that the statute does not specify any required mental state, however, does not mean that none exists. We have repeatedly held that "mere omission from a criminal enactment of any mention of criminal intent" should not be read "as dispensing with it." *Morissette* v. *United States*, 342 U.S. 246, 250, 72 S. Ct. 240, 96 L. Ed. 288 (1952). This rule of construction reflects the basic principle that "wrongdoing must be conscious to be criminal." *Id.*, at 252, 72 S. Ct. 240, 96 L. Ed. 288.... Although there are exceptions, the "general rule" is that a guilty mind is "a necessary element in the indictment and proof of every crime." *United States v. Balint*, 258 U.S. 250, 251, 42 S. Ct. 301, 66 L. Ed. 604, T.D. 3375 (1922). We therefore generally "interpret[ ] criminal statutes to include broadly applicable scienter requirements, even where the statute by its terms does not contain them." *United States* v. *X-Citement Video, Inc.*, 513 U.S. 64, 70, 115 S. Ct. 464, 130 L. Ed. 2d 372 (1994).

. . . .

## C

Section 875(c), as noted, requires proof that a communication was transmitted and that it contained a threat. The "presumption in favor of a scienter requirement should apply to *each* of the statutory elements that criminalize otherwise innocent conduct." *X-Citement Video,* 513 U.S., at 72, 115 S. Ct. 464, 130 L. Ed. 2d 372 (emphasis added). The parties agree that a defendant under Section 875(c) must know that he is transmitting a communication. But communicating *something* is not what makes the conduct "wrongful." Here "the crucial element separating legal innocence from wrongful conduct" is the threatening nature of the communication. *Id.,* at 73, 115 S. Ct. 464, 130 L. Ed. 2d 372. The mental state requirement must therefore apply to the fact that the communication contains a threat.

Elonis's conviction, however, was premised solely on how his posts would be understood by a reasonable person.... Having liability turn on whether a "reasonable person" regards the communication as a threat—regardless of what the defendant thinks—"reduces culpability on the all-important element of the crime to negligence," *Jeffries,* 692 F. 3d, at 484 *(Sutton, J., dubitante)* and we "have long been reluctant to infer that a negligence standard was intended in criminal statutes," *Rogers v. United States*, 422 U.S. 35, 47, 95 S. Ct. 2091, 45 L. Ed. 2d 1 (1975)....

In light of the foregoing, Elonis's conviction cannot stand. The jury was instructed that the Government need prove only that a reasonable person would regard Elonis's communications as threats, and that was error. Federal criminal liability generally does not turn solely on the results of an act without considering the defendant's mental state....

There is no dispute that the mental state requirement in Section 875(c) is satisfied if the defendant transmits a communication for the purpose of issuing a threat, or with knowledge that the communication will be viewed as a threat....

The judgment of the United States Court of Appeals for the Third Circuit is reversed, and the case is remanded for further proceedings consistent with this opinion.

## Mary Graw Leary, Symposium: *Emerging Issues in Crime Victims' Rights: The Third Dimension of Victimization*
13 Ohio St. J. Crim. L. 139 (Fall 2015)

. . . .

### I. INTRODUCTION

The criminal law serves unique and critical purposes in society. It defines minimal conduct and safeguards commonly shared social interests. It has the potential to protect members of the community, prevent victimization, and punish those when such protection and prevention fail. Crime itself has been defined as a voluntary act that causes a social harm. . . .

New social values emerge as society evolves, as do to novel methods of victimizing people. Ideally, the criminal law identifies these new forms of victimization and, if they compromise a socially valuable interest, the law condemns such behavior as criminal. . . . At times, this evolution has been the result of changed social values. For example, prohibition, the criminalization of adultery, and the non-criminalization of marital rape reflect formerly held social values that are no longer prevalent in modem society.

However, criminal law does not change only because of evolving social values. The criminal law must also respond to more structural changes in society that lead to innovative forms of victimization. . . . While such structural changes are not commonplace, they demand significant shifts in the criminal law to protect the community and socially valued interests that emerge.

The time has come for such a shift. Traditionally, when addressing individual victims, the criminal law functions in two dimensions: crimes against the person and crimes against property. This modality is outdated. With the advent of the Internet, electronic commerce, and numerous digital platforms at the very core of modern American existence, modern American criminal law must recognize a third dimension of victimization of individuals: crimes against the digital extension of the person.

. . . States must review criminal codes and restructure them to recognize the many new forms of victimization that are achieved digitally. Because of the uniquely pernicious harms of digital victimization, current criminal codes are insufficient. They fail to capture both the social value being protected and the harms accomplished through these digital victimizations. This article argues that one's digital presence can, in fact, be an extension of oneself. As such, one's digital self can be harmed in ways that are distinct from our current understanding of personal or property crimes. . . .

## III. THE UNIQUE HARMS TO THE DIGITAL SELF

A. *The Digital Self is an Extension of the Physical Self*

... The concept of the "digital self" or "digital person" arose from the early days of the Internet and the increased role of the digital world in everyday life. This concept, referred to as one's "digital footprint," that leaves traces throughout the digital world. It includes information individuals themselves have placed into the digital world through social networking profiles, blog posts, and other forms of self-created digital content that combine to form a "digital profile." It also includes, however, information collected about individuals without their consent, even including information placed on the Internet connected to the individual's identity hut not endorsed by the individual. Examples of this type of information include false information, incorrect information, or intentionally hurtful information. While the individual's physical self and the individual's digital self were at one time two distinct personas, over time, the digital and physical selves have arguably merged—becoming somewhat indistinguishable.

The overlap and blurring of the individual's digital and physical selves have manifested in a number of ways. For example, teens primarily communicate not through in person connections or even through a telephone, but through texting. One of the most primary forms of communication is through social media—one digital profile sharing information with a whole network of digital profiles. Usually, individuals voluntarily create social profiles and place these digital versions of themselves online. However, employers often require their employees to place profiles through social platforms such as LinkedIn or Facebook for employment purposes. In this way, an employee's "professional self" takes on a digital form, as well as a physical one, in the business world.

Basic components of daily life now occur online, including bill paying, banking, and video and audio communications. In short, our digital selves are no longer compartmentalized from our physical selves; they are, in fact, extensions of ourselves. ...

B. *The Harms to the Digital Self are Uniquely Pernicious and Inadequately Recognized in the Criminal Law*

Given the examples above, one might argue that the criminal law already recognizes harms to the person, and there is no need to alter the criminal law to recognize an entirely new category of victimization. However, such a view fails to recognize that the harms to the digital person, as an extension of oneself, are uniquely pernicious and deserve a separate and distinct category.

When crime was limited to the physical world, it was limited to the finite world. For example, a physical restraint, legal protective order, or the relocation of the victim could thwart a stalker. Today, that stalker can now utilize the Internet to find the victim, continue to stalk the victim online, and effectively always be within reach of the victim.... While a stalking victim in the past may have *felt* as though the stalker was omnipresent, today the stalker *is* virtually omnipresent. This kind of "omnipresent" harm is distinctly different and unique from traditional concepts of stalking. . . .

## IV. THE CRIMINAL LAW ADAPTS

It is not novel for the criminal law to embark on such a fundamental shift. Given some of the aforementioned purposes of the criminal law, it is necessary that the criminal law reflects the contemporarily shared values of the present. That said, the criminal law is not the only social structure to address social ills, and legislatures are wise to move cautiously when considering significant alterations. The law cannot respond to every social ill through criminalization. Given the slow progress of legislative efforts, many forms of victimization will have changed between the time of the legislation's conception and its passage, thus making the law obsolete before it takes effect. This reality is compounded when the need for change is driven by rapidly evolving technologies.

Nonetheless, when the societal landscape has gone through substantial changes, the criminal law must do so as well. This has occurred many times in history on very fundamental levels. It has also occurred with more minor but still significant changes with technology, such as theft, stalking and harassment, and reputational harm. . . .

Just as a call for a change in the criminal law to recognize a new societal harm is not novel, the notion that technology drives some fundamental changes is also not new. Defamation law, although not criminal, offers a clear example. This body of law began in feudal times, expanded with the advent of the printing press, and later was constitutionalized by the Supreme Court with the emergence of broadcast and mass media. . . .

While not categorized as a crime, defamation law is not wholly unrelated to the crimes of cyber stalking/harassment or threats. The traditional versions of these crimes were once limited to the physical world; however, new technologies such as online and digital communications have altered the landscape with the criminal law following. Before the 1990s, stalkers victimized people, mostly women, but law enforcement was without a mechanism to respond. These victims suffered profound harms relating to stress, fear, and financial cost of relocation or trying to escape the reach of the stalkers. However, since these offenders had not physically harmed the victims, no remedy was available to the victims or to law enforcement. This example demonstrates a situation in which the victims were clearly harmed, but because such harms were previously only conceptualized as bodily harm, the law was inadequate and provided no relief or redress for the victims. Therefore, the first anti-stalking laws emerged in the 1990s, and subsequently, forty-nine states and the federal government had an anti-stalking or anti-harassment crime by 1996. Thus, the law adapted to a new reality of the crime of stalking through understanding the crime's parameters and recognizing that the motive of offenders was not always violence but also included elements of obsession, real or imagined relationships, and control. . . .

Therefore, the idea that society should consider significantly altering the criminal code by recognizing the digital person as an extension of oneself through which the actual person can be profoundly harmed, is not revolutionary. Similar transformational shifts occurred, such as expanding the concept of crime, which was previously limited to include crimes against a person to include crimes against property. Such alterations have also taken place in smaller contexts, such as understanding the societal harms of crimes like harassment, stalking or threats, and how the criminal law has adjusted to recognize such harms. Finally, technological shifts, such as mass media, the Internet, cellular devices, can create new harms experienced by victims as well as new socially-protected interests. As such, the criminal law should recognize this third dimension of victimization within the context of personal crime.

## V. THE LAW RECOGNIZES EXTENSIONS OF THE SELF IN A VARIETY OF CONTEXTS

The suggestion of recognizing the digital person as an extension of the physical person is not as radical as it may first seem. The criminal law has a rich history of understanding harms to the person that occur outside the physical realm. Crimes, such as sexually-abusive images of children, stalking and harassment, and identity theft, to name a few, are instances where the criminal law has recognized a relationship between the person and the extension of the person beyond his or her physical body. Accordingly, recognizing a separate category of personal crime, i.e. that the digital person is an extension of the person, is a natural outgrowth of this precedent. The distinction between these isolated cases of the past and the need for a more contemporary, comprehensive approach highlight the nature of our inter-connected world. With each of these aforementioned changes in the criminal law, the law was responding to a new, but narrow, form of victimization. With the advent of the Internet and digital communications, all people have the potential to create a digital presence as an extension of themselves where this presence has emotional, financial, and commercial implications. As such, its protection, particularly when understood as an avenue to the actual self, is a socially-valuable interest. . . .

### B. *Non-Consensual or "Revenge" Pornography*

A rapidly emerging area of the criminal law that clearly demonstrates this recognition of the harm to the person through the targeting of the digital person is the area of non-consensual or "revenge" pornography. "Revenge pornography" refers to a nude or sexually explicit image that is shared publicly without the consent of the victim. It often references an intimate image or video that was initially shared between two people in an intimate relationship with the expectation that it will remain private. However, the images are not always produced with the consent of the victim, or with the knowledge of any of the subjects depicted. They can be shared by the victim or taken from her by a hacker.

Regarding distribution, this dissemination can take many forms including sharing the image with other people; posting the image on a web site designed to injure such victims; posting the image and accompanying it with identifying and/or disparaging remarks regarding the victim; mass sharing to communities such as classmates, cities and towns, groups; or targeting its distribution to specific persons such as employers, family members, and paramours. Often such a distribution occurs after the end of an intimate relationship. However, non-consensual pornography events have occurred when an offender hacks into an account of the victim and shares the pictures.

Of particular concern are situations in which the images are posted on websites designed for public sharing such as IsAnyoneUp.com, UGotPosted.com or MyEx.com. One such website owner actually required the subject's identifying information for submission of images to UGotPosted.com, and then charged victims hundreds of dollars to remove them through changemyreputation.com.

Regardless of the exact form of the victimization, the harm is very tangible and unique to these victims. Victims experience extreme invasions of privacy which cause them to suffer severe psychological trauma, emotional trauma, personal trauma, professional ruin, and property losses. Ultimately, victims' reputations are destroyed. Similar to victims of sexually abusive images of children, victims of revenge pornography suffer the perpetual harm of their explicit images being available on the Internet for eternity without an ability to retrieve or delete them. This brings the psychological trauma of wondering whether every person with whom they interact has seen these images.

When the images are also connected with a phone number or other identifying information, the harm becomes more profound as they then contend with cyber harassment and stalking. Victims are often stalked both in person and electronically, being subjected to receiving massive amounts of pornography or obscene messages. Additionally, these victims suffer property losses. They report having lost their jobs and being unable to obtain new positions. They suffer other forms of property loss including the costs of moving, changing their names, telephone numbers, and lives.

As this trend grew, as well as the public discovery of websites such as IsAnyoneUp.com dedicated to this anti-social behavior, the criminal law adjusted. Although not a crime against the physical body or property *per se*, many states clearly recognize the social harm of revenge pornography. As a result, approximately fourteen states have adopted legislation to criminalize this behavior. This body of statutes is a clear example of the criminal law recognizing the abuse of the digital person as an abuse of the actual person because that image or persona is an extension of the self.

These statutes vary widely. Some statutes require the intent to cause harm at the time of dissemination. Others do not do so. Some statutory reforms include a private right of action, while others respond with a purely criminal reaction. Some of the statutes limit criminal liability to the initial distributor. However, there is one common theme amongst these varying state statutes: implicit in many of these statutes is the recognition of the digital extension of the person. For example, New Jersey's legislature recognized that "people have a right to control the observation of their most intimate behavior under circumstances where a reasonable person would not expect to be observed."²³ California's law recognizes the "extreme humiliation of victims."²⁴ Delaware's statute also recognizes the property loss and notes the "person depicted unwillingly becomes sexual entertainment for strangers and the person's career and standing within the community can be negatively impacted."²⁵ All of these state findings exemplify an understanding that images are an extension of the victims, which by themselves, cause measurable social harms when exploited.

C. *Stalking, Harassment, and Cyber Bullying*

Within the context of crimes such as stalking, harassment, bullying, and threats, the criminal law has recognized harm to the person beyond the victim's physical person. It recognized the harm to the more intangible extension of the person. As society migrates to more digital existences, the criminal law has adapted to modify crimes, such as cyber stalking and harassment, cyber bullying, and online threats. The criminal law's recognition of the digital extension of self as a source of harm becomes clearer. It also officially recognizes this form of harm, and creates more support for the proposal of this article.

. . . The purpose of engaging in stalking is not always to cause physical harm to the victim. It can be driven by anger or a desire for contact. It has been found that defendants engage in this behavior for a variety of reasons including revenge, control, contact, or mental health issues. The harms experienced by victims of this relentless activity can include fear, hypervigilance, disrupted sleep, helplessness, anxiety, and PTSD.

In a post-digital world, the commission of these crimes has migrated to cyberspace. "Cyberstalking" refers to situations in which the offender uses technologies such as email, texting, or devices to create a level of intimidation, harassment, and fear in his victims. While it may manifest within a different medium than stalking and bullying in the physical world, it is driven by the same factors and causes similar harms. However, these harms are more acute when they occur through the Internet because these attacks "transcend all physical boundaries, borders, and limitations."

The advent of the Internet also provided the platform for increased incidents of stalking because the Internet provides both anonymity and access to many potential victims. The anonymity allows the perpetrators to engage in more behaviors, to utilize more means such as email or cellular connections, and to do it at all times. . . .

Notwithstanding these more pernicious harms, the criminal law responded by enacting legislation that criminalized these specific forms of stalking and harassment. All fifty states have some form of such legislation. Furthermore, the federal law has made it illegal to transmit threats across state lines using telephone or communication devices to harass or engage in interstate stalking.

---

23. [n82] *See* Sen. Judiciary Comm. Statement to Sen. Comm. Substitute for Sen. No. 1031, 1 (N.J. 1998).
24. [n83] *See generally* S.B. 1255, 2013–2014 Gen. Assemb., Reg. Sess. (Cal. 2014).
25. [n84] H.B. 260, 147th Gen. Assemb., Reg. Sess. (Del. 2014).

Thus, the evolution of the law reflects an implicit recognition of the extension of self and the need to criminalize harming that extension. The migration from stalking and harassment model to a cyberstalking model also endorses the concept that the social harm is distinct and arguably greater in the digital world than in the physical. . . .

## VII. CONCLUSION

The law is organic and nowhere is this felt more acutely than the criminal law. The number of methods that can be used to victimize a person is limited only by the imagination of the deviant mind seeking to cause such social harm. Therefore, this body of law is constantly adapting to new forms of victimization. Technology has permanently altered how Americans live. The criminal law should reflect this fundamental shift as well.

The purpose of the criminal law is to protect socially valuable interests. Jurisprudence in other areas indicates that the law has recognized crimes that protect interests beyond the person or property, but extensions of the self. It has further acknowledged the unique harms experienced by the victim when that extension is the target of misdeeds. The criminal law must explicitly convey that by abandoning the two dimensional construct of crimes against the individual and embrace this third dimension. By recognizing the social harms caused by targeting the online extensions of ourselves, criminal codes will advance the very purpose of the criminal law to protect citizens.

# III. Fighting Back

Women who are driven to kill abusive husbands are entitled to assert the same laws of self-defense and justification available to others who perceive they are under a grave threat of imminent danger. Under these laws, unless she is inside her own home, a victim has a "duty to retreat" prior to using deadly physical force. In addition, deadly physical force may be used only to meet what one reasonably believes to be a deadly attack. Over the years, however, some court decisions have weakened the "duty to retreat" rule. As of the fall of 2015, 33 states have enacted so-called "Stand Your Ground" laws, in which the "duty to retreat" has been eliminated under certain circumstances, which has implications in domestic violence killings where a couple shares a home.[26]

In October 2005, Florida became the first state to enact a statute allowing deadly physical force to prevent a "forcible felony," without requiring the actor to first retreat if it was safe to do so. Supporters laud these laws. Wayne La Pierre of the National Rifle Association has said: "If you're going to empower someone, empower the crime victim." Sarah Brady, chairwoman of the Brady Campaign to Prevent Gun Violence and wife of the late James Brady, the press secretary permanently maimed by a bullet

---

26. American Bar Association, National Task Force on Stand Your Ground Laws, *Final Report and Recommendations,* 10 (September 2015).

in the 1981 assassination attempt against President Reagan, derided the laws as a "license to kill."[27]

The Stand Your Ground law in Florida captured national headlines in February 2012 after a young, unarmed African American, 17-year-old Trayvon Martin, was shot to death by George Zimmerman, a security guard in a housing community. Zimmerman was indicted for the killing and in July 2013 found not guilty.[28] The American Bar Association formed a task force to study the impact of Stand Your Ground laws and in the fall of 2015, it recommended that states that have not yet enacted Stand Your Ground Laws refrain from doing so and that where states have already passed such laws, they repeal them.[29]

The following is Florida's "Stand Your Ground" statute.

## Fla. Stat. § 776.013 (2016) Home protection; use or threatened use of deadly force; presumption of fear of death or great bodily harm.

(1) A person is presumed to have held a reasonable fear of imminent peril of death or great bodily harm to himself or herself or another when using or threatening to use defensive force that is intended or likely to cause death or great bodily harm to another if:

(a) The person against whom the defensive force was used or threatened was in the process of unlawfully and forcefully entering, or had unlawfully and forcibly entered, a dwelling, residence, or occupied vehicle, or if that person had removed or was attempting to remove another against that person's will from the dwelling, residence, or occupied vehicle; and

(b) The person who uses or threatens to use defensive force knew or had reason to believe that an unlawful and forcible entry or unlawful and forcible act was occurring or had occurred.

(2) The presumption set forth in subsection (1) does not apply if:

(a) The person against whom the defensive force is used or threatened has the right to be in or is a lawful resident of the dwelling, residence, or vehicle, such as an owner, lessee, or titleholder, and there is not an injunction for protection from domestic violence or a written pretrial supervision order of no contact against that person. . . .

(3) A person who is attacked in his or her dwelling, residence, or vehicle has no duty to retreat and has the right to stand his or her ground and use or threaten to use force, including deadly force, if he or she uses or threatens to use force in accordance with s. 776.012(1) or (2) or s. 776.031(1) or (2) .

---

27. Adam Liptak, *15 States Expand Right to Shoot in Self-Defense,* N.Y. TIMES, August 7, 2006.
28. *Travon Martin Shooting Fast Facts,* CNN LIBRARY, February 11, 2015.
29. American Bar Association, National Task Force on Stand Your Ground Laws, *Final Report* (2015).

(4) A person who unlawfully and by force enters or attempts to enter a person's dwelling, residence, or occupied vehicle is presumed to be doing so with the intent to commit an unlawful act involving force or violence.

(5) As used in this section, the term:

(a) "Dwelling" means a building or conveyance of any kind, including any attached porch, whether the building or conveyance is temporary or permanent, mobile or immobile, which has a roof over it, including a tent, and is designed to be occupied by people lodging therein at night.

(b) "Residence" means a dwelling in which a person resides either temporarily or permanently or is visiting as an invited guest. . . .

## § 776.032. Immunity from criminal prosecution and civil action for justifiable use or threatened use of force.

(1) A person who uses or threatens to use force as permitted in . . . s. 776.013 . . . is justified in such conduct and is immune from criminal prosecution and civil action. . . .

### Bartlett v. State
Court of Appeal of Florida, First District
993 So. 2d 157 (2008)

BROWNING, C.J.

Laurie Lynn Bartlett (Appellant) was charged with the second-degree murder of her live-in boyfriend, Ernest Lamar, arising from the stabbing of the victim with a knife. Pursuant to Florida Rule of Criminal Procedure 3.201, the defense filed notice of intent to rely on self-defense based on the "battered-spouse syndrome." The jury found Appellant guilty of the lesser-included offense of manslaughter, and she was sentenced to ten years' incarceration, to be followed by five years' probation. Appellant argues that the trial court abused its discretion in allowing the primary detective in this case to testify that before he obtained a warrant for Appellant's arrest, he ruled out the possibility that the killing was done in self-defense. Concluding that it was error to allow the detective to opine to the jury that he had ruled out self-defense, and that the State has not met its burden under *State v. DiGuilio*, 491 So. 2d 1129, 1139 (Fla. 1986), to show there is no reasonable possibility that the error affected the verdict, we are constrained to reverse Appellant's conviction and sentence and remand for a new trial.

Investigator Mark Walton was the Bay County Sheriff's Department case agent responsible for investigating Appellant's case. Walton observed Appellant and briefly spoke to her at the trailer where the stabbing occurred. Appellant was crying and seemed to be upset but did not appear to have any physical injuries. A number of photos were taken of the stabbing scene, which were published without an objection. With Appellant's permission, Walton looked inside the trailer where Mr. Lamar's body was located. At the trial, Walton was shown photos of the crime scene. He identified a single stab wound in the victim's chest as the apparent cause of death. He explained certain details relating to the crime scene and the location of Mr. Lamar's body. The prosecutor asked Walton if he is the individual who had signed the complaint, and he answered "yes." Walton testified that he had written "murder" on the complaint as the crime in question. When questioned as to whether he had to rule out self-defense in signing the complaint, Walton answered "yes." When the State asked Walton why he had ruled out self-defense, Appellant's attorney objected because the question called for "opinion, speculation." The court sustained the objection. Next, the State approached the bench and argued as follows:

> The new self-defense law requires them to make that particular finding before they sign the complaint, they have to rule it out before, so it's part of the statutory requirement for him to be able to sign that complaint. He should be able to testify what went into his thinking process before he made that decision.

The trial judge changed his mind, stating:

> That is a requirement, then as long as you are going to ask him the facts that he relied on, not just as to his speculation, then the objection is overruled, so rephrase your question.

The State then asked Walton what facts and evidence he had observed that led him to rule out self-defense. He testified:

> When I first got to the scene I went in and looked at Mr. Lamar's body. The stab wound, which is located about here, you could look at it and see with the naked eye it was a very significant downward angle. The knife would have had to go in at an angle like this, just sort of common sense. Anybody looking at it would have been able to deduce that. The original explanation for the wound was that he had been walking down the hallway, he had tripped, and that the knife had gone into his [sic], that he had basically accidentally fallen on the knife. He was supposed to have been carrying a plate of pizza with the knife in one hand and that's when this was supposed to have occurred as he walked down the hallway. This would have meant that he would have taken the knife and gone at a severe downward angle into his own chest and that did not match that statement. So I had this to begin with, this story which was inconsistent with the facts at the scene. We started working from there and, in fact, later found the knife that was used to cut the pizza that night, which was a completely separate knife from the one that stabbed Mr. Lamar. There were no traces of the pizza on the knife that stabbed Mr. Lamar. Only his own blood up to the hilt of the knife.
>
> In my experience, um, with the numerous occasions that I have been called for fights involving weapons or any kind of altercation between people, someone who is simply trying to ward off an aggressor with a knife—

Defense counsel objected because the State was "going into war stories" that were not relevant. The objection was overruled. Walton continued testifying:

> [I]n my experience the knife is held out to ward someone off. This wouldn't explain this wound. This wound came from someone who brought the knife down into his chest with a great deal of force, making it not an accident. The inconsistent stories with the evidence, which continued up until the end to be inconsistent with the evidence. The evidence would show that a knife, that someone took a knife and used a great deal of force to enter it into Mr. Lamar's body at a downward angle and the absence of any kind of wounds that I observed on [Appellant] led me to believe that this was not a self-defense situation. In addition to the fact that we had two witnesses that advised in their statements—

After defense counsel objected on hearsay grounds, the prosecutor cut off any further statement by Walton on direct examination.

On cross-examination, Investigator Walton reiterated that he had observed a single stab wound in the upper chest area. He noted that at the autopsy, several "poke" wounds were described. Walton testified that these wounds indicated that someone had poked Mr. Lamar with some type of instrument that did not break the victim's skin. These poke wounds were not evident to Walton at the crime scene. Two knives were found at the site, one on the living-room coffee table and the other between the couch cushions. One of the knives had pizza sauce on it, and the other had what appeared to be blood on it. Walton acknowledged that in ruling out self-defense, he had assumed that Mr. Lamar was standing upright when he was stabbed. When he was asked whether the downward angle of the wound could be explained if Mr. Lamar, as the aggressor, had lunged or leaned forward toward Appellant, with a level extension of the knife, Walton testified he did not believe that was the case. . . .

Before the enactment of sections 776.032 and 776.013, Florida Statutes, in 2005, "a person was justified in using deadly force when the person was attacked in his or her home and 'reasonably believed deadly force was necessary to prevent "imminent death or great bodily harm to himself or herself or another or to prevent the imminent commission of a forcible felony."'" *State v. Heckman*, 993 So. 2d 1004, 2007 Fla. App. LEXIS 19316, 2007 WL 4270594, *2 (Fla. 2d DCA Dec. 7, 2007) (quoting Note, *Florida Legislation — The Controversy Over Florida's New "Stand Your Ground" Law — Fla. Stat. § 776.013 (2005)*, 33 Fla. St. U.L. Rev. 351, 354 (Fall 2005)). "The creation of section 776.013 eliminated the burden of proving that the defender had a reasonable belief that deadly force was necessary by providing a conclusive presumption of such." *Heckman*, 2007 Fla. App. LEXIS 19316, 2007 WL 4270594 at *2. . . .

In the testimony at issue, Appellant preserved the objections based on "opinion, speculation," relevancy, and hearsay grounds. Addressing the first ground for objection, Appellant argues on appeal that Investigator Walton's testimony that he had ruled out self-defense essentially foreclosed the jury from making a finding on this critical, ultimate issue: "It is for the lawyers to argue and the jury to decide whether Ms. Bartlett killed Lamar in self-defense. It was illegal evidence, properly characterized as lay opinion testimony because Walton was never qualified as an expert." Even though the defense did not express its objection this artfully in the trial court, we conclude that the "opinion" objection was sufficient to invoke section 90.701, *supra*. Appellant concedes that it was proper to allow Walton to testify regarding what he had seen at the crime site, including the victim's wounds. However, the jury did not need the investigator's opinion for the jury to determine whether Appellant had acted in self-defense. The error occurred in allowing Walton to opine to the jury that the nature of the stab wound led him to rule out self-defense. Appellant correctly asserts that the mere fact that section 776.032(2) required the investigator(s) to determine whether "there is probable cause that the force that was used was unlawful" does not automatically bootstrap this information into admissible evidence. On this record, the factual matter of what the investigator personally observed at the crime scene is quite distinct from his opinion regarding what had happened before his arrival, *i.e.*, the circumstances of the stabbing death. . . .

We note too that the jury could have held the opinions of the lead investigator in higher regard than the testimony of any other lay witness, thereby reinforcing the prejudice caused by Investigator Walton's conclusions. Also, the jury could have inferred that Walton knew certain information that had not been disclosed to the jury, leading the jury impermissibly to speculate as to matters outside the record. *See Martinez v. State*, 761 So. 2d 1074, 1080 (Fla. 2000) . . . we are constrained to REVERSE the conviction and sentence and REMAND for a new trial.

## IV. Consequences of the Criminalization of Domestic Violence

In a federally-funded experiment in Minnesota in 1984, police exercised three options in response to calls for help involving domestic violence—arrest, mediation or separation. Among those arrested, 10 percent repeated their violence; for those mandated to mediation, there was a 19 percent recidivism rate; and for the merely separated, the number rose to 24 percent. Although subsequent studies did not yield such dramatic results, within five years of the experiment, 84 percent of all police departments in the country with populations over 100,000 adopted pro-arrest policies in D.V. cases.[30]

Beyond the question of whether mandatory arrest works, is one of whether criminal prosecution and conviction has any impact on the future safety of a D.V. victim. The following study by two researchers from the University of Toledo found that criminal convictions reduced the likelihood of future battering.

---

30. Judith McFarlane, Pam Willson, Dorothy Lemmey & Ann Malecha, *Women Filing Assault Charges on an Intimate Partner: Criminal Justice Outcome and Future Violence Experienced*, 6 Violence Against Women 396, 398 (April 2000).

## Lois A. Ventura & Gabrielle Davis, *Domestic Violence: Court Case Conviction and Recidivism*

11(2) VIOLENCE AGAINST WOMEN 255, 261–62, 264–273 (2005)

. . . .

STUDY SITE

The site of the study was a Midwestern urban area with a population of approximately 300,000. The city police were legally required to conform to a preferred arrest policy. There was one police officer on a force of approximately 300 assigned to serve as the designated domestic violence liaison to the city prosecutor's office. That police officer was also assigned to track all felony domestic violence charges handled by the county prosecutor's office. Court advocates were available to assist domestic violence victims. One city prosecutor was designated to handle domestic violence cases exclusively, and other city prosecutors were assigned to work on domestic violence cases as part of their general caseloads. Evidence-based prosecution had been endorsed by city officials and city prosecutors, but it was not yet routinely practiced. Victim testimony was generally regarded to be necessary to achieve a conviction in domestic violence cases.

SAMPLE

This research sample was drawn from the population of a larger study. The larger study tracked data from all (N = 1,982) domestic violence charges filed in the municipal court from April 1, 2000 to March 31, 2001. Of the 1,982 cases tracked, 67.6% resulted in dismissal. Only 23.8% of the cases resulted in conviction, whereas 8.6% of the cases were still pending.

The current study selected random samples of convicted and dismissed cases from the complete data set for further data collection, recidivism tracking, and analysis. . . . The objective was for the two sample groups to jointly approximate 500 cases with no less than 200 cases in either group. . . . This random selection procedure resulted in a sample of 315 dismissed cases and 204 convicted cases, totaling 519 cases.

. . . .

Three hundred and fifteen of the domestic violence cases in the sample were dismissed. The reasons for the dismissal, as stated in the court records, were as follows: 220 (69.8%) victims failed to appear, for 89 (28.2%) no specific explanation was given, 4 (1.3%) victims recanted, and 2 (0.6%) were referred to anger management. Based on the court records, the most common reason a judge dismissed a domestic violence case was that at some point in the process, "the victim failed to appear." At the time of this study, the municipal court did not usually pursue domestic violence prosecutions unless the victims appeared in court and testified. Evidence-based prosecution was not the common practice for this jurisdiction at the time of the study.

Two hundred and four of the sample cases resulted in conviction. The types of convictions were as follows: 120 (58.8%) pleas to a lesser amended charge, 75 (36%)

pleas to the original charge (domestic violence misdemeanor), and 9 (4.4%) convictions at trial.

Women composed 452 (87.1%) of the domestic violence victims in the sample. Men were the accused batterers in 454 (87.5%) of the domestic violence cases. Two hundred and twenty-three (43.1%) of the batterers were Caucasian. Of the remaining 295 (56.9%) 272 were African American, 22 were Hispanic, and 1 was Asian. The average age of a batterer was 32.70 (SD=9.48). Two hundred and twenty (42.5%) of the batterers were younger than 30 years old. Only 143 (28.4%) of the batterers reported being married at the time of their arrest. Two hundred and eighty-nine (57.5%) of the batterers reported being employed. The average educational level for the sample of batterers was 11.86 years (SD=1.376). Most, 349 (69.5%), of the batterers reported completing high school. Slightly more than half of the batterers, 252 (54.1%) were represented by a public defender, and 214 (45.9%) were represented by private counsel.

. . . .

BATTERERS' CRIMINAL HISTORIES AND CASE DISPOSITIONS

Three hundred and eight (59.3%) of the batterers had a history of one or more prior arrests for domestic violence. In addition to domestic violence arrests, many batterers had other types of charges in their criminal histories. One hundred and thirty-seven (26.4%) had a history of one or more violent felony charges in their history, 358 (69%) had violent misdemeanor charges (including and in addition to domestic violence) in their history, and 462 (89%) had one or more nonviolent misdemeanor charges in their history. . . .

Violent felonies were the only types of offenses in which a statistically significant difference existed. Batterers whose domestic violence cases resulted in dismissals had, on average, more violent felony charges in their criminal history than did batterers whose domestic violence cases resulted in convictions. A longer history of serious violent charges was associated with an increased likelihood of having domestic violence cases dismissed.

COURT CASE OUTCOMES AND DOMESTIC VIOLENCE RECIDIVISM

In the year following the disposition of the domestic violence cases being tracked, 169 (32.6%) of the batterers were arrested on another domestic violence charge. . . .

One hundred eighty-nine (92.6%) of the 204 convicted offenders received one or more of the following sanctions: jail time, work release sentence, electronic monitoring, and probation. Fifteen (7.4%) of the 204 convicted batterers received only a suspended jail sentence or fines and court costs. The most common sanction for a convicted batterer was probation with all or part of a jail sentence suspended. Seventy-three (35.8%) of the 204 convicted batterers were sentenced to and actually spent some time in jail. The minimum length of jail time was 5 days, and the maximum was 180 days. The 73 batterers sentenced to jail served an average of less than 2 months (58.42 days) in jail.

. . . .

It is important to note that of the factors this study found to be associated with domestic violence recidivism, the only one that is the result of an external intervention rather than an offender characteristic is court case disposition. Conviction, similar to arrest, appears to have at least a modest deterrent influence on domestic violence recidivism.

This study's findings suggest that any deterrent value of conviction may be negated when the sanctions imposed are only suspended sentences or fines. Such sanctions may have little impact on the convicted batterer. If a convicted batterer receives only a fine or a suspended jail sentence without probation, the offender has no specific rules or treatment requirements to complete to avoid incarceration. There is no ongoing monitoring of the batterer. This lack of monitoring and lack of accountability may be interpreted by a batterer as the equivalent of receiving a free pass to do as he pleases.

. . . .

Most studies show the hours immediately after arrest or separation can be the most dangerous for a woman who is in an abusive relationship. Following arrest, a suspect must be brought before a judge, usually within as brief a period of time as possible, so that he may be informed of the charges against him, and whether the prosecution is seeking to hold him in jail pending trial.

At this time, which is known as the arraignment, the defendant will have an attorney present — either retained or appointed by the court — and will enter a plea of guilty or not guilty. Whether he remains in jail or is released is based on a number of factors; seriousness of the charges, the defendant's prior criminal history, the strength of the case, and the likelihood the defendant might flee the jurisdiction.

In the federal courts and in some states, the danger the defendant presents to his victim or others in the community is also a factor for consideration. And, in a minority of jurisdictions, if the crime charged concerns an incident of domestic violence, that in and of itself, is enough to require the court to set at least some bail to ensure the defendant will return and to protect the victim and the community from harm. Moreover, in some jurisdictions, apparently in deference to the factors present in lethality assessments, those charged with crimes of domestic violence are not eligible for release unless they have spent a so-called "cooling off" period in jail.

## A. Bail Considerations

A defendant charged with a federal crime of domestic violence, such as traveling across state lines to commit an act of domestic violence, or using a firearm in the commission of domestic violence, could end up remanded without any opportunity for release pending trial.

## 18 USCS § 3142 (2015) Release or detention of a defendant pending trial

(a) In general. Upon the appearance before a judicial officer of a person charged with an offense, the judicial officer shall issue an order that, pending trial, the person be—

(1) Released on personal recognizance or upon execution of an unsecured appearance bond, under subsection (b) of this section;

(2) released on a condition or combination of conditions under subsection (c) of this section;

(3) temporarily detained to permit revocation of conditional release, deportation, or exclusion under subsection (d) of this section; or

(4) detained under subsection (e) of this section.

. . . .

(e) Detention.

(1) If, after a hearing . . . the judicial officer finds that no condition or combination of conditions will reasonably assure the appearance of the person as required and the safety of any other person and the community, such judicial officer shall order the detention of the person before trial. . . .

## United States v. Rogers

United States Court of Appeals, Tenth Circuit

371 F.3d 1225 (2004)

Murphy, Circuit Judge. . . .

### II. BACKGROUND

Rogers was indicted by a federal grand jury for possession of a firearm while subject to a protection order, in violation of 18 U.S.C. § 922(g)(8), and possession of a firearm following a misdemeanor conviction of domestic violence, in violation of 18 U.S.C. § 922(g)(9). At the government's request, a detention hearing was held pursuant to 18 U.S.C. § 3142(f)(1). After reviewing the Pretrial Services Report and considering the arguments of the parties presented at the detention hearing, a magistrate judge ordered Rogers detained pending trial. The magistrate judge specifically found that there was "a serious risk that the defendant will endanger the safety of another person or the community" based on Rogers' outstanding domestic protective orders.

. . . .

Shortly thereafter, Rogers moved for further review of the detention order. In his motion, Rogers asserted that the district court had erred in holding a detention hearing in the first instance because none of the six conditions precedent set out in § 3142(f)(1) and (2) to the holding of such a hearing were present in this case. In response, the government asserted that the district court should adopt the reasoning of the Second Circuit in *United States v. Dillard*, 214 F.3d 88 (2d Cir. 2000) and conclude that each of the weapon-possession crimes set out in Rogers' indictment were "crimes of violence" pursuant to §3142(f)(1)(A). Concluding that *Dillard* was unpersuasive, the district court rejected the government's position that possessing a weapon while subject to a protection order or possessing a weapon following a misdemeanor conviction of domestic violence were "crimes of violence" for purposes of §3142(f)(1)(A). Instead, the district court relied on the D.C. Circuit's decision in *United States v. Singleton*, 337 U.S. App. D.C. 96, 182 F.3d 7 (D.C. Cir. 1999) for the proposition that weapon-possession crimes are not crimes of violence. In particular, the district court concluded that "'nothing inherent in a §922(g) offense creates a "substantial risk" of violence warranting pretrial detention.'" Dist. Ct. Order at 6 (quoting *Singleton*, 182 F.3d at 15).

## III. ANALYSIS

On appeal, the government contends the district court erred in concluding that possession of a firearm while subject to a domestic protection order and possession of a firearm following a misdemeanor conviction of domestic violence are not "crimes of violence" for purposes of the Bail Reform Act. "This is a question of the construction and applicability of a federal statute that we review de novo." *United States v. Cisneros*, 328 F.3d 610, 613 (10th Cir. 2003).

Section 3142(f)(1)(A) of the Bail Reform Act provides that a detention hearing shall be held "upon motion of the attorney for the Government" in a case that involves a "crime of violence." . . .

We likewise conclude that possession of a firearm while subject to a domestic protection order and possession of a firearm following a misdemeanor conviction of domestic violence both involve a substantial risk, resulting from the nature of the offense, that physical force may be used against the person or property of another. "It [is] undeniable that possession of a gun gives rise to *some* risk that the gun may be used in an act of violence. . . . Possession of a gun greatly increases one's ability to inflict harm on others and therefore involves some risk of violence." *Dillard*, 214 F.3d at 93. This is particularly true with regard to the crimes at issue in this case. A defendant whose background includes domestic violence which advances to either a criminal conviction or the imposition of a protection order has a demonstrated propensity for the use of physical violence against others. . . .

"The dangerousness of guns and their adaptability to use in violent crime is why Congress has prohibited their possession" by individuals subject to a domestic protection order or convicted of a misdemeanor crime of domestic violence. *See Dillard*, 214 F.3d at 93. "Without possession of guns such persons are far less capable of committing acts of violence." *Id.* Furthermore, the prohibitions set out in §922(g)(8) and (9) seek to protect society in general, and the intimate partners of persons with a background of domestic violence in particular, by reducing the risk of violence that may result from the possession of guns by persons with a proven propensity for violence. *Cf. id.* The possession of guns in violation of §922(g)(8) and (9) increases the risk that individuals subject to a domestic protection order or convicted of a misdemeanor crime of domestic violence may engage in violent acts. *Cf. id.* That risk results from the nature of the offense and is undoubtedly substantial. Cf. id.

This court recognizes that Rogers asserts such a conclusion is completely at odds with the decision of the D.C. Circuit in *United States v. Singleton*, 337 U.S. App. D.C. 96, 182 F.3d 7 (D.C. Cir. 1999) and the Seventh Circuit in *United States v. Lane*, 252 F.3d 905 (7th Cir. 2001). Contrary to Rogers' assertions, however, this conclusion is not completely inconsistent with *Singleton* and *Lane*. *Singleton*, *Lane*, and *Dillard* all involve the question whether 18 U.S.C. § 922(g)(1), possession of a firearm by a convicted felon, is a crime of violence under the definition set out in § 3156(a)(4)(B). *Lane*, 252 F.3d at 906; *Dillard*, 214 F.3d at 89; *Singleton*, 182 F.3d at 9–10. This case, on the other hand, focuses on whether § 922(g)(8) and (9) are crimes of violence. This differing context is key.

In concluding that § 922(g)(1) is not a crime of violence under the terms of the Bail Reform Act, both *Singleton* and *Lane* conclude, *inter alia,* that § 922(g)(1) is not a crime of violence because the mere possession of a firearm by a convicted felon does not create a substantial risk that physical force will be used against the property or person of another. *Lane*, 252 F.3d at 906–07; *Singleton*, 182 F.3d at 14–15. In reaching this conclusion, both courts noted that large numbers of felonies involve economic, regulatory, or other crimes that do not entail physical violence at all. *Lane*, 252 F.3d at 906; *Singleton*, 182 F.3d at 14–15. Thus, both courts noted that although there might be *some* increased chance of violence flowing from the possession of a weapon by a felon, that risk could simply not be classified as *substantial*. *Lane*, 252 F.3d at 906–07; *Singleton*, 182 F.3d at 14–15.

As set out at some length above, however, the underlying actions leading to the prohibitions in § 922(g)(8) and (9) necessarily involve actual violence or credible threats of violence. This distinction is key to this court's conclusion that possession of a firearm while subject to a domestic protection order and possession of a firearm following a misdemeanor conviction of domestic violence both involve a substantial risk, resulting from the nature of the offense, that physical force may be used against the person or property of another. This court recognizes that the calculus of risk and whether that risk results from the nature of the offense may well be different with regard to § 922(g)(1). We offer no opinion on that question, however, because it is not before the court. Instead, we limit our analysis to § 922(g)(8) and (9). Accordingly, read in context, this opinion is not necessarily inconsistent with the decisions in *Singleton* and *Lane*.

The more difficult question is whether the substantial risk of physical force created by the possession of a firearm in violation of § 922(g)(8) and (9) occurs in "the course of committing" the weapon-offense. As to this question, we conclude that the analysis of the court in *Dillard* is quite persuasive:

> If one uses a gun in an act of violence, that violence necessarily occurs during the possession of the gun. Whether the person has possession of the gun

only for a few seconds—the seconds during which it is used for violent purposes—or has possession for years, but uses it violently only for a few seconds, the violent use in either case necessarily occurs during—or in the course of—the possession. If that possession is illegal because the possessor is a [prohibited person] who is forbidden from possessing a gun, the violent use will inevitably have occurred in the course of the commission of the offense of illegal possession.

214 F.3d at 93–94; *see also id.* at 94 n.5 ("The offense proscribed by section 922(g)(1) is not the felon's 'acquisition' of a firearm; it is the felon's possession of a firearm. The offense continues to be committed as long as the felon continues to be in possession.")

Our conclusion that possession of a firearm in violation of §922(g)(8) and in violation of §922(g)(9) are crimes of violence for purposes of the Bail Reform Act is not contrary to this court's decision in *United States v. Lucio-Lucio*, 347 F.3d 1202 (10th Cir. 2003). The defendant in *Lucio-Lucio* pleaded guilty to illegally re-entering the United States in violation of 8 U.S.C. §1326. 347 F.3d at 1203. He had previously been deported twice. *Id.* The United States Sentencing Guidelines manual in effect at the time Lucio-Lucio was sentenced provided for an eight-level enhancement if the defendant had committed an "aggravated felony" prior to being deported. *See* U.S.S.G. §2L1.2 (2002). The applicable definition of "aggravated felony" included a "crime of violence" as defined by 18 U.S.C. §16. Section 16(b), in turn, defines crime of violence identically to the definition of crime of violence set out in 18 U.S.C. §3156(a)(4)(B). Prior to his deportation, Lucio-Lucio had been convicted of driving while intoxicated. 347 F.3d at 1203. Thus, the issue in *Lucio-Lucio* was whether felony driving while intoxicated was a "crime of violence."

In answering that question in the negative, *Lucio-Lucio* highlighted the requirement that the risk of physical force be used "in the course of committing the offense." *Id.* at 1205....

The crimes at issue in this case, violations of §922(g)(8) and (9), are much more like burglary, an example *Lucio-Lucio* identified as the "paradigmatic offense that falls under §16(b)," than they are like driving while intoxicated. According to *Lucio-Lucio*, in a burglary "what is risked is not just injury, but intentional violence committed by the offender in connection with the same general course of action. The burglar thus risks *committing* an act of violence in connection with the commission of the offense." 347 F.3d at 1206. *Lucio-Lucio* further explained that in the case of burglary, the defendant "is reckless with respect to the risk that *intentional* physical force will be used in the course of committing the offense." *Id.* at 1206. Similarly, a person who has previously committed domestic violence and thereafter possesses a weapon is reckless with respect to the risk that he might use the weapon as a means to inflict intentional physical force. That is, in the words of *Lucio-Lucio*, "A [person possessing a weapon in violation of §922(g)(8) or (9)] is reckless of the risk of committing an intentional act of violence; a drunk driver is reckless of the risk that he will accidently cause harm." *See id.* at 1206.

For those reasons set out above, this court concludes that § 922(g)(8) and (9) are crimes of violence for purposes of the Bail Reform Act. Thus, in contrast to the conclusion of the district court, the government was entitled to a detention hearing upon its request. 18 U.S.C. § 3142(f)(1)(A). Although the district court ultimately concluded that the government was not entitled to a detention hearing, it originally held such a hearing and found, by clear and convincing evidence, that Rogers presented a danger to another person or the community. Rogers does not challenge that finding on appeal, relying instead exclusively on the assertion that the government was never entitled to a hearing because the offenses at issue are not crimes of violence for purposes of the Bail Reform Act. Having rejected that contention, this court REVERSES the district court and REMANDS the matter to the district court to reinstate its original findings and to order Rogers detained pending trial pursuant to the terms of 18 U.S.C. §§ 3142 and 3143.

---

State laws establishing bail conditions vary widely. Some states have bail statutes specifically tailored to address domestic violence. These may include requiring a defendant to go before a judge prior to setting bail as opposed to permitting a defendant to be released directly from the police precinct or following an appearance before a magistrate; allowing a judge to consider a victim's safety in any bail decision or to set a minimum mandatory bail amount prior to release. Some states authorize a "cooling-off" period during which time a person charged with a crime of domestic violence cannot be released. Elsewhere, such as in New York, danger to the community or to a crime victim is not a statutory factor to be considered in setting bail, although there is a provision allowing judges to consider whether domestic abusers have violated orders of protection before making a bail determination. Selected bail statutes follow.

## NY Criminal Procedure Law § 510.30 (2016) Application for recognizance or bail; rules of law and criteria controlling determination

1. Determinations of applications for recognizance or bail are not in all cases discretionary but are subject to rules, prescribed in article five hundred thirty and other provisions of law relating to specific kinds of criminal actions and proceedings, providing (a) that in some circumstances such an application must as a matter of law be granted, (b) that in others it must as a matter of law be denied and the principal committed to or retained in the custody of the sheriff, and (c) that in others the granting or denial thereof is a matter of judicial discretion.

2. To the extent that the issuance of an order of recognizance or bail and the terms thereof are matters of discretion rather than of law, an application is determined on the basis of the following factors and criteria:

(a) With respect to any principal, the court must consider the kind and degree of control or restriction that is necessary to secure his court attendance when required. In determining that matter, the court must, on the basis of available information, consider and take into account:

(i) The principal's character, reputation, habits and mental condition;

(ii) His employment and financial resources; and

(iii) His family ties and the length of his residence if any in the community; and

(iv) His criminal record if any; and

(v) His record of previous adjudication as a juvenile delinquent, as retained pursuant to section 354.2 of the family court act, or, of pending cases where fingerprints are retained pursuant to section 306.1 of such act, or a youthful offender, if any; and

(vi) His previous record if any in responding to court appearances when required or with respect to flight to avoid criminal prosecution; and

(vii) Where the principal is charged with a crime or crimes against a member or members of the same family or household as that term is defined in subdivision one of section 530.11 of this title, the following factors:

(A) any violation by the principal of an order of protection issued by any court for the protection of a member or members of the same family or household as that term is defined in subdivision one of section 530.11 of this title, whether or not such order of protection is currently in effect; and

(B) the principal's history of use or possession of a firearm; and

(viii) If he is a defendant, the weight of the evidence against him in the pending criminal action and any other factor indicating probability or improbability of conviction; or, in the case of an application for bail or recognizance pending appeal, the merit or lack of merit of the appeal; and

(ix) If he is a defendant, the sentence which may be or has been imposed upon conviction. . . .

## 18 Pennsylvania Consolidated Statutes § 2711 (2016)
## Probable cause arrests in domestic violence cases.

. . . .

(c) *Bail.*

(1) A defendant arrested pursuant to this section shall be afforded a preliminary arraignment by the proper issuing authority without unnecessary delay. In no case shall the arresting officer release the defendant from custody rather than taking the defendant before the issuing authority.

(2) In determining whether to admit the defendant to bail, the issuing authority shall consider whether the defendant poses a threat of danger to the victim. If the issuing authority makes such a determination, it shall require as a condition of bail

that the defendant shall refrain from entering the residence or household of the victim and the victim's place of employment and shall refrain from committing any further criminal conduct against the victim and shall so notify the defendant thereof at the time the defendant is admitted to bail. Such condition shall expire at the time of the preliminary hearing or upon the entry or the denial of the protection of abuse order by the court, whichever occurs first. A violation of this condition may be punishable by the revocation of any form of pretrial release or the forfeiture of bail and the issuance of a bench warrant for the defendant's arrest or remanding him to custody or a modification of the terms of the bail. The defendant shall be provided a hearing on this matter....

## Suraji R. Wagage, *When the Consequences Are Life and Death: Pretrial Detention for Domestic Violence Offenders*

7 Drexel L. Rev. 195 (Winter 2015)

### INTRODUCTION

Jennifer Martel was twenty-seven years old, vivacious and out-going. "She didn't have a mean bone in her body," according to her uncle. She was studying to become a teacher while working at a grocery store to make ends meet. She shared an apartment in Waltham, Massachusetts with her boyfriend of five or six years, Jared Remy, and their four-year-old daughter. On Tuesday, August 13, 2013, Jennifer and Jared got into an argument. Jared slammed Jennifer's head against a mirror. Waltham police arrested him that night, and he was charged with assault and battery. The next day, Jared was released on his personal recognizance. The judge had issued Jennifer a temporary restraining order against Jared on Tuesday, but Jennifer declined to extend it on Wednesday in court. Jared's mother had importuned her not to seek a permanent restraining order, saying it would ruin his life. Two former girlfriends had taken out restraining orders against him in the past and he had been arrested and charged with beating a former girlfriend in 2005.

The next day, Thursday, Waltham police were again called to Jennifer's apartment. When they arrived, they found Jared covered in blood. Jennifer's body lay lifeless on the couple's patio. She had been stabbed to death. Neighbors allegedly saw Jared on top of her and attempted to intervene.

"Neighbors tried to help, we tried to stop it. We couldn't," said a witness. The muscular Jared, who had been fired from his job as a security guard at Fenway Park for steroid use, allegedly swung his knife at a neighbor trying to interfere. Jared and Jennifer's four-year-old daughter was home at the time. "I always used to say [Jennifer] was going to end up dead ... He was always hitting her," said her uncle. Jared would eventually plead guilty to Jennifer's murder, receiving a life sentence without the possibility of parole.

A Massachusetts law would have enabled prosecutors to hold Jared without bail for up to ninety days following a dangerousness hearing if the court concluded that no conditions of release could assure Jennifer's safety.[31] However, prosecutors opted against this route, most likely due to Jennifer's reluctance to seek a restraining order: "Officials with the Middlesex prosecutor's office . . . . [s]a[id] their conversations with Martel were a prominent factor in how they pursued charges against Remy."

However, in retrospect, the risk factors pointing toward a violent denouement in Jennifer's tragic case seem all too clear. Commentators observe that Jared's steroid abuse, grabbing Jennifer by the neck in the past, history of battering, and control over her social life are all signs of "increased risk" of homicidal violence. These factors are all noted in the empirically-derived *Danger Assessment* created by Jacquelyn Campbell, a leader in the study of violence against women, to determine the "likelihood of lethality or near lethality occurring in a case of intimate partner violence." Jennifer's family also reported that she was attempting to leave Jared in those final days. Jennifer sent emails to friends and family telling them she was frightened, and on the day of her death, she changed her Facebook relationship status from "In a Relationship" to "It's Complicated." Her mother stated, "I talked to her on Wednesday; she said she was planning her escape." If Jared had known Jennifer was planning to leave him, Campbell's assessment would have rated her risk as "severe." The system in place, even in a jurisdiction with a law allowing a domestic violence offender to be held without bail, largely leaves to the victim the discretion to decide whether a dangerousness hearing is pursued. And "victims tend to badly underestimate the risks," according to Campbell's findings.

Middlesex District Attorney Marian T. Ryan has opened an internal investigation into her office's decision not to seek a dangerousness hearing for Jared. Jared was no stranger to such a proceeding, having been held without bail for eighty-one days in 2005 following charges of assaulting and threatening a former girlfriend (including "threatening to kill her . . . cutting up her clothing and pictures, and punching and kicking her until she ran to a neighbor's house"). She survived. Unfortunately, the findings of the District Attorney's Office can do nothing to reverse Jennifer's fate. The Massachusetts legislature has already sprung into action on behalf of Jennifer and future similar cases by introducing a bill on April 1, 2014 that would strengthen domestic violence laws and require judges to undergo biannual training on domestic violence issues. This overhaul signals the willingness of lawmakers to take domestic violence crimes seriously and consider sweeping changes to existing policies in this area.

. . . .

## I. DOMESTIC VIOLENCE PREVALENCE AND INTERVENTIONS

### A. Domestic Violence Statistics

Statistics on domestic violence underscore the prevalence of this societal issue and its need for legal attention. . . .

---

31. [n22] *See* Mass. Guidelines for Judicial Practice: Abuse Prevention Proceedings § 8:06 (2014).

Intimate partner homicide has been declining for the past two decades, but it continues to be a significant concern. Though there has been a decrease in marital homicide, there has been an increase in the rate of unmarried males killing their partners, as in the case of Jennifer Martel. The majority of female homicide victims are killed by men with whom they have been romantically involved. The decline in overall intimate partner homicide rates has been attributed to a decline in spousal homicide and female-perpetrated homicides. Domestic violence research indicates two large sex differences: in cases of women killing an intimate partner, the woman is likely to have been the victim of abuse, while this is uncommon in cases of men killing their partner. Also, women are far more likely to incur serious bodily injury from intimate violence than men, though surveys indicate that women and men are equally likely to be physically aggressive toward their partners. The U.S. Department of Justice's National Crime Victimization Survey found that 72% of the victims of intimate partner homicide and 85% of the victims of non-lethal intimate partner violence were women. Researchers posit that declining rates of intimate partner homicide are due to: a decline in domesticity (increase in divorce rates and decrease in marriage rates) leading to decreased exposure to violence by partners; the increasing economic status of women leading to reduced financial dependence on men; and domestic violence interventions and resources.

B. *Domestic Violence Laws and Interventions*

. . . .

*1. Mandatory arrest*

Mandatory arrest policies require police to arrest a suspect if there is probable cause to believe the suspect committed a domestic violence offense. Prior to the advent of these policies, police were reluctant to arrest for domestic violence offenses. Statutes in most jurisdictions enabled police to arrest for a misdemeanor offense only if the offense had been committed in the officer's presence or if an arrest warrant was issued, which gave police "de facto legal backing to do nothing" in domestic violence cases. Police also continued to favor mediation, trying to "cool down" violent offenders and leave them at the scene rather than removing them. Mediation techniques treated domestic violence as a "family dispute" where both parties were at fault. Furthermore, officers commonly believed that the victims likely provoked the abuse or should not be assisted if they were unwilling to seek legal recourse against the abusers. As one police chief explained, "if the woman didn't do anything after she was hit, then why should we do anything[?]"

Mandatory arrest policies were developed to combat these views, particularly on the heels of several highly publicized lawsuits against police for egregious cases of non-intervention. These policies have been moderately successful in reducing the recidivism of domestic violence offenders. Randomized trials studying the efficacy of mandatory domestic violence interventions are scarce due to the difficulty of (and potential equal protection concerns involved with) randomly assigning defendants to different outcomes. The studies that do exist are typically conducted under the aegis of the National Institute of Justice (NIJ). An early study funded by the NIJ to determine the efficacy of mandatory arrest policies in reducing recidivism was promising. This landmark study randomly assigned defendants in domestic violence cases in Minneapolis to mandatory arrest followed by at least one night in jail, physical separation for eight hours, or police mediation, and discovered that mandatory arrest resulted in significantly lower recidivism rates over the following six months.

Former U.S. Attorney General William French Smith cited the results of this study when he recommended that mandatory arrest be implemented as the standard response in domestic violence cases. However, follow-up replication studies in six more cities funded by the NIJ had mixed results. These studies uncovered a potential interaction effect at play wherein arrest led to a deterrent effect in employed or married offenders but had the opposite effect on unemployed or unmarried offenders. Researchers theorized that arrest could deter offenders who were likely to be stigmatized by the arrest, but would be less likely to deter offenders who were unlikely to be stigmatized by arrest. However, these studies are susceptible to the criticism that they did not successfully replicate the original study because the arrested abuser did not necessarily have to spend a night in jail.

Regardless of the efficacy of mandatory arrest policies in deterring recidivism, such policies compelled police to take domestic violence seriously, and helped to shape public perception of domestic violence as a crime and not a private dispute. These policies also provide ancillary benefits, such as ensuring more equitable police action across the races and socioeconomic statuses of offenders. However, one drawback to mandatory arrest policies is victim arrest, wherein the victim is arrested either as a result of the same event that caused the arrest of the abuser (dual arrest), or as a result of a false or exaggerated complaint filed by the abuser (retaliatory arrest). These policies have also been criticized for limiting police discretion; however, police still have discretion to determine whether probable cause exists to believe a domestic violence offense has occurred.

*2. No-drop prosecution*

No-drop prosecution policies require prosecutors to pursue domestic violence cases regardless of the victim's unwillingness to proceed. Victims' desire not to press charges or testify, stemming from fear of or attachment to their abusers, had frequently hindered prosecution. Prosecutors, however, can use alternative evidence such as photographs, physical evidence, medical reports, victim statements, and 911 tapes when a victim is unwilling to testify. Studies of recidivism as a function of prosecution policy have found mixed results. There has only been one randomized study, funded by the NIJ, that measured the efficacy of no-drop prosecution in reducing recidivism.

This study found that women who had the option to drop the charges, but continued regardless, had the lowest rate of re-abuse, while women who had the option to drop the charges, and did so, had the highest rate of re-abuse (higher than women with no-drop charges). However, for safety reasons, this study excluded many important groups of defendants: those with previous records of violence against the victim, those with criminal histories of violence, and those who posed serious threats of imminent danger. Therefore, the results may not reflect the efficacy of no-drop prosecution policies with respect to all domestic violence defendants.

Correlational studies have been conducted on rearrest likelihood depending on various prosecutorial outcomes, such as *nolle prosequi*, dismissals, probation with treatment, and jail sentences, and have reached conflicting conclusions. Notably, these studies did not compare no-drop prosecution to drop-permitted prosecution.

. . . .

*3. Mandatory medical reporting*

Some states have called for policies that would require routine screening of women for intimate partner violence during emergency room visits. Health care providers may be statutorily required to report such domestic violence to the police. Generally, studies show that the majority of women—in some studies, the great majority of women—support screening for domestic violence during hospital visits and mandatory reporting. Women's support varies by whether they have been (or are being) abused. Abused women are typically less likely to support mandatory reporting than non-abused women, with exceptions.

The benefits of such policies include facilitating the prosecution of abusers and encouraging health care personnel to identify domestic violence, thereby helping to prevent serious domestic violence assaults and homicides. Medical screening could also furnish victims with documentation for future court cases and potential referrals to community resources for education on prevention, safety planning, and options for leaving. Drawbacks include potential retaliator violence by perpetrators, reducing patients' autonomy, and compromising doctor-patient confidentiality.

*4. GPS monitoring*

Many states have statutes allowing judges to order that the defendant be monitored by a global positioning system (GPS) as a condition of bail, and a majority of states either have passed, or are considering, statutes that require pre-trial GPS monitoring in cases of domestic violence. Use of a GPS device is often limited to cases in which the defendant has violated a protection order, committed a crime of domestic violence, or has been deemed "high-risk." Defendants may be statutorily required to pay the cost of GPS monitoring, estimated at around ten dollars per day. Also, GPS systems can be designed to only transmit information about the defendant's location when a protective order violation has taken place, thereby mitigating Fourth Amendment privacy concerns. GPS monitoring is often "bilateral," monitoring both offenders and their victims in order to ensure victim safety. Research shows that GPS monitoring is effective at reducing offenders' likelihood of reoffending, both in the short and long term. GPS monitoring has been lauded for allowing victims to re-enter society by enabling them to remain in their homes instead of relocating to shelters and to perform daily tasks without fear due to mobile monitoring. Potential disadvantages reported by victims include worries of over-dependence on the monitoring, psychological debilitation when the monitors are removed, and fear caused by false alarms.

## 5. Bail statutes

Bail statutes can serve as a domestic violence intervention in two main ways: the defendant may be released on conditional bail, or the bail statute may authorize pretrial detention (denial of bail). The legal system has not widely considered denial of bail as a source of domestic violence intervention, but this approach covers a potentially lethal gap in the coverage left by other interventions. A domestic violence offender may be arrested and prosecuted, but in the meantime he or she may be set free to seek out and attack the victim; to "finish[] the job," as Jennifer Martel's mother said. Conditional bail does not rectify this danger because a determined defendant will not be deterred by mere judicial stipulations that he or she should stay away from the victim. Assaults and intimate partner homicides that take place while a defendant is under a protection order illustrate this grim reality. Protective orders have been shown to reduce the risk of violence but do not eliminate it by any means, and can sometimes spur retaliatory violence.

Bail statutes that authorize denial of bail or pretrial detention could prevent such tragedies, and such statutes carry congressional and Supreme Court approval. Denial of bail on the basis of future dangerousness was enabled in the federal system by the Bail Reform Act of 1984: "If, after a hearing ... the judicial officer finds that no condition or combination of conditions will reasonably assure the appearance of the person as required and the safety of any other person and the community, such judicial officer shall order the detention of the person before trial." The statute requires a clear and convincing standard of proof to hold a defendant on the basis of future dangerousness. A detention hearing must be held in a case involving certain offenses. Such offenses include: crimes of violence that carry a maximum sentence of life imprisonment or death, controlled substance offenses for which the maximum term of imprisonment is ten years or more, a felony if the defendant has been convicted of two or more of the preceding offenses, or any felony involving a minor victim or possession of a dangerous weapon. The First, Third, and Fifth Circuits have determined that defendants may not be detained unless their charges fit one of the above four categories. However, since most domestic violence cases are brought at the state, not federal, level, these policies are not dispositive. Therefore, the Bail Reform Act of 1984 serves to open the door to pretrial detention based on future dangerousness in the context of domestic violence.

The Bail Reform Act of 1984 followed the Bail Reform Act of 1966, which attempted to restrict "needless [] ... det[ention]" of defendants prior to trial. The Bail Reform Act of 1966 even moved "towards eliminating 'bail' from the glossary of criminal procedure" by creating a "presumption" of non-monetary release before trial. This was followed in 1969 by President Nixon's exhortation for legislation to "permit 'temporary pretrial detention' of criminal defendants whose 'pretrial release presents a clear danger to the community.'"

The denial of bail potentially implicates three main constitutional issues: violation of the Eighth Amendment, violation of the presumption of innocence, and violation of due process. The Eighth Amendment guarantees that "[e]xcessive bail shall not be required, nor excessive fines imposed, nor cruel and unusual punishments inflicted." The presumption of innocence has been held to follow from the Fifth, Sixth, and Fourteenth Amendments. The right to due process guarantees that "no person shall... be deprived of life, liberty, or property, without due process of law."

The United States Supreme Court considered the constitutionality of committing defendants to pretrial detention on the basis of future dangerousness under the Bail Reform Act of 1984 in *United States v. Salerno*.[32] The Court determined that the Bail Reform Act was constitutional. In an opinion written by Chief Justice Rehnquist, the Court held that the Bail Reform Act did not violate substantive or procedural due process, did not constitute "impermissible punishment before trial," and did not violate the Eighth Amendment. The Act did not violate the right to due process because it had a "legitimate and compelling... purpose" to prevent danger and offered procedural protections. Procedural protections included reserving detention for serious crimes, ensuring a prompt hearing, and limiting the length of detention. The Court considered the Act stringent enough to overcome the argument that it could lead to unjust incapacitation of those "merely suspected" of committing crimes because it required not only a finding of probable cause to believe the crime had been committed by the defendant, but also a "full-blown adversary hearing" with a clear and convincing evidentiary standard before the defendant could be detained.

The Court also indicated that pretrial detention did not violate the Eighth Amendment's ban on "cruel and unusual punishments" because it was not conceived by Congress as a punishment for dangerous individuals, but as a "potential solution to a pressing societal problem." The Bail Reform Act's goal was therefore not punitive but regulatory, and "preventing danger to the community is a legitimate regulatory goal." The Court backed this reasoning with precedents in which it had "repeatedly" held that such a regulatory interest in safety may outweigh an individual's liberty interest. Therefore, the Supreme Court found pretrial detention of dangerous individuals constitutionally justified, a decision substantiated by a long line of precedents.

The Supreme Court of Massachusetts, one of the only states with a specific pretrial detention statute for domestic violence offenders, considered the constitutionality of this procedure in reference to domestic violence in *Mendonza v. Commonwealth* and *Commonwealth v. Callender*.[33] Mendonza, while being served by police with a

---

32. [n123] 481 U.S. 739 (1987).
33. [n133] 673 N.E.2d 22 (Mass. 1996) (both cases are combined in one opinion). Due to the rarity of pretrial detention of more than a few days for domestic violence offenses, no other cases that specifically consider the constitutionality of this intervention have been found. *See also* State v. Jones, 130 So. 3d 1 (La. Ct. App. 2013) (holding that pretrial detention for domestic violence does not trigger the attachment of jeopardy, but "pretrial detention" in this case only constituted holding the defendant for six hours); State v. Malette, 509 S.E.2d 776 (N.C. 1999) (holding that North Carolina's statute on bail and pretrial release for individuals accused of domestic violence offenses was constitutional as applied to the defendant (North Carolina does not have a policy of pretrial detention as

protection order obtained by his wife which would require him to move out of the family home, barricaded himself in the bedroom with gasoline and threatened to burn the house down. Callender was arrested for banging on the door of an apartment he was forbidden to visit, while on probation for three violations of protective orders. In both cases, the Commonwealth moved for a dangerousness hearing. The Supreme Court of Massachusetts determined that pretrial detention on the grounds of dangerousness for domestic violence offenses did not offend substantive due process rights or equal protection, following the precedent and reasoning of *Salerno*. The court observed that "[t]he Federal statute followed extensive legislative fact-finding that tended to show that a surprising number of crimes are committed by persons awaiting trial." The court further noted that the lengthy periods of time between arrest and conclusion of a trial demonstrate the need for some preliminary means for the government to "incapacitat[e] persons who pose a particular danger to the public." The necessity for probable cause to believe the person had committed a serious crime and the conclusion of the trial as an "inevitable end point to the State's preventive authority" provide protections for the defendant. Therefore, the United States Supreme Court and the Supreme Court of Massachusetts have given their imprimatur to pretrial detention on the basis of future dangerousness and pretrial detention for domestic violence offenders on the basis of future dangerousness respectively.

a. Bail statutes for domestic violence offenses nationwide

Bail statutes vary widely across the United States. Some states have a specific provision or provisions for bail in domestic violence (or "family violence") cases, and some do not. States with a specific domestic violence provision fall into three categories. In the first and most common type, there is a presumption of conditional bail (not pretrial detention), and the defendant is required to go before a judge or magistrate. Conditions of bail may include: avoiding the alleged victim's home, school, and place of employment; visitation limitations with any children; refraining from damaging specifically identified property and from assaulting the alleged victim; abstaining from consumption of alcohol; and even GPS monitoring. Twenty-two states have provisions of this nature. Provisions in four of these states suggest bail denial or revocation for repeat domestic violence offenders or for violations of conditions of protective orders or bail.

In the second type of domestic violence bail provision, however, the statute explicitly suggests pretrial detention (denial of bail) for domestic violence offenses without reference to repeat offenses. Five states have provisions of this nature. Some of these provisions list various serious offenses that may qualify for denial of bail and include

---

considered herein, but allows holding a defendant for up to forty-eight hours pending a bail hearing)); State v. Thompson, 508 S.E.2d 277 (N.C. 1998) (holding that North Carolina's statute allowing a domestic violence offender to be held for up to forty-eight hours did not facially violate substantive due process, procedural due process, or double jeopardy, but that the statute as applied to the defendant violated procedural due process because the magistrate scheduled the bail hearing for forty-eight hours after the defendant's commitment even though there were judges available earlier).

domestic violence among the list, while others, including Massachusetts and New Hampshire, have several statutes or even chapters devoted to bail for domestic violence offenses alone. . . .

In the third type of domestic violence bail provision, the defendant need not go before a judge or can avoid it if certain conditions are met, and denial of bail is not mentioned. Seven states have provisions of this nature. In California, for example, the defendant need not go before a judge if the "arresting officer determines that there is not a reasonable likelihood that the offense will continue." This statute directs each city and county to "develop a protocol to assist officers to determine when arrest and release is appropriate." In these states, the police officer may set bail and impose conditions on release.

States without a specific domestic violence provision for bail follow one of two approaches. In the first, denial of bail is not mentioned and the defendant is often not required to go before a judge. Bail may be assigned by a law enforcement officer or bail commissioner based upon a bail schedule stipulating monetary amounts for different offenses. If the defendant must go before a judge, the judge has discretion to set conditions of the release that will ensure the defendant's appearance in court. Nine states have provisions of this nature.

In the second approach, statutes provide for pretrial detention or denial of bail for serious offenses, though domestic violence offenses are not mentioned specifically. Seven states have provisions of this nature. In these states, denial of bail may only be available if serious aggravating factors are present. In states where pretrial detention for serious offenses is possible but its application to domestic violence offenses is not statutorily authorized, judges may be unlikely to extend the statute to domestic violence cases. However, such statutes may serve as the foundation for extension to domestic violence offenses.

In total, nine states reference denial of bail for domestic violence offenses, either initially or after repeat offenses.

## II. BAIL STATUTES ARE A CRITICAL FOCAL POINT FOR DOMESTIC VIOLENCE INTERVENTIONS

An analysis of the practical utility of pretrial detention in deterring domestic violence is complicated by the fact that there is no empirical research on this topic given the rarity of pretrial detention statutes for domestic violence offenders. However, the importance of this intervention can be imputed from existing research on mandatory arrest and no-drop prosecution policies and the danger of assault following victims' attempted separation from their abusers.

*A. The Effects of Mandatory Arrest Policies and No-Drop Prosecution Extended to Pretrial Detention*

As discussed in Part I, research on violence recidivism rates following use of mandatory arrest or no-drop prosecution is promising, if qualified. Contrary to concerns that violence could increase following mandatory state intervention, violence tended to decrease. This result may be extended to pretrial detention in that reducing the defendant's exposure to the victim reduces violence.

However, as noted, mandatory arrest and prosecution policies may spur retaliatory effects. In this regard, pretrial detention would carry the additional benefit of physically preventing a domestic violence offender from accessing his or her intended victim. Empirical research is required to determine whether pretrial detention could spur a retaliatory effect upon the defendant's release for reasons distinct from mandatory arrest or no-drop prosecution policies, but small sample sizes may impede such research.

*B. Pivotal Juncture Covered by Bail Statutes: Recognition of the Phenomenon of Separation Assault*

Pretrial detention also covers a critical gap left by mandatory arrest and no-drop prosecution policies: the period between arrest and disposition, which is often lengthy. As observed by the Court in *Salerno*, the risk of offenders committing dangerous acts post-arrest and pre-sentencing is high, as determined by congressional findings. These findings indicated that anywhere from one in six to one in four defendants were rearrested during the pretrial period, a third of whom were rearrested more than once.

This risk is particularly relevant to domestic violence offenses, in which research has consistently shown that the period of separation from one's abuser is the most dangerous. The need for pretrial detention may commonly arise in such circumstances, when the victim is attempting to leave his or her abuser, as Jennifer Martel was — according to her family — attempting to leave Jared Remy when she was murdered. . . .

Research on separation assault belies past common assumptions that victims who did not leave their abusive mates were masochists who had a "conscious or unconscious need for pain and punishment." Rather, in addition to psychological and sociological factors (learned helplessness, victim blaming, institutional sexism, patriarchal norms), research shows that victims in abusive relationships have a compelling reason not to leave their abusive partners: explicit or implicit and well-founded threats of violence. Bail statute reform has the potential to alter this calculus in the victim's favor by providing protection not found in other domestic violence interventions. . . .

Mandatory arrest and no-drop prosecution policies have made great strides in converting domestic violence from a private affair in which the state feared to intrude into a public matter of societal concern. The further step of categorizing domestic abuse as a serious offense that may require pretrial detention will push the sociological conception of abuse still further by legitimizing its seriousness as a crime on par with those singled out for pretrial detention.

. . . .

*E. Means of Encouraging Enactment of Statutes*

Domestic violence pretrial detention statutes could be federally encouraged via the Violence Against Women Act ("VAWA"). VAWA, as passed in 1994 and reauthorized in 2013, comprehensively reformed legal strategies surrounding crimes of gendered violence. It strengthened federal penalties for certain offenses and, through extensive grants, supported training of police officers, prosecutors, and judges to increase understanding of gendered offenses. VAWA grants could be used to incentivize statutes that enable pretrial detention of domestic violence offenders and to educate legal actors as to the importance of such policies.

## CONCLUSION

Domestic violence and intimate partner homicide continue to be serious concerns that are insufficiently addressed by current policies of mandatory arrest, no-drop prosecution, and mandatory medical reporting. Pretrial detention of domestic violence offenders could serve as a potent intervention that protects victims during the period of separation from an abusive partner when such protection is most needed. . . . Such a system would minimize infringement of the defendant's constitutional rights with multiple safeguards. If pretrial detention hearings are mandatory when a certain number of risk factors are met, tragedies like Jennifer Martel's case could be prevented. The outlook for men and women like Jennifer is optimistic: legislators are taking note of the need to reform domestic violence laws, suggesting overhauls of existing systems. The proposals made herein warrant consideration as legislators move forward with domestic violence law reform, as pretrial detention and mandatory detention hearings could provide protection that domestic violence victims lack under current policies.

## *Notes and Questions*

- **HIGH TECHNOLOGY**

In 1993, the National Criminal Justice Association (NCJA) proposed a model anti-stalking statute for states to adopt. But many of the new technologies used by stalkers did not exist at the time. Given that some of these high-tech stalking mechanisms allow for long-distance stalking, the law as drafted, which used terms like "maintaining a visual or physical proximity to a person" has become obsolete. "The challenge is to enact laws that address stalking perpetuated through all of the currently known technologies, as well as through future technologies not yet developed or available to stalkers." *See* National Center for Victims of Crime, *The Model Stalking Code Revisited: Responding to the New Realities of Stalking*, June, 2007 at 16.

Meanwhile, cell phone technology has become so sophisticated that stealth applications are available that monitor the whereabouts of their users without their knowledge—a boon to stalkers everywhere. Editorial: *Sneaky Apps That Track Cell Phones*, N.Y. TIMES. Dec. 23, 2012 Sen. Al Franken, a Minnesota Democrat, reintroduced in November 2015 Senate Bill 2270, the Location Anti-Tracker Act, which would require the permission of cellphone users before companies could sell or share their location information. As of early 2016, the bill had been referred to the Senate Judiciary Committee for further study. How might you craft a law to encompass technologies, known and not yet invented?

There are now laws against so-called "revenge-porn" in 34 states and the District of Columbia. For a full listing, see https://www.cybercivilrights.org/revenge-porn-laws, accessed October 9, 2016. One example from Arizona, Arizona Revised Stat. 13-1425, *Unlawful distribution of images depicting nudity or sexual activities*, makes it unlawful to "intentionally disclose an image of another person who is identifiable from the image itself or from information displayed in connection with the image" if the person depicted is either nude or engaged in a specific sexual activity; if the depicted person had a reasonable expectation of privacy (the mere fact the depicted person sent the image to another by means of an electronic devise does not "remove the person's reasonable expectation of privacy for that image"); and if the image was disclosed with the intent to "harm, harass, intimidate or coerce the depicted person."

- **STRANGULATION**

In spite of stronger laws, strangulation remains a tough charge for prosecutors to prove. According to an article in the New York Times, although thousands of defendants have been charged under the state's strangulation law that went into effect in 2010, as of three years later, fewer than 20 went to trial. In addition, according to the article, prosecutors, police and medical personnel had not been fully trained on how to gather evidence to support the charge insofar as asking the right questions of victims and recognizing the tell-tale signs of strangulation such as broken blood vessels in the eye causing redness, known as "petechaiae." Julie Besonen, *A New Crime, But Convictions Are Elusive; Choking Someone is Now a Felony in New York City, but Evidence Can Be Ambiguous,* N.Y. TIMES, February 17, 2013. Go through each of the headings in this chapter describing the various kinds of crimes that are considered domestic violence and ask yourself what evidence would you need to support a criminal conviction for each.

- **BAIL**

Advocates for victims of domestic violence and sexual assault have long called for bail statutes that allow judges to take into account victim safety at the time of making initial bail determinations following arrest. In 2008, California passed Proposition 9, or Marsy's Law, named for Marsalee Nicholas who was stalked and murdered by an ex-boyfriend in 1983. Shortly thereafter, her family saw the accused murderer at a local grocery store, unaware he had been released on bail. *About Marsy's Law: Justice with Compassion,* https://marsyslaw.us/about-marsys-law, accessed March 22, 2017. The law requires judges to consider when setting bail both victims' safety and protection of the public. Cal. Const. Art.1, Sec. 28(b).

But in recent years, the trend has gone in the opposition direction with defense lawyers, criminal justice reformers, as well as some politicians and courts expressing concern about the size of the pre-trial bail population in the United States and the impact setting bail has on the poor and minority population. As many as 750,000 persons sit in local jails in this country—60 percent of them awaiting trial. Nick Pinto, *The Bail Trap,* N.Y. TIMES MAGAZINE, August 13, 2015. The New York Center for Court Innovation noted in 2015: "The use of money bail places a significant burden on indigent defendants and their families." Elise White, et al., *Navigating the Bail Payment System in New York City: Findings and Recommendations* 1, December 2015. The CCI report found that in 2014, there were 48,816 cases in criminal court in which bail was set at initial arraignments, one half of which could not immediately post bail. *Id.,* at 2.

Bail reform measures in New Jersey took effect on January 1, 2017, and allow both sides in this debate to declare victory. On the one hand, changes in the law permit courts to order preventive detention for the most dangerous, violent defendants awaiting trial. At the same time, cash bail for low level offenders has been replaced with a "risk-based" formula that would in most instances allow low-risk, non-violent defendants to remain free without posting cash bail pending trial. New Jersey's bail reform law also mandates faster trial, which would be achieved by imposing deadlines on police and prosecutors to move cases more swiftly to completion. *Attorney General Law Enforcement Directive No. 2016-6;* 8-10, www.nj.gov/oag/dcj/agguide/directives/2016-6_Law-Enforcement.pdf, accessed March 21, 2017. This puts New Jersey in line with the vast majority of states that allow judges to consider public safety when determining whether to set bail on a person accused of a crime. James C. McKinley Jr., *Released Man's Murder Charge Stokes a Bail Debate,* N.Y. TIMES, March 22, 2017.

Chapter 4

# Evidentiary Issues in Domestic Violence Cases

> **CONSIDER AS YOU READ ABOUT EVIDENCE**
> 1. The impact of the *Crawford, Davis and Giles* decisions on domestic violence prosecutions
> 2. What constitutes "testimonial" evidence
> 3. How to determine evidence of propensity vs. evidence of motive, intent, absence of mistake and common scheme or plan in domestic violence cases
> 4. The impact on due process of allowing children to testify via videotape, closed circuit TV or in the presence of service animals

The trial of a criminal domestic violence case moves like any other. The prosecutor, who bears the burden of proof beyond a reasonable doubt, usually places in evidence testimony of the victim, any eyewitnesses to the crime, copies of calls to 911, photographs of the victim's injuries, testimony of police officers who observed those injuries, hospital records and admissions to police by the defendant. The defense attorney, with no burden of proof, will sometimes attempt to show the incident was more of a marital spat in which the victim got the worst of it. Or, that she has a motive to lie because the accused is not paying child support, or has left her for another woman.

The challenge for prosecutors comes when the victims are dead or refuse to testify against their abusers. Recognizing that pursuing criminal trials in domestic violence cases without the assistance of the survivors—perhaps over their vehement objections and recantations—is controversial, this chapter focuses not on the controversy, but on the evidentiary problems this presents for litigators and the courts, particularly in the light of the past decade of decisions of the United States Supreme Court.[1]

Beginning in the 1990s, district attorneys began so-called "evidence based," or "victimless prosecutions." Thus, even if a victim refused to testify, the prosecutor

---

1. The emphasis in this chapter will be on evidentiary issues arising in criminal trials in the state and federal courts. However, many of the issues addressed are relevant to the trial of domestic violence cases in the civil and family courts as well.

would introduce her frantic call to the 911 operator as a "present sense impression," her initial statement to police as an "excited utterance," and any comment she made to a doctor as a "statement for the purpose of obtaining medical treatment." This evidence was admissible under the rubric of "firmly rooted" exceptions to the rule against hearsay or because it bore "particularized guarantees of trustworthiness" as articulated by the United States Supreme Court in *Ohio v. Roberts*, 448 U.S. 56 (1980). But these prosecutions appeared ready to grind to a dead halt when the Supreme Court overturned *Roberts* in *Crawford v. Washington*, 541 U.S. 36 (2004).

The Court in *Crawford* held that interrogations of witnesses by police could not be used at trial unless the persons questioned were available for cross-examination because their statements were "testimonial," and the use of them at a criminal trial violated the Confrontation Clause of the United States Constitution. Unfortunately, the Court provided no guidance to the lower courts about how to evaluate which statements were "testimonial." The ruling sent a chill through district attorneys' offices, provided hope to defense lawyers and generated confusion among judges who had more questions than answers about how to apply the new rule in domestic violence trials. Eventually, the Court was called upon to clarify.

## I. *Crawford* and the Fate of Victimless Prosecutions

### Crawford v. Washington
United States Supreme Court
541 U.S. 36 (2004)

SCALIA, J., delivered the opinion of the Court, in which STEVENS, KENNEDY, SOUTER, THOMAS, GINSBURG, and BREYER, JJ., joined. REHNQUIST, C.J., filed an opinion concurring in the judgment, in which O'CONNOR, J., joined.

Petitioner Michael Crawford stabbed a man who allegedly tried to rape his wife, Sylvia. At his trial, the State played for the jury Sylvia's tape-recorded statement to the police describing the stabbing, even though he had no opportunity for cross-examination. The Washington Supreme Court upheld petitioner's conviction after determining that Sylvia's statement was reliable. The question presented is whether this procedure complied with the Sixth Amendment's guarantee that, "[i]n all criminal prosecutions, the accused shall enjoy the right ... to be confronted with the witnesses against him."

I

On August 5, 1999, Kenneth Lee was stabbed at his apartment. Police arrested petitioner later that night. After giving petitioner and his wife *Miranda* warnings, detectives interrogated each of them twice. Petitioner eventually confessed that he and Sylvia had gone in search of Lee because he was upset over an earlier incident in which Lee had tried to rape her. The two had found Lee at his apartment, and a fight ensued in which Lee was stabbed in the torso and petitioner's hand was cut. . . . Sylvia generally corroborated petitioner's story about the events leading up to the fight, but her account of the fight itself was arguably different — particularly with respect to whether Lee had drawn a weapon before petitioner . . . .

The State charged petitioner with assault and attempted murder. At trial, he claimed self-defense. Sylvia did not testify because of the state marital privilege, which generally bars a spouse from testifying without the other spouse's consent. See Wash. Rev. Code § 5.60.060(1) (1994). In Washington, this privilege does not extend to a spouse's out-of-court statements admissible under a hearsay exception, see *State v. Burden,* 120 Wn. 2d 371, 377, 841 P.2d 758, 761 (1992), so the State sought to introduce Sylvia's tape-recorded statements to the police as evidence that the stabbing was not in self-defense. Noting that Sylvia had admitted she led petitioner to Lee's apartment and thus had facilitated the assault, the State invoked the hearsay exception for statements against penal interest, Wash. Rule Evid. 804(b)(3) (2003).

Petitioner countered that, state law notwithstanding, admitting the evidence would violate his federal constitutional right to be "confronted with the witnesses against him." Amdt. 6. According to our description of that right in *Ohio v. Roberts,* 448 U.S. 56, 65 L. Ed. 2d 597, 100 S. Ct. 2531 (1980), it does not bar admission of an unavailable witness's statement against a criminal defendant if the statement bears "adequate 'indicia of reliability.'" *Id.*, at 66, 65 L. Ed. 2d 597, 100 S. Ct. 2531. To meet that test, evidence must either fall within a "firmly rooted hearsay exception" or bear "particularized guarantees of trustworthiness." *Ibid.* The trial court here admitted the statement on the latter ground. . . . The jury convicted petitioner of assault.

The Washington Court of Appeals reversed. . . .

The Washington Supreme Court reinstated the conviction, unanimously concluding that, although Sylvia's statement did not fall under a firmly rooted hearsay exception, it bore guarantees of trustworthiness. . . .

## II

The Sixth Amendment's Confrontation Clause provides that, "[i]n all criminal prosecutions, the accused shall enjoy the right . . . to be confronted with the witnesses against him." We have held that this bedrock procedural guarantee applies to both federal and state prosecutions. *Pointer v. Texas,* 380 U.S. 400, 406, 13 L. Ed. 2d 923, 85 S. Ct. 1065 (1965). . . .

### A

. . . . The right to confront one's accusers is a concept that dates back to Roman times. See *Coy v. Iowa,* 487 U.S. 1012, 1015, 101 L. Ed. 2d 857, 108 S. Ct. 2798 (1988); Herrmann & Speer, *Facing the Accuser: Ancient and Medieval Precursors of the Confrontation Clause,* 34 Va. J. Int'l L. 481 (1994). The founding generation's immediate source of the concept, however, was the common law. . . . See 3 W. Blackstone, Commentaries on the Laws of England 373–374 (1768).

. . . .

Pretrial examinations became routine under two statutes passed during the reign of Queen Mary in the 16th century, 1 & 2 Phil. & M., c. 13 (1554), and 2 & 3 *id.*, c. 10 (1555). These Marian bail and committal statutes required justices of the peace to examine suspects and witnesses in felony cases and to certify the results to the court. It is doubtful that the original purpose of the examinations was to produce evidence admissible at trial. See J. Langbein, Prosecuting Crime in the Renaissance 21–34 (1974)....

### B

....

Many declarations of rights adopted around the time of the Revolution guaranteed a right of confrontation.... The proposed Federal Constitution, however, did not. At the Massachusetts ratifying convention, Abraham Holmes objected to this omission precisely on the ground that it would lead to civil-law practices: "The mode of trial is altogether indetermined;... whether [the defendant] is to be allowed to confront the witnesses, and have the advantage of cross-examination, we are not yet told.... [W]e shall find Congress possessed of powers enabling them to institute judicatories little less inauspicious than a certain tribunal in Spain,... the *Inquisition.*" 2 Debates on the Federal Constitution 110–111 (J. Elliot 2d ed. 1863).... The First Congress responded by including the Confrontation Clause in the proposal that became the Sixth Amendment.

....

### III
### A

First, the principal evil at which the Confrontation Clause was directed was the civil-law mode of criminal procedure, and particularly its use of *ex parte* examinations as evidence against the accused.....

Accordingly, we once again reject the view that the Confrontation Clause applies of its own force only to in-court testimony, and that its application to out-of-court statements introduced at trial depends upon "the law of Evidence for the time being." 3 Wigmore § 1397, at 101; accord, *Dutton v. Evans,* 400 U.S. 74, 94, 27 L. Ed. 2d 213, 91 S. Ct. 210 (1970) (Harlan, J., concurring in result)....

The text of the Confrontation Clause reflects this focus. It applies to "witnesses" against the accused—in other words, those who "bear testimony." 1 N. Webster, An American Dictionary of the English Language (1828). "Testimony," in turn, is typically "[a] solemn declaration or affirmation made for the purpose of establishing or proving some fact." *Ibid.* An accuser who makes a formal statement to government officers bears testimony in a sense that a person who makes a casual remark to an acquaintance does not. The constitutional text, like the history underlying the common-law right of confrontation, thus reflects an especially acute concern with a specific type of out-of-court statement.

....

B

The historical record also supports a second proposition: that the Framers would not have allowed admission of testimonial statements of a witness who did not appear at trial unless he was unavailable to testify, and the defendant had had a prior opportunity for cross-examination. The text of the Sixth Amendment does not suggest any open-ended exceptions from the confrontation requirement to be developed by the courts. Rather, the "right . . . to be confronted with the witnesses against him," Amdt. 6, is most naturally read as a reference to the right of confrontation at common law, admitting only those exceptions established at the time of the founding. See *Mattox v. United States,* 156 U.S. 237, 243, 39 L. Ed. 409, 15 S. Ct. 337 (1895). . . .

IV

Our case law has been largely consistent with these two principles. Our leading early decision, for example, involved a deceased witness's prior trial testimony. *Mattox v. United States,* 156 U.S. 237, 39 L. Ed. 409, 15 S. Ct. 337 (1895). In allowing the statement to be admitted, we relied on the fact that the defendant had had, at the first trial, an adequate opportunity to confront the witness: "The substance of the constitutional protection is preserved to the prisoner in the advantage he has once had of seeing the witness face to face, and of subjecting him to the ordeal of a cross-examination. This, the law says, he shall under no circumstances be deprived of . . . ." *Id.*, at 244, 39 L. Ed. 409, 15 S. Ct. 337. . . . . Even our recent cases, in their outcomes, hew closely to the traditional line. *Ohio v. Roberts,* 448 U.S., at 67–70, 65 L. Ed. 2d 597, 100 S. Ct. 2531, admitted testimony from a preliminary hearing at which the defendant had examined the witness. . . .

V

Although the results of our decisions have generally been faithful to the original meaning of the Confrontation Clause, the same cannot be said of our rationales. *Roberts* conditions the admissibility of all hearsay evidence on whether it falls under a "firmly rooted hearsay exception" or bears "particularized guarantees of trustworthiness." 448 U.S., at 66, 65 L. Ed. 2d 597, 100 S. Ct. 2531. This test departs from the historical principles identified above in two respects. First, it is too broad: It applies the same mode of analysis whether or not the hearsay consists of *ex parte* testimony. . . . At the same time, however, the test is too narrow: It admits statements that *do* consist of *ex parte* testimony upon a mere finding of reliability. . . .

A

Where testimonial statements are involved, we do not think the Framers meant to leave the Sixth Amendment's protection to the vagaries of the rules of evidence, much less to amorphous notions of "reliability." . . . Admitting statements deemed reliable by a judge is fundamentally at odds with the right of confrontation. To be sure, the Clause's ultimate goal is to ensure reliability of evidence, but it is a procedural rather than a substantive guarantee. It commands, not that evidence be reliable, but that reliability be assessed in a particular manner: by testing in the crucible of cross-examination....

## C

*Roberts'* failings were on full display in the proceedings below. Sylvia Crawford made her statement while in police custody, herself a potential suspect in the case. Indeed, she had been told that whether she would be released "depend[ed] on how the investigation continues." App. 81. In response to often leading questions from police detectives, she implicated her husband in Lee's stabbing and at least arguably undermined his self-defense claim. Despite all this, the trial court admitted her statement, listing several reasons why it was reliable. In its opinion reversing, the Court of Appeals listed several *other* reasons why the statement was *not* reliable. Finally, the State Supreme Court relied exclusively on the interlocking character of the statement and disregarded every other factor the lower courts had considered. The case is thus a self-contained demonstration of *Roberts'* unpredictable and inconsistent application.

Each of the courts also made assumptions that cross-examination might well have undermined. The trial court, for example, stated that Sylvia Crawford's statement was reliable because she was an eyewitness with direct knowledge of the events. But Sylvia at one point told the police that she had "shut [her] eyes and ... didn't really watch" part of the fight, and that she was "in shock." App. 134. The trial court also buttressed its reliability finding by claiming that Sylvia was "being questioned by law enforcement, and, thus, the [questioner] is ... neutral to her and not someone who would be inclined to advance her interests and shade her version of the truth unfavorably toward the defendant." *Id.*, at 77. The Framers would be astounded to learn that *ex parte* testimony could be admitted against a criminal defendant because it was elicited by "neutral" government officers. But even if the court's assessment of the officer's motives was accurate, it says nothing about Sylvia's perception of her situation. Only cross-examination could reveal that.

The State Supreme Court gave dispositive weight to the interlocking nature of the two statements—that they were both ambiguous as to when and whether Lee had a weapon. The court's claim that the two statements were *equally* ambiguous is hard to accept. Petitioner's statement is ambiguous only in the sense that he had lingering doubts about his recollection.... Moreover, Sylvia specifically said Lee had nothing in his hands after he was stabbed, while petitioner was not asked about that.

The prosecutor obviously did not share the court's view that Sylvia's statement was ambiguous—he called it "damning evidence" that "completely refutes [petitioner's] claim of self-defense." Tr. 468 (Oct. 21, 1999). We have no way of knowing whether the jury agreed with the prosecutor or the court. Far from obviating the need for cross-examination, the "interlocking" ambiguity of the two statements made it all the more imperative that they be tested to tease out the truth.

. . . .

Where nontestimonial hearsay is at issue, it is wholly consistent with the Framers' design to afford the States flexibility in their development of hearsay law—as does

*Roberts*, and as would an approach that exempted such statements from Confrontation Clause scrutiny altogether. Where testimonial evidence is at issue, however, the Sixth Amendment demands what the common law required: unavailability and a prior opportunity for cross-examination. We leave for another day any effort to spell out a comprehensive definition of "testimonial." Whatever else the term covers, it applies at a minimum to prior testimony at a preliminary hearing, before a grand jury, or at a former trial; and to police interrogations. These are the modern practices with closest kinship to the abuses at which the Confrontation Clause was directed.

In this case, the State admitted Sylvia's testimonial statement against petitioner, despite the fact that he had no opportunity to cross-examine her. That alone is sufficient to make out a violation of the Sixth Amendment. *Roberts* notwithstanding, we decline to mine the record in search of indicia of reliability. Where testimonial statements are at issue, the only indicium of reliability sufficient to satisfy constitutional demands is the one the Constitution actually prescribes: confrontation.

The judgment of the Washington Supreme Court is reversed, and the case is remanded for further proceedings not inconsistent with this opinion.

---

Chief Justice Rehnquist's concurrence in *Crawford* warned that Justice Scalia's decision offered no assistance to the lower courts to determine what constituted testimonial evidence and that inconsistency and confusion would reign in the nation's criminal courts. His was right. During the two years following the *Crawford* decision, the case was cited in lower court opinions more than 3,000 times.[2] And those courts were widely divided over how to apply *Crawford*. The Supreme Court eventually clarified some of those issues—whether to admit a 911 recording of a victim of domestic violence and statements made by a victim to the police shortly after a domestic assault.

## Davis v. Washington
### United States Supreme Court
### 126 S. Ct. 2266 (2006)

SCALIA, J., delivered the opinion of the Court, in which ROBERTS, C.J., and STEVENS, KENNEDY, SOUTER, GINSBURG, BREYER, and ALITO, JJ., joined. THOMAS, J., filed an opinion concurring in the judgment in part and dissenting in part.

. . . .

### I
### A

The relevant statements in *Davis v. Washington*, No. 05-5224, were made to a 911 emergency operator on February 1, 2001. When the operator answered the initial call,

---

2. As an aside, by the end of 2016, Lexis listed more than 20,000 citing references to the *Crawford* decision.

the connection terminated before anyone spoke. She reversed the call, and Michelle McCottry answered. In the ensuing conversation, the operator ascertained that McCottry was involved in a domestic disturbance with her former boyfriend Adrian Davis, the petitioner in this case:

"911 Operator: Hello.

"Complainant: Hello.

"911 Operator: What's going on?

"Complainant: He's here jumpin' on me again.

"911 Operator: Okay. Listen to me carefully. Are you in a house or an apartment?

"Complainant: I'm in a house.

"911 Operator: Are there any weapons?

"Complainant: No. He's usin' his fists.

"911 Operator: Okay. Has he been drinking?

"Complainant: No.

"911 Operator: Okay, sweetie. I've got help started. Stay on the line with me, okay?

"Complainant: I'm on the line.

"911 Operator: Listen to me carefully. Do you know his last name?

"Complainant: It's Davis.

"911 Operator: Davis? Okay, what's his first name?

"Complainant: Adran

"911 Operator: What is it?

"Complainant: Adrian.

"911 Operator: Adrian?

"Complainant: Yeah.

"911 Operator: Okay. What's his middle initial?

"Complainant: Martell. He's runnin' now." App. in No. 05-5224, pp. 8–9.

As the conversation continued, the operator learned that Davis had "just run out the door" after hitting McCottry, and that he was leaving in a car with someone else. *Id.*, at 9–10. McCottry started talking, but the operator cut her off, saying, "Stop talking and answer my questions." *Id.*, at 10. She then gathered more information about Davis (including his birthday), and learned that Davis had told McCottry that his purpose in coming to the house was "to get his stuff," since McCottry was moving. *Id.*, at 11–12. McCottry described the context of the assault, *id.*, at 12, after which the operator told her that the police were on their way. "They're gonna check the area for him first," the operator said, "and then they're gonna come talk to you." *Id.*, at 12–13.

The police arrived within four minutes of the 911 call and observed McCottry's shaken state, the "fresh injuries on her forearm and her face," and her "frantic efforts to gather her belongings and her children so that they could leave the residence." 154 Wn. 2d 291, 296, 111 P.3d 844, 847 (2005) (en banc).

The State charged Davis with felony violation of a domestic no-contact order. "The State's only witnesses were the two police officers who responded to the 911 call. Both officers testified that McCottry exhibited injuries that appeared to be recent, but neither officer could testify as to the cause of the injuries." *Ibid*. McCottry presumably could have testified as to whether Davis was her assailant, but she did not appear. Over Davis's objection, based on the Confrontation Clause of the Sixth Amendment, the trial court admitted the recording of her exchange with the 911 operator, and the jury convicted him. The Washington Court of Appeals affirmed, 116 Wn. App. 81, 64 P.3d 661 (2003). The Supreme Court of Washington, with one dissenting justice, also affirmed, concluding that the portion of the 911 conversation in which McCottry identified Davis was not testimonial, and that if other portions of the conversation were testimonial, admitting them was harmless beyond a reasonable doubt. 154 Wash. 2d, at 305, 111 P.3d, at 851. . . .

B

In *Hammon v. Indiana*, No. 05-5705, police responded late on the night of February 26, 2003, to a "reported domestic disturbance" at the home of Hershel and Amy Hammon. 829 N.E.2d 444, 446 (Ind. 2005). They found Amy alone on the front porch, appearing "'somewhat frightened,'" but she told them that "'nothing was the matter,'" *id.*, at 446, 447. She gave them permission to enter the house, where an officer saw "a gas heating unit in the corner of the living room" that had "flames coming out of the . . . partial glass front. There were pieces of glass on the ground in front of it and there was flame emitting from the front of the heating unit." App. in No. 05-5705, p. 16.

Hershel, meanwhile, was in the kitchen. He told the police "that he and his wife had 'been in an argument' but 'everything was fine now' and the argument 'never became physical.'" 829 N.E.2d, at 447. By this point Amy had come back inside. One of the officers remained with Hershel; the other went to the living room to talk with Amy, and "again asked [her] what had occurred." *Ibid.;* App. in No. 05-5705, at 17, 32. Hershel made several attempts to participate in Amy's conversation with the police, see *id.*, at 32, but was rebuffed. The officer later testified that Hershel "became angry when I insisted that [he] stay separated from Mrs. Hammon so that we can investigate what had happened." *Id.*, at 34. After hearing Amy's account, the officer "had her fill out and sign a battery affidavit." *Id.*, at 18. Amy handwrote the following: "Broke our Furnace & shoved me down on the floor into the broken glass. Hit me in the chest and threw me down. Broke our lamps & phone. Tore up my van where I couldn't leave the house. Attacked my daughter." *Id.*, at 2.

The State charged Hershel with domestic battery and with violating his probation. Amy was subpoenaed, but she did not appear at his subsequent bench trial. The State called the officer who had questioned Amy, and asked him to recount what Amy told him and to authenticate the affidavit. Hershel's counsel repeatedly objected to the admission of this evidence. See *id.*, at 11, 12, 13, 17, 19, 20, 21. At one point, after hearing the prosecutor defend the affidavit because it was made "under oath," defense counsel said, "That doesn't give us the opportunity to cross examine [the] person who allegedly drafted it. Makes me mad." *Id.*, at 19. Nonetheless, the trial court admitted the affidavit as a "present sense impression," *id.*, at 20, and Amy's statements as "excited utterances" that "are expressly permitted in these kinds of cases even if the declarant is not available to testify." *Id.*, at 40. . . .

The trial judge found Hershel guilty on both charges, *id.*, at 40, and the Indiana Court of Appeals affirmed in relevant part, 809 N.E.2d 945 (2004). The Indiana Supreme Court also affirmed, concluding that Amy's statement was admissible for state-law purposes as an excited utterance, 829 N.E.2d, at 449; that "a 'testimonial' statement is one given or taken in significant part for purposes of preserving it for potential future use in legal proceedings," where "the motivations of the questioner and declarant are the central concerns," *id.*, at 456, 457; and that Amy's oral statement was not "testimonial" under these standards, *id.*, at 458. It also concluded that, although the affidavit was testimonial and thus wrongly admitted, it was harmless beyond a reasonable doubt, largely because the trial was to the bench. *Id.*, at 458–459. . . .

## II

The Confrontation Clause of the Sixth Amendment provides: "In all criminal prosecutions, the accused shall enjoy the right . . . to be confronted with the witnesses against him." In *Crawford v. Washington,* 541 U.S. 36, 53–54, 124 S. Ct. 1354, 158 L. Ed. 2d 177 (2004), we held that this provision bars "admission of testimonial statements of a witness who did not appear at trial unless he was unavailable to testify, and the defendant had had a prior opportunity for cross-examination." A critical portion of this holding, and the portion central to resolution of the two cases now before us, is the phrase "testimonial statements." Only statements of this sort cause the declarant to be a "witness" within the meaning of the Confrontation Clause. See *id.*, at 51, 124 S. Ct. 1354, 158 L. Ed. 2d 177 . . .

Without attempting to produce an exhaustive classification of all conceivable statements — or even all conceivable statements in response to police interrogation — as either testimonial or nontestimonial, it suffices to decide the present cases to hold as follows: Statements are nontestimonial when made in the course of police interrogation under circumstances objectively indicating that the primary purpose of the interrogation is to enable police assistance to meet an ongoing emergency. They are testimonial when the circumstances objectively indicate that there is no such ongoing emergency, and that the primary purpose of the interrogation is to establish or prove past events potentially relevant to later criminal prosecution.

## III

### A

. . . .

The difference between the interrogation in *Davis* and the one in *Crawford* is apparent on the face of things. In *Davis,* McCottry was speaking about events *as they were actually happening*, rather than "describing past events," *Lilly v. Virginia*, 527 U.S. 116, 137, 119 S. Ct. 1887, 144 L. Ed. 2d 117 (1999) (plurality opinion). Sylvia Crawford's interrogation, on the other hand, took place hours after the events she described had occurred. Moreover, any reasonable listener would recognize that McCottry (unlike Sylvia Crawford) was facing an ongoing emergency. Although one *might* call 911 to provide a narrative report of a crime absent any imminent danger, McCottry's call was plainly a call for help against bona fide physical threat. Third, the nature of what was asked and answered in *Davis*, again viewed objectively, was such that the elicited statements were necessary to be able to *resolve* the present emergency, rather than simply to learn (as in *Crawford*) what had happened in the past. That is true even of the operator's effort to establish the identity of the assailant, so that the dispatched officers might know whether they would be encountering a violent felon. See, *e.g.*, *Hiibel v. Sixth Judicial Dist. Court of Nev., Humboldt Cty.*, 542 U.S. 177, 186, 124 S. Ct. 2451, 159 L. Ed. 2d 292 (2004). And finally, the difference in the level of formality between the two interviews is striking. Crawford was responding calmly, at the station house, to a series of questions, with the officer-interrogator taping and making notes of her answers; McCottry's frantic answers were provided over the phone, in an environment that was not tranquil, or even (as far as any reasonable 911 operator could make out) safe.

We conclude from all this that the circumstances of McCottry's interrogation objectively indicate its primary purpose was to enable police assistance to meet an ongoing emergency. She simply was not acting as a *witness*; she was not *testifying*. . . .

. . . .

### B

Determining the testimonial or nontestimonial character of the statements that were the product of the interrogation in *Hammon* is a much easier task, since they were not much different from the statements we found to be testimonial in *Crawford*. It is entirely clear from the circumstances that the interrogation was part of an investigation into possibly criminal past conduct—as, indeed, the testifying officer expressly acknowledged, App. in No. 05-5705, at 25, 32, 34. There was no emergency in progress; the interrogating officer testified that he had heard no arguments or crashing and saw no one throw or break anything, *id.*, at 25. When the officers first arrived, Amy told them that things were fine, *id.*, at 14, and there was no immediate threat to her person. When the officer questioned Amy for the second time, and elicited the challenged statements, he was not seeking to determine (as in *Davis*) "what is happening," but rather "what happened." Objectively viewed, the primary, if not indeed the sole, purpose of the interrogation was to investigate a possible crime—which is, of course, precisely what the officer *should* have done.

. . . .

### IV

Respondents in both cases, joined by a number of their *amici*, contend that the nature of the offenses charged in these two cases—domestic violence—requires greater flexibility in the use of testimonial evidence. This particular type of crime is notoriously susceptible to intimidation or coercion of the victim to ensure that she does not testify at trial. When this occurs, the Confrontation Clause gives the criminal a windfall. We may not, however, vitiate constitutional guarantees when they have the effect of allowing the guilty to go free. Cf. *Kyllo v. United States,* 533 U.S. 27, 121 S. Ct. 2038, 150 L. Ed. 2d 94 (2001) (suppressing evidence from an illegal search). But when defendants seek to undermine the judicial process by procuring or coercing silence from witnesses and victims, the Sixth Amendment does not require courts to acquiesce. While defendants have no duty to assist the State in proving their guilt, they *do* have the duty to refrain from acting in ways that destroy the integrity of the criminal-trial system. We reiterate what we said in *Crawford:* that "the rule of forfeiture by wrongdoing ... extinguishes confrontation claims on essentially equitable grounds." 541 U.S., at 62, 124 S. Ct. 1354, 158 L. Ed. 2d 177 (citing *Reynolds,* 98 U.S., at 158–159, 25 L. Ed. 244). That is, one who obtains the absence of a witness by wrongdoing forfeits the constitutional right to confrontation.

We take no position on the standards necessary to demonstrate such forfeiture, but federal courts using Federal Rule of Evidence 804(b)(6), which codifies the forfeiture doctrine, have generally held the Government to the preponderance-of-the-evidence standard, see, *e.g., United States v. Scott,* 284 F.3d 758, 762 (CA7 2002). State courts tend to follow the same practice, see, *e.g., Commonwealth v. Edwards,* 444 Mass. 526, 542, 830 N.E.2d 158, 172 (2005). Moreover, if a hearing on forfeiture is required, *Edwards,* for instance, observed that "hearsay evidence, including the unavailable witness's out-of-court statements, may be considered." *Id.,* at 545, 830 N.E.2d, at 174. The *Roberts* approach to the Confrontation Clause undoubtedly made recourse to this doctrine less necessary, because prosecutors could show the "reliability" of *ex parte* statements more easily than they could show the defendant's procurement of the witness's absence. *Crawford,* in overruling *Roberts,* did not destroy the ability of courts to protect the integrity of their proceedings.

We have determined that, absent a finding of forfeiture by wrongdoing, the Sixth Amendment operates to exclude Amy Hammon's affidavit. The Indiana courts may (if they are asked) determine on remand whether such a claim of forfeiture is properly raised and, if so, whether it is meritorious.

. . . .

---

The *Crawford/Davis* holdings have no impact in situations where the absence of the witness is procured by the misconduct of the accused. But that misconduct must be intended to prevent a witness from appearing in court as the following case involving a crime of domestic violence demonstrates.

## Giles v. California
Supreme Court of the United States
554 U.S. 353 (2008)

JUSTICE SCALIA delivered the opinion of the Court....

On September 29, 2002, petitioner Dwayne Giles shot his ex-girlfriend, Brenda Avie, outside the garage of his grandmother's house. No witness saw the shooting, but Giles' niece heard what transpired from inside the house. She heard Giles and Avie speaking in conversational tones. Avie then yelled "Granny" several times and a series of gunshots sounded. Giles' niece and grandmother ran outside and saw Giles standing near Avie with a gun in his hand. Avie, who had not been carrying a weapon, had been shot six times. One wound was consistent with Avie's holding her hand up at the time she was shot, another was consistent with her having turned to her side, and a third was consistent with her having been shot while lying on the ground. Giles fled the scene after the shooting. He was apprehended by police about two weeks later and charged with murder.

At trial, Giles testified that he had acted in self-defense. Giles described Avie as jealous, and said he knew that she had once shot a man, that he had seen her threaten people with a knife, and that she had vandalized his home and car on prior occasions. He said that on the day of the shooting, Avie came to his grandmother's house and threatened to kill him and his new girlfriend, who had been at the house earlier. He said that Avie had also threatened to kill his new girlfriend when Giles and Avie spoke on the phone earlier that day. Giles testified that after Avie threatened him at the house, he went into the garage and retrieved a gun, took the safety off, and started walking toward the back door of the house. He said that Avie charged at him, and that he was afraid she had something in her hand. According to Giles, he closed his eyes and fired several shots, but did not intend to kill Avie.

Prosecutors sought to introduce statements that Avie had made to a police officer responding to a domestic-violence report about three weeks before the shooting. Avie, who was crying when she spoke, told the officer that Giles had accused her of having an affair, and that after the two began to argue, Giles grabbed her by the shirt, lifted her off the floor, and began to choke her. According to Avie, when she broke free and fell to the floor, Giles punched her in the face and head, and after she broke free again, he opened a folding knife, held it about three feet away from her, and threatened to kill her if he found her cheating on him. Over Giles' objection, the trial court admitted these statements into evidence under a provision of California law that permits admission of out-of-court statements describing the infliction or threat of physical injury on a declarant when the declarant is unavailable to testify at trial and the prior statements are deemed trustworthy. Cal. Evid. Code Ann. § 1370 (West Supp. 2008).

A jury convicted Giles of first-degree murder. He appealed. While his appeal was pending, this Court decided in *Crawford v. Washington*, 541 U.S. 36, 53-54, 124 S. Ct. 1354, 158 L. Ed. 2d 177 (2004), that the Confrontation Clause requires that a defendant have the opportunity to confront the witnesses who give testimony against him, except in cases where an exception to the confrontation right was recognized at the time of the founding. The California Court of Appeal held that the admission of Avie's unconfronted statements at Giles' trial did not violate the Confrontation Clause as construed by *Crawford* because *Crawford* recognized a doctrine of forfeiture by wrongdoing. 123 Cal. App. 4th 475, 19 Cal. Rptr. 3d 843, 847 (2004) (officially depublished). It concluded that Giles had forfeited his right to confront Avie because he had committed the murder for which he was on trial, and because his intentional criminal act made Avie unavailable to testify. The California Supreme Court affirmed on the same ground. 40 Cal. 4th 833, 837, 55 Cal. Rptr. 3d 133, 152 P.3d 433, 435 (2007). We granted certiorari. 552 U.S. 1136, 128 S. Ct. 976, 169 L. Ed. 2d 800 (2008).

II

... The State does not dispute here, and we accept without deciding, that Avie's statements accusing Giles of assault were testimonial. But it maintains (as did the California Supreme Court) that the Sixth Amendment did not prohibit prosecutors from introducing the statements because an exception to the confrontation guarantee permits the use of a witness's unconfronted testimony if a judge finds, as the judge did in this case, that the defendant committed a wrongful act that rendered the witness unavailable to testify at trial. We held in *Crawford* that the Confrontation Clause is "most naturally read as a reference to the right of confrontation at common law, admitting only those exceptions established at the time of the founding." *Id.*, at 54, 124 S. Ct. 1354, 158 L. Ed. 2d 177. We therefore ask whether the theory of forfeiture by wrongdoing accepted by the California Supreme Court is a founding-era exception to the confrontation right.

A

We have previously acknowledged that two forms of testimonial statements were admitted at common law even though they were unconfronted. See *id.*, at 56, n. 6, 62, 124 S. Ct. 1354, 158 L. Ed. 2d 177. The first of these were declarations made by a speaker who was both on the brink of death and aware that he was dying.... Avie did not make the unconfronted statements admitted at Giles' trial when she was dying, so her statements do not fall within this historic exception.

A second common-law doctrine, which we will refer to as forfeiture by wrongdoing, permitted the introduction of statements of a witness who was "detained" or "kept away" by the "means or procurement" of the defendant....

This Court first addressed forfeiture in *Reynolds v. United States*, 98 U.S. 145, 25 L. Ed. 244 (1879), where, after hearing testimony that suggested the defendant had kept his wife away from home so that she could not be subpoenaed to testify, the trial court permitted the government to introduce testimony of the defendant's wife from the defendant's prior trial. See *id.*, at 148-150, 25 L. Ed. 244. On appeal, the Court held that admission of the statements did not violate the right of the defendant to confront witnesses at trial, because when a witness is absent by the defendant's "wrongful procurement," the defendant "is in no condition to assert that his constitutional rights have been violated" if "their evidence is supplied in some lawful way." *Id.*, at

158, 25 L. Ed. 244. *Reynolds* invoked broad forfeiture principles to explain its holding. The decision stated, for example, that "[t]he Constitution does not guarantee an accused person against the legitimate consequences of his own wrongful acts," *ibid.*, and that the wrongful-procurement rule "has its foundation" in the principle that no one should be permitted to take advantage of his wrong, and is "the outgrowth of a maxim based on the principles of common honesty," *id.*, at 159, 25 L. Ed. 244.

*Reynolds* relied on these maxims (as the common-law authorities had done) to be sure. But it relied on them (as the common-law authorities had done) to admit prior testimony in a case where the defendant had engaged in wrongful conduct designed to prevent a witness's testimony. The Court's opinion indicated that it was adopting the common-law rule. It cited leading common-law cases—*Lord Morley's Case, Harrison's Case,* and *Scaife*—described itself as "content with" the "long-established usage" of the forfeiture principle, and admitted prior confronted statements under circumstances where admissibility was open to no doubt under *Lord Morley's Case. Reynolds, supra,* at 158-159, 25 L. Ed. 244.

If the State's rule had an historical pedigree in the common law or even in the 1879 decision in *Reynolds*, one would have expected it to be routinely invoked in murder prosecutions like the one here, in which the victim's prior statements inculpated the defendant. It was never invoked in this way.

. . . .

In 1997, this Court approved a Federal Rule of Evidence, entitled "Forfeiture by wrongdoing," which applies only when the defendant "engaged or acquiesced in wrongdoing that was intended to, and did, procure the unavailability of the declarant as a witness." Fed. Rule of Evid. 804(b)(6). . . .

[T]he dissent issues a thinly veiled invitation to overrule *Crawford* and adopt an approach not much different from the regime of *Ohio v. Roberts*, 448 U.S. 56, 100 S. Ct. 2531, 65 L. Ed. 2d 597 (1980), under which the Court would create the exceptions that it thinks consistent with the policies underlying the confrontation guarantee, regardless of how that guarantee was historically understood. The "basic purposes and objectives" of forfeiture doctrine, it says, require that a defendant who wrongfully caused the absence of a witness be deprived of his confrontation rights, whether or not there was any such rule applicable at common law. . . .

The dissent closes by pointing out that a forfeiture rule which ignores *Crawford* would be particularly helpful to women in abusive relationships—or at least particularly helpful in punishing their abusers. Not as helpful as the dissent suggests, since only *testimonial* statements are excluded by the Confrontation Clause. Statements to friends and neighbors about abuse and intimidation, and statements to physicians in the course of receiving treatment would be excluded, if at all, only by hearsay rules, which are free to adopt the dissent's version of forfeiture by wrongdoing. In any event, we are puzzled by the dissent's decision to devote its peroration to domestic abuse cases. Is the suggestion that we should have one Confrontation Clause (the one the Framers adopted and *Crawford* described) for all other crimes, but a special, improvised, Confrontation Clause for those crimes that are frequently directed against women? Domestic violence is an intolerable offense that legislatures may choose to combat through many means—from increasing criminal penalties to adding resources for investigation and prosecution to funding awareness and prevention campaigns. But for that serious crime, as for others, abridging the constitutional rights of criminal defendants is not in the State's arsenal.

The domestic-violence context is, however, relevant for a separate reason. Acts of domestic violence often are intended to dissuade a victim from resorting to outside help, and include conduct designed to prevent testimony to police officers or cooperation in criminal prosecutions. Where such an abusive relationship culminates in murder, the evidence may support a finding that the crime expressed the intent to isolate the victim and to stop her from reporting abuse to the authorities or cooperating with a criminal prosecution—rendering her prior statements admissible under the forfeiture doctrine. Earlier abuse, or threats of abuse, intended to dissuade the victim from resorting to outside help would be highly relevant to this inquiry, as would evidence of ongoing criminal proceedings at which the victim would have been expected to testify....

The state courts in this case did not consider the intent of the defendant because they found that irrelevant to application of the forfeiture doctrine. This view of the law was error, but the court is free to consider evidence of the defendant's intent on remand.

. . . .

We decline to approve an exception to the Confrontation Clause unheard of at the time of the founding or for 200 years thereafter. The judgment of the California Supreme Court is vacated, and the case is remanded for further proceedings not inconsistent with this opinion.

---

In the aftermath of the Supreme Court trilogy of *Crawford, Davis and Giles* well-known domestic violence advocate and law professor Sarah Buel wrote the following article suggesting how the doctrine of forfeiture should work in cases involving intimate partner violence.

## Sarah M. Buel, *Putting Forfeiture to Work*
43 U.C. Davis L. Rev. 1295 (April 2010)

### Introduction

Intimate partner violence ("IPV") offenders commit astonishing levels of witness tampering with such apparent impunity as to suggest that they act with community and state approval. All fifty states, the District of Columbia, and the Commonwealth of Puerto Rico have codified prohibitions against witness tampering, including a broad range of defendant conduct that deters or attempts to deter a witness from taking part in legal proceedings. Because witness tampering sabotages the legal system by impeding an IPV victim's ability to access remedies needed to achieve safety, and because it enables guilty batterers to go free, a more robust forfeiture doctrine is necessary to fulfill its legislative intent.

As early as 1666, the forfeiture concept was cited in American case law for the proposition that if a defendant caused a witness's unavailability, prior victim statements were permitted to prevent the defendant from benefitting from his own wrongdoing. Many of the reasons that animated the Founders to sanction forfeiture have only grown more numerous with recognition of IPV as a crime and the state's concomitant benefits from its prevention.

Situating IPV within the criminal realm was intended to clarify the state's responsibility for public safety—including that of victims—while bringing to the court's attention the full range of batterers' harmful and illegal conduct. Witness tampering includes an array of deleterious coercion, ranging from bribery, threats, and stalking, to assault, rape, and murder. In response to prolific witness tampering, the doctrine of forfeiture by wrongdoing evolved as a necessary equitable remedy. The gist is that when a defendant coerces, threatens, or harms a witness with the intention of preventing her testimony against him, the forfeiture doctrine should permit admission of the witness's hearsay statements at trial. Despite recognition of the doctrine in American jurisprudence for centuries, a vast schism exists between the legislative intent of witness tampering and forfeiture laws and their implementation in the courts.

In a trilogy of recent cases, *Crawford v. Washington* and its progeny, *Davis v. Washington*, and *Giles v. California*, the U.S. Supreme Court has directly addressed the problem of unavailable witnesses vis-a-vis defendants' Sixth Amendment right to confront their accusers....

In 2008, the Supreme Court granted certiorari in *Giles v. California* to resolve lingering confusion regarding confrontation and offender motives. The *Giles* majority held that even if a batterer kills his victim, he can invoke his confrontation rights to keep her past statements out of the trial unless the state can prove he killed with the intent of preventing her testimony....

After the case was appealed to the Supreme Court, Justice Scalia invoked sweeping originalist claims in his majority opinion to buttress the Court's decision requiring lower courts to specifically address the defendant's intent in killing Avie.[3] Although Justice Scalia had acknowledged in *Davis* that domestic violence is "notoriously susceptible to intimidation or coercion of the victim to ensure that she does not testify at trial," this recognition is noticeably absent from his final formulation of a confrontation paradigm. Justice Scalia held that it was necessary to vacate the California Supreme Court's *Giles* ruling because the Sixth Amendment's Framers did not recognize a forfeiture exception absent specific intent to silence.

The *Giles* Court acknowledged that "the absence of a forfeiture rule covering this sort of conduct would create an intolerable incentive for defendants to bribe,

---

3. Avie was Brenda Avie, the victim in this case. [Ed. Note.]

intimidate, or even kill witnesses against them." In a majority opinion imbued with the rhetoric of originalism, the Court required the state to prove with what purpose the offender acted, but did not clarify the evidence needed to substantiate that the offender "expressed the intent" to silence a witness. In this Article, I urge that offender conduct causing an IPV victim not to testify should result in forfeiture of the right to confront his accuser, as referenced in *Crawford*, *Davis*, and *Giles*, but not be given the stature intended by the Framers in those cases.

Rarely are abusers held responsible, precisely because their victims are too frightened to testify about both the initial crime and subsequent witness tampering. Based on prior harm, victims understand, all too well, the likelihood of batterers' threats being realized. As a result, witness tampering persists, with victims, legal scholars and practitioners alike lamenting the paucity of options and the law's sparse enforcement. The immediate result of successful witness tampering is that the victim opts not to testify against the menacing abuser. Moreover, after *Crawford*, *Davis*, and *Giles*, it is far more difficult for prosecutors to prove their cases absent the victim's in-court testimony.

Indeed, batterers are not only incentivized to make their victims unavailable, but are now rewarded for doing so. Although Justice Scalia recognized this state-created danger, it is puzzling that in all three decisions he appears to identify the peril, but not to offer a realistic remedy. Justice Scalia's restricted standard in *Giles* brought renewed focus to the issue of mens rea when he said that if a defendant's prior abuse "expressed the intent" to prevent a victim's testimony, that evidence may be admissible "where such an abusive relationship culminates in murder." Thus, prior to *Giles*, conceptions of witness tampering focused solely on those acts committed after the charged crime but before a court proceeding. In *Giles*, Justice Scalia acknowledged that the defendant's previous harm can substantially contribute to silencing a victim. However, under a more just conception of the law, the forfeiture doctrine must presume admission of all conduct indicating the offender's intent to silence the witness, including conduct in nonhomicide cases, to fulfill its normative and doctrinal purpose. The practices in most courts do not reflect an awareness of domestic violence dynamics when faced with offenders who have unlawfully silenced their victims. Batterers often successfully shift the attention from themselves to the victim's conduct, mischaracterizing recantation and refusal to participate in prosecutorial proceedings as indicative of fabrication or stupidity. Victim blaming has proven an effective weapon in the offender's arsenal, allowing the batterer to skillfully reframe his violence away from the crime on which the court should be focused and, instead, onto the victim's agency interfering with orderly case handling.

This Article illuminates the law on witness tampering and the largely failed application of forfeiture as a remedy in intimate partner violence cases. It offers two main arguments: first, the forfeiture doctrine's application in IPV cases has been woefully inadequate; and second, there is an immediate need to clarify the "intent-to-silence" calculus. The forfeiture doctrine advances significant jurisprudential and public policy interests, in part by furthering what one court characterized as "the truth-seeking function of the adversary process, allowing factfinders access to valuable evidence no longer available through live testimony." The loss of a victim's statements as a result of witness tampering is often fatal for the case because the typical batterer has ensured that insufficient corroborative evidence exists — such as 911 calls, medical records, additional witnesses, forensic corroboration, and police or emergency personnel testimony on victim injuries — to sustain a conviction. . . .

I. Forfeiture as Intended Remedy

The doctrine of forfeiture by wrongdoing predates the Constitution. Its equitable foundation lies in not permitting the accused to benefit from his misconduct and encompasses coercion that thwarts IPV victims from truthfully testifying against their perpetrators. Judge Jeffrey Atlas affirmed its sound social policy basis in *People v. Santiago*, a case in which a particularly violent batterer terrorized, coerced, and controlled his girlfriend over a ten year period: "No class of cases seems more worthy of the protections afforded by the public policy which dictated this evidentiary rule [of forfeiture by wrongdoing] than matters involving domestic violence."[4] *Santiago* demonstrates that at least some courts are acknowledging not only the prevalence of witness tampering in IPV cases, but also the apt fit of forfeiture analysis in these matters. Although higher courts reiterate that it is "well established, as a matter of simple equity" and "common sense" that the right to confrontation is forfeited if the defendant has "wrongfully procured the witnesses' silence through threats, actual violence or murder," lower courts face the impractical requirements of the present approach to forfeiture. These burdensome procedural demands imperil the legal framework for abuse prevention and offender accountability.

Current interpretations of the forfeiture doctrine require an often unrealistic, rare confluence of empowered, tenacious survivors and engaged state actors if victims are to access such legal remedies. In an archetypal case in which I was involved as counsel, Mary S. had been brutally beaten by her ex-husband, John, throughout their marriage, including during each of her three pregnancies, and even post-divorce while a protective order was in place. Soon after Mary was forced to let the protective order lapse because she could not afford to miss any more work to attend yet another hearing, her ex-husband broke into her home and assaulted her as she tried to call the police. He smashed her cell phone and fled, telling her and their children that they had better not report him or he would return to "finish the job." Because Mary was terrified of increased violence, she did not call the police until John later slashed her car tires, stalked her at all hours, and screamed threats at her from the street. Although the prosecutor initially subpoenaed several neighbors and me to testify, he later said

---

4. [n71] *People v. Santiago*, No. 2725-02, 2003 N.Y. Misc. LEXIS 829, at 51 (N.Y. Sup. Ct. Apr. 7, 2003). In this forfeiture hearing, the prosecutor sought admission of a battered woman's out-of-court and grand jury testimony alleging ten years of severe violence by her common law husband. The judge found that because the defendant's blatant witness intimidation caused her recantation, the victim's prior statements would be allowed at trial under the doctrine of forfeiture by wrongdoing. *Id.*

that the case would not go forward because Mary was too afraid to testify due to John's threats of retaliation if she did so.

I explained forfeiture doctrine to the prosecutor, but he assured me that, after *Davis*, the judge would allow neither Mary's statements to the police nor any witness testimony about prior abuse to be introduced at trial. Subsequently, Mary's depression worsened as her nine-year-old daughter began bedwetting and her twelve-year-old son was suspended from school for assaulting other children and his teacher. After the Attorney General's Office told John he would have to pay child support, Mary saw John throw a large rock through her living room window, after which he and his girlfriend raced off in a new truck. Mary cried as she explained the history of abuse to yet another police officer, adding that the abuse would only worsen if she testified against John. As the officer prepared to leave, Mary's six year-old son asked if he could borrow the officer's gun. When the officer asked why he wanted the gun, the child replied, "I need to scare my Daddy from hurting us anymore. Nobody else will stop him, but I can." The young police officer said to me, "Ma'am, you need to fix these laws. Look what this guy is allowed to get away with as long as he keeps them scared enough!" Mary's case epitomizes the conundrum faced by those seeking to bring IPV cases forward and prevent ongoing abuse as relentless offenders intimidate witnesses with seeming impunity. Current interpretations of the forfeiture doctrine are unlikely to bring relief because many victims are understandably too scared to testify. In *Giles*, Justice Scalia made clear that in order to trigger a forfeiture claim, the state must prove that when the defendant committed the offense rendering the witness unavailable, the accused intended to deter the victim from testifying in a legal proceeding. Seemingly consistent with basic criminal law requirements for proof of mens rea prior to conviction, this narrow reading ignores the need for a more nuanced analysis of intent, at least in cases involving current or former intimate partners. . . .

A. Doctrinal Premise of Forfeiture

. . . .

To determine whether forfeiture is an available remedy, most states require an evidentiary hearing, outside the presence of a jury, in which the prosecutor must prove four elements: (1) unavailability of the declarant; (2) the defendant's intent to silence the witness with his actions; (3) knowledge that the witness had sought to or had reported the crime, was to be a witness, or both; and (4) that the offender was the cause of the declarant's absence. In dicta, the *Davis* Court specified that it took no stance on the necessary standard of proof required, but instead cited federal courts' use of the preponderance of the evidence standard and noted state courts' general adherence to the same. Some states require a clear and convincing standard, notably Washington and New York.

In their concurrence in *Giles*, Justices Souter and Ginsburg were troubled by what they called "near circularity" when the court decides both whether the accused committed the underlying crime (here, murder) and simultaneously whether he is guilty of witness tampering. In nearly all cases, however, separate proceedings—with different standards of proof—are held to determine if forfeiture applies, and then, whether this defendant is guilty of the underlying offense....

Much case law supports the principle that the forfeiture-by-wrongdoing exception permits admission of missing witnesses' statements in trials for crimes against them, as well as in trials charging defendants for the underlying offenses about which they worried that murdered witnesses would testify. This concept of reflexive forfeiture should apply in murder and nonhomicide cases alike based on principles of equity....

Although its purpose is to protect the accused in criminal cases, the Sixth Amendment right to confront one's accuser is not without exception and must flex to accommodate compelling rule of law concerns. A defendant's own disruptive behavior, absence from trial, misconduct, or instigation of a witness's unavailability for trial may constitute a waiver of this right. Courts have been clear that defendants must not be allowed to benefit from their unlawful witness tampering, whether achieved by threats, chicanery, violent assaults, or murder. To reward batterers for their deleterious crimes is counter to the very essence of equitable law.

B. Historical Conceptions of Confrontation

Increasingly, scholars are questioning both longstanding and newly created assumptions about confrontation, with *Crawford*, *Davis*, and *Giles* offering surprisingly little guidance on its purpose. In *Crawford*, Justice Scalia offered that the "ultimate goal" is to admit only reliable evidence, while in other cases, he emphasized the symbolic importance of "face-to-face confrontation between accused and accuser as 'essential to a fair trial in a criminal prosecution.'" Contrary to Justice Scalia's originalist assertions, the Framers of the Confrontation Clause left few clues as to its mandates, with previous Justices noting that it comes to us "on faded parchment." Yet John Henry Wigmore asserted that cross-examination was the critical and necessary purpose of confrontation; the Supreme Court has since adopted this position as its own. Writing for a splintered court in *Giles*, Justice Scalia traversed the historical terrain he covered in *Crawford* and *Davis*, analyzing treatises and common law while locating the absence of cases on point as indicative of the Framers' assent. Justice Breyer, dissenting, countered by stating that "I know of no instance in which this Court has drawn a conclusion about the meaning of a common-law rule solely from the absence of cases showing the contrary—at least not where there are other plausible explanations for that absence." Justice Souter's concurrence, joined by Justice Ginsburg, addressed why the rhetoric of originalism did not square with today's recognition of domestic violence:

> The historical record ... simply does not focus on what should be required for forfeiture when the crime charged occurred in an abusive relationship or was its culminating act; today's understanding of domestic abuse had no apparent significance at the time of the Framing, and there is no early example of the forfeiture rule operating in that circumstance.

Imposing originalist analysis on the Confrontation Clause, and thereby the forfeiture doctrine, seems further ill advised because of the nascent state of evidence law when the Sixth Amendment was drafted. At the *Giles* oral argument, Justices Kennedy and Breyer noted that given the array of witness restrictions in place during the Founding era, the *Giles* case would not have been heard at that time. In that era, the categories of those unable to testify included spouses, children, atheists, "interested persons" in a case, and convicted felons. Because domestic violence was not viewed as a crime, the archetypal Confrontation Clause case involving prior statements to police by a recanting victim was not within their realm of possibility.

Justices Souter and Ginsburg insisted that the presence of domestic violence gives rise to an inference of intent to silence. Because Justices Souter and Ginsburg were critical members of the majority, a state seeking to introduce an unavailable victim's previous statements should be able to successfully invoke their—the Souter-Ginsburg—argument. Professor Deborah Tuerkheimer convincingly argued, "At least in 'the classic abusive relationship,' the Court's rule effectively allows forfeiture to be presumed without a specific inquiry into the defendant's intent." Although Justice Scalia did not reference this Souter-Ginsburg test, he recognized that domestic violence perpetrators, through their abuse, often intend to prevent victims from accessing help and testifying in criminal cases. Taking the text of Justices Souter and Scalia together, lower courts should permit an absent victim's statements once the prosecutor has provided evidence of prior abuse or a classic abusive relationship.

. . . .

Professor Richard Freidman offered that instead of applying the confrontation right presumptively to all hearsay statements, the historically supported rule should limit it to those made in expectation of future prosecution. A more coherent doctrine is one in which a domestic violence victim's statements are only deemed testimonial if made with a nefarious intent. An abuse victim who has been terrorized by her partner for a duration may understand that her outcry could become part of the state's case against her batterer, but this in no way impinges on the credibility of her rendition of events.

Regardless of whether statements are made to a police officer or doctor, the investigation should focus on verifying the veracity of those statements, not on discarding all evidence that might help get to the truth. To do so rewards the recidivist offender who has forced his victim to have prior contact with the criminal justice system, making her unwittingly familiar with the process. The judge or jury with a more accurate picture of the incident before them—in the context of the "classic abusive relationship"—can then decide how much weight to accord the statements. Historical and current notions of equity require that courts concentrate on the perpetrator's unlawful actions that caused a witness's unavailability, not on whether the victim knows how the legal system works and whether the defendant admits intentional obstruction of justice.

Although Giles finally acknowledged the crucial role of domestic violence context in assessing forfeiture, it failed to resolve the conflicting textual ambiguities inherent in the insistence that cross-examination is always the best means to discern the truth. Again writing for the majority in *Crawford*, Justice Scalia emphasized that the

Confrontation Clause is a substantive guarantee demanding that reliability of evidence be tested "in the crucible of cross-examination." *Crawford*'s citing to Blackstone's Commentaries of 1768 and a British historical analysis from 1713 is a stark reminder that domestic violence was neither recognized nor criminalized when those tomes were written. Thus, reliance on their unequivocal determinations of how best to seek the truth is of little use here. . . .

Because trial court judges serve as the gatekeepers in determining what evidence is admissible, they look to the Supreme Court for guidance on evolving jurisprudential norms. When the Court leaves gaps in definition, analysis, practical application, and explanation, the bench and bar fill them. That five Justices agreed on the relevance of the domestic violence context in determining forfeiture reflects an intuitive logic that ought to change the implementation dynamic.

C. Due Diligence

Forfeiture hearings are a burdensome process for all parties, particularly at the misdemeanor level where high case volume hinders the court's ability to schedule trials, let alone additional hearings, in a timely manner. However, because delays most often benefit defendants in criminal cases, this unwieldy process can easily be manipulated to their advantage. Because many victims cannot safely testify against their abusers, diligent prosecutors flag IPV cases to "fast-track" them, including setting an early date for the forfeiture hearing. This means that in addition to setting a hearing as quickly as possible, prosecutors oppose continuances as this only gives an offender more time to intimidate witnesses.

Absent a victim's testimony regarding her batterer's witness tampering, the prosecutor can provide the court with documentation ranging from jail phone calls, letters, and e-mail or phone messages to eyewitness accounts and medical records. . . .

To further aid in expediting forfeiture hearings and trials, training for medical personnel should include recording the perpetrator's identity in their records and fully describing their diagnoses (including a list of injuries and their causes, as well as a diagramed body map). Law enforcement training must also specify the importance of documenting the full history of abuse as a means of creating a paper trail and identifying other potential witnesses. All jail calls should be recorded, with high-risk cases flagged to catch those perpetrators engaging in witness tampering. Finally, victim-witness advocates should be involved in every IPV case to maintain contact with the victim, provide her with ongoing safety planning, and keep the prosecutor informed of past and ongoing abuse.

Importantly, some courts have said that the defendant's actions need not rise to the level of a crime to trigger forfeiture provisions as long as the conduct resulted in the witness being made unavailable to testify. Success in preventing a witness from testifying is also not necessarily a required element of this crime. Federal Rule of Evidence 804(b)(6) requires that the witness's unavailability was procured to trigger forfeiture, but not to secure an underlying witness tampering conviction. . . .

Increasingly, courts admit expert testimony to explain victim behavior that may seem irrational to a layperson, but is, in fact, typical, necessary, and logical when framed within the context of the abusive relationship. Jurors may not understand why a victim stayed with the offender after being beaten, delayed her help-seeking actions (e.g., calling the police or a shelter), or why these attempts failed. An expert can either describe general characteristics of IPV victims or those specific to the instant case, including whether the survivor speaks English, suffers depression, knows of the available community resources, or lacks the job skills necessary to support her children. An expert can make clear that given evidence of a batterer's far-reaching power, an IPV survivor may accurately, and thus reasonably, perceive that her only option is to comply with his demands, thus explaining her absence from court.

Although it is not always feasible, use of an expert can be enormously helpful in forfeiture hearings and in trials to explain the dynamics and impact of abuse. In the *Santiago* forfeiture hearing, a domestic violence expert elucidated why the victim repeatedly sought police help then returned to her abuser after he alternately professed his love and threatened to kill her if she took part in the prosecutions for his violent assaults. . . .

## II. Predicate Witness Tampering

Despite being the most common crime committed by batterers, witness tampering is the least charged, prosecuted, and sentenced offense. As the frequency and severity of the coercive conduct increases, the batterer gains greater control of the court-centric legal process, enabling him not only to subvert the law and avoid sanctions, but also to increase the likelihood of his recidivist harm to the victim. For victims, the consequences of perpetrator intimidation are often so dire that lingering traumatic effects interfere with almost every aspect of their lives. . . .

### A. The Aftermath of *Crawford*, *Davis*, and *Giles*

With the *Crawford*, *Davis*, and *Giles* cases, the Supreme Court muddied the troubled waters of IPV prosecution, exacerbating the already prolific incidence of witness tampering. Because IPV victims may be unable or unwilling to testify against their perpetrators, the ability to convict offenders often turns on the use of hearsay exceptions, usually excited utterances. . . .

Ignoring the prolific witness tampering occurring in IPV cases implies that critical contextual analysis is missing—an omission so great that it renders the *Crawford*, *Davis*, and *Giles* trilogy an unworkable albatross for truth-seeking courts. The devastating impact of these cases is evidenced by prosecutors across the country being forced to dismiss domestic violence cases because batterers have coerced victims not to testify at trial.

. . . .

#### 1. Endangered and Discouraged Victims

*Crawford*'s insistence that IPV victims be present to testify gives offenders greater incentive to threaten, coerce, or kill them as a means of ensuring case dismissal. That batterers' witness tampering is such a successful enterprise poses great danger for abuse victims. The latest data from the U.S. Department of Justice on homicide trends suggest that while fewer men are being murdered by an intimate partner, the corresponding rate for women has held steady for at least two decades and increased in areas lacking sophisticated medical trauma centers. Victim safety, however, must not be measured solely in terms of homicide rates, for abusers commit a wide range of heinous though nonfatal crimes against their current or former intimate partners.

Largely absent from the world of criminal adjudication are gang members who commit IPV offenses. They are often brutal in their assaults, and are proficient at intimidating their victims and the community. In many of these cases, Baltimore Judge Videtta Brown observed that, first, IPV victims are increasingly younger; second, their batterers are frequently gang-affiliated; and, third, that established IPV resources and research have generally not contemplated such victims. Intimidation is an effective means of silencing gang partner-victims if they are under eighteen, as they are usually unsure of whom to trust and lack access to protective orders. . . .

Although it is beyond the scope of this Article to discuss in detail the means and impact of batterers' use of children in their witness tampering schemes, at least a cursory mention is necessary to comprehend the scope of harm. Children may be deterred from reporting IPV abuse because of the perpetrators' continuing intimidation, which offenders sometimes couch in terms of loyalty to the family. Professor Margaret Drew stated that in her twenty-four years of family law practice, the most common witness tampering she has seen is a batterer's manipulation of his children, including telling them that their mother is going to put him in jail and that they will not be able to see him unless she dismisses the charges. The children then relentlessly beg the mother to let Dad come home and not make him suffer in prison until the mother is worn down and decides she cannot testify. The typical offender may also threaten to kill the children or their mother if the case proceeds, and makes unremitting, harassing phone calls to the victim's family, friends, and coworkers, telling her he will only stop if she either returns to him or drops the charges.

. . . Professor Drew also reported that numerous abusers use the court system to intimidate victims by filing (1) false, retaliatory complaints with child protective services, triggering invasive investigations and records for victims, (2) unsubstantiated cross petitions for civil protective orders, (3) unfounded criminal complaints, and (4) baseless civil lawsuits to harass victims into agreeing to dismiss the criminal case. Batterers may say they will kill themselves if the children report the abuse to authorities or testify in court. If victims persist in their quest for safety and justice, perpetrators seek vengeance in means as desperate as slashing victims' tires to prevent court appearances.

Survivors are likely to be discouraged from even reporting domestic violence offenses if they experience added obstacles once they turn to the courts for safety. Since the *Crawford-Davis-Giles* rulings, a great number of victims have revealed that their batterers actually explain to them that if they do not appear in court, the case must be dismissed. Armed with the knowledge that many courts have opted for dismissal rather than navigating the confusing forfeiture process, offenders are hyper-motivated to silence their victims. Thus, even when prosecutors attempt to hold batterers responsible for their crimes, witness tampering can readily sabotage prosecutors' best efforts. Most victims thus view the batterer as victor, for he has successfully manipulated the criminal justice system to ensure she cannot utilize it to achieve safety.

2. Race and Socioeconomic Status

Given that the largest national studies indicate that low-income women of color are disproportionately victimized by intimate partners, it is essential to fashion remedies that specifically address criminal justice system bias and structural inequalities. Absent sufficient financial resources, women of color are further constrained in their efforts to flee abuse. Those victims who are economically dependent on their batterers are less apt to contact the police or courts for help, and if they did so initially, would be more likely to later recant under duress.

. . . .

Compounding racial, ethnic, and socioeconomic factors, IPV victims of color often face cultural bans against seeking help with larger criminal justice entities, especially beyond the familial milieu. For example, undocumented immigrant victims fear deportation and even those here legally may have no knowledge of their rights or resources, further isolating them from possible legal remedies such as protective orders and prosecution of their abusers. Numerous IPV survivors of color face the challenge of competing loyalties rooted in race and gender, with ethnic identity prevailing because socialized oppression leaves no other choice. Prior negative experiences with domestic violence shelters, police, and courts make it more difficult for them to trust the largely white criminal justice system. Since African-American and Hispanic men are disproportionately imprisoned, victims of color also cite not wanting to feel responsible for incarcerating another man from their community and seeking to keep their family together.

The narrative on witness tampering and forfeiture would be deficient if it minimized the role that race and class play in the paradigm of proffered remedies. Indeed, the irrefutable evidence of the criminal justice system's disparate treatment of victims and offenders of color raises serious questions about the sincerity of proposed reforms that fail to address such concerns. A more vigorous forfeiture doctrine can improve victim safety and offender accountability while decreasing the understandable trepidation prevalent among those who are low-income, of color, or both.

3. Community Backlash Against IPV Victims

Too often, police and court responses to witness tampering are permeated with excuses, denial, and overt backlash against IPV victims. For at least the past two decades, a widespread, media-hyped backlash has unfurled against female victims. The sources of this vitriol sometimes label themselves feminists who contest "victim feminism" and argue that abuse victims must instead embrace "power feminism." This position assumes a notion of volition, that IPV survivors can simply choose to be empowered agents and their victimization will cease. The truth is that victimized survivors cannot stop the abuse. Only the community, when possessing collective will, has the power to make it worth the perpetrators' while to stop.

Some have voiced backlash against those seeking recognition for men as IPV victims, arguing for gender-neutral definitions and law enforcement. Absolute conceptualization is not necessary, for neither gender's IPV victimization is diminished by recognition of the other. Across the country, IPV victim advocates also report increasing backlash against victims by those in the legal system. Repeatedly over the past few years, police officers, judges, prosecutors, and law professors have expressed some version of "The pendulum has swung too far in favor of victims." That any person holds this view is troublesome. But it is unethical, and perhaps unlawful, when those whose job it is to enforce laws use this view as an excuse to justify conduct that further endangers IPV victims. The backlash must be named and its resulting harm publicized, identifying those engaging in unethical behavior and ending complicity under the guise of equal treatment of all parties.

. . . .

4. Misuse of Chronic Nuisance Laws

In addition to problematic court rulings, recently enacted chronic nuisance laws—meant to penalize repeat callers for police assistance—have further victimized some IPV survivors. Although initially designed to hold landlords and tenants responsible for drug distribution on their premises, the newer statutes include crimes of violence. The statutes protect businesses and victims from stranger violence, but there is no such provision for those victimized by an intimate partner. For example, the chronic nuisance law of Coaldale, Pennsylvania, enacted in 2006, targets domestic violence victims who request help but do not subsequently agree to take part in the offender's prosecution. . . .

Penalizing victims for repeat police calls ignores the role of witness tampering in domestic violence cases. Survivors opting not to take part in criminal prosecutions are usually doing what they believe is necessary to keep their children and themselves alive. . . . The chronic nuisance laws vary as to whether they trigger an automatic fine or arrest, but all specify that the victim incurs civil liability for failing to stop the offender's problematic behavior. Yet it is common knowledge among IPV experts that the victim cannot stop the abuse; only the community's holding the offender accountable for his crimes accomplishes that end. Given the proliferation of chronic nuisance laws adversely impacting abuse survivors, a batterer can now threaten not only his own violent retaliation for her seeking help, but can count on the state to punish the victim as well. In the process, the identity of wrongdoer becomes transposed, further alienating the true victim from the legal system and quite effectively sabotaging abuse prevention laws and rational public policy.

### B. Abusive Control

Domestic violence is characterized by intentional harms perpetrated against an intimate partner as a planned pattern of coercive control. By ascribing negative connotations of abandonment, shame, jealousy, and rejection to their victim's conduct, offenders justify inflicting abuse. It is not surprising, then, that batterers feel outraged when their crimes are reported to authorities, for then their victims are challenging their absolute power. Rarely does an IPV perpetrator take responsibility for his abuse; instead, he blames the victim for betraying him by being disobedient, assertive, or behaving in any manner that most would consider ordinary. To avoid accountability within the legal system and to regain control of his partner, the batterer typically begins his campaign of witness tampering. If this IPV offender is not in custody and his nonviolent, coercive tactics have failed to deter the victim from proceeding with legal action, then he may resort to physical attacks. Experts theorize that as the perpetrator senses he is losing control of his victim, he may escalate the violence, and even murder her. . . .

Paradoxically, leaving the abuser does not bring the victim safety because batterers frequently increase the severity of abuse during that time, including committing crimes against the victim's children, family, pets, and property. Although some victims remain with the batterers in the immediate aftermath of abuse, most flee at least temporarily, thus greatly increasing the likelihood of more dangerous forms of witness tampering later. One study found that seventy-three percent of battered women requesting emergency medical care were injured by a violent partner after leaving him. Separation abuse is thus typically part of a batterer's campaign to make accessing legal assistance too risky for the victim.

When perpetrators are not deterred by termination of the relationship or the presence of a protective order, survivors feel frustrated, vulnerable, and unsure how to achieve safety. Yet most well-intentioned professionals, friends, and family are puzzled when victims will not or cannot leave the batterer. Given that leaving the abuser often does not achieve safety, it is remarkable that little effort is made to warn victims of this likely impending danger.

. . . .

### C. Coercive Threats Implying Violence

IPV perpetrators employ an array of oppressive schemes to silence witnesses, sometimes ably conveying their threats without directly contacting the victims. Batterers who use violence to deter witnesses from testifying against them are guilty of witness intimidation, and often make good on prior threats to the victim. In the Texas capital murder case of *Hartfield v. State*,[5] prosecutors presented evidence that the defendant had been previously acquitted of sexually assaulting his wife, and that during that trial, he had publicly threatened to kill her when he was released from jail. His wife obtained a protective order, but her husband strangled her and then burned her home, for which

---

5. [n273] 28 S.W.3d 69 (Tex. App. 2000).

a court later found him guilty. The legal system's denial of the existence of IPV danger is evident in this 2000 case where the defendant Hartsfield made his death threat in open court yet was charged with neither witness intimidation nor retaliation.....

1. Nonverbal Threats

Incessant violence is sufficient but not necessary to ensure near total control, for astute batterers use tone of voice, a look, and other more subtle forms of threatening communication to ensure victim compliance. Though most people can understand the threat implicit in the simple presence of a previously harmful actor in the organized crime context, they have not been sufficiently educated to similarly analogize a batterer's impact on his victim. In The Godfather Part II, Mafioso Michael Corleone brought a long-lost brother from rural Italy to a New York hearing in which another brother was about to testify about the family's organized crime activities. Words were unnecessary to assure that no testimony was forthcoming, for the Corleone brothers knew from past experience that Michael would not hesitate to use violence to ensure that they did not cooperate with authorities. Similarly, IPV victims have learned that a batterer's frown, raised eyebrows, or seemingly innocuous comment may signal impending harm.

In some cases, the frequency and type of violence are so severe that even if the batterer is unable to directly contact the victim post arrest, she is terrorized enough so that cooperation with authorities seems implausible to her....

A defendant may resort to nonviolent means of coercion that are nonetheless quite effective, particularly if he is incarcerated. For example, Jeffrey Stillman assaulted his live-in girlfriend and was charged with attempted murder, assault, rape, and kidnapping.[6] The emergency room physician who saw the victim on the night of the attack testified: "[She] was clearly beaten about the face; her face was swollen; it was black and blue ... [and] she had scratches and abrasions here and there; she had a cut on her hand. She seemed quite upset." Another physician examined the victim the following day and diagnosed "facial bruising, ecchymosis, and trauma to the eye; perforated right ear drum," as well as a right shoulder strain and symptoms from post-traumatic strangulation. The victim testified that she passed out repeatedly from the beatings, including after being strangled by the defendant. From jail, Stillman sent several letters directing the victim to change her testimony: "Say you were drunk when they questioned you [and] the officers got you all confused.... Call my attorney [and] tell him you were drunk/confused when you gave statements [and] now you remember that I didn't hit you, rape you, or kidnap you.... Please think about a way to get me out.... You'll be glad you did!" and "I really wish you'd reconsider fixing the story." The jury found Stillman guilty of the felonious assault, rape, kidnapping, tampering

---

6. [n284] Stillman v. Moore, No. 2:05-CV-1119, 2006 WL 2787112, at 2 (S.D. Ohio Sept. 6, 2006). The jury found Stillman guilty of felonious assault, rape, kidnapping, tampering with evidence, intimidation of a witness, and the domestic violence offense, and not guilty of attempted murder. The judge ordered that the eight years on the felonious assault and the four years on the tampering be served consecutively for a total of twelve years. *Id.*

with evidence, intimidation of a witness, and the domestic violence, but not guilty of attempted murder.

2. Harming Victims' Helpers

Some batterers also retaliate against those they perceive as helping the victim in any capacity. A few prototypical case narratives may be helpful here. In the first, Vaughn Jones engaged in a terrorizing campaign of retaliation against those close to his ex-girlfriend because the San Francisco police arrested him for assaulting her.[7] Strong evidence indicated that Jones committed sixteen arson-type felonies on the homes of his ex-girlfriend's friends and relatives, and that he sent a threatening letter to the ex's ten-year-old daughter. Jones had previously said that he would "get" her and her friends if she reported the abuse and sought help from the Daly City police. Jones was subsequently convicted of domestic violence crimes and served time in the San Mateo County Jail. Upon his release, Jones distributed flyers in the neighborhoods of four friends and relatives of his ex-girlfriend, stating that child pornographers and drug dealers lived in these four person's homes. Cars and homes at those four addresses were then firebombed or otherwise subjected to arson-type crimes.

. . . .

Some perpetrators also target counsel for victims intending to deprive them of access to legal remedies. Attorney Julie Porzio was handling Donna Bochicchio's divorce from Michael Bochicchio, an abusive retired state trooper, with whom Donna had two children.[8] As Porzio and Donna pulled into the Middletown, Connecticut, court parking lot for a hearing, Bochicchio murdered his estranged wife and severely injured Porzio . . . Several prosecutors who routinely handle domestic violence cases describe incidents in which batterers attempted or threatened to harm them. These threatened lawyers expressed shock, humility, fear, and renewed compassion for their abused clients after being subjected to the perpetrators' control tactics. One attorney— whose office was trashed by a wealthy, violent defendant in a divorce case—said she will think twice before knowingly representing another battered wife. Advocates in two large American cities said they felt forced to ask abused residents to leave their shelters after their partners threatened and attempted to harm staff. Most of these lawyers explained their desire for anonymity based on fear of batterer reprisal and embarrassment, notably, the same sentiments voiced by IPV victims. . . .

3. Third Party Accomplices

Batterers also enmesh third parties in their witness tampering schemes. Some accomplices willingly collude with the batterer while others do so only under duress or significant coercion. In a recent domestic violence witness intimidation case involving high-level officials over time, New York Governor David Paterson and several of his top aides were accused of pressuring an IPV victim to drop her requests

---

7. [n290] Jaxon Van Derbeken, *Man Charged in Series of Arson Attacks on Homes of Ex's Friends*, S.F. Chron., Mar. 6, 2008, at B3.

8. [n302] 20/20: *Divorce Case Takes a Shocking Turn* (ABC television broadcast Aug. 30, 2007).

for protection orders. David Johnson, a top advisor to Governor Paterson, was alleged to have severely beaten his live-in girlfriend, Sherr-una Booker, on October 31, 2009. Staff said the Governor directed his press secretary, Marissa Shorenstein, to persuade the victim to characterize the incident as nonviolent. The same sources told the New York Times that another state employee, Deneane Brown, was directed to contact Booker and "tell her the governor wants her to make this go away." Brown also arranged a phone call between the Governor and Booker the day before Booker was to appear in court for a permanent protection order against David Johnson. The case was dismissed when Booker did not appear, although she had twice before obtained temporary protective orders, and at the first hearing, the judge had noted bruising on her arms. Booker subsequently asserted that the state police (who lacked legal authority in the case) had bullied her to refrain from seeking the protective order against Johnson. Although state police superintendent Harry Corbitt resigned in the wake of his admissions that state troopers did contact Booker, he depicted their intent as only to explain her "options." Whatever the alleged motivations for Governor Paterson and his staff's repeated contact with Booker, sufficient evidence from their own admissions existed to indicate that unlawful witness tampering occurred.

. . . .

### D. Nonviolent Coercion

Sometimes offenders resort to less overt means of victim tampering, including bribes, endearments, pleas for forgiveness, apologies, threats, and property damage. Judge Jeffrey Atlas astutely noted that although the Santiago defendant's endearments and pleas for forgiveness may have appeared innocuous, his "promises [were] not to be trusted . . . [because they] always contained the implicit threat that the complainant's unwillingness to cooperate with him [would] result in dire consequences for her." Thus, although the accused may engage in conduct that does not otherwise constitute criminal behavior, it can nonetheless be improper if it results in the complainant being dissuaded from testifying at trial.

. . . .

### III. Intent-to-Silence Calculus

Given the sea changes wrought by the *Crawford*, *Davis*, and *Giles* cases, courts are scrambling to disentangle the morass of conflicting common and statutory law. The disorder is puzzling and unnecessary because the imposed regime is contrary even to originalist views. Giles verified that at common law the two types of unconfronted statements deemed admissible were dying declarations and those made by a witness whom the defendant had prevented from appearing. Because every state has promulgated witness tampering and intimidation statutes, irrefutable legislative intent exists to justify fashioning a workable framework through which offenders can be held accountable.

In recognition of profuse witness tampering, the Federal Rules of Evidence Advisory Committee codified forfeiture in Federal Rule of Evidence 804(b)(6) as a hearsay exception. Although the rule creates a Confrontation Clause exception, its intent requirement rewards a defendant who lies about his goal in harming a witness. Similarly, insisting that the defendant must be successful in keeping the witness from testifying only places the cooperating victim in greater danger. Mandating intent and completion of unavailability is also contrary to many states' laws and unnecessarily burdens Rule 804(b)(6) with roadblocks to cessation of witness tampering.

While noting the adverse societal impact of witness tampering in domestic violence cases, Judge Jeffrey Atlas asserted that it was time to move from excuses to remedial action. He posited:

> Clearly, the nature of this syndrome and the cost to the families involved, the police, medical professionals, the courts and society in general cry out for a solution. It is simply unacceptable for our process to turn a blind eye to the dangers of such abuse by shrugging our shoulders and saying that nothing can be done within the framework of existing law.

The inquiry into whether an offender's animus rises to a level meriting forfeiture requires evaluation of the intent-to-silence standard. Every nuance has potential significance, giving currency to the argument that case factors and context can be dispositive. By definition, in IPV cases, the victim and offender have a prior or current relationship which has given the defendant access to much personal and otherwise confidential information about the victim, and her family, employment, children, habits, home, and resources. This knowledge gives an offender the means to coerce a victim under the state's radar screen, necessitating inferences in certain circumstances if justice is to be served. Because *Giles* created a new standard requiring the state to prove a defendant's animus when he committed the crime, and the offender is not likely to admit his intent, it is necessary to provide guidance for inference standards. An IPV offender does not need to specify intent for the victim to implicitly know why she is being targeted. In *Illinois v. Allen*, the U.S. Supreme Court asserted that specific intent is not required when the defendant engages in wrongdoing. Citing other precedent, the Court reasoned, "We accept instead the statement of Mr. Justice Cardozo who ... said: 'No doubt the privilege (of personally confronting witnesses) may be lost by consent or at times even by misconduct.'"

One premise of criminal law holds that if conduct is reckless enough, intent is inferred. Some courts have held that as long as a witness's unavailability is a foreseeable result of the defendant's actions, intent can be inferred or presumed. Permitting a defendant to both cause a witness's nonappearance and preclude that witness's previous statements makes the court complicit with that offender's misconduct. Since *Crawford*, *Davis*, and *Giles* did not provide much guidance in determining sufficient intent, I offer some case factors as dispositive. As discussed below, such facets range from those directly involving the court and offender crimes to those specific to the victim and overall relationship context. As is true in applying a "totality of the circumstances" standard, here, too, these considerations must flex with appropriate weight given to achieve an equitable result.

A. Murder

Capturing the thrust of the argument in favor of presuming intent to silence with murder is the following statement from a case out of the Second Circuit:

> It is hard to imagine a form of misconduct more extreme than the murder of a potential witness.... We have no hesitation in finding, in league with all circuits to have considered the matter, that a defendant who wrongfully procures the absence of a witness or potential witness may not assert confrontation rights as to that witness.[9]

Courts should presume that when a defendant commits murder, a rebuttable presumption or inference of intent to silence applies. In *Giles*, Justice Scalia stated that when an abusive relationship ends in murder, "the evidence may support a finding that the crime expressed the intent to isolate the victim and to stop her from reporting abuse to the authorities or cooperating with a criminal prosecution—rendering her prior statements admissible under the forfeiture doctrine."...

Linda Greenhouse, legal reporter for the New York Times, stated, "It is therefore likely that the Justices accepted the new case, *Giles v. California*, to make it clear that as long as the victim's unavailability as a witness was a foreseeable consequence of the murder, the Sixth Amendment does not require the state to prove the actual motive for the murder was to make the victim unavailable."...

Consistent with *Reynolds v. United States*, the 1898 case enshrining the forfeiture doctrine, federal common law has held that murdering a witness presumes the defendant intended to prevent the testimony and was successful in doing so, thereby admitting the declarant's statements....

It is a stretch to take from *Reynolds* a premise that confrontation can be denied only by conduct specifically intending to prevent a witness's testimony. The *Reynolds* Court makes no reference to the defendant's intent, seemingly disinterested in his reasons for preventing witnesses from testifying against him, only in the unjust result. Similarly, reported cases from the era in which the Sixth Amendment was drafted focus entirely on the nexus between the offender's conduct and a witness's unavailability. The forfeiture doctrine means to hold defendants responsible for setting in motion actions that prevent witness testimony, regardless of whether they were initially intended to achieve that outcome. Particularly with domestic violence murders, a defendant would be hard pressed to argue that he could neither foresee that his actions would result in great harm to the victim, nor that the injury would prevent the victim's testimony. If the protective covenant of the Sixth Amendment is stretched to protect batterers who murder their partners, the motive to ensure silence appears obvious.

---

9. [n374] *United States v. Dhinsa*, 243 F.3d 635, 652 (2d Cir. 2001) (quoting *United States v. White*, 116 F.3d 903, 911 (D.C. Cir. 1997), *cert. denied*, 522 U.S. 960 (1997)), *cert. denied*, 534 U.S. 897 (2001).

### B. Pending Legal Proceedings

Temporal proximity between a defendant's unlawful conduct and a legal proceeding could support a prima facie case for witness tampering. In *Giles*, Justice Scalia deemed "evidence of ongoing criminal proceedings at which the victim would have been expected to testify" as "highly relevant to this inquiry." A factfinder may reasonably conclude that preventive or retaliatory animus was a factor motivating the defendant to coerce the witness in part because it can be assumed that at arraignment the offender received notice that his conduct was unlawful, that he is not to commit any crimes during the pendency of his case, and that he is not to contact the victim by any means. Thus provided with specific information about prohibited conduct as part of being afforded due process, the offender has heightened knowledge of the legal system and can no longer claim to be victimized by the courts. It does not seem too much to ask that he refrain from committing crimes.

. . . .

### C. Present Protective Order

If an IPV victim obtains a protective order, and the respondent recidivates against her during its pendency, the court should presume the intent to silence. In order to obtain a protective order, an applicant must prove to a court that a domestic violence offense was committed against her and that it is likely to happen again. Meeting these elements helps document evidence of the "classic abusive relationship" that should give rise to an inference, Justice Souter argued in his *Giles* concurrence, of the perpetrator's goal of victim compliance. Most victims are reluctant to seek protective orders; the majority of those who do cite serious abuse ranging from assault and threats to kill, to kidnapping and harming children. With the infliction of repeated trauma, the offender seeks to instill such fear that the victim will be unable to fathom facing him in court or taking any action that could bring further harm to herself and her children.

The legislative intent of protective order laws is to prevent further harm to IPV victims and create a rational mechanism for enforcement. In practice, however, oversight of protective orders is left to an array of societal actors, such as police, judges, prosecutors, advocates, employers, family, and community members, who impose their own arbitrary biases about which victims deserve attention. An IPV perpetrator's willingness to violate a protective order signals disrespect for the court's authority as well as for the safety and privacy rights of the victim. This type of brazen disregard for the rule of law compounded by lax police enforcement caused all states to append criminal charges to violation of protective orders. Some courts and law enforcement accord a minimal level of deference to their own protective orders, thus emboldening offenders to perpetuate the "classic abusive relationship."

### D. Classic Abusive Relationship

Whether a batterer murders his victim or engages in other coercive conduct, *Giles* also stated, "Earlier abuse, or threats of abuse, intended to dissuade the victim from resorting to outside help would be highly relevant to this inquiry, as would evidence of ongoing criminal proceedings at which the victim would have been expected to testify." Under this standard, the state must be prepared to show not only that prior abuse occurred, but also that its intent was to deter the victim from seeking assistance. Absent the victim's testimony to assert this causal connection, the prosecutor may need to offer an expert or empirical data explaining that an offender need not utter a word to discourage a victim from contacting authorities for aid. However, such complicating and unnecessary impediments should be removed because the defendant's confrontation rights can be preserved without rewarding him for silencing his victim.

Notably, Justice Souter argued in his *Giles* concurrence that intent to silence should be inferred with proof of a "classic abusive relationship." The Court has signaled that evidence of prior abuse should be admissible if it deterred the witness from testifying. Many facets of the *Giles* decision seemingly beckon the state to prove intent through use of substantive evidence other than a victim's direct testimony, be it circumstantial, based on acceptable hearsay, or otherwise performing the function of truth-seeking.

The *Giles* decision mistakenly implied that it is relatively easy to obtain documentation of the scope, severity, duration, and type of prior abuse to meet this standard. There are many reasons why a victim does not contact authorities to report previous harm, thereby depriving the state of a paper trail by which to document the dangerous history that the court could interpret as expressing the intent to silence. Consistent with state evidentiary rules, a prosecutor should be afforded latitude in the means by which she proves evidence of a "classic abusive relationship."

. . . .

E. Recantation

. . . .

Several courts have found that when a victim recants her earlier story of abuse, prior domestic violence between the parties is, in the words of one of these courts, "relevant to show the trier of fact the context of the relationship between the victim and the defendant, where . . . that relationship is offered as a possible explanation for the victim's recantation."[10] By creating and exploiting victim vulnerabilities, IPV offenders make recantation as typical in this context as in gang, organized crime, and drug cases. It is estimated that between eighty and ninety percent of domestic violence victims decline to participate in the prosecution or recant their allegations. This astonishingly high number demands a rethinking of the structural, cognitive, and psychological basis of the witness tampering-forfeiture paradigm.

F. Mixed Purpose

In most jurisdictions, the forfeiture rule requires neither that the declarant be a witness at the time of the tampering nor that the defendant's sole intent was to silence her. . . . Because the rule of forfeiture is designed to prevent precisely the outcome of

---

10. [n415] *State v. Arakawa*, 61 P.3d 537, 545 (Haw. Ct. App. 2002).

rewarding offender misconduct, a batterer's claim that he lacked intentionality cannot control whether testimonial statements are admissible.

. . . .

G. Admissibility of Nontestimonial Hearsay

. . . .

After *Giles*, an IPV victim's statements made to a physician as part of her medical care should presumptively be admitted. Since the 2004 *Crawford* decision, prosecutors have lamented that some judges have mistakenly redacted from medical records a victim's identification of the defendant as her assailant. It is often relevant to the provision of care for the medical provider to know who caused an IPV victim's injuries. For instance, in order to determine an effective discharge plan, the physician must know if the patient has a safe place to live and strategies to avoid recurrent harm. By directly asking the identity of the IPV perpetrator and documenting his name in the medical record, the present doctor and all subsequent medical providers will be in a better position to assist that victim with safety planning and abuse prevention. *Davis* allowed that a 911 operator's questions regarding the perpetrator's identity can be "necessary to be able to resolve the present emergency" because law enforcement en route to the scene need to "know whether they would be encountering a violent felon." Along these same lines, physicians can assert that effective patient care necessitates their having a complete picture of a battered patient's immediate and future danger risks.

Healthcare professionals also need to know if the perpetrator came to the hospital with the victim and is in the waiting room where he can cause further harm to the victim and staff. Because IPV perpetrators generally engage in chronic and repeat abuse, it is foreseeable that victims will remain in danger. Also, medical providers may be the only persons to whom the victim discloses this information, making it particularly important that they implement effective interventions.

. . . .

In addition to the use of medical records, friends, neighbors, coworkers, fellow parishioners, and other nongovernmental agents should be interviewed to determine if the victim told them about the abuse. These people are sometimes willing to testify about their knowledge of the abuse, but are often too frightened of the perpetrator to assist. They are understandably intimidated because they either have seen that the defendant is quite willing to carry out his threats of pre-emptive or retaliatory violence, or have already been direct targets of his witness tampering.

It should be noted that hearsay and testimonial evidence are not completely excluded from criminal trial proceedings. Hearsay and testimonial statements are admissible in probation revocation and restitution hearings, for example. Reliable hearsay and testimonial statements are admissible in probation revocation hearings because these proceedings not intended to be adversarial. Restitution hearings are viewed in a similar light, allowing the state to meet its burden of proof (regarding costs to the victim) through the introduction of relevant evidence, including hearsay.

H. Context

While most courts do not acknowledge the forfeiture doctrine in IPV cases, some have correctly inferred forfeiture from examining cumulative circumstances and the history of abuse in each case. *Giles* appears to have adopted this position—that the state should not have to prove a defendant said he intended to dissuade a witness from testifying if it can be presumed from the totality of his actions. Legal scholars and prosecutors agree that, most often, the abuser's ongoing coercive behavior is the direct cause of the victim not appearing for trial. It is thus imperative that when judges make forfeiture determinations, they hear the complete history of abuse, including that which occurred prior to the charge before the court. In *Santiago*, Judge Atlas conducted a forfeiture hearing in which he allowed the victim, her counselor, a responding New York City police officer, a prosecutor with whom the victim had spoken, and a domestic violence expert to testify about the full history of mistreatment. In finding that the defendant Victor Santiago's ongoing abuse caused his girlfriend's absence, Judge Atlas clarified:

> I do not believe that the cases admitting prior testimony of an unavailable witness should be read to hold that prior evidence given by an unavailable witness is admissible only when the defendant's misconduct causing the unavailability occurs between the defendant's arrest and the date of trial. While that may occur in the usual case, domestic violence matters are of such a different character as to justify a broader application of the rule.

In rejecting the limited post-arrest timeframe, Judge Atlas provided the basis on which prosecutors can rest when arguing for admission of relevant history of abuse between the parties at bar. Although recognition of defendants' longstanding abusive courses of conduct is just gaining traction within criminal law, its civil corollary is the doctrine of continuing tort. If abuse occurs over a prolonged period and forms "a continuous and unbroken wrong," the doctrine permits courts to toll the statute of limitations as a means of holding batterers responsible for the full range of harm they have inflicted. Just as continuing tort enables courts to consider the cumulative effect of batterer harm in its liability calculus, so, too, should forfeiture analysis weigh the same comprehensive scope of coercive conduct.

An IPV defendant's prior bad acts should also be subject to contextual analysis. The case of *Gardner v. State*[11] provides an example. Married six times, John Steven Gardner shot his second wife, Rhonda, early in her pregnancy, causing a miscarriage and permanent paraplegia. Convicted of aggravated assault, he served eight years in prison, but while there, Gardner met this third wife, Margaret, and soon started threatening to kill her and her family. When Margaret fled, Gardner kidnapped her at work and was sent back to prison after leading police on a high-speed chase. Because Gardner

---

11. [n451] No. AP-75582, 2009 WL 3365652 (Tex. Crim. App. Oct. 21, 2009).

repeatedly threatened to "hunt her down" if she ever left him, Margaret remained in fear of him. Gardner subsequently murdered his sixth wife, Tammy, after a terrorizing campaign of life-threatening assaults and threats against Tammy and her family—while in the presence of her young daughter.

*Gardner* illustrates the reasons why a more robust forfeiture doctrine must be embraced to further the construct of IPV as criminal conduct. Had Gardner been apprehended and prosecuted when intimidating Mary, perhaps Tammy would still be alive. With its intent-based doctrinal standard, the *Giles* majority constrained lower courts from serving their gate-keeping function. Absent specific guidance about the kind of evidence needed to find intent, lower courts are struggling to make sense of this mandate. In his concurrence, Justice Souter noted that the historical precedent on which the majority relies lacks consideration of intent in the context of domestic violence because the Framers did not have the benefit of today's awareness. More importantly, Justice Souter argued that there is no basis to suspect that the Framers would have disagreed with the inference that forfeiture's requisite intent could be met with evidence of a "classic abusive relationship." He concluded emphatically, stating, "If the evidence for admissibility shows a continuing relationship of this sort, it would make no sense to suggest that the oppressing defendant miraculously abandoned the dynamics of abuse the instant before he killed his victim, say in a fit of anger."

Given the importance of context, a prosecutor should be permitted to use explicit, implicit, and circumstantial evidence to prove that the batterer caused a witness's unavailability. Professor Melissa Hamilton's empirical research documents judicial discourse that is critical of battered women who do not fight back against their abusers, do not leave violent relationships, and fail to resist reconciliation. This important recent scholarship notes that judges continue to assume that fleeing a batterer is logical, safe, and simple, while ignoring the powerful role of intimidation. In IPV cases, an expansive notion of threats must be employed to accurately take account of the deleterious intent of offender coercion.

Courts could well apply what Harvard Business School professors Nitin Nohria and Anthony Mayo call "contextual intelligence"—the use of intuitive analytic skills to understand the tactics and objectives at play in an evolving IPV relationship, and to recognize the victim's behavior as her adaptive strategies. Victims must use contextual intelligence—adapting to knowledge of batterers' behavioral patterns—in attempting to survive batterers' often-changing, oppressive tactics. In *Santiago*, Judge Atlas modeled contextual intelligence by hearing the full extent of defendant Victor Santiago's coercion and violence against his girlfriend, and then weaving context into his richer forfeiture analysis.

Because some judges do not understand the power of a batterer's coercive control over time, even absent violence, they are unable to appreciate its importance when evaluating causation with an unavailable abuse victim. Judge Atlas's opinion in *Santiago* makes clear that in order to conduct a meaningful forfeiture hearing, the court must take into account the full history of perpetrator abuse. Evidencing a highly sophisticated understanding of witness tampering, Judge Atlas notes that the batterer's coercive conduct permeates every facet of the relationship, necessitating a contextual analysis of each party's actions.

Rather than place a temporal restriction on proffered evidence, the standard from the continuing tort doctrine offers a more equitable alternative. With continuing tort, courts admit all evidence of abuse that is part of an ongoing course of conduct. An expanded forfeiture doctrine thus connotes significance not only for the harm from individual acts of abuse, but also for the cumulative physical and emotional effects of that abuse. Batterers frequently inflict many forms of trauma, each intensifying the harm of previous injuries.

. . . .

Knowledge of past abuse is vital to appreciating the contextual basis of a victim's reasonable perception that a batterer's imminent retaliation is likely. Professor Elizabeth Schneider explained that intimate partner violence is "premised on an understanding of coercive behavior and of power and control—including a continuum of sexual and verbal abuse, threats, economic coercion, stalking, and social isolation—rather than 'number of hits.'" Several courts have found that particularly when a victim recants her earlier story of abuse, prior domestic violence between the parties is "relevant to show the trier of fact the context of the relationship between the victim and the defendant, where . . . that relationship is offered as a possible explanation for the victim's recantation."

Judge Atlas articulated a necessarily broader standard that specifically included conduct prior to the arrest for the case presently before the court. Judge Atlas's position specifically included conduct prior to the arrest for the case presently before the court. Professor Myrna Raeder believes that when dealing with domestic abuse forfeiture cases, a greater evidentiary standard is warranted. She proposed a wider evidentiary relevance spectrum, including information regarding prior domestic violence arrests, previous victim recantations, post-traumatic stress disorder, and history of abuse. This proposal also provides the specific language and rationales to facilitate admission of relevant evidence that assist the factfinder in determining whether witness tampering occurred and forfeiture should result.

Often, single pieces of evidence fail to indicate abusers' intent to silence; rather, viewing the cumulative evidence in its totality forms the picture. This more nuanced analysis requires that the factfinder be fully aware of typical domestic violence dynamics in order to accurately assess the tipping point as to how much prior abuse, recantation, crime scene evidence, or other factors are enough to warrant forfeiture.

. . . .

## Conclusion

For those IPV victims who do take part in the court process, retaliation is highly likely, and yet it is rarely addressed adequately by the legal system. Batterers' overt reprisals serve to punish victims for cooperating with authorities and to warn them not to do so again. The current scheme the Supreme Court provided in the *Giles-Davis-Crawford* triad is largely unworkable, at least in part because of confusing mandates and contrary opinions. In his *Giles* dissent, Justice Breyer expressed "the need for a rule that can be applied without creating great practical difficulties and evidentiary anomalies." By identifying the most equitable approaches specified in well-reasoned decisions, untenable results should be minimized. As officers of the court sworn to ensure that justice is served, lawyers must not lose hope that witness tampering can be eradicated by implementing reforms that serve normative criminal law goals. . . .

## II. Evidence of Prior Acts of Domestic Violence in Homicide and Other Domestic Violence Cases

All of the confrontation issues inherent in domestic violence cases involving reluctant victims are, of course, present in domestic violence homicide prosecutions where there is no survivor to testify. Obviously, as noted in *Giles*, the admissibility of statements made by the deceased to friends or physicians as opposed to law enforcement are not testimonial and would be governed by local evidentiary rules. Some of this type of evidence helped the prosecutors convict in *People v. Bierenbaum,* a New York homicide case, where the body of the victim was never found. The state's intermediate appellate court, in a decision reprinted in part below, upheld the conviction. That case is followed by *People v. Dorm,* a recent case from the New York Court of Appeals that discusses the use of prior acts of domestic violence to place current charges in context.

Given the dynamic of escalating violence inherent in so many domestic violence cases, the question of how much evidence will be presented to the trier of fact of prior incidents of abuse and for what purpose they will be offered becomes one of critical importance to both sides. To understand some of the nuances of the *Bierenbaum* and *Dorm* cases, readers must appreciate what in New York is called "Molineux evidence." There is a similar rule in other states and in federal law. Molineux evidence consists of other crimes or bad acts that is introduced by prosecutors when it tends to establish motive, intent, absence of mistake, a common scheme or plan or the identification of the perpetrator. *See People v. Molineux,* 168 N.Y. 264 (1901).

### People v. Bierenbaum

New York Supreme Court, Appellate Division, First Department

301 A.D.2d 119 (2002)

Marlow, J.

A jury convicted Robert Bierenbaum of second-degree murder based on circumstantial evidence that on July 7, 1985 he intentionally killed his wife, Gail Katz Bierenbaum, in their Manhattan apartment; transported her body to a New Jersey airport the same day; loaded it onto a small private plane; and piloted it over the Atlantic

Ocean where he discarded her remains. Neither her body nor her remains has ever been found.

. . . .

## THE CIRCUMSTANTIAL EVIDENCE

That the victim died July 7, 1985 is conceded. That defendant was the last person who saw her, and who was known to have been alone with her until 11:00 A.M. that day, cannot be persuasively disputed on the basis of this record. Contested are the way and reason her life ended, the way her killer disposed of her body immediately thereafter, and her killer's identity and state of mind.

The trial testimony and physical exhibits revealed the following:

In 1982 defendant and the victim married. From the beginning, they quarreled frequently. No witness disputed that their discord and fighting reached a level characterized by threats against the victim and at least one previous violent act by defendant against her. Defendant essentially admitted as much, and was heard to say, more than once, that during one argument there was "physical contact," that their last argument was "explosive" and "severe," and that he was frustrated in his marriage because they argued constantly. He also said that he hated the victim so much, and that she would get him so upset, that he wanted to kill her.

They both complained many times to many people that their marriage was loveless and their life together was stormy. On one occasion a coworker overheard defendant in a common work area arguing loudly with his wife over the telephone. The victim would complain also that defendant tried to exert excessive control over her, and she expressed fear of him more than once. The record is replete with evidence depicting events and statements which motivated the victim to end her marriage. In 1984, she was so unhappy that she consulted a divorce lawyer.

One day in the fall of 1983, at about 3:00 P.M., the victim called her cousin, Hillard Wiese, an attorney, at his office. "Speaking in very hushed tones and very rapidly" and "sounding extremely upset," she told him that she and defendant had a fight the night or day before. She said that he, not for the first time, had choked her, although this was the first time she was thereby rendered unconscious. When she came to, he begged her forgiveness and promised it would never happen again. She told Wiese she was speaking quickly and softly because she was expecting defendant. She called Wiese again the following day to let him know she took his advice and was staying with her grandfather. . . .

The trial record also makes it clear — notwithstanding the victim occasionally vacillated about terminating her marriage — this couple was on the verge of divorce in July 1985. While married to defendant, the victim had an affair with at least one other man; just before the day she disappeared she stated to a friend she was about to tell defendant she wanted a divorce; she had borrowed money to prepare to leave; she said she was seeing one or two other men and that she loved one of them; she was looking for an apartment and was seen with circled newspaper ads for apartment rentals the day before she disappeared and her friend had offered her a place in Connecticut to stay while she got herself resettled. Defendant himself said his wife told him she wanted a divorce.

The proof is most telling that on the very day the victim disappeared, she intended to confront defendant with her decision to leave him. She was also determined to make it clear to defendant that she would use a letter, written to her by his psychiatrist warning her of the danger he posed to her, in order to humiliate him with his professional peers should he refuse to meet her divorce settlement demands. To that same end, she also planned to threaten to expose his and his father's alleged multimillion-dollar Medicare fraud.

At the time the deceased disappeared, defendant was a surgical resident at Maimonides Hospital and a licensed pilot. On July 7, 1985, at 4:30 P.M., he rented a Cessna 172 plane at Caldwell Airport in Fairfield, New Jersey. He returned it after one hour and 56 minutes, giving him time enough to fly round trip approximately 165 miles over a part of the Atlantic Ocean. From the rental office's vantage point, one would not have been able to see defendant on the tarmac getting ready to board—and possibly load luggage or other items onto—the plane, which was in a position readily accessible by automobile for such purposes.

Later the same day, around 6:30 P.M., defendant arrived alone at his sister's Montclair, New Jersey home for his nephew's birthday party. There he told his father that he and his wife had an argument earlier that day, that she left for Central Park, and she had not returned by the time he left Manhattan. Significantly, he omitted telling his father that he had flown an airplane for nearly two hours that very afternoon.

That evening, he went to the home of his friend, Dr. Scott Baranoff. From there, he telephoned his apartment more than once. A seemingly distraught defendant also told Baranoff about the argument, adding that his wife had not yet returned after having left their apartment wearing shorts, a halter top and sandals. However, he again omitted to mention that he had rented and flown an airplane for almost two hours that same afternoon, a consistent omission whenever he told others about the events of July 7.

When defendant returned to their Manhattan apartment, he telephoned his wife's friend and former psychology teacher, Dr. Yvette Feis. He told her of the argument and that the victim had left for Central Park with a blanket for sunbathing. Defendant and Dr. Feis spoke daily that first week, but during the first few calls she urged him to contact the police and to speak to the doorman.

At 9:00 P.M. the next night (July 8), he finally spoke to Detective Vergilio Dalsass, telling him that his wife left their apartment at 11:00 A.M. on July 7 to sunbathe in Central Park wearing pink shorts and a white t-shirt. He stated he had remained behind in their apartment until 5:30 P.M. before leaving for his sister's New Jersey home.

. . . .

Defendant called a number of the deceased's friends voicing expressions of concern that she may have harmed herself, specifically attributing that notion to comments made to him by her therapist, Dr. Sybil Baran. However, Dr. Baran unequivocally denied she had ever said anything like that to defendant or that she ever discussed anything with him on that subject. To the contrary, it was her professional opinion, based on three years of treating the deceased once or twice weekly, that she was not suicidal. . . .

Furthermore, on July 14, while with his wife's friend Maryann DeCesare and a group of friends who were searching for her and posting missing person signs in Central Park and elsewhere, defendant quipped that he thought his wife—who was missing for a full week—was on a shopping spree at Bloomingdale's, adding, "You know what a JAP[12] she was." When the search party returned to the marital apartment— only seven days after his wife's disappearance—defendant volunteered to his mother-in-law, in DeCesare's presence, "I wonder why the cat got sick. I had to take the rug out to be cleaned."

Later on July 14, at a meeting at Detective Dalsass' office arranged by the deceased's sister Alayne Katz, and with her parents and defendant's father also present, Dalsass interviewed defendant again face-to-face. The detective specifically made it clear to defendant the importance of omitting nothing in describing and detailing for him the last three days his wife and he spent together. . . .

Notwithstanding these and other direct, uncomplicated admonitions, defendant omitted telling Detective Dalsass that he and his wife had argued that Sunday morning. However, in the July 8 interview, he had specifically denied that the reason she left the apartment at 11:00 A.M. to sunbathe in Central Park was related to an argument that morning. In addition, he had, the day before (July 13), told Detective O'Malley that he and his wife had argued the night before she "disappeared" and continued arguing on the morning of July 7, prompting her to go to Central Park at 11:00 A.M. to "cool off."

He again omitted on July 14 to tell Dalsass—and O'Malley as well the day before— that he was a licensed pilot, rented a plane in New Jersey, and flew it for two hours from 4:30 P.M. to 6:30 P.M. on July 7. Instead, he falsely told both detectives, on a total of at least three occasions, that he stayed in his Manhattan apartment all day until 5:30 P.M., emphasizing to Dalsass that he was "positive" that "he left [his apartment] at 5:30 [P.M.]." He also changed his claim that on July 7 he had spoken to the doorman who, he had originally maintained, said he saw the victim leave the building Sunday shortly after 11:00 A.M. In fact, the doorman did not speak to defendant July 7 and could not recall seeing either defendant or the deceased that day.

. . . .

---

12. [n*] "*Offensive Slang* A Jewish-American girl or woman regarded as being pampered or over-indulged" (American Heritage Dictionary of the English Language 935 [4th ed 2000]).

The record also reveals that, although in July defendant told Detective Dalsass he would respond to his request to view the apartment, defendant in fact did not contact Dalsass until September 12, 1985, and he did not permit entry until September 30. When Dalsass arrived, the crime scene unit was only allowed to search for fingerprints, the victim's diary and her address book. The investigators were not permitted to check for blood or hair samples or to search for "anything that we could document that a crime took place."

In the days, weeks, months and years following his wife's disappearance, defendant made several inconsistent, unfounded or otherwise suspect and incriminating statements. Among them are the following examples: he told Detective Dalsass that he and his wife had no argument on July 7, but he told Detective O'Malley that they argued on July 6 and continued on the morning of July 7. He told her friend, Dr. Feis, that they had a severe argument the day of her disappearance, more severe than he had originally described to her and to various other people. He admitted that during the July 7 argument he failed to heed his psychiatrist's advice to try to defuse the situation and that this argument on the day she disappeared became "explosive." He told others that he and the victim argued just before she left for Central Park "to cool off"; another that a private investigator he had hired found evidence she was living in California probably with financial help from her family; others that she had a drug problem, that she may have disappeared with drug dealers and that she probably was murdered by her "druggie friends"; others that she may have run off to live with someone in the Caribbean; and others that his missing wife was seen after July 7, 1985 "in some type of fugue state" in the Central Park area and that it was unlikely she would return.

. . . .

A few weeks after his wife disappeared, defendant began dating a nurse whom he knew from Maimonides Hospital where they were employed. In late July or early August, defendant asked her out, and they became intimate on their first date. They saw each other socially about five times over the next six weeks, until she abruptly ended their relationship because, in her view, he unjustifiably "attacked" her verbally one evening in a restaurant. Early in that period, before they began dating, and therefore significantly before the end of September, he falsely told her the police had searched his apartment and car and found him to be "clean." Furthermore, she testified that, during that early period, he expressed no concern about his wife's disappearance.

Thereafter, commencing in September 1985 and continuing for a period just under one year, defendant invited a medical student, Dr. Roberta Karnofsky, who worked under his direct supervision at Coney Island Hospital, to live with him in the marital apartment. They began dating a month before she moved in. During their entire relationship, she did not observe him make any efforts to locate his missing wife.

. . . .

At one point while they lived together, on a day that Dr. Karnofsky was angry or annoyed with defendant, and, having heard a number of accusatory answering machine messages directed at defendant, she confronted him "to see what his reaction [would be]":

> "What I said to him was, well, I think that if you did this and if it really happened as some people seem to think it did, that perhaps something happened in the apartment and you intentionally or unintentionally — Gail was hurt, you could have put her in one of those big flight bags or duffel bags and carried her out of the apartment since she was very small, put her in the back of your car, drive out to the airport and thrown her body out of the plane."

Defendant displayed no reaction, "he didn't say anything."

About midway through their one-year relationship, defendant gave his approval to have Dr. Karnofsky's girlfriend, Sharon, also move into the apartment temporarily. She expressed this homicide theory to Sharon one day while defendant was not home. Together, the two women looked for and found defendant's flight log. In it, they located a handwritten entry which appeared to have been changed from the original notation of July 7, 1985 to the substituted date of August 7, 1985. The jury saw this altered document.

. . . .

Through the testimony of several witnesses, including four expert witnesses — New York City's Chief Medical Examiner, an experienced New York City police pilot, an aviation safety inspector, and an airline transport pilot/flight instructor/FAA flight test examiner — the People established that it was physically possible for defendant, a surgical resident and pilot, unassisted, to disarticulate a recently expired body of the victim's size (5 feet, 3 inches tall, weighing 110 pounds) within 10 minutes, pack her dismembered torso and limbs into a flight/duffel bag and carry them through an unmonitored rear exit of his apartment building for a distance of two blocks to his garaged car. They also proved that it was also feasible for him to so transport the bag containing the decedent's remains — whether disarticulated or intact — to Caldwell Airport in Fairfield, New Jersey, and load it aboard a Cessna 172 plane directly from the car parked alongside on the tarmac, all unnoticed. They further established that it was possible for defendant, also alone, to pilot the Cessna 172 over the Atlantic Ocean as much as 85 miles east of the shoreline, maintain sufficient control of this relatively easy-to-operate plane so as to singlehandedly throw these human remains from the air into the ocean, and then land back at the same airport, all in less than two hours of flight time. . . .

## DISCUSSION

*1. Reasonable Doubt*

. . . .

To begin with, any notion that the victim disappeared in some way other than her actual demise on July 7, 1985 is utterly dispelled by a combination of the legitimate inferences raised by all the proof and by defendant's concession that his wife died, and that she died that day. There is every reason in this record to find that defendant was the last person to see her alive at 11:00 A.M. that Sunday morning. Apart from the fact that there is no reliable evidence that anyone else saw or heard from her thereafter, defendant repeatedly admitted to several people, including his father, that he last saw her then. In fact, defendant even misstated to Detective O'Malley that the building doorman said he last saw her leave the building shortly after 11 o'clock on July 7. Defendant later retracted that claim.

Second, he admitted that their marriage was unhappy and virtually over, and that his own anger had reached a level tempting him toward violence against her because he was so frustrated by the strife between them. Moreover, he told Dr. Feis—after withholding the whole truth from others, and from her during their many earlier conversations subsequent to July 7—that his last encounter with his wife on July 7 ended in an argument more "severe" than he had previously let on, that it "had become explosive," and that in its midst he had failed to heed his psychiatrist's advice to "defuse the situation." More specifically, he also admitted to his father that they had "difficulty in adjusting to each other," and in 1983 "that they had an argument, had some physical contact." By way of corroboration, Dr. Leigh McCullough testified that in November 1983 she saw "finger shaped" bruises on the victim's neck, and the latter told her that defendant choked her when he became angry at seeing her smoking a cigarette.

By 1985, the parties' three-year-old marriage can fittingly be described as an emotional battleground. Verbal strife plagued it, express and implied threats uttered by defendant aggravated it, and defendant's admitted violence against his victim during at least one episode surely worsened it. By July, it was against this backdrop that a divorce was virtually inevitable—a situation exacerbated further by defendant's knowledge of his wife's adultery.

Armed with circled apartment rental ads the day before she disappeared, the victim declared to her close friend, Denise Kasenbaum, that she was leaving defendant that weekend. The evidence is also strong that she was determined to confront defendant with her divorce demands. Her stated intentions, should defendant refuse to accede to those demands, were plain. First, she would threaten to humiliate him by publishing to his professional colleagues and superiors a warning letter she had received from defendant's treating psychiatrist; and, second, she would threaten to expose an alleged Medicare fraud in which she claimed he and his father were allegedly involved. As discussed at greater length elsewhere in this opinion, notwithstanding defendant's contentions to the contrary, this evidence is clearly relevant not only to motive, but to intent and identity.

. . . .

In addition to the foregoing powerful circumstantial evidence, the People contend that the interplay between certain items of evidence also supports the verdict. . . . Therefore, in the aggregate, the People convincingly advance the conclusion that the jury's verdict was correct. Illustrative—but not exhaustive—are the following examples:

1. Defendant misstated that the doorman told him he saw the victim on the afternoon of July 7, when in fact the doorman made it clear he saw her last on July 6 and he could not remember whether he saw either the victim or defendant at all on July 7;

2. Defendant described differently to different people the items the victim took and the clothes she wore when she purportedly left to sunbathe in Central Park, and whether she was then wearing shoes and her engagement ring;

3. Defendant gave contradictory accounts about whether and why he sent the living room rug out to be cleaned immediately following the decedent's disappearance, but completely withheld that information from the police;

4. He was inconsistent about his purported knowledge of his wife's post-July 7 whereabouts, alluding to different theories and purported sightings to different people . . . ;

5. Perhaps defendant's most damning omission was his repeated, false claim to the police and to others that he remained in the apartment all afternoon on July 7 and then went directly to his nephew's birthday party in New Jersey. However, the evidence also conclusively establishes that he rented and flew a Cessna 172 airplane beginning at 4:30 P.M. that day from Caldwell Airport in Fairfield, New Jersey and returned two hours later at 6:30 P.M. He can hardly claim with any credibility that an interlude of that nature and length slipped his mind when he spoke to the police and others on the first day, or, indeed, at least four times during the first week, following his wife's "unexplained" disappearance.

Compounding the significance of that devastating omission — an omission which concealed the very means and opportunity to dispose permanently of his victim's body — is the documentary evidence found in his home several months after July 1985 showing clearly that his written flight log entry for July 7 was changed from July 7 to August 7.

Furthermore, he said to at least two people, not including the police, that he had searched for his inexplicably missing wife in Central Park on the afternoon of July 7 and there allegedly found the suntan oil and towel she had taken with her when she left the apartment at 11:00 A.M.

However, notwithstanding that, initially, the police carefully explained to him at least three times their critical need to know every detail he was able to recall in order to aid their search efforts, he withheld all of this information during their interviews with him — one encounter a mere 34 hours, and the others all within seven days — following his wife's disappearance. It is beyond cavil that this information was relevant and that it was exactly the type they implored him to convey. Instead, he consistently told the police and others that he remained in the marital apartment from the time the victim had left at 11:00 A.M. until 5:30 P.M., then going directly to his nephew's birthday party at his sister's New Jersey home;

6. During the first police interview of defendant on July 8 at 9:00 P.M., lasting 45 minutes, Detective Dalsass asked defendant for a list of the names and phone numbers of the victim's friends, relatives and others to facilitate the search efforts. Because defendant did not have a list with him, Dalsass said he would call defendant's home for it that evening. However, defendant said he would not be home until later, as he had plans to dine out—after an interview which had focused on his wife's sudden "disappearance" just 34 hours earlier. Dalsass waited until 12:30 A.M. and left the first of approximately eight messages on defendant's home answering machine and at his work number during the ensuing week. Defendant responded to none of them. Consequently, although defendant had contact with Detective O'Malley in the interim, Detective Dalsass could not speak to defendant to obtain that vital information until the July 14 interview. Furthermore, he did not turn over the victim's telephone/address book until more than two weeks after her disappearance;

7. He told several people that, just before his wife left the apartment for the last time, they argued. Nevertheless, he contradicted himself among various versions and aspects of those statements. Furthermore, when defendant spoke to Detective Dalsass on Monday, July 8 and again on Sunday, July 14, he never said—indeed on July 8 he denied—that he and his wife argued that morning, even though Dalsass did acknowledge that defendant, on July 14, said the victim was "pissed" the morning she left. However, apparently also on July 8, defendant told the victim's therapist, Dr. Sybil Baran, that he and the victim had argued and that "she'd gone off in a huff";

8. Although defendant would not allow any police officers to view or inspect his apartment until September 30, 1985—and then only with severe restrictions—he, long before that day, falsely stated to others that the police had searched his home and car and found him to "be clean"; and

9. Defendant falsely attributed to Dr. Baran the opinion that the victim was depressed and might have committed suicide. Dr. Baran unequivocally denied she had ever made either of those statements to defendant or that she had even held these opinions. In fact, several witnesses, including Dr. Baran, described the victim's state of mind during the period before July 7 as being "happy," "jovial" and the like.

Defendant's lies, misstatements and omissions powerfully bespeak his consciousness of guilt. We recognize that the law most often views consciousness of guilt evidence as weak—but not always. The Court of Appeals has made that clear. In *People v. Cintron* (95 NY2d 329, 333, 740 N.E.2d 217, 717 N.Y.S.2d 72), the Court said that the "probative weight" of evidence of consciousness of guilt is "highly dependent upon the facts of each particular case." . . . .

In light of the foregoing, this verdict is supported by legally sufficient evidence and it is thoroughly consistent with the evidentiary weight.

## 2. *Psychiatrist's Warning Letter and Other Hearsay*

The Trial Justice rejected the People's pretrial request to call defendant's treating psychiatrists and psychologist as witnesses to testify about factual matters and opinions connected to their treatment of defendant, including the conversations they had with the victim and defendant's parents, after defendant's consent was procured. The court did, however, permit the prosecution to adduce testimony that the victim had received a letter from one of these psychiatrists warning her of the danger defendant posed to her, although the Justice prohibited the People from introducing the letter itself. . . .

The psychiatrist communicated the consented-to warning by sending a letter, sometimes referred to as a *Tarasoff* letter (*see Tarasoff v. Regents of Univ. of California,* 17 Cal. 3d 425, 131 Cal. Rptr. 14, 551 P.2d 334), to the victim. The Justice allowed the jury to learn only of its existence and nature, but not of its specific contents beyond its warning to the victim that defendant posed a threat to her. That ruling was correct, first, because defendant waived his CPLR 4504(a) privilege by consenting that the warning be communicated; second, because a warning under these circumstances is an exception to the principle of confidentiality since the psychiatrist is under a duty to warn the intended target of a patient's violence; third, because the nature and existence of the warning letter were relevant to the state of the parties' marriage and defendant's motive to kill his wife in light of her stated intent to use it as leverage in her contemplated divorce action against defendant by confronting him with it and threatening to reveal its contents if he refused to meet her divorce settlement demands; and, finally, because it was relevant to prove, in addition to motive and the state of the parties' marriage, the interrelated issues of his intent to kill her and his identity as her killer.

. . . .

One of the prosecution's key assertions was that defendant was motivated to kill his wife because she threatened to destroy him by exposing the letter's contents should he fail to meet her divorce demands. It was therefore highly relevant to the question of defendant's motive that the jury be allowed to know and consider the consequences the victim intended by threatening defendant with such a disclosure to his superiors and peers, a disclosure which would likely compromise severely his professional status, his personal reputation and standing, and his economic future. While defendant understandably argues that this ruling prejudiced him at trial, we hold that under these circumstances it did not unduly do so.

. . . .

Turning next to defendant's hearsay claims, he argues that the Trial Justice erroneously allowed several People's witnesses to testify that the victim had told them that, inter alia, her marriage was stormy, that she was afraid of defendant, that he was very controlling, that there was much verbal strife between them, that her husband had occasionally made threatening statements to her, that he once choked her in 1983 rendering her unconscious, that she had taken steps to prepare to leave him, and that she had used and intended again to use the *Tarasoff* letter to threaten him if he failed to meet her divorce demands.

. . . .

We hold that the reliability of this evidence, initially a question for the court to resolve, is amply supported by this record. . . . In *Nucci,* the Court set forth the factors relevant to a trial justice's assessment of the reliability of out-of-court-statements which the People proffer as hearsay exceptions. The Court said (at 603):

> "Reliability is the sum of the circumstances surrounding the making of the statement that render the declarant worthy of belief. Relevant factors include 'spontaneity, repetition, the mental state of the declarant, absence of motive to fabricate, . . . unlikelihood of faulty recollection and the degree to which the statement was against the declarant's . . . interest' (*see People v. James,* 93 NY2d 620, 642, 717 N.E.2d 1052, 695 N.Y.S.2d 715 [citing *Idaho v. Wright,* 497 U.S. 805, 821, 111 L. Ed. 2d 638, 110 S. Ct. 3139; *Dutton v. Evans,* 400 U.S. 74, 89, 27 L. Ed. 2d 213, 91 S. Ct. 210]). Courts have also 'considered the status or relationship to the declarant of the person to whom the statement was made . . . , whether there was a coercive atmosphere, whether it was made in response to questioning and whether the statements reflect an attempt to shift blame or curry favor' (*James, supra,* 93 N.Y.2d at 642–643 [citing *United States v. Matthews,* 20 F3d 538, 546, other citations omitted])."

The victim's contested statements meet virtually all these enumerated criteria. She was speaking spontaneously; she repeated the statements separately to various people in her life; her statements about the troubled side of their marriage were a natural consequence of corroborated facts about their marriage; she was, by all indications, in good mental health; there appears no reason for her to have fabricated the matters she discussed at the time of her utterances; and her statements largely concerned private matters that some would be embarrassed or otherwise reluctant to disclose. Furthermore, the statements were made mostly to those close to her, in contexts completely devoid of coercion, not in response to anyone's questioning, nor under circumstances at all suggestive of any attempt to curry anyone's favor.

. . . .

### 3. Excited Utterances and Prior Violence

Defendant contends that the court improperly allowed the prosecution to adduce testimony, and otherwise refer to evidence, that defendant was violent, and that he choked his wife to the point of unconsciousness in late 1983. As a part of that contention, defendant also asserts that the Trial Justice erred in allowing Hillard Wiese, an attorney and the victim's cousin, to testify about the victim's purported "excited utterances" describing the choking event. . . .

Defendant correctly argues that the victim's statements during her telephone call to Hillard Wiese do not constitute "excited utterances." . . . .

To begin with, Wiese was unable to reliably estimate how long before his cousin called him that the choking incident occurred. Based on what he said at trial, the interval could have been as long as 24 hours, hardly a typical time span to qualify as an "excited utterance." Second, the record is totally devoid of evidence about what transpired during these many intervening hours to enable the trier of fact to determine, based on "'the activities of the declarant in the interim,'" whether the "declarant had the opportunity to reflect . . ." (*id.*). Finally, the victim chose to call an attorney, rather than a layperson, one with whom she did not have an especially close, personal and confidential relationship. . . .

Therefore, the Trial Justice should not have admitted the victim's statements to Hillard Wiese as "excited utterances." However, we hold that this error was harmless, because, as we noted earlier, the jury otherwise properly learned that the victim claimed defendant had committed a violent act against her in the fall of 1983, as evidence relevant to the state of their marriage, to defendant's motive, to his intent, and relevant evidence of identity. Indeed, defendant himself told his father in 1983 that their strife had reached the point of "some physical contact," and there is credible testimony that in 1985 defendant was so filled with hostility that he was tempted toward violence against his wife. . . .

Defendant counters this reasoning, contending that the 1983 choking incident and all the other evidence and references to threats and marital strife should have been precluded because they bespeak propensity and because the People improperly used the choking incident to suggest that defendant had a propensity for violence. Therefore, he argues such evidence unduly prejudiced him, outweighing any of its probative value.

This complaint—apart from ignoring or underestimating the appropriate, limiting language the court carefully chose to caution and instruct the jury—misconstrues the rationale underlying *People v. Molineux* (168 NY 264, 61 N.E. 286, 10 N.Y. Ann. Cas. 256, 16 N.Y. Cr. 120) and its progeny. *Molineux* authorizes a trial justice to consider allowing a jury to hear about a defendant's prior bad acts—be they violent or otherwise—if they shed light on the issues of intent, identity, motive, absence of accident or mistake, or common plan and scheme (*id.* at 293). In other words, they "may be admitted only if the acts help establish some element of the crime under consideration . . ." (*People v. Lewis*, 69 N.Y.2d 321, 325, 514 N.Y.S.2d 205, 506 N.E.2d 915). In this case his behavior and threats were admitted because they revealed the former three of these five potentially relevant items.

Often, evidence of prior assaults and threats manifests general aggressiveness, i.e., a general propensity to act aggressively against other people. It is this inappropriate and distracting inference which the *Molineux* ruling and its progeny aim to bar. However, the proof here evinces defendant's intent to focus his aggression on one person, namely, his wife—his victim. That key factor in the context of marital or other intimate relationships frequently differentiates domestic violence assaults and homicides—wherein prior bad acts have often been deemed admissible during the People's direct case—from other cases wherein evidence of past assaultive behavior against people other than the victim has most properly been precluded. In the former, the previous aggression principally indicates intent, or motive, or identity; whereas in the latter it can predominantly give rise to an inference of propensity. This logic and rationale accords with well-settled law in New York in these matters (*People v. Angel*, 238 A.D.2d 210, 656 N.Y.S.2d 256, *lv. denied* 90 NY2d 1009, 688 N.E.2d 1387, 666 N.Y.S.2d 104; *People v. Bonilla, supra*; *People v. LaFrance, supra*).

Finally, this evidence shows that this defendant was motivated and had an intent to harm this victim. There is little or nothing by way of circumstantial evidence that is more relevant or more probative in a circumstantial murder case—especially one involving domestic violence—than the type of evidence at issue on this appeal...

## People v. Dorm
New York Court of Appeals
12 N.Y. 3d 16 (2009)

JONES, J.

Defendant and victim had been involved in a romantic relationship for three months when the charged crimes occurred. On January 1, 2005, after a New Year's Eve party, defendant and victim returned to victim's apartment where an argument erupted during which defendant blocked victim's attempts to leave and bolted the door. The altercation escalated from pushing and shoving, to throwing of a phone, and ultimately to victim punching defendant and defendant manually choking victim on her bed. The couple unsuccessfully attempted to reconcile in the weeks that followed and the relationship terminated. On January 18, 2005, victim informed the police about the New Year's Eve incident. Defendant appeared uninvited at victim's place of employment on January 20, 2005 and after speaking with her at a nearby cafe, defendant grabbed victim's hand so as to prevent her from leaving. Victim again contacted the police and defendant was arrested the next day when he returned to that location.

Defendant was charged with assault in the second and third degrees, unlawful imprisonment in the first degree, and stalking in the fourth degree. As probative of intent, motive, and the nature and background of the relationship, the People sought to introduce evidence of defendant's prior conduct toward victim, and similar conduct against other women which resulted in prior arrests of defendant. The People were precluded from introducing such evidence at the first trial and the jury acquitted defendant of assault in the third degree and stalking in the fourth degree. The jury was deadlocked on the remaining charges.

Defendant was retried on the two remaining charges before a different justice. Unlike the first trial, the court in the second trial allowed the People to introduce evidence of defendant's prior and subsequent conduct toward victim and gave limiting instructions to the jury explaining the proper use of such evidence. The court did not allow evidence of defendant's similar conduct against other women. The jury subsequently convicted defendant of unlawful imprisonment in the first degree and assault in the second degree. The Appellate Division unanimously affirmed the conviction, reasoning that the trial court properly permitted "evidence of conflicts between defendant and the victim before and after the incident at issue" because the evidence was "relevant to defendant's motive, and it provided necessary background regarding the couple's relationship that tended to explain aspects of the victim's testimony that might otherwise have been unbelievable or suspect" (47 AD3d 503, 849 NYS2d 548 [2008]). A Judge of this Court granted leave to appeal (10 NY3d 862 [2008]) and we now affirm. . . .

Contrary to defendant's arguments, the evidence in this case was not propensity evidence, but was probative of his motive and intent to assault his victim; it provided necessary background information on the nature of the relationship and placed the charged conduct in context (*see People v Resek*, 3 NY3d 385, 389, 821 NE2d 108, 787 NYS2d 683 [2004]; *People v Till*, 87 NY2d 835, 837, 661 NE2d 153, 637 NYS2d 681 [1995]). We cannot say that the trial court abused its discretion when it allowed only the evidence of prior conduct relating to victim and gave proper limiting instructions to the jury.

Furthermore, the fact that two justices ruled differently on the admissibility of such evidence does not suggest an abuse of discretion. Both rulings are legitimate exercises of discretion notwithstanding the fact that the first trial resulted in acquittals and a hung jury when the subject evidence was precluded and the second trial resulted in convictions when it was admitted. The outcome of a trial has no bearing on whether the court properly exercised its discretion in admitting evidence.

Accordingly, the order of the Appellate Division should be affirmed.

---

The following is the appeal of the civil trial in which the plaintiffs, the surviving families of Nicole Brown Simpson and Ronald Goldman, sought damages for their murders from the defendant, former football star O.J. Simpson. The jury found in favor of the plaintiffs. The defendant cited numerous errors in the court's evidentiary rulings on appeal. Among those cited was the admission of evidence of the couple's long and sorry history of domestic violence.

## Rufo v. Simpson
California Court of Appeal
86 Cal. App. 4th 573 (2001)

Vogel (C.S.), P.J.

### INTRODUCTION

These consolidated civil actions arise from the murders of Nicole Brown Simpson and Ronald Lyle Goldman. A jury found that defendant Orenthal James (O.J.) Simpson committed these homicides willfully and wrongfully, with oppression and malice. Sharon Rufo and Fredric Goldman, the parents and heirs of Ronald Goldman, were awarded $8.5 million compensatory damages on their cause of action for wrongful death. (Code Civ. Proc., §§ 377.60, 377.61.) Fredric Goldman as personal representative of the estate of Ronald Goldman was awarded minor compensatory damages and $12.5 million punitive damages on the survival action, the cause of action Ronald Goldman would have had if he survived. (Code Civ. Proc., §§ 377.30, 377.34.) Louis H. Brown as personal representative of the estate of Nicole Brown Simpson was awarded minor compensatory damages and $12.5 million punitive damages on the survival action, the cause of action Nicole Brown Simpson would have had if she survived. Defendant Simpson appeals from the judgments.

. . . .

Nicole and Ronald were stabbed to death on the night of June 12, 1994, in front of Nicole's home on Bundy Drive in Los Angeles.

Plaintiffs contended that Simpson, Nicole's ex-husband, had the motive to kill Nicole in a rage. On several prior occasions during their marriage Simpson had physically abused Nicole. In 1992 they separated. In May 1993 they agreed to try for a year to see if they might reconcile. In April 1994 Simpson was encouraged they would reconcile. But on May 22, 1994, Nicole terminated the relationship. Simpson retaliated by threatening to cause serious income tax problems for Nicole concerning their arrangement regarding his residence on Rockingham Avenue in Los Angeles. On June 7, 1994, Nicole telephoned a battered women's shelter hotline and stated she was frightened because her ex-husband was stalking her, and she sought advice whether it might be safer to move back in with him. By the end of that conversation she decided not to move back with him. On June 12, 1994, Simpson's and Nicole's young daughter performed in a dance recital. Simpson flew from New York to Los Angeles to attend it. Simpson was in a foul mood that day. At the dance recital, Simpson and Nicole sat apart and did not interact. When the recital ended, Nicole excluded Simpson from a post-recital family dinner.

Ronald was a waiter at the restaurant where the dinner occurred. Afterwards, Nicole telephoned the restaurant about a pair of eyeglasses left at the dinner. Ronald may have been killed because he encountered the murder of Nicole while delivering the eyeglasses to her home.

Shortly after the killings, Nicole's and Ronald's bodies were found in front of her residence. Police responded to the scene and collected physical evidence. Numerous drops of blood at the scene were proved by DNA evidence to be Simpson's. There was a left-hand leather glove, of a rare make that Nicole had previously purchased for Simpson, that matched the right-hand glove later found at Simpson's residence. Bloody footprints at the scene were made by distinctive luxury shoes similar to those worn by Simpson in the past. A knit cap at the scene contained hair fibers matching Simpson's hair. Ronald's shirt contained hair fibers matching Simpson's hair, and cloth fibers matching bloodstained socks found at Simpson's residence.

Other physical evidence from Simpson's Ford Bronco and Simpson's home on Rockingham pointed to Simpson as the murderer. The Bronco contained blood from Simpson, Nicole, and Ronald. Simpson's freshly dripped blood was found on his driveway. Simpson had recent cuts and abrasions on his hands. The right-hand glove matching the left-hand glove from the crime scene was found on a path next to Simpson's house. This glove contained Simpson's blood, Nicole's blood, Ronald's blood, Nicole's hair, and Ronald's hair. A pair of socks found in Simpson's bedroom contained Simpson's and Nicole's blood.

Faced with overwhelming physical evidence, the defense suggested that some evidence was planted by police officers or ineptly contaminated during collection, storage, or testing.

Simpson testified and claimed that he was at home on Rockingham during the time of the killings, prior to being picked up by a limousine driver for a ride to the airport to fly to a previously scheduled event in Chicago. Plaintiffs presented evidence that Simpson had time to commit the murders, go home, catch his ride to the airport, and dispose of evidence in a small bag that he would not allow the limousine driver to handle and which was never seen again. On the flight back to Los Angeles after being notified of Nicole's death, Simpson told a passenger that there were two victims killed in the garden area of Nicole's house, although those details had not been provided to him in the notification. After being informed that police were going to arrest him, Simpson and a friend fled in Simpson's Bronco. Simpson had his passport, a fake goatee and mustache, $8,000 to $9,000 in cash, and a loaded gun. Simpson talked about committing suicide.

. . . .

## ADMISSIBILITY OF SIMPSON'S PRIOR ABUSE OF NICOLE

Simpson contends the trial court erred in admitting evidence of five instances of Simpson's prior abuse of Nicole. This evidence showed: (1) outside a veterinary clinic around the spring of 1983, Simpson approached Nicole's car, tried to pull off Nicole's fur coat, and hit Nicole in the face, saying he "didn't buy this fur coat for you to go fuck somebody else"; (2) in 1984, Simpson lost his temper and struck Nicole's Mercedes with a baseball bat; (3) at a public beach in July 1986, Simpson slapped Nicole and she fell to the sand; (4) on New Year's Day 1989, Simpson and Nicole had a violent argument during which he pulled her hair and struck her on the face or head, for which Simpson pleaded nolo contendere to spousal abuse; and (5) during a rage in October 1993, Simpson broke a door of Nicole's residence.

Simpson contends this evidence showed nothing more than bad character or a propensity for violence, which is inadmissible under Evidence Code section 1101, subdivision (a). But that section further provides, "Nothing in this section prohibits the admission of evidence that a person committed a crime, civil wrong, or other act when relevant to prove some fact (such as motive, opportunity, intent, preparation, plan, knowledge, identity, absence of mistake or accident . . . ) other than his or her disposition to commit such an act." (Evid. Code, § 1101, subd. (b); *People v. Ewoldt* (1994)

7 Cal. 4th 380, 393 [27 Cal. Rptr. 2d 646, 867 P.2d 757].) The trial court denied Simpson's motion in limine to exclude this evidence. The court ruled the evidence was admissible to show motive, intent, and identity.

. . . .

Here the trial court correctly concluded the evidence of Simpson's prior abuse of Nicole was relevant to motive, intent, and identity. (*People v. Linkenauger, supra*, 32 Cal. App. 4th at pp. 1613–1614.) The court did not abuse its discretion under Evidence Code section 352 in concluding that the probative value of this evidence outweighed the potential prejudicial effect. (*People v. Linkenauger, supra*, 32 Cal. App. 4th 1603, 1614; *People v. McCray, supra*, 58 Cal. App. 4th 159, 173.) The fact that the prior instances occurred several years before the killings did not preclude their admission into evidence. (*People v. McCray, supra*, 58 Cal. App. 4th at p. 173.) This fact merely affected the weight that the jury would accord to this evidence.

HEARSAY ISSUES REGARDING VARIOUS STATEMENTS BY NICOLE

. . . .

*Statements at the Times of the Prior Incidents*

Concerning the 1984 incident in which Simpson struck Nicole's automobile with a baseball bat, Mark Day testified that he was a security patrol officer who was called to the Simpson residence on Rockingham in response to a disturbance. As he approached the front door Nicole came running across the front yard. She was very upset. She stated that "he" (Simpson) had lost his temper and that she was afraid. Day then observed the damage to the Mercedes and spoke to Simpson who admitted he had lost his temper.

Concerning the 1989 incident, Los Angeles Police Detective John Edwards went to the Rockingham residence in response to a 911 call. When Edwards buzzed at the gate of the residence, he observed Nicole, wearing only a bra and sweat pants, run from the bushes across the driveway to a control box and collapse onto it. She appeared to push on a button repeatedly while yelling to Edwards, "he's going to kill me, he's going to kill me." She then ran to the gate and when it opened she "came flying through that open area of the gate, ran directly to [Edwards] and collapsed onto [Edwards]." She was cold, wet, and shivering. "She was crying, she was hysterical, and appeared to be very frightened and exhausted." She repeated "he's going to kill me, he's going to kill me," and when Edwards inquired, who, she said O.J. Simpson. Edwards observed multiple injuries on her forehead, eye, cheek, lips, and neck and asked what happened. Nicole answered "O.J. had hit her, kicked her, slapped her, and pulled her hair."

*Telephone Call to Battered Women's Shelter*

After considering Simpson's motion to exclude the following evidence entirely, the court admitted it for the limited purpose of showing Nicole's state of mind.

Nancy Ney was a director of Sojourn House, a battered women's shelter. She had training regarding domestic abuse. She was on duty receiving calls on the shelter's telephone hot line on June 7, 1994, five days before the murders. She received a call from a woman who stated that her name was Nicole, she was Caucasian, she was in her 30's, she had been married eight years but was divorced, she had two children under age 10, she was living in West Los Angeles, and her ex-husband was famous. Nicole stated that she was frightened. Her ex-husband had been calling her begging her to come back to him and he had been stalking her. She related that she found him staring at her in a restaurant and a market and following her when she drove. This unnerved her and she was frightened by it. Upon questioning by Ney whether her ex-husband had ever beaten her or threatened her, Nicole replied he had beaten her throughout the marriage and told her a few different times that if he ever caught her with another man he would kill her. Nicole asked for Ney's opinion whether it might be safer for her and the children to move back in with him. Ney and Nicole discussed this, and by the end of the conversation Nicole came to the conclusion that in the long run it would not be best for her to move back in with him. Nicole indicated she did not wish to come to the shelter. She thanked Ney for helping her and letting her express her feelings. Ney invited her to call back in a week but did not hear from her again.

*Written Statements*

*Diary Entries*

After considering Simpson's objection to the following evidence in its entirety, the court admitted it for the limited purpose of showing Nicole's state of mind.

Edited pages from Nicole's diary were admitted into evidence as exhibit No. 735. The entry for May 22, 1994, states "we[']ve officially split," and then describes the intended arrangements for child visitations. The entry for June 3, 1994, states that when Simpson came over to her residence at 8:30 p.m. to pick up the children for visitation, he commented to her, "You hung up on me last nite, you're gonna pay for this bitch, you're holding money from the IRS, you're going to jail you fucking cunt. You think you can do any fucking thing you want, you've got it coming—I've already talked to my lawyers about this bitch—they'll get you for tax evasion bitch I'll see to it. You're not gonna have a fucking dime left bitch." Nicole's entry adds, "I just turned around and walked away."

*Letter*

Portions of an undated letter in Nicole's handwriting addressing Simpson were introduced into evidence for the limited purpose of showing Nicole's state of mind. The redacted version, exhibit No. 732, includes the following: "O.J.[:] I think I have to put this all in a letter. A lot of years ago I used to do much better in a letter. I'm gonna try it again now. I'd like you to keep this letter if we split, so that you'll always know why we split. I'd also like you to keep it if we stay together, as a reminder.... There was also that time before Justin [was born and a few months] after Sydney [was born] I felt really good about how I got back in shape [and] we were out[,] you beat the holy hell out of me [and] we lied at the x-ray lab [and] said I fell off a bike. Remember!?? And since Justin[']s birth is the mad New Years Eve beat up.... I just don't see how that compares to infidelity, wife beating, verbal abuse.... And if I wanted to hurt you or had it in me to be anything like the person you are I would have done so after the New Year incident. But I didn't even do it then. I called the cops to save my life whether you believe it or not. But I didn't pursue anything after that. I didn't prosecute, I didn't call the press [and] didn't make a big charade out of it. I waited for it to die down and asked for it to. But I've never loved you since or been the same."

. . . .

*Spontaneous Statements to Police*

As discussed in the previous section, the prior incidents of abuse were relevant and admissible to show motive, intent, and identity. Nicole's statements describing those incidents were therefore relevant, and they were admissible if they came within an exception to the hearsay rule. Nicole's statements to responding officers on the dates of the 1984 and 1989 incidents were properly admitted under the spontaneous statement exception to the hearsay rule. . . .

Simpson contends "a period of time had transpired between the event and the statements," and Nicole "had an opportunity to 'contrive and misrepresent' and to regain her 'reflective powers.'" The record supports the trial court's contrary conclusion. Whether the requirements of the spontaneous statement exception are satisfied in any given case is largely a question of fact. The determination of this question is vested in the trial court. . . . The trial court here did not abuse its discretion in concluding Nicole's statements to the officers satisfied the spontaneous statement exception. . . .

*State of Mind Evidence*

Hearsay is a statement made other than while testifying as a witness, which statement is *offered in the trial to prove the truth of the matter asserted in the statement*. (Evid. Code, § 1200, subd. (a) [fn. 3, *ante*].) Unlike the two statements to officers concerning prior incidents which were admitted to prove the truth of the matters asserted, the statements made in the telephone call to the battered women's shelter, the diary entries, and the letter were expressly limited to the purpose of showing Nicole's state of mind. Most of the statements were not hearsay at all, because they were not admitted to prove the truth of the matters asserted.

Thus, under plaintiffs' offers of evidence and the trial court's rulings and instructions limiting the purpose of the evidence, the statements made in the telephone call to the battered women's shelter were *not* admitted *to prove*: (a) that her ex-husband had been calling her, begging her to come back to him; (b) that he was stalking her; (c) that she found him staring at her in a restaurant and a market and following her vehicle; (d) that he had beaten her throughout the marriage; and (e) that he had told her different times that if he ever caught her with another man he would kill her. The statements in the diary were *not* admitted *to prove* that Nicole evaded taxes. The statements in the letter were *not* admitted *to prove*: (a) that Simpson beat Nicole and they lied to the X-ray lab that she fell off her bike; (b) that the "mad New Years Eve beat up" occurred; and (c) that Simpson committed "infidelity, wife beating, verbal abuse."

Rather, these statements were offered or admitted only as circumstantial evidence from which inferences could be drawn concerning how Nicole felt about the nature of the relationship between her and Simpson. They were offered to explain her conduct in finally terminating the relationship, which in turn was alleged to have provoked Simpson to murder. As such, they were not hearsay. (*People v. Ortiz* (1995) 38 Cal. App. 4th 377, 389–390 [44 Cal. Rptr. 2d 914]; 1 Witkin, Cal. Evidence (4th ed. 2000) Hearsay, §§ 37-39, 198, pp. 719–721, 915.)

. . . .

To avoid the force of plaintiffs' argument that all this evidence had a limited admissible purpose to show Nicole's state of mind, Simpson contends Nicole's state of mind was irrelevant. He is wrong.

This argument was raised early by Simpson's pretrial motion in limine to exclude all of the out-of-court statements by Nicole. Goldman's opposition to the motion in limine answered it as follows: "Here, Goldman contends that particular 'acts or conduct' of Nicole motivated Simpson to murder her: breaking off their relationship for good in May 1994, ignoring Simpson at their daughter's June 12 recital, and refusing to include Simpson in a family dinner and celebration immediately following the recital, after he had flown thousands of miles to be at the recital. Of course, Simpson's motive is a highly relevant issue because it is probative of the identity of the killer. See *People v. Zack*, 184 Cal. App. 3d 409, 413–14[, *supra*]. Moreover, at his deposition, Simpson denied all of this conduct, contending that he (not Nicole) broke off the relationship, that he was not rejected by Nicole, that he interacted pleasantly with Nicole at the recital, and that he chose not to go out to dinner with the family. Thus, Nicole's state of mind—her fear of Simpson and intense hostility toward him for threatening to turn her [in to] the Internal Revenue Service and forcing her and their children to move out of their house—not only proves and explains why she engaged in the conduct that plaintiffs contend motivated Simpson to kill her, but also serves to rebut Simpson's claims to the contrary."

. . . .

Simpson contends that because he denied being the perpetrator, *the defense* did nothing to put into issue Nicole's state of mind or conduct immediately before the killings. This does not show the evidence was irrelevant. Even without an opening statement by Simpson's counsel or testimony by Simpson, plaintiffs were entitled to present evidence tending to establish motive. Without persuasive evidence from plaintiffs regarding motive, the jurors might believe there was nothing in the relationship between Simpson and Nicole which would precipitate a murder. (See *People v. Zack, supra*, 184 Cal. App. 3d 409, 415 [prior assaults on wife admissible, husband "was not entitled to have the jury determine his guilt or innocence on a false presentation that his and the victim's relationship and their parting were peaceful and friendly"]; *People v. Linkenauger, supra*, 32 Cal. App. 4th 1603, 1615 [same].)

. . . .

The judgments are affirmed.

## Peters-Riemers v. Riemers
Supreme Court of North Dakota
2001 ND 62 (2001)

Neumann, Justice.

Roland C. Riemers appeals a domestic violence protection order restraining him from contact with Jenese A. Peters-Riemers. We affirm the protection order.

I

On March 6, 2000, Peters-Riemers applied for domestic violence protection from Riemers. In her application, Peters-Riemers attested that she and Riemers had been involved in a verbal and physical confrontation on March 4, 2000. She packed a bag and told Riemers she was taking their two-year-old son with her to stay in a hotel. Riemers told her she could not take their son, and the parties began struggling. During the struggle, Peters-Riemers dialed 911, but Riemers held her from the telephone. They struggled until Riemers hit Peters-Riemers in the face, and she fell to the floor. Riemers went to another room, and Peters-Riemers picked up her bag and left the house. As she was leaving, a patrol car drove into the driveway. Peters-Riemers explained she had placed the 911 call. After showing the officers she needed medical attention, she drove herself to a hospital. Peters-Riemers' injuries included bone fractures, bruising, and swelling around her eye.

The district court granted Peters-Riemers a temporary domestic violence protection order on the day of her application. A hearing was held on March 14, 2000, to determine whether to issue a permanent protection order. During the hearing, Riemers attempted to testify about alleged previous incidents of abuse by Peters-Riemers and about his state of mind at the time of the March 4, 2000, confrontation. Riemers also attempted to cross-examine Peters-Riemers regarding the alleged incidents of previous abuse. Peters-Riemers objected to both lines of inquiry based on relevance. The district court sustained Peters-Riemers' relevancy objections. After the hearing, the district court issued a one-year protection order against Riemers. Riemers appeals.

II

. . . .

A

Riemers argues the district court abused its discretion by ruling his testimony about alleged previous incidents of abuse by Peters-Riemers and about Riemers' state of mind was irrelevant in deciding whether to grant Peters-Riemers' petition for a domestic violence protection order under N.D.C.C. § 14-07.1-02.

When asked why he feared for his personal safety at the time of the confrontation, Riemers began testifying about a previous incident involving him and Peters-Riemers. Peters-Riemers objected based on relevance. The district court sustained the objection. Riemers' attorney told the court they had offered the testimony to show Riemers' state of mind as it pertained to self-defense. The district court reiterated the objection was sustained.

Relevant evidence is evidence that reasonably and actually tends to prove or disprove any fact in issue. N.D.R.Ev. 401; *Schaefer v. Souris River Telecom.*, 2000 ND 187, P10, 618 N.W.2d 175. We review a district court's admission or exclusion of evidence based on relevance grounds by applying an abuse of discretion standard. *Schaefer*, at P 10. A district court abuses its discretion when it acts in an arbitrary, unreasonable, or unconscionable manner or when it misinterprets or misapplies the law. *Mellum v. Mellum*, 2000 ND 47, P21, 607 N.W.2d 580. . . .

Because acts committed in self-defense are statutorily excluded from the definition of domestic violence, testimony about previous incidents of abuse by Peters-Riemers and about Riemers' state of mind was clearly relevant because of its bearing on whether Riemers acted in self-defense. . . . Accordingly, the district court misapplied the law and abused its discretion in excluding this evidence.

Under Rule 103(a), N.D.R.Ev., error may not be predicated upon the erroneous exclusion of evidence unless a substantial right of the party is affected. *State v. Hart*, 1997 ND 188, P21, 569 N.W.2d 451. *See also* N.D.R.Civ.P. 61 . . . . In *Hart*, the defendant argued the trial court abused its discretion in excluding evidence supporting his claim of self-defense. *Id.* at P 18. Hart attempted to testify about a statement allegedly made by an unavailable witness, and the trial court ruled the proffered testimony was hearsay. *Id.* at P 19. Hart offered the statement to show his state of mind. *Id.* at P 20. Hart's self-defense evidence and evidence about his state of mind were admitted in other portions of his testimony. *Id.* at P 21. Accordingly, we held the exclusion of Hart's testimony did not affect Hart's substantial rights and did not require reversal. *Id.* at P 21. We reach the same conclusion here.

Riemers was allowed to testify as to his state of mind:

Q At—during this altercation, did you—were you in fear for your personal safety at that point in time?

A Very much so.

When asked why he feared for his personal safety, the court sustained Peters-Riemers' relevancy objection. However, at another point in his testimony, Riemers testified as to alleged previous incidents of abuse by Peters-Riemers:

A At that point she attacked me—

Q In what manner?

A Her usual manner. Starting off with tearing off my shirt, ripping it to pieces—

Q Usual manner? You mean she's done this in the past?

A A number of occasions. She scratched up my chest and face, she would try to kick me in the testicles and the leg or hit me any place she could. And then—

Q And this was happening this evening—that evening in question?

A Yes, it was happening that evening.

Q She attempted to kick you in the testicles?

A Yes, you see—

Q Has she done that before?

A Yes. She's tried to rip them off at times.

Because Riemers was allowed to testify both about alleged previous incidents of abuse by Peters-Riemers and about his state of mind, the district court's error in excluding relevant evidence was not prejudicial and did not affect Riemers' substantial rights. Nonprejudicial mistakes by the district court constitute harmless error and are not grounds for reversal. *Huesers v. Huesers*, 1998 ND 54, P11, 574 N.W.2d 880.

B

Riemers argues the district court violated his and the parties' son's due process rights by denying him the opportunity to cross-examine Peters-Riemers about alleged previous incidents of abuse by Peters-Riemers.

In *Sandbeck v. Rockwell*, 524 N.W.2d 846, 848-49 (N.D. 1994), a majority of this Court held that the scope of a hearing often depends on whether the procedure is an action or a special proceeding, and that N.D.C.C. § 14-07.1-02(1) makes it clear that a domestic violence proceeding is not a plenary action that requires a full-blown trial. Rather, the statute creates a special summary proceeding and directs a motion hearing noticed by order of the court. *Sandbeck*, 524 N.W.2d at 849.

Under N.D.R.Civ.P. 43(e), for a motion "based on facts not appearing of record[,] the court may hear the matter on affidavits presented by the respective parties, but the court may direct the matter be heard wholly or partly on testimony or depositions." For the summary proceeding of a protection order, the trial court is thus authorized under the rules to hear the evidence on affidavits or partly on affidavits or, as in *Sandbeck*, partly on affidavits and partly by cross-examination of each affiant. 524 N.W.2d at 850.

On March 6, 2000, Peters-Riemers filed a petition for protective relief and an affidavit supporting her petition. The district court heard the matter on Peters-Riemers' affidavit on March 14, 2000. Riemers did not submit an opposing affidavit. At the hearing, the district court, exercising its discretion, allowed the cross-examination of Peters-Riemers as to the contents of her affidavit. Peters-Riemers did not present direct testimony in addition to her affidavit testimony. During cross-examination, Riemers' attorney asked Peters-Riemers, "Ever hit [Riemers] in the past?" Peters-Riemers objected based on relevancy. The court sustained Peters-Riemers' relevancy objection.

In the previous subsection, we concluded testimony about alleged previous incidents of abuse by Peters-Riemers was relevant because of its bearing on whether Riemers acted in self-defense. However, Peters-Riemers' affidavit discusses only the events of the night of the confrontation, March 4, 2000, and an affair Riemers had in Honduras during the parties' marriage. Thus, although Peters-Riemers' testimony about alleged previous incidents of abuse by Peters-Riemers was relevant, it was beyond the scope of the affidavit. *See* N.D.R.Evid. 611(b) (specifying "cross-examination should be limited to the subject matter of the direct examination and matters affecting the credibility of the witness").  . . .

The district court here, exercising its discretion, also allowed Riemers to testify. After Riemers testified, the court asked Riemers' attorney, "Do you have anything further?" Riemers' attorney replied, "I have nothing further, Your Honor." Riemers did not ask the court to allow him to call Peters-Riemers as part of his own case to question her about relevant issues beyond the scope of her affidavit. Had Riemers asked to call Peters-Riemers as an adverse witness to question her about alleged previous incidents of abuse, and had his request been denied after he had already been forbidden to pursue these matters on cross-examination, Riemers would have been denied every possible opportunity to elicit this relevant evidence from Peters-Riemers. *See* N.D.R.Civ.P. 43(b) . . . . That almost certainly would have been an abuse of discretion, but that is not what happened in this case.

The district court appropriately controlled the presentation of evidence during Peters-Riemers' case, and Riemers failed to call Peters-Riemers as part of his case. The district court did not violate Riemers and the parties' son's due process rights. . . .

We affirm the district court's order.

# III. Evidentiary Tools Unique to Domestic Violence Cases

## A. Propensity for Intimate Partner Abuse

The following is an article explaining the rationale behind allowing propensity evidence in domestic violence cases followed by examples of several state statutes permitting this evidence at trial.

### Andrew King-Ries, *Responding: Two New Solutions: True to Character: Honoring the Intellectual Foundations of the Character Evidence Rule in Domestic Violence Prosecutions*
23 St. Louis U. Pub. L. Rev. 313 (2004)

. . . .

2. The Importance of the Character Evidence Rule in Domestic Violence Prosecutions

No other evidence rule goes to the heart of a particular crime the way that the character evidence rule does with domestic violence. The fundamental nature of domestic violence is that it is behavior repeated over time. In the domestic violence context, the character evidence ban denies the nature of domestic violence, creates an unlevel playing field that reinforces negative and inaccurate stereotypes about women, and perpetuates violence against women.

### i. Denial of Women's Realities

One troubling statistic in domestic violence cases is that, on average, women do not involve the police until after the seventh incident of violence within the relationship. This statistic tells us that by the time women are involved in the criminal justice system as domestic violence victims, they have already been victimized repeatedly. Women do not enter courtrooms as victims of isolated incidents of violence. Rather, they suffer a pattern of violence meant to accomplish subjugation and control. Each incident of violence is critical to creating the pattern and accomplishing the control. Further, the repetition of violence committed by intimate partners changes the nature of the victims' stories; their stories are fundamentally different from the stories of victims of isolated, random violence at the hands of strangers.

. . . .

The character evidence rule denies the domestic violence victim's reality on two levels. First, the fact of repetitive violence does not exist within the courtroom. Second, the victim must discuss an isolated incident without its larger context of repetitive violence. Isolating the incident from its context denies that which gives it a substantial part of its meaning. A kick in the crotch is a significant violation of personal autonomy. However, a kick in the crotch in context of past forced sexual activities may convey a different meaning. The current construction of the character evidence rule precludes the victim from discussing her more nuanced reality of the kick in the crotch.

This denial of the victim's reality within the courtroom has profound impact on the victim. When victims are prevented from discussing their reality, they often become frustrated, confused, and disenfranchised. The system that the victim turned to for protection mimics the abusive patterns of the relationship from which she is seeking refuge. The purpose of battering is to create an altered reality for the victim so that she will bear the abuse. One of the most powerful tools in the batterer's arsenal is the ability to engage the societal stigma against victims by convincing the victim that if she reports the violence, she will either not be believed or will be blamed for not leaving the relationship. When the legal system denies the victim's reality, it contributes to the social stigma against victims and directly reinforces the victim's sense that her story is not believable, that it is not important.

### ii. Hides True Nature of Domestic Violence

Because it suppresses the reality of the relationship, the character evidence rule also hides the true nature of domestic violence from the public. When the victim is not permitted to place the charged incident into the pattern of abuse, the jury is permitted to believe that domestic violence incidents are isolated incidents, stemming primarily from conflict within the relationship. In addition, the jury members—as representatives of society—are allowed only a limited view into what constitutes domestic violence. The true nature of the problem is hidden from the jurors. . . .

### 1. Traditional Policy Arguments Are Unpersuasive

The traditional policy arguments in favor of the character evidence rule are not persuasive in the context of a modern domestic violence trial. The concern over unfair surprise has largely been addressed by procedural rules requiring notice of the charges and pre-trial recitation of all prior bad act evidence. The claim that a person will have to defend against his whole life is exaggerated. The defendant is aware of his past and aware that the only relevant portion of his past is that which relates to violence against women. Because the prosecution is limited in its knowledge of the defendant's private life, its main source of information comes from prior police reports and from the victim. Prior police reports are readily accessible to both the prosecution and the defense. The victim is generally subjected to a grueling interview with the defense prior to trial, during which the defense is free to investigate prior instances of violence of which the victim knows. In addition, the prosecution is under a continuing duty to provide pre-trial discovery and therefore must inform the defense of any acts of misconduct which the prosecution intends to present. Finally, the question of whether a prior bad act is admissible can be established pre-trial. The concept of unfair surprise does not exist in the typical domestic violence trial today.

. . . .

### 2. The Current Rule Never Contemplated Domestic Violence

. . . [T]he character evidence ban was well established in the American common law before the American Revolution. Domestic violence has been expressly or tacitly sanctioned since the formation of the United States. The character evidence rule, therefore, was established at a time when the legal position of women was subordinate to men, and it was legal for a husband to beat his wife.

Overlapping the history of the character evidence rule with the history of domestic violence highlights several significant issues and calls into question the continued validity of the character evidence rule in the domestic violence context. The character evidence rule developed to deal with specific sets of problems relating to character and the effort to achieve fair trials and just verdicts. Because domestic violence was not a crime, the unique issues surrounding domestic violence were not considered in the set of problems that the character evidence rule was developed to address. The character evidence rule should, therefore, reflect changed understandings.

. . . .

It is important to recognize that the rejection of the character evidence rule in the domestic violence context does not equate with a return to a focus on character. The defendant's prior acts of domestic violence are not character, they are context. Consistent with modern conceptions of battering relationships, the prior acts are simply part of the pattern, not isolated incidents. The jury will have to assess the entire pattern, not simply the isolated charged incident. The function of the jury will still be the assessment of objective actions. The focus of the trial remains on the objective actions of the defendant, not on whether the defendant is a good person or a bad person. Jurors have the ability to determine objective actions even when confronted with evidence of prior misconduct. As has been discussed, juries have historically been presented with evidence of the domestic violence victim's "character." The addition of admission of prior acts of the defendant may add to the jury's task but not substantially alter it.

. . . .

## Minn. Stat. 634.20 (2015) Evidence of Conduct

Evidence of domestic conduct by the accused against the victim of domestic conduct, or against other family or household members, is admissible unless the probative value is substantially outweighed by the danger of unfair prejudice, confusion of the issue, or misleading the jury, or by considerations of undue delay, waste of time, or needless presentation of cumulative evidence. "Domestic conduct" includes, but is not limited to, evidence of domestic abuse, violation of an order for protection . . . violation of a harassment restraining order . . . .

## C.R.S. (Colorado) 18-6-801.5 (2015) Domestic violence — evidence of similar transactions

(1) The general assembly hereby finds that domestic violence is frequently cyclical in nature, involves patterns of abuse, and can consist of harm with escalating levels of seriousness. The general assembly therefore declares that evidence of similar transactions can be helpful and is necessary in some situations in prosecuting crimes involving domestic violence.

(2) In criminal prosecutions involving domestic violence in which the defendant and the victim named in the information have engaged in an intimate relationship as of the time alleged in the information, evidence of any other acts of domestic violence between the defendant and the victim named in the information, and between the defendant and other persons, constitute other acts or transactions for the purposes of this section, and the court may authorize the admission of evidence as provided in subsection (3) of this section.

(3) The proponent of evidence of other acts or transactions under this section shall advise the trial court by offer of proof of such evidence and shall specify whether the evidence is offered to show a common plan, scheme, design, identity, modus operandi, motive, or guilty knowledge or for some other purpose.

(4) Upon the offer of proof under subsection (3) of this section, the trial court shall determine whether the probative value of the evidence of similar acts or transactions is substantially outweighed by the danger of unfair prejudice to the defendant, confusion of the issues, or misleading of the jury if the evidence is allowed or by considerations of undue delay, waste of time, or needless presentation of cumulative evidence.

(5) Upon admitting evidence of other acts or transactions into evidence pursuant to this section and again in the general charge to the jury, the trial court shall direct the jury as to the limited purpose for which the evidence is admitted and for which the jury may consider it.

## B. Medical Record Evidence in Domestic Violence Cases

Medical records can be an important evidentiary tool in domestic violence trials. The extent of the diagnosed injuries will determine whether the prosecution will be able to prove the essential elements of assault charges. Conversely, if the victim informs a doctor the injuries were the result of an accident, the records will go a long way in impeaching her testimony and may contribute to an acquittal.

### People v. Benston
Court of Appeals of New York
15 N.Y. 3d 610 (2010)

CHIEF JUDGE LIPPMAN.

. . . .

Defendant, who was without another place to live, had been residing in the spare bedroom in complainant's apartment, at her invitation. Although their relationship was platonic at that time, they had been involved in a romantic relationship many years prior, beginning when complainant was 14 years old and lasting until she was 20 or 21.[13] . . .

On October 3, 2004, defendant informed complainant that he had taken five dollars in quarters from her coin purse for laundry and had replaced them with a five dollar bill. Complainant, upset because she suspected defendant had been going through her personal belongings, asked him to move out. Defendant became angry and threatened to kill complainant. He assaulted her and choked her—using first a scarf and then a leather belt. Complainant was able to free herself and called 911. After defendant fled the apartment, complainant finished packing his belongings and brought them to his brother's house. By the time complainant returned to her apartment, the police had arrived. One of the officers discovered defendant crouched in a corner of complainant's apartment. Defendant was then arrested and complainant was taken to the hospital.

Complainant reported to medical personnel that she had been strangled by an old boyfriend and that he had used a black leather belt. She was diagnosed by the attending physician with "domestic violence [and] asphyxiation." Prior to the introduction of the medical records at trial, defense counsel moved to redact, among other things,

---

13. [n1] Complainant was 36 years old at the time of the crimes.

references to domestic violence, to the perpetrator's status as a former boyfriend and to the existence of a safety plan for complainant. The court ordered certain portions of the records to be redacted—specifically, any references to a history of abuse and to statements that complainant had asked the perpetrator to leave her home and that she had filed a complaint against him. The court did, however, permit references to domestic violence, the perpetrator's relationship to complainant, the description of the weapon and the existence of a safety plan. The court also denied defendant's motion in limine to preclude the attending physician from making repeated references to "domestic violence," instead requiring defense counsel to make specific objections if and when necessary.

In addition to the charges stemming from the October 3 incident, defendant was also indicted on charges pertaining to three subsequent episodes. On February 12, 2005, defendant, in violation of an order of protection, telephoned complainant repeatedly and showed up outside the door to her apartment.[14] Defendant allegedly caused a disturbance by kicking complainant's door and yelling for her male houseguest to leave the apartment. On February 16, 2005, defendant again approached complainant in violation of an order of protection by meeting her on the street when she got off the bus on her way home from work. During this encounter, defendant allegedly asked complainant not to testify against him and threatened to kill her. The following morning, defendant was waiting for complainant outside her apartment, again in violation of an order of protection, and accompanied her part of the way to work until she was able to elude him at a subway station. Defendant allegedly told her that he had had a razor with him the night before and thought about killing her and killing himself.

Defendant was acquitted of attempted murder in the second degree, but was convicted of assault in the second degree, attempted assault in the second degree, criminal possession of a weapon in the fourth degree, four counts of criminal contempt in the first degree, two counts of criminal contempt in the second degree, intimidating a victim or witness in the third degree, aggravated harassment in the second degree and harassment in the second degree.

The Appellate Division affirmed, finding that it was a proper exercise of discretion for the court to allow limited references in medical records and testimony to the effect that complainant "was diagnosed as having been subjected to domestic violence involving a former boyfriend," as those references were relevant to the proposed treatment (70 AD3d 479, 479, 895 NYS2d 370 [1st Dept 2010]). A Judge of this Court granted defendant leave to appeal, and we now affirm.

. . . .

---

14. [n2] A telephone company representative testified that defendant called complainant's home and cell phone numbers a combined total of 93 times that day.

Business Records Exception

Under the business records exception to the hearsay rule,

> "[a]ny writing or record ... made as a memorandum or record of any act, transaction, occurrence or event, shall be admissible in evidence in proof of that act, transaction, occurrence or event, if the judge finds that it was made in the regular course of any business and that it was the regular course of such business to make it, at the time of the act, transaction, occurrence or event, or within a reasonable time thereafter" (CPLR 4518[a]).

This exception applies to criminal proceedings through Criminal Procedure Law § 60.10.

Generally, business records are deemed trustworthy both because they reflect routine business operations and because the person making the particular entry has the responsibility to keep accurate records that can be relied upon for business purposes (*see Williams v Alexander*, 309 NY 283, 286, 129 NE2d 417 [1955]). Hospital records, in particular, are trustworthy as they are "designed to be 'relied upon in affairs of life and death'" (*Williams*, 309 NY at 288, quoting 6 Wigmore, Evidence § 1707, at 36 [3d ed 1940]) and as they reflect the condition of a patient who has the clear motivation to report accurately. Hospital records fall within the business records exception when they "reflect[] acts, occurrences or events that relate to diagnosis, prognosis or treatment or are otherwise helpful to an understanding of the medical or surgical aspects of ... [the particular patient's] hospitalization" (*Williams*, 309 NY at 287 [internal quotation marks and citations omitted]). . . .

We noted in *Williams* that, in certain situations, how the patient was injured "may be helpful to an understanding of the medical aspects of his [or her] case" (309 NY at 288). To that end, the analysis of some lower courts addressing the admissibility of medical records in domestic violence or child abuse situations may be instructive here. The Second Department found admissible medical records containing a statement by a complainant that she was attacked by friends of her former boyfriend who were trying to stop her from testifying against him in a domestic violence proceeding (*see People v Greenlee*, 70 AD3d 966, 897 NYS2d 132 [2d Dept 2010], *lv denied* 14 NY3d 888, 929 NE2d 1011, 903 NYS2d 776 [2010]). The information was found relevant to treatment because it could be used to develop a discharge plan that would ensure the victim's safety (*Greenlee*, 70 AD3d at 967). Moreover, in a case involving child abuse, a nurse's testimony that an abused foster child told her that his foster mother caused his bruises was found proper because it was germane to diagnosis and treatment (*see People v Caccese*, 211 AD2d 976, 977, 621 NYS2d 735 [3d Dept 1995], *lv denied* 86 NY2d 780, 655 NE2d 723, 631 NYS2d 626 [1995]). At least one trial court has found medical records containing a diagnosis of domestic violence admissible due, in part, to the close association between the physical and psychological injuries typically involved (*see People v Swinger*, 180 Misc 2d 344, 349, 689 NYS2d 336 [Crim Ct, NY County 1998]; *see also People v Anonymous*, 192 Misc 2d 570, 573-574, 746 NYS2d 894 [Sup Ct, Bronx County 2002] [medical records containing the identity of an abuser in a child abuse case found relevant to treatment of the victim, including potential mental health referrals]).

The inquiry ... remains whether the statements at issue were relevant to diagnosis and treatment. In *Benston*, defendant argues that several statements from complainant's medical records should not have been admitted. The specific statements that defendant contests are references to an "old boyfriend" as the perpetrator, the description of the case as involving "domestic violence," references to a "safety plan" for complainant and the description of the weapon as a "black" leather belt. Defendant also argues that this is not a case of domestic violence because he and complainant were living together in a platonic, landlord-tenant-type relationship.

The latter argument is without merit. Neither cohabitation nor a current romantic relationship is necessary for one individual to subject another to acts that will be considered domestic violence. Rather, domestic violence is characterized by a current, or former, intimate relationship between the parties (*see e.g.* CPL 530.11[1][e] [for family offense matters, "members of the same family or household" are defined to include "persons who are not related by consanguinity or affinity and who are or have been in an intimate relationship regardless of whether such persons have lived together at any time. Factors the court may consider in determining whether a relationship is an 'intimate relationship' include but are not limited to: the nature or type of relationship, regardless of whether the relationship is sexual in nature; the frequency of interaction between the persons; and the duration of the relationship"]; Family Ct Act § 812[1]; *see also* Social Services Law § 459-a[2]). The relationship between these two individuals, considering both their former relationship and their living situation at the time of the assault, is clearly one that is subject to classification as involving domestic violence. In this context, it is relevant for purposes of diagnosis and treatment that complainant's assault was at the hands of a former boyfriend.

The references to "domestic violence" and to the existence of a safety plan were admissible under the business records exception. Not only were these statements relevant to complainant's diagnosis and treatment, domestic violence was part of the attending physician's diagnosis in this case. With all that has been learned about the scourge of domestic violence in recent decades, we now recognize that it differs materially, both as an offense and a diagnosis, from other types of assault in its effect on the victim and in the resulting treatment. In this context, a doctor faced with a victim who has been assaulted by an intimate partner is not only concerned with bandaging wounds. In addition to physical injuries, a victim of domestic violence may have a whole host of other issues to confront, including psychological and trauma issues that are appropriately part of medical treatment. Developing a safety plan, including referral to a shelter where appropriate, and dispensing information about domestic violence and necessary social services can be an important part of the patient's treatment. Therefore, it was not error to admit references to domestic violence and a safety plan in complainant's medical records.

Contrary to defendant's argument, references to domestic violence and a safety plan do not lead to the conclusion that there has been a history of abuse. It is worth noting that the trial court here did not admit the medical records in their entirety. Rather, the court exercised its discretion by redacting certain portions of the records, most significantly the references to any history of abuse. . . .

Accordingly . . . the order of the Appellate Division should be affirmed.

———

Even without a statement from a patient pointing to an intimate partner as the cause of injuries, the medical records themselves, if properly prepared, are invaluable in assisting the prosecution in obtaining a conviction of the perpetrator in domestic violence cases. But the key is to insure they are carefully documented.

## Nancy E. Isaac & V. Pualani Enos, *Documenting Domestic Violence: How Health Care Providers Can Help Victims*
(U.S. Dep't Justice, Nat'l Inst. Justice, Sept. 2001)

. . . .

It appears that at present, many medical records are not sufficiently well-documented to provide adequate legal evidence of domestic violence. A study of 184 visits for medical care in which an injury or other evidence of abuse was noted revealed major shortcomings in the records:[15]

- For the 93 instances of an injury, the records contained only 1 photograph. There was no mention in any records of photographs filed elsewhere (for example, with the police).

- A body map documenting the injury was included in only 3 of the 93 instances. Drawings of the injuries appeared in 8 of the 93 instances.

- Doctors' and nurses' handwriting was illegible in key portions of the records in one-third of the patients' visits in which abuse or injury was noted.

- All three criteria for considering a patient's words an excited utterance were met in only 28 of the more than 800 statements evaluated (3.4%). Most frequently missing was a description of the patient's demeanor, and often the patient was not clearly identified as the source of the information.

On the plus side, although photographs and body maps were rare, injuries were otherwise described in detail. And in fewer than 1 percent of the visits were negative comments made about the patient's appearance, manner, or motive for stating that abuse had occurred. . . .

———

15. [To complete this study, researchers examined the charts of approximately 100 domestic violence victims from a Boston-area legal advocacy program, which examined the medical records of clients. The other sources of records were from two Boston-area hospitals. In total, 96 medical charts of 86 women who made 772 visits to health care providers were examined. Medical professionals, social workers, lawyers, judges, and researchers analyzed the records and focused on 184 visits because the records contained one or more indicators of domestic violence.—Eds.]

What health care providers can do

- Medical records could be much more useful to domestic violence victims in legal proceedings if some minor changes were made in documentation. Clinicians can do the following:
- Take photographs of injuries known or suspected to have resulted from domestic violence.
- Write legibly. Computers can also help overcome the common problem of illegible handwriting.
- Set off the patient's own words in quotation marks or use such phrases as "patient states" or "patient reports" to indicate that the information recorded reflects the patient's words. To write "patient was kicked in abdomen" obscures the identity of the speaker.
- Avoid phrases such as "patient claims" or "patient alleges," which imply doubt about the patient's reliability. If the clinician's observations conflict with the patient's statements, the clinician should record the reason for the difference.
- Use medical terms and avoid legal terms such as "alleged perpetrator," "assailant," and "assault."
- Describe the person who hurt the patient by using quotation marks to set off the statement. The clinician would write, for example: *The patient stated, "My boyfriend kicked and punched me."*
- Avoid summarizing a patient's report of abuse in conclusive terms. If such language as "patient is a battered woman," "assault and battery," or "rape" lacks sufficient accompanying factual information, it is inadmissible.
- Do not place the term "domestic violence" or abbreviations such as "DV" in the diagnosis section of the medical record. Such terms do not convey factual information and are not medical terminology. Whether domestic violence has occurred is determined by the court.
- Describe the patient's demeanor, indicating, for example, whether she is crying or shaking or seems angry, agitated, upset, calm, or happy. Even if the patient's demeanor belies the evidence of abuse, the clinician's observations of that demeanor should be recorded.
- Record the time of day the patient is examined and, if possible, indicate how much time has elapsed since the abuse occurred. For example, the clinician might write, *Patient states that early this morning his boyfriend hit him.*

. . . .

## IV. Special Evidentiary Considerations with Child Witnesses in Family Violence or Sexual Abuse Cases

Where children are court witnesses about their own physical or sexual abuse or about violence transpiring in their home, special rules apply. The courts must take into account the age of the child testifying and the ability of that child to understand and appreciate the need for truth and accuracy. The evidentiary rules about child witnesses vary among jurisdictions. The ages at which children are deemed to be able to testify under oath are determined by statute. State laws also determine whether children may testify via closed-circuit television or, in cases involving sex crimes, with the assistance of anatomically correct dolls.

In cases involving physical abuse, bodily injuries speak volumes about what harm has befallen a child. More difficult are sex abuse allegations made by children, some too young to understand exactly what wrong has been done to them. Sexual abuse of children, by its very nature, takes place in a private setting where the perpetrator often extracts promises from the child not to reveal the incident to a grown up.

The legal system faces the dilemma of either believing the child too readily or dismissing the child's statements too quickly. The former could result in an innocent person spending many years in jail and being labeled for life as a child sex offender. The latter could allow child predators to remain unpunished and leave children in serious danger.

Although mental health professionals routinely debate whether children are easily misled into telling lies or are routinely believed to be fabricating when truthfully making allegations of sexual abuse, the laws governing evidence provided by children are written by legislators and applied by judges. What follows are some of the issues surrounding this important and controversial topic.

## A. The Ability to Testify Under Oath

The United States Supreme Court in 1895 in *Wheeler v. United States,* 159 U.S. 523, 524–25 (1895), held a child as young as five was capable of being sworn as a witness, as long as he had sufficient "capacity and intelligence" to understand the difference between a truth and a lie, appreciated the consequences of lying and comprehended what was required by an oath. Under current federal law [F.R.E. 601 and 18 U.S.C. § 3509] children are presumed competent until the party seeking to bar their testimony proves otherwise by compelling evidence. Most state laws establishing child witness competency either make reference to the minimum age at which a child may be sworn or establish a standard for determining the level of the child's understanding of the proceedings.

### Fla. Stat. 90.605 (2015) Oath or affirmation of witness.

(1) Before testifying, each witness shall declare that he or she will testify truthfully, by taking an oath or affirmation....

(2) In the court's discretion, a child may testify without taking the oath if the court determines the child understands the duty to tell the truth or the duty not to lie.

## B. Accomodations for Child Witnesses

Recognizing that child victims of domestic violence and sex abuse are particularly vulnerable and may be traumatized by facing their alleged perpetrators in the courtroom, special rules have been adopted for them ranging from permitting their testimony via video-tape or allowing them to use anatomically correct dolls to explain what happened to them. These laws, while of use to children, are not without controversy, particularly when they involve the use of anatomically correct dolls in pre-trial interviews with forensic examiners and law enforcement personnel.

### N.J. Stat. Sec. 2A:84A-16.1 (2016) Dolls as testimonial aids

In prosecutions for those crimes described in sections 2C:14-2, 2C:14-3 and 2C:24-4 of the New Jersey Statutes, where the complaining witness is a child under the age of 16, the court shall permit the use of anatomically correct dolls, models or similar items of either or both sexes to assist the child's testimony.[16]

### 42 Pa. C.S. Sec. 5987 (2016) Use of dolls

In any criminal proceeding charging physical abuse, indecent contact or any of the offenses enumerated in 18 Pa.C.S. Ch. 31 [relating to sexual offenses], the court shall permit the use of anatomically correct dolls or mannequins to assist a child in testifying on direct examination and cross-examination.

### A.C.A. Sec. 16-44-203 (Arkansas 2015) Videotaped deposition of alleged victim under 17 years of age in sexual offense prosecution.

(a) As used in this section, the term "videotaped deposition" means the visual recording on a magnetic tape, together with the associated sound, of a witness testifying under oath in the course of a judicial proceeding, upon oral examination and where an opportunity is given for cross-examination in the presence of the defendant and intended to be played back upon the trial of the action in court.

(b) In any prosecution for a sexual offense or criminal attempt to commit a sexual offense against a minor, upon motion of the prosecuting attorney and after notice to the opposing counsel, the court may, for good cause shown, order the taking of a videotaped deposition of any alleged victim under the age of seventeen (17) years. The videotaped deposition shall be taken before the judge in chambers in the presence of the prosecuting attorney, the defendant, and the defendant's attorneys. Examination and cross-examination of the alleged victim shall proceed at the taking of the videotaped deposition in the same manner as permitted at trial under the provisions of the Arkansas Uniform Rules of Evidence.

---

16. The cited statutes relate to the following crimes involving children; sexual contact or sexual assault, abuse and/or neglect.

(c) Any videotaped deposition taken under the provisions of this section shall be admissible at trial and received into evidence in lieu of the direct testimony of the alleged victim. However, neither the presentation nor the preparation of such videotaped deposition shall preclude the prosecutor's calling the alleged victim to testify at trial if that is necessary to serve the interests of justice.

(d) Videotapes which are a part of the court record are subject to a protective order of the court for the purpose of protecting the privacy of the alleged victim.

---

The last time the United States Supreme Court visited the issue of child testimony via videotape was more than 25 years ago—before the *Crawford, Davis* and *Giles* trio—in *Maryland v. Craig,* 497 U.S. 836 (1990). A grand jury charged Sandra Ann Craig with child abuse and various sexual offenses against a six-year-old child who attended a kindergarten Craig operated. The child testified in one room in the presence of the district attorney and the defense lawyer, while the judge, jury and defendant remained in the courtroom. Craig was convicted, which was upheld by the Maryland intermediate appellate court but reversed by the state's highest tribunal. The United States Supreme Court granted certiorari specifically to address the important Confrontation Clause issues and did so under a *Roberts* analysis. "Our precedents establish that 'the Confrontation Clause reflects a *preference* for face-to-face confrontation at trial,'" wrote Justice Sandra Day O'Connor writing for a 5-4 majority, upholding Craig's conviction. The case remains good law and is excerpted below.

## Maryland v. Craig

Supreme Court of the United States

497 U.S. 836 (1990)

Justice O'Connor delivered the opinion of the Court.

This case requires us to decide whether the Confrontation Clause of the Sixth Amendment categorically prohibits a child witness in a child abuse case from testifying against a defendant at trial, outside the defendant's physical presence, by one-way closed circuit television.

I

In October 1986, a Howard County grand jury charged respondent, Sandra Ann Craig, with child abuse, first and second degree sexual offenses, perverted sexual practice, assault, and battery. The named victim in each count was a 6-year-old girl who, from August 1984 to June 1986, had attended a kindergarten and prekindergarten center owned and operated by Craig.

In March 1987, before the case went to trial, the State sought to invoke a Maryland statutory procedure that permits a judge to receive, by one-way closed circuit television, the testimony of a child witness who is alleged to be a victim of child abuse. To invoke the procedure, the trial judge must first "determine that testimony by the child victim in the courtroom will result in the child suffering serious emotional distress such that the child cannot reasonably communicate." Md. Cts. & Jud. Proc. Code Ann. § 9-102(a)(1)(ii) (1989). Once the procedure is invoked, the child witness, prosecutor, and defense counsel withdraw to a separate room; the judge, jury, and defendant remain in the courtroom. The child witness is then examined and cross-examined in the separate room, while a video monitor records and displays the witness' testimony to those in the courtroom. During this time the witness cannot see the defendant. The defendant remains in electronic communication with defense counsel, and objections may be made and ruled on as if the witness were testifying in the courtroom.

. . . .

Craig objected to the use of the procedure on Confrontation Clause grounds, but the trial court rejected that contention, concluding that although the statute "take[s] away the right of the defendant to be face to face with his or her accuser," the defendant retains the "essence of the right of confrontation," including the right to observe, cross-examine, and have the jury view the demeanor of the witness. App. 65-66. The trial court further found that, "based upon the evidence presented . . . the testimony of each of these children in a courtroom will result in each child suffering serious emotional distress . . . such that each of these children cannot reasonably communicate." *Id.*, at 66. The trial court then found the named victim and three other children competent to testify and accordingly permitted them to testify against Craig via the one-way closed circuit television procedure. The jury convicted Craig on all counts, and the Maryland Court of Special Appeals affirmed the convictions, 76 Md. App. 250, 544 A.2d 784 (1988).

The Court of Appeals of Maryland reversed and remanded for a new trial. 316 Md. 551, 560 A.2d 1120 (1989). The Court of Appeals rejected Craig's argument that the Confrontation Clause requires in all cases a face-to-face courtroom encounter between the accused and his accusers, *id.*, at 556-562, 560 A.2d at 1122-1125 . . . .

Reviewing the trial court's finding and the evidence presented in support of the § 9-102 procedure, the Court of Appeals held that, "as [it] read *Coy* [*v. Iowa*, 487 U.S. 1012, 101 L. Ed. 2d 857, 108 S. Ct. 2798 (1988)], the showing made by the State was insufficient to reach the high threshold required by that case before § 9-102 may be invoked." *Id.*, 316 Md. at 554-555, 560 A.2d at 1121 (footnote omitted).

We granted certiorari to resolve the important Confrontation Clause issues raised by this case.

II

The Confrontation Clause of the Sixth Amendment, made applicable to the States through the Fourteenth Amendment, provides: "In all criminal prosecutions, the accused shall enjoy the right . . . to be confronted with the witnesses against him."

We observed in *Coy v. Iowa* that "the Confrontation Clause guarantees the defendant a face-to-face meeting with witnesses appearing before the trier of fact." 487 U.S. at 1016 (citing *Kentucky v. Stincer*, 482 U.S. 730, 748, 749-750, 96 L. Ed. 2d 631, 107 S.

Ct. 2658 (1987) (Marshall, J., dissenting)); see also *Pennsylvania v. Ritchie*, 480 U.S. 39, 51, 94 L. Ed. 2d 40, 107 S. Ct. 989 (1987) (plurality opinion); *California v. Green*, 399 U.S. 149, 157, 26 L. Ed. 2d 489, 90 S. Ct. 1930 (1970); *Snyder v. Massachusetts*, 291 U.S. 97, 106, 78 L. Ed. 674, 54 S. Ct. 330 (1934); *Dowdell v. United States*, 221 U.S. 325, 330, 55 L. Ed. 753, 31 S. Ct. 590 (1911); *Kirby v. United States*, 174 U.S. 47, 55, 43 L. Ed. 890, 19 S. Ct. 574 (1899); *Mattox v. United States*, 156 U.S. 237, 244, 39 L. Ed. 409, 15 S. Ct. 337 (1895). This interpretation derives not only from the literal text of the Clause, but also from our understanding of its historical roots. See *Coy, supra*, 487 U.S. at 1015-1016; *Mattox, supra*, 156 U.S. at 242 (Confrontation Clause intended to prevent conviction by affidavit); *Green, supra*, 399 U.S. at 156 (same); cf. 3 J. Story, Commentaries on the Constitution § 1785, p. 662 (1833).

We have never held, however, that the Confrontation Clause guarantees criminal defendants the *absolute* right to a face-to-face meeting with witnesses against them at trial. Indeed, in *Coy v. Iowa*, we expressly "left for another day . . . the question whether any exceptions exist" to the "irreducible literal meaning of the Clause: 'a right to *meet face to face* all those who appear and give evidence *at trial*.'" 487 U.S. at 1021 (quoting *Green, supra*, 399 U.S. at 175 (Harlan, J., concurring)). The procedure challenged in *Coy* involved the placement of a screen that prevented two child witnesses in a child abuse case from seeing the defendant as they testified against him at trial. See 487 U.S. at 1014-1015. In holding that the use of this procedure violated the defendant's right to confront witnesses against him, we suggested that any exception to the right "would surely be allowed only when necessary to further an important public policy"—*i. e.*, only upon a showing of something more than the generalized, "legislatively imposed presumption of trauma" underlying the statute at issue in that case. *Id.*, at 1021; see also *id.*, at 1025 (O'Connor, J., concurring). We concluded that "since there had been no individualized findings that these particular witnesses needed special protection, the judgment [in the case before us] could not be sustained by any conceivable exception." *Id.*, at 1021. Because the trial court in this case made individualized findings that each of the child witnesses needed special protection, this case requires us to decide the question reserved in *Coy*.

The central concern of the Confrontation Clause is to ensure the reliability of the evidence against a criminal defendant by subjecting it to rigorous testing in the context of an adversary proceeding before the trier of fact. The word "confront," after all, also means a clashing of forces or ideas, thus carrying with it the notion of adversariness. . . .

[T]he right guaranteed by the Confrontation Clause includes not only a "personal examination," 156 U.S. at 242, but also "(1) insures that the witness will give his statements under oath—thus impressing him with the seriousness of the matter and guarding against the lie by the possibility of a penalty for perjury; (2) forces the witness to submit to cross-examination, the 'greatest legal engine ever invented for the discovery of truth'; [and] (3) permits the jury that is to decide the defendant's fate to observe the demeanor of the witness in making his statement, thus aiding the jury in assessing his credibility." *Green, supra*, at 158 (footnote omitted).

The combined effect of these elements of confrontation—physical presence, oath, cross-examination, and observation of demeanor by the trier of fact—serves the purposes of the Confrontation Clause by ensuring that evidence admitted against an accused is reliable and subject to the rigorous adversarial testing that is the norm of Anglo-American criminal proceedings....

We have recognized, for example, that face-to-face confrontation enhances the accuracy of factfinding by reducing the risk that a witness will wrongfully implicate an innocent person. See *Coy, supra*, 487 U.S. at 1019-1020 ("It is always more difficult to tell a lie about a person 'to his face' than 'behind his back.'... That face-to-face presence may, unfortunately, upset the truthful rape victim or abused child; but by the same token it may confound and undo the false accuser, or reveal the child coached by a malevolent adult"); *Ohio v. Roberts*, 448 U.S. 56, 63, n.6, 65 L. Ed. 2d 597, 100 S. Ct. 2531 (1980); see also 3 W. Blackstone, Commentaries *373-*374. We have also noted the strong symbolic purpose served by requiring adverse witnesses at trial to testify in the accused's presence. See *Coy*, 487 U.S. at 1017 ("There is something deep in human nature that regards face-to-face confrontation between accused and accuser as 'essential to a fair trial in a criminal prosecution'") (quoting *Pointer v. Texas*, 380 U.S. 400, 404, 13 L. Ed. 2d 923, 85 S. Ct. 1065 (1965)).

Although face-to-face confrontation forms "the core of the values furthered by the Confrontation Clause," *Green*, 399 U.S. at 157, we have nevertheless recognized that it is not the *sine qua non* of the confrontation right. See *Delaware v. Fensterer*, 474 U.S. 15, 22, 88 L. Ed. 2d 15, 106 S. Ct. 292 (1985) *(per curiam)*....

For this reason, we have never insisted on an actual face-to-face encounter at trial in *every* instance in which testimony is admitted against a defendant. Instead, we have repeatedly held that the Clause permits, where necessary, the admission of certain hearsay statements against a defendant despite the defendant's inability to confront the declarant at trial. See, *e.g., Mattox*, 156 U.S. at 243.... In *Mattox*, for example, we held that the testimony of a Government witness at a former trial against the defendant, where the witness was fully cross-examined but had died after the first trial, was admissible in evidence against the defendant at his second trial. See 156 U.S. at 240-244....

We have accordingly stated that a literal reading of the Confrontation Clause would "abrogate virtually every hearsay exception, a result long rejected as unintended and too extreme." *Roberts*, 448 U.S. at 63. Thus, in certain narrow circumstances, "competing interests, if 'closely examined,' may warrant dispensing with confrontation at trial."...

In sum, our precedents establish that "the Confrontation Clause reflects a *preference* for face-to-face confrontation at trial," *Roberts, supra*, at 63 (emphasis added; footnote omitted), a preference that "must occasionally give way to considerations of public policy and the necessities of the case," *Mattox, supra*, at 243."... Thus, though we reaffirm the importance of face-to-face confrontation with witnesses appearing at trial, we cannot say that such confrontation is an indispensable element of the Sixth

Amendment's guarantee of the right to confront one's accusers. Indeed, one commentator has noted that "it is all but universally assumed that there are circumstances that excuse compliance with the right of confrontation." Graham, *The Right of Confrontation and the Hearsay Rule: Sir Walter Raleigh Loses Another One*, 8 Crim. L. Bull. 99, 107–108 (1972).

. . . .

That the face-to-face confrontation requirement is not absolute does not, of course, mean that it may easily be dispensed with. As we suggested in *Coy*, our precedents confirm that a defendant's right to confront accusatory witnesses may be satisfied absent a physical, face-to-face confrontation at trial only where denial of such confrontation is necessary to further an important public policy and only where the reliability of the testimony is otherwise assured. . . .

### III

Maryland's statutory procedure, when invoked, prevents a child witness from seeing the defendant as he or she testifies against the defendant at trial. We find it significant, however, that Maryland's procedure preserves all of the other elements of the confrontation right: The child witness must be competent to testify and must testify under oath; the defendant retains full opportunity for contemporaneous cross-examination; and the judge, jury, and defendant are able to view (albeit by video monitor) the demeanor (and body) of the witness as he or she testifies. Although we are mindful of the many subtle effects face-to-face confrontation may have on an adversary criminal proceeding, the presence of these other elements of confrontation—oath, cross-examination, and observation of the witness' demeanor—adequately ensures that the testimony is both reliable and subject to rigorous adversarial testing in a manner functionally equivalent to that accorded live, in-person testimony. These safeguards of reliability and adversariness render the use of such a procedure a far cry from the undisputed prohibition of the Confrontation Clause: trial by *ex parte* affidavit or inquisition, see *Mattox*, 156 U.S. at 242; see also *Green*, 399 U.S. at 179 (Harlan, J., concurring) . . . . Rather, we think these elements of effective confrontation not only permit a defendant to "confound and undo the false accuser, or reveal the child coached by a malevolent adult," *Coy, supra*, 487 U.S. at 1020, but may well aid a defendant in eliciting favorable testimony from the child witness. Indeed, to the extent the child witness' testimony may be said to be technically given out of court (though we do not so hold), these assurances of reliability and adversariness are far greater than those required for admission of hearsay testimony under the Confrontation Clause. See *Roberts*, 448 U.S. at 66. We are therefore confident that use of the one-way closed circuit television procedure, where necessary to further an important state interest, does not impinge upon the truth-seeking or symbolic purposes of the Confrontation Clause.

The critical inquiry in this case, therefore, is whether use of the procedure is necessary to further an important state interest. The State contends that it has a substantial interest in protecting children who are allegedly victims of child abuse from the trauma of testifying against the alleged perpetrator and that its statutory procedure for receiving testimony from such witnesses is necessary to further that interest.

We have of course recognized that a State's interest in "the protection of minor victims of sex crimes from further trauma and embarrassment" is a "compelling" one. *Globe Newspaper Co. v. Superior Court of Norfolk County*, 457 U.S. 596, 607, 73 L. Ed. 2d 248, 102 S. Ct. 2613 (1982); see also *New York v. Ferber*, 458 U.S. 747, 756-757, 73 L. Ed. 2d 1113, 102 S. Ct. 3348 (1982); *FCC v. Pacifica Foundation*, 438 U.S. 726, 749-750, 57 L. Ed. 2d 1073, 98 S. Ct. 3026 (1978); *Ginsberg v. New York*, 390 U.S. 629, 640, 20 L. Ed. 2d 195, 88 S. Ct. 1274 (1968); *Prince v. Massachusetts*, 321 U.S. 158, 168, 88 L. Ed. 645, 64 S. Ct. 438 (1944). "We have sustained legislation aimed at protecting the physical and emotional well-being of youth even when the laws have operated in the sensitive area of constitutionally protected rights." *Ferber, supra*, at 757. In *Globe Newspaper*, for example, we held that a State's interest in the physical and psychological well-being of a minor victim was sufficiently weighty to justify depriving the press and public of their constitutional right to attend criminal trials, where the trial court makes a case-specific finding that closure of the trial is necessary to protect the welfare of the minor. See 457 U.S. at 608-609. This Term, in *Osborne v. Ohio*, 495 U.S. 103, 109 L. Ed. 2d 98, 110 S. Ct. 1691 (1990), we upheld a state statute that proscribed the possession and viewing of child pornography, reaffirming that "'it is evident beyond the need for elaboration that a State's interest in "safeguarding the physical and psychological well-being of a minor" is "compelling."'" *Id.*, at 109 (quoting *Ferber, supra*, 458 U.S. at 756-757).

We likewise conclude today that a State's interest in the physical and psychological well-being of child abuse victims may be sufficiently important to outweigh, at least in some cases, a defendant's right to face his or her accusers in court. That a significant majority of States have enacted statutes to protect child witnesses from the trauma of giving testimony in child abuse cases attests to the widespread belief in the importance of such a public policy. See *Coy*, 487 U.S. at 1022-1023 (O'Connor, J., concurring) ("Many States have determined that a child victim may suffer trauma from exposure to the harsh atmosphere of the typical courtroom and have undertaken to shield the child through a variety of ameliorative measures"). Thirty-seven States, for example, permit the use of videotaped testimony of sexually abused children; 24 States have authorized the use of one-way closed circuit television testimony in child abuse cases; and 8 States authorize the use of a two-way system in which the child witness is permitted to see the courtroom and the defendant on a video monitor and in which the jury and judge are permitted to view the child during the testimony.

The statute at issue in this case, for example, was specifically intended "to safeguard the physical and psychological well-being of child victims by avoiding, or at least minimizing, the emotional trauma produced by testifying." *Wildermuth v. State*, 310 Md. 496, 518, 530 A.2d 275, 286 (1987)....

Given the State's traditional and "'transcendent interest in protecting the welfare of children,'" *Ginsberg*, 390 U.S. at 640 (citation omitted), and buttressed by the growing body of academic literature documenting the psychological trauma suffered by child abuse victims who must testify in court, see Brief for American Psychological Association as *Amicus Curiae* 7-13; G. Goodman et al., Emotional Effects of Criminal Court Testimony on Child Sexual Assault Victims, Final Report to the National Institute of Justice (presented as conference paper at annual convention of American Psychological Assn., Aug. 1989), we will not second-guess the considered judgment of the Maryland Legislature regarding the importance of its interest in protecting child abuse victims from the emotional trauma of testifying. Accordingly, we hold that, if the State makes an adequate showing of necessity, the state interest in protecting child witnesses from the trauma of testifying in a child abuse case is sufficiently important to justify the use of a special procedure that permits a child witness in such cases to testify at trial against a defendant in the absence of face-to-face confrontation with the defendant.

The requisite finding of necessity must of course be a case-specific one: The trial court must hear evidence and determine whether use of the one-way closed circuit television procedure is necessary to protect the welfare of the particular child witness who seeks to testify.... The trial court must also find that the child witness would be traumatized, not by the courtroom generally, but by the presence of the defendant. See, e.g., *State v. Wilhite*, 160 Ariz. 228, 772 P.2d 582 (1989); *State v. Bonello*, 210 Conn. 51, 554 A.2d 277 (1989); *State v. Davidson*, 764 S.W.2d 731 (Mo. App. 1989); *Commonwealth v. Ludwig*, 366 Pa. Super. 361, 531 A.2d 459 (1987). Denial of face-to-face confrontation is not needed to further the state interest in protecting the child witness from trauma unless it is the presence of the defendant that causes the trauma. In other words, if the state interest were merely the interest in protecting child witnesses from courtroom trauma generally, denial of face-to-face confrontation would be unnecessary because the child could be permitted to testify in less intimidating surroundings, albeit with the defendant present. Finally, the trial court must find that the emotional distress suffered by the child witness in the presence of the defendant is more than *de minimis, i.e.*, more than "mere nervousness or excitement or some reluctance to testify," *Wildermuth, supra*, at 524, 530 A.2d at 289; see also *State v. Mannion*, 19 Utah 505, 511-512, 57 P. 542, 543-544 (1899). We need not decide the minimum showing of emotional trauma required for use of the special procedure, however, because the Maryland statute, which requires a determination that the child witness will suffer "serious emotional distress such that the child cannot reasonably communicate," §9-102(a)(1)(ii), clearly suffices to meet constitutional standards.

To be sure, face-to-face confrontation may be said to cause trauma for the very purpose of eliciting truth, cf. *Coy, supra*, 487 U.S. at 1019-1020, but we think that the use of Maryland's special procedure, where necessary to further the important state interest in preventing trauma to child witnesses in child abuse cases, adequately ensures the accuracy of the testimony and preserves the adversary nature of the trial. See *supra*, at 851-852. Indeed, where face-to-face confrontation causes significant emotional distress in a child witness, there is evidence that such confrontation would in fact *disserve* the Confrontation Clause's truth-seeking goal....

In sum, we conclude that where necessary to protect a child witness from trauma that would be caused by testifying in the physical presence of the defendant, at least where such trauma would impair the child's ability to communicate, the Confrontation Clause does not prohibit use of a procedure that, despite the absence of face-to-face confrontation, ensures the reliability of the evidence by subjecting it to rigorous adversarial testing and thereby preserves the essence of effective confrontation. Because there is no dispute that the child witnesses in this case testified under oath, were subject to full cross-examination, and were able to be observed by the judge, jury, and defendant as they testified, we conclude that, to the extent that a proper finding of necessity has been made, the admission of such testimony would be consonant with the Confrontation Clause.

IV

The Maryland Court of Appeals held, as we do today, that although face-to-face confrontation is not an absolute constitutional requirement, it may be abridged only where there is a "'case-specific finding of necessity.'" 316 Md. at 564, 560 A.2d at 1126 (quoting *Coy, supra,* 487 U.S. at 1025 (O'Connor, J., concurring)). Given this latter requirement, the Court of Appeals reasoned that "the question of whether a child is unavailable to testify . . . should not be asked in terms of inability to testify in the ordinary courtroom setting, but in the much narrower terms of the witness's inability to testify in the presence of the accused." 316 Md. at 564, 560 A.2d at 1126 (footnote omitted). "The determinative inquiry required to preclude face-to-face confrontation is the effect of the presence of the defendant on the witness or the witness's testimony." *Id.*, at 565, 560 A.2d at 1127. The Court of Appeals accordingly concluded that, as a prerequisite to use of the §9-102 procedure, the Confrontation Clause requires the trial court to make a specific finding that testimony by the child in the courtroom *in the presence of the defendant* would result in the child suffering serious emotional distress such that the child could not reasonably communicate. *Id.*, at 566, 560 A.2d at 1127. This conclusion, of course, is consistent with our holding today.

In addition, however, the Court of Appeals interpreted our decision in *Coy* to impose two subsidiary requirements. First, the court held that "§9-102 ordinarily cannot be invoked unless the child witness initially is questioned (either in or outside the courtroom) in the defendant's presence." *Id.*, at 566, 560 A.2d at 1127; see also *Wildermuth*, 310 Md. at 523-524, 530 A.2d at 289 (personal observation by the judge should be the rule rather than the exception). Second, the court asserted that, before using the one-way television procedure, a trial judge must determine whether a child would suffer "severe emotional distress" if he or she were to testify by *two*-way closed circuit television. 316 Md. at 567, 560 A.2d at 1128.

Reviewing the evidence presented to the trial court in support of the finding required under §9-102(a)(1)(ii), the Court of Appeals determined that "the finding of necessity required to limit the defendant's right of confrontation through invocation of §9-102 . . . was not made here." *Id.*, at 570-571, 560 A.2d at 1129. The Court of Appeals noted that the trial judge "had the benefit only of expert testimony on the ability of the children to communicate; he did not question any of the children himself, nor did he observe any child's behavior on the witness stand before making his ruling. He did not explore any alternatives to the use of one-way closed-circuit television." *Id.*, at 568, 560 A.2d at 1128 (footnote omitted). The Court of Appeals also observed that "the testimony in this case was not sharply focused on the effect of the defendant's presence on the child witnesses." *Id.*, at 569, 560 A.2d at 1129....

The Court of Appeals appears to have rested its conclusion at least in part on the trial court's failure to observe the children's behavior in the defendant's presence and its failure to explore less restrictive alternatives to the use of the one-way closed circuit television procedure. See *id.*, at 568-571, 560 A.2d at 1128-1129. Although we think such evidentiary requirements could strengthen the grounds for use of protective measures, we decline to establish, as a matter of federal constitutional law, any such categorical evidentiary prerequisites for the use of the one-way television procedure. The trial court in this case, for example, could well have found, on the basis of the expert testimony before it, that testimony by the child witnesses in the courtroom in the defendant's presence "will result in [each] child suffering serious emotional distress such that the child cannot reasonably communicate," § 9-102(a)(1)(ii). See *id.*, at 568-569, 560 A.2d at 1128-1129; see also App. 22-25, 39, 41, 43, 44-45, 54-57. So long as a trial court makes such a case-specific finding of necessity, the Confrontation Clause does not prohibit a State from using a one-way closed circuit television procedure for the receipt of testimony by a child witness in a child abuse case. Because the Court of Appeals held that the trial court had not made the requisite finding of necessity under its interpretation of "the high threshold required by [*Coy*] before § 9-102 may be invoked," 316 Md. at 554-555, 560 A.2d at 1121 (footnote omitted), we cannot be certain whether the Court of Appeals would reach the same conclusion in light of the legal standard we establish today. We therefore vacate the judgment of the Court of Appeals of Maryland and remand the case for further proceedings not inconsistent with this opinion.

*It is so ordered.*

---

Post-*Crawford* and *Davis,* the Supreme Court reviewed a case in which a pre-school age child disclosed abuse to a teacher. In that milieu, the statements made by the child were not testimonial hearsay because they were obtained to respond to the danger of immediate and continued child abuse and not to gather evidence against the abuser in a future trial. Thus, at the abuser's later trial, they were able to be used against him. The decision is excerpted below.

## Ohio v. Clark

Supreme Court of the United States

135 S. Ct. 2173 (2015)

Justice Alito delivered the opinion of the Court.

Darius Clark sent his girlfriend hundreds of miles away to engage in prostitution and agreed to care for her two young children while she was out of town. A day later, teachers discovered red marks on her 3-year-old son, and the boy identified Clark as his abuser. The question in this case is whether the Sixth Amendment's Confrontation Clause prohibited prosecutors from introducing those statements when the child was not available to be cross-examined. Because neither the child nor his teachers had the primary purpose of assisting in Clark's prosecution, the child's statements do not implicate the Confrontation Clause and therefore were admissible at trial.

### I

Darius Clark, who went by the nickname "Dee," lived in Cleveland, Ohio, with his girlfriend, T.T., and her two children: L.P., a 3-year-old boy, and A.T., an 18-month-old girl. Clark was also T.T.'s pimp, and he would regularly send her on trips to Washington, D. C., to work as a prostitute. In March 2010, T.T. went on one such trip, and she left the children in Clark's care.

The next day, Clark took L.P. to preschool. In the lunchroom, one of L.P.'s teachers, Ramona Whitley, observed that L.P.'s left eye appeared bloodshot. She asked him "'[w]hat happened,'" and he initially said nothing. 137 Ohio St. 3d 346, 347, 2013-Ohio-4731, 999 N.E.2d 592, 594. Eventually, however, he told the teacher that he "'fell.'" *Ibid*. When they moved into the brighter lights of a classroom, Whitley noticed "'[r]ed marks, like whips of some sort,'" on L.P.'s face. *Ibid*. She notified the lead teacher, Debra Jones, who asked L.P., "'Who did this? What happened to you?'" *Id.*, at 348, 999 N.E.2d, at 595. According to Jones, L.P. "'seemed kind of bewildered'" and "'said something like, Dee, Dee.'" *Ibid*. Jones asked L.P. whether Dee is "big or little," to which L.P. responded that "Dee is big." App. 60, 64. Jones then brought L.P. to her supervisor, who lifted the boy's shirt, revealing more injuries. Whitley called a child abuse hotline to alert authorities about the suspected abuse.

When Clark later arrived at the school, he denied responsibility for the injuries and quickly left with L.P. The next day, a social worker found the children at Clark's mother's house and took them to a hospital, where a physician discovered additional injuries suggesting child abuse. L.P. had a black eye, belt marks on his back and stomach, and bruises all over his body. A.T. had two black eyes, a swollen hand, and a large burn on her cheek, and two pigtails had been ripped out at the roots of her hair.

A grand jury indicted Clark on five counts of felonious assault (four related to A.T. and one related to L.P.), two counts of endangering children (one for each child), and two counts of domestic violence (one for each child). At trial, the State introduced L.P.'s statements to his teachers as evidence of Clark's guilt, but L.P. did not testify. Under Ohio law, children younger than 10 years old are incompetent to testify if they "appear incapable of receiving just impressions of the facts and transactions respecting which they are examined, or of relating them truly." Ohio Rule Evid. 601(A) (Lexis 2010). After conducting a hearing, the trial court concluded that L.P. was not competent to testify. But under Ohio Rule of Evidence 807, which allows the admission of reliable hearsay by child abuse victims, the court ruled that L.P.'s statements to his teachers bore sufficient guarantees of trustworthiness to be admitted as evidence.

Clark moved to exclude testimony about L.P.'s out-of-court statements under the Confrontation Clause. The trial court denied the motion, ruling that L.P.'s responses were not testimonial statements covered by the Sixth Amendment. The jury found Clark guilty on all counts except for one assault count related to A.T., and it sentenced him to 28 years' imprisonment. Clark appealed his conviction, and a state appellate court reversed on the ground that the introduction of L.P.'s out-of-court statements violated the Confrontation Clause.

In a 4-to-3 decision, the Supreme Court of Ohio affirmed. It held that, under this Court's Confrontation Clause decisions, L.P.'s statements qualified as testimonial because the primary purpose of the teachers' questioning "was not to deal with an existing emergency but rather to gather evidence potentially relevant to a subsequent criminal prosecution." 137 Ohio St. 3d, at 350, 999 N.E.2d, at 597. The court noted that Ohio has a "mandatory reporting" law that requires certain professionals, including preschool teachers, to report suspected child abuse to government authorities. See *id.*, at 349-350, 999 N.E.2d, at 596-597. In the court's view, the teachers acted as agents of the State under the mandatory reporting law and "sought facts concerning past criminal activity to identify the person responsible, eliciting statements that 'are functionally identical to live, in-court testimony, doing precisely what a witness does on direct examination.'" *Id.*, at 355, 999 N.E.2d, at 600 (quoting *Melendez-Diaz v. Massachusetts*, 557 U.S. 305, 310-311, 129 S. Ct. 2527, 174 L. Ed. 2d 314 (2009); some internal quotation marks omitted).

We granted certiorari, 573 U.S. ___, 135 S. Ct. 43, 189 L. Ed. 2d 896 (2014), and we now reverse.

## II

### A

The Sixth Amendment's Confrontation Clause, which is binding on the States through the Fourteenth Amendment, provides: "In all criminal prosecutions, the accused shall enjoy the right . . . to be confronted with the witnesses against him." In *Ohio v. Roberts*, 448 U.S. 56, 66, 100 S. Ct. 2531, 65 L. Ed. 2d 597 (1980), we interpreted the Clause to permit the admission of out-of-court statements by an unavailable witness, so long as the statements bore "adequate 'indicia of reliability.'" Such indicia are present, we held, if "the evidence falls within a firmly rooted hearsay exception" or bears "particularized guarantees of trustworthiness." *Ibid.*

In *Crawford v. Washington*, 541 U.S. 36, 124 S. Ct. 1354, 158 L. Ed. 2d 177 (2004), we adopted a different approach. We explained that "witnesses," under the Confrontation Clause, are those "who bear testimony," and we defined "testimony" as "a solemn declaration or affirmation made for the purpose of establishing or proving some fact." *Id.,* at 51, 124 S. Ct. 1354, 158 L. Ed. 2d 177 (internal quotation marks and alteration omitted). The Sixth Amendment, we concluded, prohibits the introduction of testimonial statements by a nontestifying witness, unless the witness is "unavailable to testify, and the defendant had had a prior opportunity for cross-examination." *Id.,* at 54, 124 S. Ct. 1354, 158 L. Ed. 2d 177. Applying that definition to the facts in *Crawford,* we held that statements by a witness during police questioning at the station house were testimonial and thus could not be admitted. But our decision in *Crawford* did not offer an exhaustive definition of "testimonial" statements. Instead, *Crawford* stated that the label "applies at a minimum to prior testimony at a preliminary hearing, before a grand jury, or at a former trial; and to police interrogations." *Id.,* at 68, 124 S. Ct. 1354, 158 L. Ed. 2d 177.

Our more recent cases have labored to flesh out what it means for a statement to be "testimonial." In *Davis v. Washington* and *Hammon v. Indiana,* 547 U.S. 813, 126 S. Ct. 2266, 165 L. Ed. 2d 224 (2006), which we decided together, we dealt with statements given to law enforcement officers by the victims of domestic abuse. The victim in *Davis* made statements to a 911 emergency operator during and shortly after her boyfriend's violent attack. In *Hammon,* the victim, after being isolated from her abusive husband, made statements to police that were memorialized in a "'battery affidavit.'" *Id.,* at 820, 126 S. Ct. 2266, 165 L. Ed. 2d 224.

We held that the statements in *Hammon* were testimonial, while the statements in *Davis* were not. Announcing what has come to be known as the "primary purpose" test, we explained: "Statements are nontestimonial when made in the course of police interrogation under circumstances objectively indicating that the primary purpose of the interrogation is to enable police assistance to meet an ongoing emergency. They are testimonial when the circumstances objectively indicate that there is no such ongoing emergency, and that the primary purpose of the interrogation is to establish or prove past events potentially relevant to later criminal prosecution." *Id.,* at 822, 126 S. Ct. 2266, 165 L. Ed. 2d 224 . Because the cases involved statements to law enforcement officers, we reserved the question whether similar statements to individuals other than law enforcement officers would raise similar issues under the Confrontation Clause. See *id.,* at 823, n. 2, 126 S. Ct. 2266, 165 L. Ed. 2d 224.

In *Michigan v. Bryant,* 562 U.S. 344, 131 S. Ct. 1143, 179 L. Ed. 2d 93 (2011), we further expounded on the primary purpose test. The inquiry, we emphasized, must consider "all of the relevant circumstances." *Id.,* at 369, 131 S. Ct. 1143, 179 L. Ed. 2d 93. And we reiterated our view in *Davis* that, when "the primary purpose of an interrogation is to respond to an 'ongoing emergency,' its purpose is not to create a record for trial and thus is not within the scope of the [Confrontation] Clause." 562 U.S., at 358, 131 S. Ct. 1143, 179 L. Ed. 2d 93. At the same time, we noted that "there may be *other* circumstances, aside from ongoing emergencies, when a statement is not procured with a primary purpose of creating an out-of-court substitute for trial testimony." *Ibid.* "[T]he existence *vel non* of an ongoing emergency is not the touchstone of the testimonial inquiry." *Id.,* at 374, 131 S. Ct. 1143, 179 L. Ed. 2d 93. Instead, "whether an ongoing emergency exists is simply one factor... that informs the ultimate inquiry regarding the 'primary purpose' of an interrogation." *Id.,* at 366, 131 S. Ct. 1143, 179 L. Ed. 2d 93.

One additional factor is "the informality of the situation and the interrogation." *Id.,* at 377, 131 S. Ct. 1143, 179 L. Ed. 2d 93. A "formal station-house interrogation," like the questioning in *Crawford,* is more likely to provoke testimonial statements, while less formal questioning is less likely to reflect a primary purpose aimed at obtaining testimonial evidence against the accused. *Id.,* at 366, 377, 131 S. Ct. 1143, 179 L. Ed. 2d 93. And in determining whether a statement is testimonial, "standard rules of hearsay, designed to identify some statements as reliable, will be relevant." *Id.,* at 358-359, 131 S. Ct. 1143, 179 L. Ed. 2d 93. In the end, the question is whether, in light of all the circumstances, viewed objectively, the "primary purpose" of the conversation was to "creat[e] an out-of-court substitute for trial testimony." *Id.,* at 358, 131 S. Ct. 1143, 179 L. Ed. 2d 93. Applying these principles in *Bryant,* we held that the statements made by a dying victim about his assailant were not testimonial because the circumstances objectively indicated that the conversation was primarily aimed at quelling an ongoing emergency, not establishing evidence for the prosecution. Because the relevant statements were made to law enforcement officers, we again declined to decide whether the same analysis applies to statements made to individuals other than the police. See *id.,* at 357, n. 3, 131 S. Ct. 1143, 179 L. Ed 2d 93.

Thus, under our precedents, a statement cannot fall within the Confrontation Clause unless its primary purpose was testimonial. "Where no such primary purpose exists, the admissibility of a statement is the concern of state and federal rules of evidence, not the Confrontation Clause." *Id.,* at 359, 131 S. Ct. 1143, 179 L. Ed. 2d 93. But that does not mean that the Confrontation Clause bars every statement that satisfies the "primary purpose" test. We have recognized that the Confrontation Clause does not prohibit the introduction of out-of-court statements that would have been admissible in a criminal case at the time of the founding. See *Giles v. California,* 554 U.S. 353, 358-359, 128 S. Ct. 2678, 171 L. Ed. 2d 488 (2008); *Crawford,* 541 U.S., at 56, n. 6, 62, 124 S. Ct. 1354, 158 L. Ed. 2d 177. Thus, the primary purpose test is a necessary, but not always sufficient, condition for the exclusion of out-of-court statements under the Confrontation Clause.

B

In this case, we consider statements made to preschool teachers, not the police. We are therefore presented with the question we have repeatedly reserved: whether statements to persons other than law enforcement officers are subject to the Confrontation Clause. Because at least some statements to individuals who are not law enforcement officers could conceivably raise confrontation concerns, we decline to adopt a categorical rule excluding them from the Sixth Amendment's reach. Nevertheless, such statements are much less likely to be testimonial than statements to law enforcement officers. And considering all the relevant circumstances here, L.P.'s statements clearly were not made with the primary purpose of creating evidence for Clark's prosecution. Thus, their introduction at trial did not violate the Confrontation Clause.

L.P.'s statements occurred in the context of an ongoing emergency involving suspected child abuse. When L.P.'s teachers noticed his injuries, they rightly became worried that the 3-year-old was the victim of serious violence. Because the teachers needed to know whether it was safe to release L.P. to his guardian at the end of the day, they needed to determine who might be abusing the child. Thus, the immediate concern was to protect a vulnerable child who needed help. Our holding in *Bryant* is instructive. As in *Bryant*, the emergency in this case was ongoing, and the circumstances were not entirely clear. L.P.'s teachers were not sure who had abused him or how best to secure his safety. Nor were they sure whether any other children might be at risk. As a result, their questions and L.P.'s answers were primarily aimed at identifying and ending the threat. Though not as harried, the conversation here was also similar to the 911 call in *Davis*. The teachers' questions were meant to identify the abuser in order to protect the victim from future attacks. Whether the teachers thought that this would be done by apprehending the abuser or by some other means is irrelevant. And the circumstances in this case were unlike the interrogation in *Hammon*, where the police knew the identity of the assailant and questioned the victim after shielding her from potential harm.

There is no indication that the primary purpose of the conversation was to gather evidence for Clark's prosecution. On the contrary, it is clear that the first objective was to protect L.P. At no point did the teachers inform L.P. that his answers would be used to arrest or punish his abuser. L.P. never hinted that he intended his statements to be used by the police or prosecutors. And the conversation between L.P. and his teachers was informal and spontaneous. The teachers asked L.P. about his injuries immediately upon discovering them, in the informal setting of a preschool lunchroom and classroom, and they did so precisely as any concerned citizen would talk to a child who might be the victim of abuse. This was nothing like the formalized station-house questioning in *Crawford* or the police interrogation and battery affidavit in *Hammon*.

L.P.'s age fortifies our conclusion that the statements in question were not testimonial. Statements by very young children will rarely, if ever, implicate the Confrontation Clause. Few preschool students understand the details of our criminal justice system. Rather, "[r]esearch on children's understanding of the legal system finds that" young children "have little understanding of prosecution." Brief for American Professional Society on the Abuse of Children as *Amicus Curiae* 7, and n. 5 (collecting sources). And Clark does not dispute those findings. Thus, it is extremely unlikely that a 3-year-old child in L.P.'s position would intend his statements to be a substitute for trial testimony. On the contrary, a young child in these circumstances would simply want the abuse to end, would want to protect other victims, or would have no discernible purpose at all.

As a historical matter, moreover, there is strong evidence that statements made in circumstances similar to those facing L.P. and his teachers were admissible at common law. See Lyon & LaMagna, The History of Children's Hearsay: From Old Bailey to Post-*Davis*, 82 Ind. L.J. 1029, 1030 (2007); see also *id.,* at 1041-1044 (examining child rape cases from 1687 to 1788); J. Langbein, The Origins of Adversary Criminal Trial 239 (2003) ("The Old Bailey" court in 18th-century London "tolerated flagrant hearsay in rape prosecutions involving a child victim who was not competent to testify because she was too young to appreciate the significance of her oath"). And when 18th-century courts excluded statements of this sort, see, *e.g., King v. Brasier*, 1 Leach 199, 168 Eng. Rep. 202 (K.B. 1779), they appeared to do so because the child should have been ruled competent to testify, not because the statements were otherwise inadmissible. See Lyon & LaMagna, *supra*, at 1053-1054. It is thus highly doubtful that statements like L.P.'s ever would have been understood to raise Confrontation Clause concerns. Neither *Crawford* nor any of the cases that it has produced has mounted evidence that the adoption of the Confrontation Clause was understood to require the exclusion of evidence that was regularly admitted in criminal cases at the time of the founding. Certainly, the statements in this case are nothing like the notorious use of *ex parte* examination in Sir Walter Raleigh's trial for treason, which we have frequently identified as "the principal evil at which the Confrontation Clause was directed." *Crawford*, 541 U.S., at 50, 124 S. Ct. 1354, 158 L. Ed. 2d 177; see also *Bryant*, 562 U.S., at 358, 131 S. Ct. 1143, 179 L. Ed. 2d 93.

Finally, although we decline to adopt a rule that statements to individuals who are not law enforcement officers are categorically outside the Sixth Amendment, the fact that L.P. was speaking to his teachers remains highly relevant. Courts must evaluate challenged statements in context, and part of that context is the questioner's identity. See *id.*, at 369, 131 S. Ct. 1143, 179 L. Ed. 2d 93. Statements made to someone who is not principally charged with uncovering and prosecuting criminal behavior are significantly less likely to be testimonial than statements given to law enforcement officers. See, *e.g., Giles*, 554 U.S., at 376, 128 S. Ct. 2678, 171 L. Ed. 2d 488. It is common sense that the relationship between a student and his teacher is very different from that between a citizen and the police. We do not ignore that reality. In light of these circumstances, the Sixth Amendment did not prohibit the State from introducing L.P.'s statements at trial.

### III

Clark's efforts to avoid this conclusion are all off-base. He emphasizes Ohio's mandatory reporting obligations, in an attempt to equate L.P.'s teachers with the police and their caring questions with official interrogations. But the comparison is inapt. The teachers' pressing concern was to protect L.P. and remove him from harm's way. Like all good teachers, they undoubtedly would have acted with the same purpose whether or not they had a state-law duty to report abuse. And mandatory reporting statutes alone cannot convert a conversation between a concerned teacher and her student into a law enforcement mission aimed primarily at gathering evidence for a prosecution.

It is irrelevant that the teachers' questions and their duty to report the matter had the natural tendency to result in Clark's prosecution. The statements at issue in *Davis* and *Bryant* supported the defendants' convictions, and the police always have an obligation to ask questions to resolve ongoing emergencies. Yet, we held in those cases that the Confrontation Clause did not prohibit introduction of the statements because they were not primarily intended to be testimonial. Thus, Clark is also wrong to suggest that admitting L.P.'s statements would be fundamentally unfair given that Ohio law does not allow incompetent children to testify. In any Confrontation Clause case, the individual who provided the out-of-court statement is not available as an in-court witness, but the testimony is admissible under an exception to the hearsay rules and is probative of the defendant's guilt. The fact that the witness is unavailable because of a different rule of evidence does not change our analysis.

Finally, Clark asks us to shift our focus from the context of L.P.'s conversation with his teachers to the jury's perception of those statements. Because, in his view, the "jury treated L.P.'s accusation as the functional equivalent of testimony," Clark argues that we must prohibit its introduction. Brief for Respondent 42. Our Confrontation Clause decisions, however, do not determine whether a statement is testimonial by examining whether a jury would view the statement as the equivalent of in-court testimony. The logic of this argument, moreover, would lead to the conclusion that virtually all out-of-court statements offered by the prosecution are testimonial. The prosecution is unlikely to offer out-of-court statements unless they tend to support the defendant's guilt, and all such statements could be viewed as a substitute for in-court testimony. We have never suggested, however, that the Confrontation Clause bars the introduction of all out-of-court statements that support the prosecution's case. Instead, we ask whether a statement was given with the "primary purpose of creating an out-of-court substitute for trial testimony." *Bryant, supra*, at 358, 131 S. Ct. 1143, 179 L. Ed. 2d 93. Here, the answer is clear: L.P.'s statements to his teachers were not testimonial.

IV

We reverse the judgment of the Supreme Court of Ohio and remand the case for further proceedings not inconsistent with this opinion.

It is so ordered.

## V. Courthouse Dogs

A long-time Seattle prosecutor, Ellen O'Neill Stephens, in an effort to assist her disabled son, obtained a companion animal for him, Jeeter, a Labrador-Golden Retriever mix. She thought the many benefits the dog provided her son would be valuable to children caught up in the stress of the justice system. She brought her son's dog with her to the King County Prosecuting Attorney's Office, where Stephens was a juvenile drug court prosecutor, one day a week. When she saw how easily the dog soothed the young drug court participants, she convinced the office to get a dog of its own in 2004. Four years later, she and a veterinarian formed Court House Dogs, which in 2012 became the Courthouse Dogs Foundation. Today there are 100 successful courthouse dog programs across the country. At the Southern Arizona Children's Advocacy Center, a dog helps calm nervous children during forensic interviews and will go to court with them if necessary. Courthouse dogs get two years of training and respond to at least 80 commands. They are sociable, patient and tolerate petting. Their job is not to interfere with or influence the court process but to be "legally neutral." *See* Linda Drake,

Russell, *The Courthouse Dog*, THE WRIT, November 2012, 5, www.courthousedogs.com /pdf/courthousedog:Russell_pdf, and www.courthousedogs.com, accessed October 20, 2016. These dogs, used by the prosecution and the defense, "dial down the stress and trauma that is the result of our adversarial system," says Stephens.[17] What follows is an article about Stephens and a case from Washington's highest court upholding the decision of a trial judge to allow a dog to comfort a highly vulnerable witness.

### Casey Holder, Comment: *All Dogs Go to Court: The Impact of Court Facility Dogs as Comfort for Child Witnesses on a Defendant's Right to a Fair Trial*
50 HOUS. L. REV. 1155 (Symposium 2013)

. . . .

The number of cases involving child witnesses has increased dramatically in the past two decades. The testimony of victims and witnesses is often crucial to the successful prosecution of a criminal case. This is especially true in cases where a child has been sexually abused or assaulted. If a child witness is also an abuse victim, the "testimony becomes imperative in proving the guilt of the defendant." These cases present even greater challenges to the prosecution because the child is likely the only witness, and the child's testimony is central to the successful prosecution of the case. . . .

A. Impact of Testifying on Child Witnesses

Child victims often feel guilty and ashamed about their experiences, and prosecutors can retraumatize children when questioning them in a courtroom. Before a child ever gets to court, he or she has already endured a number of potentially traumatic experiences in the legal system. The child likely has been interviewed by police or by a forensic investigator and may have met with a therapist or psychologist. Even when children want to testify against their abusers, the courtroom and the trial process can intimidate them and make them feel anxious. Judges have recognized that a child is likely to suffer compounded fear and anxiety when participating in a trial, effectively being retraumatized.

A child's fear of the defendant and apprehension in an unfamiliar setting can inhibit the child's ability to testify, preventing all facts in the case from being included in the trial. In some cases, a child may be completely unable to speak due to fear. Additionally, the judge, lawyers, and jury can overwhelm child witnesses, making them feel nervous or anxious. A child "may feel intimidated or embarrassed" when the defense attorney conducts cross-examination and questions his testimony. Often, prosecutors have to drop cases when children will not testify against the defendant. . . .

B. Special Circumstances for Child Witnesses

Both federal and state legislation acknowledge the unique position of child witnesses and implement protective measures for children testifying in court. For instance,

---

17. Ellen O'Neill-Stephens telephone interview with the author.

the Victims of Child Abuse Act of 1990 recognizes the traumatic impact a trial can have on a child.[18] This law outlines alternative methods of testimony for when a child is unable to testify in court because of fear, likelihood of trauma, incapacity, or conduct of the defendant or defense counsel. Additional protections for children stipulated in the Act include allowing testimony via closed-circuit television or videotaped deposition, closing the courtroom, use of a guardian ad litem, allowing a child witness to be accompanied to the witness stand by an adult attendant for emotional support, and allowing the use of testimonial aids such as puppets or drawings to assist a child's testimony.

Another attempt to relieve the trauma of child testimony is the Uniform Child Witness Testimony by Alternative Methods Act.[19] This model legislation provides further safeguards for child witnesses by creating procedures for states to adopt that authorize alternative methods of testimony. If clear and convincing evidence indicates that a child is particularly vulnerable to emotional harm, the child may testify by an alternative method.

In addition to the legislature, many courts have recognized the unique nature of cases involving child witnesses. Trial courts have broad discretion within the law to allow nontraditional techniques that help child witnesses clearly communicate sensitive and critical information. . . .

Crawford v. Washington precludes the introduction of testimonial, out-of-court statements unless (1) the witness is unavailable to testify in court; and (2) the defendant previously had an opportunity for cross-examination. Regardless of whether the court finds the testimonial statement reliable through other means, the testimony can be excluded as a violation of the Confrontation Clause if actual face-to-face confrontation is not satisfied.

Prior to the Crawford decision, most child witnesses were never called to the stand because their testimonial statements could be introduced under exceptions to the hearsay rule. However, post-Crawford, statements made to police, therapists, or forensic interviewers may no longer be introduced as evidence of what a child experienced or witnessed. As a result, more children will be forced to testify face-to-face with the defendant, increasing their apprehension in the courtroom. . . .

Defendants routinely object to child witnesses carrying items with them to the witness stand, citing undue prejudice, juror empathy, and an appearance of credibility. Defendants claim that comfort items engender a jury's sympathy toward a child witness, but sympathy does not necessarily deprive the defendant of a fair trial. Courts are careful to balance the defendant's right to a fair trial with the child's interest in being

---

18. [n39] 18 U.S.C. § 3509 (2006 & Supp. V 2012).

19. [n42] Unif. Child Witness Testimony by Alt. Methods Act (2002), available at http://www.uniformlaws.org/shared/docs/child_witness_testimony/child_witness_final_02.pdf (outlining model legislation to protect child witnesses). The Act was created after the 1999 Rules of Evidence removed a provision allowing alternative testimony methods for child victims. 81 Am. Jur. 2d Witnesses ß 188 (2004).

free from fear and intimidation before allowing a comfort item. Most often, the benefit of a calm and articulate witness outweighs any potential prejudicial effects on the defendant. A judge can further safeguard the defendant's rights by instructing the jury to "not allow any bias, passion, prejudice, sympathy or pity to interfere with [the] verdict" to prevent this sympathy from impacting the jury's decision.

. . . .

C. Current Court Facility Dog Programs

Much like comfort items and support persons, dogs help children throughout the judicial process. Court facility dogs work in initial meetings with prosecutors, during preparations for trial, and even during trial. The first known use of a court facility dog occurred in Mississippi in 1992.[20] A German shepherd named Vachss worked with an abused seven-year-old girl in therapy. As the trial drew near, the girl asked if Vachss could accompany her to the witness stand. The judge conducted a witness voir dire and concluded that allowing Vachss to accompany the child in the witness box would serve the best interest of justice.

After Vachss entered that Mississippi courtroom, attorneys in other states began exploring the benefits of court facility dogs. In 2003, Ellen O'Neill-Stephens, a prosecutor in King County, Washington, created "Courthouse Dogs," a program that educates and advocates specifically for court facility dogs. The program seeks to teach the legal system about the benefits of court facility dogs when used properly. . . .

Since the experience in King County, prosecutors across the country are recognizing the benefits of using dogs to calm and support victims and witnesses, especially children. In Carroll County, Maryland, a dog works with prosecutors as they meet with children and prepare for trial. The prosecutors hope that in the future the dog will be able to accompany children in the courtroom. A program in Harris County, Texas called "Paw and Order SDU" works with the Children's Assessment Center (CAC) to connect therapy dogs with victims of abuse. Volunteer handlers bring therapy dogs to the CAC to calm and relax young victims of domestic violence. Similar programs exist in Florida and New York, where dogs work with child victims in diverse legal settings. Currently, seventeen states allow dogs into the courtroom.[21] The benefits that these court facility dogs provide to child witnesses and to the justice system should encourage courts to utilize them in the courtroom, despite opponents' objections to the practice. . . .

A. Prejudice Generally

Defendants oppose court facility dogs based on various alleged prejudicial effects. The actual impact of a certain method of presenting evidence on the jury and the

---

20. [n99] Dan Wiessner, *U.S. Courtroom Dogs Spark Legal Debate*, Reuters (Sept. 12, 2011, 12:21 PM), http://www.reuters.com/article/2011/09/12/us-usa-courtoom-dogs-idUSTRE78B4KN20110912.

21. [n115] Christine Clarridge, *Courthouse Dogs Calm Victims' Fears About Testifying*, Seattle Times (Sept. 24, 2012, 4:35 PM), http://seattletimes.com/seattle-news-/courthouse-dogs-calm-victims-fears.

verdict cannot be measured with complete accuracy, and a prejudicial practice may go unnoticed by jurors. The jury will not always perceive prejudicial practices as such, so the trial court must exercise vigilance in observing whether a practice reduces the fairness of the trial. A defendant is not necessarily guilty, nor is any witness necessarily a victim, at least not until a defendant is convicted of the charged offense. However, allowing a dog to comfort and support a child on the witness stand could signal to the jury that the child is a victim and needs the dog because of some underlying trauma. A dog cannot discern if a witness is stressed because she is afraid of the defendant or because she is lying on the stand. Either way, a dog will react to that stress and comfort the witness, potentially lending to the appearance that the witness is a victim. Even a proper jury instruction may not completely eliminate a dog's influence on the jury. A jury might still conclude that the dog was protecting the frightened witness or comforting the vulnerable witness, and both conclusions presuppose that the defendant is guilty....

### IV. Using Dogs in the Courtroom Is a Logical Step Forward

Despite objections to the use of dogs in the courtroom, the practice is a logical extension of current protections for child witnesses. Judicial precedent and statutory law support the use of added protections for testifying children, and court facility dogs serve as a form of protection. Court facility dogs can enhance the trial process both for child witnesses and for the justice system by facilitating the delivery of calm and coherent testimony. Additionally, the court can initiate certain safeguards to ensure that the defendant retains the right to a fair trial. By requiring the child to demonstrate a substantial need for the dog, implementing a jury instruction regarding the dog, and specifying the appropriate guidelines for court facility dogs, a court can preserve the integrity of the trial....

### D. Policies to Protect Defendants' Rights During Trial

Certain precautions reduce the potential for prejudice to the defendant and ensure that the use of a court facility dog is beneficial to all parties. These protections start when a dog is selected to work with a child and continue through the trial process. Requiring that the child witness have a substantial need for emotional support ensures that prosecutors incorporate court facility dogs only as needed. Additionally, judges can issue a special jury instruction to mitigate any potential inferences the jury could draw from the dog's presence. Furthermore, specific guidelines for court facility dogs reduce the possibility of distraction....

### V. Conclusion

The use of court facility dogs to comfort child witnesses during testimony is a logical step toward protecting child witnesses while, at the same time, recognizing a defendant's right to a fair trial. Children are increasingly likely to testify in the courtroom—face-to-face with the defendant. These witnesses will undoubtedly feel apprehension about testifying and will likely seek comfort and support in the courtroom. Court facility dogs can fill a gap for witnesses when traditional comfort items and support persons fail to ease their anxiety. Although opponents may raise a variety of objections to a dog being present in the courtroom, an array of precautionary measures effectively combat any prejudice. With a properly trained dog and an appropriately tailored jury instruction, a defendant's right to a fair trial will not be compromised.

## State v. Dye
### Supreme Court of Washington
### 178 Wn. 2d 541 (2013)

En Banc

Wiggins, J. — This case requires us to determine whether a court may allow a witness to be accompanied by a comfort animal, here a dog, when testifying during trial. Generally, we give trial courts wide discretion to control trial proceedings, including the manner in which testimony will be presented. We recognize that some trial procedures, such as providing a child witness with a toy on the stand or shackling a defendant at trial, may risk coloring the perceptions of the jury. But trial courts are capable of addressing these risks. Here, the trial court acted within its broad discretion when it determined that Ellie, the facility dog provided by the prosecutor's office to the victim Douglas Lare, was needed in light of Lare's severe developmental disabilities in order for Lare to testify adequately. We affirm the Court of Appeals.

### FACTS
#### I. Background

Douglas Lare suffers from significant developmental disabilities, including cerebral palsy, Kallman Syndrome, and mild mental retardation. He has an IQ (intelligence quotient) of 65, and although he is 56 years old, he functions at a mental age ranging from 6 to 12 years old. While he lives independently and has been working for the Veteran's Hospital for 23 years, Lare has difficulty with daily household activities, reading, and writing, and he uses a payee service to handle his finances.

In 2005, Lare became romantically involved with his neighbor Alesha Lair. Alesha was also dating the defendant, Timothy Dye, a fact that she did not reveal to Lare. In 2007, Alesha moved into Lare's apartment, along with Alesha's sister, her mother, and her mother's boyfriend. Alesha opened several credit cards in Lare's name and charged them to their limits, using them to buy herself and her family clothing, shoes, computers, beer, cigarettes, a DVD (digital video disk) player, and cell phones. Alesha also withdrew money from Lare's retirement account.

When Alesha and her family moved out of Lare's apartment, Alesha used Lare's money to furnish her new apartment, and Dye moved in with Alesha. Alesha took a key to Lare's apartment with her. In total, Alesha borrowed approximately $42,000 against the credit cards in Lare's name and withdrew $59,000 from Lare's retirement account.

On January 19, 2008, Lare called 911 to report a DVD player and DVD missing. On January 24, Lare woke up to find Dye rummaging through his apartment. Dye asked Lare if he could take a DVD player and VCR (videocassette recorder), but Lare refused. Dye nonetheless took some DVDs and a shelving unit. The following day, Lare came home from work to find his front door propped open. His television, VCR, DVD player, microwave, and a collectible knife were missing. In a telephone interview with a police detective, Dye admitted that he had pawned Lare's DVD player but claimed that Lare had voluntarily offered it to him. After the detective stopped the recording, Dye told her that "he didn't have anything to worry about because his name wasn't on any of the pawn slips and so there was no way to pin it on him." Report of Proceedings (RP) (Dec. 6, 2010) at 6.

After the burglaries, Lare became very fearful. He installed three locks on his front door and began sleeping with mace, a frying pan, and two knives in his bedroom for protection.

II. Trial and Appellate Proceedings

The State charged Dye with residential burglary in connection with the January 24 incident, alleging as an aggravator that Lare was a vulnerable victim.

During Lare's defense interview, he was accompanied by a facility dog, Ellie. Ellie is a golden retriever used by the King County Prosecuting Attorney's Office to comfort children who are giving statements and testimony. Ellie was trained by, and lives with, the prosecutor at Dye's trial.

Lare then requested Ellie's presence during his testimony at trial. The State moved to allow Ellie to accompany Lare during his testimony, arguing that Lare needed Ellie's assistance because of his "significant anxiety regarding his upcoming testimony" and because he "functions at the level of a child and is fearful of the defendant." Clerk's Papers (CP) at 104. The State further added during a pretrial hearing that Lare was a "complete dog fan" and that Ellie had provided Lare "tremendous comfort" during the previous interview. RP (Nov. 18, 2010) at 28.

Dye's counsel said that she did not object to Ellie's presence "if [Dye] gets to hold his baby while he is testifying," arguing that "the prejudice is extreme, allowing the alleged victim in this case to pet the dog." *Id.* The trial court disagreed, noting that Lare was a "developmentally disabled individual who has ... significant emotional trauma." *Id.* at 29. The court found that Ellie "would be very unobtrusive, will just simply be next to the individual, not be laying [sic] in his lap, and if we can accommodate somebody who has a developmental disability when they're testifying in the courtroom I think it's appropriate to do so." *Id.* The court then suggested that if Dye had a similar disability, the court might be receptive to allowing Dye to hold his baby on the stand.

Dye's counsel also argued that Ellie's presence might inflame Dye's allergies or distract the jury. The court offered to accommodate Dye's allergies so long as he could provide medical documentation of them. There is no indication in the record that Dye did so.

At trial, Ellie sat with Lare during his testimony and accompanied him to the restroom. Lare also fed Ellie treats and used Ellie as a table while reading an exhibit. Ellie's presence is not otherwise indicated in the record except for her introduction at the beginning of Lare's testimony:

Q. ... Who's your friend there with you?

A. This is Ellie.

Q. And why is Ellie there with you?

A. Ellie is to help me and to make it easier for me. And I have treats here.

RP (Dec. 1, 2010) at 10. At the end of the trial, the court instructed the jury not to "make any assumptions or draw any conclusions based on the presence of this service dog." CP at 53.

The jury convicted Dye of residential burglary but did not find that Lare was a vulnerable victim. *State v. Dye*, 170 Wn. App. 340, 344, 283 P.3d 1130 (2012). Dye appealed his conviction, and the Court of Appeals affirmed the trial court. . . .

## ANALYSIS

### I. Standard of Review

The trial court is generally in the best position to perceive and structure its own proceedings. Accordingly, a trial court has broad discretion to make a variety of trial management decisions, ranging from "the mode and order of interrogating witnesses and presenting evidence," to the admissibility of evidence, to provisions for the order and security of the courtroom. In order to effectuate the trial court's discretion, we grant the trial court broad discretion: even if we disagree with the trial court, we will not reverse its decision unless that decision is "manifestly unreasonable or based on untenable grounds or untenable reasons." *In re Marriage of Littlefield*, 133 Wn.2d 39, 46-47, 940 P.2d 1362 (1997). . . .

### A. Applicable legal standard

No controlling authority in Washington decides whether a dog may accompany a witness during testimony. We have found only two on-point published cases from other jurisdictions: *People v. Tohom*, 969 N.Y.S.2d 123, 109 A.D.3d 253 (N.Y. App. Div. 2013), and *People v. Spence*, 212 Cal. App. 4th 478, 151 Cal. Rptr. 3d 374 (2012). In both cases, the witness at issue was a young girl who had been raped by her father. *Tohom*, 969 N.Y.S.2d 123; *Spence*, 212 Cal. App. 4th at 485. The witness in *Spence* was crying and upset as she recounted the events to health workers. 212 Cal. App. 4th at 485-86. Accordingly, the prosecutor moved for a "therapy dog" to be present on the witness stand with the victim, citing concerns that the witness might have an "emotional meltdown and refuse to testify." *Id*. at 512. The trial court granted the motion, ruling that "it was reasonably probable that testifying might be an intimidating situation for [the witness]," *id*., and that the dog was known to be nondisruptive. The appellate court agreed, deferring without analysis to the trial court's "implied findings of necessity." *Id.* at 518. Similarly, in *Tohom*, the witness was experiencing symptoms of posttraumatic stress disorder and did not feel comfortable testifying because her family members blamed her for the situation. 969 N.Y.S.2d at 126-27. The trial court permitted the dog to be present during the witness's testimony and the appellate division affirmed, citing the trial court's discretion to "fashion an appropriate measure to address a testifying child witness's emotional or psychological stress, based upon the particular needs of that child." *Id.* at 132-33.

The Court of Appeals has held that a child witness may hold a doll during testimony. In *State v. Hakimi*, 124 Wn. App. 15, 18, 98 P.3d 809 (2004), the two witnesses were young girls who had been allegedly molested by their babysitter, Morteza Hakimi. Hakimi moved to prohibit the witnesses from carrying a doll to the witness stand. The trial court heard argument on the motion, including testimony by an expert in child interviewing that "girls in particular in the 9-year-old age range may find security and comfort by holding a toy while answering questions posed to them during examination at trial." *Id.* at 21. The trial court weighed the interests of the witnesses against the potential prejudice to Hakimi and denied Hakimi's motion. . . . *Id.* at 20. The Court of Appeals affirmed the trial court, joining the many other jurisdictions that have permitted child witnesses to hold a doll, toy, or other comfort item on the witness stand or to be accompanied by a parent, victim advocate, or other trusted individual.

Upon examining those cases that have allowed a child witness to use a comfort item or support person, a few important similarities and differences become clear. First, the cases are in largely universal agreement that abuse of discretion is the correct standard. *See, e.g., State v. Perovich*, 2001 SD 96, 632 N.W.2d 12, 17-18. . . .

Second, many of these cases involved highly egregious facts. *See, e.g., Holmes v. United States*, 84 U.S. App. D.C. 168, 171 F.2d 1022, 1023 (1949) ("The child was a little girl of nine who had been subjected to a most terrible and horrifying experience [being raped, beaten and disfigured, and left unconscious under some leaves] to a degree which might well influence the balance of her life.").

Third, the courts are split on whether the prosecution must prove that the special measure is necessary to secure the witness's testimony. A number of courts have declined to require that the prosecution make a showing of necessity, instead putting the onus on the defendant to prove prejudice or impropriety. . . .

Two states explicitly require the prosecution to show that a special measure is necessary to facilitate the witness's testimony. Delaware has adopted a "substantial need" standard, *Gomez v. State*, 25 A.3d 786, 798-99 (Del. 2011), and Hawaii has adopted a similar "compelling necessity" standard. *State v. Palabay*, 9 Haw. App. 414, 417, 844 P.2d 1 (1992).

Finally, several states have shied away from an explicit necessity test but nevertheless relied on a record that clearly indicated that the witness would have difficulty testifying in the absence of the comfort item or support person. . . .

In a different vulnerable-witness setting, Washington and United States Supreme Court jurisprudence has required a showing of necessity to allow testimony via closed-circuit television. In *Maryland v. Craig*, 497 U.S. 836, 840, 110 S. Ct. 3157, 111 L. Ed. 2d 666 (1990), the prosecution sought to have the witness—a young girl who had been allegedly molested by the owner of her kindergarten—examined and cross-examined in a separate room while those in the courtroom watched on video. The Court held that in order to overcome the defendant's confrontation clause right of "face-to-face confrontation," the trial court must make a case-specific finding of necessity. *Id.* at 855-56. That is, the trial court must hear evidence and "find that the child witness would be traumatized, not by the courtroom generally, but by the presence of the defendant." *Id.* at 856. We adopted the same rule in *State v. Foster*, 135 Wn.2d 441, 469, 957 P.2d 712 (1998), agreeing with the Court's reasoning in full.

Our confrontation clause analysis in *Foster*, 135 Wn.2d at 466-70, and our fair trial analysis ... show that where special courtroom procedures implicate constitutional rights, it is not the defendant's burden to prove that he or she has been prejudiced, but the prosecution's burden to prove that a special dispensation for a vulnerable witness is necessary. The present context is no different. However, we do not require a showing of "substantial need" or "compelling necessity".... Trial courts have a unique perspective on the actual witness that an appellate court reviewing a cold record lacks; because the trial court is in the best position to analyze the actual necessity of a special dispensation, we will not overrule the trial court's exercise of discretion unless the record fails to reveal the party's reasons for needing a support animal or if the record indicates that the trial court failed to consider those reasons. Using this standard, we now analyze whether the trial court's decision was based on untenable grounds, based on untenable reasons, or manifestly unreasonable.

*B. Untenable grounds*

A trial court's decision is based on untenable grounds "if the factual findings are unsupported by the record." *Littlefield*, 133 Wn.2d at 46-47. Here, the trial court found that Lare was a "developmentally disabled individual who has ... had some significant emotional trauma" and that in contrast, Dye was "under no disability whatsoever." RP (Nov. 18, 2010) at 29. These findings are well supported by the record. Lare's sister testified as to the nature and extent of Lare's conditions. Lare himself testified to how the burglaries made him feel "very vulnerable and very scared." RP (Dec. 1, 2010) at 41.

The trial court also found that Ellie would be "very unobtrusive, will just simply be next to the individual, not be lying in his lap...." RP (Nov. 18, 2010) at 29. Indeed, Ellie's conduct at trial supports the trial court's finding. The record does not indicate that Ellie ever disrupted proceedings, left Lare's side, or made any gestures toward Dye (growling, for instance) that would have made him look dangerous or untrustworthy. Because the trial court's decision to allow Ellie to be present was predicated on findings based in the record, the trial court did not rely on untenable grounds.

*C. Untenable reasons*

A trial court's decision is made for untenable reasons if "it is based on an incorrect standard or the facts do not meet the requirements of the correct standard." *Littlefield*, 133 Wn.2d at 47. Under the standard discussed above, the trial court's "implicit" finding of necessity was sufficient. *Dye*, 170 Wn. App. at 348. . . . The trial court clearly understood that Ellie was needed in order to facilitate Lare's testimony, in light of his mental state. The trial court did everything but explicitly state on the record that Lare would not testify *but for* Ellie's presence, and the failure to do so does not constitute error. Our precedent does not call for magic words, but for "'a hearing with a record evidencing the reasons for the action taken . . . .'" Because the trial court held a hearing on the permissibility of Ellie's presence, and because the record showed why Ellie's presence was needed to facilitate Lare's testimony, the trial court did not rely on untenable reasons.

*D. Manifestly unreasonable*

A manifestly unreasonable decision is one that is "outside the range of acceptable choices, given the facts and the applicable legal standard . . . ." *Littlefield*, 133 Wn.2d at 47 (citing *State v. Rundquist*, 79 Wn. App. 786, 793, 905 P.2d 922 (1995)). As we have noted above, the applicable legal standard gives broad discretion to the trial court, and the trial court based its decision on Lare's vulnerable mental state. Furthermore, there is no actual evidence on the record that Ellie had the effect of distracting the jury, damaging the presumption of Dye's innocence, or otherwise tainting the proceedings. . . .

Furthermore, whatever subconscious bias may have befallen the jury was cured by the trial court's limiting instruction, which cautioned the jury not to "make any assumptions or draw any conclusions based on the presence of this service dog." CP at 53. Juries are presumed to follow instructions absent evidence to the contrary. *State v. Kirkman*, 159 Wn.2d 918, 928, 155 P.3d 125 (2007). . . .

### III. Conclusion

Dye has failed to establish that his fair trial rights were violated. Any prejudice that resulted from Ellie's presence was minor and largely mitigated by the limiting instruction that the trial court gave. In contrast, the trial court ruled that Ellie's presence would be helpful in reducing Lare's anxiety and eliciting his testimony, and no evidence to the contrary appears on the record. Both the general trend of courts to allow special procedural accommodations for child witnesses and the deference built into the abuse of discretion standard require us to respect the trial court's decision in how to structure its own proceedings. While the possibility that a facility dog may incur undue sympathy calls for caution and a conscientious balancing of the benefits and the prejudice involved, the trial court balanced the competing factors appropriately. The trial court did not abuse its discretion, and the Court of Appeals is affirmed.

# VI. Evidentiary Privileges in Domestic Violence Cases

## A. The Marital Privilege

Since 1628, the marital privilege, prohibiting a wife from testifying against her husband, has been part of the common law. The rule against spouses testifying against one another continued into the nineteenth century. In *Trammel v. United States*, 445 U.S. 40, 44 (1980), Chief Justice Burger described the modern rationale for the privilege as "fostering the harmony and sanctity of the marriage relationship." In *Trammel*, the Court held the privilege was no longer applicable in situations where a wife willingly testified against her husband in a criminal prosecution, under the rationale that if she were willing to testify, "there is probably little in the way of marital harmony for the privilege to preserve." *Id.* at 52.

It is important to understand there are two types of marital privileges. One involves invoking the marital privilege to prevent one spouse from testifying at a criminal trial against the other. The other prevents the disclosure of communication between spouses. In many states, the privilege does not exist where one spouse is charged with committing an act of domestic violence against the other. In those few states where the privilege remains intact, even in the face of domestic violence, a spouse maintains the option of voluntarily testifying against her abuser.[22] Below is a sample of a marital privilege statute from Utah.

### Utah R. Evid. Rule 502 (2016) Husband-wife

(a) *Definition.*

    (1) "Confidential communication" means a communication:

        (A) made privately by any person to his or her spouse; and

        (B) not intended for disclosure to any other person.

(b) *Privilege in criminal proceedings.*—In a criminal proceeding, a wife may not be compelled to testify against her husband, nor a husband against his wife.

(c) *Statement of the privilege.*—An individual has a privilege during the person's life:

    (1) to refuse to testify or to prevent his or her spouse or former spouse from testifying as to any confidential communication made by the individual to the spouse during their marriage; and

    (2) to prevent another person from disclosing any such confidential communication.

(d) *Who may claim privilege.*—The privilege may be claimed by:

---

22. *See* Heather Fleniken Cochran, *Improving Prosecution of Battering Partners: Some Innovations in the Law of Evidence*, 7 Tex. J. Women & L. 89, 90 and n.3. (1997).

(1) the person who made the confidential communication;

(2) the person's guardian or conservator;

(3) the non-communicating spouse to whom the confidential communication was made may claim the privilege on behalf of the person who made the confidential communication during the life of the communicating spouse.

(e) *Exceptions to the privilege.* — No privilege exists under paragraph (c) in the following circumstances....

(3) *Spouse charged with crime or tort.* — In a proceeding in which one spouse is charged with a crime or a tort against the person or property of:

(A) the other spouse;

(B) the child of either spouse;

(C) a person residing in the household of either spouse; or

(D) a third person if the crime or tort is committed in the course of committing a crime or tort against any of the persons named above....

## B. Domestic Violence Counselor/Social Worker

In many states, what a victim of domestic violence or sexual assault tells a counselor, victim advocate, or social worker is protected by statutory privilege from having to be divulged.

### People v. Turner
Colorado Supreme Court
109 P.3d 639 (2005)

Justice Kourlis delivered the Opinion of the Court.

. . . .

### I. BACKGROUND

On November 20, 2003, the Chaffee County District Attorney brought two domestic violence charges of assault and harassment against Robert Turner, Jr., stemming from allegations that he battered his girlfriend, M.P.

During pretrial discovery, defense counsel discovered that M.P. had contacted the Alliance, a private, nonprofit domestic violence victim advocacy center located in Salida, Colorado, in connection with the charges.

On April 14 and 16, 2004, defense counsel served the Alliance with two separate subpoenas duces tecum demanding production of records of M.P.'s contact with the Alliance. The first subpoena required the Alliance to produce "any and all records, notes and files regarding any and all assistance provided to [M.P.]." The second requested the same information "pursuant to [M.P.'s] reports of domestic violence/abuse on or about November 20, 2003 and thereafter."

On April 20, relying on section 13-90-107, the Alliance noted its refusal to comply with the subpoena in a letter to defense counsel. In response, defense counsel filed a Motion to Compel with the county court, arguing that records of assistance provided by the Alliance to M.P. were properly discoverable because the victim-advocate privilege only applies to communications made by a victim of domestic abuse, and not to "assistance" provided by the organization. On April 29, 2004, contending that the plain language and underlying purpose of the statute attaches the privilege to records of assistance provided, the Alliance moved to quash the subpoena.

The county court conducted an evidentiary hearing on May 5, 2004, taking arguments from the defendant and the Alliance on the question of whether the defendant's request for records or reports of the kinds of assistance the Alliance provided M.P. fell within statutorily privileged "communications" made to victim advocates by a victim of domestic violence.

The court agreed with the defendant that the victim-advocate privilege was not intended to protect records of assistance provided by a domestic abuse agency. The court held that although evidence of housing assistance had "marginal relevance," it was nonetheless not protected by the privilege and was therefore discoverable. Although the court did deny the defendant full access to all records of M.P.'s contact with the agency, it nonetheless ordered the Alliance to "provide a broad outline as to the type of assistance," provided to M.P., including for example, "emergency financial assistance."

The Alliance petitioned from that decision and we accepted original jurisdiction.

. . . .

### III. ANALYSIS

We are asked to interpret section 13-90-107(1)(k)(I), which reads as follows:

> A victim's advocate shall not be examined as to any communication made to such victim's advocate by a victim of domestic violence, as defined in section 18-6-800.3(1), C.R.S., or a victim of sexual assault, as described in sections 18-3-401 to 18-3-405.5, 18-6-301, and 18-6-302, C.R.S., in person or through the media of written records or reports without the consent of the victim.

. . . We hold that the plain language of the statute must be construed in a manner designed to serve the underlying objective of the privilege. Accordingly, the defendant may not obtain records of any assistance, advice or other communication provided by a victim's advocate unless he demonstrates that the victim has waived the privilege-which burden he has not here met. We also reject the defendant's contention that his right to compulsory process and confrontational rights are violated by our construction of the statute.

A. Nature of Domestic Violence and Need for Privilege

. . . .

Maintaining and handling client records and collecting information from and about victims of domestic violence are a critical function of any victim advocacy program. See Ronald B. Adrine & Alexdria M. Ruden, Confidentiality and Liability Concerns, Oh. Domestic Violence L. § 16:4 (2004). The disclosure of the victim's residence or location can make the victim accessible to an abuser from whom he or she is hiding. *Id.*

It is within this unique societal setting that the General Assembly acted to create the victim-advocate privilege. Much like the psychologist-patient privilege, the assumption of confidentiality is essential to fostering trust between the parties to the relationship. Hearing on SB 95153 . . . .

B. The Victim-Advocate Privilege

. . . .

The victim-advocate privilege was adopted in 1994, see Ch. 327, sec. 7, § 1390-107, 1994 Colo. Sess. Law, 2031, in furtherance of "the policy of the law to encourage confidences and to preserve them inviolate," see section 13-90107(1)(k)(I). The privilege provides that the victim's advocate shall not be examined "as to any communication made to such victim's advocate by a victim of domestic violence . . . in person or through the media of written records or reports." The statute provides no exceptions and requires no balancing of competing interests. . . .

Furthermore, the statute recognizes the "victim advocate" as a person "whose primary function is to render advice, counsel, or assist victims of domestic violence," see section 13-90-107(1)(k)(II)(A). . . .

The legislative history supports a conclusion that the General Assembly intended a broad construction of "communications." Representative DeGette, one of the cosponsors of the bill explained that the privilege was intended to protect treatment by victim-advocates in the same manner as protections offered treatment by psychologists and psychotherapists. See Hearing on HB 941253.

More importantly, the clear language of the statute extends the privilege so as to prohibit the disclosure of information contained in records or reports, such that "examined" is not a restrictive term making the privilege effective only at trial. . . .

Accordingly, the plain language of the statute leads us to conclude that the privilege extends to services or assistance provided by the agency to the victim.

. . . .

Of course, in the face of any privilege, the defendant may still discover records or reports of assistance by demonstrating waiver. At this point in the proceeding, the defendant has made no such showing.

. . . .

C. The Defendant's Due Process Argument

. . . .

The United States Supreme Court has identified two types of confrontation clause protections afforded the defendant: the right physically to face those who testify against him, and the right to conduct cross-examination. *Delaware v. Fensterer*, 474 U.S. 15, 18–19, 88 L. Ed. 2d 15 (1985). Here, the defendant argues in essence that the Alliance's argument that the privilege protects records of assistance provided the victim interferes with his ability to prepare his defense adequately because he would be hampered in cross-examining the alleged victim by probing her motive and credibility....

[T]he defendant's right to cross-examination is not absolute, explaining that under appropriate circumstances, the trial court may limit the defendant's right of confrontation. *Id.* ...

A year after our decision in District Court, the Supreme Court decided *Pennsylvania v. Ritchie*, 480 U.S. 39, 94 L. Ed. 2d 40, 107 S. Ct. 989 (1987). The Court dealt with the question of whether and to what extent the State's interest in the confidentiality of its investigative files concerning child abuse must yield to the defendant's confrontational rights. *Id.* at 43. There, the defendant was charged with sexually assaulting his 13-year-old daughter who had been placed in a state created protective service agency. *Id.* The agency was charged with investigating the abuse of children in its custody. *Id.* The statute made investigative reports by the agency confidential, subject to eleven exceptions. *Id.* The defendant issued a subpoena to the agency to produce its files. *Id.* The Agency refused to comply. *Id.* at 44. The state supreme court reversed the trial court decision denying the defendant access to the files, on grounds that the decision violated the defendant's right to cross-examine witnesses and his right to compulsory process. *Id.* at 46. The Supreme Court ultimately rejected the former position and held that the right to question adverse witnesses does not include the power to require the pretrial disclosure of any and all information that might be useful in contradicting unfavorable testimony. Rather, the Court concluded that "the right is satisfied if defense counsel receives wide latitude at trial to question witnesses." *Id.* at 53.

. . . .

Here, the victim-advocate privilege excludes from the definition of "victim advocate" "an advocate employed by any law enforcement agency." § 13-90-107(1)(k)(II). Unlike the state statute in *Ritchie*, moreover, our statute defines the privilege without exceptions. As noted in *Clark*, we reject the application of an ad hoc regime to determine the scope of the victim's rights under a statute that creates such a privilege. Accordingly, the defendant's compulsory process claim fails.

We hold that neither the defendant's right to cross-examine witnesses, nor his right to compulsory process is violated by withholding records of any assistance the Alliance may have provided M.P.

## III. CONCLUSION

We conclude that the underlying purpose of the victim-advocate privilege and the plain language of the statute forbid the disclosure of records or reports of assistance provided the victim by the Alliance in this case. We recognize that the strong public policy underlying the statute requires that records of assistance or services offered to victims be kept confidential. To interpret the statute otherwise would betray that clear intent. Further, we find nothing in the record to support the defendant's contention that M.P. has at present waived the privilege either expressly or by implication. Lastly, we reject the defendant's contention that his Sixth Amendment right to confrontation and his right to compulsory process entitle him to the Alliance's records. We therefore conclude that the trial court abused its discretion by compelling the Alliance to produce records pursuant to the subpoena in this case. We make our Rule absolute, reverse the decision of the trial court and remand for further proceedings consistent with this opinion.

## *Notes and Questions*

- **PROPENSITY EVIDENCE**

Cal. Evid. Code § 1109 allows in evidence at a domestic violence trial prior acts of intimate partner abuse under certain circumstances. In *People v. Johnson,* 77 Cal. App. 4th 410 (2000), a mid-level appellate court upheld the statute. The rationale for the statute, articulated in the legislative history, was that "the propensity inference is particularly appropriate in the area of domestic violence because on-going violence and abuse is the norm in domestic violence cases. Not only is there a great likelihood that any one battering episode is part of a larger scheme of dominance and control, that scheme usually escalates in frequency and severity. Without the propensity inference, the escalating nature of domestic violence is likewise masked. If we fail to address the very essence of domestic violence, we will continue to see cases where perpetrators of this violence will beat their intimate partners, even kill them, and go on to beat or kill the next intimate partner. Since criminal prosecution is one of the few factors which may interrupt the escalating pattern of domestic violence, we must be willing to look at that pattern during the criminal prosecution, or we will miss the opportunity to address this problem at all." (Assem. Com. Rep. on Public Safety (June 25, 1996) pp. 3–4.)

- **POST-*CRAWFORD* EVIDENTIARY ISSUES**

Over the years, Dr. Bierenbaum has continued to protest his innocence, without success. After exhausting his direct appeals, he filed a number of post-conviction proceedings. His latest effort, a petition for a writ of habeas corpus citing ineffective assistance of counsel, also failed. For a full recounting of the court's rationale for rejecting the claim, see *Bierenbaum v. Graham,* 607 F.3d 36 (2d Cir. 2010). Go through the *Bierenbaum* decision in the text and address each of the statements sought to be introduced by the prosecutor in light of *Crawford.* Is anything inadmissible today that was admissible at the original trial in light of the post-*Crawford* view on confrontation?

Chapter 5

# Expert Testimony & Syndrome Evidence[1]

> **CONSIDER AS YOU READ EXPERT TESTIMONY**
> 1. The use by the defense and the acceptance in the courts of the Battered Women's Syndrome to show why abused women would react with deadly force against their batterers
> 2. The use by the prosecutor of Battered Women's Syndrome to show why victims of domestic violence might remain with their abusers or recant their claims of abuse
> 3. The development and legal acceptance of other syndrome evidence

## Introduction

Battered Women's Syndrome is the focus of much of this chapter. It will explore the use of this evidence by defense attorneys and prosecutors, its expansion to child abuse cases and the policy questions raised by the increasing reliance on experts in the court system. One of two legal tests are applied to determine whether to admit scientific expert testimony. One, the *Frye* test, arises from the 1923 case, *Frye v. United States*, 293 F. 1013 (D.C. Cir. 1923), which involved a request by a defendant to introduce the results of a systolic blood pressure deception test, a predecessor of the current polygraph or lie-detector machine. In upholding the trial court's decision not to allow it, the appellate court in *Frye* gave great deference to scientific expert witnesses and required the trial judge to determine whether the test had been generally accepted in the applicable scientific community; it had not.

Almost 70 years later, the Supreme Court established the *Daubert* test, concluding that the *Frye* test had, in fact, been displaced by the Federal Rules of Evidence. Section 702 of the Federal Rules reads: "If scientific, technical or other specialized knowledge will assist the trier of fact to understand the evidence or determine a fact in issue, a witness qualified as an expert by knowledge, skill, experience, training or education, may testify thereto in the form of an opinion or otherwise." The Federal Rule

---

1. This chapter was written for the first edition of the text by the Hon. Rosalyn Richter and has been updated by the author with her permission.

further provides the evidence or testimony must "assist the trier of fact to understand the evidence or to determine a fact in issue."

In *Daubert v. Merrell Dow Pharmaceuticals*, 509 U.S. 579 (1993), the Supreme Court held the trial court must determine whether the proposed scientific expert evidence will assist the trier of fact in determining a fact at issue, and whether the evidence is relevant. The trial court must determine whether the scientific testimony is reliable and in making this decision, *Daubert* provides a list of factors for the trial court to consider including: a) whether the theory or technique can be (and has been) tested; b) whether it has been subjected to peer review and publication; c) its known or potential error rate; d) the existence and maintenance of standards controlling its operation and e) whether it has attracted widespread acceptance within the scientific community.

The Supreme Court in *Kumho Tire Co. v. Carmichael*, 526 U.S. 137 (1999), clarified that the *Daubert* holding not only applied to testimony about "hard science," which includes areas in which precise calculation is possible such as mathematics, chemistry, and the physical sciences, but also applied to the "soft sciences." Although no absolute definition of "soft science" exists, it includes testimony about psychology, sociology, the behavioral sciences, anthropology and cultural issues. "Soft science" is the primary focus of expert testimony in domestic violence and child abuse cases.

Some states still use the *Frye* test, others follow *Daubert,* and some use a combination of both. Still others have obviated the need for individualized determinations as to the scientific validity or reliability of such expert testimony by adopting statutes allowing for the use of syndrome evidence in cases involving claims of battering.

# I. Use of Syndrome Evidence by Defendants in Self-Defense Cases

As advocates began to focus on the response of the criminal justice system to domestic violence, attorneys looked at the treatment of women who fought back or killed their abusers. These women, who were being prosecuted for murdering their abusers, raised self-defense claims, but in so doing encountered obstacles. For a killing to be in complete self-defense (sometimes referred to as "perfect self-defense"), the defendant must actually and reasonably believe in the need to use force to defend herself. Where the defendant's subjective beliefs are objectively unreasonable, there is "imperfect self-defense" and the defendant cannot be convicted of murder but can be convicted of the lesser crime of manslaughter.

In assessing the reasonableness of a defendant's beliefs, the law had been based on the "reasonable man" standard, which required the court to evaluate the defendant's perceptions and actions from the perspective of the hypothetical person of "ordinary firmness." This standard, which is historically based on a man's response to an attack by a stranger, did not take into account the experience and perspective of women in general and battered women in particular. A battered woman may have developed certain behavior patterns and psychological reactions in response to years of abuse and may not react the way a man would if a stranger assaulted him.

Judges and juries have long questioned why battered women did not leave their abusers, suggesting a "reasonable person" in such a situation would not have resorted to deadly force, but would have left the relationship instead. Attorneys representing women charged with murder sought to present expert testimony to explain why they did not feel they could safely leave and to establish that their reactions to the situation were, in fact, reasonable.

The defense of self-defense or justification also traditionally involves a response to an "immediate" threat. Yet some battered women have killed their abusers in non-confrontational situations, such as when the batterer is sleeping or when he is distracted. Attorneys also sought to introduce expert testimony to explain why a battered woman might perceive the risk of danger as "imminent" even if she was not actually being threatened.

Section 3.04 of the Model Penal Code, Use of Force in Self-Protection, states:

> [T]he use of force upon or toward another person is justifiable when the actor believes that such force is immediately necessary for the purpose of protecting himself against the use of unlawful force by such other person on the present occasion. . . . The use of deadly force is not justifiable under this Section unless the actor believes such force is necessary to protect himself against death, serious bodily harm, kidnapping or sexual intercourse compelled by force or threat. . . .

Battered women's syndrome is not a separate affirmative defense to a homicide charge or an element of a justification defense, but rather is the basis for psychological testimony offered to explain the behavior of a battered woman, which might not otherwise be understandable to the jury. One of the earliest cases to discuss this syndrome evidence was *State v. Kelly*.

## State v. Kelly
### 97 N.J. 178 (1984)

WILENTZ, J.

. . . .

On May 24, 1980, defendant, Gladys Kelly, stabbed her husband, Ernest, with a pair of scissors. He died shortly thereafter at a nearby hospital. The couple had been married for seven years, during which time Ernest had periodically attacked Gladys. According to Ms. Kelly, he assaulted her that afternoon, and she stabbed him in self-defense, fearing that he would kill her if she did not act.

Ms. Kelly was indicted for murder. At trial, she did not deny stabbing her husband, but asserted that her action was in self-defense. To establish the requisite state of mind for her self-defense claim, Ms. Kelly called Dr. Lois Veronen as an expert witness to testify about the battered-woman's syndrome. After hearing a lengthy voir dire examination of Dr. Veronen, the trial court ruled that expert testimony concerning the syndrome was inadmissible on the self-defense issue under *State v. Bess*, 53 N.J. 10 (1968)....

Ms. Kelly was convicted of reckless manslaughter. In an unreported decision relying in part on *Bess*, the Appellate Division affirmed the conviction. We granted certification, 91 N.J. 539 (1983), and now reverse.

....

The Kellys had a stormy marriage. Some of the details of their relationship, especially the stabbing, are disputed. The following is Ms. Kelly's version of what happened—a version that the jury could have accepted and, if they had, a version that would make the proffered expert testimony not only relevant, but critical.

The day after the marriage, Mr. Kelly got drunk and knocked Ms. Kelly down. Although a period of calm followed the initial attack, the next seven years were accompanied by periodic and frequent beatings, sometimes as often as once a week. During the attacks, which generally occurred when Mr. Kelly was drunk, he threatened to kill Ms. Kelly and to cut off parts of her body if she tried to leave him. Mr. Kelly often moved out of the house after an attack, later returning with a promise that he would change his ways. Until the day of the homicide, only one of the attacks had taken place in public.

The day before the stabbing, Gladys and Ernest went shopping. They did not have enough money to buy food for the entire week, so Ernest said he would give his wife more money the next day.

The following morning he left for work. Ms. Kelly next saw her husband late that afternoon at a friend's house. She had gone there with her daughter, Annette, to ask Ernest for money to buy food. He told her to wait until they got home, and shortly thereafter the Kellys left. After walking past several houses, Mr. Kelly, who was drunk, angrily asked "What the hell did you come around here for?" He then grabbed the collar of her dress, and the two fell to the ground. He choked her by pushing his fingers against her throat, punched or hit her face, and bit her leg.

A crowd gathered on the street. Two men from the crowd separated them, just as Gladys felt that she was "passing out" from being choked. Fearing that Annette had been pushed around in the crowd, Gladys then left to look for her. Upon finding Annette, defendant noticed that Annette had defendant's pocketbook. Gladys had dropped it during the fight. Annette had retrieved it and gave her mother the pocketbook.

After finding her daughter, Ms. Kelly then observed Mr. Kelly running toward her with his hands raised. Within seconds he was right next to her. Unsure of whether he had armed himself while she was looking for their daughter, and thinking that he had come back to kill her, she grabbed a pair of scissors from her pocketbook. She tried to scare him away, but instead stabbed him.

The central question in this case is whether the trial court erred in its exclusion of expert testimony on the battered-woman's syndrome. That testimony was intended to explain defendant's state of mind and bolster her claim of self-defense.

. . . .

As the problem of battered women has begun to receive more attention, sociologists and psychologists have begun to focus on the effects a sustained pattern of physical and psychological abuse can have on a woman. The effects of such abuse are what some scientific observers have termed "the battered-woman's syndrome," a series of common characteristics that appear in women who are abused physically and psychologically over an extended period of time by the dominant male figure in their lives. . . . Dr. Lenore Walker, [is] a prominent writer on the battered-woman's syndrome. . . .

According to Dr. Walker, relationships characterized by physical abuse tend to develop battering cycles. Violent behavior directed at the woman occurs in three distinct and repetitive stages that vary both in duration and intensity depending on the individuals involved. . . .

Some women may even perceive the battering cycle as normal, especially if they grew up in a violent household. *Battered Women, A Psychosociological Study of Domestic Violence* 60 (M. Roy ed. 1977); D. Martin, *Battered Wives*, 60 (1981). Or they may simply not wish to acknowledge the reality of their situation. T. Davidson, *Conjugal Crime*, at 50 (1978) ("The middle-class battered wife's response to her situation tends to be withdrawal, silence and denial . . .").

Other women, however, become so demoralized and degraded by the fact that they cannot predict or control the violence that they sink into a state of psychological paralysis and become unable to take any action at all to improve or alter the situation. There is a tendency in battered women to believe in the omnipotence or strength of their battering husbands and thus to feel that any attempt to resist them is hopeless.

. . . .

Finally, battered women are often hesitant to leave a battering relationship because, in addition to their hope of reform on the part of their spouse, they harbor a deep concern about the possible response leaving might provoke in their mates. They literally become trapped by their own fear. Case histories are replete with instances in which a battered wife left her husband only to have him pursue her and subject her to an even more brutal attack. D. Martin, *supra*, at 76–79.

The combination of all these symptoms—resulting from sustained psychological and physical trauma compounded by aggravating social and economic factors—constitutes the battered-woman's syndrome. Only by understanding these unique pressures that force battered women to remain with their mates, despite their long-standing and reasonable fear of severe bodily harm and the isolation that being a battered woman creates, can a battered woman's state of mind be accurately and fairly understood.

The voir dire testimony of Dr. Veronen, sought to be introduced by defendant Gladys Kelly, conformed essentially to this outline of the battered-woman's syndrome. Dr. Vernonen, after establishing her credentials, described in general terms the component parts of the battered-woman's syndrome and its effects on a woman's physical and mental health. The witness then documented, based on her own considerable experience in counseling, treating, and studying battered women, and her familiarity with the work of others in the field, the feelings of anxiety, self-blame, isolation, and, above all, fear that plagues these women and leaves them prey to a psychological paralysis that hinders their ability to break free or seek help.

Dr. Veronen stated that the problems of battered women are aggravated by a lack of understanding among the general public concerning both the prevalence of violence against women and the nature of battering relationships. She cited several myths concerning battered women that enjoy popular acceptance—primarily that such women are masochistic and enjoy the abuse they receive and that they are free to leave their husbands but choose not to.

. . . .

Whether expert testimony on the battered-woman's syndrome should be admitted in this case depends on whether it is relevant to defendant's claim of self-defense, and, in any event, on whether the proffer meets the standards for admission of expert testimony in this state. . . .

Self-defense exonerates a person who kills in the reasonable belief that such action was necessary to prevent his or her death or serious injury, even though this belief was later proven mistaken. "Detached reflection cannot be demanded in the presence of an uplifted knife," Justice Holmes aptly said, *Brown v. United States*, 256 U.S. 335, 343, 41 S. Ct. 501, 502, 65 L. Ed. 961, 963 (1921); and the law accordingly requires only a reasonable, not necessarily a correct, judgment. See *State v. Hipplewith*, 33 N.J. 300, 316–17 (1960); *State v. Mount*, 73 N.J.L. 582, 583 (E. & A. 1905); *State v. Lionetti*, 93 N.J.L. 24 (Sup. Ct. 1919).

While it is not imperative that *actual* necessity exist, a valid plea of self-defense will not lie absent an actual (that is, honest) belief on the part of the defendant in the necessity of using force. While no case in New Jersey has addressed the point directly, the privilege of self-defense does not exist where the defendant's action is not prompted by a belief in its necessity: "He has no defense when he intentionally kills his enemy in complete ignorance of the fact that his enemy, when killed, was about to launch a deadly attack upon him." W. LaFave & A. Scott, *Criminal Law* § 53, at 394 (1972).

. . . .

Honesty alone, however, does not suffice. A defendant claiming the privilege of self-defense must also establish that her belief in the necessity to use force was reasonable. See, e.g., *State v. Mellillo*, 77 N.J.L. 505 (E. & A. 1908); *State v. Mark Len*, 108 N.J.L. 439, 440 (Sup. Ct. 1932).

. . . .

Thus, even when the defendant's belief in the need to kill in self-defense is conceded to be sincere, if it is found to have been unreasonable under the circumstances, such a belief cannot be held to constitute complete justification for a homicide. As with the determination of the existence of the defendant's belief, the question of the reasonableness of this belief "is to be determined by the jury, not the defendant, in light of the circumstances existing at the time of the homicide." *State v. Hipplewith, supra*, 33 N.J. at 316; *see State v. Bess, supra*, 53 N.J. at 16; *State v. Fair, supra*, 45 N.J. at 93; *State v. Jayson*, 94 N.J.L. 467, 471 (E. & A. 1920). It is perhaps worth emphasizing here that for defendant to prevail, the jury need not find beyond a reasonable doubt that the defendant's belief was honest and reasonable. Rather, if any evidence raising the issue of self-defense is adduced, either in the State's or the defendant's case, then the jury must be instructed that the State is required to prove beyond a reasonable doubt that the self-defense claim does not accord with the facts; acquittal is required if there remains a reasonable doubt whether the defendant acted in self-defense. *State v. Abbott*, 36 N.J. 63, 72 (1961). *See generally State v. Chiarello*, 69 N.J. Super. 479 (App. Div. 1961).

. . . .

Gladys Kelly claims that she stabbed her husband in self-defense, believing he was about to kill her. The gist of the State's case was that Gladys Kelly was the aggressor, that she consciously intended to kill her husband, and that she certainly was not acting in self-defense.

The credibility of Gladys Kelly is a critical issue in this case. If the jury does not believe Gladys Kelly's account, it cannot find she acted in self-defense. The expert testimony offered was directly relevant to one of the critical elements of that account, namely, what Gladys Kelly believed at the time of the stabbing, and was thus material to establish the honesty of her stated belief that she was in imminent danger of death.

The State argues that there is no need to bolster defendant's credibility with expert testimony concerning the battering because the State did not attempt to undermine defendant's testimony concerning her prior mistreatment at the hands of her husband. The State's claim is simply untrue. In her summation, the prosecutor suggested that had Ernest Kelly lived, he might have told a different story from the one Gladys told. . . .

On the facts in this case, we find that the expert testimony was relevant to Gladys Kelly's state of mind, namely, it was admissible to show she *honestly* believed she was in imminent danger of death. . . . Moreover, we find that because this testimony was central to the defendant's claim of self-defense, its exclusion, if otherwise admissible, cannot be held to be harmless error.

. . . .

Since a retrial is necessary, we think it advisable to indicate the limit of the expert's testimony on this issue of reasonableness. It would not be proper for the expert to express the opinion that defendant's belief on that day was reasonable, not because this is the ultimate issue, but because the area of expert knowledge relates, in this regard, to the reasons for defendant's failure to leave her husband. Either the jury accepts or rejects that explanation and, based on that, credits defendant's stories about the beatings she suffered. No expert is needed, however, once the jury has made up its mind on those issues, to tell the jury the logical conclusion, namely, that a person who has in fact been severely and continuously beaten might very well reasonably fear that the imminent beating she was about to suffer could be either life-threatening or pose a risk of serious injury. What the expert could state was that defendant had the battered-woman's syndrome, and could explain that syndrome in detail, relating its characteristics to defendant, but only to enable the jury better to determine the honesty and reasonableness of defendant's belief. Depending on its content, the expert's testimony might also enable the jury to find that the battered wife, because of the prior beatings, numerous beatings, as often as once a week, for seven years, from the day they were married to the day he died, is particularly able to predict accurately the likely extent of violence in any attack on her. That conclusion could significantly affect the jury's evaluation of the reasonableness of defendant's fear for her life.

Having determined that testimony about the battered-woman's syndrome is relevant, we now consider whether Dr. Veronen's testimony satisfies the limitations placed on expert testimony by Evidence Rule 56(2) and by applicable case law. *State v. Cavallo*, 88 N.J. 508, 516 (1982). Evidence Rule 56(2) provides that an expert may testify "as to matters requiring scientific, technical or other specialized knowledge if such testimony will assist the trier of fact to understand the evidence or determine a fact in issue." . . .

In a relatively new field of research, such as that of the battered-woman's syndrome, there are three ways a proponent of scientific evidence can prove its general acceptance and thereby its reliability: (1) by expert testimony as to the general acceptance, among those in the profession, of the premises on which the proffered expert witness based his or her analysis; (2) by authoritative scientific and legal writings indicating that the scientific community accepts the premises underlying the proffered testimony; and (3) by judicial opinions that indicate the expert's premises have gained general acceptance. *State v. Cavallo*, 88 N.J. at 521. Applying those methods to the case at bar, we note that judicial opinions thus far have been split concerning the scientific acceptability of the syndrome and the methodology used by the researchers in this area. On the other hand, Dr. Veronen, the proffered expert, testified that the battered-woman's syndrome is acknowledged and accepted by practitioners and professors in the fields of psychology and psychiatry. Dr. Veronen also brought to the court's attention the findings of several researchers who have published reports confirming the presence of the battered-woman's syndrome. She further noted that the battered-woman's syndrome has been discussed at several symposia since 1977, sponsored by such organizations as the Association for the Advancement of Behavior Therapy and the American Sociological Association. Briefs submitted to this Court indicate that there are at least five books and almost seventy scientific articles and papers about the battered-woman's syndrome.

Thus, the record before us reveals that the battered woman's syndrome has a sufficient scientific basis to produce uniform and reasonably reliable results as required by *State v. Cavallo*, and Evid. R. 56(2).... However, while the record before us could require such a ruling, we refrain from conclusively ruling that Dr. Veronen's proffered testimony about the battered-woman's syndrome would satisfy New Jersey's standard of acceptability for scientific evidence. This is because the State was not given a full opportunity in the trial court to question Dr. Veronen's methodology in studying battered women or her implicit assertion that the battered-woman's syndrome has been accepted by the relevant scientific community....

---

Today, all 50 states allow defendants to present expert testimony on battered women's syndrome, at least when the issue of self-defense is raised. States differ, however, on the circumstances under which the evidence is admissible and the scope of the expert's testimony.

## State v. Hanks
### Supreme Court of Minnesota
### 817 N.W.2d 663 (2012)

Meyer, Justice.

....

### I.

Betsy Marie Hanks first met Matthew Albert in 2001, when she was 17 years old. Over the next 8 years, Hanks and Albert lived together, considered marriage, and had four children together. Hanks and Albert had a troubled relationship....

Albert was a construction worker, working out of town most of the summer of 2009. That summer Hanks met L.G., who worked on a nearby cattle ranch. Hanks and her sons spent a great deal of time with L.G., assisting him with his work on the ranch and riding horses with him. L.G. and Hanks became very good friends, but both denied at trial that they were romantically involved....

On October 19, 2009, the day before the murder, Hanks went to visit L.G. When Albert discovered that Hanks was with L.G., he drove around looking for L.G. He eventually found L.G. and allegedly attempted to hit L.G. with his vehicle. Albert was cited for reckless driving for the incident. Albert told the two officers who responded to the incident that Albert was considering leaving Hanks because Hanks was "messing around." Albert asked the officers if he could remove his belongings from the home he shared with Hanks. Later in the day, Hanks's father attempted to mediate a reconciliation of sorts between Hanks and Albert. The three of them talked past midnight and came to an agreement that Albert would spend less time away from home and Hanks would stop spending time with L.G.

The morning of October 20, Albert got the two older children ready for school, ran an errand, fed the youngest two children, and then went back to bed. Hanks lay on the bed with Albert for awhile, then got up and placed the two youngest children in her vehicle. She then returned to the house to retrieve a pair of boots for one of the children. Hanks would later tell investigators that she "paced around the house trying to figure out what to do" and "decided that it was the time to make things right." She then retrieved Albert's gun from under the bed and shot him in the head. When interviewed by investigators, Hanks said she was not thinking about shooting Albert when she left the house to put the children in the vehicle, and did not think about it until she returned to the house. When asked how long she contemplated shooting Albert, Hanks repeatedly asserted that it was "[n]ot very long."

After shooting Albert, Hanks left the house, drove to her father's house, and discarded the gun in a ditch before returning home. When Hanks returned home, Albert was still alive. Hanks called 911 and told the dispatcher that she had found her husband with a gunshot wound to his head, she did not know what had happened, and Albert's gun was missing. Albert was taken to the hospital and died later that day as a result of the gunshot wound.

After Albert was taken to the hospital, Hanks spoke with an investigator from the Beltrami County Sheriff's Department. Hanks explained the events of the previous day. . . . Two days later she was again questioned by an investigator, who challenged the story Hanks had earlier given. In response, Hanks first said that her three-year-old had been holding the gun and it discharged as she attempted to take it from him. On further questioning, Hanks told a different story—she admitted shooting Albert but claimed Albert was suicidal and asked Hanks to end his life for him. When the investigator told Hanks he did not believe this story either, Hanks said she shot Albert because she wanted a better father for her children who "treated them like people." Hanks also told the investigator that Albert said if Hanks ever took their children "he'd make sure that was the last time I'd see 'em." As a result of this threat, Hanks wanted to "make it so [Albert] can't interfere." Hanks told the investigator that she dropped the gun in a ditch after the shooting. Hanks also said that when she returned after disposing of the gun and discovered Albert alive, she called 911 because she wanted Albert to live.

On October 26, 2009, the State charged Hanks with second-degree intentional murder, Minn. Stat. §609.19, subd. 1(1) (2010). A grand jury later indicted Hanks for both first-degree premeditated murder and second-degree intentional murder, Minn. Stat. §609.185(a)(1) (2010); Minn. Stat. §609.19, subd. 1(1). Before trial, the district court granted Hanks's motion for an award of fees to hire a psychiatrist to examine her and assist in her defense. The district court later granted Hanks's motion for fees for an expert witness on battered woman syndrome. In January 2011, prior to trial, the State filed a motion to prohibit the battered woman syndrome expert from testifying, arguing that Hanks had not shown she was a battered woman, making battered woman syndrome expert testimony irrelevant and highly prejudicial.

The court addressed the State's motion on the first day of trial. . . . The next day the court ruled that "the testimony of an expert [about battered woman syndrome] in this case [does not] fit[] any of the prior decisions that the Courts of Minnesota have held that such testimony is admissible." The court explained that because Hanks was not claiming she acted in self-defense, the testimony could not come in under *State v. Hennum,* 441 N.W.2d 793, 797-99 (Minn. 1989). The court distinguished *State v. Grecinger,* 569 N.W.2d 189, 196-97 (Minn. 1997), noting that the testimony in that case explained "why a woman would keep returning to an abuser and why a woman would change her story in order to maintain that relationship." Because Hanks was neither returning to an abusive relationship nor attempting to maintain an abusive relationship, the court found *Grecinger* likewise inapplicable. Therefore, the court ruled, "I just don't see that expert testimony should be allowed, and I am not going to allow it."

. . . .

The jury found Hanks guilty of both first- and second-degree murder. The district court adjudicated Hanks guilty of both first- and second-degree murder. The court sentenced Hanks to life imprisonment without the possibility of release for first-degree murder. On appeal, Hanks claims: (1) the district court committed reversible error when it excluded expert testimony on battered woman syndrome. . . .

II.

. . . .

We have recognized that battered woman syndrome expert testimony is admissible in at least two contexts: when a battered woman claims self-defense for the murder of her abuser, *State v. Hennum,* 441 N.W.2d 793, 797-99 (Minn. 1989), and when the State seeks to rehabilitate the credibility of a battered woman in the prosecution of her batterer, *State v. Grecinger,* 569 N.W.2d 189, 196-97 (Minn. 1997). Generally, battered woman syndrome expert testimony may be helpful to juries because battered woman syndrome "is beyond the understanding of the average person," and expert testimony may "help to explain a phenomenon not within the understanding of an ordinary lay person." *Hennum,* 441 N.W.2d at 798.

In *Hennum,* we noted that battered woman syndrome testimony is admissible

> (1) to dispel the common misconception that a normal or reasonable person would not remain in such an abusive relationship, (2) for the specific purpose of bolstering the defendant's position and lending credibility to her version of the facts, and (3) to show the reasonableness of the defendant's fear that she was in imminent peril of death or serious bodily injury.

*Id.* . . .

The district court in this case ruled that the proffered battered woman syndrome expert testimony was inadmissible, stating: "I am not convinced that the testimony of an expert in this case fits any of the prior decisions that the Courts of Minnesota have held that such testimony is admissible." The court determined that *Hennum* did not apply because Hanks did not raise self-defense. The court also determined that *Grecinger* "permitted expert testimony as helpful to a jury in understanding" "the dynamics of abusive relationships and why a woman would keep returning to an abuser and why a woman would change her story in order to maintain that relationship." The court concluded that *Grecinger* did not apply because Hanks was neither returning to an abusive relationship nor trying to maintain it. Instead, the court stated that Hanks sought admission of the battered woman syndrome testimony to "prove self serving changes in her statement."

. . . .

In determining the relevance of battered woman syndrome evidence, we consider whether the proffered evidence demonstrated that the proponent had the type of relationship about which the expert will testify. *MacLennan*, 702 N.W.2d at 235 (holding that the defendant had not established the relevance of expert testimony on battered child syndrome because there was "little demonstrable evidence of the type of relationship described by [the defendant's] expert that would give rise to battered child syndrome").[2] The defendant in *MacLennan* testified that he was afraid of the victim (his father) and that the victim had physically abused him on one occasion. The majority of MacLennan's offer of proof consisted of evidence that the victim had a bad temper and had neglected MacLennan. We concluded that such evidence of a "tense relationship" was insufficient to establish the type of relationship that would give rise to battered child syndrome, and so the expert testimony was irrelevant. *Id.*

It was not an abuse of discretion for the district court to conclude that the evidence in Hanks's offer of proof was similarly deficient in failing to establish the type of relationship that would give rise to battered woman syndrome. Hanks's offer of proof asserted the following: Albert was not involved in the lives of his children. Albert preferred that Hanks stay at home with the children rather than work outside the home. Albert controlled the family finances and did not give Hanks money. Albert got angry when Hanks went out socially and "wanted [Hanks] socially isolated." Albert disabled Hanks's vehicle so she could not drive it. Albert made threats to kill L.G., Hanks, his children, and himself. One of Hanks's children stated that "Dad hit mom!"

Hanks's expert defined battering as "a pattern of physical and psychological coercion that may create ongoing fear of safety among victims" and stated that battered woman syndrome explains "how women react to ongoing battering." We conclude that Hanks's offer of proof established that Albert was controlling and had a bad temper, but the proof was insufficient to establish that Hanks was a victim of battered woman syndrome. Notably, Hanks never claimed that Albert physically abused her or even that she was afraid of Albert. At most, she was afraid that Albert would hurt her children if she left him. The district court did not abuse its discretion in finding that the evidence of a troubled relationship between Hanks and Albert was insufficient to establish the type of relationship that would give rise to battered woman syndrome and that, therefore, the expert testimony was irrelevant. The district court thus did not err in excluding the testimony. . . .

---

2. The full cite is *State v. MacLennan*, 702 N.W. 2d 219 (Minn. 2005) [Eds. Note].

## II. Use of Expert Testimony by Prosecutors

Until 1990, only a few state appellate courts had ruled on whether prosecutors could use expert testimony on battering in a domestic violence case except in response to a self-defense claim raised by a defendant. Prosecutors sought to call experts to explain why victims stay in abusive relationships and why victims recant. Expert testimony also might explain a delay in reporting or a victim's inconsistent descriptions of the incident.

In *State v. Ciskie*, 751 P.2d 1165 (Wash. 1988), one of the earliest cases allowing the use of such testimony by prosecutors, the defendant was charged with multiple rapes over a two-year period of a woman with whom he had been involved. In response to the defense claim that the sexual encounters were consensual because the victim never broke off the relationship after the rape allegedly occurred, the prosecution sought to offer testimony about battered women's syndrome. The Washington Supreme Court, which in an earlier case had allowed the use of expert testimony by a defendant, concluded the prosecution should be allowed to introduce this testimony. The Court noted that the potential prejudice to the defendant could be minimized because the expert would only be allowed to testify in a hypothetical manner, and could not express an opinion as to whether or not the victim had been raped.

Although courts generally allow the introduction of expert testimony in rebuttal when the victim's credibility has been challenged based on a delay in reporting or where the victim has recanted, the more difficult question is whether the prosecution should be allowed to call an expert witness on its direct case. The concern is that by allowing such testimony on the prosecutor's case in chief, the expert may improperly bolster the victim's testimony. The following case was cited by the Minnesota Supreme Court in *Hanks* printed above. Here, it stands for the proposition that with proper limitations to ensure the defendant gets a fair trial, expert testimony also may be introduced by the state.

### State v. Grecinger
Minnesota Supreme Court
569 N.W.2d 189 (1997)

Tomljanovich, Justice.

. . . .

Grecinger had been in an on-and-off relationship with the victim, Barbara Skoglund for about three years, during which they lived together at various times. On September 28, 1991, Grecinger and Skoglund attended a memorial run for the BPM motorcycle club and a party that took place afterward. The events that took place on that day and the day before are in drastic dispute. At trial, Skoglund testified that on the night before the party, Grecinger grabbed her by her hair, slapped her, threw her to the floor, and choked her until she lost consciousness. The next day, Skoglund said that she did not want to attend the party but, according to her testimony, Grecinger insisted that she go. Once at the party, Skoglund found Grecinger kissing a woman who was sitting on his lap. She testified that she threw the woman off his lap but did not get into a fight with the woman. Skoglund then told Grecinger that their relationship was over and went into the bathroom.

Skoglund further testified that Grecinger followed her into the bathroom, closed the door, and beat her. Grecinger grabbed her by the hair, threw her to the floor, kicked her, and choked her until she lost consciousness. During this time, Grecinger allegedly told her, "If you leave me, I'm gonna kill you; if I can't have you, * * * no one's gonna." When Skoglund regained consciousness, she started screaming for help, and Grecinger choked her again until she lost consciousness. When she regained consciousness a second time, Grecinger demanded that she get on her knees, hug him, and apologize for making him angry. Grecinger then told her to walk out of the bathroom with her head up high without crying or looking at anyone. Grecinger followed Skoglund outside and told her to get on his motorcycle. Skoglund started to run away from Grecinger, but he caught her and dragged her back over the dirt road to his motorcycle. Again, he told her to get on the motorcycle. She complied, and they drove off.

Skoglund testified that during the motorcycle ride, Grecinger slapped her in the face. Upon arriving at Grecinger's house, Skoglund broke away and ran down the street, screaming for help. Two women stopped and let her into their car. Skoglund asked them to take her to the home of her friend, Char Copiskey, where she spent the night. The next morning, Copiskey suggested that they go to the Battered Women's Coalition ("Coalition"). At the Coalition, pictures were taken of Skoglund. Skoglund was then taken to the emergency room because she was fading in and out of consciousness.

Skoglund was admitted to the hospital under an assumed name out of concern for her safety, and she remained there for five days. She suffered from numerous injuries, including swelling and bruising around both eyes; a fracture in her left orbital bone; bleeding in her right eye; bruising and abrasions on her face, ear, and neck; a swollen lip; swelling around her vocal cords consistent with choking; bruising and swelling on her shoulders, chest, arms, and legs; an abrasion on her abdomen; and a tender scalp.

Two law enforcement officers visited Skoglund in the hospital and tried to get a statement from her. Initially, Skoglund refused to talk to them because she did not want to involve the police; however, after being assured that Grecinger would not be arrested except upon her request, she agreed to give a statement. She told one of the officers that the night before the party, Grecinger had choked her until she passed out, and that at the party, he followed her into the bathroom, where he threw her to the floor, slapped her, and again choked her into unconsciousness. When she gave the statement to police, Skoglund asked them not to press charges against Grecinger at that time.

. . . .

In her testimony, Skoglund admitted that she lied to some people about the cause of her injuries because she was afraid of Grecinger. However, Skoglund also testified that she had previously identified Grecinger as her assailant to others, including Copiskey, a police investigator, a worker from the Coalition, and two of her sisters. On several occasions in 1992 and 1993, Skoglund petitioned for orders for protection against Grecinger; however, she either sought to have the petitions dismissed or failed to follow through on them, because she feared that Grecinger would harm her. Finally, in June 1994, Skoglund sought to reopen the investigation against Grecinger for the alleged September 1991 assault, because she was afraid he was going to kill her. . . .

Grecinger testified that at the party following the memorial run, a woman was sitting on his lap when Skoglund walked into the kitchen, grabbed the woman by her hair, and pulled her off of him. Although Grecinger tried to break up the fight, Skoglund wound up with her shirt torn, hair pulled out, scratches on her face, and a bloody lip. After fighting with the woman, Skoglund grabbed Grecinger by his hair and dragged him to the bathroom. According to Grecinger, Skoglund "went completely bananas" in the bathroom and kicked the toilet seat off the toilet, hit him with the toilet tank cover, and ripped the medicine cabinet off the wall. Skoglund then asked him to hug her and tell her he loved her. Grecinger denied hitting or choking Skoglund in the bathroom and maintained that he only tried to prevent her from hurting him and herself.

. . . .

In response to the defense's attack on Skoglund's credibility, the prosecution sought to introduce expert testimony on battered woman syndrome. The court admitted the expert testimony over Grecinger's objection. As foundation for the expert testimony, a psychologist testified that she first treated Skoglund in October 1992. The psychologist testified that Skoglund reported symptoms of anxiety stemming from a physically abusive episode with her boyfriend one year earlier. The psychologist subsequently diagnosed Skoglund as suffering from posttraumatic stress disorder.

After Skoglund and the psychologist who treated her had testified, an expert witness testified regarding battered woman syndrome, which she described as a subset of posttraumatic stress disorder. The expert further testified that the symptoms of a woman suffering from battered woman syndrome can include feelings of terror, acceptance of blame for the battering, a negative self-image, isolation, denial or minimization of the abuse, and depression. She explained that many battered women do not report the abuse out of fear for their safety, denial of the abuse, fear that no one will listen, or hope that the batterer will change.

The jury convicted Grecinger of attempted murder in the second degree and assault in the third degree, and he was sentenced to 153 months in prison. On appeal to the court of appeals, Grecinger argued that the expert testimony should have been excluded because it was irrelevant and lacked proper foundation. The court of appeals affirmed Grecinger's conviction, holding that expert testimony on battered woman syndrome was properly admitted because it helped the jury understand the delay in reporting and the inconsistencies in the victim's testimony. On appeal to this court, Grecinger argues that the expert testimony was improperly admitted, because it was not helpful to the jury and because it was merely duplicative of other witnesses' testimony about the reasons for the delayed prosecution.

. . . .

Under Minn. R. Evid. 608(a), the credibility of a witness can be supported by evidence in the form of an opinion only when the character of that witness has been attacked in that respect. *See State v. Fader*, 358 N.W.2d 42, 47 (Minn. 1984). Because the victim's credibility can be attacked during cross-examination of the victim or even during opening statements, the prosecution need not wait until rebuttal to present expert testimony on battered woman syndrome. Rather, such testimony may be presented as rehabilitative evidence during the state's case-in-chief. *Cf., e.g., People v. Sanchez,* 208 Cal. App. 3d 721, 256 Cal. Rptr. 446, 454 (Cal. Ct. App.) . . . .

Consequently, the admission of battered woman syndrome testimony during the state's case-in-chief in this case was proper under Minn. R. Evid. 608(a). By the time the expert testimony on battered woman syndrome was presented, Skoglund's credibility regarding her delay in seeking prosecution of Grecinger was already at issue. During opening statements, Grecinger's attorney suggested that during the gap in time, Skoglund used the alleged incident to control Grecinger. Furthermore, when cross-examining Skoglund, Grecinger's attorney briefly questioned Skoglund regarding her delay in seeking prosecution.

Although the prosecutor asserted only that battered woman syndrome testimony was being offered to explain the delay in prosecution, such testimony arguably was responsive to other attacks against Skoglund's credibility. For instance, Grecinger's attorney stated that Skoglund was a liar because of the various stories she had told to explain her injuries. Furthermore, Grecinger's attorney questioned Skoglund about why she returned to her relationship with Grecinger after the alleged assault, and why she recanted statements she had made when seeking an order for protection against Grecinger.

Having concluded that expert testimony about battered women syndrome could properly be admitted to rehabilitate Skoglund's credibility under Rule 608(a), we must ascertain whether it is admissible under Minn. R. Evid. 702 when introduced as part of the prosecution's case-in-chief. In *State v. Hennum*, this court considered the admissibility of expert testimony on battered woman syndrome to support a defendant's self-defense claim for the shooting death of her husband. We decided two important issues in *Hennum*. First, we held that battered woman syndrome has gained sufficient scientific acceptance to warrant admissibility as expert testimony. *Hennum*, 441 N.W.2d at 798–99. We held that such testimony satisfied the helpfulness test of Minn. R. Evid. 702, because it helped to explain a phenomenon that was not understood by the average person. 441 N.W.2d at 798. Second, this court held that expert testimony on battered woman syndrome should be limited to a description of the syndrome and its characteristics. *Id.* at 799. We held that the expert should not be permitted to testify on the ultimate fact of whether the particular defendant actually suffers from battered woman syndrome. *Id.*

. . . .

In this case, Grecinger contends that the expert testimony did not meet the helpfulness test because it was cumulative of other evidence in the case. He observes that prior to the expert witness' testimony, several other witnesses had testified as to why the prosecution was delayed. For example, Skoglund testified that she did not immediately pursue prosecution because Grecinger forced her to recant her statement to the sheriff's department. Furthermore, a deputy sheriff testified that he did not pursue prosecution at the time of the alleged incident because he had promised Skoglund he would not arrest Grecinger unless she requested that he do so.

However, such testimony does not explain why Skoglund did not seek prosecution at the time of the assault. Instead, the jury might believe that a woman who is beaten by her mate would immediately seek to have him arrested and that such a woman would not recant such a statement despite threats made by the batterer. Consequently, the expert testimony on battered woman syndrome was not duplicative of prior testimony; rather, it was necessary to explain the complexity of Skoglund's behavior and the reasons for her behavior.

. . . .

Grecinger also argues that the admission of expert testimony on battered woman syndrome was unfairly prejudicial because such testimony shifted attention away from the case and focused on the problem of domestic violence. Unlike circumstances in which expert testimony on battered woman syndrome is presented to support a defendant's claim of self-defense, prosecutorial use of such testimony raises the added concern for the rights of the alleged batterer in such a proceeding. Because of the special knowledge that expert witnesses possess, we are concerned about the potential for expert testimony on battered woman syndrome to influence a jury unduly, particularly in cases such as this where there are two entirely different accounts of the events in controversy. Thus, to minimize the potential for unfair prejudice to the defendant, we caution trial judges that careful inquiry and balancing must be made under Minn. R. Evid. 403.

. . . .

Thus, a defendant need not be unfairly prejudiced by the prosecution's use of expert testimony on battered woman syndrome, if adequate limitations are placed on the presentation thereof. In *Hennum,* this court held that an expert testifying on battered woman syndrome may not testify as to whether the defendant actually suffers from the syndrome. *Hennum,* 441 N.W.2d at 799. This holding similarly applies to expert testimony on battered woman syndrome presented by the prosecution. Such a limitation provides one means of ensuring that such testimony will not unfairly prejudice the alleged batterer.

In addition, because of our concern about the impact expert testimony on battered woman syndrome may have on the jury, we emphasize that the expert may not suggest that the complainant was battered, was truthful, or fit the battered woman syndrome. Likewise, the expert may not express an opinion as to whether the defendant was in fact a batterer.

In the case at hand, the expert testimony was adequately limited and was not unfairly prejudicial to Grecinger.... The expert did not testify as to whether Skoglund suffered from battered woman syndrome, whether or when Skoglund had told the truth, or whether Grecinger was a batterer. Consequently, the issue of Skoglund's credibility remained in the hands of the jury, and Grecinger was not unfairly prejudiced.

...Affirmed.

## III. Other Uses of Syndrome Evidence by Defendants

### A. Duress

Defendants have sought to introduce syndrome evidence in support of their claims that they have been coerced into committing crimes by their abusive spouse or partner. The Model Penal Code defines duress as follows:

### Model Penal Code § 2.09. Duress.

(1) It is an affirmative defense that the actor engaged in the conduct charged to constitute an offense because he was coerced to do so by the use of, or a threat to use, unlawful force against his person or the person of another, that a person of reasonable firmness in his situation would have been unable to resist.

(2) The defense provided by this Section is unavailable if the actor recklessly placed himself in a situation in which it was probable that he would be subjected to duress. The defense is also unavailable if he was negligent in placing himself in such a situation, whenever negligence suffices to establish culpability for the offense charged.

(3) It is not a defense that a woman acted on the command of her husband, unless she acted under such coercion as would establish a defense under this Section. [The presumption that a woman acting in the presence of her husband is coerced is abolished.]

## State v. B.H

New Jersey Supreme Court

183 N.J. 171 (2005)

JUSTICE LAVECCHIA delivered the opinion of the Court.

....

### I.

In March of 2001, B.H. left her husband, S.H., and took their two young daughters to a women's shelter. While there, she informed a counselor that in 1999 her husband had forced her to have sexual intercourse with her then seven-year-old stepson, L.H. At the counselor's urging, she reported the incident to the Division of Youth and Family Services (DYFS); however, she reunited with her husband when she left the shelter.

DYFS promptly conducted an investigation of the home, and an investigator from the Ocean County Prosecutor's Office contacted B.H. At the investigator's request, B.H. agreed to be interviewed. She appeared voluntarily at police headquarters and was administered *Miranda* warnings. She then talked with investigators for approximately an hour before making a taped statement in which she admitted to having engaged in sexual intercourse with her stepson while her husband watched.

In her statement, B.H. told the investigators that her husband, S.H., had physically and sexually assaulted her on other occasions but she denied that he had threatened her with any violence on the day that the incident with her stepson took place.

According to B.H., S.H. justified the intercourse as something that would be "good" for her to do with L.H., "that it would help [them] get along better." B.H. was arrested and charged with first-degree aggravated sexual assault, N.J.S.A. 2C:14-2a(1) (count I), and second-degree endangering the welfare of a child, N.J.S.A. 2C:24-4a (count II).

At trial it was brought out that in July of 1999, B.H. and S.H. were living in a motel with their infant daughter. S.H.'s son, L.H., was spending the weekend with them, as he frequently did. Sometime during the afternoon, L.H. entered the motel room and discovered his father and B.H. having sexual intercourse on the bed. S.H., having noticed that his son was observing them, told L.H. to lower his pants and placed the child on top of B.H., who lay naked with her legs apart. In accordance with S.H.'s directions, L.H. engaged in sexual intercourse with B.H. for several minutes. B.H. did not protest or attempt to leave, although she claimed that she remained passive during the sexual act. However, in her trial testimony, her description of what had happened that afternoon differed from her prior statement to police. She now claimed that S.H. had threatened her.

> He had his hand at my throat. He wouldn't let me off the bed. And I told him that I didn't want to do this, that I was not going to do this. And he said that if I didn't go through with this, that he would make me pay and that I would never see my daughter again.

B.H. said that she lied in her earlier statement about S.H. because "at that point [S.H.] had already gotten into [her] head again," and he had instructed her not to reveal his role in the incident.

B.H. also testified about earlier incidents of physical, sexual, and emotional abuse that S.H. inflicted on her. She described a relationship with S.H. that involved physical violence (she claimed to be beaten about her breasts where bruises would not be visible to others, and choked until she would almost pass out) and sexually violent practices that involved recurrent incidents of rape in various forms (described by one expert who interviewed her as "bizarre" sexual practices). The violence began early in the relationship. B.H. was nineteen years of age when she met S.H. She claimed that the first abusive incident occurred not long thereafter, when the two began to live together. In that encounter, S.H. held an ax to B.H.'s throat and, over an extended period of time, repeatedly raped her and performed other acts of a humiliating nature on her. Other incidents that need not be detailed similarly involved threats, physical violence, and violent sexual practices that B.H. also claimed to have endured from S.H. According to B.H., the abuse continued throughout their relationship, except for a short period of time when S.H. was on medication and in therapy.

Defense counsel informed the trial court that B.H. intended to present a duress defense and that she would rely on the testimony of Dr. Roger Raftery, a licensed psychologist with expertise in forensic psychology. . . .

In rebuttal, the State presented Dr. Timothy J. Michals, a licensed physician specializing in psychiatry and forensic psychiatry. He explained to the jury that battered woman syndrome is not a disease or disorder recognized as a psychiatric diagnosis, but rather is a theory employed in legal contexts to explain the interaction between the batterer and the battered woman. He stated that in his thirty years of practice he was unaware of any circumstance in which a battered woman had assaulted a third party at the direction of her batterer and that the syndrome was not useful in situations in which the woman harms a third person. In his view, it is helpful only in those cases in which an abused woman reacts to her abuser by harming him. Dr. Michals opined that B.H. was not suffering from battered woman syndrome in respect of the incident involving L.H. because: 1) there was a third party victim involved in this crime; 2) B.H. did not mention in her statement to police that she was being battered at the time of the incident; and 3) when interviewed by Dr. Michals, B.H.'s description of what had happened differed from what she had told the police. Moreover, he testified that he could not even form the conclusion that B.H. was a "battered woman" at the time the incident with L.H. occurred.

When it was time to instruct the jury on the defense of duress, the trial court identified the following factors from the model charge for the jury to consider: 1) the immediacy of the threat, specifically whether the force or threat of force posed a danger of present, imminent, and impending harm to the defendant or her daughter; 2) the gravity of the harm; 3) the seriousness of the crime that was committed; 4) the age, health, size, and mental and physical condition of both the defendant and the person alleged to have coerced her; 5) the possibility for escape or resistance; and

6) the opportunity for seeking assistance from officials. The dispute in this matter focuses on the following limitation that the court placed on the jury's consideration of the expert testimony on battered woman syndrome....

> Now with regard to this issue, that is whether the defendant recklessly placed herself in the situation, I have allowed testimony concerning battered woman syndrome. You may or may not determine that the defendant was afflicted with this condition. That is one of the many factual issues that are solely within your province.
>
> Should you determine that she was so afflicted, that does not establish that she acted under duress. The sole purpose for which that evidence is offered to you is to explain why the defendant continued to live with her husband and why she hadn't left him. It may be considered, if you find it credible, on the issue of recklessness.
>
> *The experts' testimony, then regarding battered woman syndrome was not offered to establish that a person of reasonable firmness in the defendant's situation would have been unable to resist, but, rather, to clear up any misconceptions that you may have concerning the activities of battered women, and to understand a battered woman's state of mind.* [(Emphasis added).]

B.H. objected to the limitation on the battered woman syndrome evidence. The court declined to adjust its charge and, as noted, the jury convicted B.H. of first-degree aggravated sexual assault (Count One) and third-degree endangering the welfare of a child (as a lesser-included charge on Count Two). She was sentenced on Count One as if she had been convicted of a second-degree offense, and given a custodial term of seven years. She was sentenced to a concurrent five-year custodial term on Count Two.

. . . .

Under N.J.S.A. 2C:2-9a, a successful duress claim must satisfy two distinct components. *See generally* 2 Paul H. Robinson, *Criminal Law Defenses* § 177 (1984). The first is that the defendant must be coerced into the criminal action by the asserted "excusing condition." *Ibid.* The "excusing condition" has been described as subjective because the defendant actually must have been influenced by it. *Ibid.* That assessment necessarily takes into account the defendant's state of mind. The defendant actually must believe in and be frightened by the likelihood of the threatened harm because the defense rests on principles of necessity. *See Commission Report,* cmt. 2 on 2C:2-9 at 70 (stating "[t]he present section gives the principle of necessity application where the evil apprehended comes from another person rather than from the perils of the physical world."). In effect, for duress to be present, "[the] defendant [must] claim[] to be psychically incapable of not acting, and therefore excused." *Id.* at 71....

The second component of the defense is objective in nature: a defendant's level of resistance to the particular threat must meet community standards of reasonableness. The jury must evaluate a defendant's response to the threat by applying the standard of the "person of reasonable firmness." N.J.S.A. 2C:2-9a. The norm presupposes an ordinary person without "serious mental and emotional defects." *See McAllister, supra,*

41 N.J. at 353–54, 196 A.2d at 792; *State v. Van Dyke*, 361 N.J. Super. 403, 417, 825 A.2d 1163, 1172 (App. Div.) .... *certif. denied,* 178 N.J. 35, 834 A.2d 407 (2003). It is an objective standard against which to measure the defendant's response to the "threat."

### B.

... [T]he defense of duress will fail if the defendant acted recklessly. To allow the jury to assess whether defendant, in fact, was reckless, the trial court admitted the testimony on battered woman syndrome. The court permitted the expert testimony to dispel any commonly held misconception that the jury might have about whether a battered woman should be regarded as having acted recklessly (and thereby be deprived of access to a duress defense) simply because she did not leave the relationship with her abuser. N.J.S.A. 2C:2-9b. ...

Assuming we do not have recklessness by the defendant, we turn to the two components of duress required by N.J.S.A. 2C:2-9a.

First, there is the requirement that the jury be convinced of the sincerity of a defendant's perception that she is being threatened, that is to say, that she honestly believes that there is an imminent threat of danger. To the extent that the jury must be persuaded that defendant perceived herself to be threatened, expert testimony about battered woman syndrome is also relevant on that question. ...

Expert testimony can be useful to a jury assessing the sincerity of a defendant's perception of a threat in connection with a duress defense. Our duress statute, by adopting the MPC standard that dispensed with an absolute threshold requirement of immediacy, allows the subjective imminence of the threat to the defendant to be but one of several factors to be considered, and thus renders syndrome evidence about the unique perceptions of a battered woman relevant to this subjective aspect of the duress calculus. *See* Dore, *supra*, 56 Ohio St. L.J. at 720, 738 (noting overlap between self-defense and duress in respect of use of syndrome evidence to understand defendant's subjective perception of imminent threat).

. . . .

In this matter, the trial court's instruction did not inform the jury that the expert testimony could be considered for such purpose, although at the close of the court's instruction on the battered woman syndrome evidence there was a reference to the testimony being used "to understand a battered woman's state of mind." That fleeting reference, however, came on the heels of the court's direction to the jury that the evidence could only be used for the recklessness assessment and did not give clear direction to the jury.

In sum, in respect of the first component of duress under N.J.S.A. 2C:2-9a, we conclude that battered woman syndrome expert evidence is relevant and admissible on the question of the sincerity of defendant's claim that she perceived a threat of harm from S.H. when she engaged in sexual intercourse with her seven-year-old stepson. It was error not to have permitted the jury to hear evidence about battered woman syndrome in connection with that subjective state-of-mind component of defendant's claim of duress. The jury instruction similarly was flawed because the jury was not informed that it could consider battered woman syndrome expert testimony when assessing the sincerity of defendant's perception of a coercive threat.

### D.

Last, we turn to the second component of duress established by N.J.S.A. 2C:2-9a. The ultimate determination for the jury is the reasonableness of a defendant's conduct. A jury must be convinced that the defendant experienced a coercion that a person of reasonable firmness in that situation would have been unable to withstand.

Because N.J.S.A. 2C:2-9a embodies an objective standard for the evaluation of a defendant's conduct in response to a threat by another, we can discern no place for battered woman syndrome evidence in that assessment.

. . . .

As to the second and objective component of the duress defense then, we agree with the trial court. The trial court correctly instructed the jury that the battered woman syndrome evidence was not to be used when it determined whether "a person of reasonable firmness" in the defendant's situation would have been unable to resist.

### V.

We hold that in light of the particular requirements of our statute, courts must apply the standard of a "person of reasonable firmness" in determining whether duress excuses criminal conduct, and battered woman syndrome expert testimony is not relevant to that analysis. The evidence is relevant, however, to a defendant's subjective perception of a threat from her abuser and, in that respect, can be relevant to her credibility. It also helps in explaining why she would remain with her abuser and, therefore, why such a defendant ought not to be perceived as acting recklessly. In those important latter respects, our decision today permits the syndrome expert testimony to expand a juror's general knowledge about a battered defendant's circumstances. Moreover, if the complete defense of duress is rejected, the syndrome evidence may be relevant in connection with sentencing where it may be applicable to a defendant's mitigation argument under N.J.S.A. 2C:44-1b(4).

. . . .

The jury charge must properly and completely explain how battered woman syndrome evidence may be considered in this matter. The charge here did not fulfill its obligation to be a complete and clear "road map" for the jury. *See State v. Martin*, 119 N.J. 2, 15, 573 A.2d 1359, 1366 (1990). For that reason, we are compelled to conclude that defendant's conviction cannot stand. We cannot treat the shortcoming in the charge as the equivalent of harmless error, particularly in light of the content restriction placed on the testimony of defendant's expert. Defendant's credibility was critical to her defense. Both the State and its expert called her credibility into question precisely because B.H. initially did not describe the coercive role that allegedly was played by S.H. (*i.e.*, that his hand was on her throat as he forced her to engage in the sexual act with L.H.). The limitation imposed on defendant's expert's testimony as it related to questions about defendant's credibility was significant.

## VI.

The judgment of the Appellate Division is affirmed as modified. The matter is remanded for further proceedings consistent with this opinion.

## B. Competency

### Commonwealth v. Conaghan

Supreme Judicial Court of Massachusetts

433 Mass. 105 (2000)

ABRAMS, J.

We granted the defendant's application for further appellate review, see *Commonwealth v. Conaghan*, 48 Mass. App. Ct. 304, 720 N.E.2d 48 (1999), to determine, among other issues, whether Conaghan's motion for a competency examination or examinations pursuant to G.L. c. 123, § 15 (a), was erroneously denied. Conaghan filed her motion four and one-half years after she pleaded guilty to manslaughter in the death of her minor son.

. . . .

We conclude that Conaghan's motions cannot be decided without the examination or examinations by an expert in the field of battered woman syndrome. We therefore vacate the order denying her an examination or examinations pursuant to G.L. c. 123, § 15(a), on the issue of competence to assist her counsel and to enter a voluntary plea of guilty. *Dusky v. United States*, 362 U.S. 402, 80 S. Ct. 788, 4 L. Ed. 2d 824 (1960). We remand this matter to the Superior Court which should order an examination or examinations pursuant to G.L. c. 123, § 15(a), by an expert in battered woman syndrome and for such further proceedings as are needed in light of the expert's opinion.

2. Conaghan's plea hearing.

At the plea hearing, the assistant district attorney read Conaghan's statement to the police concerning the events surrounding her son's death. Conaghan told the police that no one else was in the house when she pushed her son and that she previously had pushed him in the same manner four or five other times. Additionally, she stated that these punishments had begun in September, 1991, and that there was no one else present when they took place. Conaghan also stated twice in response to the judge's questions that she was pleading guilty out of her own free will. The trial judge specifically asked her whether anybody had threatened her or made promises in order to get her to plead guilty and she replied, "No."

(a) Materials in support of motion to withdraw guilty plea and for new trial.

In support of her motion to withdraw the guilty plea and for a new trial, Conaghan filed supplementary materials regarding Paul Haynes's violent conduct with other women and children; an affidavit narrating her own history of physical and psychological abuse, and some of her psychiatric and medical records since her incarceration. The judge concluded that there was nothing in Conaghan's affidavit creating a substantial issue that would require a psychiatric examination or examinations and an evidentiary hearing.

(b) Conaghan's affidavit.

In 1991, Conaghan met Paul Haynes. Shortly after beginning a relationship with Haynes, he moved in with her. Because Haynes was unemployed, Conaghan used her earnings and child support payments to pay his rent and bills. Haynes told Conaghan that he worked for an individual named "Tony" who was affiliated with the mafia. Haynes would often threaten Conaghan with Tony if she did not obey him or if she displeased him in any way. While she was living with Haynes, she learned that Haynes also owned a gun.

Haynes ordered Conaghan to punish her son physically in order to cure his behavioral problems and illnesses. Haynes also physically punished Conaghan's son. At Haynes's direction, Conaghan assisted him. According to Conaghan, prior to Haynes's moving in she had only punished her son through nonphysical means.

Conaghan stated in her affidavit that Haynes instructed her to lie to the authorities about her son's death. Haynes told her to "cover for him" because, if charged, he would receive life imprisonment given his prior criminal record. Haynes also instructed Conaghan to kill herself. When she refused, Haynes instructed her to turn herself in to the authorities, Conaghan did so. In addition, Haynes continued to instruct her on what to tell her lawyer and the authorities. According to Conaghan, Haynes also told her to plead guilty in order to avoid further investigation which might result in his being charged.

(c) Conaghan's psychiatric records.

Conaghan submitted some of her mental treatment records since her incarceration. She has received extensive therapy for severe bipolar disorder. These records also make references to her "past tendencies to be lorded over by abusive males." Conaghan has not been evaluated for battered woman syndrome while at the Massachusetts Correctional Institution at Framing-ham, because diagnosis of and treatment for battered woman syndrome is beyond the mandate of the prison's medical services department.

(d) Evidence at Paul Haynes's trial.

One year and eleven months after Conaghan's plea, Haynes was convicted by a jury of forcible rape of a child, indecent assault and battery on a child under fourteen years of age, assault and battery, and assault and battery by means of a dangerous weapon in connection with his abuse of James and Joyce Sanford. The partial transcript of that trial submitted by Conaghan in support of her motion to withdraw her guilty plea and for a new trial reveals the violent and abusive personality of Paul Haynes.

Haynes moved in with Rebekah Sanford. He brought Conaghan with him and told Sanford that Conaghan was his sister. The testimony reveals that the Sanford children, especially James, were continually "disciplined" by Haynes. The testimony revealed the Sanfords' fear of Haynes and fear of being killed. Conaghan's affidavit expressed the same fear.

Conaghan testified at Haynes's trial. She said Haynes would beat the Sanford children and afterward show her the bruises to humiliate the children. According to Conaghan, Haynes was particularly violent toward James.

. . . .

3. Delay.

The Commonwealth asserts that Conaghan's delay makes her claim not credible. The Commonwealth also asserts that Conaghan is not credible because she did not come forward until after Haynes's trial. Where, as here, the claim is that Conaghan was not competent rationally to assist her counsel in her defense or to meet the constitutional requirement that a plea must be voluntary with "sufficient present ability to consult with [her] lawyer with a reasonable degree of rational understanding and whether [she] has a rational as well as factual understanding of the proceedings against [her]," *Dusky v. United States*, 362 U.S. 402, 4 L. Ed. 2d 824, 80 S. Ct. 788 (1960); *Commonwealth v. Robbins*, 431 Mass. 442, 445, 727 N.E.2d 1157 (2000), expert testimony is required. *See Commonwealth v. Crawford*, 429 Mass. 60, 64–65, 706 N.E.2d 289 (1999).

Evidence of battered woman syndrome is "material to the issue whether [Conaghan] could assist her counsel in preparing a defense that served her best interests." *McMaugh v. State*, 612 A.2d 725, 732 (R.I. 1992). A common characteristic of battered women is a learned helplessness which manifests itself in the inability to perceive herself as abused and to communicate the abuse to others. *Commonwealth v. Pike*, 431 Mass. 212, 222, 726 N.E.2d 940 (2000). Evidence of battered woman syndrome may be considered newly discovered evidence warranting a new trial because usually there is delay in coming forward with information on the abuse, even if there were some knowledge of the abuse at trial. *Id. See United States v. Brown*, 891 F. Supp. 1501, 1509–1510 (D. Kan. 1995) (granting new trial because there was no way trial counsel would have discovered defendant suffered from battered woman syndrome because victims usually do not come forward with information on abuse); *McMaugh v. State, supra* (noting that it was not until after defendant began serving her sentence that she was able to reveal she was victim of extreme abuse and domination). Therefore, the fact that Conaghan was not able to come forward with claims of abuse at the hands of Haynes until 1997 does not render her allegations less credible, if she suffered from battered woman syndrome.

4. Conclusion.

Conaghan's motion raises a serious question as to her mental competency to assist her attorney in establishing a defense and to plead guilty voluntarily. On this record, Conaghan is entitled to an examination or examinations by an expert in battered woman syndrome under G.L. c. 123, §15(a), as to her competency to assist counsel in her defense and to enter a voluntary plea due to battered woman syndrome. G.L. c. 123, § 15(a), provides that "[w]henever a court of competent jurisdiction doubts whether a defendant in a criminal case is competent to stand trial or is criminally responsible by reason of mental illness or mental defect, it may *at any stage of the proceedings* . . . order an examination of such defendant to be conducted by one or more qualified . . . psychologists . . . when an examination is ordered, the court shall instruct the examining physician or psychologist in the law for determining mental competence to stand trial and criminal responsibility" (emphasis added). Nothing in the statute limits the time within which this must be done. . . .

The order denying Conaghan's motion for a court-appointed expert under G. L. c. 123, § 15 (a), is vacated, the case is remanded to the Superior Court for an examination or examinations by an expert on battered woman syndrome to determine (1) whether Conaghan was suffering from battered woman syndrome; (2) whether, if she were suffering from battered woman syndrome, Conaghan had the ability at the time of that plea to assist her attorney in preparing her defense; (3) whether, if she were suffering from battered woman syndrome, Conaghan was competent voluntarily to plead guilty; and (4) whether, if she were suffering from battered woman syndrome, Conaghan pleaded "with a reasonable degree of rational understanding" and with a "rational as well as factual understanding of the proceedings against [her]." *Dusky v. United States, supra* at 402. *Commonwealth v. Robbins, supra* at 445. See *McMaugh v. State, supra* at 732. The order denying the motion for a competency examination or examinations is vacated. The matter is remanded to the Superior Court proceeding consistent with this opinion and for such further proceedings as may be needed after the expert has rendered an opinion.

So ordered.

## IV. Syndrome Evidence in Cases Involving Children

### A. Battered Child Syndrome

In cases where the defendant claims that injuries to a child occurred by accident, courts have allowed experts to testify about battered child syndrome to show that the injuries could not have occurred accidentally.

Some experts have incorporated the psychological effects of child abuse under the term "battered child syndrome," and others, in an effort to distinguish it from the physical symptoms identified by Dr. C. Henry Kempe in his landmark article describing battered children, have used the term "child abuse syndrome."

Defendants who are charged with killing a parent (parricide) have sought to introduce evidence of their psychological responses to years of abuse in support of self-defense claims. The landmark case of *State v. Janes* is one of the earliest cases on this subject.

The following article proposes that a broad "domestic abuse syndrome" be permitted by the courts with a particular emphasis on allowing abused children to rely on this evidence in their defense when charged with killing parents they claim to be abusive. It is followed by the *Janes* decision.

## Nancy Wright, *Voice for the Voiceless: The Case for Adopting the "Domestic Abuse Syndrome" for Self-Defense Purposes for All Victims of Domestic Violence Who Kill Their Abusers*

4 Crim. L. Brief 76 (Spring, 2009)

Introduction

. . . .

When victims of domestic abuse are charged with the murder of their abusers, they frequently claim that they acted in self-defense. Attorneys for these victims of domestic abuse ask courts to admit expert testimony regarding various "syndromes" to describe the devastating psychological impact of a lifetime of severe physical, sexual and psychological violence, as part of the self-defense plea. These various syndromes, detailed below, are referred to collectively in this article as "domestic abuse syndrome" (or DAS) whether the victim is a battered woman or a battered child. Without the opportunity to present this expert testimony, victims of domestic abuse syndrome will not be able to demonstrate to the jury the reasonableness of their perceptions of imminent danger or the concomitant reasonableness of their use of lethal force to defend themselves. Unless all victims of domestic abuse syndrome are able to present this evidence, it is likely that their already broken lives will be completely shattered by a murder conviction, and they will once again find themselves trapped with no ability to escape; only this time it will be in a prison cell.

. . . .

Following the lead of attorneys offering expert testimony regarding the effects of domestic abuse on adult victims, lawyers representing children, who have killed their abusive parents, have tried to introduce expert testimony regarding the impact of domestic abuse on child victims as part of a self-defense plea. In the case of physical abuse, attorneys have proffered expert testimony regarding "battered child syndrome" (or BCS) to describe the psychological effects on the child as part of a self-defense plea. Medical evidence of BCS has long been admissible in dependency hearings to remove children from abusive homes and in criminal trials to prosecute the abusive parents. . . . However, as used in those cases, BCS referred only to severe abuse of infants or very young children, usually under the age of five. Use of the same term "battered child syndrome" as part of a self-defense plea for parricide is, therefore, clearly a misnomer and has led to considerable confusion, since obviously, very young children are not capable of killing their abusers. Thus, the psychological effects of physical, sexual and psychological abuse of children who are old enough to kill their abusers might more appropriately be termed "battered child syndrome of an older child."

Whatever term is used, courts have been far more reluctant to allow expert testimony regarding the psychological effects of battering on children than on adults as part of a self-defense plea. This reluctance is hard to understand since BWS (and its various iterations) and BCS of an older child are the functional and psychological equivalents of each other. Therefore, there seems to be little basis for courts to deny battered children the right to present expert testimony regarding their abuse to help the jury understand why, like battered adults, abused children could be justified in killing their abusers based on self-defense....

### Admitting Expert Testimony Regarding the Domestic Abuse Syndrome as Part of a Self-Defense Plea For All Victims of Domestic Violence

....

The psychological impact of domestic abuse is the same on all of the victims of DAS. Both women and children display "hypervigilance" in monitoring the abuse and "learned helplessness" in trying, usually unsuccessfully, to cope with the battering. Moreover, many of the women and children who are victims of DAS are impoverished, which exacerbates the psychological effects of their abuse....

Like a battered woman, a battered child develops "a heightened sensitivity" during the tension-building stage and is able to anticipate when an "acute explosion" phase is about to begin. This helps explain why child-victims of abuse tend to kill most often during the tension-building stage because they lack the physical strength to defend themselves during the acute explosion stage when the abuse occurs.

Battered children often kill their abusive parents while the abusers are in apparently non-threatening situations, such as being asleep or incapacitated. The Minnesota Supreme Court noted in *State v. McLennan* that an attack on a parent by a child "does not occur at the time of the conflict; rather, it occurs when the child has the opportunity to attack."[3]

....

The reasons why a battered child might ultimately resort to parricide are also understandable based on the psychological effects of prolonged abuse. As nationally known child abuse expert Leonard P. Edwards explained, if a "child believes there is no escape and that he or she will continue to be abused, the child may take desperate action. Some children run away from home. In a few cases a child may finally fight back by killing the abuser." An example of a child finally fighting back by committing parricide occurred in *Maricopa County*.[4] In that case, after "years of severe physical, psychological and emotional abuse and neglect, twelve year old K.T. shot her mother in the back of the head, while her mother was sleeping." Defense expert Dr. Frank Miller testified at K.T.'s trial that he had "only seen a few cases" in his career approaching "the heinous treatment" and "the terrible and degrading physical and emotional abuse

---

3. [n 134] State v. MacLennan, 702 N.W.2d 219, 227 (Minn. 2005)....
4. [n 192] [In re Appeal in] Maricopa County, 893 P.2d [60,] 62 [(Ariz. Ct. App. 1994)].

suffered by [K.T.] and her younger sister." Dr. Miller commented that the "only ones that have exceeded that that I've seen are always postmortem of the child." He explained that K.T. lived in "constant fear of imminent irrational punishment" which had been "worsening in intensity and severity to the point of possible death, punctuated by the presence of a casket in the house in which, it was threatened by [the mother that] K.T. and her sister could find themselves. This was underscored by the fact that both K.T. and her sister had been choked to the point of unconsciousness" by their "'sadistic'" mother. K.T., and other people acting on her behalf, had "without success, sought help numerous times from state, police and school officials." . . .

Because battered woman's syndrome and battered child's syndrome of an older child, are the "functional and legal equivalent" of one another, it seems only logical that courts that admit expert testimony re BWS as part of a woman's self-defense plea, should also admit expert testimony regarding BCS as part of a child's self-defense plea. . . .

Nevertheless, although an increasing number of courts have found that expert testimony regarding the psychological impact of BWS is admissible on the issue of self defense, surprisingly few courts have found that similar expert testimony regarding BCS is also admissible. In the context of an abused woman, according to a 1996 report from the National Institute of Justice, expert testimony on "battering and its effects is admissible, at least to some degree, or has been admitted . . . in each of the 50 states plus the District of Columbia." . . .

It was not until five years after the *Janes* case, that the Ohio Supreme Court in *State v. Nemeth* became the second state supreme court to admit expert testimony regarding BCS as part of a self-defense plea in a parricide case.[5] *Nemeth* involved the prosecution of sixteen-year-old Brian Nemeth for the murder of his abusive mother with a bow and arrow. Like Andrew Janes, Brian had suffered years of abuse at the hands of his alcoholic mother, including being hit with a stick, burned on his hand with a cigarette and cut on his side with a coat hanger. In the six months before her death, Brian's mother's drinking, and the abuse that went with it, escalated until it was a nightly occurrence. On the evening of her death, Brian spent most of the night in his bedroom with the door locked, listening to his mother cursing him and threatening to "beat his face in" and kill him. Finally, when Brian heard his mother walk away, he got his bow and arrows, found his mother lying on the couch, and shot her five times in the head and neck. The therapist who examined Brian diagnosed him as suffering from BCS and noted that he had "very compatible symptoms as do women in abusive relationships." In finding the expert testimony regarding BCS to be admissible, the *Nemeth* court stated that such evidence would help to show that a child's behavior was "consistent with that of an abused child and would lend support to his testimony that he had been abused both generally and just prior to the killing."

---

5. [n 255] [Eds. Note: The footnote is missing in the original article. The official cite for this case is *State v. Nemeth*, 82 Ohio St. 3d 202 (1998).]

In the decade since the *Nemeth* case was decided, no other state supreme court has upheld the admissibility of expert testimony in a parricide case although the Minnesota Supreme Court indicated in *dicta* in *MacLennan* that such testimony might be allowed in an appropriate case....

In order for expert testimony regarding the psychological effects of domestic abuse syndrome to be admissible as part of a self defense plea, the testimony must meet several legal requirements. There is little doubt that expert testimony regarding the psychological effects of domestic abuse syndrome meets the threshold requirements that the evidence is both relevant and reliable regardless of whether the abuse victim is a woman or a child. The state of mind of the woman or child at the time they killed their abusers is clearly relevant and numerous cases have held that both battered woman's syndrome and battered child's syndrome meet the requisite level of reliability for admission.

In addition, in order to be admissible, expert testimony regarding the psychological effects of DAS on both women and children must be "[r]elated to a subject that is sufficiently beyond common experience that the opinion of an expert would assist the trier of fact." Expert testimony regarding the psychological effects of domestic abuse syndrome clearly meets this threshold requirement as well. This type of evidence is sometimes referred to as "social framework testimony" since it provides "a social and psychological context in which the trier can understand and evaluate claims about the ultimate fact."...

Finally, in order for expert testimony regarding the psychological effects of DAS on women and children to be admissible, it must also be determined that the probative value of the evidence is not substantially outweighed by its prejudicial effect. There can be little doubt that the critical importance of allowing the jury to fully understand the abusive relationship and its psychological impact outweighs any potentially prejudicial animosity which the jury might feel towards the abuser. It is also clear that, rather than being a pretext to explain unlawful behavior, expert testimony regarding DAS would be offered to help the jury come to a full understanding of the factual and psychological context in which the homicide occurred, so that they can reach a fair and informed verdict....

### The Psychological Impact of Domestic Abuse Syndrome on Children Is Beyond the Common Experience of the Jury

The reasons given by courts as to why the expert testimony regarding the psychological manifestations of BWS on a woman should be admitted to help the jury "place [her] behavior in an understandable light" are even more compelling when considering whether to admit evidence of BCS to explain the psychological effects of DAS on an abused child....

### Very Few Jurors Have Been Battered Children

There are some legal experts who opine that, although expert testimony regarding battered woman's syndrome is necessary to counter the common sense conclusion of jurors that a reasonable woman would have left the abusive situation, this need does not apply in the case of a battered child. The rationale for this view is that the vast majority of jurors have not been battered adults and, without the expert testimony, could not understand why a grown woman would choose to remain in an abusive situation, especially with the availability of support services. However, because every juror has been a child, who has been dependent on a parent or guardian to provide for their care, the inability of a child to leave his or her home is within the common experience of the jury and expert testimony regarding BCS is not required for the jury to fully understand the child's situation.

This rationale misses some crucial aspects of why expert testimony is necessary to help jurors understand the perspective of a battered child. Even if lay jurors might have experienced and, therefore, might be able to understand the financial support that a child receives from his or her parents, this does not mean that expert testimony is not needed. Financial dependence is only a part of the explanation for why a battered child does not leave an abusive home. Expert testimony is needed to assist lay jurors in fully comprehending the strong psychological and emotional reasons that keep a battered child from seeking help or escaping from the abuser. This is also the reason why simply hearing extensive testimony from the child regarding the kinds of abuse that the child has suffered is not enough to understand the child's perspective. It is not the fact that the child has been abused, or even the *physical effect* of that abuse, that expert testimony will help the jury understand. Rather, it is the *psychological effect* of the abuse that makes expert testimony necessary....

Moreover, the fact that battered children grow up in an environment "wholly different from the safe and nurturing home depicted by traditional values and social expectations" seems to confirm that BCS is, fortunately, beyond the common experiences most jurors have encountered. Children who spend their formative years in unsafe, abusive homes often find it nearly impossible to develop any non-violent methods of problem solving.... Usually, such children have seen only violence used to solve problems in the home, and "[u]nlike the battered adult, [have] no outside context with which to compare the abusive reality." Because abused children are unaware of other problem-solving methods, they begin to pattern their behavior after that of their abusive parents. This effect of growing up in a violent environment may help the jury understand why abused children might resort to using violence against their abusers rather than leaving the abusive situation or reporting the abuse....

Very Few Battered Children Can Provide Corroborating Testimony Regarding Their Abuse

Expert testimony regarding battered child syndrome may also be necessary to establish that the abuse could have occurred without anyone outside of the immediate family knowing about it. Unlike a battered woman, who may be able to corroborate her physical abuse by the testimony of other witnesses, in most cases an abused child will not be able to provide any similar corroborating testimony....

Compounding the problem is the fact that a battered child will frequently maintain the secrecy and remain silent about both the fact that the abuse is occurring and the identity of the perpetrator. Battered children are often directly threatened by their abusers regarding the consequences of telling anyone about the abuse.

. . . .

### The Probative Value of Expert Testimony Regarding the Psychological Impact of Domestic Abuse Syndrome on Children

Like expert testimony regarding the psychological impact of domestic abuse syndrome on battered women, similar evidence on behalf of battered children has high probative value and is not outweighed by any prejudicial effect. There are two main concerns regarding the potential prejudicial effects of expert testimony regarding the battered child syndrome. Neither of these concerns is sufficiently prejudicial that it should outweigh the high probative value of expert testimony regarding the psychological effects of DAS on children.

The first concern is that expert testimony regarding battered child's syndrome will lead the jury to develop animosity towards the abusive parent, shifting the jury's attention from the proper inquiry of whether the child was justified in killing the parent to the irrelevant issue of the parent's relative worth as a mother or father. . . .

Clearly, if this concern has any merit, it applies with equal force to battered woman's syndrome and does not explain why a court that admits expert testimony regarding BWS would not admit expert testimony regarding BCS. Moreover, in both cases, it seems cruelly ironic to essentially be arguing that, because a parent was so abusive that a jury may feel animosity towards the batterer, that evidence should be kept from the jury. It seems as though the court would be rewarding abusive parents for their bad conduct by keeping their behavior from the jury, while punishing the battered child by not giving the jury all of the information which might assist them in determining why the child might have been acting in self defense in killing the abusive parent.

Moreover, the results of a 1996 U.S. Department of Justice study of both state and federal cases involving battered women should help allay any potential concerns that admitting expert testimony regarding domestic abuse syndrome would mean that the abused women and children would not be convicted or that any convictions would be overturned on appeal. The study analyzed the state court appeals of 152 battered women who were convicted of killing their abusive partners. On appeal, 63% of the convictions or sentences were affirmed. This result occurred even though expert testimony regarding BWS was admitted in 71% of the affirmances. Similarly, 75% of the appeals in federal court resulted in affirmances of the battered women's convictions or sentences. The researchers considered these findings "strong evidence that, contrary to the contention of some critics, admitting expert testimony on battering and its effects, is not tantamount to an acquittal." Although their study involved expert testimony regarding battered women, there seems to be little doubt that a similar study regarding expert testimony about battered child syndrome, would lead to the same results.

The second concern regarding the prejudicial effect of expert testimony regarding battered child's syndrome is that the testimony will impermissibly infringe on the role of the jury in determining the child's credibility. Some courts have opined that, if an expert testifies to the same facts as the abused child and explains them using technical terms like "learned helplessness" and "hypervigilance," the child's testimony may be bolstered and embellished with an "aura of special reliability and trustworthiness" making it more likely that the jury will believe the child.

The reasoning behind this concern seems circular and misguided. Part of the reason why courts allow expert testimony in the first place is precisely because experts have specialized knowledge which jurors can rely on to reach their verdicts. It is axiomatic to say that, because jurors might rely on the testimony, it should be excluded. If this was the case, then all expert testimony would either need to be excluded or the jury would need to be told not to rely on the testimony, in which case it would be hard to fathom why the testimony was admitted in the first place. . . .

### Developing Acceptable Legal Standards for Self-Defense Pleas by Victims of Domestic Abuse Syndrome

. . . .

In the traditional confrontational setting, a majority of jurisdictions apply an objective standard of reasonableness in establishing justification for homicide and reject a purely subjective standard whether the defendant has been the prior victim of abuse by the decedent or not. In most cases involving DAS victims who kill their abusers in a confrontational setting, this standard of reasonableness is sufficient to assure that the battered women or children can establish a self defense plea.

However, in a non-confrontational setting, such as where the abusers are passive or asleep, a hybrid standard of reasonableness, which combines both a subjective prong and an objective prong, is essential to assure that the psychological effects of DAS can be properly considered by a jury. The subjective prong of the hybrid standard assures that the jury can understand the perception of DAS victims when evaluating whether they were justified in killing their abusers. The objective prong provides an external criterion against which the reasonableness of the defensive actions of DAS victims can be measured.

In addition, in a non-confrontational setting, the time frame in which DAS victims must fear grievous bodily harm in order to plead self defense must be broadly construed. The use of an expansive time frame enables the jury to consider the unique ability of DAS victims to anticipate severe attacks by their abusers when evaluating whether the danger from the abuser was immediate or imminent.

### An Objective Standard of Reasonableness for Victims of Domestic Abuse Syndrome Who Claim Self-Defense in a Confrontational Context

. . . It is estimated that about 75% of the cases involving a battered woman killing her abusive spouse occur in a confrontational setting "where the [homicide] victim was usually the initial aggressor who provoked the final confrontation that ended up lethal." In these cases, even if a court admits expert testimony regarding DAS, it would do so only to establish the woman or child's *subjective honesty* in believing that he or she was in danger of grievous bodily harm at the time of the homicide. However, the court would not admit the expert testimony to establish the *objective reasonableness* of the woman or child's defensive actions. . . .

Unlike battered women who frequently kill their abusive spouses in a confrontational setting, most battered children kill their abusive parents in non-confrontational settings. . . .

Evaluating Whether the Women or Children Were Acting in Objectively Reasonable Manners

There are valid reasons for imposing a hybrid standard, which incorporates both the subjective and the objective standards of reasonableness, to prove self-defense in a non-confrontational setting regarding both women and children who are victims of domestic abuse syndrome. . . .

The Subjective Prong Enables a Jury to Consider Whether Victims of Domestic Abuse Syndrome Were Justified in Killing Their Abusers

The subjective prong of the hybrid standard is essential to place the jury in the position of the DAS victim, so that the jury can "then properly assess the reasonableness of the defendant's perceptions of imminence and danger." Traditional self-defense law is premised on isolated encounters between two strangers; a situation where no history exists and no connection needs to be made between an abusive past and a violent response. However, this is not the situation where the defendant has a prolonged history of abuse by the decedent. An abusive family is by definition an unreasonable situation. Battered women have frequently suffered from years of abuse which resulted in the psychological effects detailed above. Battered children, who have often been abused since infancy, have never had the opportunity to develop the perspective of the "objectively reasonable person" because they have never experienced a "normal" person's reaction to danger. Thus, they have no basis for understanding what a "reasonable" reaction to threats on their lives would be. "Because the abused child's psyche has been altered by physical, sexual or emotional abuse, it is inappropriate to judge the child's fear [solely] against the rational person standard."

Imposing a purely objective standard of reasonableness and refusing to admit the expert testimony regarding the subjective perspective of a victim of domestic abuse syndrome would thus mean that the jury would have to disregard this crucial evidence of years of abuse in the case of a battered woman or, perhaps, a lifetime of abuse in the case of a battered child. Rather than looking at the facts that occurred immediately prior to the killing with the same understanding as the battered woman or child, the jury would have to look at the same facts from the perspective of a detached reasonable person. This might make sense in the traditional situation where the defendant was, in fact, a detached person, and the only issue was whether the actions of that detached person were reasonable; however, it makes no sense where the defendant was anything but a detached person and where the actions of that person can only be fairly examined with the battered woman's or child's psychological background in mind....

### A Broad Time Frame for Victims of Domestic Abuse Syndrome Who Claim Self Defense

Most justifiable homicide statutes include the terms "imminent" or "immediate" to describe the time frame in which the defendant must fear grievous bodily harm in order to claim self defense. At the present time, there is a split of authority as to whether justifiable homicide, in the context of a victim of DAS who kills his or her abuser, requires that the terms immediate or imminent be narrowly defined, as meaning something happening right away, or more broadly defined, as meaning something that might or is about to occur.

Jurisdictions which define the terms narrowly refuse to permit self-defense instructions where a victim of domestic abuse syndrome kills his or her abuser during a pause in the violence, feeling that a narrow time frame best comports with the traditional policy that self-defense in a homicide case should only be allowed in the most dire circumstances. These courts opine that holding that the use of deadly force is justified by a danger of death or serious injury that is merely about to occur is equivalent to holding such force is justified even when it is not absolutely necessary....

Once expert testimony is admitted to illuminate this characteristic of hypermonitoring, the jury will be able to understand how, even in an ostensibly non-confrontational situation, the DAS victim can honestly and reasonably believe that the abusive spouse or parent poses an imminent threat of grievous bodily harm. Understanding a domestic abuse syndrome victim's "acute discriminatory powers," would therefore give the jury a basis for recognizing how, at the time of the killing, the abuser's violence had, "in the [DAS victim's] mind, passed from the 'normal' and tolerable into the 'abnormal' and life threatening." Use of a broader time frame is, thus, essential to enable the jury to consider the domestic abuse syndrome victim's unique ability to anticipate that grievous harm from the abuser is, in fact, immediate or imminent.

### The Heightened State of Terror of Victims of Domestic Abuse Syndrome

The use of a broad time frame will also enable juries to consider the domestic abuse syndrome victim's build up of terror and fear that DAS victims experience as a result of the prolonged history of abuse....

Moreover, the jurisdictions that require a narrow time frame fail to recognize that it is only when the abuser is incapacitated that a battered person may have an opportunity to fight back. This is especially true of abused children, who are "generally unable to protect themselves during a confrontation, because of obvious physical and less apparent psychological reasons. If they are to be able to relieve themselves of their plight, the most inappropriate time may be during a beating." It is only by using a broad time frame that a jury can consider a child's history of abuse and the build-up of fear and terror that culminate in the need to commit parricide before the violence escalates and the child becomes the homicide victim. . . .

Conclusion

. . . .

Often living in poverty, and lacking any financial resources, most victims of domestic abuse syndrome come to feel that they are trapped into remaining with their abusers. When in desperation, often after many years of abuse, they take matters into their own hands and kill their abusers, they are silenced victims once again if they are unable to get the expert help they need to present their stories and the psychological impact that a lifetime of abuse has had on them.

This final victimization can be prevented by allowing expert testimony regarding domestic abuse syndrome. Obviously, in the ideal world the battering would never have been allowed to escalate to the point where killing the abuser would appear to be the only way out to the abuse victim. In the ideal world, the war on poverty would be won and the abject poverty that makes leaving the abuser an economic impossibility for domestic violence victims would no longer exist. But these abused women and children do not live in an ideal world. At least, by allowing them to present expert testimony about their abuse, these victims of DAS can be provided with a just world, where the psychological impact of their years of suffering is considered and where they will receive the fair trial that every defendant deserves.

## State v. Janes
### Supreme Court of Washington
### 121 Wn. 2d 220 (1993)

Opinion by Durham

. . . .

Each of the residents of the Jaloveckas/Janes home could readily be identified as a victim. Certainly, Walter Jaloveckas was the victim of homicide; there is also indication that his childhood was traumatic. The defendant, 17-year-old Andrew Janes, was abandoned by an alcoholic father at age 7, and then sporadically abused by Walter for 10 years. Andrew's mother, Gale, and his brother, Shawn, were also abused and shared the pain of these traumatic times. The abuse ended when Andrew shot and killed Walter. Yet, there is no doubt that the suffering continues and is in many ways greatly amplified by Walter's death.

In 1978, Walter began living with Gale, a single mother, and her young sons, Shawn and Andrew. The relationship was difficult from the beginning. Walter attempted to be a father figure to the boys and he helped support them financially. However, he was also subject to frequent outbursts of temper which sometimes resulted in severe physical and emotional abuse. As one of the trial experts testified, throughout his association with Walter, Andrew experienced "chronic and enduring abuse that he received as a child and as an adolescent", Report of Proceedings (RP), at 602, and "an unremitting pattern of episodic terror", RP, at 1495. Some of these incidents will be detailed below.

On August 30, 1988, Walter was shot and killed by Andrew. The events immediately leading to Walter's death began on the evening of August 29. Walter became upset after learning that one of his friends had been arrested and he began yelling at Gale. Andrew was present for a while, but then left to listen to music in his room. After tiring of the confrontation, Gale went to Andrew's room and told him to take his dirty clothes to the laundry room. Walter appeared shortly thereafter, and according to Gale's testimony, leaned his head into Andrew's room and spoke to him in a low voice. Gale could not hear Walter's comments, but remarked that the low tone used by Walter was one usually reserved for threats. Andrew later told a psychiatrist that Walter criticized him but that he couldn't remember exactly what Walter had said. On the witness stand, Andrew was completely unable to recall the contents of Walter's comment.

When Andrew awoke at 5 a.m. on August 30, Walter had already gone to work. Gale mentioned to Andrew that Walter was still mad. One of Andrew's classmates, Eric Haukap, dropped by the Janes' home about 6:30 in the morning. Andrew showed Haukap a shotgun, and his friend watched as Andrew loaded it with five shells. Andrew then said that he was going to kill Walter. This threat was familiar to Andrew's friend, as he had made it several times before. Andrew hid the loaded shotgun and the two left to catch the bus to school. At school, Andrew smoked marijuana with some other students. He attended only two classes before leaving school to return home. No one else was at home.

. . . .

When Walter returned home at his normal time, around 4:30 p.m., Andrew shot him with the pistol as he came through the front door. According to the medical examiner, two shots hit Walter Jaloveckas: the first through his right eye and the second through his head as he fell.

Andrew then punched the buttons on the house alarm system to summon the police, the fire department, and a medical unit. When the police arrived, he began firing upon them. He also fired several random shots, hitting the house, the telephone, and Walter's car. In the course of these actions, Andrew wounded Mrs. Eve Flores, a passerby, and Mountlake Terrace police officer James Blackburn. After about 5 minutes, Andrew surrendered.

. . . .

Andrew never disputed that he shot and killed Walter. Instead, at his jury trial, he offered two distinct defenses: First, that the homicide was justifiable self-defense, based on the history of abuse by Walter. Second, that his capacity to premeditate and to form intent was diminished by the abuse he had suffered and from his use of drugs and alcohol.

In support of Andrew's request for a self-defense instruction, Dr. Christopher Varley, a child psychiatrist, was called for an offer of proof. This testimony, in large part, was repeated later before the jury. Dr. Varley testified that Andrew suffered from, *inter alia*, post-traumatic stress disorder (PTSD). This disorder was the result of "the chronic and enduring abuse that he received". RP, at 602. Dr. Varley testified that the number of physically abusive events over the 10-year period was difficult to define, and set the range at between 20 and 500 incidents. Emotional abuse in the form of criticism and rebuke extended over the life of the family. Dr. Varley testified that the PTSD impaired Andrew's capacity to premeditate.

. . . .

The trial court denied the request for a self-defense instruction. The court specifically found that Walter's confrontation with Gale the night before, his unknown comment to Andrew that same night, and Gale's statement the next morning that Walter was still mad were insufficient to establish imminent danger. . . .

The defense also proposed a diminished capacity instruction. The judge noted the acceptance of PTSD within the medical community and ruled that he would so instruct the jury. The court allowed additional expert testimony on this subject as well as the family history of abuse. The witnesses were limited to events personally observed and also witnessed by the defendant. The court also permitted testimony as to the effects of alcohol and drugs on the defendant.

At trial, the defense presented 14 witnesses in an extensive defense. The testimony documented a litany of abusive behavior by Walter toward Andrew and his family. This abuse began when Andrew was still a young child. For example, at the age of 9, Andrew was caught shoplifting. Walter beat both Andrew and his brother Shawn with a belt or wire hanger, and a plastic piggy bank. The next day, a neighbor noticed welts on Andrew and contacted Child Protective Service (CPS). No action was taken. In approximately the same period, Walter hit Andrew in the mouth with a mop as punishment for improperly wringing it out. A week after Andrew's 10th birthday, in another incident, Walter smashed Andrew's stereo with a sledgehammer.

On several occasions, Walter assaulted Andrew in front of nonfamily members. For instance, testimony by Robin Miller, a family friend, indicated that in 1985 Walter punched Andrew in the face for failing to properly complete a homework assignment. CPS was again called, but no action was taken. Miller saw other similar incidents where Walter "slugged" and "manhandled" Andrew, as well as "roughed him up."

. . . .

In connection with the diminished capacity instruction, the defense presented expert testimony from Dr. Bruce Olson and Dr. Christopher Varley. Dr. Olson is a clinical psychologist who examined Andrew over 10 hours, and spoke with Gale, Shawn, and others. Dr. Olson testified with reasonable medical certainty that Andrew suffered from PTSD. It was Dr. Olson's opinion that Andrew's capacity to premeditate on August 30, 1988, was impaired, but not absent. However, Dr. Olson testified that, in his opinion, at the time of the shooting, Andrew intended to do it. Dr. Olson stated that Andrew was also impaired by the use of alcohol and drugs, but that Andrew took these drugs to get himself "psyched up" to shoot Walter. Dr. Olson testified at length about PTSD and its relation to child abuse, about Andrew's history of abusive treatment, and about the events of August 29 and 30. Dr. Olson's testimony lasted over a day and a half.

. . . .

In rebuttal, the State called Dr. Carl Redick, a psychologist at Western State Hospital. Dr. Redick testified that he evaluated Andrew pursuant to a court order as to his competency, sanity, diminished capacity, and capacity to premeditate. Dr. Redick also spoke to Gale and Shawn and reviewed the case history as well as the reports of the other doctors. He spent 8 to 10 hours with the defendant. Dr. Redick concluded that Andrew suffered from long-term substance abuse, including alcohol, LSD, and marijuana. Dr. Redick further testified that Andrew had the capacity to premeditate on August 30, 1988, and that he did not suffer from PTSD.

In accord with its earlier ruling, the trial court did not give a self-defense instruction. The jury found Andrew not guilty of first degree murder, but found him guilty of second degree murder, and guilty of two counts of second degree assault. The court imposed a reduced exceptional sentence of 120 months confinement on the murder count, and 20 months confinement for each of the assault counts, to be served concurrently. . . .

The Court of Appeals reversed Andrew's second degree murder conviction. It held that the trial court erred in failing to instruct the jury on self-defense. *State v. Janes*, 64 Wn. App. 134, 136, 822 P.2d 1238 (1992). We accepted review.

### Battered Child Syndrome

The first question raised in this case is if expert testimony regarding the "battered child syndrome" is generally admissible in appropriate cases to aid in the proof of self-defense. . . . The admissibility of the battered child syndrome is a question of first impression in Washington.

. . . .

Originally developed as a physical diagnosis for describing child abuse, the "battered child syndrome" has come to describe both the physiological and psychological effects of a prolonged pattern of physical, emotional and sexual abuse. *See generally* Steven R. Hicks, *Admissibility of Expert Testimony on the Psychology of the Battered Child*, 11 L. & Psychol. Rev. 103, 108–11 (1987). Such abuse typically lasts over a significant period of time and tends to operate in recurring patterns.

Victims of chronic abuse suffer from a general psychological disorder known as post-traumatic stress disorder. PTSD is an anxiety-related disorder which occurs in response to traumatic events outside the normal range of human experience. As Dr. Olson testified at trial, child abuse "is an extreme stressor that exceeds a child's capacity to cope with it or integrate it into their personality, their awareness, their consciousness." RP, at 781. Although PTSD is classified as a mental disorder, "it is one of the few kinds of psychiatric disorders that is considered a *normal response* to an *abnormal situation.*" Paul A. Mones, *When a Child Kills: Abused Children Who Kill Their Parents* 63 (1991).

The resulting psychological response to abuse-induced PTSD is often referred to as the "battered child syndrome." One principal characteristic of the syndrome is hypervigilance. . . .

Children who suffer from prolonged abuse develop "a very finely tuned antenna for impending violence [which] . . . picks up low-level cues that people who have not been traumatized would not see." Mones, at 63 (quoting Dr. Lenore Walker). . . .

Although this court has not ruled on the admissibility of the battered child syndrome,[6] we have previously allowed another related syndrome which presents a particularly close parallel to the battered child syndrome. In *State v. Allery*, 101 Wn.2d 591, 682 P.2d 312 (1984), we recognized the battered woman syndrome. Both syndromes find their basis in abuse-induced PTSD and elicit a similar response from the abuse victim. For purposes of the *Frye* test, we can see no reason to treat these two syndromes differently. Given the close relationship between the battered woman and battered child syndromes, the same reasons that justify admission of the former apply with equal force to the latter.

. . . .

We hold, therefore, that as a general matter, evidence of the battered child syndrome is admissible to help prove self-defense whenever such a defense is relevant. The underlying principles of the battered child syndrome are generally accepted in the scientific community and satisfy the ER 702 requirements by helping the trier of fact to understand a little-known psychological problem.

### Self-Defense

The second question before us is, given the history of abuse and other circumstances, was there sufficient evidence that the defendant was in imminent danger of grievous bodily harm so as to warrant a self-defense instruction. The defense relied on expert testimony that Andrew suffered from battered child syndrome. It also pointed to Walter's argument with Gale the night prior to the shooting, Walter's comments to Andrew in a "low voice", and Gale's warning to Andrew on the following morning that Walter was still mad. The trial court ruled, as a matter of law, that a

---

6. [n6] Washington courts have admitted the "battered child syndrome" for purposes of proving a physical pattern of child abuse. *See State v. Toennis*, 52 Wn. App. 176, 758 P.2d 539, *review denied*, 111 Wn.2d 1026 (1988); *State v. Mulder*, 29 Wn. App. 513, 629 P.2d 462 (1981). However, this case is the first in our jurisdiction to address the use of this syndrome for demonstrating the psychological effects of prolonged abuse in a self-defense context.

justifiable homicide instruction was unavailable because the events of the prior night and the morning of the killing were too far removed and lacked sufficient aggressiveness to constitute imminent danger.

. . . .

By learning of the defendant's perceptions and the circumstances surrounding the act, the jury is able to make the "*critical determination* of the 'degree of force which . . . a reasonable person in the same situation . . . seeing what [s]he sees and knowing what [s]he knows, then would believe to be necessary.'" (Italics ours.) *Wanrow*, at 238 (quoting *State v. Dunning*, 8 Wn. App. 340, 342, 506 P.2d 321 (1973)); *see also State v. Hughes*, 106 Wn.2d 176, 189, 721 P.2d 902 (1986); *State v. Theroff*, 95 Wn.2d 385, 390, 622 P.2d 1240 (1980). . . . .

This approach to self-defense provides balance to our jurisprudence. The subjective aspects ensure that the jury fully understands the totality of the defendant's actions from the defendant's own perspective. Such a consideration is especially important in battered person cases. . . . The objective portion of the inquiry serves the crucial function of providing an external standard. Without it, a jury would be forced to evaluate the defendant's actions in the vacuum of the defendant's own subjective perceptions. In essence, self-defense would always justify homicide so long as the defendant was true to his or her own internal beliefs.

. . . .

In evaluating the reasonableness of the defendant's belief in imminent danger, the battered child syndrome is of considerable assistance in helping the jury understand the circumstances surrounding the homicide. . . . Nonetheless, testimony that a defendant suffers from the battered child syndrome, standing alone, does not ensure that the defendant's belief in imminent harm was reasonable. . . .

Applying these concepts to the case before us, we conclude that the trial court's consideration of the motion for a self-defense instruction was incomplete. The trial court denied the requested instruction because it believed that the comments of Walter the night prior to, and the warning of Andrew's mother the morning of, the homicide were not sufficiently aggressive and were too far removed from the homicide to justify a self-defense instruction. However, there is nothing in the record before us which indicates that the trial court considered the defense evidence in light of Andrew's subjective knowledge and perceptions. In the defendant's offer of proof, there was considerable evidence as to the interaction between long-term abuse, self-defense and the battered child syndrome. Also, the trial court may have given undue consideration to the length of time between the alleged threat and the homicide; the justifiable homicide statute requires imminence, not immediacy.

Thus, we are unable to determine if this evidence was properly considered and evaluated by the trial court in denying the proposed instruction. We therefore remand this case to the trial court. On remand, the trial court is to reconsider its ruling denying the self-defense instruction in light of the principles discussed in this opinion. If the trial court determines that some evidence existed to justify a self-defense instruction, then it should order a new trial. Otherwise, Andrew's conviction stands, subject to a continuation of the normal appeals process.

## B. Child Sexual Abuse Accommodation Syndrome

The more complicated and controversial legal question is whether expert testimony on child sexual abuse accommodation syndrome (CSAAS) should be admitted at trial. CSAAS was first identified by Roland Summit in 1983 and was designed to teach clinicians why children may be reluctant to disclose abuse. *See* Roland C. Summit, *Child Abuse Accommodation Syndrome*, 7 CHILD ABUSE & NEGLECT 177 (1983). He contended that child victims of sexual abuse exhibit a set of behaviors that allow them to "accommodate" the abuser as part of their daily life. His model has five components, of which two are preconditions to the occurrence of sexual abuse and the remaining three are sequentially contingent on it. The categories are: (1) secrecy, (2) helplessness, (3) entrapment and accommodation, (4) delayed unconvincing disclosure, and (5) retraction. Later, Summit wrote that he did not intend to imply that CSAAS is present in all abused children or that it should be treated as a scientific instrument that could be used in every case to diagnose abuse. *See* R. Summit, *Abuse of the Child Sexual Abuse Accommodation Syndrome*, J. CHILD SEXUAL ABUSE 1, 153–163 (1992). Summit's model has, in fact, been used as a basis for proposed expert testimony in child abuse cases.

### State v. Chauvin
Louisiana Supreme Court
846 So. 2d 697 (2003)

KNOLL, JUSTICE

This criminal case concerns the admissibility of expert testimony with regard to Post-Traumatic Stress Disorder (PTSD) of a sexually abused victim. After a jury trial, defendant was convicted of two counts of indecent behavior with juveniles. On appeal, his convictions were reversed and the case remanded to the trial court for a new trial..... We granted the State's application for a writ of certiorari to consider the admissibility of this type of expert testimony as substantive evidence bearing on the credibility of the victim's testimony and the question of the accused's guilt or innocence.

On June 20, 1999, A.C., who was fifteen years old, attended a Father's Day gathering at her friend A.L.'s family home. A.L. was fourteen years old. A.C. testified that A.L. was seated using the computer in the living room, and A.C. was standing behind her. A.L.'s parents and A.L.'s aunt were outside. The defendant, who was the fiancé of A.L.'s aunt, was also present at A.L.'s family home. A.C. testified that while she was standing behind A.L., watching A.L. use the computer, the defendant came into the room, knelt next to A.C. on her right side and behind A.L., and touched her behind, put his hand inside her panties and put one of his fingers in her vagina. The defendant then left the room, but returned and repeated these actions. A.C. also testified that the defendant French-kissed her on that same day in the living room, when no one was present. She further testified that at a prior time at A.L.'s house, when passing the defendant in the hallway, the defendant had touched her breasts through her clothing.

Later on Father's Day, A.C. accompanied A.L. and A.L.'s parents to have supper at A.L's grandmother house. A.L.'s aunt and the defendant were also present. A.L. testified that at her grandmother's house, the defendant asked for a good-by hug and kiss. A.L. was surprised when the defendant kissed her by sticking his tongue in her mouth. The defendant was 34 years old at the time of these incidents.

On this same day, after these incidents, A.C. told A.L. what defendant had done to her. A.L. also told A.C. what defendant had done to her. The next day, A.L. told A.C.'s older sister, Mandy, about these incidents. Detective Ashli Richardson of the Houma Police Department testified that these incidents were reported to the police department approximately four days after they occurred. Detective Dawn Gautreaux testified that a report was made to the Terrebonne Sheriff's Office by the victims on July 26, 1999.

At trial, over the objection of the defendant, the State was allowed to introduce the expert testimony of Renee Thompson Ring, a licensed clinical social worker. The State wanted to use Ms. Ring's expert opinion to establish that A.C.'s clinical symptoms were consistent with a sexual abuse victim; in other words, to use her testimony as substantive evidence of sexual abuse. The trial court allowed Ms. Ring to testify as an expert without conducting a *Daubert* hearing to test the reliability of PTSD in the diagnosis of sexual abuse.

Ms. Ring testified before the jury that she saw A.C. as a patient at "The Haven," "a safe place for persons of sexual assault and domestic violence to come in for individual counseling or group counseling...." She treated A.C. clinically for emotional problems. Based upon objective and subjective symptomatology, she diagnosed A.C. with PTSD. Ms. Ring's testimony described PTSD in layman's terms and the symptomatology that she saw that led her to diagnose A.C. as suffering from PTSD. On cross-examination, Ms. Ring was questioned as to whether these same symptoms might be seen in a child that was having problems other than sexual abuse. Ms. Ring responded that one would rule out any other reasons for the disorder and this how one would make a diagnosis. Also, on cross-examination, Ms. Ring acknowledged that the diagnosis was her opinion, and also acknowledged that experts make mistakes.

. . . .

We begin by noting that child sexual abuse cases are not easy to prosecute. Dara Loren Steele, Note, *Expert Testimony: Seeking an Appropriate Admissibility Standard for Behavioral Science in Child Sexual Abuse Prosecutions*, 48 Duke L.J. 933, 938 (1999). Child sexual abuse is difficult to prove because it most often occurs in private, often the perpetrator is a member of the victim's family, and physical evidence of the abuse is rare. *Id.* The problems with prosecuting child sexual abuse cases are increased by the fact that most children fail to report the abuse, and, if they do report, there is often a significant lapse in time between the actual occurrence and the ultimate reporting of the abusive incident by the child. *Id.*, pp. 938–939. Even then, the child may not include details in her revelation and often children recant or alter their allegations of abuse. *Id.*, p. 939.

Expert testimony can assist a trier of fact in understanding the significance of a child-witness's demeanor, inconsistent reports, delayed disclosure, reluctance to testify, and recantation. Veronica Serrato, Note, *Expert Testimony in Child Abuse Prosecutions: A Spectrum of Uses*, 68 B.U. L. Rev. 155, 156 (1988). An expert witness can explain to jurors that a child-witness's seemingly abnormal behavior—delayed reporting, inconsistent statements, and recantation—is in fact normal for children who have been sexually abused and can also dispel inaccurate perceptions held by jurors, allowing them to better assess a child-witness's testimony. *Id.* p. 163. Expert testimony becomes problematic when it infringes upon other interests: for example, when it is unduly prejudicial, when it invades the province of the jury, when it bolsters a child-witness's testimony, or when it leads to a "battle of the experts." *Id.* p. 156. . . .

## Reliability of PTSD

With regard to testimony from mental health professionals, it is important to note the distinction between substantive evidence and evidence designed to rehabilitate witness credibility. 1 John E.B. Myers, *Evidence in Child Abuse and Neglect Cases*, § 5.1, p.412 (3d ed. 1997). Expert testimony in child sexual abuse litigation falls into two categories: (1) expert testimony offered as substantive proof that a child was sexually abused, and (2) expert testimony offered for the more limited purpose of rehabilitating a child's impeached credibility. *Id.*, § 5.12, p.459. Expert testimony offered as substantive evidence takes several forms, including testimony that in the expert's opinion, the child's symptoms are consistent with sexual abuse. *Id.*, § 5.34, p.527. When such testimony is offered by the prosecution, the purpose is to prove that abuse occurred. . . .

In many child sexual abuse prosecutions, prosecutors offer expert PTSD-based testimony that the child complainant's behavior is consistent with being sexually abused. Lisa Askowitz & Michael Graham, *The Reliability of Expert Psychological Testimony in Child Sexual Abuse Prosecutions*, 15 Cardozo L. Rev. 2027, 2046 (1994). Because evidence of PTSD is admissible in other contexts, prosecutors of child sexual abuse cases might attempt to capitalize on PTSD's legacy of admissibility by offering testimony which refers explicitly to PTSD. *Steele*, p. 946. The expert explains the diagnostic category, and then matches the behavioral characteristics of the child with the PTSD criteria. Askowitz, p. 2046. In its true form, testimony based on PTSD suggests only that sexual abuse may be the cause of the child's behavior, but it does not rule out other traumatic causes of the behavior. Id. PTSD assumes the presence of a stressor and then attaches a diagnosis to the child's reactions to it. *Id.* PTSD merely is a therapeutic tool; it is not designed to determine sexual abuse. *Id. See also* Steele, p. 946.

. . . .

Several other state courts have considered the admissibility of expert testimony regarding PTSD in a criminal prosecution for child sexual abuse. Almost every court that has addressed this issue has concluded that PTSD is admissible to explain a victim's behavior that is apparently inconsistent with having been sexually abused if the defense has made it an issue. As to the more difficult issue of whether evidence of PTSD is admissible to prove sexual abuse, the courts are divided. Some jurisdictions allow PTSD testimony to show that the victim was sexually abused. Other jurisdictions forbid PTSD testimony for the purpose of proving that sexual abuse in fact occurred. In addition, some courts recognize that PTSD is founded upon good science, but conclude it will not assist the trier of fact to determine whether sexual abuse occurred because it is a therapeutic method that was not intended to be used as forensic tool. *See State v. Cressey*, 628 A.2d at 699; *State v. Hall*, 412 S.E.2d at 889.

. . . .

We are concerned about the use of PTSD evidence as substantive evidence that sexual abuse has occurred, when such evidence is not limited to explaining "superficially bizarre" reactions common to victims of child sexual abuse but which are uncommon to the experience of jurors. First, the psychiatric procedures used in developing the diagnosis of PTSD are designed for therapeutic purposes and are not reliable as fact-finding tools to determine whether sexual abuse has in fact occurred. *See Hall*, 412 S.E.2d at 889. And secondly, the potential for prejudice looms large because the jury may accord too much weight to expert opinions stating medical conclusions which were drawn from diagnostic methods having limited merit as fact-finding devices. *Id.*

Although PTSD is widely accepted among professionals as an anxiety disorder attributable to some type of trauma, it has not been proven to be a reliable indicator that sexual abuse is the trauma underlying the disorder or that sexual abuse has even occurred. The principal diagnostic criteria for PTSD "includes persistent reexperiencing of the traumatic event . . . persistent avoidance of stimuli associated with the trauma and numbing of general responsiveness. . . ." DSM-IV at 463. The diagnostic criteria for PTSD are thus not intended to provide clinical or forensic tools for determining whether child sexual abuse has occurred but for dealing with the aftermath of severe traumatic events that have occurred in a variety of contexts.

. . . .

In the matter before us, there was no evidence in the record that A.C. or A.L. recanted their allegations. Nor were they young children who were cognitively unable to testify coherently or incapable of providing details. We find Ms. Ring's expert testimony went beyond the limited purpose of explaining the superficially bizarre behavior of a victim of child sexual abuse. We further find Ms. Ring's testimony deprived defendant of a fair trial by imbuing the girls' testimony with an undeserved scientific aura of truth.

For the foregoing reasons, the ruling of the appellate court is affirmed. This case is remanded to the district court for a new trial consistent with the views expressed herein.

## V. Jurors as Experts

### People v. Arnold

Court of Appeals of New York

96 N.Y. 2d 358 (2001)

CHIEF JUDGE KAYE.

. . . .

Defendant was convicted of assault for stabbing his former girlfriend. His defense at trial was that he had acted in self-defense after she had attacked him with a razor blade. During voir dire, defense counsel asked a panel of prospective jurors if anyone was "thinking in the back of your mind maybe this is not the case that I ought to be sitting on because of my own personal background, my own personal experience, my own personal feelings about certain situations." Prospective Juror Number 4, who had a bachelor's degree in sociology and had minored in women's studies, answered, "Yes," stating that she had done "a lot of research" on domestic violence and battered women's syndrome. She added, "I have a problem with that." Defense counsel then asked whether if, in the jury room, "would you be saying, well, I minored in this in college, and I've done all of this research and in effect become another witness in the case, an expert if you will, on that area with the other jurors. Do you think that might be a problem?" The prospective juror answered, "I think so." Counsel then asked whether she would feel more comfortable sitting on another kind of case, such as a bank robbery. She responded, "I think I would."

Later in the voir dire, defense counsel asked the entire panel whether they could follow the law as instructed by the court, and whether they agreed that they would not use this case as a "referendum" on crime, domestic abuse or violence in the streets. Without stating how, the transcript reads, "Prospective jurors indicating yes."

Defense counsel moved to excuse Prospective Juror Number 4 for cause, arguing she had indicated that she could not be fair in this case because of her background in women's studies. Counsel noted she did not give an unequivocal assurance that she could be fair, and added the juror had admitted the possibility that, because of her background, she might become an "unsworn witness in the jury room." The prosecutor opposed the challenge, arguing that although the prospective juror said that she would "feel more comfortable with another kind of case," and that she had "experience with issues concerning conjugal violence and women's studies," she did not say that she "wouldn't be able to listen to the law and would be unfair." The prosecutor contended that the juror "can be advised as to what she can or cannot do."

The trial court denied the challenge for cause, after which defense counsel used a peremptory challenge to excuse Prospective Juror Number 4. During the course of the voir dire, defendant exhausted his peremptory challenges.

A divided Appellate Division reversed. The majority reasoned that once "the prospective juror expressed doubt regarding her ability to be impartial or indicated that she might be an unsworn expert witness in the jury room, it was incumbent upon the court to ascertain that her prior state of mind would not influence her verdict and that she would render an impartial verdict based on the evidence." (272 AD2d 857, 858.) In addition, the majority noted that "the later general acknowledgment by all prospective jurors that they would follow the law" did not establish "the impartiality of the prospective juror in question." Two Justices dissented, arguing that the prospective juror indicated no "predisposition to rule a certain way," and also "indicated that she would base her decision on the evidence alone and that she would follow the law as instructed by the court." (272 AD2d, at 858-859.) A Judge of this Court granted leave, and we affirm.

## Analysis

One of the important rights afforded a criminal defendant under our system of justice is the right to a fair trial before an unbiased fact finder. But ours is a human process, and just as there are no "perfect" trials, there are no "perfect" juries.

While the goal is utter impartiality, each juror inevitably brings to the jury room a lifetime of experience that will necessarily inform her assessment of the witnesses and the evidence. This is a reality we simply cannot deny. Nor would we want a jury devoid of life experience, even if that were possible, because it is precisely such experience that enables a jury to evaluate the credibility of witnesses and the strength of arguments. What we can — and do — ask, however, is that every juror enter the trial with an open mind, that every juror not be prejudiced from the outset against any particular party, and that every juror be willing to decide the case solely on the evidence presented and the law instructed by the Trial Judge.

In order to achieve that goal, Criminal Procedure Law § 270.20(1)(b) provides that a party may challenge a prospective juror for cause if the juror "has a state of mind that is likely to preclude him from rendering an impartial verdict based upon the evidence adduced at trial." Upon such a challenge, a juror who has revealed doubt, because of prior knowledge or opinion, about her ability to serve impartially must be excused unless the juror states unequivocally on the record that she can be fair. While the CPL, unlike the former Code of Criminal Procedure, does not require any particular expurgatory oath or "talismanic" words (*see, People v Johnson,* 94 NY2d 600, 611; *People v Culhane,* 33 NY2d 90, 106), jurors must clearly express that any prior experiences or opinions that reveal the potential for bias will not prevent them from reaching an impartial verdict. If there is any doubt about a prospective juror's impartiality, trial courts should err on the side of excusing the juror, since at worst the court will have "replaced one impartial juror with another" (*People v Culhane, supra,* at 108 n 3).

. . . .

Prospective jurors who make statements that cast serious doubt on their ability to render an impartial verdict, and who have given less-than-unequivocal assurances of impartiality, must be excused (*see, People v Blyden,* 55 NY2d 73, 78; *see also, People v Torpey,* 63 NY2d 361, 367-369). By contrast, where prospective jurors unambiguously state that, despite preexisting opinions that might indicate bias, they will decide the case impartially and based on the evidence, the trial court has discretion to deny the challenge for cause if it determines that the juror's promise to be impartial is credible (*see, People v Williams,* 63 NY2d 882, 884-885).

Here, as the Appellate Division correctly held, the trial court should not have seated Prospective Juror Number 4 without obtaining her unequivocal assurance that she could be fair. In response to defense counsel's questioning, the prospective juror volunteered that she did not think she should be sitting on this case because of her experience. Specifically, she stated that she had studied domestic violence extensively and that she had a "problem." Those statements revealed that, because of her background, the juror herself questioned whether she could be impartial in any domestic violence case. Thus, the juror's own statements cast serious doubt on her ability to serve. Accordingly, the trial court should have granted the challenge for cause unless the juror unequivocally indicated that she could be fair despite her background.

Furthermore, we agree with the Appellate Division that the collective acknowledgment by the entire jury panel that they would follow the Judge's instructions and would not use this case as a "referendum" on crime or domestic violence was insufficient to constitute an unequivocal declaration of impartiality from Prospective Juror Number 4. The group answer by the entire panel did not address her personal attitudes, nor did it force her to confront the crucial question whether she could be fair to this defendant in light of her expressed predisposition. Indeed, nothing less than a personal, unequivocal assurance of impartiality can cure a juror's prior indication that she is predisposed against a particular defendant or particular type of case.

Defendant also contends that further inquiry was required of Prospective Juror Number 4 after she admitted that, because of her knowledge on domestic violence issues, she might, in the jury room, become an unsworn "expert" witness on the subject. This too is a recurring issue and a matter of serious concern. Indeed, even more so than defining "bias," courts have struggled to draw the line between permissible "life" experience and impermissible juror "expertise." . . .

Most recently, in *People v Maragh* (94 NY2d 569), we reversed a conviction and ordered a new trial where two jurors — both nurses — used their professional expertise to calculate the victim's blood loss and reach conclusions about the cause of death, reaching findings that contravened the expert testimony and theories both sides presented at trial. The nurses then shared their findings with the rest of the jury, which used them in its deliberations. While noting that a verdict generally "may not be impeached by probes into the jury's deliberative process," we recognized that a narrow exception exists where there has been a showing of "improper influence" on the jury (*id.,* at 573). . . .

Here, relying on *Maragh*, defendant argues that the trial court was required to conduct further inquiry of Prospective Juror Number 4 after she indicated that, because of her background in women's studies, she might become an unsworn expert witness on the issue of domestic violence.

We readily agree that when the juror concurred with defense counsel's suggestion that she might, in the jury room, become another expert witness in the case, the trial court — to avoid *Maragh*-type problems — should immediately have reminded, and cautioned, her that she was required to decide the case solely on the evidence presented. Trial Judges are strongly encouraged to follow that practice *whenever* a prospective juror indicates a possible motivation to inject non-record facts into the deliberations. The more difficult question is whether at that point the Trial Judge's refusal to allow a challenge for cause based on that ground alone would constitute reversible error. Under the facts before us, we cannot say that it would.

None of the requirements identified in *Maragh* as necessary to create reversible error were met here. The juror obviously did not conduct any "personal specialized assessments" of the evidence outside the common ken of juror experience (*see*, 94 NY2d, at 574) — she was excused on a peremptory challenge by the defense. Even more fundamentally, the record does not demonstrate that Prospective Juror Number 4 could have injected any knowledge outside the common realm of juror experience into the deliberations, or that she stood in a position of expertise comparable to the jurors in *Maragh*. The fact that the juror had studied domestic violence in college did not demonstrate that she had specialized knowledge that would enable her to exert undue influence on her fellow jurors. Indeed, all jurors bring their background, education and "predispositions, of varying intensity, when they enter the jury box" (*People v Williams, supra,* 63 NY2d, at 885). We do not require jurors to check their life experiences at the courtroom door, nor could we. In fact, one of the goals of New York's jury reform was to eliminate all automatic exemptions from service, bringing to the jury room a wide array of individuals with specialized knowledge and training. *Maragh* should not be read as requiring trial courts automatically to excuse them.

What *Maragh* and our other precedents do require, however, is that jurors not engage in experimentation, investigation and calculation that necessarily rely on facts outside the record and beyond the understanding of the average juror. This applies equally if the jury conducts unauthorized experiments at the crime scene, or if an "expert" juror performs "expert" scientific analysis — requiring knowledge of facts beyond those presented at trial — and convinces the other jurors to disregard the trial testimony and instead rely on his expertise. Of course no such thing happened here.

In addition, under *Maragh*, there is no reversible error unless a juror has specialized knowledge "concerning a material issue in the case" (94 NY2d, at 574). Here, while defendant was charged with assaulting his former girlfriend, he points to no material contested issue in the case particular to Prospective Juror Number 4's research. Finally, *Maragh* states that reversible error will occur only where the juror communicates an "expert opinion to the rest of the jury panel with the force of private, untested truth as though it were evidence" (94 NY2d, at 574). Again, since Prospective Juror Number 4 was not seated, she did not communicate any specialized knowledge to the other jurors. On this record, we decline to hold that the trial court's failure to take action, at the voir dire stage, to prevent potential jury misconduct constituted immediate reversible error.

While a finding of reversible error on that ground would be premature here, we caution trial courts to investigate and address potential jury misconduct problems as early as possible. Jurors should be instructed from the outset that they must decide the case based on the evidence presented and that evidence alone. Further, if any juror indicates a willingness to consider facts outside the record, the court should remind the juror what is and is not permissible. Indeed, in *Maragh,* we suggested that trial courts may wish to "modify their standard instructions differentiating between ordinary and professional opinions of jurors, and directing that jurors may not use their professional expertise to insert facts and evidence outside the record with respect to material issues into the deliberation process" (94 NY2d, at 576). We urge trial courts to give such a charge, in order to alleviate the potential for improper activity. In fact, a pattern charge has been devised for use in civil cases (*see,* PJI 1:25A). And, of course, if a juror upon inquiry in voir dire indicates an inability or unwillingness to follow the Judge's instructions, that would provide grounds for a challenge for cause.

In sum, we conclude that the Appellate Division correctly reversed defendant's conviction. After Prospective Juror Number 4 volunteered that she had a predisposition that might prevent her from being impartial in a domestic violence case, the trial court should have granted the challenge for cause unless the juror stated unequivocally that she would be able to render an unbiased decision.

Accordingly, the order of the Appellate Division should be affirmed.

## *Notes and Questions*

- **OTHER EXPERT TESTIMONY ISSUES**

    In *State of New Jersey v. Townsend*, 186 N.J. 473 (2006), in a decision issued more than 20 years after the *Kelly* case, the New Jersey Supreme Court upheld the use of expert testimony by the prosecution on battered women's syndrome to convince the jury that the victim's dying declaration exonerating the defendant was not credible. The expert offered testimony about the general habits of battered women, such as lying to protect their abusers. The court noted, however, that the jury should have been instructed that the testimony was admitted for the limited purpose of assessing the victim's credibility, though it concluded that the failure to give this instruction was harmless error. If protecting a batterer is part of a victim's survival mechanism, what possible reason might she have for doing so with her dying breath?

    The term "rape trauma syndrome" (RTS) is traced to Ann Wolbert Burgess & Lynda Lyttle Holmstrom, *Rape Trauma Syndrome*, 131 AM. J. PSYCHIATRY 981 (1974). One of the earliest appellate cases to discuss the admission of expert testimony on RTS is *People v. Bledsoe*, 36 Cal. 3d 236 (1984), in which the court held that the state improperly admitted expert testimony by a rape counselor who stated that the victim suffered from rape trauma syndrome. The court suggested in *dicta,* however, that such testimony could be admitted to rebut misconceptions about the presumed behavior of rape victims. Courts have allowed the admission of RTS to rebut a defense that the alleged rape was consensual, a common claim raised in marital rape cases, or to explain a victim's actions that might be inconsistent with rape. *See, e.g., State v. Kinney,* 171 Vt. 239 (2000) (RTS testimony admitted where defense claimed sex was consensual); *People v. Taylor,* 75 N.Y.2d 277 (1990) (RTS testimony admitted where victim, who knew her assailant, initially told police she could not identify the perpetrator).

- **RETROACTIVE APPLICATION OF BATTERED WOMEN'S SYNDROME**

Battered women, many of whom were convicted before BWS was accepted in the legal community, have sought to gain release from jail by applying for parole or by filing clemency and *habeas corpus* petitions alleging they were suffering from the syndrome when they committed their crimes. The petitioners rarely prevail.

California amended its Penal Code to provide that a writ of habeas corpus can be filed on the basis that expert testimony relating to intimate partner battering and its effects was not received in evidence at trial, and had it been received, there is a reasonable probability, sufficient to undermine confidence in the judgment of conviction, that the result of the proceedings would have been different. Cal. Pen. Code § 1473.5. The law only covers individuals who were convicted of violent felonies before Aug. 29, 1996, and that resulted in judgments of conviction after a plea or trial as to which expert testimony may be probative on the issue of culpability.

Using the amended statute, Hudie Joyce Walker who was in jail 14 years for the murder of her abusive husband, had her conviction vacated by a California intermediate appellate court and was granted a new trial. *See In re Walker,* 147 Cal. App. 4th 533 (2007). Walker claimed a long history of domestic abuse, and said she killed her husband only after he threatened her with a gun and told her: "This will be your last goddamned day on Earth." Walker waited before she killed him; first fleeing her home and reporting the threat to the local sheriff. After returning to the marital home to retrieve her belongings, she shot her husband. The prosecutor said the killing was premeditated and deliberate; Walker said it followed further threats by her husband. In vacating Walker's conviction, the court ruled that BWS testimony might have led to her acquittal.

Expert testimony also is admissible in civil cases as evidenced by *Soutiere v. Soutiere,* 163 Vt. 265 (1995). The trial court in this divorce action admitted expert testimony to explain why the victim stayed in the abusive marriage, to show the long-term effects of abuse on the plaintiff-victim, and to help the court understand the property distribution issues. Most divorce actions are heard to a court rather than a jury. Is there any reason why an expert should not be permitted to testify at a bench trial?

- McMARTIN PRESCHOOL CASE

The extent to which treatment modalities for sexually abused children were used to conduct a large-scale sex abuse investigation is at the heart of the fiasco surrounding the McMartin Preschool sex abuse trial in Los Angeles early in the 1980s. A parent who was later determined to have been emotionally troubled was concerned about her three-year-old son, a student at McMartin, who she claimed had been anally raped by the school's only male teacher, Ray Buckey. The teacher was arrested, prompting police to send a form letter to the parents of approximately 200 students asking if they knew about other instances of child sex abuse at the school. Needless to say, the parents were distraught; they questioned their children, talked to one another and corrupted any future investigation. Before long, children were recounting outlandish tales of anal penetration, naked foreplay, animal sacrifices and satanic rituals "to the point that police seemed to be dealing with a set of crimes that could not possibly have gone unnoticed by the other teachers at McMartin." RICHARD BECK, WE BELIEVE THE CHILDREN: A MORAL PANIC IN THE 1980s 37 (New York: Public Affairs, 2015). In putting together its case against Buckey, the prosecutor relied in part on interviews conducted by Children's Institute International, a child advocacy organization, in the hope the alleged victims could be interviewed in a therapeutic, as opposed to law enforcement, setting. *Id.* at 41. In his book, Beck is highly critical of the investigation. In his view, the techniques used during the interviews, that were influenced by Summit's writings on CSAAS, were inappropriate for forensic examinations. *Id.* 49-51. A Grand Jury returned a 105-count indictment against five teachers at the pre-school. The McMartin case led to the longest and most expensive trial in American criminal history up to that point; with the case costing Los Angeles County $15 million to prosecute. Buckey spent five years in jail awaiting trial. The first trial, which lasted two years, ended in acquittals on some counts and a jury deadlock on others. A second trial against Buckey ended in a hung jury. *Id.* at 61; David Stout, *Virginia McMartin Dies at 88; Figure in Case on Child Abuse,* N.Y. TIMES, December 19, 1995.

- THE MENENDEZ BROTHERS

One of the most notorious murder trials in which the defendants alleged they suffered a delayed reaction to years of sexual, physical and emotional abuse by their father involved 18-year-old Erik Menendez and his brother, 21-year-old Lyle. They were accused of shooting their parents on August 20, 1989 while they were watching television at their Beverly Hills mansion. The brothers' first trial in 1993 ended in a hung jury; three years later, they were convicted of first-degree murder and sentenced to life in prison without the possibility of parole. Crimesider Staff, *The Menendez Brothers: 25 Years Later,* L.A. TIMES, August 20, 2014; www.cbsnews.com/news/the-menendez-brothers-murdered-their-parents-25-years-ago, accessed September 11, 2016. The brothers' defense at trial was that their Hollywood executive father, Jose, had molested the younger son for a dozen years while their mother, Kitty, did nothing to stop it. The last straw for the sons was when their father bullied Lyle by removing his hairpiece, which led them to plot to end their lifelong torture by killing their parents. The trial in the Van Nuys, California Superior Court gripped the nation; it was one of the early gavel-to-gavel trials covered by the fledgling Court TV station. Spectators lined up outside the courthouse at 4 in the morning to snare seats. Prosecutors—and ultimately the jurors—did not buy the brothers' abuse defense. The District Attorney asserted the brothers were not suffering from PTSD but instead were anxious to get their hands on their parents' $14 million estate so they ended their lives prematurely. Immediately after their parents' funeral, the Menendez brothers went on a luxury buying spree. Dominick Dunne, *Courtroom Notebook: The Menendez Murder Trial*, Vanity Fair, October 1993, www.vanityfair.com/magazine/1993/10/dunne199310, accessed September 11, 2016.

# Chapter 6

# The Violence Against Women Act—Fighting Domestic Violence on a Federal Level

> **CONSIDER AS YOU READ FIGHTING DOMESTIC VIOLENCE ON A FEDERAL LEVEL**
>
> 1. The history behind the Violence Against Women Act
> 2. The Supreme Court's rejection of the civil remedies provision of VAWA
> 3. The new federal crimes of domestic violence under VAWA
> 4. The ability of the government to regulate gun ownership by domestic violence perpetrators

During the holiday season of 1990, former Vice President Joseph R. Biden, Jr., then a senator and chairman of the Judiciary Committee, met with reporters to discuss the Violence Against Women Act, which he had introduced earlier that year. Although Christmas is a time of peace and good will, for victims of domestic violence, it is just another dangerous day at home. As the senator said: "During this holiday season, in the six weeks between Thanksgiving and New Year's, about 450,000 women will be violently abused in their homes . . . most tragically, every week between now and Christmas, about 30 women will be killed by their spouses."[1]

After nearly five years of legislative hearings around the country in which battered women, domestic violence advocates, and members of law enforcement testified, the bill passed in the summer of 1994 and was signed into law by President Clinton on September 13, 1994 as part of the Violent Crime Control and Law Enforcement Act. Re-authorized in 2000 and again in 2005, it has revolutionized the way domestic

---

1. *Domestic Violence Is Target of Bill*, N.Y. Times, Dec. 16, 1990.

violence is addressed in the United States.² The latest version was signed into law by President Obama on March 7, 2013.³

The Act created federal criminal laws against domestic violence and stalking. It made it a federal crime to use firearms in domestic violence incidents and barred persons convicted of misdemeanor domestic assaults from having access to guns. It provided for out-of-state recognition and enforcement of orders of protection issued by sister-state courts. It required local jurisdictions to implement mandatory arrest policies to be eligible for federal funds for domestic violence programs. It established civil remedies allowing victims to sue their batterers for damages; and established a pool of federal funds to support state and local programs against sexual assault and domestic abuse. Although the civil penalties provision was struck down by the U.S. Supreme Court in 2000, the criminal sanctions and restrictions on firearms remain useful tools in the arsenals of prosecutors and victims in their fight against domestic violence.

The Act also changed immigration laws so many foreign battered women could leave their abusive husbands without having to fear immediate deportation. It created the federal Office on Violence Against Women, responsible for disbursing the money to domestic violence organizations and for coordinating legal and policy positions on domestic violence.⁴

## I. Setting the Stage for VAWA

During hearings on VAWA, Sen. Biden, after reviewing dismal statistics on injuries to women and the lack of effective state law enforcement responses, said: "Something is seriously wrong."⁵ In session after session, at the Capitol and around the country, legislators were inundated with true-life horror stories about domestic violence. At a hearing in Salt Lake City, Terri Orr, domestic violence survivor and editor of *The Park Record*, a Park City, Utah newspaper, described her pain after an attack by an intimate partner as, "a throbbing kind of hurt you feel when you try to pat makeup on an eye that is blackened and swollen. It is a sharp hurt, like when you breathe in too quickly and feel the spot on your rib cage where you were hit."⁶ In Washington, D.C., law

---

2. *Ten Years of Extraordinary Progress: The Violence Against Women Act: S. Subcomm. On Crime, Corrections, and Victims' Rights* at 4 (Sept. 2004) (Report of Sen. Joseph R. Biden, Jr.) [hereinafter *Biden Report*].

3. Violence Against Women Act (VAWA) Reauthorization 2013, www.justice.gov/tribal/violence-against-women-act-vawa-reauthorization-2013-0, accessed February 23, 2016.

4. *Biden Report, supra*, at 27.

5. *Violence Against Women: Hearing before the H. Subcomm. on Crime and Criminal Justice*, 102nd Cong. 8 (1992) (statement of Sen. Biden, Feb. 6, 1992) [hereinafter *Violence Against Women Hearing*].

6. *Violent Crimes Against Women: Hearing before the Sen. Judiciary Comm.*, 103rd Cong. 6 (1993) (statement of Terri Orr, Apr. 19, 1993, Salt Lake City, UT).

professor and domestic violence survivor Sarah Buel said, "Women are taught about street violence but no one said to me, 'You need to be careful about who you marry.'"[7] At the same hearing, Charlotte Fedders, a nurse and ex-wife of John M. Fedders, the former chief of enforcement for the Securities and Exchange Commission, told of years of verbal abuse from her husband that battered her self-esteem and paved the way for escalating physical violence.[8]

The need for federal legislation to stop the problem was crucial because of discrepancies in how domestic violence was handled by state and local law enforcement. In jurisdictions without mandatory arrest policies, the accountability for batterers, as measured by arrests, was shockingly low. In 1986 in Washington D.C., there were 19,000 calls to police alleging domestic violence offenses and only 42 arrests.[9]

Nonetheless, the call for federal legislation was not universal. Then Chief Justice William H. Rehnquist spoke on behalf of the Judicial Conference, the policy-making body of the federal courts, in opposing it. "Although supporting the underlying objective ... to deter violence against women ... [t]he broad definition of criminal conduct is so open-ended, and the new private right of action so sweeping, that the legislation could involve the federal courts in a whole host of domestic relations disputes." The Conference of Chief Justices, which is composed of the chief justices of the state courts, also opposed it.[10] Sen. Robert Dole, Republican of Kansas, derided it as part of the Democrats' "excessive social spending."[11]

## II. Violence Against Women Act Becomes Law

The Violence Against Women Act was first signed into law on September 13, 1994.[12] Several months after signing it President Clinton said:

> [D]omestic violence is now the number one health risk for women between the ages of 15 and 44 in our country. If you think about it, it's a bigger threat than cancer or car accidents.... The FBI estimates that a woman is beaten

---

7. *Domestic Violence Is Target of Bill*, N.Y. TIMES.

8. *Id.*

9. *Violence Against Women Hearing, supra,* at 98 (statement of Sandra Jean Sands, Office of the Gen. Counsel, Dep't of Health & Human Services and past-president of the DC Coalition Against Domestic Violence).

10. Chief Justice William H. Rehnquist, 1991 YEAR-END REPORT ON THE FEDERAL JUDICIARY 5 (1992). The Judicial Conference eventually backed away from that position. Justice Rehnquist did not. Six years *after* VAWA was signed into law, Justice Rehnquist voted with the majority to overturn a substantial portion of the Act. *See* Judith Resnik & Theodore Ruger, *One Robe, Two Hats,* N.Y. TIMES, July 17, 2005, at 13.

11. Resnick & Ruger, *id.*

12. The Violence Against Women Act of 1994, Pub. L. No. 103-322, 108 Stat. 1902-55 (codified as amended at 18 U.S.C., 28 U.S.C., and 42 U.S.C.).

in this country once every 12 seconds. And we know, too, that often when a spouse is beaten, the children are beaten as well. For too long, domestic violence has been considered purely a private matter. From now on, it is a problem we all share. . . .[13]

## A. The *Morrison* Decision

Aspects of the 1994 law were quickly challenged in the federal courts, but no provision caused as much controversy as the one permitting a private right of civil action in the federal courts by victims against their sexual or domestic abusers. That section of the law was considered landmark because of the new way it defined domestic violence and sexual assault against women.

Defendants who were sued for damages asserted that Congress exceeded the limits of the Commerce Clause in enacting the private remedies provision of VAWA. Prior to the case coming to the Supreme Court, the majority of the federal trial courts upheld the constitutionality of the civil remedies provision. *See, e.g., Kuhn v. Kuhn,* 1999 U.S. Dist. LEXIS 11010 (N.D. Ill.). But, in an *en banc* decision in 1999, *Brzonkala v. Virginia Polytechnic Inst.,* 169 F.3d 820 (4th Cir. 1999), the court ruled against the plaintiff. A petition for a writ of certiorari was brought to the United States Supreme Court. In a 5-to-4 decision, the Supreme Court struck down the most widely touted and novel aspect of VAWA. The case had been closely watched by Congress, the White House, state officials, the media and women's groups. The Clinton Administration entered the case on behalf of the petitioner, a young woman who had been the victim of a campus rape. Thirty-six states and Puerto Rico filed briefs in support of her.

### United States v. Morrison
United States Supreme Court
529 U.S. 598 (2000)

Chief Justice Rehnquist delivered the opinion of the Court.

In these cases we consider the constitutionality of 42 U.S.C. § 13981, which provides a federal civil remedy for the victims of gender-motivated violence. The United States Court of Appeals for the Fourth Circuit, sitting en banc, struck down § 13981 because it concluded that Congress lacked constitutional authority to enact the section's civil remedy. Believing that these cases are controlled by our decisions in *United States v. Lopez,* 514 U.S. 549, 131 L. Ed. 2d 626, 115 S. Ct. 1624 (1995), *United States v. Harris,* 106 U.S. 629, 27 L. Ed. 290, 1 S. Ct. 601 (1883), and the *Civil Rights Cases,* 109 U.S. 3, 27 L. Ed. 835, 3 S. Ct. 18 (1883), we affirm.

---

13. Press Release, The White House, Office of the Press Secretary, Remarks by the President at Violence Against Women Act Event (March 21, 1995).

## I

Petitioner Christy Brzonkala enrolled at Virginia Polytechnic Institute (Virginia Tech) in the fall of 1994. In September of that year, Brzonkala met respondents Antonio Morrison and James Crawford, who were both students at Virginia Tech and members of its varsity football team. Brzonkala alleges that, within 30 minutes of meeting Morrison and Crawford, they assaulted and repeatedly raped her. After the attack, Morrison allegedly told Brzonkala, "You better not have any . . . diseases." Complaint P22. In the months following the rape, Morrison also allegedly announced in the dormitory's dining room that he "liked" to get girls drunk and . . . ." *Id.*, P31. The omitted portions, quoted verbatim in the briefs on file with this Court, consist of boasting, debased remarks about what Morrison would do to women, vulgar remarks that cannot fail to shock and offend. . . .

In early 1995, Brzonkala filed a complaint against respondents under Virginia Tech's Sexual Assault Policy. During the school-conducted hearing on her complaint, Morrison admitted having sexual contact with her despite the fact that she had twice told him "no." After the hearing, Virginia Tech's Judicial Committee found insufficient evidence to punish Crawford, but found Morrison guilty of sexual assault and sentenced him to immediate suspension for two semesters.

Virginia Tech's dean of students upheld the judicial committee's sentence. However, in July 1995, Virginia Tech informed Brzonkala that Morrison intended to initiate a court challenge to his conviction under the Sexual Assault Policy. University officials told her that a second hearing would be necessary to remedy the school's error in prosecuting her complaint under that policy, which had not been widely circulated to students. The university therefore conducted a second hearing under its Abusive Conduct Policy, which was in force prior to the dissemination of the Sexual Assault Policy. Following this second hearing the Judicial Committee again found Morrison guilty and sentenced him to an identical 2-semester suspension. This time, however, the description of Morrison's offense was, without explanation, changed from "sexual assault" to "using abusive language."

Morrison appealed his second conviction through the university's administrative system. On August 21, 1995, Virginia Tech's senior vice president and provost set aside Morrison's punishment. She concluded that it was "'excessive when compared with other cases where there has been a finding of violation of the Abusive Conduct Policy,'" 132 F.3d 949, 955 (CA4 1997). Virginia Tech did not inform Brzonkala of this decision. After learning from a newspaper that Morrison would be returning to Virginia Tech for the fall 1995 semester, she dropped out of the university.

In December 1995, Brzonkala sued Morrison, Crawford, and Virginia Tech in the United States District Court for the Western District of Virginia. Her complaint alleged that Morrison's and Crawford's attack violated § 13981 and that Virginia Tech's handling of her complaint violated Title IX of the Education Amendments of 1972, 86 Stat. 373-375, 20 U.S.C. §§ 1681-1688. Morrison and Crawford moved to dismiss this complaint on the grounds that it failed to state a claim and that § 13981's civil remedy is unconstitutional. The United States, petitioner in No. 99-5, intervened to defend § 13981's constitutionality.

The District Court dismissed Brzonkala's Title IX claims against Virginia Tech for failure to state a claim upon which relief can be granted. See *Brzonkala v. Virginia Polytechnic and State Univ.*, 935 F. Supp. 772 (WD Va. 1996). It then held that Brzonkala's complaint stated a claim against Morrison and Crawford under § 13981, but dismissed the complaint because it concluded that Congress lacked authority to enact the section under either the Commerce Clause or § 5 of the Fourteenth Amendment. *Brzonkala v. Virginia Polytechnic and State Univ.*, 935 F. Supp. 779 (WD Va. 1996).

A divided panel of the Court of Appeals reversed the District Court, reinstating Brzonkala's § 13981 claim and her Title IX hostile environment claim. *Brzonkala v. Virginia Polytechnic and State Univ.*, 132 F.3d 949 (CA4 1997). The full Court of Appeals vacated the panel's opinion and reheard the case en banc. The en banc court then issued an opinion affirming the District Court's conclusion that Brzonkala stated a claim under § 13981 because her complaint alleged a crime of violence and the allegations of Morrison's crude and derogatory statements regarding his treatment of women sufficiently indicated that his crime was motivated by gender animus. Nevertheless, the court by a divided vote affirmed the District Court's conclusion that Congress lacked constitutional authority to enact § 13981's civil remedy. *Brzonkala v. Virginia Polytechnic and State Univ.*, 169 F.3d 820 (CA4 1999). Because the Court of Appeals invalidated a federal statute on constitutional grounds, we granted certiorari. 527 U.S. 1068 (1999).

Section 13981 was part of the Violence Against Women Act of 1994, § 40302, 108 Stat. 1941-1942. It states that "persons within the United States shall have the right to be free from crimes of violence motivated by gender." 42 U.S.C. § 13981(b). To enforce that right, subsection (c) declares:

> "A person (including a person who acts under color of any statute, ordinance, regulation, custom, or usage of any State) who commits a crime of violence motivated by gender and thus deprives another of the right declared in subsection (b) of this section shall be liable to the party injured, in an action for the recovery of compensatory and punitive damages, injunctive and declaratory relief, and such other relief as a court may deem appropriate."

. . . .

## II

. . . As we observed in *Lopez*, modern Commerce Clause jurisprudence has "identified three broad categories of activity that Congress may regulate under its commerce power." 514 U.S. at 558 (citing *Hodel v. Virginia Surface Mining & Reclamation Assn., Inc.*, 452 U.S. 264, 276-277, 69 L. Ed. 2d 1, 101 S. Ct. 2352 (1981); *Perez v. United States*, 402 U.S. 146, 150, 28 L. Ed. 2d 686, 91 S. Ct. 1357 (1971)). "First, Congress may regulate the use of the channels of interstate commerce." 514 U.S. at 558 (citing *Heart of Atlanta Motel, Inc. v. United States*, 379 U.S. 241, 256, 85 S. Ct. 348, 13 L. Ed. 2d 258

(1964); *United States v. Darby*, 312 U.S. 100, 114, 85 L. Ed. 609, 61 S. Ct. 451 (1941)). "Second, Congress is empowered to regulate and protect the instrumentalities of interstate commerce, or persons or things in interstate commerce, even though the threat may come only from intrastate activities." 514 U.S. at 558 (citing *Shreveport Rate Cases*, 234 U.S. 342 (1914); *Southern R. Co. v. United States*, 222 U.S. 20, 32 S. Ct. 2, 56 L. Ed. 72 (1911); *Perez, supra*, at 150). "Finally, Congress' commerce authority includes the power to regulate those activities having a substantial relation to interstate commerce,... *i.e.*, those activities that substantially affect interstate commerce." 514 U.S. at 558-559 (citing *Jones & Laughlin Steel, supra*, at 37)....

Since *Lopez* most recently canvassed and clarified our case law governing this third category of Commerce Clause regulation, it provides the proper framework for conducting the required analysis of § 13981. In *Lopez*, we held that the Gun-Free School Zones Act of 1990, 18 U.S.C. § 922(q)(1)(A), which made it a federal crime to knowingly possess a firearm in a school zone, exceeded Congress' authority under the Commerce Clause. See 514 U.S. at 551. Several significant considerations contributed to our decision.

First, we observed that § 922(q) was "a criminal statute that by its terms has nothing to do with 'commerce' or any sort of economic enterprise, however broadly one might define those terms." 514 U.S. at 561....

The second consideration that we found important in analyzing § 922(q) was that the statute contained "no express jurisdictional element which might limit its reach to a discrete set of firearm possessions that additionally have an explicit connection with or effect on interstate commerce." *Id.*, at 562. Such a jurisdictional element may establish that the enactment is in pursuance of Congress' regulation of interstate commerce.

Third, we noted that neither § 922(q) "'nor its legislative history contains express congressional findings regarding the effects upon interstate commerce of gun possession in a school zone.'" *Ibid.* (quoting Brief for United States, O.T. 1994, No. 93–1260, pp. 5-6)....

Finally, our decision in *Lopez* rested in part on the fact that the link between gun possession and a substantial effect on interstate commerce was attenuated. *Id.*, at 563-567....

Like the Gun-Free School Zones Act at issue in *Lopez*, § 13981 contains no jurisdictional element establishing that the federal cause of action is in pursuance of Congress' power to regulate interstate commerce. Although *Lopez* makes clear that such a jurisdictional element would lend support to the argument that § 13981 is sufficiently tied to interstate commerce, Congress elected to cast § 13981's remedy over a wider, and more purely intrastate, body of violent crime.

In contrast with the lack of congressional findings that we faced in *Lopez*, § 13981 *is* supported by numerous findings regarding the serious impact that gender-motivated violence has on victims and their families. See, *e.g.*, H. R. Conf. Rep. No. 103-711, p. 385

(1994); S. Rep. No. 103-138, p. 40 (1993); S. Rep. No. 101-545, p. 33 (1990). But the existence of congressional findings is not sufficient, by itself, to sustain the constitutionality of Commerce Clause legislation. As we stated in *Lopez*, "'Simply because Congress may conclude that a particular activity substantially affects interstate commerce does not necessarily make it so.'" 514 U.S. at 557, n. 2 (quoting *Hodel*, 452 U.S. at 311 (REHNQUIST, J., concurring in judgment))....

We accordingly reject the argument that Congress may regulate noneconomic, violent criminal conduct based solely on that conduct's aggregate effect on interstate commerce. The Constitution requires a distinction between what is truly national and what is truly local. *Lopez*, 514 U.S. at 568 (citing *Jones & Laughlin Steel*, 301 U.S. at 30)....

### III

Because we conclude that the Commerce Clause does not provide Congress with authority to enact § 13981, we address petitioners' alternative argument that the section's civil remedy should be upheld as an exercise of Congress' remedial power under § 5 of the Fourteenth Amendment. As noted above, Congress expressly invoked the Fourteenth Amendment as a source of authority to enact § 13981.

. . . .

Shortly after the Fourteenth Amendment was adopted, we decided two cases interpreting the Amendment's provisions, *United States v. Harris*, 106 U.S. 629, 27 L. Ed. 290, 1 S. Ct. 601 (1883), and the *Civil Rights Cases*, 109 U.S. 3, 27 L. Ed. 835, 3 S. Ct. 18 (1883). In *Harris*, the Court considered a challenge to § 2 of the Civil Rights Act of 1871. That section sought to punish "private persons" for "conspiring to deprive any one of the equal protection of the laws enacted by the State." 106 U.S. at 639. We concluded that this law exceeded Congress' § 5 power because the law was "directed exclusively against the action of private persons, without reference to the laws of the State, or their administration by her officers." 106 U.S. at 640....

We reached a similar conclusion in the *Civil Rights Cases*. In those consolidated cases, we held that the public accommodation provisions of the Civil Rights Act of 1875, which applied to purely private conduct, were beyond the scope of the § 5 enforcement power. 109 U.S. at 11....

Petitioners alternatively argue that, unlike the situation in the *Civil Rights Cases*, here there has been gender-based disparate treatment by state authorities, whereas in those cases there was no indication of such state action. There is abundant evidence, however, to show that the Congresses that enacted the Civil Rights Acts of 1871 and 1875 had a purpose similar to that of Congress in enacting § 13981: There were state laws on the books bespeaking equality of treatment, but in the administration of these laws there was discrimination against newly freed slaves....

But even if that distinction were valid, we do not believe it would save § 13981's civil remedy. For the remedy is simply not "corrective in its character, adapted to counteract and redress the operation of such prohibited state laws or proceedings of state officers." *Civil Rights Cases*, 109 U.S. at 18. Or, as we have phrased it in more recent cases, prophylactic legislation under §5 must have a "'congruence and proportionality between the injury to be prevented or remedied and the means adopted to that end." *Florida Prepaid Postsecondary Ed. Expense Bd. v. College Savings Bank*, 527 U.S. 627, 639, 144 L. Ed. 2d 575, 119 S. Ct. 2199 (1999); *Flores*, 521 U.S. at 526. Section 13981 is not aimed at proscribing discrimination by officials which the Fourteenth Amendment might not itself proscribe; it is directed not at any State or state actor, but at individuals who have committed criminal acts motivated by gender bias. . . .

For these reasons, we conclude that Congress' power under §5 does not extend to the enactment of §13981.

IV

Petitioner Brzonkala's complaint alleges that she was the victim of a brutal assault. But Congress' effort in §13981 to provide a federal civil remedy can be sustained neither under the Commerce Clause nor under §5 of the Fourteenth Amendment. If the allegations here are true, no civilized system of justice could fail to provide her a remedy for the conduct of respondent Morrison. But under our federal system that remedy must be provided by the Commonwealth of Virginia, and not by the United States. The judgment of the Court of Appeals is

*Affirmed.*

. . . .

JUSTICE SOUTER, with whom JUSTICE STEVENS, JUSTICE GINSBURG, and JUSTICE BREYER join, dissenting.

The Court says both that it leaves Commerce Clause precedent undisturbed and that the Civil Rights Remedy of the Violence Against Women Act of 1994, 42 U.S.C. §13981, exceeds Congress's power under that Clause. I find the claims irreconcilable and respectfully dissent.

. . . .

One obvious difference from *United States v. Lopez*, 514 U.S. 549, 131 L. Ed. 2d 626, 115 S. Ct. 1624 (1995), is the mountain of data assembled by Congress, here showing the effects of violence against women on interstate commerce. Passage of the Act in 1994 was preceded by four years of hearings, which included testimony from physicians and law professors; from survivors of rape and domestic violence; and from representatives of state law enforcement and private business. The record includes reports on gender bias from task forces in 21 States, and we have the benefit of specific factual findings in the eight separate Reports issued by Congress and its committees over the long course leading to enactment. . . .

With respect to domestic violence, Congress received evidence for the following findings:

"Three out of four American women will be victims of violent crimes sometime during their life." H. R. Rep. No. 103-395 p. 25 (1993) (citing U.S. Dept. of Justice, Report to the Nation on Crime and Justice 29 (2d ed. 1988)).

"Violence is the leading cause of injuries to women ages 15 to 44 . . . ." S. Rep. No. 103-138, p. 38 (1993) (citing Surgeon General Antonia Novello, From the Surgeon General, U.S. Public Health Services, 267 JAMA 3132 (1992)).

"As many as 50 percent of homeless women and children are fleeing domestic violence." S. Rep. No. 101-545, p. 37 (1990) (citing E. Schneider, Legal Reform Efforts for Battered Women: Past, Present, and Future (July 1990)).

"Since 1974, the assault rate against women has outstripped the rate for men by at least twice for some age groups and far more for others." S. Rep. No. 101-545, at 30 (citing Bureau of Justice Statistics, Criminal Victimization in the United States (1974) (Table 5)).

"Battering 'is the single largest cause of injury to women in the United States.'" S. Rep. No. 101-545, at 37 (quoting Van Hightower & McManus, Limits of State Constitutional Guarantees: Lessons from Efforts to Implement Domestic Violence Policies, 49 Pub. Admin. Rev. 269 (May/June 1989).

"An estimated 4 million American women are battered each year by their husbands or partners." H. R. Rep. No. 103-395, at 26 (citing Council on Scientific Affairs, American Medical Assn., Violence Against Women: Relevance for Medical Practitioners, 267 JAMA 3184, 3185 (1992).

"Over 1 million women in the United States seek medical assistance each year for injuries sustained [from] their husbands or other partners." S. Rep. No. 101-545, at 37 (citing Stark & Flitcraft, Medical Therapy as Repression: The Case of the Battered Woman, Health & Medicine (Summer/Fall 1982).

"Between 2,000 and 4,000 women die every year from [domestic] abuse." S. Rep. No. 101-545, at 36 (citing Schneider, *supra*).

"Arrest rates may be as low as 1 for every 100 domestic assaults." S. Rep. No. 101-545, at 38 (citing Dutton, Profiling of Wife Assaulters: Preliminary Evidence for Trimodal Analysis, 3 Violence and Victims 5-30 (1988)).

"Partial estimates show that violent crime against women costs this country at least 3 billion—not million, but billion—dollars a year." S. Rep. No. 101-545, at 33 (citing Schneider, *supra,* at 4).

"Estimates suggest that we spend $5 to $10 billion a year on health care, criminal justice, and other social costs of domestic violence." S. Rep. No. 103-138, at 41 (citing Biden, Domestic Violence: A Crime, Not a Quarrel, Trial 56 (June 1993)). . . .

Based on the data thus partially summarized, Congress found that

"crimes of violence motivated by gender have a substantial adverse effect on interstate commerce, by deterring potential victims from traveling interstate, from engaging in employment in interstate business, and from transacting with business, and in places involved, in interstate commerce . . . [,] by diminishing national productivity, increasing medical and other costs, and decreasing the supply of and the demand for interstate products . . . ." H.R. Conf. Rep. No. 103-711, p. 385 (1994). . . .

Indeed, the legislative record here is far more voluminous than the record compiled by Congress and found sufficient in two prior cases upholding Title II of the Civil Rights Act of 1964 against Commerce Clause challenges. In *Heart of Atlanta Motel, Inc. v. United States,* 379 U.S. 241, 13 L. Ed. 2d 258, 85 S. Ct. 348 (1964), and *Katzenbach v. McClung,* 379 U.S. 294, 13 L. Ed. 2d 290, 85 S. Ct. 377 (1964), the Court referred to evidence showing the consequences of racial discrimination by motels and restaurants on interstate commerce. Congress had relied on compelling anecdotal reports that individual instances of segregation cost thousands to millions of dollars. See Civil Rights—Public Accommodations, Hearings on S. 1732 before the Senate Committee on Commerce, 88th Cong., 1st Sess., App. V, pp. 1383–1387 (1963). . . .

II

The Act would have passed muster at any time between *Wickard* in 1942 and *Lopez* in 1995, a period in which the law enjoyed a stable understanding that congressional power under the Commerce Clause, complemented by the authority of the Necessary and Proper Clause, Art. I. § 8 cl. 18, extended to all activity that, when aggregated, has a substantial effect on interstate commerce. As already noted, this understanding was secure even against the turmoil at the passage of the Civil Rights Act of 1964, in the aftermath of which the Court not only reaffirmed the cumulative effects and rational basis features of the substantial effects test, see *Heart of Atlanta, supra,* at 258; *McClung, supra,* at 301-305, but declined to limit the commerce power through a formal distinction between legislation focused on "commerce" and statutes addressing "moral and social wrongs," *Heart of Atlanta, supra,* at 257.

The fact that the Act does not pass muster before the Court today is therefore proof, to a degree that *Lopez* was not, that the Court's nominal adherence to the substantial effects test is merely that. Although a new jurisprudence has not emerged with any distinctness, it is clear that some congressional conclusions about obviously substantial, cumulative effects on commerce are being assigned lesser values than the once-stable doctrine would assign them. These devaluations are accomplished not by any express repudiation of the substantial effects test or its application through the aggregation of individual conduct, but by supplanting rational basis scrutiny with a new criterion of review. . . .

## B. After *Morrison*—What Remains

Following the Supreme Court's decision in *Morrison,* there was an unsuccessful effort in Congress to amend a VAWA authorization bill to reinstate the civil remedies provision provided there was a proven nexus to interstate commerce. In addition, several states in response to the decision enacted mini-VAWAs allowing for civil causes of action to be brought in state courts.[14]

New York City in 2000 was the first jurisdiction to enact its own civil remedies provision for victims of gender violence after *Morrison*. California followed in 2002 and Illinois in 2004.[15]

Other VAWA provisions have been routinely upheld by the federal courts. Congress enacted these provisions, not based on its ability to regulate those activities having a "substantial relation" to interstate commerce, but pursuant to its power to regulate the use of the channels of interstate commerce — the first *Lopez* category.

The federal criminal statutes that apply to crimes of domestic violence that remain untouched by *Morrison* include, 18 U.S.C. § 2261 (interstate domestic violence, making it a crime to cross state lines or Indian country with the intent to kill or injure an intimate partner; to cause an intimate partner to cross state lines by force or duress or fraud); 18 U.S.C. § 2261A (stalking, making it a crime to cross state lines to kill, injure or harass or place another under surveillance and in the course of so doing place that person or his or her immediate family member or intimate partner in reasonable fear of death or injury or cause or attempt to cause emotional distress); 18 U.S.C. § 2262 (interstate violation of a protection order) and 18 U.S.C. § 2265 (full faith and credit given to state orders of protection provided they were issued with certain due process guarantees). To facilitate 18 U.S.C. § 2265, the FBI and state criminal justice agencies manage the National Crime Information Center — Protection Order File, (NCIC-POF), which is accessible by law enforcement and court staffs and includes a record of all orders of protection issued by courts around the country. The National Instant Criminal Background Check (NICS) also has access to the registry so it can be searched prior to selling any guns at licensed federal gun dealers.[16]

## United States v. Larsen
### 615 F.3d 780 (7th Cir. 2010)

SYKES, *Circuit Judge*.

David Larsen brutally beat Teri Jendusa-Nicolai, his ex-wife, at his home in Wisconsin. He then bound her with duct tape, stuffed her in a garbage can filled with snow, put the can in the back of his truck, and drove to a self-storage facility in Illinois. He left her there — still bound and in the snow-filled garbage can — in an unheated rented storage locker. She was discovered the next day, about an hour from death.

---

14. *See* Julie Goldscheid, *The Second Circuit Addresses Gender Based Violence: A Review of Violence Against Women Act Cases,* 66 BROOK. L. REV. 457, 461 nn.26, 27 (2000).

15. Edward S. Synder & Laura W. Morgan, *Domestic Violence Ten Years Later,* ABA SEC. FAM. L., 1(4) LAW TRENDS & NEWS 7 (2005).

16. National Network to End Domestic Violence, *Protection Order Registries and Databases,* nnedv.org/downloads/SafetyNet/OVW/NNEDV_ProtectionOrder_tipsheet_2011.pdf, accessed November 13, 2016.

Larsen was charged with state and federal crimes; the state charges were resolved first. *See State of Wisconsin v. Larsen*, 2007 WI App 147, 302 Wis. 2d 718 736 N.W.2d 211. Thereafter in federal court, Larsen waived his right to a jury and after a trial to the court was convicted of two counts: kidnapping in violation of 18 U.S.C. § 1201(a)(1), and interstate domestic violence in violation of 18 U.S.C. § 2261(a)(2) and (b)(2) (the Interstate Domestic Violence Act). The district judge sentenced him to life in prison, which exceeded the recommended sentencing-guidelines range.

Larsen challenges both his convictions and his sentence. His first claim on appeal is a Commerce Clause challenge to the Interstate Domestic Violence Act; he contends that the Act unconstitutionally federalizes purely local violent crime with an insufficient nexus to interstate commerce. He next argues that his convictions for kidnapping and interstate domestic violence are multiplicitous in violation of the Double Jeopardy Clause....

We reject these arguments and affirm. The Interstate Domestic Violence Act punishes those who use "force, coercion, duress, or fraud" to cause a domestic partner to travel in interstate commerce and who commit a violent crime against the victim "in the course of, as a result of, or to facilitate" that interstate travel. 18 U.S.C. § 2261(a)(2). This statute lies well within the scope of Congress's power to regulate the channels or instrumentalities of, or persons in, interstate commerce. We further conclude that Larsen's convictions are not multiplicitous; the crimes of kidnapping and interstate domestic violence contain different elements, and each requires proof of a fact that the other does not.... Finally, Larsen's life sentence was not unreasonable, either on its own terms or because the judge's decision to impose it was based primarily on Jendusa-Nicolai's miscarriage.

### I. Background

On January 31, 2004, David Larsen brutally attacked Teri Jendusa-Nicolai, his ex-wife, when she came to his home in Racine County, Wisconsin, to pick up their two young daughters. The couple had divorced three years earlier after an abusive marriage, and Jendusa-Nicolai had recently taken Larsen to court for nonpayment of child support. Larsen lured her into his home and began to beat her with a baseball bat, strangle, and smother her. When she did not succumb, he bound her head, ankles, and wrists with duct tape and placed her in a garbage can filled with snow. He then put the garbage can, with Jendusa-Nicolai inside, in the back of his pick-up truck and drove to a self-storage facility in Illinois where he had a rented storage locker. He left her there to die, in a cold storage locker, in the snow-filled garbage can with boxes wedged around it to prevent her from climbing out.

During the drive to Illinois, Jendusa-Nicolai managed to free her hands and call 911 from her cell phone. She gave Larsen's home address, and local law enforcement and rescue personnel broke into Larsen's home around 11 a.m. in an attempt to find Jendusa-Nicolai. They remained inside for about 15 minutes—just long enough to ascertain that she was not there. Jendusa-Nicolai was able to make two more calls from her cell phone: She called her husband at noon and called 911 a second time around

2 p.m. At one point along the route to Illinois, she tried to extend her hand outside the garbage can in an effort to attract the attention of passing motorists. Larsen saw this, hit her again, and confiscated her cell phone.

From the second and third phone calls, the police learned that Jendusa-Nicolai was bound and in the back of Larsen's truck. They also learned that Jendusa-Nicolai's two daughters were missing. At about 3:30 p.m., law-enforcement officers and a rescue team reentered Larsen's home after the Racine County District Attorney concluded that exigent circumstances existed for a warrantless search. The police searched the house thoroughly for six hours looking for the two missing children as well as clues about Jendusa-Nicolai's where-abouts. They went through papers, played back voicemail messages, and searched through Larsen's computer files. During this search, they observed a large quantity of blood in the front hall, as well as an overturned chair, a blood-stained bucket, sweatpants with duct tape around the ankles, and blood-stained gloves and socks. In the meantime other officers prepared a search-warrant application.

Police arrested Larsen around 6 p.m. that evening when he reported for work. He told investigators that his daughters were at his girlfriend's house but claimed he did not know anything about Jendusa-Nicolai's disappearance. Police recovered the two girls at about 9:45 p.m. and suspended the search of Larsen's home without any further information about Jendusa-Nicolai's location. The search warrant was issued at about 11 p.m.

The next morning, the police searched Larsen's wallet and found two business cards for a storage facility in Illinois. Police called the storage facility, and an employee checked Larsen's unit and heard moaning inside. Local police immediately responded and recovered Jendusa-Nicolai from inside the garbage can. Doctors later said she was about an hour from death: Her body temperature had dropped to 84 degrees, renal failure had begun, and she was frostbitten about her body. She was hospitalized and suffered a miscarriage two days later while still at the hospital; she estimated that she had been pregnant for about five weeks. All her toes had to be amputated due to frostbite, and her hearing was damaged because of the blows to her head.

Larsen was charged in state court with attempted first-degree intentional homicide and two counts of interference with child custody. *See Larsen*, 2007 WI App 147, P 1, 302 Wis. 2d 718, 736 N.W.2d 211. A federal grand jury indicted Larsen on two counts: kidnapping, *see* 18 U.S.C. § 1201(a)(1), and forcibly causing a former spouse to travel in interstate commerce while committing a crime of violence in the course of and to facilitate the travel, *see id.* § 2261(a)(2), (b)(2) (the Interstate Domestic Violence Act). Larsen moved to suppress the evidence recovered in the warrantless search of his home, but the district court denied the motion. Larsen pleaded no contest to the state charges, *see Larsen*, 2007 WI App 147, P 13, 302 Wis. 2d 718, 736 N.W.2d 211, and after sentencing he returned to federal court and opted for a bench trial. The case was tried to the court, and at the close of the evidence, Larsen moved to dismiss on two constitutional grounds. He argued first that the Interstate Domestic Violence

Act exceeded Congress's legislative power under the Commerce Clause, and second, that the kidnapping and interstate domestic violence charges were multiplicitious in violation of the Double Jeopardy Clause. The district court rejected these arguments and convicted him on both counts.

The sentencing guidelines suggested a sentence of 292 to 365 months, but the judge sentenced Larsen to life imprisonment on the kidnapping charge and a concurrent term of ten years (the statutory maximum) on the interstate domestic-violence charge. In imposing this above-guidelines sentence, the judge emphasized that Jendusa-Nicolai's miscarriage just days after the assault was a severe aggravating factor that the guidelines had not taken into consideration.

## II. Discussion

### A. Commerce Clause Challenge to the Interstate Domestic Violence Act

Larsen first argues that the Interstate Domestic Violence Act is unconstitutional because it exceeds Congress's legislative power under the Commerce Clause. Specifically, he claims that the Act impermissibly regulates purely local, noneconomic conduct that does not have a substantial effect on interstate commerce.... We conclude, in line with four other circuits, that the Interstate Domestic Violence Act is a proper exercise of Congress's Commerce Clause power. *See United States v. Lankford*, 196 F.3d 563 (5th Cir. 1999); *United States v. Page*, 167 F.3d 325 (6th Cir. 1999); *United States v. Gluzman*, 953 F. Supp. 84 (S.D.N.Y. 1997), *aff'd*, 154 F.3d 49 (2d Cir. 1998); *United States v. Bailey*, 112 F.3d 758 (4th Cir. 1997).

The Supreme Court's "modern Commerce Clause jurisprudence has 'identified three broad categories of activity that Congress may regulate under its commerce power.'" *United States v. Morrison*, 529 U.S. 598, 608, 120 S. Ct. 1740, 146 L. Ed. 2d 658 (2000) (quoting *United States v. Lopez*, 514 U.S. 549, 558, 115 S. Ct. 1624, 131 L. Ed. 2d 626 (1995)). The Court has held that the Commerce Clause authorizes Congress to regulate the "use of the channels of interstate commerce"; the "instrumentalities of interstate commerce, or persons or things in interstate commerce, even though the threat may come only from intrastate activities"; and "those [intrastate] activities that substantially affect interstate commerce." *Lopez*, 514 U.S. at 558-59; *see also Morrison*, 529 U.S. at 608-09; *Perez v. United States*, 402 U.S. 146, 150, 91 S. Ct. 1357, 28 L. Ed. 2d 686 (1971). Congress's legislative authority in the first and second categories is plenary. *Cleveland v. United States*, 329 U.S. 14, 19, 67 S. Ct. 13, 91 L. Ed. 12 (1946) ("The power of Congress over the instrumentalities of interstate commerce is plenary...."); *Caminetti v. United States*, 242 U.S. 470, 491, 37 S. Ct. 192, 61 L. Ed. 442 (1917) ("[T]he authority of Congress to keep the channels of interstate commerce free from immoral and injurious uses has been frequently sustained, and is no longer open to question."). Congressional power in the third category, however, extends only to *economic activity* that substantially affects interstate commerce. *Morrison*, 529 U.S. at 611....

Larsen conceptually locates his argument in the third Commerce Clause category. The Act is unconstitutional, he contends, because Congress lacks the authority to punish domestic violence, which is wholly intrastate conduct, noneconomic in nature, and does not substantially affect interstate commerce. This argument is misplaced. The Interstate Domestic Violence Act regulates the channels or instrumentalities of interstate commerce and persons in interstate commerce—not purely intrastate activity—and therefore falls within *Lopez's* first and second categories, in which Congress has plenary authority to legislate. The Act punishes only those who cause a spouse or intimate partner to "travel in interstate or foreign commerce" and who commit a crime of violence "in the course of, as a result of, or to facilitate" that interstate travel. It is the victim's movement in interstate commerce—not the intrastate crime of violence—that implicates the Interstate Domestic Violence Act.

The Supreme Court has long held that movement of persons across state lines is sufficient to permit congressional regulation under the Commerce Clause. *See Camps Newfound/Owatonna, Inc. v. Town of Harrison, Me.*, 520 U.S. 564, 573, 117 S. Ct. 1590, 137 L. Ed. 2d 852 (1997) (reaffirming that the movement of persons across state lines is a form of commerce); *Heart of Atlanta Motel, Inc. v. United States*, 379 U.S. 241, 256, 85 S. Ct. 348, 13 L. Ed. 2d 258 (1964) (holding that the act of crossing state lines need not be commercial in character); *Caminetti*, 242 U.S. at 491. In *Cleveland* the Supreme Court upheld the Mann Act against a challenge by polygamists who transported their wives across state lines. 329 U.S. 14. The defendants had argued that the Mann Act unconstitutionally regulated marriage, a purely intrastate matter. The Court rejected this argument: "The power of Congress over the instrumentalities of interstate commerce is plenary; it may be used to defeat what are deemed to be immoral practices; and the fact that the means used may have 'the quality of police regulations' is not consequential." *Id*. at 19 (quoting *Hoke v. United States*, 227 U.S. 308, 323, 33 S. Ct. 281, 57 L. Ed. 523 (1913)). And in *Caminetti* the Court upheld the White Slave Act of 1910, which prohibited the transportation of women in interstate commerce for purposes of debauchery or prostitution. 242 U.S. at 491. . . .

Larsen relies heavily on *Morrison*, but that pivotal case hurts rather than helps his argument. *Morrison* invalidated, on Commerce Clause grounds, a provision in the Violence Against Women Act that provided a civil remedy to victims of gender-related violence. The Supreme Court analyzed the provision under *Lopez's* third category—as a regulation of wholly intrastate activity—"[g]iven [its] focus on gender-motivated violence wherever it occurs (rather than violence directed at the instrumentalities of interstate commerce, interstate markets, or things or persons in interstate commerce) . . . ." *Morrison*, 529 U.S. at 609. The Court noted in particular that the statute lacked any jurisdictional element that would "lend support" to the argument that the provision was sufficiently tied to interstate commerce. *Id*. at 613.

There is nothing in *Morrison* that limits Congress's authority to regulate the use of the channels or instrumentalities of, or persons in, interstate commerce. *See, e.g., Cleveland*, 329 U.S. at 16. To the contrary, the Court specifically distinguished the civil remedy in the Violence Against Women Act, which regulated wholly intrastate conduct, from § 2261(a)(1), the criminal-penalty provision at issue here. The Court took note of the "interstate travel" element of the criminal offense and the difference that the presence of this element made in the Commerce Clause analysis: "The Courts of Appeals have uniformly upheld th[e] criminal sanction [§ 2261(a)(1)] as an appropriate exercise of Congress' Commerce Clause authority, reasoning that '[t]he provision properly falls within the first of *Lopez's* categories as it regulates the use of channels of interstate commerce.'" *Morrison*, 529 U.S. at 613 n.5 (quoting *Lankford*, 196 F.3d at 571-72) (alteration in *Morrison*).

This language, of course, cannot be taken as an explicit endorsement of the conclusion that § 2261(a)(1) survives Commerce Clause challenge as a regulation of the channels or instrumentalities of, or persons in, interstate commerce; *Morrison* addressed only the civil-remedy provision in the Violence Against Women Act. But the Court's language undermines Larsen's position that § 2261(a)(1) regulates purely intrastate activity and must be analyzed as such under *Lopez* and *Morrison*. Accordingly, we join the Second, Fourth, Fifth, and Sixth Circuits in holding that the Interstate Domestic Violence Act is a valid exercise of Congress's power under the Commerce Clause to regulate the channels or instrumentalities of, or persons in, interstate commerce. . . . .

AFFIRMED.

## III. Federal Firearms Restrictions

The statistics on guns and domestic violence provide shocking evidence on how deadly this combination is for women. Having a gun in the home makes a woman 7.2 times more likely to be the victim of a domestic violence homicide.[17]

As part of Congress' effort to combat the use of guns in domestic violence, it passed amendments to the 1968 Gun Control Act restricting access to keep firearms out of the hands of domestic violence offenders. In 1996, the Lautenberg Amendment, after then New Jersey Sen. Frank Lautenberg, made it a federal crime to possess a firearm after having been convicted of a misdemeanor crime involving domestic violence. The Lautenberg law contains no exemption from the firearms ban for members of the military or persons in law enforcement. Effectively, conviction of a misdemeanor means the end of one's career in these fields.

### Darren Mitchell & Susan B. Carbon, *Firearms and Domestic Violence: A Primer for Judges*
39(2) Ct. Rev.: J. Am. Judges Ass'n 32 (2002)

. . .

In 1994, along with the passage of the original Violence Against Women Act (VAWA), Congress enacted the first federal legislation to address this issue directly.

---

17. Women and Firearms Fact Sheet, Violence Policy Center, www.vpc.org/fact_sht/womenfs.htm.

The new law, which amended the Gun Control Act of 1968 and is codified at 18 U.S.C. section 922(g)(8), makes it a federal crime for a person who is subject to a qualifying order to possess a firearm or ammunition, or to ship or receive a firearm or ammunition in interstate or foreign commerce. To qualify under section 922(g)(8), a protection order must:

1. have been issued after a hearing of which the respondent received actual notice, and at which the respondent had an opportunity to participate;

2. restrain the respondent from harassing, stalking, or threatening an intimate partner of the respondent or child of such intimate partner of the respondent or child of such intimate partner or the respondent, or engaging in other conduct that would place an intimate partner in reasonable fear of bodily injury to the partner or child; and

3. either include a finding that the respondent represents a credible threat to the physical safety of such intimate partner *or* child or by its terms explicitly prohibit the use, attempted use, or threatened use of physical force against such intimate partner or child that would reasonably be expected to cause bodily injury.

. . . .

Provided that these requirements have been satisfied, mere possession of a firearm or ammunition will subject a defendant to prosecution under section 922(g)(8). The order itself need not prohibit possession of firearms, and the respondent need not have violated the order itself in any way. The federal law does, however, require that the possession be "knowing" to support a prosecution. Section 922(g)(8) applies only for the duration of the qualifying protection order.

In addition to section 922(g)(8), the 1994 amendments to the Gun Control Act included 18 U.S.C. section 922(d)(8), which makes it a federal crime to sell or transfer a firearm or ammunition to a person knowing or having reasonable cause to believe that the person is subject to a qualifying protection order. The same requirements discussed above in reference to section 922(g)(8) apply to protection orders under section 922(d)(8). . . .

A limited exception to sections 922(g)(8) and 922(d)(8) exists for law enforcement officers, armed forces personnel, and other local, state, and federal employees who are required to use weapons as part of their official duties. Under 18 U.S.C. section 925(a)(1), sometimes referred to as the "official-use exemption," the prohibitions in sections 922(g)(8) and 922(d)(8) do not apply to firearms that are received or possessed by such individuals for use in performing official duties on behalf of a federal, state, or local agency. Personal weapons, however, are not covered by the exemption.

In 1996, Congress enacted the second important amendment to the Gun Control Act related to domestic violence. Known as the "Lautenberg Amendment," the new law added persons who have been convicted of certain misdemeanor crimes of domestic violence to the list of those barred by the federal law from purchasing or possessing firearms and ammunition. The prohibition, found at 18 U.S.C. section 922(g)(9), has been particularly controversial because it applies to misdemeanors and does not include an official-use exemption for law enforcement and military personnel. Despite several court challenges, section 922(g)(9) has withstood judicial scrutiny and remains good law.

Which misdemeanor crimes qualify under section 922(g)(9)? The definition of a misdemeanor crime of domestic violence requires that the offense be a misdemeanor under federal or state law and have, as an element, the use or attempted use of physical force or the threatened use of a weapon....

The federal law also imposes two due-process-related requirements, namely that the perpetrator must have been represented by counsel (or have knowingly waived that right) and that if the perpetrator was entitled to a jury trial, either the case was tried by a jury or the perpetrator knowingly and intelligently waived that right.

It is important to note that only a "conviction" triggers the section 922(g)(9) prohibition.... By regulation, the question of whether a qualifying "conviction" exists is made by reference to the governing *state* law....

Although section 922(g)(8) imposes a lifetime ban on firearm possession following a qualifying misdemeanor conviction, the statute does provide that firearms possession rights may be restored under limited circumstances. Specifically, the conviction must be "expunged or set aside" or it must be "an offense for which the person has been pardoned or has had civil rights restored" (if the law of the applicable jurisdiction provides for the loss of civil rights under such offense).

Federal courts have consistently held that section 922(g)(9) applies to misdemeanor convictions that occurred prior to the 1996 enactment of the Lautenberg Amendment....

As part of the Lautenberg Amendment, Congress also enacted 18 U.S.C. section 922(d)(9), which prohibits the sale or transfer of a firearm or ammunition to a person if the transferor knows or has reasonable cause to believe that the person has been convicted of a misdemeanor crime of domestic violence. The definition of misdemeanor crime of domestic violence is the same as that which applies to section 922(g)(9).

. . . .

### State Judges' Role with Respect to Federal Firearms Laws

. . . .

Perhaps the most common misunderstanding about the relationship between the federal and state firearm prohibitions arises when the two sets of laws address similar situations but differ significantly in their approach. For instance, we have seen that under the federal Gun Control Act (18 U.S.C Sec. 922(g)(8)), a person subject to a domestic violence protection order meeting specific statutory criteria is not permitted to possess a firearm while the order is in effect. By contrast, many states impose such a ban only if the issuing court exercises its discretion to prohibit firearm possession as part of the order's terms and conditions. In such a state, the question arises whether a respondent legally can possess a firearm when the order does not include a state-law firearm prohibition yet otherwise satisfies the federal Gun Control Act requirements....

In fact, this is neither a situation that triggers the Supremacy Clause nor one that enables the state court judge to abrogate the federal firearm laws. Rather, both sets of laws remain in full force and both apply to this situation. The respondent would not be subject to a state-law firearm prohibition, because the judge opted not to invoke her authority to prohibit gun possession, but the respondent nonetheless would be subject to federal prosecution under the federal gun law, because the federal prohibition is independent of state law. This analysis holds true for all of the federal firearm statutes discussed above.

Confusion also arises over a state court judge's role in the *enforcement* of the 18 U.S.C. section 922(g)(8) prohibition when it is a state court order of protection that triggers the federal law. Especially in states where the protection order form provides a space for the issuing judge to indicate whether the federal prohibitions apply, some judges misunderstand their role. For instance, some judges are under the misimpression that they can "override" the operation of 18 U.S.C. section 922(g)(8) simply by not checking the appropriate space on a protection order form, or by including language in the order to the effect that the federal law does not apply against the respondent.

In fact, section 922(g)(8) does not rely on state law definitions or standards to determine whether a person is prohibited from possessing a firearm. Rather, the question of whether a protection order issued by a state court triggers the section 922(g)(8) prohibition is determined solely by reference to the specific requirements of the *federal* statute. In practice, this means that the particular findings and terms of the order must be assessed against the federal requirements enumerated in section 922(g)(8), and inquiry must be made into whether the federal notice and hearing requirements were satisfied.

. . . .

All of this is not to say, however, that the actions of state court judges do not profoundly affect the operation of the federal law. In fact, the nature of the conduct proscribed by the order or of the findings of fact included therein determines whether the federal law applies. For instance, by ensuring that their orders hew to the specific requirements of section 922(g)(8) (that is, that they contain the requisite findings or prohibitory language or both), judges can facilitate subsequent enforcement of the federal firearm laws. In addition, judges can promote the deterrent effect of the federal law by providing the respondent with both written and oral notice that they will be in violation of section 922(g)(8) if they possess or purchase a firearm while the protection order is in effect. By indicating on the order the relationship between the parties as well as the order's compliance with due process requirements of section 922(g)(8), judges can also make it clear that a protection order triggers the federal prohibition. . . .

---

In June 2008, the United States Supreme Court in *District of Columbia v. Heller*, 128 S. Ct. 2783 (2008), ended years of debate between handgun advocates and those favoring gun control measures, by holding that the Second Amendment protects an individual's right to bear arms. The case arose out of a challenge to a District of Columbia law that restricted gun ownership by individuals—even in their own homes. In striking down the measure, Justice Scalia emphasized the Court was not outlawing all gun regulation. Like most legal rights, the right secured by the Second Amendment is not unlimited. The Court did not list among the possible appropriate regulatory measures that of keeping firearms away from domestic violence offenders. Thus, the Court created a situation similar to the one it created when it issued the *Crawford* decision. In the seven years after *Heller* was decided, the Supreme Court was asked no less than 70 times to weigh in to challenges to gun regulations.[18] In 2010, in *McDonald v. City of Chicago*, 130 S. Ct. 3020 (2010), the Supreme Court held that the Second Amendment right to bear arms is applicable to the states. Notwithstanding, the Supreme Court has never subsequently ruled that the government is without power to impose appropriate restrictions on who has the right to possess a gun. On more than one occasion, the Court has addressed the legality of imposing firearms restrictions on those convicted of domestic violence.

## United States v. Hayes
United States Supreme Court
555 U.S. 415 (2009)

Justice Ginsburg delivered the opinion of the Court

. . . .

### I

In 2004, law enforcement officers in Marion County, West Virginia, came to the home of Randy Edward Hayes in response to a 911 call reporting domestic violence. Hayes consented to a search of his home, and the officers discovered a rifle. Further investigation revealed that Hayes had recently possessed several other firearms as well. Based on this evidence, a federal grand jury returned an indictment in 2005, charging Hayes, under §§ 922(g)(9) and 924(a)(2), with three counts of possessing firearms after having been convicted of a misdemeanor crime of domestic violence.

The indictment identified Hayes's predicate misdemeanor crime of domestic violence as a 1994 conviction for battery in violation of West Virginia law. The victim of that battery, the indictment alleged, was Hayes's then-wife—a person who "shared a child in common" with Hayes and "who was cohabitating with . . . him as a spouse."

---

18. The Editorial Board, *An Opening to Restrict Guns*, N.Y. Times, December 9, 2015.

Asserting that his 1994 West Virginia battery conviction did not qualify as a predicate offense under § 922(g)(9), Hayes moved to dismiss the indictment. Section 922(g)(9), Hayes maintained, applies only to persons previously convicted of an offense that has as an element a domestic relationship between aggressor and victim. The West Virginia statute under which he was convicted in 1994, Hayes observed, was a generic battery proscription, not a law designating a domestic relationship between offender and victim as an element of the offense. The United States District Court for the Northern District of West Virginia rejected Hayes's argument and denied his motion to dismiss the indictment. 377 F. Supp. 2d 540, 541-542 (2005). Hayes then entered a conditional guilty plea and appealed.

In a 2-to-1 decision, the United States Court of Appeals for the Fourth Circuit reversed. A § 922(g)(9) predicate offense, the Court of Appeals held, must "have as an element a domestic relationship between the offender and the victim." 482 F.3d 749, 751 (2007). In so ruling, the Fourth Circuit created a split between itself and the nine other Courts of Appeals that had previously published opinions deciding the same question. According to those courts, § 922(g)(9) does not require that the offense predicate to the defendant's firearm possession conviction have as an element a domestic relationship between offender and victim. We granted certiorari, 552 U.S. 1279, 128 S. Ct. 1702, 170 L. Ed. 2d 512 (2008), to resolve this conflict.

II

Section 922(g)(9) makes it "unlawful for any person ... who has been convicted in any court of a misdemeanor crime of domestic violence ... [to] possess in or affecting commerce, any firearm or ammunition." Section 921(a)(33)(A) defines "misdemeanor crime of domestic violence" as follows:

"[T]he term 'misdemeanor crime of domestic violence' means an offense that—

"(i) is a misdemeanor under Federal, State, or Tribal law; and

"(ii) has, as an element, the use or attempted use of physical force, or the threatened use of a deadly weapon, committed by a current or former spouse, parent, or guardian of the victim, by a person with whom the victim shares a child in common, by a person who is cohabitating with or has cohabitated with the victim as a spouse, parent, or guardian, or by a person similarly situated to a spouse, parent, or guardian of the victim." (Footnote omitted.)

... We note as an initial matter that § 921(a)(33)(A) uses the word "element" in the singular, which suggests that Congress intended to describe only one required element. Immediately following the word "element," § 921(a)(33)(A)(ii) refers to the use of force (undoubtedly a required element) and thereafter to the relationship between aggressor and victim, *e.g.*, a current or former spouse. The manner in which the offender acts, and the offender's relationship with the victim, are "conceptually distinct attributes." *United States v. Meade*, 175 F.3d 215, 218 (CA1 1999)....

Treating the relationship between aggressor and victim as an element of the predicate offense is also awkward as a matter of syntax. It requires the reader to regard "the use or attempted use of physical force, or the threatened use of a deadly weapon" as an expression modified by the relative clause "committed by." In ordinary usage, however, we would not say that a person "commit[s]" a "use." It is more natural to say that a person "commit[s]" an "offense." . . .

Had Congress placed the "committed by" phrase in its own clause, set off from clause (ii) by a semicolon or a line break, the lawmakers might have better conveyed that "committed by" modifies only "offense" and not "use" or "element." Congress' less-than-meticulous drafting, however, hardly shows that the legislators meant to exclude from § 922(g)(9)'s firearm possession prohibition domestic abusers convicted under generic assault or battery provisions.

As structured, § 921(a)(33)(A) defines "misdemeanor crime of domestic violence" by addressing in clause (i) the meaning of "misdemeanor" and, in turn, in clause (ii), "crime of domestic violence." Because a "crime of domestic violence" involves both a use of force and a domestic relationship, joining these features together in clause (ii) would make sense even if Congress had no design to confine laws qualifying under § 921(a)(33)(A) to those designating as elements both use of force and domestic relationship between aggressor and victim. See *id.*, at 761 (Williams, J., dissenting). See also *United States v. Barnes*, 353 U.S. App. D.C. 87, 295 F.3d 1354, 1358-1360, 1361 (CADC 2002) ("The fact that the Congress somewhat awkwardly included the 'committed by' phrase in subpart (ii) (instead of adding a subpart (iii)) is not significant in view of the *un*natural reading that would result if 'committed by' were construed to modify 'use of force.'").

A related statutory provision, 25 U.S.C. § 2803(3)(C), indicates that Congress did not ascribe substantive significance to the placement of line breaks and semicolons in 18 U.S.C. § 921(a)(33)(A). In 2006, Congress amended § 921(a)(33)(A)(i) to include misdemeanors under "[t]ribal law" as predicate offenses. As a companion measure, Congress simultaneously enacted § 2803(3)(C), which employs use-of-force and domestic-relationship language virtually identical to the language earlier placed in § 921(a)(33)(A)(i), except that § 2803(3)(C) uses no semicolon or line break.

Section 2803(3)(C) authorizes federal agents to "make an arrest without a warrant for an offense committed in Indian country if—

> "the offense is a misdemeanor crime of domestic violence . . . and has, as an element, the use or attempted use of physical force, or the threatened use of a deadly weapon, committed by a current or former spouse, parent, or guardian of the victim, by a person with whom the victim shares a child in common, by a person who is cohabitating with or has cohabitated with the victim as a spouse, parent, or guardian, or by a person similarly situated to a spouse, parent or guardian of the victim . . . ."

At the time Congress enacted § 2803(3)(C), the Courts of Appeals uniformly agreed that § 921(a)(33)(A) did not limit predicate offenses to statutory texts specifying both a use of force and a domestic relationship as offense elements. Congress presumably knew how § 921(a)(33)(A) had been construed, and presumably intended § 2803(3)(C) to bear the same meaning. See *Merrill Lynch, Pierce, Fenner & Smith Inc.* v. *Dabit*, 547 U.S. 71, 85-86, 126 S. Ct. 1503, 164 L. Ed. 2d 179 (2006) ("[W]hen 'judicial interpretations have settled the meaning of an existing statutory provision, repetition of the same language in a new statute indicates, as a general matter, the intent to incorporate its . . . judicial interpretations as well.'"). . . . Relying on spacing and punctuation to hem in § 921(a)(33)(A), while reading § 2803(3)(C) to contain no similar limitation, would create a disjunction between these two provisions that Congress could not have intended.

As a second justification for its construction of § 921(a)(33)(A), the Court of Appeals invoked the "rule of the last antecedent," under which "a limiting clause or phrase . . . should ordinarily be read as modifying only the noun or phrase that it immediately follows." *Barnhart v. Thomas*, 540 U.S. 20, 26, 124 S. Ct. 376, 157 L. Ed. 2d 333 (2003). . . .

Most sensibly read, then, § 921(a)(33)(A) defines "misdemeanor crime of domestic violence" as a misdemeanor offense that (1) "has, as an element, the use [of force]," and (2) is committed by a person who has a specified domestic relationship with the victim. To obtain a conviction in a § 922(g)(9) prosecution, the Government must prove beyond a reasonable doubt that the victim of the predicate offense was the defendant's current or former spouse or was related to the defendant in another specified way. But that relationship, while it must be established, need not be denominated an element of the predicate offense.

### III

Practical considerations strongly support our reading of § 921(a)(33)(A)'s language. Existing felon-in-possession laws, Congress recognized, were not keeping firearms out of the hands of domestic abusers, because "many people who engage in serious spousal or child abuse ultimately are not charged with or convicted of felonies." 142 Cong. Rec. 22985 (1996) (statement of Sen. Lautenberg). By extending the federal firearm prohibition to persons convicted of "misdemeanor crime[s] of domestic violence," proponents of § 922(g)(9) sought to "close this dangerous loophole." *Id.*, at 22986.

Construing § 922(g)(9) to exclude the domestic abuser convicted under a generic use-of-force statute (one that does not designate a domestic relationship as an element of the offense) would frustrate Congress' manifest purpose. Firearms and domestic strife are a potentially deadly combination nationwide. See, *e.g.*, Brief for Brady Center To Prevent Gun Violence et al. as *Amici Curiae* 8-15; Brief for National Network To End Domestic Violence et al. as *Amici Curiae* 2-8. Yet, as interpreted by the Fourth Circuit, § 922(g)(9) would have been "a dead letter" in some two-thirds of the States from the very moment of its enactment. 482 F.3d, at 762 (Williams, J., dissenting).

As of 1996, only about one-third of the States had criminal statutes that specifically proscribed *domestic* violence. See Brief for United States 23, n 8. Even in those States, domestic abusers were (and are) routinely prosecuted under generally applicable assault or battery laws. See Tr. of Oral Arg. 19. And no statute defining a distinct federal misdemeanor designated as an element of the offense a domestic relationship between aggressor and victim. Yet Congress defined "misdemeanor crime of domestic violence" to include "misdemeanor[s] under Federal . . . law." § 921(a)(33)(A)(i). Given the paucity of state and federal statutes targeting *domestic* violence, we find it highly improbable that Congress meant to extend § 922(g)(9)'s firearm possession ban only to the relatively few domestic abusers prosecuted under laws rendering a domestic relationship an element of the offense. . . .

IV

The rule of lenity, Hayes contends, provides an additional reason to construe §§ 922(g)(9) and 921(a)(33)(A) to apply only to predicate offenses that specify a domestic relationship as an element of the crime. "[T]he touchstone of the rule of lenity is statutory ambiguity." *Bifulco v. United States*, 447 U.S. 381, 387, 100 S. Ct. 2247, 65 L. Ed. 2d 205 (1980) (internal quotation marks omitted). We apply the rule "only when, after consulting traditional canons of statutory construction, we are left with an ambiguous statute." *United States v. Shabani*, 513 U.S. 10, 17, 115 S. Ct. 382, 130 L. Ed. 2d 225 (1994). Section 921(a)(33)(A)'s definition of "misdemeanor crime of domestic violence," we acknowledge, is not a model of the careful drafter's art. See *Barnes*, 295 F.3d, at 1356. But neither is it "grievous[ly] ambigu[ous]." *Huddleston v. United States*, 415 U.S. 814, 831, 94 S. Ct. 1262, 39 L. Ed. 2d 782 (1974). The text, context, purpose, and what little there is of drafting history all point in the same direction: Congress defined "misdemeanor crime of domestic violence" to include an offense "committed by" a person who had a specified domestic relationship with the victim, whether or not the misdemeanor statute itself designates the domestic relationship as an element of the crime.

. . . .

For the reasons stated, the judgment of the United States Court of Appeals for the Fourth Circuit is reversed, and the case is remanded for further proceedings consistent with this opinion. . . .

## United States v. Castleman

United States Supreme Court

134 S. Ct. 1405 (2014)

Justice Sotomayor delivered the opinion of the Court.

Recognizing that "[f]irearms and domestic strife are a potentially deadly combination," *United States v. Hayes*, 555 U.S. 415, 427, 129 S. Ct. 1079, 172 L. Ed. 2d 816 (2009), Congress forbade the possession of firearms by anyone convicted of "a misdemeanor crime of domestic violence." 18 U.S.C. § 922(g)(9). The respondent, James Alvin Castleman, pleaded guilty to the misdemeanor offense of having "intentionally or knowingly cause[d] bodily injury to" the mother of his child. App. 27. The question before us is whether this conviction qualifies as "a misdemeanor crime of domestic violence." We hold that it does.

I

. . . .

B

In 2001, Castleman was charged in a Tennessee court with having "intentionally or knowingly cause[d] bodily injury to" the mother of his child, in violation of Tenn. Code Ann. § 39-13-111(b) (Supp. 2002). App. 27. He pleaded guilty. *Id.,* at 29.

In 2008, federal authorities learned that Castleman was selling firearms on the black market. A grand jury in the Western District of Tennessee indicted him on two counts of violating § 922(g)(9) and on other charges not relevant here. *Id.,* at 13-16.

Castleman moved to dismiss the § 922(g)(9) charges, arguing that his Tennessee conviction did not qualify as a "misdemeanor crime of domestic violence" because it did not "ha[ve], as an element, the use . . . of physical force," § 921(a)(33)(A)(ii). The District Court agreed, on the theory that "the 'use of physical force' for § 922(g)(9) purposes" must entail "violent contact with the victim." App. to Pet. for Cert. 40a. The court held that a conviction under the relevant Tennessee statute cannot qualify as a "misdemeanor crime of domestic violence" because one can cause bodily injury without "violent contact"—for example, by "deceiving [the victim] into drinking a poisoned beverage." *Id.,* at 41a.

A divided panel of the U.S. Court of Appeals for the Sixth Circuit affirmed, by different reasoning. 695 F.3d 582 (2012). The majority held that the degree of physical force required by § 921(a)(33)(A)(ii) is the same as required by § 924(e)(2)(B)(i), which defines "violent felony." *Id.,* at 587. . . . Applying our decision in *Johnson v. United States,* 559 U.S. 133, 130 S. Ct. 1265, 176 L. Ed. 2d 1 (2010), which held that § 924(e)(2)(B)(i) requires "*violent* force," *id.,* at 140, 130 S. Ct. 1265, 176 L. Ed. 2d 1, the majority held that Castleman's conviction did not qualify as a "misdemeanor crime of domestic violence" because Castleman could have been convicted for "caus[ing] a slight, nonserious physical injury with conduct that cannot be described as violent." 695 F.3d, at 590. . . .

The Sixth Circuit's decision deepened a split of authority among the Courts of Appeals. Compare, *e.g., United States v. Nason,* 269 F.3d 10, 18 (CA1 2001) (§ 922(g)(9) "encompass[es] crimes characterized by the application of *any* physical force"), with *United States v. Belless,* 338 F.3d 1063, 1068 (CA9 2003) (§ 922(g)(9) covers only "the violent use of force"). We granted certiorari to resolve this split, 570 U.S. ___, 134 S. Ct. 49, 186 L. Ed. 2d 962 (2013), and now reverse the Sixth Circuit's judgment.

II

A

. . . .

*Johnson* resolves this case in the Government's favor—not, as the Sixth Circuit held, in *Castleman's*. In *Johnson*, we considered whether a battery conviction was a "violent felony" under the Armed Career Criminal Act (ACCA), §924(e)(1). As here, ACCA defines such a crime as one that "has as an element the use . . . of physical force," §924(e)(2)(B)(i). We began by observing that at common law, the element of force in the crime of battery was "satisfied by even the slightest offensive touching." 559 U.S., at 139, 130 S. Ct. 1265, 176 L. Ed. 2d 1 (citing 3 W. Blackstone, Commentaries on the Laws of England 120 (1768)). . . . [H]ere, the common-law meaning of "force" fits perfectly: The very reasons we gave for rejecting that meaning in defining a "violent felony" are reasons to embrace it in defining a "misdemeanor crime of domestic violence."

First, because perpetrators of domestic violence are "routinely prosecuted under generally applicable assault or battery laws," *Hayes*, 555 U.S., at 427, 129 S. Ct. 1079, 172 L. Ed. 2d 816, it makes sense for Congress to have classified as a "misdemeanor crime of domestic violence" the type of conduct that supports a common-law battery conviction. Whereas it was "unlikely" that Congress meant to incorporate in the definition of a "'violent felony' a phrase that the common law gave peculiar meaning only in its definition of a misdemeanor," *Johnson*, 559 U.S., at 141, 130 S. Ct. 1265, 176 L. Ed. 2d 1, it is likely that Congress meant to incorporate that misdemeanor-specific meaning of "force" in defining a "misdemeanor crime of domestic violence."

Second, whereas the word "violent" or "violence" standing alone "connotes a substantial degree of force," *id.,* at 140, 130 S. Ct. 1265, 176 L. Ed. 2d 1, that is not true of "domestic violence." "Domestic violence" is not merely a type of "violence"; it is a term of art encompassing acts that one might not characterize as "violent" in a nondomestic context. . . . Indeed, "most physical assaults committed against women and men by intimates are relatively minor and consist of pushing, grabbing, shoving, slapping, and hitting." DOJ, P. Tjaden & N. Thoennes, Extent, Nature and Consequences of Intimate Partner Violence 11 (2000).

Minor uses of force may not constitute "violence" in the generic sense. For example, in an opinion that we cited with approval in *Johnson*, the Seventh Circuit noted that it was "hard to describe . . . as 'violence'" "a squeeze of the arm [that] causes a bruise." *Flores v. Ashcroft*, 350 F.3d 666, 670 (2003). But an act of this nature is easy to describe as "domestic violence," when the accumulation of such acts over time can subject one intimate partner to the other's control. If a seemingly minor act like this draws the attention of authorities and leads to a successful prosecution for a misdemeanor offense, it does not offend common sense or the English language to characterize the resulting conviction as a "misdemeanor crime of domestic violence."

. . . .

A third reason for distinguishing *Johnson*'s definition of "physical force" is that unlike in *Johnson*—where a determination that the defendant's crime was a "violent felony" would have classified him as an "armed career criminal"—the statute here groups those convicted of "misdemeanor crimes of domestic violence" with others whose conduct does not warrant such a designation. Section 922(g) bars gun possession by anyone "addicted to any controlled substance," § 922(g)(3); by most people who have "been admitted to the United States under a nonimmigrant visa," § 922(g)(5)(B); by anyone who has renounced United States citizenship, § 922(g)(7); and by anyone subject to a domestic restraining order, § 922(g)(8). Whereas we have hesitated (as in *Johnson*) to apply the Armed Career Criminal Act to "crimes which, though dangerous, are not typically committed by those whom one normally labels 'armed career criminals,'" *Begay v. United States*, 553 U.S. 137, 146, 128 S. Ct. 1581, 170 L. Ed. 2d 490 (2008), we see no anomaly in grouping domestic abusers convicted of generic assault or battery offenses together with the others whom § 922(g) disqualifies from gun ownership.

An additional reason to read the statute as we do is that a contrary reading would have rendered § 922(g)(9) inoperative in many States at the time of its enactment. The "assault or battery laws" under which "domestic abusers were...routinely prosecuted" when Congress enacted § 922(g)(9), and under which many are still prosecuted today, *Hayes*, 555 U.S., at 427, 129 S. Ct. 1079, 172 L. Ed. 2d 816, fall generally into two categories: those that prohibit both offensive touching and the causation of bodily injury, and those that prohibit only the latter. See Brief for United States 36-38. Whether or not the causation of bodily injury necessarily entails violent force—a question we do not reach—mere offensive touching does not. See *Johnson*, 559 U.S., at 139-140, 130 S. Ct. 1265, 176 L. Ed. 2d 1. So if offensive touching did not constitute "force" under § 921(a)(33)(A), then § 922(g)(9) would have been ineffectual in at least 10 States—home to nearly thirty percent of the Nation's population—at the time of its enactment. See *post*, at ___, 188 L. Ed. 2d, at 443 and n. 5 (Scalia, J., concurring in part and concurring in judgment)....

B

Applying this definition of "physical force," we conclude that Castleman's conviction qualifies as a "misdemeanor crime of domestic violence." In doing so, we follow the analytic approach of *Taylor v. United States*, 495 U.S. 575, 110 S. Ct. 2143, 109 L. Ed. 2d 607 (1990), and *Shepard v. United States*, 544 U.S. 13, 125 S. Ct. 1254, 161 L. Ed. 2d 205 (2005). We begin with *Taylor*'s categorical approach, under which we look to the statute of Castleman's conviction to determine whether that conviction necessarily "ha[d], as an element, the use or attempted use of physical force, or the threatened use of a deadly weapon," § 921(a)(33)(A).

The Tennessee statute under which Castleman was convicted made it a crime to "commi[t] an assault...against" a "family or household member"—in Castleman's case, the mother of his child. Tenn. Code Ann. § 39-13-111(b). A provision incorporated by reference, § 39-13-101, defined three types of assault: "(1) [i]ntentionally, knowingly or recklessly caus[ing] bodily injury to another; (2) [i]ntentionally or knowingly caus[ing] another to reasonably fear imminent bodily injury; or (3) [i]ntentionally or knowingly caus[ing] physical contact with another" in a manner that a "reasonable person would regard...as extremely offensive or provocative." § 39-13-101(a)....

First, a "bodily injury" must result from "physical force." Under Tennessee law, "bodily injury" is a broad term: It "includes a cut, abrasion, bruise, burn or disfigurement; physical pain or temporary illness or impairment of the function of a bodily member, organ, or mental faculty." Tenn. Code Ann. § 39-11-106(a)(2) (1997)....

Second, the knowing or intentional application of force is a "use" of force. Castleman is correct that under *Leocal v. Ashcroft*, 543 U.S. 1, 125 S. Ct. 377, 160 L. Ed. 2d 271 (2004), the word "use" "conveys the idea that the thing used (here, 'physical force') has been made the user's instrument." Brief for Respondent 37. But he errs in arguing that although "[p]oison may have 'forceful physical properties' as a matter of organic chemistry, . . . no one would say that a poisoner 'employs' force or 'carries out a purpose by means of force' when he or she sprinkles poison in a victim's drink," *ibid*. The "use of force" in Castleman's example is not the act of "sprinkl[ing]" the poison; it is the act of employing poison knowingly as a device to cause physical harm. That the harm occurs indirectly, rather than directly (as with a kick or punch), does not matter. . . . *Leocal* held that the "use" of force must entail "a higher degree of intent than negligent or merely accidental conduct," 543 U.S., at 9, 125 S. Ct. 377, 160 L. Ed. 2d 271; it did not hold that the word "use" somehow alters the meaning of "force."

Because Castleman's indictment makes clear that the use of physical force was an element of his conviction, that conviction qualifies as a "misdemeanor crime of domestic violence."

### III

. . .

### A

First, Castleman invokes § 922(g)(9)'s legislative history to suggest that Congress could not have intended for the provision to apply to acts involving minimal force. But to the extent that legislative history can aid in the interpretation of this statute, Castleman's reliance on it is unpersuasive.

Castleman begins by observing that during the debate over § 922(g)(9), several Senators argued that the provision would help to prevent gun violence by perpetrators of severe domestic abuse. Senator Lautenberg referred to "serious spousal or child abuse" and to "violent individuals"; Senator Hutchison to "'people who batter their wives'"; Senator Wellstone to people who "brutalize" their wives or children; and Senator Feinstein to "severe and recurring domestic violence." 142 Cong. Rec. 22985-22986, 22988. But as we noted above, see *supra*, at ___, 188 L. Ed. 2d, at 434, the impetus of § 922(g)(9) was that even perpetrators of severe domestic violence are often convicted "under generally applicable assault or battery laws." *Hayes*, 555 U.S., at 427, 129 S. Ct. 1079, 172 L. Ed. 2d 816. So nothing about these Senators' isolated references to severe domestic violence suggests that they would not have wanted § 922(g)(9) to apply to a misdemeanor assault conviction like Castleman's.

Castleman next observes that § 922(g)(9) is the product of a legislative compromise. The provision originally barred gun possession for any "crime of domestic violence," defined as any "felony or misdemeanor crime of violence, regardless of length, term, or manner of punishment." 142 Cong. Rec. 5840. Congress rewrote the provision to require the use of physical force in response to the concern "that the term crime of violence was too broad, and could be interpreted to include an act such as cutting up a credit card with a pair of scissors," *id.,* at 26675. See *Hayes,* 555 U.S., at 428, 129 S. Ct. 1079, 172 L. Ed. 2d 816. Castleman would have us conclude that Congress thus meant "to narrow the scope of the statute to convictions based on especially severe conduct." Brief for Respondent 24. But all Congress meant to do was address the fear that §922(g)(9) might be triggered by offenses in which no force at all was directed at a person. As Senator Lautenberg noted, the revised text was not only "more precise" than the original but also "probably broader." 142 Cong. Rec. 26675.

### B

We are similarly unmoved by Castleman's invocation of the rule of lenity. Castleman is correct that our "construction of a criminal statute must be guided by the need for fair warning." *Crandon v. United States,* 494 U.S. 152, 160, 110 S. Ct. 997, 108 L. Ed. 2d 132 (1990). But "the rule of lenity only applies if, after considering text, structure, history, and purpose, there remains a grievous ambiguity or uncertainty in the statute, such that the Court must simply guess as to what Congress intended." *Barber v. Thomas,* 560 U.S. 474, 488, 130 S. Ct. 2499, 177 L. Ed. 2d 1 (2010) (citation and internal quotation marks omitted). That is not the case here.

### C

Finally, Castleman suggests—in a single paragraph—that we should read §922(g)(9) narrowly because it implicates his constitutional right to keep and bear arms. But Castleman has not challenged the constitutionality of §922(g)(9), either on its face or as applied to him, and the meaning of the statute is sufficiently clear that we need not indulge Castleman's cursory nod to constitutional avoidance concerns.

. . . .

Castleman's conviction for having "intentionally or knowingly cause[d] bodily injury to" the mother of his child qualifies as a "misdemeanor crime of domestic violence." The judgment of the United States Court of Appeals for the Sixth Circuit is therefore reversed, and the case is remanded for further proceedings consistent with this opinion. . . .

## Voisine v. United States

United States Supreme Court

136 S. Ct. 2272 (2016)

JUSTICE KAGAN delivered the opinion of the Court.

. . . .

### I

Congress enacted §922(g)(9) some 20 years ago to "close [a] dangerous loophole" in the gun control laws. *United States v. Castleman,* 572 U.S. ___, ___, 134 S. Ct. 1405,

188 L. Ed. 2d 426, 432 (2014) (quoting *United States v. Hayes*, 555 U.S. 415, 426, 129 S. Ct. 1079, 172 L. Ed. 2d 816 (2009)). An existing provision already barred convicted felons from possessing firearms. See § 922(g)(1) (1994 ed.). But many perpetrators of domestic violence are charged with misdemeanors rather than felonies, notwithstanding the harmfulness of their conduct. . . .

Petitioner Stephen Voisine pleaded guilty in 2004 to assaulting his girlfriend in violation of § 207 of the Maine Criminal Code, which makes it a misdemeanor to "intentionally, knowingly or recklessly cause[ ] bodily injury or offensive physical contact to another person." Me. Rev. Stat. Ann., Tit. 17-A, § 207(1)(A). Several years later, Voisine again found himself in legal trouble, this time for killing a bald eagle. See 16 U.S.C. § 668(a). While investigating that crime, law enforcement officers learned that Voisine owned a rifle. When a background check turned up his prior misdemeanor conviction, the Government charged him with violating 18 U.S.C. § 922(g)(9).

Petitioner William Armstrong pleaded guilty in 2008 to assaulting his wife in violation of a Maine domestic violence law making it a misdemeanor to commit an assault prohibited by § 207 (the general statute under which Voisine was convicted) against a family or household member. See Me. Rev. Stat. Ann., Tit. 17-A, § 207-A(1)(A). A few years later, law enforcement officers searched Armstrong's home as part of a narcotics investigation. They discovered six guns, plus a large quantity of ammunition. Like Voisine, Armstrong was charged under § 922(g)(9) for unlawfully possessing firearms.

Both men argued that they were not subject to § 922(g)(9)'s prohibition because their prior convictions (as the Government conceded) could have been based on reckless, rather than knowing or intentional, conduct. The District Court rejected those claims. Each petitioner then entered a guilty plea conditioned on the right to appeal the District Court's ruling.

The Court of Appeals for the First Circuit affirmed the two convictions, holding that "an offense with a *mens rea* of recklessness may qualify as a 'misdemeanor crime of violence' under § 922(g)(9)." *United States v. Armstrong*, 706 F.3d 1, 4 (2013); see *United States v. Voisine*, 495 Fed. Appx. 101, 102 (2013) (*per curiam*). Voisine and Armstrong filed a joint petition for certiorari, and shortly after issuing *Castleman*, this Court (without opinion) vacated the First Circuit's judgments and remanded the cases for further consideration in light of that decision. See *Armstrong v. United States*, 572 U.S. ___, 134 S. Ct. 1759, 188 L. Ed. 2d 590 (2014). On remand, the Court of Appeals again upheld the convictions, on the same ground. See 778 F.3d 176, 177 (2015).

We granted certiorari . . . .

## II

The issue before us is whether § 922(g)(9) applies to reckless assaults, as it does to knowing or intentional ones. To commit an assault recklessly is to take that action with a certain state of mind (or *mens rea*)—in the dominant formulation, to "consciously disregard[]" a substantial risk that the conduct will cause harm to another. ALI, Model Penal Code § 2.02(2)(c) (1962); Me. Rev. Stat. Ann., Tit. 17-A, § 35(3) (Supp. 2015) (adopting that definition); see *Farmer v. Brennan*, 511 U.S. 825, 836-837, 114 S. Ct. 1970, 128 L. Ed. 2d 811 (1994) (noting that a person acts recklessly only when he disregards a substantial risk of harm "of which he is aware"). . . . Statutory text and background alike lead us to conclude that a reckless domestic assault qualifies as a "misdemeanor crime of domestic violence" under § 922(g)(9). Congress defined that phrase to include crimes that necessarily involve the "use . . . of physical force." § 921(a)(33)(A). Reckless assaults, no less than the knowing or intentional ones we addressed in *Castleman*, satisfy that definition. Further, Congress enacted § 922(g)(9) in order to prohibit domestic abusers convicted under run-of-the-mill misdemeanor assault and battery laws from possessing guns. Because fully two-thirds of such state laws extend to recklessness, construing § 922(g)(9) to exclude crimes committed with that state of mind would substantially undermine the provision's design.

### A

Nothing in the word "use"—which is the only statutory language either party thinks relevant—indicates that § 922(g)(9) applies exclusively to knowing or intentional domestic assaults. Recall that under § 921(a)(33)(A), an offense counts as a "misdemeanor crime of domestic violence" only if it has, as an element, the "use" of force. Dictionaries consistently define the noun "use" to mean the "act of employing" something. Webster's New International Dictionary 2806 (2d ed. 1954) ("[a]ct of employing anything"); Random House Dictionary of the English Language 2097 (2d ed. 1987) ("act of employing, using, or putting into service"); Black's Law Dictionary 1541 (6th ed. 1990) ("[a]ct of employing," "application"). On that common understanding, the force involved in a qualifying assault must be volitional; an involuntary motion, even a powerful one, is not naturally described as an active employment of force. See *Castleman*, 572 U.S., at ___, 134 S. Ct. 1405, 188 L. Ed. 2d 426, 438 ("[T]he word 'use' conveys the idea that the thing used (here, 'physical force') has been made the user's instrument" (some internal quotation marks omitted)). But the word "use" does not demand that the person applying force have the purpose or practical certainty that it will cause harm, as compared with the understanding that it is substantially likely to do so. Or, otherwise said, that word is indifferent as to whether the actor has the mental state of intention, knowledge, or recklessness with respect to the harmful consequences of his volitional conduct. . . .

In sum, Congress's definition of a "misdemeanor crime of violence" contains no exclusion for convictions based on reckless behavior. A person who assaults another recklessly "use[s]" force, no less than one who carries out that same action knowingly or intentionally. The relevant text thus supports prohibiting petitioners, and others with similar criminal records, from possessing firearms.

B

So too does the relevant history. As explained earlier, Congress enacted § 922(g)(9) in 1996 to bar those domestic abusers convicted of garden-variety assault or battery misdemeanors—just like those convicted of felonies—from owning guns. See *supra*, at 1-2; *Castleman*, 572 U.S., at ___, ___, 134 S. Ct. 1405, 188 L. Ed. 2d 426, 432; *Hayes*, 555 U.S., at 426-427, 129 S. Ct. 1079, 172 L. Ed. 2d 816. Then, as now, a significant majority of jurisdictions—34 States plus the District of Columbia—defined such misdemeanor offenses to include the reckless infliction of bodily harm. See Brief for United States 7a-19a (collecting statutes). That agreement was no coincidence. Several decades earlier, the Model Penal Code had taken the position that a *mens rea* of recklessness should generally suffice to establish criminal liability, including for assault. See § 2.02(3), Comments 4-5, at 243-244 ("purpose, knowledge, and recklessness are properly the basis for" such liability); § 211.1 (defining assault to include "purposely, knowingly, or recklessly caus[ing] bodily injury"). States quickly incorporated that view into their misdemeanor assault and battery statutes. So in linking § 922(g)(9) to those laws, Congress must have known it was sweeping in some persons who had engaged in reckless conduct....

What is more, petitioners' reading risks rendering § 922(g)(9) broadly inoperative in the 35 jurisdictions with assault laws extending to recklessness—that is, inapplicable even to persons who commit that crime knowingly or intentionally. Consider Maine's statute, which (in typical fashion) makes it a misdemeanor to "intentionally, knowingly or recklessly" injure another. Me. Rev. Stat. Ann., Tit. 17-A, § 207(1)(A). Assuming that provision defines a single crime (which happens to list alternative mental states)—and accepting petitioners' view that § 921(a)(33)(A) requires at least a knowing *mens rea*—then, under *Descamps v. United States*, 570 U.S. ___, 133 S. Ct. 2276, 186 L. Ed. 2d 438 (2013), *no* conviction obtained under Maine's statute could qualify as a "misdemeanor crime of domestic violence." See *id.*, at ___, 133 S. Ct. 2276, 186 L. Ed. 2d 438, 451 (If a state crime "sweeps more broadly" than the federally defined one, a conviction for the state offense "cannot count" as a predicate, no matter what *mens rea* the defendant actually had)....

And anyway, we would not know how to resolve whether recklessness sufficed for a battery conviction at common law. Recklessness was not a word in the common law's standard lexicon, nor an idea in its conceptual framework; only in the mid- to late-1800's did courts begin to address reckless behavior in those terms. See Hall, Assault and Battery by the Reckless Motorist, 31 J. Crim. L. & C. 133, 138-139 (1940). The common law traditionally used a variety of overlapping and, frankly, confusing phrases to describe culpable mental states—among them, specific intent, general intent, presumed intent, willfulness, and malice. See, *e.g.*, *Morissette v. United States*, 342 U.S. 246, 252, 72 S. Ct. 240, 96 L. Ed. 288 (1952); Model Penal Code § 2.02, Comment 1, at 230. Whether and where conduct that we would today describe as reckless fits into that obscure scheme is anyone's guess: Neither petitioners' citations, nor the Government's competing ones, have succeeded in resolving that counterfactual question. And that indeterminacy confirms our conclusion that Congress had no thought of incorporating the common law's treatment of *mens rea* into § 921(a)(33)(A). That provision instead corresponds to the ordinary misdemeanor assault and battery laws used to prosecute domestic abuse, regardless of how their mental state requirements might—or, then again, might not—conform to the common law's.

### III

The federal ban on firearms possession applies to any person with a prior misdemeanor conviction for the "use . . . of physical force" against a domestic relation. § 921(a)(33)(A). That language, naturally read, encompasses acts of force undertaken recklessly—*i.e.,* with conscious disregard of a substantial risk of harm. And the state-law backdrop to that provision, which included misdemeanor assault statutes covering reckless conduct in a significant majority of jurisdictions, indicates that Congress meant just what it said. Each petitioner's possession of a gun, following a conviction under Maine law for abusing a domestic partner, therefore violates § 922(g)(9). We accordingly affirm the judgment of the Court of Appeals. . . .

---

Among the more controversial aspects of the domestic violence related firearms restrictions is the Lautenberg Amendment's failure to carve out a law enforcement or military exception. Conviction of a misdemeanor related to domestic violence bars persons in these professions from possessing guns, without exception. The measure was upheld by the District of Columbia Circuit in 1999, and the United States Supreme Court declined to review the decision [528 U.S. 928 (1999)].

## Fraternal Order of Police v. United States
United States Court of Appeals, District of Columbia Circuit
173 F.3d 898 (1999)

Williams, Circuit Judge. . . .

### I. Background

In *Fraternal Order of Police v. United States*, 332 U.S. App. D.C. 49, 152 F.3d 998 (D.C. Cir. 1998) ("*FOP I*"), this panel addressed two provisions of the 1996 amendments to the Gun Control Act of 1968, 18 U.S.C. § 921 et seq. The first was § 922(g)(9), which adds domestic violence misdemeanants—"any person who has been convicted in any court of a misdemeanor crime of domestic violence"—to the list of those for whom it is unlawful to possess a firearm "in or affecting interstate commerce" or to receive a firearm that has been shipped in interstate or foreign commerce. . . . Thus, domestic violence misdemeanants, unique among persons forbidden to possess guns under the Act, are not allowed to possess even government-issued firearms.

The Fraternal Order of Police challenged the amendments on a variety of grounds, including the equal protection element of the Fifth Amendment's due process clause. See *Bolling v. Sharpe*, 347 U.S. 497, 500, 98 L. Ed. 884, 74 S. Ct. 693 (1954). We found such a violation, holding that the amendments failed "rational basis" review because of their harsher treatment of domestic violence misdemeanants as compared to domestic violence felons. See 152 F.3d at 1002-03.

The United States petitioned for rehearing on two grounds: that FOP had not properly raised an argument based on the irrationality of the relative treatment of misdemeanants and felons, and that we were incorrect to find the difference irrational. We granted the petition, and requested briefing and heard oral argument on both points. See *Fraternal Order of Police v. United States*, 159 F.3d 1362 (1998).

We now determine that although it was likely improvident to address the felon-misdemeanant equal protection question in our original opinion, it has now become appropriate to do so. We also reverse our previous position and hold that the challenged provisions do satisfy rational basis review....

III. The rationality of the felon/misdemeanant distinction

The analysis of standing on this issue is unchanged from our prior opinion. 152 F.3d at 1001-02. On the merits, it is plain that §§ 922(g)(9) and 925(a)(1) impose a harsher sanction on domestic violence misdemeanants than on felons. Whereas gun possession by persons convicted of a crime punishable by at least one year of imprisonment is subject to § 925(a)(1)'s exemption for government-issued firearms, gun possession by domestic violence misdemeanants is not. See §§ 922(g)(1) & (9), 925(a)(1).

Such domestic violence misdemeanants are not a suspect class for equal protection analysis, and we assume for the purposes of this section that the regulation does not infringe a fundamental right.... Thus, the classification "must be upheld against equal protection challenge if there is any reasonably conceivable state of facts that could provide a rational basis for the classification." *FCC v. Beach Communications, Inc.*, 508 U.S. 307, 313, 124 L. Ed. 2d 211, 113 S. Ct. 2096 (1993).

Treating misdemeanants more harshly than felons seems irrational in the conventional sense of that term. After all, "what is uniform and undisputed is that the presence of some aggravating circumstance (or perhaps the absence of a mitigating one) is necessary to establish a felony." *FOP I*, 152 F.3d at 1003. In the standard equal protection case the legislature is fully entitled to weigh one characteristic more heavily than another, even though the balance may seem baffling to the court. But here Congress has incorporated a set of classifications made by state legislators who clearly regarded the felons' conduct as calling for greater severity than the misdemeanants'—whether because of moral opprobrium, risk to society, or whatever criteria may have guided their judgment. Yet Congress inverted this adopted classification, imposing a lesser disability on the felons, whom the state legislators had singled out for more severe treatment. Thus the usual proposition that Congress is entitled to address a problem "one step at a time" is not self-evidently applicable. See *id*.

But on reflection it appears to us not unreasonable for Congress to believe that existing laws and practices adequately deal with the problem of issuance of official firearms to felons but not to domestic violence misdemeanants—adequately at least in the sense of explaining how Congress might have found that as to felons the net benefit of federal prohibition (and non-exemption) fell below the net benefit of prohibition and non-exemption as to misdemeanants. Although state laws do not uniformly ban felons from possessing guns, as we observed in *FOP I*, see 152 F.3d at 1003, nonlegal restrictions such as formal and informal hiring practices may, as the government argues, prevent felons from being issued firearms covered by §925(a)(1) in a large measure of the remaining cases. In the absence of evidence negating these propositions, they indicate that there is a reasonably "conceivable state of facts" under which it is rational to believe that the felon problem makes a weaker claim to federal involvement than the misdemeanant one. When the government is faced with a practical determination like this one, we are obliged to accept "rough," even "illogical," solutions with an "imperfect fit between means and ends." See *Heller v. Doe*, 509 U.S. 312, 321, 125 L. Ed. 2d 257, 113 S. Ct. 2637 (1993).

. . . .

Finally, we reaffirm the determination in our original opinion that a special focus on domestic violence misdemeanants, as opposed to other misdemeanants, was not irrational under the norms of equal protection jurisprudence. See *id*. at 1002-03. . . .

*Commerce Clause*

FOP argues that §922(g)(9) is beyond Congress's power to enact under the commerce clause. We join all the numbered circuits[19] in rejecting this argument because §922(g)(9) contains a "jurisdictional element": in any prosecution under the provision for possession, the government must prove that the defendant possessed the firearm "in or affecting commerce."

. . . .

The district court's order granting summary judgment for the defendant is *Affirmed*.

---

Keeping guns out of the hands of batterers requires the efforts of everyone in the justice system. The following article addresses what happens when prosecutors are less than zealous about charging perpetrators with crimes that will insure the spirit of the Lautenberg Amendment is upheld.

---

19. [n2] See *United States v. Smith*, 101 F.3d 202, 215 (1st Cir. 1996); *United States v. Sorrentino*, 72 F.3d 294, 296 (2d Cir. 1995); *United States v. Gateward*, 84 F.3d 670, 672 (3d Cir. 1996); *United States v. Wells*, 98 F.3d 808, 811 (4th Cir. 1996); *United States v. Rawls*, 85 F.3d 240, 242 (5th Cir. 1996); *United States v. Turner*, 77 F.3d 887, 889 (6th Cir. 1996); *United States v. Lewis*, 100 F.3d 49, 52 (7th Cir. 1996); *United States v. Barry*, 98 F.3d 373, 378 (8th Cir. 1996); *United States v. Nguyen*, 88 F.3d 812, 820-21 (9th Cir. 1996); *United States v. Bolton*, 68 F.3d 396, 400 (10th Cir. 1995); *United States v. McAllister*, 77 F.3d 387, 390 (11th Cir. 1996).

## Tom Lininger, *An Ethical Duty to Charge Batterers Appropriately*
22 Duke J. Gender L. & Pol'y 173 (Spring 2015)

Introduction

On June 5, 2008, Utah prosecutors charged Ronald Lee Haskell with a misdemeanor crime of domestic violence. Records show that he hit his wife in the head and dragged her by her hair while their children were watching. In plea negotiations, Haskell's attorney persuaded the prosecution to reduce the charge to simple assault. The prosecution agreed to recommend that the court hold Haskell's plea "in abeyance" so that it would not appear on his record if he avoided further convictions in the next year. This disposition allowed Haskell to evade the gun ban for convicted domestic abusers under 18 U.S.C. § 922(g)(9), known as the Lautenberg Amendment.

Haskell's conviction disappeared, but his violence continued. After his wife divorced him and fled with their children, he went on a rampage. On July 2, 2014, he tied his mother to a chair and choked her after he learned that she had spoken with his ex-wife. He then drove to Texas on July 9, 2014, to find his ex-wife at her sister's residence near Houston. He disguised himself as a deliveryman for Federal Express. He became outraged when he discovered that his ex-wife was not there. He approached the house disguised as a deliveryman for Federal Express, and asked to see his ex-wife under the pretense of delivering a package. When he learned she was not there, he became enraged, brandished a gun, and ordered the six occupants of the residence—most of them children—to lie facedown on the floor. Then he tied them up and shot each of them in the head. All but one of the victims, a fifteen-year-old girl, died in the shooting. Next, he drove to the residence of his ex-wife's parents, where the death toll would likely have increased, had it not been for police intervention after the fifteen-year-old survivor of the shooting called 911.

The Haskell case demonstrates the urgent need for, and the limited effectiveness of, the federal gun ban for convicted domestic abusers. Convicted batterers are much more likely than the general population to commit homicide when allowed access to firearms. Yet the federal government has rarely enforced the gun ban, prosecuting approximately thirty to seventy each year among hundreds of thousands of potentially eligible defendants. Critics ranging from the U.S. Senate Judiciary Committee to columnists for the New York Times and U.S.A. Today have bemoaned the ineffectual enforcement of the federal gun ban.

Why is the federal gun ban utilized so infrequently? Advocates seeking to enhance its effectiveness have focused on the Supreme Court's interpretation of the Lautenberg Amendment, and have claimed that the lack of clarity in the interpretation of the statute has hindered its application. These advocates won a commendable victory in *United States v. Castleman* on March 26, 2014, and improved the uniformity of court decisions interpreting the ban. Yet, the last decade has shown that the most important limitation on the gun ban is not jurisprudential. It is the reluctance of local prosecutors to charge domestic violence in a way that would maximize the applicability of the federal gun ban. Until local prosecutors charge domestic violence appropriately, the vast majority of convicted batterers will dodge the gun ban with impunity.

This article proposes an ethical duty for prosecutors to charge batterers to the full extent of the law. The duty would obligate prosecutors to seek all possible enhancements based on the relationship of the accused to the victim and/or any witnesses, and to oppose any proposed dispositions that would lead to expunction. The new rule would increase the recognition that convicted abusers are ineligible to possess guns. The appropriate charging of domestic violence would also have ancillary benefits, allowing employers to recognize abusers, allowing victims to demonstrate their eligibility for certain government benefits, and increasing the odds that batterers will receive necessary counseling.

. . . .

## I. The Lautenberg Amendment and Its Rationale

When Senator Lautenberg first sought to disarm convicted domestic violence misdemeanants nearly twenty years ago, his purpose was clear: to decrease the grave risk that batterers with guns will kill their victims. Research subsequent to the passage of the Lautenberg Amendment has strengthened the evidence that perpetrators of fatal shootings are more likely to have a history of domestic violence

### A. Firearms and Domestic Violence

Today, there are a significant number of convicted domestic abusers in the United States. In fact, offenders convicted of domestic violence account for about 25% of violent offenders in local jails and 7% of violent offenders in state prison. Justice Sotomayor noted that more than a million acts of domestic violence occur in the U.S. every year. Given that 40% of U.S. households have guns, it is likely that hundreds of thousands of convicted domestic violence misdemeanants possess firearms.

Domestic violence is much more likely to result in the victim's death if the abuser owns a firearm. The risk of violence increases by 500% when batterers have access to firearms. Domestic violence assaults involving a gun are twenty three times more likely to result in death than those involving other weapons or bodily force. In 2011, intimate partners committed nearly two-thirds of fatal shootings in which women were the victims. Between 1980 and 2008, firearms were the cause of death for more than two-thirds of homicide victims who were spouses or ex-spouses of the assailants.

The single most accurate predictor of homicide with a firearm is a background of domestic violence. Mary Fan at the University of Washington School of Law analyzed recently released data in the National Violent Death Reporting System, and sought to identify common denominators among people who killed others with firearms. She found that one characteristic was more likely than any other to correspond with fatal shootings: a history of domestic abuse. Domestic violence also correlates with mass shootings, as 57% of shootings with four or more victims included a family member or current or former intimate partner of the shooter.

The dangers posed by armed domestic abusers extend beyond fatal shootings. Domestic abusers also use firearms to commit non-fatal assaults and to threaten homicides. In 2004, among residents of battered women's shelters in California, 37% reported that their abusers had threatened to shoot them or had otherwise harmed them with firearms. In the same study, 65% of respondents who had lived in households with a firearm reported that their abusers had used firearms against them, usually threatening to shoot them.

Conversely, domestic violence fatalities decrease when jurisdictions restrict batterers' access to firearms. When police increase enforcement of state statutes denying firearms to domestic abusers, the rate of homicides committed against intimate partners goes down significantly.

B. Passage of Lautenberg Amendment

On March 21, 1996, Senator Frank Lautenberg introduced S. 1632, "a bill to prohibit persons convicted of a crime involving domestic violence from owning or possessing firearms." As originally introduced, the bill prohibited the possession of firearms by any person who had committed a "crime involving domestic violence," whether the charged offense was a felony or misdemeanor. The bill created a disability not only for defendants who had been convicted of such an offense, but also for defendants who had been indicted and were awaiting trial. The original version of the bill did not require that the predicate offenses include specific elements, so long as they involved domestic violence.

Senator Lautenberg's intent was evident in a number of his 1996 floor statements. He explained that, "we proposed that no wife beater, no child abuser ... ought to be able to have a gun, because we learned one thing—that the difference between a murdered wife and a battered wife is often the presence of a gun." In addition, he noted that approximately two million cases of domestic abuse are reported each year, and that approximately 150,000 of these cases involve a firearm. He also discussed the fatal consequences of gun possession by batterers: "there is no question that the presence of a gun dramatically increases the likelihood that domestic violence will escalate into murder." According to Senator Lautenberg, "for many battered women and abused children, whether their abuser gets access to a gun will be nothing short of a matter of life and death." If abusers are permitted to retain their guns, "the end result, without any question, would be more shootings, more injuries, and more death."

. . . .

Senator Lautenberg made a number of concessions to win the support of Republicans in the Senate. They insisted that he drop the language creating a firearms disability based solely on an indictment for a misdemeanor crime of domestic violence. The Republicans also required that no predicate would qualify under the Lautenberg Amendment unless the defendant had been represented by counsel in the misdemeanor proceeding or had knowingly and intelligently waived his right to counsel.

After these revisions, the Senate approved the Lautenberg Amendment by a voice vote on July 25, 1996. The Senate approved it again by a resounding 97-2 vote when Senator Lautenberg added it to a new vehicle, the Treasury, Postal and General Appropriations Act.

Senator Lautenberg faced a tougher challenge in overcoming the opposition of the Republicans in the House of Representatives. They sought sweeping changes to the Lautenberg Amendment as a price for their approval. They proposed, inter alia, limiting the ban to misdemeanants who had been entitled to a jury trial, were notified of the law at the time of their conviction, and had abused their intimate partners (as opposed to only their children).

In order to fend off these major changes, which he felt would "gut" his bill, Senator Lautenberg agreed to other changes that he deemed to be less significant. He reached a compromise with the Republican negotiators in the early morning hours on September 28, 1996, the very day when the House voted on the bill. Senator Lautenberg accepted eleventh-hour amendments that, according to Lautenberg, had been authored by "enemies of the ban—lawmakers who oppose any curbs on guns."

The most significant of the revisions incorporated a new "use-of-force" requirement. As Lautenberg would later recount, "some argued that the term 'crime of violence' [in the original bill] was too broad, and could be interpreted to include an act such as cutting up a credit card with a pair of scissors. Although this concern seemed far-fetched to me, I did agree to a new definition." The Republican negotiators proposed, and Senator Lautenberg accepted, a version of the use-of-force requirement that was more restrictive than the typical definition in the federal gun laws.

One final amendment by Republican Representative Bob Barr added language that subjected police officers and military personnel to the new gun ban. Senator Lautenberg later indicated that Representative Barr inserted this amendment after Senator Lautenberg had gone to sleep on September 28, 1996. Senator Lautenberg did not object to the revision when he learned of it the next day, but he had concerns about Representative Barr's motives; Senator Lautenberg suspected that the amendment was part of a strategy to make the bill less attractive to fellow Republicans and decrease the likelihood of its passage.

Even with Representative Barr's last-minute amendment, the House approved the conference report on September 28, 1996, by a vote of 370-37. The Senate passed the bill on September 30, 1996, by a vote of 84–15. The President signed the bill into law on September 30, 1996.

Two themes emerged in the legislative record that culminated in the passage of the Lautenberg Amendment. First, Congress expressed its intent that the new gun ban be applied broadly. Second, Congress intended for the new law to be applied uniformly so that it would reach any conviction for an act involving domestic violence, notwithstanding the vagaries of state statutory definitions.

### C. Definition of Predicate Offenses

Section 922(g)(9) of Title 18 ("Lautenberg Amendment") creates a firearms disability for any person convicted of "a misdemeanor crime of domestic violence." The Lautenberg Amendment also criminalizes the act of selling or otherwise disposing of a firearm by giving it to a person who has been convicted of a misdemeanor crime of domestic violence. Only convictions—not indictments—for a misdemeanor crime of domestic violence can result in a firearms disability under § 922(g)(9). Like the rest of 18 U.S.C. § 922(g), § 922(g)(9) has a jurisdictional predicate: the government must prove that the firearm or ammunition in question has traveled in interstate commerce. A violation of the Lautenberg Amendment is punishable by a prison term of up to ten years and a fine of up to $250,000.

The term "misdemeanor crime of domestic violence" is defined in 18 U.S.C. § 921(a)(33)(A):

> "Misdemeanor crime of domestic violence" means an offense that—
>
> (i) is a misdemeanor under Federal or State law; and
>
> (ii) has, as an element, the use or attempted use of physical force, or the threatened use of a deadly weapon, committed by a current or former spouse, parent, or guardian of the victim, by a person with whom the victim shares a child in common, by a person who is cohabiting with or has cohabited with the victim as a spouse, parent, or guardian, or by a person similarly situated to a spouse, parent, or guardian of the victim.

In addition to these definitional requirements for the predicate offense, § 921(a)(33)(B)(i) also imposes procedural requirements:

> A person shall not be considered to have been convicted of such an offense for purposes of this chapter, unless—
>
> (I) the person was represented by counsel in the case, or knowingly and intelligently waived the right to counsel in the case; and
>
> (II) in the case of a prosecution for an offense described in this paragraph for which a person was entitled to a jury trial in the jurisdiction in which the case was tried, either
>
> (aa) the case was tried by a jury, or
>
> (bb) the person knowingly and intelligently waived the right to have the case tried by a jury, by guilty plea or otherwise.

The Lautenberg Amendment includes other language allowing an exception to the gun ban for defendants whose civil rights were forfeited as a result of the misdemeanor conviction and then restored at a later time. For purposes of the Lautenberg Amendment, the forfeiture and restoration of civil rights will be evaluated under state, not federal, law. A defendant seeking to invoke the exception for restoration of civil rights bears the burden of proof on this issue. A defendant who appeals a conviction for a misdemeanor crime of domestic violence is still subject to the gun ban until the conviction is vacated.

One unique provision of the Lautenberg Amendment is its coverage of military and law enforcement personnel, who are exempted from all the other gun bans under 18 U.S.C. §§ 922(g)(1)-922(g)(8). These personnel are subject to the same criminal penalties that apply to ordinary citizens who possess firearms after a misdemeanor crime of domestic violence.

Congress revisited the Lautenberg Amendment in 2006 as part of reauthorization of the Violence Against Women Act. At that time, Congress amended the definition of the predicate offense under 18 U.S.C. § 921(a)(33)(A) to indicate that a conviction under tribal law would also be subject to the gun ban.

## II. The Supreme Court's Review of the Lautenberg Amendment

In the last decade, the Supreme Court has interpreted the Lautenberg Amendment twice. In 2009, the Court considered the statute's requirement of a current or past intimate relationship between the offender and the victim (the "relational requirement"). In 2014, the Court considered the statute's requirement that the predicate offense involve the use of force against the victim (the "use-of-force requirement"). . . .

### A. *Hayes* and the Relational Requirement

In 2004, police in West Virginia responded to the home of Randy Edward Hayes after receiving a 911 call reporting domestic violence. Upon arrival, police found that Hayes possessed several weapons. The federal grand jury returned an indictment of Hayes for violating the Lautenberg Amendment by possessing firearms after a 1994 conviction for a misdemeanor crime of domestic violence. Hayes had committed the 1994 assault against his wife, but the local prosecutor had charged Hayes under a generic battery statute that did not require proof of any particular relationship between the assailant and the victim. Hayes entered a conditional guilty plea to the federal charges in 2004 so that he could appeal.

When the case reached the Fourth Circuit, Hayes argued that his previous misdemeanor conviction did not meet the relational requirement for a predicate offense under the Lautenberg Amendment. He insisted that the definition of "misdemeanor crime of domestic violence" in 18 U.S.C. § 921(a)(33)(A) requires that the statute defining the predicate offense include, as a discrete and indispensable element, the relationship between the assailant and the victim. Hayes also argued that the rule of lenity should favor the defendant when a criminal statute is ambiguous. The Fourth Circuit reversed Hayes' conviction, agreeing with his narrow interpretation of § 921(a)(33)(A).

The United States petitioned for certiorari, and the Supreme Court granted review. The United States argued that § 921(a)(33)(A) does not require that the relationship between abuser and victim to be an element of the predicate offense; rather, the United States contended that the relationship need only have existed at the time of the offense, whether or not the charging instrument mentioned the relationship. In support of this argument, the United States offered technical arguments of statutory construction and also relied heavily on the legislative history of the Lautenberg Amendment, particularly the comments of sponsors who sought universal application of the gun ban. The United States argued that the Supreme Court's broad interpretation of § 921(a)(33)(A) would make a real difference in protecting battered women from homicide.

Various amici suggested that the *Hayes* ruling would be vital in determining the efficacy of the Lautenberg Amendment. Senators Lautenberg, Feinstein, and Murray—the most ardent supporters of the Lautenberg Amendment in 1996—submitted an amicus brief indicating that the Court's decision in *Hayes* would determine whether the Lautenberg Amendment would be a "dead letter." Other amici urged a ruling in favor of the United States in order to ensure effective enforcement of the Lautenberg Amendment and to protect "victims of thousands of domestic violence abusers."

By a 7–2 vote, the Supreme Court adopted the Government's position. Justice Ginsburg wrote for the majority, opining that the most "sensible" interpretation of § 921(a)(33)(A) did not require that the statute defining the underlying offense must include the relationship as an element. "Practical considerations strongly support our reading of § 921(a)(33)(A)'s language," the majority opinion observed. The Court emphasized the importance of effectuating, rather than thwarting, congressional intent to disarm convicted batterers throughout the United States.

Advocacy groups hailed the Court's decision as a major victory for battered women. The National Network to End Domestic Violence issued a press release commending the Hayes ruling for "keeping guns out of the hands of batterers." The Brady Campaign to Prevent Handgun Violence praised the Court's decision to "protect domestic violence victims." It appeared that the Supreme Court cleared away the hurdles to effective enforcement of the Lautenberg Amendment.

B. *Castleman* and the Use-of-Force Requirement

Five years later, in 2014, the United States and a long list of amici were once again asking the Supreme Court to breathe life into the Lautenberg Amendment. The 2014 case involved a defendant in Tennessee, James Alvin Castleman, who had possessed firearms in 2008 after a 2001 conviction for "intentionally or knowingly causing bodily injury to" the mother of his child. Charged in federal court with violating the Lautenberg Amendment, he moved to dismiss the indictment on the ground that the predicate offense did not meet the use-of-force requirement in § 921(a)(33)(A). He claimed that the act at issue in his 2001 conviction was simply an offensive touching, not an act of violence within the meaning of the use-of-force requirement in § 921(a)(33)(A). The Sixth Circuit agreed with Castleman and reversed his conviction.

The United States petitioned for certiorari to make the argument that an offensive touching involves a sufficient use of force to qualify as a predicate under the Lautenberg Amendment. According to the United States, the phrase "domestic violence" is a term of art that means something broader than mere "violence," and spans a range of harmful conduct that does not necessarily involve a forceful blow. As in *Hayes*, the United States highlighted comments in the legislative history of the Lautenberg Amendment to support their position that the sponsors' intent that the gun ban apply broadly irrespective of variations in states' definitions of domestic violence.

The government's position attracted support from several amici. For example, Mayors Against Gun Violence filed a brief asserting that a ruling for the United States in *Castleman* would "keep guns out of the hands of convicted abusers." The National Network to End Domestic Violence beseeched the Court to support the United States' position and "allow Section 922(g)(9) to do the important work that Congress enacted it to do." The Brady Center to Prevent Gun Violence filed a brief contending that the proper interpretation of the Lautenberg Amendment would make "[gun-related] violence less likely by punishing—and thus deterring—such conduct."

The Supreme Court ruled in favor of the government. The Court explained that while minor uses of force may not amount to "violence" in the generic sense, they do suffice for the use-of-force requirement in the Lautenberg Amendment. Within the unique context of domestic violence, offensive touching can be very harmful, especially when continued over a prolonged period. The Court was mindful that a broad reading of the use-of-force requirement could facilitate the more effective implementation of the Lautenberg Amendment because many local prosecutors charge domestic violence under statutes that do not require use of force in the strictest sense.

Advocates for the government's position celebrated the *Castleman* ruling as a huge step forward for battered women. Jonathan Lowy, a lawyer for the Brady Center to Prevent Gun Violence, described it as "an important victory for women, children and families across the nation who will continue to be protected by strong, sensible federal laws that keep domestic-violence abusers from obtaining guns." The White House issued a press release expressing confidence in the efficacy of the *Castleman* ruling: "this week the Supreme Court decided a case that will save women's lives."

C. The Fallacy That Judicial Interpretations Constrain Lautenberg

There is a widespread belief that judicial interpretation of the Lautenberg Amendment played a significant role in determining the effectiveness of the gun ban for convicted domestic abusers. For example, one commentator predicted that the Supreme Court's holding in *Hayes* would "effectuate the purpose" of the Lautenberg Amendment and deny firearms to batterers. Another commentator wrote that a broad judicial interpretation of Lautenberg would "give full effect to Congress's intent," but that "the wrong decision by the Court could leave abused women and children vulnerable to gun violence." A press release from Mayors Against Illegal Guns in 2014 summed up the prevailing belief about the importance of the judiciary in implementing the gun ban for convicted abusers: "we're counting on the Supreme Court to keep Americans safe."

This faith is misplaced. The Supreme Court's interpretations of the Lautenberg Amendment matter very little if federal prosecutors rarely utilize the statute.

Favorable interpretations of the relational requirement or the use-of-force requirement do not put gun-toting batterers in prison. The Court's willingness to construe 18 U.S.C. § 921(a)(33)(A) in accordance with congressional intent is a necessary, but not sufficient, condition for successful prosecution of gun possession by convicted domestic violence misdemeanants. The most important variable for effective enforcement is the number of charges filed by federal prosecutors under the Lautenberg Amendment.

Charging rates remained low after the *Hayes* ruling in 2009. The year before it was decided, federal prosecutors charged 67 defendants under the Lautenberg Amendment. The Supreme Court decided *Hayes* in February 2009, and one might have expected an increase in the number of charges filed thereafter. But the number of defendants charged under the Lautenberg Amendment in 2009 actually dropped to 49. The number rose to 56 in 2010, dropped to 40 in 2011, and dropped further to 32 in 2012. In none of the four years following the *Hayes* ruling did the number of defendants charged under the Lautenberg Amendment exceed the number charged in the year immediately prior to the *Hayes* ruling. These data cast doubt on the assumption that the *Hayes* ruling fixed a jurisprudential problem that had constrained the enforcement of the gun ban for domestic abusers. The commentators who predicted that the *Hayes* ruling would increase prosecutors' use of the Lautenberg amendment were mistaken.

There is no cause for optimism that *Castleman* will make more of a difference. Indeed, very few jurisdictions had interpreted the use-of-force requirement restrictively before the Court overruled this interpretation in *Castleman*, so there is little reason to expect that it will bring increased prosecutions under the Lautenberg Amendment.

Some advocates who defend the efficacy of the gun ban for convicted abusers point to the total number of background checks that led to denials due to a prior conviction for domestic violence. For example, Senator Lautenberg himself referred to thousands of purchases prevented by his amendment. Background checks do not deny guns to all convicted batterers, however. One problem is that the background checks rely on an incomplete database of convictions that undercounts misdemeanor crimes of domestic violence. Even when a background check thwarts an attempted purchase by a convicted domestic violence misdemeanant, the hindrance is usually only momentary. Purchasers disqualified in background checks easily buy guns from sellers who are not federally licensed, and who do not need to run background checks on purchasers. For example, neighbors and vendors at gun shows are exempt from running background checks. Further, the black market provides many options to a determined purchaser. Enforcement that consists primarily of background checks by licensed dealers, as opposed to prosecution for unlawful possession, provides scant protection for victims of domestic violence.

In sum, the sanguine commentary on *Hayes* and *Castleman* masks a more basic problem that limits the effectiveness of the Lautenberg Amendment. Federal prosecutors simply do not utilize the Lautenberg Amendment very much, and their willingness to use the statute does not seem sensitive to the Supreme Court's construction of the language in § 921(a)(33)(A). . . .

### III. The Real Culprit: Undercharging by Local Prosecutors

Why do federal prosecutors file so few charges under the Lautenberg Amendment? These charges are fairly easy to prove—the evidence need only show the fact of possession and the fact of the prior qualifying conviction (a task made easier by the Supreme Court's favorable jurisprudence). The low number of federal prosecutions filed under the Lautenberg Amendment is not due to the difficulty of proving such cases, but rather to the lack of opportunity to charge them. In other words, federal law enforcement agents are not referring many cases that meet the requirements of 18 U.S.C. § 922(g)(9).

Why do federal law enforcement officers refer so few prosecutable cases under the Lautenberg Amendment? The explanation lies in the difficulty of finding such convictions in federal databases such as the National Instant Criminal Background Check System (NICS). Underreporting of qualifying convictions to NICS remained a significant problem even in 2014. Even when local jurisdictions enter qualifying convictions into NICS, they are not conspicuous as predicates for 18 U.S.C. § 922(g)(9), because most are under generic assault statutes that do not require proof of domestic abuse. . . .

The challenge of discerning domestic violence is particularly difficult when the defendant enters a guilty plea—the most common type of conviction under simple assault statutes. There may be an abundance of misdemeanor convictions that could qualify under the Lautenberg Amendment, but these convictions are difficult to recognize in federal databases.

The lack of clarity is due in large part to local prosecutors' practice of undercharging domestic violence in the first place. Local prosecutors rarely charge defendants under the specialized statutes that clearly indicate the commission of domestic violence, even though these statutes now exist in half the states. Prosecutors are presently under no obligation to invoke the specialized statutes, and they prefer to file more general assault charges or reduced charges. The following subsections consider the reasons why prosecutors undercharge domestic violence, the harmful effects of such undercharging, and the inadequacy of current safeguards designed to ensure appropriate charging.

#### A. Reasons for Undercharging

Undercharging of domestic violence can take several forms. Sometimes, local prosecutors select a lenient charge, or a charge without an enhancement based on the relationship between the offender and the victim. Other times, prosecutors dismiss the case altogether. Even when they file strict charges at the outset, they might later engage in "charge bargaining" as part of plea negotiations. Prosecutors might agree to dispose of charges by means of pretrial diversion, such that the defendant would avoid punishment if he keeps a clean record. Sometimes the prosecution might agree to expunction or restoration of gun rights after conviction and service of the sentence. This subsection will refer to all of the foregoing strategies by the shorthand "undercharging."

The reasons for undercharging are manifold. Some prosecutors simply do not take domestic violence seriously. One author discussed an old-fashioned view that is "disdainful of prosecuting domestic violence cases" because of the perception that such cases are "trivial." A prosecutor with such a view might sympathize with defendants and not want to take away their rights to possess firearms, especially if the defendants are law enforcement officers or military personnel whose loss of gun rights might cause them to lose their jobs.

Alternatively, some local prosecutors might choose to "deal down" cases for the sake of expediency. These prosecutors may believe that they will accomplish more good by charging a large volume of domestic violence cases and disposing of them quickly through plea agreements. The prosecutors might also choose to accept guilty pleas because judges want to clear their dockets. Defendants are eager to plead when presented with the alternative of a reduced charge less likely to result in a firearms disability.

Some prosecutors undercharge domestic violence because they believe it is difficult to take such cases to trial. Complainants in domestic violence cases often recant or refuse to testify. Their reluctance can create major problems for the prosecution, especially after the Supreme Court's rulings under the Confrontation Clause that an accuser's hearsay statement might be inadmissible unless cross-examination is possible. For all these reasons, undercharging is attractive.

Ironically, the *Hayes* and *Castleman* decisions may hinder enforcement of the Lautenberg Amendment by decreasing local prosecutors' reliance on specialized domestic violence statutes. The Court's recent jurisprudence might breed overconfidence among local prosecutors that a generic assault conviction with a scant record is all that federal prosecutors need to charge the Lautenberg Amendment. While *Hayes* and *Castleman* may improve the likelihood that federal prosecutors can use simple assaults as predicates, these decisions may have also decreased the likelihood that federal law enforcement officials can recognize the predicates in databases.

B. Effects of Undercharging

. . . .

Even if undercharging did not impede the detection of defendants who violate Lautenberg, another significant problem would remain: defendants convicted of simple assault sometimes lack notice of the gun ban. As Chief Justice Roberts noted in his *Hayes* dissent, "an individual should not go to jail for failing to conduct a 50-state survey or comb through obscure legislative history." The notice problem is an important issue of fairness, which also erodes the protection of victims because armed abusers may not know of their firearm disability. By contrast, if local prosecutors were to utilize the specialized statutes for domestic assault, courts could develop protocols for informing defendants that they have lost their gun rights.

A third adverse consequence of undercharging is that the applicability of the gun ban may turn on prosecutorial discretion. Some commentators welcome a high level of discretion for prosecutors, but other commentators note that discretion invites arbitrariness or vindictiveness in the selection of charges. The application of the gun ban should not turn on whether a local prosecutor liked or disliked the defendant at the time the prosecutor charged the predicate offense. The elimination of discretion would ensure that all similarly situated defendants receive the same treatment.

Undercharging of domestic violence has many harmful effects unrelated to the Lautenberg Amendment. Undercharging thwarts the intent of state legislatures to match certain punishments to the crime of domestic violence. Undercharging also diminishes the protection of battered women. An accused returning home from jail shortly after a complaint may increase the complainant's vulnerability by demonstrating the futility of calling the police. Other harms result from the mislabeling of domestic violence as general assault. An employer who is considering whether to hire an abuser convicted of simply assault for a sensitive job might not be able to discern from a background check that the defendant is a domestic abuser. A survivor of domestic violence might have difficulty demonstrating her eligibility for government benefits and resources that state legislatures have made available for battered women. In short, undercharging is a dishonest characterization of domestic violence that redounds to the detriment of battered women and society as a whole.

C. Inadequacy of Safeguards

There are several safeguards designed to prevent, or mitigate the harms of, prosecutors' tendency to undercharge cases involving domestic violence....

One safeguard is the reporting requirement imposed by Congress in 2005 as a condition for states to receive funding under the Violence Against Women Act. The statute required states to improve their processes for providing information to the FBI about the facts underlying misdemeanor convictions involving domestic violence, so that federal law enforcement officials could recognize convicted abusers even if local prosecutors had filed charges that did not require proof of domestic violence. Notwithstanding these improvements, there are still significant gaps in the reporting system. Many jurisdictions are not completing the questionnaires used to determine whether ambiguous misdemeanor convictions might qualify as predicates under the Lautenberg Amendment. As a result, a significant number of convicted batterers are able to escape accountability in background checks because domestic violence is not conspicuous in their conviction records. The greater use of factual questionnaires for the FBI's databases has not offset the harm caused by local prosecutors' reluctance to charge batterers appropriately.

A second safeguard, the U.S. Department of Justice's requirement that prosecutors must charge the most serious offense, has not solved the problem of undercharging in the context of domestic violence. The requirement applies at the federal level, but the federal government handles very few misdemeanors involving domestic violence. State agencies and local district attorneys' offices prosecute the lion's share of domestic violence offenses, but these offices generally have not imposed such requirements. Further, the U.S. Department of Justice altered its charging policy in 2010 due to concerns about overcharging of drug cases, so now even federal prosecutors have more discretion in selecting charges.

A third safeguard against undercharging is sentencing based on the conduct underlying an offense, rather simply the conviction. The goal behind this approach is to sentence offenders based on what they actually did, irrespective of how prosecutors charged them. Proponents of sentencing based on offense conduct have suggested that it might reduce some of the incentives for undercharging and might promote uniformity in the disposition of cases. Sentencing based on offense conduct has fallen far short of this goal. State courts—which handle the vast majority of cases involving domestic violence—did not embrace the new sentencing system to the same extent as federal courts. Even at the federal level, prosecutors were able to limit their presentation of offense conduct to judges in order to ensure that sentences aligned with the charges actually filed. An even more fundamental problem with sentencing based on offense conduct arose when the Supreme Court held that the right to trial by jury limits the ability of judges to sentence defendants for conduct not charged in the indictment. In short, sentencing reform has not been a viable means of reining in prosecutorial discretion in charging.

Some states allow crime victims to express their views when prosecutors are contemplating plea agreements with perpetrators of violent crime. One rationale for the involvement of victims is that their input might limit the willingness of prosecutors to offer overly generous terms to defendants. Yet, research does not indicate that victims exert much influence over plea offers. Survivors of domestic violence are particularly unlikely to insist on strict charges, because 80 percent of these survivors will change their stories or refuse to cooperate with the prosecution.

In sum, there is little reason for confidence in the various safeguards that purport to limit the harmful effects of undercharging. The only way to solve the problem is to impose a specific obligation on local prosecutors to file the right charges in cases involving domestic violence.

### IV. A Proposed Ethical Duty to Charge Batterers Appropriately.

. . . .

### A. Nature of the Ethical Duty

An ethical duty to charge domestic violence appropriately must include several elements. It must include an obligation to bring the most serious applicable charge, and to invoke all statutes and enhancements specifically tailored to cases involving intimate partners as victims or witnesses. The ethical duty to charge appropriately must include an obligation to avoid dispositions that will hinder the subsequent detection of a qualifying predicate under the Lautenberg Amendment. The ethical duty must include a "safety valve" that permits adjustment of charges in extraordinary circumstances, so long as the disposition remains proportionate to the offense and accords adequate protection to victims and witnesses.

Here is one possible formulation of an ethical duty to charge batterers appropriately:

> In a case involving an allegation of domestic violence, a prosecutor must charge the most serious offense readily supported by evidence accessible at the time of the charging decision. The charging instrument must include any possibly applicable offense or enhancement that specifies the intimate or familial relationship between the assailant and victims and/or witnesses, assuming that such offense or enhancement is readily supported by evidence accessible at the time of the charging decision. The prosecutor shall not consent to any negotiated disposition involving dismissal or expunction except under extraordinary circumstances, and in any event, the prosecutor must seek a disposition reflecting the gravity of the offense and ensuring reasonable protection of all victims from further violence. In a case involving a misdemeanor crime of domestic violence, a prosecutor shall file thorough records with the court and shall submit, or cause to be submitted, thorough information to the National Instant Criminal Background Check System (NICS) in order to ensure that the defendant is subject to any applicable firearms disability under federal and state law.

The proposed rule rests on compelling principles. Prosecutors should not subordinate the interests of accusers just because the United States' adversarial system puts the primary emphasis on the conflict between the government and the accused. Prosecutors sometimes exploit victims instrumentally to secure convictions in cases that proceed to trial, regarding victims as nuisances hindering the efficient disposition of cases through plea bargains or dismissals. The ethical duty to charge domestic violence cases appropriately would align with the deontological imperative that every person, including a crime victim, has inherent dignity and moral autonomy; no person is simply a means to an end. Deontological philosophy also posits that violent crime is a lapse of moral duty deserving a particular punishment irrespective of prosecutors' concerns about efficiency and streamlining caseloads. Put a different way, the gravity of domestic violence does not vary depending on a prosecutor's workload.

The proposed duty would also result in several other tangible benefits. The rule would increase the odds that local prosecutors would select charges that clearly signal the defendant's commission of domestic violence. Convictions for such offenses would be more easily recognizable in NCIS and other law enforcement databases, leading to greater accuracy in background checks and greater detection of § 922(g)(9) violators when police consult the databases after search warrants and traffic stops. More generally, the new duty proposed here would promote consistency in the treatment of cases involving domestic violence, thereby increasing deterrence of prospective offenders. Victims would gain greater confidence to file complaints without fear of reprisals after abrupt dismissals. The proper charging of domestic violence would lead to greater precision and clarity in court records. When prosecutors explicitly label domestic violence as such, there is a great likelihood that judges in marital dissolution cases will not award custody to batterers, that battered women will be able to qualify for special government benefits, and that prospective employers will not hire batterers for jobs in sensitive settings.

B. Codifying the Duty

There are several bodies of authority regulating the ethics of prosecutors. Which would be the best vehicle for the proposed rule requiring prosecutors to charge batterers appropriately? This Subpart will consider four options: the ABA Model Rules of Professional Conduct, the ABA Standards for Practice (Prosecution Function), the internal rules of prosecuting agencies, and state statutes.

The optimal home for the new ethical rule would be the ABA Model Rules of Professional Conduct, because they provide a template adopted in virtually all states' ethical codes. State bars enforce their ethics codes through disciplinary proceedings. Harmful consequences, ranging from censure to disbarment, could befall violators of the state ethical codes, so attorneys are more attentive to these codes than to hortatory, nonbinding guidelines. Another advantage of regulating prosecutors under state bars' ethical codes is that the panels evaluating bar complaints consist primarily of attorneys who are not prosecutors. These "outsiders" bring a degree of accountability that an in-house review by fellow prosecutors would lack.

The proposed rule would insert a new topic into the ABA Model Rules. But the rule would fit well alongside other existing rules. Many of these rules take account of third-party interests when such interests might not otherwise attract sufficient attention. One example is the Rule 1.6(b) list of exceptions to attorney-client confidentiality, allowing disclosure of client information when necessary to avert "reasonably certain death of substantial bodily harm to a third party," among other categories of harm to third parties. Rule 1.6(b)(7) also allows attorneys to reveal client information when necessary to comply with statutes that mandate reporting of child abuse. Another relevant example is Rule 4.4(a), which directs that a lawyer representing a client shall not unduly "embarrass, delay or burden a third person." The most on-point example is Rule 3.8, which sets forth several duties of prosecutors with respect to both the accused and third parties, including a subpoint that regulates the charging decision. A new ethical rule to charge batterers appropriately is a reasonable extension of principles that already underlie the ABA Model Rules in general, and Rule 3.8 in particular.

A less desirable option for codifying the new duty would be to include it in the Standards for Criminal Practice (Prosecution Function). Approved by the ABA House of Delegates in 1993, these standards set forth specific guidance for both prosecutors and defense attorneys. The standards for prosecutors include a list of considerations to take into account when charging a case initially, and other considerations to bear in mind when considering a negotiated disposition. On first examination, the

Standards might seem to be a good home for the new duty to charge batterers appropriately: after all, they treat the issues of charging and plea negotiation in more detail than do the ABA Model Rules. But no state bar has adopted the Standards for Criminal Practices as part of mandatory regime subject to enforcement through bar discipline. At best, the Standards for Criminal Practice are precatory and aspirational, and prosecutors would be less likely to follow such nonbinding guidelines than to obey the first-tier authority in the state ethics codes based on the ABA Model Rules.

Some prosecutorial agencies have extensive in-house rules and guidelines for their attorneys. For example, the U.S. Attorneys' manuals span nine volumes. However, the ethical duty to charge batterers appropriately deserves to be codified universally, and in-house regulation would lead to a patchwork approach. The local jurisdictions that handle the great bulk of domestic violence misdemeanors are the least likely to have in-house ethical codes. Even if all prosecutorial agencies had ethics codes, the relegation of an ethical matter to this level of authority would result in a wide disparity of approaches, thwarting the intent of Congress to treat domestic abusers uniformly. Another problem with in-house regulation is the apparent conflict of interest when prosecutors sit in judgment of other prosecutors within the same agency.

State statutes deserve consideration as a vehicle for the regulation of prosecutorial ethics, but this approach might be too radical. State bars are generally reluctant to cede their self-regulation to legislatures. In fact, the legislative branch has rarely taken up the regulation of the legal profession at all. Examples of statutes regulating the legal profession are most noteworthy for their infrequency. A proposal to legislate new standards for lawyers might provoke backlash in state bars at a time when it is important to build a consensus in favor of appropriate charging for cases involving domestic violence.

. . . .

C. Foreseeable Objections

Several objections to this Article's proposal are possible. The first is that limits on prosecutorial discretion are generally undesirable. When Attorney General John Ashcroft instructed federal prosecutors to charge the most serious offense in all categories of cases (subject to very limited exceptions), critics complained that the policy led to draconian sentences and failed to account for unique circumstances that might warrant leniency in a particular case. The zealous charging of drug cases—which federal prosecutors handle more commonly than cases involving spousal abuse—drew especially strong condemnation. Eventually Attorney General Eric Holder heeded the critics and revised the Ashcroft guidelines to allow federal prosecutors greater discretion in charging. The criticism of overcharging in federal drug cases, however, does not apply with the same force to this article's proposal. The punishments prescribed by federal drug statutes were extremely harsh during the era of obligatory charging. By contrast, the punishments for misdemeanor crimes of domestic violence are generally lenient. Drug prosecutions do not present the same practical challenges as domestic violence prosecutions, such as unavailable witnesses, lack of cooperators and lack of physical evidence. Moreover, the history of prosecutorial reluctance to charge domestic violence is unique to this category of crime. Simply put, the need to mandate prosecutorial zeal is greater, and the effects are less dangerous, in the context of domestic violence.

Some might argue that a requirement of strict charging could reduce opportunities for cooperation by defendants in cases involving domestic violence. But batterers typically have little value in cooperating as government witnesses against co-defendants, because domestic violence is generally a single-defendant crime. It is true that prosecutors might want batterers to agree to participate in treatment programs, but lenient initial charges are not necessary to entice such participation; the court can require it as part of the sentence, or the prosecutor can incentivize it by recommending a reduced sentence, if not a reduced charge. A stricter initial charge might actually increase the likelihood of cooperation by the defendant, because he would have more to lose if he were uncooperative.

Another possible criticism is that this article's proposal might have a "chilling effect" on prosecutors or victims of domestic violence. Perhaps prosecutors might prefer to forego charges altogether for fear that dismissals and charge bargaining would not be possible if a particular prosecution proved difficult. Or perhaps victims of domestic violence would not complain to police in the first place if the only possible outcome were a strict charge. These concerns are not new, however. The same concerns arose in response to prior initiatives to treat domestic violence more seriously. The concerns seem to lack merit with respect to prosecutors, who are under political pressure to charge domestic violence even if lenient dispositions are no longer possible. Victims need to summon police and extricate themselves from danger even if the consequences befalling the batterers will be more serious due to the new rules. Enlightened policy makers have long ago realized that the victims' sympathy for the abusers cannot lead to lower sanctions; punishment is not less urgent just because a victim fearing reprisals urges leniency for the offender.

One last foreseeable objection is that the proposed rule is too specific for the ABA Model Rules. Yet Rule 3.8 already includes many rules that impose highly specific duties on prosecutors, such as the duty to refrain from calling lawyers before the grand jury except in certain limited circumstances. The general trend is for ethical rules to become more specific, and specificity is particularly important for rules governing prosecutors. Some critics might argue that that a unique ethical rule for charging cases involving domestic violence does not make sense when the ABA Model Rules do not regulate the charging of other cases, but the uniqueness of domestic violence justifies this special treatment. In any event, it is certainly possible to add ethical rules for charging other categories of cases in the future.

In sum, the advantages of establishing an ethical rule for the charging of domestic violence outweigh the possible disadvantages. While prosecutors might resent limitations on their discretion, it is more important to promote uniformity in charging and to protect battered women from potentially lethal violence.

### Conclusion

Many commentators hailed the Supreme Court's ruling in *Castleman* as an important step forward in the reduction of gun-related violence by convicted batterers. The reality is more complicated.

. . . .

The best way to ensure the appropriate punishment of gun possession by convicted domestic batterers is to charge them appropriately in the first instance. Local prosecutors who handle cases involving domestic violence should not select generic charges in order to simplify and hasten disposition of these cases. Local prosecutors should not consent to reduced charges, dismissals or expunctions that allow defendants to gain access to firearms.

. . . As Senator Lautenberg urged nearly 20 years ago, no convicted batterer should be able to evade firearms the disability under 18 U.S.C. § 922(g)(9), because "there is no margin of error when it comes to domestic abuse and guns."

## *Notes and Questions*

- **SURVIVORS SHARE THEIR STORIES**

When Congress was building its record for the need for federal legislation to combat domestic violence, it conducted hearings around the country. In an effort to determine whether domestic violence crossed all socio-economic barriers, it heard the testimony of domestic violence survivors who came from unlikely places. One of those was Charlotte Fedders, who had elicited a public firestorm in the mid-eighties—a time when domestic violence was still not widely discussed—when she revealed in divorce proceedings that she had long been a victim of serious domestic violence. The 5' 9" Mrs. Fedders described abuse at the hands of her 6' 10" husband, who was respected in the Washington, D.C. legal community as the powerful enforcement chief of the U.S. Securities and Exchange Commission. Unlike his public persona, Mrs. Fedders described her husband in his private life as a man who suffered from dark moods and eruptions of frightening rages. She told of incidents in which he blackened her eye, broke her eyeglasses and attempted to toss her over the banister of a staircase. Their relationship made front-page news at the time and resulted in part in Fedders resigning from his SEC position. *See* Brooks Jackson, *Storm Center: John Fedders of SEC is Pummeled by Legal and Personal Problems—Enforcement Chief is Figure in New Southland Trial, Defendant in Divorce Case—A Letter to the White House*, WALL ST. J., Feb. 25, 1985. Today, stories of family violence among the rich and famous, as noted elsewhere in this book, are not so rare.

- **OTHER ASPECTS OF VAWA**

VAWA was originally passed as Title IV of the Violent Crime Control and Law Enforcement Act of 1994 (P.L. 103-322). Most of this chapter in your book has dealt with the federal criminal laws against domestic violence created by VAWA, but in fact, the statute established many programs to help local communities address the problem. Between 1995 and 2014, some $6 billion in grants have been awarded to state and local governments, courts, and non-profit organizations to fight domestic violence and sexual assault under VAWA. VAWA funded the National Domestic Violence Hotline and established the federal Office on Violence Against Women. VAWA 2013 made numerous changes to the original law, including expanding the definition of domestic violence to encompass "intimate partners," rather than just current or formerly married couples. It also added language forbidding discrimination in awarding grants. Underserved populations such as women over 50, those in same-sex relationships or the transgendered are specifically included in VAWA 2013. The new law addresses cyberstalking and insures that public housing is not denied to victims of domestic violence. There are also programs to stop sex-trafficking and violence against women on college campuses and to engage more men in the fight against domestic violence. For a detailed comparison of all the VAWA statutes over the last 20 years, see Lisa N. Sacco, *The Violence Against Women Act: Overview, Legislation, and Federal Funding,* Report to the Congressional Research Service, May 26, 2015, https://www.fas.org/sgp/crs/misc/R42499.pdf, accessed October 23, 2016. Review the Sacco report and decide how you design a future version of VAWA. Keeping in mind that reduced government spending is always a political promise, are there programs under the law you might eliminate or change?

The U.S. Department of Justice issues guidelines on how to handle cases to each of the offices of the United States Attorneys. One section, addressing the Violence Against Women Act, offers the following with respect to federal prosecutions of domestic violence offenses: "While domestic violence remains primarily a matter of state and local jurisdiction, prosecutors are encouraged to use the criminal provisions of VAWA in appropriate cases." The suggested criteria include: whether state sanctions for domestic violence offenses are adequate; whether the nature of a perpetrator's crime will make it difficult for local prosecutors to prove and whether the state in which the particular United States Attorney is located has bail provisions for batterers that include allowing for pre-trial detention. United States Department of Justice, U.S. ATTORNEYS' MANUAL Sec. 9.60.1100—Violence Against Women Act.

- **LAUTENBERG STATUTE AND LAW ENFORCEMENT**

Is it fair to deprive a member of law enforcement of his or her livelihood because of a conviction of an act of misdemeanor domestic violence under the Lautenberg Amendment? Before forming an opinion on this issue, you should be aware that "studies show that law enforcement officials have significantly higher tendencies to commit abuse against their intimate partners than the 'non-police population.'" *See* Carrie Chew, *Domestic Violence, Guns, and Minnesota Women: Responding to New Law, Correcting Old Legislative Need, and Taking Cues from Other Jurisdictions,* 25 HAMLINE J. PUB. L. & POL'Y 115, 137 (2003). Refer back to the section on domestic violence in law enforcement in Chapter 2 as well. That having been said, there have been instances around the country where prosecutors and judges have agreed to allow police perpetrators of domestic violence offenses to enter "no contest" pleas or have their records expunged so they could continue to carry firearms. The Lautenberg ban has made it even more likely that domestic abusers will have their convictions expunged. First, the Lautenberg Amendment makes it more worthwhile to seek an expungement. Second, it may increase the odds of receiving one, since courts may sympathize more with persons convicted of domestic violence offenses that subject them to the federal sanction. In one case, a California judge agreed to grant a police officer an expungement so he could keep his firearm and his job, despite the fact he had brutally and repeatedly raped his estranged wife. "'[I]nstead of taking away the guns,' one commentator suggests, 'the courts have taken away the convictions.'" Notably, thousands of convicted domestic abusers have had their records expunged since 1996, including many who would not have qualified for or sought an expungement prior to the passage of the Lautenberg Amendment. In Rhode Island, for example, state courts expunged over 1,300 domestic assault convictions and nolo contendere pleas obtained in the five years following passage of the Lautenberg Amendment (1997–2001), compared to fewer than 350 in the previous five years (1992–1996). Other states have experienced similar trends. Robert A. Mikos, *Enforcing State Law in Congress's Shadow,* 90 CORNELL L. REV. 1411, 1463–64 (2005) (citations omitted).

- **MORE ON GUNS**

The *New York Times* reported that in 2010 nearly 80,000 people were denied gun permits nationally because they provided inaccurate information about their criminal histories during mandatory background checks. Although intentional misrepresentation on these forms is a felony, only 44 of those who failed to provide accurate information were prosecuted. Michael S. Schmidt, *Both Sides in Gun Debate Agree: Punish Background-Check Liars,* NEW YORK TIMES, January 14, 2013. How likely would it be to get Congress to strengthen laws against those who lie about their domestic violence history to get guns?

The New York Court of Appeals in *People v. Havrish,* 8 N.Y.3d 389 (2007), held that a domestic violence perpetrator required by law to surrender his handgun, could not later be prosecuted for the separate crime of criminal possession of a weapon once the authorities learned he had it. The court ruled that the act of turning over the weapon was testimonial because, but for the court-ordered surrender the government would not have been aware of the defendant's possession of the weapon. Further, the act of turning over the gun was clearly incriminating. The United States Supreme Court denied *certioriari* to address the matter further. *New York v. Havrish,* 552 U.S. 886 (2007).

California has led the nation on keeping guns out of the hands of batterers. In 2013, the legislature approved a bill that helped keep firearms out of the hands of some 20,000 criminals, domestic abusers and mentally ill individuals. It was signed into law by Gov. Jerry Brown in May of that year and allocated $24 million to pay the cost of confiscating 39,000 handguns and 1,670 assault rifles in the hands of Californians considered dangerous. Editorial, *Real Gun Control From Sacramento,* N.Y. TIMES, May 6, 2013.

On Election Day, 2016 voters in California passed Proposition 63, a strict gun control measure that limits ammunition magazines to 10 rounds, requires background checks to buy bullets, makes it a crime for a gun-owner to fail to report to police when the weapon is stolen and makes it easier to remove guns from felons. Patrick McGreevy, *California Voters Approve Gun Control Measure Proposition 63*, L.A. TIMES, November 8, 2016, www.latimes.com/nation/politics/trailguide/la-na-election-day-2016-proposition-63-gun-control-1478280771-htmlstory.html, accessed November 17, 2016. The measure was approved by 63 percent of the state's voters. Bryan Schatz, *The NRA is Already Aiming at California's Big New Gun Proposition; Gun Rights' Advocates Lost a Battle, But They're Already Preparing for a Much Longer War*, MOTHER JONES, November 9, 2016, www.motherjones.com/politics/2016/11/proposition-gun-ammunition-newsom-california-nra, accessed November 17, 2016.

- **DOMESTIC VIOLENCE, GUNS AND TERROR**

There may be a correlation between violence at home and terrorism; a deadly combination when fueled by easy access to high-powered guns and explosives. After a series of horrifying terrorist attacks in 2016, the *New York Times* examined the connection between those acts and a personal history of domestic violence. After looking at the relationships the terrorists had with their intimate partners, analyzing statistics provided by a gun control group, and interviewing social scientists, the paper came up with shocking results. Omar Mateen, the suspect in the Orlando, Florida nightclub massacre; Cedric Ford, who killed 17 Kansas co-workers and Man Haron Monis, who killed two and injured others in a Sydney, Australia hostage taking, all allegedly had one thing in common—they were batterers. *Everytown for Gun Safety*, a gun control organization, reported that 57 percent of mass shootings from 2009 to 2015 included among the victims a spouse or family member of the perpetrator. Sixteen percent of the shooters had been charged at some point with an act of domestic violence. Amanda Taub, *The Interpreter: Mass Attacks, Domestic Abuse and a Pattern of Total Control,* N.Y. TIMES, June 16, 2016. What dynamic at work in domestic violence relationships might be at work in the minds of terrorists?

In early 2017 federal prosecutors charged the widow of Mateen with aiding and abetting her late husband's terrorist act, a charge that could carry life in prison. In addition, she allegedly misled law enforcement officials when she was interviewed following the mass shooting. Erin Marie Daly, Richard Perez-Pena and Adam Goldman, *'She Knew,' Prosecutor Says of Orlando Gunman's Wife; In a Rare Move in a Terrorism Case, the Spouse of an Attacker is Charged with Complicity,* N.Y. TIMES, January 18, 2017. At the time of publication, it was unknown to what extent her claim she was a battered spouse would be relevant to her defense. What information about the domestic life of Mateen and his wife, Noor Zahi Salman, would be relevant in the event this case went to trial? Would a battered woman's defense be relevant to an alleged crime that went well beyond family violence? Consider the arguments for and against this defense in the context of this case.

# Chapter 7

# Children, the Elderly and Domestic Violence

> **CONSIDER AS YOU READ ABOUT CHILDREN, THE ELDERLY AND DOMESTIC VIOLENCE**
>
> 1. The history of child abuse and child protective services
> 2. Mandated reporter statutes
> 3. Child abuse by commission and omission
> 4. The impact of domestic violence on child custody
> 5. International child abduction
> 6. Special challenges in fighting elder abuse

Children and the elderly are among the most vulnerable victims of domestic violence. Government agencies charged with protecting children—removing them from parents and caregivers if necessary to save their lives—keep statistics that tell the story of unacceptable levels of abuse in a civilized society. The number of seniors who suffer violence in their own homes is more difficult to track. The elderly who are abused by their children or spouses are particularly vulnerable. That includes physical and verbal abuse as well as theft. Retirement accounts and social security checks are tempting to elder abusers. Fearing the loss of the companionship and necessary care from family members, and generational embarrassment about being victimized by domestic violence, older victims often do not report abuse to police, prosecutors or social work agencies. In fact, only one in 24 cases of elder abuse are reported to the authorities. Not surprisingly, most of the perpetrators of elder abuse are men and most of the victims are women.[1]

Approximately 702,000 children were victims of abuse or neglect in 2014 and in that year there were 1,580 deaths as a result of child abuse.[2] As many as 275 million children worldwide are exposed to family violence. Experts maintain that children

---

1. NCADV (2015), *Domestic Violence National Statistics,* www.ncadv.org, accessed March 9, 2016.
2. *Child Maltreatment 2014,* Children's Bureau, U.S. Department of Health & Human Services, http://www.acf.hhs.gov/programs/cb/research-data-technology/statistics-research/child-maltreatment, accessed March 10, 2016.

exposed to domestic violence are more likely to be physically or sexually abused themselves, to suffer from impaired social development and to become violent and aggressive children or adults.[3]

# I. The History of Abuse Against Children and the Emergence of Child Welfare Groups

## A. Ten Centuries of Child Abuse

### Martin Ventrell, *Evolution of the Dependency Component of Juvenile Court*

4 Juvenile & Fam. Ct. J. (1998)

. . . .

Child maltreatment is not a recent phenomenon, nor is it unique to certain nations and cultures. It appears children have always been abused and neglected. A number of studies of the history of child maltreatment have begun with the now familiar quote by psycho-historian Lloyd De Mause:

> The history of childhood is a nightmare from which we have only recently begun to awake. The further back in history one goes, the lower the level of child care and the more likely children are to be killed, abandoned, beaten, terrorized and abused.[4]

History seems to bear out De Mause. Evidence of infanticide (the practice of intentional killing of a child condoned by parents and society), for example, exists in much of ancient history. Infanticide had been an accepted procedure for disposing of undesirable children. Robert Ten Bensel notes evidence of infanticide in 7000 BC with the finding of remains of infants interred in the walls at the city of Jericho. Siculus, a Greek historian of the first century, reported the putting to death of weak, infirm and those who lacked courage. A second century Greek physician instructed midwives to examine children and dispose of the unfit. The Roman Law of Twelve Tables prohibited the raising of defective children. Infanticide, which existed as late as the 19th century in parts of Europe, was justified in two ways. First, because children were considered parental "property," parents, as property owners, were entitled to destroy that property. Second, infancy (historically—birth to age seven) was by definition a period of time before the right to live vested.

Illegitimacy is another historical cause of child maltreatment. Many societies outlawed illegitimacy, and illegitimate children were ostracized, abandoned and killed.

---

3. *Behind Closed Doors: The Impact of Domestic Violence on Children* (New York: UNICEF, Child Protection Division, 2006), 5, 7, www.unicef.org/media/files/behindcloseddoors.pdf, accessed March 10, 2016.

4. [n23] De Mause, The History Of Childhood (1974).

Child maltreatment must be defined in historical context. [Twentieth] century definitions of maltreatment include previously accepted child-rearing practices. Severe physical punishment of children is part of our history of the family. Severe beatings by parents and teachers have been considered effective moral training. Likewise, that which clearly constitutes sexual abuse in 20th century America, may have been accepted practice. As fathers were property owners of their children, daughters could be lent to guests for sexual purposes, and sons and daughters could be sent to the streets to raise family income through prostitution. It was not unlawful to engage in sexual intercourse with a young girl in 16th century England unless she was under age ten.

. . . .

2. Protection

. . . .

The development of American family law most likely has its origins in the 16th and 17th centuries when society moved from communal living arrangements to family groups. From there, it is argued that the relationship of those family groups to the church and state, and the institutions that resulted therefrom, form the basis of the law which led to the creation of the juvenile court. This period is characterized by non-intervention into the family except to the extent a driving social policy warranting intervention arose. The two driving policies which justified intervention were the regulation of poverty and the regulation of wealth.

. . . .

1. Family Law System One — Wealth

Under system one, the wealthy experienced no family intervention except to the extent it was necessary to insure the passage of wealth. The state had an interest in taxing the transfer of property from one generation to the next. Under primogeniture, court or crown involvement was generally unnecessary. However, where a patriarch died prior to his heir's majority or where there was a dispute as to the identity of the heir, or the character of land tenure, the crown became interested in the child to ensure proper passage of wealth and to collect tax on the property. It is in these proceedings that we first see the appointment of a representative for the child in the form of a guardian *ad litem*.

2. Family Law System Two — Poverty

As the chancery court was deciding the property and custody issues of the aristocracy, a statutory scheme dealing with the custody of poor children was developing. Two concepts which began to emerge in 16th century England out of what became the Elizabethan Poor Laws, which serve to connect this period in history to juvenile court. The first is the government's assumption of the authority and obligation to care for poor children as a kind of ultimate parent. The second is the mechanism of apprenticeships as a means of that parentage.

At the decline of the feudal age, motivated by the emergence of an under-class of poor children, and the vagrancy and crime attributed to the poor, combined with the post reformation decline of the church as an instrument of social welfare, Parliament passed the Statute of Artificers in 1562 and later the Poor Law Act of 1601. The Statute of Artifices provided that poor children could be involuntarily taken from their parents and apprenticed. The Poor Laws were a series of statutes authorizing removal of poor children from their parents at the discretion of overseer officials and the "bounding out" of children to a local resident as an apprentice until the age of majority. In addition to this forced labor, the Poor Laws also provided cash for those unable to work. These laws resulted in considerable family intervention and are seen as the beginning of "state-run welfare."

. . . .

D. Colonial America: Transplanting and Developing the English System

The English dual system of family law was transplanted with the colonists into 17th and 18th century America and then modified in a number of ways. For the majority of colonists, there continued to be little or no intervention into patriarchal, autonomous family life. Only the rich and poor were effected, and the rich only minimally.

. . . .

System number two, however, English Poor Law, was transplanted firmly into the colonies and even enhanced.

. . . .

Involuntary apprenticeship of poor children became an integral part of colonial North American Poor Law. . . . In 18th century Virginia, for example, children could be removed and apprenticed not only because of their poverty but because their parents were not providing "good breeding, neglecting their formal education, not teaching a trade, or were idle, dissolute, unchristian or uncapable."

. . . .

While governmental intervention due to child abuse per se was exceptionally rare in colonial America, Robert Bremmer has recorded three 17th century American cases. The 1655 Massachusetts case of twelve-year-old apprentice John Walker who was killed by his master may be the first recorded American case of child abuse. John was brutally beaten and neglected until his death. His master was convicted of manslaughter. In addition, in Massachusetts, Samuel Morrison in 1675 and Robert Styles in 1678 had their children removed by the court for failure to provide suitable homes.[5]

In summary, the developing American system of intervention into the life of the child was characterized by the absence of intervention except on very rare occasions or where the very poor were concerned. Family autonomy for the self-sufficient was paramount. The majority of children in Colonial America received no protection from abuse and neglect. The Massachusetts Stubborn Child Law of 1646, for example, even allowed parents to classify their child as stubborn and seek state punishment, including capital punishment. In the case of the poor, the state felt authorized to remove poor children

---

5. [n.63] 1 R. Bremner, Children and Youth in America 123–124; 41–42 (1970).

and apprentice them for the common good. It was in no way, however, a system designed to protect maltreated children, and little welfare was actually provided to children and their families in exchange for lost autonomy. This doctrine remained intact and was emulated in the states and territories of the west through the 18th century.

. . . .

## B. Emergence of Modern Child Protective Measures

In the mid-19th century wealthy, socially conscious, middle-class reformers inspired primarily by liberal religious organizations, began to appreciate it was appropriate to spare the rod *without* spoiling the child. The prominence of the persons involved in the movement caused newspapers to report on the deplorable acts committed in the name of child discipline. In New York City, as early as 1833, the city charter permitted certain officials to remove children from abusive or neglectful parents or guardians and "commit [them] to the almshouse, or other suitable place."[6]

The world's first child protective agency, the New York Society for the Prevention of Cruelty to Children (NYSPCC), was founded in 1875 by Henry Bergh, a philanthropist who nine years earlier had created the American Society for the Prevention of Cruelty to Animals (ASPCA). Bergh was a wealthy businessman who became interested in the plight of abused animals while traveling abroad where he intervened on behalf of overworked horses. He based his American organization against animal cruelty on one that had developed in the 1820s in England.[7]

Bergh created the NYSPCC following the sensational 1874 New York case of the child "Mary Ellen." The child was born in 1864 to Francis and Thomas Wilson. After Thomas Wilson died, Francis Wilson was forced to work and sent her child to board with a babysitter. Once Francis could no longer afford to pay her, the sitter gave little Mary Ellen to the city's Department of Charities. The department illegally placed her with a couple named Mary and Thomas McCormack. Mr. McCormack claimed to be Mary Ellen's biological father. When he died a short time later, his widow remarried, turning into the archetypal wicked stepmother.

Perhaps angry because she thought the child was the illegitimate offspring of her late husband, the stepmother routinely beat and starved Mary Ellen and imprisoned her in their apartment. A concerned neighbor who heard the abuse contacted a social worker, Etta Angell Wheeler, who reached out to Henry Bergh for help. By then, Bergh was the president of the New York Society for the Prevention of Cruelty to Animals. He cleverly sent a bogus census taker to Mary Ellen's apartment to verify the allegations of abuse. Together with Elbridge Gerry, a prominent attorney, Bergh filed a petition in the New York Supreme Court to have the child produced before a judge to testify about

---

6. J. Robert Shull, Note, *Emotional and Psychological Child Abuse: Notes on Discourse, History, and Change*, 51 STAN. L. REV. 1665, 1685 (quoting HOMER FOLKS, THE CARE OF DESTITUTE, NEGLECTED, AND DELINQUENT CHILDREN 97 (1900)).

7. ROSWELL C. MCCREA, THE HUMANE MOVEMENT 5, 147–48 (1910)

Little Mary Ellen Wilson, victim of child abuse and inspiration for the world's first child protective agency.

her torture. The judge issued what was then known as a "special warrant," which allowed for the child's immediate removal from her home. The child confirmed what Bergh feared. Her stepmother was indicted for felonious assault, convicted by a jury after trial, and sentenced to a year in jail.[8]

---

8. The full story of Mary Ellen Wilson is discussed on the website of the NYSPCC. *See* The New York Society for the Prevention of Cruelty to Children, *History—1870-1874: The Catalyst*, www.nyspcc.org

Mary Ellen and her story were front-page news. The *New York Times,* quoted the child's description of her bleak home life:

> I am never allowed to play with other children or to have any company whatever. Mamma has been in the habit of whipping and beating me almost everyday. She used to whip me with a twisted whip—a rawhide. The whip always left a black and blue mark on my body.... I have no recollection of ever having been kissed by anyone—I have never been kissed by mamma.... I never dared speak to anybody, because if I did I would get whipped....[9]

The NYSPCC was instrumental in the development of laws against child labor, as well as child abuse and neglect. It assisted in the development of the juvenile and family court system, and lobbied for the enactment of child support collection and enforcement laws. The NYSPCC also acted as an arm of the government to investigate cases of child abuse and to operate shelter systems for abused or abandoned children.

By 1900, there were 161 agencies established for the prevention of cruelty to children in the United States.[10] Notwithstanding, the situation for children during the late 19th and early 20th centuries was dire. Poor immigrant families flooded East Coast urban areas and were forced by dire circumstances to abandon their children while they earned money, or to exploit them by denying them schooling to work long hours in unsafe factories. In so doing, they caused the advantaged classes to become concerned enough to create the beginnings of a child protective system.[11] Its evolution was slow. In 1899, the first juvenile court was established in Illinois and other states followed. Early in the 20th century the United States Children's Bureau was established to develop government programs to promote child welfare.[12]

---

/about-the-new-york-society-for-the-prevention-of-cruelty-to-children/history/, accessed March 5, 2017. *See also The Real Story of Mary Ellen Wilson,* www.americanhuman.org. After the trial ended, Mary Ellen went on to live a long, quiet, and happy life. She was placed with a loving family, married and had two daughters—one named Etta, after Etta Wheeler, the social worker who saved her. Her daughters described her as gentle. She died in 1956 at age 92.

9. *Mr. Bergh Enlarging His Sphere of Usefulness: Inhuman Treatment of a Little Waif—Her Treatment—A Mystery to be Cleared Up,* N.Y. TIMES, Apr. 10, 1874. *See also*, Barbara W. Boat, *Abuse of Children and Abuse of Animals: Using the Links to Inform Child Assessment and Protection, in* CHILD ABUSE, DOMESTIC VIOLENCE, AND ANIMAL ABUSE: LINKING THE CIRCLES OF COMPASSION FOR PREVENTION AND INTERVENTION 83 (Frank R. Ascione & Phil Arkow eds., 1999), in which the author quotes the 19th century reformer and newspaper reporter, Jacob Riis, describing the scene when "Mary Ellen," was brought to court:

> I saw a child brought in, carried in a horse blanket, at the sight of which men wept aloud, and I heard the story of Mary Ellen again, that stirred the soul of a city and roused the conscience of a world that had forgotten; and, as I looked, I knew I was where the first chapter of the children's rights was being written.

10. Sara J. Klein, Note, *Protecting the Rights of Foster Children: Suing Under § 1983 to Enforce Federal Child Welfare Law,* 26 CARDOZO L. REV. 2611, 2617 n.39. (2005).

11. Murray Levine, *A Therapeutic Jurisprudence Analysis of Mandated Reporting of Child Maltreatment by Psychotherapists,* 10 N.Y.L. SCH. J. HUM. RTS. 711, 715 (1993).

12. LELA B. COSTIN, HOWARD JACOB KARGER & DAVID STOESZ, THE POLITICS OF CHILD ABUSE IN AMERICA 83 (1996).

As the political climate changed throughout the 20th century, so did the role of public agencies in guarding child welfare. During the Great Depression, social welfare agencies spread to help entire families in need, including children. During the periods following both world wars, a conservative climate caused the government to retreat from interfering with private family matters.[13]

## II. The Modern Fight Against Child Abuse

The rediscovery of the scourge of child abuse came about largely because of Dr. C. Henry Kempe's seminal article, published in 1962, about the "battered-child syndrome." Written with several colleagues, *The Battered-Child Syndrome* 181(1) J. AM. MED. ASS'N 17 (1962), revealed the dirty secret with which most emergency room physicians were well aware, that a significant number of children were being seriously injured by their parents and caretakers. The children showed up in doctor's offices and hospital emergency rooms with broken bones, burns, cuts or black and blue marks — many times these injuries happened repeatedly and often, when the children presented to doctors, these wounds were in various stages of healing. When asked about their origin, doctors were given explanations from the children's caretakers that did not have the ring of truth. Unfortunately, many physicians feared initiating any action against the parents because they did not want to face law suits if they were mistaken.

This article described in excruciating detail the type of injuries these children — many of them only toddlers who could not communicate — had suffered. "The bones tell a story the child is too young or frightened to tell," Kempe wrote. These abused children often showed additional signs of abuse — malnutrition and poor hygiene. The article outlined what doctors should look for in these children and what probing questions to ask parents and caretakers. It also advised health care professionals to observe whether children kept away from their parents — in a safe atmosphere like a hospital setting — stopped continued to suffer the same "accidents" their parents claimed they suffered at home.

Most importantly, the article urged health care practitioners to get involved in the fight against child abuse by contacting hospital officials, child welfare authorities and the police, if their suspicions were aroused. Once Dr. Kempe encouraged doctors to be courageous in calling out child abuse, it paved the way for future mandated reporter statutes that broadened the circle of those expected to be responsible for the frontline protection of children. So influential was the Kempe piece that a year after his article was published, California became the first state to enact a law mandating that doctors report suspected child abuse to the authorities and within four years all 50 states and the District of Columbia enacted mandated reporter laws.[14] Congress

---

13. *Id.* at 89–90, 97–99.
14. Richard Beck, WE BELIEVE THE CHILDREN: A MORAL PANIC IN THE 1980's, 6 (New York, Public Affairs, 2015).

assisted in the proliferation of these statutes by enacting the Child Abuse Prevention and Treatment Act, signed into law by President Nixon on January 31, 1974. These laws are considered the modern turning point in the fight against child abuse.

## A. Mandated Reporters

Statistically, it is a family member who is the most likely culprit when it comes to child abuse.[15] This creates the unusual problem of making the outside world responsible for protecting abused children. Accordingly, child protective laws now exist in each state mandating that child abuse be reported to the authorities. Most of the laws are addressed to those most likely to come into contact with children, such as health care workers and teachers. Maryland's law is one such example. New Jersey's law is the broadest; everyone is a potential mandated reporter.

### Maryland Family Law Code Ann. § 5-704 (2016)

. . . .

(a) In general.—Notwithstanding any other provision of law, including any law on privileged communications, each health practitioner, police officer, educator, or human service worker, acting in a professional capacity in this State:

(1) who has reason to believe that a child has been subjected to abuse or neglect, shall notify the local department or the appropriate law enforcement agency; and

(2) if acting as a staff member of a hospital, public health agency, child care institution, juvenile detention center, school, or similar institution, shall immediately notify and give all information required by this section to the head of the institution or the designee of the head.

(b) Oral and written reports; cooperation among departments and agencies.—

(1) An individual who notifies the appropriate authorities under subsection (a) of this section shall make:

(i) an oral report, by telephone or direct communication, as soon as possible to the local department or appropriate law enforcement agency; and

(ii) a written report:

1. to the local department not later than 48 hours after the contact, examination, attention, or treatment that caused the individual to believe that the child had been subjected to abuse or neglect; and

2. with a copy to the local State's Attorney.

. . . .

(c) Contents of report.—Insofar as is reasonably possible, an individual who makes a report under this section shall include in the report the following information:

---

15. Beck, WE BELIEVE THE CHILDREN, 96.

(1) the name, age, and home address of the child;

(2) the name and home address of the child's parent or other person who is responsible for the child's care;

(3) the whereabouts of the child;

(4) the nature and extent of the abuse or neglect of the child, including any evidence or information available to the reporter concerning possible previous instances of abuse or neglect. . . .

## N.J. Stat. § 9:6-8.10. Report of Abuse (2016)

Any person having reasonable cause to believe that a child has been subjected to child abuse or acts of child abuse shall report the same immediately to the Division of Child Protection and Permanency by telephone or otherwise. Such reports, where possible, shall contain the names and addresses of the child and his parent, guardian, or other person having custody and control of the child and, if known, the child's age, the nature and possible extent of the child's injuries, abuse or maltreatment, including any evidence of previous injuries, abuse or maltreatment, and any other information that the person believes may be helpful with respect to the child abuse and the identity of the perpetrator.

## B.H. v. County of San Bernardino

Supreme Court of California

62 Cal. 4th 168 (2015)

CHIN, J.

. . . .

Plaintiff, B.H., was born in August 2006. At all times after plaintiff's birth, mother Lauri H. and father Louis Sharples lived apart. Starting in February or March 2008, Lauri H. and Sharples informally agreed that Sharples could begin to take physical custody of plaintiff for periods of a few days, which eventually occurred every weekend.

In July 2008, Lauri H. and Sharples began to have custody disputes over plaintiff. Over the Fourth of July holiday, Sharples was scheduled to take plaintiff for five days. After plaintiff was dropped off, Sharples called the Sheriff's Department on July 2 and reported he noticed plaintiff frequently had bruises when he arrived for his visits. Sharples also reported that on this particular visit, plaintiff "ha[d] bruises around his neck" and "it look[ed] like somebody choked him." This prompted Lauri H. to call the county department of children and family services (DCFS) the following day to report that Sharples had made a false report of child abuse. Lauri H. reported that she noticed that plaintiff often returned from visits with various injuries.

Both Sharples's report to the Sheriff's Department and Lauri H.'s report to DCFS were subsequently investigated. The officer responding to Sharples's report interviewed both parties and found the allegations inconclusive. Likewise, DCFS social worker Leann Ashlock met with both parties and urged them to reconcile their differences. Ashlock coordinated a supervised visit so Lauri H. could see plaintiff on July 28. The parties decided to continue sharing custody of plaintiff until they could settle their matters before a family law court.

On September 17, 2008, a family law court granted Sharples one midweek visit and custody of plaintiff every weekend. During the following weekend, on September 22, Lauri H. picked up plaintiff after a visit with Sharples and noticed a scratch and bruises on his face. When Lauri H. returned home with plaintiff, she discussed the injuries with Christy Kinney, the woman who raised Lauri H. and with whom she and plaintiff [were] living. Kinney advised Lauri H. to photograph plaintiff's injuries. Lauri H. took photographs of plaintiff's face and body before she left for school. At 10:14 that evening, while Lauri H. was out for an evening class and party, and without Lauri H.'s knowledge, Kinney called 911 to report her suspicions of child abuse to the Sheriff's Department. . . .

Deputy Sheriff Kimberly Swanson responded to the residence shortly before midnight and spoke with Kinney. At this time, plaintiff was asleep and in Kinney's care. Kinney woke plaintiff for Deputy Swanson to observe him. For about 20 minutes, Swanson spoke with Kinney and attempted to examine plaintiff, who was crying and unresponsive because Kinney had just awakened him. . . .

Three days later, Deputy Swanson wrote a report about the incident. Deputy Swanson cleared the case, concluding that there was an ongoing custody dispute between plaintiff's parents, and that the case was "for information only at this time and forward to station files." Swanson noted that Kinney saw that plaintiff "had a cut and bruising above his right eye" when he returned from his weekend visit with his father. Swanson also noted that plaintiff "had small bruises, which appeared to be old, on his upper right arm and on his back" and that Kinney had contacted Sharples, who told her plaintiff had fallen and bumped his head. Sergeant Jeff Bohner, Deputy Swanson's supervisor, reviewed and approved the report.

Lauri H. did not allow plaintiff to visit Sharples again until October 10 or 11, 2008. During the following weekend's visit, Sharples called his girlfriend and said that plaintiff had fallen, hit his head, and would not wake up. Sharples's girlfriend rushed home, noticed that plaintiff was "stiff," and asked if Sharples had called 911. When Sharples responded that he had not, his girlfriend instructed him to call 911, while she notified Lauri H. Emergency personnel responded and transported plaintiff to Loma Linda University Medical Center. Plaintiff, unconscious and suffering from seizures, was treated for severe head trauma and was given a craniectomy, in which a portion of the skull is removed in order to relieve pressure on the brain caused by swelling. Plaintiff suffered subdural hematoma, cerebral edema, and subfalcine herniation caused by intracranial pressure. A consulting forensic pediatrician determined that the injuries were caused by child abuse, most likely "shaken baby syndrome."

Plaintiff filed a complaint, through his mother Lauri H. as guardian ad litem, against the County of San Bernardino, the City of Yucaipa, Deputy Swanson, Sergeant Bohner (collectively, defendants), and Sharples. The complaint alleged two causes of action against defendants: (1) breach of a public entity's mandatory duty to report or cross-report child abuse allegations, under Government Code section 815.6, and (2) negligence by an employee within the scope of employment, under Government Code section 815.2, subdivision (a).

Defendants filed a motion for summary judgment on the ground they did not breach a mandatory statutory duty owed to plaintiff and were entitled to governmental immunities under Government Code sections 815.2, subdivision (b), 820.2, and 821.6. The trial court found that because the decision not to cross-report was based on the officer's investigatory findings and her discretionary determination of no child abuse, defendants were immune from liability. It granted the motion for summary judgment.

In an unpublished opinion, the Court of Appeal affirmed the trial court's order granting the summary judgment motion....

We granted plaintiff's petition for review to decide whether Deputy Swanson and the Sheriff's Department had mandatory duties to report and to cross-report under section 11166, subdivisions (a) and (k).

## DISCUSSION

CANRA[16] sets forth several different reporting requirements once child abuse or neglect is suspected. (§ 11166.) Certain types of professionals known as "mandated reporters" (§ 11165.7) "shall" report to law enforcement agencies or county welfare departments any known or suspected instance of child abuse or neglect. (§§ 11165.9, 11166, subd. (a).) "Any other person" "may" report to law enforcement agencies or county welfare departments any known or suspected instance of child abuse or neglect. (§ 11166, subd. (g); see § 11165.9.) Certain designated agencies, such as a police department, sheriff's department, or county welfare department, "shall" accept such reports made by a "mandated reporter or another person." (§ 11165.9.) In addition, law enforcement agencies "shall" cross-report to the county welfare or probation department "every known or suspected instance of child abuse or neglect reported to it which is alleged to have occurred as a result of the action of a person responsible for the child's welfare." (§ 11166, subd. (k).) Reciprocal duties of cross-reporting to law enforcement agencies are imposed on the county welfare or probation department. (§ 11166, subd. (j).)

. . . .

---

16. The initials stand for "Child Abuse and Neglect Reporting Act." [Eds.]

B. *California's Government Claims Act*

Under the Government Claims Act (Gov. Code, § 810 et seq.), governmental tort liability must be based on statute.... Relevant to this case, Government Code section 815.6 provides a statutory exception to the general rule of public entity immunity: "Where a public entity is under a mandatory duty imposed by an enactment that is designed to protect against the risk of a particular kind of injury, the public entity is liable for an injury of that kind proximately caused by its failure to discharge the duty unless the public entity establishes that it exercised reasonable diligence to discharge the duty." (Gov. Code, § 815.6.) ....

The first element of liability under Government Code section 815.6 requires that "'the enactment at issue be *obligatory*, rather than merely discretionary or permissive, in its directions to the public entity; it must *require*, rather than merely authorize or permit, that a particular action be taken or not taken. It is not enough, moreover, that the public entity or officer have been under an obligation to perform a function if the function itself involves the exercise of discretion.'" . . .

Section 11166, subdivision (k) provides:

> "A law enforcement agency *shall immediately, or as soon as practicably possible, report* by telephone, fax, or electronic transmission to the agency given responsibility for investigation of cases under Section 300 of the Welfare and Institutions Code and to the district attorney's office *every known or suspected instance* of child abuse or neglect *reported to it*, except acts or omissions coming within subdivision (b) of Section 11165.2, which shall be reported only to the county welfare or probation department. A law enforcement agency *shall report* to the county welfare or probation department *every known or suspected* instance of child abuse or neglect *reported to it which is alleged* to have occurred as a result of the action of a person responsible for the child's welfare, or as the result of the failure of a person responsible for the child's welfare to adequately protect the minor from abuse when the person responsible for the child's welfare knew or reasonably should have known that the minor was in danger of abuse. A law enforcement agency also *shall* send, fax, or electronically transmit a written report thereof *within 36 hours of receiving the information concerning the incident* to any agency to which it makes a telephone report under this subdivision." (Italics added.) ....

Second, within section 11166 itself, the Legislature used both the words "shall" and "may," depending on the duties imposed on various persons and governmental agencies. For example, section 11166, subdivision (a) provides that mandated reporters, various designated professionals (§ 11165.7), "shall" report to law enforcement agencies, county probation departments, or county welfare departments any known or suspected instance of child abuse or neglect. (§§ 11165.9, 11166, subd. (a).)....

The purpose of CANRA ... is to protect children from abuse and neglect. (§ 11164, subd. (b).) California's child abuse reporting law was reenacted in 1980 to overhaul an earlier reporting scheme, with the goal of "increasing the likelihood that child abuse victims would be identified. (Stats. 1980, ch. 1071, § 4, pp. 3420 et seq.)" (*Ferraro v. Chadwick* (1990) 221 Cal. App. 3d 86, 90 [270 Cal. Rptr. 379].). . . .

The Court of Appeal improperly linked the duties designated in section 11166, subdivision (k) with those designated in subdivision (a) of that section. Subdivision (a) requires mandated reporters, which includes a police officer or sheriff's deputy (§ 11165.7, subd. (a)(34)), to report any known or suspected instance of child abuse or neglect to law enforcement agencies or child welfare agencies (§ 11165.9).

The Court of Appeal concluded that a law enforcement agency's duty to cross-report under section 11166, subdivision (k) depends, not just on the receipt of a child abuse or neglect report, but on its employee's fulfillment of its duties under section 11166, subdivision (a). . . .

The Court of Appeal incorrectly determined that a law enforcement agency's duty to cross-report under section 11166, subdivision (k) is contingent on its employee's duty, arising as a mandated reporter, to report and investigate under subdivision (a). First, the language of section 11166, subdivisions (k) and (a) reflects that the duties specified in each provision are not dependent on each other and are not the same. Section 11165.9 specifies that law enforcement agencies and the county welfare department "shall accept a report of suspected child abuse or neglect whether offered by a mandated reporter or another person, or referred by another agency." In turn, section 11166, subdivision (k) requires law enforcement agencies to cross-report to other agencies those reports *received* by them from mandated reporters or another person (i.e., nonmandated reporters). (§ 11166, subds. (a), (k), (g).)

On the other hand, section 11166, subdivision (a) requires mandated reporters to *make* reports of known or suspected instances of child abuse or neglect to the agencies specified in section 11165.9. The definition of a mandated reporter consists of a list of 44 classes of professionals, including teachers, health practitioners, coroners, clergy members, and police officers, who are, broadly, "individuals whose professions bring them into contact with children." . . . .

Second, nothing in section 11166, subdivision (k) indicates that a law enforcement agency must first investigate the matter before cross-reporting an initial report of abuse. Neither subdivision (a) nor subdivision (k) of section 11166 states that the duty to report and cross-report arises only after the completion of an investigation. . . .

Third, other provisions of CANRA specify different obligations and procedures for the reporting of investigations. (§§ 11166.3, subd. (a), 11169, subd. (a).) These provisions indicate that a law enforcement agency's duty to cross-report the receipt of an initial child abuse or neglect report is separate from its investigative duties.

. . . .

The parties' and the court's underlying assumption — that section 11166, subdivision (a) applies when an officer follows up on a reported incident of child abuse — is based on *Alejo v. City of Alhambra* (1999) 75 Cal.App.4th 1180 [89 Cal. Rptr. 2d 768] (*Alejo*). There, the plaintiff sued the City of Alhambra and one of its police officers for the negligent failure to investigate or report child abuse under CANRA. The plaintiff's father, suspecting that the plaintiff's mother and her boyfriend were abusing the plaintiff, went to the police to report the matter. The police department and the officer who spoke with the father failed to cross-report the father's initial report to other governmental agencies and to conduct any investigation into the alleged abuse. Six weeks later, the mother's boyfriend severely beat the plaintiff. (*Alejo*, at pp. 1183–1184.)

. . . .

*Alejo* conflates an officer's mandatory reporting duties with those of an officer investigating a reported instance of alleged child abuse or neglect. It failed to recognize that there is "a dichotomy between reporter and reportee, i.e., differentiating between those who make the initial report and the officials who come later" in performing their investigatory or prosecutorial functions. (*James W. v. Superior Court*, *supra*, 17 Cal.App.4th at p. 257.) . . .

In regard to investigating whether child abuse or neglect has occurred, the assessments of mandated reporters and the agencies receiving child abuse reports are not the same and are governed by different standards. As explained below, Deputy Swanson did not have a duty to report under section 11166, subdivision (a). Deputy Swanson, acting on behalf of the Sheriff's Department—as the recipient of a child abuse report made by a third party—was dispatched to fulfill the Sheriff's Department's function of investigating a specific reported incident of child abuse. Deputy Swanson's findings, observations, and duties regarding the investigation of the reported incident of abuse were not governed by section 11166, subdivision (a), but were instead governed by CANRA's provisions setting forth various obligations and procedures related to investigations. . . .

CANRA defines "[a]n employee of any police department, county sheriff's department, county probation department, or county welfare department" as a "'mandated reporter,'" without any express exceptions. (§ 11165.7, subd. (a)(34).) Also, there is no dispute that Deputy Swanson was an employee of a county sheriff's department. Because Deputy Swanson is designated a mandatory reporter, but was dispatched to investigate a third party report of an instance of suspected child abuse (a task that most mandated reporters do not perform), there is an ambiguity in Deputy Swanson's role within CANRA's comprehensive statutory scheme. . . . . .

The statutory provisions reflect that when an employee of a child protective agency is dispatched to investigate a child abuse incident report received by the agency, the various provisions governing reporting by child protective agencies apply. The child protective agency then has a duty to report to other child protective agencies that it is investigating the case within 36 hours after *starting* its investigation. (§ 11166.3, subd. (a).) Under the version of CANRA in effect at the time of the incident at issue here, the investigating agency was required to report its investigative findings to the Department of Justice if it determined the child abuse or neglect allegations not to be "unfounded, as defined in Section 11165.12." (§ 11169, former subd. (a), as amended by Stats. 2004, ch. 842, § 17, p. 6410). Section 11165.12 defines reports as unfounded, substantiated, or inconclusive in terms of the investigator's subjective findings. . . .

The Legislature imposed an objective standard—while granting concomitant broad immunities for those mandated reporters who report suspected instances of child abuse—to rectify the problem of inadequate child abuse reporting, to broaden the circumstances under which reporting is required, and to encourage mandated reporters to report reasonable suspicions of child abuse. . . . After commenting on the problem of underreporting, Deputy Attorney General Gates testified that "we have to rely on third parties reporting child abuse who come into contact with children and are able to observe potential injuries and potential cases of child abuse. So, it is imperative that third parties report, and it is imperative that they report completely and not just subjectively or let their own philosophy interfere with their legal duties." (Transcript of Assem. Public Hearing, *supra*, p. 4.)

We conclude that Deputy Swanson did not have a duty to file a report of a suspected incident of child abuse in this case for several reasons. First, imposing section 11166, subdivision (a)'s reporting duties on Deputy Swanson in the circumstance of this case would not further CANRA's goals. The Legislature intended that all reasonably suspected *instances* of child abuse be identified and reported to the designated local authorities and that they in turn be cross-reported to other designated agencies. . . .

Here, Kinney's 911 report notified the Sheriff's Department of the suspected *instance* or *incident* of child abuse. If the Sheriff's Department had cross-reported the incident to DCFS and the district attorney's office, as it was required to, all of the proper authorities would have been notified of that operative incident. In her investigation in response to the report, Deputy Swanson did not identify a different instance of child abuse, but gathered information concerning the one that had already been reported. Thus, the child welfare agency lacked awareness of the suspected incident of child abuse, not because it failed to receive Deputy Swanson's investigative report, but because the Sheriff's Department had failed in its cross-reporting duties. The Sheriff's Department was further required to notify the child welfare agency of its investigation within 36 hours after its inception. (§ 11166.3, subd. (a).) Once notified of the suspected child abuse incident, the child welfare agency was required to evaluate the report within 10 calendar days. (Welf. & Inst. Code, § 16501, subd. (f).) If DCFS had been notified of Kinney's initial report and the Sheriff's Department's investigation, it could have readily requested Deputy Swanson's investigative report as part of its evaluation.

Second, there would be other oddities in the statutory scheme if we were to conclude that a law enforcement officer investigating a report of suspected child abuse must file a report under section 11166, subdivision (a). Section 11170, subdivision (b)(2) requires that on completion of the investigation, the investigating agency shall inform the mandated reporter of the results of the investigation and of any action the agency is taking with regard to the child or family. Certainly in some cases multiple actors and multiple agencies may be involved in an investigation and in the ultimate decision about what steps to take with regard to the child or family. But at least where an officer sees an investigation of a previously reported incident of child abuse through to its conclusion, the officer presumably would know the results of his or her own investigation and would not need notification by his or her own agency.

Third, Courts of Appeal have held that preliminary determinations of the potential risk to the child and the necessity of intervention made by employees of child protective agencies based on their investigative findings are not ministerial duties; these decisions are subjective, "involve a formidable amount of discretion" and are entitled to immunity.... We recognize that B.H.'s claim is based on an allegation that Deputy Swanson failed to make a *mandatory* report under a standard of *objective reasonableness*. But the difference between the subjective, discretionary nature of decisions made in the course of following up on a reported incident of child abuse and the mandatory, objective nature of the section 11166, subdivision (a) reporting duty reinforces the point that Deputy Swanson was not required to report under subdivision (a) when she was dispatched in response to a previously reported incident of suspected child abuse.

Fourth, the different statutory immunities conferred on mandated reporters and on investigators demonstrate that the Legislature distinguished between the two separate functions of reporting and investigating an incident of abuse. (See § 11172, subd. (a) [providing absolute immunity for mandated reporters from liability based on filing a report].)....

Finally, although Deputy Swanson did not have a duty to report in this case, we note that in other circumstances a law enforcement officer would have that duty with the concomitant obligations, liabilities, and immunities. Law enforcement officers, although considered to be employees of child protective agencies, have numerous duties other than investigating child abuse reports and determining a child's best interest based on that investigation. Deputy Swanson would be required to report in the first instance if she encountered a child while patrolling the streets or working a case for whom no report of suspected abuse or neglect had been made in a situation that would sustain an objectively reasonable suspicion of child abuse or neglect. For example, if Deputy Swanson were dispatched to investigate a reported residential burglary and observed evidence that would sustain an objective suspicion of child abuse, she would be required to report under section 11166, subdivision (a). Deputy Swanson also would have been required to report were she dispatched to investigate a report of a suspected incident of child abuse and observed evidence that would sustain an objective suspicion that a different, previously unreported incident or instance of child abuse had occurred....

## CONCLUSION

The Court of Appeal erred in affirming the trial court's grant of summary judgment as to the cause of action relating to Government Code section 815.6 and Penal Code section 11166, subdivision (k). However, the Court of Appeal correctly affirmed the trial court's grant of summary judgment as to the cause of action relating to section 11166, subdivision (a). Accordingly, we reverse its judgment in part, affirm its judgment in part, and remand to that court for further proceedings consistent with this opinion.

---

If mandated reporters do not take decisive and swift action, they may be setting themselves up for civil suits in the event a child is injured.

## L.A. and L.A. v. D.Y.F.S.

Supreme Court of New Jersey

217 N.J. 311 (2014)

Justice LaVecchia delivered the opinion of the Court.

. . . .

### I.

### A.

The summary judgment record reveals the following. On January 13, 2001, at about 8:00 p.m., two-year-old S.A. was brought to the emergency room of the Jersey Shore University Medical Center (JSMC) by two men who identified themselves as her relatives. They informed the triage nurse that they had been called to S.A.'s home by S.A.'s stepmother because S.A. was vomiting and unable to walk. The nurse noted that S.A. was lethargic and weak, and that she had an unusual odor on her breath.

S.A. was examined by Dr. Daniel Yu, M.D., a board-certified Emergency Medicine specialist who was then an attending physician in JSMC's Emergency Department. Dr. Yu noted that S.A.'s mouth smelled of "cologne" and "chemical alcohol." Dr. Yu conducted a full examination of S.A., including checking her breathing, pulse, blood sugar, mucous membranes, neck, heart, lungs, abdomen, extremities, and skin. He also performed a thorough set of diagnostic tests, including a urinalysis, a blood test, and chest x-rays, as well as checking for metabolic disorders and internal bleeding. Dr. Yu treated S.A. with an intravenous saline drip to prevent dehydration. The blood test results revealed that S.A. had a blood alcohol concentration of 0.035 percent.

S.A.'s father, K.L., arrived at the hospital around 8:30 p.m. He presented JSMC staff with a bottle of cologne and stayed with S.A. while she was at JSMC. Dr. Yu noted that the cologne had a similar odor to S.A.'s breath. Taking into account the low body weight of this child when assessing the impact of ingesting cologne containing chemical alcohol, Dr. Yu diagnosed S.A. with accidental cologne ingestion. Dr. Yu did not record information about the cologne such as the size of the bottle, how much cologne remained in the bottle, the brand of cologne, or the ingredients of the cologne, although he testified that he understood cologne to have a high ethanol content. Dr. Yu also did not inquire as to how S.A. had come to consume the cologne. While she was at

JSMC, S.A. also was assessed by a pediatric resident and several nurses. Neither Dr. Yu nor any of the JSMC staff noted any signs that S.A. had been abused or neglected, and the Division of Youth and Family Services (DYFS) was not contacted.

S.A. became more alert and was able to stand by 9:30 p.m. She was discharged to K.L. at 11:20 p.m., at which time she was walking steadily and was able to tolerate fluids.

Subsequent to S.A.'s treatment at JSMC, S.A. received medical treatment at another physician's office for a chemical burn on her foot. She was seen by that doctor on February 23, February 27, and March 1, 2001, and he made no reports to DYFS in connection with the incident. On March 15, 2001, DYFS received a report of suspected child abuse concerning S.A. The caller informed DYFS that S.A. had burn marks over her body and a belt mark on her chest, and that she was being beaten by her stepmother. A DYFS case worker examined S.A. and determined that S.A.'s injuries were the result of abuse and neglect. Nevertheless, DYFS did not remove S.A. from the care of K.L. and his wife. On April 5, 2001, DYFS received a report that S.A. had been found hanging from a hook on a door with her hands bound. DYFS's investigation revealed numerous injuries inflicted on S.A.: multiple burns including ones located on her private parts, numerous bruises on her body, and a welt on her chest. She was removed from K.L.'s care, taken into DYFS's custody, and ultimately placed with L.A., who adopted her in April 2006.

### B.

.... In April 2007, L.A. filed the instant complaint individually and on behalf of S.A. against several parties, including Dr. Yu and JSMC. The complaint alleged that Dr. Yu had committed medical malpractice and had breached the standard of care set forth in N.J.S.A. 9:6-8.10 by failing to notify DYFS after treating S.A. for accidental cologne ingestion. With the exception of Dr. Yu and JSMC, all defendants settled out of court.

Following the exchange of discovery, Dr. Yu and JSMC filed motions for summary judgment. On August 13, 2010, the trial court granted summary judgment in favor of defendants, holding that no reasonable jury could find that Dr. Yu had reasonable cause to believe that child abuse had been committed against S.A. The trial court concluded that the ingestion of any type of substance by a two-year-old child, in and of itself, does not create reasonable cause to believe that child abuse has been committed. . . .

On appeal from the grant of summary judgment to defendants, the Appellate Division reversed and remanded the matter for trial. *L.A. ex rel. S.A. v. N.J. Div. of Youth & Family Servs.*, 429 N.J. Super. 48, 56 A.3d 890 (App.Div.2012).

. . . .

We granted the petitions for certification filed by Dr. Yu and JSMC. 213 N.J. 535, 65 A.3d 261 (2013). We also granted amicus curiae status to Legal Services of New Jersey (LSNJ).

## II.

### A.

Before this Court, Dr. Yu asserts that the Appellate Division's decision misconstrues N.J.S.A. 9:6-8.10 and improperly increases the reporting requirements imposed on physicians. Citing the explicit imposition of different standards for DYFS personnel to report suspected abuse in N.J.S.A. 9:6-8.36a and for doctors to take children into protective custody in N.J.S.A. 9:6-8.16, Dr. Yu argues that the Legislature intended N.J.S.A. 9:6-8.10's "reasonable cause to believe" standard to apply equally to *all* persons. Dr. Yu maintains that "reasonable cause" has been used in numerous statutes and long defined as "reasonable grounds for thought supported by circumstances sufficiently strong to warrant the ordinarily prudent person to believe." . . . . Further, from a policy perspective Dr. Yu argues that the Appellate Division created an unworkably open-ended reporting requirement that in practice will have the undesirable result of obligating physicians to report any child injuries where an inference of abuse or neglect could be made, even when the parents offer an explanation and the physician thinks abuse or neglect is unlikely.

### B.

. . . .

Citing this Court's decision in *G.S. v. Department of Human Services*, 157 N.J. 161, 723 A.2d 612 (1999), which held that accidental ingestion of a foreign substance may be indicative of child abuse, L.A. argues that the Appellate Division did not create a new rule by holding that Dr. Yu may have had a duty to report under the circumstances. L.A. also disputes the argument by Dr. Yu and LSNJ that the Appellate Division's interpretation of N.J.S.A. 9:6-8.10 will result in over-reporting. . . . .

## III.

. . . .

On its face, the language of this provision clearly indicates that the reporting requirement is applicable to all persons. In referring to "any" person, the provision carves out no one. The statute also states plainly that the reporting requirement is only triggered by a "reasonable cause to believe" that child abuse has been committed. . . .

Thus, based on a plain language reading of the statute, we perceive that the Legislature intended that "reasonable cause to believe" that a child has been subjected to child abuse requires a reasonable belief based on the facts and circumstances known to the person on the scene. The reasonableness of forming that belief, or, as here, the reasonableness of not forming that belief, must be tested based on the circumstances of the case and requires an individualized assessment of what the person on the scene observed or discerned. In that review, the actions of the person on the scene must be objectively reasonable given the facts and circumstances known to that person.

. . . .

## B.

In 1964, when the Legislature first enacted a statute providing for mandatory reporting of child abuse, that statute applied only to physicians and hospitals. . . .

A physician making such a report to a prosecutor was given immunity from liability, civil or criminal, that might be incurred as a result of making the report, *id.* at §6, and "knowingly and wilfully" failing to report was made a misdemeanor, *id.* at §7. That provision was repealed by the Legislature in 1974. *See* L. 1974, c. 119, §54.

In amending Title 9 in 1971, the Legislature studied and created a new requirement for reporting to child welfare authorities. *See* L. 1971, c. 437, §3. The originally proposed bill provided that "[a]ny person may report suspicion or knowledge of child abuse," while a number of specifically listed individuals (including household members, prosecutors, social workers, school officials, and medical personnel) "shall report suspicion or knowledge of child abuse." S. 747, 194th Leg. (Apr. 6, 1970). Although the proposed bill passed both houses of the Legislature, Governor Cahill exercised his conditional veto power in respect of the reporting requirement, amending it to provide that "[a]ny person having reasonable cause to believe that a child has been subjected to child abuse or acts of child abuse shall report the same promptly to the Bureau of Children's Services by telephone or otherwise." *See Governor's Conditional Veto to Senate Bill No. 747*, at 2 (Nov. 15, 1971). In justifying the change included in the conditional veto, Governor Cahill explained that

> Section 3 deals with the reporting of "suspicion or knowledge of child abuse"; as to some persons the reporting of "suspicion of child abuse" is made mandatory. The meaning and connotation of the word "suspicion" is legally too ill-defined to be helpful or appropriate in this context. What is desired is that a report should be made whenever there is reasonable cause to believe an offense has been committed. Imposing an absolute requirement that "suspicion" be reported provides an invitation to abuse, harassment and litigation, none of which will assist in the alleviation of this serious problem.

Governor Cahill's conditional veto language was adopted by both Houses of the Legislature. *See* L. 1971, c. 437, §3. . . . Subsequent amendments to the provision have merely updated the name of the agency to which reports shall be made. *See* L. 1987, c. 341, §4; L. 2012, c. 16, §21.

A governor's conditional veto of a bill is a significant source of insight into the legislative intent underlying a provision affected by the conditional veto. *See Fisch v. Bellshot*, 135 N.J. 374, 386, 640 A.2d 801 (1994). . . . Thus, we have recognized that a governor's conditional veto provides legitimate information to be "considered in determining legislative intent, and may be 'strong evidence' of that intent when the veto directly affects that part of the legislation to be construed." *DiProspero v. Penn*, 183 N.J. 477, 503, 874 A.2d 1039 (2005). . . .

## C.

That legislative history, read in connection with the entirely straightforward language of N.J.S.A. 9:6-8.10, supports the conclusion that "reasonable cause to believe" was intended as a standard that would be understandable on its face, and that would be applicable to all persons who come into contact with children who may be victims of child abuse. The "any persons" language in N.J.S.A. 9:6-8.10 and the Legislature's failure to enact a reporting requirement specific to physicians after N.J.S.A. 9:6-8.1 was repealed indicate that the standard set forth in N.J.S.A. 9:6-8.10 is presently intended to apply to physicians. . . . .

We hold that the phrase "reasonable cause to believe," as used in N.J.S.A. 9:6-8.10, imposes a requirement that is subject to the test for objective reasonableness. The statutory duty to report child abuse requires a reasonable belief based on the facts and circumstances known to the person on the scene. In other words, was it reasonable for the person who must decide whether to report to believe that abuse has occurred, taking into account the background of that person and the facts and circumstances known to him or her at the time? In each instance, the reasonableness of forming, or not forming, a belief that an incident of child abuse has occurred must be tested based on the circumstances of the case. In that review, the judgment and actions of the person on the scene must survive the test of objective reasonableness.

## V.

. . . .

Based on the record before us, we agree with the trial court that, objectively viewed, the circumstances surrounding S.A.'s presentation at the hospital were insufficient to give rise to a finding that Dr. Yu behaved unreasonably in failing to report an incident of suspected child abuse. As all the courts reviewing this matter have noted, there was no evidence of intentional behavior by S.A.'s parents or legal guardians in connection with what Dr. Yu reasonably perceived to be an accidental ingestion of cologne.

To the extent . . . we recognized that grossly negligent or reckless conduct can sustain an abuse and neglect finding and, therefore, can provide the underpinnings to a potentially reportable event, we cannot ignore the fact that the liquid two-year-old S.A. ingested was a common item found in many homes. It was not an inherently dangerous item such as an acid, a poison, a gun, or a non-household, sharp cutting instrument that no reasonable adult would allow in any accessible proximity to a child of such tender age. While child-proofing of homes is not a new or revolutionary precaution in modern life, the idea that a toddler might find a way to get her hands on a common cosmetic or toiletry item is not equivalent to grossly negligent or reckless behavior on the part of a parent. Were that to be so, every accidental ingestion case presenting at a hospital emergency room would risk becoming a mandatory child abuse reporting incident. We do not believe that the reporting obligation was meant to operate in such fashion. Indeed, it would foster over-reporting, something the Legislature and Governor Cahill cast a wary eye toward when fashioning the standard for requiring reporting.

We add only that later tragic events in the life of this child cannot cloud the analysis when considering the objective reasonableness of Dr. Yu's first and only interaction with two-year-old S.A. Given that S.A. had no prior history of hospital involvement at JSMC, the circumstances support Dr. Yu's diagnosis and treatment of S.A.'s symptoms and do not render objectively unreasonable his failure to report suspected child abuse. That later episodes of child abuse transpired in this child's life does not mean that Dr. Yu erred in not detecting something prescient of those subsequent events based on his emergency room interaction with S.A. involving her ingestion of a common household item like cologne.

---

Among the many goals of mandatory child abuse reporting statutes was to alleviate the fear of liability on behalf of a person who mistakenly, yet in good faith, reports child abuse, and thereby eliminate the concern of professionals about the possible legal consequences of "getting involved."

## Brown v. Pound
Alabama Supreme Court
585 So. 2d 885 (1991)

ADAMS, JUSTICE.

This case involves the suspicion of child abuse reported by a doctor, pursuant to the Child Abuse Reporting Act, § 26-14-1 et seq., Code of Ala. 1975. Vadine Brown appeals from the dismissal of her claim against Dr. Daniel Pound and others, on the ground of immunity, as provided for by § 2614-9, Code of Ala. 1975. We affirm.

On March 6, 1988, Mrs. Brown took her grandson to Decatur Medical Surgical Center to be treated for a burn. Dr. Daniel Pound, who was in charge of the emergency room, examined the burn. As a result of his examination, he suspected child abuse and reported his suspicions to the Morgan County Department of Human Resources, as mandated by § 26-14-3, Code of Ala. 1975. The Department of Human Resources investigated and determined that there was no evidence of child abuse.

On January 10, 1989, Mrs. Brown filed a complaint in the Circuit Court of Morgan County, against Dr. Daniel Pound and Decatur Medical Associates, Ltd., a partnership doing business as Decatur Medical Surgical Center, on the theory of respondeat superior. She alleged that the report made by Dr. Pound was groundless and in violation of the Child Abuse Reporting Act. She further alleged that, as a result of the report, she had suffered mental and emotional damages, as well as an invasion of privacy.

In response to her complaint, Dr. Pound and Decatur Medical Associates filed a motion to dismiss on the ground of absolute immunity, citing § 26-14-9. The trial court dismissed the case. Vadine Brown filed a notice of appeal on November 1, 1990.

The sole issue presented is whether the trial court erred in dismissing the case on the ground that § 26-14-9, Code of Ala. 1975, provides absolute immunity to the doctor and to the medical center.

The Alabama Child Abuse Reporting Act was passed in 1965 for the purpose of protecting children who may be subjected to abuse or neglect....

The failure of any of the persons named in the statute to report suspected child abuse subjects them to criminal sanctions. Because it requires that these individuals report child abuse, it also provides immunity to those who report....

Mrs. Brown contends that § 26-14-9 is not, and should not be, an absolute grant of immunity. She alleges in her complaint that because of Dr. Pound's groundless report, she was subjected to embarrassment, humiliation, and mental and emotional stress.

Only one case to date has thoroughly addressed the issue of immunity in suspected child abuse or neglect cases. In *Harris v. City of Montgomery*, 435 So. 2d 1207 (Ala. 1983), the examining physician filed a report with the Montgomery Police Department after diagnosing the child's injury as a case of suspected child abuse or neglect. After an investigation, the police department determined that the case was not one of child abuse or neglect. Thereafter, the child's mother filed a complaint against the treating physician, the hospital, the police officers, and the City of Montgomery. The trial court granted the physician and the hospital's motion to dismiss, pursuant to the immunity provision of § 26-14-9. See 435 So. 2d at 1212. This Court stated that the immunity was absolute. *Id.*

In *Harris*, the allegations against the officers, however, included false imprisonment, false arrest, defamation, and other tortious conduct not protected by the statute. *Harris*, at 1212. This Court determined that the officers' alleged actions were not protected by the immunity provision and reversed the dismissal as to those allegations and remanded the case for further proceedings. *Id.*

Mrs. Brown argues that *Harris* indicates that the immunity provided by § 24-14-9, is not absolute if there are allegations of other torts. While mere compliance with the statute is not an automatic grant of immunity, this case does not present any allegations of injury or damage not related to the reporting of the suspected child abuse. See, *Harris*, at 1215. There is no evidence that Dr. Pound did anything more than comply with the mandates of the statute in reporting his suspicions. Because the action of Dr. Pound and the Decatur Medical Surgical Center were within the requirements of the Child Abuse Reporting Act, § 26-14-9 provides them with absolute immunity.

. . . .

Mrs. Brown has failed to allege any claims for which § 26-14-9 does not provide immunity; therefore, the dismissal was proper.

The judgment of dismissal is due to be affirmed.

---

Not every professional who comes into contact with a child has a duty to report abuse or neglect to state authorities under most mandated reporter statutes. Nor do the mandated reporter laws undermine other certain privileges under the law. The following case addresses the tensions between disclosure requirements and recognized privileges under the law—here, the clergy-penitent privilege.

## Wilson v. Darr
Iowa Supreme Court
553 N.W.2d 579 (1996)

CARTER, JUSTICE.

Plaintiff, Megan Wilson, challenges an order granting summary judgment for certain defendants in the action. . . .

This case arises out of physical and sexual abuse allegedly perpetrated upon plaintiff by her father. He is also a defendant in the case, but not involved with the issues contained in this appeal. Plaintiff's family were members of Sacred Heart Church of Valley Junction from 1987 to 1989. Father Kottas was the associate pastor of that church from 1987 to 1989. Plaintiff and her parents met with him in late April and early May of 1988 for family counseling. Father Kottas holds a Masters Degree in Human Development but is not a licensed counselor. Plaintiff, in her deposition and the affidavits that were used as part of the summary judgment record, stated that she did not tell Father Kottas that her father had sexually abused her but did tell him that he had "hurt" her. She expressed the view that the counseling with Father Kottas focused too strongly on efforts to reunite the family unit rather than on efforts to alleviate the emotional problems that plaintiff was suffering as a result of past child abuse.

Plaintiff completed the seventh and eighth grades at Sacred Heart School during the 1986–87 and 1987–88 school years. Kimary Darr was a counselor employed by the school at this time. Plaintiff met with Darr for one-half hour each week while attending Sacred Heart School. During the 1988–89 school year, at which time plaintiff was attending Dowling High School, she met with Darr every other week for approximately forty-five minutes. The physical and sexual abuse of plaintiff by her father stopped in December of 1988 when he moved from the family home. Darr maintains that she did not know of the physical or sexual abuse perpetrated upon plaintiff by her father until plaintiff told her of the abuse in the spring of 1989. Plaintiff could not recall telling Darr about the abuse prior to the latter date.

Plaintiff and her family met with Ellen Taylor, a licensed counselor employed by Catholic Social Services, on several occasions between January of 1989 and March of 1989. During some of these sessions, everyone in the family was present, including plaintiff's father. At other sessions, Taylor talked only with the plaintiff or only with the parents. Plaintiff attempted suicide in late February of 1989. In her deposition and affidavits, plaintiff contends that the counseling sessions with Taylor were focused too strongly on efforts to reunite the family unit rather than efforts to alleviate plaintiff's emotional harm as a result of past child abuse.

In early April of 1989, plaintiff began counseling with Mindy Levine, a licensed social worker employed by Iowa Methodist Medical Center in Des Moines. Levine's area of expertise included the detection of children who have suffered sexual abuse based on all available indicia. In Levine's affidavit, filed in opposition to the motions for summary judgment, she indicated that during the time she counseled plaintiff the symptoms of an abused child were obvious. She further stated that the desirability of preserving the family unit was outweighed by the need to deal directly with the emotional problems of an abused child. . . .

II. *The Claim Against Father Kottas.*

Plaintiff's argument of this claim is based on the contention that Father Kottas failed to report to proper authorities a child abuse situation involving plaintiff and her father. There is no claim that Father Kottas had been made aware of any sexual abuse involving those persons. Plaintiff urges, however, that Father Kottas should have been aware of past physical abuse based on her statement to him that her father had hurt her. The district court did not decide this issue on the extent of Father Kottas's knowledge but, rather, dismissed the claim against him on the basis he had no duty to report child abuse even if he suspected it.

The record presented on the summary judgment motion reflects that Father Kottas met with the Wilson family on several occasions for purposes of assisting them in their familial relationship. It appears, however, that his role in these discussions was that of a clergyman counseling the family to work out their differences in accordance with the teachings of the church. We agree with the conclusions of the district court that this involvement in the Wilsons' familial conflicts did not render him a mandatory reporter of suspected child abuse under the requirements of Iowa Code section 232.69 (1989). To the extent that subpart (1) of that statute makes a "counselor" a mandatory reporter of child abuse, this is limited to a reasonable belief actually formed by the counselor "in the scope of professional practice." Father Kottas's professional practice, as it related to the Wilson family, was that of clergyman. In *State v. Motherwell*, 114 Wash. 2d 353, 788 P.2d 1066 (1990), the court held that members of the clergy counseling their parishioners in the religious context were not mandatory reporters under that state's statute.

The legislature did not include members of the clergy among those that are required to report child abuse under section 232.69. Because it is common knowledge that clergymen engage in activities within a religious context that might unearth abusive situations, that omission must be deemed to have been a conscious choice to exclude this profession from the reporting requirements of the statute.

The district court was correct in concluding that Father Kottas had no statutory duty to report child abuse visited upon plaintiff. Plaintiff does not suggest that he had a common-law duty to report such matters. Consequently, the district court's grant of summary judgment in favor of Father Kottas will not be disturbed.

. . . .

And finally, while there may be a moral duty to protect a child from serious abuse, unless the statute imposes a universal duty to report child abuse, as New Jersey law does, there is no legal duty to make such reports for which one may be held accountable.

## State v. Wilson
### Kansas Supreme Court
### 267 Kan. 550 (1999)

LARSON, J.:

This is an appeal by Steven and Gloria Wilson of their convictions for endangering a child in violation of K.S.A. 21-3608. The Wilsons challenge (1) the constitutionality of K.S.A. 21-3608(a) on grounds of being vague, overbroad, and beyond the scope of the State's police power, (2) the trial court's interpretation of K.S.A. 21-3608(a), and (3) the sufficiency of the evidence.

All charges in this case arose from the events surrounding the abuse and neglect of then 5-year-old L.O. (born October 24, 1991), the daughter of S.O. and J.R. Several adults, many of whom were siblings or related by marriage, lived with their respective children in the same house as L.O. in Kansas City, Kansas. Among the adults living there in various rooms on different floors of the house were Gloria and Steven Wilson, who are married; Norman and Linda Randall, who are married; S.O. who stayed there with her boyfriend (who was not J.R.); and J.R. who lived there with his girlfriend. Gloria Wilson, Norman Randall, and J.R. are all siblings.

Gloria and Steven Wilson began living in the house in late February 1997 and were there in April 1997 when L.O. was removed by employees of the Department of Social and Rehabilitation Services (SRS). During that time, L.O. was neglected and verbally and physically abused by her mother and, to a lesser extent, Norman Randall, on a regular basis in various violent and sadistic ways. The abuse occurred on a daily basis and in Steven and Gloria's presence.

Linda Randall testified that on one occasion, when S.O. was beating L.O. with a board, Steven took the board away and stomped on it and threatened to beat up S.O. Linda also testified that on one occasion, when S.O. had beaten L.O., Gloria beat up S.O. Gloria also testified she called SRS several times to report the abuse of L.O., but SRS records did not substantiate this claim.

Although Gloria was L.O.'s paternal aunt, there was no evidence that Steven or Gloria ever took or were given responsibility for caring for L.O.

On April 28, 1997, SRS employees went to the house in response to a report made that day that L.O. had been severely abused. When the social workers arrived and asked about L.O.'s whereabouts, several individuals, including Gloria Wilson, falsely claimed that L.O. was not there. Someone in the group stated L.O. was in California, and no one attempted to correct this statement. When the social workers asked L.O.'s parents, S.O. and J.R., how long L.O. had been in California, the parents gave inconsistent responses. When the social workers asked for clarification, Gloria falsely asserted that L.O. had been gone for about a week to visit an aunt.

After determining they were not going to get any more information about L.O.'s whereabouts, the social workers left. However, they returned with the police and a warrant the next day to search the home for L.O.

L.O. was found upstairs, sitting quietly on the floor. Her head had been shaved, and there were patches on her head where no hair was growing. Her feet were extremely red and swollen. She was frail, extremely thin, very dirty, and reeked of urine. She had various scratches, bruises, and burn marks from head to toe, and all her fingers were swollen. L.O.'s feet hurt so much she had difficulty standing. She kept asking for water and something to eat. After an officer carried L.O. downstairs, Steven Wilson began arguing with the police, either telling them they should not be there or asking why they were there. When asked by the police why he had not reported L.O.'s condition to anyone, Steven responded that it was not his problem.

L.O. was taken to the hospital for treatment. She was underweight and ravenously hungry. She said the swelling in the joints of her fingers was from her mother bending back her fingers. The rest of her injuries L.O. described as variously attributable to blows, belt-beatings, scratches, cigarette burns, and paddling, primarily by her mother and to a lesser extent, by Norman Randall and "Big Linda" (an apparent reference to Linda Randall). Some injuries were in various stages of healing. There were also possible indications of sexual abuse. Testimony at trial further indicated that S.O. forced L.O. to stand in corners with her arms in the air for hours at a time, and that S.O. and Norman Randall handcuffed L.O. to a bed at night.

In a 22-count information, 11 defendants, including the Wilsons, were charged with various crimes in relation to the treatment of L.O. The Wilsons were each charged with one count of endangering a child in violation of K.S.A. 21-3608. Norman Randall pled guilty to attempted child abuse and Linda Randall pled guilty to child endangerment; the Randalls testified at the Wilsons' trial on behalf of the State.

Steven moved to dismiss and asserted he could not be convicted under the child endangerment statute, K.S.A. 21-3608, for failing to report L.O.'s abuse because he had no duty to report it under the child abuse and neglect reporting statute, K.S.A. 38-1522. At the hearing on the motion, Steven also argued that the language of K.S.A. 21-3608(a) which speaks of an offender "causing or permitting" a child to be placed in a situation of jeopardy presumes that the offender has some degree of charge or custody of the child, which he did not.

Steven's motion was denied by Judge Dexter Burdette, who noted, among other comments, that under *State v. Walker*, 244 Kan. 275, 281, 768 P.2d 290 (1989), there is no requirement that one charged under K.S.A. 21-3608 have an independent legal duty to the child.

Gloria moved to dismiss on grounds the language of the child endangerment statute is vague, overbroad, and exceeds the scope of the police power. This motion was argued before Judge Thomas L. Boeding. At that time Steven joined in Gloria's motion and she incorporated the arguments from his earlier motion in her own. The trial court denied the motion to dismiss, and the case proceeded to a bench trial.

The State called seven witnesses at trial, including SRS workers, police officers, the hospital staff who treated L.O., and Norman and Linda Randall. Neither defendant presented evidence. After motions for acquittal were denied, the trial court rendered a memorandum decision, finding both Wilsons guilty.

The trial court found the Wilsons were adults living in the same house with L.O. and the abusers; Gloria is L.O.'s paternal aunt but neither defendant was a parent, stepparent, child care provider, or babysitter of L.O.; the continuous course of substantial and serious abuse occurred around them on a daily basis; the child's abused and deteriorated condition was obvious; and, on at least one occasion, each defendant stepped in to halt the abuse, but SRS records showed no evidence either ever reported it.

The trial court found the child endangerment statute focuses on the reasonableness of a defendant's actions rather than on any independent legal duty to the child. The court concluded the Wilsons had a responsibility under the unique circumstances of the case to "do something" to protect L.O. and a reasonable person under the circumstances would have reported the situation to the authorities and stopped the abuse sooner.

The Wilsons were each sentenced to 1-year in county jail and placed on 24 months' probation. As restitution, each was held jointly and severally responsible with the other house occupants for $614 of L.O.'s medical bills.

Steven and Gloria each appeal, raising identical issues.

Is K.S.A. 21-3608(a) unconstitutionally vague, overbroad, or beyond the scope of the State's police power?

. . . .

The Wilsons were convicted under K.S.A. 21-3608(a), which states:

> "Endangering a child is intentionally and unreasonably causing or permitting a child under the age of 18 years to be placed in a situation in which the child's life, body or health may be injured or endangered."

. . . .

The Wilsons argue the endangering a child statute criminalizes omissions based on markedly indefinite standards. They also argue that because the phrase "endangering of life" was found vague and ambiguous in *State v. Kirby*, 222 Kan. 1, 563 P.2d 408 (1977), the existence of the word "endangering" causes K.S.A. 21-3608(a) to be likewise unconstitutionally vague.

The State more persuasively argues this issue has been determined by this court in *State v. Fisher*, 230 Kan. 192, 200, 631 P.2d 239 (1981), where we upheld the present language of K.S.A. 21-3608(a) (which was at that time found in subsection [b]) and concluded it was not unconstitutionally vague. . . . .

We disagree with the Wilsons' contention that their argument differs from that made in *Fisher*. They argue a distinction without a difference. The *Fisher* rationale is still good law in Kansas. K.S.A. 21-3608(a) requires that the prohibited acts be unreasonable, the holdings from other states cited in *Fisher* upheld similar statutes against void for vagueness arguments, and the *Fisher* language dealing with the word "endangering" is controlling.

K.S.A. 21-3608(a) is not void for vagueness.

. . . .

The Wilsons claim that the statute prohibits conduct and activities which are lawful. Their example is of children being permitted by their parents to play football despite the great likelihood of injury.

The Wilsons' argument seems to relate more to vagueness than overbreadth. In any event, the argument is without merit. As noted in *Fisher*, child endangerment statutes like K.S.A. 21-3608 are necessarily drawn with broad language because they are designed to cover a broad range of conduct and circumstances. See *Fisher*, 230 Kan. at 198, 631 P.2d 239, quoting with approval *Commonwealth v. Mack*, 467 Pa. 613, 359 A.2d 770 (1976).

As to the argument about permitting football to be played, our court in *Fisher*, 230 Kan. at 197, looked to the *People v. Beaugez*, 232 Cal. App. 2d 650, 658, 43 Cal. Rptr. 28 (1965), response that courts will not give strained meanings to legislative language through a process of imaginative hypothesizing; a common-sense interpretation of the statute is the guiding principle.

. . . .

We hold K.S.A. 21-3608(a) is not unconstitutionally overbroad.

. . . .

Having found K.S.A. 21-3608(a) constitutional we now turn to the Wilsons' argument that, properly construed, the statute's terms do not apply to them under the facts of this case. . . .

The Wilsons' second argument in favor of their interpretation of K.S.A. 213608 relates to the limited duties imposed by the child abuse and neglect reporting statute, K.S.A. 38-1522. Because they had no duty to report the abuse of L.O. under the reporting statute, they reason the legislature could hardly have intended to criminalize their failure to prevent or report abuse under K.S.A. 21-3608(a).

K.S.A. 38-1522(a) requires certain categories of professional persons (ranging from doctors and nurses to teachers and law enforcement officers) to report suspected abuse or neglect to SRS, a law enforcement agency, or the attorney general. Failure to report is a class B misdemeanor. K.S.A. 38-1522(f). . . . The Wilsons were not among those required to report the abuse and, therefore, under K.S.A. 38-1522(b), their reporting would have been merely permissive and their failure to report would not subject them to criminal liability under K.S.A. 38-1522(f).

The State contends the Wilsons' duty to do "something" to stop the abuse of L.O., whether by reporting or otherwise, is derived from the child endangerment statute. The State argues the fact the Wilsons had no duty to report the abuse under the reporting statute is completely irrelevant to the question of the interpretation of K.S.A. 21-3608.

We are not prepared to adopt the arguments of either party as being conclusive. The provisions of the reporting statute are not irrelevant but do not require the result the Wilsons suggest. It is presumed that legislative enactments are intended to operate in harmony. It is therefore troubling that the Wilsons would be criminally liable for failure to report abuse under K.S.A. 21-3608 when the legislature expressly avoided imposing such liability under

K.S.A. 38-1522.

. . . .

This court does not question that the goal of K.S.A. 21-3608 is to protect children from abuse and neglect, but this does not mean we should expand criminal liability to every circumstance which would arguably protect children despite the statute's express or implied limitations or the factual situations which the legislature expressly declined to reach when it had the opportunity of doing so. If we carry the State's requested interpretation of the statute in this case to its logical extension, anyone without any authority, custody, or control over a child or its abuser is criminally liable for failing to attempt to stop or report known abuse.

. . . .

In arriving at this holding, we are not unsympathetic to the plight of children like L.O., nor do we condone the inaction of the Wilsons. While we conclude in this opinion that some of Gloria's conduct was criminal, the Wilsons' actions prior to the SRS visit, though morally reprehensible, were not criminal as K.S.A. 21-3608 is now written. Courts must interpret the law as written rather than deciding what the law ought to be.

Was there sufficient evidence that Steven or Gloria Wilson violated K.S.A. 21-3608?

. . . .

Based on our interpretation of K.S.A. 21-3608, the Wilsons' failure to act was not in itself sufficient to create criminal liability because they had neither authority nor control over either L.O. or her abuser, *i.e,* they were not in a position to "permit" L.O.'s placement in the abusive situation. Accordingly, Steven's conviction must be reversed.

However, there was evidence that when SRS first came to investigate L.O.'s circumstances, Gloria was a leader among those who falsely asserted that L.O. was not in the house and, in fact, had gone to California. The trial court made specific findings of fact to this effect. This action by Gloria had the effect of "causing" a situation where the abuse could be continued.

SRS had to secure a search warrant. This resulted in L.O. remaining in an abusive situation for an additional day. Gloria's conduct was an act of commission, not a mere omission. Her interference with the earliest intervention by SRS places her in a different position than Steven. When Gloria stepped into the active role of hiding the abuse and effectively turning away the only help L.O. was going to receive, she participated in creating, sustaining, and causing the endangering circumstances of the child. Accordingly, Gloria's conviction is affirmed.

Affirmed in part and reversed in part.

## B. Scope and Limit of Duties to Protect Children

The language of child endangerment statutes often imposes liability on those who "permit" a child to be placed in harm's way, as the example from Colorado, with its fairly standard language, demonstrates.

### Col. Rev. Stats. § 18-6-401 (2015) Child abuse

(1) (a) A person commits child abuse if such person causes an injury to a child's life or health, or permits a child to be unreasonably placed in a situation that poses a threat of injury to the child's life or health, or engages in a continued pattern of conduct that results in malnourishment, lack of proper medical care, cruel punishment, mistreatment, or an accumulation of injuries that ultimately results in the death of a child or serious bodily injury to a child. . . .

---

The following case involves the killing of Lisa Steinberg in New York City by her father, Joel. The defendant was an attorney; his live-in girlfriend, Hedda Nussbaum, who failed to intervene to save little Lisa, was herself horribly battered by him, and the level of cruelty and torture he inflicted on the child outraged the public. It was front-page news for months. Legally, the case revealed the difficulties in prosecuting child fatalities where no witnesses observed the actual killing and it clarified the extent of one's liability for acts of omission leading to a child's death. From a public health and policy perspective, it demonstrated the dangers for children of living in homes where severe domestic violence was present.

### People v. Steinberg
New York Court of Appeal
79 N.Y.2d 673 (1992)

KAYE, J.

. . . .

I.

In the evening of November 1, 1987, defendant and Hedda Nussbaum were at home in their one-bedroom Greenwich Village apartment, with their two "adopted" children,

Lisa, then six years old, and Mitchell, 16 months old. Nussbaum was in the kitchen with Lisa while defendant dressed in the bedroom for his dinner appointment with a friend. Lisa went into the bedroom to ask defendant to take her with him. Moments later, defendant carried Lisa's limp body out to Nussbaum, who was then in the bathroom, and they laid the child on the bathroom floor. Lisa was unconscious, having experienced blunt head trauma of great force, and her breathing was raspy. According to Nussbaum, defendant later admitted that he had "knocked [Lisa] down and she didn't want to get up again."

While Nussbaum attempted to revive Lisa, defendant continued dressing. Defendant told Nussbaum to let her sleep, promised to awaken the child upon his return, and then left for dinner. Nussbaum did not seek medical care for Lisa because she believed defendant had supernatural healing powers, and felt that calling for assistance would be considered a sign of disloyalty.

Defendant returned about three hours later, at 10:00 P.M., retrieved a file relating to his oil well investments, and left again. When he came back a few minutes later, Nussbaum urged him to revive the still-unconscious child. Defendant declined—explaining that they "ha[d] to be relating when she wakes up"—and he instead freebased cocaine for the next several hours. Finally, at 4:00 A.M., after Nussbaum's repeated urgings, defendant carried Lisa from the bathroom floor to the bedroom, where her breathing seemed to sound better. Defendant rested his arm on Lisa, and continued talking to Nussbaum.

At 6:00 A.M., when Nussbaum left the room, defendant called out that Lisa had stopped breathing. Defendant initially rejected Nussbaum's offer to call 911, but finally acceded when his attempts to resuscitate the child failed. Police and paramedics arrived shortly after being summoned, administered oxygen, and rushed Lisa to the hospital.

At the hospital, defendant explained that Lisa had gone to bed complaining of a stomach ache, and had vomited during the night, but that he believed she was otherwise all right until he checked on her around 6:00 A.M. and discovered that her breathing was coarse. In fact, the doctors determined that Lisa, who was in a coma, was suffering from severe head injuries—a result of blunt trauma—and placed her on life support equipment. Lisa's condition did not improve, and neurological tests performed on November 3 indicated that she was brain dead. Life support was discontinued on November 5.

Defendant was indicted for second degree (depraved indifference) murder, first degree manslaughter, and seven charges that were severed or dismissed. Defendant was acquitted of murder but convicted of manslaughter, and the Appellate Division affirmed the conviction. We find no error and accordingly also affirm.

II.

First degree manslaughter requires proof that defendant, with intent to cause serious physical injury, caused death (Penal Law § 125.20[1]). The People's theory, as charged to the jury, was that defendant performed both acts of commission (striking

Lisa) and acts of omission (failure to obtain medical care), each with intent to cause serious physical injury, and that such acts caused Lisa's death. Defendant contends that failure to obtain medical care for a child cannot, as a matter of law, support the *mens rea* element of first degree manslaughter — intent to cause serious physical injury — unless defendant has medical expertise, and would thereby know that serious injury will result from a lack of medical attention. That contention — which he characterizes as the core question on this appeal — is meritless.

The Penal Law provides that criminal liability may be based on an omission *(see,* Penal Law § 15.05), which is defined as the failure to perform a legally imposed duty (Penal Law § 15.00[3]). Parents have a nondelegable affirmative duty to provide their children with adequate medical care *(Matter of Hofbauer,* 47 NY2d 648, 654-655; Family Ct Act § 1012[f][i][A]). Thus, a parent's failure to fulfill that duty can form the basis of a homicide charge *(see, People v. Flayhart,* 72 NY2d 737; *People v. Henson,* 33 NY2d 63).

. . . .

Contrary to defendant's claim, even a person without specialized medical knowledge can have the intent to cause serious physical injury by withholding medical care. If the objective is to cause serious physical injury, the mental culpability element of first degree manslaughter is satisfied — whether or not defendant had knowledge that the omission would in fact cause serious injury or death.

Defendant argues that "everyone" knows that failure to supply food to a child will lead to death, and thus intentional homicide is a proper charge under those circumstances *(see, e.g., Zessman v. State,* 94 Nev. 28, 573 P2d 1174; *Harrington v. State,* 547 SW2d 616 [Tex Crim App]), but that the need for medical care is often a matter of opinion, and a layperson could not be expected to know the gravity of the situation. The distinction defendant would have us draw, as a matter of law, between defendants who have a medical background and those who do not, is unsupportable.

Putting aside defendant's attempt to import a knowledge requirement into a statute that has none, and putting aside that the *mens rea* for first degree manslaughter is intent to cause serious physical injury, not death — it is plain that defendant's argument centers on factual, not legal, distinctions. Certainly there are situations where the need for prompt medical attention would be obvious to anyone — a child bleeding profusely, for example, or a six-year-old girl laying unconscious after a blunt head trauma. Thus, defendant's argument that the failure to obtain medical care for a child may not, as a matter of law, support a homicide charge that requires intent must be rejected.

### III.

Having found no defect in the prosecution's legal theory, we next consider whether the evidence is legally sufficient to sustain the conviction. In undertaking this review, the evidence must be viewed in a light most favorable to the People *(People v. Contes,* 60 NY2d 620, 621) to determine whether there is a valid line of reasoning and permissible inferences from which a rational jury could have found the elements of the crime proved beyond a reasonable doubt (*People v. Bleakley,* 69 NY2d 490, 495)....

There was no dispute at trial that Lisa's death was a homicide. Even the defense expert agreed that the child's death was caused by brain trauma as a result of abuse. The medical testimony, including Lisa's treating physicians and the postmortem examination, confirmed beyond a reasonable doubt that Lisa's death was a consequence of an assault and a failure to obtain prompt medical attention.

The evidence was also legally sufficient to support the jury's determination that the assault was administered by defendant—and not Nussbaum, as the defense had argued. Nussbaum herself testified that she did not strike Lisa that night; that moments after Lisa went into the bedroom, defendant carried her unconscious body out; and that defendant admitted to knocking Lisa down.

There was also evidence that defendant had physically abused Lisa several days before her death, and that defendant's knuckles had fresh bruises on November 2. Moreover, there was evidence of Nussbaum's debilitated physical condition on November 1 from which a jury could infer that she did not deliver the fatal injury. Thus, based on the evidence, a rational jury could have concluded, beyond a reasonable doubt, that it was defendant who caused the head trauma that led to Lisa's death.

The evidence was also sufficient to support the jury's determination that defendant struck Lisa and thereafter failed to summon medical assistance, each with the intent to cause serious physical injury. Intent may be inferred from conduct as well as the surrounding circumstances (*see, People v. Smith,* 79 NY2d 309, 315; *People v. Bracey,* 41 NY2d 296, 301). The expert testimony described the tremendous force necessary to inflict the head trauma that caused Lisa's death. Moreover, after Lisa was rendered unconscious, defendant left for dinner, and when he returned three hours later, free-based cocaine while the child lay on the bathroom floor. Additionally, when defendant admitted to Nussbaum during the night that he knocked Lisa down, he explained that "the staring business had gotten to be too much for her." This is relevant because there was evidence that defendant was convinced that the children were staring at him to induce hypnotic trances. Thus, the jury could have inferred from the evidence that defendant's objective in assaulting Lisa and failing to summon medical assistance was to cause serious physical injury, perhaps in response to Lisa's purported staring. That defendant acceded to Nussbaum's request to telephone 911 when Lisa stopped breathing might demonstrate that defendant did not intend to cause the child's death, but does not militate against the jury finding that he intended to cause serious injury.

In sum, the evidence was sufficient to establish the elements of first degree manslaughter.

Similarly, there is no merit in defendant's claim that Nussbaum's testimony was insufficiently corroborated. Although many States, and the Federal courts, permit a conviction to rest solely on the uncorroborated testimony of an accomplice (*see, People v. Moses,* 63 NY2d 299, 310–311 [Jasen, J., dissenting]), our Legislature requires that accomplice testimony be corroborated by evidence "tending to connect the defendant with the commission" of the crime (CPL 60.22[1])....

The Trial Judge enumerated specific items of independent, corroborative evidence for the jury's consideration: (i) defendant's presence at the apartment at 6:30 A.M. on November 2, as confirmed by police and paramedics; (ii) defendant's own statements that placed him in the apartment during the hours prior to the 911 call, and indicated that he and Nussbaum were the only adults in the apartment; (iii) the medical testimony indicated that the injuries to Lisa were inflicted by a man of defendant's stature, and that Nussbaum was so debilitated that she was physically incapable of inflicting the injuries; (iv) hairs, forcibly removed from Lisa's head, were found on defendant's clothing; and (v) defendant had fresh bruises on his hand.

This evidence, if credited by the jury—as was their prerogative—was sufficient to meet the "tending to connect" standard of CPL 60.22(1). Thus, we reject defendant's assertions that there was insufficient corroboration as a matter of law.

....

## C. Shaken Baby Syndrome

As an outgrowth of the legal obligation that requires medical professionals to report suspected cases of child abuse and neglect to law enforcement, doctors and hospital personnel became increasingly involved in testifying on behalf of prosecutors in trials involving child abuse.

Convictions for a type of child abuse in which perpetrators shake infants so hard the babies develop internal head trauma resulting in death were based almost solely on the observations, diagnosis and in-court testimony of doctors. This particular type of abuse, called "shaken-baby syndrome," formed the basis for several high profile prosecutions, most notably the Massachusetts case of British nanny Louise Woodward.[17] Recently, the reliability of the science that is the underpinning of shaken-baby convictions has been called into question.

### Deborah Tuerkheimer, *The Next Innocence Project: Shaken Baby Syndrome and the Criminal Courts*
87 Wash. U.L. Rev. 1 (2009)

Every year in this country, hundreds of people are convicted of having shaken a baby, most often to death. In a prosecution paradigm without precedent, expert medical testimony is used to establish that a crime occurred, that the defendant

---

17. Louise Woodward was a teenage nanny from Britain who in 1997 was alleged to have murdered her eight-month-old charge, Matthew Eappen, by shaking him to death. Although convicted of second degree murder and given a sentence that could have lasted the rest of her life, a post-conviction proceeding resulted in a reduction to involuntary manslaughter and a sentence of time served, which amounted to less than a year. *Former British Nanny Tops U.S. Criminals List*, Apr. 13, 2007, www.dailymail.co.uk; *Commonwealth v. Woodward*, 427 Mass. 659 (1998).

caused the infant's death by shaking, and that the shaking was sufficiently forceful to constitute depraved indifference to human life. Shaken Baby Syndrome (SBS) is, in essence, a medical diagnosis of murder, one based solely on the presence of a diagnostic triad: retinal bleeding, bleeding in the protective layer of the brain, and brain swelling.

New scientific research has cast doubt on the forensic significance of this triad, thereby undermining the foundations of thousands of SBS convictions....

## 1. Introduction

Natalie Beard died on October 16, 1995. That morning, her mother had brought the seven-month-old to the home of her day care provider, Audrey Edmunds. The baby was by all accounts fussy. According to the caregiver's account, shortly after the baby was delivered to her, Edmunds propped Natalie in her car seat with a bottle, left the room, and returned a half-hour later to discover her limp. Edmunds—herself a mother—immediately called 911 to report that Natalie appeared to have choked and was unresponsive. Rescue workers responded minutes later and flew the baby to the hospital, where she died that night.

Prosecutors charged Edmunds with murder based on the theory that Natalie had been shaken to death. No witness claimed to have seen the defendant shake the baby. There were no apparent indicia of trauma. Edmunds maintained her innocence throughout. Yet a jury convicted Edmunds on the sole basis of expert testimony that Natalie suffered from Shaken Baby Syndrome (SBS). A court sentenced Edmunds to eighteen years in prison.

In important respects, this case falls squarely within the shaken baby prosecution paradigm that developed in the early 1990s. The infant had no external injuries suggestive of abuse. The accused was unable to provide an explanation for the child's condition. The medical evidence against the defendant consisted of the three diagnostic symptoms comprising the classic triad: retinal hemorrhages (bleeding of the inside surface of the back of the eye); subdural hemorrhages (bleeding between the hard outer layer and the spongy membranes that surround the brain); and cerebral edema (brain swelling). The presence of these three signs was understood to be pathognomic— or exclusively characteristic—of SBS.

At trial, the prosecution's experts testified that only shaking, possibly accompanied by impact could explain the injuries. Regarding the force necessary to cause these injuries, jurors heard the explanation typically offered in these cases: the force was equivalent to a fall from a second- or third-story window, or impact by a car moving at twenty-five to thirty miles an hour. The prosecution's experts concluded that the shaking necessarily occurred while the baby was in the defendant's care, since the trauma of the shaking would have caused immediate unconsciousness. The scientific basis for SBS was not challenged by the defense. And indeed, at the time of Edmunds's trial, the medical consensus on this issue was overwhelming.

. . . .

Edmunds is a representative shaken baby case in every respect but one. On January 31, 2008, Audrey Edmunds was granted a new trial on the basis of an evolution in scientific thinking. For the first time, a court examining the foundation of SBS concluded that it had become sufficiently eroded that a new jury probably would have a reasonable doubt as to the defendant's guilt. According to the court, a shift in mainstream medical opinion had undermined the basis of the SBS diagnosis, raising the distinct possibility that Edmunds, who was still serving her eighteen-year sentence in Wisconsin, had done nothing whatsoever to harm the child. As is true of an unknown number of convictions like it, the science upon which the defendant's conviction rested had advanced, raising the specter of innocence. . . .

The Age of SBS

The first appeal of an SBS-related conviction was reported in 1984.[18] Based on the presence of bilateral retinal hemorrhages and subdural hematoma, the prosecution's expert concluded that a four-month-old infant had been shaken to death, and the appellate court affirmed the sufficiency of the evidence to convict. Over the next five years, less than fifteen appeals of convictions based on an SBS diagnosis were reported.

Beginning in 1990, however, the number of appeals grew dramatically. In five-year increments, published appellate decisions increased from 74 (January 1, 1990-December 31, 1994), to 160 (January 1, 1995-December 31, 1999), to 315 (January 1, 2000-December 31, 2004). The numbers from the first half of the current five-year period suggest that this trend toward rising SBS appeals is continuing: from January 1, 2005 to June 30, 2008, 259 written opinions in this category were issued.

. . . .

### III. Scientific Evolution

. . . .

In the past, the mere presence of retinal hemorrhaging, subdural hematoma, and cerebral edema was taken to mean that a baby had been shaken hard enough to produce what were conceptualized as whiplash forces. According to the conventional understanding of SBS, [t]he application of rotational acceleration and deceleration forces to the infant's head causes the brain to rotate in the skull. Abrupt deceleration allows continuing brain rotation until bridging veins are stretched and ruptured, causing a thin layer of subdural hemorrhage on the surface of the brain.[19] Retinal hemorrhages were thought to result from a similar causal mechanism. Most significantly, the triad of symptoms was believed to be distinctly characteristic—in scientific terms, pathognomonic—of violent shaking.

Despite its lingering presence in the popular imagination, the scientific underpinnings of SBS have crumbled over the past decade as the medical establishment

---

18. [n44] *Ohio v. Schneider,* No. L-84-214, 1984 Ohio App. LEXIS 11988 (Ohio Ct. App. Dec. 21, 1984). . . .

19. [n62] Brian Harding, R. Anthony Risdon, & Henry F. Krous, Letter, *Shaken Baby Syndrome,* 328 BRIT. MED. J. 720, 720 (2004).

has deliberately discarded a diagnosis defined by shaking. Although no single nomenclature has emerged in its place, doctors are now in widespread agreement that SBS is an unhelpful characterization, and that the presence of retinal hemorrhages and subdural hematoma cannot conclusively prove that injury was inflicted.

. . . .

A. Flawed Science

. . . .

A logical fallacy of profound importance was uncovered by a close examination of the pre-1999 SBS literature: researchers had chosen subjects for study based on the presence of subdural hematomas and retinal hemorrhages and, with little or no investigation into other possible causes of these symptoms, simply concluded that the infants were shaken. . . .

Other studies purporting to support the validity of the SBS diagnosis relied on confessions to establish the mechanism of injury. Here, too, a number of problems undermined the validity of the research. Putting aside momentarily the possibility that a suspected abuser would be less than candid with doctors and investigators, the classification of an account as a confession in these studies was highly problematic from a methodological perspective: where caretakers said that they shook the baby, it was never detailed how much they shook the baby, how long they shook the baby, and did the baby's symptoms precede the shaking or did they follow the shaking.

. . . .

Around the same time, magnetic resonance imaging (MRI) revolutionized the field of radiology and significantly altered the diagnostic universe. Compared to its precursor, computed tomography (CT), MRI enabled a far more detailed assessment of the pattern, extent, and timing of central nervous system injuries. New radiological findings challenged what had become akin to scientific gospel, revealing the presence of triad symptoms in the mimics of abuse: accidental injury and medical disorders manifesting as SBS. And as technology and scientific methodology advanced, researchers questioning the basis for SBS reached a critical mass.

This momentum was catalyzed by the high-profile prosecution of British au pair Louise Woodward, which in 1997 brought shaken baby syndrome into the international spotlight.[20] The case was widely perceived as one of the more intriguing legal dramas of the age—one that [left] unresolved a mystery of sickening fascination to parents everywhere. In its wake, an already divided scientific community became even more polarized. . . .

2. Lucid Intervals

In the past, defendants prosecuted for SBS were identified by the science—that is, by the certainty of doctors that the perpetrator of abuse was necessarily the person

---

20. [n91] *Commonwealth v. Woodward,* No. CRIME. 97-0433, 1997 WL 694119 at *1 (Mass. Sup. Ct. Nov. 10, 1997). . . .

with the infant immediately prior to the loss of consciousness. However, studies have since shown that children suffering fatal head injury may be lucid for more than seventy-two hours before death. Because the prospect of a lucid interval lessens the ability to pinpoint when an injury was inflicted, this research dramatically alters the forensic landscape. Without other evidence, the identity of a perpetrator—assuming a crime has occurred—simply cannot be established.

. . . .

### 3. Removing the Shaking from the Syndrome

New debate has emerged regarding whether shaking can generate the force levels sufficient to cause the injuries associated with SBS. Those who believe it cannot point to a number of biomechanical studies, as well as research using animal and computer models. Many of these scientists assume arguendo that rotational acceleration-deceleration forces can, in theory, cause retinal hemorrhage and subdural hematoma, but contend that shaking an infant with sufficient force to do so would necessarily damage the neck and cervical spinal cord or column. Since most infants diagnosed with SBS do not present this type of injury, they could not have been simply shaken.

. . . .

Once this fact is acknowledged, the question of how much force is required to generate the types of injury associated with SBS becomes critical to whether trauma was inflicted, accidental, or undeterminable. The latest thinking about force thresholds complicates this inquiry. New research shows that relatively short-distance falls may cause fatal head injury that looks much like the injury previously diagnosed as SBS. Moreover, these signs and symptoms may not appear immediately. . . .

## IV. SBS and the Law

Given the scientific developments described, we may surmise that a sizeable portion of the universe of defendants convicted of SBS-based crimes is, in all likelihood, factually innocent. . . .

The criminal justice implications of all of this are staggering. To put the scope of the problem in a more familiar framework, it is helpful to consider the number of known exonerations in the United States over the past thirty years. From 1989 through 2007, there were 210 DNA exonerations, mostly for rape. It is reasonable to suspect that this number of SBS-based convictions after trial occurred in the past year alone. Additional (non-DNA) exonerations include those of 111 inmates on death row, 135 other individuals, and perhaps another 200 or so defendants whose convictions were overturned based on a mass scandal implicating widespread systemic corruption. Unlike SBS cases, none of these exonerations involve a set of paradigmatic facts later determined to be a faulty basis for prosecution.

. . . .

### A. Investigation and Prosecution

. . . .

It is worth noting the considerable deference given to child-abuse doctors—who, as a general rule, remain believers in the diagnosis. Accordingly, prosecutors may exhibit a disinclination to interrogate the science upon which these physicians' opinions rest. There is nothing novel about the observation that prosecutors tend to defer to their experts; but, in this context, the relationship between the prosecutor and the allied medical professionals is a particularly close one. In the typical SBS case, the expert is the case: there is no victim who can provide an account, no eyewitness, no corroborative physical evidence, and no apparent motive to kill. Doctors identify both the occurrence of a crime and its perpetrator, and their assurance regarding each is essential for a conviction. These dynamics may well contribute to a prosecutorial reluctance to challenge the validity of an SBS diagnosis. But they do not fully explain a continued willingness to pursue charges in cases built entirely on contested expert testimony....

1. Prosecutorial Training

Training is especially critical in this area, where a complex and evolving body of science is outcome determinative. As one prominent instructor recently urged, investigators and prosecutors should obtain a basic education on medical issues common to all of these cases. Since most prosecutors encounter SBS cases infrequently, few become experts in the issues they raise. It is unsurprising, then, that a nationwide training apparatus has developed to disseminate information about the basic structure of an SBS prosecution. For instance, the American Prosecutors Research Institute of the National District Attorneys Association transmits newsletters, organizes conferences, and provides other support for prosecuting the SBS case. The National Center on Shaken Baby Syndrome, an organization dedicated in part to training law enforcement officers, has hosted and collaborated on nine conferences since 2000. And prosecutors who have become leaders in the field have published book chapters with instruction in handling SBS cases from investigation through trial.

These training materials present a view of the science refracted through an advocate's lens. For instance, a 2001 publication asserts: the [prosecution] expert can testify that the forces the child experiences are the equivalent of a 50-60 m.p.h. unrestrained motor vehicle accident, or a fall from 3-4 stories on a hard surface; and current research and professional consensus within the medical literature clearly supports the conclusion that ... there is no lucid interval. Similarly, from a chapter published in 2006: there is emerging consensus among credible medical experts that when children have suffered serious or potentially fatal head injuries, they will start to experience symptoms almost immediately after injury; [t]he collection of ocular damage, subdural or subarachnoid bleeding over the brain, axonal damage, and severe brain swelling is not seen in the same patterns in any forms of accidental trauma, but is seen in cases involving severe and violent shaking; and the medical field has reached substantial consensus concerning many of the issues pertinent to criminal [SBS] cases.

. . . .

### 2. Caregiver Accounts

Prosecutorial confidence in guilt is augmented by statements on the part of SBS suspects—statements which are inevitably perceived as incriminatory. The three accounts most often offered to explain an infant's loss of consciousness or other obviously severe neurological symptoms are that: (i) their onset was unprovoked/without explanation, (ii) the infant fell from a short distance, and (iii) the infant was shaken playfully or in the course of revival efforts. Research over the past decade has made each of these explanations newly plausible. But because law enforcement officers interrogating the SBS suspect know that the infant's injuries were caused by violent shaking—the science is believed to prove this definitively—the narratives are all perceived as false and, therefore, incriminating. . . .

## B. Evidentiary Challenges

Defense motions to exclude expert testimony regarding SBS have, almost without exception, proven unsuccessful. Despite new challenges to the scientific underpinnings of the diagnosis, the admission of SBS testimony is facilitated by its once-uncontroversial nature. Even recently, and in cases involving triad symptoms alone, courts in both Daubert and Frye jurisdictions have rejected arguments that SBS is not generally accepted in the medical community and that it is not based on reliable scientific methods.

. . . .

## C. Jury Verdicts

Little is known about the operation of juries in shaken baby cases. One national trial consultant who assists the defense in this area has estimated a conviction rate of 95%; a prosecutor widely recognized as a national authority on SBS has suggested that the figure is closer to 50%; and a forensic pathologist who has consulted on many hundreds of cases for the defense places the figure somewhere between the two. In the absence of meaningful empirical documentation, the impressionistic data of those who see the largest number of these cases—and have done so for at least a decade—becomes a helpful source of information. . . .

Enormous procedural and substantive hurdles confront defendants at the post-conviction stage. Although the law differs depending on jurisdiction, a number of generalizations can be made about the SBS defendant's burden of proof. Put simply, there are tensions between the governing framework for collateral relief and the issues presented by SBS cases.

First, the evidence presented at the post-conviction stage must be deemed new, or discovered after the trial. One problem for the defense is that the proffered evidence is less definitive than past scientific improvement[s]—DNA typing, primarily.

Second, the evidence must be material to the case and not merely cumulative. . . .

Finally, the evidence must probably have resulted in a different verdict at trial. This is the most difficult burden for the defense. . . .

Beyond onerous post-conviction relief standards, defendants seeking collateral relief in SBS cases confront the likelihood that, in coming years, the current scientific controversy will be suspended in a kind of equilibrium. At some point, unless a revolutionary breakthrough fatally undermines SBS, defendants convicted in this era of uncertainty will be hard-pressed to claim that evidence of the diagnosis's invalidity is new. Newly discovered evidence motions will be effectively foreclosed without ever having become truly viable.

. . . .

## State v. Edmunds
Wisconsin Court of Appeals
308 Wis. 2d 374 (2008)

Dykman, J.

. . . .

### *Background*

Audrey Edmunds was charged with first-degree reckless homicide following the death of seven month old Natalie on October 16, 1995, while Edmunds was caring for Natalie at Edmunds's home. At trial, the State presented numerous medical expert witnesses who testified to a reasonable degree of medical certainty that the cause of Natalie's death was violent shaking or violent shaking combined with impact that caused a fatal head injury. The State's witnesses also testified that after being injured, Natalie would have had an immediate and obvious response and would not have appeared normal. Natalie's mother, and the father of another child in Edmunds's care who observed Natalie, testified that Natalie was acting normally when she was dropped off at Edmunds's home on the morning of her death.

Edmunds presented one medical expert witness who agreed with the State's witnesses that Natalie was violently shaken before her death but who opined that the injury occurred before Natalie was brought to Edmunds's home. The defense witness testified that Natalie had a lucid interval following the shaking and then suffered a seizure at Edmunds's home that resulted in her death. Edmunds testified that after Natalie was dropped off in the morning, Natalie was crying very hard and refused her bottle. After trying unsuccessfully to console Natalie, Edmunds left Natalie in a bedroom in her car seat with a propped bottle. After tending to her own children and the other children in her care, Edmunds observed that Natalie had stopped crying. Edmunds testified that she picked Natalie up and realized Natalie was limp and liquid was coming out of her nose and mouth. Edmunds called 911, and rescue personnel arrived and tried to resuscitate Natalie. Natalie was pronounced dead later that night at University Hospital.

The State presented another medical expert witness in rebuttal who disagreed with the defense expert and who stated that the medical evidence established that Natalie was violently shaken immediately before reacting and could not have had a lucid interval. In closing arguments, the defense tried to create reasonable doubt as to whether one of Natalie's parents had shaken her before leaving her with Edmunds, and the State reiterated that the medical testimony established that Natalie had been violently shaken immediately before requiring medical attention, which had to have been while in Edmunds's care. Edmunds was convicted of first-degree reckless homicide.

Edmunds filed a post conviction motion in 1997, arguing insufficiency of the evidence, multiple trial errors, sentencing errors, and that the real controversy was not tried because the issue should have been *whether* Natalie was shaken, not *who* had shaken Natalie. In her reply brief, Edmunds also claimed that she was entitled to a new trial on newly discovered evidence. In support, Edmunds submitted a proffer of expert medical testimony, including expert reports from two doctors. The first doctor was expected to testify that impact is necessary to cause fatal injuries in an infant, thus questioning whether "shaken baby syndrome" exists; that there was no evidence of an impact in Natalie's case; that, even assuming head trauma, there is a possibility of a significant lucid interval in infants after receiving a traumatic head injury; and that Natalie's acute brain injury may have been the result of a spontaneous re-bleeding of an older, minor injury, without a new trauma. The second doctor was expected to testify that Natalie was subject to intentional trauma that caused her death, but that there was no way within a reasonable degree of medical certainty to time the injury prior to her death and that a layperson would not be able to identify whether Natalie had undergone neurological damage. The circuit court denied Edmunds's motion. . . .

Edmunds filed this motion for a new trial in 2006, asserting that there were significant developments in the medical community around "shaken baby syndrome" in the ten years since her trial that amounted to newly discovered evidence. The circuit court held an evidentiary hearing, and Edmunds presented expert medical testimony from six doctors who explained that there is now a significant debate in the medical community as to whether Natalie's symptoms were necessarily indicative of shaking or shaking combined with head trauma in infants. The experts explained that there was not a significant debate about this issue in the mid-1990s and that the opinions offered in Edmunds's first post conviction motion would have been considered minority or fringe medical opinions. The State presented four medical experts, who testified that the medical evidence available in 1996 was still valid, despite the emergence of a debate about shaking and traumatic head injuries in infants and small children. The State's experts disagreed with the defense experts and maintained that the evidence at trial established that Natalie had been violently injured while in Edmunds's care.

The circuit court found that Edmunds had presented newly discovered evidence but denied her motion because it concluded that Edmunds had not established that there was a reasonable probability of a different result with the new evidence. The court explained that while both parties had presented credible evidence, the State's evidence was more convincing. Edmunds appeals.

. . . .

## Discussion

Edmunds contends that she is entitled to a new trial because the developments in medical research and literature in the ten years since her trial have provided new evidence that creates a reasonable probability that a different result would be reached in a new trial. *See State v. Armstrong,* 2005 WI 119, PP157-162, 283 Wis. 2d 639, 700 N.W.2d 98. The State asserts that Edmunds's claims are procedurally barred because they are identical to the claims she raised in her 1997 post conviction motion and that, if not barred, the claims do not meet the test for newly discovered evidence entitling Edmunds to a new trial. We conclude that Edmunds's claims are not procedurally barred and that she has established she is entitled to a new trial based on newly discovered evidence.

### Newly discovered evidence

To obtain a new trial based on newly discovered evidence, a defendant must establish by clear and convincing evidence that "(1) the evidence was discovered after conviction; (2) the defendant was not negligent in seeking evidence; (3) the evidence is material to an issue in the case; and (4) the evidence is not merely cumulative." *Armstrong,* 2005 WI 119, 283 Wis. 2d 639, P161, 700 N.W.2d 98 (citation omitted). Once those four criteria have been established, the court looks to "whether a reasonable probability exists that a different result would be reached in a trial." *Id.* (citation omitted). The reasonable probability factor need not be established by clear and convincing evidence, as it contains its own burden of proof. *Id.,* PP160-62 (abrogating *State v. Avery,* 213 Wis. 2d 228, 234-37, 570 N.W.2d 573 (Ct. App. 1997)).

The circuit court found that Edmunds had established the first four criteria by clear and convincing evidence....

We agree with the circuit court that Edmunds established the first four factors of the newly discovered evidence test by clear and convincing evidence. Edmunds presented evidence that was not discovered until after her conviction, in the form of expert medical testimony, that a significant and legitimate debate in the medical community has developed in the past ten years over whether infants can be fatally injured through shaking alone, whether an infant may suffer head trauma and yet experience a significant lucid interval prior to death, and whether other causes may mimic the symptoms traditionally viewed as indicating shaken baby or shaken impact syndrome. Edmunds could not have been negligent in seeking this evidence, as the record demonstrates that the bulk of the medical research and literature supporting the defense position, and the emergence of the defense theory as a legitimate position in the medical community, only emerged in the ten years following her trial. The evidence is material to an issue in the case because the main issue at trial was the cause of Natalie's injuries, and the new medical testimony presents an alternate theory for the source of those injuries. This evidence is not merely cumulative, in that it differs from the substance and quality of the defense evidence at trial. We find no erroneous exercise of discretion in the circuit court's findings as to these factors, as they are supported by the medical expert testimony at the post conviction hearing motion as contrasted with the medical expert testimony at trial.

The real crux of the dispute in this case is whether the new expert medical testimony Edmunds offers establishes a reasonable probability that a different result would be reached in a new trial. The circuit court found that there was not a reasonable probability of a different result following a new trial after weighing Edmunds's new evidence against the State's rebuttal evidence. The court said that although Edmunds had presented credible testimony from medical experts challenging the medical opinions presented at trial, the State's countering evidence was more convincing. Thus, the court explained, the State's case was as strong or stronger than it had been at the time of trial, so that there was not a reasonable probability a new result would be reached with a new trial. Again, we review this finding for an erroneous exercise of discretion. *See McCallum,* 208 Wis. 2d at 473. . . .

Here, the circuit court expressly found that Edmunds's new evidence and the State's new evidence were both credible. The court then weighed the evidence and concluded that the State's evidence was stronger. Under *McCallum,* the court applied the wrong legal standard. After determining that both parties presented credible evidence, it was not the court's role to weigh the evidence. Instead, once the circuit court found that Edmunds's newly discovered medical evidence was credible, it was required to determine whether there was a reasonable probability that a jury, hearing all the medical evidence, would have a reasonable doubt as to Edmunds's guilt. This question is not answered by a determination that the State's evidence was stronger. As explained in *McCallum,* a jury could have a reasonable doubt as to a defendant's guilt even if the State's evidence is stronger. . . .

The newly discovered evidence in this case shows that there has been a shift in mainstream medical opinion since the time of Edmunds's trial as to the causes of the types of trauma Natalie exhibited. We recognize, as did the circuit court, that there are now competing medical opinions as to how Natalie's injuries arose and that the new evidence does not completely dispel the old evidence. Indeed, the debate between the defense and State experts reveals a fierce disagreement between forensic pathologists, who now question whether the symptoms Natalie displayed indicate intentional head trauma, and pediatricians, who largely adhere to the science as presented at Edmunds's trial. However, it is the emergence of a legitimate and significant dispute within the medical community as to the cause of those injuries that constitutes newly discovered evidence. At trial, and on Edmunds's first post conviction motion, there was no such fierce debate. Thus, the State was able to easily overcome Edmunds's argument that she did not cause Natalie's injuries by pointing out that the jury would have to disbelieve the medical experts in order to have a reasonable doubt as to Edmunds's guilt. Now, a jury would be faced with competing credible medical opinions in determining whether there is a reasonable doubt as to Edmunds's guilt. Thus, we conclude that the record establishes that there is a reasonable probability that a jury, looking at both the new medical testimony and the old medical testimony, would have a reasonable doubt as to Edmunds's guilt. Accordingly, we reverse and remand for a new trial. Order reversed and cause remanded with directions.

## III. Teen Dating Violence

Teenage romance is filled with tumult; besides the hormonal fluctuations of adolescence, the young and in love must navigate fickle hearts, foolish crushes and high-school jealousies. Parents often take these relationships, to the extent adults even consider them as such, with a grain of salt. But one aspect of the youthful dating game that must be taken seriously is the violence that sometimes goes along with it — which is largely hidden from surrounding adults. But as this topic emerges from the shadows, adults are paying attention. In Arizona, an organization called Purple Ribbon Council, an anti-domestic violence group, visits high schools to instruct teens on how to recognize abusive relationships. As former Cleveland Heights Municipal Court Judge Lynn Toler, who is now a volunteer with the organization, has said: "Early intervention is the key to getting out in front of domestic violence. It can't just be the courts responding afterward."[21]

In 2007, the Centers for Disease Control surveyed 15,000 teens; 10 percent of them reported some form of physical abuse by a dating partner.[22] In Rhode Island in 2007, the state legislature passed the Lindsay Ann Burke Act in honor of a 23-year-old woman murdered by her abusive boyfriend. R.I. Gen. Laws Ann §§ 16-85-1, 16-85-2 and 16-21-30, 16-22-24 require that school districts establish policies to recognize and respond to dating violence and that they incorporate anti-violence lessons into health classes.[23] The following article, written for domestic violence advocates, seeks to explain the challenges that accompany representing young victims mired in abusive relationships.

### Andrew Sta. Ana & Stephanie Nilva,
### *Teen Victims of Intimate Partner Violence*
LAWYER'S MANUAL ON DOMESTIC VIOLENCE, REPRESENTING THE VICTIM, 254 (6th ed. 2015)

. . . .

Teen Dating Violence is Not Domestic Violence Light

Advocates unfamiliar with the complexity or scope of teen dating violence may incorrectly dismiss violence perpetrated by young people as less severe than violence perpetrated by adults. Indeed, according to one study, up to 80% of parents do not

---

21. Lynn Toler, *Personal Best/My Cause: Street Justice: Lynn Toler Helps Teens Fight Domestic Violence*, AARP THE MAGAZINE 66, August/September 2015.

22. Elizabeth Olson, *Killings Prompt Efforts to Spot and Reduce Abuse of Teenagers in Dating*, N.Y. TIMES, January 4, 2009.

23. Marybeth Sullivan, *OLR Research Report: Summary of Rhode Island's Lindsay Ann Burke Act*, webserver.rilin.state.ri.us/PublicLaws/law07/law07490.htm, accessed October 3, 2016.

perceive dating violence as a serious concern for their children and consequently have few conversations with their children about it. Despite the misleading label, teens inflict violence at rates that belie this common misconception. In fact, one in three teens knows someone whose dating partner has abused them. Women aged 16 to 24 suffer the highest rates of intimate partner violence of any age group. A 2013 study found that, among students who dated, 21% of female students and 10% of male students were abused by a dating partner in the preceding 12 months.

When working with young clients, the phrase "domestic violence" can be clumsy and inaccurate. "Domestic" may not resonate with youth who are being abused by a partner, and can be a barrier to screening and intervention. For young people in romantic relationships, dating violence may be far from "domestic," committed in schools, public places, online and sometimes their homes. Young people may not describe their relationship with their partner as "dating," but as "hanging out," "messing around," "fooling around," or as a "friend with benefits." . . .

### Adolescence and Dating Violence

During the span of adolescence, young people experience profound changes in mental, emotional and physical development. Developing senses of self-identity, community, family and culture, along with exposure to new levels of stress, emotion and conflict, combine to impact teens' responses to and perceptions of dating violence. These developmental responses can include boundary-testing, defying authority, increasing reliance on friends, exploring risky behaviors and rejecting family and community standards. For example, a survivor seeking to determine her own identity separate and apart from her family and community may not disclose that she is in a romantic relationship at all, let alone an abusive one. She may fear judgment, or even punishment, from her family members. She may not disclose that she is sexually active, or that she has exchanged intimate pictures with her partner. In other cases, she may only disclose a select portion of her experience, withholding details to protect herself or her abusive partner. Another young survivor may rely heavily on a peer group for advice on his relationships, or idealize and confuse images of relationships in the media and through culture as demonstrative of actual relationships. He may not disclose that his dating partner may be of the same sex, or that he is exploring his emerging sense of sexual orientation or gender identity. Other young people may substitute the influence of their families with the influence of an abusive partner before they have developed independent decision-making skills in a safe and supportive environment. In all of these scenarios, as counsel the ability to offer nonjudgmental understanding will enhance open communication with the client and improve advocacy on behalf of young people. . . .

### Disclosures of Dating Violence

Given their developmental stage and their mistrust of authority figures, young people may engage in what at first seems to be risky or self-destructive behavior. The ability to reserve judgment and focus on the support you can provide to a young survivor may make all the difference in encouraging help-seeking behavior. Some teen survivors may not fully appreciate future and long-term implications of their behaviors. These can include engaging in risky sexual behaviors or unprotected sex, the exchange of sexually suggestive or explicit text messages ("sexts"), or revealing personal or family secrets, all without a full appreciation of the consequences of those behaviors. Given the response they can reasonably expect from adults, teens are much more likely to disclose an incident of dating violence to a friend than to a parent or an attorney.

. . . .

Technology: A tool of power and control, a tool for survival

Young people actively use technology to discover new and innovative ways to connect, communicate and explore their identities and relationships. Some popular forms of communication include apps and social media that did not exist even a few years ago, yet seem essential for communication today. In appreciating these rapid advances, attorneys must adapt and learn how young survivors use and experience technology.

Technology abuse can take the form of monitoring messages and calls; forced sharing of passwords; threatening to release intimate messages or pictures; shooting videos of a sexual assault; anonymously posting secrets and rumors on social media; the use of tracking software to monitor the movement of a partner; and creating fake profiles to manipulate a survivor. Young people and their online or digital connections to others, whether intimate, casual, fleeting, friendly, surreptitious, experimental or meaningful, should be taken seriously. Whether made abruptly or deliberately, these communications provide an opportunity for genuine connection, intimacy, and independence. Online and through social media, young people flirt, joke, fight, make up, fall in love and experience a full range of emotions. Occasionally, these communications can include casual and intimate sexual encounters, inducing the exchange and use of pictures, the use of webcams and explicit text messages. . . .

Just a few years ago, when an abuser contacted the victim through email, social media, or even telephone, a common response was to advise a survivor to delete an account, change a password, "block" the abuser or change a phone number. In many cases this can be an effective and powerful strategy. However, for many young survivors, disconnecting from their online community and friends can mean cutting them off from sources of support, resistance and resilience. A survivor's disappearance from online communities also might trigger renewed or increased abuse. Staying online can serve as an important tool to document evidence and maintain connections through apps and social media. Some receive information about their abuser's location through friends and family, and others refuse to compromise their lives and online presence because of harassment. . . .

Despite their intimacy, online exchanges come with tremendous risk to the survivor should they be exposed. In some instances, the non-consensual release and distribution of intimate encounters is seen as a form of sexual violence and can result in trauma to a survivor. Trauma from the violence could be coupled with feelings of shame and embarrassment in spaces outside the digital world. Furthermore, these communications are rarely private, if ever. Through the use of screenshots, third-party apps and spyware, the sharing of passwords and numerous recording devices, the most personal and intimate connections can be corrupted and spread very quickly. Abusers and use disclosure of intimate messages or pictures to keep survivors in a relationship or to coerce them to engage in non-consensual sex. Images can be manipulated digitally or shared with peers and family members to shame a survivor. . . .

## Advocacy

### Criminal Justice System

Teen survivors of dating violence seeking safety from an abuser are supported by various legal systems, including the criminal legal system. In the criminal system, the rights of both the survivor and those of the abuser will differ significantly. . . .

The issues of statutory rape and child pornography arise for teen survivors of dating violence, who may have partners their own age or far older. Courts will seriously examine allegations that relate to sexual intercourse and contact between an adult and a minor. . . . Serious legal issues are also triggered in cases involving the possession, creation or distribution of sexually explicit images of minors. Possession of child pornography violates both state and federal law. The release or distribution of these images is often referred to as "Revenge Porn," and many states around the country are seeking to find ways to protect victims, and to be responsive to the complicated circumstances under which these images are created or distributed. . . .

### Safety Planning

Inevitably, safety planning—in which a step-by-step strategy for keeping safe is developed with the client will play a critical role for survivors. Assisting teens successfully mean understanding the world of youth. A relationship between two young people may appear to you to be more ambiguous than one between adults, which may be defined by marriage or a shared household. A successful safety plan for a teen will probably be designed for the routines and schedules of a young person, which can encompass a school setting, neighborhood and a young person's presence online. Be aware that your client's relationship status with the abuser may change many times between appointments or before court dates. . . .

Because a teen's social circle or schedule may vary by day or by week, the safety plan must adapt to those circumstances. A sixteen-year-old survivor with an abusive partner in the same school will have different needs than one involved with a twenty-five-year-old. A teen may fear the abuser's gang or circle of friends. Young people can feel hopeless about pursuing help because the abuser will likely remain in the same school. A client involved with an older abusive partner will be particularly subject to such person's controlling behavior. . . .

Remind your client to alter his or her route to school, know the location of local police stations, travel with friends or family, and keep a charged cell phone or change for a phone call on hand. If he abusive partner is in the same school, you might offer to speak to the school principal or other school contacts about alerting security personnel, changing a student's schedule or locker location or obtaining a safety transfer....

## IV. Family Violence as a Form of Child Abuse

Children are not only harmed as the direct victims of abuse, they also suffer by witnessing violence in the home. Although experts vary in their opinions about the extent of the harm suffered by children who witness family violence, courts view the problem as a dangerous one.

### People v. Johnson
### New York Court of Appeals
### 95 N.Y. 2d 368 (2000)

WESLEY, J.

On March 7, 1997, defendant Theodore Johnson violently attacked his ex-girlfriend Vanessa Parker as she walked home from the supermarket with her three daughters. Defendant approached Parker and struck her in the back of the head, knocking her against a fence. The baby carriage Parker was wheeling, carrying their child, was also knocked over. Parker's two older children, 7 and 12 years old, immediately began to cry. Defendant yelled and cursed at Parker about previously putting him in jail (Parker already had an order of protection against defendant in connection with a prior harassment incident). He grabbed her by the back of the neck, dragged her to her apartment entrance, ordered her to unlock the apartment and knocked her head against the door.

Parker's 12-year-old daughter picked up the baby carriage and the children followed them inside. Once inside, defendant pushed Parker up the steps into the apartment, again causing her to fall. He continued his cursing, telling her that he would "leave [her] in the house for dead" and then she would "see how [her] children would like being motherless." After entering the apartment, the children went directly to their bedroom. Defendant followed Parker into the living room, and continued to beat her with his hands, feet and a metal pipe. Defendant also threw cups, plates and glasses at the walls and at Parker.

He continued his verbal abuse, cursing and yelling at Parker for calling the police about past incidents of abuse. Trapped in their room, the children could hear the glass breaking, Parker's screams and defendant's yelling. Defendant's reign of terror lasted for over 10 hours. Parker was finally able to sneak out of the apartment and call the police. Only after defendant's arrest did the children emerge from the bedroom, where they were exposed to broken glass and debris strewn around the living room. Later, when defendant was in jail awaiting trial, he threatened to beat Parker if she did not drop the charges against him.

After a nonjury trial, defendant was convicted of two counts of endangering the welfare of a child, intimidating a victim or witness, menacing and a number of felonies related to the order of protection. With regard to the felonies, Supreme Court sentenced defendant as a second felony offender. The Appellate Division modified the judgment by reversing defendant's convictions for endangering the welfare of a child, holding that the evidence was legally insufficient, while sustaining defendant's second felony offender adjudication. A Judge of this Court granted both the People and defendant leave to appeal.

On the People's appeal, we are asked to determine whether the evidence was legally sufficient to support defendant's conviction for endangering the welfare of a child when his actions were not specifically directed at the children. The People contend that the statute is written broadly enough to cover conduct directed at others that is likely to cause harm to children. Under the facts of this case, we agree.

Penal Law § 260.10(1) provides that a person endangers the welfare of a child when "[h]e knowingly acts in a manner likely to be injurious to the physical, mental or moral welfare of a child less than seventeen years old." Actual harm to the child need not result for criminal liability; it is "sufficient that the defendant act in a manner which is *likely* to result in harm to the child, *knowing* of the likelihood of such harm coming to the child" (*People v. Simmons*, 92 NY2d 829, 830 [emphasis added]).

Nothing in the statute restricts its application solely to harmful conduct directed at children (*see, People v. Bergerson*, 17 NY2d 398, 401 [noting that the prior version of statute was intended to be broad in scope]). The statute is broadly written and imposes a criminal sanction for the mere "likelihood" of harm. Moreover, the language provides that defendant "knowingly" act in such a manner, further suggesting that the statute does not require that the conduct be specifically directed at a child; rather, a defendant must simply be *aware* that the conduct may likely result in harm to a child, whether directed at the child or not (*see*, Penal Law § 15.05[2]).

Defendant would rewrite the statute. We have previously noted that when a statute imposes criminal liability for knowingly disregarding a risk, it does not require a particular outcome or actions aimed at a specific individual; the crime is solely defined by the risk of injury produced by defendant's conduct (*see, People v. Davis*, 72 NY2d 32, 36-37). The same can be said here. Endangering the welfare of a child is not defined by specifically targeted acts or individuals, but by conduct which a defendant knows will present a "likelihood" of harm to a child (i.e., with an awareness of the potential for harm).

We reject defendant's contention that applying the statute to conduct not specifically directed at children will result in a wild proliferation of prosecutions based on bad parenting or the exposure of children to inappropriate behavior. Here, defendant's conduct could hardly be characterized as bad parenting—or indeed parenting at all. Moreover, the statute has been in place for over 30 years. The Legislature specifically recognized that behavior that was *likely* to produce harm to a child's physical, mental or moral well-being fell within its sweep as long as the defendant was *aware* of its potential for harm to a child. The Legislature's response to conduct that could cause harm to children has not produced a clarion call for legislative reform of the statute; we will not supplant that function by judicial stitchery.

The adverse effects of domestic violence on children have been well documented over the past two decades and have been recognized by all branches of our government in New York. In 1996, the Governor approved an act to amend the Domestic Relations Law and the Family Court Act to require courts to consider domestic violence when rendering child custody and visitation determinations. He noted that "[t]he victims of domestic violence are not limited to those who are actually battered by spouses, for the evidence is overwhelming that those who batter their spouses inflict tremendous harm on their children. . . . [D]omestic violence causes great psychological and developmental damage to children even when they are not themselves physically abused" (Governor's Approval Mem to L 1996, ch 85, 1996 McKinney's Session Laws of NY, at 1858, 1859). Some trial courts in child endangerment prosecutions have also explicitly recognized the overwhelming evidence of harm to children exposed to domestic violence (*see, e.g., People v. Malone*, 180 Misc 2d 744).

Viewing all the evidence and the inferences which may be drawn in the light most favorable to the People, as we are obliged to do, we conclude that a rational trier of fact could have reasonably determined that defendant's assaultive conduct in this case created a likelihood of harm to the children of which he was aware. Here, the children saw defendant approach their mother and strike her down in the street, whereupon they immediately started crying. In their immediate presence, the defendant then threatened to kill their mother. For over 10 hours they hid in their bedroom, listening to defendant's yelling and cursing, their mother's screams and the sounds of breaking glass.

To the extent that some courts have determined that section 260.10(1) requires that a defendant's conduct must be directly focused upon the child, or that evidence of a child witnessing a severe act of violence is insufficient as a matter of law to support a conviction under this statute, those decisions are not to be followed (*see, People v. Carr,* 208 AD2d 855, *appeal after new trial* 229 AD2d 446, *lv. denied* 88 NY2d 1067; *People v. Suarez,* 133 Misc 2d 762). We reiterate, however, that each case is fact specific (*see, People v. West,* 271 AD2d 806; *People v. Brooks,* 270 AD2d 206, *lv. denied* 95 NY2d 794; *People v. Parr,* 155 AD2d 945, *lv. denied* 75 NY2d 870 [all holding that a defendant who performs a significant act of domestic violence against a mother in the presence of a child is guilty of endangering the welfare of that child]).

. . . .

# V. Family Violence and Child Custody

## A. Should Batterers Be Custodial Parents?

In *Stanley v. Illinois,* 405 U.S. 645 (1972), the Supreme Court held that the custody, care and nurturing of a child is a fundamental right under the Constitution and that a parent is entitled to due process before he or she loses that right. In proceedings held by courts to determine whether a parent is fit to obtain—or maintain—custody, the impact of domestic violence on that decision varies. In some states, there is a legal presumption against granting custody of children to batterers. In others, domestic violence is one of many factors to be given serious weight in making a custody decision. Examples of each approach follow.

### Ala. Code § 30-3-131 (2015) Presumption against perpetrator of violence.

In every proceeding where there is at issue a dispute as to the custody of a child, a determination by the court that domestic or family violence has occurred raises a rebuttable presumption by the court that it is detrimental to the child and not in the best interest of the child to be placed in sole custody, joint legal custody, or joint physical custody with the perpetrator of domestic or family violence. Notwithstanding the provisions regarding rebuttable presumption, the judge must also take into account what, if any, impact the domestic violence had on the child.

### Ind. Code Ann. § 31-17-2-8 (2016) Factors considered—Standard.

The court shall determine custody and enter a custody order in accordance with the best interests of the child. In determining the best interests of the child, there is no presumption favoring either parent. The court shall consider all relevant factors, including the following:

(1) The age and sex of the child.

(2) The wishes of the child's parent or parents.

(3) The wishes of the child, with more consideration given to the child's wishes if the child is at least fourteen (14) years of age.

(4) The interaction and interrelationship of the child with:

    (A) the child's parent or parents;

    (B) the child's sibling; and

    (C) any other person who may significantly affect the child's best interests.

(5) The child's adjustment to the child's:

    (A) home;

    (B) school; and

    (C) community.

(6) The mental and physical health of all individuals involved.

(7) Evidence of a pattern of domestic or family violence by either parent.

(8) Evidence that the child has been cared for by a de facto custodian, and if the evidence is sufficient, the court shall consider the factors described in section 8.5(b) [IC 31-17-2-8.5(b)] of this chapter.

## Nancy Ver Steegh, *Differentiating Types of Domestic Violence: Implications for Child Custody*

65 La. L. Rev. 1379 (2005)

### I. Introduction

Family Courts have traditionally turned a blind eye to domestic violence or have minimized its significance. Custody disputes involving domestic violence have been forced into a one-size-fits-all paradigm, an erroneous and potentially life-threatening approach. What is required is a differentiated approach based on careful screening of cases for the presence of domestic violence and thoughtful consideration of the clinical and legal implications.

. . . .

### II. Differentiating Types of Violence

A. Contradictory Research Suggests the Existence of Different Types of Domestic Violence

. . . .

Researcher Michael P. Johnson[24] has taken the process of integrating competing studies to its conclusion by developing a comprehensive typology that accounts for contradictory research and connects contrasting perspectives. Based on his analysis of the "family conflict" and the "feminist" studies discussed above, he concludes that women's advocates and service providers are primarily observing one type of domestic violence, Intimate Terrorism, while family conflict researchers are predominantly measuring another type of violence, Situational Couple Violence.

Johnson identifies four types of domestic violence based on the motivation of the aggressor and the overall pattern of the violence. The two most common forms are Intimate Terrorism, which involves an escalating pattern of coercive control, and Situational Couple Violence, which involves isolated conflict-based incidents. These two forms are the subject of this article. A third form, Violent Resistance, which involves self-defense, will be discussed only as it relates to Intimate Terrorism and Situational Couple Violence.

. . . .

---

24. [n15] Michael P. Johnson, Ph.D., is an Associate Professor of Sociology, Women's Studies, and African and African American Studies at Pennsylvania State University.

1. Intimate Terrorism

   a. The Johnson Typology: Intimate Terrorism

Intimate Terrorism (IT) is the type of violence observed in battered women's shelters and measured by crime and clinical studies. In Intimate Terrorism, violence is one tactic in a larger pattern of power and control. Control is exerted by making threats, wielding economic control, applying privilege and punishment, manipulating and threatening children, isolating the victim, and inflicting emotional and sexual abuse. As compared with other types of violence, Intimate Terrorism involves more frequent per couple incidents, more severe violence, and results in more serious injury. This type of violence is quite likely to escalate over time.

Intimate Terrorism is nearly always perpetrated by men upon women, and female victims are more likely to suffer from Post Traumatic Stress Syndrome (PTSD), depression, and poor health. These women actively seek formal help and are likely to leave the abuser. Intimate Terrorism accounts for somewhere between eleven percent and thirty-five percent of domestic violence situations.

. . . .

      i. Victims of Intimate Terrorism

. . . The most commonly held view of "battered women" is based on "the traumatization model" which includes themes such as "learned helplessness" and "battered women's syndrome." Some women who are victims of Intimate Terrorism suffer from Post Traumatic Stress Disorder as a result of the abuse. Victims experience painful and serious physical injuries, as well as depression, PTSD, suicide attempts, and substance abuse. Victimization is also related to difficulty maintaining employment and a permanent residence.

However, contrary to popular belief, many victims of domestic violence leave the violent relationship. In fact, Richard Gelles reports that women who experience the most frequent and severe violence (arguably victims of Intimate Terrorism) are more likely to leave. This is consistent with research demonstrating victims' use of a "vast array of personal strategies and help resources." For example, in one study, researcher Lee Bowker found that women used seven personal strategies (such as talking to or avoiding their partner, hiding or running away, threatening to call police or file divorce, or fighting back physically) to end the abuse, after which they accessed informal and formal resources (including police, clergy, physicians, and lawyers). Victims, therefore, are not necessarily passive but may be active survivors of abuse.

. . . .

      iii. Intimate Terrorists as Parents

. . . First, these fathers are likely to be rigidly authoritarian. They expect to be obeyed without question, are highly irritable, show little empathy for children, and spank children more than twice as often. Second, battering fathers tend to be under-involved parents who view children as an annoying hindrance and are unwilling to accommodate their needs. This pattern of neglect may be punctuated with brief periods of fatherly interest in the children during which he will attempt to win their favor. Third, batterers continually undermine the parenting efforts of the mother by ridiculing her, overruling her decisions, and physically attacking her. Finally, battering fathers tend to be self-centered, viewing the children as extensions of themselves and believing that the children should meet their needs.

Cycles of terror and kindness can lead to traumatic bonding with the battering parent. The child may crave positive contact with the batterer and be unable to separate love and abuse. Children may conclude that their safety depends upon sustaining close ties with the batterer.

Evan Stark[25] describes the batterer's extension of coercive tactics to the children as "tangential spouse abuse." Batterers are able to control the mother by manipulating or threatening the children, even after divorce. Unfortunately, fathers with a history of Intimate Terrorism are also likely to continue their previous inappropriate parenting practices after divorce....

2. Situational Couple Violence

   a. The Johnson Typology: Situational Couple Violence

. . . .

Situational Couple Violence is the type of domestic violence measured in the epidemiological "family conflict" studies, and it is initiated nearly equally by men and women. However, there is evidence that men and women are differently motivated and that women suffer more injury and negative consequences resulting from the violence. These consequences include higher levels of depression, low self-esteem, and substance abuse. This type of violence usually does not escalate and may in fact de-escalate or stop altogether. Situational Couple Violence is the most common form of domestic violence accounting for an estimated fifty-one percent of cases.

. . . .

   i. Victims of Situational Couple Violence

There is a common assumption that all victims of domestic violence should want to leave their relationships. Obviously, many should and do leave, including some victims of Situational Couple Violence. However, others want to live safely in their current relationships, seeking only an end to the violence. As compared to victims of Intimate Terrorism, victims of Situational Couple Violence are more likely to voluntarily choose to work on the relationship rather than leave it....

   ii. Perpetrators of Situational Couple Violence

Johnson believes that one of the Holtzworth-Munroe and Stuart batterer types, family-only perpetrators, are involved in Situational Couple Violence. These family-only perpetrators inflict less severe violence with less psychological and sexual abuse.

---

   25. [n86] Evan Stark, Ph.D., is an Associate Professor of Public Administration, Director of the Masters in Public Health Program at Rutgers-Newark and Director of Urban Health Administration at the UMDNJ School of Public Health.

They evidence little or no psycho pathology and are usually not violent outside the home. Their violence results from stress, anger, and lack of relationship skills such that a marital conflict becomes violent. Their violence is not likely to escalate over time, and they generally have positive attitudes toward women. Holtzworth-Munroe and Stuart hypothesize that family-only perpetrators make up fifty percent of violent men.

### iii. Situational Couple Violence and Parenting

Bancroft and Silverman report that some perpetrators parent quite responsibly after divorce, leading one to speculate that these are cases of Situational Couple Violence rather than Intimate Terrorism. According to them, these fathers did not undermine the mother or use the children against her during the marriage. They were less psychologically abusive, they accepted the termination of the relationship, and they showed the ability to elevate the children's needs over their own. After five years, their former partners reported few problems. If indeed these were cases of Situational Couple Violence, this is an indication that carefully structured parenting plans may work in such situations and that ongoing contact with both parents would be in the children's best interest....

In cases involving Situational Couple Violence, children remain at risk but are likely to benefit from parental education regarding the impact of high conflict on children and enhanced conflict resolution skills....

### iv. Violent Resistance

Violent Resistance involves situations where a female victim defends herself against her aggressive male partner. In one study, researchers found that victims who resist violence, either physically or verbally, were twice as likely to be injured.

While some perpetrators of Situational Couple Violence are female, they must be carefully distinguished from women who are violent resisters of Intimate Terrorism. Confusing a woman defending herself from Intimate Terrorism with a woman perpetrator of Situational Couple Violence could be a deadly mistake for her and her children. A woman resisting Intimate Terrorism (and her children) needs immediate protection, not anger management techniques. The possibility of such a mistake illustrates a danger inherent in the creation and use of typologies. At the same time, "a monolithic etiological model of marital aggression is inadequate to capture the diversity of relationship and individual dynamics in physically aggressive marriages."

. . . .

## III. Using Differentiated Case Management to Match Families with Appropriate Court Procedures and Services

For too long, courts and legislatures have taken a one-size-fits-all approach to domestic violence and very real differences among families have been overlooked. As a result of this lack of scrutiny, the most acute cases (arguably those involving Intimate Terrorism) are not taken seriously enough, resulting in batterers being given unrestricted access to children and sometimes even custody. At the same time, in other cases (potentially those involving Situational Couple Violence) families are discouraged from accessing services, such as parent education and mediation which would be helpful to them. Families experiencing domestic violence are in need of special care and handling, and it is time for professionals from all disciplines to work together to provide it, rather than shaking their heads over the complexity and intransigence of the problem.

A. Current Failure to Differentiate Cases Involving Different Types of Domestic Violence

1. Misidentifying Cases: All Domestic Violence Viewed as Situational Couple Violence

. . . .

The tendency to view all cases of domestic violence as Situational Couple Violence takes place in family court as well as in criminal cases. As will be discussed in later sections, this propensity is encouraged by statutory definitions that target Situational Couple Violence rather than Intimate Terrorism. The failure to understand the dynamic of coercive control present in Intimate Terrorism places victims and children in extreme danger and discourages them from seeking help. At the same time, hesitancy to acknowledge the existence of Situational Couple Violence allows the mischaracterization of cases to continue and is used by some to justify it. All cases of domestic violence are "real," but they should not all be handled the same way. . . .

C. Regulating Perpetrator Contact with Children

The type of violence experienced also has implications for structuring post-decision relationships with children.

1. Supervised Visitation

Because parental rights are not terminated in divorce proceedings, the perpetrator of domestic violence will have continued access to the children in the form of visitation. As discussed above, this may be appropriate in cases of Situational Couple Violence, assuming the parties have improved their conflict resolution skills and have been informed about the harm to children resulting from ongoing conflict.

However, in cases of Intimate Terrorism visitation can be dangerous. The batterer may harm the children through acts of violence or psychological abuse. In addition, the abuser is likely to use visitation to assault or manipulate the mother in an attempt to reassert the pattern of domination and control. Unfortunately, some intimate terrorists are granted unrestricted visitation of their children.

. . . .

Certainly an argument can be made that in some cases, Intimate Terrorists should not be allowed visitation, especially if the child strongly objects. However, many experts believe that children benefit from ongoing but limited contact with the abusive parent. This is because the visits provide a "reality check" for the child and help the child come to terms with the abuser.

Supervised visitation centers provide a safe location for visits under the oversight of trained personnel who can intervene if problems arise. Parents arrive and depart at different times so that there is no opportunity for contact. Staff members observe the visits and interact with parents to provide informal advice and education. Visiting parents are prohibited from whispering to children, forcing physical contact, or making negative comments about family members. Most families view the program favorably, and there is some indication that parental attitudes are positively affected.

. . . .

2. Parent Coordinators

Because cases involving violence or high conflict require extra oversight and monitoring, some courts have created the role of parent coordinator. Parent coordinators are analogous to special masters used in federal civil cases where judges appoint professionals with particular subject matter expertise and delegate limited decision making power to them. In 2000, the American Bar Association Family Law Section held an interdisciplinary conference on high conflict cases and the conferees recommended appointing parenting coordinators or masters to manage recurring child custody and access disputes. By 2003, at least fourteen states had implemented this new professional role.

Parent coordinators assist parents in creating, implementing, and monitoring parenting plans. Some states limit appointment of parent coordinators to post-decree matters while other states involve them in the divorce process. During the divorce process, parent coordinators may function as the leader of an interdisciplinary team assisting the family. More typically parent coordinators make decisions or recommendations about day-to-day matters such as scheduling, activities, transportation, child care, discipline, education, and health care. They generally cannot modify custody, allow relocation, or make any other major changes to court orders. Rather, they settle more routine parenting disputes outside of the court setting. Thus, depending on the needs of the family, parent coordinators may perform assessments, provide education, serve as case coordinator, assist with conflict management, and potentially make binding decisions or recommendations to the court. . . .

IV. Implications for Substantive Law Reform

Courts can more effectively meet the needs of children by differentiating between cases of Situational Couple Violence and Intimate Terrorism. With support, education, and careful planning, children may be parallel parented by parents with a history of Situational Couple Violence. However, children who are exposed to Intimate Terrorism need additional protection. They require physical and emotional safety, structure and predictability, and a strong bond with the nonviolent parent. Without intensive intervention, perpetrators of Intimate Terrorism are incapable of meeting these needs and awarding them custody or unsupervised visitation endangers the children.

. . . .

### B. Domestic Violence and "Best Interests"

#### 1. Domestic Violence as a Single Factor

Because courts historically failed to recognize the nexus between domestic violence and parenting, during the 1980s, women's advocates lobbied for the inclusion of domestic violence as a factor in determining the best interests of the child. This effort was bolstered by mounting empirical evidence concerning the harm to children from witnessing abuse and the prevalence of concurrent child abuse. Currently nearly every state includes domestic violence as an explicit factor to be considered in determining custody.

In cases of Situational Couple Violence, case-by-case evaluation of the children's needs is likely to be appropriate, and a best interests analysis can be useful in creating a highly structured parenting plan that requires little contact between the parents. Of course, this assumes that the court will give sufficient weight to the domestic violence factor.

However, in cases involving Intimate Terrorism, inclusion of domestic violence as one factor among many may not provide adequate protection for children. Judges who are unfamiliar with the dynamics of Intimate Terrorism may discount the seriousness of the abuse and give the factor too little weight....

#### 2. Use of Experts

In addition to amending relevant statutory sections, custody evaluators and guardians ad litem can effectively assist the court by taking into account the dynamics of Situational Couple Violence and Intimate Terrorism when making risk assessments and custody and access recommendations. Unfortunately, both groups have been criticized for failing to identify domestic violence and for viewing all domestic violence as conflict-based (Situational Couple Violence), and consequently overlooking control-based violence (Intimate Terrorism).

The custody evaluator should make an in-depth investigation, which includes obtaining relevant police and court records, interviewing all parties with information, making home visits, and completing any psychological testing. He or she should inform the court concerning the frequency and severity of the violence, the type of violence, and the impact of the violence on the children.

Multi-disciplinary teams including guardians ad litem and custody evaluators are ideally situated to assist families with a history of Situational Couple Violence in reducing conflict levels and developing parenting plans. In contrast, these professionals can provide important protection to children exposed to Intimate Terrorism by alerting courts to the pattern of coercive control and by strongly recommending the use of supervised visitation and parenting coordinators.

### C. "Friendly Parent" Provisions and Joint Custody

#### 1. "Friendly Parent" Provisions

During the 1980s, public policy shifted to encourage continued involvement by both parents after divorce. This led to the passage of best interest factors favoring the parent most willing to encourage contact with the other parent, commonly referred to as "friendly parent" provisions. Twenty-eight states have enacted such provisions.

"Friendly parent" provisions should not be used in cases involving domestic violence. Exercise of such provisions is especially dangerous in cases of Intimate Terrorism for several reasons: (1) the batterer may appear to be the more cooperative parent and thus gain custody or unrestricted access to the children; (2) the victim may be coerced into agreeing to unrestricted visitation in order to keep custody; (3) the victim may be forced to have additional ongoing contact with the batterer; and (4) the batterer is likely to use the provision as a means to control and manipulate the process.

"Friendly parent" provisions are counterproductive in cases of Situational Couple Violence as well because they encourage cooperative parenting in cases where increased contact may exacerbate conflict levels. While parents with a history of Situational Couple Violence may be able to parallel parent under a carefully drafted parenting plan, they should not be encouraged to coparent or share joint physical custody. States with "friendly parent" provisions should explicitly provide that they do not apply in cases of domestic violence.

2. Joint Custody

The movement supporting continued involvement by both parents after divorce led to increased use of various forms of joint custody and, consequently, nearly every state has adopted joint custody in some form. Like "friendly parent" provisions, joint legal or physical custody is dangerous for victims of Intimate Terrorism because continued contact provides the opportunity for manipulation, control, and additional violence by the batterer. Joint physical custody is ill-advised for parents with a history of Situational Couple Violence, although in some cases, it is possible that parents may be able to share joint legal custody pursuant to a carefully drafted parenting plan. States should explicitly provide that joint legal and physical custody is inappropriate in cases of domestic violence. For example, Minnesota has adopted a rebuttable presumption against ordering joint legal or physical custody in cases of domestic abuse.

D. Presumptions Against Custody Awards to Batterers

Concern about the application of "friendly parent" provisions and joint custody in domestic violence cases led several influential bodies to encourage states to adopt rebuttable presumptions against custody awards to batterers. In 1990, Congress urged creation of such presumptions and in 1994 the National Council of Juvenile and Family Court Judges drafted a Model Code on Domestic Violence that contains a rebuttable presumption. The presumption states, "it is detrimental to the child and not in the best interest of the child to be placed in sole custody, joint legal custody, or joint physical custody with the perpetrator of family violence." Similarly the American Bar Association recommends that "[w]here there is proof of [domestic violence], batterers should be presumed by law to be unfit custodians for their children." . . .

1. Triggering the Presumption

When viewed through the lens of a domestic violence typology, rebuttable presumption statutes are both over and under inclusive. Specifically, they are likely to include cases of Situational Couple Violence (which arguably they should not) and at the same time, they fail to reliably capture cases of Intimate Terrorism (which should fall under their umbrella of coverage).

In cases of Intimate Terrorism, rebuttable presumptions against custody awards to batterers are quite appropriate and they were likely written with that scenario in mind. As previous sections have discussed, Intimate Terrorists are dangerous and unsuitable parents who manipulate the court system to continue a pattern of abuse and control.

However, in contrast, invoking a rebuttable presumption regarding custody is inappropriate in cases of Situational Couple Violence where enhanced conflict resolution skills and counseling might enable both parents to remain more substantially involved in the child's life. Cases of Situational Couple Violence require careful but discretionary handling. Not only is the nature of the violence very different, but it is possible that both parents may initiate Situational Couple Violence. Automatic operation of a presumption could be quite harmful to a child in such a case.

Unfortunately, presumption statutes are not carefully drafted to target Intimate Terrorists. Just as definitions of domestic abuse fail to include identification of a pattern of domination and control, behaviors triggering presumption statutes may not distinguish between Intimate Terrorism and Situational Couple Violence.

For example, Louisiana has one of the most comprehensive rebuttable presumption statutes. It is presumed that "no parent who has a history of perpetrating family violence shall be awarded sole or joint custody of children." The court may find "a history of perpetrating family violence," triggering the presumption, if there is one incident involving "serious bodily injury" or a finding of more than one incident of violence. This trigger could include cases of Situational Couple Violence where there had been two occurrences of relatively "mild" violence spaced over a long period of time. However, the statute could (at least theoretically) exclude cases of Intimate Terrorism where the pattern of domination and control was maintained primarily through means other than repeated physical violence. Even if most cases of Intimate Terrorism are found to fall within the purview of the statute, the court is not clearly directed toward identifying them.

Rebuttable presumption statutes should be amended so that they are triggered by patterns of coercive control. This will maximize their application in cases of Intimate Terrorism and make it less likely that cases of Situational Couple Violence will fall within them.

2. Operation of the Presumption When Violence Is Alleged Against Both Parents

States are divided about the application of presumptions against custody awards to perpetrators in cases where both parents are alleged to have a history of violence.

The Louisiana statute addresses situations where both parents have a history of violence by awarding custody "solely to the parent who is less likely to continue to perpetuate family violence." Viewed through the typology lens, this is troubling for two reasons. First, as discussed previously, in cases of Intimate Terrorism the male is nearly always the perpetrator. Consequently, in cases of Intimate Terrorism, this provision could be construed against women who are violent resisters engaging in self defense. Second, it is more likely that both parents may initiate violence in cases of Situational Couple Violence. However, as previously discussed, in Situational Couple Violence cases neither parent should be automatically presumed to be unfit.

The Nevada statute is even more troubling. It provides that "if it is not possible for the court to determine which party is the primary aggressor, the presumption applies to both parties." As noted above, this section could defeat custody awards to victims of Intimate Terrorism who defend themselves. However, it is most likely to be invoked in cases involving Situational Couple Violence. In such a case, the statute could work to deprive a child of two potentially fit parents.

In direct contrast to Nevada, the courts in North Dakota have held that when both parents have an equivalent history of violence, the presumption does not apply. In cases of Situational Couple Violence, this is the most sensible solution. However, in a case involving Intimate Terrorism, the victim could be penalized for defending herself.

When both parents have a history of domestic violence, the first step should be to determine the type of violence involved. The presumption should apply to perpetrators who evidence a pattern of coercive control. As discussed previously, in cases of Intimate Terrorism it is very likely that any violence perpetrated by the female victim is in the nature of self defense (Violent Resistance). Equally initiated violence is only likely to occur in cases involving Situational Couple Violence and, for the foregoing reasons, rebuttable presumptions against custody awards to perpetrators should not apply in those cases.

3. Overcoming the Presumption

Questions also arise concerning when presumptions against custody have been rebutted. For example, the North Dakota statute provides that the "presumption may be overcome only by clear and convincing evidence that the best interests of the child require that parent's participation as a custodial parent." Such language gives the court little guidance and makes it more likely that cases of Intimate Terrorism will be erroneously viewed as Situational Couple Violence. Not surprisingly, this statutory section has resulted in numerous appellate cases.

On its face, the Louisiana rebuttable presumption statute appears to be more informative. The presumption can be overcome by showing the following by a preponderance of the evidence: completion of a treatment program; lack of alcohol and drug use; and proof that the parent's participation is in the best interest of the child or children. While all of these factors are useful, they are not specifically directed at cessation of a pattern of domination and control. Although the statute requires a treatment program "designed specifically for perpetrators of family violence," it does not differentiate between treatment programs for Intimate Terrorists and those for perpetrators of Situational Couple Violence. Consequently, a perpetrator of Intimate Terrorism could meet the requirements of the statute while continuing to engage in coercive control and dangerous parenting practices. For example, in *D.O.H. v. T.L.H.*,[26] completion of anger management therapy was deemed sufficient to rebut the statute even though no determination concerning the type of violence was made. As discussed above, anger management classes are not appropriate for perpetrators of Intimate Terrorism, although they are likely to be quite helpful to perpetrators of Situational Couple Violence.

Rebuttable presumption statutes should be amended to require greater court scrutiny in situations where the perpetrator seeks to overcome the presumption. Ideally a treatment plan based on an assessment by an interdisciplinary team should be developed for each batterer and compliance should be monitored for a year or more. In addition to taking concrete steps to end the violence and improve parenting skills, attitudinal change should be evaluated by experts before a court finding that the presumption is overcome.

E. Termination of Parental Rights

In extreme cases of Intimate Terrorism where services such as supervised visitation, parent coordination, and even incarceration are not sufficient to keep the former partner and children safe, the state should proceed with termination of the batterer's parental rights. As Joan Meier explains, "TPR actions—send a clear message that batterers have lost their 'rights' to their children—might actually impact many abusers more powerfully than the more common civil or criminal justice restraining orders or criminal adjudications."

V. Conclusions and Recommendations

Differentiating among types of domestic violence has practical implications for court procedure and for substantive child custody law. The one-size-fits-all approach endangers children and victims because the failure to differentiate among families means that cases of Intimate Terrorism are often mischaracterized as cases of Situational Couple Violence. As a result, neither group is adequately protected or referred to appropriate court procedures and services. Unfortunately, the language contained in most family law statutes supports the mistaken view that domestic violence is a single phenomenon.

. . . .

# B. Failure to Protect Children from Witnessing Violence

One of the more controversial issues involving the exposure of children to domestic violence emerged in New York City in early 2000 when a group of mothers alleged

---

26. [n278] *D.O.H. v. T.L.H*, 01-0174 (La. App. 3d Cir. 10/31/01), 799 So. 2d 714, 718 . . . .

that their children were being removed from their custody and control solely because they failed to contact the authorities when they were victims of domestic violence. Whether this was actually the case was hotly contested. Be that as it may, there is certainly a legitimate concern for the well-being of children in these situations—given the evidence that it is highly likely that if a mother is abused at home, the children are likely to suffer from the same treatment. In addition, studies consistently show battering is learned behavior, and boys who grow up to be batterers are likely to have been boys who witnessed their mothers' beatings as they were growing up.

Nonetheless, the practice of punishing women who do not leave their batterers by taking away their children is a controversial one. It has been criticized as cruel, dangerous, and ineffectual. And now, in New York at least, it is in most instances, illegal. The case that finally spoke to the issue was *Nicholson v. Scoppetta*, 3 N.Y.3d 357 (2004). The matter began as a class action suit in the federal court in the Eastern District of New York brought pursuant to 42 U.S.C. § 1983 against the New York City Administration for Children's Services (ACS) by three mothers who maintained their children were removed from them without probable cause or due process of law solely because the mothers were victims of domestic violence. The federal judge granted a preliminary injunction barring ACS from removing children and placing them in foster care under these circumstances in early 2002. On appeal, the United States Court of Appeals for the Second Circuit certified three questions to the highest court of New York in order to be better able to resolve the issues before it. Those questions were (1) whether the definition of a neglected child under New York law included instances where the person legally responsible for the child's care allowed that child to witness domestic violence against the caretaker; (2) whether the injury or possible injury to a child witness to domestic violence by one parent against another constituted a danger or risk to the child's health and (3) whether the mere fact a child has witnessed domestic violence between her parents demonstrates it is necessary to remove that child from the home. The answer to those questions were, in essence, it depends. Exposing a child to domestic violence was not presumptively neglectful, the New York court opined. Only if a petitioner demonstrated by a fair preponderance of the evidence that the mother had been exposing her children to repeated domestic violence that had been shown to have caused fear and anxiety in the exposed children might state protective workers be justified in removing those children from her care. The court must weigh the balance between the harm to a child of being exposed to domestic violence versus the harm of being removed from a loving, albeit abused mother.

# VI. Domestic Violence and Interjurisdictional Custody Disputes

## A. The Uniform Child Custody and Jurisdiction Enforcement Act

Most states have adopted the Uniform Child Custody and Jurisdiction Enforcement Act (UCCJEA) which helps to establish where jurisdiction lies in a multi-state, and in some instances, multi-national custody dispute. Following separation, many custody disputes span multiple jurisdictions, particularly in situations where one party flees the jurisdiction with the child or children to escape domestic violence. Therefore, the fact the UCCJEA requires the court to consider domestic violence when determining custody, is of critical importance.

### Joan Zorza, *The UCCJEA: What Is It and How Does It Affect Battered Women in Child-Custody Disputes?*
27 Fordham Urb. L.J. 909 (2000)

Introduction

The Uniform Child-Custody Jurisdiction and Enforcement Act ("UCCJEA" or "Act") is the revised version of The Uniform Child Custody Jurisdiction Act ("UCCJA"), which states are now being asked to adopt immediately in its stead. The UCCJA was the original model act for states to determine when they have jurisdiction to decide a custody case and when they must give full faith and credit to the custody decrees of other states. When the National Conference of Commissioners on Uniform State Laws ("NCCUSL" or "Conference") wrote the UCCJA in 1968, it sought to correct two major problems of its day: child abductions by family members and jurisdictional disputes arising in interstate custody or visitation matters. While these issues can arise independently, the NCCUSL correctly saw the two problems as often interrelated. Indeed, more than half of the nation's 350,000 annual child abductions occur in the context of domestic violence, most of them perpetrated by abusive fathers. These abductions have been found to be as traumatic to children as when they are abducted by strangers, with many developing post-traumatic stress disorder.

. . . .

I. History of Jurisdictional Debate

A. The Supreme Court's Refusal to Resolve Important Jurisdictional Disputes

The jurisdictional problems that arise in interstate custody disputes and the inability to have custody decrees enforced by other states became increasingly prevalent throughout the last century. Attempts by lawyers to get the

U.S. Supreme Court to resolve the matter failed, beginning with its 1947 decision in *Halvey v. Halvey*, [330 U.S. 610, 612 (1947)] which refused to require states to give full faith and credit to another state's custody decree. This refusal was based on the notion that every custody determination, whether issued as a "temporary" or "permanent" order, was actually only a temporary order, always modifiable, and that moving to another state constituted a change in circumstances warranting modification.

Effectively, the *Halvey* decree rewarded losing contestants who abducted their children and relocated across state lines. At a minimum, an abducting family member was guaranteed a de novo trial in the new state to try to gain lawful custody. Further, because any prior custody decree could not be enforced beyond the issuing state's borders, abductors were also safe from contempt or abduction charges so long as the abductors never returned to the state from which they had fled.

. . . This decision was followed by *May v. Anderson*, [345 U.S. 528 (1953)] in a second attempt to require states to honor and enforce the custody decrees of other states. Despite the *May*'s dissenter's serious reservations, this later attempt proved just as unsuccessful as the first. At the time of the U.S. Supreme Court's decision in *Halvey*, most abductors were fathers or grandparents, who were far better situated than mothers to win custody in a new state for a number of reasons. Women of the time faced even greater gender bias discrimination, which impacted them financially and socially, thereby rendering them less able to litigate their interests or be seen as financially or socially fit. In addition, the United States had no awareness of domestic violence, further impeding women's efforts to force courts to recognize abusive situations, and the need to protect them and not to be blamed for the abuse or receive help in becoming independent both financially and emotionally from the abuse. In light of these circumstances, the Conference probably never guessed how the UCCJA would be used to hurt so many mothers who later fled to protect themselves or their children from abuse.

B. Enactment of the Parental Kidnapping Prevention Act

Although the UCCJA was introduced in 1968, states were slow to adopt it throughout the next twelve years. Those states that did adopt the UCCJA often made alterations—some quite substantial—in their own versions. These practices produced conflicting judicial decisions about whether a state had to recognize another state's decree, even when both states' UCCJA versions differed only slightly. As a result, far too few custody decisions were being honored and enforced by courts of other states.

To correct this problem, Congress enacted the PKPA.[27] The PKPA forced every state to give full faith and credit to any custody decree, no matter in which state the decision was rendered, provided it met due process and the PKPA jurisdictional requirements. The PKPA also prevented other states from modifying a custody order issued by any other state, with only a few exceptions. It also added various enforcement

---

27. [n13] See *id*. When Congress enacted the PKPA in December of 1980, 43 states had adopted the UCCJA. By 1980 there was enough awareness of domestic violence that Congress could and should have taken it into account. However, domestic violence issues were never raised or considered in it. See Patricia M. Hoff, *The ABC's of the UCCJEA: Interstate Child-Custody Practice Under the New Act*, 32 Fam. L.Q. 267, 268 (1998).

mechanisms for use against abductors, including: (1) the use of the Federal Parent Locator Service to locate abductors; and (2) provision for issuing federal Unlawful Flight to Avoid Prosecution ("UFAP") arrest warrants under the Fugitive Felon Act, for child abductors fleeing across state or international lines to avoid prosecution on state felony abduction charges.

. . .

Specifically, the PKPA preempts the UCCJA by not allowing courts making initial custody decisions to consider significant connection jurisdiction in cases when there is a home state jurisdiction. It prevents any state from exercising modification jurisdiction when there is already a pending proceeding in a state in accordance with the PKPA/UCCJA, and further gives the original state the right to exclusive jurisdiction to modify any of its orders provided the child or one of the contestants continued to reside in that state.

## II. The UCCJEA

### A. Re-Examination of the UCCJA

While the Conference knew that the UCCJA would have to be amended to conform with the PKPA, it was ironically the Uniform Interstate Family Support Act, which governs paternity establishment and child support determinations, collection and enforcement, that was the impetus for the reexamination of the UCCJA. The Conference began reexamination of the UCCJA in 1994, and soon realized it must harmonize the UCCJA with the full faith and credit mandate of the Violence Against Women Act ("VAWA"), which was enacted on September 13, 1994, and requires states to honor and enforce orders of protection, including ex parte orders. The Conference would also need to decide whether to cover tribal court orders, resolve the ambiguities about which custody proceedings are covered, clarify that the "best interests" language in the UCCJA was not meant to open up the merits of the case, resolve whether orders of protection trigger emergency jurisdiction, determine when courts have declined jurisdiction, resolve confusion about how long temporary jurisdiction lasts and finally, determine how to effectively enforce orders quickly and uniformly throughout the country. While the NCCUSL continued to ignore the problems of domestic violence for anyone except those involving the particular child, domestic violence advocates forced the Commissioners to make a number of concessions in its final version to include some protections for victims of domestic violence. While these changes are rather minimal, in part because of PKPA limitations, they will help battered women and their children. . . .

### B. The UCCJEA Notice Requirements

The UCCJEA provides that any first child-custody determination made concerning a particular child under age 18—as long as the jurisdictional requirements are met—binds all parties with notice. This specifically includes child custody provisions in orders of protection. This notice should be given to any parent whose rights have not been terminated and to any other person having physical custody of the child or who had physical custody of the child barring temporary absences for six consecutive months within the year prior to beginning the custody proceeding and has either been awarded legal custody by a court or claims a right under the law of the state to legal custody. Notice, in a way that is reasonably likely to give actual notice, can be given to any person outside of the state under either state's notice laws, "but may be by publication if other means are not effective." This change will enable a fleeing battered woman to protect herself against her abuser by being able to serve him and causing him to be bound by any decision later made in the case. It should also prevent her from being subject to federal kidnapping charges in cases where he has filed an action in the home state without ever giving her notice, but the court nevertheless defaults her and awards him custody.

C. UCCJEA Initial Jurisdictional Criteria

Except in emergencies, an initial custody determination must be made by a court having one of the UCCJEA's four jurisdictional criteria, some of which are new and all of which are statutorily prioritized. Parties cannot confer jurisdiction on a court that does not otherwise meet one of these criteria; however, emergency jurisdiction, while largely eliminated for initial permanent determinations, can often be used to obtain temporary orders and modifications. The four types of jurisdiction are "home state," "significant connection," "appropriate forum," and "no other state."

Home State Jurisdiction: As required by the PKPA, the UCCJEA states that if the child involved in the custody dispute has a home state, only that state may make the initial custody determination, unless the home state declines jurisdiction. A child's temporary absences from the state are not relevant to this determination. A child's home state keeps its status for six months after a child leaves, regardless of why the child has left, provided a parent or person acting as a parent remains in the home state. Unless acting as a parent, grandparents possessing visitation are not considered "contestants" for purposes home state retention.

Significant Connection Jurisdiction: As under the PKPA, when there is no home state or the home state court has declined jurisdiction, a state with significant connection jurisdiction is permitted to preside over a custody determination. In contrast to the old UCCJA, the child's presence is not required for there to be significant connection jurisdiction, and the "best interests" and "present or future care" language has been eliminated.

More Appropriate Forum Jurisdiction: A court in a state that is the appropriate forum may do so only if courts having home state or significant connection jurisdiction have decided to exercise it.

No Other State Jurisdiction: Only if no court of any other state has jurisdiction on any of the three previous jurisdictional criteria may a court exercise no other state jurisdiction to deal with these "vacuum" situations. This type of jurisdiction would enable a court to take jurisdiction in a custody action between the parents who work for a traveling circus, whose child has never spent, for example, more than two weeks per year in the same state.

Once a state court has made an initial child-custody determination consistent with one of these four jurisdictional requirements, the issuing court retains exclusive continuing jurisdiction with the following exceptions: (1) under certain exceptions when a court of another state has temporary emergency jurisdiction; (2) when the issuing court "or the court of another State determines that the child, the child's parents, and any person acting as a parent do not presently reside in" the issuing state; or (3) when a court of this state finds "that neither the child, the child and one parent nor the child and a person acting as a guardian have a significant connection with this state and that substantial evidence is no longer available in this state concerning the child's care, protection, training and personal relationships." This section is necessary to bring this act in compliance with section 1738(d) of the PKPA, which prevents any other state from modifying an issuing state's custody decree except when all of the parties and child have left the state, unless the issuing state has declined jurisdiction.

D. Temporary Emergency Jurisdiction

Temporary emergency jurisdiction only arises in the extraordinary circumstances where a child is present in a state and it permits that state's court to issue only short-term orders. However, the UCCJEA does permit a court to exercise this type of jurisdiction in an emergency to protect the child, its siblings or its parents who are subjected to or threatened with mistreatment or abuse. This is a major improvement over the comparable sections in both the UCCJA and the PKPA, which only permit jurisdiction to be assumed to protect the particular child in question, and not a parent or sibling.

If no previous custody determination has been made, and no child-custody proceeding is commenced in a court having jurisdiction to make an initial child-custody determination, the temporary order made under the temporary emergency jurisdiction can become a final order, but only if it so provides, once the deciding state becomes the child's home state. However, if there is a prior custody decree that is entitled to be enforced or an action is filed in a court having jurisdiction to make an initial child-custody determination, the court with emergency jurisdiction must do two things. First, it must specify in the temporary emergency order a period of time that the court considers adequate to allow the person seeking the emergency order to obtain an order from the state having initial custody jurisdiction. Second, the court "shall immediately communicate with the court of that State to resolve the emergency, protect the safety of the parties and the child, and determine a period for the duration of the temporary order."

Once factual findings or rulings of law have been made after notice and opportunity to be heard in a custody or other proceeding entitled to full faith and credit, for example, in an order of protection case, no court may re-litigate the issues decided. Thus, a temporary emergency jurisdiction can make a final ruling as to the underlying abuse. It also will halt the practice of re-litigating the abuse finding on the theory that the allegation was only made for tactical advantage or to alienate the child from the other parent.

This new language in the UCCJEA is a significant improvement for battered women over treatment allotted under the original UCCJA. For example, it permits a court of another state to assume temporary jurisdiction when a parent removes herself to another state when she is being battered or threatened with abuse, and enables her to protect all of the children when only one is being abused. In addition, it tells both courts that safety of the parties and child is the first consideration.

However, there are serious deficiencies as well. Forcing women to rely on a judge to decide whether the temporary order may become permanent leaves the battered woman or protective parent at the mercy of a judge, who may fail to find that an emergency exists, or may fail to finalize the order because he or she believes there is a minimal likelihood of future danger, a common judicial failing. Nor will she be protected if her abuser initiates (or re-initiates) litigation before she has been gone for six months, and it may not protect her if she is forced to flee to yet another state. Similarly, the new language will not help in all emergency situations where she acts to protect someone who is not her and the abuser's child. For example, siblings are not defined in the statute, and only in a state that otherwise adopts a broad construction of that term would half-and step-siblings be included. Without a broad construction, emergency jurisdiction will not be able to protect a mother from being treated as a wrongful abductor in a case filed by her current husband when she has fled with all of her children because her prior husband was sexually abusing his child. It is even less likely to protect her if she fled with all children in an attempt to protect an abused niece, nephew, grandchild or foster child in her care, or her own parent or sibling who is being severely abused by her husband. Regardless of whether the emergency is covered under section 204, including the state's definition of "sibling," it may still be possible for her to convince the court that issued the initial decree to decline jurisdiction in a case where the abuse is particularly severe.

Unfortunately, although the comments make it clear that section 208 of the UCCJEA should not be used to harm protective parents, section 208(c) makes it extremely risky for a battered woman who has fled abuse to seek protection under the court's temporary emergency jurisdiction. This is because the court may assess her with all of the opponent's "necessary and reasonable expenses" if the court declines jurisdiction or stays her proceeding. Her risk may be exacerbated because many batterers deliberately threaten to, and in some instances, drive their victims into poverty or even homelessness, even if it also may make them destitute themselves. Such an abuser, though taking a calculated risk, may deliberately escalate the violence to force his victim to flee, and then purposely drive up his expenses to further punish and control her. Even if she ultimately prevails, she will have been further emotionally drained by the flight and litigation, possibly impairing her parenting abilities.

. . . .

### G. Declining Jurisdiction

As under the UCCJA, the UCCJEA provides that a court with jurisdiction may decline to exercise it for two reasons: inconvenient forum, which can be done at any time, and unjustifiable conduct. However, both grounds have been altered, in part to take domestic violence into account.

### 1. Declining Jurisdiction for Inconvenient Forum

A court can decline jurisdiction because it is an inconvenient forum upon a motion of a party, the court's own motion, or at the request of another court (but no longer at the request of a guardian ad litem). Declining jurisdiction in the custody matter does not mean that the court would have to decline jurisdiction in the divorce or another proceeding, or all aspects of the proceeding; however, once a court has declined custody jurisdiction, it should stay the custody matter upon condition that it is commenced in the appropriate designated state, imposing any other conditions that the court considers reasonable. In deciding whether to decline jurisdiction, a court is required to permit the parties to submit information and consider all relevant factors, including: (1) whether domestic violence has occurred and is likely to continue, and which state could best protect the parties and child; (2) how long the child has lived outside this state; (3) how far it is between the courts; (4) the relative finances of the parties; (5) any agreement of the parties as to which state should hear the case; (6) the nature and location of the evidence needed to resolve the case (including the child's testimony); (7) the ability of the court to decide the issues expeditiously and the procedures necessary to present the evidence; and (8) how familiar each court is with the facts and issues in the pending litigation.

. . . .

### 2. Declining Jurisdiction for Reason of Conduct

In contrast to the UCCJA, the UCCJEA mandates that if a state court has jurisdiction, except in temporary emergency jurisdiction situations, the court must decline jurisdiction when a person seeking to invoke its jurisdiction has engaged in unjustifiable conduct, with three exceptions. The court need not decline jurisdiction by reason of conduct if the parents and all persons acting as parents agree to the acceptance of jurisdiction, no court of any other state would have initial, exclusive continuing or modification jurisdiction, or the court of the state otherwise having jurisdiction determines that this state is the more appropriate forum. Even if jurisdiction is declined, the court may retain it until jurisdiction is assumed in the other court, or so that it can issue temporary orders to prevent a repetition of the unjustifiable conduct or to ensure the safety of the child.

Unjustifiable conduct includes "removing, secreting, retaining or restraining" a child. However, in language specifically favorable to battered women, the comment to the statute reads:

> A technical illegality or wrong is insufficient to trigger the applicability of this section. This is particularly important in cases involving domestic violence and child abuse. Domestic violence victims should not be charged with unjustifiable conduct for conduct that occurred in the process of fleeing domestic violence, even if their conduct is technically illegal. Thus, if a parent flees with a child to escape domestic violence and in the process violates a joint

custody decree, the case should not be automatically dismissed under this section. An inquiry must be made into whether the flight was justified under the circumstances of the case. However, an abusive parent who seizes the child and flees to another state to establish jurisdiction has engaged in unjustifiable conduct and the new state must decline to exercise jurisdiction under this section.

Following the International Child Abduction Remedies Act, a state court must assess all reasonable costs and fees to be paid to the parent who establishes that jurisdiction was based on unjustifiable conduct. In cases where a fleeing victim sought the court's temporary emergency jurisdiction but the court declined jurisdiction or stayed its action, the court should presumptively assess all costs against the wrongful party (i.e., the parent who wrongfully fled, as determined by the court's denial of accepting temporary emergency jurisdiction), unless the party from whom the fees are sought can establish that the assessment would be clearly inappropriate. This puts a battered woman or mother of an abused child at enormous risk when she attempts to claim temporary emergency jurisdiction. It greatly increases the chance that an abusive father, particularly if he has greater resources, will be encouraged to aggressively litigate, in his effort to make her liable for all of his "reasonable expenses including costs, communication expenses, attorney's fees, investigative fees, expenses for witnesses, travel expenses, and child care during the courts of the proceedings." Batterers, who are known to retaliate by abusing the judicial process to further control and demoralize their victims or drive them into economic ruin, may well use this penalty to drive their victims into flight or hiding, and then have the judicial system simultaneously reward themselves and punish their victims. California has attempted to decrease this possibility for abuse of this section by batterers.

H. Affidavit and Address Confidentiality

The UCCJEA attempts to get each party in its first pleading to provide under oath essentially the same information that section 9 of the UCCJA required: (1) a child's present address or whereabouts; (2) places where the child lived during the last five years and the names and present addresses of the persons with whom the child lived; (3) whether the party has ever participated in any capacity in any custody proceeding concerning the child and, if so, which court, docket number and date of any child-custody determination; (4) information about any other related proceeding, including those for enforcement, protective orders, termination of parental rights and adoptions; and (5) the names and addresses of anyone not a party who has physical custody of the child or claims rights to legal or physical custody or visitation with the child. Likewise, it places a continuing duty on each party to update the information about "any proceeding in this or any other State that could affect the current proceeding."

However, the UCCJEA notice requirements make two changes, the first in partial response to those advocates asking for protections for battered women. That change is an option, which if taken by a state, can help victims of domestic violence by incorporating "local law providing for the confidentiality of procedures, addresses, and other identifying information," including procedures to seal the information and not release it until "after a hearing in which the court takes into consideration the health, safety, or liberty of the party or child and determines that the disclosure is in the interest of justice." The commentary to section 209 urges states that do not have procedures to keep sensitive identifying information confidential to adopt such statutory protections. . . .

The second change overturns roughly half of the existing case law that held that failure to comply with the affidavit requirements or knowingly submitting false information was a jurisdictional defect, allowing jurisdiction to be declined and the case dismissed, and that any resulting custody decree be considered void. Instead, section 209(b) of the UCCJEA permits the court on its own motion or that of a party to stay the proceeding until the information is furnished. Abusers are most likely to manipulate courts by falsifying information, and this change in the statute removes the possibility of having a case dismissed from victims faced with blatant fraud or deception.

I. Option to Recognize Tribal Orders

Unlike the UCCJA and PKPA, which never addressed tribal court custody proceedings, the UCCJEA gives states the option of doing so. Furthermore, by taking this option, states help to bring custody law in greater conformity with the VAWA full faith and credit mandate and better protect abused victims. It is likely that reluctance of some states to recognize tribal custody decrees in the past prevented the Conference from including a provision requiring that all states honor and enforce tribal court orders and clarifying that "state" does include tribal lands. The UCCJEA does, however, clarify that it is not trying to diminish the protections of Indian children under the Indian Child Welfare Act ("ICWA"), noting that any proceeding subject to ICWA is not governed by the UCCJEA to the extent it is governed by ICWA. In addition, the commentary observes that the UCCJEA "does not purport to legislate custody jurisdiction for tribal courts," but tells Tribes how they can adopt the UCCJEA.

### III. Enforcing and Registering Custody Decrees

The UCCJEA has made many changes so that it can be better enforced to ensure return of the abducted child, including situations governed by the International Child Abduction Remedies Act (ICARA), implementing the Hague Convention. The enforcement section of the UCCJEA specifically covers situations before any party has commenced a custody action in any court, so that a court can order speedy return of the child to the petitioner. In addition, the UCCJEA requires states to enforce and not modify the child-custody determinations of other states or countries, or registered orders that were made in accordance with both the UCCJEA and the PKPA. The determinations entitled to enforcement specifically include temporary emergency jurisdiction orders and the custody provisions after notice of domestic violence orders. Enforcement remedies under the UCCJEA are in addition to any other remedies available under state law.

A. Registration of Decrees

The UCCJEA creates a registration process for custody decrees. However, unlike the registration process required by VAWA's full faith and credit mandate, which does not require giving notice a second time to register a protection order in another jurisdiction, the UCCJEA does require giving notice to any parent or person acting as a parent who has been awarded custody or visitation as part of the registration process before a custody decree can be registered. Furthermore, very naively, the UCCJEA requires that notice must be given in each state where the order must be registered, further endangering those who are already at most risk of retaliation and very likely causing them further delay, uncertainty and expense.

The UCCJEA's registration process unfortunately ignored the urgings of the battered women's advocates submitted through Roberta Valente, former staff director of the American Bar Association's Domestic Violence Commission, who suggested that all custody decrees, particularly those entered in cases involving domestic violence, could be registered statewide, and ultimately national registry for orders of protection. This would immediately afford full protection for battered woman and endangered children throughout the United States no matter where they must flee, and without imposing time delays and endangerment resulting from further slow judicial processes and notification to their abusers. If custody decrees were all nationally registered, so would be any subsequent orders to vacate, stay or modify the prior order, so any enforcing court would have access to information about the validity of the decree.

Although NCCUSL ignored most of the suggestions concerning registration, it did provide for protecting the fleeing family in those few cases where a court has denied all custody or visitation to an abusive parent, by not requiring notice to be given to the abuser. However, since virtually no courts prohibit all contact by the abuser with the children, the fleeing family will be placed in great danger by having to reveal to which state they have fled as part of the notice given to the abusive parent.

In cases where her batterer has already abducted the child, the mother can file a petition to register the child-custody decree with an accompanying request for a warrant to pick up the child, and will not have to notify the abductor until the child has actually been recovered. This provision for protection shows that the NCCUSL takes protection of children far more seriously than it does of that involving battered women, and still does not recognize that in about a quarter of cases where male batterers killing their intimate female partners, they also kill their children.

However, in the typical registration case requiring advance notice (i.e., when no abduction is involved), a victim of domestic violence must notify her abuser when she files to register the order, and he, like any other respondent, has twenty days to contest the validity of the order. The UCCJEA permits a respondent to challenge the order on only three grounds: (1) the issuing court did not have jurisdiction;

(2) respondent did not have any notice and opportunity to be heard in the issuing court; or (3) the custody determination was vacated, stayed or modified. It would also be hoped that any finding of fraud, whether notice or the order itself had been faked or fraudulently obtained, will be reduced to a written finding that can later be used to impeach the respondent. Once any custody order is registered, the only permissible grounds for challenge is that it has subsequently been vacated, stayed or modified, although due process considerations and statutory ones should permit a challenge if the matter could not have been asserted previously.

. . . .

C. Enforcement Mechanisms

For a battered woman with a custody decree in one state who must allow visitation to her out-of-state abuser, it might be wise for her to have the court condition the out-of-state (or country) visitation on the prior registration of the child-custody decree so that it will be immediately enforceable. However, prior registration is not actually needed — though may still be desirable — for orders issued from other Hague Child Abduction Convention signatory countries since that treaty provides for similar swift return of abducted or wrongfully retained children and enforcement of custody orders from those countries.

1. Issuing Warrants

Another remedy under the UCCJEA permits courts to enforce orders by issuing warrants to take immediate physical custody of the child. Section 311 permits the court to issue such a "pick up" warrant upon credible testimony "that the child is imminently likely to suffer serious physical harm or be removed from this State." Courts are directed to hear such petitions on the next judicial day after the warrant is executed, and may only delay if the next court date is "impossible." Not only may law enforcement officers be directed to take physical custody of the child immediately, but if "a less intrusive remedy is not effective, it may authorize law enforcement officers to enter private property to take physical custody of the child including, in exigent circumstances, by forcibly entering at any hour." The court must also provide for the placement of the child pending final relief.

2. Enforcing Visitation

Although the UCCJEA forbids courts to modify the custody order of another state or permanently change custody, Section 305 does allow enforcing courts to enforce visitation rights in two limited situations. The first exception permits a court to provide for make-up visitation time when visitation time has been obstructed. Although the language only talks of visitation (which undoubtedly shows that the language was inserted at the request of fathers' rights groups), custodial parents should be likewise entitled to make-up time if their time with the child has been obstructed. The second exception allows courts to temporarily designate specific visitation times when orders do "not provide for a specific visitation schedule" (e.g., "reasonable visitation.") In a "reasonable visitation" case, the court must set an expiration date unless, as a result of judicial communication, the issuing court has deferred jurisdiction on this issue to the enforcing court on the grounds it is a more convenient forum, or, although not suggested under the UCCJEA, the order is issued simultaneously by both courts. Otherwise, the enforcing court's order expires on whichever date occurs first, the expiration date set by the enforcing court or the date of a new order by the issuing court.

3. Prosecutor's Role in Enforcement

Probably the most important addition to the enforcement section, unless a state opts out, is the creation in sections 315–317 of an interstate network of prosecutors modeled after California's prosecutors who, for twenty years, have had authority to enforce child-custody orders from other states and countries. These officials will be able to help locate and return missing children, as well as seek enforcement in the state's criminal and civil courts. As a practical matter, they can also help contact their counterparts in other states when the child is in another state. For left-behind battered women, and especially those who have little access to funding, these remedies should greatly help them in retrieving children who are wrongfully taken to other states.

The danger is that these public officials, acting on behalf of the court, either fail to act because they do not take the abuse sufficiently seriously or they act against fleeing battered women without raising any domestic violence justifications. Furthermore, they may be subject to manipulation by abusers, especially if they are not very knowledgeable about domestic violence. They may also further endanger battered women and their children by either revealing confidential addresses or workplace locations. Consequently, courts will normally assess expenses pursuant to sections 312 and 317 against the losing party (including all direct expenses and costs incurred by the public officials). It is also likely that this section will be used to hurt fleeing battered women and protective mothers. In contrast, section 208(b), prevents fees, costs or expenses from being assessed against a state under the UCCJEA, although it does not prohibit recovery authorized by other laws.

## Conclusion

The UCCJEA has fixed several problems of its predecessor, the UCCJA, with the result that the UCCJEA is more effective than the old UCCJA and better reconciled with other federal laws. For the first time courts that are making child-custody determinations are encouraged to look at domestic and family violence to protect the rest of the family from an abuser when a parent, the child or any sibling of the child is being abused. In addition, the UCCJEA makes clear that protective parents should not be punished for fleeing incidents or patterns of domestic violence, and that any judicial finding or determination that parental or child abuse occurred is res judicata as to each party who had notice of that proceeding.

A number of improvements in the UCCJEA are left as options to the states, and it is hoped that battered women's advocates will urge states to adopt these options on behalf of their clients: addressing confidentiality provisions, granting full faith and credit to tribal child-custody determinations and designating prosecutors or other state officials to enforce child-custody determinations. In addition, advocates for battered women should urge their states to adopt the changes made by California for denying jurisdiction by reason of conduct in its version of the UCCJEA.

The biggest problem with the UCCJEA for battered women is that it requires notice to be given all over again to register a custody decree in any other jurisdiction. It is likely that this problem can only be rectified by federal legislation amending the PKPA, the VAWA full faith and credit mandate, and requiring the state and federal registries for orders of protection to also register child-custody decrees.

Overall, the UCCJEA is an improvement over the UCCJA, and should be supported by battered women and their advocates, especially with the proposed changes.

## B. International Child Abduction

The Hague Convention on the Civil Aspects of International Child Abduction, approved by 23 nations on October 24, 1980, including the United States, was implemented by Congress through the passage of the International Child Abduction Remedies Act, 42 U.S.C. § 11601 *et seq.* Today there are 74 signatory nations to the convention.[28] It was enacted to prevent parents involved in custody disputes from kidnaping their children and removing them to a foreign jurisdiction. In the event a child *is* taken from the United States to another country, or from a signatory or ratifying country to any other in the course of a custody battle, the aggrieved parent may petition for the child to be returned.[29]

Although the local court cannot adjudicate the underlying custody matter, it can determine a child was wrongfully removed and order that child to be returned to the country of residence, unless one of four exceptions can be established by the responding parent—one of which is that the child would be harmed by being forced to return.

### Souratgar v. Fair
United States Court of Appeals for the Second Circuit
818 F. 3d 72 (2016)

KATZMANN, *Chief Judge*:

The International Child Abduction Remedies Act ("ICARA") provides that the prevailing petitioner in a child abduction case shall be awarded expenses incurred in connection with the petition "unless the respondent establishes that such order would be clearly inappropriate." 22 U.S.C. § 9007(b)(3). That determination requires district courts to weigh relevant equitable factors, including intimate partner violence.

---

28. Department of State, *International Parental Child Abduction; U.S. Hague Convention Treaty Partners,* https://travel.state.gov/content/childabduction/en/country/hague-party-countries-html, accessed October 23, 2016.

29. *See* Elisa Perez-Vera, *Explanatory Report on the 1980 Hague Child Abduction Convention,* HCCH Publications, Hague Conference on Private International Law (1982).

Respondent-appellant Lee Jen Fair ("Lee") appeals from a February 27, 2014 judgment following a February 20, 2014 order of the United States District Court for the Southern District of New York (Castel, *J.*), which awarded $283,066.62 in expenses to Petitioner-Appellee Abdollah Naghash Souratgar ("Souratgar"). Previously, Souratgar had petitioned for the return of Shayan, the son whose custody he and Lee shared in Singapore, under the Hague Convention on the Civil Aspects of International Child Abduction ("Hague Convention"), Oct. 25, 1980, T.I.A.S. No. 11670, 1343 U.N.T.S. 89, *reprinted in* 51 Fed. Reg. 10494 (Mar. 26, 1986), and its domestic implementing legislation, ICARA, 22 U.S.C. §§ 9001-9011. The district court granted that petition, and a panel of our Court affirmed. . . . Souratgar then sought an order directing Lee to pay the "necessary expenses" related to his successful petition pursuant to 22 U.S.C. § 9007(b)(3). Notwithstanding Lee's arguments that her indigence and Souratgar's acts of violence against her rendered the requested award clearly inappropriate, the district court ordered Lee to pay Souratgar $283,066.62. *See Souratgar v. Fair* (*Souratgar III*), No. 12-cv-7797, 2014 U.S. Dist. LEXIS 22167, 2014 WL 704037, at *9-12 (S.D.N.Y. Feb. 20, 2014).

In resolving whether it was clearly inappropriate to order Lee to pay expenses to Souratgar, our consideration is grounded in the record, which reveals that Souratgar committed intimate partner violence against Lee but Lee did not commit any violence against Souratgar. The district court was correct in considering this unilateral intimate partner violence as a relevant equitable factor, but, after reviewing the record, we find that the district court erred in its assessment of the relationship between the intimate partner violence and Lee's decision to remove Shayan from the country of habitual residence and thus erred in its weighing of the equitable factors. Because Lee established that Souratgar had committed multiple, unilateral acts of intimate partner violence against her, and that her removal of the child from the habitual country was related to that violence, an award of expenses to Souratgar, given the absence of countervailing equitable factors, is clearly inappropriate. Accordingly, we REVERSE the order and VACATE the judgment.

## BACKGROUND

Lee, a Malaysian national, and Souratgar, an Iranian national, married in 2007 and resided in Singapore. In 2008, Lee became pregnant, which is when, on her account, Souratgar began abusing her. Lee gave birth to their son, Shayan, in January 2009. After several years of marital discord, Lee eventually departed the marital home with Shayan in May 2011 and left Singapore with Shayan one year later.

After Lee departed Singapore, Souratgar filed a petition in the Southern District of New York seeking the return of Shayan to Singapore as provided by the Hague Convention and ICARA. In considering the petition, the district court conducted a nine-day evidentiary hearing at which both Lee and Souratgar testified. The district court ultimately granted the petition after concluding that Souratgar had established a prima facie case under the Hague Convention and that Lee had failed to prove either of her two asserted affirmative defenses. *See Souratgar I*, 2012 U.S. Dist. LEXIS 181989, 2012 WL 6700214, at *4-17. Lee appealed, and a panel of this Court affirmed the judgment. *Souratgar II*, 720 F.3d at 100.

Souratgar then moved in the district court for an order directing Lee to pay his expenses related to Shayan's return to Singapore. ICARA provides that, if the petitioner succeeds, a district court "shall order the respondent to pay necessary expenses incurred by or on behalf of the petitioner, including court costs, legal fees, foster home or other care during the course of proceedings in the action, and transportation costs related to the return of the child, unless the respondent establishes that such order would be clearly inappropriate." 22 U.S.C. § 9007(b)(3). The district court, in a finding not challenged by Souratgar, determined that only $283,066.62 of his requested $618,059.61 constituted necessary expenses related to the return of Shayan. *See Souratgar III*, 2014 U.S. Dist. LEXIS 22167, 2014 WL 704037, at *2-8, *12. Lee argued that an order directing her to pay Souratgar's expenses would be clearly inappropriate for two reasons: (1) "Souratgar's past abusive behavior" against Lee and (2) Lee's "inability to pay." 2014 U.S. Dist. LEXIS 22167, [WL] at *9. The district court determined that neither argument was persuasive.

As to Lee's first argument, the district court acknowledged that it had, in considering the merits of Souratgar's petition for the return of Shayan, made detailed factual findings "that Souratgar engaged in abusive conduct" against Lee. *Id.* The district court made those findings in the course of evaluating Lee's affirmative defense under Article 13(b) of the Hague Convention. Under that provision, a signatory state need not order the return of the child if the respondent establishes that "there is a grave risk that his or her return would expose the child to physical or psychological harm or otherwise place the child in an intolerable situation." Hague Convention art. 13(b), 1343 U.N.T.S. at 101.

Lee had argued that Article 13(b) should apply because, if returned to Singapore, Shayan would face a grave risk of physical and psychological harm due to Souratgar's violence. The district court ultimately disagreed, finding no risk of physical harm to Shayan because "there is no credible evidence that petitioner physically abused the child." *Souratgar I*, 2012 U.S. Dist. LEXIS 181989, 2012 WL 6700214, at *11. The district court also found psychological harm unlikely because Souratgar and Lee would probably never live together again, diminishing the prospect that Shayan would "bear witness to petitioner's abuse of respondent." *Id.* The district court further found that there was no evidence that Shayan "himself suffers from [post-traumatic stress disorder] or will have a negative reaction to being repatriated to Singapore" and "that Singapore is well-equipped to mitigate any risk of harm to the child pending a final custody determination." *Id.*

In coming to this conclusion, the district court considered and made numerous factual findings about each party's allegations of abuse at the hands of the other. The district court was generally skeptical of many of the allegations, but was most inclined to credit those that were contemporaneously documented, explaining:

Based upon an assessment of credibility and available corroboration or lack thereof, the Court finds that both parties have exaggerated their claims. The Court recognizes that victims of spousal abuse often do not come forward to report instances of domestic violence for many reasons and, therefore, a lack of near-contemporaneous documentation does not necessarily render a victim's claims unbelievable. In this particular case, however, the respondent did report instances of domestic abuse to the police or to the court. But these police and medical reports do not identify the most severe acts of violence claimed before this Court.

2012 U.S. Dist. LEXIS 181989, [WL] at *7.

Specifically, the district court considered Lee's allegations that Souratgar: (1) on May 31, 2008, when Lee was pregnant, "hit and kicked her on her head and body," *id.*; (2) in March 2009, "struck her multiple times on her right shoulder while the child was breastfeeding in her arms," 2012 U.S. Dist. LEXIS 181989, [WL] at *8; (3) during an argument in late 2009 or early 2010, "took the child out of her arms and started to beat her on the head and back," *id.*; (4) on January 5, 2010, followed Lee to a neighbor's house and pulled her back into the marital home, where Souratgar "continued to beat her" causing "scratches and redness on her arms where he had grabbed her," *id.* (internal quotation marks and alterations omitted); (5) on August 15, 2011, when Lee met Souratgar at his office to pick up packages that belonged to her, "pulled [Lee's] hands and also pushed" her, from which she "suffered some bruises and scratches on" her chest and hands, 2012 U.S. Dist. LEXIS 181989, [WL] at *9 (internal quotation marks omitted); (6) on November 22, 2011, chased Lee by car, attempting to overtake her vehicle "in a reckless and dangerous manner," *id.* (internal quotation marks omitted); and (7) "forced [Lee] to engage in certain sexual acts," 2012 U.S. Dist. LEXIS 181989, [WL] at *10. The district court discredited some of these allegations, including the allegation of sexual assault, but found most of them to be credible. In short, the district court made a factual finding that Souratgar perpetrated repeated acts of intimate partner violence against Lee.

By contrast, the district court considered Souratgar's allegation that Lee "had tried to attack him with a knife and chopper a few times," but found Souratgar's "account to be exaggerated and not credible." 2012 U.S. Dist. LEXIS 181989, [WL] at *8. Nowhere in the district court's decision is there any other suggestion that Lee had committed any violence, nor have we found any in our independent review of the record.

Despite these findings that Souratgar had committed violence but that Lee had not, the district court ordered Lee to pay Souratgar for his expenses because she "has not established that the past abuse in this case makes an award of fees clearly inappropriate." *Souratgar III*, 2014 U.S. Dist. LEXIS 22167, 2014 WL 704037, at *9. In so doing, the district court acknowledged that other district courts had found awards of expenses to perpetrators of intimate partner violence to be clearly inappropriate, but nevertheless found Lee's case distinguishable. *See id.* Reasoning that Lee's departure from the marital home in May 2011 eliminated the dilemma faced by other victims who continued to reside with their abusers, the district court concluded that Lee "has not established that the past abuse of her was causally related to her decision to leave Singapore with her son." *Id.*

As to Lee's second argument against an order awarding expenses—that her indigence rendered such an order clearly inappropriate—the district court was likewise unpersuaded, because Lee had "not provided the Court with any documentation of her assets or income beyond the [pension] account and the deed of her interest in her family's home." 2014 U.S. Dist. LEXIS 22167, [WL] at *11. The district court found that these documents undermined Lee's assertion of indigence, noting that she had approximately $150,000 in a Singaporean pension account that she may be able to access in the future and concluding that she would probably be able to sell her one-third interest in a family home to satisfy the judgment. 2014 U.S. Dist. LEXIS 22167, [WL] at *10. Notwithstanding Lee's sworn affidavit that she had been unemployed for five years and earned money by selling cakes "for $10 or $20, primarily to her friends," the district court expressed disappointment that Lee had "not provided the Court with any other information regarding her current income." *Id.* It concluded that an award "reduction in this case would neither remedy [Lee's] inability to pay nor serve the purposes of" ICARA. 2014 U.S. Dist. LEXIS 22167, [WL] at *12.

Accordingly, by Memorandum and Order of February 20, 2014, the district court ordered Lee to pay Souratgar $283,066.62 in expenses. *Id.* The Clerk of Court entered judgment on February 27, 2014, and Lee filed notice of this appeal on March 26, 2014.

## DISCUSSION

. . . .

### II. ICARA's "Clearly Inappropriate" Standard

We review for abuse of discretion a district court's award of expenses under the Hague Convention. *See Ozaltin v. Ozaltin*, 708 F.3d 355, 374-75 (2d Cir. 2013). A district court abuses its discretion "if it base[s] its ruling on an erroneous view of the law or on a clearly erroneous assessment of the evidence, or render[s] a decision that cannot be located within the range of permissible decisions." *Id.* at 375 (quoting *In re Sims*, 534 F.3d 117, 132 (2d Cir. 2008)).

ICARA's presumption of an award of expenses to a prevailing petitioner is "subject to a broad caveat denoted by the words, 'clearly inappropriate.'" *Whallon v. Lynn*, 356 F.3d 138, 140 (1st Cir. 2004). This caveat retains "the equitable nature of cost awards," so that a prevailing petitioner's presumptive entitlement to an award of expenses is "subject to the application of equitable principles by the district court." *Ozaltin*, 708 F.3d at 375 (quoting *Moore v. Cnty. of Delaware*, 586 F.3d 219, 221 (2d Cir. 2009)). "Absent any statutory guidance to the contrary, the appropriateness of such costs depends on the same general standards that apply when 'attorney's fees are to be awarded to prevailing parties only as a matter of the court's discretion.'" *Id.* (quoting *Fogerty v. Fantasy, Inc.*, 510 U.S. 517, 534, 114 S. Ct. 1023, 127 L. Ed. 2d 455 (1994)).

Generally, in determining whether expenses are "clearly inappropriate," courts have considered the degree to which the petitioner bears responsibility for the circumstances giving rise to the fees and costs associated with a petition. *See, e.g., Whallon v. Lynn*, No. Civ.A. 00-11009-RWZ, 2003 U.S. Dist. LEXIS 6501, 2003 WL 1906174, at *4 (D. Mass. Apr. 18, 2003) (reducing fees, among other reasons, "because both parties bear responsibility for the degree of enmity between them"), *aff'd*, 356 F.3d 138; *Aly v. Aden*, No. 12-1960, 2013 U.S. Dist. LEXIS 19981, 2013 WL 593420, at *20 (D. Minn. Feb. 14, 2013); *Silverman v. Silverman*, No. 00-cv-2274, 2004 U.S. Dist. LEXIS 18439, 2004 WL 2066778, at *4 (D. Minn. Aug. 26, 2004). Where, as here, the respondent's removal of the child from the habitual country is related to intimate partner violence perpetrated by the petitioner against the respondent, the petitioner bears some responsibility for the circumstances giving rise to the petition. In line with this reasoning, district courts in other circuits have concluded that "family violence perpetrated by a parent is an appropriate consideration in assessing fees in a Hague case." *Guaragno v. Guaragno*, No. 09-cv-187, 2010 U.S. Dist. LEXIS 139576, 2010 WL 5564628, at *2 (N.D. Tex. Oct. 19, 2010) (finding that a prevailing petitioner's physical abuse of the respondent "is a significant factor in the determination of the assessment of fees and expenses"), *adopted by* 2011 U.S. Dist. LEXIS 8312, 2011 WL 108946 (N.D. Tex. Jan. 11, 2011); *see also Aly*, 2013 U.S. Dist. LEXIS 19981, 2013 WL 593420, at *20 (finding any award of expenses to the prevailing petitioner clearly inappropriate in part because the petitioner "was physically and verbally abusive toward respondent"); *Silverman*, 2004 U.S. Dist. LEXIS 18439, 2004 WL 2066778, at *4 ("[That the petitioner] had been physically and mentally abusive toward respondent . . . is appropriately considered in determining fees.").

This concept is analogous to the equitable doctrine of unclean hands. The American legal system rightfully "closes the doors of a court of equity to one tainted with inequitableness or bad faith relative to the matter in which he seeks relief." *Precision Instrument Mfg. Co. v. Auto. Maint. Mach. Co.*, 324 U.S. 806, 814, 65 S. Ct. 993, 89 L. Ed. 1381, 1945 Dec. Comm'r Pat. 582 (1945); *see also Moore v. Cnty. of Delaware*, 586 F.3d 219, 221 (2d Cir. 2009) (per curiam) (holding that under Rule 39 of the Federal Rules of Appellate Procedure, the denial of otherwise properly taxable costs "may be appropriate where a losing party can demonstrate misconduct by a prevailing party").

Furthermore, considering intimate partner violence as an equitable factor in the determination of whether an award of expenses is "clearly inappropriate" is not contrary to the legislative purpose of ICARA's fee-shifting provision. The sparse legislative history of the provision reveals that it was "intended to provide an additional deterrent to wrongful international child removals and retentions." H.R. Rep. No. 100-525, at 14 (1988), *as reprinted in* 1988 U.S.C.C.A.N. 386, 395. In general, treating the fee-shifting provision as an additional deterrent furthers ICARA's overall purpose of discouraging parents from taking their custody battles across international borders. *See id.* at 5. But Congress did not provide that the provision's added deterrence was so overriding that courts *must* award fees regardless of the circumstances of a particular case. Rather, a common sense interpretation of the text indicates that, *even if* an award of fees would serve a deterrent purpose, that purpose must give way if awarding fees would be "clearly inappropriate." This is in contrast to a determination of the merits of an ICARA petition, where courts may only consider intimate partner violence between a respondent and petitioner if it relates to the potential for grave risk of physical or psychological harm to the child or would otherwise place the child in an intolerable situation. Hague Convention art. 13(b), 1343 U.N.T.S. at 101. In the fee-shifting context, Congress built a safety valve directly into the statute, leaving it to courts to determine when an award of expenses would be clearly inappropriate, notwithstanding the additional deterrence value such expenses might provide.

The district court was therefore correct to consider Souratgar's unilateral violence in its determination of whether to order Lee to pay expenses under ICARA. *See Souratgar III*, 2014 U.S. Dist. LEXIS 22167, 2014 WL 704037, at *9. However, we respectfully conclude that the able district court exceeded its discretion in awarding expenses to Souratgar in light of its fact-finding and its related analysis of the relevant equitable factors. In the course of reviewing the petition, the district court made explicit factual findings that Lee had not committed the violent acts alleged by Souratgar but that Souratgar had repeatedly perpetrated violence against her. *Souratgar I*, 2012 U.S. Dist. LEXIS 181989, 2012 WL 6700214, at *11. But because Lee had fled the marital home to her sister's home within Singapore before fleeing the country, the district court found that she "ha[d] not established that the past abuse of her was causally related to her decision to leave Singapore." *Souratgar III*, 2014 U.S. Dist. LEXIS 22167, 2014 WL 704037, at *9. We differ with the district court's conclusion on this point. First, this finding is belied by the record: The district court found that Souratgar's violence toward Lee did not stop when she left their home. *See Souratgar I*, 2012 U.S. Dist. LEXIS 181989, 2012 WL 6700214, at *9, *11 (discussing violent incidents in August 2011 and November 2011, after her May 2011 departure from the marital home). Second, we find that Lee's testimony shows, and Souratgar does not genuinely dispute, that her departure was related to Souratgar's history of intimate partner violence. Therefore, we find that Souratgar bears some responsibility for the circumstances giving rise to the petition.

Accordingly, having reviewed all relevant equitable factors, because the respondent has shown that the petitioner engaged in multiple, unilateral acts of intimate partner violence against her and that her removal of the child from the habitual country was related to that violence, and because there are no countervailing factors in the record in favor of the petitioner, an award of expenses would be "clearly inappropriate."

In so holding, we express no opinion about circumstances beyond the facts of this appeal, particularly where countervailing equitable factors are present. We also do not attempt to catalog the possible countervailing equitable factors that a district court may properly weigh. This task is better left to the district courts to develop on a case-by-case basis so that they retain "broad discretion" in applying equitable principles to implement "the Hague Convention consistently with our own laws and standards." *Whallon*, 356 F.3d at 140. Here, the district court assessed two potential countervailing equitable factors—psychological abuse and abuse of the child—but neither was present in this case. *See Souratgar I*, 2012 U.S. Dist. LEXIS 181989, 2012 WL 6700214, at *11 (discussing Souratgar's "abusive conduct . . . [that] included shouting and offensive name-calling"); 2012 U.S. Dist. LEXIS 181989, [WL] at *7 ("The Court finds that both parties have deep love for Shayan and care greatly about his wellbeing.").

As a matter of clarification, we agree with the district court that a respondent's inability to pay an award is a relevant equitable factor for courts to consider in awarding expenses under ICARA. *See, e.g., Rydder v. Rydder*, 49 F.3d 369, 373-74 (8th Cir. 1995) (reducing an ICARA award to a "more equitable" amount in light of the respondent's "straitened financial circumstances"). However, this relevant equitable factor can never be a *countervailing* factor to intimate partner violence in a case like the one before us—it would remain clearly inappropriate to order a victim of intimate partner violence to pay an expenses award to the perpetrator, absent countervailing equitable factors, even where the victim is wealthy.

Finally, we note that intimate partner violence in any form is deplorable. It can include a range of behaviors, from a single slap to a lethal blow. However, we need not determine in the matter at hand what quantum of violence must have occurred to warrant a finding that fees are "clearly inappropriate," given the repeated violence established in the record here. Those determinations we leave to be resolved as they arise in future cases.

Here, after assessing all relevant equitable factors, because of the clarity of the factual record, the nature of the multiple, unilateral acts of violence, and the absence of countervailing equitable factors in favor of petitioner, we conclude that an award of expenses to Souratgar is clearly inappropriate. In the ordinary course, we would remand the case to the district court to assess the petitioner's request for fees and costs consistent with our opinion. However, given the record in this case, we cannot envision any scenario where an award of expenses would not be clearly inappropriate. Accordingly, a remand would serve no useful purpose. *Cf. Rydder*, 49 F.3d at 373-74 (reducing fee award without remanding for consideration by the district court).

For these reasons, we REVERSE the order and VACATE the judgment of the district court.

. . . .

## VII. Domestic Violence and the Elderly

Elderly victims of intimate partner abuse share much in common with youthful victims—embarrassment in front of their peers, fear of loneliness, and concern nobody will believe their stories. The federal government estimates that hundreds of thousands of elders are abused in this drastically under-reported crime. On June 15, 2006, the International Network for the Prevention of Elder Abuse and the World Health Organization launched the first World Elder Abuse Awareness Day (WEAAD) at the United Nations to promote better understanding of this serious problem and to search for ways to solve it. Each year on that date local governments are encouraged to sponsor awareness programs and events calling attention to elder abuse.³⁰ The author of an article in the *AARP Magazine* described the painful, personal impact of elder abuse; a brief excerpt follows.

## David France, *And Then He Hit Me*
AARP Magazine 73 (Jan. & Feb. 2006)

Almost from the start of her second marriage, Hedy Schweitzer felt she had to choose between two painful options. She could endure her husband's violent beatings and hurricanes of criticism, which shook her confidence and left her self-doubting despite the fact that she was a successful health-care professional. Or she could do something she considered far worse: admit she'd made a huge mistake by marrying him in the first place. So from 1993 until a year ago, she tried to cover up the abuse, even from her own grown children. She lied when friends and colleagues saw the cheeks enlarged by blows and the ankles gnarled from being slammed in car doors, or when doctors inquired about her shattered eardrums and broken fingers, now healed at awkward angles. She pretended nothing was amiss. Unfortunately, so did almost everyone else. All the while, Hedy . . . thought she was probably among the world's oldest victims of domestic violence. "I thought this is something that happens to young and inexperienced girls. Not somebody in their 50s, not a grandmother," she says one morning as sun spills through the stained glass windows of her living room in Milwaukee. She glances at pictures of her children and grandchildren, crowded on a bookshelf. "The overwhelming thing for me, as an older person, was being ashamed, because this shouldn't be happening to me. I should know better."

---

Federal and state lawmakers have started to take a closer look at this problem as special interest groups have begun to step up their efforts at addressing elder abuse. The U.S. Department of Justice Office on Violence Against Women Enhanced Training and Services to End Abuse in Later Life in early 2016 announced it was prepared to make nine grants around the country, totaling $3.2 million to support a coordinated community response to fighting elder abuse. The goal was to "help provide victims across the life span with the protection and services they need to pursue safe and healthy lives, while improving communities' capacity to hold offenders accountable for their crimes."³¹

District Attorneys' offices have put enhanced resources into stopping elder abuse. The popular conception is that only those seniors without family are vulnerable, usually at the hands of professional caregivers. Studies show that is not correct. The

---

30. U.S. Department of Health and Human Services, Administration for Community Living, *What is World Elder Abuse Day?* www.aoa.acl.gov/AoA_Programs/Elder_Rights/EA_Prevention/weaad.aspx, accessed October 6, 2016.

31. U.S. Department of Justice, Office on Violence Against Women, *OVW Enhanced Training and Services to End Abuse in Later Life Program,* https://www.justice.gov/ovw/file/797701/download, accessed October 5, 2016.

National Center on Elder Abuse reports that only 15 percent of seniors who are abused are abused by a caregiver, while nearly 60 percent of all elderly victims are abused by a family member.[32]

The Office of the New York County District Attorney, which has had a specialized unit to address economic crimes against the elderly for more than 20 years, has expanded it beyond financial fraud to include neglect and physical abuse under current District Attorney Cyrus Vance. That office now has more than two-dozen prosecutors specially trained to protect the elderly. Unit Chief Catherine Christian reports that 900 defendants were arraigned in 2015 in which their alleged victims were 60 years of age or older. She states: "The exact same thing you hear from a young victim, you hear from an older person. The older women, particularly, are embarrassed by having to talk about sexual things and do not feel comfortable speaking to a younger district attorney." She counsels patience to her staff when dealing with elderly victims, and warns against ageism when evaluating their concerns. Although some victims have dementia and limited resources, others are wealthy, educated and sophisticated. Elder abuse prosecutors in the New York County District Attorney's office do outreach in senior centers, and with geriatric social workers, financial institutions and civil attorneys to educate them about the problem.

---

Some states have enacted laws specifically addressing domestic violence against children, the elderly or the vulnerable. Some examples follow.

### Tex. Penal Code § 22.04 (2016) Injury to a Child, Elderly Individual, or Disabled Individual.

(a) A person commits an offense if he intentionally, knowingly, recklessly, or with criminal negligence, by act or intentionally, knowingly, or recklessly by omission, causes to a child, elderly individual, or disabled individual:

    (1) serious bodily injury;

    (2) serious mental deficiency, impairment, or injury; or

    (3) bodily injury.

. . . .

(c) In this section:

    (1) "Child" means a person 14 years of age or younger.

    (2) "Elderly individual" means a person 65 years of age or older.

    (3) "Disabled individual" means a person:

        . . . .

---

32. National Center on Elder Abuse, *Research: Statistics/Data*, https://ncea.acl.gov/whatwedo/research/statistics.html#perpetrators, accessed September 25, 2016.

(B) who otherwise by reason of age or physical or mental disease, defect, or injury is substantially unable to protect the person's self from harm or to provide food, shelter, or medical care for the person's self. . . .

(e) An offense under Subsection (a)(1) or (2) or (a-1)(1) or (2) is a felony of the first degree when the conduct is committed intentionally or knowingly. When the conduct is engaged in recklessly, the offense is a felony of the second degree.

(f) An offense under Subsection (a)(3) or (a-1)(3) is a felony of the third degree when the conduct is committed intentionally or knowingly, except that an offense under Subsection (a)(3) is a felony of the second degree when the conduct is committed intentionally or knowingly and the victim is a disabled individual residing in a center, as defined by Section 555.001, Health and Safety Code, or in a facility licensed under Chapter 252, Health and Safety Code, and the actor is an employee of the center or facility whose employment involved providing direct care for the victim. When the conduct is engaged in recklessly, the offense is a state jail felony.

(g) An offense under Subsection (a) is a state jail felony when the person acts with criminal negligence. An offense under Subsection (a-1) is a state jail felony when the person, with criminal negligence and by omission, causes a condition described by Subsection (a-1)(1), (2), or (3).

(h) A person who is subject to prosecution under both this section and another section of this code may be prosecuted under either or both sections. Section 3.04 does not apply to criminal episodes prosecuted under both this section and another section of this code. If a criminal episode is prosecuted under both this section and another section of this code and sentences are assessed for convictions under both sections, the sentences shall run concurrently. . . .

## Cal. Pen. Code § 368 (2016) Crimes against elders and dependent adults; Legislative findings; Infliction of pain, injury, or endangerment; Theft, embezzlement, forgery, fraud, or identity theft; False imprisonment; Restraining order

(a) The Legislature finds and declares that crimes against elders and dependent adults are deserving of special consideration and protection, not unlike the special protections provided for minor children, because elders and dependent adults may be confused, on various medications, mentally or physically impaired, or incompetent, and therefore less able to protect themselves, to understand or report criminal conduct, or to testify in court proceedings on their own behalf.

(b)

(1) Any person who knows or reasonably should know that a person is an elder or dependent adult and who, under circumstances or conditions likely to produce great bodily harm or death, willfully causes or permits any elder or dependent adult to suffer, or inflicts thereon unjustifiable physical pain or mental suffering, or having the care or custody of any elder or dependent adult, willfully causes or permits the

person or health of the elder or dependent adult to be injured, or willfully causes or permits the elder or dependent adult to be placed in a situation in which his or her person or health is endangered, is punishable by imprisonment in a county jail not exceeding one year, or by a fine not to exceed six thousand dollars ($6,000), or by both that fine and imprisonment, or by imprisonment in the state prison for two, three, or four years.

(2) If, in the commission of an offense described in paragraph (1), the victim suffers great bodily injury, as defined in Section 12022.7, the defendant shall receive an additional term in the state prison as follows:

(A) Three years if the victim is under 70 years of age.

(B) Five years if the victim is 70 years of age or older.

(3) If, in the commission of an offense described in paragraph (1), the defendant proximately causes the death of the victim, the defendant shall receive an additional term in the state prison as follows:

(A) Five years if the victim is under 70 years of age.

(B) Seven years if the victim is 70 years of age or older.

(c) Any person who knows or reasonably should know that a person is an elder or dependent adult and who, under circumstances or conditions other than those likely to produce great bodily harm or death, willfully causes or permits any elder or dependent adult to suffer, or inflicts thereon unjustifiable physical pain or mental suffering, or having the care or custody of any elder or dependent adult, willfully causes or permits the person or health of the elder or dependent adult to be injured or willfully causes or permits the elder or dependent adult to be placed in a situation in which his or her person or health may be endangered, is guilty of a misdemeanor. A second or subsequent violation of this subdivision is punishable by a fine not to exceed two thousand dollars ($2,000), or by imprisonment in a county jail not to exceed one year, or by both that fine and imprisonment.

(d) Any person who is not a caretaker who violates any provision of law proscribing theft, embezzlement, forgery, or fraud, or who violates Section 530.5 proscribing identity theft, with respect to the property or personal identifying information of an elder or a dependent adult, and who knows or reasonably should know that the victim is an elder or a dependent adult, is punishable as follows:

(1) By a fine not exceeding two thousand five hundred dollars ($2,500), or by imprisonment in a county jail not exceeding one year, or by both that fine and imprisonment, or by a fine not exceeding ten thousand dollars ($10,000), or by imprisonment pursuant to subdivision (h) of Section 1170 for two, three, or four years, or by both that fine and imprisonment, when the moneys, labor, goods, services, or real or personal property taken or obtained is of a value exceeding nine hundred fifty dollars ($950).

(2) By a fine not exceeding one thousand dollars ($1,000), by imprisonment in a county jail not exceeding one year, or by both that fine and imprisonment, when the

moneys, labor, goods, services, or real or personal property taken or obtained is of a value not exceeding nine hundred fifty dollars ($950).

(e) Any caretaker of an elder or a dependent adult who violates any provision of law proscribing theft, embezzlement, forgery, or fraud, or who violates Section 530.5 proscribing identity theft, with respect to the property or personal identifying information of that elder or dependent adult, is punishable as follows:

(1) By a fine not exceeding two thousand five hundred dollars ($2,500), or by imprisonment in a county jail not exceeding one year, or by both that fine and imprisonment, or by a fine not exceeding ten thousand dollars ($10,000), or by imprisonment pursuant to subdivision (h) of Section 1170 for two, three, or four years, or by both that fine and imprisonment, when the moneys, labor, goods, services, or real or personal property taken or obtained is of a value exceeding nine hundred fifty dollars ($950).

(2) By a fine not exceeding one thousand dollars ($1,000), by imprisonment in a county jail not exceeding one year, or by both that fine and imprisonment, when the moneys, labor, goods, services, or real or personal property taken or obtained is of a value not exceeding nine hundred fifty dollars ($950).

(f) Any person who commits the false imprisonment of an elder or a dependent adult by the use of violence, menace, fraud, or deceit is punishable by imprisonment pursuant to subdivision (h) of Section 1170 for two, three, or four years.

. . . .

(*l*) Upon conviction for a violation of subdivision (b), (c), (d), (e), or (f), the sentencing court shall also consider issuing an order restraining the defendant from any contact with the victim, which may be valid for up to 10 years, as determined by the court. It is the intent of the Legislature that the length of any restraining order be based upon the seriousness of the facts before the court, the probability of future violations, and the safety of the victim and his or her immediate family. This protective order may be issued by the court whether the defendant is sentenced to state prison or county jail, or if imposition of sentence is suspended and the defendant is placed on probation.

## N.Y. Penal Law § 260.32 (2015) Endangering the welfare of a vulnerable elderly person, *or an incompetent or physically disabled person* in the second degree

A person is guilty of endangering the welfare of a vulnerable elderly person, *or an incompetent or physically disabled person* in the second degree when, being a caregiver for a vulnerable elderly person, *or an incompetent or physically disabled person*:

1. With intent to cause physical injury to such person, he or she causes such injury to such person; or

2. He or she recklessly causes physical injury to such person; or

3. With criminal negligence, he or she causes physical injury to such person by means of a deadly weapon or a dangerous instrument; or

4. He or she subjects such person to sexual contact without the latter's consent. Lack of consent under this subdivision results from forcible compulsion or incapacity to consent, as those terms are defined in article one hundred thirty of this chapter, or any other circumstances in which the vulnerable elderly person, *or an incompetent or physically disabled person* does not expressly or impliedly acquiesce in the caregiver's conduct. In any prosecution under this subdivision in which the victim's alleged lack of consent results solely from incapacity to consent because of the victim's mental disability or mental incapacity, the provisions of section 130.16 of this chapter shall apply. In addition, in any prosecution under this subdivision in which the victim's lack of consent is based solely upon his or her incapacity to consent because he or she was mentally disabled, mentally incapacitated or physically helpless, it is an affirmative defense that the defendant, at the time he or she engaged in the conduct constituting the offense, did not know of the facts or conditions responsible for such incapacity to consent.

Endangering the welfare of a vulnerable elderly person, *or an incompetent or physically disabled person* in the second degree is a class E felony.

---

Despite statutes making elder abuse a crime, it remains a difficult crime to prosecute as the following article indicates.

## Lisa Fischel-Wolovick, *Police Response: Mandatory Arrest & Primary Physical Aggressor*
### in Lawyer's Manual of Domestic Violence: Representing the Victim 52 (6th ed. 2015)

. . . .

### Elder Abuse

Despite inclusion in the definition of a household, elder abuse remains a difficult crime to prosecute, particularly where the victims may have difficulty recalling the incidents. Careful reviewing of other family members, caretakers, and medical personnel, evidence of medical documentation, and sudden withdrawals of savings may be indicative of identity theft and grand larceny.

In cases where the elderly person is a poor historian and unable to accurately recall the times and dates of the incidents, they remain at risk of elder abuse. For the prosecutor and family court attorney, there are significant symptoms of abuse in the elderly, including bruising and marks on the wrists or ankles, indicating that the victim had been restrained for long periods of time. Medical evidence that the victim did not have access to necessary medication can be documented through collaboration with physicians, homemaker service agencies, and public health nurses. Increasingly, research has indicated that victims of intimate partner violence seek medical treatment not simply in the emergency rooms, but also in relationship to chronic stress related illnesses. These somatic complaints can be found in the elderly, and the general population, and are frequently found in women who are abused. Having clients sign HIPPAA released at intake, and screening to determine if medical attention has ever been obtained for injuries or stress related illnesses, is essential in building a case for prosecution in either criminal or Family Court.

Significantly, civil guardianship proceedings in New York State Supreme Court continue to be the primary forum where safety concerns for the elderly are heard. A guardianship proceeding under the Mental Hygiene Law is a proceeding in which the petitioner seeks to strip the allegedly incompetent person of their rights to determine how they manage their finances, where they will live, and who will care for them. This application should be a last resort, increasing advocacy for victims of elder abuse to assist them in removing the batterer from their home—without taking away the victim's civil rights—is essential....

## *Notes and Questions*

- **MORE ON MANDATED REPORTERS.**

At Penn State University, a school known nationwide for its success on the football field, a scandal in 2011 in which one-time assistant coach Gerald "Jerry" Sandusky was charged with sexually abusing multiple boys during a 15-year-period rocked the institution to its core and ignited a national conversation on whether mandatory reporting laws needed to be broadened. If this were to happen, mandated reporter statutes nationwide might resemble New Jersey's. In her thought-provoking article, published in *Washington Lawyer* magazine, author Anna Stolley Persky asked: "Should all American adults be responsible for calling the authorities when they suspect a child is being neglected or abused? Do adults want to take on that level of responsibility toward their fellow citizens and, if so, how should they be held accountable for failing to do so?" Anna Stolley Persky, *The Penn State Scandal: Child Abuse Reporting Laws,* Washington Lawyer, June 2013, 23–24. Discuss the pros and cons of making every adult a mandated reporter.

Mandated reporter statutes have been lauded for the role they have played in protecting battered children. But what about the toll they have taken on the lives of those wrongfully accused of child abuse and permanently tagged as a danger to children? *In the Matter of Mary L. v. Dep't of Social Services,* 244 A.D.2d 133 (N.Y. App. Div. 1998), concerned a legal challenge to a 1996 amendment to § 422 of the state's Social Services Law, known as "Elisa's Law," for a child who had been horribly abused by a mother long known to child welfare workers. Prior to the child's death, unfounded reports of suspected child abuse were routinely expunged. Following that tragedy, these unfounded reports (which meant that "some credible evidence of the alleged abuse or maltreatment" was not found to exist) were retained for the purpose of detecting a "pattern of abuse." The unfounded reports could not be divulged to employers or admitted in judicial or administrative proceedings and were expunged from the New York State Central Register 10 years after the youngest child referred to in the report turned 18 years old. The petitioner, Mary L., was informed by the Department of Social Services (DSS) she was "the subject of a report of suspected child abuse or maltreatment." The report was later determined to be unfounded. The petitioner and her employee union sought to have the record expunged and to permanently enjoin DSS from retaining unfounded reports under the theory that retaining the records violated petitioner's state and federal constitutional rights to due process and equal protection. The court found there was little, if any, stigma attached to the maintenance of sealed unfounded reports. Future employers would not have access to them and maintaining them was rationally related to the goal of the statute, which was to protect the health and safety of children.

There has been criticism of Child Abuse Prevention and Treatment Act (CAPTA) amendments for being overly deferential to those named in unfounded reports of child abuse. Since CAPTA first became law in 1974, it has been amended several times. In reviewing the legislative history surrounding those amendments, one writer drew the conclusion the changes were being driven by legislators and lobbyists who feared mandatory reporting laws were too intrusive into the privacy of the family and too fraught with the possibility of error:

> Other testimony, however, and congressional reports presented by the bill's sponsors focused extensively on the numbers of parents injured by "false" reports. Senator Dan Coats, one of the bill's cosponsors, acknowledged that one million reports of child abuse are substantiated each year, but emphasized the nearly two million "false or unsubstantiated reports... that are filed wrongfully and in some cases maliciously...."
>
> Several problems exist with Senator Coats's assessment. First he fails to distinguish meaningfully between erroneous and unsubstantiated reports. Second, he seems to assume that any unsubstantiated report is "unnecessary," which illustrates his conflation of unsubstantiated reports with those that are in fact erroneous. This conflation ignores the fact that reporting statutes deliberately place the degree of suspicion required for reporting at a very low level to encourage reporting and protect as many children as possible. Establishing a high standard of proof, on the other hand, ensures that some actual cases of abuse will ultimately be considered "unsubstantiated." Third, he provides absolutely no support for his allegation that many reports are filed "maliciously"—in fact, malice is rarely alleged. Fourth, Senator Coats omits the fact that nearly every state has "good faith" immunity, which begs the question of what effect the CAPTA Amendments' new "good faith" immunity provision is intended to have outside of directly targeting the few states that provide absolute immunity....

Caroline T. Trost, Note, *Chilling Child Abuse Reporting: Rethinking the CAPTA Amendments*, 51 Vand. L. Rev. 183, 206–08 (1998).

- **ANIMAL ABUSE**

The connection between the abuse of animals, the abuse of children, and domestic violence is well known to researchers and social scientists. In her chapter, *Abuse of Children and Abuse of Animals*, in CHILD ABUSE, DOMESTIC VIOLENCE, AND ANIMAL ABUSE: LINKING THE CIRCLES OF COMPASSION FOR PREVENTION AND INTERVENTION 83 (F.R. Ascione & P. Arkow eds., 1999), Barbara W. Boat writes:

> Our awareness of the child abuse-animal abuse connection is being heightened in regard to domestic violence settings. . . . In a national survey of over 6,000 U.S. families, researchers found that 50 percent of men who frequently assaulted their wives also frequently abused their children. Many men who resort to violence to control women can enhance their control by harming or killing family animals or by threatening to do so. Persons who counsel battered women report that dogs and cats have been stabbed, shot, hanged and otherwise mutilated by abusive spouses. Sometimes the animals simply disappear or die mysteriously. . . . In a study of 38 battered women who were consecutive intakes in a shelter, 71 percent who owned pets reported that their violent partners had threatened or actually harmed their pets. Equally disturbing is that 32 percent of the women reported that their children were perpetrating abusive acts against the pets as well. . . .

In March 2006, Gov. John Balducci of Maine signed the first law in the country giving judges the authority to include pets on domestic violence orders of protection. The law authorizes penalties for violations, including jail time, if appropriate. In signing the law, the governor called it "'unconscionable' that 76 percent of victims who seek safety at domestic violence shelters report that their abusers either harmed or threatened their pets as a tool to control and intimidate them. The new law can help break that cycle of violence." Sharon Kiley Mack, *Law Protects Pets of Abuse Victims; Maine Legislation to Curb Cycle of Violence Against Animals 1st in Nation*, BANGOR DAILY NEWS, Apr. 1, 2006. Today 32 states plus the District of Columbia and Puerto Rico have laws allowing courts to issue orders of protection for companion animals, with Alaska being the latest jurisdiction to enact such a law in January of 2017. *See* Rebecca F. Wisch, University of Michigan, Animal League and Historical Center, *Domestic Violence and Pets: List of States That Include Pets in Protection Orders,* https://www.animallaw.info/article/domestic-violence-and-pets-list-states-include-pets-protection-orders, accessed October 23, 2016.

- **BATTERERS AND CHILD CUSTODY**

In her effort to determine which parent actually obtains custody in the face of allegations of domestic violence, Georgetown University Law Professor Joan S. Meier obtained disturbing results:

> . . . In 1989, the Supreme Judicial Court of Massachusetts' Gender Bias Study found that more than 70% of fathers received sole or joint custody regardless of whether there was a history of abuse. . . . *See also* Linda Neilson, *Partner Abuse, Children and Statutory Change: Cautionary Comments on*

*Women's Access to Justice,* 18 WINDSOR Y.B. ACCESS JUST. 115, 144 (2000) (reporting that a study of 1147 randomly selected court files in a Canadian jurisdiction found that "not only do abusers obtain unrestricted access to their children, they also obtain custody in a significant number of cases.... Joint, split or full custody was granted to, or obtained by abusers in 16% of the court-filed cases....").

My own (and research assistant's) admittedly unscientific survey of many of the United States cases ... found that, of thirty-eight cases in which mothers alleged abuse and sought to limit fathers' access to children, *only two trial courts* agreed with the mother; the remaining thirty-six courts awarded at least joint, and often sole, custody to the father. Thirteen of these decisions were upheld on appeal; one of the two favoring the mother was reversed on appeal. *See Dinius v. Dinius,* 564 N.W.2d 300 (N.D. 1997). Most of these cases were decided in states with a presumption against custody to the batterer.... However, it is also clear that, in those few cases where appeal is possible, appellate courts are more likely to recognize the validity and significance of domestic violence for child custody decisions....

Joan S. Meier, *Domestic Violence, Child Custody, and Child Protection: Understanding Judicial Resistance and Imagining the Solutions,* 11 J. GENDER SOC. POL'Y & L. 657, 662 n.19 (2003).

- **UNWANTED CHILDREN**

In Texas in 1999 the nation's first "safe haven" law was passed permitting a birth mother to abandon her unwanted baby at a safe location without fear of prosecution. The Texas law specifies the abandoned child be given to an emergency medical services provider, a hospital or child protective service at any time during the child's first two months of life to avoid prosecution. Tex. Family Code § 262.302 (2016). The law reads:

(a) A designated emergency infant care provider shall, without a court order, take possession of a child who appears to be 60 days old or younger if the child is voluntarily delivered to the provider by the child's parent and the parent did not express an intent to return for the child.

(b) A designated emergency infant care provider who takes possession of a child under this section has no legal duty to detain or pursue the parent and may not do so unless the child appears to have been abused or neglected. The designated emergency infant care provider has no legal duty to ascertain the parent's identity and the parent may remain anonymous. However, the parent may be given a form for voluntary disclosure of the child's medical facts and history.

(c) A designated emergency infant care provider who takes possession of a child under this section shall perform any act necessary to protect the physical health or safety of the child. The designated emergency infant care provider is not liable for damages related to the provider's taking possession of, examining, or treating the child, except for damages related to the provider's negligence.

Under Tex. Family Code 262.301, a "designated emergency infant care provider" includes an emergency services worker, a hospital or medical facility or child placement agency.

Today, all 50 states have Safe Haven laws. Since 1999, 3,245 children have been safely left at hospitals, police stations, child welfare agencies and fire houses, according to the Save Abandoned Babies Foundation, www.saveabandonedbabies.org, accessed March 5, 2017.

The many ways batterers have to abuse women know no bounds and sabotaging birth control is apparently a popular one. The National Domestic Violence Hotline reported in 2011 that one in four women surveyed said they had been pressured by an intimate partner not to use birth control or forced into having unprotected sexual intercourse. More than 3,000 women responded to the survey between August 16 and September 26, 2010. In a newspaper interview, Dr. Elizabeth Miller, a professor at the University of California, Davis, School of Medicine who devised the survey, said coercion against using contraception was "another mechanism for control in an unhealthy relationship." Roni Caryn Rabin, *Report Details of Sabotage of Birth Control,* N.Y. TIMES, February 15, 2011.

# Chapter 8

# Divorce and Domestic Violence

> **CONSIDER AS YOU READ ABOUT DIVORCE**
> 1. Difficulty of obtaining divorce due to domestic violence
> 2. Emergence of no-fault divorce
> 3. Impact of no-fault divorce on division of assets where domestic violence is present

Although he would one day be known as the architect of the conservative political revolution in America, in 1969, then-Governor Ronald Reagan of California started one of the 20th century's great liberalizing movements by signing the nation's first no-fault divorce law. No-fault divorce allows one party to end a marriage without the consent of the other party, with no reason given other than the vague terms "irreconcilable differences" or "irretrievable breakdown." Today, every state has some form of no-fault divorce.

Divorce statutes can be complex and arcane. The goal in this chapter is not to dissect the states' various divorce laws, but to examine their impact on dissolving a marriage plagued by domestic violence. Two issues are of importance to the intersection of divorce and domestic violence. The first is whether in this era of no-fault divorce, domestic violence is still considered during the fault phase of a matrimonial proceeding. The second is, what role, if any, fault plays in splitting marital assets.

Before moving to that discussion, however, it is helpful to review the history of divorce. In medieval England, to the extent divorce was allowed at all, it was controlled by the canon laws of the church. Professor R.H. Helmholz explores the rigid sanctity of marriage in his book MARRIAGE LITIGATION IN MEDIEVAL ENGLAND (1974). For example, he writes that one Robert Handenby was sued for divorce in 1390 in York, England by his wife, Margaret, because "[d]iscord has recently arisen." No elaboration on what constituted "discord" was provided, but the wife's request for separation (which was the extent of most divorces at the time) was denied. Mrs. Handenby was, however, told by the court she could petition again if she were mistreated by her husband in the future, intimating abuse was the "discord" driving her to seek to get away from him. However, the success of her application would depend on her ability to present "two legitimate witnesses." *Id.* at 101.

Even the presence of serious domestic violence did not merit separation or divorce. In 1395, also in York, Margaret Neffeld sued her husband because he "had once attacked her with a knife, forcing her to flee into the street 'wailing and in tears.' Another time he had set upon her with a dagger, wounding her in the arm and breaking one of her bones...." *Id.* at 105. The husband denied the allegations and said whatever he *may* have done was "for the purpose of 'reducing her from errors.'" Divorce denied. *Id.*

Prior to the mid-19th century, divorce in England was available to the upper classes through a costly act of Parliament, and then only to a cuckolded husband. First, a husband had to sue the object of his wife's affections for adultery in court, and if he prevailed, he recovered damages and could then seek a divorce from Parliament. The Divorce Act of 1857 was introduced to ameliorate the injustices of the country's divorce system. In debates about the wisdom of passing the Divorce Act, a "standard, reiterated argument in favor of divorce dealt with the responsibility of the legislative body to protect working-class women who were plagued by brutal, drunken husbands. Significantly, Parliament did not consider upper-class men to be a danger to their wives. Rather, only in 'the humbler ranks of life [was] some prompt remedy' necessary."[1] When ultimately passed, the act allowed women to be divorced only on three grounds — incest, bigamy and gross physical cruelty.[2]

---

1. Marlene Tromp, The Private Rod: Marital Violence, Sensation, and the Law in Victorian Britain 72–73 (2000).
2. Mary Lyndon Shanley, Feminism, Marriage, and the Law in Victorian England, 1850–1895, 44 (1989).

In most of the British colonies, divorce was permitted on the grounds of adultery or desertion. But, like the situation in the states today, divorce law varied greatly from colony to colony, and in any event, was rare.[3] After the Revolutionary War, divorce laws were liberalized, particularly in the Northeast. But not all states followed the trend, New York being the primary example.[4] The first New York divorce law was enacted in New York in 1787 and the only ground was adultery.[5] Wife beating, widely practiced and ignored in the law, was eventually addressed through the vague ground of "cruelty."

In the western states, divorce laws were enacted that were "wide-ranging in their grounds, lax in their operation, and whose minimal residency requirements seemed to invite migrants in search of divorce."[6] Meanwhile, the number of divorces was increasing. Between 1880 and 1890, divorces grew by 70 percent, and between 1890 and 1900 by another 67 percent.[7]

Divorce continued to escalate in the United States through the 1980s.[8] Once no-fault divorce was enacted in California in 1969, other states rapidly followed. Within five years, more than half of the states had passed some form of no-fault divorce. After California enacted it, the National Conference of Commissioners on Uniform State Laws drafted the Uniform Marriage and Divorce Act (UMDA), which eliminated *all* grounds for divorce, simply allowing marriages to end on demand. Few states have adopted the UMDA.[9]

## I. Domestic Violence as a Ground for Divorce

New York was the last holdout against unilateral, no-fault divorce. Until 2010, the parties could end a marriage without asserting grounds, but only if both husband and wife wanted it. Otherwise, to obtain a divorce in New York, the plaintiff had to prove any of the following grounds against the defendant: cruel and inhuman treatment; abandonment for more than one year; defendant's imprisonment for three or more consecutive years or adultery. If the parties agreed, no grounds were necessary, but they had to live apart for a year pursuant to a written separation agreement. N.Y. Dom. Rel. Law § 170(1)-(6).

---

3. Roderick Phillips, Untying the Knot: A Short History of Divorce 39–40 (1991).

4. *Id.* at 43, 146.

5. 1787 N.Y. Laws Ch. 69. The law forbade any party convicted of adultery under the Act from ever remarrying "and that every such remarriage shall be null and void." Adultery remained the *only* ground available in that state until 1967. *See* Myrna Felder, *Family Law: P.K. v. R.K.: When Is Abandonment Justified?*, N.Y.L.J., Aug. 14, 2006.

6. Phillips, *supra*, at 146.

7. *Id.* at 153.

8. *Id.* at 224, 225.

9. Gary H. Nichols, Note, *Covenant Marriage: Should Tennessee Join the Noble Experiment?*, 29 U. Mem. L. Rev. 397, 416–17 (1999).

Obtaining a divorce pursuant to a separation agreement, the least painful of the options, was unlikely if a marriage was marred by domestic violence. The only recourse for a married victim of domestic abuse who wanted out of the relationship often was to allege cruel and inhuman treatment. The ground required proof of a pattern of behavior, which was no easy task.

## Echevarria v. Echevarria
Court of Appeals of New York
40 N.Y.2d 262 (1976)

Gabrielli, J.

In this matrimonial action, plaintiff wife sued for divorce on grounds of "cruel and inhuman treatment" (Domestic Relations Law, § 170, subd [1]), alleging that, within the four-year period of their marriage, her husband had beaten her twice by repeatedly striking her with his hands and causing bruises and black and blue marks on her face, head and body. The first alleged beating occurred just after the parties were married in 1970. Following the second beating in 1974, plaintiff obtained an order of protection from the Family Court at which time she was compelled to move out of the marital residence for fear of her life. Plaintiff testified that her husband frightened and harassed her and made her "very nervous" to the point of rendering her unable to work. At the conclusion of plaintiff's case, the Trial Judge dismissed the complaint, holding that, as a matter of law, two beatings within a four-year period were insufficient grounds for a judgment of divorce. He noted that the wife might have grounds for divorce based upon "constructive abandonment" (Domestic Relations Law, § 170, subd [2]) but that the action would not accrue until a year of separation had elapsed. We conclude that the Trial Judge erred in dismissing the complaint as a matter of law.

This case involves more than a single act of violence resulting from momentary anger, "transient discord" or mere incompatibility (see *Johnson v. Johnson*, 43 AD2d 842, affd 36 NY2d 667; *Rios v. Rios*, 34 AD2d 325, affd 29 NY2d 840; *Hessen v. Hessen*, 33 NY2d 406, 410–411; Single Act as Basis of Divorce or Separation on Grounds of Cruelty, Ann., 7 ALR3d 761). Rather, there is testimony as to two fierce beatings within the brief four-year period of this marriage (cf. *Hessen v. Hessen, supra*, pp 411–412), the last of such severity that the Family Court deemed it necessary to grant the wife an order of protection. Even one beating constitutes more than a single act of violence when it is composed of repeated and prolonged acts of physical abuse. Despite his dismissal of the complaint, the Trial Judge found that the wife "had to flee the [marital] premises for her life and obtain an order of protection." As we noted in *Hessen v. Hessen (supra*, p 411), "[objective] proof of physical or mental injury to the complainant spouse would certainly be a decisive basis for granting the divorce." The plaintiff in this case has made out a prima facie case that it would be "unsafe or improper" for her to cohabit with defendant *(Johnson v. Johnson, supra; Hessen v. Hessen, supra*, pp 409–410; *Barnier v. Barnier*, 43 AD2d 568). She testified that she was frightened and harassed by defendant who made her "too nervous to work," thus raising the issue of harm to her mental as well as physical well being (see *Johnson v. Johnson, supra*).

As noted in the dissenting opinion at the Appellate Division, it would serve no purpose to require plaintiff to delay her action for divorce until the statutory period for "constructive abandonment" had elapsed (Domestic Relations Law, § 170, subd [2]), as suggested by the Trial Judge. It would be pointless to allow this obviously defunct marriage to be needlessly prolonged in light of the evidence of physical abuse and its effect on the physical and mental well being of the plaintiff (see 1 Foster & Freed, Law and the Family, § 6:11, p 296).

Accordingly, the order of the Appellate Division should be reversed and the matter remitted for a new trial. . . .

## Brady v. Brady

Court of Appeals of New York

64 N.Y.2d 339 (1985)

WACHTLER, J.

Plaintiff Edward Brady has brought this matrimonial action against his wife, defendant Dorothy Brady, seeking a divorce and sale of the marital residence. The complaint alleged, as grounds for obtaining a divorce, that Mrs. Brady committed acts constituting cruel and inhuman treatment and constructively abandoned plaintiff by refusing to engage in sexual relations with him (*see*, Domestic Relations Law § 170). . . .

The parties married in 1956 and have four children, who were born between 1957 and 1966. From May 1977 to September 1979, Mr. Brady lived in the marital residence on an infrequent basis and since September or October 1979 he has not resided there at all. Mr. Brady commenced this action for a divorce in 1981. . . . Among the allegations relating to the claim of cruel and inhuman treatment were that Mrs. Brady, during 1976, struck him with objects, including a lamp and a vase, threatened him with a knife, attempted to choke him and frequently berated him. Her answer denied all of these allegations and set forth counterclaims for maintenance and child support, but not for a judgment of divorce.

At trial, plaintiff, with minimal corroboration, testified to the allegations in the complaint. Mrs. Brady, supported in much of her testimony by one of the Brady children, again denied the charges of constructive abandonment and cruel and inhuman treatment, and stated that she did not seek a divorce. The trial court, apparently rejecting most of plaintiff's specific claims of cruel and inhuman treatment, granted him a divorce on that cause of action. The court termed the marriage a "dead" one, and concluded that based on the marital breakdown and the separation of the parties further cohabitation was improper. . . .

The Appellate Division unanimously modified the trial court judgment. The court found that plaintiff had not made out a cause of action for divorce based on cruel and inhuman treatment, and thus deleted the portions of the judgment granting plaintiff a divorce and ordering the sale of the marital residence upon the emancipation of the remaining infant child. We now affirm.

. . . .

In *Hessen v. Hessen* (33 NY2d 406, *supra*), we held that a plaintiff seeking a divorce under the cruel and inhuman treatment subdivision must show serious misconduct, and not mere incompatibility. Subsequent cases have established that a plaintiff, relying on this subdivision, must generally show a course of conduct by the defendant spouse which is harmful to the physical or mental health of the plaintiff and makes cohabitation unsafe or improper (*Forcucci v. Forcucci*, 96 AD2d 751; *Kennedy v. Kennedy*, 91 AD2d 1200; *Warguleski v. Warguleski*, 79 AD2d 1107). . . .

At the time the *Hessen* case was decided, only a wife was able to collect alimony following a divorce. If, however, her "misconduct" entitled the husband to obtain a divorce on a ground such as cruel and inhuman treatment, she was precluded under Domestic Relations Law § 236 from receiving alimony or exclusive possession of the marital home. (*Hessen v. Hessen*, supra, 410–411; *Barry v. Barry*, 93 AD2d 797). Thus, the effect of granting a husband a divorce on the ground of his wife's cruel and inhuman treatment was a potential financial catastrophe to the wife. In *Hessen*, we noted that this negative effect could be particularly harmful where the defendant, as was the case therein, was a "dependent older woman" (*Hessen v. Hessen*, supra, p 412), and this fact served as one of the bases for requiring a higher degree of proof of cruel and inhuman treatment in a long-term marriage.

In 1980, the Equitable Distribution Law was enacted and Domestic Relations Law § 236 was amended to provide, in part, that either spouse could be required to pay alimony ("maintenance"), and to eliminate the rule that misconduct by a spouse precludes receiving an award of alimony or exclusive possession of the marital home. The change with respect to the person who could be required to pay alimony was constitutionally required in light of the Supreme Court's 1979 decision in *Orr v. Orr* (440 U.S. 268), which held that the Alabama statutory scheme which imposed alimony obligations on husbands only violated the equal protection clause of the 14th Amendment to the United States Constitution. Plaintiff argues that the *Hessen* rule, as to long-term marriages, was designed to protect only women and thus can no longer be followed in view of the *Orr* decision. He also argues that there is no longer any reason to require a higher showing of misconduct in a long-term marriage as the spouse against whom the divorce is granted can receive alimony payments and exclusive possession of the marital home, and thus there is no danger that granting a divorce will be financially ruinous to a "dependent older woman."

If the evidentiary requirement set forth in *Hessen* with respect to marriages of long duration were applied only where the plaintiff was the husband, then there would likely be an equal protection violation. *Hessen*, however, has been . . . and should be followed whether the plaintiff is the husband or the wife. Thus, plaintiff's constitutional argument is without merit. Plaintiff's contention that the rationale for the *Hessen* rule has been eliminated by the 1980 amendments to Domestic Relations Law

§ 236 is also unconvincing. That financial problems could have faced a middle aged woman against whom a cruelty divorce was granted was merely one of the bases for requiring a higher degree of proof of cruel and inhuman treatment in a long-term marriage. The fundamental reason for such a rule was, and remains, the common-sense notion that the conduct which a plaintiff alleges as the basis for a cause of action must be viewed in the context of the entire marriage, including its duration, in deciding whether particular actions can properly be labeled as cruel and inhuman.

. . . .

It is not clear, which, if any, of plaintiff's allegations were credited by the trial court. The trial court did conclude that plaintiff had not made a sufficient showing of cruel and inhuman treatment under *Hessen* in view of the duration of the marriage (26 years), but concluded that "the *Hessen* rule must be considered as no longer retraining its authority." The court went on to find that the Bradys' marriage was a "dead" one, and, "in its discretion," granted Mr. Brady a divorce on his cause of action for cruel and inhuman treatment. While the trial court does have broad discretion as to whether to grant a cruelty divorce (*see, e.g., Forcucci v. Forcucci*, 96 AD2d 751, *supra*), such a divorce cannot be granted simply because the court concludes that there is a "dead marriage." . . .

Order affirmed. . . .

---

Notwithstanding the fact no-fault divorce is now entrenched in our society, there is a small move in the opposite direction. In what is claimed to be an effort to strengthen marriage, a movement inspired largely by religious conservatives has been championing the so-called "covenant marriage." Louisiana in 1997 passed a "covenant marriage" law. The law permits spouses to voluntarily elect a more binding marriage by pledging to engage in pre-marital counseling about the purpose and seriousness of marriage and to take all reasonable steps to remain married for life. The law provides for limited grounds for divorce, but it specifically states domestic violence as one of them, and the counseling is not required if there are allegations of domestic violence or sexual abuse.

## Louisiana R.S. 9:307 (2016) Divorce or separation from bed and board in a covenant marriage; exclusive grounds.

A. Notwithstanding any other law to the contrary and subsequent to the parties obtaining counseling, a spouse to a covenant marriage may obtain a judgment of divorce only upon proof of any of the following:

(1) The other spouse has committed adultery.

(2) The other spouse has committed a felony and has been sentenced to death or imprisonment at hard labor.

(3) The other spouse has abandoned the matrimonial domicile for a period of one year and constantly refuses to return.

(4) The other spouse has physically or sexually abused the spouse seeking the divorce or a child of one of the spouses.

(5) The spouses have been living separate and apart continuously without reconciliation for a period of two years.

(6) (a) The spouses have been living separate and apart continuously without reconciliation for a period of one year from the date the judgment of separation from bed and board was signed.

(b) If there is a minor child or children of the marriage, the spouses have been living separate and apart continuously without reconciliation for a period of one year and six months from the date the judgment of separation from bed and board was signed; however, if abuse of a child of the marriage or a child of one of the spouses is the basis for which the judgment of separation from bed and board was obtained, then a judgment of divorce may be obtained if the spouses have been living separate and apart continuously without reconciliation for a period of one year from the date the judgment of separation from bed and board was signed. . . .

C. The counseling referenced in Subsections A and B of this Section, or other such reasonable steps taken by the spouses to preserve the marriage, as required by the Declaration of Intent signed by the spouses, shall occur once the parties experience marital difficulties. If the spouses begin living separate and apart, the counseling or other intervention should continue until the rendition of a judgment of divorce.

D. Notwithstanding the provisions of Subsection C of this Section, the counseling referenced in Subsections A and B of this Section shall not apply when the other spouse has physically or sexually abused the spouse seeking the divorce or a child of one of the spouses.

## II. Domestic Violence, Economic Issues and the Distribution of Marital Assets

One criticism of no-fault divorce has been that it alleviates responsibility for domestic violence in a marriage and, therefore, could have negative financial implications for a victim during the division of marital assets. However, in most no-fault states, fault grounds remain as an option. In addition, judges in many jurisdictions retain discretion to apportion assets with marital "fault" in mind.

### A. California's Divorce Law

Although California is a no-fault state, and marital assets upon divorce are divided in the community property tradition[10] it is a state that specifically provides

---

10. ALISON CLARKE-STEWART & CORNELIA BRENTANO, DIVORCE: CAUSES AND CONSEQUENCES 15 (2006).

that courts must consider the existence of domestic violence when determining asset allocations.[11]

## Cal. Fam. Code § 4320 (2016) Circumstances to be considered in ordering spousal support

In ordering spousal support under this part, the court shall consider all of the following circumstances:

(a) The extent to which the earning capacity of each party is sufficient to maintain the standard of living established during the marriage, taking into account all of the following:

(1) The marketable skills of the supported party; the job market for those skills; the time and expenses required for the supported party to acquire the appropriate education or training to develop those skills; and the possible need for retraining or education to acquire other, more marketable skills or employment.

(2) The extent to which the supported party's present or future earning capacity is impaired by periods of unemployment that were incurred during the marriage to permit the supported party to devote time to domestic duties.

(b) The extent to which the supported party contributed to the attainment of an education, training, a career position, or a license by the supporting party.

(c) The ability of the supporting party to pay spousal support, taking into account the supporting party's earning capacity, earned and unearned income, assets, and standard of living.

(d) The needs of each party based on the standard of living established during the marriage.

(e) The obligations and assets, including the separate property, of each party.

(f) The duration of the marriage.

(g) The ability of the supported party to engage in gainful employment without unduly interfering with the interests of dependent children in the custody of the party.

(h) The age and health of the parties.

(i) Documented evidence, including a plea of nolo contendere, of any history of domestic violence, as defined in Section 6211, between the parties or perpetrated by either party against either party's child, including, but not limited to, consideration of

---

11. There are eight community property states: Arizona, California, Idaho, Louisiana, Nevada, New Mexico, Texas and Washington. Their laws were influenced by the Spanish-Catholic traditions. In these states each party owns one-half of the income and property that are acquired during the marriage. The rest of the states, influenced by the English common law, divide marital property upon dissolution of the marriage under what is known as an "equitable distribution" system, using a set of factors to determine how to fairly split the parties' financial assets. *See* Lenore J. Weitzman, The Divorce Revolution 5 (1985).

emotional distress resulting from domestic violence perpetrated against the supported party by the supporting party, and consideration of any history of violence against the supporting party by the supported party.

(j) The immediate and specific tax consequences to each party.

(k) The balance of the hardships to each party.

(l) The goal that the supported party shall be self-supporting within a reasonable period of time. Except in the case of a marriage of long duration as described in Section 4336, a "reasonable period of time" for purposes of this section generally shall be one-half the length of the marriage. However, nothing in this section is intended to limit the court's discretion to order support for a greater or lesser length of time, based on any of the other factors listed in this section, Section 4336, and the circumstances of the parties.

(m) The criminal conviction of an abusive spouse shall be considered in making a reduction or elimination of a spousal support award in accordance with Section 4324.5 or 4325.

(n) Any other factors the court determines are just and equitable.

## Cal. Fam. Code § 4325 (2016) Rebuttable presumption for conviction of domestic violence

(a) In any proceeding for dissolution of marriage where there is a criminal conviction for an act of domestic violence perpetrated by one spouse against the other spouse entered by the court within five years prior to the filing of the dissolution proceeding, or at any time thereafter, there shall be a rebuttable presumption affecting the burden of proof that any award of temporary or permanent spousal support to the abusive spouse otherwise awardable pursuant to the standards of this part should not be made.

(b) The court may consider documented evidence of a convicted spouse's history as a victim of domestic violence, as defined in Section 6211, perpetrated by the other spouse, or any other factors the court deems just and equitable, as conditions for rebutting this presumption.

(c) The rebuttable presumption created in this section may be rebutted by a preponderance of the evidence.

---

In addition, if before the final entry of divorce, one spouse wins a civil judgment against the other for an act of domestic violence, then the court may order that payment of that judgment come out of the abuser's share of the community property.

## Cal. Fam. Code § 2603.5 (2016) Judgment of spousal abuse enforced against abusive spouse's community property

The court may, if there is a judgment for civil damages for an act of domestic violence perpetrated by one spouse against the other spouse, enforce that judgment against the abusive spouse's share of community property, if a proceeding for dissolution of marriage or legal separation of the parties is pending prior to the entry of final judgment.

## In re Marriage of Cauley
### California Court of Appeal
### 138 Cal. App. 4th 1100 (2006)

MIHARA, J.

Under Family Code section 4325, there is a rebuttable presumption that an award of spousal support not be made to a spouse who has been convicted of intraspousal domestic violence. Appellant Eileen J. Cauley has been convicted of domestic violence against respondent Gerald W. Cauley. The parties' settlement agreement provided that spousal support was not subject to modification or termination. The trial court found that the presumption of section 4325 applied here and had not been rebutted. It then granted respondent's motion to terminate spousal support to appellant. We find no merit to appellant's contentions and affirm.

### I. Statement of Facts

On November 25, 2002, respondent filed a petition for dissolution of marriage. The parties had been married for 18 years. In March 2003, respondent requested a temporary restraining order. His declaration stated that appellant had threatened his life in numerous telephone messages and calls and had physically attacked him several times during the prior year. The court issued the temporary restraining order, which was due to expire in July 2003.

On June 25, 2003, the parties signed a stipulation for judgment. It provided in relevant part: "Husband shall pay Wife for her support and maintenance $5,250.00 per month, payable via direct deposit on the 10th day of each calendar month commencing immediately after the effective date of this Agreement. These spousal support payments shall continue until Wife's remarriage or the death of either Husband or Wife, whichever occurs first, or until further order of the court. These payments shall be non-modifiable with the following exceptions which may form the basis for a modification of the above amount: 1) Wife's cohabitation with a partner; 2) Husband's loss of income either due to disability, or job loss." The trial court retained jurisdiction as to spousal support until March 31, 2010. Respondent also agreed to take his request for a restraining order off calendar with prejudice.

On August 6, 2003, appellant flew to Florida where respondent was living with his girlfriend and her son. During the next couple of days, appellant removed items from the exterior of respondent's house, sprayed herbicide in the garden, ripped out plants, killed his fish, stole personal property, and threw numerous items in the bay behind the house. At some point during appellant's crime spree, respondent opened his door, and she sprayed herbicide in his face. When his girlfriend arrived, appellant sprayed her as well. Appellant was eventually arrested for domestic battery.

On August 12, 2003, respondent obtained a temporary restraining order in Florida. On September 10, 2003, appellant did not appear at the hearing, and the trial court made the restraining order effective for one year. It ordered appellant to have no contact with respondent.

On August 15, 2003, appellant sent respondent's attorney a letter in which she threatened to accuse respondent of rape if he did not have the domestic battery charges dropped. A few days later, appellant contacted the police department and reported that respondent had raped her.

Appellant also repeatedly violated the restraining order. She sent written and electronic correspondence to respondent. She made telephone calls, and left messages on his voicemail. Appellant threatened respondent, his wife, members of their families, and his employer. Between September 2003 and March 2004, appellant made more than 1,000 calls, and left nearly 500 messages, which totaled almost 70 hours of recordings. Though respondent changed his home telephone to an unlisted number, appellant was able to obtain his new cell phone number within a few weeks, and the calls continued. In February 2004, appellant threatened the president of the company that employed respondent. On March 22, 2004, appellant left over 52 messages on respondent's voice mail.

Since appellant had left Florida, the prosecutor was seeking her extradition from California for violations of the restraining order. In the meantime, on March 30, 2004, respondent requested a restraining order in California so that California authorities could prosecute her if she continued to harass him. On the same date, respondent filed a motion for modification and termination of spousal support based on appellant's acts of domestic violence.

In the spring of 2004, Florida issued a warrant for appellant's arrest on the charge of felony aggravated stalking and a $1,000,000 bond was set. On April 16, 2004, appellant was arrested in San Jose and eventually extradited to Florida. On May 17, 2004, she pleaded guilty to felony aggravated stalking and was placed on five years probation. Appellant's conditions of probation required her to attend anger management training, receive alcoholic/ psychiatric treatment, and not contact the victims.

Meanwhile, on April 26, 2004, the court in California ordered a temporary cessation in spousal support under section 4325, and set the case for a review hearing on October 18, 2004. The court also granted respondent's request for a restraining order. Appellant was ordered to have no contact with respondent, his wife, and her son for three years.

On May 17, 2004, appellant was released from custody in Florida. Less than two weeks later, appellant again began making telephone calls in which she threatened to harm respondent and his coworkers. She made over 91 calls between May 28 and October 11, 2004. Though the trial court had set spousal support temporarily at $0, appellant repeatedly threatened respondent if he did not pay her. Based on this conduct, Florida again charged appellant with felony aggravated stalking as well as violation of the conditions of her probation.

On October 13, 2004, the review hearing on the spousal support order was held. Appellant did not attend. The trial court then set a hearing for appellant to present evidence to rebut the presumption that she was not entitled to spousal support. Counsel agreed to provide declarations and to use the hearing for cross-examination and argument. Later that same afternoon, appellant was arrested on the Florida charges.

Prior to the hearing on December 15, 2004, respondent submitted two declarations. Though appellant did not submit a declaration, her counsel made an offer of proof on her behalf at the hearing. He stated that there was a nonmodifiable settlement agreement that provided for spousal support, that appellant was a convicted felon who was an alcoholic with no job and no training, and that appellant made the telephone calls to find out when she would receive her support payments. Respondent's counsel argued that respondent and his family had lived through "two years of sheer hell," that appellant had been in numerous alcohol treatment programs, and that appellant had violated court orders in both Florida and California.

## II. Discussion

### A. Termination of Spousal Support

. . . .

Relying on section 3591, appellant contends that the trial court erred in applying section 4325 in the present case. Section 3591, subdivision (c) states in relevant part that "[a]n agreement for spousal support may not be modified or revoked to the extent that a written agreement . . . specifically provides that the spousal support is not subject to modification or termination." Here the parties agreed that spousal support would not be modified or terminated unless appellant cohabited with a partner or appellant suffered a loss of income. Respondent counters that enforcement of the settlement agreement would violate the public policy against domestic violence.

. . . .

In this case, we conclude that the public policy against enforcement of the nonmodifiable spousal support provision clearly outweighs any interest in its enforcement. Though there is a strong public policy in favor of enforcing the spousal support provisions of the parties' settlement agreement and appellant would forfeit a substantial amount of spousal support if there were no enforcement, the parties could not have reasonably expected that respondent would finance his own abuse by appellant. Balanced against these factors, we note that there is a significant public policy against domestic violence. . . . Refusal to enforce the spousal support provision will further this policy against domestic violence, because appellant will have fewer financial resources to continue her harassment of respondent. We must also emphasize that appellant's misconduct is extremely serious and has continued despite incarceration and court orders in California and Florida. Moreover, there is a direct connection between appellant's misconduct and the nonmodifiable spousal support provision. As previously stated, appellant has relied on respondent's obligations to provide her with the financial ability to harm him. While we acknowledge the fundamental principle that former spouses are free to specify the terms of their settlement agreement, we decline to enforce the spousal support provision in the present case. Accordingly, the trial court did not err in concluding that appellant failed to rebut the presumption of section 4325.

Appellant also claims that respondent has other remedies. She points out that she has 83 counts of contempt pending against her in California and is facing additional charges in Florida, and thus she could potentially be incarcerated. This factor has no relevance. The fact that appellant has continued to threaten and harass respondent despite court orders does not render section 4325 inapplicable. Moreover, appellant's references to termination of spousal support as punishment misconstrue the effects of section 4325. Section 4325 embodies a legislative determination that victims of domestic violence not be required to finance their own abuse.[12]

... The order is affirmed. ...

## B. The Consideration of Domestic Violence in the Awarding of Marital Assets in Other Jurisdictions

Elsewhere, marital dissolution statutes leave open the door to apportion property based on a "fault" standard, with the criteria on which to base the division left to the discretion of the court. In describing the various methods courts use to distribute marital assets and property, Prof. Barbara Bennett Woodhouse, in an article, *Sex, Lies and Dissipation: The Discourse of Fault in a No-Fault Era*, 82 Geo. L.J. 2525, 2532–33 (1994), categorized them as "fault-blind," "fault-driven," and "fault-regarding."

> Fault-blind jurisdictions completely embrace the theory that merit and blame within marriage are unknowable or irrelevant to divorce. At every opportunity, fault-blind systems close the door on allegations of bad behavior. Fault-driven systems, by contrast, single out specific types of conduct—usually adultery or abandonment—and make them not only relevant but dispositive of spousal rights and obligations. In such jurisdictions, a spouse who commits one act of adultery may be barred from receiving alimony, no matter how severe the need or disparate the parties' resources.
>
> Occupying the middle ground, fault-regarding states continue to weigh issues of merit and blame, but expand their focus from the traditional grounds such as adultery and abandonment to the wider context of the couple's particular marriage, general situation, and shared social norms. In contrast to fault driven systems, a fault-regarding system adopts notions of comparative blame. When the balance of fault is truly lopsided, taking into account all the circumstances, a fault-regarding system uses an award of alimony or a

---

12. [n5] Appellant argues that when respondent entered into a nonmodifiable support agreement, he gambled that she would not engage in domestic violence and lost. However, we remain unpersuaded that victims must be required to financially support those who have been convicted of harming them.

larger share of the marital property to compensate the victim and punish the wrongful conduct.

In New York, judges have eschewed basing property awards on marital fault, unless the acts of the fault-bearing spouse were so blatantly egregious they "shocked the conscience" of the court.

---

## Havell v. Islam

New York Supreme Court, Appellate Division, First Department

301 A.D.2d 339 (2002)

WILLIAMS, P.J.

Plaintiff wife commenced this divorce action in May 1999. The facts elicited at trial show that the parties had been married for 21 years and parented six children, four of whom are minors. Both hold Bachelor of Arts and Master of Arts degrees; the husband from Cambridge University in England, the wife from Manhattanville College and New York University, respectively.

The couple met while working at Citibank, the wife from 1970–1978, the husband from 1970–1988. At the time of their marriage, he was earning $45,000 a year and she was earning $40,000 a year at Lehman Brothers in the international banking and securities trading group. The wife left Lehman Brothers in late 1983, at which time she was earning $150,000–175,000 a year; at the time, the husband was earning about the same. The husband's annual income at Citibank peaked at $300,000–350,000 before his position was eliminated in 1988. He received a salary of $110,000 from Citibank until 1990 and was unemployed thereafter. Subsequently, the wife was the family's sole economic support.

After leaving Lehman Brothers, the wife took a position in 1984 with Neuberger Berman in order to launch a fixed income department. Her starting salary was $150,000 plus a percentage of fees of assets managed. In four years, she was earning over $1 million per year. In 1996, she was released from Neuberger and received a compensation package of $6,841,427 plus a refund of her investment which exceeded $500,000. She proceeded to start her own company, Havell Capital Management, specializing in the management of fixed income assets. By the time of trial, December 2000, her company had approximately $250 million of assets under management, she was a 50.5% owner receiving a draw of $320,000 per year and an estimated income of $879,167.

In the course of the marriage, the couple acquired valuable real estate, including a brownstone on East 78th Street in Manhattan, a country home in Sandisfield, Massachusetts and a second country home in North Salem, New York. The family took several vacations a year and entertained at the brownstone and the North Salem home.

Meanwhile, despite plaintiff wife's alleged encouragement, defendant declined to seek any business opportunities and instead gardened, read and attempted several writing projects. He claimed to be engaged in running the household and child-rearing. Throughout the marriage, defendant was verbally and/or physically abusive to plaintiff and his children on numerous occasions.

On April 15, 1999, plaintiff advised defendant that she would seek a divorce. Several days later, on April 21, 1999, he broke the locks on the door to her bedroom, where she slept separately from him. On April 22, 1999, their daughter Chloe's birthday, he set his alarm clock to waken him at 4:00 A.M. and entered his wife's bedroom at approximately 5:00 A.M. The wife awoke to the sight of him entering her bedroom, taking a seat in a chair at the foot of her bed, and wearing yellow rubber gloves and carrying a barbell. When she sat up, he went over, pinned the wife to the bed with his knee and began beating her viciously on the head, face, neck and hands with the barbell. Plaintiff, who was conscious during the incident, observed her blood, teeth and bone spattering everywhere. Her screams brought their three young daughters, Chloe, Clarissa and Georgina, aged 15, 12 and 10 respectively, into the room where defendant told Chloe that he had killed her mother. As Chloe tried to call 911 for assistance, defendant twice attempted to renew his attack on plaintiff, first with a long piece of pipe and then with a large towel over her face. The daughters held him off her until the police arrived and arrested defendant.

Plaintiff's injuries were severe. She suffered, among other things, multiple contusions, a broken nose and jaw, broken teeth, multiple lacerations, and neurological damage. Her medical treatment included the surgical installation of a titanium plate over her eye, over 20 hours of painful dental procedures, and many other oral and facial surgical procedures over the next several months. Afterwards, she has suffered pain, dizziness, headaches, nightmares, sleeplessness and post-traumatic stress syndrome. Despite these problems plus horrible bruises and scarring, plaintiff was back at work on a part-time basis three weeks after the attack.

Defendant was indicted for attempted murder, pleaded guilty to assault in the first degree on August 11, 2000 and was sentenced subsequently to 8 1/4 years in prison. Prior to that, on August 13, 1999, defendant was held in contempt by Justice Silbermann [sic] for entering the North Salem residence in violation of orders of protection. He pleaded guilty to that charge on December 7, 2000 and was sentenced to a 30-day jail term to run concurrently with the sentence in the assault case.

Plaintiff wife commenced this divorce action in May 1999. In a pendente lite order dated June 17, 1999, the court granted her motion for distribution of 100% of the proceeds from the sale of the East 78th Street residence to the extent of ordering that all but $150,000 of the expected proceeds, $3.9 million, be retained by the wife to purchase a new residence and for ordinary living expenses. The $150,000 was awarded to the unemployed husband for his living expenses. This Court affirmed that order (*Havell v. Islam*, 273 A.D.2d 164, 710 N.Y.S.2d 51). Prior to trial, the husband was awarded additional monies from that sale to bring his total award to $377,500. This additional award was also affirmed by this Court (*Havell v. Islam*, 288 A.D.2d 160, 734 N.Y.S.2d 841).

The net value of the marital assets is not in question, as the parties are in substantial agreement that it is in the area of $13 million.

. . . .

The court's decision after trial granted plaintiff a divorce, denied defendant counsel fees and equitable distribution beyond the pendente lite award, and distributed all other marital assets to plaintiff. . . .

The court held that defendant's vicious assault on plaintiff was so egregious as to "shock the conscience" and relied on its equitable powers to render justice between the parties. It specifically rejected defendant's contention that a spouse's egregious conduct should not be considered as a factor in equitable distribution unless the behavior had some economic impact. The court denied defendant counsel fees, reasoning that under the circumstances, it would be inequitable to require plaintiff to pay them. The court also declined to award defendant a setoff, in the amount of the marital property denied him, against plaintiff's potential judgment in her personal injury action against him.

. . . .

The general rule in New York is that marital fault should not be considered in determining equitable distribution (Scheinkman, Practice Commentaries, McKinney's Cons Laws of NY, Book 14, Domestic Relations Law C236B:27, at 437–440). However, the leading New York cases on when and how marital fault may be considered are *O'Brien v. O'Brien* (66 N.Y.2d 576, 589–590, 498 N.Y.S.2d 743, 489 N.E.2d 712) and *Blickstein v. Blickstein* (99 A.D.2d 287, 290–293, 472 N.Y.S.2d 110, *appeal dismissed* 62 N.Y.2d 802; *see also McMahan v. McMahan*, 100 A.D.2d 826, 474 N.Y.S.2d 974). These cases hold that Domestic Relations Law § 236(B)(5)(d), the statute listing the 13 factors to be considered in awards of equitable distribution, provides that marital fault may be taken into consideration pursuant to the statute's catchall provision (formerly clause [10], now clause [13] pursuant to a 1986 amendment), which allows consideration of "any other factor" which may be "just and proper." They go on to specify that marital fault only be taken into consideration where "the marital misconduct is so egregious or uncivilized as to bespeak of a blatant disregard of the marital relationship—misconduct that 'shocks the conscience' of the court thereby compelling it to invoke its equitable power to do justice between the parties" (*Blickstein* 99 A.D.2d at 292; *see also O'Brien* 66 N.Y.2d at 589).

On this appeal, defendant contends that subsequent cases regarding the consideration of fault have added a second, economic component to the *Blickstein* test: whether the spouse's misconduct has "such adverse physical and/or psychological effect upon the innocent spouse so as to interfere with her ability to be, or to become self-supporting" (*Wenzel v. Wenzel*, 122 Misc 2d 1001, 1002, 472 N.Y.S.2d 830 [husband, without provocation, attacked wife with a knife inflicting multiple stab wounds and leaving her for dead]; *see also Thompson v. Thompson*, NYLJ, Jan. 5, 1990, at 28, col 3 [husband raped his 17-year-old stepdaughter]). . . .

It is our view that *McCann v. McCann* (156 Misc 2d 540, 593 N.Y.S.2d 917) best explains what the appellate courts mean by "egregious" and offers a framework that harmonizes those decisions with *Wenzel* and *Thompson*. The *McCann* court found a husband's conduct to be nonegregious where he deceitfully entered into a marriage based upon his promise to make every effort to have children with his wife and he subsequently refused to fulfill that promise after several years of lying, resulting in the wife, who relied on his promise, passing the age of child-bearing without having a child. *McCann*, discussing the *Blickstein* formulation, explained that "egregious" and "conscience-shocking" have no meaning outside of a specific context, and that conduct is "conscience-shocking, evil, or outrageous" only when "the act in question grievously injures some highly valued social principle." (*Id.* at 545.) Therefore, the court concluded, conduct no matter how violent or repugnant is "egregious" only where it substantially implicates an important social value. The court further noted that the cases that have taken marital fault into consideration involved the paramount social values: preservation of human life and "the integrity of the human body" (*McCann* 156 Misc. 2d at 547).

Thus, the *McCann* court, unlike the *Wenzel* and *Thompson* courts, does not include impairment of economic independence in the definition of "egregious," but does explain the effort on the part of those courts to lend meaning to the term in the marital fault context and to identify a harm to a significant social value. Its reading of *Blickstein* also invokes the important rule in equity that a person should not be allowed to profit from his own wrongdoing, as defendant here callously seeks to do.

. . . .

As for the assault on plaintiff, we find that the trial court gave the incident its due consideration. The cases defendant cites in this regard as comparably egregious to his own are readily distinguishable factually. For instance, he relies on *Brancoveanu v. Brancoveanu* (145 A.D.2d 395, 535 N.Y.S.2d 86, *lv. dismissed* 73 NY2d 994, 538 N.E.2d 358, 540 N.Y.S.2d 1006), where the husband contracted for the wife's murder, abandoned the scheme prior to implementation and, upon equitable distribution, recovered, among other things, 40% of the proceeds from the sale of the marital residence. Obviously defendant's conduct herein was far more shocking and despicable. The authorities that plaintiff cites in this regard, such as *Venkursawmy v. Venkursawmy* (NYLJ, Mar. 16, 1990, at 22, col 5 [husband poured gasoline on wife and struck match]) and *Wenzel v. Wenzel (supra* [husband stabbed wife numerous times with knife and left her for dead]), are far more indicative of the circumstances at bar; in those cases the court awarded no marital property to the attempted murderer/spouse. Moreover, it is precisely the type of "egregious," "conscience-shocking" conduct defined in *McCann*.

. . . .

Accordingly, the judgment of the Supreme Court, New York County . . . should be affirmed. . . .

---

In contrast, Nevada, a community property state, does not permit property division or a child support award to be determined on whether either party has engaged in marital misconduct or abuse absent proof the conduct had some economic impact on the community property.

## Wheeler v. Upton-Wheeler
Nevada Supreme Court
113 Nev. 1185 (1997)

### FACTS

Appellant John Wheeler and respondent Ruthann Upton-Wheeler were married on December 21, 1982. The parties have one child, Lindsay Wheeler, born on August 28, 1978. On July 21, 1993, Ruthann filed a complaint for divorce. A trial was held on September 30, 1994. At the trial, photographs of Ruthann depicting numerous bruises allegedly inflicted by John were admitted into evidence over the objection of John's counsel. The district court indicated that the photographs would be admitted for the limited purpose of determining whether Ruthann's request for an unequal division of community property should be granted.

A judgment was entered on February 24, 1995, granting joint legal custody of Lindsay to both parties and physical custody of Lindsay to John. Ruthann was granted liberal visitation rights. The court further ordered that Ruthann's child support obligation would be $436 per month, payable until Lindsay turned eighteen in two years. The parties' residence was awarded to John, with John paying Ruthann $18,500 for her fifty-percent portion of the net equity in the house. John was ordered to pay Ruthann $10,000 by November 15, 1994. Regarding the remaining $8,500, the court stated that "[Ruthann] shall additionally receive credit from [John] in an amount equivalent to [Ruthann's] obligation to pay child support determined at the rate of $436.00 per month which would otherwise have been paid until the parties' child emancipates." The district court further stated:

> The Court finds that a compelling reason exists to make an unequal disposition of the community property. The Court bases this finding on a review of the evidence and finds that an abusive relationship existed between the parties in which the Plaintiff suffered from Defendant's conduct. Therefore, the Court makes the following division of property . . . .

As an additional consequence to John for the alleged abuse, the district court determined that whatever child support obligation remained after the $8,500 payment for the house was satisfied, Ruthann would not be required to pay. Thus, Ruthann would pay absolutely no child support.

On March 6, 1995, John filed a proper person motion to set aside the judgment and order a new trial pursuant to NRCP 59 and 60. Ruthann filed an opposition to John's motion. On April 11, 1995, the district court entered an order denying John's motion to set aside the judgment and order a new trial. John appeals from the final judgment and the order denying his motion for a new trial.

## CHILD SUPPORT

John contends that the district court abused its discretion by not following the mandatory guidelines for a determination of child support. Specifically, John contends that based upon Ruthann's wage statement, child support should have been awarded at the maximum amount of $500 per month, rather than $436 per month. John further contends that the district court abused its discretion in releasing Ruthann from any support obligation because of alleged fault of John, specifically, his alleged abuse of Ruthann. John argues that this is in clear violation of Nevada statutes.

. . . .

The district court . . . erred in releasing Ruthann from any support obligation because of John's alleged abuse. NRS 125B.080(4) states that "the minimum amount of support that may be awarded by a court in any case is $100 per month per child, unless the court makes a written finding that the obligor is unable to pay the minimum amount." NRS 125B.080(9) provides a number of factors which the court may consider when adjusting the amount of child support, but does not include one parent's physical abuse of the other parent. The child support portion of the district court judgment in this case states as follows:

> The Court finds that based upon Plaintiff's income, child support pursuant to the statutory formula would be approximately $436.00 per month, payable until the child is emancipated. However, Plaintiff is released from this obligation as part of the unequal distribution of property justified by the Defendant's abusive conduct towards Plaintiff.

The district court did not cite an appropriate reason to deviate from the mandatory child support guidelines.

Even if a legitimate compelling reason existed to support an unequal distribution of property, such unequal distribution could not be accomplished by reducing or eliminating Ruthann's obligation to pay child support. In *Westgate v. Westgate*, 110 Nev. 1377, 887 P.2d 737 (1994), the district court reduced the father's child support obligation in half to penalize the mother for violating the father's visitation rights. We determined that the district court erred in reducing the father's child support obligation because NRS 125B.080 does not list punishment for failure to comply with a visitation agreement as a reason to reduce child support. *Id.* at 1380, 887 P.2d at 739.

Similarly, in the case at hand, the district court did not simply reduce, but completely eliminated Ruthann's child support obligation because John allegedly abused Ruthann. NRS 125B.080 does not list punishment for alleged abuse of a spouse as a reason to decrease the child support obligation of the abused spouse. Additionally, by completely releasing Ruthann from any child support obligation, the district court violated NRS 125B.080(4), which requires that child support be awarded at a minimum of $100 per month per child, unless the court finds that the obligor is unable to pay the minimum amount. The district court did not cite any reason, other than the alleged abuse, for releasing Ruthann from her child support obligation. Consequently, the district court erred in releasing Ruthann from her obligation.... We conclude that, although the district court erred in calculating the amount of child support to be awarded, a new trial is not warranted. Accordingly, the district court did not abuse its discretion in denying John's motion for a new trial on this issue. We remand this issue to the district court for a determination, based on the evidence presented at trial, of the appropriate amount of child support to be awarded pursuant to the mandatory child support guidelines.

## UNEQUAL DISTRIBUTION OF COMMUNITY PROPERTY

John contends that the district court violated NRS 125.150 by making an unequal distribution of community property based on its assessment that John had physically abused Ruthann during the course of their marriage. NRS 125.150(1)(b) provides that:

In granting a divorce, the court:

> (b) Shall, to the extent practicable, make an equal disposition of the community property of the parties, except that the court may make an unequal disposition of the community property in such proportions as it deems just if the court finds a compelling reason to do so and sets forth in writing the reasons for making the unequal disposition.

... Thus, the issue in this case is whether spousal abuse constitutes a "compelling reason" to make an unequal distribution of property.

In 1993, the legislature amended NRS 125.150(1)(b) to provide for an equal division of community property, rather than an equitable division. See 1993 Nev. Stat., ch. 135, § 1, at 240. It appears that in amending NRS 125.150(1)(b), the legislature wanted to ensure that Nevada would remain a no-fault divorce state....

Accordingly, we conclude that, except for a consideration of the economic consequences of spousal abuse or marital misconduct, evidence of spousal abuse or marital misconduct does not provide a compelling reason under NRS 125.150(1)(b) for making an unequal disposition of community property. If spousal abuse or marital misconduct of one party has had an adverse economic impact on the other party, it may be considered by the district court in determining whether an unequal division of community property is warranted.

Consequently, to the extent that it relied on evidence of spousal abuse as it related to the respective merits of the parties, rather than whether the abuse had an economic impact, the district court erred in making an unequal division of property. We therefore remand this issue to the district court for a determination, based on the evidence presented at trial, of whether spousal abuse had an adverse economic impact on Ruthann which would warrant an unequal distribution of the community property....

## C. Economic Issues for Domestic Violence Survivors

As the Sarah Buel article in the introductory chapter noted, one of the many reasons victims of domestic violence remain with their abusers is financial. A lack of funds in the pocket of a domestic violence victim may make the prospect of divorce overwhelming, if not impossible. In 2009, the New York State Office for the Prevention of Domestic Violence recognized this and issued a Bulletin describing the problem and suggestions to deal with it.

> Economic abuse is a means of control used against many victims of domestic violence by their partners. Tactics of economic abuse include: the abuser taking complete control of the couple's money, making a victim account for every penny spent, discontinuing the payment of bills (such as the mortage or utilities) without the victim's knowledge, defaulting on loans in the victim's name, and identity theft. Financial self-sufficiency is a critical factor in a victim's ability to escape abuse and maintain independence for themselves and their children.[13]

The New York State OPDV suggested that domestic violence victims check credit reports to be sure they are not being secretly saddled with debt by their abusive partners. Each of the major credit reporting agencies will provide consumers with one free credit report annually. In addition, victims of domestic violence must be careful to protect against identity theft through which an abuser can obtain credit cards, access to bank accounts and perpetuate financial mischief.[14]

Since 2005, the Allstate Foundation has focused on assisting victims of domestic violence attain financial independence and empowerment. The foundation commissioned a study in 2014, which showed that 78 percent of all Americans had no idea of the connection between domestic violence and financial abuse. While only eight percent of Americans claimed to be victims of economic abuse, its most common victims, 40 percent, were single mothers.[15]

The National Network to End Domestic Violence (NNEDV) reports that financial abuse is present in a staggering 98 percent of all abusive relationships. "As with other forms of abuse, financial abuse may begin subtly and progress over time. It may even look like love initially as abusers have the capacity to appear very charming and are masterful at manipulation," notes the NNEDV on its website.[16]

---

13. New York State Office for the Prevention of Domestic Violence, *Financial Issues and Domestic Violence,* OPDV BULLETIN/WINTER 2009.

14. *Id.*

15. Purple Purse: The Allstate Foundation, *Financial Abuse Survey,* www.purplepurse.com/get-the-facts/about-the-allstate-foundation/financial-abuse-survey, accessed November 22, 2016.

16. National Network to End Domestic Violence, *About Financial Abuse,* www.nnedv.org/resources/ejresources/about-financial-abuse.html, accessed November 22, 2016.

## III. Divorce Mediation and Domestic Violence

Accompanying the no-fault divorce revolution has been the growing reliance on mediation to settle divorce cases. It is considered faster, cheaper and less stressful than litigation, particularly when issues of fault are removed from the table. Mediation is described as "an alternative dispute resolution process... wherein the parties, with the assistance of a neutral person or persons, isolate disputed issues in order to consider options and alternative to reach consensual settlement."[17] Mediation is highly controversial where couples have domestic violence issues. In some states, it is forbidden by statute when domestic violence is present. What follows are three essays showing the evolving views about whether litigation, mediation or some combination of the two are best for divorcing couples when domestic violence is involved.

### CONNIE J.A. BECK & BRUCE D. SALES, FAMILY MEDIATION: FACTS, MYTHS AND FUTURE PROSPECTS 7, 12–13, 28–31 (2001)

....

Legislation mandating mediation for certain classes of cases (i.e., custody or visitation disputes) was first passed in Massachusetts and Connecticut in 1980, and California soon followed in 1981 (D.G. Brown, 1982). By 1991, there were at least 205 court-related divorce mediation programs, and in 1997 there were estimated to be at least 2,000 programs, many of which offered divorce mediation....

[T]here is a growing literature concerning specific instances when airing concerns face-to-face in mediation can be extremely detrimental to one or both parties and to their children. (Bryan, 1992; Fischer, Vidmar & Ellis, 1993; Grillo, 1991; Treuthart, 1993). Cases that include spousal abuse that are characterized by a "culture of violence" provide one example. Culture of violence relationships include three main characteristics. First, a pattern of abuse is present, which can include physical, emotional, familial (e.g., abuse to children and/or extended family), sexual, or financial abuse (e.g., the abuser controls all money and financial resources) or a combination of these. Second, a pattern of domination and control is present wherein the abuser maintains control over every aspect of the abused person's life. The abuser makes the rules for the family and enforces them by threats of future violence against the abused person as well as the person's children or extended family and friends. Emotional abuse and social isolation are common and eventually lead the abused person to feel depressed, alone, and fearful that no one will support her[21] or help her if she leaves. Eventually, the abused person is led to feel responsible for the abuse because of minor violations of the rules, even though the rules are seldom explicit and may change

---

17. CONNIE J.A. BECK & BRUCE D. SALES, FAMILY MEDIATION: FACTS, MYTHS, AND FUTURE PROSPECTS 3 (2001).

from day to day. Third, the culture of violence relationships include a pattern of denial and minimization of the abuse. Even when questioned, the abused spouse will deny the abuse or make excuses for why it must be her fault. Ellis (1990) explained that the family is regarded socially as a "private domain" where outsiders are extremely hesitant to intervene in disturbances within the family or come to the aid of even an assaulted wife or partner. In addition, privacy norms governing family relations dictate that observers' or victims' reporting spousal abuse is a deviation from these norms or "snitching." Thus, privacy norms surrounding families support and encourage abused spouses to keep the abuse a secret.

There is also empirical support in other disciplines for the notion that there are different types of marital violence. . . .

The notion that there are different types of marital violence and that these couples find their way into mediation is also supported in the mediation research. . . . [In one study] about 50% of the women reported that there was violence in the marriage and that the violence impaired their ability to communicate with the ex-spouse on an equal basis (Pearson, 1991, 1993). Of this 50%, approximately 33% of these women also reported that they felt they had less bargaining power in mediation (Pearson, 1991, 1993). The Alaska Judicial Council conducted a study in 1992 concerning visitation mediation and found that 68% of the parents who request mediation were ineligible because of a statutory requirement that excludes all cases involving domestic violence (Alaska Judicial Council, 1992). . . .

There are also documented security problems found at mediation program sites. Of the 56 court-mandated mediation programs in California, 33 reported that security problems or incidents had occurred in mediation sessions or related family court services ranging from physical violence directed at spouses and other family members to violence toward attorneys and mediators (Ricci et al., 1991). Although 14 of these programs reported having both bailiffs nearby to intervene in the event of violence or other security measures in place, 15 of these 33 had no provisions for security. . . . The programs reporting security problems also noted that they commonly confiscated weapons brought into their offices (Ricci et al., 1991).

The second reason why meeting face-to-face may be extremely detrimental is the actual communication pattern of the couple. Fischer et al. (1993) argued that all couples develop idiosyncratic modes of communication. Single words, facial expressions, gestures or tones of voice go unnoticed by outsiders but convey clear meaning to the couple. An abuser, therefore, is able to intimidate and control the abused person through hidden symbols that even the most astute mediator may not identify (Fischer et al., 1993). Such illicit communication stymies all meaningful airing of concerns.

. . . Mediators, like everyone, are incapable of identifying abusers' hidden signals; thus current screening procedures are useless for this population of abused women. At best, these screening procedures give legislators, program administrators, and mediators a sense of security that spousal abuse victims will be identified, and these procedures probably do identify a number of women who are willing to disclose their abuse. At worst, the screening fails to identify a number of abused women — the women who are most at risk of future violence. Therefore, the culture of violence victim is placed in a no-win situation. Identify the abuse and risk heightened future violence; refuse to identify the abuse and place herself in danger by simply attending a court-mandated, face-to-face session; or not respond or not attend the mediation sessions and risk contempt charges and possible sanctions for failing to appear at the sessions.

. . . .

## Nancy Ver Steegh, *Yes, No, and Maybe: Informed Decision Making About Divorce Mediation in the Presence of Domestic Violence*
9 Wm. & Mary J. Women & L. 145 (2003)

. . . .

### VI. Divorce Mediation When Domestic Violence Is an Issue

Although mediation provides a desirable alternative for many families, there are serious concerns about its use in cases of domestic violence. Some of these concerns arise from the mediation process itself and others stem from the varying quality of the conducted mediation.

A. Reasons Why Mediation Might Never Be Appropriate

1. Is Mediation Too Private?

Privacy and confidentiality are critical aspects of the mediation process. Both are necessary to encourage full disclosure and candid problem solving. Some women's advocates, however, are troubled by the private nature of mediation. After years of working to have domestic violence dealt with as a crime, they see mediation as potentially returning the issue "back into the shadows." Because criminal prosecution sends a public message to the abuser that his behavior is unacceptable, advocates fear that the abusers in mediation will not be held accountable for the abuse. Similarly, they fear that if these cases are removed from the courts, new favorable legal precedents will not be established.

Two factors mitigate these concerns. First, divorce mediation need not supplant the use of the criminal system. If an abuse survivor chooses to do so, she can file criminal charges, pursue a protective order, and mediate the divorce.... Consequently, each victim must make an individual assessment of whether the abuser will be deterred from further violence by criminal prosecution. Either way, she could proceed with mediation.

Proponents of mediation argue that the privacy of the process and the neutrality of the mediator increase the likelihood that the abuser will admit the abuse and accept help.

The adversarial approach to spousal abuse often actually encourages the husband to deny his past abusive behavior because his defense attorney will assist him in denying the offense.... In mediation, the mediator and the couple can immediately deal with the abuse because the neutral role of the mediator takes away the need for the mediator to be a judge determining what happened in the past and allows the mediator to focus on steps to remove any possibility of future allegations or occurrences of abuse....

Although more research is needed in this area, there is some evidence that mediation prevents future violence. Researchers Ellis and Stuckless report that voluntary multi-session mediation is more effective in preventing future violence than either coerced mediation or lawyer negotiations. Interestingly, they found that the preparation of affidavits with "hurtful" content may have undermined lawyers' efforts to end the abuse.

Some mediators specifically recommend that a protective order be pursued simultaneously with mediation and that the mediation sessions be used to reinforce the boundaries set in the order.

. . . .

### b. The Problem of Power Imbalance in Cases of Domestic Violence

In cases where domestic violence has taken place, there has already been a severe abuse of power and the consequent power imbalance can make mediation impossible. Barbara Hart argues that cooperation between spouses when domestic abuse had occurred is "an oxymoron." Others agree that especially where there has been a culture of battering coupled with severe abuse, the power imbalance is too great to be overcome in mediation. Victims may fear retaliatory violence if they disagree with the abuser, thus making negotiation impossible.

. . . .

Each couple differs with respect to power imbalance and relative power levels may change throughout the relationship. The power imbalance inherent in domestic violence will render some abuse survivors unable to mediate. However, this assumption cannot be made for all couples who have had violent incidents. Capacity to mediate can only be assessed on an individual level. However, if the couple and the mediator proceed with the mediation, the mediator needs to remain especially alert for power imbalances and be prepared to deal with them.

. . . .

### c. Dealing with Power Imbalances

In some cases, the power imbalance is too severe for mediation to take place. However, in less extreme cases, skilled mediators are equipped to deal with moderate power differentials....

Mediators watch for specific behaviors that indicate power imbalances. These include but are not limited to tone of voice, glaring, insults, passivity, threats, outbursts, and refusal to speak. In addition to behavioral cues, mediators watch for lopsided agreements....

Additional safeguards in such situations include independent legal advice and, to some extent, judicial review. If necessary, the mediator can end the mediation "on behalf" of the less empowered person.

....

3. Do Mediators Know What They Are Doing?

....

Mediators are expected to provide information to clients about their training, education, and expertise. Mediators are cautioned not to undertake domestic abuse cases without "appropriate and adequate" training. However, this language is very general and fails to specify anything about the desired training. Similarly, the American Law Institute requires that mediators be qualified to identify abuse....

Abuse survivors need to exercise special care in selecting a mediator because in some states, no training or credentials are required for mediators. In fact, only 70% of mediation programs surveyed report that mediators regularly attend domestic violence training programs. Families who have experienced domestic violence should only consider mediating with someone who has specialized domestic violence training and experience. Mediators should only undertake such cases if they are trained to understand the dynamics of domestic violence and have been taught special techniques for working with abusive families such as power balancing, screening, special safeguards, safety planning, and community referrals. This training should be followed up with experiential requirements including the co-mediation of cases and a lengthy period of case supervision....

## Dafna Lavi, *Divorce Involving Domestic Violence: Is Med-Arb Likely to be the Solution?*
14 Pepp. Disp. Resol. L.J. 91 (2014)

### Chapter One: Introduction

....

In recent decades we are unhappily witnessing an increase in two social phenomena: One, a dramatic increase in the incidence of domestic violence against women and the second, an increase in the rate of divorce. There are cases in which a couple may be part of both trends....

The academic discourse regarding this issue, examining whether divorce cases involving violence can suitably be handled in mediation proceedings, compares how such cases are handled by the mediation process and how they are handled by the judicial process. In effect, this discourse has developed against the background of the disappointment with the judicial process and from the manner of handling such cases. Proponents of mediation and its suitability for handling divorce cases involving violence point to the disadvantages of the judicial process while opponents of mediation point to its disadvantages. The problem arising from this discourse is precisely the fact that it is convincing! In other words, an examination of the discourse discloses that those who express serious reservations regarding the efficacy of the judicial process in handling such cases are correct, but those opposing the use of mediation, pointing out its failures and serious disadvantages in terms of handling such cases are also correct. These failures and disadvantages have not yet been satisfactorily resolved, in spite of empirical attempts at improvement, alongside a great deal of writing being done in the field. This article proposes, therefore, a third solution: Med-arb.

Med-arb is a hybrid process of two stages for dispute resolution that integrates mediation with arbitration and combines the advantages of both processes. This process, one of the most innovative methods of ADR, has been gaining in popularity in recent years in various countries around the world and in the various areas of applicability. . . .

### Chapter Two: Divorce Cases Involving Violence

. . . .

The judicial system operates upon the assumption that the judge can make an objective determination as to who is right and who is not, what the best outcome is for the family and what the correct solution is. However, according to its critics, in divorce cases this process ignores the emotional and psychological aspects of the conflict and puts the judges in an untenable position because most of them have not undergone sufficient training in such subjects. In effect, the judges are expected to solve problems within the family that neither the parties nor even professionals in the field would be able to solve.

Regarding the litigants themselves, a recent study found that 50 to 70 percent of couples involved in divorce litigation assert that the judicial system is "impersonal" and threatening. Their dissatisfaction focuses on the fact that the judicial process served to increase their feelings of anger and hostility towards their spouse. Divorcing couples described the litigation process as lengthy, expensive, inefficient and disempowering. . . .

B. Divorce Cases Involving Domestic Violence

. . . .

Firstly, in divorce cases complicated by domestic violence, the conflict is likely to be escalated in a particularly severe manner. The increased hostility between the parents has, in extreme cases, led to the murder of the parent who has been the victim of the abuse, or of the children, followed by suicide of the violent parent.

Secondly, in such cases, the traditional fault-based inquiry of the courts, focusing on whether domestic violence has indeed occurred, often fails to arrive at an accurate determination. Batterers often appear to be more credible witnesses, while victims may lack credibility. Moreover, emotional abuse is extremely difficult to prove in accordance with the rules of evidence, and cognitive dissonance makes it difficult to accept horrific allegations. Furthermore, many domestic violence cases come before the courts as contested custody and child support cases, with the element of violence being concealed by these labels. The adversarial system has been widely recognized as ineffective in promoting justice in such cases....

It seems that the fact that violence exists is not adequately taken into account by the courts in rendering decisions regarding child custody or visitation rights. Studies demonstrate that the abusive parent sometimes prevails in custody battles. However, even when the victim is awarded sole custody, the visitation rights of the other parent are likely to constitute a problem. At times the courts do not pay sufficient attention to questions of security related to such visits, giving the violent party the opportunity to manipulate the family. Moreover, many victims of domestic violence are reluctant to take legal recourse against their attackers due to concerns about the attendant publicity, the implications for their family's reputation, and the ability to keep the family together....

Chapter Four: Is Mediation Likely to Provide a Solution?
The Existing Academic Discussion

A. Divorce Mediation in General

Mediation is a process in which a neutral person assists disputing parties in identifying and discussing issues of concern, exploring various solutions, and guiding parties toward a settlement agreeable to all of them. The process is volitional and confidential. In cases involving divorce and related issues, many courts regard mediation as preferable to litigation.

. . . .

It must be remembered that the fundamental premise of mediation is that it is a process of interests-based negotiation, as contrasted with a discussion of positions that at times leads each party to become "locked into" his own position. In divorce cases, the main advantage of this interests-based focus over the position-based focus, or rights-based focus, of the judicial process is that the mediator is more likely to focus upon the concealed needs and interests of the parties and their children. In this manner, shared interests are often discovered, particularly regarding the children's welfare, which may constitute a basis for a mediation settlement....

B. Divorce Mediation Where Violence is Involved

On the face of things, all of the advantages of the mediation process in divorce cases—enumerated in the previous section—exist, and even more so, in divorce cases involving violence. The increased popularity of ADR methods, such as mediation in custody disputes involving domestic violence, is due to ADR's less adversarial nature, the enhanced ability of parents to keep their children out of the conflict, the protection ADR affords for the parents' rights, negotiation that is client-centered, and the focus of ADR on settlement without court involvement....

### (a) The Opponents' Position

I was forced to sit down with a man who for the past twelve years has abused me, intimidated me, controlled me by threats and scare tactics, emotionally tore me down and whom I truly fear....

#### i. The Component of Danger

The assertion is that the mediation process inherently endangers the woman. The danger of serious, even life-threatening physical harm is at issue. The very fact that the violent husband knows the precise time when the wife will be present at mediation meetings exposes her to serious danger. This danger may also await the mediator. Those raising this assertion point to legislation in twenty states of the United States that explicitly forbid the use of the mediation process in divorce cases involving violence. The argument is that mediation is not equipped to provide the woman with the protection she needs in the course of the process itself or afterwards. The periods of the most serious violence occur in response to the victim's attempt to leave the violent husband. At that point, the husband becomes desperate, feels his loss of control over his victim, and as a result is "pushed" to the use of desperate measures, in an attempt to retain his control over the wife. While the courts can issue protective orders where there is threat of violence from the husband, such tools are not available in the mediation process. Additionally, one should remember that it is not always possible to evaluate, in advance, the existence of present danger or its extent. Even the most violent of husbands is almost always equipped with a "public face." A mediator can never acquire precise information regarding the conduct of the violent husband the moment the mediation session ends.

Studies have found that mediation is less successful in preventing repeat violence than is the traditional judicial process. While 17% of violent husbands resorted to violence again after a mediation process, only 10% of violent husbands who had gone through a legal process, such as arrest, returned to the use of violence against their wives or former wives. Studies point to the fact that the phenomenon of violence after a mediation process is more common as opposed to violence after a judicial process. It seems that judicial processes permit the operation of two mechanisms of deterrence: preventing the violent husband's access to his wife and an effective sanction. Mediation does not permit this deterrent. The assertion, therefore, is that in comparison to the judicial process, the mediation process puts the woman at a greater risk of physical harm.....

#### ii. Disparity of Power between the Parties

. . . .

Once violence enters into the picture, the parties cannot approach the mediation table on an equal basis. Violence, by its very definition, includes a component of disparity of power and imbalance between the violent party and his victim. The presumption is that disparities of power between the parties in mediation are likely to lead to negative results, which would not be the same in a judicial process....

1) One of the serious concerns noted in the academic literature is that the victim will act out of fear and tend to make too many concessions due to the power

disparity. The assertion is that a mediation settlement based on fear lacks the necessary element of truly free consent, and, is consequently defective and inappropriate. If the victim and her violent husband arrive at a divorce settlement in a mediation process, the probability increases that provisions will be included that are unfair to the woman, with respect both to child custody and to financial matters. . . .

The wife's fear is even likely to bring about concessions in advance regarding relevant topics such as financial matters. Alternatively, the fear may cause the wife's "agreement" to discuss matters that are normally subject to a "procedural veto" in this type of dispute (e.g., the husband's visitation rights or joint custody of children, which present a real danger to her and the children). Beyond the wife's rights, which are likely to be infringed upon, the rights of the third party—the children—should be taken into account. A defective settlement that is arrived at due to disparity of powers between the parties, fear and negation of the truly free will of the wife, may have dire implications for the children as well.

2) Moreover, it must be remembered that abuse is also likely to include financial abuse, when the husband has absolute control of all of the financial means and deprives the wife of any information concerning their financial circumstances or access to means of payment. . . .

3) The violent husband weakens the wife, which is sometimes manifested by a isolation of the woman from the outside world. With the objective of retaining his total control over her and maintaining her absolute dependence (physical, emotional, financial, etc.) on him, the violent husband often isolates his wife from any outside environment whatsoever. Professionals talk about the fact that in an ironic manner, it is precisely in such a situation that the wife often develops absolute and exclusive dependency upon her violent husband. This is a direct result of years of isolation from the outside world, of prohibitions and distance from relatives and friends, sanctions for leaving the house without the husband's approval, etc. All of these strengthen the violent husband's means of control over the wife and, in a paradoxical manner, heightens the wife's dependence on him, increasing the disparity of power between them and the absolute denial of her freedom of choice.

4) At times the disparity of power between the parties is so great that it is no longer possible to speak only of denial of the wife's free choice or of her independence, but rather of annulment of her very being. . . .

In view of all of the above, the assertion is that in a situation where there is such a disparity of power and in view of the psychological-emotional state of the wife (and as a result of it), the wife is not capable of negotiating in a mediation process, and even if she does so, the quality of the settlement arrived at is pre-determined. . . .

### iii. The Mediator's Limitations

Various scholars throughout the world, as well as people working in the field (such as attorneys who represent women who have been victims of violence in divorce cases in the courts), raise concerns regarding the quality of the handling of such cases that can be provided by mediation. These concerns are raised both with respect to the various mediation programs (under the auspices of the courts as well as community or other kinds of mediation) and with respect to the mediator himself. The doubts relate to the very ability of the programs as well as the mediator to identify and screen cases involving violence and to handle them appropriately. One of the assertions is that mediation programs often operate under time pressures and deal with a heavy caseload. Community mediation programs are based, for the most part, on the work of volunteer mediators who have received only minimal training. These conditions make the handling of divorce disputes involving violence nearly impossible, and in any case certainly inappropriate, therefore carrying with them the potential for disastrous results. The mediator himself is even likely to fail to identify the extent of the violent party's influence on the victim during the mediation itself, right under the nose of the mediator. Often a violent husband has the ability to control his wife with a word, a movement or a hint of a movement, noticed or understood only by himself and his wife (like a code or hidden threat of violence). The wife may then easily agree to terms that will put her and her children's lives in danger, simply in order to get out of the room....

### iv. Additional Reasons for Objection

Additional reasons for objection to the use of mediation in divorce cases involving domestic violence cited in the scholarly literature with less frequency are that it "preserves the power paradigm," "it cheapens and distorts the phenomenon of domestic violence," "it creates a clash between concepts," and "the feminist argument."...

Additionally, mediation is even likely to contribute to a distorted perspective regarding the phenomenon of domestic violence: The phenomenon of domestic violence is not caused due to conflict of any kind between the husband and the wife. Focusing on the conflict as the "source" of the problem (as mediation does), creates a mistaken representation for which wife is also responsible (to some extent) for the abuse. In addition, the critics make the point that the failure to impose legal sanctions on a batterer conveys a message to society that domestic violence is merely a private matter and not a crime....

A further reason for opposition is "the clash between concepts." The autonomy of free will (of the parties to mediation) is one of the fundamental principles of the mediation process. "Violence," on the other hand, as it is broadly defined, includes any act that causes the victim to do something that she does not want to do, or to refrain from doing something that she wants to do, or causes her to be subject to scare tactics and threats.....

A further reason for opposition is "the feminist argument." Feminism contributed to the fact that domestic violence was removed from the private sphere, became the subject of legislation, and entered into public discourse. It also helped mold the way it is dealt with, including by the courts. "The private is public" is the central argument of second wave feminism. The feminist demand is, therefore, to turn the "private" into the "public" and to expose "private" oppression to public criticism in order to expand the scope of social and legal protection of women. . . .

Mediation, to a great extent, does the opposite. In other words, it transforms what is "public" into the "private." It may be said that the justice spoken of in the mediation process is individual justice. In other words, as distinguished from the judicial process, in which the results are determined according to the application of the law—legal norms of a general objective nature based upon principles considered important by those determining such norms—in the mediation process, the settlement agreement between the parties is fashioned according to individual norms, chosen by the parties, which are consistent with their personal feeling of justice (e.g., accepted custom, the rules of the market, ethical rules, religious law, etc.). This often happens as a result of the parties intentionally ignoring the general law (of course, where the law is dispositive and not cognitive). Here the feminist argument comes into play. According to the feminist argument, there are certain issues, such as family disputes on a background of violence, when it is not acceptable to permit the individual sense of justice of the parties to determine how they will end. The feminists did not struggle to transfer such issues from the private to the public realm and to enact general objective norms regarding them only to have such norms ignored and to return these issues to the private realm or to the realm of the individual sense of justice of any particular person. The opposition to mediation based on this reason argues that it is unacceptable to allow the violent party to be protected from public scrutiny and legal sanctions. There is the additional concern that by virtue of transferring the handling of the subject of domestic violence from the court to the privacy of the mediation process, new legal precedents will not be established. . . .

(b) The Proponents' Position

Those who support mediation in divorce cases involving violence assert that the mediation process should not be automatically ruled out for every divorce case in which there is some kind of domestic violence. Cases involving extreme levels of violence will indeed not be suitable for mediation, but in general the mediation process does have advantages over the judicial process even in divorce cases involving violence.

i. Elimination of the Component of Danger

Proponents of the use of mediation in divorce cases involving violence argue that "litigation is also dangerous." In effect, this proposal centers on the argument that there is relatively greater security provided by the judicial system when compared to the mediation process. Proponents say that this proposition is fundamentally erroneous. . . . .

Moreover, there are those who assert that the judicial process is even more dangerous than mediation. In the judicial process in general, particularly in the legal pleadings, the parties (under the influence of their attorneys) usually take extreme positions with the objective of portraying the opposing party in the most negative light possible. This is likely to escalate the danger when the violent husband discovers that a complaint of violence has been filed against him or when he is served with a complaint including allegations that he used violence....

Supporters of mediation argue that in comparison to the judicial process, mediation limits the component of danger and is likely to make a greater contribution to preventing violence by the former spouse.

### ii. The Mediator's Skills

....

Those supporting mediation propose the mediator's skills, acquired through specific training, are an answer to the assertions regarding his limitations. In other words, the assertion is that proper training of mediators is likely to resolve many of the reservations expressed by the opponents to mediation in divorce cases involving domestic violence....

The Model Standards of Practice for Divorce and Family Mediators provides that a mediator must have knowledge of family law and the psychological impact of a family crisis on the parents and the children. In addition to special training in the mediation process itself, mediators must also undergo training and education in the field of domestic violence and the subject of child abuse and neglect.

Empirical studies have given merit to the assumption of proponents of mediation that victims of violence are able to carry out negotiations efficiently instead of from a position of inferiority that is a result of power inequality between the parties engaged in mediation. These positive findings are attributed to the skills of the mediator regarding the mediator's ability to identify, screen, and gage the component of violence at the outset as well as appropriately deal with the problem of the power disparities and any other difficulties that such situation creates.

### iii. Screening and Adopting Appropriate Coping Strategies

Proponents of mediation in divorce cases involving violence assert that not all divorce cases involving violence are alike and that there are certainly many such cases that are can be dealt with appropriately through mediation. The proponents of mediation object to the sweeping generalization that any dispute between a separated couple that involves violence is unsuited for mediation. According to these proponents, screening at the outset should be preferable to exclusion from the outset. As a result of screening, disputes that are not appropriate for mediation will be removed from the agenda of the process (and the parties will be referred for different treatment), whereas those cases appropriate for mediation can receive appropriate treatment within the mediation process, from a wide spectrum of means of dealing with this issue, when the element of violence has been picked up in the preliminary screening....

A number of possible means of dealing with violence within the mediation process (to the extent that an element of violence has been identified during the screening but the case was not disqualified from being handled in mediation), are enumerated in the literature: the use of separate legal advice for each party (with the attorney for the victim being someone who has expertise in both the mediation process and the subject of domestic violence); the participation of additional experts in the process (including professionals and therapists); screening that accompanies the entire mediation process; frequent use of caucusing (with the content remaining confidential from the other party); the presence of armed guards during all of the mediation sessions alongside the accompaniment of a security guard to the parking area; the use of co-mediators (two mediators, one male and one female); the use of separate waiting areas and separate entrances for men and women; stopping the process when necessary; and, referring the victim to appropriate shelters or to programs for advice and assistance that specialize in domestic violence, when problems of security arise. The mediator always has the option to receive assistance from the court through referral of the parties for emergency interrogation or through evaluation of the case and its legal aspects. . . .

Additionally, knowledgeable mediators and mediation program administrators may also introduce both victims and abusers to other community and professional resources available to them. . . . Mediators can educate participants about a variety of options that may be available, including: batterers' treatment and anger management programs; alcohol and drug treatment; dual-diagnosis consultants and treatment; victim support and treatment; posttraumatic stress groups; therapy; supervised access and exchange facilities; reunification therapists; parenting coordination; assistance in implementing court-ordered parenting plans; treatment for traumatized children; parenting without violence classes; parenting education, skills training, and coaching; custody evaluation; child protection services; protective orders; removal of weapons; criminal penalties; court orders with triggers; suspended or supervised visitation; case management; interpreter services; housing and employment assistance; immigration services; establishing child support and paternity; child care; and advocacy.

### iv. Efficiency

The fact that the mediation process is less expensive and quicker than litigation has additional value in divorce cases involving violence, and this is a significant advantage a victim of domestic violence, who is naturally interested in concluding the dispute as quickly as possible (and at minimal financial cost).

### v. "Giving a Voice" and Empowerment of the Woman—the Feminist Argument

. . . .

Current critical feminist insights regarding the law assert, as mentioned above, that the judicial process does not faithfully fulfill its function of "giving women a voice" and therefore, a better alternative for dispute resolution is necessary. In comparison to the legal process, which is geared towards the competition and struggle identified with the male style, the mediation process is perceived as the "home court" of women. One of the advantages attributed to mediation from the feminist perspective is empowerment of the woman who participates in mediation, in view of the opportunity it gives her to express herself and to address the emotional aspects of the dispute (because women tend to speak about feelings with greater ease)....

Indeed, in the field as well, women who went through mediation for divorce disputes report that the mediation enabled them to voice their concerns and to express their point of view. Studies demonstrate that these women feel that they had an equal amount of influence on fashioning the terms of the settlement agreement at the conclusion of the mediation process. Battered women note that the mediation empowered them, enabling them to stand up for themselves and to take responsibility for their decisions, actions and future, to present their position and to solve their problems. One study shows that only 15% of battered women left the mediation process before its conclusion. In a process that places the parties at the center and which emphasizes the "empowerment" of the parties, it is not surprising that women feel this "empowerment" more strongly. Victims of violence are particularly likely to benefit from this empowerment, which constitutes part of the process of healing from the crisis that they went through....

C. The problems of the current situation

Two central problems are raised both by the scholarly discourse and the existing practice with respect to divorce cases involving violence....

(a) "Practical Problems"

....

One of the solutions proposed by the proponents of mediation to deal with the problems created by the use of mediation in divorce cases involving violence is screening. However, this solution is far from perfect and may frequently result in disappointment. Firstly, the findings point to the fact that only about 80% of mediation programs formerly attempt to identify violence and only about half of such programs conduct personal interviews in addition to filling out questionnaires....

Another solution offered by the proponents of mediation for dealing with its disadvantages is training the mediator and ensuring that he has the requisite skills to deal with these cases. According to their assertion, only mediation carried out by a skilled and experienced mediator who specializes in the subject of domestic violence, understands the unique dynamic of such cases, and uses special techniques to deal with them will be able to address many of the assertions of the opponents of mediation. Indeed, many mediation programs provide training for mediators to recognize signs of domestic violence and be able to manage situations where it becomes an issue. However, in some states there is still no requirement for special training for mediators. In effect, only 70% of the mediation programs that were surveyed report that mediators participated in training programs regarding domestic violence.

Moreover, the concern is that training the mediator, regardless of how extensive such training may be, will not enable him to discern all of the signs of control and exploitation in the couple's relationship. More importantly, the assertion is that no person can be talented enough so as to put the victim in a position of equal power opposite the exploitative and violent party, no matter the degree to which the mediator is attuned to the dynamics of the relationship. Similarly, although the Model Standards provide that mediators should undergo training that includes familiarity with family law and insight about how family issues can affect all members of the family, "there is no specific description of what appropriate training in domestic violence issues might entail." The effectiveness of existing mediator training programs should be studied in order to ascertain how much training is necessary, at what frequency mediators should be required to undergo additional training, and the topics that should be included in the training programs. Until such time, according to this assertion, relying on the mediator's training and skills is simply insufficient....

Another solution that has been proposed in the scholarly literature for dealing with the failures of the mediation process, especially the "danger component," is online dispute resolution (ODR). ODR is simply any form of ADR that takes place through use of the internet. Online mediation enables the parties to be physically separated, unlike traditional mediation where the physical presence of the parties and mediator is central to the process. Where there is a basis for concern that mediation in the presence of both parties would jeopardize a victim's safety, the elimination of the potential for physical contact through the use of ODR might enable the use of mediation. However, this solution is also not perfect and is intended primarily to deal with the danger component while not resolving the other disadvantages created by the process....

### Chapter Five: Med-Arb — The Proposed Solution

. . . .

#### A. The Substance, Development and Sphere of Application of Med-Arb

Med-arb is a combination of the words "mediation" and "arbitration." It is a hybrid, two-stage process for dispute resolution, combining mediation with arbitration. Classic med-arb is carried out by one neutral mediator, who was agreed upon by all of the parties, and who, only if the mediation does not succeed, will then wear the hat of an arbitrator will carry out arbitration between the parties, rending a binding arbitration award with respect to all of the issues that were not resolved in the course of the mediation process. The goal of med-arb is to combine the advantages of mediation and arbitration in one forum. Med-arb attempts to combine the consensual nature of mediation with the component of "finality of the judgment" of arbitration. By agreeing to med-arb, the parties express their prior consent to attempt to arrive at a volitional agreement during the first stage—mediation—and if this is not successful (or is only partially successful because some issues continue to be disputed) accept the binding award of the mediator-arbitrator in the second stage. The two stages of the process are clearly separated from one another. There are those who call med-arb "mediation with muscle" or "mediation with a bite" since it prevails over what is considered, in the opinion of various scholars, to be one of the central weaknesses of the mediation process: the mediator's lack of authority to impose a binding award on the parties. The mediator-arbitrator, on the other hand, is chosen by the parties and their attorneys. He must have experience in carrying out mediations and arbitrations as well knowledge of the dispute subject. Clearly, this complex role must be filled by someone the parties (and their attorneys) trust. Additionally, prior to the beginning of the process, the mediator-arbitrator must apprise the parties of the risks involved in the use of the process and have them sign a waiver of the right to replace the mediator-arbitrator (or disqualify him) and of the right to appeal his award. The med-arb agreement also includes the basic rules of the process and details of the issues to be deliberated.

Med-arb originally appeared as a reaction to the need for resolution of labor disputes through binding arbitration in place of strikes and lock-outs of factories. At the beginning of the 20th century there were two main methods for a neutral person to make a decision. The first—"the independent chairman method"—developed in 1911 in a factory in Chicago. The second method—"the arbitrator method"—developed in 1903 in the wake of the protest of coal miners. In effect, the theoretical underpinnings of med-arb can be found somewhere prior to World War II, and its formal structure was formed in the wake of the bombing of Pearl Harbor in December 1941. The term "med-arb" was coined in 1970. Sam and John Kagel, the first ones to develop this process, used it for the first time to settle a nurses' strike in a San Francisco hospital. According to the Kagels' model, the parties waived their right to strike and undertook a commitment to accept the final settlement. In this manner authority was accorded to the mediator-arbitrator to arrive at a settlement if the parties failed to arrive at a settlement by themselves.

Until this point med-arb developed in four central arenas: labor disputes, international arbitration, corporate disputes, and family and estate disputes. Various countries, such as China, Germany, and Switzerland, use various forms of med-arb in international disputes. Countries such as Brazil, China and Hong Kong have even enacted arbitration legislation including provisions relating to med-arb. In the arena of corporate disputes, med-arb has proven itself to be effective for certain kinds of disputes. A survey of ADR habits among conglomerates that was conducted in 1997 demonstrates the importance of med-arb in this sector....

In the fourth arena of family disputes, which is the area relevant to this article—med-arb is developing because the judicial process cannot provide an appropriate solution due to the emotional nature of the disputes, and the long-term and expensive qualities of the disputes.... Med-arb is perceived as appropriate in disputes of this nature since it saves time and money, is carried out privately and is suitable for sensitive subjects, as it encourages the building of relationships instead of destroying them and escalating conflict. The additional value of med-arb over the mediation process (which also has these advantages) is that it contributes to the finality of the deliberations and the determination. Although in the arena of family disputes med-arb is still in its initial stages, and there has not yet been any in-depth study regarding its application, voices regarding its alleged advantages are already being heard. . . .

B. The Advantages of Med-Arb, its Disadvantages and Means of Dealing with Them

. . . .

(a) Efficiency and Finality of the Proceedings as Opposed to Impairment of Neutrality

Efficiency is perceived as one of the obvious advantages of med-arb. The dual role of the mediator-arbitrator makes the process more efficient than separate mediation and arbitration processes since the single mediator-arbitrator does not have to begin from the starting point and the same issues do not have to be raised again. Unlike mediation alone, in med-arb, the mediator-arbitrator can use his understandings of the relationship between the parties and their interests that he acquired during the mediation process in reaching a suitable solution during arbitration. Moreover, the finality of the proceeding is one of the prominent advantages of the med-arb process. Unlike "pure" mediation, the med-arb process, like arbitration, ensures a final determination. The settlement agreement that the parties reach at the end of the mediation stage of the process is binding and can be legally enforced. The certain knowledge that the dispute will end constitutes an enormous advantage from the perspective of the parties and in terms of the process.

However, just as it contributes to efficiency, the duality of the role of the mediator-arbitrator also leads to criticism regarding the potential impairment of his neutrality. In pure mediation, confidentiality is one of the basic principles of the process. There are legislative enactments that regulate the behavior of the mediators and even impose serious restrictions on the use that may be made of information disclosed during the process. In the arbitration proceeding, the arbitrator must base his award solely upon facts that are considered relevant to his award. By contrast, in med-arb, the mediator-arbitrator is exposed to a variety of information during the mediation stage. This includes confidential information pertaining not just to the case but also regarding the parties' interests, that is not disclosed in the course of ordinary arbitration, such as intimate, emotional or personal information, which is not relevant in the strictly legal sense, as well as privileged information provided to the mediator-arbitrator, without the presence of the other party, in the caucuses that take place during the mediation stage. While this does not create a problem for the mediator in a pure mediation proceeding, which does not end with an award by the mediator, in med-arb the exposure to this kind of information is likely to sway the mediator-arbitrator in favor of one party and to adversely affect the results of the proceeding since it is not realistic to expect him to block out (consciously or sub-consciously) all critical information provided during the mediation stage. . . .

Moreover, one must remember that the parties are entitled to fashion the proceeding as they see fit, and they have the means to use protective measures or various models of med-arb in order to deal with the issue of confidentiality. The parties may choose the model of med-arb according to which a different person serves in each role of mediator and arbitrator. Proponents of med-arb assert that the model of "same-neutral med-arb" (using the same person as mediator and arbitrator) is not mandatory. There is no necessity that the mediator also serve as the arbitrator in the case. The parties may decide on a different model of med-arb, such as "opt-out med-arb," in which, at the conclusion of the mediation stage and prior to the beginning of the arbitration stage, each of the parties is entitled to request that someone else be appointed as arbitrator. In this manner, many of the concerns and ethical dilemmas regarding the issue of neutrality of the mediator-arbitrator are likely to be resolved.

(b) Flexibility of the Process as Opposed to Impairment of its Fairness

The flexibility of the process is one of its most significant advantages, and there are those who believe that med-arb is the most flexible of all of the existing ADR processes. The med-arb process is considered flexible since it enables the transition from mediation to arbitration, a return to mediation and again going on to arbitration. Even at the arbitration stage the arbitrator can go back to his role as a mediator in order to deal with specific issues. All of this is according to the med-arb model that the parties choose at the outset of the process. The combination of arbitration and mediation enables the parties to fashion a process that is custom-made for the circumstances of the dispute between them and to choose a suitable neutral mediator-arbitrator as they desire....

(c) Incentive for Settlement as Opposed to Coercion

Studies show a further advantage of the med-arb process is that it provides an incentive for the parties to reach a settlement agreement. There are proponents who believe that the authority of the mediator-arbitrator in effect reduces the risk that issues will remain unresolved after the stage of mediation, when he will have to render an arbitration judgment. In other words, the presence of the mediator-arbitrator and the threat of an arbitration judgment create a tremendous incentive for the parties to resolve their difficulties in mediation. A further positive influence of med-arb is the conduct of the parties during the phase of mediation. Aside from the incentive to reach a settlement agreement, med-arb also provides an incentive to behave honestly and fairly during the stage of mediation, knowing that if they fail to reach a settlement agreement they will forfeit their control of the outcome. There are even those who assert that using direct "force" serves as an incentive for the parties to relate with greater seriousness to the mediation stage and to cooperate in the hope that they can impress the mediator-arbitrator.

However, and precisely on this point, criticism is raised with respect to the coercive aspect of the process, which is the product of the "power" of the mediator-arbitrator. The assertion is that the authority accorded to the same person who is trying to mediate between the parties to render a coerced judgment, as well his ability to threaten terminating the mediation process at any time (e.g., if the parties are not making progress and in order to move onto the arbitration phase), grants him a great deal of power. The critics assert that this combination is likely to result in the mediator-arbitrator forcing his opinion on the parties, and that the end result of the mediation phase is likely to be a forced settlement agreement, thereby compromising the volitional nature of the process and the parties' participation and genuine satisfaction. The assertion is that the component of coercion in the med-arb process is an inherent flaw in the process, and that the agreements that the parties arrive at during the mediation phase are the product of pressure applied by the mediator-arbitrator and therefore they cannot be volitional. According to one response voiced against this alleged disadvantage, empirical studies of the med-arb process have demonstrated that most of the mediators-arbitrators who were observed were not especially directive during the mediation phase. They concentrated their pressure tactics at the end of the sessions, more as a last ditch effort to rescue a failed mediation than as a policy of aggressive facilitation. . . .

(d) Conduct of the Parties to the Proceeding

Another contention against med-arb relates to the conduct of the parties. The critics assert that during mediation the parties will be afraid to disclose information that they would disclose in a pure mediation proceeding, because of the arbitration proceeding looming in the future. They assume that unlike mediation, which requires openness and sincerity, the arbitration proceeding requires parties to act in a calculated manner. Unlike the mediator, who builds the process in reliance upon the openness of the parties, their true intentions, their interests, their preferences, and their business background, the arbitrator is supposed to render a judgment between them. Because the parties are aware of the judicial power of the mediator-arbitrator, and out of their fear lest at the stage of the ruling he uses the information that they disclosed during the mediation stage against them, they will refrain from fully cooperating during the mediation stage. Countering this contention, the proponents of med-arb assert that there is no empirical basis for this concern, and that quite the opposite, there are empirical studies that point to the openness of the parties in the med-arb proceeding. Other criticism relating to the parties' conduct in the med-arb proceeding, concerns the manipulative behavior of the parties. The assertion is that if one of the parties wishes to end the mediation phase and to go on to the arbitration phase, he is likely to force this on the other party through his lack of cooperation in carrying out the negotiations during the mediation phase. Such manipulation can also be used in pure mediation in order to bring the proceeding to its conclusion, but the studies show that the risk that such manipulation will occur is greater in the med-arb proceeding. Proponents of med-arb respond by stating that the volitional nature of the proceeding demonstrates that the parties are familiar with the process, trust the mediator-arbitrator and intend to cooperate with him, and that they understand that a lack of integrity on their part or any other manipulative strategy is first and foremost harmful to themselves, insofar as these are strategies that harm the proceeding itself. If this answer is insufficient, and the concern regarding manipulation still exists, the parties are likely to include in the med-arb agreement a provision pursuant to which each party must disclose before the other party and before the mediator-arbitrator all relevant information and must refrain from strategies of disinformation.

One of the solutions scholars have proposed as a general solution to the criticism of the med-arb process and to address many of the disadvantages attributed to it is prior to starting the proceeding, the parties sign an informative document regarding the risks and ethical dilemmas involved in such a hybrid process. In California, the ADR Practice Guide includes an informative document of this nature. The parties who sign it prior to beginning the med-arb declare that it has been brought to their attention that the mediator-arbitrator may be influenced by the confidential information brought before him during the mediation phase and that: "The parties understand that this process will likely cause the arbitrator to receive information that might not otherwise have been received as evidence in the arbitration and to receive information confidentially from each of the parties that may not be disclosed to the other side."

Similarly, in this document, the parties undertake not to sue the mediator-arbitrator or to attack the results of the med-arb on the basis of these risks. My proposal is, therefore, that the parties sign a med-arb document that will attest to their informed consent to the process and to the mediator-arbitrator's consent to serve at the outset as a mediator, and to act according to the principles of med-arb detailed above and set forth in such a document. The importance of this document is in its assurance that if the parties are interested in the med-arb process, it is only after all of the risks and ethical dilemmas that may arise during this hybrid process were brought to their knowledge and understood prior to giving their informed consent to them. The document is also important because it affords protection to the mediator-arbitrator due to the parties' waiver of the right to file an action against the mediator-arbitrator, and limits the mediator-arbitrator's liability to instances in which he has breached his duty to act with neutrality and in good faith. The parties similarly waive the right to challenge the results of the med-arb—both the mediation settlement agreement and the arbitration agreement—as part of strengthening the objective of finality of the process. . . .

C. The Potential Contribution of Med-Arb to the Issue of Divorce Mediation in the Presence of Domestic Violence

(a) Med-arb as a Real Remedy: Addressing the Practical Problem

The mediation process, as stated above, in dealing with divorce cases in the presence of violence presents (or is likely to present) various disadvantages, which, in many cases cannot be completely resolved, even through the spectrum of solutions offered by its proponents, as we termed this above, "the practical problems." In many cases, med-arb is likely to address these advantages, as detailed below:

(1) Solutions such as screening disputes, ensuring the mediator's skill, caucusing, and expanding a new definition of the mediator's "duty of neutrality," etc. were proposed to address the failure of "disparity of power between the parties." With respect to "the fairness of the mediation settlement," solutions are limited and questionable.

It seems that med-arb is likely to provide a better solution. Firstly, the mediator's duty of neutrality in the classic mediation proceeding (which the opponents of mediation fear will be breached if the mediator intervenes on behalf of the victim) no longer constitutes a problem in the case of med-arb. The mediator-arbitrator is likely to terminate the mediation phase of the proceeding when he feels parties are arriving at a settlement that is unfair to the victim or are making decisions that do not reflect an appropriate balance of power between the parties. During the arbitration phase, the arbitrator relies upon his discretion to render the award only as for those matters, which include the balance of power that is appropriate in his opinion. In this manner, med-arb achieves both goals: it preserves neutrality during the mediation phase, and it preserves the fairness of the settlement and the victim's rights during the arbitration phase. In fact, what is presented in general med-arb literature as a disadvantage of the process—"a mediator with muscle"—is not such a great disadvantage (if at all) regarding med-arb in divorce cases involving violence. In this type of case, a certain element of coercion in the process is not necessarily negative and can even be advantageous (in comparison to classic mediation).

Secondly, even though it is not always possible to completely remove the imbalance of power between the parties, the mediator-arbitrator's options to intervene and render an award is likely to prevent the degree of power from being the dominant factor influencing the final results. The very knowledge that the proceeding grants the victim an option for third-party intervention to render a determination gives the victim a power, which she does not have in the classic mediation proceeding. In other words, the weak party has an additional option to settle in med-arb. In this manner, med-arb contributes to resolving the problem of the disparity of power between the parties that exists in classic mediation.

(2) The fact that the mediator-arbitrator is a mediator with muscle, as stated in the previous paragraph, is likely to be an advantage in divorce cases involving violence with respect to another problem attributed to mediation—the component of danger. This problem, as stated, cannot be completely eradicated, in spite of the attempts to do so (such as the solution of ODR). The mediator-arbitrator's muscle is likely to influence the violent party to restrain himself, because if he does not do so, there may no longer have control over the results once the mediation phase is abandoned for the arbitration phase, with the attendant binding award of the arbitrator. Med-arb is even likely to reduce the force of this problem when the victim asks to withdraw from the mediation proceeding after it has already begun. In the classic mediation proceeding, such a situation is likely to increase the danger awaiting the victim, both because of her refusal to continue the dialogue in the mediation setting, and because in most cases, the handling of the case is transferred to the court for a judicial proceeding. As stated above, some assert that it is precisely the judicial proceeding that escalates the conflict between the parties and in effect, increases the danger awaiting the wife from her violent husband. In the med-arb proceeding, even where the mediation phase ends, the proceeding itself is not terminated and certainly is not transferred to the court; rather, the parties

continue to the arbitration phase. Thus, the problem of the danger component is weakened.

(3) An additional problem is the preservation of the power paradigm. Some argue that mediation, being a volitional process throughout, is likely to contribute to preserving the mold of the abuser-victim relationship because it provides a platform for the aggressive party. Med-arb is not a volitional process all the way through, but rather, includes the coercive arbitration phase where needed, resolving this problem by definition.

(4) The common denominator of additional problems existing in classic mediation—cheapening and distorting the phenomenon of domestic violence, as well as the feminist argument, as set forth above—is the wrong message of tolerance that society supposedly transmits by allowing divorce cases involving domestic violence to be handled in a mediation process. As one of the scholars stated, this sends a message to the specific parties and to the general public that domestic violence is acceptable, and that it is the fault of both of the parties, or it is simply a private matter between a man and his wife within the privacy of their own home.

Med-arb constitutes a balancing solution that is beneficial all around. It transmits a strong and uncompromising message in the form of the arbitrator's decision rendered by a third party, instead of the tolerant message that classic mediation transmits. It also contributes to the empowerment of the victim during the mediation phase and assists her "to have more of a voice in what happens to her future." This addresses the feminist argument of the opponents of mediation with its own feminist argument.

However, this is not sufficient. In this article I argue that beyond dealing with the disadvantages of mediation, med-arb has distinct advantages of its own that have added value precisely in divorce cases involving domestic violence, as detailed below:

(1) The first advantage is the finality of the proceeding. . . .

(2) The advantage of efficiency in med-arb, expressed in findings in the field as well, is that it saves time and money as compared to independent and separate mediation and arbitration proceedings because the same person serves as mediator and as arbitrator, and due to the continuity between the two proceedings. Med-arb results in relatively quick results and the price that the parties are required to pay is fair. The economic advantage for the victim in divorce cases is important because, in many cases, she was subject to financial abuse in addition to the physical or psychological abuse. Additionally, the speed with which the bond is dissolved is likely to have practical implications in terms of limiting the element of danger to the victim. This advantage is certainly significant for the victim of domestic violence seeking divorce.

(3) A further advantage of the med-arb process is the flexibility of the process that enables a transition from mediation to arbitration, back to mediation, and so forth.

This advantage is particularly valuable in divorce cases involving domestic violence because the terms of the mediation settlement are likely to change according to the shift in circumstances: unexpected behavior of the violent party, a varying level of violence, a varying balance of powers between the parties, the confidence that the victim is likely to acquire or lose in the course of the proceeding, etc. As one of the scholars points out: "As a couple moves through the mediation process or other legal proceedings, the situation could quickly change."

Therefore, preserving flexibility is of the utmost importance. The possibility of a prior agreement, in which the mediator will be authorized to go from the mediation phase to the arbitration phase and back again, is a special advantage that does not exist in the normal mediation proceeding. In the scholarly literature of recent years, it is repeatedly expressed that there is no one correct solution for every divorce case involving violence, and that each case must be considered on its merits. . . . The transition between mediation and arbitration and back again, which is possible in a med-arb proceeding, is, therefore, a significant advantage precisely for divorce cases involving violence.

(b) Exchanging the Safety Net—Addressing the Conceptual Problem

. . . .

One part of the argument points to the need to look for a third solution in divorce cases involving violence, in view of the problems arising from making do with the two customary alternatives—the judicial process or mediation. The argument is that in view of the substantive disadvantages of both of these alternatives, a third, more appropriate, alternative is necessary.

The answer to this can be found in the med-arb process and adapting it to deal with divorce cases involving violence. In other words, med-arb is likely to provide a third, more appropriate solution. Firstly, it seems that for the most part the med-arb process constitutes a more appropriate solution than the judicial process. As the advanced scholarly literature demonstrates, in a comparison between the judicial process and the mediation process for dealing with divorce cases involving violence, it seems that the general balance tips towards the latter. Moreover, studies show that the rate of success of mediation in divorce cases involving violence is quite similar to the rate of success of mediation in other kinds of cases. The data demonstrates a rate of success in dispute resolution that varies from 51% to 76%. Additionally, couples in both violent and nonviolent relationships report satisfaction from the mediation process, the settlement agreement that was reached, and the level at which agreements were carried out. . . .

The second part of the argument points to the problem inherent in viewing the judicial process as the "safety net" of the mediation process (when the inherent disadvantages of the mediation process that cannot be completely resolved, arise). In order to resolve one problem, another one has been created. In other words, mediation was initially proposed as an alternative to the judicial process in divorce cases involving violence, due to the limitations of the latter. How, therefore, can returning to the judicial process be presented as a remedy for the disadvantages of mediation? Is it appropriate for a limited process that was abandoned (at least partially) in favor of an alternative, to be used to correct the disadvantages of that same alternative?

The response to the first part of this argument can also be found in med-arb. Med-arb substitutes arbitration for the safety net of the judicial process offered in mediation. In med-arb, if the mediation phase fails, the parties automatically go on to the arbitration phase, which is structured within the process, and do not avail themselves of the judicial process. The victim knows in advance that even if the mediation does not succeed, then arbitration will serve as her safety net and she will not be forced to pay the price of returning to the judicial process (as a safety net). Such knowledge is likely to encourage her to try the mediation process without fear of the risk of failure, or the further risk accompanying such failure—the return to the judicial process.

Further, the importance of the safety net for the victim in the case of total or partial failure of the mediation cannot be overemphasized; to the safety net increases the spectrum of cases in which victims find the strength to turn to this process as the most appropriate means to dissolve their connection to their abusers. . . .

Moreover, instead of referring parties to the judicial process from the outset or as a result of the failure of the mediation, this article proposes the option of remaining entirely within the sphere of ADR by choosing med-arb. The med-arb process is composed both of mediation and arbitration, both of which are defined as types of ADR. As scholars note: "Empowerment and self-determination, hallmarks of alternative dispute resolution, are an appealing option for those who prefer to rely on their own decision-making capacities, in lieu of those of a judge."

It would be impossible to exaggerate the importance of empowerment and the return of control over the process and over her life in general for victims of domestic violence. The med-arb proceeding, therefore, opens the possibility of being totally removed from the judicial process and remaining within ADR! Even if the mediation phase fails, the victim will still remain within the field of ADR, under the umbrella of the arbitration process. Moreover, many victims do not wish to press criminal charges against their attackers due to concerns about privacy and the impact such a step will have on their family. Victims of domestic violence might consider the med-arb process a way to address the problem without exposing themselves and their family to the polarizing dynamic inherent in the judicial process. . . .

## Chapter Six: Recommendations

. . . The recommendation is to apply med-arb only to those cases where there is informed consent of the victim to adopt it, and only for those cases where a mediation proceeding is suitable (i.e., to the exclusion of cases of extreme violence).

Moreover, our proposal is to adopt med-arb as an addition to mechanisms (derived both from the academic discourse and from actual practice) that were developed and adopted in recent years in order to improve the mediation process and its results. These mechanisms—screening, training of mediators, adding security measures, caucusing frequently, integrating professionals into the process, etc.—have been found, despite their importance, to be insufficient in many cases, not to say disappointing. This article seeks, therefore, to add med-arb to the existing mechanisms.

We also propose on-going and empirical follow-up of the conduct, as well as the results of the med-arb proceeding in divorce cases involving violence. The idea is to try to examine the degree of efficiency of the process as well as its efficacy in such cases, through questionnaires and surveys of the parties who participated in med-arb proceedings. The questions must be addressed to both parties as well as to the mediator-arbitrator, and they should include questions pertaining to the parties' level of satisfaction from the proceeding, its fairness, and the fairness of the result as they perceive it. The survey should include questions about the short and long term implications and the results of the med-arb (such as post med-arb violence or threats of violence), the victim's sense of security in the course of the med-arb proceeding, the transitions between the mediation and the arbitration phases of the process, the autonomy of the parties during these phases, regarding the degree of parties' cooperation, the degree to which the mediator-arbitrator conveyed neutrality, the degree of effectiveness of the results (the mediation settlement together with the arbitration decision), the procedures or mechanisms that should have been used in the process and were not, etc.

The promise that med-arb holds for divorce cases involving violence must be put to the test in the field. Naturally, the med-arb process not only offers the advantages of mediation and arbitration, but also brings with it the disadvantages of each. Nevertheless, the holistic approach has already instructed us that the whole is always greater than the sum of its parts.

## Chapter 7: Conclusion

So, why should we be writing about domestic violence again?

We should write about domestic violence because of its growing phenomenon and seriousness, and in the name of truth, which requires us to state that the judicial process, in most cases, is not equipped to provide a solution in such cases. Mediation, which serves as an alternative to litigation, does not constitute a perfect alternative; there are still substantial disadvantages, which cannot be completely corrected, despite the developing literature in the field, and significant efforts for improvement in the field.

Therefore, this article proposes a third option—med-arb. Along with the presentation of the med-arb process, its development, its advantages, and its implementation, this article has also presented its disadvantages and possible ways of dealing with them. One of them is prior informed consent of the parties to the process and its results, which, even if it does not necessarily provide 100% assurance of the propriety of the process, it can still greatly reduce its dangers and actualize the parties' right to self-determination and the development of their personal autonomy through the choice of a flexible process fashioned to meet their needs, the advantages of which would seem to greatly outweigh its disadvantages. Some of the disadvantages of med-arb (such as the element of coercion) are not necessarily a disadvantage when dealing with divorce cases involving violence, whereas some of its advantages (particularly the potential for self-determination and empowerment) are likely to accord added value in such cases and to make a significant contribution for the victims. . . .

The importance of the trend, coming both from the academic world and from the field, seems to find more humane and appropriate solutions for divorce cases involving violence and the experience of pain for the victims and their children as far as possible. This article seeks to be part of this positive trend.

## Alaska Stat. 25.24.060 (2015) Mediation

(a) Except as provided in (f) and (g) of this section, at any time within 30 days after a complaint or cross-complaint in a divorce action is filed, a party to the action may file a motion with the court requesting mediation, for the purpose of achieving a mutually agreeable settlement in termination of the marriage. When a party moves for settlement mediation, the other party shall answer the motion on the record, and the judge may order mediation. When no request for mediation is made, the court may at any time order the parties to submit to mediation if it determines that mediation may result in a more satisfactory settlement between the parties.

. . . .

(f) The court may not order or refer parties to mediation in a divorce proceeding if a protective order issued or filed under AS 18.66.100—18.66.180 is in effect. The court may not order or refer parties to mediation if a party objects on the grounds that domestic violence has occurred between the parties unless the court finds that the conditions of (g)(1)-(3) of this section are met. If the court proposes or suggests mediation under this subsection,

(1) mediation may not occur unless the victim of the alleged domestic violence agrees to the mediation; and

(2) the court shall advise the parties that each party has the right to not agree to mediation and that the decision of each party will not bias other decisions of the court.

(g) A mediator who receives a referral or order from a court to conduct mediation under (a) of this section shall evaluate whether domestic violence has occurred between the parties. A mediator may not engage in mediation when either party has committed a crime involving domestic violence unless

(1) mediation is requested by the victim of the alleged domestic violence, or proposed by the court and agreed to by the victim;

(2) mediation is provided by a mediator who is trained in domestic violence in a manner that protects the safety of the victim and any household member, taking

into account the results of an assessment of the potential danger posed by the perpetrator and the risk of harm to the victim; and

(3) the victim is permitted to have in attendance a person of the victim's choice, including an attorney.

## *Notes and Questions*

- **WOMEN WHO LEAVE.**

Contrary to the popular myth, typified by the question often asked by those without knowledge of the issues inherent in domestic violence—"Why does she stay?"—the answer is, "She doesn't." In a 10-year study of 201 couples in which the wife was the victim of domestic violence, psychologists Neil Jacobson and John Gottman found that 38 percent of the women divorced their husbands within two years of the inception of the study. *See* NEIL JACOBSON & JOHN GOTTMAN, WHEN MEN BATTER WOMEN: NEW INSIGHTS INTO ENDING ABUSIVE RELATIONSHIPS 24, 49 (1998). Serious economic issues face some women who leave their marriages and, in fact, lack of economic resources is an oft-cited reason for remaining with an abusive husband. In her book, THE DIVORCE REVOLUTION (1985), Lenore J. Weitzman reported a woman's standard of living declined by 73 percent after divorce, while a man's standard climbed 42 percent. She blamed California's no-fault divorce laws and other divorce reforms. Her conclusions came from a study sample drawn from the divorce dockets of the Los Angeles County courts in 1977. Several subsequent studies did not replicate her results. For example, using her methodology, sociologist Richard R. Peterson determined a woman's standard of living post-divorce declined 27 percent while a man's increased by 10 percent. *See* Richard R. Peterson, *A Re-Evaluation of the Economic Consequences of Divorce,* 61(3) AM. SOCIOLOGICAL REV. 528–36 (1996). Notwithstanding this discrepancy in numbers, would you consider that the threat of a 27 percent decline in living standard—still sizable—might contribute to a woman remaining in an abusive marriage?

# Chapter 9

# Civil Actions and Domestic Violence

> **CONSIDER AS YOU READ ABOUT CIVIL ACTIONS**
> 1. Historical bars against tort recovery for domestic violence; interspousal tort immunity, statutes of limitations
> 2. Expansion of liability for acts of domestic violence
> 3. Insurers and domestic violence; the impact of Obamacare
> 4. Lack of success by victims of domestic violence against third party actors

The concept of suing in tort for the physical, emotional, or economic pain of domestic violence is a recent development. For many years, traditional legal barriers firmly blocked a victim's ability to sue for civil damages.

If a victim was married to the abuser, civil claims were barred by inter-spousal tort immunity. If a relationship was a long one, and the battering consisted of the well-known escalating cycle of violence, a victim faced a short statute of limitations. Most states required married victims to seek civil redress for domestic violence solely within the context of any divorce action. Given the only source for obtaining financial recovery was often a homeowner's insurance policy, and the language of most policies barred payment for intentional torts between spouses, these claims were meaningless. Adding to the problems for financial redress was the lack of sympathy from the courts or from employers who penalized employees for taking time off from work to pursue their claims.

With the passage of the Violence Against Women Act in 1994, which included provisions for civil recovery for victims of gender-based violence, advocates for battered women hoped to bypass the patchwork of the statutory and common law limitations imposed by the states. In fact, in the six years following passage of the act, there were 73 reported cases, mostly involving intentional torts.[1] But in 2000, the Supreme Court in *United States v. Morrison*, struck down the civil remedies provisions of VAWA. Thus, victims seeking to sue their batterers in tort must navigate a legal roadmap with different terrain in each jurisdiction. What follows is an overview of the historical obstacles faced by victims considering tort actions against their abusers.

---

1. Jennifer Wriggins, *Domestic Violence Torts,* 75 S. Cal. L. Rev. 121, 134 n.64 (2001).

# I. Interspousal Tort Immunity

The earliest legal barrier against recovering damages for assaults by a spouse was the well-entrenched doctrine of interspousal tort immunity. Although its validity was questioned early in the 20th century, in some states, it lasted beyond the 21st. In a minority of states, some vestiges still remain. And even where it has been outlawed, insurance policies, in failing to cover intentional torts perpetrated by family members, keep the doctrine alive *de facto*.

### Thompson v. Thompson
United States Supreme Court
218 U.S. 611 (1910)

Mr. Justice Day delivered the opinion of the court.

This case presents a single question, which is involved in the construction of the statutes governing the District of Columbia. That question is, Under those statutes may a wife bring an action to recover damages for an assault and battery upon her person by the husband?

The declaration of the plaintiff is in the ordinary form, and in seven counts charges divers assaults upon her person by her husband, the defendant, for which the wife seeks to recover damages in the sum of $70,000. As issue of law being made by demurrer to the defendant's pleas, the Supreme Court of the District of Columbia held that such action would not lie under the statute. Upon writ of error to the Court of Appeals of the District of Columbia the judgment of the Supreme Court was affirmed. 31 App. D.C. 557.

At the common law the husband and wife were regarded as one. The legal existence of the wife during coverture was merged in that of the husband, and, generally speaking, the wife was incapable of making contracts, of acquiring property or disposing of the same without her husband's consent. They could not enter into contracts with each other, nor were they liable for torts committed by one against the other. In pursuance of a more liberal policy in favor of the wife, statutes have been passed in many of the State looking to the relief of a married woman from the disabilities imposed upon her as a femme covert by the common law....

It is insisted that the Code of the District of Columbia has gone so far in the direction of modifying the common law relation of husband and wife as to give to her an action against him for torts committed by him upon her person or property. The answer to this contention depends upon a construction of §1155 of the District of Columbia Code, 31 Stat. 1189, 1374, March 3, 1901. That section provides:

> "SEC. 1155. Power of Wife to Trade and Sue and be Sued.—Married women shall have power to engage in any business, and to contract, whether engaged in business or not, and to sue separately upon their contracts, and also to sue separately for the recovery, security, or protection of their property, and

for torts committed against them, as fully and freely as if they were unmarried; contracts may also be made with them, and they may also be sued separately upon their contracts, whether made before or during marriage, and for wrongs independent of contract committed by them before or during their marriage, as fully as if they were unmarried, and upon judgments recovered against them execution may be issued as if they were unmarried; nor shall any husband be liable upon any contract made by his wife in her own name and upon her own responsibility, nor for any tort committed separately by her out of his presence without his participation or sanction: Provided, That no married woman shall have power to make any contract as surety or guarantor, or as accommodation drawer, acceptor, maker, or indorser."

... By this District of Columbia statute the common law was changed, and, in view of the additional rights conferred upon married women in § 1155 and other sections of the Code, she is given the right to sue separately for redress of wrongs concerning the same. That this was the purpose of the statute, when attention is given to the very question under consideration, is apparent from the consideration of its terms. Married women are authorized to sue separately for "the recovery, security or protection of their property, and for torts committed against her as fully and freely as if she were unmarried." That is, the limitation upon her right of action imposed in the requirement of the common law that the husband should join her was removed by the statute, and she was permitted to recover separately for such torts, as freely as if she were still unmarried. The statute was not intended to give a right of action as against the husband, but to allow the wife, in her own name, to maintain actions of tort which at common law must be brought in the joint names of herself and husband.

... It is suggested that the liberal construction insisted for in behalf of the defendant in error in this case might well be given, in view of the legislative intent to provide remedies for grievous wrongs to the wife; and an instance is suggested in the wrong to a wife rendered unable to follow the avocation of a seamstress by a cruel assault which might destroy the use of hand or arm; and the justice is suggested of giving a remedy to an artist who might be maimed and suffer great pecuniary damages as the result of injuries inflicted by a brutal husband.

Apart from the consideration that the perpetration of such atrocious wrongs affords adequate grounds for relief under the statutes of divorce and alimony, this construction would at the same time open the doors of the courts to accusations of all sorts of one spouse against the other, and bring into public notice complaints for assault, slander and libel, and alleged injuries to property of the one or the other, by husband against wife or wife against husband. Whether the exercise of such jurisdiction would be promotive of the public welfare and domestic harmony is at least a debatable question. The possible evils of such legislation might well make the lawmaking power hesitate to enact it. But these and kindred considerations are addressed to the legislative, not the judicial branch of the Government. In cases like the present, interpretation of the law is the only function of the courts. ...

We do not believe it was the intention of Congress, in the enactment of the District of Columbia Code, to revolutionize the law governing the relation of husband and wife as between themselves. We think the construction we have given the statute is in harmony with its language and is the only one consistent with its purpose.

The judgment of the Court of Appeals of the District of Columbia will be affirmed.

Mr. Justice Harlan, with whom concur Mr. Justice Holmes and Mr. Justice Hughes, dissenting.

This is an action by a wife against her husband to recover damages for assault and battery. The declaration contains seven counts. The first, second and third charge assault by the husband upon the wife on three several days. The remaining courts charge assaults by him upon her on different days named—she being at the time pregnant, as the husband then well knew.

. . . .

The action is based upon §§ 1151 and 1155 of the Code of the District, which are as follows:

> "SEC. 1151. All the property, real, personal, and mixed, belonging to a woman at the time of her marriage, and all such property which she may acquire or receive after her marriage from any person whomsoever, by purchase, gift, grant, devise, bequest, descent, in the course of distribution, by her own skill, labor, or personal exertions, or as proceeds of a judgment at law or decree in equity, or in any other manner, shall be her own property as absolutely as if she were unmarried, and shall be protected from the debts of the husband and shall not in any way be liable for the payment thereof: Provided, That no acquisition of property passing to the wife from the husband after coverture shall be valid if the same has been made or granted to her in prejudice of the rights of his subsisting creditors.

> "SEC. 1155. Married women shall have power to engage in any business, and to contract, whether engaged in business or not, and to sue separately upon their contracts, and also to sue separately for the recovery, security or protection of their property, and for torts committed against them, as fully and freely as if they were unmarried; contracts may also be made with them, and they may also be sued separately upon their contracts, whether made before or during marriage, nd for wrongs independent of contract committed by them before or during their marriage, as fully as if they were unmarried, and upon judgments recovered against them execution may be issued as if they were unmarried; nor shall any husband be liable upon any contract made by his wife in her own name and upon her own responsibility, nor for any tort committed separately by her out of his presence without his participation or sanction: Provided, That no married woman shall have power to make any contract as surety or as guarantor, or as accommodation drawer, acceptor, maker or indorser."

The court below held that these provisions did not authorize an action for tort committed by the husband against the wife.

In my opinion these statutory provisions, properly construed, embrace such a case as the present one. If the words used by Congress lead to such a result, and if, as suggested, that result be undesirable on grounds of public policy, it is not within the functions of the court to ward off the dangers feared or the evils threatened simply by a judicial construction that will defeat the plainly-expressed will of the legislative department. With the mere policy, expediency or justice of legislation the courts, in our system of government, have no rightful concern. Their duty is only to declare what the law is, not what, in their judgment, it ought to be—leaving the responsibility for legislation where it exclusively belongs, that is, with the legislative department, so long as it keeps within constitutional limits. Now, there is not here, as I think, any room whatever for mere construction—so explicit are the words of Congress. Let us follow the clauses of the statute in their order. The statute enables the married woman to take, as her own, property of any kind, no matter how acquired by her, as well as the avails of her skill, labor or personal exertions, "as absolutely as if she were unmarried." It then confers upon married women the power to engage in any business, no matter what, and to enter into contracts, whether engaged in business or not, and to sue separately upon those contracts. If the statute stopped here, there would be ground for holding that it did not authorize this suit. But the statute goes much farther. It proceeds to authorize married women "also" to sue separately for the recovery, security or protection of their property; still more, they may sue, separately, "for torts committed against them, as fully and freely as if they were unmarried." No discrimination is made, in either case, between the persons charged with committing the tort. No exception is made in reference to the husband, if he happens to be the party charged with transgressing the rights conferred upon the wife by the statute. In other words, Congress, by these statutory provisions, destroys the unity of the marriage association as it had previously existed. It makes a radical change in the relations of man and wife as those relations were at common law in this District. In respect of business and property the married woman is given absolute control; in respect of the recovery, security and protection of her property, she may sue, separately, in tort, as if she was unmarried; and in respect of herself, that is, of her person, she may sue, separately, as fully and freely, as if she were unmarried, "for torts committed against her." So the statute expressly reads. But my brethren think that notwithstanding the destruction by the statute of the unity of the married relation, it could not have been intended to open the doors of the courts to accusations of all sorts by husband and wife against each other; and, therefore, they are moved to add, by construction, to the provision that married women may "sue separately . . . for torts committed against them as fully and freely as if they were unmarried" these words: "Provided, however, that the wife shall not be entitled, in any case, to sue her husband separately for a tort committed against her person." If the husband violently takes possession of his wife's property and withholds it from her she may, under the statute, sue him, separately, for its recovery. But such a civil action will be one in tort. If he injures or destroys her property she may, under the statute, sue him, separately, for damages. That action would also be one in tort. If these propositions are disputed, what becomes of the words in the statute to the effect that she may "sue separately for the recovery, security and protection" of her property? But if they are conceded — as I think they must be — then Congress, under the construction now placed by the court on the statute, is put in the anomalous position of allowing a married woman to sue her husband separately, in tort, for the recovery of her property, but denying her the right or privilege to sue him separately, in tort, for damages arising from his brutal assaults upon her person. I will not assume that Congress intended to bring about any such result. I cannot believe that it intended to permit the wife to sue the husband separately, in tort, for the recovery, including damages for the detention, of her property, and at the same time deny her the right to sue him, separately, for a tort committed against her person.

I repeat that with the policy, wisdom or justice of the legislation in question this court can have no rightful concern. It must take the law as it has been established by competent legislative authority. It cannot, in any legal sense, make law, but only declare what the law is, as established by competent authority.

My brethren feel constrained to say that the present case illustrates the attempt, often made, to effect radical changes in the common law by mere construction. On the contrary, the judgment just rendered will have, as I think, the effect to defeat the clearly expressed will of the legislature by a construction of its words that cannot be reconciled with their ordinary meaning.

I dissent from the opinion and judgment of the court. . . .

## Brown v. Brown

Connecticut Supreme Court of Errors

88 Conn. 42 (1914)

THAYER, J.

The plaintiff by this action seeks to recover damages from her husband for an assault and battery and false imprisonment. The parties were married in October, 1877. If she has a cause of action against her husband it is not questioned that the suit is well brought. The complaint is demurred to, the only ground of demurrer assigned being that by reason of her coverture she has no cause of action against him for the personal injuries alleged in the complaint. The Superior Court sustained the demurrer, and the only question presented by this appeal is whether that ruling was correct.

By the common law the husband might restrain the wife of her liberty and might chastise her. 1 Blackstone's Commentaries, 444. "The law which attached such subjection to the legal status of a married woman has been abolished, but not by direct legislation; it has disappeared under the continuous pressure of judicial interpretation or indirect legislation." *Mathewson v. Mathewson*, 79 Conn. 23, 27, 63 A. 285. It is now as unlawful for him to beat or falsely imprison his wife as for another to do so, and he is amenable to the criminal law for such an offense. If another, prior to the recent statutes, committed these offenses against her, he was liable in an action for the injuries inflicted upon her by such torts, but the action had to be brought in the name of her husband and herself jointly, the real purpose of the action being to reduce the chose into the possession of the husband. The wife was joined because, if her husband should die pending the suit, the damages would survive to her. 1 Blackstone's Commentaries, 443; 1 Chitty on Pleading, 64. The common law regarded husband and wife as but one person, and the husband was that person. Being but one person, they could not contract with or sue one another. This resulted logically from the legal identity of husband and wife. If this were the present status of the parties, the plaintiff could have no action for the recovery of damages for the torts alleged.

Chapter 114 of the Public Acts of 1877, p. 211, entitled An Act in Alteration of the Act concerning Domestic Relations, but commonly called the Married Women's Act, established a new legal status for persons thereafter married. It took effect April 20th, 1877, and is embodied in the present revision of the General Statutes. §§ 4545, 4546, 391, 392. The purpose and effect of the Act were in question in *Mathewson v. Mathewson*, 79 Conn. 23, 63 A. 285. In the opinion, written by JUDGE HAMERSLEY, after a review of the previously-existing law relating to the status of married persons, it is held that "in enacting this law the State adopted a fundamental change of public policy"; that by it "the unity in the husband of his own and his wife's legal identity and capacity to own property, was removed, and a new foundation, namely, equality of husband and wife in legal identity and capacity of owning property, was laid"; and that since the Act took effect "husband and wife alike retain the capacity of owning, acquiring and disposing of property, which belongs to unmarried persons." . . .

In *Marri v. Stamford Street R. Co.*, 84 Conn. 9, 23, 24, 78 A. 582, we held that, as the result of the legal status created by the Act of 1877, the wife may now, by an action in her own name, recover for physical injuries tortiously inflicted upon her as fully and to the same extent as a husband may when he is the person injured, and that the wife's right of recovery for her injuries is exclusive. . . .

By these two cases it is established that a wife, married since April 20th, 1877, may contract with her husband or other person, and may in her own name sue her husband or such other person for breach of such contract; also that she has a cause of action upon which she may recover in a suit brought in her own name for personal injuries wrongfully inflicted upon her by others than her husband. If a cause of action in her favor arises from the wrongful infliction of such injuries upon her by another, why does not the wrongful infliction of such injuries by her husband now give her a cause of action against him? If she may sue him for a broken promise, why may she not sue him for a broken arm? The defendant's answer is that a wise public policy forbids it, that no right of action accrued to her from such a tort prior to the statute of 1877, that none is expressly given her by that statute, and that none can be implied; and that this is the holding of courts in other jurisdictions in cases which have arisen under similar statutes.

It is true that courts in some of the States have held that statutes more or less similar to the one here in question give a married woman no right of action against her husband for a tort. They find in the statutes construed no legislative intent to change the legal status of husband and wife as regards the legal identity of the two, but simply an intent to ameliorate the condition of the wife by permitting her to retain and deal with her own property, and to contract with, and sue and be sued by, others than her husband. . . . [T]he legislative intent in the Act of 1877 was to change the foundation of the legal status of husband and wife, and that the statute effects that change. In marriages which have occurred since the Act took effect the parties retain their legal identity, and their civil rights are to be determined in accordance with the status thus established. These rights, except so far as they are modified by the statute itself or by other statutes, or are necessarily affected by the reciprocal rights and obligations which are inherent in the relation of husband and wife, are the same as they were before marriage. The statute leaves nothing to implication. The right to contract with the husband, and to sue him for breach of contract, and to sue for torts, is not given to the wife by the statute. These are rights which belonged to her before marriage, and, because of the new marriage status created by the statute, are not lost by the fact of marriage, as they were under the common-law status. The status of the parties after marriage being fixed, there was no occasion for providing in express terms what the consequences would be. They followed logically.

. . . .

In the fact that the wife has a cause of action against her husband for wrongful injuries to her person or property committed by him, we see nothing which is injurious to the public, or against the public good, or against good morals. This is the usual test for determining whether a statute or a contract is against public policy. When a wife is allowed to possess and deal with her own property and carry on business in her own name like a *feme sole*, she ought to have the same right to contract and enforce her contracts, and the same remedies for injuries to her person and property, which others have, and to be liable upon her contracts and for her torts the same as others are. This is the position in which she now stands. The danger that the domestic tranquility may be disturbed if husband and wife have rights of action against each other for torts, and that the courts will be filled with actions brought by them against each other for assault, slander and libel, as suggested in some of the cases cited in behalf of the defendant, we think is not serious. So long as there remains to the parties domestic tranquility, while a remnant is left of that affection and respect without which there cannot have been a true marriage, such actions will be impossible. When the purposes of the marriage relation have wholly failed by reason of the misconduct of one or both of the parties, there is no reason why the husband or wife should not have the same remedies for injuries inflicted by the other spouse which the courts would give them against other persons. . . .

There is error, the judgment is set aside and the cause remanded for further proceedings according to law.

## Townsend v. Townsend

Missouri Supreme Court

708 S.W.2d 646 (1986)

. . . .

Appellant Diana Townsend filed action against her husband seeking damages for personal injuries suffered when he shot her in the back with a shotgun as he attempted to enter her residence. It was alleged the shooting was "intentional and malicious in that defendant acted with a purpose to seriously injure or kill the plaintiff by means of a deadly weapon," causing injuries which entitled her to compensatory and punitive damages.

Respondent moved for summary judgment, raising as a bar the doctrine of interspousal immunity. . . .

Interspousal tort immunity flowed as a by-product from the common law concept of oneness or the "identity of spouses." . . . Missouri, as did other states in varying degrees, modified the rule in 1855 by granting a married woman her legal identity. This was first accomplished through exception to joinder rules in our civil procedure statutes. Thirty-four years later the Married Women's Act more substantively defined the scope of a married woman's legal identity. Chapter 109, RSMo 1889. Section 6864 of the act deemed a married woman a "femme sole" for the purposes of "transact[ing] business . . . . to contract and be contracted with, *to sue and be sued*, and to enforce and have enforced against her property such judgments as may be rendered for and against her, and may *sue and be sued at law* or in equity, *with or without* her husband being joined as a party. . . ." (emphasis added).

The crucial question never squarely addressed by the Court was whether that language abrogated the common law unity fiction for purposes of interspousal torts. In *Rogers v. Rogers*, 265 Mo. 200, 177 S.W. 382 (1915), the act was only nominally construed in dismissing a wife's false imprisonment action against her husband. Though sometimes characterized as procedural and on other occasions as substantive, § 8304, RSMo 1909, was found to be a definitive declaration of women's rights as a "femme sole." However, the entrenched unity doctrine played a continuing role in the narrow "statutory construction" resulting in this Court's refusal to depart from the archaic doctrine absent express legislative authority. . . .

The narrow statutory construction of *Rogers*, flowing from the unity fiction, persists in Missouri, despite a thirty-year trend away from strict application of interspousal immunity. Following the 1915 decision in *Rogers* the bar to interspousal tort actions was classified as substantive, the Court finding that no cause of action for personal injuries between husband and wife arose at common law. *Willott v. Willott*, 333 Mo. 896, 62 S.W.2d 1084, 1085 (1933). Yet legislative inaction in the face of *Rogers*, was in the end analysis given as justification for the decision. *Id.* at 1085–86.

However, in *Mullally v. Langenberg Bros. Grain Co.*, 339 Mo. 582, 98 S.W.2d 645 (1936), a wife was allowed to sue her husband's employer for her injuries suffered as a result of acts by the husband in the course of his employment. . . .

In *Hamilton v. Fulkerson*, 285 S.W.2d 642 (Mo. 1955), the narrow statutory construction of *Rogers* was again circumvented to allow a wife to sue her husband for injuries sustained by his negligent operation of an automobile *before* their marriage. There the Court construed a Married Women's Act provision making rights of action possessed by a woman at marriage separate property as an abrogation of the unity doctrine for antenuptial torts. Section 451.250.1, RSMo 1978....

The unity fiction was also found inapplicable where a wife sought to sue the administrator of her deceased husband's estate for the negligent acts of her husband during their marriage. *Ennis v. Truhitte*, 306 S.W.2d 549 (Mo. banc 1957) (overruled in *Ebel v. Ferguson*, 478 S.W.2d 334, 336 (Mo. banc 1972)). With the husband dead, there was no marital relationship to disturb and thus no policy basis for applying the rule.

The trend toward liberalization came to a halt in *Brawner v. Brawner*, 327 S.W.2d 808 (Mo. banc 1959), *cert. denied*, 361 U.S. 964, 4 L. Ed. 2d 546, 80 S. Ct. 595 (1960). Distinguishing earlier cases of interspousal tort recoveries as special circumstances, the Court found itself "in [no] better position to interpret the legislative intent of these statutes than the courts that decided the *Rogers* case in 1915 and the *Willott* case in 1933." *Id.* at 811. Against the confusing backdrop of the *Rogers, Hamilton, Ennis* and *Brawner* cases, this Court in its most recent decision on the issue retreated further, refusing to "*create* a cause of action" where, due to the unity fiction, "no cause of action [comes] into existence during the marriage." *Ebel v. Ferguson*, 478 S.W.2d 334, 336 (Mo. banc 1972).

. . . .

Today we reject the archaic doctrine embraced in *Ebel* and *Rogers*. Those decisions as well as related cases employing the doctrine of interspousal immunity in intentional tort actions are disapproved and are no longer to be followed. It "belies reality and fact to say there is no tort when the husband either intentionally or negligently injures his wife" or vice versa. *Brawner*, 327 S.W.2d at 819–20 (Hollingsworth, J., dissenting).

. . . .

Turning to the unity fiction itself, our construction today does not *create* a right but rather constitutes an overdue *recognition* that our General Assembly attempted to abrogate this common law doctrine in the Married Women's Act. The derivative sections of the act by their terms authorize married women to transact business, convey property, contract, sue and be sued in the same manner as a single woman. Sections 451.250, 451.290, RSMo 1978; 507.010, RSMo Cum. Supp. 1984. A husband is relieved of liability for his wife's torts. Section 537.040, RSMo 1978....

As to public policy, it is little comfort to the victim of an intentional shooting at the hands of her husband that her recovery is barred by a common law doctrine having as its basis "her protection and benefit: so great a favorite is the female sex in the laws of England." 1 W. Blackstone, Commentaries 445. By the same token, we no longer indulge the notion that this doctrine is needed to preserve the sanctity of the home. In cases such as this, there can be little sanctity remaining when the relationship becomes the source of wanton violence. Nor can we foresee that personal injury suits between spouses will be any more damaging to marital harmony than the multiplicity of property and contract actions currently permitted. Indeed, to frustrate recovery where warranted arguably contributes to violent domestic disturbances. . . .

The judgment is reversed and the cause remanded to the trial court with direction to reinstate plaintiff's petition.

. . . .

### Ill. Comp. Stat. Ann (2016) 750 ILCS 65/1
### Rights to sue and be sued

A married person may, in all cases, sue and be sued without joining his or her spouse as if unmarried. A husband or wife may sue the other for a tort committed during the marriage. No finding by any court under Section 401 of the Illinois Marriage and Dissolution of Marriage Act [750 ILCS 5/401] shall be admissible or be used as prima facie evidence of a tort in any civil action brought under this Act. An attachment or judgment in an action may be enforced by or against a married person as if unmarried.

## II. Statutes of Limitations

Statutes of limitations exist to assure fairness and promote justice by "preventing surprises through the revival of claims that have been allowed to slumber until evidence has been lost, memories have faded, and witnesses have disappeared." *Order of Railroad Telegraphers v. Railway Express,* 321 U.S. 342, 348–49 (1944). Statutes of limitations act as a barrier to tort actions for victims of domestic violence. Although they vary from state to state, the statute of limitations on intentional assault tends to be no more than a year or two from the incident giving rise to the claim; for negligence, it is generally three years, and for a claim of infliction of emotional distress, the period could be as long as six years.

Unfortunately, for complex emotional, economic, psychological and legal reasons discussed throughout this book, battered women do not necessarily involve themselves in legal actions immediately after suffering a domestic assault. Government studies show women, on average, suffer approximately seven incidents of abuse before they ever pick up the telephone to call police or venture to court to seek a restraining order. Therefore, it is highly unlikely they will contemplate civil litigation within the strikingly narrow available legal window.

## Lisa Napoli, *Tolling the Statute of Limitations for Survivors of Domestic Violence Who Wish to Recover Civil Damages Against Their Abusers*

5 Circles Bu. W. J. L. & Soc. Pol'y 53 (1997)

### I. Introduction

Plaintiffs who wish to recover civil damages for assault and battery must do so within a prescribed period of time, usually one to three years depending on the jurisdiction. . . .

Violence between intimates is not comprised of singular incidents of violence. It is composed of ongoing abuse, both physical and mental, having the purposes of isolating, intimidating, and controlling the abused. Moreover, violence between intimates, unlike other types of violence, is buttressed by the systemic devaluation of its victims. Devaluation is precisely what entraps the abused and permits such violence to continue. A heightened understanding of this type of violence, and the belief system supporting it, is key to appropriately tolling the statute of limitations.

Statutes of limitations can be tolled if the plaintiff gives a legitimate reason as to why she could not have brought her action within the prescribed time. There are three main sources of tolls of a limitations period: statute, common law, and equity. Statutory tolls for civil claims typically include insanity, the statutory toll that is most appropriate in the context of domestic violence. "Insanity" means that, by reason of some mental defect, the plaintiff was incapable of bringing a timely action.

The relevant common law toll is duress. Duress is based on a lack of capacity because of coercion: requiring that the plaintiff was being coerced by the defendant to refrain from bringing a timely action. The relevant equitable toll is estoppel, which is premised on the principle that "no man may take advantage of his own wrong." Under the estoppel theory, the defendant is estopped from benefitting from the plaintiff's failure to bring a timely action because of the sequelae of the defendant's own violent conduct.

. . . .

### II. Policies Behind Limitations Statutes and Tolling

Statutes of limitations are premised on various policy considerations:

Limitation statutes are intended to provide the wrongfully injured party with a reasonable opportunity to secure compensation while protecting potential defendants from the risk of perpetual liability for past actions. Additionally, these statutes are designed to maximize judicial fairness and reliability of outcome by disfavoring stale suits where "evidence has been lost, memories have faded, and witnesses have disappeared."

All jurisdictions provide for tolling (or suspending) statutes of limitations. The policy underlying these tolls is the rectifying of the arbitrary or unjust results arrived at when statutes of limitations are applied in certain cases. The toll for infancy, for example, is based on the presumption that a child does not have the capacity to protect her legal rights. Another toll is the delayed discovery rule, which is designed to relieve victims of "toxic torts" whose injuries may not be discernible until a much later date.

The arguments against allowing tolls of statutes of limitations center around the fear of prejudice to the defendant because of "stale" evidence and, to a lesser extent, that a defendant will be subjected to long-term liability. The preoccupation with "stale" evidence is unfounded as "[t]he modern exclusionary and hearsay rules exclude evidence which are unreliable or may create substantial danger of undue prejudice. The function and effect of the modern rules of evidence supplant the evidentiary function of date-of-injury accrual."

Additionally, both the concerns of "stale" evidence and long-term liability do not, in practice, bar the application of rules which toll a statute of limitations for substantial periods of time. For example, the application of the delayed discovery rule can potentially lead to a very long period of time between the tort and the legal proceedings. The same is true for cases tolled by infancy.

. . . .

### III. Insanity

In New York, the statutory exception to the statute of limitations is CPLR 208, which tolls the limitations period, if a person is insane, for as long as the disability lasts. The basic standard for "insanity" within the meaning of CPLR 208 is an inability "to protect [one's] legal rights because of an over-all inability to function in society."[5] "Insanity" is "largely a factual question."

. . . .

### IV. Duress

Duress originated in the common law, but is sometimes referred to as justifying the application of estoppel and as constituting inequitable conduct. Thus, although duress is properly a common law doctrine, sources of authority for duress can also be found in cases dealing with equitable estoppel. The standard for duress is subjective: "The condition of mind produced by threats which render a person incapable of exercising his free will is and should be the only inquiry." Duress must be an element of the underlying cause of action, and "where duress is part of the cause of action, it tolls the statute of limitations for as long as the duress continues."

The case law around duress has developed primarily in the context of parties who are not intimates. Sex abuse survivors, who are considered to manifest a form of post-traumatic stress disorder as do survivors of domestic violence, have argued duress with mixed success. The main sticking point appears to be that courts cannot understand that duress would continue even though the abuse creating the duress has a finite beginning and end. Nonetheless, duress is a potentially useful exception for some survivors where the facts of the case support its use: for example, where there is evidence that an abuser has continued to harass or stalk her or his partner. Since duress is so often folded in with estoppel, it can be used to bolster an estoppel argument despite being doctrinally separate.

Duress places its focus on coercion by the defendant and the prevention of the plaintiff from acting in a timely manner because of this coercion. Courts have found themselves somewhat at ease with the conception of an abused person as degraded to the point of utter passivity and duress requires only a slight adjustment to that view. Duress straddles a middle area: courts will have to change their conception of "duress" to accommodate the reality of domestic violence, but they can still maintain the comfortable view of the abused as requiring the protection of the court because she is fearful and weak. Duress, is therefore, a mixed solution to the question of how best to toll the statute of limitations.

## V. Equitable Estoppel

The principle that forms the basis for equitable estoppel is that one cannot benefit from one's wrong. New York has codified equitable estoppel in the General Obligations Law: the court has the power "to find that by reason of conduct of the party to be charged it is inequitable to permit him to interpose the defense of the statute of limitation." Estoppel focuses on the actions of the tortfeasor as opposed to the victim, which from a policy standpoint, is preferable since the blame is not placed on the victim. The elements of estoppel generally do not make sense when applied to the case of violence between intimates — but this does not mean that estoppel should not be used. Litigation around violence between intimates is comparatively recent and the doctrine of estoppel should change accordingly to encompass these recent developments in the law.

. . . .

Many courts have not allowed the use of equity to toll the statute of limitations for domestic violence and sex abuse cases, the body of litigation most closely analogous to domestic violence. Courts are inconsistent on what prevents them from doing so: some say too much time has passed, while others cannot understand the nature of an abused person's capacity to function after trauma. Still others recommend that the Legislature address the issue.

Battering has the purpose of eroding the abused's physical and mental ability to function — to isolate the abused and to make her or him dependent on the abuser. Since the abuser's wrong created the situation where the abused is unable — because he or she is too afraid, or mentally, emotionally, or physically degraded — to bring an action, the abuser should not be allowed to benefit from having created those circumstances. The estoppel doctrine concentrates on the abuser's behavior as opposed to the insanity exception, which focuses exclusively on the abused's capacity. The use of estoppel, in lieu of the insanity exception, would ameliorate the pattern and practice of "blaming the victim."

. . . .

An infamous New York case from 30 years ago cast light on the horrifying level of domestic violence that took place in the home of Joel Steinberg and Hedda Nussbaum. On November 1, 1987 six-year-old Lisa Steinberg was gravely injured by her guardian, Joel Steinberg, who together with Nussbaum, failed to obtain any medical attention for her until the following morning, even though the child was injured and unconscious. Lisa died several days later when she was removed from a life support system at the hospital.

Steinberg was a criminal defense lawyer, and his live-in companion, Nussbaum, was a former children's book editor. Both were initially charged in Lisa's death until it was determined that for most of their 10-year relationship, Steinberg had been brutally beating Nussbaum, rendering her, in the view of the prosecutors, unable to intervene to save her child's life. Or to protect herself, for that matter.

In late 1988, in the midst of the criminal trial against Steinberg, Nussbaum filed a $3 million civil suit against him. In it, Nussbaum alleged Steinberg "engaged in a course of conduct which included but was not limited to hitting, smacking, punching, choking, shoving and otherwise assaulting" her intermittently from 1977 to Nov. 2, 1987.[2]

One of the threshold issues of the Nussbaum civil suit was whether she was barred by the New York statute of limitations, or whether the statute was tolled by reason of the fact Steinberg's numerous acts of brutality rendered her legally insane.

## Nussbaum v. Steinberg
New York Supreme Court
Ind. No. 23416/88 (March 6, 1997)

STEVEN E. LIEBMAN, SPECIAL REFEREE

. . . .

The notorious and rather dismal circumstances underlying this lawsuit have been widely publicized, both in the context of this action and a prior highly infamous criminal case involving the parties. The criminal case resulted in the defendant's incarceration for the death of his "adopted" daughter Lisa. The plaintiff, Hedda Nussbaum, instituted this action against the named defendant, Joel Steinberg, to recover money damages from him for the extensive physical and psychological injuries he inflicted upon her during their lengthy personal relationship. The plaintiff's Complaint alleges causes of action for assault, battery, intentional infliction of emotional distress and prima facia tort, based upon acts that occurred from 1978 through November 2, 1987. Plaintiff initiated this action in October 1988, and concedes that almost all of the events alleged in the complaint occurred more than one year before the action commenced. However, it is plaintiff's position that the process by which the defendant effectively achieved his psychological dominance over her actually occurred in the first years of their relationship, from 1975 through 1978, even before

---

2. Ronald Sullivan, *Steinberg Hit Lisa in Face, Witness Says*, N.Y. TIMES, Nov. 29, 1988.

the defendant ever physically assaulted the plaintiff. By that time, the consequence to the plaintiff was that she believed that she was incapable of existing without him. . . .

The defendant moved for summary judgment dismissing the Complaint upon the ground that the causes of action alleged therein were barred by the one year Statute of Limitations, pursuant to CPLR § 215(3). In response, the plaintiff contends that the Statute of Limitations was tolled on the grounds afforded by CPLR § 208, which permits a tolling of the Statute of Limitations as a result of plaintiff's alleged qualifying incapacity. Plaintiff argues that the defendant's physical and psychological abuse rendered her incapable of independent thought or conduct, and that she thereby suffered from insanity within the statutory meaning of CPLR § 208. . . . It is plaintiff's assertion that it was not until her permanent separation from Joel Steinberg in November 1987, and a year thereafter of intensive in-patient psychiatric treatment, that she was able to comprehend her true circumstances and perceive the wrongs Joel Steinberg had done to her so as to permit her to pursue legal redress by the commencement of this action.

. . . .

Where the evidence shows that an individual is generally able to care for oneself and is aware of any possible claims that might exist, courts will disallow the tolling of the applicable Statute of Limitations. (*McBride v. County of Westchester*, 211 AD2d 792 [1995]). However, the law cannot presently exclude or blindly ignore domestic violence cases from the tolling provisions under CPLR § 208, where the allegations of such domestic violence can be proven to constitute in an individual an overall inability to function in society as a result. The argument that applying CPLR § 208 to victims of domestic violence, so as to potentially enlarge the group of plaintiffs, is not a valid basis for denying application of the tolling statute to such victims of domestic violence. The application of the current statutory insanity standard to these victims will not require any more detailed or different attention than other plaintiffs, in that they will still have to meet the requirements of CPLR § 208, as would any other tort claimant. . . .

It must be recognized that domestic violence, by its very nature, is much more insidious and complex than even other intentional torts or crimes involving assault, or other abuse, in that the abuser and the victim are generally found to be in a close or intimate relationship. The destructive impact of violence in such an intimate relationship may be so complete that the victim is rendered incapable of independent judgment even to save one's own life. In various forms, the victim may very well turn to the tormentor for connection and support. Significantly, because the usual close proximity and/or relationship of the domestic violence abuser and the victim, the abused and battered person is often less able than intentional tort victims to obtain legal protection or recourse after being abused or assaulted. The emotional commitments and the psychological attachments that domestic violence victims usually have to their abusers provides a significant impediment to the victims being capable of seeking help or assistance, even where the abuser does not appear to be actively restraining them from seeking aid. These factors, in various combinations, confirm the devastating effect that such prolonged psychological and physical abuse can have on the victims; including a demonstration that such a person would be clearly incapacitated and incapable of recognizing or asserting their legal rights. In instances where a batterer's primary goal is often absolute control over every aspect of the victim's life, the combination of such extensive control and violence may disable one's independent judgment and functioning so as to place that person within the insanity definition of CPLR § 208.

Plaintiff testified on her own behalf detailing, through her own testimony, her story of her relationship with Joel Steinberg for over a ten-year period, that only ended because of the intervening and tragic death of Lisa Steinberg. Plaintiff's testimony recounted the years of the horrific physical abuse and violence and total emotional and psychological domination by the defendant over every aspect of her life and being. The magnitude of this traumatic, brutal and destructive relationship was dramatically illustrated by the New York City Police Department videotape of the plaintiff, shortly after her arrest, evidencing physical injuries to virtually every part of her body. No less evident than the condition of her ravaged and mutilated body were her significant psychological disorders and mental defects that undoubtedly were the consequences of her relationship with Joel Steinberg.

Plaintiff also offered the testimony of her treating psychiatrist Dr. Samuel C. Klagsbrun and a prominent expert in psychological trauma Professor Bessel van der Kolk, M.D. The defendant relied on the offer of the expert testimony of Dr. Daniel Schwartz, a retired forensic psychiatrist.

Dr. Schwartz offered his opinion that throughout the entire period of 1975 through 1987, the plaintiff never became incapable of protecting her legal rights or functioning overall in society. Dr. Schwartz characterized plaintiff as having made bad choices or used very poor judgment, but that she still retained the ability to exercise her free will and make decisions. . . . Dr. Schwartz described his former practice as primarily examining criminal defendants to establish their competency to stand trial under CPL § 730. He admitted that he had no clinical knowledge about the psychology or life experience of battered women, nor received any training in physical or psychological trauma. Dr. Schwartz conceded that he had never worked with any professionals who treated victims of domestic violence; and he was unaware of his own former institution's protocols for the treatment of battered women. He eventually concluded that plaintiff suffered from what he described as a dependent personality disorder, and that she retained power to extricate herself from the control of the defendant if she had desired to.

The testimony offered by Dr. Klagsbrun and Dr. van der Kolk confirmed their respective expert opinions that Hedda Nussbaum decisively demonstrated that her behavior was consistent with prolonged and extensive psychological and physical abuse. The result of such exposure, they concluded, made the plaintiff incapable of functioning independently of the defendant to the extent of making her unable to make her own judgments about her life or the protection of her interests. Dr. Klagsbrun testified that at the time the plaintiff was admitted to his hospital for treatment she was still delusional and still suffering from a psychotic disorder. He also described Ms. Nussbaum as continuing to display "robotic" impaired functioning and to even talk about the defendant in an adoring manner. Dr. Klagsbrun further stated that the plaintiff believed that she was responsible for her abuse; a perception confirmed as common among trauma victims by Dr. van der Kolk. The testimony of Dr. Klagsbrun emphasized that the impact on Hedda of the defendant's violence so impaired her judgment that she was unable to make judgments and decisions which were basic to human life. Dr. van der Kolk concluded that the plaintiff had even lost her capacity to escape or take independent action; and for all intents and purposes, the plaintiff was "dead to the world." Both physicians maintained that the plaintiff's process to recovery was slow and painful. Notwithstanding the opinion of Dr. Schwartz in this case, it appears that every competent psychiatrist who had examined the plaintiff found that she was not functioning in society, and that this incapacity was the result of chronic trauma inflicted upon her by the defendant. . . .

Upon review of the testimony offered by the parties' expert witnesses, I find the testimony offered by Dr. Schwartz without substance or probative weight. In the instant case, the opinion of Dr. Schwartz, as to the plaintiff's disability condition during the period at issue, is unsupported by any objective evidence, and therefore fails to provide any basis upon which the Statute of Limitations should not be tolled. The court fully credits the testimony of Drs. Klagsbrun and van der Kolk, as well as their findings and expert opinions regarding the plaintiff's physical, mental and emotional status to the extent that the plaintiff was rendered incapable of pursuing her legal rights until late in 1988, and that the plaintiff established a sufficient basis that she continuously suffered from an overall inability to function in society. The court further credits the unrebutted testimony of the plaintiff with respect to her overall mental condition and circumstances of her relationship with the defendant, that made her unable to protect her legal rights because of her over-all inability to function. In light of the foregoing, the weight of the evidence adduced at the hearing clearly establishes that the plaintiff suffered from the disability of insanity, up to and through September 1988, and is therefore entitled to the benefits of the tolling provisions set forth in CPLR § 208, permitting her to proceed in her civil action against the defendant . . .

## Nussbaum v. Steinberg

New York Supreme Court, Appellate Division

269 A.D.2d 192 (2000)

Order, Supreme Court, New York County (Steven Liebman, Spec. Ref.), entered March 13, 1997, which denied defendant's motion for summary judgment seeking dismissal of the action as time-barred. . . .

The evidence adduced at the hearing and credited by the Special Referee amply demonstrated that, during the 10-year period preceding the commencement of this action, plaintiff was unable to protect her legal rights because of an overall inability to function in society, which tolled the one-year Statute of Limitations for intentional torts pursuant to CPLR 208 (*see, McCarthy v. Volkswagen of Am.,* 55 NY2d 543, 548).

## III. Expanding Tort Liability for Domestic Violence

### A. Battered Women's Syndrome

Recognition by the courts that suffering multiple assaults during the course of a long relationship or marriage can result not only in physical harm but in emotional distress was a tremendous breakthrough for plaintiffs. The New Jersey judiciary, often on the cutting edge in tort actions, recognized early that the battered women's syndrome—besides providing justification to what would otherwise be criminal acts on the part of a victim of domestic violence—could also be the basis for a victim's civil claim.

**Cusseaux v. Pickett**

New Jersey Superior Court

279 N.J. Super. 335 (1994)

Napolitano, J.S.C.

### I. INTRODUCTION

This matter is before the court on defendant's motion to dismiss the first count of plaintiff's complaint for failure to state a cause of action pursuant to R. 4:6-2(e). The defendant argues that the "battered-woman's syndrome" is not recognized as an affirmative cause of action by the courts of this State. This court denies the motion to dismiss and holds that the "battered-woman's syndrome" is now a cognizable cause of action under the laws of New Jersey.

### II. FACTS

Plaintiff, Jean Marie Cusseaux, lived with the defendant, Wilson Pickett, Jr., for a period of about ten years, from 1982 to 1992. Plaintiff alleges that, during this time period, defendant severely mistreated her, jeopardized her health and well-being, and caused her physical injuries on numerous occasions. Plaintiff further alleges that defendant's actions were part of a continuous course of conduct and constituted a pattern of violent behavior, frequently associated with his being intoxicated. Plaintiff alleges that the acts of abuse and violence are too numerous to detail with specificity; however, on a number of occasions, she was required to seek medical attention. As a result of the defendant's behavior, plaintiff alleges that she was caused to suffer the condition of the battered woman's syndrome, which includes serious personal and emotional injuries that will require medical and other attention. On April 15, 1992, defendant's final assault allegedly caused plaintiff finally to end the relationship.

## III. LAW

. . . .

*B. Battered-Woman's Syndrome*

The battered-woman's syndrome was first recognized by the courts in New Jersey in *State v. Kelly,* 97 N.J. 178, 478 A.2d 364 (1984), where the Court acknowledged it as an element of self-defense. The Court held that expert testimony on the battered-woman's syndrome was admissible because it is relevant and material to establish the honesty and reasonability of the defendant's belief that she was in imminent danger of serious bodily injury or death. *Kelly, supra,* 97 N.J. at 201, 478 A.2d 364; *see also State v. Myers,* 239 N.J. Super. 158, 169, 570 A.2d 1260 (App. Div. 1990).

. . . .

Notwithstanding, there has yet to be a civil case in New Jersey that has recognized the battered-woman's syndrome. Thus, it is this case of first impression which now addresses whether the battered-woman's syndrome is a cognizable cause of action under the laws of New Jersey.

## IV. ANALYSIS

It is well established in this State that an injured party may sustain a cause of action for serious personal and emotional injuries that are directly and causally related to the actions of another person. *Eyrich for Eyrich v. Dam,* 193 N.J. Super. 244, 473 A.2d 539 (App. Div.), *certif. denied, Eyrich v. Dam,* 97 N.J. 583, 483 A.2d 127 (1984), *appeal after remand,* 203 N.J. Super. 144, 495 A.2d 1375 (App. Div. 1984). As discussed above, the Legislature has specifically found domestic violence to be a serious crime against society. N.J.S.A. 2C:25-18. More importantly, in enacting the Prevention of Domestic Violence Act, the Legislature recognized that our judicial and law enforcement system was insufficient to address the problem. If this Act had never become law, the ubiquitous deficiency of our legal system would continue in spite of the fact that the acts listed among those classified as "domestic violence" under the statute were already criminal offenses.

. . . .

[T]his court will recognize the battered-woman's syndrome as an affirmative cause of action under the laws of New Jersey. In order to state a cause of action for the battered-woman's syndrome, the plaintiff must allege the following elements. The plaintiff must show 1) involvement in a marital or marital-like intimate relationship; and 2) physical or psychological abuse perpetrated by the dominant partner to the relationship over an extended period of time; and 3) the aforestated abuse has caused recurring physical or psychological injury over the course of the relationship; and 4) a past or present inability to take any action to improve or alter the situation unilaterally.[3]

. . . .

---

3. [n7] Nothing in this opinion should be construed to limit the application of these principles only to women in traditional marital or marital-like relationships. Indeed, in any domestic intimate partnership, the victim, whether female or male, whether the union is heterosexual or homosexual, may plead a battered-person syndrome so long as the aforementioned requirements are met. It is the

## V. CONCLUSION

This court holds that the battered-woman's syndrome constitutes an affirmative cause of action under the laws of New Jersey. Defendant's motion to dismiss Count One of the complaint for failure to state a cause of action is denied.

## B. The Tort of Domestic Violence

The legislative creation of the tort of domestic violence eliminates proof problems as to whether the continued conduct of the defendant in a civil action caused the victim to suffer from battered women's syndrome as well as the stigma for domestic violence victims of having to claim a mental disability or insanity in order to toll statutes of limitation. California's domestic violence tort statute follows.

### California Civil Code § 1708.6 (2016) Tort of domestic violence; Damages

(a) A person is liable for the tort of domestic violence if the plaintiff proves both of the following elements:

(1) The infliction of injury upon the plaintiff resulting from abuse, as defined in subdivision (a) of Section 13700 of the Penal Code.

(2) The abuse was committed by the defendant, a person having a relationship with the plaintiff as defined in subdivision (b) of Section 13700 of the Penal Code.

(b) A person who commits an act of domestic violence upon another is liable to that person for damages, including, but not limited to, general damages, special damages, and punitive damages . . . .

### California Penal Code § 13700 (2016)

. . . .

(a) "Abuse" means intentionally or recklessly causing or attempting to cause bodily injury, or placing another person in reasonable apprehension of imminent serious bodily injury to himself or herself, or another.

(b) "Domestic violence" means abuse committed against an adult or a minor who is a spouse, former spouse, cohabitant, former cohabitant, or person with whom the suspect has had a child or is having or has had a dating or engagement relationship. For purposes of this subdivision, "cohabitant" means two unrelated adult persons living together for a substantial period of time, resulting in some permanency of relationship. Factors that may determine whether persons are cohabiting include, but are not limited to, (1) sexual relations between the parties while sharing the same living quarters, (2) sharing of income or expenses, (3) joint use or ownership of

---

unhappy history of domestic violence against women in traditional marital relationships which has given this tort its name.

property, (4) whether the parties hold themselves out as husband and wife, (5) the continuity of the relationship, and (6) the length of the relationship. . . .

## California Code of Civil Procedure § 340.15 (2016)
## Action for damages resulting from domestic violence

(a) In any civil action for recovery of damages suffered as a result of domestic violence, the time for commencement of the action shall be the later of the following:

(1) Within three years from the date of the last act of domestic violence by the defendant against the plaintiff.

(2) Within three years from the date the plaintiff discovers or reasonably should have discovered that an injury or illness resulted from an act of domestic violence by the defendant against the plaintiff.

## C. Infliction of Emotional Distress

Even without the legislative creation of a new tort of domestic violence, judicial understanding that domestic violence constitutes more than the infliction of physical injuries makes it easier for survivors to seek civil redress.

### Feltmeier v. Feltmeier
Illinois Supreme Court
207 Ill. 2d 263 (2003)

JUSTICE RARICK delivered the opinion of the court:

Plaintiff, Lynn Feltmeier, and defendant, Robert Feltmeier, were married on October 11, 1986, and divorced on December 16, 1997. The judgment for dissolution of marriage incorporated the terms of a December 10, 1997, marital settlement agreement. On August 25, 1999, Lynn sued Robert for the intentional infliction of emotional distress. According to the allegations contained in the complaint, Robert engaged in a pattern of domestic abuse, both physical and mental in nature, which began shortly after the marriage and did not cease even after its dissolution.

On October 20, 1999, Robert filed a motion to dismiss the suit under sections 2-615 and 2-619 of the Code of Civil Procedure (735 ILCS 5/2-615, 2-619 (West 1998)), maintaining that the complaint failed to allege facts that give rise to an action for intentional infliction of emotional distress and that, even if the conduct alleged was actionable, the claim was not viable because the statute of limitations had run on most of the alleged misconduct. The circuit court denied Robert's motion to dismiss on February 14, 2000. Robert then filed an amended motion to dismiss under section 2-619, arguing that provisions contained in the marital settlement agreement released him from the claim presented in Lynn's lawsuit. The circuit court denied this motion on June 23, 2000.

. . . .

The first matter before us for review is whether Lynn's complaint states a cause of action for intentional infliction of emotional distress. . . .

According to the allegations contained in Lynn's complaint, since the parties' marriage in October 1986, and continuing for over a year after the December 1997 dissolution of their marriage:

"[Robert] entered into a continuous and outrageous course of conduct toward [Lynn] with either the intent to cause emotional distress to [Lynn] or with reckless disregard as to whether such conduct would cause emotional distress to [Lynn], said continuing course of conduct, including but not limited to, the following:

A. On repeated occasions, [Robert] has battered [Lynn] by striking, kicking, shoving, pulling hair and bending and twisting her limbs and toes.

* * *

B. On repeated occasions, [Robert] has prevented [Lynn] from leaving the house to escape the abuse.

* * *

C. On repeated occasions, [Robert] has yelled insulting and demeaning epithets at [Lynn]. Further, [Robert] has engaged in verbal abuse which included threats and constant criticism of [Lynn] in such a way as to demean, humiliate, and degrade [Lynn]. * * *

D. On repeated occasions, [Robert] threw items at [Lynn] with the intent to cause her harm.

* * *

E. On repeated occasions, [Robert] attempted to isolate [Lynn] from her family and friends and would get very upset if [Lynn] would show the marks and bruises resulting from [Robert's] abuse to others.

F. On repeated occasions since the divorce, [Robert] has engaged in stalking behavior.

* * *

G. On at least one occasion, [Robert] has attempted to interfere with [Lynn's] employment by confiscating her computer. Additionally, [Robert] broke into [Lynn's] locked drug cabinet for work on or about March 23, 1997."

The complaint further alleged, as examples of conduct within the categories set forth above, dozens of episodes of abusive behavior, including specific details and time frames for the various physical and emotional attacks.

In *McGrath v. Fahey*, 126 Ill. 2d 78, 127 Ill. Dec. 724, 533 N.E.2d 806 (1988), this court set forth the three elements necessary to state a cause of action for intentional infliction of emotional distress, stating:

> "First, the conduct involved must be truly extreme and outrageous. Second, the actor must either *intend* that his conduct inflict severe emotional distress, or know that there is at least a high probability that his conduct will cause severe emotional distress. Third, the conduct must in fact cause *severe* emotional distress. (*Public Finance Corp. v. Davis* (1976), 66 Ill. 2d 85, 90, 4 Ill. Dec. 652, 360 N.E.2d 765.)" (Emphases in original.) *McGrath*, 126 Ill. 2d at 86.

In the case at bar, Robert first contends that the allegations of Lynn's complaint do not sufficiently set forth conduct which was extreme and outrageous when considered "[i]n the context of the subjective and fluctuating nature of the marital relationship." . . .

One policy concern that has been advanced is the need to recognize the "mutual concessions implicit in marriage," and the desire to preserve marital harmony. See *Henriksen v. Cameron*, 622 A.2d 1135, 1138–39 (Me. 1993). However, in this case, brought after the parties were divorced, "there is clearly no marital harmony remaining to be preserved." *Henriksen*, 622 A.2d at 1139. Moreover, we agree with the Supreme Judicial Court of Maine that "behavior that is 'utterly intolerable in a civilized society' and is intended to cause severe emotional distress is not behavior that should be protected in order to promote marital harmony and peace." *Henriksen*, 622 A.2d at 1139, quoting *Vicnire v. Ford Motor Credit Co.*, 401 A.2d 148, 154 (Me. 1979).

. . . .

A second policy concern is the threat of excessive and frivolous litigation if the tort is extended to acts occurring in the marital setting. Admittedly, the likelihood of vindictive litigation is of particular concern following a dissolution of marriage, because "the events leading to most divorces involve some level of emotional distress." *Henriksen*, 622 A.2d at 1139. However, we believe that the showing required of a plaintiff in order to recover damages for intentional infliction of emotional distress provides a built-in safeguard against excessive and frivolous litigation. . . .

Another policy consideration which has been raised is that a tort action for compensation would be redundant. However, as earlier noted, while our legislature has recognized the inadequacy of our legal system in allowing abusers to escape financial liability for domestic violence, the laws of this state provide no compensatory relief for injuries sustained. An action for dissolution of marriage also provides no compensatory relief for domestic abuse. See *Merenoff v. Merenoff*, 76 N.J. 535, 556, 388 A.2d 951, 962 (1978). . . . In Illinois, as in most other states, courts are not allowed to consider marital misconduct in the distribution of property when dissolving a marriage. See 750 ILCS 5/503(d) (West 2002).

After examining case law from courts around the country, we find the majority have recognized that public policy considerations should not bar actions for intentional infliction of emotional distress between spouses or former spouses based on conduct occurring during the marriage. See *Henriksen*, 622 A.2d at 1140 (and cases cited therein). Additionally, our appellate court, while only considering the *res judicata* and collateral estoppel effects of such suits, has found that a plaintiff's intentional infliction of emotional distress action against her former husband for conspiring to murder her was not barred by their prior dissolution proceeding. See *Vance v. Chandler*, 231 Ill. App. 3d 747, 753, 173 Ill. Dec. 525, 597 N.E.2d 233 (1992).

. . . .

Therefore, we conclude that neither the policy considerations commonly raised nor the law of this state support a conclusion that an action for intentional infliction of emotional distress based upon conduct occurring in the marital setting should be barred or subject to any heightened threshold for establishing outrageousness. With this background in mind, we now examine the allegations set forth in Lynn's complaint to determine whether Robert's conduct satisfies the "outrageousness" requirement.

. . . .

The issue of whether domestic abuse can be sufficiently outrageous to sustain a cause of action for intentional infliction of emotional distress is apparently one of first impression in Illinois. . . . In the instant case, we must agree with the appellate court that, when the above-summarized allegations of the complaint are viewed in their entirety, they show a type of domestic abuse that is extreme enough to be actionable:

> "It combines more than a decade of verbal insults and humiliations with episodes where freedom of movement was deprived and where physical injury was often inflicted. The alleged pattern of abuse, combined with its duration, worked a humiliation and loss of self-esteem. Regardless of the form in which it arrived, violence was certain to erupt, and when seasons of spousal abuse turn to years that span the course of a decade, we are unwilling to dismiss it on grounds that it is unworthy of outrage." 333 Ill. App. 3d at 1176.

Therefore, where we find that a reasonable trier of fact could easily conclude that Robert's conduct was so outrageous as to be regarded as intolerable in a civilized community, we reject his contention that the complaint fails to sufficiently allege this element.

It is equally clear, and Robert does not argue to the contrary, that Lynn's complaint adequately pleads the second element necessary to state a cause of action for intentional infliction of emotional distress, *i.e.*, that Robert either intended to inflict, or knew that his conduct was likely to inflict, severe emotional distress upon Lynn. However, Robert does contest the adequacy of the complaint as to the third necessary element, that his conduct in fact caused severe emotional distress. He argues that Lynn's complaint "contains no factual allegations from which the level of severity of the emotional distress could be inferred." We must disagree.

Lynn's complaint specifically alleges that, "[a]s a direct and proximate result of the entirety of [Robert's] course of conduct, [she] has sustained severe emotional distress including, but not limited to[,] loss of self-esteem and difficulty in forming other relationships, and a form of Post Traumatic Stress Disorder sustained by battered and abused women as a result of being repeatedly physically and verbally abused and harassed over a long period of time." The complaint also alleges that Lynn has suffered depression and a "fear of being with other men," and that her enjoyment of life has been substantially curtailed. Finally, it is alleged that Lynn has incurred, and will continue to incur, medical and psychological expenses in an effort to become cured or relieved from the effects of her mental distress.

Emotional distress includes all highly unpleasant mental reactions, such as fright, horror, grief, shame, humiliation, embarrassment, anger, chagrin, disappointment, worry, and nausea. See Restatement (Second) of Torts § 46, Comment *j*, at 77 (1965). . . . Here, we find that Lynn has sufficiently alleged that as a result of enduring Robert's physical and psychological abuse for the duration of their 11-year marriage and beyond, she suffered severe emotional distress. Therefore, where the complaint sets forth sufficient facts which, if proven, could entitle Lynn to relief, we conclude that she has stated a cause of action for intentional infliction of emotional distress. We, of course, express no opinion on the substantive merits of Lynn's complaint. We simply hold that, taking the allegations of the complaint as true, as we are required to do for purposes of our review, the complaint is sufficient to survive a motion to dismiss.

The second certified question we examine is whether Lynn's claim for intentional infliction of emotional distress based on conduct prior to August 25, 1997, is barred by the applicable statute of limitations. Robert contends that each separate act of abuse triggered a new statute of limitations so that "all claims by Lynn based upon incidents occurring prior to August 25, 1997," or more than two years before the date on which Lynn filed her complaint, would be time-barred. Lynn responds that Robert's actions constitute a "continuing tort" for purposes of the statute of limitations and that her complaint, filed within two years of the occurrence of the last such tortious act, is therefore timely. The appellate court majority agreed with Lynn. 333 Ill. App. 3d at 1181.

. . . .

Generally, a limitations period begins to run when facts exist that authorize one party to maintain an action against another. *Sundance Homes, Inc. v. County of Du Page*, 195 Ill. 2d 257, 266, 253 Ill. Dec. 806, 746 N.E.2d 254 (2001), quoting *Davis v. Munie*, 235 Ill. 620, 622, 85 N.E. 943 (1908). However, under the "continuing tort" or "continuing violation" rule, "where a tort involves a continuing or repeated injury, the limitations period does not begin to run until the date of the last injury or the date the tortious acts cease." *Belleville Toyota, Inc. v. Toyota Motor Sales, U.S.A., Inc.*, 199 Ill. 2d 325, 345, 264 Ill. Dec. 283, 770 N.E.2d 177 (2002).

. . . .

In the instant case, Robert cites *Belleville Toyota* and maintains that "each of the alleged acts of abuse inflicted by Robert upon Lynn over a 12 year period are separate and distinct incidents which give rise to separate and distinct causes of action, rather than one single, continuous, unbroken, violation or wrong which continued over the entire period of 12 years." We must disagree. While it is true that the conduct set forth in Lynn's complaint could be considered separate acts constituting separate offenses of, *inter alia*, assault, defamation and battery, Lynn has alleged, and we have found, that Robert's conduct *as a whole* states a cause of action for intentional infliction of emotional distress....

. . . .

The purpose behind a statute of limitations is to prevent stale claims, not to preclude claims before they are ripe for adjudication (*Guzman v. C.R. Epperson Construction, Inc.*, 196 Ill. 2d 391, 400, 256 Ill. Dec. 827, 752 N.E.2d 1069 (2001)), and certainly not to shield a wrongdoer (*Tom Olesker's Exciting World of Fashion, Inc. v. Dun & Bradstreet, Inc.*, 61 Ill. 2d 129, 137, 334 N.E.2d 160 (1975))....

Thus, we find that the two-year statute of limitations for this action began to run in August 1999, because Lynn's complaint includes allegations of tortious behavior by Robert occurring as late as that month. Applying the continuing tort rule to the instant case, Lynn's complaint, filed August 25, 1999, was clearly timely and her claims based on conduct prior to August 25, 1997, are not barred by the applicable statute of limitations.

... *Affirmed.*

## Kloepfel v. Bokor

Washington Supreme Court

149 Wn. 2d 192 (2003) (en banc)

SANDERS, J.

The Court of Appeals affirmed a $60,000 judgment in favor of Judy Kloepfel against Joseph Bokor for intentional infliction of emotional distress. The issue here is whether the tort of outrage requires proof of severe emotional distress by objective symptomatology and a medical diagnosis....

Mr. Bokor and Ms. Kloepfel began a relationship in 1986, moved in together to share expenses in 1994, and separated in July 1997 when Kloepfel moved out. Bokor, a former police officer, claimed their relationship became romantic when Kloepfel and he lived together. But she claims it was merely platonic. In any case, Kloepfel sought a restraining order against Bokor in August 1997. The court ordered Bokor to stay away from Kloepfel, and to not call her, threaten her, or go to her home or place of business. Bokor ignored this and every subsequent court order to stay away from Kloepfel.

Bokor's violations of no contact orders led to his conviction for several misdemeanors and a felony. He was convicted in January 1998 and again in March 1999 of "harassment, domestic violence." In September 1999 he was found guilty of making harassing phone calls and felony stalking. Bokor admitted he had repeatedly violated these no-contact orders to stay away from Kloepfel. The violations continued until at least October 2000.

While under a no-contact order he threatened to kill Kloepfel. He threatened to kill the man she was dating if he kept seeing her. While watching her house, he saw the truck of another man in her driveway and called that man's wife to inform her where her husband was, implying an affair. In all he called Kloepfel's home 640 times, her work 100 times, and the homes of men she knew numerous times as well. Kloepfel began spending weekends away from home to avoid Bokor. Her employer made various arrangements to protect Kloepfel from Bokor at work.

The court found Bokor's conduct severely disrupted Kloepfel's life and made it impossible for her to carry on a normal dating relationship with anyone else. His repeated phone calls and his driving by her house at all hours disturbed her privacy. Although she did not seek professional care of a doctor or counselor, her physical symptoms of emotional distress included nervousness, sleeplessness, hyper-vigilance, and stomach upset.

In December 1999 Kloepfel sued Bokor for invasion of privacy, malicious harassment, and intentional and negligent infliction of emotional distress. A bench trial was held on the claim for intentional infliction of emotional distress only. Kloepfel prevailed on her claim of intentional infliction of emotional distress. The court awarded Kloepfel $60,265, including a judgment for $60,000, costs, interest, and statutory attorney fees. . . .

This issue requiring us to interpret the meaning of "severe emotional distress" for purposes of the third element of outrage is a question of law, and our review is de novo. *State v. Johnson,* 128 Wn. 2d 431, 443, 909 P.2d 293 (1996).

I

The tort of outrage requires the proof of three elements: (1) extreme and outrageous conduct, (2) intentional or reckless infliction of emotional distress, and (3) actual result to plaintiff of severe emotional distress. *Reid v. Pierce County,* 136 Wn. 2d 195, 202, 961 P.2d 333 (1998) (citing *Dicomes v. State,* 113 Wn. 2d 612, 630, 782 P.2d 1002 (1989) (quoting *Rice v. Janovich,* 109 Wn. 2d 48, 61, 742 P.2d 1230 (1987))). These elements were adopted from the *Restatement (Second) of Torts* § 46 (1965) by this court in *Grimsby v. Samson,* 85 Wn. 2d 52, 59–60, 530 P.2d 291 (1975).

. . . .

Bokor argues, however, that the court should have required evidence of "objective symptomatology" and a medical diagnosis to establish severe emotional distress. Pet. for Review at 2. The term "objective symptomatology" emerged as a requirement for proof of *negligent* infliction of emotional distress in *Hunsley v. Giard,* 87 Wn. 2d 424, 553 P.2d 1096 (1976), just one year after the adoption of the tort of outrage in *Grimsby.*

For negligent infliction of emotional distress, a plaintiff must prove he has suffered emotional distress by "objective symptomatology," and the "emotional distress must be susceptible to medical diagnosis and proved through medical evidence." *Hegel v. McMahon,* 136 Wn. 2d 122, 135, 960 P.2d 424 (1998). The symptoms of emotional distress must also "constitute a diagnosable emotional disorder." *Id.*

Bokor argues the same requirement applies to claims for outrage, relying on *Haubry v. Snow,* 106 Wn. App. 666, 31 P.3d 1186 (2001). *Haubry* held, with respect to an outrage claim, "[t]here is no doubt that [the defendant's] actions were outrageous and inappropriate. However, as with the claim of negligent infliction of emotional distress, to survive summary judgment [the plaintiff] necessarily had to establish that the emotional distress is manifested by objective symptoms." *Haubry,* 106 Wn. App. at 680–81.

. . . .

Bokor also argued in the Court of Appeals that *Benoy v. Simons,* 66 Wn. App. 56, 831 P.2d 167 (1992) supported an objective symptomatology requirement for intentional infliction of emotional distress. *Kloepfel v. Bokor,* noted at 110 Wn. App. 1059, slip op. at 7. *Benoy* does suggest severe emotional distress should be proved by objective physical symptoms, 66 Wn. App. at 63, but the cases cited in *Benoy* provide no more support than those cited in *Haubry. Benoy* cites *Lawson v. Boeing Co.,* 58 Wn. App. 261, 792 P.2d 545 (1990), and *Spurrell v. Block,* 40 Wn. App. 854, 701 P.2d 529 (1985), but *Lawson* and *Spurrell* did not require proof by objective symptomatology; rather they held plaintiffs had not shown severe emotional distress on the facts. *Lawson,* 58 Wn. App. at 270; *Spurrell,* 40 Wn. App. at 862–63. These cases appear to have followed the Restatement's requirement that to be severe emotional distress must be more than "transient and trivial emotional distress" which is "a part of the price of living among people." *Restatement (Second) of Torts* § 46 cmt. j.

We have never applied the objective symptomatology requirement to intentional infliction of emotional distress. *Berger v. Sonneland,* 144 Wn. 2d 91, 113, 26 P.3d 257 (2001) ("Washington cases have limited the objective symptom requirement to negligent infliction of emotional distress claims."); *see also Brower v. Ackerley,* 88 Wn. App. 87, 99–100, 943 P.2d 1141 (1997) ("No Washington case has incorporated [the objective symptomatology requirement] into the tort of outrage."). The basic elements remain unchanged since their adoption from the *Restatement* in *Grimsby,* and we have not grafted an objective symptomatology requirement to them. *See Robel v. Roundup Corp.,* 148 Wn. 2d 35, 51, 59 P.3d 611 (2002).

Quite simply, objective symptomatology is not required to establish intentional infliction of emotional distress. "The general rule is firmly established that physical injury or bodily harm — 'objective symptomology' — is not a prerequisite to recovery of damages where intentional (and, in most states, reckless) emotional harm has been inflicted." 4 Stuart M. Speiser, Charles F. Krause & Alfred W. Gans, The American Law of Torts § 16:17, at 1076 (1987). Many states, including this one, have distinguished negligent infliction of emotional distress from intentional infliction of emotional distress by making bodily harm or objective symptomatology a requirement of negligent but not intentional infliction of emotional distress. *See id.*

II

The intentional tort of outrage was recognized by this court in 1975 in *Grimsby* while the objective symptomatology requirement was first applied to *negligent* infliction of emotional distress a year later in *Hunsley.* Notably, there was no mention of objective symptomatology in *Grimsby.* The question posed in *Hunsley* was whether a plaintiff who suffered emotional distress when a negligently driven car crashed into her house could collect for negligent infliction of emotional distress when she suffered no physical impact and stood outside the zone of immediate danger. *See Hunsley,* 87 Wn. 2d at 425. *Hunsley* held that the plaintiff could recover if she proved negligence, i.e., duty, breach, proximate cause, and damage, and proved the additional requirement of objective symptomatology. *Id.* at 435–36.

The court carefully placed this requirement within the framework of negligence law. The court was mindful of the "view that a negligent act should have some end to its legal consequences." *Hunsley,* 87 Wn. 2d at 435. Though it recognized defendants have a duty to avoid negligent infliction of emotional distress and plaintiffs are to be compensated for damages following a breach of that duty, the court balanced the plaintiff's right of recovery against the policy in negligence cases that liability should be limited where a defendant's act was merely negligent and not reckless or intentional. *See id.* The courts' interest in limiting liability for negligence has a long history. *See, e.g., Palsgraf v. Long Island R.R.,* 248 N.Y. 339, 162 N.E. 99 (1928)....

*Hunsley* similarly limited its holding to cases of *negligence,* recognizing that "[i]ntentional or willful acts, even those involving no physical impact and leading only to mental stress, usually resulted in a cause of action." *Hunsley,* 87 Wn. 2d at 427–28 (citing *Gadbury v. Bleitz,* 133 Wash. 134, 233 P. 299, 44 A.L.R. 425 (1925)). This court in *Bleitz* said, "we have adopted the rule that if such [mental] suffering is the direct result of a wilful wrong as distinguished from one that is merely negligent, then there may be a recovery." *Bleitz,* 133 Wash. at 136. *Hunsley* added, "[f]rom early in its history, this court has allowed recovery of damages for mental distress, even without physical impact or injury, when the defendant's act was willful or intentional." *Hunsley,* 87 Wn. 2d at 431–32 (citing *Willson v. N. Pac. R.R.,* 5 Wash. 621, 32 P. 468, 34 P. 146 (1893); *Davis v. Tacoma Ry. & Power Co.,* 35 Wash. 203, 77 P. 209 (1904); *McClure v. Campbell,* 42 Wash. 252, 84 P. 825 (1906); *Wright v. Beardsley,* 46 Wash. 16, 89 P. 172 (1907); *Nordgren v. Lawrence,* 74 Wash. 305, 133 P. 436 (1913)).

The distinction in treatment between negligence and intentional torts is related to the difference in fault. Society through its courts has a "definite tendency to impose greater responsibility upon a defendant whose conduct was intended to do harm, or was morally wrong." Prosser and Keeton on The Law of Torts § 8, at 37 (W. Page Keeton et al. eds., 5th ed. 1984). Courts generally establish rules which make liability more likely to attach to intentional wrongdoers than to those who are merely negligent. *Id.* Washington is no exception to this rule.

. . . .

We continue to be more likely to allow recovery of emotional distress damages for intentional acts than for negligent ones. *See, e.g., White River Estates v. Hiltbruner,* 134 Wn. 2d 761, 766, 953 P.2d 796 (1998) (holding that emotional distress damages may be a remedy for a statutory violation only if that violation sounds in intentional tort); *Birchler v. Castello Land Co.,* 133 Wn. 2d 106, 942 P.2d 968 (1997) (allowing recovery of emotional distress damages where there was an intentional interference with property interests); *Nord v. Shoreline Sav. Ass'n,* 116 Wn. 2d 477, 483, 805 P.2d 800 (1991) (emotional distress damages have been allowed as part of the recovery for intentional wrongdoing without reference to whether the emotional distress claimed was severe); *Cagle v. Burns & Roe, Inc.,* 106 Wn. 2d 911, 916, 726 P.2d 434 (1986) (damages for emotional distress available upon proof of an intentional tort).

Bokor has not suggested any reason to abandon the long-standing distinction between torts of intention and torts of negligence. In fact, if we were to apply objective symptomatology to outrage claims, we would make it more difficult to recover for an intentional act than for a negligent one. This is contrary to common sense as well as established law.

III

The elements of outrage sufficiently limit recovery of emotional distress damages without necessity to prove severe emotional distress by objective symptomatology. Unlike causes of action based on negligence, a plaintiff claiming intentional or reckless infliction of emotional distress must show extreme and outrageous conduct intended to cause emotional distress to the plaintiff. Once these have been shown, it can be fairly presumed that severe emotional distress was suffered. An analogous example can be found in this court's decision in *Carmody v. Trianon Co.,* 7 Wn. 2d 226, 109 P.2d 560 (1941). *Carmody* upheld an award of damages for mental anguish without requiring direct proof of the mental anguish because "'[n]o one could receive a beating, such as was rendered the plaintiff in this case, without suffering insult and humiliation therefrom.'" *Carmody,* 7 Wn. 2d at 235 (quoting *Stewart v. Watson,* 133 Mo. App. 44, 112 S.W. 762, 764 (1908)). No rational person could endure the constant harassment suffered by Kloepfel without suffering severe emotional distress.

. . . .

Even without the objective symptomatology requirement, outrage's third element requires evidence of severe emotional distress. "Emotional distress" includes "all highly unpleasant mental reactions, such as fright, horror, grief, shame, humiliation, embarrassment, anger, chagrin, disappointment, worry, and nausea." *Restatement (Second) of Torts, supra,* cmt. j at 77. Severe emotional distress is, however, not "transient and trivial" but distress such "that no reasonable man could be expected to endure it." *Id.*; *Grimsby,* 85 Wn. 2d at 59. The elements of outrage provide sufficient limitation on claims, and there is no need to graft the objective symptomatology requirement to intentional infliction of emotional distress.

The Court of Appeals is affirmed.

## IV. Tort Actions in Divorce

For many years, courts would not permit married individuals to raise tort claims against a spouse outside of a divorce action. Since most matrimonial actions are commenced under an equitable "no-fault" theory, married plaintiffs often are unable to obtain jury trials or take advantage of the full range of financial recovery available in a traditional tort trial. Therefore, concerned with the immediate necessities of alimony, equitable distribution, child custody and support, the wife would be barred by concepts of *res judicata* from seeking civil redress for marital torts in a subsequent legal action if she failed to address those issues in the divorce proceeding.

Today, only a few states still bar a spouse from suing separately in tort for incidents that took place during the marriage. The judicial philosophy in these states is that the tort action is related to the dissolution proceedings and the distribution of the marital assets, and therefore should not be severed. The majority of courts appreciate that relief sought in a tort action is different than that sought in a divorce proceeding. In some of these states, such as New York, which overruled the prohibition on bringing tort actions against a former spouse outside of a matrimonial matter more than a decade ago, litigants are given the option of determining in which forum they wish to proceed. Other states prohibit litigants from pursuing tort claims in divorce actions under the theory the relief sought in each is vastly different. Below are cases illustrating the widely varying judicial philosophies on the inter-relationship between divorce actions and tort suits.

### Chen v. Fischer
New York Court of Appeals
6 N.Y.3d 94 (2005)

CIPARICK, J.:

Plaintiff Xiao Yang Chen and defendant Ian Ira Fischer were married on March 11, 2001. Shortly thereafter, Fischer commenced an action for divorce on the ground of cruel and inhuman treatment. Chen counterclaimed for divorce—also alleging cruel and inhuman treatment—and asserted an additional cause of action for fraudulent inducement. Specifically, as grounds for divorce, Chen alleged that on May 6, 2001, Fischer "grabbed [her] and violently slapped her across the face and ear causing [her] to suffer bruising, pain and swelling" and that he threw her on the ground and attempted to suffocate her. As a result of that incident, each party filed a family offense petition against the other in Family Court and received a temporary order of protection. The parties agreed to consolidate these petitions with the matrimonial action.

At the conclusion of the matrimonial trial, they further agreed to withdraw the petitions without prejudice on the record in open court.

On October 15, 2001, prior to trial of the matrimonial action, the parties entered into a stipulation on the issue of fault. "In satisfaction of the stipulation," the parties agreed to withdraw all their fault allegations—including those related to the May 6 incident—save one. After trial on the remaining issues—including equitable distribution and a fraudulent inducement cause of action—on May 8, 2002 a dual judgment of divorce was granted on the ground of cruel and inhuman treatment based on each party's sole remaining fault allegation.

Chen allegedly commenced the instant personal injury action on January 18, 2002, while the matrimonial action was pending. The complaint asserted two causes of action—one for intentional infliction of emotional distress and a second for assault and battery. As to the second cause of action, the complaint alleged that on May 6, 2001, Fischer slapped her in the face and ear, causing permanent injury, necessitating continuing medical treatment and rendering her unable to perform her usual and customary activities. Fischer answered, raising several affirmative defenses, including res judicata and various theories of estoppel.

Fischer moved to dismiss the complaint pursuant to CPLR 3211 (a)(5) and Chen cross-moved to dismiss several of Fischer's affirmative defenses. Supreme Court granted Fischer's motion and denied Chen's cross motion. The court found that the allegations in Chen's personal injury action were "virtually identical" to those in her counterclaim for divorce and arose out of the same transaction or series of transactions. Thus, the court determined that the tort action was barred by res judicata.

The Appellate Division affirmed, agreeing that the action was barred because the tort claim could have been litigated with the divorce action and Chen did not expressly reserve the right to bring that claim when she withdrew her fault allegations for purposes of the stipulation.... We granted Chen leave to appeal and now reverse.

Typically, principles of res judicata require that "once a claim is brought to a final conclusion, all other claims arising out of the same transaction or series of transactions are barred, even if based upon different theories or if seeking a different remedy" (*O'Brien v. City of Syracuse*, 54 N.Y.2d 353, 357, 429 N.E.2d 1158, 445 N.Y.S.2d 687 [1981]). In the context of a matrimonial action, this Court has recognized that a final judgment of divorce settles the parties' rights pertaining not only to those issues that were actually litigated, but also to those that could have been litigated (*Rainbow v. Swisher*, 72 N.Y.2d 106, 110, 527 N.E.2d 258, 531 N.Y.S.2d 775 [1988]; see also *O'Connell v. Corcoran*, 1 N.Y.3d 179, 184–185, 802 N.E.2d 1071, 770 N.Y.S.2d 673 [2003])....

It is not always clear whether particular claims are part of the same transaction for res judicata purposes. A "pragmatic test" has been applied to make this determination—analyzing "whether the facts are related in time, space, origin, or motivation, whether they form a convenient trial unit, and whether their treatment as a unit conforms to the parties' expectations or business understanding or usage" (Restatement [Second] of Judgments § 24[2]; see *Smith v. Russell Sage College,* 54 N.Y.2d 185, 192–193, 429 N.E.2d 746, 445 N.Y.S.2d 68 [1981]; *Reilly,* 45 N.Y.2d at 29).

Applying these principles, it is apparent that personal injury tort actions and divorce actions do not constitute a convenient trial unit. The purposes behind the two are quite different. They seek different types of relief and require different types of proof. Moreover, a personal injury action is usually tried by a jury, in contrast to a matrimonial action, which is typically decided by a judge when the issue of fault is not contested. Further, personal injury attorneys are compensated by contingency fee, whereas matrimonial attorneys are prohibited from entering into fee arrangements that are contingent upon the granting of a divorce or a particular property settlement or distributive award (see Code of Professional Responsibility DR 2-106[c][2][I] [22 NYCRR 1200.11(c)(2)(I)]).

. . . .

Significant policy considerations also support this conclusion. To require joinder of interspousal personal injury claims with the matrimonial action would complicate and prolong the divorce proceeding. This would be contrary to the goal of expediting these proceedings and minimizing the emotional damage to the parties and their families. Delaying resolution of vital matters such as child support and custody or the distribution of assets to await the outcome of a personal injury action could result in extreme hardship and injustice to the families involved, especially for victims of domestic violence. In addition, parties should be encouraged to stipulate to, rather than litigate, the issue of fault (see *Blickstein v. Blickstein,* 99 A.D.2d 287, 293–294, 472 N.Y.S.2d 110 [2d Dept 1984]; see also *O'Brien v. O'Brien,* 66 N.Y.2d 576, 589–590, 489 N.E.2d 712, 498 N.Y.S.2d 743 [1985] [noting that fault should only be considered "in egregious cases" for purposes of equitable distribution, in part, "because fault will usually be difficult to assign and because introduction of the issue may involve the courts in time-consuming procedural maneuvers relating to collateral issues"]).

Unlike the Appellate Division, we decline to adopt the reasoning of the New Jersey Supreme Court in *Tevis v. Tevis* (79 N.J. 422, 400 A.2d 1189 [1979]). In *Tevis,* the Court held that under that State's "single controversy" rule, the interspousal personal injury claim should have been brought with the matrimonial action so that the issues between the parties could be decided in one proceeding in order to prevent protracted litigation (see *Tevis,* 79 N.J. at 434, 400 A.2d at 1196). However, that view is decidedly the minority view and the New Jersey Supreme Court has recently acknowledged the potential drawbacks to litigating an interspousal tort claim prior to the divorce proceeding—noting that it "may have a negative psychological impact on parties by prolonging the uncertainty of their marital status" (*Brennan v. Orban,* 145 N.J. 282, 303, 678 A.2d 667, 678 [1996]). Indeed, other states to address the issue have reached the conclusion we reach today, emphasizing the fundamental differences between the two types of actions and noting the complications that could result from the rigid application of res judicata principles (see *Delahunty v. Massachusetts Mut. Life Ins. Co.,* 236 Conn 582, 590–594, 674 A.2d 1290, 1295–1297 [1996]; *Henriksen v. Cameron,*

622 A.2d 1135, 1141–1142 [Me 1993]; *Heacock v. Heacock*, 402 Mass 21, 23–24, 520 N.E.2d 151, 153 [1988]).

Here, although the personal injury claim could have been litigated with the matrimonial action — as the facts arose from the same transaction or series of events — it was not, as all of Chen's fault allegations, save one, were withdrawn by stipulation for the salutary purpose of expediting the matrimonial action. She is therefore not precluded from litigating that claim in a separate action.

Parties are free, of course, to join their interspousal tort claims with the matrimonial action (see CPLR 601[a]) and the trial court retains discretion to sever the claims in the interest of convenience, if necessary (see CPLR 603). If a separate interspousal tort action is contemplated, however, or has been commenced, the better practice would be to include a reservation of rights in the judgment of divorce. Finally, if fault allegations are actually litigated in a matrimonial action, res judicata or some form of issue preclusion would bar a subsequent action in tort based on the same allegations.

Accordingly, the order of the Appellate Division should be reversed, with costs, and the case remitted to Supreme Court for further proceedings in accordance with this opinion.

## Lord v. Shaw

Utah Supreme Court

665 P.2d 1288 (1983)

Howe, Justice.

Appellant seeks the reversal of a summary judgment in which the trial court dismissed her complaint against her former husband, respondent, for torts he allegedly committed during their marriage.

Appellant and respondent, after nearly twenty years of marriage, were divorced in October of 1978. In September of 1980 appellant brought this suit consisting of six causes of action. Briefly summarized, she alleged:

(1) That in July of 1977 respondent willfully, maliciously and wrongfully seized her by the throat, choked her into semiconsciousness, then pushed her out the door and off the porch;

(2) That in August of 1977 the respondent seized her by the throat and strangled her into semi-consciousness;

(3) That in November of 1977 the respondent struck her and pushed her into a wall;

(4) That in June of 1976 the respondent willfully, maliciously and wrongfully struck and beat her. He also struck their minor child who attempted to intervene. Later that same evening, respondent threatened suicide and lay on top of appellant preventing her from calling for help;

(5) That in September of 1977 the respondent beat her, tore her clothes from her body, and forced her to submit to sexual intercourse against her will;

(6) That throughout the course of their marriage, the respondent "engaged in a course of conduct (including but not limited to the events and incidents outlined above), designed and calculated to cause [appellant] to suffer . . . . [Respondent's] conduct was willful, wanton, negligent, vicious, intentional, violent, and malicious, . . . .

The court found that "neither party was under any disabilities nor are there any other circumstances which would stop the statutes of limitations from running." Among its conclusions of law, the trial court held:

> The first five causes of action are actions based on the torts of assault, battery, or false imprisonment and are therefore barred by the appropriate statute of limitations, Utah Code Annotated Section 78-12-29 . . . .
>
> That the sixth cause of action is also governed by the same statute of limitations and is therefore barred.

U.C.A., § 78-12-29(4) requires that actions for "libel, . . . slander, assault, battery, false imprisonment or seduction" must be commenced within one year of their accrual. Assuming appellant's allegations to be true for purposes of summary judgment, clearly the first five causes of action arose from various assaults and batteries suffered by the appellant during marriage. She was choked, hit, beaten, lain on, stripped of her clothes and forced to submit to sexual intercourse. However, this suit (filed September of 1980) was not filed within one year of even the most recent (November of 1977) of those events.

Slightly different is the sixth cause of action. In it, appellant does not allege one specific incident. Rather, the gravamen of the cause of action is "a course of conduct (including but not limited to the events and incidents outlined above) [referring to the first five causes of action], designed and calculated to cause [appellant] to suffer . . . ." The allegation that respondent's "course of conduct" was "designed and calculated" suggests that his acts were intentional. Further, in parentheses appellant indicates that some of the specific acts comprising the course of conduct were "(including but not limited to the events and incidents outlined above) . . . ." The acts charged in the first five causes of action are intentional torts and, more specifically, arise from assaults and batteries suffered by appellant.

. . . .

Appellant argues that the statute of limitations should have been tolled because the doctrine of interspousal tort immunity disabled her from suing on these causes of action until the case of *Stoker v. Stoker*, Utah, 616 P.2d 590 (1980) was decided on August 8, 1980. That case held that the Legislature had abolished that common law doctrine insofar as it barred a wife's action for personal injuries intentionally inflicted upon her by her husband prior to their divorce.

The state of the law which foreclosed interspousal suit for an intentional tort prior to our decision in *Stoker v. Stoker, supra*, did not *disable* a wife from bringing an action against her husband for the torts he committed upon her. Interspousal immunity is not comparable to disabilities such as minority, mental incompetency, and imprisonment which are statutorily delineated. See generally U.C.A., 1953, § 78-12-36. Compare *Vana v. Elkins*, 20 Ariz. App. 557, 514 P.2d 510 (1973) (regarding disability and the marriage relationship under a married women statute). In the present case the appellant was no more under a disability than was the plaintiff in *Stoker v. Stoker, supra*, who did bring suit and effected a change in the law. Both Mrs. Stoker and appellant had access to the courts at all times to seek a judicial recognition of the lifting of the immunity which prevented their recovery at common law. It was incumbent upon the appellant, as it was upon Mrs. Stoker, to file her action within the statutory period and if necessary, to seek a change in the case law which stood in her path to recovery.

. . . .

As an additional ground for the summary judgment against the plaintiff, the trial court held that the plaintiff was barred by res judicata from suing her ex-husband for torts which occurred during the marriage, because his liability for any tort should have been litigated in the divorce action. We do not comment on this ruling other than to observe that actionable torts between married persons should not be litigated in a divorce proceeding. We believe that divorce actions will become unduly complicated in their trial and disposition if torts can be or must be litigated in the same action. A divorce action is highly equitable in nature, whereas the trial of a tort claim is at law and may well involve, as in this case, a request for trial by jury. The administration of justice will be better served by keeping the two proceedings separate. See *Windauer v. O'Connor,* 107 Ariz. 267, 485 P.2d 1157 (1971) where the Supreme Court of Arizona arrived at the same conclusion because of "the peculiar and special nature of a divorce action."

. . . .

# V. Insurance Issues in Domestic Violence Tort Litigation

Given the purpose of civil litigation is to make injured parties whole through monetary compensation, it is appropriate to ask in situations where domestic abusers are either poor, middle or working class—who pays? In many instances, the answer is nobody. This may explain, in part, why most domestic violence actions are brought in the family courts or prosecuted criminally.

To the extent individuals are insured against possible tortious conduct, prevailing parties may seek compensation through policies held by the tortfeasor. However, restrictions on insurance coverage for intentional torts strictly limit the amount available for recovery.

## A. Lack of Coverage for Acts of Domestic Violence

### Jennifer Wriggins, *Interspousal Tort Immunity and Insurance "Family Member Exclusions": Shared Assumptions, Relational and Liberal Feminist Challenges*

17 Wis. Women's L.J. 251 (2002)

. . . .

### II. The Persistence of De Facto Interspousal Tort Immunity

. . . .

[D]e facto interspousal tort immunity persists in the form of insurance exclusions. Insurance companies for decades have included "family member exclusions" in homeowner and automobile liability policies. . . . These provisions are ubiquitous in homeowners liability policies and were widespread in automobile policies until fairly recently. The reason for the exclusions is . . . to protect against collusive suits. Court decisions in both homeowners and automobile contexts have struck some of these exclusions down as against public policy, particularly in the automobile context. An additional common insurance provision, the "intentional acts exclusion," also bars claims for some intentional torts between spouses.

These insurance exclusions have a similar effect to common law inter-spousal tort immunity. They inhibit and discourage litigation seeking redress for tortious injury. . . .

Interspousal immunity has reappeared in a new guise—the guise of private insurance. The archaic mechanism for protecting actors who cause harm within families has been replaced by a new, more subtle mechanism. That mechanism is private liability insurance contracts which exclude coverage for intentional torts between family members.

The new mechanism, liability insurance, is significant. Liability insurance operates through contracts purchased by individuals and couples from private insurance companies. Some might argue that unlike blanket common-law immunity, these liability insurance exclusions reflect market demand and, as such, are not subject to the same criticisms as the common law rule. If the exclusions simply reflect individual choice, there is no valid basis to critique them, according to some. However, it is debatable whether insurance markets simply reflect consumer demand; moreover, problems such as imperfect information plague such markets. People are not very good risk estimators, as much research has shown, and may tend to make suboptimal insurance decisions. Thus, arguments that markets reflect consumer demand and consumer demand reflects rational decision-making are weak in the insurance context. Moreover, insurance is not accurately referred to as "private." Insurance is heavily regulated by the states, although state regulators are often very influenced by the insurance industry. Insurance contracts are far from individually bargained-for contracts. Automobile insurance is mandatory in almost every state, and homeowners insurance is required as a condition for getting a mortgage.

State legislation mandates specific provisions of insurance contracts and specific insurance markets. Thus, the state, through insurance regulation, maintains an active role in the de facto persistence of interspousal immunity.

### III. Feminist Approaches

The prevalence of injury from domestic violence and the lack of compensation for injuries from domestic violence would probably be recognized by feminists across a wide spectrum as an example of law's failure. Domestic violence injuries are to some extent a "gender-specific harm." After all, in the United States, "domestic violence is the most common cause of nonfatal injury to women."[4] Interspousal immunity was, and insurance family member exclusions are, ways that law "legitimates gender-specific harms." The striking contrast between widespread injury and lack of recognition or compensation seems to present a powerful example of law devaluing injuries to women. . . .

A liberal feminist critique of family member exclusions in insurance might go as follows. First, a liberal feminist perspective might consider the problem of the persistence of de facto interspousal tort immunity as important because family member and other exclusions operate to "underdeter and undercompensate" harms particularly suffered by women. Although liberal feminism takes the principle of individual autonomy as foundational, when harms are focused on particular groups, those harms become of particular concern.

Further, such a critique would take the position that people actually are individuals and it should be assumed that they will act as such. To assume that they would collude and defraud insurance companies with other family members, much more than they would with nonfamily members, is a stereotype and thus mistaken. Therefore, the same insurance rules should be applied to claims made by one family member against another as to claims made by a stranger against a family member. This is indeed what some courts have claimed in striking down family member exclusions in the automobile context. . . . Stereotyping is one of the enemies of liberal feminism. The exclusions, since simply based on stereotypes, should be abolished. If that happens, there are likely to be many consequences. Among them are more litigation, more compensation, and more deterrence.

. . . .

A relational feminist perspective presents a broad critique, which arguably may conflict with the idea of private insurance itself. If we had a system which valued community and relationship more, we might conclude that private insurance itself, which by definition extends coverage to only some members of a community, is anathema. . . .

---

4. [n23] Demetrios N. Kyriacous et al., Risk Factors of Injury to Women from Domestic Violence, 23 New Eng. J. Med. No. 25, Dec. 16, 1999, at 1892.

But we currently live in a world where private liability insurance has much to do with what claims get brought and who gets compensated for their injuries. Liability insurance is based on probabilistic behavior predictions that people are less likely to collude with those outside the private realm of their families than with those inside the family realm. . . .

Relational feminists probably would have responses to this, as follows: even if it is true, as indeed it may be, that family members are more likely to collude with one another than with others, that does not justify the wholesale exclusion. The wholesale exclusion is unacceptable given the harm that the exclusion does to women. Claims investigation and rate-setting should be able to deal with the collusion concern. The increased valuation of community and relationship is precisely what makes the family member exclusion unacceptable. Valuing relationships means that we recognize the potential for both harm and good in relationships, and that when there is harm, we find ways to heal it and compensate for it. Once intentional torts take place in relationships and family communities, liability insurance should be there to help with compensation and deterrence. Moreover, valuing community and relationship means that more loss-sharing should take place through the mechanism of insurance than currently takes place. All policyholders should, as part of valuing community and relationship, help compensate (through insurance premiums) those injured by intentional torts of family members. In this way, the state would take injuries to women more seriously and begin to counter, rather than legitimate, these injuries.

. . . .

## B. The Patient Protection and Affordable Care Act and Domestic Violence

On March 23, 2010, Public Law 111-148, the Patient Protection and Affordable Care Act, 42 U.S.C. § 18001, *et. seq.* was signed into law. More commonly known as "Obamacare," after President Obama who championed the bill, the law recognizes the special health care needs of domestic violence victims. Accordingly, as of January 1, 2014, insurance companies nationwide cannot use a domestic or sexual violence history as a pre-existing health condition to refuse insurance coverage. Whether to retain Obamacare, and if so in what form, was the subject of much debate during the presidential campaign of 2016. As of the time this book went to press, the law remained intact. It allows recent domestic violence victims to apply for a hardship exemption to avoid the financial penalty for failing to buy insurance and requires insurers to cover mental health and substance abuse services for victims of domestic violence. The following article discusses Obamacare in the context of domestic violence.

## Maggie Jo Buchanan, *Fighting Domestic Violence Through Insurance: What the Affordable Care Act Does and Can Do for Survivors*

23 Tex. J. Women & L. 77 (Fall 2013)

Domestic violence survivors have continuously faced discrimination by insurance companies through denial of coverage or through expensive premiums. . . .

The Patient Protection and Affordable Care Act (ACA) has been a hotly contested political issue since its introduction. Even after the United States Supreme Court upheld the Act's constitutionality, 2012 Republican candidates frequently vowed to repeal the law. However, the GOP failed to win either the presidency or enough seats in Congress to overturn the ACA, allowing it to continue protecting domestic violence survivors.

The ACA contains two provisions that have the potential to ease discrimination among insurance companies. First, the ACA makes it illegal for insurance companies—and the government through Medicaid or other public health programs—to consider a history of domestic violence when setting premium rates. Second, the ACA requires domestic violence screenings and counseling to be covered by all insurance plans without copay. These provisions, when paired with the individual mandate requiring Americans either to have insurance or to face a tax, could pave the way toward better insurance and better treatment for survivors. . . .

### I. Financial Challenges Facing Domestic Violence Survivors in Accessing Healthcare

. . . .

#### A. Insurance Discrimination

Insurance companies frequently use evidence of domestic violence in deciding whether to offer an applicant insurance coverage and at what cost. While some states have enacted laws prohibiting the use of domestic violence information in insurance determinations, these laws have not provided an adequate remedy to the problem.

. . . .

Insurance companies justify their use of this information on the grounds that they believe the survivors are living "risky" lifestyles. The companies' representatives claim that survivors chose to be in an abusive relationship and insurance companies should not be held responsible for covering the injuries that result from that "choice." These same companies, however, have been unable to produce any statistical evidence to justify their claim that domestic violence survivors cost more to insure. A State Farm representative conceded that the company had no empirical evidence to back up such a claim and admitted that the classification was "just sort of a logical conclusion."

Further, even in states that have limited this practice by law, insurance companies can find ways around the prohibition. State statutes frequently prohibit insurance companies from making coverage decisions "solely" or "only" on a history of domestic violence. Despite these statutes, insurance companies are still allowed to use a history of domestic violence in setting premiums. The companies can examine preexisting medical conditions that suggest a history of domestic violence, or simply consider the violence in conjunction with other undefined factors. . . .

B. Inability to Access Domestic Violence Screenings and Counseling

. . . .

1. Screenings

Insurance companies are largely silent on physicians' providing (or not providing) screenings, but the Department of Health and Human Services (HHS) projects that many survivors can access screenings only through out-of-pocket or cost-sharing means. Adding to this problem, physicians themselves seem reluctant to screen their patients for domestic violence regardless of insurance concerns. In a nationwide survey of over 5,000 women, "only 7 percent said a health professional had ever asked them about domestic or family violence." . . . .

In a column published in The New York Times, Dr. Erin Marcus, a physician and associate medical director of the Institute for Women's Health at the University of Miami Miller School of Medicine, explained why many physicians feel uncomfortable screening patients for abuse. Among these reasons, Dr. Marcus lists the frustration doctors feel with patients who do not immediately leave their abusive relationships. In addition, physicians see domestic violence as a criminal justice issue, and in general doctors "take umbrage at being expected to delve into a difficult, messy topic."

2. Counseling

Insurance coverage for general counseling, let alone counseling for domestic violence, varies considerably across insurance plans and many plans do not cover any type of counseling at all. . . . survivors are frequently either denied insurance altogether or offered more expensive, less comprehensive plans because they were abused. Because of this, obtaining a plan that includes coverage for general counseling is more difficult for survivors when compared to the rest of the population. Without adequate coverage, the financial hurdles to accessing treatment are steep. The National Directory of Marriage & Family Counseling explains that counseling costs range from $75 to $200 an hour. An average six- to twelve-session treatment can cost upwards of $1,200. For those struggling to start a life away from their abusive partners, the cost of healing will often simply be too high.

II. The Pronounced Harm to Survivors Created by Barriers to Healthcare

. . . .

A. Insurance Denials and High Premiums

Insurance discrimination contributes significantly to the cycle of abuse because of the resulting economic sanctions against survivors. Abusers frequently have financial control over their survivors. . . . Because insurance is either unavailable or too expensive, survivors become more dependent on their partners to meet their—and their children's—healthcare needs. And when survivors are aware of the effects that calling the police or seeking medical help may have on their ability to buy insurance, they will be even more unlikely to leave the relationship and find help.

B. Cost Prohibitive Domestic Violence Screening and Counseling

. . . .

1. Screening

Survivors are forced to pay out-of-pocket for screening services causing greater difficulty in identifying individuals in need of help. By choosing not to screen regardless of coverage, or only screening irregularly, medical professionals are allowing important opportunities to combat domestic violence lapse as well. Significant evidence demonstrates that domestic violence screenings as part of an annual checkup could have a strong preventative impact on domestic violence. Further, the director of the Center for Health Improvement and Prevention Studies explains that even a medical professional's discussion about domestic violence can plant the seed for change. . . .

2. Counseling

Similar to screenings, the lack of coverage for counseling has severe consequences. Counseling can interrupt the cycle of abuse inherent in domestic violence for those who enter into therapy while in the abusive relationship. Moreover, effective counseling helps survivors recover after being in an abusive relationship. The need for counseling can be pronounced: "The psychological trauma of abuse can be so severe that twenty-five percent of all suicide attempts and twenty-six percent of all suicide attempt-related injuries treated . . . are attributable to an abusive relationship."

C. Those Most Affected

. . . .

Many studies suggest that, despite the need for holistic screening methods, the fact remains that those suffering most frequently from abusive relationships are low-income women. The evidence on this point is pronounced—"Women receiving TANF [Temporary Assistance for Needy Families] are current survivors of domestic violence at rates about ten times higher than women in the general population." Gender of the survivors aside, "[households] with incomes between $7,500 and $25,000 experience nearly three times the amount of domestic violence as those with incomes above $50,000." For those with incomes below $7,000, that rate rises to five times as much.

Regardless of the socioeconomic status of the survivor, abusers frequently have financial control over their victims. Even for those survivors from higher income brackets, financial dependence on abusive partners causes some survivors to stay in abusive relationships. Abused persons who live under the financial control of their abuser are no more able to access care if they live in a mansion as opposed to a shack. . . .

Insurance agencies, through their discriminatory practices and lack of coverage for necessary treatment, contribute to survivors staying in abusive relationships. In addition, medical professionals' discomfort with the subject furthers the isolation of domestic violence survivors in the healthcare system. However, the ACA has provisions addressing both prongs of this problem.

### III. How the ACA Could Help Ease the Challenges Domestic Violence Survivors Face

Some of the ACA has gone into effect, but beginning in 2014, all the major provisions—including the provision requiring Americans to carry health insurance—will become effective. As a result, many survivors who previously lacked insurance will be enrolled in coverage and able to access medical care more frequently. Additionally, the ACA has two provisions that specifically address domestic violence. First, it prohibits insurance companies from considering the abuse in their coverage determinations. Second, insurance must cover screenings and counseling for domestic violence without copayment. These provisions demonstrate a growing consciousness towards the need for reform but continue to remain problematic.

#### A. How the ACA Will Increase the Number of Survivors Eligible for Care

Beginning at the start of 2014, the individual mandate will take effect and all Americans will be required to have health insurance or face a penalty in the form of a tax. As a way to ensure all Americans have health insurance in 2014, the ACA has enacted several provisions to lessen the burden of buying health insurance.

First, insurance through an employer can satisfy the ACA health insurance requirement. Moreover, states will be able to expand eligibility for Medicaid starting in 2014. In addition to the Medicaid expansion, subsidies to buy insurance will be available to individuals with financial hardship who cannot otherwise afford insurance. Further, a new way of obtaining insurance will be available through insurance exchanges. These exchanges, run by either the state or the federal government, will provide a way to compare and select from among different private plans designed for families and individuals not otherwise insured. . . .

#### B. Prohibition of Insurance Discrimination

The ACA specifically prohibits insurance companies from discriminating against domestic violence survivors. The applicable language reads:

> . . . .
>
> A group health plan and a health insurance issuer offering group or individual health insurance coverage may not establish rules for eligibility (including continued eligibility) of any individual to enroll under the terms of the plan or coverage based on any of the following health status-related factors in relation to the individual or a dependent of the individual:

(7) Evidence of insurability (including conditions arising out of acts of domestic violence.

. . . The phrase "conditions arising out of acts of domestic violence" is broad enough that the prohibition could dodge the problems that plague some of the more limited state laws. Instead of only prohibiting discrimination against those that an insurance company can clearly label from medical or police records, the provision could be understood to prevent discrimination against survivors on the basis of a medical history suggestive of abuse or through the other, more creative means insurance companies have developed over the years. At the same time, while the language is promising it does not itself mandate this interpretation of the law.

. . . .

### IV. Recommendations on How to Best Implement the Domestic Violence Provisions

The domestic violence insurance provisions have created a foundation for ridding discrimination, but guidelines that better define the provisions, clarify the requirements of medical professionals, and expand provisions past the current guidelines must be enacted at either a state or federal level.

A. Goals for Implementation

With robust implementation of the law, domestic violence survivors will be able to access the healthcare services they need. The primary goal of the recommendations that follow is to ensure more survivors become less financially dependent on their abusers and receive the physical and mental treatment they need to heal from the abuse. But a secondary goal exists as well within these recommendations. If broad and proper implementation is successful, the provisions of the ACA focused on domestic violence have the potential to promote awareness of the prevalence of domestic violence in America and help combat dangerous stereotypes of survivors. Four basic steps, instituted through federal or state guidance, could help achieve these goals.

B. Necessary First Steps

First, HHS must specifically define the discrimination provision to prohibit practices insurance companies have used to avoid similar state prohibitions. Second, either HHS or state officials must expand the screening and counseling provision to men. Third, HHS must require screenings and brief counseling during a patients' yearly checkup. Finally, to ensure medical professionals are able to carry out the screenings and counseling effectively, states must require training for medical professionals on domestic violence, and the federal government should issue a best-practices guide for those providing the services.

1. Define Insurance Discrimination Broadly

HHS should enact guidelines better defining the phrase "conditions arising out of" to mean injuries suggestive of domestic violence for all insurance plans in all states. If HHS remains inactive, insurance companies are likely to interpret the requirement narrowly and stop discriminating only against those survivors who can be labeled as such through specific language in police and medical reports. Insurance companies will continue to deny coverage for those who have any documentation of medical or personal conditions suggestive of domestic violence.

### 2. Expand Provision to Apply to Men

A major problem with the screening and counseling provision is that it is listed only under "women's preventative health" instead of under the general preventative health section which applies to all patients. While women are the majority of survivors, they are not the only people abused. It is extremely important for men to be screened for domestic violence as well; heterosexual and homosexual men are, for a variety of reasons, reporting abuse by their partners in increasing numbers, and screening and counseling will give men an additional safe place for reporting abuse. Congress should fix this problem through legislation. If, however, political gridlock on a federal level proves insurmountable, states could include these services for men as part of their own benchmark plans.

. . . .

### 3. Define When Screenings and Counseling Will be Covered

Screenings and counseling should be covered as a required part of all annual checkups—for everyone—and medical professionals must be trained in these practices. Doing so will remove the problem of healthcare providers' opting not to address domestic violence. These services are not currently required to be covered annually, though regulations open the door for screenings to be included in the annual well-woman visits also required to be covered without copayment . . . .

While brief counseling after an initial screening conducted by any medical professional can be beneficial, it can hardly be comprehensive enough to help patients with all the feelings and issues they may have regarding their abusive relationships. In-depth counseling conducted by trained professionals for domestic violence should be covered under the ACA as part of the extended mental health services package. Care should be taken to specifically define counseling for domestic violence as a covered service, allowing survivors coverage even though they are unable to present a specific mental health disease as the law currently requires.

### 4. Prepare Professionals to Frequently Conduct Screenings and Counseling

States must take proactive steps to ensure all medical professionals in their state are equipped to effectively provide these services as they become more common. Studies demonstrate that physicians with past domestic violence training already institute the most effective screening policies for their practices and are less likely to judge certain patients as "at-risk." Only a few states, however, require training of medical professionals on domestic violence. . . .

Finally, states and the HHS should set baseline "best practices" for the brief screenings and counseling that would occur during checkups—these materials also must help medical professionals address the limits of patient confidentiality in regard to domestic violence. While states could prepare such materials, HHS should develop a nationwide guide to complement work the federal government has already started. . . .

## Conclusion

Insurance discrimination and inadequate practices in regard to screening and counseling can amount to a denial of treatment that could be vital to a survivor's decision to leave an abusive relationship and ability to heal afterward. The Affordable Care Act's domestic violence provisions provide the skeleton framework that could be used to help these individuals obtain better and more complete insurance coverage, while also promoting awareness and prevention. Officials, however, still must take many proactive steps to bring these provisions to life in a way that can create long-lasting change.

# VI. Tort Actions Against Police and Public Agencies

Third party suits provide another source for recovery in tort litigation. There had been some early success for domestic violence victims suing police departments and the cities that employed them for failing to fulfill a duty to protect against violent domestic abusers, particularly when the police agency was aware of the existence of court orders of protection and when a victim repeatedly reached out for help. One particularly egregious case came out of the federal court in Connecticut, where police were aware a woman's husband was stalking her and yet, despite her many attempts in obtaining help from law enforcement, she was nearly killed. In *Thurman v. City of Torrington,* 595 F. Supp. 1521 (D.D.C. 1984), Tracey Thurman, a battered woman, complained of repeated threats on her life and the life of her child by her estranged husband. Her repeated attempts to get her husband arrested after he either threatened to physically attack her or actually did so, fell on deaf ears. She sued, alleging that the failure of the city police department to act to protect her violated her constitutional rights to equal protection under the laws. Although the city tried to get the case dismissed, the federal district court allowed it to go forward.

But in the more than 30 years since the *Thurman* case, the tide has turned against the ability to state a cause of action against public officials for failure to protect an individual from domestic assault.

## DeShaney v. Winnebago County Department of Social Services
### 489 U.S. 189 (1989)

CHIEF JUSTICE REHNQUIST delivered the opinion of the Court.

Petitioner is a boy who was beaten and permanently injured by his father, with whom he lived. Respondents are social workers and other local officials who received complaints that petitioner was being abused by his father and had reason to believe that this was the case, but nonetheless did not act to remove petitioner from his father's custody. Petitioner sued respondents claiming that their failure to act deprived him of his liberty in violation of the Due Process Clause of the Fourteenth Amendment to the United States Constitution. We hold that it did not.

I

The facts of this case are undeniably tragic. Petitioner Joshua DeShaney was born in 1979. In 1980, a Wyoming court granted his parents a divorce and awarded custody of Joshua to his father, Randy DeShaney. The father shortly thereafter moved to Neenah, a city located in Winnebago County, Wisconsin, taking the infant Joshua with him. There he entered into a second marriage, which also ended in divorce.

The Winnebago County authorities first learned that Joshua DeShaney might be a victim of child abuse in January 1982, when his father's second wife complained to the police, at the time of their divorce, that he had previously "hit the boy causing marks and [was] a prime case for child abuse." App. 152–153. The Winnebago County Department of Social Services (DSS) interviewed the father, but he denied the accusations, and DSS did not pursue them further. In January 1983, Joshua was admitted to a local hospital with multiple bruises and abrasions. The examining physician suspected child abuse and notified DSS, which immediately obtained an order from a Wisconsin juvenile court placing Joshua in the temporary custody of the hospital. Three days later, the county convened an ad hoc "Child Protection Team"—consisting of a pediatrician, a psychologist, a police detective, the county's lawyer, several DSS caseworkers, and various hospital personnel—to consider Joshua's situation. At this meeting, the Team decided that there was insufficient evidence of child abuse to retain Joshua in the custody of the court. The Team did, however, decide to recommend several measures to protect Joshua, including enrolling him in a preschool program, providing his father with certain counseling services, and encouraging his father's girlfriend to move out of the home. Randy DeShaney entered into a voluntary agreement with DSS in which he promised to cooperate with them in accomplishing these goals.

Based on the recommendation of the Child Protection Team, the juvenile court dismissed the child protection case and returned Joshua to the custody of his father. A month later, emergency room personnel called the DSS caseworker handling Joshua's case to report that he had once again been treated for suspicious injuries. The caseworker concluded that there was no basis for action. For the next six months, the caseworker made monthly visits to the DeShaney home, during which she observed a number of suspicious injuries on Joshua's head; she also noticed that he had not been enrolled in school, and that the girlfriend had not moved out. The caseworker dutifully recorded these incidents in her files, along with her continuing suspicions that someone in the DeShaney household was physically abusing Joshua, but she did nothing more. In November 1983, the emergency room notified DSS that Joshua had been treated once again for injuries that they believed to be caused by child abuse. On the caseworker's next two visits to the DeShaney home, she was told that Joshua was too ill to see her. Still DSS took no action.

In March 1984, Randy DeShaney beat 4-year-old Joshua so severely that he fell into a life-threatening coma. Emergency brain surgery revealed a series of hemorrhages caused by traumatic injuries to the head inflicted over a long period of time. Joshua did not die, but he suffered brain damage so severe that he is expected to spend the rest of his life confined to an institution for the profoundly retarded. Randy DeShaney was subsequently tried and convicted of child abuse.

Joshua and his mother brought this action under 42 U.S.C. § 1983 in the United States District Court for the Eastern District of Wisconsin against respondents Winnebago County, DSS, and various individual employees of DSS. The complaint alleged that respondents had deprived Joshua of his liberty without due process of law, in violation of his rights under the Fourteenth Amendment, by failing to intervene to protect him against a risk of violence at his father's hands of which they knew or should have known. The District Court granted summary judgment for respondents.

The Court of Appeals for the Seventh Circuit affirmed, 812 F.2d 298 (1987), holding that petitioners had not made out an actionable § 1983 claim for two alternative reasons. First, the court held that the Due Process Clause of the Fourteenth Amendment does not require a state or local governmental entity to protect its citizens from "private violence, or other mishaps not attributable to the conduct of its employees." *Id.*, at 301. In so holding, the court specifically rejected the position endorsed by a divided panel of the Third Circuit in *Estate of Bailey by Oare v. County of York*, 768 F.2d 503, 510–511 (1985), and by dicta in *Jensen v. Conrad*, 747 F.2d 185, 190–194 (CA4 1984), cert. denied, 470 U.S. 1052 (1985), that once the State learns that a particular child is in danger of abuse from third parties and actually undertakes to protect him from that danger, a "special relationship" arises between it and the child which imposes an affirmative constitutional duty to provide adequate protection. 812 F.2d, at 303–304. Second, the court held, in reliance on our decision in *Martinez v. California*, 444 U.S. 277, 285 (1980), that the causal connection between respondents' conduct and Joshua's injuries was too attenuated to establish a deprivation of constitutional rights actionable under § 1983. 812 F.2d, at 301–303. The court therefore found it unnecessary to reach the question whether respondents' conduct evinced the "state of mind" necessary to make out a due process claim after *Daniels v. Williams*, 474 U.S. 327 (1986), and *Davidson v. Cannon*, 474 U.S. 344 (1986). 812 F.2d, at 302.

Because of the inconsistent approaches taken by the lower courts in determining when, if ever, the failure of a state or local governmental entity or its agents to provide an individual with adequate protective services constitutes a violation of the individual's due process rights, see *Archie v. Racine*, 847 F.2d 1211, 1220–1223, and n. 10 (CA7 1988) (en banc) (collecting cases), cert. pending, No. 88-576, and the importance of the issue to the administration of state and local governments, we granted certiorari. 485 U.S. 958 (1988). We now affirm.

## II

The Due Process Clause of the Fourteenth Amendment provides that "[n]o State shall . . . deprive any person of life, liberty, or property, without due process of law." Petitioners contend that the State deprived Joshua of his liberty interest in "free[dom] from . . . unjustified intrusions on personal security," see *Ingraham v. Wright*, 430 U.S. 651, 673 (1977), by failing to provide him with adequate protection against his father's violence. The claim is one invoking the substantive rather than the procedural component of the Due Process Clause; petitioners do not claim that the State denied Joshua protection without according him appropriate procedural safeguards, see *Morrissey v. Brewer*, 408 U.S. 471, 481 (1972), but that it was categorically obligated to protect him in these circumstances, see *Youngberg v. Romeo*, 457 U.S. 307, 309 (1982).

But nothing in the language of the Due Process Clause itself requires the State to protect the life, liberty, and property of its citizens against invasion by private actors. The Clause is phrased as a limitation on the State's power to act, not as a guarantee of certain minimal levels of safety and security. It forbids the State itself to deprive individuals of life, liberty, or property without "due process of law," but its language cannot fairly be extended to impose an affirmative obligation on the State to ensure that those interests do not come to harm through other means. Nor does history support such an expansive reading of the constitutional text....

Petitioners contend, however, that even if the Due Process Clause imposes no affirmative obligation on the State to provide the general public with adequate protective services, such a duty may arise out of certain "special relationships" created or assumed by the State with respect to particular individuals. Brief for Petitioners 13–18. Petitioners argue that such a "special relationship" existed here because the State knew that Joshua faced a special danger of abuse at his father's hands, and specifically proclaimed, by word and by deed, its intention to protect him against that danger. *Id.*, at 18–20. Having actually undertaken to protect Joshua from this danger—which petitioners concede the State played no part in creating—the State acquired an affirmative "duty," enforceable through the Due Process Clause, to do so in a reasonably competent fashion. Its failure to discharge that duty, so the argument goes, was an abuse of governmental power that so "shocks the conscience," *Rochin v. California*, 342 U.S. 165, 172 (1952), as to constitute a substantive due process violation. Brief for Petitioners 20.

We reject this argument.

. . . .

It may well be that, by voluntarily undertaking to protect Joshua against a danger it concededly played no part in creating, the State acquired a duty under state tort law to provide him with adequate protection against that danger. See Restatement (Second) of Torts § 323 (1965) (one who undertakes to render services to another may in some circumstances be held liable for doing so in a negligent fashion); see generally W. Keeton, D. Dobbs, R. Keeton, & D. Owen, Prosser and Keeton on the Law of Torts § 56 (5th ed. 1984) (discussing "special relationships" which may give rise to affirmative duties to act under the common law of tort). But the claim here is based on the Due Process Clause of the Fourteenth Amendment, which, as we have said many times, does not transform every tort committed by a state actor into a constitutional violation. See *Daniels v. Williams*, 474 U.S., at 335–336; *Parratt v. Taylor*, 451 U.S., at 544; *Martinez v. California*, 444 U.S. 277, 285 (1980); *Baker v. McCollan*, 443 U.S. 137, 146 (1979); *Paul v. Davis*, 424 U.S. 693, 701 (1976). A State may, through its courts and legislatures, impose such affirmative duties of care and protection upon its agents as it wishes. But not "all common-law duties owed by government actors were ... constitutionalized by the Fourteenth Amendment." *Daniels v. Williams, supra*, at 335. Because, as explained above, the State had no constitutional duty to protect Joshua against his father's violence, its failure to do so—though calamitous in hindsight—simply does not constitute a violation of the Due Process Clause.

Judges and lawyers, like other humans, are moved by natural sympathy in a case like this to find a way for Joshua and his mother to receive adequate compensation for the grievous harm inflicted upon them. But before yielding to that impulse, it is well to remember once again that the harm was inflicted not by the State of Wisconsin, but by Joshua's father. The most that can be said of the state functionaries in this case is that they stood by and did nothing when suspicious circumstances dictated a more active role for them. In defense of them it must also be said that had they moved too soon to take custody of the son away from the father, they would likely have been met with charges of improperly intruding into the parent-child relationship, charges based on the same Due Process Clause that forms the basis for the present charge of failure to provide adequate protection.

The people of Wisconsin may well prefer a system of liability which would place upon the State and its officials the responsibility for failure to act in situations such as the present one. They may create such a system, if they do not have it already, by changing the tort law of the State in accordance with the regular lawmaking process. But they should not have it thrust upon them by this Court's expansion of the Due Process Clause of the Fourteenth Amendment.

*Affirmed.*

## Town of Castle Rock v. Gonzales
### 545 U.S. 748 (2005)

JUSTICE SCALIA delivered the opinion of the Court.

We decide in this case whether an individual who has obtained a state-law restraining order has a constitutionally protected property interest in having the police enforce the restraining order when they have probable cause to believe it has been violated.

I

The horrible facts of this case are contained in the complaint that respondent Jessica Gonzales filed in Federal District Court. . . . Respondent alleges that petitioner, the town of Castle Rock, Colorado, violated the Due Process Clause of the Fourteenth Amendment to the United States Constitution when its police officers, acting pursuant to official policy or custom, failed to respond properly to her repeated reports that her estranged husband was violating the terms of a restraining order.

The restraining order had been issued by a state trial court several weeks earlier in conjunction with respondent's divorce proceedings. The original form order, issued on May 21, 1999, and served on respondent's husband on June 4, 1999, commanded him not to "molest or disturb the peace of [respondent] or of any child," and to remain at least 100 yards from the family home at all times. 366 F.3d 1093, 1143 (CA10 2004) (en banc) (appendix to dissenting opinion of O'Brien, J.). The bottom of the preprinted form noted that the reverse side contained "IMPORTANT NOTICES FOR RESTRAINED PARTIES AND LAW ENFORCEMENT OFFICIALS." *Ibid.* (emphasis deleted). The preprinted text on the back of the form included the following "**WARNING**":

> "**A KNOWING VIOLATION OF A RESTRAINING ORDER IS A CRIME** . . . . A VIOLATION WILL ALSO CONSTITUTE CONTEMPT OF COURT. **YOU MAY BE ARRESTED** WITHOUT NOTICE IF A LAW ENFORCEMENT OFFICER HAS PROBABLE CAUSE TO BELIEVE THAT YOU HAVE KNOWINGLY VIOLATED THIS ORDER." *Id.,* at 1144.

The preprinted text on the back of the form also included a "**NOTICE TO LAW ENFORCEMENT OFFICIALS**," which read in part:

> "YOU SHALL USE EVERY REASONABLE MEANS TO ENFORCE THIS RESTRAINING ORDER. YOU SHALL ARREST, OR, IF AN ARREST WOULD BE IMPRACTICAL UNDER THE CIRCUMSTANCES, SEEK A WARRANT FOR THE ARREST OF THE RESTRAINED PERSON WHEN YOU HAVE INFORMATION AMOUNTING TO PROBABLE CAUSE THAT THE RESTRAINED PERSON HAS VIOLATED OR ATTEMPTED TO VIOLATE ANY PROVISION OF THIS ORDER AND THE RESTRAINED PERSON HAS BEEN PROPERLY SERVED WITH A COPY OF THIS ORDER OR HAS RECEIVED ACTUAL NOTICE OF THE EXISTENCE OF THIS ORDER." *Ibid.*

On June 4, 1999, the state trial court modified the terms of the restraining order and made it permanent. The modified order gave respondent's husband the right to spend time with his three daughters (ages 10, 9, and 7) on alternate weekends, for two weeks during the summer, and, "'upon reasonable notice,'" for a mid-week dinner visit "'arranged by the parties'"; the modified order also allowed him to visit the home to collect the children for such "parenting time." *Id.,* at 1097 (majority opinion).

According to the complaint, at about 5 or 5:30 pm. on Tuesday, June 22, 1999, respondent's husband took the three daughters while they were playing outside the family home. No advance arrangements had been made for him to see the daughters that evening. When respondent noticed the children were missing, she suspected her husband had taken them. At about 7:30 pm., she called the Castle Rock Police Department, which dispatched two officers. The complaint continues: "When [the officers] arrived . . . , she showed them a copy of the TRO and requested that it be enforced and the three children be returned to her immediately. [The officers] stated that there was nothing they could do about the TRO and suggested that [respondent] call the Police Department again if the three children did not return home by 10:00 pm." App. to Pet. for Cert. 126a.

At approximately 8:30 pm., respondent talked to her husband on his cellular telephone. He told her "he had the three children at amusement park in Denver." *Ibid.* She called the police again and asked them to "have someone check for" her husband or his vehicle at the amusement park and "put out an [all points bulletin]" for her husband, but the officer with whom she spoke "refused to do so," again telling her to "wait until 10:00 pm. and see if" her husband returned the girls. *Id.,* at 126a–127a.

At approximately 10:10 pm., respondent called the police and said her children were still missing, but she was now told to wait until midnight. She called at midnight and told the dispatcher her children were still missing. She went to her husband's apartment and, finding nobody there, called the police at 12:10 a.m.; she was told to wait for an officer to arrive. When none came, she went to the police station at 12:50 a.m. and submitted an incident report. The officer who took the report "made no reasonable effort to enforce the TRO or locate the three children. Instead, he went to dinner." *Id.,* at 127a.

At approximately 3:20 a.m., respondent's husband arrived at the police station and opened fire with a semiautomatic handgun he had purchased earlier that evening. Police shot back, killing him. Inside the cab of his pickup truck, they found the bodies of all three daughters, whom he had already murdered. *Ibid.*

On the basis of the foregoing factual allegations, respondent brought an action under Rev. Stat. § 1979, 42 U.S.C. § 1983, claiming that the town violated the Due Process Clause because its police department had "an official policy or custom of failing to respond properly to complaints of restraining order violations" and "tolerate[d] the non-enforcement of restraining orders by its police officers." App. to Pet. for Cert. 129a. The complaint also alleged that the town's actions "were taken either willfully, recklessly or with such gross negligence as to indicate wanton disregard and deliberate indifference to" respondent's civil rights. *Ibid.*

Before answering the complaint, the defendants filed a motion to dismiss under Federal Rule of Civil Procedure 12(b)(6). The District Court granted the motion, concluding that, whether construed as making a substantive due process or procedural due process claim, respondent's complaint failed to state a claim upon which relief could be granted.

A panel of the Court of Appeals affirmed the rejection of a substantive due process claim, but found that respondent had alleged a cognizable procedural due process claim. 307 F.3d 1258 (CA10 2002). On rehearing en banc, a divided court reached the same disposition, concluding that respondent had a "protected property interest in the enforcement of the terms of her restraining order" and that the town had deprived her of due process because "the police never 'heard' nor seriously entertained her request to enforce and protect her interests in the restraining order." 366 F.3d at 1101, 1117. We granted certiorari. 543 U.S. 955, 160 L. Ed. 2d 316, 125 S. Ct. 417 (2004).

## II

The Fourteenth Amendment to the United States Constitution provides that a State shall not "deprive any person of life, liberty, or property, without due process of law." Amdt. 14, § 1. In 42 U.S.C. § 1983, Congress has created a federal cause of action for "the deprivation of any rights, privileges, or immunities secured by the Constitution and laws." Respondent claims the benefit of this provision on the ground that she had a property interest in police enforcement of the restraining order against her husband; and that the town deprived her of this property without due process by having a policy that tolerated nonenforcement of restraining orders.

As the Court of Appeals recognized, we left a similar question unanswered in *DeShaney v. Winnebago County Dep't of Social Servs.*, 489 U.S. 189, 103 L. Ed. 2d 249, 109 S. Ct. 998 (1989), another case with "undeniably tragic" facts: Local child-protection officials had failed to protect a young boy from beatings by his father that left him severely brain damaged. *Id.*, at 191–193, 103 L. Ed. 2d 249, 109 S. Ct. 998.

. . . .

### A

Our cases recognize that a benefit is not a protected entitlement if government officials may grant or deny it in their discretion. See, *e.g.*, *Kentucky Dep't of Corrections v. Thompson*, 490 U.S. 454, 462–463, 104 L. Ed. 2d 506, 109 S. Ct. 1904 (1989). The Court of Appeals in this case determined that Colorado law created an entitlement to enforcement of the restraining order because the "court-issued restraining order . . . specifically dictated that its terms must be enforced" and a "state statute command[ed]" enforcement of the order when certain objective conditions were met (probable cause to believe that the order had been violated and that the object of the order had received notice of its existence). 366 F.3d at 1101, n. 5; see also *id.*, at 1100, n. 4; *id.*, at 1104–1105, and n 9.

. . . .

### B

The critical language in the restraining order came not from any part of the order itself (which was signed by the state-court trial judge and directed to the restrained party, respondent's husband), but from the preprinted notice to law-enforcement personnel that appeared on the back of the order. . . . That notice effectively restated the statutory provision describing "peace officers' duties" related to the crime of violation of a restraining order. . . .

The Court of Appeals concluded that this statutory provision—especially taken in conjunction with a statement from its legislative history, and with another statute restricting criminal and civil liability for officers making arrests—established the Colorado Legislature's clear intent "to alter the fact that the police were not enforcing domestic abuse retraining orders," and thus its intent "that the recipient of a domestic abuse restraining order have an entitlement to its enforcement." 366 F.3d at 1108.

Any other result, it said, "would render domestic abuse restraining orders utterly valueless." *Id.,* at 1109.

. . . .

We do not believe that these provisions of Colorado law truly made enforcement of restraining orders *mandatory*. A well established tradition of police discretion has long coexisted with apparently mandatory arrest statutes.

. . . .

Against that backdrop, a true mandate of police action would require some stronger indication from the Colorado Legislature than "shall use every reasonable means to enforce a restraining order" (or even "shall arrest . . . or . . . seek a warrant"), §§ 18-6-803.5(3)(a), (b). That language is not perceptibly more mandatory than the Colorado statute which has long told municipal chiefs of police that they "shall pursue and arrest any person fleeing from justice in any part of the state" and that they "shall apprehend any person in the act of committing any offense . . . and, forthwith and without any warrant, bring such person before a . . . competent authority for examination and trial." Colo. Rev. Stat. § 31-4-112 (Lexis 2004). It is hard to imagine that a Colorado peace officer would not have some discretion to determine that—despite probable cause to believe a restraining order has been violated—the circumstances of the violation or the competing duties of that officer or his agency counsel decisively against enforcement in a particular instance.[5] The practical necessity for discretion is particularly apparent in a case such as this one, where the suspected violator is not actually present and his whereabouts are unknown. Cf. *Donaldson v. Seattle,* 65 Wash. App. 661, 671–672, 831 P.2d 1098, 1104 (1992) ("There is a vast difference between a mandatory duty to arrest [a violator who is on the scene] and a mandatory duty to conduct a follow up investigation [to locate an absent violator]. . . . A mandatory duty to investigate would be completely open-ended as to priority, duration and intensity").

. . . .

Respondent does not specify the precise means of enforcement that the Colorado restraining-order statute assertedly mandated-whether her interest lay in having police arrest her husband, having them seek a warrant for his arrest, or having them "use every reasonable means, up to and including arrest, to enforce the order's terms," Brief for Respondent 29–30. Such indeterminacy is not the hallmark of a duty that is mandatory. Nor can someone be safely deemed "entitled" to something when the identity of the alleged entitlement is vague. See *Roth,* 408 U.S., at 577, 33 L. Ed. 2d 548, 92 S. Ct. 2701 (considering whether "certain benefits" were "secure[d]" by rule

---

5. [n8] Respondent in fact concedes that an officer may "properly" decide not to enforce a restraining order when the officer deems "a technical violation" too "immaterial" to justify arrest. Respondent explains this as a determination that there is no probable cause. Brief for Respondent 28. We think, however, that a determination of no probable cause to believe a violation has occurred is quite different from a determination that the violation is too insignificant to pursue.

or understandings); cf. *Natale v. Ridgefield,* 170 F.3d 258, 263 (CA2 1999) ("There is no reason ... to restrict the 'uncertainty' that will preclude existence of a federally protectable property interest to the uncertainty that inheres in the exercise of discretion")....

Even if the statute could be said to have made enforcement of restraining orders "mandatory" because of the domestic-violence context of the underlying statute, that would not necessarily mean that state law gave *respondent* an entitlement to *enforcement* of the mandate. Making the actions of government employees obligatory can serve various legitimate ends other than the conferral of a benefit on a specific class of people. See, *e.g., Sandin v. Conner,* 515 472, 482, 132 L. Ed. 2d 418, 115 S. Ct. 2293 (1995) (finding no constitutionally protected liberty interest in prison regulations phrased in mandatory terms, in part because "[s]uch guidelines are not set forth solely to benefit the prisoner"). The serving of public rather than private ends is the normal course of the criminal law because criminal acts, "besides the injury [they do] to individuals, ... strike at the very being of society; which cannot possibly subsist, where actions of this sort are suffered to escape with impunity." 4 Blackstone, Commentaries on the Laws of England 5 (1769); see also *Huntington v. Attrill,* 146 U.S. 657, 668, 36 L. Ed. 1123, 13 S. Ct. 224 (1892). This principle underlies, for example, a Colorado district attorney's discretion to prosecute a domestic assault, even though the victim withdraws her charge. See *People v. Cunefare,* 102 P.3d 302, 311–312 (Colo. 2004) (Bender, J., concurring in part, dissenting in part, and dissenting in part to the judgment).

Respondent's alleged interest stems only from a State's *statutory* scheme—from a restraining order that was authorized by and tracked precisely the statute on which the Court of Appeals relied. She does not assert that she has any common-law or contractual entitlement to enforcement. If she was given a statutory entitlement, we would expect to see some indication of that in the statute itself. Although Colorado's statute spoke of "protected person[s]" such as respondent, it did so in connection with matters other than a right to enforcement. It said that a "protected person shall be provided with a copy of [a restraining] order" when it is issued, § 18-6-803.5(3)(a); that a law enforcement agency "shall make all reasonable efforts to contact the protected party upon the arrest of the restrained person," § 18-6-803.5(3)(d); and that the agency "shall give [to the protected person] a copy" of the report it submits to the court that issued the order, § 18-6-803.5(3)(e). Perhaps most importantly, the statute spoke directly to the protected person's power to "initiate contempt proceedings against the restrained person if the order [was] issued in a civil action or request the prosecuting attorney to initiate contempt proceedings if the order [was] issued in a criminal action." § 18-6-803.5(7). The protected person's express power to "initiate" civil contempt proceedings contrasts tellingly with the mere ability to "request" initiation of criminal contempt proceedings—and even more dramatically with the complete silence about any power to "request" (much less demand) that an arrest be made.

....

### III

We conclude, therefore, that respondent did not, for purposes of the Due Process Clause, have a property interest in police enforcement of the restraining order against her husband. It is accordingly unnecessary to address the Court of Appeals' determination (366 F.3d at 1110–1117) that the town's custom or policy prevented the police from giving her due process when they deprived her of that alleged interest. See *American Mfrs. Mut. Ins. Co. v. Sullivan*, 526 U.S. 40, 61, 143 L. Ed. 2d 130, 119 S. Ct. 977 (1999).

. . . .

The judgment of the Court of Appeals is reversed.

# VII. Domestic Violence Torts at the Workplace

Domestic violence is not left inside the front door of a woman's home. In fact, homicide is the number one cause of death for women in the workplace. Besides causing real danger to victims, domestic violence is a financial disaster—as well as a dilemma for employers. If a victim of domestic violence informs her employer that she is afraid of her stalking spouse, and the employer fails to take the warning seriously, that employer risks a civil suit if the employee or other workers are injured by him. But, if the threat is taken so seriously the employee is discharged to insure the safety of the other workers, the threat of an unfair termination suit looms.

For many victims of domestic violence, the only hope of escape is to become financially independent of the abuser. But, that is unlikely to happen if she faces loss of her job—either due to the above-mentioned safety issue or to the negative impact on her productivity from domestic violence-related injury and stress.

The issue is examined below, first, from the employer's point of view.

### John E. Matejkovic, *Which Suit Would You Like? The Employer's Dilemma in Dealing With Domestic Violence*
33 Cap. U. L. Rev. 309 (2004)

#### I. INTRODUCTION

Unfortunately, all too often violence has become part of the American working environment. It is estimated that between 1.7 and 2 million violent acts occur each year in the workplace. Workplace violence is experienced by 13 of every 1,000 workers. Approximately 1% of all workplace violence was committed by an intimate partner—a current or former spouse, boyfriend, or girlfriend—in what would normally be classified as an incident of domestic violence.

While workplace violence decreased between 1993 and 1999, there were still too many incidents of violence, especially homicides occurring in the workplace, with 651 homicides in 1999 alone. With regard to instances of domestic violence, while the numbers in and out of the workplace also declined, the numbers are still significant.

In 1993, 1.1 million females were victims of nonfatal domestic violence, dropping to 588,490 such victims in 2001. Additionally, intimates killed 1,247 females and 440 males in 2000. Thirty-three percent of all female homicides are due to acts of domestic violence.

Homicides are the second leading cause of death in the workplace generally. According to the National Institute for Occupational Safety and Health (NIOSH), homicide is the leading cause of death for females in the workplace, accounting for 40% of all female workplace deaths. Twenty-five percent of female victims were assaulted by people known to them, and 16% of women workplace homicides are a result of domestic violence. In nearly two-thirds of work place assaults, women were the victims.

. . . Seventy-four percent of female victims of domestic violence are harassed by their abusers on the job, 56% are late for work on several occasions per month, 28% leave work early at least five times per month, 54% miss a minimum of three days per month, and 75% use company time to handle domestic violence-related matters. It has been reported that domestic violence costs employers approximately $5 billion per year in absenteeism, lost productivity, and increased health care costs. It is estimated that one quarter to one half of female victims lose their jobs due to domestic violence.

. . . .

## II. TORT-BASED LIABILITY

. . . .

Most tort claims that an employer might face in the circumstances discussed herein would probably be based on some form of negligence — the failure to act as a reasonable person under the circumstances that leads to (causes) an injury. In the employment setting, the employer must keep in mind that often the injured parties (the potential plaintiffs) may not only be the target of the domestic violence, but, as indicated above, targets may also be co-workers or other bystanders. From an employer's perspective, it might seem unfair to make them liable for the actions of third parties who commit acts of domestic violence in the workplace; but, it is clear that domestic violence does occur in the workplace, sometimes for no other reason than the perpetrator knows where the victim is going to be at some particular point in time — at work.

For the most part, the law does not recognize a duty to protect persons from the acts of third parties, as there is no liability for the acts of those third parties. However, there are exceptions to this general rule. Where "special relations" exist between the parties, a duty to protect may arise. Employment has been noted to create such a "special relation." Moreover, when parties voluntarily assume a duty to protect another, they may be liable for their failure to do so.

Finally, a duty to protect against the acts of a third party may arise where an injury or harm is foreseeable. While the existence of duty is normally a question of law to be determined by a judge in the first instance, courts have discretion to determine duty as a matter of policy as to whether an employee is entitled to protection. Forseeability is generally a question of fact for a jury's determination, decided as an issue of law only if reasonable minds can come to only one conclusion. There is also authority imposing a duty to act on an employer where there is a known threatened harm that the employee might encounter within the scope of his or her employment.

. . . .

For the most part, tort-based claims against employers are based on the following three main theories: (1) failure to protect and provide adequate security; (2) negligent retention; and (3) failure to warn. . . .

## III. STATUTORY CONSIDERATIONS

Employers should also be aware of potential statutory concerns and claims that might arise as a result of domestic violence spilling into the workplace. As all employers are increasingly aware, statutory regulations at the state and federal level play a substantial role in defining employment rights and responsibilities. In fact, as discussed below, state legislatures are taking an increasingly active role in providing protections to victims of domestic violence, especially protections with regard to their employment. . . .

### A. *Federal Statutes*

Every employer is undoubtedly aware of the numerous federal statutes affecting the employment relationship. Everything from the Immigration Reform and Control Act of 1986 (IRCA) to the Worker Adjustment and Retraining Notification Act of 1988 (WARN) to the Employee Retirement Income Security Act of 1974 (ERISA) describes how employers must interact with employees or potential employees. In the context discussed herein, probably the most significant concerns would arise under Title VII of the Civil Rights Act of 1964. However, other statutes may become increasingly important. For example, while not yet achieved as an amendment to the Americans with Disabilities Act (ADA), several states have adopted statutes establishing that status as a victim of domestic violence is a "disability." Similarly, the Occupational Safety and Health Administration (OSHA) may eventually become more important in the domestic violence context, although at the current time it is only marginally applicable. For the most part, however, an employer's main concern in the domestic violence context should arise out of Title VII liability exposure.

Under Title VII, there are two areas of concern: a claim based on straight sex discrimination and a claim based upon sexual harassment, which is a form of sex discrimination. The sex discrimination claim might take one of two forms: disparate treatment or disparate impact. A disparate treatment claim might arise where a female employee is treated differently than a similarly-situated male employee, although after nearly forty years, most employers would, presumably, know better.

Disparate impact claims might be more problematic from the employer's perspective. In light of the statistics discussed at the beginning of this Article demonstrating that more females than males are victims of domestic violence, any employer that adopts a policy disfavoring domestic violence victims could arguably be sued on the basis of disparate impact....

B. *State Statutes*

Perhaps the greatest area of concern for employers dealing with domestic violence in the workplace arises from the variety of state laws that provide some protection to victims of domestic violence, especially in the employment context. It is at the state level that most protections come and restriction on employment actions have occurred....

1. *Unemployment Compensation*

Most states have adopted some form of unemployment compensation—a public policy insurance benefit provided to employees who lose their jobs through no fault of their own. For the most part, these protections apply to individuals who are laid off due to an economic down turn, for example. However, most of these statutes also provide some type of protection to employees who are terminated unjustly or who quit for "good cause." In the context of this Article, a number of states have adopted statutes providing some protection to employees who are either terminated or required to quit due to domestic violence concerns.... In addition to the already enacted statutes, a number of states have legislative proposals currently pending, and an employer would be wise to consult the status of these proposals when considering any unemployment compensation exposure.... Perhaps of some comfort to employers is the fact that in most instances, the unemployment compensation benefits available to domestic violence victims are not usually charged against the employer's account.

2. *Workers' Compensation*

All states have some form of workers' compensation benefits available to persons who are injured on the job or as a result of their employment. In most instances, to be eligible for workers' compensation, the injury must occur at or "arise out of" the claimant's employment. Thus, in order to be eligible for benefits, injured employees may have to prove, in the domestic violence context, that the violence "arose out of their employment," or occurred "in the course of employment." In most instances, if an employee qualifies for workers' compensation or the injury "arose out of" or "in the course of" their employment, workers' compensation is the exclusive remedy available to an injured employee (which would, presumably, bar any tort claim by the injured employee against the employer). There are instances where victims of domestic violence occurring in the workplace have been awarded workers' compensation benefits.[6] However, the greater weight of authority seems to indicate that domestic violence occurrences in the workplace do not "arise out of" the victim's employment

---

6. [n305] *See, e.g.,* Weiss v. City of Milwaukee, 559 N.W.2d 588, 595 (Wis. 1997); Tampa Maid Seafood Prods. v. Porter, 415 So. 2d 883, 885 (Fla. Dist. Ct. App. 1982); Murphy v. Workers' Comp. Appeals Bd., 150 Cal. Rptr. 561, 564–65 (Cal. Ct. App. 1978).

and therefore are not covered by workers' compensation.[7] In fact, in some instances, courts addressing the availability of workers' compensation specifically note that workers' compensation benefits may not be available, but instead hold that the injured employee may have a claim for inadequate security.[8] In any instance where the domestic violence occurs at work, it is strongly suggested that an employer immediately check with workers' compensation counsel, and if the state has ruled that workers' compensation benefits are available, those benefits may be the injured employee's exclusive remedy, thus shielding the employer from any tort-liability exposure.

### 3. Anti-Discrimination Provisions

Many states have current statutes providing protection to domestic violence victims, whether the statute specifically addresses domestic violence or not. Many of the statutes provide protections to victims of crimes, generally, without specific reference to the employee's status as a domestic violence victim. However, Illinois has a statute that specifically protects and addresses concerns related to domestic violence. . . .

. . . .

### 4. Leaves of Absence

A number of states have enacted statutes providing victims of domestic violence the ability to take unpaid leave from their employment and provide employees with protection of re-employment. Again, the details of each state's statute vary significantly, so employers should very carefully review what their state might require. . . .

### 5. Restraining/Protective Orders

A number of states have proposed or enacted statutes allowing employers to seek for protective or restraining orders, where violence, harassment, or stalking of employees has occurred. Many states that provide this protection allow a protective order or restraining order to be issued when the employer shows that the employee has experienced some form of violence or stalking or that a credible threat of violence or stalking can be demonstrated. In a few of the states, the employer must demonstrate that the employee involved is in imminent danger, or that irreparable harm will befall the employee if the protective order is not granted. Some of the statutes allow the employer to obtain a restraining or protective order in its own name, rather than on behalf of the employee, and some require that an employee who is the target of violence must be consulted prior to the employer's seeking the order. . . .

Which lawsuit would you like?

---

7. [n306] *See, e.g.*, Peavler v. Mitchell & Scott Mach. Co., 638 N.E.2d 879, 882 (Ind. Ct. App. 1994); Johnson v. Drummond, Woodsum, Plimpton & MacMahon, P.A., 490 A.2d 676, 676 (Me. 1985); *In re* Colas v. Watermain, 744 N.Y.S.2d 229, 231 (N.Y. App. Div. 2002); Panpat v. Owens-Brockway Glass Container, Inc., 49 P.3d 773, 778 (Or. 2002).

8. [n307] *See, e.g.*, Arceneaux v. K-Mart Corp., No.Civ.A.94-3720, 1995 WL 479818, at *2 (E.D. La. Aug. 11, 1995).

## Carroll v. Shoney's, Inc.
Alabama Supreme Court
775 So. 2d 753 (2000)

MADDOX, JUSTICE.

Willie Gene Carroll, as administrator of the estate of Mildred K. Harris, deceased, filed a wrongful-death action against Shoney's Inc., d/b/a Captain D's Restaurant (hereinafter "Captain D's"), and Ronnie Harris, Mildred Harris's husband. Willie Gene Carroll is Mildred Harris's father. The trial judge dismissed the claim against Ronnie Harris, and entered a summary judgment for Captain D's. . . .

### Facts

The facts, viewed in the light most favorable to Carroll, as the nonmovant, suggest the following: On the evening of September 22, 1995, Mildred Harris was working at Captain D's. Adrian Edwards, the relief manager, was also working that evening. Ms. Harris told Edwards that, the night before, her husband, Ronnie Harris, had beaten and choked her and that he had threatened her. Ms. Harris told Edwards that she was afraid of Ronnie Harris and that she did not want to talk to him. Ms. Harris asked Edwards to telephone the police if Ronnie Harris appeared at the restaurant that evening.

Around 10 o'clock that evening, while Ms. Harris was working in the rear of the restaurant, Ronnie Harris came in. He pushed his way past Edwards and went to the back of the restaurant, where he confronted Ms. Harris. He told Ms. Harris that he was going to "get her." Edwards and another employee repeatedly told Ronnie Harris to leave, but he continued yelling at Ms. Harris. Edwards telephoned the police; the officer who responded to the call escorted Ronnie Harris from the restaurant. The police detained him briefly; they released him after learning that Captain D's was not going to press charges. Evidence was presented indicating that after that confrontation Ms. Harris asked employees of Captain D's to help her hide from her husband; there was evidence indicating that she was taken to a motel in Montgomery and that her fellow employees lent her enough money to pay for the motel room.

The next day, September 23, 1995, Edwards reported for work and told the restaurant manager, Rhonda Jones, about the incident that had occurred the night before. . . . Edwards also told Jones that Ms. Harris had said that she was afraid to return to work. At some point after the conversation, Ms. Harris telephoned Jones and asked to be excused from work that evening. Ms. Harris told Jones that she and her husband had been fighting and that she was afraid of him. Jones told Ms. Harris to come into work; and she also told Ms. Harris that if Ronnie Harris showed up, she would telephone the police. Ms. Harris went to work that evening, and was working at the front counter. At some point during her shift, Ronnie Harris walked into the restaurant, pulled out a pistol, and shot Ms. Harris in the back of the head. Ms. Harris died as a result of the gunshot wound.

. . . .

## III.

It is well settled that absent a special relationship or special circumstances a person has no duty to protect another from criminal acts of a third person. See *Ex parte McRae's of Alabama, Inc.*, 703 So. 2d 351 (Ala. 1997)....

We believe that Carroll has failed to show how this case falls outside the general rule that a person has no duty to protect another from criminal acts of a third person. Alabama law requires a plaintiff to show three elements to establish a duty that would be the basis for a cause of action such as the one presented in this case.... First, the particular criminal conduct must have been foreseeable. Second, the defendant must have possessed "specialized knowledge" of the criminal activity. Third, the criminal conduct must have been a probability.

> Viewing the facts most favorably to Carroll, as we are required to do, and applying the law to those facts, we conclude that the plaintiff has not presented evidence creating a genuine issue of material fact as to Captain D's liability. The particular criminal conduct in this case was a murder. Unlike *Hail v. Regency Terrace Owners Ass'n*, [Ms. 1981397, December 22, 1999] So. 2d, 1999 Ala. LEXIS 328 (Ala. 1999), there was no evidence in this case that any employee of Captain D's was told, or should have reasonably foreseen, that Ronnie Harris would enter the Captain D's restaurant and murder his wife. Admittedly, there was evidence that Mildred Harris and her husband had been fighting, and that she had requested permission to be away from work for that reason, but the evidence also indicated that she had made similar requests on other occasions for the same reason. During his deposition, Carroll, who is Mildred Harris's father, admitted that he had no reason to think that Ronnie Harris would shoot Mildred Harris. Based on the foregoing, we fail to see how Captain D's can be held responsible for Ms. Harris's death. Consequently, we affirm the judgment of the trial court.

---

Employers can lessen the risk of domestic violence following their employees to work by taking advantage of laws that have been enacted in several states allowing them to apply for restraining orders to keep domestic abusers from stalking, harassing or harming their victims on the job. An employer seeking such an order in most states where available need only show the employee has experienced either violence or a credible threat of violence at work.

## Georgia Code. Ann. § 34-1-7 (2016)

....

(b) Any employer whose employee has suffered unlawful violence or a credible threat of violence from any individual, which can reasonably be construed to have been carried out at the employee's workplace, may seek a temporary restraining order and an injunction on behalf of the employer prohibiting further unlawful violence or threats of violence by that individual at the employee's workplace or while the employee is acting within the course and scope of employment with the employer. Nothing in this Code section shall be construed as authorizing a court to issue a temporary restraining order or injunction prohibiting speech or other activities that are protected by the Constitution of this state or the United States. . . .

---

Domestic violence affects both the worker and the employer at the office. Studies show the following: Between 2005 and 2006, 130,000 employees reported getting fired because they were victims of stalking; in 2005, a survey in Maine showed 96 percent of domestic violence victims said they could not perform as required at the jobsite; domestic violence cost employers in Tennesee $174 million in 2006 in lost wages and productivity; two-thirds of the nation's corporate executives think domestic violence is a problem for employers, and 55 percent of them believe it lowers productivity.[9]

## Green v. Bryant
### United States District Court, Eastern District of Pennsylvania
### 887 F. Supp. 798 (1995)

DITTER, J.

. . . .

### I. FACTS

Defendant, Dr. Winston Murphy Bryant, employed plaintiff, Philloria Green, from December 1992 through August 1993. Plaintiff asserts that during her last week of work, her estranged husband raped and severely beat her with a pipe at gun point. She received medical treatment and returned to work shortly thereafter. Ms. Green informed another doctor in the office about the attack. The doctor informed defendant, who then terminated plaintiff's employment. Ms. Green asserts that Dr. Bryant told her that the discharge had nothing to do with plaintiff's performance at work, but was based solely upon her being the victim of a violent crime.[10] Plaintiff alleges that defendant retroactively terminated her health insurance so that none of her medical expenses were covered. She also alleges that she has suffered migraine headaches and post-traumatic stress disorder as a result of her being fired.

. . . .

---

9. Workplaces Respond to Domestic and Sexual Violence, *The Facts on the Workplace and Domestic Violence,* www.workplacerespond.org, accessed March 6, 2017.

10. [n2] Presumably, defendant's concerns stemmed from the physical or emotional danger to other employees or patients if plaintiff's estranged husband came to the workplace and engaged in further violent behavior directed primarily at plaintiff.

## II. PLAINTIFF'S STATE-LAW CLAIMS

### A. Wrongful Discharge

Plaintiff asserts in count II that defendant wrongfully discharged her from employment in violation of Pennsylvania public policy. Plaintiff admits she was an at-will employee of Dr. Bryant's. The general rule in Pennsylvania is that an at-will employee may be dismissed with or without cause, for good reason, bad reason, or no reason. *Clark v. Modern Group, Ltd.*, 9 F.3d 321, 327 (3d Cir. 1993)....

Ms. Green argues that her dismissal violates dual public policies: protecting an employee's right to privacy and protecting victims of crime or spousal abuse.[11] In support of her first contention, plaintiff notes that the Third Circuit has recognized a strong policy favoring a right to privacy. *Borse v. Piece Goods Shop, Inc.*, 963 F.2d 611 (3d Cir. 1992). There is little connection between *Borse* and this case. *Borse* involved an employee whose employment was terminated for refusing to submit to urinalysis screening and personal property searches conducted by her employer. *Id.* at 612. In this case, plaintiff states that she revealed to another employee, Dr. Brown, that she had been raped and severely beaten. There is no allegation that defendant initiated the conversation, required disclosure of the information, questioned plaintiff about her marital situation, inquired into personal or private details, or in any way sought to intrude upon plaintiff's privacy in a substantial and highly offensive manner. See *Borse*, 963 F.2d at 625. I find that defendant's discharge of plaintiff did not violate the public policy favoring a right to privacy.

Plaintiff also argues that her discharge is in violation of Pennsylvania's policy to protect victims of crime and domestic abuse, as embodied in the state's criminal code, Protection from Abuse Act, 23 Pa. C.S.A. § 6101 et seq., and the establishment of the Crime Victim's Compensation Board, 71 P.S. § 180-7 et seq. The flaw in plaintiff's argument is that while these statutes provide certain procedures and protections, they do not thereby create a protected employment class. In the statutes to which plaintiff refers, the legislature included certain programs or safety measures, but excluded others. For example, the Protection from Abuse Act specifies that a defendant may be directed to pay a plaintiff for economic losses incurred as a result of the abuse. 23 Pa. C.S.A. § 6108(a)(8). It does not, however, say that a complainant is entitled to any kind of employment rights or benefits. Similarly, a crime victim may be eligible for compensation pursuant to 71 P.S. § 180-7.3, but the statute does not create employment rights or privileges.... Therefore, in the absence of any indication that Pennsylvania has established a clear mandate that crime victims generally, or spousal abuse victims specifically, are entitled to benefits or privileges beyond those enumerated in the laws, I must conclude that plaintiff's dismissal was not in violation of public policy. Because plaintiff has not alleged facts sufficient to state a

---

11. [n3] Plaintiff's complaint also mentions "protection of employment of crime victims and witnesses." She has not, however, alleged any facts indicating that she was fired for appearing as a witness or for participating in court proceedings against her assailant.

claim that her discharge from at-will employment was in violation of public policy, defendant's motion to dismiss count II must be granted.

. . . .

## NYC Administrative Code 8-107.1 Victims of Domestic Violence, Sex offenses or Stalking.

. . . .

1. (a) It shall be an unlawful discriminatory practice for an employer, or an agent thereof, because of any individual's actual or perceived status as a victim of domestic violence, or as a victim of sex offenses or stalking:

(1) To represent that any employment or position is not available when in fact it is available;

(2) To refuse to hire or employ or to bar or to discharge from employment; or

(3) To discriminate against an individual in compensation or other terms, conditions, or privileges of employment.

(b) Requirement to make reasonable accommodation to the needs of victims of domestic violence, sex offenses or stalking. Except as provided in subparagraph (d), any person prohibited by paragraph 1 from discriminating on the basis of actual or perceived status as a victim of domestic violence or a victim of sex offenses or stalking shall make reasonable accommodation to enable a person who is a victim of domestic violence, or a victim of sex offenses or stalking to satisfy the essential requisites of a job provided that the status as a victim of domestic violence or a victim of sex offenses or stalking is known or should have been known by the covered entity. . . .

## R.I. Gen. Laws § 12-28-10 (2016) Victims of domestic abuse — Employment discrimination

(a) No employer, employment agency or licensing agency shall refuse to hire any applicant for employment, or discharge an employee or discriminate against him or her with respect to any matter related to employment, solely by reason of his or her seeking or obtaining a protective order pursuant to chapter 15 of title 15 or chapter 8.1 of title 8 or refusing to seek or obtain a protective order.

(b) In any civil action alleging a violation of this chapter, the court may:

(1) Award to a prevailing applicant or employee actual damages, and reasonable attorneys' fees and costs, and, where the challenged conduct is shown to be motivated by malice or ill will, punitive damages; provided, punitive damages shall not be available against the state or its political subdivisions; and

(2) Afford injunctive relief against any employer, employment agency or licensing agency who commits or proposes to commit a violation of this chapter.

## VIII. False Arrest Claims

Tort actions have also been undertaken by those charged with domestic violence who think they have been treated unfairly by law enforcement.

### Wildoner v. Borough of Ramsey
New Jersey Supreme Court
162 N.J. 375 (2000)

GARIBALDI, J.

. . . .

I.

Plaintiff, seventy years old at the time of his arrest, resided with his wife in the Woodlands Senior Home, a senior citizens' complex in Ramsey. On September 15, 1993, plaintiff's neighbor, Helen Gannon, reported to the apartment complex's manager, Margaret Diefert, that she had heard plaintiff using loud and abusive language and that he was threatening to throw knives at his wife. Diefert called the police.

A short while later, Officers Zuhone and O'Donahue arrived at the complex in response to Diefert's complaint. The officers first spoke with Gannon and Diefert. At that time Gannon confirmed her initial report. The officers then proceeded to plaintiff's apartment, which Mrs. Wildoner allowed them to enter. The officers observed a knife on the kitchen floor and a red mark on Mrs. Wildoner's arm. The officers arrested plaintiff and wheeled him out of the apartment in a wheelchair, covered by a blanket. He was transported to the police station in an ambulance.

A criminal complaint charging simple assault pursuant to N.J.S.A. 2C:121(a) was signed by Officer Zuhone against plaintiff. Because Cecilia Wildoner refused to sign a domestic violence complaint against her husband, Officers O'Donahue and Zuhone applied to the Ramsey Municipal Court for a temporary restraining order ("TRO") pursuant to N.J.S.A. 2C:25-21 of the Domestic Violence Act. By order dated September 15, 1993, the Municipal Court granted a TRO restraining plaintiff from going back to his home, and ordered the Wildoners to appear for a formal hearing in the Superior Court. Plaintiff was released that same day to his son, Arthur Wildoner, Jr., a Garfield police officer, who was allowed to take his father home without having to post bail.

The next day, after hearing testimony from Mrs. Wildoner only, the Law Division vacated the TRO. On the order vacating the TRO, the court made a hand-written notation: "Testimony in Court. No Complaint filed by Plaintiff. Police improperly obtained TRO." The assault complaint filed in the municipal court was dismissed at the end of the State's case.

On December 8, 1993, plaintiff filed a timely Notice of Claim pursuant to N.J.S.A. 59:8-4. On September 14, 1995, plaintiff filed this action against the Borough, the Department, and Officers O'Donahue and Zuhone, alleging false arrest and imprisonment, mistreatment, and malicious prosecution, in violation of his federal constitutional and state common-law rights. He also sought compensatory and punitive damages. Both Gannon and Diefert initially were also named as defendants, but plaintiff executed stipulations dismissing them both. . . .

A. *The Officers' Account*

According to the officers, Mrs. Wildoner informed the police that plaintiff had been drinking and that an argument had ensued between them because Mrs. Wildoner did not want her husband to drive. Consistent with Gannon's report, the officers observed a knife in plain view on the kitchen floor. They also saw a red mark on Mrs. Wildoner's arm that she stated her husband had caused. Mrs. Wildoner also informed the officers that there had been a pattern of abuse throughout the forty-eight years of the couple's marriage.

Plaintiff was then arrested for a domestic violence assault. . . . Plaintiff was charged with simple assault and released that same day to his son, Arthur Wildoner, Jr.

B. *The Wildoners' Account*

Plaintiff concedes that Gannon made a report to police claiming that she had heard plaintiff being loud and abusive and threatening to throw a knife at his wife. According to Mrs. Wildoner's deposition (which was taken in her husband's presence), however, the couple had not been arguing that day. Instead, plaintiff was, at times, "talking loud" about their grandchildren and, later, he was angry and shouting because Gannon had telephoned three times that day out of concern for Mrs. Wildoner's safety. Gannon's third call was to let Mrs. Wildoner know that she had called the police.

When the police arrived, one officer told Mrs. Wildoner to wait in the bedroom; when the officer returned he indicated that they were going to arrest plaintiff. According to Mrs. Wildoner, the police had her husband's hands behind his back and he was saying, "You're hurting me, you're hurting me."

Mrs. Wildoner attempted to help her husband put on his pants. In attempting to do so, she bruised her arm on the edge of a table. At some point, Mrs. Wildoner gave up trying to get her husband's pants on and the police took her husband away in a wheelchair, clad only in a t-shirt and his underwear. Mrs. Wildoner denied having told police that her husband had been drinking, slapped her with a cane, verbally abused her, or thrown a knife at her. She admitted having told police that her husband was angry. She also conceded that a knife was in plain view, but said that it was on the table, not the floor. Finally, Mrs. Wildoner testified that her husband could not possibly have beaten her "because I'd run like hell."

Plaintiff, in his deposition, stated that when the police arrived, he was seated at the kitchen table tapping a knife on the table. He agreed that at one point it may have flown out of his hands and landed on the kitchen floor, but he stated that his wife was in the bedroom at that time. According to plaintiff, one of the officers said "we don't have nothing here," and was going to leave, but one officer then abruptly returned, said "I'm going to try something," read plaintiff his rights, and twisted his hands behind his back to handcuff him. Aside from trying to get his arms behind his back to handcuff him, plaintiff concedes that the police did nothing else to him physically. Moreover, although plaintiff claims the police told him that he was "bluffing" about being unable to walk, he also concedes that the police did get him a wheelchair and did not try to force him to walk. An ambulance transported him to the police station.

Plaintiff, who was seventy years old, testified that he had been wounded in the knee in World War II and had never recovered the full use of his legs. For the last eight to nine years he had had trouble bending the knee and had developed arthritis in the other leg, making it difficult for him to walk. He testified that he needed a cane and it took him a long time to get out of a chair. According to plaintiff, he could not possibly have attacked his wife because "[s]he could give me a shove and that would be the end of it."

In March, 1997, Arthur Wildoner, Jr. was deposed by defendants' attorneys concerning his knowledge of the incident. Wildoner, Jr., a Garfield police officer for twenty-one years, testified that at the time of the September 1993 incident, his parents had resided at the Ramsey apartment for approximately one to two years. Prior to that time, they had resided in a private residence in Garfield for approximately twenty-one years. Wildoner, Jr. worked as a Garfield police officer for about the last nineteen of his parents' twenty-one years' residence in Garfield. During that time, Wildoner, Jr. testified, the Garfield police had been called to his parents' home in connection with domestic disturbances on approximately five occasions....

Wildoner, Jr. also stated that, when asked what happened, plaintiff told him that "he had a fight with mommy and a couple of other choice words out of his mouth and he said they arrested me." That same evening Wildoner, Jr. asked his mother what happened. She told him that "they were fighting, he is drinking, she took his keys away and ... he threw a knife at her."

Wildoner, Jr. testified that his mother had reported that plaintiff had "hit her a few times" over the years, but Wildoner, Jr. stated that he was not concerned about the altercations because his mother was in better physical condition and his father could not throw a knife "with any velocity or substance behind it." Asked whether he, in his experience responding to domestic violence complaints, would have arrested a "frail" elderly man such as his father who had reportedly assaulted a "woman that's basically strong and healthy," Wildoner, Jr. replied, "Yes. If the law states that there is a victim who claims she was assaulted with a knife that was thrown at her, whether the guy is frail or not, he was arrested for domestic violence."

II.

. . . .

The Law Division granted defendants' motion and dismissed plaintiff's complaint. The court found that the facts not in dispute—that the police had acted in response to a citizen's complaint, and that when they arrived at the apartment they observed, consistent with Gannon's report, a knife in plain view and a red mark on

Mrs. Wildoner's arm-not only supported the officers' objective good faith but also established probable cause for them to believe that plaintiff had committed an offense. The court observed that Mrs. Wildoner's declining to sign a complaint did not preclude the officers' action; to the contrary, the court found that the Domestic Violence Act was specifically designed to protect victims in the not uncommon situation in which an alleged victim says "I don't want him out of the house." . . . Accordingly, the court held that defendants were immune from liability under Section 1983 and N.J.S.A. 59:2-1, 3-3, and 9-2(d).

Plaintiff appealed, and the Appellate Division reversed, in part, the dismissal of plaintiff's claims. 316 N.J. Super. 487, 720 A.2d 645 (1998). . . .

The Appellate Division held, however, that the punitive damages claims against the individual officers could go forward on remand. *Id.* at 508, 720 A.2d 645.

The Appellate Division based its conclusion that plaintiff submitted evidence sufficient to allow a jury reasonably to find that the police lacked probable cause to arrest plaintiff principally upon the Wildoners' denials that any act of domestic violence had occurred and the differing versions of the police investigation presented by defendants and the Wildoners. . . .

We granted defendants' petition for certification. 158 N.J. 75, 726 A.2d 938 (1999).

### III.

. . . .

A. *Section 1983*

Section 1983 provides in pertinent part:

> Every person who, under color of any statute, ordinance, regulation, custom, or usage of any State . . . subjects, or causes to be subjected, any citizen of the United States . . . to the deprivation of any rights, privileges, or immunities secured by the Constitution and laws, shall be liable to the party injured in an action at law, suit in equity, or other proper proceeding for redress.

. . . .

B. *N.J.S.A. 59:3-3 of the Tort Claims Act*

Plaintiff also claims damages under the New Jersey Tort Claims Act, N.J.S.A. 59:1-1 to -12-3, N.J.S.A. 59:3-3 states:

> A public employee is not liable if he acts in good faith in the execution of enforcement of any law. Nothing in this section exonerates a public employee from liability for false arrest or false imprisonment.

The same standard of objective reasonableness that applies in Section 1983 actions also governs questions of good faith arising under the Tort Claims Act, N.J.S.A. 59:9-3. *Lear v. Township of Piscataway*, 236 N.J. Super. 550, 553, 566 A.2d 557 (App. Div. 1989); *Hayes v. Mercer County*, 217 N.J. Super. 614, 621–22, 526 A.2d 737 (App. Div.) (holding marked similarities between facts known about indicted man and facts known about plaintiff coupled with plaintiff's refusal to submit to photographic identification established objective reasonableness of investigator's initiating investigation against wrong man), *certif. denied,* 108 N.J. 643, 532 A.2d 227 (1987).

C. *N.J.S.A. 2C:25-22 of the Domestic Violence Act*

In addition to the good-faith immunity provided by the Tort Claims Act, defendants also are shielded by the specific immunity provided under N.J.S.A. 2C:25-22 of the Domestic Violence Act. Plaintiff's arrest was made pursuant to the Domestic Violence Act. Domestic violence remains a serious problem in our society. *Cesare v. Cesare,* 154 N.J. 394, 397, 713 A.2d 390 (1998)....

The purpose of the Domestic Violence Act is "to assure the victims of domestic violence the maximum protection from abuse the law can provide." N.J.S.A. 2C:25-18. The Legislature specifically addressed the need to counter prevailing societal views regarding acts of domestic violence. *Ibid.* The Legislature particularly sought to cure the reluctance on the part of police to arrest alleged perpetrators of domestic violence that had contributed to the under enforcement of the domestic violence laws. *Ibid.* ...

As part of the Act the Legislature encouraged the training of police and judicial personnel "in the procedures and enforcement of the Act, and about the social and psychological context in which domestic violence occurs." *Ibid.*

The Act also broadened the discretion of a police officer to arrest an alleged perpetrator, even when the victim did not corroborate the incident, provided that the officer had probable cause to believe the incident occurred. N.J.S.A. 2C:25-21(b). The purpose of this broadened authority to arrest was not to punish the perpetrator, but to protect the victim. *Carfagno v. Carfagno,* 288 N.J. Super. 424, 434, 672 A.2d 751 (Ch. Div. 1995). With those provisions, the Legislature attempted to assure that more arrests would be made, and more victims protected, from domestic violence.

To ensure protection for law enforcement officers and others who in good faith report a possible incident of domestic violence, the Legislature enacted N.J.S.A. 2C:25-22, which provides:

> A law enforcement officer or a member of a domestic crisis team or any person who, in good faith, reports a possible incident of domestic violence to the police shall not be held liable in any civil action brought by any party for an arrest based on *probable cause, enforcement in good faith of a court order, or any other act or omission in good faith* under this act.

. . . .

V.

. . . .

Under the circumstances of this case, the officers properly placed substantial reliance on Gannon's statement. Gannon did not phone in an anonymous tip; rather, she waited at the scene and confirmed her report to police, conduct that eventually led to her also being named as a defendant in this suit. There was no allegation that

Gannon reported the incident out of any motivation other than concern for Mrs. Wildoner's safety. . . .

Similarly, the arrest in this case was effected for the principal purpose of removing the alleged perpetrator from the victim's presence and to allow the parties time to cool off. It is well documented that, for a number of reasons, victims of domestic violence often do not report their abuse to law enforcement officers. Many victims deny the abuse when questioned. . . .

Courts, too, have recognized that victims of domestic violence do not often report their abuse to law enforcement agencies. Indeed, this Court has noted "the high incidence of unreported abuse [and that] . . . the FBI and other law enforcement experts believe that wife abuse is the most unreported crime in the United States." *State v. Kelly*, 97 N.J. 178, 191, 478 A.2d 364 (1984). *See also Tierney v. Davidson*, 133 F.3d 189, 198–99 (2d Cir. 1998) (finding police officers had acted reasonably in conducting limited search of premises of alleged domestic violence incident even though victim's statements suggested that she did not want police to pursue their investigation, the court finding that victim's statements were contradicted by neighbors' independent reports of dispute and that victim's statements were self-contradictory); *United States v. Bartelho*, 71 F.3d 436, 442 (1st Cir. 1995) (recognizing that "the police were not required to take [the victim's] statements at face value, given her demeanor, their training regarding domestic violence, and [a neighbor's] report."). *See, e.g.,* Lawrence W. Sherman, *Policing Domestic Violence* 226–230 (1992) (discussing role of neighbors in reporting and countering domestic violence in chronic cases).

We find that the failure of the victim and the alleged perpetrator to corroborate the allegations did not create a material issue of fact defeating probable cause. In certain cases, lack of corroboration can defeat the reliability of an informant's tip as a basis for probable cause. In the totality of circumstances here, however, Gannon's report was sufficient. She was plaintiff's neighbor who heard plaintiff yelling and threatening to throw knives at his wife, and she reported those specific details directly to the police. Moreover. although plaintiff and his wife did not corroborate Gannon's report to the police, the police were able to corroborate adequately the details of the report through their independent investigation. It is undisputed that when the police were at the apartment, they saw a knife in plain view and a red mark on Mrs. Wildoner's arm. Combined with Gannon's report, the officers had, at a minimum, an objectively reasonable belief in the existence of probable cause. That the police acted in good faith is underscored by the fact that, unlike in *Kirk,* where the plaintiff remained incarcerated for four days until bail was posted, plaintiff was merely held until his son arrived to take him home, with no bail having been imposed.

. . . .

Indeed, if probable cause to arrest cannot be based upon the reliable report of a concerned citizen, as supported by an officer's review of the totality of the circumstances, then law enforcement officers' willingness to make such arrests may be chilled by fear of civil liability for their actions. Such a chilling effect would not further the goals of the Domestic Violence Act. The Act is remedial in nature, and "is to be liberally construed to achieve its salutary purposes." *Cesare, supra*, 154 N.J. at 400, 713 A.2d 390. A broad interpretation of the Act better conforms to the public policy against domestic violence and is in accordance with New Jersey's place "in the forefront of states that have sought to curb domestic violence." *Brennan v. Orban*, 145 N.J. 282, 299, 678 A.2d 667 (1996).

VI.

Given the dynamics of domestic violence and the frequency with which victims themselves do not reach out to the police for assistance, it is critical that law enforcement officers be able to rely on concerned citizens' reports of domestic violence, as verified by a review of the totality of the circumstances, in order to arrest an alleged abuser. Certainly, an officer should consider the statement of a victim when reviewing the totality of the circumstances. However, where the officers investigating an alleged incident of domestic violence observe a weapon at the scene and an injury to the victim, and where statements other than that of the victim support a belief that a domestic violence incident occurred, the law enforcement officer could reasonably conclude that there is probable cause to arrest the alleged batterer.

We reverse the judgment of the Appellate Division and reinstate the order of the trial court dismissing the complaint.

## Notes and Questions

- **THE STEINBERG TRIAL**

Although Hedda Nussbaum won the preliminary round in her effort to toll the statute of limitations for her civil action against her batterer, Joel Steinberg, she ultimately dropped the case, citing Steinberg's claim of indigency following imposition of his 8 1/3-to-25 year sentence for killing Lisa. *See* HEDDA NUSSBAUM, SURVIVING INTIMATE TERRORISM 461–66 (2005). Consider whether Nussbaum's victory on an insanity argument might impact on whether she could protect her child from abuse by Steinberg. Would you as a family court judge grant custody of Lisa Steinberg to Hedda Nussbaum knowing what you know about the facts of this case?

Nussbaum was a highly controversial figure. Acting New York Supreme Court Justice Harold J. Rothwax charged the jury that she was an accomplice in the death of Lisa Steinberg and therefore, under New York law, Joel Steinberg could not be convicted solely on her testimony. *See* Ronald Sullivan, *Steinberg Jury Will Consider All Four Charges of Homicide*, N.Y. TIMES, Jan. 18, 1989. *See also* Nadine Brozan, *Unresolved Issue: Is Nussbaum Culpable?*, N.Y. TIMES, Jan. 24, 1989, in which the reporter interviewed Ann Jones, author of a book on battered women, who said: "I am firmly in the camp of those who believe she is not culpable. It is as unreasonable to say that Hedda Nussbaum should have left as it is to say that the Iranian hostages should have escaped." In the same article, Susan Brownmiller, author of the seminal work on rape, AGAINST OUR WILL: MEN, WOMEN AND RAPE, as well as WAVERLY PLACE, a novel inspired by the Steinberg case, said: "Hedda Nussbaum first collaborated in her own destruction and then became incapable of acting to save her child. There are those who feel that once she was battered, she became so demoralized that she lost all willpower, but that is not good enough for me."

- **PARENT-CHILD TORT IMMUNITY**

Parent-child tort immunity existed throughout much of the late 19th and early 20th centuries. *See, e.g., Foley v. Foley,* 61 Ill. App. 577 (1895), where a child, upon the death of his father, was adopted by an uncle who cruelly beat him and neglected to provide proper medical care. The court held the child could not maintain a civil action against parents, adoptive or biological, for injuries: "[T]he child shall not contest with the parent the parent's right to govern the child." *Id.* at 579. It was not until some 60 years later that Illinois courts recognized the right of a child to sue a parent where willful and wanton parental misconduct was alleged. *See Nudd v. Matsoukas,* 7 Ill. 2d 608 (1956). Assume Lisa Steinberg had survived her father's treatment of her. What causes of action might she have considered bringing against him? Would she have any claims against Hedda Nussbaum? Would the fact that Nussbaum was battered by Steinberg provide her immunity from a suit brought by their child? Should it?

- **WRONGFUL DEATH**

The families of domestic violence victims can, and do, recover from their loved-ones' abusers through wrongful death actions. Not only do these suits permit families to obtain compensation for the loss of the earning power and companionship of the deceased, but closure and personal satisfaction may be possible through the award of punitive damages. These suits generally contain no legal issues unique to the fact they arise out of domestic violence situations. The most famous wrongful death claim is probably that brought by the families of Ronald Goldman and Nicole Brown Simpson against O.J. Simpson. Although O.J. Simpson was acquitted in less than 4 hours for the 1994 deaths of Goldman and his ex-wife, in 1997, a Santa Monica civil jury awarded the families $33.5 million in compensatory and punitive damages after being convinced by a preponderance of the evidence that O.J. Simpson had killed them.

The differences in the two actions were the lesser standard of proof and the fact O.J. Simpson had no right to remain silent in a civil action. He was forced to sit for depositions, testified on the witness stand four days and was believed by the jury to have lied about many of the facts surrounding the murder. *See* Stephanie Simon, *Simpson Liable in Slayings; Compensatory Damages Put at $8.5 Million; Trial: The Defendant Gives No Show of Emotion as the Verdicts Against Him are Read. Tearfully, Kim Goldman Shouts Out at Him, 'Oh My God, You're a Murderer!',* L.A. TIMES, Feb. 5, 1997; Stephanie Simon, *Simpson Verdict: $25 Million; Punitive Damages Bring Total to $33.5 Million; Trial: Jury in Civil Case Awards $12.5 Million to the Heirs of Each Victim. The Huge Judgments Leave No Doubt That Most Panelists Were Outraged by the Slayings,* L.A. TIMES, Feb. 11, 1997.

Juries in wrongful death actions are not bound by acquittals in previous criminal trials. Acquittals may have a preclusive impact under insurance laws in jurisdictions that have enacted so-called "slayer statutes." These laws bar those who have caused the death of a decedent from inheriting any portion of that person's estate or from obtaining the insurance benefits of the victim. *See generally* David T. Austern, *Strategies for Recovery in Domestic Violence Tort Cases*, 33(8) TRIAL 26 (1997) (discussing California statute entitling wife to insurance proceeds after acquittal of her husband's death and Oklahoma statute reaching different result where defendant-wife acquitted of first degree murder of her husband).

- **HELPING DOMESTIC VIOLENCE SURVIVORS IN THE WORKPLACE**

The *Carroll v. Shoney's* and *Bryant v. Green* cases make it clear that the workplace can be an inhospitable place for women suffering domestic violence; either because employers do not take it seriously enough or because employers are so fearful that batterers will stalk their victims to the office that they want no part of it. One woman who has spent the last 16 years trying to open office doors to domestic violence victims is Ludy Green, who founded *Second Chance Employment Services*, a Washington, D.C.-based non-profit organization that helps battered women get back on their professional feet. In addition to Washington, *Second Chance* also operates in Los Angeles, New York City, Atlanta, Columbus and West Palm Beach.

Dr. Green holds a doctorate in industrial organization psychology from George Washington University and is the author of ENDING DOMESTIC VIOLENCE CAPTIVITY: A GUIDE TO ECONOMIC FREEDOM (Volcano Press, 2014). Her interest in domestic violence began while she was working for a Florida congressman and volunteered at a local domestic violence shelter. It disturbed her that many of the shelter clients returned to their abusive husbands and lovers. She took an informal survey to figure out why. She learned these women were trapped by a lack of job skills or hurt by remaining out of the workforce for a lengthy period raising children which prevented them from being able to support themselves sufficiently to break out of the cycle of violence. With the help of 40 of her colleagues in the human resources field, Green partnered with local businesses to lend their support to battered women by hiring them or contributing in some other way to getting them started on the road to financial independence.

Today, *Second Chance* has a $3.7 million budget funded by federal and local grant money as well as business and personal contributors that supports a small office with eight paid staff members and 500 volunteers. The group hosts two major fund-raising galas each year and monthly events to raise money and social awareness about the economic impact on women of being battered. *Second Chance* clients are seen by appointment and referred by domestic violence shelters, government social work departments and faith-based organizations. Business partners include hairdressers who provide free shampoos and blow-outs so job interviewees can look their best and retail partners that provide two new free suits to each client on the job hunt.

As of late 2016, the group had placed 8,235 women in jobs around the country ranging from entry-level receptionists and sales women positions to posts as professors in community colleges and management consultants. It even helped an obstetrician-gynecologist escape domestic violence and get back on the high-level career track. *Second Chance* has partnered with 230 organizations over the years including Morgan Stanley, IBM, Macy's, Sun Trust Bank and Saks Fifth Avenue. Dr. Green thinks the reluctance by some employers to hiring a woman who has suffered domestic violence comes from ignorance about those who are impacted by it. "They think it is just uneducated or homeless women and that is totally wrong," she said. Part of her work includes education and consciousness raising about domestic violence—and she sees a ray of hope. "Attitudes have totally changed. People once laughed at me when I said employment was a solution to end domestic violence," she said. Now, they understand she was right. In fact, even the 2013 Violence Against Women Act recognizes the connection between employment and ending domestic violence. *Dr. Ludy Green, interview with the author*, November 21, 2016.

Clearly, not all workplaces are enlightened when it comes to domestic violence. In 2015 the New York Attorney General reached a settlement with Bon-Ton Stores, with some 200 retail outlets across the northern part of the country, over a claim filed by a woman who alleged she was retaliated against by the store because she was a victim of domestic violence. The woman was a Bon-Ton saleswoman who arrived for her regular shift telling store security officers that her husband had threatened to kill her. Her manager sent her home telling her she was not permitted to return until she obtained an order of protection against her estranged husband. She contacted the attorney general who commenced an investigation that led to the settlement, which required the company to educate employees that domestic violence victims cannot be discriminated against. The store also put into effect a safety plan that allowed this particular employee to park her car closer to the store, use her cellphone while on duty in case of an emergency, and give her access to a safe place in the event her husband came to stalk her at the workplace. Noam Scheiber, *Settlement in New York Domestic Abuse Case May Set Broader Precedent,* N.Y. Times, November 19, 2015.

Chapter 10

# Domestic Violence and Family Law

> **CONSIDER AS YOU READ ABOUT FAMILY LAW**
> 1. The distinction between civil and criminal orders of protection
> 2. The procedure by which a victim of domestic violence secures a protective order
> 3. The efficacy of orders of protection
> 4. Double Jeopardy concerns when seeking sanctions for violations of civil orders of protection

Despite mandatory arrest laws, victims of domestic violence remain free to seek their own protective orders in state, family or civil courts. At one time, it was the *only* place battered wives could go to receive court protection from their abusive husbands, because the law considered domestic violence a private, family matter. But today all victims—female, male or transgendered—as well as those in same sex relationships have the option of seeking civil protective orders whether or not their abusers face criminal charges.

The rationale for proceeding in the civil courts for a protective order is that instead of being a witness for the prosecution, a victim who petitions in the family courts maintains a modicum of control over her case. A victim will usually come to court *ex parte,* and if the court determines she faces danger from an intimate partner, an order of protection will be issued. Later, if the victim decides she no longer needs or wants the protection of the court, under most circumstances, she may withdraw her petition without prejudice to renew.

In theory, allowing the victim to control access to court proceedings could be considered empowering. But some criticize the civil protective order system because it treats domestic violence as a family matter, rather than as a crime punishable by the state. Although domestic violence is a crime, civil orders of protection are nonetheless available in all 50 states and the District of Columbia for those victims who want this protection. Pennsylvania started the trend more than 40 years ago.[1]

---

1. Emilie Meyer, Civil Protection Orders: A Guide for Improving Practice 2 (National Council of Juvenile and Family Court Judges, 2010).

As this chapter unfolds, keep in mind the goals of the civil protective order system and the criminal justice system are vastly different. Civil protective orders are designed to protect a victim from harm and to help stop family violence. The prosecution of domestic violence in the criminal courts is to protect individual safety as well, but it also seeks to hold batterers accountable for their behavior and to signal societal outrage at domestic violence.

The need for protection against domestic violence is enormous. Between 1994 and 2005, 1.4 million orders of protection were obtained in New York State.[2] In Cook County, Illinois, in 2006, courts issued 18,447 civil protective orders.[3] The need is everywhere; even in rural Montana, 3,905 orders of protection were issued in domestic relations courts in 2008.[4] Nationwide, 1.2 million victims of domestic violence flood the courts each year seeking civil restraining orders against their abusers.[5]

When seeking an order of protection against a family member, litigants go to the family divisions of civil court in most jurisdictions. After obtaining an order of protection *ex parte*, the petitioner, as the victim is known in family court, serves the respondent, and a hearing is held. Because the proceedings are civil in nature, the standard of proof is a preponderance of the evidence.

Many issues that fall under the rubric of family law have been discussed elsewhere in this book. The impact of domestic violence on child custody determinations, for example, was covered in Chapter 8. The requirement that each state give Full Faith and Credit to the civil protective orders issued by every other state was examined in the chapter on the Violence Against Women Act. The adjudication of domestic violence allegations in matrimonial actions was discussed in the chapter on divorce. Here, the emphasis is on whether the civil protective order system keeps victims safe and what statutes, cases and procedures have developed to facilitate this area of domestic violence law.

### Catherine F. Klein & Leslie E. Orloff, *Protective Orders and Other Injunctive Relief: Civil Protection Orders*

THE IMPACT OF DOMESTIC VIOLENCE ON YOUR LEGAL PRACTICE 200–02, 210 (2d ed. 2004)

Civil protection orders are available to domestic violence victims by statute in all fifty states, the District of Columbia, Puerto Rico, and all U.S. Territories. Civil protection orders that are properly drafted and consistently enforced can offer effective

---

2. New York Office for the Prevention of Domestic Violence, N.Y. STATE'S RESPONSE TO DOMESTIC VIOLENCE: SYSTEMS AND SERVICES MAKING A DIFFERENCE, 5, www.opdv.ny.gov/whatisdv/about_dv/nyresponse/nysdv.pdf, accessed October 30, 2016.

3. E. Kenneth Wright, Jr., *President's Page: Helping Victims of Domestic Violence,* 23 CBA RECORD 12 (January 2009).

4. Diana E. Garrett & Shannon Fuller, *Domestic Violence: Orders of Protection Myths Dispelled; Practical Tips for All Montana Lawyers,* 40 MONTANA LAWYER 6 (May 2015).

5. MEYER, CIVIL PROTECTION ORDERS, *supra*, at 3.

protection for many victims of domestic violence. In most jurisdictions, protection orders offer broad relief and may be used with or instead of more traditional domestic relations remedies or criminal court proceedings. Protection orders can also offer crucial protection against continued violence for victims who are not ready to separate from their abusers.

There are generally two types of protection orders available to victims of abuse. Most states authorize emergency, or temporary orders of protection, issued after an *ex parte* hearing if the victim can show that there is immediate danger of future violence. Such orders are short-lived (typically 14–30 days) and are intended to protect victims of domestic violence until a full hearing can be scheduled. Courts also issue protection orders after a full hearing, by consent, or by default. Full protection orders are of longer duration, typically for one to three years. These protection orders can also be modified or extended by written motion for good cause. The National Council of Juvenile and Family Court Judges' Model Code on Domestic Violence recommends that protection orders last indefinitely. Progressive jurisdictions are adopting this approach.

. . . .

### Obtaining a Protection Order

Generally, there is no statute of limitations within which a victim of domestic violence must file for a protection order. Some courts, however, may not grant an order if the most recent threat or incident of abuse took place more than several months prior to the filing of a petition for a civil protection order. When courts adopt this approach, attorneys representing battered women can often argue successfully that current circumstances warrant issuance of a protection order now because the victim will be taking steps that are likely to trigger escalation of abuse (i.e., separation, initiation of a court case, divorce, child custody, support or an immigration case) and/or because there have been attempts to kidnap the children. Victims should be able to get protection orders when there has been past abuse without the court requiring them to await another beating.

. . . .

States condition the issuance of a protection order on an underlying act of abuse which generally constitutes a criminal act, including: battery, assault, kidnapping, burglary, criminal trespass, interference with child custody, rape, sexual assault, interference with personal liberty, destruction of property, criminal threats, harm to pets, stalking and attempts to do any of these actions. Some states authorize the issuance of protection orders for behavior that has not physically harmed the petitioner, including specified forms of emotional abuse and harassment.

Most jurisdictions allow an abused adult to file on his or her own behalf. Most states allow an adult to file on behalf of a child or an incompetent adult. Some states allow minors to petition for protection on their own behalf. . . . A few of these states also permit minors in dating relationships to petition against other minors. Abused elderly individuals may petition the court for protection orders as well. . . .

Jurisdiction for protection orders generally exists in the state where the underlying acts of abuse have taken place or where the victim is present. The immigration status of the victim is not relevant for a protection order or any family court jurisdiction.

. . . .

Many jurisdictions provide form pleading to facilitate the process of petitioning for a protection order. Some innovative jurisdictions provide for a comprehensive domestic violence intake center, through which the victim can fill out and file a petition for a protection order as well as receive counseling and other information from victim's rights advocates all in one location. The Violence Against Women Act prohibits states from charging victims of domestic violence court filing fees or service of process fees in connection with protection order cases.

### Relief Available

Be careful to include in the petition all forms of relief necessary to protect the victim. When the parties have children, obtaining custody and an initial child support order are essential. Gaps in the relief provided or a lack of specificity in the drafting of the order can lead to future violence and make enforcement of the order difficult, if not impossible. Because batterers often are also abusive to the petitioner's children, it is important to include the children specifically by name in all appropriate provisions.

Courts have broad authority to issue any form of relief that may deter violence. Orders need not be limited to only those forms of relief specifically listed in the state statute. Be creative, and ask for all the relief you think will help the victim.

. . . .

Batterers often file retaliatory petitions for civil protection orders (in addition to false criminal charges) after victims take legal action against them. Some batterers do not file petitions, but allege during the civil protection order hearing that they have been abused. Under these circumstances, some courts may issue mutual orders in the mistaken belief that such orders will prevent future violence against either party. When mutual protection orders are entered against innocent victims, both batterers and victims learn that the system can be manipulated, and that courts are unwilling to determine who has been abused and order appropriate legal protection. Mutual protection orders violate due process and are not afforded full faith and credit under the Violence Against Women Act of 1994. . . .

Since mutual protection orders became unenforceable, abusers seeking to use the legal system against their victims have begun to file criss-cross protection order petitions. This occurs in two ways. In many instances, the victim will file for a protection order against the abuser and when he is served with the temporary protection order, he files one against the victim in retaliation. In other instances, the abuser will beat the victim to the courthouse and file for a protection order against the victim alleging that the victim is the perpetrator and the abuser the victim. However the abuser initiates the case, the victim should not agree to the issuance of a protection order against her. The victim should go to trial and offer evidence that the initiator is the abuser. If the victim agrees to the issuance of an order against her, the abuser is quite likely to also be able to convince a court that she violated the order in some way (e.g. contact), even if she does not. . . .

# I. Who Is Part of the Family?

The protective order statutory scheme is designed to stop violence among family members. Therefore, only those who fit the definition of "family" are protected. Spouses and children have long been considered family everywhere. As times changed, and society's acceptance of alternative lifestyles has grown, the definition of "family" has expanded to include unmarried couples with children, same sex couples and dating partners. With the 2015 United States Supreme Court decision in *Obergefell v. Hodges,* 135 S. Ct. 2584 (2015), that recognized a constitutional right for gay couples to marry, there can be no question that the concept of "family" has grown. The New York Family Court Act, quite restrictive until 2008, when it added "intimate relationship" as one qualifying for family protection, is an example.

## N.Y. Family Ct. Act § 812 (2016) Procedures for Family Offense Proceedings

1. . . . For purposes of this article, "members of the same family or household" shall mean the following:

(a) persons related by consanguinity or affinity;

(b) persons legally married to one another;

(c) persons formerly married to one another *regardless of whether they still reside in the same household*;

(d) persons who have a child in common regardless *of* whether such persons have been married or have lived together at any time; *and*

(e) persons who are not related by consanguinity or affinity and who are or have been in an intimate relationship regardless of whether such persons have lived together at any time. Factors the court may consider in determining whether a relationship is an "intimate relationship" include but are not limited to: the nature or type of relationship, regardless of whether the relationship is sexual in nature; the frequency of interaction between the persons; and the duration of the relationship. Neither a casual acquaintance nor ordinary fraternization between two individuals in business or social contexts shall be deemed to constitute an "intimate relationship". [Emphasis added.]

## II. The Legality of *Ex Parte* Orders of Protection

*Ex parte* orders of protection, issued to meet an ongoing domestic violence emergency, have their own set of unique legal issues. In the New Jersey case excerpted below, the question was how far the state's courts could go in providing protection to a domestic violence victim who fled from a violent home in another jurisdiction.

### Shah v. Shah

Supreme Court of New Jersey

184 N.J. 125 (2005)

Justice RIVERA-SOTO delivered the opinion of the Court.

. . . .

I.

In 2001, plaintiff Gayatri Shah and defendant Mayank K. Shah married in India. Shortly after the marriage, defendant returned to Illinois, where he is licensed to practice medicine and, almost eighteen months later, plaintiff joined him there. After four months, plaintiff, who was then pregnant, left the marital home in Illinois and sought refuge with family friends in Bergen County where, on August 22, 2003, she filed a complaint against defendant under the Prevention of Domestic Violence Act of 1991, N.J.S.A. 2C:25-17 to -33 (Domestic Violence Act). An *ex parte* temporary restraining order issued on the filing of the complaint. . . .

The *ex parte* temporary restraining order was made returnable for a final hearing on September 4, 2003. Although both plaintiff and her counsel appeared on that date, defendant appeared only through his counsel. . . . . The amended temporary restraining order was then made returnable on September 23, 2003, on which date the trial court entered a second amended temporary restraining order that provided that "[a]ll other provisions of the TRO entered on 8/22/03 and amended TRO entered on 9/4/03 remain in effect," and further ordered that defendant pay plaintiff "emergent support" of $ 1,500, to be followed by "an additional $300/wk until final hearing." . . . The second amended temporary restraining order was made returnable on October 9, 2003. Coincidentally, also on September 23, 2003, while in New Jersey, plaintiff was served with a complaint for divorce filed by defendant in his home state of Illinois.

Defendant commenced a two-tiered attack on the second amended temporary restraining order. First, he filed a notice of appeal challenging the trial court's exercise of both subject matter and personal jurisdiction. Second, defendant, through counsel, moved before the trial court to dismiss the domestic violence complaint for want of both subject matter and personal jurisdiction, *see* R. 4:6-2(a) and (b), and on *forum non conveniens* grounds, *see generally Kurzke v. Nissan Motor Corp.*, 164 N.J. 159, 164-66, 752 A.2d 708 (2000), as well as to stay the final restraining order hearing scheduled for October 9, 2003. Defendant asserted, before both the trial court and the Appellate Division, that because he had no contacts whatsoever with New Jersey, New

Jersey's courts could not exercise personal jurisdiction over him. Plaintiff did not challenge defendant's factual assertions concerning the lack of minimum contacts.

By an order dated October 8, 2003, the trial court denied all of defendant's objections, clearing the path for the final restraining order hearing scheduled for the following day. Defendant immediately sought leave to appeal from the denial of his motion to dismiss and, therefore, the trial court adjourned its hearing on the final restraining order until October 20, 2003, continued in effect "[a]ll provisions of the Temporary Restraining Order entered on 8/22/03 [and] amended TRO's of 9/4/03 [and] 9/23/03," and noted that there would be "no further adjournments." On October 20, 2003, defendant sought emergent relief from the Appellate Division. That same day, the Appellate Division granted defendant's motion for leave to appeal, consolidated defendant's appellate applications, and ordered that "[a] stay is granted of any further proceedings in the trial court pending disposition of the appeal or the further order of the court, except that the temporary order remains in effect pending the appeal."

In a published opinion, the Appellate Division affirmed in part and reversed in part the second amended temporary restraining order, vacated its stay, and remanded the cause to the Family Part. *Shah v. Shah*, 373 N.J. Super. 47, 860 A.2d 940 (App.Div.2004). As an overarching proposition, the panel held that the trial court possessed both subject matter and personal jurisdiction to issue the protective or prohibitory portions of the second amended temporary restraining order because "plaintiff, having a lawful presence in New Jersey and residing here, at least for the time being, is entitled to seek and expect the full protection of our laws." *Id.* at 52, 860 A.2d 940. The panel reasoned that once "a factual basis [to the domestic violence complaint] is found to exist, the court must be seen to have the authority to enter any reasonable order required to protect plaintiff's safety and her personal integrity[,]" concluding that "[t]his State's lack of jurisdiction over defendant's person cannot be seen as a reason for denying or limiting plaintiff in respect of the protections our laws afford to her." *Ibid.*

The Appellate Division then distinguished between the propriety of issuing protective or prohibitory relief versus affirmative relief, noting that "[i]t is another thing entirely, however, to enter an order that acts upon defendant personally, in the sense of imposing affirmative obligations on him, in the absence of any conduct on his part subjecting himself to the jurisdictional sway of this State." *Ibid.* The panel grounded that distinction on the principle that "a court is without the power to effect a mandate when it lacks personal jurisdiction over defendant." *Id.* at 53, 860 A.2d 940....

Although it endorsed the trial court's power to issue this hybrid order, the Appellate Division cautioned that "that order can be enforced to require defendant to perform the acts mandated *only by a court that has personal jurisdiction over him.*" *Id.* at 54, 860 A.2d 940 (emphasis supplied).

We originally granted defendant's petition for certification. 182 N.J. 630, 868 A.2d 1032 (2005). However, because defendant sought review of an interlocutory judgment and on our own motion, we vacated the grant of certification and, treating defendant's petition for certification as an application for leave to appeal, *see, e.g., Butler v. Bonner & Barnewall, Inc.*, 56 N.J. 567, 573 n.3, 267 A.2d 527 (1970), granted defendant leave to appeal the interlocutory disposition of the Appellate Division. 183 N.J. 259, 872 A.2d 1050 (2005). We also granted *amicus curiae* status to Legal Services of New Jersey (LSNJ) and to Partners for Women and Justice (Partners).

## II.

### A.

In *State v. Reyes*, 172 N.J. 154, 160-61, 796 A.2d 879 (2002), we explained the purposes of the Domestic Violence Act as follows:

> The Legislature enacted the Domestic Violence Act "to assure victims of domestic violence the maximum protection from abuse the law can provide." Because it is remedial in nature, the Legislature directed that the Act be liberally construed to achieve its salutary purposes.
>
> . . . .

Because *Reyes* also thoughtfully marshaled the strong public policy considerations that undergird both the Domestic Violence Act as well as the decisional authority resulting from it, *id.* at 163-64, 860 A.2d 879, we need not address them again here. Instead, we turn directly to the assertions of the parties and *amici* in this case.

### B.

Defendant has never set foot in New Jersey, either literally or figuratively. Based on defendant's utter lack of contact with this State, he asserts that New Jersey courts lack both subject matter and *in personam* jurisdiction over him sufficient to allow a final restraining order hearing to proceed. Although defendant concedes that New Jersey courts have jurisdiction to issue *ex parte* temporary restraining orders upon the filing of a domestic violence complaint, defendant maintains that, in addition to defeating any attempt to secure a final restraining order, New Jersey's want of jurisdiction over him also requires that the temporary restraining order, although properly entered in the first instance, must be vacated.

Plaintiff recognizes the constitutional limitations imposed on the exercise of *in personam* jurisdiction. She argues, however, that the distinction drawn by the Appellate Division is both constitutional and entirely consonant with the purposes of the Domestic Violence Act: protective or prohibitory restraints (or, in some instances, "hybrid" restraints) are permissible, but affirmative obligations cannot be entered in the absence of personal jurisdiction over the defendant. . . .

We address first whether there was proper subject matter jurisdiction in New Jersey for this domestic violence action or whether, as defendant asserts, this action should have been brought only in Illinois. We highlight that the Domestic Violence Act specifically provides that a domestic violence complaint can be brought "in a court having jurisdiction over the place . . . where the plaintiff resides or is sheltered." N.J.S.A. 2C:25-28a. . . . . The fundamental logic of that statutory provision is unassailable: a victim of domestic abuse who seeks a place of refuge must be able to engage the protections of the law of the jurisdiction in which she is sheltered. To state otherwise flies in the face of plain common sense....

Although two states statutorily prohibit the filing of a domestic violence complaint against a non-resident defendant when there has been no proof of any in-state domestic violence, *see* Ga. Code Ann. § 19-13-2 (2004); 750 Ill. Comp. Stat. Ann. 60/208 (West 2005), the overwhelming majority of states protect a victim of domestic violence while she is in the state, regardless of where the abuse occurred....

Consistent with the express terms of our own statute and the broad protections it provides for victims of domestic abuse, we hold that, as long as one of the statutorily enumerated subject matter jurisdiction conditions precedent to the filing of a domestic violence complaint is present and the action is venued either "where the alleged act of domestic violence occurred, where the defendant resides, or where the plaintiff resides or is sheltered," N.J.S.A. 2C:25-28a, New Jersey courts have all requisite subject matter jurisdiction to adjudicate a complaint seeking relief under the Domestic Violence Act.

B.

A determination that plaintiff was entitled to bring her domestic violence complaint in New Jersey does not, however, answer the question raised here, that is, if personal jurisdiction cannot be exercised over the defendant, what limitations, if any, exist on the power of the court to grant temporary or final relief in a domestic violence case. In that respect, we agree with the distinction made by the Appellate Division between prohibitory orders that serve to protect the domestic violence victim, and affirmative orders that require that a defendant undertake an action....

A different result obtains, however, when a court attempts to exercise its coercive power to compel action by a defendant over whom the court lacks personal jurisdiction. Although we have made clear that "a state may regulate conduct occurring outside its borders," we have also made clear that

> the test for "due process requires only that in order to subject a defendant to a judgment in personam, if he [or she] be not present within the territory of the forum, he [or she] have certain minimum contacts with it such that the maintenance of the suit does not offend 'traditional notions of fair play and substantial justice.'" *Int'l Shoe Co. v. Washington*, [326 U.S. 310, 316, 66 S. Ct. 154, 158, 90 L. Ed. 95, 102 (1945)] (quoting *Milliken v. Meyer*, 311 U.S. 457, 463, 61 S. Ct. 339, 343, 85 L. Ed. 278, 283 (1940)). Those unchanging commands of due process govern every foray into the realm of long-arm jurisdiction over non-residents. *Jacobs v. Walt Disney World, Co.*, 309 N.J. Super. 443, 452, 707 A.2d 477 (App.Div.1989) (citing *Avdel Corp. v. Mecure*, 58 N.J. 264, 268, 277 A.2d 207 (1971)).

*Blakey v. Cont'l Airlines, Inc.*, 164 N.J. 38, 66, 751 A.2d 538 (2000).

. . . .

Once an examination of the defendant's minimum contacts with the State is complete, the policy question whether "the assertion of jurisdiction affect[s] traditional notions of fair play and substantial justice[,]" *Blakey v. Cont'l Airlines, Inc., supra,* 164 N.J. at 69, 751 A.2d 538, must be addressed. That requires the consideration of a number of factors that comprise "the flip-side of the purposeful availment doctrine, [that is] whether the offending party could reasonably anticipate that the forum state would have a substantial interest in vindicating the personal rights of the injured party." *Ibid.*

Under the circumstances present here, no New Jersey court can exercise personal jurisdiction over defendant in a manner consonant with due process. It is conceded that defendant has zero contacts with the State of New Jersey. Thus, he has not "purposefully availed" himself of the laws of New Jersey. Indeed, this case presents the very circumstances condemned in *Lebel v. Everglades Marina, Inc., supra,* 115 N.J. at 323, 558 A.2d 1252: "The 'minimum contacts' requirement [cannot be] satisfied [by] the unilateral activities of the plaintiff." Viewed that way, there can be no doubt that subjecting defendant to a final order in New Jersey would "offend 'traditional notions of fair play and substantial justice.'" *Blakey v. Cont'l Airlines, Inc., supra,* 164 N.J. at 66, 751 A.2d 538 (citing *Int'l Shoe Co. v. Washington, supra,* 326 U.S. at 316, 66 S. Ct. at 158, 90 L. Ed. at 102). Therefore, in Domestic Violence Act matters, New Jersey courts lack the power to enter an order requiring the performance of any affirmative act by a defendant over whom in personam jurisdiction cannot be asserted.

### C.

The minimum contacts considerations that forbid the entry of an order granting affirmative relief against a defendant over whom the court lacks personal jurisdiction also forbid the entry of a final restraining order within the context of a domestic violence complaint. A final restraining order must, by statutory definition, include affirmative relief. *See, e.g.,* N.J.S.A. 2C:25-29b (requiring the surrender of firearms and permits), -29.1 (requiring the payment of a civil penalty) and -29.4 (requiring the payment of a surcharge). In addition, a final restraining order may well have severe collateral consequences, including registration in a central registry, *N.J.S.A.* 2C:25-34, a registration that is not subject to expungement. *In re M.D.Z.,* 286 N.J. Super. 82, 668 A.2d 423 (App.Div.1995). For those reasons, we also hold that when personal jurisdiction over a defendant is lacking, New Jersey courts do not have the power to enter a final restraining order against that defendant.

### D.

That said, although we endorse the distinction drawn by the Appellate Division between prohibitory and affirmative orders, we reject the panel's characterization of that "portion of the trial court's order that requires defendant to turn over plaintiff's personal papers—her work permit, social security card, immigration documents and mail" as a "hybrid." *Shah v. Shah,* 373 N.J. Super. 47, 53, 860 A.2d 940 (App.Div.2004). We see no principled difference between affirmatively requiring that defendant turn over documents, albeit documents with legal significance to plaintiff, and requiring that defendant pay money to plaintiff. If, consonant with due process, a court wanting jurisdiction over the person of a defendant cannot order that defendant to pay money, then it surely follows that the court similarly cannot order that defendant to take any other affirmative act.

E.

Defendant's final argument remains. According to defendant, even if a temporary restraining order of some form is properly entered in the absence of personal jurisdiction over the defendant, it must come to an end at some point due to its very nature as a temporary order. Thus, reasons defendant, because the trial court is required to hold a hearing "within 10 days of the filing of a complaint [under the Domestic Violence Act] in the county where the ex parte restraints were ordered," N.J.S.A. 2C:25-29a, temporary restraining orders cannot continue without end.

There is, no doubt, a superficial appeal to defendant's plea. That appeal, however, does not withstand close scrutiny. Much like the incarcerated civil contemnor who "carries the keys to freedom in his willingness to comply with the court's directive," *Catena v. Seidl*, 68 N.J. 224, 232, 343 A.2d 744 (1975) (Schreiber, J., dissenting) (citing *Green v. United States*, 356 U.S. 165, 197, 78 S. Ct. 632, 650, 2 L. Ed. 2d 672, 696 (1958) (Black, J. dissenting)), defendant easily can rid himself of the entire parade of horribles he cites as flowing from the continued pendency of the temporary restraining order: he can either come into New Jersey and substantively defend against the domestic violence complaint, or he can request that both matters — the divorce action and the domestic violence complaint — be heard in Illinois and seek a resolution favorable to him there. What defendant disingenuously urges simply cannot be done: we cannot, at defendant's whim, deny plaintiff the protection against domestic violence the Legislature intended, particularly when defendant is not prejudiced by the continued pendency of an order that requires that he do absolutely nothing.

. . . .

IV.

In sum, we hold that, upon the filing of a complaint by a plaintiff "alleging the commission of an act of domestic violence with the Family Part of the Chancery Division of the Superior Court [venued either] in a court having jurisdiction over the place where the alleged act of domestic violence occurred, where the defendant resides, or where the plaintiff resides or is sheltered," N.J.S.A. 2C:25-28a, New Jersey courts have the authority to issue *ex parte* relief, in the form of a temporary restraining order, upon a showing both that "the plaintiff is in danger of domestic violence," N.J.S.A. 2C:25-28g, and that the temporary restraining order is "necessary to protect the life, health or well-being of a victim on whose behalf the relief is sought." N.J.S.A. 2C:25-28f. We further hold that, if personal jurisdiction cannot be exercised over a defendant within constitutional due process limits, the temporary restraining order may only provide for prohibitory relief, and no final restraining order may issue. Finally, in the event personal jurisdiction cannot be exercised over a defendant, we also hold that, once issued, "[a]n order for emergency, ex parte relief... shall remain in effect until a judge of the Family Part issues a further order." N.J.S.A. 2C:25-28i.

As modified by this opinion, the judgment of the Appellate Division is affirmed and the matter is remanded to the Family Part of the Chancery Division for further proceedings consistent with this opinion.

---

The Georgia statute referred to by the New Jersey court in *Shah v. Shah* is reprinted below.

## Official Code of Georgia Annotated § 19-13-2 (2016)
## Jurisdiction of superior court

(a) Except for proceedings involving a nonresident respondent, the superior court of the county where the respondent resides shall have jurisdiction over all proceedings under this article.

(b) For proceedings under this article involving a nonresident respondent, the superior court where the petitioner resides or the superior court where an act involving family violence allegedly occurred shall have jurisdiction, where the act involving family violence meets the elements for personal jurisdiction provided for under paragraph (2) or (3) of Code Section 9-10-91.

## Anderson v. Deas
Court of Appeals of Georgia
279 Ga. App. 892 (2006)

PHIPPS, Judge.

In *Anderson v. Deas*,[6] Jonita Anderson charged Raymond Deas with having committed acts of family violence (i.e., making terroristic threats and stalking) by placing harassing and intimidating telephone calls to her in Georgia from another state. We held that because any such acts would not have occurred in Georgia, Anderson's charges did not give the Superior Court of DeKalb County personal jurisdiction over Deas under § 2(b) of the Family Violence Act (FVA). The Supreme Court of Georgia granted certiorari and remanded the case to us for reconsideration of our holding in light of *Innovative Clinical & Consulting Svcs. v. First Nat. Bank &c.*[7] Upon reconsideration, we adhere to our original decision.

Section 2(b) of the FVA, codified at OCGA § 19-13-2(b), gives superior courts of Georgia jurisdiction over a nonresident charged with commission of an act of family

---

6. [n1] 273 Ga. App. 770 (615 SE2d 859) (2005).
7. [n2] 279 Ga. 672 (620 SE2d 352) (2005).

violence where the act meets the elements of personal jurisdiction under paragraphs (2) or (3) of the Georgia long arm statute, codified at OCGA § 9-10-91. Paragraph (2) of the long arm statute authorizes a court of this state to exercise personal jurisdiction if the nonresident "[c]ommits a tortious act or omission within this state." Jurisdiction exists under paragraph (3) if the nonresident, either in person or through an agent, "[c]ommits a tortious injury in this state caused by an act or omission outside this state if the tort-feasor regularly does or solicits business, or engages in any other persistent course of conduct, or derives substantial revenue from goods used or consumed or services rendered in this state."

We held that although Deas may have committed a tortious injury in this state, Georgia courts clearly do not have jurisdiction over him under paragraph (3) of the long arm statute, because he has not met any of the other requirements (such as regularly doing or soliciting business or engaging in any other persistent course of conduct in the state) set forth in paragraph 3.

We further concluded that jurisdiction was not sustainable under paragraph (2) based on Deas's commission of a tortious act within this state. We based this conclusion on *Gust v. Flint*'s[8] disapproval of *Coe & Payne Co. v. Wood-Mosaic Corp.*'s[9] interpretation of paragraph (2). Finding no essential difference between paragraphs (2) and (3), *Coe & Payne* held that a tortious act may be said to have been committed in this state within the meaning of paragraph (2) based either on occurrence of the tortious conduct or commission of the injury in this state. *Gust v. Flint* held that where a person commits a tortious act outside this state causing injury in the state, paragraph (3) rather than (2) applies—thereby requiring the presence of one of the contacts set forth in paragraph (3) before long arm jurisdiction may be exercised if the tortious injury but not the act occurs in this state.

The Supreme Court in *Innovative Clinical* adhered to the approach adopted in *Gust*. But *Innovative Clinical* disapproved other cases to the extent that they engrafted requirements similar to those set forth in paragraph (3) onto paragraph (1) of the long arm statute, which extends jurisdiction to a nonresident who "[t]ransacts any business within this state." OCGA § 9-10-91(1). *Innovative* found *Gust*'s construction of paragraphs (2) and (3) mandated by the plain language of the long arm statute. *Innovative*, however, found the disapproved cases' application of paragraph (3)-type requirements to paragraph (1) inconsistent with the policy of our long arm statute "to exercise jurisdiction over nonresident defendants to the maximum extent permitted by procedural due process."

In remanding this case to us, the Supreme Court raised the question of whether Anderson's claim that daily telephone calls Deas had placed to Georgia to allegedly terrorize and stalk her were sufficient to show that he had engaged in a "persistent course of conduct" in this state under paragraph (3).

---

8. [n4] 257 Ga. 129 (356 SE2d 513) (1987).
9. [n5] 230 Ga. 58 (195 SE2d 399) (1973).

Anderson testified that, in September 2004, Deas had made three threatening and harassing telephone calls to her and that, as far back as August, he had been threatening to kill her and hurt her child. In his testimony, Deas acknowledged that, during August and September 2004, he had made daily telephone calls to his daughter, but he denied making any threats.

When a person commits the offense of stalking by placing a harassing or intimidating telephone call to another person, the offense is deemed to occur at the place where the communication is received. Nonetheless, the conduct giving rise to the offense occurs at the place where the maker of the call speaks into the telephone. The effect is transmission of the voice along the telephone line or otherwise and receipt by its listener at the other end. We, therefore, conclude that Deas did not engage in any conduct, persistent or otherwise, in Georgia, either when he made his daily phone calls to speak to his daughter or when he made the calls that allegedly threatened and harassed Anderson.

As recognized in *Innovative Clinical*, consistent with due process, paragraph (3) of the long arm statute might provide for a Georgia court's exercise of personal jurisdiction over a nonresident who has committed a tortious injury in the state caused by an act outside the state without also requiring the nonresident to have engaged in a persistent course of conduct here. But by its plain language, paragraph (3) does not do that. And, by its plain language, the FVA gives Georgia superior courts jurisdiction over a nonresident only where the act with which he is charged meets the requirements of paragraphs (2) or (3) of the long arm statute.

Prior to the Supreme Court's grant of certiorari, we affirmed an order of the superior court concluding that it lacked jurisdiction over Deas under the FVA and dismissing a protective order previously entered. Upon reconsideration in light of *Innovative Clinical*, we must adhere to our decision.

## III. Relief Provided Under Protective Orders

The scope of the relief that may be ordered as part of an order of protection proceeding is very broad. The court has the power to do what is necessary to stop the family violence and keep the victims safe.

### Maldonado v. Maldonado
District of Columbia Court of Appeals
631 A.2d 40 (1993)

KING, ASSOCIATE JUDGE:

On January 30, 1992, the trial court issued a Civil Protection Order ("CPO") at the request of appellant ("wife") against her husband, the appellee. In January 1993, the wife's motion to extend the CPO for a period of one year was denied. This appeal followed. We reverse and remand.

## I.

In January 1992, the wife sought a civil protection order because of the husband's abusive behavior which included beatings with the hands, a belt, a thick cable, threats with a gun, and other physical force which on at least one occasion caused the wife to lose consciousness. The abuse culminated in a severe beating on January 13, 1992, which required hospital treatment. Thereafter, the wife and the couple's two daughters went into hiding. In order to provide protection for herself and her daughters, the wife obtained, on January 17, 1992, a Temporary Protective Order which expired after fourteen days. A hearing on her request for a CPO, which could be in effect for up to one year, was scheduled for January 30, 1992. On that date the husband consented to the issuance of a CPO to expire on January 30, 1993.

The court approved the CPO. . . .

Meanwhile, in a separate criminal proceeding, the husband was indicted for armed assault with intent to kill, threats, and obstruction of justice for conduct which arose from one of his attacks on the wife. The husband subsequently pleaded guilty in that case, and on December 30, 1992, Judge Wolf imposed an aggregate sentence of not less than two years and not more than eight years. The husband began serving that sentence immediately.

On December 21, 1992, the wife moved to extend the CPO which was scheduled to expire on January 30, 1993. The motion alleged that the husband violated the CPO on a number of occasions, including: waiting for the wife outside her place of employment and attempting to induce her to allow him to see the children; approaching the children and their babysitter outside of the school; and approaching the wife and one of the children as they were walking down the street. Prior to the hearing the husband consented to and signed an extended CPO which contains terms substantially the same as those set forth in the CPO which was scheduled to expire January 30, 1993.

The wife's request for an extension came before Judge Wolf for a hearing on January 26, 1993, with the husband, the wife, and the latter's attorney all being present. The trial judge, noting that since the husband was serving a prison sentence he would not be able to physically assault the wife, concluded that no CPO would be necessary: "I don't think there's good cause when he's locked up." Accordingly he denied the motion to extend. We hold that the trial judge erred in so doing.

## II.

Under the Intrafamily Offenses Act, a CPO may be extended "for good cause shown." *See* D.C. Code § 16-1005(d) (1989). The determination of good cause is committed to the sound discretion of the trial court which is subject to reversal only upon a showing of abuse of that discretion. *See Cruz-Foster v. Foster,* 597 A.2d 927, 931–32 (D.C. 1991); *Johnson v. United States,* 398 A.2d 354, 362 (D.C. 1979). This case presents the issue of whether the trial court abused discretion by denying an extension of a CPO solely because the respondent was serving a sentence which, unless modified, would apparently not result in release on parole until after the date the extended CPO would itself expire. We conclude that, under the circumstances, the husband's incarceration was a factor which may and should have been considered by the trial judge; however, that factor may not be the sole determinate as to whether the CPO should or should not be extended. *See Cruz-Foster, supra,* 597 A.2d at 928 (remanding to permit trial judge to take into account the effect a stay-away order, in a criminal case involving the same two parties, could have upon the question of whether the CPO should be extended). In relying upon the husband's incarceration as the sole basis for denying the extension of the CPO, the trial judge abused his discretion. *See In re J.D.C.,* 594 A.2d 70, 75 (D.C. 1991) (trial court abuses its discretion when it rests its legal conclusion on incorrect legal standards).

The Intrafamily Offenses Act is a remedial statute and as such should be liberally construed for the benefit of the class it is intended to protect. *See Cruz-Foster, supra,* 597 A.2d at 930; *United States v. Harrison,* 149 U.S. App. D.C. 123, 124, 461 F.2d 1209, 1210 (1972). Here the wife sought an extension that would have preserved the custody status of her children, required the husband to pay regular child support, and ordered the husband not to telephone the wife and not to molest, assault or in any manner threaten or physically abuse the wife or her children. The proposed extension also required the husband to stay away from the wife's home, work place, and the children's schools. Only the latter directive would be fully rendered moot by the husband's incarceration and that would be so only if the sentences imposed in the criminal case assured that the husband remained in custody around-the-clock throughout the duration of any extended CPO. We are not persuaded that such necessarily would be the case.

For a variety of reasons, we cannot conclude with certainty that the husband would remain incarcerated through January 30, 1994 — the expiration date for the requested extended CPO. The wife proffered to the trial judge that the husband could be eligible, if certain events were to occur, for a furlough program that could result in some form of release as soon as one year after the service of sentence began. The husband was sentenced on December 30, 1992. Thus one year later — December 1993 — would be one month before the expiration date of the requested extended CPO. Indeed the twelve month waiting period might expire even earlier than December 1993, since appellant was held in lieu of bond for a period of time before he was sentenced, and he is entitled to credit on his sentence for the time served before he was sentenced. *See* D.C. Code § 24-431(a) (1989). Whether the credit for time served before sentencing would also shorten the twelve month period before appellant might be eligible for the furlough program is unknown; however, the uncertainty on that point should have put the trial judge on notice of the possibility that the husband might be at large sooner than anticipated.

Furthermore, as the trial judge himself recognized, appellant could be released to a half-way house as early as January 25, 1994 — five days before the expiration of the requested extended CPO. Whether appellant would in fact be paroled when he was first eligible, and whether, if paroled, he would be placed in a half-way house at the earliest possible date, is far from certain. The possibility of this occurrence, however, cannot be ignored. Finally, appellant is incarcerated at a nearby facility and if he were to escape he would likely be able to locate the wife and their children if he wished to do so. A CPO, of course, does not guarantee protection under those circumstances; however, that is not the standard for its issuance. Rather, its existence serves as a potential deterrent and provides a measure of peace of mind for those for whose benefit it was issued.

Moreover, with respect to the portion of the original order barring threats directed at the wife and children and the telephoning of the wife, the wife would be left open to harassment or threatening communications from the husband should he gain access to a telephone. In addition, threats can be communicated by mail or through third parties. Although threats to commit physical harm by one incarcerated may, in some instances, not rise to the level of seriousness that physical abuse does, such conduct nonetheless can have significant adverse affects upon the victim. Congress recognized that reality in 1968 when it provided that a threat to injure the person of another is punishable for a term of up to twenty years. *See* D.C. Code § 22-2307 (1989). At a minimum, the wife is entitled to be free of abuse or threats by the husband whether committed by telephone or the mail. Further, although the husband has apparently acted in person in his previous assaults upon the wife, during the period he is incarcerated he could act through others to molest or assault her or the children. Again, although a CPO does not guarantee that such conduct will not occur, it nonetheless serves as some deterrent. Thus, we conclude that even if the husband remained incarcerated, that circumstance would not prevent him from engaging in conduct, either alone, through others, or both, that would be barred by the CPO if it had been extended.

. . . .

Finally, the husband consented to the extension of the CPO. Although the trial court made no findings concerning the voluntariness of that consent, the inquiries made of the husband by the trial judge suggest that the husband was freely agreeing to the extension. We believe the purpose of the statute is served by encouraging respondents' consent to these agreements. *See* Super. Ct. Intra-Fam. R. 11(b). We think, therefore, that if the consent is voluntary a trial judge ordinarily should issue the CPO when requested. *See United States v. City of Jackson,* 519 F.2d 1147, 1151 (5th Cir. 1975) (court should approve consent decree so long as its terms are not unlawful, unreasonable, or inequitable); *see also Moore v. Jones,* 542 A.2d 1253, 1254 n.1 (1988) ("court approval of a consent decree means the court has concluded that the terms of the decree are not unlawful, unreasonable, or inequitable"). If the trial court declines to issue a CPO freely consented to by a respondent, we believe that a strong statement of reasons for not doing so should be set forth. Here, the trial judge gave no reason for declining to accept the respondent's agreement to be bound by the extension of the CPO, and we conclude for that reason and the other reasons set forth above that he abused his discretion. Accordingly, we reverse and remand for further proceedings on the wife's motion to extend the CPO.

*Reversed and remanded.*

---

The extent of the powers of the family court in protecting victims includes issuing an order removing a batterer from the home. This case, nearly 20 years old, is still good law and illustrates the broad powers of the court in keeping victims safe.

## V.C. v. H.C.

New York Supreme Court, Appellate Division, First Department

257 A.D.2d 27 (1999)

Ellerin, P.J.

At issue on this appeal is whether the Family Court, having found that a victim of domestic violence who has fled the marital home for her safety is entitled to an order of protection, should also have provided a remedy that could restore the victim to her home and exclude her abusers instead of leaving the home in the sole possession of the abusers.

On January 3, 1995, petitioner, a middle-aged deaf woman, filed petitions for orders of protection, alleging that she had fled her home in December 1994 because of escalating violence and abuse by her husband and their adult son and requesting that the orders provide that respondents be excluded from their common residence. Specifically, she alleged, *inter alia,* that her husband physically and verbally abused and threatened her, changed the locks on the marital home and refused to give her a key, and forced her to take drugs against her will, and that their son was verbally and physically abusive.

Following an initial ex parte proceeding, the Family Court denied the request that respondents be excluded from the home and issued temporary orders of protection pursuant to Family Court Act §828 requiring respondents not to "assault, menace, harass or recklessly endanger petitioner" and "not to exclude petitioner from the [marital] residence".

At the fact-finding hearing, petitioner testified that she fled to her daughter's home in December 1994 after two incidents in which her husband, who is confined to a wheelchair, pointed a loaded gun at her and threatened to kill her. On November 18, 1994, while her husband was high on cocaine, he pulled a loaded gun out from under the seat of his wheelchair, pointed it at her, and said, "I am going to kill you". She ran into the bathroom and locked the door. On another day, he reached into the drawer in the couple's bedroom, placed his hand on his gun, and cursed at her. She called for their son to come help her, but when he entered the room he blocked the bedroom door and trapped her in the room.

Petitioner also testified that, in 1975, her husband, while intoxicated, shot her in the heat of a dispute, grazing her chest. He was not arrested because he told the police that someone else had shot her, and he threatened those present, including petitioner's oldest son, who is his stepson, not to contradict his story.

In addition to these specific incidents, petitioner testified that her husband constantly abused her by punching her in the face and pulling her hair. She also testified that he hit her twice on the back with a stick.

As to the petition against her younger adult son, petitioner testified that he punched and slapped her when she refused his demands to cook meals or do other errands for him, made at all hours of the day and night. On numerous occasions, father and son acted together to abuse her. In November 1994, they changed the locks on the home and refused to give her a key. It was only after she had left home, retained counsel, and obtained an ex parte order of protection that they eventually provided her with a key.

Petitioner's adult daughter corroborated her mother's account of her stepfather's abuse, providing details as to other incidents, including one in which he attempted to stab petitioner with a machete, and confirming that her stepfather always kept a gun near him. She also testified that when her mother arrived at her home in December 1994, she noticed that her mother, who said she was frightened, was severely bruised. Although petitioner's daughter's testimony was cut short, she also testified briefly to certain incidents during her childhood, including her stepfather's use of herself and her brothers and cousins to assist him in selling drugs until, as a teenager, she was placed in foster care.

Petitioner's oldest son also corroborated the abuse against his mother, stating that it was often precipitated by drinking. He recounted witnessing the 1975 shooting, and he also testified that his stepfather had sexually abused him from the time he was seven or eight until he was in ninth grade, at which time he left home to live on the streets to escape the abuse.

On August 18, 1995, the court informed counsel that it was terminating the fact-finding hearing because sufficient evidence had already been presented to show that respondents had committed the family offense of harassment. Petitioner's counsel objected, arguing that the remainder of the evidence would establish far graver offenses. The court overruled the objection and instead offered respondents the option of admitting to harassment, in which case they could remain in the marital residence pending disposition. In the alternative, it informed them that it would make a finding of harassment and would exclude them from the apartment pending disposition. Respondents admitted to harassment. The court thereupon extended the ex parte order of protection requiring them not to harass petitioner and ordered Mental Health Services (MHS) to evaluate the parties and render a recommendation as to disposition.

Although that report was prepared, it failed to make a recommendation as to disposition. The matter was set down for disposition, but was transferred several times to different Judges for various reasons, including the failure of the court to provide an appropriate interpreter for petitioner, and the transfer to another county of an assigned Judge. Ultimately, on July 17, 1996, 18 months after petitioner had fled her home to escape from the abuse and filed petitions, the matter appeared before Judge Cohen for a dispositional hearing. However, rather than hearing testimony, the court issued a ruling summarily denying a three-year order of protection and denying the request that the order of protection exclude the respondents from the marital home, and instead issued a one-year order of protection merely requiring respondents to stay away from petitioner. The court stated:

> "[I]t is my understanding that the main issue at this dispositional hearing is the apartment. I want it clear I am not ruling on who gets the apartment. I won't even consider it.
>
> "At this point my understanding is that the mother moved out and is living somewhere else and she wants the apartment back. . . .
>
> "If the petitioner wants the apartment she will have to take appropriate action in the appropriate court. This is not the court for this. You can have a hearing for 20 months and I will never rule on who gets this apartment. It's not before me."

We reverse.

Among the purposes of a family offenses proceeding under article 8 of the Family Court Act is to protect victims of domestic violence by providing "a civil, non-criminal alternative to a criminal prosecution" (Besharov, Practice Commentaries, McKinney's Cons Laws of NY, Book 29A, Family Ct Act § 812, at 181) when family members commit certain designated criminal offenses.

. . . .

If the petitioner is able to establish the allegations in the petition and demonstrate that the respondent has committed a family offense, the court will generally hold a dispositional hearing (Family Ct Act § 835). A broader standard of admissibility of evidence is available on the dispositional hearing than at the fact-finding hearing, and evidence may be admitted as long as it is "material and relevant" (Family Ct Act § 834), including hearsay and other evidence otherwise incompetent (Besharov, Practice Commentaries, McKinney's Cons Laws of NY, Book 29A, Family Ct Act § 834, at 240).

Following the dispositional hearing, the Family Court may dismiss the petition if the allegations in the petition are not established, suspend judgment for up to six months, place respondents on probation for up to one year and require them to participate in an educational program, issue an order of protection, or order restitution (Family Ct Act § 841). The order of protection may set forth "reasonable conditions of behavior to be observed . . . by the petitioner or respondent", including, but not limited to, requiring them "to stay away from the home . . . [of] the other spouse"

(Family Ct Act § 842[a]). Such a condition may be imposed not only where the parties are already living apart at the time the order is issued but, where necessary, it may also be imposed where it will require a party to stay away from what has heretofore been his or her own home (*see, Merola v. Merola,* 146 AD2d 611; *Kilmer v. Kilmer,* 109 AD2d 1004; *Matter of Leffingwell v. Leffingwell,* 86 AD2d 929).

Initially, we reject respondents' argument that petitioner's appeal is academic because the one-year order of protection has expired and has not been renewed. Petitioner's argument that the court improperly failed to exclude respondents from the marital home as a condition of the order of protection is obviously not academic. Petitioner, who has shown that she remains unable to return to her home based upon the court's failure to address the issue of whether respondents should be excluded, is clearly continuing to suffer harm. Moreover, by removing herself from the family home for her own safety, petitioner obviated the need for a further order of protection, so her failure to seek one does not render academic her argument that the order was inadequate (*cf., Matter of Alice C. v. Joseph C.,* 212 AD2d 698 [issue of whether court improperly refused to issue order of probation as part of order of protection without holding dispositional hearing is academic, since order of protection has expired]).

Moreover, we find that Family Court erred in failing to hold a dispositional hearing to consider the issues of whether the order of protection should have included a provision excluding respondents from the marital apartment and whether it should have extended for three years.

We find no basis in law for the Family Court's action in refusing to even consider whether respondents should be excluded from the apartment as a condition of the order of protection, which it had found to be clearly warranted by respondents' behavior. As noted above, the Family Court is unquestionably permitted to order a nonresident party to stay away from the home of the other spouse or to exclude a resident party from the common home (*Matter of Ross v. Ross,* 152 AD2d 580; *Matter of Quintana v. Quintana,* 237 AD2d 130; *Merola v. Merola, supra; Kilmer v. Kilmer, supra; Matter of Leffingwell v. Leffingwell, supra*). There is no logical rationale to limit the power of the court by prohibiting it from excluding a resident abusive spouse merely because the victim of the abuse has been forced by her abuser to flee their common home. Such a holding would reward the worst of abusers, i.e., those whose behavior was so violent or threatening that it forced their family members to leave home, with automatic possession of the home, and would obviously frustrate the intent of the statutory scheme, which seeks to protect, not punish, the victims of domestic violence.

For these reasons, it was clearly error for the Family Court to base its decision, as it intimated it was doing, on the fact that petitioner could theoretically seek exclusive occupancy of the marital home in a divorce action commenced in Supreme Court. The issue before the Family Court was not, as claimed by respondents, a permanent award of exclusive possession of the marital property incident to the divorce (*cf., Handa v. Handa,* 103 AD2d 794, *appeal dismissed* 64 NY2d 1040; *Matter of Roy v. Roy,*

109 AD2d 150), but instead, the propriety of an exclusion order to prevent further family disturbance (*see, Kilmer v. Kilmer, supra*). Regardless of the fact that the petitioner had already moved out, the Family Court not only has jurisdiction to determine this issue, but it is its very mandate to provide for this type of relief in matters involving family violence. Clearly, recourse to a divorce proceeding was of little or no use to petitioner. Not only would she not be entitled to counsel in a divorce proceeding, but the commencement of a new action would cause further delay, during which time petitioner would remain excluded from her home by the threat of violence.

Further, while we must remain sensitive to the fact that the Family Court must deal with the practical realities of the impact of its decisions on the safety and well-being of the litigants before it, we note that the court should not base its decision solely on the fact that one party has found another place to stay and the other has not. A victim of the outrageous and life-threatening sort of abuse set forth in this matter cannot be held hostage to the potential homelessness of her abuser, who created the intolerable situation in the first instance.

Moreover, in addition to its failure to consider excluding respondents from the home, we find that the Family Court erred in not considering whether the order of protection should extend for three years. Section 842 of the Family Court Act sets out the conditions which may be granted under an order of protection, and it provides that a final order of protection may extend for one year "or for a period not in excess of three years upon a finding by the court on the record of the existence of aggravating circumstances as defined in paragraph (vii) of subdivision (a) of section eight hundred twenty-seven of this act", which provides, in pertinent part, that "aggravating circumstances shall mean physical injury or serious physical injury to the petitioner caused by the respondent, the use of a dangerous instrument against the petitioner by the respondent, a history of repeated violations of prior orders of protection by the respondent, prior convictions for crimes against the petitioner by the respondent or the exposure of any family or household member to physical injury by the respondent and like incidents, behaviors and occurrences which to the court constitute an immediate and ongoing danger to the petitioner, or any member of the petitioner's family or household."

We categorically reject respondents' argument that a petitioner must specifically state in the petition that "aggravating circumstances" exist in order for the court to issue a three-year order of protection upon disposition. There is certainly no such requirement in the statute. Clearly, it is for the court to determine, on the evidence before it, whether such circumstances exist, and the court is in no way barred from doing so merely because the petitioner did not use certain special language in her petition.

Respondents also argue that, regardless of whether the court erred in determining that it did not have the power to grant petitioner the relief she requested, petitioner has not demonstrated that she was entitled to a dispositional hearing because all of the facts relevant to her claim were presented in the fact-finding hearing and those facts demonstrate that the order issued by the court was the appropriate relief under the circumstances.

However, it is clear that, under the circumstances of this case, petitioner was entitled to present further evidence on the issue of disposition (*cf., Matter of Quintana v. Quintana, supra* [Family Court was not required to hold dispositional hearing "where the court did receive and consider the type of evidence that would have been admitted at a dispositional hearing had the court formally chosen to bifurcate the matter"]). In particular, we note that petitioner has demonstrated that the fact-finding hearing, which was held before a different Judge from the one determining disposition, was abbreviated by respondent's admission to the family offense of harassment prior to petitioner having had an opportunity to present evidence that she claims would have been crucial to disposition. Most significantly, at the fact-finding hearing, the court terminated the case prior to the planned testimony of an expert on battered women's syndrome, who, according to petitioner's offer of proof, would have helped explain her delayed reaction to the abuse inflicted upon her, her inability to leave the marital home on her own, and the impact of her deafness on her ability to function under hostile circumstances. These were factors relevant not only to fact finding but to disposition as well. While the court had already ruled that the expert's testimony was germane to the issues presented, it apparently concluded that it was able to reach a conclusion as to the fact-finding portion of the proceeding without the testimony. Under these circumstances, petitioner has demonstrated that she had further evidence relevant to disposition that she should have been permitted to set before the court.

Nor was the necessity of a hearing obviated by the existence of the MHS report. In the appropriate case, it is not impossible that the evidence presented at the fact-finding hearing, if sufficiently broad in scope, could be an adequate basis for a disposition along with a MHS report. However, an MHS report in and of itself does not take the place of the parties' right to present evidence on disposition.

Finally, we note the absurdity of the argument set forth by respondents that there was no need for a dispositional hearing to explore whether an order of exclusion was necessary because the record is clear that respondents ceased harassing petitioner when ordered to do so in the original temporary order of protection. We can hardly require evidence of continuing harassment to be a condition to an order of exclusion in a situation where the respondents, who were found to have committed harassment, remain in the home while their victim has been forced to flee, thereby eliminating both their motivation and opportunity to further abuse her.

Under these circumstances, it is clear that a dispositional hearing was necessary in this matter. We therefore remand for a dispositional hearing before a different Judge of the Family Court (*see, Matter of Eames v. Eames,* 147 AD2d 696), to determine whether an order of protection excluding respondents from the apartment is warranted and whether it should extend for three years.

. . . .

## Stuckey v. Stuckey

Colorado Supreme Court

768 P.2d 694 (1989)

We granted certiorari to review the judgment of a district court affirming a permanent injunction issued by a county court forbidding the father of a minor child from having any contact with that child. We elected to limit our review to the narrow issue of whether the county court had jurisdiction to enter such an order. We conclude that it did and therefore affirm the judgment of the district court.

### I.

Charles L. Stuckey (father) and Carol K. Stuckey (mother) were formerly married and had a child, Benjamin. Prior to the time this action was commenced, the marriage had been dissolved and the mother had been awarded custody of Benjamin. On December 5, 1986, when Benjamin was fourteen years old, the mother, acting without counsel, filed a verified motion for a temporary restraining order in the county court for Jefferson County. She sought to prevent the father from contacting her or Benjamin, and in support of that relief averred that the father by his past threats and conduct had caused her to be fearful of him. She averred that the father was afflicted with organic brain syndrome and outlined several past incidents that had given rise to her fears for her own safety and that of Benjamin. The last such incident took place on November 22, 1986, and consisted of "a comment threatening Ben with physical violence."

The mother appeared on December 5 without counsel and presented testimony at a hearing at which the father was not present or represented by counsel. At the conclusion of the hearing, the county court issued a temporary restraining order preventing the father from "calling, approaching, threatening, molesting, or injuring" the mother or Benjamin. The court relied upon section 14-4-102, 6B C.R.S. (1987), authorizing restraining orders to prevent domestic abuse, as the source of authority to issue the restraining order. The order required the father to appear on December 19, 1986, to show cause why the temporary restraining order should not be made permanent.

On December 19 both the father and the mother appeared without counsel. The court heard evidence, including the testimony of Benjamin, and found that unless permanently restrained, the father was likely to cause harm to the mother and Benjamin and therefore permanently enjoined the father from threatening, molesting, injuring, calling or approaching the mother or Benjamin.

The father appealed, asserting among other things that the county court lacked jurisdiction to restrain him from access to his minor child. The Jefferson County District Court affirmed the permanent injunction, concluding that section 14-4-102 does authorize the relief granted by the county court and reasoning that the statute "does not expressly or impliedly limit the jurisdiction of the District Court which has continuing jurisdiction over custodial matters." We granted certiorari to review the district court's conclusion that the county court had jurisdiction to issue the permanent injunction insofar as it purports to restrain the father from contact with his minor child.

## II.

. . . .

### B.

. . . .

To ensure that violence within a family can be promptly curbed, the Domestic Abuse Act provides for a judge to be available in each judicial district to issue emergency protection orders by telephone at all times when the courts are closed. § 14-4-103(1). During these times a judge may issue a written or verbal ex parte emergency protection order upon the assertion by a peace officer of "reasonable grounds to believe that an adult is in immediate and present danger of domestic abuse, based upon an allegation of a recent incident of actual domestic abuse or threat of domestic abuse." § 14-4-103(2). An oral order must be supported by a judicial finding that "an imminent danger in close proximity exists to the life or health of one or more persons." § 14-4-103(5). The officer obtaining such a verbal order must reduce it to writing, sign it, and include a statement of "the grounds for the order asserted by the officer." § 14-4-103(5).

The emergency protection order may extend protection to children of either of the parties as well as to an adult. . . .

### C.

The father argues that to construe the Domestic Abuse Act so broadly as to permit county courts to prevent a parent from contacting his child trenches on the exclusive jurisdiction of district courts in custody matters. *See, e.g.,* § 19-1-104(1)(c), 8B C.R.S. (1988 Supp.) . . . The father also urges that such a construction of the Domestic Abuse Act is inconsistent with the denial of jurisdiction to county courts in "matters affecting children, including custody, support, guardianship, adoption, dependency, or delinquency," § 13-6-105(1)(d), 6A C.R.S. (1987). When the scope of the relief that can be awarded by the county court under the Domestic Abuse Act is properly understood, however, we do not believe that the father's arguments have merit.

We recognize that the legislature has expressly denied county courts subject matter jurisdiction in matters affecting children. *See* § 13-6-105(1)(d). We also acknowledge that the legislature has specifically granted the district courts exclusive jurisdiction in particular matters concerning children. . . . The Children's Code also specifies that the juvenile court can issue temporary protective custody orders with respect to dependent or neglected children. §§ 19-3-204, 19-3-401, 8B C.R.S. (1988 Supp.). The Children's Code further authorizes the juvenile court to issue an order of protection in assistance of, or as a condition of, any decree authorized by the code. § 19-1-114, 8B C.R.S. (1988 Supp.).

The Uniform Dissolution of Marriage Act, §§ 14-10-101 to 14-10-133, 6B C.R.S. (1987 & 1988 Supp.), provides another source of statutory authority for exclusive district court jurisdiction in matters concerning children. Child custody proceedings initiated by petitions for dissolution of marriage or legal separation are exclusively within the jurisdiction of the district courts. § 14-10-123, 6B C.R.S. (1987). Once a child custody proceeding has been initiated, the district court has jurisdiction to provide injunctive relief to regulate contact among the parties including "enjoining a party from molesting or disturbing the peace of the other party or of any child." § 14-10-108(2)(b), 6B C.R.S. (1987); *see also* § 14-10-108(3), (4), (5), (6), 6B C.R.S. (1987). Custody proceedings result in determinations of custody, *see* § 14-10-124, 6B C.R.S. (1987), and delineation or denial of visitation rights, *see* § 14-10-129, 6B C.R.S. (1987). Custody determinations and visitation provisions are subject to modification in district court proceedings pursuant to statutory procedures and criteria. §§ 14-10-131, 14-10-131.5, 14-10-129, 6B C.R.S. (1987 & 1988 Supp.).

We believe that a construction of the Domestic Abuse Act is available that will obviate conflict between the remedies available thereunder and the traditional exclusive jurisdiction of district courts in juvenile and domestic relations matters. Prior to the enactment of the Domestic Abuse Act, no single procedure was explicitly provided to restrain intra-family violence directed at both adults and minor children. Although such relief could be obtained in the county court as to adults only, in the juvenile court as to delinquent or dependent or neglected children only, and through the Uniform Dissolution of Marriage Act when a dissolution of marriage action or other custody proceeding had been initiated, there was no single statutory procedure affording protection to both adults and children in family disturbances where initiation of dissolution of marriage proceedings was not desired. More importantly, the restraint of domestic violence necessitates a rapid response to a possibly volatile situation whenever it occurs, and no provisions existed for obtaining restraining orders promptly enough to provide effective immediate relief to both adults and children involved in family disturbances. It was to fill these voids that the Domestic Abuse Act was adopted. *See* Walker, *Legislative Activities in Family Law,* 11 Colo. Law. 1560, 1567 (1982). The Act had the effect of specifying two forums, the county court and district court, in which relief from domestic abuse might be sought at any time of the day or night, and had the additional benefit of consolidating into a single set of procedures the statutory authority for protecting both adults and children in situations involving domestic abuse. There is no indication, however, that the legislature intended by enactment of the Domestic Abuse Act to intrude on the traditional jurisdiction of the district courts in juvenile and domestic relations matters to make long-term provisions for custody or visitation rights concerning minor children.

For the foregoing reasons, we conclude that emergency protection orders and restraining orders issued under §§ 14-4-102 and -103 implicitly are subject to modification or termination in proceedings under the Colorado Children's Code, the Uniform Dissolution of Marriage Act, and other traditional bases of district court jurisdiction over the restrained conduct. Once the issues concerning the appropriateness of contacts between the parties have been posed in proceedings under these statutes, resolution of custody, visitation, and permissible contact between parents and between parent and child can be evaluated and resolved in light of full information, including the information that led up to the issuance of the emergency protection order or restraining order under the Domestic Abuse Act.

Turning to the facts of the present case, we conclude that the county court had jurisdiction to enjoin the father from contacting his minor son. The allegations in the mother's verified motion for temporary restraining order that the father threatened violence to her and her minor child, and the evidence presented in the hearings on the appropriateness of injunctive relief supported a finding of domestic abuse as defined in section 14-4-101(2). The provisions of sections 14-4-102 and -103 therefore provided the jurisdictional basis for the relief granted by the county court.

This relief is consistent with the provisions of section 13-6-105 denying jurisdiction to the county court as to certain matters. With respect to the denial of the power to issue injunctions, a specific exception is recognized for injunctions authorized by the Domestic Abuse Act. § 13-6-105(1)(f); § 13-6-104(5). By enactment of the Domestic Abuse Act the General Assembly has affirmatively granted county courts jurisdiction to provide injunctive relief, including protection for minor children, in domestic abuse situations. §§ 14-4102 to -103. Moreover, the denial of county court jurisdiction in matters affecting children, § 13-6-105(1)(d), was amended by the same legislative bill that enacted the Domestic Abuse Act to permit county courts to exercise jurisdiction to the extent authorized in the Domestic Abuse Act. See § 13-6-105(1)(f) and n. 3, above. The Domestic Abuse Act itself provides that restraining orders to prevent domestic abuse can be issued notwithstanding the availability of such relief in a domestic relations action filed in district court. § 14-4-102(1), 6B C.R.S. (1987).

Furthermore, as discussed earlier the relief accorded here does not prevent the district court from determining matters of custody, visitation, and permissible contact between the parties should such matters be properly presented in proceedings under the Colorado Children's Code, the Uniform Dissolution of Marriage Act, or some other source of district court jurisdiction.

We affirm the judgment of the district court.

# IV. Assessing the Effectiveness of Protective Orders

## Susan L. Keilitz, Paula L. Hannaford & Hillery S. Efkeman, *Civil Protective Orders: The Benefits and Limitations for Victims of Domestic Violence*

National Center for State Courts Research Report vii–xiv (1997)

In 1994 the National Center for State Courts initiated a study of civil protection orders under a grant from the National Institute of Justice....

The National Center's study examined the civil protection order process and the environments in which the process takes place in three jurisdictions with different processes and service models. These jurisdictions are the Family Court in Wilmington, Delaware; the County Court in Denver, Colorado; and the District of Columbia Superior Court. . . .

Across the three project sites, 554 women agreed to participate in the study . . . (Delaware, 151; Denver, 194; District of Columbia, 209). . . .

Summary of Key Findings and Implications for Practice

- Civil protection orders are valuable for helping victims regain a sense of well-being.

For nearly three-quarters of the study participants, the short-term effects of the protection order on three aspects (whether their lives have improved, whether they felt better about themselves, and whether they felt safer) of the participants' well being were positive. These positive effects improved over time, so that by the time of the six-month follow-up interview, the proportion of participants reporting life improvement increased to 85 percent. More than 90 percent reported feeling better about themselves, and 80 percent of those with a protection order in effect felt safer. Furthermore, in both the initial and follow-up interviews, 95 percent of the participants stated that they would seek a protection order again.

- In the vast majority of cases, civil protection orders deter repeated incidents of physical and psychological abuse.

A majority of the participants in both the initial and the follow-up interviews reported having no problems (72.4 percent and 65.3 percent, respectively . . . ). Repeat occurrences of physical abuse were reportedly rare, but varied greatly across the study sites. At the initial interviews, 2.6 percent of the participants reported repeated physical abuse. In the six-month follow up, that proportion more than tripled to 8.4 percent. The incidence of repeated physical abuse was much higher, however, in Delaware (10.9 percent) and the District of Columbia (11.9 percent) than in Denver, where only about 2 percent of the participants reported being reabused physically.

Psychological abuse was reported by 4.4 percent of the study participants initially, but after six months the reported incidents rose to 12.6 percent. As for the reports of repeated physical abuse, there was a high level of variance across the sites. Psychological abuse was highest in Delaware (23.6 percent) and lowest in the District of Columbia (1.7 percent), with Denver falling in the middle (13.3 percent).

The most frequently reported problem in both the initial and follow-up interviews involved respondents calling the victim at home or work (16.1 percent and 17.4 percent, respectively). In both the initial and follow-up interviews, about 9 percent of the participants reported that the respondents came to their homes. Stalking was infrequently reported. In the initial interviews about 4 percent of the participants reported being stalked by the respondent, and this figure rose to about 7 percent in the follow-up interviews.

- The study participants experienced severe abuse.

More than one-third of the study participants had been threatened or injured with a weapon; more than half the participants had been beaten or choked, and 84 percent had suffered milder physical abuse, such as slapping, kicking, and shoving. While the use of weapons to threaten or injure the participants occurred for most women only once or twice, more than 40 percent of the participants experienced severe physical abuse at least every few months, and 10 percent experienced such abuse weekly. About 10 percent of the participants sought a protection order after only a week, but 15 percent of the women experienced abuse for one to two years, and nearly one-quarter had endured the respondent's abusive behavior for more than five years.

Most significantly, the longer the woman experienced abuse, the more intense the abusive behavior became; consequently, the longer a victim stays in a relationship, the more likely it is that she will be severely injured by the abuser. . . .

- The majority of the abusive partners have a criminal record.

Sixty-five percent of the respondents had a prior criminal arrest history. These charges consisted of a variety of offenses including violent crime (domestic violence, simple assault, other violence and weapons charges), drug and alcohol-related crimes (drug and DUI offenses), and other categories of crimes (property, traffic and miscellaneous offenses). Of the 129 respondents with any history of violent crime, 109 had prior arrests for violent crimes other than domestic violence. These findings are generally consistent with a study conducted in Quincy, Massachusetts, that found that "80 percent of abusers have prior criminal histories . . . and half have prior violence records."

If the woman's abuser had an arrest record for violent crime, she was significantly less likely to have been available for a second interview. Furthermore, respondents with arrest histories for drug-and alcohol-related crimes and for violent crime tended to engage in more intense abuse of their partners than did other respondents. . . .

- The criminal record of the respondent is associated with improvements in well being and in curbing abusive conduct.

For the Well-being Index, participants are more likely to report positive outcomes when the respondent has a record of violent crime. Protection orders therefore can be particularly helpful for improving the well-being of women when their abusers have been sufficiently (and probably publicly) violent in the past to be arrested for the behavior. For the Problems Index, in the initial interviews, the participants whose abuser had a higher number of arrests tended to report a greater number of problems with the protection order. In the follow-up interviews, the participants whose abuser had at least one arrest for a violent crime other than domestic violence were more likely to experience a greater number of problems with the protection order. . . .

- Temporary protection orders can be useful even if the victim does not follow through to obtain a permanent order.

The most commonly cited reason for not returning for a permanent order was that the respondent had stopped bothering the petitioner (35.3 percent), which suggests that being the subject of the court's attention can influence the abuser's behavior. Also, one-fourth of the study participants who obtained only a temporary protection order engaged in safety planning at that time. The court process thus offered an opportunity for educating victims about the actions they could take to protect themselves. . . .

- The court process can influence the victim's active participation in deterring further violence in her life.

A more centralized process and direct assistance to petitioners for protection orders may encourage women with a temporary order to return to court for a permanent order. The proportion of women who returned to court for a permanent order following a temporary order was significantly higher in Denver (60 percent) than in the District of Columbia (44 percent). In addition, a higher proportion of women developed a safety plan in Denver, where each petitioner is assisted by an advocate from Project Safeguard, in comparison to Delaware and the District of Columbia. Study participants in Denver also reported far fewer repeated occurrences of physical violence compared to the participants in Delaware and Denver.

. . . .

- Victims do not use the contempt process to enforce orders.

Few of the study participants filed contempt motions for violations of the protection order. In 130 cases (89.7 percent), no contempt motions were filed. Thirteen cases (9.0 percent) had one contempt motion and only two cases (1.4 percent) had more than one contempt motion. Of the cases in which contempt motions were filed, the court held a hearing on the matter in nine cases and granted the motion in five of these cases. . . .

- The potential for linking victims to services through the court process has not been achieved.

Overall, more than three-fourths (77.5 percent) of the study participants received some type of service or assistance, either before or after they obtained a protection order. However, the participants' private circle of friends and relatives accounted for a large proportion of the assistance the victims received. . . .

- Law enforcement agencies can do more to assist prosecutors in developing cases for prosecution, to arrest perpetrators, and to help victims access the civil protection order process.

The reported use of police services varied across the sites, as did the response of the police. In Delaware, for example, a higher proportion of the participants had called the police following the incident that spurred them to seek a protection order (Delaware, 97 percent; Denver, 93 percent; District of Columbia, 90 percent), but the police came to the scene of the incident in a lower proportion of the cases (Delaware, 79 percent; Denver 89 percent; District of Columbia, 94 percent). Once at the scene, however, the police in Delaware (Wilmington Police and New Castle County Police) were more likely to take notes and interview witnesses. The police arrested the respondent in Denver in a considerably higher proportion of the cases, particularly in comparison to the District of Columbia (87 percent compared with 41 percent). In each of the sites, however, the proportion of the participants who reported that the police had told them how to obtain a civil protection order was too low for good practice (Delaware, 57 percent; Denver, 54 percent; District of Columbia, 71 percent)....

## V. Sanctions for Violations

Since most jurisdictions now permit litigants to pursue family offense civil matters and criminal cases simultaneously, the question of constitutional double jeopardy arises. Normally, it is not a problem, because the relief sought differs. In the family offense proceeding, which is civil in nature, the litigant wants an order of protection to keep her safe, while the prosecutor in the criminal case wants jail or a probationary sentence.

A problem arises if the abuser who is subject to a civil protective order ignores it and assaults the victim who is protected by the order. Such assault would permit the victim to petition the civil court to have the abuser held in contempt of the original protective order. Meanwhile, the local district attorney may also want the abuser prosecuted criminally. If the civil court judge on the original protective order finds the abuser in contempt for violating the court's order, that judge retains the power to jail him. What follows is an excerpt from a consolidated case before the United States Supreme Court that included the dual prosecution of a domestic violence incident. The Court held that such dual prosecution and/or punishment for contempt violated constitutional principles against double jeopardy. Prosecution of the underlying offenses, however, may go forward.

### United States v. Dixon

United States Supreme Court

509 U.S. 688 (1993)

JUSTICE SCALIA announced the judgment of the Court and delivered the opinion of the Court with respect to Parts I, II, and IV, and an opinion with respect to Parts III and V, in which JUSTICE KENNEDY joins.

....

I

[Eds. Note—The fact pattern of the first respondent, Alvin Dixon, relates to allegations that he committed a drug offense while he was out on bond for a charge of second-degree murder. Because his case is not related to domestic violence, the facts of his case have been omitted.]

Based on [Michael] Foster's alleged physical attacks upon her in the past, Foster's estranged wife Ana obtained a civil protection order (CPO) in Superior Court of the District of Columbia. See D.C. Code Ann. § 16-1005(c) (1989) (CPO may be issued upon a showing of good cause to believe that the subject "has committed or is threatening an intrafamily offense"). The order, to which Foster consented, required that he not "'molest, assault, or in any manner threaten or physically abuse'" Ana Foster; a separate order, not implicated here, sought to protect her mother. 598 A.2d at 725–726.

Over the course of eight months, Ana Foster filed three separate motions to have her husband held in contempt for numerous violations of the CPO. Of the 16 alleged episodes, the only charges relevant here are three separate instances of threats (on November 12, 1987, and March 26 and May 17, 1988) and two assaults (on November 6, 1987, and May 21, 1988), in the most serious of which Foster "threw [his wife] down basement stairs, kicking her body[,] . . . pushed her head into the floor causing head injuries, [and Ana Foster] lost consciousness." 598 A.2d at 726.

After issuing a notice of hearing and ordering Foster to appear, the court held a 3-day bench trial. Counsel for Ana Foster and her mother prosecuted the action; the United States was not represented at trial, although the United States Attorney was apparently aware of the action, as was the court aware of a separate grand jury proceeding on some of the alleged criminal conduct. As to the assault charges, the court stated that Ana Foster would have "to prove as an element, first that there was a Civil Protection Order, and then [that] . . . the assault as defined by the criminal code, in fact occurred." Tr. in Nos. IF-630-87, IF-631-87 (Aug. 8, 1988), p. 367; accord, *id.*, at 368. At the close of the plaintiffs' case, the court granted Foster's motion for acquittal on various counts, including the alleged threats on November 12 and May 17. Foster then took the stand and generally denied the allegations. The court found Foster guilty beyond a reasonable doubt of four counts of criminal contempt (three violations of Ana Foster's CPO, and one violation of the CPO obtained by her mother), including the November 6, 1987, and May 21, 1988, assaults, but acquitted him on other counts, including the March 26 alleged threats. He was sentenced to an aggregate 600 days' imprisonment. See § 161005(f) (authorizing contempt punishment); Super. Ct. of D.C. Intrafamily Rules 7(c), 12(e) (1987) (maximum punishment of six months' imprisonment and $300 fine).

The United States Attorney's Office later obtained an indictment charging Foster with simple assault on or about November 6, 1987 (Count I, violation of § 22-504); threatening to injure another on or about November 12, 1987, and March 26 and May 17, 1988 (Counts II-IV, violation of § 22-2307); and assault with intent to kill on or about May 21, 1988 (Count V, violation of § 22-501). App. 43-44. Ana Foster was the complainant in all counts; the first and last counts were based on the events for which Foster had been held in contempt, and the other three were based on the alleged events for which Foster was acquitted of contempt. Like Dixon, Foster filed a motion to dismiss, claiming a double jeopardy bar to all counts, and also collateral estoppel as to Counts II-IV. The trial court denied the double jeopardy claim and did not rule on the collateral-estoppel assertion.

The Government appealed the double jeopardy ruling in *Dixon*, and Foster appealed the trial court's denial of his motion. The District of Columbia Court of Appeals consolidated the two cases, reheard them en banc, and, relying on our recent decision in *Grady v. Corbin*, 495 U.S. 508, 109 L. Ed. 2d 548, 110 S. Ct. 2084 (1990), ruled that both subsequent prosecutions were barred by the Double Jeopardy Clause. 598 A.2d at 725. . . . We granted certiorari, 503 U.S. 1004 (1992).

II

. . . .

The Double Jeopardy Clause, whose application to this new context we are called upon to consider, provides that no person shall "be subject for the same offence to be twice put in jeopardy of life or limb." U.S. Const., Amdt. 5. This protection applies both to successive punishments and to successive prosecutions for the same criminal offense. See *North Carolina v. Pearce*, 395 U.S. 711, 23 L. Ed. 2d 656, 89 S. Ct. 2072 (1969). It is well established that criminal contempt, at least the sort enforced through nonsummary proceedings, is "a crime in the ordinary sense." *Bloom, supra*, at 201. Accord, *New Orleans v. Steamship Co.*, 87 U.S. 387, 20 Wall. 387, 392, 22 L. Ed. 354 (1874).

. . . .

In both the multiple punishment and multiple prosecution contexts, this Court has concluded that where the two offenses for which the defendant is punished or tried cannot survive the "same-elements" test, the double jeopardy bar applies. See, *e.g.*, *Brown v. Ohio*, 432 U.S. 161, 168–169, 53 L. Ed. 2d 187, 97 S. Ct. 2221 (1977); *Blockburger v. United States*, 284 U.S. 299, 304, 76 L. Ed. 306, 52 S. Ct. 180 (1932) (multiple punishment); *Gavieres v. United States*, 220 U.S. 338, 342, 55 L. Ed. 489, 31 S. Ct. 421 (1911) (successive prosecutions).

The same-elements test, sometimes referred to as the "*Blockburger*" test, inquires whether each offense contains an element not contained in the other; if not, they are the "same offence" and double jeopardy bars additional punishment and successive prosecution. . . .

We recently held in *Grady* that in addition to passing the *Blockburger* test, a subsequent prosecution must satisfy a "same-conduct" test to avoid the double jeopardy bar. The *Grady* test provides that, "if, to establish an essential element of an offense charged in that prosecution, the government will prove conduct that constitutes an offense for which the defendant has already been prosecuted," a second prosecution may not be had. 495 U.S. at 510.

III

A

The first question before us today is whether *Blockburger* analysis permits subsequent prosecution in this new criminal contempt context, where judicial order has prohibited criminal act. If it does, we must then proceed to consider whether *Grady* also permits it. See *Grady, supra*, at 516.

We begin with *Dixon*. The statute applicable in Dixon's contempt prosecution provides that "[a] person who has been conditionally released . . . and who has violated a condition of release shall be subject to . . . prosecution for contempt of court." § 23-1329(a). Obviously, Dixon could not commit an "offence" under this provision until an order setting out conditions was issued. The statute by itself imposes no legal obligation on anyone. . . .

In this situation, in which the contempt sanction is imposed for violating the order through commission of the incorporated drug offense, the later attempt to prosecute Dixon for the drug offense resembles the situation that produced our judgment of double jeopardy in *Harris v. Oklahoma*, 433 U.S. 682, 53 L. Ed. 2d 1054, 97 S. Ct. 2912 (1977) (*per curiam*). There we held that a subsequent prosecution for robbery with a firearm was barred by the Double Jeopardy Clause, because the defendant had already been tried for felony murder based on the same underlying felony. . . . So too here, the "crime" of violating a condition of release cannot be abstracted from the "element" of the violated condition. The *Dixon* court order incorporated the entire governing criminal code in the same manner as the *Harris* felony-murder statute incorporated the several enumerated felonies. . . .

To oppose this analysis, the Government can point only to dictum in *In re Debs*, 158 U.S. 564, 594, 599–600, 39 L. Ed. 1092, 15 S. Ct. 900 (1895), which, to the extent it attempted to exclude certain nonsummary contempt prosecutions from various constitutional protections for criminal defendants, has been squarely rejected by cases such as *Bloom*, 391 U.S. at 208. The Government also relies upon *In re Chapman*, 166 U.S. 661, 41 L. Ed. 1154, 17 S. Ct. 677 (1897), and *Jurney v. MacCracken*, 294 U.S. 125, 79 L. Ed. 802, 55 S. Ct. 375 (1935), which recognize Congress' power to punish as contempt the refusal of a witness to testify before it. But to say that Congress can punish such a refusal is not to say that a criminal court can punish the same refusal *yet again*. Neither case dealt with that issue, and *Chapman* specifically declined to address it, noting that successive prosecutions (before Congress for contemptuous refusal to testify and before a court for violation of a federal statute making such refusal a crime) were "improbable." 166 U.S. at 672.

Both the Government, Brief for United States 15-17, and Justice Blackmun, *post*, at 743, contend that the legal obligation in Dixon's case may serve "interests . . . fundamentally different" from the substantive criminal law, because it derives in part from the determination of a court rather than a determination of the legislature. That distinction seems questionable, since the court's power to establish conditions of release, and to punish their violation, was conferred by statute; the legislature was the ultimate source of both the criminal and the contempt prohibition. More importantly, however, the distinction is of no moment for purposes of the Double Jeopardy Clause, the text of which looks to whether the *offenses* are the same, not the interests that the offenses violate. And this Court stated long ago that criminal contempt, at least in its nonsummary form, "is a crime in every fundamental respect." *Bloom, supra,* at 201; accord, *e.g., Steamship Co.,* 20 Wall. at 392. Because Dixon's drug offense did not include any element not contained in his previous contempt offense, his subsequent prosecution violates the Double Jeopardy Clause.

The foregoing analysis obviously applies as well to Count I of the indictment against Foster, charging assault in violation of § 22-504, based on the same event that was the subject of his prior contempt conviction for violating the provision of the CPO forbidding him to commit simple assault under § 22-504. The subsequent prosecution for assault fails the *Blockburger* test, and is barred.

The remaining four counts in *Foster,* assault with intent to kill (Count V; § 22-501) and threats to injure or kidnap (Counts II-IV; § 22-2307), are not barred under *Blockburger*. As to Count V: Foster's conduct on May 21, 1988, was found to violate the Family Division's order that he not "molest, assault, or in any manner threaten or physically abuse" his wife. At the contempt hearing, the court stated that Ana Foster's attorney, who prosecuted the contempt, would have to prove, first, knowledge of a CPO, and, second, a willful violation of one of its conditions, here simple assault as defined by the criminal code. See, *e.g.,* 598 A.2d at 727–728; *In re Thompson,* 454 A.2d 1324, 1326 (D.C. 1982); accord, *Parker v. United States,* 373 A.2d 906, 907 (D.C. 1977) (*per curiam*). On the basis of the same episode, Foster was then indicted for violation of § 22-501, which proscribes assault with intent to kill. Under governing law, that offense requires proof of specific intent to kill; simple assault does not. See *Logan v. United States,* 483 A.2d 664, 672–673 (D.C. 1984). Similarly, the contempt offense required proof of knowledge of the CPO, which assault with intent to kill does not. Applying the *Blockburger* elements test, the result is clear: These crimes were different offenses, and the subsequent prosecution did not violate the Double Jeopardy Clause.

Counts II, III, and IV of Foster's indictment are likewise not barred. These charged Foster under § 22-2307 (forbidding anyone to "threaten . . . to kidnap any person or to injure the person of another or physically damage the property of any person") for his alleged threats on three separate dates. Foster's contempt prosecution included charges that, on the same dates, he violated the CPO provision ordering that he not "in any manner threaten" Ana Foster. Conviction of the contempt required willful violation of the CPO—which conviction under § 22-2307 did not; and conviction under § 22-2307 required that the threat be a threat to kidnap, to inflict bodily injury, or to damage property—which conviction of the contempt (for violating the CPO provision that Foster not "in any manner threaten") did not. Each offense therefore contained a separate element, and the *Blockburger* test for double jeopardy was not met.

## IV

Having found that at least some of the counts at issue here are not barred by the *Blockburger* test, we must consider whether they are barred by the new, additional double jeopardy test we announced three Terms ago in *Grady v. Corbin*. They undoubtedly are, since *Grady* prohibits "a subsequent prosecution if, to establish an essential element of an offense charged in that prosecution [here, assault as an element of assault with intent to kill, or threatening as an element of threatening bodily injury], the government will prove conduct that constitutes an offense for which the defendant has already been prosecuted [here, the assault and the threatening, which conduct constituted the offense of violating the CPO]." 495 U.S. at 510.

We have concluded, however, that *Grady* must be overruled. Unlike *Blockburger* analysis, whose definition of what prevents two crimes from being the "same offence," U.S. Const., Amdt. 5, has deep historical roots and has been accepted in numerous precedents of this Court, *Grady* lacks constitutional roots. The "same-conduct" rule it announced is wholly inconsistent with earlier Supreme Court precedent and with the clear common-law understanding of double jeopardy. See, *e.g., Gavieres v. United States*, 220 U.S. at 345 (in subsequent prosecution, "[w]hile it is true that the conduct of the accused was one and the same, two offenses resulted, each of which had an element not embraced in the other"). We need not discuss the many proofs of these statements, which were set forth at length in the *Grady* dissent. See 495 U.S. at 526 (opinion of Scalia, J.). . . .

. . . *Grady* was not only wrong in principle; it has already proved unstable in application. Less than two years after it came down, in *United States v. Felix*, 503 U.S. 378, 118 L. Ed. 2d 25, 112 S. Ct. 1377 (1992), we were forced to recognize a large exception to it. There we concluded that a subsequent prosecution for conspiracy to manufacture, possess, and distribute methamphetamine was not barred by a previous conviction for attempt to manufacture the same substance. We offered as a justification for avoiding a "literal" (*i.e.*, faithful) reading of *Grady* "longstanding authority" to the effect that prosecution for conspiracy is not precluded by prior prosecution for the substantive offense. *Felix, supra,* at 388–391. Of course the very existence of such a large and longstanding "exception" to the *Grady* rule gave cause for concern that the rule was not an accurate expression of the law. This "past practice" excuse is not available to support the ignoring of *Grady* in the present case, since there is no Supreme Court precedent even discussing this fairly new breed of successive prosecution (criminal contempt for violation of a court order prohibiting a crime, followed by prosecution for the crime itself).

. . . .

Having encountered today yet another situation in which the pre-*Grady* understanding of the Double Jeopardy Clause allows a second trial, though the "same-conduct" test would not, we think it time to acknowledge what is now, three years after *Grady*, compellingly clear: The case was a mistake. We do not lightly reconsider a precedent, but, because *Grady* contradicted an "unbroken line of decisions," contained "less than accurate" historical analysis, and has produced "confusion," we do so here. *Solorio v. United States*, 483 U.S. 435, 439, 442, 450, 97 L. Ed. 2d 364, 107 S.

Ct. 2924 (1987). Although *stare decisis* is the "preferred course" in constitutional adjudication, "when governing decisions are unworkable or are badly reasoned, 'this Court has never felt constrained to follow precedent.'" *Payne v. Tennessee*, 501 U.S. 808, 827, 115 L. Ed. 2d 720, 111 S. Ct. 2597 (1991) (quoting *Smith v. Allwright*, 321 U.S. 649, 665, 88 L. Ed. 987, 64 S. Ct. 757 (1944), and collecting examples). We would mock *stare decisis* and only add chaos to our double jeopardy jurisprudence by pretending that *Grady* survives when it does not. We therefore accept the Government's invitation to overrule *Grady*, and Counts II, III, IV, and V of Foster's subsequent prosecution are not barred.

. . . .

## Walker v. Walker
### New York Court of Appeals
### 86 N.Y.2d 624 (1995)

Bellacosa, J.

The sole issue in this case is the discretionary authority of the Family Court to impose consecutive six-month incarcerations for three separate violations of an order of protection. The respondent former husband in the Family Court proceeding is the appellant before this Court on an appeal as of right taken on the dissent of two Justices at the Appellate Division.

By a dispositional order in 1993, Family Court committed appellant to jail for multiple violations of a Family Court order of protection secured by his former wife. In the same order, the court suspended an additional nine-month commitment for other discrete violations. The court then issued a new order of protection, essentially directing Fred Walker to refrain from any contact whatsoever with Emma Walker. While jailed, he nevertheless sent three separate written communications to her. As the protected and aggrieved party, she filed two further petitions alleging these three new, willful failures to obey the latest order of protection and seeking appropriate relief. After a hearing, Family Court found that appellant disobeyed the new order by the three separate acts of communication.

In adjudicating the latest round of violations, Family Court issued a dispositional order revoking the suspension of the prior commitment and, pursuant to Family Court Act § 846-a, also ordered defendant jailed for six months for each of the new violations. The combined period of incarceration accumulated to 27 months. Only the consecutive six-month jail commitments imposed by Family Court for these three violations are at issue here. The dispositive legal question on this appeal emanates from the commitment authorization in Family Court Act § 846-a and particularizes to whether Family Court is authorized to impose consecutive commitments for separate, multiple violations of one order of protection.

The Appellate Division, with two Justices dissenting in part, affirmed Family Court's dispositional order, holding that consecutive periods of incarceration are authorized.

In affirming, we hold that the Family Court is not generally precluded from imposing, in the exercise of prudent and appropriate discretion, a maximum six-month jail commitment for each separate and distinct violation of an order of protection, to be served consecutively.

. . . .

Sections 841 and 842 of the Family Court Act authorize the inclusion of orders of protection as part of dispositional orders in family offense proceedings. Family Court Act § 846-a prescribes the procedure and penalty for failure to obey such an order:

> "If a respondent is brought before the court for failure to obey any lawful order issued under this article and if, after hearing, the court is satisfied by competent proof that the respondent has willfully failed to obey any such order, the court may . . . commit the respondent to jail for a term not to exceed six months."

Appellant claims that the statute allows a maximum of six months' incarceration only, regardless of the number of willful acts of disobedience against the same order. That limitation finds no support, however, in the statute or its purpose.

Under appellant's argument, a violator already penalized for willfully failing to obey an order of protection would garner immunity from further official sanction for persistent, separate violations (*see, Carmille A. v. David A.,* 162 Misc 2d 22, 26). Such an approach is in no way compelled or warranted by the governing statutes, sentencing principles or reasonable statutory analysis. Its incongruous and untenable result would also constitute an invitation to violate and no incentive to obey.

That appellant disobeyed the court's order from jail serves only to underscore the need for an effective judicial option for appropriate punishment and deterrence. To disallow consecutive penalties under these circumstances would also elevate form over substance and frustrate the core purpose of Family Court Act article 8, which is designed to provide reasonable means and methods of protection and enforcement for victims of domestic violence. We thus reject this construction and constriction of the statutory authority of Family Court Judges in dealing with such situations and agree with the resolution of this matter by both courts below.

In 1980, the Legislature amended the Family Court Act to provide new focus and direction for more aggressive measures that would protect victims of domestic violence (L 1980, ch 530; Besharov, Practice Commentary, McKinney's Cons Laws of NY, Book 29A, Family Ct Act art 8, at 128). The statute unequivocally and firmly declares that a proceeding under article 8 "is for the purpose of attempting to stop the violence, end the family disruption and obtain protection" (Family Ct Act § 812[2][b]; *see also,* Governor's Prog Mem, L 1980, ch 530, 1980 Legis Ann, at 212; L 1994, ch 222). Indeed, victims are given the option of proceeding in Family Court or Criminal Court (Family Ct Act §§ 812, 813[1]). Private aggrieved parties may petition for protection by way of a violator's incarceration for violations of Family Court orders under the corresponding punishment section, section 846-a (L 1980, ch 530, § 10; Family Ct Act

§§ 846, 846-a [as renum]; *see also,* L 1994, ch 222). Stricter enforcement of orders of protection thus became the statutory order of the day and continues as the prevailing policy today. Importantly, no restriction on consecutive punishment for separate acts is statutorily expressed. We conclude also that no such limitation may be reasonably inferred from the diametrically opposite thrust of the legislative intent.

Our conclusion drawn from direct statutory analysis is supplemented and supported by common-law principles dealing with consecutive punishments in the criminal realm. The familiar canon of construction that "legislative enactments in derogation of common law . . . are deemed to abrogate the common law only to the extent required by the clear import of the statutory language" is a useful directional signal (*Morris v. Snappy Car Rental,* 84 NY2d 21, 28; *see,* McKinney's Cons Laws of NY, Book 1, Statutes § 153). The Family Court, as a court of limited jurisdiction created by constitutional amendment effective in 1962 (NY Const, art VI, § 1[a]), does not enjoy our customary common-law tradition and building blocks (*see,* Besharov, Practice Commentary, McKinney's Cons Laws of NY, Book 29A, Family Ct Act § 115, at 23). In light of the punitive nature of Family Court Act § 846-a, however, it is helpful to look to analogous common-law rules relating to concurrent and consecutive sentencing regimens for penal violations (*see,* McKinney's Cons Laws of NY, Book 1, Statutes § 273).

Courts have long enjoyed sentencing discretion to impose consecutive penalties for multiple crimes *(see, People v. Ingber,* 248 NY 302, 305 [Cardozo, Ch. J.]). In upholding this general power when a pertinent sentencing statute neither specifically authorizes nor prohibits consecutive sentences, Chief Judge Cardozo declared that "[w]e think the discretionary power of the court to impose a cumulative [consecutive] sentence in cases not covered by the mandatory statute remains, undiminished, as it was at common law" *(id.,* at 304-305; *see also, Matter of Browne v. New York State Bd. of Parole,* 10 NY2d 116, 120; *Ponzi v. Fessenden,* 258 US 254, 265). Indeed, at the time of *Ingber* and still today, when the Legislature intends to circumscribe judicial authority to impose consecutive punishments, it does so explicitly *(see, e.g.,* Penal Law § 70.25[2]; *compare, People ex. rel Maurer v. Jackson,* 2 NY2d 259, 264).

Instead of appellant's inverted focus—that section 846-a does not specifically authorize consecutive sentences—we advert to Chief Judge Cardozo's teaching that "[n]othing short of obvious compulsion will lead us to a reading of the statute whereby the pains and penalties of crimes are shorn of all terrors more poignant than a form of words" *(People v. Ingber,* 248 NY 302, 306, *supra).* That reasoning and eloquent expression apply with equal force to the Family Court's enforcement and punishment authority with respect to orders of protection pursuant to section 846-a. The three consecutive penalties imposed on appellant for his willful flouting (from jail, while serving time for prior violations of an earlier order of protection) of the most recent order of protection fit within the authorization of Family Court Act § 846-a. That also helps to insure that the statute and the order are not "shorn of all terrors" and relegated to merely "a form of words" *(People v. Ingber, supra,* at 306).

Accordingly, the order of the Appellate Division should be affirmed, without costs.

## Notes and Questions

- **WHO IS FAMILY?**

In a truly expansive interpretation of term "household member," a New Jersey court, in *Hamilton v. Ali*, 350 N.J. Super. 479 (2001), determined that a pair of warring college suite mates were household members for the purposes of being covered by the state's domestic violence act and thus the victim of their dispute could receive a civil order of protection from the chancery court. The parties were freshman undergraduate students assigned to the same nine-student suite, with a common bathroom and sitting area. The defendant kicked in the plaintiff's bedroom door while he was out to get the plaintiff's stash of beer. When the plaintiff confronted him about it, the defendant put his finger to the plaintiff's nose and slammed him against the wall. The court determined the suite mates were covered by the act because the relationship was continual and included living together in close proximity and resulted in daily contact. Do you think this an over-expansion of the definition of "household member"? Under this definition, would a live-in nanny qualify for a civil order of protection? What about the concierge in an apartment building? The dog-walker who comes each day to feed and walk the pets? Is this what you think was intended in providing protection to household and family members?

- **STANDARDS OF PROOF**

In the criminal trial of an A misdemeanor in New York state, which is a crime punishable by one year or less, the defendant has a right to a jury trial and, of course, the standard of proof is beyond a reasonable doubt. In a contempt proceeding before the New York Family Court, there is no jury and the standard of proof is a mere preponderance of the evidence. Are you surprised that a person held in contempt for multiple violations of a civil protective order could theoretically spend years in jail, while the most time a defendant convicted in criminal court for multiple violations of a protective order would get is two years? Do you agree with Judge Bellacosa's reasoning in the *Walker* case?

- **HOUSING ISSUES AND DOMESTIC VIOLENCE**

There are serious negative housing consequences for victims of domestic violence, as this recent article by Jenny Kutner shows. In *Domestic Violence Victims Can Be Evicted for Calling Police. Here's Why*, the article, which was published in the on-line publication, Connections.Mic, on July 14, 2016, Kutner wrote:

> Ashley Rousey hadn't planned to call the police when her ex-boyfriend showed up at her apartment in late February 2008.
>
> A month before, Rousey had reached out to a local domestic violence advocacy group, saying her ex had abused her, and moved into her own apartment in King County, Washington. When Rousey asked her abuser to leave, she said he grew agitated, refused and threw a rock at her window. Rousey called the police, who issued a trespass notice barring him from the property.

What Rousey didn't realize was that by reaching out for help, she ran the risk of being evicted. . . . Victims of domestic abuse like Rousey face homelessness at elevated rates. The National Network to End Domestic Violence reported 38% of domestic abuse victims are homeless at some point in their lives, and between 22% and 57% of homeless women say domestic violence has been the immediate cause of their loss of housing. . . .

A key part of the problem is that victims of domestic violence can be evicted from their homes for being involved in domestic disturbances, particularly ones that require police intervention. Estimates from the American Civil Liberties Union indicate that in hundreds of municipalities across the country, victims can be thrown out of their homes for calling the police repeatedly. The problem disproportionately impacts poor women and women of color, who face high rates of intimate partner violence and have fewer options if they are evicted.

"It's unconscionable that [victims] are removed from their homes and face repeated discrimination simply because of the heinous crimes committed against them," Sen. Jeanne Shaheen (D-N.H.) said in a statement to *Mic.*

To address the problem, this week Shaheen introduced the Fair Housing for Domestic Violence and Sexual Assault Survivors Act, which would amend the Fair Housing Act to classify abuse survivors as a protected class. It would make it illegal for landlords to discriminate against someone because of a history of sexual or domestic violence, and would prohibit private property owners from evicting victims if they call for help. . . .

Not only does evicting survivors of domestic abuse pose the immediate threat of homelessness, it can also make it difficult for tenants to secure housing in the future. If victims try to seek new housing with an eviction record, potential landlords can reject a lease application without considering the context.

Can landlords do that?

The practice of kicking out victims sounds like it should be illegal, but survivors often lack legal protections preventing this type of housing discrimination. Landlords can, and often do, include lease provisions stipulating that criminal activity of any kind on the property is grounds for removal, giving them the power to evict entire households if they believe tenants are disruptive. . . .

The full article is available at https://mic.com/articles/148484/domestic-violence-victims-can-be-evicted-for-calling-police-here-s-why#zQRqkpyYI, accessed November 2, 2016.

The bill introduced by Sen. Shaheen, S.3164, that was discussed in the Kutner article, was referred to the Senate Committee on Banking, Housing and Urban Affairs, where as of November 2016, it has remained. https://www.congress.gov/bill/114-congress/senate-bill/3164/all-actions?overview=closed#tabs, accessed November 3, 2016.

In addition to being kicked out of an apartment because of victimization by an abuser, some tenants must flee an apartment to *get away* from one. Under those circumstances, a tenant with a lease could be subject to penalties for breaking it. What follows is a Texas law designed to protect domestic violence victims under those circumstances.

## Tex. Prop. Code § 92.016 (2016) Right to Vacate and Avoid Liability Following Family Violence

(a) For purposes of this section:

(1) "Family violence" has the meaning assigned by Section 71.004, Family Code.

(2) "Occupant" means a person who has the landlord's consent to occupy a dwelling but has no obligation to pay the rent for the dwelling.

(b) A tenant may terminate the tenant's rights and obligations under a lease and may vacate the dwelling and avoid liability for future rent and any other sums due under the lease for terminating the lease and vacating the dwelling before the end of the lease term if the tenant complies with Subsection (c) and provides the landlord or the landlord's agent a copy of one or more of the following orders protecting the tenant or an occupant from family violence:

(1) a temporary injunction issued under Subchapter F, Chapter 6, Family Code;

(2) a temporary ex parte order issued under Chapter 83, Family Code; or

(3) a protective order issued under Chapter 85, Family Code.

(c) A tenant may exercise the rights to terminate the lease under Subsection (b), vacate the dwelling before the end of the lease term, and avoid liability beginning on the date after all of the following events have occurred:

(1) a judge signs an order described by Subsection (b);

(2) the tenant provides a copy of the relevant documentation described by Subsection (b) to the landlord;

(3) the tenant provides written notice of termination of the lease to the landlord on or before the 30th day before the date the lease terminates;

(4) the 30th day after the date the tenant provided notice under Subdivision (3) expires; and

(5) the tenant vacates the dwelling.

(c-1) If the family violence is committed by a cotenant or occupant of the dwelling, a tenant may exercise the right to terminate the lease under the procedures provided by Subsection (b)(1) or (3) and Subsection (c), except that the tenant is not required to provide the notice described by Subsection (c)(3).

(d) Except as provided by Subsection (f), this section does not affect a tenant's liability for delinquent, unpaid rent or other sums owed to the landlord before the lease was terminated by the tenant under this section.

(e) A landlord who violates this section is liable to the tenant for actual damages, a civil penalty equal in amount to the amount of one month's rent plus $ 500, and attorney's fees.

(f) A tenant who terminates a lease under Subsection (b) is released from all liability for any delinquent, unpaid rent owed to the landlord by the tenant on the effective date of the lease termination if the lease does not contain language substantially equivalent to the following:

> (f) "Tenants may have special statutory rights to terminate the lease early in certain situations involving family violence or a military deployment or transfer."

(g) A tenant's right to terminate a lease before the end of the lease term, vacate the dwelling, and avoid liability under this section may not be waived by a tenant.

# Chapter 11

# Immigration and Domestic Violence

> **CONSIDER AS YOU READ ABOUT IMMIGRATION**
> 1. The history of immigration law
> 2. Impact of VAWA on the ability of battered immigrant women to remain in the United States
> 3. Increased likelihood of removal for non-citizen perpetrators of domestic violence
> 4. Domestic violence as an international human rights issue and whether it can form the basis for asylum for a victim from a country that does not recognize the dangers of domestic abuse

Rodi Alvarado, known only as "R.A." in a series of administrative law decisions determining her fate, fled Guatemala in 1995 to escape a decade of brutal beatings by her husband, a former soldier. For more than a decade, her fate in the United States was in limbo and her case made new law—and gave a small measure of hope—for the most desperate victims of domestic violence. Alvarado had been granted asylum in the United States by an immigration judge who ruled she had been a victim of severe abuse and that the Guatemalan government would not protect her from her husband if she were forced to return home. The Board of Immigration Appeals reversed the decision, which became a rallying point for human-rights groups, 100 members of Congress, and more than 50,000 people who wrote to the Attorney General in support of her asylum request.[1] Unfortunately, her fate got tangled up in election year politics.

Her story, discussed more fully later in this chapter, is one of the more egregious examples of how foreign women who are victims of domestic violence suffer—not only at the hands of their batterers, but also under laws and regulations that guided—and continue to guide—United States immigration policy for the last century. The reality is grim for immigrant women who are victims of domestic violence.

---

1. *AG Ashcroft Sends Domestic Violence Case Back to Appeals Board: Partial Victory—But Rodi Alvarado's Life Remains in Limbo*, ASYLUM PROTECTION NEWS 35, Jan. 24, 2005, *available at* www.humanrightsfirst.org/asylum/torchlight/newsletter/newslet_35.htm.

## I. The History of Women and Immigration Law

The immigration laws and policies in effect for most of the 20th century reflect a shockingly outmoded view of married women as chattel. Until mid-century, unless a woman was married to a United States citizen or legal resident alien, she could neither enter nor remain in this country. The direct route to immigration required a special skill, which necessitated advanced education or training, which most women did not possess. Thus, an immigrant woman's link to the United States was generally through her husband or other male relative. And, if she had the misfortune to be married to an abusive man, she had no choice but to stay in the marriage if she hoped to become a lawful resident or citizen, or if she hoped to raise her children in the United States. The following law review excerpt provides an overview of the immigration situation for women.

### Leslye E. Orloff & Janice V. Kaguyutan, *Offering a Helping Hand: Legal Protections for Battered Immigrant Women: A History of Legislative Responses*
10 Am. U. J. Gender Soc. Pol'y & L. 95 (2001)

. . . .

II. United States Immigration Laws Historically Fostered Domestic Abuse

A. U.S. Immigration Law's Roots in Coverture

Early United States immigration laws incorporated the concept of coverture, which was "a legislative enactment of the common law theory that the husband is the head of the household." Immigration laws in the 1920s gave male citizens and lawful permanent residents control over the immigration status of their immigrant wives and children. The law required a husband to either file a petition for his wife or accompany her when she applied for immigration status. Female citizens or lawful permanent residents could not, however, file petitions for their male immigrant spouses. This approach grew out of the doctrine of "coverture" that was a part of United States common law at that time. Coverture was defined as the legal principle under which "the very being or legal existence of the woman is suspended during the marriage, or at least incorporated and consolidated into that of the husband, under whose wing, protection, and cover, she performs everything." Coverture was so much a part of United States law that from 1907 through 1922, when a United States citizen woman married a man from another country, she lost her United States citizenship. Between 1907 and 1922, all American women acquired their husband's nationality upon marriage. . . .

Although subsequent legislation, particularly the Immigration and Nationality Act of 1952 ("INA"), changed the statutory language to make the immigration laws gender-neutral giving the same women ability to confer legal immigration status on her spouse as men had, the impact of the spousal sponsorship laws is still rooted in the coverture mentality. Since the power of sponsorship and autonomous action lies with the citizen or lawful permanent resident spouse, and because the majority of immigrant spouses and victims of domestic violence are women, the ramifications of spousal sponsorship are most serious for women.

B. Enhanced Danger to Battered Immigrants: The Immigration Marriage Fraud Amendments of 1986

In 1986, Congress codified a number of immigration law changes that further jeopardized the safety of battered immigrant women and their children. The Immigration Marriage Fraud Amendments of 1986 ("IMFA") significantly enhanced the control a citizen or lawful permanent resident spouse had over his alien spouse's immigration status. The IMFA re-confirmed the original power of the lawful permanent resident or citizen spouse to control the immigration status of his alien spouse by allowing her to become a lawful permanent resident only if he petitions for her. The IMFA created a presumption in immigration law that all marriages were fraudulent until proven to be valid. In an effort to ensure that lawful permanent resident status was granted only to spouses in valid marriages to United States citizens or lawful permanent residents, the IMFA required that immigrant spouses who gained residency based on a marriage to a United States citizen or lawful permanent resident fulfill a two-year conditional residency requirement before being granted full lawful permanent residency.

To prove that the marriage was valid, the law required a joint petition to be filed ninety days before the expiration of two years from when the immigrant spouse first gained her legal status, possibly followed by a scheduled joint interview with an INS official. The law did not require the citizen or lawful permanent resident spouse to file immigration papers for her, or to follow through with the joint petition. Nor did the law oblige him to stay in the marriage for the two-year period during which his wife was dependent on him for her immigration status. This legislative attempt to "curb fraud" and expose "sham marriages" did, however, place battered immigrant women at the mercy of their husbands. It also placed in jeopardy the immigration status of any children whose avenue to attain lawful permanent resident status was based on their mother's marriage to a citizen or lawful permanent resident. If the mother's legal immigration status terminated, so did the children's status terminate.

The IMFA contained two provisions that allowed the Attorney General to change the immigrant spouse's conditional resident status to a permanent resident status without satisfying the requirements of the joint petition and interview if she satisfied the criteria for "extreme hardship" or "good faith/good cause." . . .

In the case of the "extreme hardship waiver," the immigrant spouse had to demonstrate that extreme hardship would result from deportation, considering only those circumstances that arose during the period that the alien spouse was admitted for permanent residence on a conditional basis. Even if successful in demonstrating these facts, the immigrant spouse was not guaranteed a waiver; discretion was left to the INS. Some INS officials interpreted the extreme hardship waiver as not really applying to battered immigrant women because they suffered hardship in the United States and deportation would not likely increase the hardship they may suffer. This misguided view was prevalent among INS officials at the time who had no understanding of the dynamics of domestic violence and who had received no training on the issue. This INS opinion ignored the extreme hardship inherent in being a victim of ongoing and often escalating instances of domestic violence and the additional difficulties deportation posed for battered women. This approach did not recognize the extreme psychological harm that domestic violence causes, the effect that carrying out the abuser's threats of deportation can have on the victim and her children, and the harm to the battered immigrant survivor of domestic violence that can come from severing her from the counseling, support systems and legal protections she needs to overcome the physical and psychological injuries she has suffered as a result of the domestic violence perpetrated against her by her citizen or lawful permanent resident spouse.

Such views were also premised on the erroneous belief that deportation would bring an end to the domestic violence. This perception ran counter to experts' understanding of the dynamics of domestic violence. First, carrying out the deportation of an abused immigrant spouse or child made the government an accomplice in the abuse. Abusers of immigrant women use threats of deportation to prevent their victims from reporting the abuse and cooperating in prosecutions. When the government deports an abused spouse, government officials are in effect carrying out the abuser's threats.

Second, deporting an immigrant domestic violence victim does not keep the victim safe from ongoing abuse. Abusers who are citizens and lawful permanent residents may freely travel abroad at any time to any place. In many instances, these abusers will follow their victims to their home countries and continue the abuse in a place where there are often no laws or law enforcement efforts to stop them. In other cases, the abuser's family members in the home country continue to abuse and terrorize the domestic violence victim and her family members.

Finally, the societal cost of deporting immigrant domestic violence victims is high. . . . if battered immigrant spouses who report abuse are deported, word of these deportations will spread and will have a chilling effect on other immigrant victims of domestic violence, making them reluctant to seek any help from the justice system.

Adopting a similarly restrictive and arbitrary approach, the INS insisted that for an immigrant spouse to obtain lawful permanent residency under the "good faith, good cause" criterion, the immigrant spouse would have had to initiate divorce proceedings herself. This promoted a "race to the courthouse" between the immigrant wife seeking a waiver and the husband trying to block her ability to attain the waiver by being the one to initiate divorce proceedings. The immigrant spouse who married in good faith, but who had good cause to divorce because of the domestic violence could not obtain this waiver unless she won the race to the courthouse. This waiver, as implemented by the INS, did not take into consideration the difficulties involved in leaving an abusive marriage, finding a lawyer, and locating the financial resources to finance divorce litigation. If the battered immigrant lost the race to the courthouse, neither the fact that the battered immigrant woman lived in a state with no-fault divorce laws nor the fact that the husband was ultimately found to be at fault played any role in the immigration case if she did not initiate the divorce proceeding. . . .

### III. Recent Changes in United States Immigration Laws That Attempt to Decrease the Frequency of Domestic Abuse

#### A. 1990 Battered Spouse Waiver: Congress' First Attempt to Reform Immigration Laws to Offer Protection For Battered Immigrants

In 1990, Congress enacted the "battered spouse waiver," which was the first piece of legislation that recognized domestic violence as a problem experienced by immigrant wives dependent on their spouses for immigration status. . . . IMFA was amended to no longer require the immigrant spouse to be the one initiating divorce and to not require marriage termination for a "good cause." The battered spouse waiver further exempted immigrants, who were battered or subjected to extreme cruelty by their citizen or permanent resident spouse and who had already acquired their conditional residency, from the joint petitioning process.

The battered spouse waiver defined domestic violence as "battering or extreme cruelty." This definition of domestic violence was derived from the evolving international law definition of domestic violence, which included some forms of emotional abuse. This definition was more inclusive than the domestic violence definition used in most state protection orders and criminal domestic violence statutes, which only covered actions that violated criminal laws including threats, attempts, and violation of civil protection orders. The battered spouse waiver's definition of domestic violence was based on international rather than United States law. This is similar to the approach United States immigration law has taken in other contexts where protections are being offered for humanitarian reasons.

While the battered spouse waiver helped battered immigrant women and their children who were locked in abusive marriages for two years by the IMFA, problems remained. The 1990 law allowed the coverture-based control of the earlier immigration legislation to continue. An immigrant spouse still could become only a resident if her citizen or resident spouse sponsored her. If the citizen or resident spouse never initiated the immigration process for his immigrant spouse, or if he began the process and later withdrew the application, the battered immigrant spouse was barred from attaining legal immigration status without her abuser's help.

Additionally, the INS implemented the battered spouse waiver in an extremely narrow way. The INS required battered immigrants applying for battered spouse waivers based on extreme cruelty to submit, along with their application, evidence from a licensed mental health professional. Since the number of mental health professionals with training on domestic violence is very low, and the number who also are bilingual and bicultural are even lower, few battered immigrant spouses were able to obtain the required mental health professional evaluation. Those living in communities where such mental health services existed were often barred access because they could not muster the financial resources to pay for the required mental health evaluation. This mental health expert requirement focused on the victim's injuries rather than abuser's actions and severely limited the number of battered immigrants who had suffered extreme cruelty to be granted the relief.

. . . .

## II. The Violence Against Women Act and Immigration Reform

With the passage of the first Violence Against Women Act in 1994, Congress brought improvements to the lives of battered immigrant women. Most importantly, it became the first step in the long process of severing the tie linking the immigration status of domestic violence sufferers to their abusers. The following article explains the impact on immigration issues of the early versions of VAWA.

### Sarah M. Wood, Note: *Queer Theory, Feminism, and the Law: VAWA's Unfinished Business: The Immigrant Women Who Fall Through the Cracks*
11 Duke J. Gender L. & Pol'y 141 (2004)

. . . .

E. The Violence Against Women Act

With the Violence Against Women Act of 1994 (VAWA 1994), Congress sought to address some of the inequities inherent in U.S. Immigration law as part of its larger goal of preventing violence against women. The immigration provisions of VAWA 1994 were specifically directed toward offering greater protection and benefits for battered immigrant women and children than the 1990 amendments provided. First . . . the new law allowed battered immigrants married to citizens or lawful permanent residents to self-petition for permanent resident status, provided the marriage was entered into in good faith and deportation would result in extreme hardship to the immigrant or her child. In addition, the immigrant must have demonstrated good moral character. During the marriage, the petitioning immigrant or her child must have been battered by a spouse who is a U.S. citizen or permanent resident, and the battered immigrant must have resided with the battering spouse.

Second, another provision lowered the evidentiary burden placed on the immigrant when submitted a petition. Prior to VAWA, battered spouses were required by federal regulations to submit an "evaluation of a professional recognized by the Service as an expert in the field." While that requirement remains in the Code of Federal Regulations, in VAWA 1994 Congress directed the Attorney General, as head of the INS, to "consider any credible evidence relevant to the application. The determination of what evidence is credible and the weight to be given that evidence shall be within the sole discretion of the Attorney General."

Third, VAWA 1994 also created a special means of suspension of deportation for battered spouses and children. The statute provided that deportation be suspended for an immigrant who:

> has been physically present in the United States for a continuous period of not less than 3 years immediately preceding the date of such application; has been battered or subjected to extreme cruelty in the United States by a spouse or parent who is a United States citizen or lawful permanent resident (or is the parent of a child of a United States citizen or lawful permanent resident parent); and proves that during all of such time in the United States the alien was and is a person of good moral character; and is a person whose deportation would, in the opinion of the Attorney General, result in extreme hardship to the alien or the alien's parent or child.

Other noncitizens seeking to cancel removal (suspend deportation) must demonstrate that deportation will result in hardship to the noncitizen's U.S. citizen or permanent resident child or parent. Battered immigrants, however, may demonstrate hardship to themselves or to immediate relatives who need not be citizens or lawful permanent residents.

. . . .

### III. VAWA 2000 Reforms

. . . .

#### A. Expanded Availability of Self-Petition

VAWA 2000 addressed the problem of battered immigrants who were no longer married to their batterers by allowing divorced women and widows to self-petition within two years of divorce or death. In the case of divorce, the noncitizen must demonstrate a connection between the abuse and the termination of the marriage. VAWA 2000 also amended the immigration statute to allow for self-petition by women who married bigamists in good faith, provided that the bigamist spouse is a U.S. citizen. If the batterer lost his citizenship or permanent resident status as a result of the abuse, through a criminal conviction, for example, the statute permits the battered spouse to self-petition if her "spouse lost or renounced citizenship status within the past 2 years related to an incident of domestic violence." All of these provisions have enabled greater numbers of battered immigrants to seek relief through self-petition.

#### B. Lower Burden of Proof and Removal of the "Extreme Hardship" Requirement

VAWA 2000 reiterated the provision of VAWA 1994 that required the Attorney General to consider "any credible evidence relevant to the application. . . ." The Senate conference report on VAWA 2000 explains that this provision of the statute:

> allows abused spouses and children who have already demonstrated to the INS that they have been the victims of battery or extreme cruelty by their spouse or parent to file their own petition for a lawful permanent resident visa without also having to show they will suffer "extreme hardship" if

forced to leave the U.S., a showing that it is not required if their citizen or lawful permanent resident spouse or parent files the visa petition on their behalf. . . .

### C. Modified "Good Moral Character" Requirement

VAWA 2000 authorizes the Attorney General to consider that a battered immigrant has shown "good moral character" despite having been convicted of crimes related to her abuse, provided that she has not been the "primary perpetrator of violence in the relationship[,]" that she has acted in self-defense, that she has not violated a protective order designed to protect her, and that the crime did not result in serious bodily injury. This provision allows a battered spouse to defend herself against abuse without the fear that by doing so she is jeopardizing her immigration status.

### D. Creation of the U Visa

Finally, Congress created the U visa in VAWA 2000 in order to facilitate prosecution of crimes of domestic violence and in order to protect "trafficked, exploited, victimized, and abused aliens who are not in lawful immigration status" from removal as long as they cooperate with law enforcement. The visa is available to those noncitizens who have "suffered substantial physical or mental abuse" as a result of criminal activities including rape, torture, trafficking, incest, domestic violence, sexual assault, prostitution, kidnaping, or murder, among many others. The U visa petitioner must obtain a certification from law enforcement that he or she "has been helpful, is being helpful, or is likely to be helpful in the investigation or prosecution of criminal activity." . . .

## III. Further VAWA Improvements

In yet another version of VAWA, passed at the end of 2005 and signed into law by President Bush on January 5, 2006, additional improvements were implemented in immigration law and policy for battered women. Under the Act, the U.S. Department of Homeland Security, which now oversees immigration matters, can no longer seize victims of domestic violence from shelters, rape crisis centers and courts where orders of protection are issued, in order to deport them. It provided that removal of a victim of domestic violence would be stayed pending final disposition of her case — including exhaustion of all appeals — as long as her moving papers establish a *prima facie* case.

Further, VAWA 2005 extended U Visa protection to children of U Visa recipients without having to obtain government certification that a criminal investigation would be hindered without the assistance of the child. It also extends self-petitioning rights to elder abuse victims and adoptive children who have not resided with the parents who battered them for two years prior to their applications, and it continues VAWA immigration protection to abused children beyond age 21. VAWA 2005 protected the confidentiality of domestic violence victims so their abusers would not learn of their efforts to self-petition. In addition, the law assured that attorneys paid through the federal Legal Services Corporation would be permitted to represent domestic violence victims in immigration proceedings.

The latest version of VAWA, signed into law by President Obama on March 7, 2013, further strengthens the Visa protections by retroactively allowing derivative child U Visa applicants to continue to be classified as children, even if they turn 21 during the application process; the retroactivity period goes back to the creation of the U Visa in 2000. It expands the opportunity to apply for U Visas to victims of stalking. Normally, those seeking permanent entrance in the United States must certify they will not become public charges; that requirement is not necessary for victims of domestic violence who are self-petitioners, U Visa filers or seekers of battered spouse waivers. Additionally, the new law regulates international marriage brokers for so-called "Mail-Order Brides," by requiring that anyone seeking a foreign wife be subject to criminal background checks. Whatever information is obtained pursuant to that check must be made available to the immigrant fiancée.

## IV. Immigration Law in Context

As you read the following materials, keep in mind the volume of cases the Bureau of Immigration and Customs Enforcement (BICE), formerly known as the Immigration and Naturalization Service (INS), is responsible for overseeing. In 2014, there were 1,016,518 immigrants who entered the United States. Immigration officials apprehended 679,996 immigrants who were subject to removal in 2014 and ultimately 414,481 were removed.[2]

Before reading the cases about immigration and domestic violence issues, you must consider first whether the definition of "extreme cruelty" is considered discretionary or non-discretionary. The answer depends on the jurisdiction in which the case is being heard.

### Johnson v. Attorney General
United States Court of Appeals, Third Circuit
602 F.3d 508 (2010)

SLOVITER, CIRCUIT JUDGE.

Petitioner Wilfred Johnson, a citizen of Guyana, petitions for review of an order of the Board of Immigration Appeals ("BIA") affirming the decision by the Immigration Judge ("IJ") to deny his application for cancellation of removal under 240A(b)(2) of the Immigration and Nationality Act, 8 U.S.C. § 1229b(b)(2). We will dismiss for lack of jurisdiction.

#### I.
#### BACKGROUND

Johnson is a native and citizen of Guyana who entered the United States in or about March 1995, without inspection. In February 2003, Johnson married a United States

---

2. U.S. Dep't of Homeland Security, YEARBOOK OF IMMIGRATION STATISTICS: 2014, at 5, 91, and 103.

citizen, with whom he has two young children. Johnson's wife filed and obtained approval of an Alien Relative Petition, which permitted his presence in the United States.

After briefly returning to Guyana, Johnson returned and was paroled into the United States in July 2005 as an applicant for legal permanent residence. However, by March 2006, Johnson's marriage began to deteriorate and he left the marital home. Meanwhile, Johnson's wife withdrew the Alien Relative Petition, commenced divorce proceedings, and obtained a restraining order preventing Johnson from visiting his young children.

Based on the allegations made by Johnson's wife in obtaining the restraining order, he was taken into custody by the Bureau of Immigration and Customs Enforcement ("ICE"). While in custody, Johnson was served with a Notice to Appear and charged with removability "in that [he] was not in possession of a valid unexpired immigrant Visa, reentry permit, border crossing card, or valid entry document required by the Immigration and Nationality Act." App. at 44. The IJ deemed Johnson "removable pursuant to the charge set forth in the Notice to Appear." App. at 47.

About one month later, Johnson filed an application in the Immigration Court for cancellation of removal under the Special Rule for Battered Spouses. *See* 8 U.S.C. § 1229b(b)(2).

Thereafter, the Immigration Court had a hearing at which Johnson testified in support of his application. He testified that his wife mistreated him by making baseless allegations against him and depriving him of access to their two children. Johnson claimed that his wife's actions amounted to extreme cruelty and that if he is subject to removal, his children will suffer.

The IJ denied Johnson's application for cancellation of removal. The BIA affirmed and dismissed Johnson's appeal. Johnson then petitioned this court to review the BIA's order.

## II.
## ANALYSIS

Johnson contends that "[t]he BIA has failed to meet its statutory duty in reviewing the IJ's decision." Pet'r's Br. at 6. The IJ found that Johnson had not established that he was battered by his wife, subjected to extreme cruelty by her, or that his removal would result in extreme hardship to himself, his children, or his wife. The BIA affirmed the IJ on the ground that Johnson "did not establish that he has been battered" by his wife. App. at 2.

Before reaching the merits of Johnson's claims, we must have jurisdiction to review the determinations of the IJ and BIA. Our jurisdiction is limited by section 242 of the INA, 8 U.S.C. § 1252(a)(2)(B)(i), which provides that "any judgment regarding the granting of relief under . . . [8 U.S.C. § 1229b]" is not subject to judicial review. Courts have interpreted a "judgment" as a discretionary decision. It is settled in this circuit that we lack jurisdiction over discretionary decisions regarding the granting of relief under 8 U.S.C. § 1229b. *See Mendez-Moranchel v. Ashcroft*, 338 F.3d 176, 178-79 (3d

Cir. 2003) (finding that "[t]he determination of whether the alien has established the requisite hardship is a quintessential discretionary judgment" and not reviewable). However, we may review "constitutional claims or questions of law raised upon a petition for review ...." 8 U.S.C. § 1252(a)(2)(D).

In his brief, the Attorney General focuses on our lack of jurisdiction to review the "inherently subjective and therefore discretionary" decisions as to "extreme cruelty." Resp't's Br. at 5. We have not yet decided whether an IJ's determination that a petitioner was subjected to "extreme cruelty" is a discretionary decision. Four of the five circuits that have addressed this precise question have held that the extreme cruelty determination is discretionary and not subject to judicial review. *See Stepanovic v. Filip*, 554 F.3d 673, 680 (7th Cir. 2009); *Wilmore v. Gonzales*, 455 F.3d 524, 528 (5th Cir. 2006); *Perales-Cumpean v. Gonzales*, 429 F.3d 977, 982 (10th Cir. 2005); *but see Hernandez v. Ashcroft*, 345 F.3d 824, 833-35 (9th Cir. 2003) (holding that the extreme cruelty determination is nondiscretionary and therefore reviewable).

We agree with the majority. Congress has not defined "extreme cruelty" or provided a legal standard for determining its existence for the purposes of 1229b(b)(2). However, the Department of Homeland Security ("DHS") promulgated a regulation that defines "battery or extreme cruelty" as:

> includ[ing], but ... not limited to, being the victim of any act or threatened act of violence, including any forceful detention, which results or threatens to result in physical or mental injury. Psychological or sexual abuse or exploitation, including rape, molestation, incest (if the victim is a minor), or forced prostitution shall be considered acts of violence. Other abusive actions may also be acts of violence under certain circumstances, including acts that, in and of themselves, may not initially appear violent but that are a part of an overall pattern of violence.

8 C.F.R. § 204.2(c)(1)(vi) (2006).

In its holding that the determination of extreme cruelty was discretionary, which deprived it of jurisdiction to review a cancellation of removal under § 1229b(b)(2), the Tenth Circuit stated that the definition of "battery or extreme cruelty" requires "consideration of many discretionary factors." *Perales-Cumpean*, 429 F.3d at 984. Of special importance to the Tenth Circuit's analysis was the language in the DHS regulation that "battery or extreme cruelty includes, but is not limited to" and "may ... be acts of violence under certain circumstances," phrases which that court concluded provided "[c]onsiderable discretion." *Id.*

Similarly the Fifth Circuit found that "[a]lthough the extreme cruelty definition provides some guidance ..., it ... does not remove the discretion afforded by Congress." *Wilmore*, 455 F.3d at 528. Following that line of authority, the Seventh Circuit found the matter discretionary, reasoning that the "IJ must determine the facts of a particular case, make a judgment call as to whether those facts constitute cruelty, and, if so, whether the cruelty rises to ... a level that it can ... be described as extreme." *Stepanovic*, 554 F.3d at 680.

These analyses are persuasive. In this case, the IJ had to determine whether the allegations Johnson's wife made against him in the divorce proceedings and in seeking a restraining order, as well as her deprivation of Johnson's access to his children, amounted to extreme cruelty. There is no objective standard by which this can be determined. "[A]n IJ does not determine extreme cruelty by simply plugging facts into a formula or applying an algorithm." *Stepanovic*, 554 F.3d at 680 (citation omitted). We also agree with the Fifth Circuit's conclusion that the term "extreme cruelty" is discretionary because it is "not self-explanatory and . . . reasonable men could differ as to its meaning." *Wilmore*, 455 F.3d at 527.

Johnson relies on *Hernandez*, where the Ninth Circuit held that extreme cruelty is nondiscretionary because it is a "measure of domestic violence that can . . . be assessed on the basis of objective standards." 345 F.3d at 834. However, that case analyzed an antecedent, albeit similar, statute that Congress has since repealed. One of the factors considered relevant by the Ninth Circuit was that the "extreme hardship" determination (as opposed to the extreme cruelty determination) was "specifically committed to 'the opinion of the Attorney General.'" *Id*. That provision does not appear in the current statute. Ultimately, though, we find the Ninth Circuit's reasoning less persuasive than that of the Tenth, Fifth, and Seventh Circuits.

Rather than focusing on whether or not "extreme cruelty" is a discretionary determination, Johnson seeks to cast his claims in legal and constitutional terms. As the Seventh Circuit stated, "[a] petitioner may not create the jurisdiction that Congress chose to remove simply by cloaking an . . . argument in constitutional garb . . . ." *Zamora-Mallari v. Mukasey*, 514 F.3d 679, 694 (7th Cir. 2008) (internal quotation marks and citation omitted). That is exactly what Johnson seeks to do. He cites no law that would support his position that the BIA's denial of his motion implicates legal or constitutional principles.

Even were we to assume jurisdiction, we would not be persuaded by Johnson's claim that merely amounts to a disagreement with the IJ's conclusion that his wife's treatment did not amount to extreme cruelty. We find nothing inadequate about the BIA's review of the IJ's decision.

Lastly, Johnson contends that the BIA's failure to address the potential hardship to his children raises a "colorable question of law." Pet'r's Br. at 13. This argument lacks merit. As the Attorney General notes, "the elements necessary to demonstrate eligibility for cancellation [of removal] are conjunctive [such that] . . . Johnson's inability to demonstrate extreme cruelty precludes him from" relief under the extreme hardship provision. Resp't's Br. at 20 n.7. Once it found the IJ's extreme cruelty determination to be sound, no further review was warranted by the BIA. . . .

---

The following case was the one found not to be persuasive by the Third Circuit in the *Johnson* case excerpted above.

## Hernandez v. Ashcroft
United States Court of Appeals, Ninth Circuit
345 F.3d 824 (2003)

PAEZ, CIRCUIT JUDGE:

While living in Mexico, Laura Luis Hernandez ("Hernandez") experienced life-threatening violence at the hands of her husband, a legal permanent resident of the United States. She fled to the United States, but her husband tracked her down, promised not to hurt her again, and begged her to return to Mexico with him. After Hernandez submitted to his demand and returned to Mexico, the physical abuse began again.

Having escaped her husband permanently, and now living without legal status in the United States, Hernandez applied for suspension of deportation under a provision of the Violence Against Women Act of 1994 ("VAWA") intended to protect immigrants who have suffered domestic violence. With the passage of VAWA, Congress provided a mechanism for women who have been battered or subjected to extreme cruelty to achieve lawful immigration status independent of an abusive spouse. However, the Board of Immigration Appeals ("BIA") affirmed the immigration judge's ("IJ's") denial of Hernandez's application because it determined that Hernandez had not "been battered or subjected to extreme cruelty *in the United States*," as the statute then required....

As a preliminary matter, we hold that we have jurisdiction to consider the BIA's determination that Hernandez was not subjected to extreme cruelty in the United States. We next turn to the merits of Hernandez's claim of eligibility for suspension of deportation. We interpret the phrase "extreme cruelty" as a matter of first impression. In so doing, we give deference to a regulation promulgated by the Immigration and Naturalization Service ("INS"), and conduct our inquiry in a manner mindful of Congress's intent that domestic violence be evaluated in the context of professional and clinical understandings of violence within intimate relationships. Although Hernandez was not battered in the United States, the interaction that took place in the United States presents a well-recognized stage within the cycle of violence, one which is both psychologically and practically crucial to maintaining the batterer's control. We conclude that an abuser's behavior during the "contrite" phase of domestic violence may, and in circumstances such as those present here does, constitute "extreme cruelty." Thus, we conclude that Hernandez suffered extreme cruelty in the United States, and we determine that the BIA erred by denying her application for suspension of deportation under VAWA....

. . . .

Accordingly, we grant the petition for review and remand for further proceedings.

### I.
### BACKGROUND

Hernandez was thirty years old when she met her future husband, Refugio Acosta Gonzalez ("Refugio"), early in 1990. Refugio frequently ate at a restaurant where

Hernandez worked in Mexicali, and after a short while they began dating. Initially, the relationship seemed idyllic. Hernandez believed that Refugio "was a marvelous person, a good person.... he used to give me flowers.... everything was marvelous." After dating for a few months, the two decided to move in together. Several months later, "we were already in love and he asked me to get married." They were married in October 1990, in a small civil ceremony with a few friends present. After the wedding, they continued living in the same apartment in Mexicali.

Following the marriage, however, Refugio's behavior changed drastically. He began drinking heavily and verbally abusing Hernandez, and ultimately began physically abusing her as well. Although the verbal and physical abuse appear to have been constant throughout the marriage, Hernandez described several specific instances of particularly serious physical assault.

On the first occasion, a few months after their marriage, Refugio and Hernandez had gone to the movies. They became separated, and Hernandez was unable to find Refugio. After searching for him without success, she returned home and went to sleep. She was awakened some time later by the shattering of the bedroom window above her head. Refugio entered the darkened room through the broken window, landing on Hernandez. Seeing her, Refugio lifted her by her hair and threw her forcefully against the wall. Hernandez lay where she fell, stunned. Refugio stumbled drunkenly into the kitchen, seized a chair, and broke it across Hernandez's back. He continued hitting and kicking her while uttering insults and other verbal abuse.

. . . .

In December of 1992 another violent assault occurred. Intoxicated, Refugio broke through the mosquito netting of the kitchen window while Hernandez was sleeping, and again attacked her. He smashed a pedestal fan over her head, breaking it on her forehead.

Hernandez was convinced that Refugio intended to kill her. She was afraid to return to her family in Mexico, because Refugio knew where they lived, and she feared he would follow her and kill her. With the help of a neighbor, Hernandez fled to the United States, to the home of her sister who lived in Los Angeles. However, after two weeks Refugio convinced the neighbor to give him the telephone number of Hernandez's sister. Refugio began calling every day. . . .

Refugio came to Los Angeles. He told Hernandez that "if I would go back with him he would look for a marriage counselor so that we could save our marriage, because he didn't want to lose me and I also didn't want to leave him." Hernandez believed him, particularly because he had never previously raised the possibility of seeking professional help. Still loving him, and believing his remorse and his promises to change, she returned to Mexico with him.

Upon their return, Hernandez found a marriage counselor. However, despite his earlier promise, Refugio refused to see the counselor. After a brief period, Refugio's violence returned.

The violence culminated several months later when Refugio came home drunk one evening. He beat Hernandez savagely, broke the windows in the house, and destroyed all of the furniture. After the beating, Hernandez "stayed in the corner sitting there in the corner, because I was very hurt." The next morning, Hernandez arose and began cooking breakfast. Behaving as though nothing had occurred, Refugio got up and began helping her. Then, suddenly, Refugio lunged at her with the knife he was using to chop vegetables. Sensing the attack, Hernandez blocked the knife thrust with her arm as Refugio attempted to stab her in the back. The knife gouged Hernandez's hand, slicing through to the bone.

Despite the severity of the wound, Hernandez was unable to go to the hospital to treat the injury. Instead, Refugio kept her trapped inside the house for two days. During these two days, Refugio stayed home with her, no longer beating her. On the third day Refugio returned to work, but he placed a padlock on the front door in order to keep Hernandez locked in the house while he was gone. However, Hernandez had an extra key to the padlock, and she was able to attract the attention of a passing neighbor. She slid the key under the door, and the neighbor unlocked the padlock and released her.

Hernandez went straight to the hospital to get treatment for her hand, but the delay in treatment had resulted in permanent damage to the nerves. The hand continues to give Hernandez great pain, and her use of it is restricted. At the hearing, Hernandez showed the IJ a scar approximately an inch and a half long on her right hand between her index finger and thumb.

In fear for her life, Hernandez again fled to the United States. She did not return to her sister's house, because Refugio knew its location....

A year later, in Salinas, she met Paulino Garcia, now her domestic partner, who "has helped me economically and morally with all the problems that I have suffered from my—from the abuse of my—the constant abuse that I suffer from my husband." In 1995, she and Paulino attempted to go to Alaska to work on a fishing boat, but Hernandez was intercepted by the INS at the airport and deportation proceedings were initiated against her.

Hernandez is still married to Refugio, but she has not had any contact with him and does not want him to find her. She believes that if she were required to return to Mexico, Refugio would find her and kill her.

. . . .

*Procedural Background*

Hernandez was served with an Order to Show Cause on June 8, 1995. She appeared before an IJ, represented by an attorney from the Northwest Immigrant Rights Project, and conceded deportability. Her attorney informed the court that she wished to seek two forms of relief: suspension of deportation under VAWA, and adjustment of status based upon an I-130 petition filed by her husband.

Following a hearing, the IJ issued a written opinion, finding Hernandez's testimony to lack credibility due to inconsistencies and the absence of corroborating testimony. The IJ denied her application for suspension of deportation because she had failed to prove she was a victim of domestic violence, and denied her application for adjustment of status because there was no evidence showing that the I-130 application had been approved.

On appeal, the BIA reversed the negative credibility determination, which it determined was unfounded. Nonetheless, the BIA affirmed the IJ's denial of both suspension of deportation and adjustment of status. With regard to the application for suspension of deportation under VAWA, the BIA determined that Hernandez met the three-year continuous physical presence requirement and the good moral character requirement. However, the BIA concluded that because the acts of physical violence occurred in Mexico, Hernandez was unable to show that she was "battered or subjected to extreme cruelty in the United States," as required by the 1994 version of the statute. Due to this conclusion, the BIA did not consider whether Hernandez had demonstrated extreme hardship.

. . . .

### III.
### SUSPENSION OF DEPORTATION UNDER VAWA

Hernandez applied for suspension of deportation under section 244(a)(3) of the Immigration and Naturalization Act (INA), 8 U.S.C. § 1254(a)(3) (1996) (now amended and recodified). The former section 244 of the INA provided a method for certain aliens to establish eligibility for a discretionary suspension of deportation and obtain a grant of lawful status. Section 244(a)(3) was added to the INA as part of the passage of the Violence Against Women Act of 1994, in order to assist certain immigrants suffering from domestic violence. This provision provided that the Attorney General had the discretion to suspend deportation proceedings against an individual who:

> 1) has been physically present in the United States for a continuous period of not less than 3 years immediately preceding the date of such application;
>
> 2) has been battered or subjected to extreme cruelty in the United States by a spouse or parent who is a United States citizen or lawful permanent resident;
>
> 3) proves that during all of such time in the United States the alien was and is a person of good moral character;
>
> 4) and is a person whose deportation would, in the opinion of the Attorney General, result in extreme hardship to the alien or the alien's parent or child.

*Id.* Hernandez bears the burden of establishing each of these four factors in order to qualify for suspension of deportation under section 244(a)(3). The BIA concluded that Hernandez had established both continuous physical presence and good moral character, the first and third prongs. Hernandez asks us to reverse the BIA's determination that she did not "suffer extreme cruelty in the United States."

A. Jurisdiction

The INS raises an initial challenge to our jurisdiction to review the BIA's determination that Hernandez did not suffer extreme cruelty in the United States. Certain prongs of the determination regarding eligibility for suspension of deportation involve nondiscretionary determinations and others involve discretionary determinations. *Kalaw v. INS*, 133 F.3d 1147, 1150–52 (9th Cir. 1997). As explained in more detail below, our jurisdiction turns upon whether the determination that an applicant was not subjected to extreme cruelty is deemed to be discretionary or nondiscretionary.

. . . .

In assessing whether a particular element is discretionary or nondiscretionary, we consider a number of factors. We have noted that determinations that "require application of law to factual determinations" are nondiscretionary. *Id.* at 1150. We concluded, for example, that continuous physical presence fell into this category, because it "must be determined from the facts, not through an exercise of discretion." *Id.* at 1151; *see also Montero-Martinez v. Ashcroft*, 277 F.3d 1137, 1141 (9th Cir. 2002) (holding that the element of the "exceptional and extremely unusual hardship" determination that involves the factual determination of whether an adult daughter is a child is nondiscretionary because it only "requires us to review the BIA's construction of the INA, which is a pure question of law. This question would not require us to review a discretionary determination by the BIA.").

Similarly, extreme cruelty involves a question of fact, determined through the application of legal standards. Section 244(a)(3) introduces battery and extreme cruelty as parallel methods by which an individual may establish that she has experienced domestic violence. *See* INA § 244(a)(3) (requiring that applicant "has been battered or subjected to extreme cruelty"). The existence or nonexistence of battery is clearly a factual determination, readily resolved by the application of a legal standard defining battery to the facts in question. Extreme cruelty provides an inquiry into an individual's experience of mental or psychological cruelty, an alternative measure of domestic violence that can also be assessed on the basis of objective standards. . . .

The text of the statute, which in some provisions "itself commits the determination to 'the opinion of the Attorney General,'" also supports our conclusion that extreme cruelty is a nondiscretionary decision. *Id.* at 1152. Unlike the inquiry into "extreme hardship," which is specifically committed to "the opinion of the Attorney General," nothing in the text of the statute indicates that the phrase at issue is discretionary. It is a basic principle of statutory construction that "where Congress includes particular language in one section of the statute but omits it in another section of the same Act, . . . Congress acts intentionally and purposely in the disparate inclusion or exclusion." *Andreiu v. Ashcroft*, 253 F.3d 477, 480 (9th Cir. 2001) (en banc) (quoting *INS v. Cardoza-Fonseca*, 480 U.S. 421, 432, 94 L. Ed. 2d 434, 107 S. Ct. 1207 (1987) (alteration omitted)). . . .

### B. Extreme Cruelty

There is no dispute that the egregious abuse that Hernandez suffered in Mexico would qualify as battery or extreme cruelty. However, it is also clear that none of the acts of battery that occurred took place in the United States. Although Congress has since removed the requirement that an alien must have suffered from domestic abuse within the United States, Hernandez's case is subject to an older version of VAWA, which did include this requirement. 8 U.S.C. § 1254(a)(3) (1996). Thus, the question presented is whether the actions taken by Refugio in seeking to convince Hernandez to leave her safe haven in the United States in which she had taken refuge can be deemed to constitute extreme cruelty.[3]

#### 1) Refugio's Behavior in the Context of Domestic Violence

Hernandez and amici argue that the interaction between Hernandez and Refugio in Los Angeles made up an integral stage in the cycle of domestic violence, and thus the actions taken by Refugio in order to lure Hernandez back to the violent relationship constitute extreme cruelty. Although according to common understanding, Refugio's actions might not be perceived as cruel, in enacting VAWA, Congress recognized that lay understandings of domestic violence are frequently comprised of "myths, misconceptions, and victim blaming attitudes," and that background information regarding domestic violence may be crucial in order to understand its essential characteristics and manifestations. H.R. Rep. No. 103-395, at 24. Thus, in order to evaluate Hernandez's argument, we must first consider the nature and effects of violence in intimate relationships.

The field of domestic violence and our own case law reflect the fact that Refugio's actions represent a specific phase that commonly recurs in abusive relationships. Abuse within intimate relationships often follows a pattern known as the cycle of violence, "which consists of a tension building phase, followed by acute battering of the victim, and finally by a contrite phase where the batterer's use of promises and gifts increases the battered woman's hope that violence has occurred for the last time." Mary Ann Dutton, *Understanding Women's Responses to Domestic Violence: A Redefinition of Battered Woman Syndrome*, 21 Hofstra L. Rev. 1191, 1208 (1993); Evan Stark, *Re-Presenting Women Battering: From Battered Woman Syndrome to Coercive Control*, 58 Alb. L. Rev. 973, 985–86 (1995).... Indeed, Hernandez's relationship with Refugio

---

3. [n10] The INS contends that neither Refugio's actions in incessantly calling Hernandez's sister's home from Mexico nor his representations in the course of his telephone conversation with Hernandez are relevant to the question of whether extreme cruelty occurred in the United States, because Refugio was in Mexico when these actions took place. However, the statutory text demonstrates that it is Hernandez's location, not Refugio's, which is significant: the question is whether *Hernandez* was "*subjected to* extreme cruelty in the United States." INA § 244(a)(3) (emphasis added). Clearly, actions taken by a person in one location may subject a person in another location to extreme cruelty. *Cf. United States v. Haggard*, 41 F.3d 1320, 1323–24, 1328 (9th Cir. 1994) (holding that family of kidnaped child in California was subjected to extreme cruelty by false claim of individual in Indiana to know location of child's dead body). Thus, we consider actions taken by Refugio in Mexico in determining whether Hernandez experienced extreme cruelty in the United States.

reflected just such a cycle: as described in Hernandez's testimony, following each violent episode, Refugio would for a time again become the man she had loved.

The literature also emphasizes that, although a relationship may appear to be predominantly tranquil and punctuated only infrequently by episodes of violence, "abusive behavior does not occur as a series of discrete events," but rather pervades the entire relationship. Dutton, *supra*, at 1208. The effects of psychological abuse, coercive behavior, and the ensuing dynamics of power and control mean that "the pattern of violence and abuse can be viewed as a single and continuing entity." *Id.*; *see also* Stark, *supra*, at 985–86. Thus, "the battered woman's fear, vigilance, or perception that she has few options may persist, . . . even when the abusive partner appears to be peaceful and calm." Dutton, *supra*, at 1208–09. The psychological role of kindness is also significant in understanding the impact of Refugio's actions on Hernandez, since in combination with the batterer's physical dominance, such kindness often creates an intense emotional dependence by the battered woman on the batterer. *Id.* at 1206, 1225. Significantly, research also shows that women are often at the highest risk of severe abuse or death when they attempt to leave their abusers. *Id.* at 1212; *see also* H.R. Rep. 103-395, at 24.

Although the INS implies otherwise, the record before the IJ and BIA contained substantial evidence regarding the cycle of violence and clinical and psychological understandings of domestic violence, evidence that was entirely unrebutted. . . .

Understood in light of the familiar dynamics of violent relationships, Refugio's seemingly reasonable actions take on a sinister cast. Following Refugio's brutal and potentially deadly beating, Hernandez fled her job, home, country, and family. Hernandez believed that if she had not fled, Refugio would have killed her. Unwilling to lose control over Hernandez, Refugio stalked her, convincing the very neighbor who helped Hernandez to escape to give him her phone number and calling her sister repeatedly until Hernandez finally agreed to speak with him. Once Refugio was able to speak with Hernandez, he emanated remorse, crying and telling Hernandez that he needed her. Refugio promised not to hurt Hernandez again, and told her that if she would go back to him he would seek counseling. Wounded both emotionally and physically by someone she trusted and loved, Hernandez was vulnerable to such promises. Moreover, Hernandez was well aware of Refugio's potential for violence. Behind Refugio's show of remorse, there also existed the lurking possibility that if Hernandez adamantly refused, Refugio might resort to the extreme violence or murder that commonly results when a woman attempts to flee her batterer. Refugio successfully manipulated Hernandez into leaving the safety that she had found and returning to a deadly relationship in which her physical and mental well-being were in danger.

2) Statutory Analysis of "Extreme Cruelty"

No court has yet interpreted the meaning of 8 U.S.C. § 1254(a)(3)'s reference to extreme cruelty. "We interpret a federal statute by ascertaining the intent of Congress and by giving effect to its legislative will." *Bedroc,* 314 F.3d at 1083 (quoting *Ariz. Appetito's Stores, Inc. v. Paradise Vill.*, 893 F.2d 216, 219 (9th Cir. 1990)). The text of the statute reveals that Congress distinguished between "battery" and "extreme cruelty," reserving the term extreme cruelty for something other than physical assault, presumably actions in some way involving mental or psychological cruelty. A contrary interpretation would render section 244's reference to "extreme cruelty" redundant, violating elementary principles of statutory construction. *See, e.g., id.* at 1088. . . .

However, because the text of the statute provides no further elucidation regarding Congress's intent, we must "look to the congressional intent revealed in the history and purposes of the statutory scheme." *Id.* (quoting *United States v. Buckland*, 289 F.3d 558, 565 (9th Cir. 2002) (en banc)). The legislative history reflects Congress's conviction that "current [immigration] law fosters domestic violence," H.R. Rep. No. 103-395, at 26, and its intent that VAWA be so interpreted as to remedy the widespread gender bias and ignorance that have resulted in governmental harm, rather than help, for survivors of domestic violence, *see* H.R. Rep. No. 103-395. However, the legislative history does not contain any explicit consideration of the phrase in question, and thus is of limited aid in interpreting Congress's intent with regard to the breadth of extreme cruelty.

. . . The INS has promulgated a regulation defining battery and extreme cruelty in the context of VAWA self petitions, a regulation that lends support to Hernandez's contention that she was subjected to extreme cruelty by Refugio's "contrite" actions. Because the statutory text at issue is subject to a number of possible interpretations, the regulation promulgated by the INS interpreting this language is accorded *Chevron* deference. *Chevron*, 467 U.S. at 843 ("If . . . the court determines Congress has not directly addressed the precise question at issue . . . the question for the court is whether the agency's answer is based on a permissible construction of the statute.").

The regulation states in relevant part:

> For the purpose of this chapter, the phrase "was battered by or was the subject of extreme cruelty" includes, but is not limited to, being the victim of any act or threatened act of violence, including any forceful detention, which results or threatens to result in physical or mental injury. Psychological or sexual abuse . . . shall be considered acts of violence. *Other abusive actions may also be acts of violence under certain circumstances, including acts that, in and of themselves, may not initially appear violent but that are a part of an overall pattern of violence.*

8 C.F.R. § 204.2(c)(1)(vi) (emphasis added).

. . . .

Here, there is no question that the relationship between Hernandez and Refugio was a violent one. Hernandez's interaction with Refugio in the United States clearly occurred within this context, an observation reaffirmed by the fact that domestic violence is not a phenomenon that appears only at brief isolated times, but instead pervades an entire relationship. *See* Dutton, *supra*, at 1208. Refugio's success in this "contrite" or "hearts and flowers" phase occurred because of Hernandez's emotional vulnerability, the strong emotional bond to Refugio necessitated by his violence, and the underlying threat that the failure to accede to his demands would bring renewed violence. Against this violent backdrop, Refugio's actions in tracking Hernandez down and luring her from the safety of the United States through false promises and short-lived contrition are precisely the type of acts of extreme cruelty that "may not initially appear violent but that are part of an overall pattern of violence." 8 C.F.R. § 204.2(c)(1)(vi). As a result, we hold that Hernandez has established that she was subjected to extreme cruelty in the United States. . . .

---

The extreme cruelty described in the *Hernandez* case was particularly egregious. And, while the judges agreed the term could encompass more than merely physical abuse, nonetheless there are limits. The following case is an example of those limits.

## Rosario v. Holder

United States Court of Appeals for the Second Circuit

627 F.3d 58 (2010)

DENNIS JACOBS, Chief Judge:

The Petitioner, Josefa Rosario, is a citizen of the Dominican Republic who seeks cancellation of removal as an abused spouse under the amended Immigration and Naturalization Act. 8 U.S.C. § 1229b(b)(2). An Immigration Judge ("IJ") found that Rosario was not "battered or subjected to extreme cruelty" within the meaning of the statute and therefore did not warrant discretionary cancellation of removal. The Board of Immigration Appeals ("BIA") affirmed. We dismiss Rosario's petition for lack of subject matter jurisdiction because the BIA's decision raises no constitutional claims or questions of law.

### BACKGROUND

Rosario was found credible by the IJ; we therefore adduce the facts to which she testified.

Rosario entered the United States on a one-month non-immigrant tourist visa in 1994. After overstaying by approximately two years, she married Pedro Martinez, a U.S. citizen, and petitioned to adjust her status to Legal Permanent Resident in 1996.

The marriage soured soon after the petition was filed, and Martinez became aggressive and insulting. There were approximately five incidents of physical abuse or intimidation in the three-month period between June 1997 and September 1997, when Martinez was jailed (for offenses unrelated to Rosario). There are no allegations of abuse after his release from prison in 2000.

During the incidents of abuse, Martinez (variously) grabbed Rosario by the arms and shoulders, shook her, verbally insulted her, and threw her on the bed. Martinez also demanded money from her and threatened to withdraw her application for a

Green Card. Rosario did not report these incidents to the police or seek medical attention.

During this time, Rosario's Green Card application languished, and, in 2000, it was denied as abandoned. In 2002, the Department of Homeland Security served Rosario with a Notice to Appear and charged her with removal.

At her Notice to Appear hearing, Rosario admitted she was in the U.S. illegally and conceded removability. Soon afterward, she filed a petition for Special Rule Cancellation of Removal under 8 U.S.C. § 1229b(b)(2)(A), which gives the Attorney General discretion to cancel the removal of an otherwise deportable alien who has been "battered or subjected to extreme cruelty" by her U.S. citizen spouse.

In 2008, an IJ denied Rosario's petition, concluding that she had not been "battered or subjected to extreme cruelty." Rosario appealed this decision to the BIA, which affirmed. Rosario now seeks review in this Court.

## DISCUSSION

### I.

As part of the 1994 Violence Against Women Act, Congress granted the Attorney General discretion to cancel the removal of otherwise deportable aliens who were found to have been "battered or subjected to extreme cruelty" by their U.S. citizen spouses. Pub. L. No. 103-322, § 40703, 108 Stat. 1796, 1955 (1994) (codified at 8 U.S.C. § 1229b(b)(2)(A))....

The determination as to whether an alien should be given this discretionary cancellation of removal is made by an IJ subject to appeal to the BIA. In 1996, Congress stripped the federal courts of jurisdiction to review these discretionary rulings. Illegal Immigration Reform and Immigrant ResponsibilityAct of 1996, Pub. L. No. 104-208, § 306, 110 Stat. 3009, 3009-607 (codified at 8 U.S.C. § 1252(a)(2)(B)(i)).

Concerned that a complete ban on judicial review of BIA determinations might violate the Suspension Clause, the Supreme Court in 2001 construed the jurisdictional ban to allow for limited federal court review of BIA decisions. *INS v. St. Cyr*, 533 U.S. 289, 307, 121 S. Ct. 2271, 150 L. Ed. 2d 347 (2001). Specifically, the Court held that even where the Attorney General had discretion over whether to grant cancellation of removal, the alien was nevertheless entitled to a determination of whether she was *eligible* for discretionary cancellation, and that this determination of eligibility was reviewable in the U.S. Circuit Courts when it was "governed by specific statutory standards." *Id.* Thus, while the federal courts retained jurisdiction to review the legal question of statutory eligibility, the Attorney General's exercise of discretion could not be second-guessed.

The REAL ID Act of 2005 amended the Illegal Immigration Reform and Immigrant Responsibility Act ("IIRIRA") to obviate the Supreme Court's Suspension Clause concerns. Pub. L. No. 109-13, § 106, 119 Stat. 231, 310 (codified in at 8 U.S.C. § 1252(a)(2)(D)); see also *Xiao Ji Chen v. Gonzales*, 471 F.3d 315, 326 (2d Cir. 2006) (describing legislative history of REAL ID Act). The REAL ID Act prescribed an exception to the general ban on judicial review of BIA decisions for Circuit Court review of "constitutional claims or questions of law." 8 U.S.C. § 1252(a)(2)(D).

In the wake of *St. Cyr* and the REAL ID Act, this Court described the scope of its jurisdiction to review BIA determinations in two ways. First, based on *St. Cyr*, we stated that we could review those "nondiscretionary decisions" by the BIA that underlie its exercise of discretion in granting or denying cancellation of removal. See, e.g., *Rodriguez v. Gonzales*, 451 F.3d 60, 62 (2d Cir. 2006) (describing scope of review as over nondiscretionary determinations underlying discretionary relief); *Sepulveda v. Gonzales*, 407 F.3d 59, 62-63 (2d Cir. 2005). Later, based on the REAL ID Act, we stated that we could review "all constitutional claims or questions of law" raised by the BIA's exercise of its discretion. See, e.g., *Argueta v. Holder*, 617 F.3d 109, 112 (2d Cir. 2010) (describing scope of review as over constitutional and legal questions). These two characterizations, which may appear to be two separate avenues of jurisdiction, are congruent: BIA statutory interpretation pursuant to an eligibility determination is nondiscretionary and therefore reviewable precisely because it presents a legal question. In contrast, the BIA's factfinding, factor-balancing, and exercise of discretion normally do not involve legal or constitutional questions, so we lack jurisdiction to review them.

II.

When the BIA's decision explicitly rests on a legal prescription or statutory interpretation, we unambiguously have jurisdiction to review it. See *Sepulveda*, 407 F.3d at 63 (holding that court has jurisdiction to review BIA determination that alien is ineligible for discretionary relief as a matter of law). Similarly, when the BIA explicitly finds an alien to be eligible for discretionary relief but then refuses to grant relief as an exercise of its discretion, such a decision is not reviewable. Determining whether we have jurisdiction to review is more difficult when the BIA is engaged in the application of law to facts.

We determine our jurisdiction by looking at the *underlying nature* of the BIA's determination rather than any gloss offered by the parties. *Argueta*, 617 F.3d at 112 ("We do not rely solely on a petitioner's description of his claims, but scrutinize a petitioner's arguments to determine whether they raise reviewable questions." (internal quotation marks omitted)); *Barco-Sandoval v. Gonzales*, 516 F.3d 35, 39 (2d Cir. 2008) . . . .

Although, in some sense, every BIA decision involves the application of law to fact, not every such decision is reviewable. See *Xiao Ji Chen*, 471 F.3d at 331 ("The mere use of the term 'erroneous application' of a statute will not, however, convert a quarrel over an exercise of discretion into a question of law."). The mixed questions of law and fact in BIA decisions are reviewable in three situations:

> (1) Where the BIA applies the wrong statute, misinterprets the correct statute, or uses an erroneous legal standard;

(2) Where the BIA's underlying factual determination is "flawed by an error of law"; and

(3) Where the BIA's conclusion is "without rational justification," meaning it is located so far outside the range of reasonable options that it is erroneous as a matter of law.

See *Mendez v. Holder*, 566 F.3d 316, 322 (2d Cir. 2009) (articulating three situations); *Barco-Sandoval*, 516 F.3d at 39 (same); *Xiao Ji Chen*, 471 F.3d at 329 (same). Except in these scenarios, the BIA's application of law to fact amounts to the exercise of its discretion and does not raise the legal or constitutional question required for our jurisdiction.

### III.

Every new petition to review a BIA decision requires us to make a jurisdictional inquiry: first asking whether the BIA's decision involves a clear legal prescription; second, where the decision only involves the application of clearly established law to a set of facts, asking whether the BIA's determination comes within any of the three specific scenarios that justify review.

This Circuit has already considered our jurisdiction to review BIA rulings on certain other aspects of abuse-based cancellation of removal. In *Rodriguez v. Gonzales*, 451 F.3d 60 (2d Cir. 2006), we held that whether an alien has been convicted of an aggravated felony always presents a legal question and is therefore nondiscretionary and reviewable. *Id*. at 62-63. Similarly, in *Sepulveda v. Gonzales*, 407 F.3d 59 (2d. Cir. 2005), we suggested, but did not hold, that whether an alien satisfies the continuous physical presence requirement also presents a legal question and its therefore reviewable. *Id*. at 63. In *Sepulveda*, we also reviewed a BIA ruling that criminal convictions legally preclude finding that the alien is of "good moral character." *Id*. at 63-64. Although the fact-specific nature of a moral character assessment ordinarily suggests that it would constitute an exercise of discretion not a legal determination, we held in *Sepulveda* that the BIA's ruling on moral character presented a legal question in that particular case because it was explicitly premised on the criminal convictions as a *matter of law. Id.*

In contrast, in *Barco-Sandoval v. Gonzales*, 516 F.3d 35 (2d Cir. 2008), and *Mendez v. Holder*, 566 F.3d 316 (2d Cir. 2009), we held that whether an alien would suffer "extreme hardship" if deported ordinarily does not require statutory interpretation but instead involves the application of the law to particular facts. Thus, we lack jurisdiction to review such determinations unless they fall into one of the three categories described in Part II.

### IV.

Now, we must decide whether we have jurisdiction to review BIA determinations as to whether a spouse has been "battered or subjected to extreme cruelty." Like "extreme hardship"—and unlike criminal conviction or continuous physical presence—whether an alien has been "battered or subjected to extreme cruelty" under the statute generally entails a factual judgment, not a legal prescription.

This conclusion finds support in the fact that Congress did not provide a specific statutory definition for the terms, and in the fact that the regulatory gloss on the terms, while requiring more than the unwanted touching of common law battery, contemplates the exercise of considerable discretion in assessing the totality of the circumstances. See 8 C.F.R. § 204.2(c)(1)(vi).

Thus, BIA determinations as to whether an alien has been "battered or subjected to extreme cruelty" require the application of law to fact, rather than statutory interpretation. As such, we have jurisdiction to review these determinations only when the BIA applies an incorrect law or legal standard, bases its decision on a factfinding premised on an error of law, or reaches a conclusion that lacks any rational justification. . . .

## V.

Rosario's petition turns on the question whether she qualifies as "battered or subjected to extreme cruelty." Therefore, the BIA's decision in this case involves the application of law to fact: a determination of whether Rosario's situation rendered her "battered or subjected to extreme cruelty" under the statute. Rosario's petition therefore does not automatically raise a legal or constitutional issue; it only does so where the BIA applied the wrong law or misapplied the appropriate law or legal standard, based its decision on a factual finding premised on a legal error, or reached a conclusion so far outside the range of reasonable options as to be without rational justification.

Here, the BIA applied the correct law, 8 U.S.C. § 1229b(b)(2)(A)(i), and the correct legal standard, 8 C.F.R. § 204.2(e)(1)(vi), to Rosario's case. There were no legal errors underlying any of the factual findings the BIA used to reach its decision. And given the level of abuse Rosario claims to have suffered, it cannot be said that the BIA's conclusion was without rational justification. Thus, the BIA's decision does not fall within any of the three scenarios where we retain jurisdiction to review.

Ultimately, the question whether the abuse Rosario suffered qualifies her for cancellation of removal is not answered by legal analysis but entails a weighing of facts and circumstances, the sort of value judgment that lies at the core of the BIA's exercise of discretion. The BIA's reasoning can be described as an application of law to fact, but that characterization cannot convert a factual determination into a legal question. Because the BIA's decision raised no question of law, we may not second-guess its discretionary factual judgment that Rosario is not eligible for cancellation of removal. Therefore, we lack jurisdiction to hear Rosario's petition. . . .

## V. The U VISA

A method for a victim of domestic violence to obtain legal status in the United States is to apply for a U Visa, which first appeared as part of VAWA 2000. The law caps the number of U Visas at 10,000 annually. Although regulations implementing the U Visa program got off to a slow start, for seven straight years, up to and including fiscal year 2015, the government has issued the maximum number permitted. As of the end of 2015, some 117,579 victims and their families have benefitted from U Visas.[4]

A non-citizen victim of domestic violence who has suffered substantial physical or mental abuse as a result of the criminal activity of her abuser is eligible to petition for U Visa status if she helps law enforcement prosecute the perpetrator. After three years, she could petition to be a lawful resident of the United States. To be eligible, the domestic violence crime must have occurred in the United States or must violate the federal or state laws of the United States. Victims may seek U Visas for themselves and for immediate family members, such as children or parents. The U Visa is important because it allows the holder to be lawfully employed in the United States. Economic dependency is one of the major reasons abused immigrants remain with their abusers.[5]

The U Visa is also valuable for the unmarried immigrant domestic violence victim who would otherwise be ineligible to self-petition for citizenship through VAWA. Keep in mind that while our focus is on the issuance of U Visas for victims of domestic violence, victims of any crime are eligible to apply.

### Hyoun Kyung Lee v. Holder
United States Court of Appeals for the Ninth Circuit
599 F.3d 973 (2010)

Per Curiam:

Hyoun Kyung Lee petitions for review of the decision of the Board of Immigration Appeals ("BIA") affirming the Immigration Judge's ("IJ") order of removal. Lee argues that the IJ erred in finding her ineligible for U visa interim relief, a temporary form of relief that was previously made available to immigrant victims of crime. Because the IJ had no authority to grant Lee U visa interim relief, we deny the petition for review.

#### BACKGROUND

Lee, a native and citizen of South Korea, was admitted to the United States at San Francisco, California in October 2003, with authorization to remain in the country

---

4. U.S. Citizenship and Naturalization Services, *USCIS Approves 10,000 U Visas for 7th Straight Fiscal Year,* December 29, 2015, https://www.uscis.gov, accessed March 6, 2017.
5. *See* Leslie Orloff & Janice V. Kaguyutan, *Offering a Helping Hand: Legal Protections for Battered Immigrant Women, supra,* 162–68.

for up to six months. She overstayed her visa, and the government commenced removal proceedings against her in July 2005. In proceedings before the IJ, Lee conceded removability, but obtained a continuance in order to seek U visa interim relief.

Congress created the "U" nonimmigrant classification for certain victims of criminal activity with the enactment of the Victims of Trafficking and Violence Protection Act of 2000, Pub. L. 106-386, 114 Stat. 1464 (2000). Under the statute, a non-citizen is entitled to a U visa if the Secretary of the Department of Homeland Security ("DHS") determines that she has suffered "substantial physical or mental abuse" as a result of qualifying criminal activity and can show that she "has been helpful, is being helpful, or is likely to be helpful" to law enforcement authorities that are investigating or prosecuting the crime. 8 U.S.C. § 1101(a)(15)(U)(i).

At the time Lee filed her application, DHS had not yet promulgated regulations implementing the U visa statute. Instead, the agency afforded individuals who established prima facie eligibility for a U visa with interim relief—in this case, deferred action—to prevent their removal from the United States pending the adoption of procedures to process their visa applications....

Lee submitted an application for interim relief to the arm of DHS responsible for issuing of visas, U.S. Citizenship and Immigration Services ("USCIS"). Lee claimed relief on the basis of her usefulness to a federal investigation of a sex trafficking ring that had victimized her. On February 2, 2006, USCIS denied Lee's application for lack of sufficient evidence of several predicates for U visa relief, including, according to the denial letter, proof of "substantial physical or mental abuse" as a result of her victimization; proof that she "possess[ed] information concerning that criminal activity;" and proof that she had been, was being, or was likely to be helpful to law enforcement authorities investigating or prosecuting the crime. Lee also failed to submit the required certification from law enforcement authorities of her assistance. USCIS indicated that Lee could submit further documentation to overcome the deficiencies in her application.

Lee obtained another continuance from the IJ to pursue her U visa application. In late March 2006, Lee sent USCIS a report from a clinical social worker attesting to the psychological harm she suffered at the hands of her sex traffickers. Lee did not submit any further evidence to USCIS.

The IJ held a merits hearing in Lee's case in April 2006. At the conclusion of the hearing, the IJ ordered Lee removed on the grounds that Lee failed to show prima facie eligibility for U visa interim relief. Although she submitted further evidence of psychological harm, she made no showing of her helpfulness to law enforcement officials. The IJ noted that "there is nothing from the United States Attorney's office where this matter is presently pending to indicate that [Lee's] testimony or information is requested or required by that agency." The BIA affirmed without opinion.

## ANALYSIS

Lee argues that the IJ erred in finding her ineligible for U visa interim relief. The appeal faces a more fundamental problem—the IJ did not have the authority to grant Lee interim relief in the first place. Rather, this decision was committed to USCIS.

The interim relief program was a DHS effort to provide temporary relief in the form of parole, deferred action, and stays of removal to individuals who showed prima facie eligibility for U visas pending issuance of the regulations. . . . At the time Lee applied for interim relief, applicants were required to submit prima facie evidence that they met each statutory requirement for eligibility, and all applications, including those filed by individuals, like Lee, who were in removal proceedings, were processed by the USCIS Vermont Service Center ("VSC"). Memorandum from William R. Yates, Assoc. Dir. of Operations to Director, VSC, USCIS ("Yates Memo 2003"), at 2-3 (Oct. 8, 2003); Memorandum from William R. Yates, Assoc. Dir., Operations to Paul E. Novak, Dir., Vermont Serv. Ctr., USCIS, at 1-2 (May 6, 2004).

The interim program afforded IJs no authority to decide applications for interim relief. Denials or termination of deferred action were not appealable. *See* Yates Memo 2003 at 6. Similarly, the U visa regulations that were ultimately issued provide USCIS with "sole jurisdiction over all petitions for U nonimmigrant status." 8 C.F.R. § 214.14(c)(1); *see also Matter of H-A-*, 22 I&N Dec. 728, 736 (BIA 1999) (noting the IJ's lack of jurisdiction to assess the evidence submitted in support of a visa petition); *Dielmann v. INS*, 34 F.3d 851, 853 (9th Cir. 1994) (upholding the Attorney General's decision to assign adjudication of immediate relative petitions to INS district directors, and not to IJs or the BIA). Even under the new regulations, petitioners who are denied U visas may appeal only to the Administrative Appeals Office of USCIS rather than the immigration court. 8 C.F.R. § 214.14(c)(5)(ii). Because USCIS, and not the IJ, had jurisdiction over Lee's request for interim relief, Lee's appeal fails.[6]

Lee also complains that the U visa regulations "fail[] to set a guideline as to the application of the 'likely to be helpful' [criterion]." The point of this argument is unclear as the validity of the regulations is not at issue in this case. In any event, Lee did not exhaust this argument in her appeal to the BIA, and thus we lack jurisdiction to review it. 8 U.S.C. § 1252(d)(1).

The petition for review is DENIED.

# VI. The Impact of Criminal Conviction on Removal

Since October 1, 1996, the types of criminal convictions that could lead to deportation have greatly expanded. Convictions for offenses involving firearms, drugs and violent felonies could all result in the perpetrator being sent back home. Included in

---

6. 2 [n2] Even if the IJ had authority to rule on the denial of interim relief, as the IJ held, Lee failed to provide sufficient documentation of her eligibility, including the required certification from a law enforcement official as to her helpfulness in the investigation or prosecution of a crime.

this list are convictions for crimes involving domestic violence, including stalking, child abuse and violation of an order of protection. Title 8 U.S.C. § 1227 (a)(2)(E)(i) & (ii), addresses domestic violence offenses.

The impact of a criminal conviction for a domestic violence offense is drastic for the immigrant. A non-citizen perpetrator may be removed from the United States, even though he may have lived in this country lawfully for years and have a job, property and a family. Unfortunately, that same conviction could have drastic and unintended consequences for the victim and the rest of the family as well. If the victim is not a citizen, has failed to self-petition to become one or is unaware of her legal right to do so, she could end up being sent back home with her dangerous batterer. And "home" may be a country that is far less troubled by violence against women than this one.

Of particular concern is the tendency on the part of inexperienced police officers to arrest both husband and wife when called to the scene of a domestic dispute. Although many state penal statutes specifically mandate that law enforcement identify which party in a domestic violence dispute is the "primary initial aggressor," and arrest accordingly, that requirement is not always followed. If an immigrant woman is arrested along with her batterer, is frightened, possesses poor language skills and has no access to an attorney with knowledge of the immigration laws, she could end up being treated no differently than the husband who beat her. And, even a *nolo contendre* plea or a plea to a lesser offense can result in deportation if the person charged has admitted facts sufficient to warrant a finding of guilt to a domestic violence crime and some sanction has been imposed.

Today it is required that a non-citizen defendant be informed of the immigration consequences of a conviction, either after trial or by pleading guilty to a crime that could result in removal from the United States.

## Padilla v. Kentucky
### Supreme Court of the United States
### 130 S. Ct. 1473 (2010)

JUSTICE STEVENS delivered the Opinion of the Court.

Petitioner Jose Padilla, a native of Honduras, has been a lawful permanent resident of the United States for more than 40 years. Padilla served this Nation with honor as a member of the U.S. Armed Forces during the Vietnam War. He now faces deportation after pleading guilty to the transportation of a large amount of marijuana in his tractor-trailer in the Commonwealth of Kentucky.

In this postconviction proceeding, Padilla claims that his counsel not only failed to advise him of this consequence prior to his entering the plea, but also told him that he "'did not have to worry about immigration status since he had been in the country so long.'" 253 S.W.3d 482, 483 (Ky. 2008). Padilla relied on his counsel's erroneous advice when he pleaded guilty to the drug charges that made his deportation virtually mandatory. He alleges that he would have insisted on going to trial if he had not received incorrect advice from his attorney.

Assuming the truth of his allegations, the Supreme Court of Kentucky denied Padilla postconviction relief without the benefit of an evidentiary hearing. The court held that the Sixth Amendment's guarantee of effective assistance of counsel does not protect a criminal defendant from erroneous advice about deportation because it is merely a "collateral" consequence of his conviction. *Id.*, at 485. In its view, neither counsel's failure to advise petitioner about the possibility of removal, nor counsel's incorrect advice, could provide a basis for relief.

We granted certiorari, 555 U.S. \_\_\_, 129 S. Ct. 1317, 173 L. Ed. 2d 582 (2009). . . . We agree with Padilla that constitutionally competent counsel would have advised him that his conviction for drug distribution made him subject to automatic deportation. Whether he is entitled to relief depends on whether he has been prejudiced, a matter that we do not address.

I

The landscape of federal immigration law has changed dramatically over the last 90 years. . . . The "drastic measure" of deportation or removal, *Fong Haw Tan v. Phelan*, 333 U.S. 6, 10, 68 S. Ct. 374, 92 L. Ed. 433 (1948), is now virtually inevitable for a vast number of noncitizens convicted of crimes. . . .

II

Before deciding whether to plead guilty, a defendant is entitled to "the effective assistance of competent counsel." *McMann v. Richardson*, 397 U.S. 759, 771, 90 S. Ct. 1441, 25 L. Ed. 2d 763 (1970); *Strickland*, 466 U.S., at 686, 104 S. Ct. 2052, 80 L. Ed. 2d 674. The Supreme Court of Kentucky rejected Padilla's ineffectiveness claim on the ground that the advice he sought about the risk of deportation concerned only collateral matters, *i.e.*, those matters not within the sentencing authority of the state trial court. 253 S.W.3d, at 483-484 (citing *Commonwealth v. Fuartado*, 170 S.W.3d 384 (2005)). In its view, "collateral consequences are outside the scope of representation required by the Sixth Amendment," and, therefore, the "failure of defense counsel to advise the defendant of possible deportation consequences is not cognizable as a claim for ineffective assistance of counsel." 253 S.W.3d, at 483. The Kentucky high court is far from alone in this view. . . .

We have long recognized that deportation is a particularly severe "penalty," *Fong Yue Ting v. United States*, 149 U.S. 698, 740, 13 S. Ct. 1016, 37 L. Ed. 905 (1893); but it is not, in a strict sense, a criminal sanction. Although removal proceedings are civil in nature, see *INS v. Lopez-Mendoza*, 468 U.S. 1032, 1038, 104 S. Ct. 3479, 82 L. Ed. 2d 778 (1984), deportation is nevertheless intimately related to the criminal process. Our law has enmeshed criminal convictions and the penalty of deportation for nearly a century, see Part I, *supra*, at 2-7. And, importantly, recent changes in our immigration law have made removal nearly an automatic result for a broad class of noncitizen offenders. Thus, we find it "most difficult" to divorce the penalty from the conviction in the deportation context. *United States v. Russell*, 686 F.2d 35, 38, 222 U.S. App. D.C. 313 (CADC 1982)....

Deportation as a consequence of a criminal conviction is, because of its close connection to the criminal process, uniquely difficult to classify as either a direct or a collateral consequence. The collateral versus direct distinction is thus ill-suited to evaluating a *Strickland* claim concerning the specific risk of deportation. We conclude that advice regarding deportation is not categorically removed from the ambit of the Sixth Amendment right to counsel. *Strickland* applies to Padilla's claim.

### III

Under *Strickland*, we first determine whether counsel's representation "fell below an objective standard of reasonableness." 466 U.S., at 688, 104 S. Ct. 2052, 80 L. Ed. 2d 674. Then we ask whether "there is a reasonable probability that, but for counsel's unprofessional errors, the result of the proceeding would have been different." *Id.*, at 694, 104 S. Ct. 2052, 80 L. Ed. 2d 674. The first prong—constitutional deficiency—is necessarily linked to the practice and expectations of the legal community....

The weight of prevailing professional norms supports the view that counsel must advise her client regarding the risk of deportation. National Legal Aid and Defender Assn., Performance Guidelines for Criminal Representation 6.2 (1995); G. Herman, Plea Bargaining 3.03, pp. 20–21 (1997); Chin & Holmes, Effective Assistance of Counsel and the Consequences of Guilty Pleas, 87 Cornell L. Rev. 697, 713-718 (2002); A. Campbell, Law of Sentencing ' 13:23, pp. 555, 560 (3d ed. 2004); Dept. of Justice, Office of Justice Programs, 2 Compendium of Standards for Indigent Defense Systems, Standards for Attorney Performance, pp. D10, H8-H9, J8 (2000) (providing survey of guidelines across multiple jurisdictions); ABA Standards for Criminal Justice, Prosecution Function and Defense Function 4-5.1(a), p. 197 (3d ed. 1993); ABA Standards for Criminal Justice, Pleas of Guilty 14-3.2(f), p. 116 (3d Ed. 1999). "[A]uthorities of every stripe—including the American Bar Association, criminal defense and public defender organizations, authoritative treatises, and state and city bar publications—universally require defense attorneys to advise as to the risk of deportation consequences for non-citizen clients...." Brief for Legal Ethics, Criminal Procedure, and Criminal Law Professors as *Amici Curiae* 12-14 (footnotes omitted) (citing, *inter alia*, National Legal Aid and Defender Assn., Guidelines, *supra*, §§ 6.2-6.4 (1997); S. Bratton & E. Kelley, Practice Points: Representing a Noncitizen in a Criminal Case, 31 The Champion 61 (Jan./Feb. 2007); N. Tooby, Criminal Defense of Immigrants § 1.3 (3d ed. 2003); 2 Criminal Practice Manual 45:3, 45:15 (2009)).

....

In the instant case, the terms of the relevant immigration statute are succinct, clear, and explicit in defining the removal consequence for Padilla's conviction. See 8 U.S.C. § 1227(a)(2)(B)(i).... Padilla's counsel could have easily determined that his plea would make him eligible for deportation simply from reading the text of the statute, which addresses not some broad classification of crimes but specifically commands removal for all controlled substances convictions except for the most trivial of marijuana possession offenses. Instead, Padilla's counsel provided him false assurance that his conviction would not result in his removal from this country. This is not a hard case in which to find deficiency: The consequences of Padilla's plea could easily be determined from reading the removal statute, his deportation was presumptively mandatory, and his counsel's advice was incorrect. . . .

Accepting his allegations as true, Padilla has sufficiently alleged constitutional deficiency to satisfy the first prong of *Strickland*. Whether Padilla is entitled to relief on his claim will depend on whether he can satisfy *Strickland*'s second prong, prejudice, a matter we leave to the Kentucky courts to consider in the first instance. . . .

IV

The Solicitor General has urged us to conclude that *Strickland* applies to Padilla's claim only to the extent that he has alleged affirmative misadvice. . . .

A holding limited to affirmative misadvice would invite two absurd results. First, it would give counsel an incentive to remain silent on matters of great importance, even when answers are readily available. Silence under these circumstances would be fundamentally at odds with the critical obligation of counsel to advise the client of "the advantages and disadvantages of a plea agreement." *Libretti v. United States*, 516 U.S. 29, 50-51, 116 S. Ct. 356, 133 L. Ed. 2d 271 (1995). When attorneys know that their clients face possible exile from this country and separation from their families, they should not be encouraged to say nothing at all. Second, it would deny a class of clients least able to represent themselves the most rudimentary advice on deportation even when it is readily available. It is quintessentially the duty of counsel to provide her client with available advice about an issue like deportation and the failure to do so "clearly satisfies the first prong of the *Strickland* analysis." *Hill v. Lockhart*, 474 U.S. 52, 62, 106 S. Ct. 366, 88 L. Ed. 2d 203 (1985) (White, J., concurring in judgment).

We have given serious consideration to the concerns that the Solicitor General, respondent, and *amici* have stressed regarding the importance of protecting the finality of convictions obtained through guilty pleas. We confronted a similar "floodgates" concern in *Hill*, see *id.*, at 58, 106 S. Ct. 366, 88 L. Ed. 2d 203, but nevertheless applied *Strickland* to a claim that counsel had failed to advise the client regarding his parole eligibility before he pleaded guilty.

A flood did not follow in that decision's wake. Surmounting *Strickland*'s high bar is never an easy task. See, *e.g.*, 466 U.S., at 689, 104 S. Ct. 2052, 80 L. Ed. 2d 674 ("Judicial scrutiny of counsel's performance must be highly deferential"); *id.*, at 693, 104 S. Ct. 2052, 80 L. Ed. 2d 674 (observing that "[a]ttorney errors . . . are as likely to be utterly harmless in a particular case as they are to be prejudicial"). Moreover, to obtain relief on this type of claim, a petitioner must convince the court that a decision to reject the plea bargain would have been rational under the circumstances. See *Roe v. Flores-Ortega*, 528 U.S. 470, 480, 486, 120 S. Ct. 1029, 145 L. Ed. 2d 985 (2000). There is no reason to doubt that lower courts—now quite experienced with applying

*Strickland*—can effectively and efficiently use its framework to separate specious claims from those with substantial merit.

It seems unlikely that our decision today will have a significant effect on those convictions already obtained as the result of plea bargains. For at least the past 15 years, professional norms have generally imposed an obligation on counsel to provide advice on the deportation consequences of a client's plea. See, *supra*, at 11-13. We should, therefore, presume that counsel satisfied their obligation to render competent advice at the time their clients considered pleading guilty. *Strickland*, 466 U.S., at 689, 104 S. Ct. 2052, 80 L. Ed. 2d 674....

Finally, informed consideration of possible deportation can only benefit both the State and noncitizen defendants during the plea-bargaining process. By bringing deportation consequences into this process, the defense and prosecution may well be able to reach agreements that better satisfy the interests of both parties. As in this case, a criminal episode may provide the basis for multiple charges, of which only a subset mandate deportation following conviction. Counsel who possess the most rudimentary understanding of the deportation consequences of a particular criminal offense may be able to plea bargain creatively with the prosecutor in order to craft a conviction and sentence that reduce the likelihood of deportation, as by avoiding a conviction for an offense that automatically triggers the removal consequence. At the same time, the threat of deportation may provide the defendant with a powerful incentive to plead guilty to an offense that does not mandate that penalty in exchange for a dismissal of a charge that does....

The judgment of the Supreme Court of Kentucky is reversed, and the case is remanded for further proceedings not inconsistent with this opinion.

---

Although it is now clear a defendant must be informed of the possibility of removal following conviction of a qualifying crime, what constitutes that crime is not always apparent.

## Singh v. Ashcroft

United States Court of Appeals, Ninth Circuit

386 F.3d 1228 (2004)

Gould, Circuit Judge:

Dalip Singh petitions for review of a decision of the Board of Immigration Appeals (BIA), affirming without opinion the order of the immigration judge (IJ). The IJ ordered Singh removed to India pursuant to 8 U.S.C. § 1227(a)(2)(E)(i) on the ground that Singh committed a "crime of domestic violence" when he committed the Oregon crime of harassment, Or. Rev. Stat. § 166.065(1)(a)(A), against his spouse. We must decide whether Oregon's harassment law, which outlaws intentionally harassing or annoying another person by subjecting that person to offensive physical contact, is a "crime of violence" as defined by 18 U.S.C. § 16(a). We have jurisdiction under 8 U.S.C. § 1252(a)(1). We grant Singh's petition and vacate the IJ's order of removal.

## I.

Singh, a native and citizen of India, entered the United States in 1990. In May of 1993, Singh was granted lawful permanent resident status based on his marriage to United States citizen Linda Olson. In June of 1998, Singh pleaded guilty to the Oregon state law crime of harassment, a class B misdemeanor. Or. Rev. Stat. § 166.065. As a result of that conviction, in February of 1999, the Immigration and Naturalization Service (INS) issued to Singh a Notice to Appear, charging that Singh was subject to removal under 8 U.S.C. § 1227(a)(2)(E)(i) because he had been convicted of a "crime of domestic violence."

A hearing was held in December of 1999. The IJ held that Singh's conviction under Oregon's harassment law was a predicate offense for removal under federal law because, as the IJ saw it, the harassment statute "necessarily encompasses by its elements that requirement of force for a crime of violence under 18 U.S.C. § 16(a)." On December 20, 1999, the IJ ordered Singh removed to India. On December 17, 2002, the BIA affirmed without opinion the IJ's order, so "we review the IJ's opinion as the final agency decision." *Tokatly v. Ashcroft*, 371 F.3d 613, 618 (9th Cir. 2004). Singh timely filed a petition for review on January 14, 2003, arguing that he was not removable under 8 U.S.C. § 1227(a)(2)(E)(i) because Oregon's harassment offense was not a "crime of violence" as defined by 18 U.S.C. § 16(a). Singh's theory was that the Oregon offense to which he pleaded guilty, and for which he was convicted, does not have as an element the use of physical force against the person of another.

. . .

## III.

Singh is removable for having committed a "crime of domestic violence" if he committed a "crime of violence" against a domestic partner. 8 U.S.C. § 1227(a)(2)(E)(i). A "crime of violence" is defined by federal law as "an offense that has as an element the use, attempted use, or threatened use of physical force against the person or property of another." 18 U.S.C. § 16(a). An element of a crime is "a constituent part of the offense which must be proved by the prosecution *in every case* to sustain a conviction under a given statute." *United States v. Innie*, 7 F.3d 840, 850 (9th Cir. 1993) (quoting *United States v. Sherbondy*, 865 F.2d 996, 1010 (9th Cir. 1988)) (internal quotation marks omitted). Thus, in assessing whether Singh is removable for committing a "crime of domestic violence," the dispositive issue becomes whether his state law conviction for harassment is a "crime of violence" under 18 U.S.C. § 16(a), when we look only at the necessary elements of the state law offense of conviction. *See Innie*, 7 F.3d at 850; *cf. Taylor v. United States*, 495 U.S. 575, 109 L. Ed. 2d 607, 110 S. Ct. 2143 (1990).

Singh pleaded guilty to the Oregon offense of harassment. The relevant portion of the harassment statute reads: "A person commits the crime of harassment if the person intentionally: Harasses or annoys another person by subjecting such other person to offensive physical contact." Or. Rev. Stat. § 166.065(1)(a)(A). Oregon's harassment law, by its terms, has three elements: (1) an intent to harass or annoy another person; (2) physical contact with that person, whether direct or indirect; and (3) offensiveness of the contact, judged by an objective standard. *See State v. Keller*, 40 Ore. App. 143, 594 P.2d 1250, 1251–52 (Or. Ct. App. 1979) (en banc).

. . . .

The necessary elements of the Oregon crime of harassment, as defined by the statute and case law, do not require sufficient "force" to constitute a "crime of violence" under 18 U.S.C. § 16(a). We have squarely held "that the force necessary to constitute a crime of violence must actually be violent in nature." *United States v. Ceron-Sanchez*, 222 F.3d 1169, 1172 (9th Cir. 2000) (quoting *Ye v. INS*, 214 F.3d 1128, 1133 (9th Cir. 2000)) (alteration in original) (internal quotation marks omitted); *see also* Black's Law Dictionary 673 (8th ed. 2004) (defining actual or physical force as "force consisting in a physical act, esp. a violent act directed against a . . . victim"). Yet the Oregon harassment offense, harkening back to the ancient common law of battery, can be made out based on an ephemeral touching, so long as it is offensive. . . . The Oregon law we confront, however, requires neither an intent to inflict a physical injury nor a resulting physical injury. . . . That Oregon requires a physical contact to be objectively offensive does not change our analysis. *Keller* held that "causing spittle to land on the person" of another may be objectively offensive. 594 P.2d at 1251. Under the most extreme case, perhaps spitting forcefully at another might be argued to constitute the use of some physical force, but 18 U.S.C. § 16(a) is not concerned with the most extreme case. Rather, 18 U.S.C. § 16(a) is concerned with the least extreme cases of an offense that nonetheless satisfy the offense's necessary elements. *See Innie*, 7 F.3d at 850. Given that "causing spittle to land on the person" of another is sufficient to sustain conviction for harassment, there are many objectively offensive physical contacts that may suffice for harassment under Oregon law, but not rise to a level of "physical force," and certainly not violent physical force satisfying the federal definition in 18 U.S.C. § 16(a) of a "crime of violence."

Oregon's harassment law reaches acts that involve offensiveness by invasion of personal integrity, but that do not amount to the use, attempted use, or threatened use of "physical force." We hold that the Oregon harassment statute, Or. Rev. Stat. § 166.065(1)(a)(A), does not require as necessary elements of conviction acts that meet the federal definition of a "crime of violence" under § 16(a). Accordingly, the respondent has not satisfied its burden to show that Singh has committed a "crime of domestic violence" under 8 U.S.C. § 1227(a)(2)(E)(i), warranting his removal.

The petition is GRANTED and the order of removal is VACATED.

## VII. Domestic Violence as Torture, a Violation of International Human Rights or the Basis for Asylum

Asylum is a form of discretionary relief for humanitarian purposes to those who, for reasons recognized in the law, would suffer if they were ejected from the asylum country and forced to return home. It is discussed most often in the context of persons fleeing civil war, racial and ethnic persecution by a corrupt government or those fearing torture for their political beliefs or activism at the hands of a totalitarian regime. It is relief that is technically available to women fleeing to the United States from abusive relationships in countries where governments are unsympathetic to spousal violence against women. But to prevail, litigants must convince immigration officials that domestic violence is a broader human rights issue rather than a problem of one man's abuse of one woman.

### Lori A. Nessel, *"Willful Blindness" to Gender-Based Violence Abroad: United States' Implementation of Article Three of the United Nations Convention Against Torture*
89 Minn. L. Rev. 71 (2004)

#### INTRODUCTION

In the Democratic Republic of the Congo (D.R.C.), D—K—found herself trapped in an abusive marriage and subjected to escalating violence.[7] She was too fearful to go to the police because of her husband's governmental ties, as well as her knowledge that the police would not intervene in domestic matters. She could not flee to a battered women's shelter because not a single shelter existed, despite the pervasive domestic violence in her country. D—K—'s status as a married woman further diminished her options. Married women are subordinated by law in the D.R.C., and are prohibited from owning property or engaging in employment without their husbands' consent. Although D—K—fled to her brother's house in search of safety on numerous occasions, her husband always found her and forced her to return home. Finally, D—K—fled to the United States to seek asylum after an extremely violent incident: her husband beat her until she lost consciousness and then raped her in front of their children.

The immigration judge who heard D—K—'s case denied her asylum claim. The judge characterized the acts of domestic violence as "atrocities," but, nevertheless, held that D—K—failed to show that her husband persecuted her on account of her membership in a "particular social group." The Board of Immigration Appeals (Board) similarly affirmed the judge's decision and D—K—was scheduled for immediate removal to the D.R.C. At the eleventh hour, the Federal Circuit Court of Appeals stayed D—K—'s removal, allowing her to pursue a newly available form of protection based

---

7. [n1] In re D—K—, slip. op. at 4 (EOIR Immigr. Ct. Dec. 8, 1998), available at http://www.uchastings.edu/cgrs/law/ij/117.html.

on Article 3 of the United Nations Convention Against Torture (Article 3 or Torture Convention).[8]

Ultimately, the same immigration judge who had denied asylum and ordered D—K— to be returned to her abuser found that the domestic violence at issue constituted "torture." Moreover, she held that the Congolese government maintained a policy of "willful blindness" because it was aware of the prevalence of domestic violence in its country, yet did not act upon that knowledge. Although U.S. asylum laws had failed to protect D—K—, the immigration judge's grant of relief under the Torture Convention freed her after two and a half years of detention and, more importantly, prohibited U.S. immigration authorities from returning her to her abuser in the D.R.C.[9]

. . . .

The *In re D—K—* decision now lies at the crossroads of what has become sharply divided interpretations of Article 3 between the Board and Attorney General on the

---

8. [n9] The United Nations General Assembly adopted the Convention Against Torture and Other Cruel, Inhuman or Degrading Treatment or Punishment in 1984. G.A. Res. 39/46, U.N. GAOR, 39th Sess., Supp. No. 51, at 197, U.N. Doc. A/39/51 (1984) [hereinafter Torture Convention]. Article 3 of the Torture Convention mandates that signatory states shall not return a person to a country in which there is a substantial likelihood that she would be tortured. Id. President Reagan signed the Torture Convention on behalf of the United States on April 18, 1988. See Michael John Garcia, Cong. Research Ctr., The U.N. Convention Against Torture: Overview of U.S. Implementation Policy Concerning the Removal of Aliens 4 (2004). In 1990, the U.S. Senate ratified the Torture Convention with a substantial number of reservations, declarations, and understandings. See 136 Cong. Rec. S17,486-92 (daily ed. Oct. 27, 1990). However, the United States did not become a full party to the Torture Convention until November 20, 1994, one month after President Clinton deposited the ratification instrument with the U.N. Secretary-General. Regulations Concerning the Convention Against Torture, 64 Fed. Reg. 8478, 8478 (Feb. 19, 1999). Because the United States adopted the position that the Torture Convention was not self-executing, see Garcia, supra, at 4, it was not until Congress enacted implementing legislation in 1998, see Foreign Affairs Reform and Restructuring Act of 1998, Pub. L. No. 105-277, 2242, 112 Stat. 2681, 2822 (1998), followed by INS and Department of Justice regulations in 1999, see 8 C.F.R. 208.16-.18 (2004); 8 C.F.R. 1208.16-.18 (2004), that the nonrefoulement provision of Article 3 of the Torture Convention became a viable defense against removal in U.S. immigration proceedings. The 1999 INS regulations specified that the Attorney General would have exclusive jurisdiction over Torture Convention claims arising under Article 3. 8 C.F.R. 208.18(c), 1208.18(c).

9. [n12] See [In re D—K—, slip. op. (EOIR Immigr. Ct. Aug. 1, 2000)] at 1–2, 6. However, unlike asylum protection, a grant of Torture Convention protection, as implemented in the United States, does not lead to permanent legal status or allow for family reunification. See infra notes 49, 333 and accompanying text. Thus, D—K—found herself in the untenable situation of having to choose between her safety and the chance to reunite with her five children. D—K—pursued her asylum appeal to the Third Circuit. See In re D—K—, No. 01-3120, slip op. at 1 (3d Cir. Jan. 15, 2002). She was ultimately granted asylum by the Board after the Justice Department agreed to withdraw its opposition in exchange for D—K—withdrawing her case from the federal court of appeals. See In re D—K—, slip op. at 1 (B.I.A. Mar. 21, 2002) (per curium). For D—K—, gaining asylum meant the possibility of reuniting with her children and obtaining permanent safety more than four years after her arrival in the United States. The Justice Department's position in this and similar cases, however, has been characterized as part of an effort to avoid federal precedent in the area of gender-based asylum jurisprudence. See Stephen M. Knight, Seeking Asylum from Gender Persecution: Progress Amid Uncertainty, 79 Interpreter Releases 689, 693–95 (2002).

one hand, and the courts of appeals on the other. The Board and Attorney General have moved toward a stringent interpretation of governmental "acquiescence" that is analogous to the nexus requirement in asylum law. The Attorney General now requires that the home government "willfully accept" the torturous activity, seemingly excluding "willful blindness" to pervasive societal problems such as domestic violence. The Board has also interpreted the Torture Convention to require a "specific intent" to inflict torture. For women fleeing intentionally inflicted "private" torture (such as domestic violence or female genital cutting), the United States' interpretation bars relief absent a showing that the abuser's intent was to inflict torture. Even in situations in which the state imprisons women with full knowledge that torture, such as rape, is prevalent under such circumstances, this interpretation forecloses relief unless the state imprisons such women with the specific intent that they be raped.

. . . .

## I. STATUTORY FRAMEWORK: A HISTORICAL PERSPECTIVE AND AN OVERVIEW OF THE REFUGEE PROTECTION REGIME IN THE UNITED STATES

. . .

The Refugee Protection Regime that exists today is based upon the 1951 United Nations Convention Relating to the Status of Refugees (Refugee Convention),[10] as amended by the 1967 United Nations Protocol on Refugees (U.N. Protocol). Pursuant to Article 33 of the Refugee Convention, a refugee was defined universally for the first time as any person who, as a result of events occurring before 1 January 1951 and owing to well-founded fear of being persecuted for reasons of race, religion, nationality, membership of a particular social group or political opinion, is outside the country of his nationality and is unable or, owing to such fear, is unwilling to avail himself of the protection of that country; or who, not having a nationality and being outside the country of his former habitual residence as a result of such events, is unable or, owing to such fear, is unwilling to return to it.

. . . .

### A. Withholding of Removal

In 1967, the United States ratified the U.N. Protocol, thereby agreeing to adhere to the international refugee protection standards. Congress, however, did not formally implement its obligations pursuant to the U.N. Protocol until 1980 when it enacted the Refugee Act. At that time, Congress set forth two different forms of relief for refugees at or within the borders of the United States: withholding of removal and asylum. To qualify for withholding of removal, a person must show that, if removed from the United States, her life or freedom would be threatened on account of her race, religion, nationality, membership in a particular social group, or political opinion.

---

10. [n33] Convention Relating to the Status of Refugees, July 28, 1951, 19 U.S.T. 6260, 189 U.N.T.S 137.

The U.S. Supreme Court has interpreted the applicable standard of proof to be "more likely than not," meaning the risk of persecution must exceed fifty percent. In keeping with the U.N. Protocol, Congress excluded various groups from protection, including criminals, those dangerous to national security, and those who have either persecuted others, engaged in genocide, or assisted in Nazi persecution.

B. Asylum

Congress's enactment of the Refugee Act of 1980 also created a more beneficial discretionary form of relief entitled "asylum." To qualify for asylum, a person must show that she is a refugee. Congress defined "refugee" as a person who has been persecuted in the past or who has a "well-founded fear of persecution" on account of race, religion, nationality, membership in a particular social group, or political opinion. In addition, a refugee must be outside of her country of nationality and be either unwilling or unable to return to that country. In sharp contrast with the mandatory nature of withholding of removal, however, asylum is discretionary. Thus, once a person demonstrates statutory eligibility, she must further show that asylum is warranted as a matter of discretion.[11] Significantly, a grant of asylum leads to familial reunification and the possibility for permanency in the United States.

. . .

Perhaps counter-intuitively, the standard of proof for asylum is significantly lower than that which is required for withholding of removal. In determining whether an individual is eligible for withholding of removal, adjudicators use a "more likely than not" standard, whereas a grant of asylum requires past persecution or a "well founded fear" of persecution. The U.S. Supreme Court has clarified that a "well founded fear" of persecution can exist if there is a one in ten chance that the feared event will happen. Stated differently, if a reasonable person in the applicant's situation would fear persecution, that fear is well-founded. Finally, the persecution suffered or feared must exist nationwide and be inflicted either directly by the government, or by forces that the government is unwilling or unable to control.

As part of the Illegal Immigration Reform and Immigrant Responsibility Act of 1996 (IIRIRA), the United States overhauled its refugee protection regime. Before 1996, detention of asylum seekers was the exception rather than the norm. Pursuant to the IIRIRA, however, any arriving alien who does not possess valid immigration documents is subjected to a new procedure entitled "expedited removal." Expedited

---

11. [Immigration and Nationality Act 208.] There are many more bars to attaining asylum than withholding of removal. For example, in addition to incorporating all of the statutory bars that apply to withholding of removal, the statutory asylum provision contains exceptions for persons who have engaged in, are suspected of engaging in, or planning to engage in terrorist activities (including espousing terrorist views). *Id.* 208(b)(2). There is also a one-year time limit in which a person must seek asylum, *Id.* 208(a)(2)(B); a bar against anyone who has firmly resettled in another country prior to arrival in the United States, *Id.* 208(b)(2)(A)(vi); a bar against anyone who can be returned to a safe third country, *id.* 208(a)(2)(A); and a bar against anyone who has previously sought asylum and been denied, *id.* 208(a)(2)(C). Finally, for asylum purposes, any aggravated felony is automatically considered a particularly serious crime and therefore, a bar to asylum. *Id.* 208(b)(2)(B)(i).

removal results in the immediate return of an "arriving alien" to her home country, unless she expresses a fear of persecution. Upon expression of such a fear, the arriving alien is then arrested and transferred to a detention facility to await a "credible fear" interview by an asylum officer. If the officer finds a credible fear of persecution, the arriving alien is permitted to seek asylum before an immigration judge during removal proceedings. While not mandated by law, the vast majority of arriving aliens that pursue asylum remain in detention throughout the proceedings.

. . . .

C. Convention Against Torture

Until 1994, asylum and withholding of removal were the only forms of relief available in the United States for those fearing persecution in their home countries. In 1994, however, the United States ratified the United Nations Convention Against Torture and Other Cruel, Inhuman or Degrading Treatment or Punishment. The drafting of the Torture Convention occurred from 1977 through 1984. The Torture Convention drew in large part upon a number of other human rights agreements that prohibit torture, and followed the earlier Declaration on the Protection of All Persons from Being Subjected to Torture and Other Cruel, Inhuman or Degrading Treatment or Punishment, adopted by the United Nations General Assembly on December 9, 1975. The Torture Convention, however, contained one entirely new provision: Article 3 required signatory states to agree not to expel, to return (refouler), or to extradite a person to another state where there are substantial grounds for believing that she would be in danger of being tortured.

. . . .

The United States' implementation of Article 3 offers protection that is at once broader and narrower than that afforded by its implementation of the Refugee Convention provisions. Most significantly, although Article 3 of the Torture Convention was based in part on Article 33 of the Refugee Convention, the Torture Convention-based relief is broader because it does not require that torture be inflicted on account of any specified protected ground. The Refugee Convention however, as interpreted in the United States and in many other signatory states, protects against persecution inflicted by either the government or "forces the government is unwilling or unable to control." In contrast, the text of the Torture Convention requires that the government inflict the torture, or that it be inflicted with governmental "acquiescence." Finally, in comparison with the Refugee Convention's "well-founded fear" requirement, the standard of proof as set forth in the Torture Convention requires "substantial grounds for believing that one would be in danger of torture." As implemented in the United States, however, the standard of proof under the Torture Convention has been elevated to the "more likely than not" standard.

. . . .

## II. WOMEN FLEEING GENDER-BASED VIOLENCE: INTERNATIONAL RECOGNITION OF A WOMEN'S HUMAN RIGHTS ISSUE

"Refugeeness" has been described as "an experience characterized by flight, force, fear, struggle for control over basic life issues, and especially ambiguity." This ambiguity is compounded for women seeking asylum protection in the United States. While the disassociative nature of the refugee experience is not unique to women, cultural norms may make it even more difficult for women to comply with the rigid standards of proof and causation all too often employed in the refugee adjudication context. Women and children constitute 80% of the estimated twelve million refugees, but the majority of applicants for asylum in the United States are men. The disproportionately small number of women seeking safety in the United States is attributable, in large part, to their severe poverty and lack of mobility.

The combination of "refugeeness" and gender may also account for the finding in recent studies that the expedited removal system that Congress implemented in 1996 has had a disparate impact on women asylum seekers. Women are more frequently removed pursuant to expedited removal (as opposed to regular immigration removal procedures) than men. The expedited removal process also presents particular obstacles to women fleeing persecution or torture and places them in grave danger of being returned to their persecutors. For example, women who have fled gender-based harm such as rape, domestic violence, honor killings, forced sterilization, female genital mutilation, or forced marriage may feel a great sense of shame and be hesitant to disclose their experiences to an immigration officer. In addition, neither women nor immigration officers may know that gender-based harm can be a basis for protection.

Indeed, based on the tumultuous history of U.S. asylum jurisprudence involving gender-based persecution, it remains unclear to what extent women fleeing gender-based harm will be protected through asylum law. Although the Refugee Convention does not set forth gender as a statutorily protected ground, the Board and the courts have developed a substantial body of jurisprudence interpreting "persecution," "membership in a particular social group," and the "nexus" requirement within the context of gender-based claims to asylum. While the Board and at least one circuit court have stated that a social group could be defined based upon the shared sex of its members, there have been no precedential decisions granting asylum protection to a woman who feared persecution based solely on her gender. Rather, the Board and the courts have charted an uneven path in gender-based asylum claims, often requiring women to articulate exceedingly narrow social groups consisting of gender in addition to other shared characteristics.

For many years, women were denied asylum based on perceptions of gender-based harm as "personal" and outside of the realm of refugee protection. However, the international reconceptualization of human rights and refugee law as inclusive of women's human rights issues impacted the development of gender-based asylum jurisprudence in the United States. For example, in 1993, the World Conference on Human Rights led to the adoption of the Vienna Declaration and Programme of Action (Declaration) by the United Nations General Assembly. The Declaration explicitly recognized women's human rights as "an inalienable, integral, and indivisible part of universal human rights." Specifically, the Declaration identified gender-specific abuses that constitute human rights violations and that must be eliminated, "including those resulting from cultural prejudice, such as violence, sexual harassment, and sexual exploitation." A few months later, in December 1993, the United Nations General Assembly adopted a Declaration on the Elimination of Violence Against Women and recognized violence against women as an important human rights issue.

. . . .

By early 1996, the United Nations Special Rapporteur on violence against women issued a report on intrafamilial violence against women. The report characterized domestic violence as a violation of human rights and recommended that states extend their refugee and asylum laws "to include gender-based claims of persecution, including domestic violence." International tribunals already had a history of granting asylum or refugee status to women based on membership in particular gender-based social groups.

. . . .

### III. THE TORTURE CONVENTION: A FRAYING SAFETY NET FOR WOMEN WHO HAVE FALLEN THROUGH THE CRACKS OF THE REFUGEE CONVENTION

. . . .

A. Text, Timing, and Intent: Defining "Torture" in an Era When Women's Human Rights Issues Were Largely Invisible

. . . .

The women's human rights movement was in its early stages at the time the Torture Convention was drafted. Just five years before the Torture Convention was finalized, the General Assembly of the United Nations adopted the Convention on the Elimination of All Forms of Discrimination Against Women (CEDAW). The CEDAW has been widely recognized as the first human rights instrument to encompass the principle that "discrimination against women is incompatible with human dignity and is detrimental to the welfare of society." There can be no doubt that the CEDAW symbolized an essential leap forward in acknowledging the human rights issues affecting women. However, because it separately addressed women's issues outside of and apart from the existing human rights treaties and conventions, the traditional male-oriented structure of the human rights regime remained intact.

. . . .

The Torture Convention's reliance on traditional international law paradigms of state responsibility to exclude private harms is evident from its definition of torture. The Torture Convention defines torture as harm "inflicted by or at the instigation of or with the consent or acquiescence of a public official or other person acting in an official capacity." The incorporation of the public/private dichotomy into this definition has been widely criticized from a gender perspective. As has been stated, "the description of the prohibited conduct relies on a distinction between public and private actions that obscures injuries to their dignity typically sustained by women." Because the Torture Convention and other human rights documents existing at that time focused on discrete violations of rights, they offer little redress in cases involving the pervasive and structural denial of rights.

. . . .

In keeping with the relative invisibility of women's human rights issues at the time of drafting, some surmise that the drafters of the Torture Convention were likely unaware of the consequences that would flow from such a narrow definition of torture that limited accountability. The drafters focused on eliminating torture carried out, or at least tolerated, by the state, reflecting the belief that the state's legal system would handle torture by private individuals. France had proposed that the definition of torture focus on the intrinsic nature of the torture without regard for who inflicts it, but its position did not gain substantial support. However, most states agreed that the Torture Convention should go beyond acts committed by public officials and also cover acts for which the state could be considered to have some responsibility.

. . . .

B. The Attorney General's and Board of Immigration Appeals' Grudging Interpretations of "Acquiescence" and "Intent" Under the Torture Convention

. . . .

1. Ratcheting Up the Standard for Governmental Acquiescence: From "Willful Blindness" to "Willful Acceptance"

Perhaps more than any other term contained in the Torture Convention, the way in which "acquiescence" is interpreted is critical to protecting against gender-based violence because it arises so often in cases involving nonstate actors. To date, the Board's interpretations of "acquiescence" have been uneven. In the three years since the Board's decision in *In re D—K—*, it has taken an increasingly formalistic and rigid approach to "acquiescence," reminiscent of the approach to nexus under asylum law.

The Board first interpreted "acquiescence" under the Torture Convention in *In re S—V—*. This case concerned a Colombian "criminal alien" who, after nearly twenty years in the United States, feared that his inability to speak Spanish combined with his family ties in America would put him at risk of being kidnaped and harmed by nongovernmental guerilla, narcotrafficking, and paramilitary groups if returned to Colombia. S—V—argued that the Colombian government's awareness of the torturous activity, combined with its inability to stop it, satisfied the Torture Convention's requirement that the torture be inflicted with governmental "acquiescence." The Board, however, held that a greater showing was required.

. . . .

However, in *Zheng v. Ashcroft*, the Ninth Circuit rejected the Board's and the Attorney General's "willful acceptance" standard as inconsistent with the intent of both the Torture Convention and the Senate.[12] In *Zheng*, the Board had relied upon its prior holding in *In re S—V—* to reverse the immigration judge's grant of Torture Convention protection to a victim of human trafficking who feared retribution for his testimony against his smugglers if returned to his native China. Although the record established that the Chinese government was aware of the smuggling operations and "condoned or at least [was] not willing to interfere" with the smugglers' conduct, the Board held that Zheng failed to prove that the Chinese government was "willfully accepting of" the smugglers' torturous activities. Relying on the Senate's clarification that "awareness," including "willful blindness," rather than "knowledge," should suffice to demonstrate a public official's acquiescence, the Ninth Circuit held that the Board's insistence on "willful acceptance" impermissibly undermined the Senate's intent.

The conflict over interpreting "acquiescence" has recently widened as the Second Circuit joined the Ninth Circuit in strongly rejecting the Board and Attorney General's utilization of a "willful acceptance" standard. In *Khouzam v. Ashcroft*, the Second Circuit expressly disapproved such a standard.[13] In keeping with the Ninth Circuit's interpretation in *Zheng*, the Second Circuit relied on the language of the Torture Convention and clear congressional intent as expressed in both the ratification and implementation processes. The court held that "torture" required "only that government officials know of or remain willfully blind to an act and thereafter breach their legal responsibility to prevent it."

. . . .

2. Between "Us" and "Them": The Familiarity of Domestic Violence

The fear of "opening the floodgates" to destitute immigrants seeking a better life in the United States permeates and influences all aspects of immigration law. However, debate as to whether gender-based violence should be recognized as a ground for protection in the United States raises this concern with particular passion. The United States' experience in protecting those fleeing gender-based violence reflects a continuum, with female genital cutting at one end, domestic violence at the other end, and a large gray area in between. American tribunals are less likely to protect against "foreign" harms that are equally prevalent in the United States. Therefore, to the extent that the feared persecution involves a foreign practice such as female genital cutting, the Board and the courts seem more inclined to offer protection.

Female genital cutting can be characterized as savage, barbaric, and "other": it is associated with tribes, it is widely practiced in African countries, and it is alien to the United States. In contrast, domestic violence-based protection claims do not fare as well, perhaps in part because no norm exists against which to judge them. Shrouded

---

12. [n214] Zheng v. Ashcroft, 332 F.3d 1186 (9th Cir. 2003). Interpreting "acquiescence" to require "willful acceptance" is also inconsistent with the term's plain meaning. As the Ninth Circuit pointed out, "acquiescence suggests passive assent because of inability or unwillingness to oppose." *Id.* at 1195 (citing American Heritage Dictionary of the English Language (4th ed. 2000)).

13. [n217] Khouzam v. Ashcroft, 361 F.3d 161, 170 (2d Cir. 2004).

in entrenched notions of "privacy," domestic violence continues to be a pervasive problem in the United States. As opposed to tribal practices, confronting domestic violence conjures up images of the "private" realm of familiar "nuclear families."[14] The U.S. government has been largely ineffective in protecting its female citizens from domestic violence. Because of the discomfort in labeling as "torture" that which is familiar and prevalent within the United States, an effort is often made to highlight the "otherness" associated with different races,cultures, or religions.

. . . .

### IV. A PROTECTION-BASED APPROACH TO "ACQUIESCENCE" UNDER THE TORTURE CONVENTION

For the Torture Convention to provide meaningful relief to women fleeing gender-based violence, "acquiescence" must be interpreted broadly to encompass either a state's failure to prosecute or its encouragement of torture by nonstate actors, including its awareness of an environment in which torture occurs. This is essential because most forms of gender-based violence are inflicted by nonstate actors in countries that condone or fail to punish in such situations. Much like the U.S. Supreme Court's narrow interpretation of the state's constitutional duty to protect against domestic violence has both immunized states from culpability for nonfeasance and left women without adequate protection, a restrictive interpretation of "acquiescence" leaves the nation state unaccountable for harm that it effectively tolerates by private actors within its borders.

A state's "willful blindness" to torture inflicted "privately" within its borders should be sufficient to establish state action under the Torture Convention. This broader, more gender-inclusive interpretation of "acquiescence" is also consistent with the international community's evolving norms concerning women's human rights. Such an interpretation would also be consistent with recent decisions by both the Second and Ninth Circuits, the Canadian model for implementating the Torture Convention, and the interpretation of "torture" under the European Convention on Human Rights.

In effect, the domestic efforts to expand the state's constitutional duty to take affirmative steps to protect women from domestic violence would hold the state as an "accomplice" when its failure to protect against domestic violence results in torture. . . .

The two major theoretical approaches to assessing responsibility in situations involving a nonstate agent of persecution are "accountability" and "protection." The accountability approach subscribed to by the minority of states requires a strong link between persecution and the state, while the protection approach focuses instead on

---

14. [n287] For example, in the recent debate as to whether domestic violence should serve as a basis for asylum protection, Ira Mehlman, a spokesman for the Federation for American Immigration Reform, remarked, "You cannot have an asylum policy that allows everybody to claim asylum based on private relationships people have with their spouses or other members of their community. . . . It makes the United States somehow responsible for everybody's marriage in the world." Emily Bazar, Asylum-Seekers Make Gender an Issue, Sacramento Bee, Feb. 9, 2004.

the absence of state protection. To protect women fleeing gender-based violence, the absence of state protection must be applied to an Article 3 analysis. Such an absence of protection could be analyzed by comparing the effectiveness of the state's protection of women with that of other groups in society.

. . . .

In the case of gender-based violence, police inaction and failure to prosecute are often documented by the U.S. Department of State. In the Democratic Republic of the Congo, for example, the State Department reports that domestic violence is pervasive. There are no shelters for battered women and domestic violence is not a crime under the penal code. Similarly, India has no law that addresses domestic violence in its entirety, as even those parts of its penal code that arguably prohibit domestic violence have been criticized as being ambiguous. Moreover, in India, marital rape is explicitly excluded from the definition of rape.[15] Thus, in those countries whose laws fail to protect adequately against domestic violence, (either because such laws do not exist or are not enforced) state nonaction can be interpreted as encouragement sufficient to satisfy a more liberal protection-based interpretation of "acquiescence" under the Torture Convention.[16]

. . . .

## CONCLUSION

. . . .

Twenty-four years after enactment of the Refugee Act in the United States, it is clear that the gender-neutral asylum law has been interpreted unevenly in protecting women fleeing gender-based harm. Because jurisprudence under Article 3 of the Torture Convention is still at a relatively formulative stage in the United States, the potential to chart a different course exists—a course which is more consistent with the intent of the Torture Convention to protect victims of torture abroad. However, in order to protect Article 3 of the Torture Convention from falling victim to the same exclusionary pattern of gender-biased interpretation, the way in which women experience torture and the state's failure to protect—or its willful blindness to the violence suffered—must, as demonstrated in *In re D—K—*, be the standard for granting Article 3 relief. This interpretation is consistent with the international community's growing recognition that

---

15. [In re D—K—, slip op. (EOIR Immigr. Ct. Aug. 1, 2000)] at 25 (citing India's Penal Code, Article 375 exemption: "Sexual intercourse by a man with his own wife, the wife not being under fifteen years of age, is not rape").

16. [n324] See Khouzam v. Ashcroft, 361 F.3d 161, 161 (2d Cir. 2004). A similar position has been advanced by Professor Rhonda Copelon, who states that if the purpose of the "consent or acquiescence" language was to cover situations where the state machinery does not work, then gender-based violence is a case in point . . . . Where domestic violence is a matter of common knowledge and law enforcement and affirmative prevention measures are inadequate, or where complaints are made and not properly responded to, the state should be held to have "acquiesced" in the continued infliction of violence. Copelon, [*Recognizing the Egregious in the Everyday: Domestic Violence as Torture*, 25 COLUM. HUM. RTS. L. REV. 291, 325 (1994),] at 355–56.

women's human rights include the right to be free from state-condoned domestic violence. Failing a correct, protection-based, interpretive approach, there is a need for specific statutory or regulatory language to alter the existing formalistic, male-biased way in which the law is interpreted, which excludes from "public" protection the more "private" harms suffered by women.

---

The difficulties inherent in convincing the federal government that private domestic violence is a human rights violation that must be redressed by a civilized society was painfully obvious in the well-publicized asylum case involving Rodi Alvarado. She was a victim of severe domestic violence whose legal journey began in 1996 when an immigration judge determined she deserved political asylum in the United States because of the horrendous domestic violence she suffered at the hands of her husband in her native Guatemala. Her legal journey is excerpted below.

## In re R—A—

United States Department of Justice, Board of Immigration Appeals

2001 BIA LEXIS 1 (2001 & 1999)

### BEFORE THE ATTORNEY GENERAL

(1) The Attorney General vacates the decision of the Board of Immigration Appeals and remands the case to the Board for reconsideration following final publication of the proposed rule published at 65 Fed. Reg. 76,588 (proposed Dec. 7, 2000).

Pursuant to 8 C.F.R § 3.1(h)(1)(iii), the Acting Commissioner of the Immigration and Naturalization Service has referred to the Attorney General for review the June 11, 1999, decision of the Board of Immigration Appeals (Board) that overturned the Immigration Judge's decision dated September 20, 1996. The June 11, 1999 decision of the Board is hereby vacated and the matter is remanded to the Board for reconsideration. I direct the Board to stay reconsideration of the decision until after the proposed rule published at 65 Fed. Reg. 76588 (Dec. 7, 2000) is published in final form. The Board should then reconsider the decision in light of the final rule.

### BEFORE THE BOARD

. . .

FILPPU, BOARD MEMBER:

In a decision dated September 20, 1996, an Immigration Judge granted the respondent's application for asylum under section 208(a) of the Immigration and Nationality Act, 8 U.S.C. § 1158(a) (1994). The Immigration and Naturalization Service has timely appealed the grant of asylum. The Service's request for oral argument before the Board has been withdrawn. The appeal will be sustained.

## I. ISSUES

The question before us is whether the respondent qualifies as a "refugee" as a result of the heinous abuse she suffered and still fears from her husband in Guatemala. Specifically, we address whether the repeated spouse abuse inflicted on the respondent makes her eligible for asylum as an alien who has been persecuted on account of her membership in a particular social group or her political opinion. We find that the group identified by the Immigration Judge has not adequately been shown to be a "particular social group" for asylum purposes. We further find that the respondent has failed to show that her husband was motivated to harm her, even in part, because of her membership in a particular social group or because of an actual or imputed political opinion. Our review is de novo with regard to the issues on appeal. See *Matter of Burbano*, 20 I. & N. Dec. 872 (BIA 1994).

## II. FACTUAL BACKGROUND

### A. Testimony and Statements of Abuse

The respondent is a native and citizen of Guatemala. She married at age 16. Her husband was then 21 years old. He currently resides in Guatemala, as do their two children. Immediately after their marriage, the respondent and her husband moved to Guatemala City. From the beginning of the marriage, her husband engaged in acts of physical and sexual abuse against the respondent. He was domineering and violent. The respondent testified that her husband "always mistreated me from the moment we were married, he was always . . . aggressive."

Her husband would insist that the respondent accompany him wherever he went, except when he was working. He escorted the respondent to her workplace, and he would often wait to direct her home. To scare her, he would tell the respondent stories of having killed babies and the elderly while he served in the army. Oftentimes, he would take the respondent to cantinas where he would become inebriated. When the respondent would complain about his drinking, her husband would yell at her. On one occasion, he grasped her hand to the point of pain and continued to drink until he passed out. When she left a cantina before him, he would strike her. As their marriage proceeded, the level and frequency of his rage increased concomitantly with the seeming senselessness and irrationality of his motives. He dislocated the respondent's jaw bone when her menstrual period was 15 days late. When she refused to abort her 3-to 4-month-old fetus, he kicked her violently in her spine. He would hit or kick the respondent "whenever he felt like it, wherever he happened to be: in the house, on the street, on the bus." The respondent stated that "as time went on, he hit me for no reason at all."

The respondent's husband raped her repeatedly. He would beat her before and during the unwanted sex. When the respondent resisted, he would accuse her of seeing other men and threaten her with death. The rapes occurred "almost daily," and they caused her severe pain. He passed on a sexually transmitted disease to the respondent from his sexual relations outside their marriage. Once, he kicked the respondent in her genitalia, apparently for no reason, causing the respondent to bleed severely for 8 days. The respondent suffered the most severe pain when he forcefully sodomized her. When she protested, he responded, as he often did, "You're my woman, you do what I say."

The respondent ran away to her brother's and parents' homes, but her husband always found her. Around December 1994, the respondent attempted to flee with her children outside the city, but her husband found her again. He appeared at her door, drunk, and as she turned to leave, he struck her in the back of her head causing her to lose consciousness. When she awoke, he kicked her and dragged her by her hair into another room and beat her to unconsciousness.

After 2 months away, her husband pleaded for the respondent's return, and she agreed because her children were asking for him. One night, he woke the respondent, struck her face, whipped her with an electrical cord, pulled out a machete and threatened to deface her, to cut off her arms and legs, and to leave her in a wheelchair if she ever tried to leave him. He warned her that he would be able to find her wherever she was. The violence continued. When the respondent could not give 5,000 quetzales to him when he asked for it, he broke windows and a mirror with her head. Whenever he could not find something, he would grab her head and strike furniture with it. Once, he pistol-whipped her. When she asked for his motivation, he broke into a familiar refrain, "I can do it if I want to."

Once, her husband entered the kitchen where the respondent was and, for no apparent reason, threw a machete toward her hands, barely missing them. He would often come home late and drunk. When the respondent noted his tardiness, he punched her. Once, he asked where the respondent had been. When she responded that she had been home waiting for him, he became enraged, struck her face, grabbed her by her hair, and dragged her down the street. One night, the respondent attempted to commit suicide. Her husband told her, "If you want to die, go ahead. But from here, you are not going to leave."

. . . .

The respondent's pleas to Guatemalan police did not gain her protection. On three occasions, the police issued summons for her husband to appear, but he ignored them, and the police did not take further action. Twice, the respondent called the police, but they never responded. When the respondent appeared before a judge, he told her that he would not interfere in domestic disputes. Her husband told the respondent that, because of his former military service, calling the police would be futile as he was familiar with law enforcement officials. The respondent knew of no shelters or other organizations in Guatemala that could protect her. The abuse began "from the moment [they] were married," and continued until the respondent fled Guatemala in May 1995. One morning in May 1995, the respondent decided to leave permanently. With help, the respondent was able to flee Guatemala, and she arrived in Brownsville, Texas, 2 days later.

. . . .

B. Country Conditions

Dr. Doris Bersing testified that spouse abuse is common in Latin American countries and that she was not aware of social or legal resources for battered women in Guatemala. Women in Guatemala, according to Dr. Bersing, have other problems related to general conditions in that country, and she suggested that such women could leave abusive partners but that they would face other problems such as poverty. Dr. Bersing further testified that the respondent was different from other battered women she had seen in that the respondent possessed an extraordinary fear of her husband and her abuse had been extremely severe.

Dr. Bersing noted that spouse abuse was a problem in many countries throughout the world, but she said it was a particular problem in Latin America, especially in Guatemala and Nicaragua. As we understand her testimony, its roots lie in such things as the Latin American patriarchal culture, the militaristic and violent nature of societies undergoing civil war, alcoholism, and sexual abuse in general. Nevertheless, she testified that husbands are supposed to honor, respect, and take care of their wives, and that spouse abuse is something that is present "underground" or "underneath in the culture." But if a woman chooses the wrong husband her options are few in countries such as Guatemala, which lack effective methods for dealing with the problem.

. . . .

### III. IMMIGRATION JUDGE'S DECISION

The Immigration Judge found the respondent to be credible, and she concluded that the respondent suffered harm that rose to the level of past persecution. The Immigration Judge also held that the Guatemalan Government was either unwilling or unable to control the respondent's husband. The balance of her decision addressed the issue of whether the respondent's harm was on account of a protected ground.

The Immigration Judge first concluded that the respondent was persecuted because of her membership in the particular social group of "Guatemalan women who have been involved intimately with Guatemalan male companions, who believe that women are to live under male domination." She found that such a group was cognizable and cohesive, as members shared the common and immutable characteristics of gender and the experience of having been intimately involved with a male companion who practices male domination through violence. The Immigration Judge then held that members of such a group are targeted for persecution by the men who seek to dominate and control them.

The Immigration Judge further found that, through the respondent's resistance to his acts of violence, her husband imputed to the respondent the political opinion that women should not be dominated by men, and he was motivated to commit the abuse because of the political opinion he believed her to hold.

. . . .

## V. THE LAW

An asylum applicant bears the burden of proof and persuasion of showing that he or she is a refugee within the meaning of section 101(a)(42)(A) of the Act, 8 U.S.C. § 1101(a)(42)(A) (1994), to be eligible for asylum under section 208(a) of the Act. The term "refugee" refers to:

> any person who is outside any country of such person's nationality ... and who is unable or unwilling to return to, and is unable or unwilling to avail himself or herself of the protection of, that country because of persecution or a well-founded fear of persecution on account of race, religion, nationality, membership in a particular social group, or political opinion.

Section 101(a)(42)(A) of the Act; see also *INS v. Cardoza-Fonseca*, 480 U.S. 421, 441 (1987).

. . . .

## VI. ANALYSIS

As noted above, we agree with the Immigration Judge that the severe injuries sustained by the respondent rise to the level of harm sufficient (and more than sufficient) to constitute "persecution." We also credit the respondent's testimony in general and specifically her account of being unsuccessful in obtaining meaningful assistance from the authorities in Guatemala. Accordingly, we find that she has adequately established on this record that she was unable to avail herself of the protection of the Government of Guatemala in connection with the abuse inflicted by her husband. The determinative issue, as correctly identified by the Immigration Judge, is whether the harm experienced by the respondent was, or in the future may be, inflicted "on account of" a statutorily protected ground.

. . . .

### A. Imputed Political Opinion

The record indicates that the respondent's husband harmed the respondent regardless of what she actually believed or what he thought she believed. The respondent testified that the abuse began "from the moment [they] were married." Even after the respondent "learned through experience" to acquiesce to his demands, he still abused her. The abuse took place before she left him initially, and it continued after she returned to him. In fact, he said he "didn't care" what she did to escape because he would find her. He also hurt her before her first call to the police and after her last plea for help.

. . . .

Nowhere in the record does the respondent recount her husband saying anything relating to what he thought her political views to be, or that the violence towards her was attributable to her actual or imputed beliefs. Moreover, this is not a case where there is meaningful evidence that this respondent held or evinced a political opinion, unless one assumes that the common human desire not to be harmed or abused is in itself a "political opinion." The record before us simply does not indicate that the harm arose in response to any objections made by the respondent to her husband's domination over her. Nor does it suggest that his abusive behavior was dependent in any way on the views held by the respondent. Indeed, his senseless actions started at the beginning of their marriage and continued whether or not the respondent acquiesced in his demands. The record reflects that, once having entered into this marriage, there was nothing the respondent could have done or thought that would have spared her (or indeed would have spared any other woman unfortunate enough to have married him) from the violence he inflicted.

. . . .

The respondent argues that, given the nature of domestic violence and sexual assaults, her husband necessarily imputed to her the view that she believed women should not be controlled and dominated by men. Even accepting the premise that he might have believed that the respondent disagreed with his views of women, it does not necessarily follow that he harmed the respondent because of those beliefs, rather than because of his own personal or psychological makeup coupled with his troubled perception of her actions at times. . . .

As we understand the respondent's rationale, it would seem that virtually any victim of repeated violence who offers some resistance could qualify for asylum, particularly where the government did not control the assailant. Under this approach, the perpetrator is presumed to impute to the victim a political opinion, in opposition to the perpetrator's authority, stemming simply from an act of resistance. Then, notwithstanding any other motivation for the original violence, the imputed political opinion becomes the assumed basis for the infliction of more harm.

It is certainly logical and only human to presume that no victim of violence desires to be such a victim and will resist in some manner. But it is another matter to presume that the perpetrator of the violence inflicts it because the perpetrator believes the victim opposes either the abuse or the authority of the abuser. We do not find that the second proposition necessarily follows from the first. Moreover, it seems to us that this approach ignores the question of what motivated the abuse at the outset, and it necessarily assumes that the original motivation is no longer the basis, at least not by itself, for the subsequent harm. We are unwilling to accept a string of presumptions or assumptions as a substitute for our own assessment of the evidence in this record, particularly when the reliability of these presumptions as genuine reflections of human behavior has not been established.

As for the record here, there has been no showing that the respondent's husband targeted any other women in Guatemala, even though we may reasonably presume that they, too, did not all share his view of male domination. The respondent was unable to set forth an accurate time frame for the great majority of the incidents she described. We are thus unable in general to link the incidents to acts of resistance in a way that might tend to support the respondent's theory. . . .

B. Particular Social Group

1. Cognizableness

. . . .

The starting point for "social group" analysis remains the existence of an immutable or fundamental individual characteristic in accordance with *Matter of Acosta*, [19 I&N Dec. 211 (BIA 1985), *modified on other grounds, Matter of Moghararrabi,* 19 I&N Dec. 439 (BIA 1987)], *supra*. We never declared, however, that the starting point for assessing social group claims articulated in *Acosta* was also the ending point. The factors we look to in this case, beyond *Acosta*'s "immutableness" test, are not prerequisites, and we do not rule out the use of additional considerations that may properly bear on whether a social group should be recognized in an individual case. But these factors are consistent with the operation of the other four grounds for asylum and are therefore appropriate, in our judgment, for consideration in the "particular social group" context.

On the record before us, we find that the respondent has not adequately established that we should recognize, under our law, the particular social group identified by the Immigration Judge.

2. Nexus

Further, we cannot agree with the Immigration Judge's nexus analysis. In analyzing "particular social group" claims, our decisions, as well as those of the Ninth Circuit, in which this case arises, require that the persecution or well-founded fear of persecution be on account of, or, in other words, because of, the alien's membership in that particular social group. . . .

In this case, even if we were to accept as a particular social group "Guatemalan women who have been involved intimately with Guatemalan male companions, who believe that women are to live under male domination," the respondent has not established that her husband has targeted and harmed the respondent because he perceived her to be a member of this particular social group. The record indicates that he has targeted only the respondent. The respondent's husband has not shown an interest in any member of this group other than the respondent herself. The respondent fails to show how other members of the group may be at risk of harm from him. . . .

. . . .

Indeed, the record does not reflect that the respondent's husband bore any particular animosity toward women who were intimate with abusive partners, women who had previously suffered abuse, or women who happened to have been born in, or were actually living in, Guatemala. There is little doubt that the respondent's spouse believed that married women should be subservient to their own husbands. But beyond this, we have scant information on how he personally viewed other married women in Guatemala, let alone women in general. On the basis of this record, we perceive that the husband's focus was on the respondent because she was his wife, not because she was a member of some broader collection of women, however defined, whom he believed warranted the infliction of harm.

The respondent's statements regarding her husband's motivation also undercut the nexus claims. He harmed her, when he was drunk and when he was sober, for not getting an abortion, for his belief that she was seeing other men, for not having her family get money for him, for not being able to find something in the house, for leaving a cantina before him, for leaving him, for reasons related to his mistreatment in the army, and "for no reason at all." Of all these apparent reasons for abuse, none was "on account of" a protected ground, and the arbitrary nature of the attacks further suggests it was not the respondent's claimed social group characteristics that he sought to overcome. The record indicates that there is nothing the respondent could have done to have satisfied her husband and prevented further abuse. Her own supposition is that he abused her because he was abused himself in the military.

The respondent was not at particular risk of abuse from her husband until she married him, at which point, given the nature of his focus, she was in a "group" by herself of women presently married to that particular man. . . .

The record in this case reflects that the views of society and of many governmental institutions in Guatemala can result in the tolerance of spouse abuse at levels we find appalling. But the record also shows that abusive marriages are not viewed as desirable, that spouse abuse is recognized as a problem, and that some measures have been pursued in an attempt to respond to this acknowledged problem. In this context, we are not convinced that the absence of an effective governmental reaction to the respondent's abuse translates into a finding that her husband inflicted the abuse because she was a member of a particular social group. The record does not support such a conclusion, as a matter of fact, when the husband's own behavior is examined. And Guatemala's societal and governmental attitudes and actions do not warrant our declaring this to be the case as a matter of law.

. . . .

The adequacy of state protection is obviously an essential inquiry in asylum cases. But its bearing on the "on account of" test for refugee status depends on the facts of the case and the context in which it arises. In this case, the independent actions of the respondent's husband may have been tolerated. But, as previously explained, this record does not show that his actions represent desired behavior within Guatemala or that the Guatemalan Government encourages domestic abuse.

. . . .

A focus on the adequacy of governmental protection would also shift the analysis in cases of refugee claims arising from civil war, as well as any other circumstance in which a government lacked the ability effectively to police all segments of society. This is not to say that the outcome of such an analysis would necessarily yield different results. The point, however, is that the existing statutory formula for assessing refugee claims would be altered. Instead of assessing the motivation of the actual persecutor, we might, for example, be focusing on the motivation or justification of the government for not intervening and affording real protection.

We reject the approach advocated by the respondent in view of the existing statutory language and the body of case law construing it. Consequently, the respondent must show more than a lack of protection or the existence of societal attitudes favoring male domination. She must make a showing from which it is reasonable to conclude that her husband was motivated to harm her, at least in part, by her asserted group membership.

. . . .

## VII. CONCLUSION

In sum, we find that the respondent has been the victim of tragic and severe spouse abuse. We further find that her husband's motivation, to the extent it can be ascertained, has varied; some abuse occurred because of his warped perception of and reaction to her behavior, while some likely arose out of psychological disorder, pure meanness, or no apparent reason at all. Absent other evidence, we accept the respondent's own assessment that the foundations of the abuse she suffered lay in the abuse her husband had experienced in his own life. We are not persuaded that the abuse occurred because of her membership in a particular social group or because of an actual or imputed political opinion. We therefore do not find the respondent eligible for asylum, and consequently, she is ineligible for withholding of deportation under section 243(h) of the Act, 8 U.S.C. § 1253(h) (1994). . . .

---

Attorney General Janet Reno remanded the case to the BIA in January 2001 with the instruction to reconsider the case in light of new asylum standards promulgated in 2000 by the U.S. Department of Justice. Those standards are excerpted below.

After George W. Bush became president in 2000, the personnel in the Justice Department changed. Incoming Attorney General John Ashcroft did not go forward to finalize the proposed Reno regulations and, in fact, they have never been finalized. Attorneys for the U.S. Department of Homeland Security, BICE's parent agency after the terrorist attacks of September 11, 2001, wrote a brief in favor of Ms. Alvarado's asylum request. But in January 2005, Attorney General Ashcroft declined to intervene on Ms. Alvarado's behalf, and the matter was returned to BIA for reconsideration without new regulations to guide it.[17]

---

17. John Files, *National Briefing Washington: Ashcroft Won't Aid Asylum Seeker,* N.Y. TIMES, Jan. 22, 2005, at A13.

## Asylum and Withholding Definitions Proposed Rules
Department of Justice (DOJ)
Immigration and Naturalization Service (INS)
8 CFR Part 208, 65 Fed. Reg. 76588 (Dec. 7, 2000)

ACTION: Proposed rule.

SUMMARY: This rule proposes to amend the Immigration and Naturalization Service (Service) regulations that govern establishing asylum and withholding eligibility. This rule provides guidance on the definitions of "persecution" and "membership in a particular social group," as well as what it means for persecution to be "on account of" a protected characteristic in the definition of a refugee. It restates that gender can form the basis of a particular social group. It also establishes principles for interpretation and application of the various components of the statutory definition of "refugee" for asylum and withholding cases generally, and, in particular, will aid in the assessment of claims made by applicants who have suffered or fear domestic violence. The Service believes these issues require further examination after the Board of Immigration Appeals (Board) decision in *In re R-A-,* Interim Decision 3403 (BIA 1999). Further, the rule clarifies that the factors considered in cases in the Court of Appeals for the Ninth Circuit regarding membership in a particular social group are not determinative. Finally, the rule clarifies procedural handling of asylum and withholding claims in which past persecution has been established. . . .

. . . .

Background

. . . .

One of these novel issues is the extent to which victims of domestic violence may be considered to have been persecuted under the asylum laws. The Board considered and rejected such a persecution claim in its decision in *In re R—A—*. This proposed rule removes certain barriers that the *In re R—A—* decision seems to pose to claims that domestic violence, against which a government is either unwilling or unable to provide protection, rises to the level of persecution of a person on account of membership in a particular social group. The proposed rule does not specify how a claim of persecution based on domestic violence should be fashioned—in particular, it does not set forth what the precise characteristics of the particular social group might be. The Department has taken this approach in part because it recognizes that the way in which a victim of domestic violence who believes she has been persecuted may characterize the particular social group of which she is a member likely will vary depending upon the social context in her country. The Department also recognizes that whether domestic violence can be so characterized in a given case will turn on difficult and subtle evaluations of particular facts. Given these realities, it seems ill-advised to try to establish a universal model for persecution claims based on domestic violence. The Department has instead decided to propose a rule that states generally applicable principles that will allow for case-by-case adjudication of claims based on domestic violence or other serious harm inflicted by individual non-state actors.

. . . .

The Meaning of Persecution

. . . .

This rule addresses the definition of persecution by clarifying that it includes both objective and subjective elements. First, the proposed rule defines persecution in § 208.15(a) as "the infliction of objectively serious harm or suffering." This general definition does not diminish the level of harm that has been recognized by the Board and generally sustained by the Courts of Appeals as sufficiently serious to constitute persecution. The definition does not preclude reference to other sources for guidance on what type of harm can constitute persecution. *See, e.g.*, United Nations High Commissioner for Refugees, Handbook on Procedures and Criteria for Determining Refugee Status (UNHCR Handbook), para. 51 (re-edited 1992) ("From Article 33 of the 1951 Convention it may be inferred that a threat to life or freedom on account of race, religion, nationality, political opinion or membership of a particular social group is always persecution. Other serious violations of human rights—for the same reasons—would also constitute persecution."). . . .

The proposed language also provides that harm is persecution only if it is "experienced as serious harm by the applicant, regardless of whether the persecutor intends to cause harm." . . . Generally, an applicant's own testimony would be the best evidence in determining whether that applicant subjectively experienced or would experience the treatment as harm.

State Action Requirement

Inherent in the meaning of persecution is the long-standing principle that the harm or suffering that an applicant experienced or fears must be inflicted by either the government of the country where the applicant fears persecution, or a person or group that government is unable or unwilling to control. . . .

Section 208.15(a)(1) of this rule provides further guidance as to what is meant by the state action requirement and, specifically, the requirement that the government be "unable or unwilling to control" non-government persecutors. The proposed rule states that "[i]n evaluating whether a government is unwilling or unable to control the infliction of harm or suffering, the immigration judge or asylum officer should consider whether the government takes reasonable steps to control the infliction of harm or suffering and whether the applicant has reasonable access to the state protection that exists." . . . Rather, the decision-maker should consider the government's policies with respect to the harm or suffering at issue, and what steps, if any, the government has taken to prevent the infliction of such harm or suffering. In addition, the decision-maker should consider what kind of access the individual applicant has to whatever protection is available, and any steps the applicant has taken to seek such protection. Any attempts by an applicant to seek protection within the country of persecution are relevant but are not determinative of the state's inability or unwillingness to control the infliction of suffering or harm. An applicant's failure to attempt to gain access to protection is not in itself determinative of the state's inability or unwillingness to control nor does this failure bar an applicant from establishing by other evidence the state's inability or unwillingness to control the infliction of suffering or harm....

The "on account of" Requirement in General

Even if it is determined that the harm an applicant has suffered or fears may constitute persecution, the applicant may qualify for asylum or withholding only if that persecution is inflicted "on account of" the applicant's race, religion, nationality, membership in a particular social group, or political opinion. The Supreme Court has held that, in order for persecution to be "on account of" one of these protected grounds, there must be evidence that the persecutor seeks to harm the victim on account of the victim's possession of the characteristic at issue. *INS v. Elias-Zacarias,* 502 U.S. 478, 482 (1992).... This rule provides guidance on several of these issues.

Under long-standing principles of U.S. refugee law, it is not necessary for an applicant to show that his or her possession of a protected characteristic is the sole reason that the persecutor seeks to harm him or her. Both the Board and the federal courts have recognized that a persecutor may have mixed motivations, and have stated that the "on account of" requirement is satisfied if the persecutor acts "at least in part" because of a protected characteristic. *See, e.g., Matter of T-M-B-,* 21 I. & N. Dec. 775 (BIA 1997), *overruled on other grounds sub nom. Borja v. INS,* 175 F.3d 732 (9th Cir. 1999) (*en banc*)....

The proposed language also incorporates the doctrine of "imputed political opinion" into the regulation. Under this doctrine, an applicant may establish persecution on account of political opinion if he or she can show that the persecutor was or is inclined to persecute because the persecutor perceives the applicant to possess a particular political opinion, even if the applicant does not in fact possess such an opinion. *See, e.g., Sangha v. INS,* 103 F.3d 1482, 1489 (9th Cir. 1997). The proposed language provides that an applicant may satisfy the "on account of" requirement by showing that the persecutor acts against him or her "on account of the applicant's race, religion, nationality, membership in a particular social group, or political opinion, or on account of what the persecutor perceives to be the applicant's race, religion, nationality, membership in a particular social group, or political opinion."...

*In re R—A—*

The proposed new language in § 208.15(b) is intended to address analytical issues that have arisen in the context of some claims based on domestic violence, and in particular in the Board's decision in *In re R—A—,* Interim Decision 3403 (BIA 1999). In that case, the Board denied asylum to a Guatemalan woman who had been the victim of severe domestic violence by her husband in Guatemala and who feared that she would be at risk of continuing violence if she returned there. Certain elements of the Board's analysis in this case affect the "on account of" inquiry in asylum and withholding cases in general, and the "particular social group" cases especially. This rule sets forth a modified statement of the principles governing the "on account of" inquiry....

[I]n some cases involving domestic violence, an applicant may be able to establish that the abuser is motivated to harm her because of her gender or because of her status in a domestic relationship. This may be a characteristic that she shares with other women in her society, some of whom are also at risk of harm from their partners on account of this shared characteristic. Thus, it may be possible in some cases for a victim of domestic violence to satisfy the "on account of" requirement, even though social limitations and other factors result in the abuser having the opportunity, and indeed the motivation, to harm only one of the women who share this characteristic, because only one of these women is in a domestic relationship with the abuser.

To allow for this possibility, this rule provides that, when evaluating whether an applicant has met his or her burden of proof to establish that the harm he or she suffered or fears is "on account of" a protected characteristic, "[b]oth direct and circumstantial evidence may be relevant to the inquiry." The rule further provides that "[e]vidence that the persecutor seeks to act against other individuals who share the applicant's protected characteristic is relevant and may be considered but shall not be required."

In every asylum or withholding case, of course, it remains the applicant's burden to establish that the specific persecutor involved in her claim is motivated to act against her because of her possession or perceived possession of a protected characteristic. As this rule underscores, both direct and circumstantial evidence may be relevant to this determination. As in any asylum or withholding case, evidence about the persecutor's statements and actions will be considered. In addition, evidence about patterns of violence in the society against individuals similarly situated to the applicant may also be relevant to the "on account of" determination....

Further, a claim involving domestic violence in which the applicant has satisfied the "on account of" requirement remains subject to the full range of generally applicable requirements under the asylum and withholding laws. For example, as in any other case, the fear of future abuse cannot be speculative, it must be "well-founded." A woman who is not in an abusive relationship, for example, would not have a "well-founded" fear of domestic violence even if there is a high incidence of domestic violence in her country of origin. The harm feared must be serious enough to constitute persecution; isolated incidents of discrimination or lesser forms of harm would not qualify as persecution. As in any asylum or withholding case in which the persecutor is not the state itself, the applicant would have to show that the state is unwilling or unable to protect her. Generally, an applicant's claim based on domestic violence will rest on personal experiences not addressed in general country conditions information. General country conditions information may, however, support such a claim. The applicant should come forward with testimony regarding her personal experience, and, if available, documentary evidence relating to her claim.

. . . .

Membership in a Particular Social Group

Once an applicant has established that the harm he or she has suffered or fears is "on account of" the characteristic asserted, the applicant must establish that the characteristic qualifies as race, religion, nationality, membership in a particular social group, or political opinion. Membership in a particular social group is perhaps the most complex and difficult to understand of these five grounds. There is relatively little precedent about the meaning of "a particular social group," and that which exists has at times been subject to conflicting interpretations. . . .

The key Board decision on the meaning of "a particular social group" requires that members of the group share a "common, immutable" trait. *Matter of Acosta,* 19 I. & N. Dec. at 233. This rule codifies this basic approach at § 208.15(c)(1), by providing that "[a] particular social group is composed of members who share a common, immutable characteristic, such as sex, color, kinship ties, or past experience, that a member either cannot change or that is so fundamental to the identity or conscience of the member that he or she should not be required to change it." The crucial aspect of this definition is that, to be immutable, the common trait must be unchangeable or truly fundamental to an applicant's identity. Gender is clearly such an immutable trait, is listed as such in *Matter of Acosta,* and is incorporated in this rule. Further, there may be circumstances in which an applicant's marital status could be considered immutable. This would be the case, for example, if a woman could not reasonably be expected to divorce because of religious, cultural, or legal constraints. Any intimate relationship, including marriage, could also be immutable if the evidence indicates that the relationship is one that the victim could not reasonably be expected to leave. Thus, this rule further provides in § 208.15(c)(1) that "[i]n determining whether an applicant cannot change, or should not be expected to change, the shared characteristic, all relevant evidence should be considered, including the applicant's individual circumstances and country conditions information about the applicant's society."

This rule also includes the principle that the particular social group in which an applicant claims membership cannot be defined by the harm which the applicant claims as persecution. It is well-established in the case law that this type of circular reasoning does not suffice to articulate a particular social group. *See Gomez v. INS,* 947 F.2d 660, 664 (2d Cir. 1991) (rejecting the applicant's claim to membership in a particular social group of women who have been previously battered and raped by Salvadoran guerrillas). It is also supported by Convention-based understandings of the definition of membership in a particular social group. *See, e.g., Islam v. Secretary of State for the Home Department,* 2 App. Cas. 629 (H.L. 1999) (United Kingdom) ("It is common ground that there is a general principle that there can only be a 'particular social group' if the group exists independently of the persecution") (Lord Steyn).

Proposed § 208.15(c)(2) provides that, "[w]hen past experience defines a particular social group, the past experience must be an experience that, at the time it occurred, the member either could not have changed or was so fundamental to his or her identity or conscience that he or she should not have been required to change it." . . .

The requirement in § 208.15(c)(1) that the persecution exist independently of the harm is equally applicable to claims of membership in a particular social group based on past experience. At least in theory, a shared past experience that defines a social group could be harm suffered by the applicant and other group members in the past. In such a claim however, the past harm that defines the social group cannot be the same harm that the applicant claims as persecution. Rather, in order for persecution to be "on account of" membership in such a group, the past experience must exist independently of the persecution. In fact, the past experience must be the reason the persecutor inflicted or is inclined to inflict the persecution on the applicant.

Finally, the proposed language in § 208.15(c)(3) provides a non-exclusive list of additional factors that may be considered in determining whether a particular social group exists. These factors are drawn from existing administrative and judicial precedent on the meaning of the "particular social group" ground. . . .

. . . .

Burden of Proof

Under U.S. law, a showing of past persecution qualifies an applicant for refugee status. Section 101(a)(42) of the Act, (8 U.S.C. 1101(a)(42)). A showing of past persecution is also strongly indicative of the possibility of future harm. Under the current regulations as modified by the final rule on asylum procedures published in conjunction with this rule, a presumption of well-founded fear applies to applicants who qualify as refugees based on past persecution. The presumption places the burden on the U.S. government to show by a preponderance of the evidence that a refugee no longer has a well-founded fear of future persecution. The Department believes that this allocation of the burden generally is appropriate in light of the applicant's refugee status.

The final rule on asylum procedures published in conjunction with this rule broadens the evidence with which the government can rebut the presumption of well-founded fear. The presumption can be rebutted by evidence of a fundamental change in circumstances, including country conditions information, or a showing of a reasonable internal relocation alternative. . . .

. . . .

In all cases of past persecution the government may rebut the presumption of well-founded fear of future persecution. The Department recognizes that, especially if the general rule concerning burden of proof is retained for cases involving individual non-state actors, some of the new types of claims based on persecution by individuals may present a question of production of evidence useful to rebuttal that may be uniquely in the hands of the applicant claiming persecution. Moreover, whether or not the burden of proof is retained in this context, the Department has concluded that it would be appropriate to codify long-standing principles of law relating to the applicant's burden of production in asylum and withholding cases. For example, in the domestic violence context, an applicant's claim will rest on direct evidence regarding her experiences with the persecutor that are not addressed in general country conditions information. Circumstantial evidence, such as general country conditions information also may support such a claim.

. . . .

Janet Reno,

*Attorney General.*

---

After 14 years and three changes in presidential administrations, Rodi Alvarado was finally granted asylum in the United States because of the severe domestic violence she endured at the hands of her husband in Guatemala.[18]

In re R—A—

Department of Justice, Board of Immigration Appeals 24 I. & N. Dec. 629 (Sept. 25, 2008)

. . . .

## OPINION

In *Matter of R-A-*, 22 I. & N. Dec. 906 (BIA 1999; A.G. 2001), the Board of Immigration Appeals denied a claim for asylum filed by an alien who had been the victim of domestic violence in Guatemala. The respondent in that case contended that the serious harm inflicted on her by her husband constituted persecution on account of her membership in a particular social group, defined as "Guatemalan women who have been involved intimately with Guatemalan male companions, who believe that women are to live under male domination." *Id*. at 911. The Acting Commissioner of the Immigration and Naturalization Service referred the decision to the Attorney General for review.

On January 19, 2001, Attorney General Reno vacated the Board's decision and directed the Board on remand to stay reconsideration of the case pending the publication in final form of a proposed rule that had been published after the Board's decision. Among other things, the proposed rule would have amended the asylum regulations relating to the meaning of the terms "persecution," "on account of," and "particular social group." *See* Asylum and Withholding Definitions, 65 Fed. Reg. 76,588 (Dec. 7, 2000). Attorney General Reno's order directed the Board to reconsider its

---

18. Associated Press, *Domestic Violence Victim Granted Asylum in U.S.,* Dec. 18, 2009, *available at* www.newsday.com/news/nation/domestic-violence-victim-granted-asylum-in-us-1.1660390, accessed March 6, 2017.

decision "in light of the final rule." The Board has continued to defer its reconsideration of *Matter of R-A-* since the issuance of that stay order.[19]

In the years since the issuance of the stay order, both the Board and courts of appeals have issued numerous decisions relating to various aspects of asylum law under the existing statutory and regulatory provisions. Although these intervening decisions may not have directly resolved the issues presented in *Matter of R-A-*, some of them have addressed, for example, the terms "persecution," "on account of," and "particular social group," and thus may have relevance to the issues presented with respect to asylum claims based on domestic violence. *See, e.g., Matter of E-A-G-*, 24 I. & N. Dec. 591 (BIA 2008); *Matter of S-E-G-*, 24 I. & N. Dec. 579 (BIA 2008); *Matter of A-M-E- & J-G-U-*, 24 I. & N. Dec. 69 (BIA 2007); *Matter of C-A-*, 23 I. & N. Dec. 951 (BIA 2006).

In addition, I have been advised that the Board has been holding not only the case of the particular alien who is the subject of the *Matter of R-A-* decision, but also a growing number of similar cases involving aliens who have alleged that they were victims of domestic violence in their home countries.[20] The stay order has prevented the Board from acting on these cases.

In light of these developments and the fact that the proposed rule cited by Attorney General Reno never has been made final, I have decided to lift the stay so that the Board can revisit the issues in *Matter of R-A-* and related cases and issue new decisions. Accordingly, the Board should now proceed as it sees fit with its reconsideration of *Matter of R-A-* and the other cases involving similarly situated aliens. This review necessarily will be based on the current regulations, because the proposed rule has not been made final. Given the passage of time, the Board may choose to request additional briefing in the pending cases or to remand cases to Immigration Judges for further factual development.

In engaging in this review (as in any review), the Board should of course consider relevant courts of appeals decisions. Insofar as a question involves interpretation of ambiguous statutory language, the Board is free to exercise its own discretion and issue a precedent decision establishing a uniform standard nationwide. Providing a consistent, authoritative, nationwide interpretation of ambiguous provisions of the immigration laws is one of the key duties of the Board. *See, e.g.*, 8 C.F.R. § 1003.1(d)(1) (2008) ("[T]he Board, through precedent decisions, shall provide clear and uniform guidance to [DHS], the immigration judges, and the general public on the proper interpretation and administration of the Act and its implementing regulations."); *see*

---

19. [n1] In 2003, Attorney General Ashcroft certified the Board's decision in *Matter of R-A-* for review and provided an opportunity for additional briefing, but ultimately remanded the case, again directing the Board to reconsider its decision "in light of the final rule." *Matter of R-A-*, 23 I. & N. Dec. 694 (A.G. 2005).

20. [n2] For aliens victimized by domestic violence in the United States, I note that the immigration laws already provide remedies in particular circumstances, including provisions for self-petitioning by battered spouses, the availability of special waivers, and the opportunity to apply for U-1 nonimmigrant status.

*also INS v. Aguirre-Aguirre*, 526 U.S. 415, 425, 119 S. Ct. 1439, 143 L. Ed. 2d 590 (1999) ("[W]e have recognized that judicial deference to the Executive Branch is especially appropriate in the immigration context where officials 'exercise especially sensitive political functions that implicate questions of foreign relations.'" (quoting *Immigration & Naturalization Service v. Abudu*, 485 U.S. 94, 110, 108 S. Ct. 904, 99 L. Ed. 2d 90 (1988))); *Jian Hui Shao v. BIA*, 465 F.3d 497, 502 (2d Cir. 2006) (noting that "only a precedential decision by the BIA—or the Supreme Court of the United States— can ensure the uniformity that seems to us especially desirable in [asylum] cases such as these"). Moreover, the Supreme Court has made clear that administrative agencies are not bound by prior judicial interpretations of ambiguous statutory provisions, because there is "a 'presumption that Congress, when it left ambiguity in a statute meant for implementation by an agency, understood that the ambiguity would be resolved, first and foremost, by the agency, and desired the agency (rather than the courts) to possess whatever degree of discretion the ambiguity allows.'" *National Cable & Telecomms. Ass'n v. Brand X Internet Servs.*, 545 U.S. 967, 982, 125 S. Ct. 2688, 162 L. Ed. 2d 820 (2005) (quoting *Smiley v. Citibank (South Dakota), N.A.*, 517 U.S. 735, 740-41, 116 S. Ct. 1730, 135 L. Ed. 2d 25 (1996) (citing *Chevron, U.S.A., Inc. v. Natural Resources Defense Council, Inc.*, 467 U.S. 837, 104 S. Ct. 2778, 81 L. Ed. 2d 694 (1984))).

## CONCLUSION

For the reasons set forth above, I remand this matter to the Board for reconsideration in accordance with this opinion.

---

In the fall of 2009, the Obama Administration recommended that Ms. Alvarado be granted asylum, which all but guaranteed it would happen. It came too late for her to enjoy raising her own children—during her 14-year odyssey they remained in Guatemala with their paternal grandparents.[21] In December of that year, she was finally granted her long-pending asylum request by an immigration judge in San Francisco.

## *Notes and Questions*

- **PRIMER ON IMMIGRATION PROCEDURE**

The Homeland Security Act of 2002 abolished the Immigration and Naturalization Service (INS). Pub. L. No. 107-296, Sec. 471, 116 Stat. 2135 (2002). The functions of the INS were transferred from the U.S. Department of Justice to the newly-formed Department of Homeland Security (DHS). The Executive Office of Immigration Review, which includes the immigration judges and the Bureau of Immigration Appeals (BIA), have remained at DOJ. The prosecutorial functions of the old INS are now the domain of the Bureau of Immigration and Customs Enforcement (BICE), which is part of DHS. Keep in mind while reading decisions that some federal court

---

21. Julia Preston, *U.S. May Be Open to Asylum for Spouse Abuse*, N.Y. TIMES, October 29, 2009.

opinions written after 2002 still refer to INS as the agency responsible for immigration matters.

The laws regarding immigration enforcement can be confusing. An immigrant first appears before an immigration judge, of which there are some 200 employed by the United States Department of Justice to review cases. If an immigrant's application to remain in this country is denied, he or she may appeal to the Board of Immigration Appeals, which is an 11-member administrative judicial body. One board member is assigned to a case. An immigrant can appeal an adverse decision to the federal appeals court. There have been legislative proposals to funnel all federal appeals of immigration cases solely to the Federal Circuit in Washington, D.C., which was created to hear only patent and trademarks cases. The theory is that such a change would alleviate the glut of immigration appeals now pending around the country and create a more uniform body of appellate law. These proposals are still pending. *See* Emma Schwartz, *Shift of Immigration Appeals to Federal Circuit Proposed,* N.Y. LAW JOURNAL, April 3, 2006, at 1.

Whether an immigrant receives asylum in the United States — for whatever reason — has been found to depend largely on where the application is heard and which judge hears it. In a study conducted by three law school professors of 140,000 decisions issued by immigration judges, it was found, for example, that in Atlanta, while only 12 percent of all refugees win asylum, in San Francisco, 54 percent do. And, in looking at individual immigration court judges in Miami, they discovered one judge granted only three percent of all asylum cases, while another judge granted 75 percent. Julia Preston, *Wide Disparities Found in Judging of Asylum Cases,* N.Y. TIMES, May 31, 2007, at A1.

Chapter 12

# Domestic Violence and the Justice System

> **CONSIDER AS YOU READ ABOUT THE JUSTICE SYSTEM**
> 1. How have the courts historically addressed domestic violence
> 2. The ethical challenges of specialized domestic violence courts
> 3. Issues that confront prosecutors and defense lawyers who handle domestic violence cases
> 4. Sanctions for lawyers and jurists who engage in domestic violence in their personal lives

Moving full circle from the introductory chapter, the justice system, which once ignored domestic violence, has now adopted laws, policies and procedures to respond to it. It is in the criminal justice arena where these changes have been most profound. As a result of mandatory arrest laws and increased advocacy for victims of domestic violence by lawyers associated with non-profit groups established for that purpose, the criminal justice system began to focus on new approaches to these cases. Prosecutors' offices formed specialized domestic violence units to work closely with complaining witnesses. They aligned themselves with court-funded social work agencies and created multi-disciplinary "family justice centers" to encourage victim cooperation with the system. In addition, with passage of VAWA, large sums of federal money became available for the nation's state court system to better meet the challenges of an increased domestic violence caseload.

But as with every response to a social problem, the pendulum swings back and forth. The conversation in recent years has shifted away from solid support of criminalizing domestic violence on the part of some victims' advocates. Some of the concerns include the high rates of incarceration of young African American men; the break-up of families if non-citizen abusers are convicted of a domestic violence offense and subsequently deported, and the loss of empowerment of victims who cede control of their cases to the prosecutor when they cooperate with the criminal justice apparatus.

# I. Problem-Solving Courts

Problem-solving courts have been in operation for nearly 30 years. Separate courts have developed to address the problem of drug addiction and juvenile crime. They have been followed by courts created to handle domestic violence cases, or cases involving defendants who suffer from mental illness and or veterans returning from multiple tours of duty fighting endless wars abroad. Problem-solving courts have two goals. The first is "to respond more effectively to social and legal problems.... And the second is to shape case resolutions that respond to the concerns of a variety of stakeholders—victims, community residents, defendants, and others—about the criminal justice process."[1]

In their book, *Good Courts,* authors Greg Berman and John Feinblatt describe how these tribunals work:

> Each shares an underlying premise: that courts should do more than just process cases, that at the end of the day, the goal is not just to make it through the calendar, but to make a difference in the lives of victims, the lives of defendants and the lives of neighborhoods. In one way or another, all of the new judicial experiments are attempting to solve the kinds of cases where social, human, and legal problems intersect.
>
> The potential implications of this shift in orientation are profound. Problem-solving courts recognize that to dispose of a case is not the same thing as to resolve it. As a consequence, they do not restrict themselves to the standard approach to case processing—a framework that often obscures the problems that brought a defendant to court, the long-term impacts of offending on a neighborhood, and the harms suffered by victims.[2]

## A. Judicial Attitude and Demeanor in Domestic Violence Cases

In a 1999 article in the *National Bulletin on Domestic Violence Prevention,* author Susan R. Paisner wrote: "Ask any domestic violence advocate where the biggest problem in the criminal justice system still resides, and that person will most likely say: judges."[3] Inappropriate judicial demeanor and the general chaos of crowded court calendars have long been cited among the many reasons victims historically have been reluctant to seek legal intervention to stop their domestic abuse.

---

1. Greg Berman, Derek Denckla & John Feinblatt, *Judicial Innovation at the Crossroads: The Future of Problem-Solving Courts,* 13 THE COURT MANAGER 28, 30 (2000).
2. GREG BERMAN & JOHN FEINBLATT, GOOD COURTS: THE CASE FOR PROBLEM-SOLVING JUSTICE 32–33 (2005).
3. Susan R. Paisner, *A Court Grows in Brooklyn: Dedicated Domestic Violence Court Serves as National Model,* 5(9) NAT'L BULL. ON DOMESTIC VIOLENCE PREVENTION 5 (1999).

JUDGE THUMB.
or — Patent Sticks for Family Correction; Warranted Lawful!

In his book about the treatment of battered women in the courtroom, BATTERED WOMEN IN THE COURTROOM: THE POWER OF JUDICIAL RESPONSES, sociology professor James Ptacek described a study of judicial responses in Boston, Massachusetts, conducted more than 30 years ago after local media reports about court insensitivity toward victims. He wrote:

... Beginning in August of 1986, the problem of judicial mistreatment of battered women was so vividly publicized in the *Boston Globe* that the Massachusetts lower criminal courts were forced to take dramatic and unprecedented actions. Within four months from the *Globe*'s first story on judicial misconduct, the crisis of public trust in the Massachusetts courts had become so serious that two judges withdrew from hearing domestic violence cases, a third judge was stripped of most of his authority, the state Judicial Conduct Commission began new investigations, separate inquiries were initiated in two courts, and the state's highest court appointed a commission to study gender bias in the court system as a whole.

. . . .

The public events of 1986 in Massachusetts actually had their origins in the previous year. The initial documentation of judicial misconduct was done in a 1985 report prepared by the Battered Women's Working Group. This body, a committee of the Governor's Anti-Crime Council, developed an imaginative study of the law in practice concerning restraining orders. The Working Group, made up of representatives of battered women's shelters, feminist attorneys, legal services representatives, police officers, and other service providers, set up a phone line at the State House to record calls presenting evidence of mistreatment of women seeking judicial protection from abuse under state law. The study design called for each complaint to be witnessed by either a shelter worker, a legal advocate or an attorney. Within six months, 250 incidents from around the state had been compiled.

The study documented "widespread patterns of noncompliance" with the law on the part of police, court clerks, and judges. The following documentation from the study illustrates the nature of the complaints:

Case #0063: Woman went to district court for temporary restraining, vacate and custody orders against her abusive boyfriend. Judge would not grant custody; he told her, "most people get married and do not have illegitimate children. These things don't happen to them."

Case #0040: When a woman was called to the bench after requesting a restraining and vacate order the judge asked her: Does your husband drink? Does he gamble? Does he run around with other women? When woman replied no, the judge asked her what reason then, did she have to be in court? Woman stammered and began to cry—advocate ended up speaking for woman. Judge has a reputation of being difficult and asking unrelated personal questions.

Case #0113: Judge granted husband and wife mutual restraining orders against each other. Judge told them to go home and behave themselves. Woman was visibly bruised, had two black eyes and many cuts and scratches on her face. Outside the court room the husband threatened to kill the wife. The woman did not feel it was safe to return home; she went into shelter.

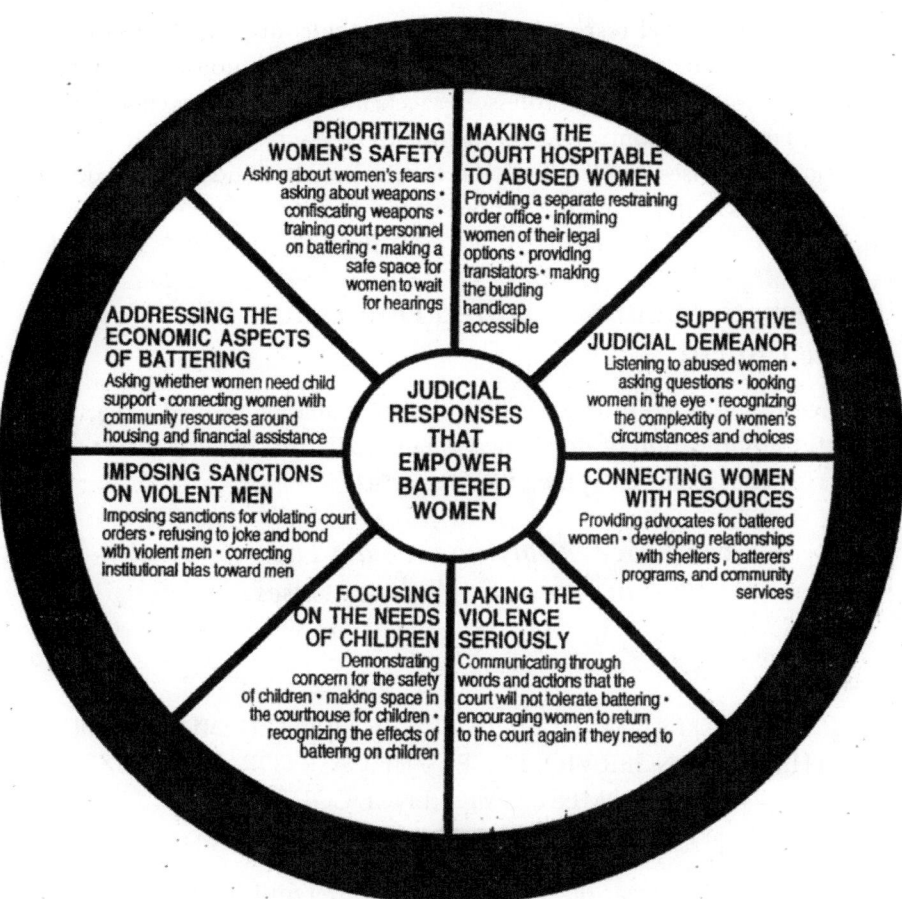

James Ptacek, Judicial Responses that Empower Battered Women.

The most common acts of noncompliance attributed to judges were incorrect applications of the law, a biased or racist attitude toward women, inappropriate denials of a temporary restraining order, and inaccurate advice or ignorance of the law....

The public spotlight on judicial hostility toward battered women created enormous public pressure for official responses. And in this scandal, the *Globe* served both as a public forum and as an instigator. In addition to the front-page articles, the *Globe* printed four editorials on judicial mistreatment of battered women. One editorial, entitled "Judicial Accountability," criticized the "conspiracy of silence" among judges, prosecutors, and defense lawyers "that allows some judges to engage in misconduct with near impunity." In a space of a few months, the power of the press forced changes that activists had sought for years.[4]

---

4. JAMES PTACEK, BATTERED WOMEN IN THE COURTROOM: THE POWER OF JUDICIAL RESPONSES 50–52, 56 (1999).

Inappropriate judicial responses re-create in the courtroom the same negative atmosphere that a battered woman faces at home. The Judicial Response wheel reprinted below, also devised by Professor Ptacek, modeled on the well-known domestic violence Power and Control Wheel included in the introductory chapter, describe those judicial responses that leave victims feeling hopeless and entrapped, and those providing victims with a sense of support.

## B. The Debate About Specialized Domestic Violence Courts

Whether a specialized problem-solving court staffed by trained judges dedicated solely to the adjudication of domestic violence cases can better address the special needs of victims is explored in the following article.

### Bruce Winick, *Applying the Law Therapeutically in Domestic Violence Cases*
69 UMKC L. Rev. 33 (2000)

. . . .

#### II. SHOULD INTIMATE VIOLENCE BE TREATED DIFFERENTLY THAN STRANGER VIOLENCE?: THE CASE FOR SPECIALIZED DOMESTIC VIOLENCE COURTS

. . . .

Is it appropriate to treat domestic violence differently than stranger violence? Should these cases be dealt with in general criminal courts or specialized domestic violence courts? Are mandatory arrest or prosecution practices warranted for domestic violence, but not for stranger violence? Are comparable penalties warranted? I believe that it is appropriate to treat domestic violence differently. Even though there is evidence that people who commit domestic violence do not specialize, but rather commit a variety of other criminal offenses, the special repetitive nature of domestic violence and of the harm it brings warrants separate treatment. Unlike stranger violence, which tends to be a onetime incident from the victim's perspective, domestic violence tends to be an on-going course of behavior involving both violence and threats of violence. Stranger violence certainly can produce intense pain, terror, and psychological distress, but on-going domestic violence can have a significantly more serious impact on the victim. That the offender often lives with the victim presents an added level of danger that brings uniqueness to the crime. The possibility of subsequent abuse is ever present after the police have left the scene, after the defendant has been released from jail if arrested, and even after the issuance of a restraining order. Once stranger violence has occurred, it rarely will be repeated. With intimate violence, however, the victim may have to live under the constant fear of repeated abuse with ever escalating force, sometimes including deadly force.

. . . .

A specialized domestic violence court is an integrated system that can handle both civil protection orders and criminal domestic violence cases. In addition to its ability to allow for integrated adjudication of all issues related to the domestic violence occurring in a victim's environment, the court can address domestic violence from a community-wide perspective by incorporating into the judicial process referrals for counseling, batterers' intervention treatment programs, substance abuse programs, and other resources for victims, batterers, and their families. Domestic violence courts can thus constitute a comprehensive community response to domestic violence that integrates multiple services into a single court-based system. . . .

Such an integrated court can offer heightened responsiveness of the judicial system to individual domestic violence victims. For example, to attempt to alleviate the economic oppression that keeps many victims in an abusing relationship, the court can order and monitor the payment of child support. A fully integrated court can also deal with related issues such as paternity and divorce.

The intake unit of a specialized domestic violence court can effectively coordinate case management by linking the present case to any related case currently pending or subsequently filed. The availability of a central court able to process all issues related to the problem provides greater access to the judicial process for victims, particularly for the majority of them who will not have the assistance of counsel because of their economic status. Rather than dealing with issues on a piecemeal basis, specialized domestic violence court judges can develop expertise in dealing with all aspects of the domestic violence problem and can improve their ability in the adjudication and disposition of these difficult issues, a difficulty enhanced by the fact that many victims and perpetrators are unrepresented.

An integrated domestic violence court also can allow effective monitoring of conditions of probation for abusers and compliance with the terms of protection orders, including treatment orders. Judges who have entered orders restraining batterers or requiring them to do various things, accepted pleas that carry various conditions, or imposed sentences that include mandated treatment or other requirements can periodically monitor the perpetrator's compliance with the court's orders and make it clear to them that the court is serious and will enforce its rulings. . . .

Domestic violence court also allows a more timely response than is possible in the typically backlogged criminal court. Time often is of the essence in these cases, and the ability of the court to act quickly may make the difference between life and death. Moreover, specialized domestic violence courts can do much to raise community consciousness about the problem of domestic violence and to marshal community resources for dealing with its prevention and treatment. Having a domestic violence court can emphasize to the community both the seriousness with which the judicial process treats domestic violence and the dedication of the courts to dealing effectively with the problem. . . .

In addition, a specialized domestic violence court can play an important role in the rehabilitation of offenders. Such an opportunity exists in cases in which offenders accept diversion or plead guilty and receive a probationary term that includes various conditions of probation, including participation in rehabilitative programs. The opportunity also exists in cases in which a variety of creative sentencing alternatives are utilized that include participation in rehabilitation.

Rehabilitative programs for batterers, involving essentially counseling, education, and cognitive restructuring, are unlikely to succeed absent the motivation of the offender to change his attitudes and behavior. There is no pill for the treatment of domestic violence. A judicial order mandating participation in a rehabilitative program may not produce the needed motivation on the part of the offender. He may simply comply with the formal requirements of the program, going through the motions, but resisting any genuine attitudinal or behavioral change. . . .

In addition, creative judicial participation in the monitoring of the offender's rehabilitative efforts, including the application of judicial praise and encouragement for positive compliance and sanctions for failure to comply, can foster continued motivation on the part of the offender to succeed in the program. In these ways, the court may be able to spark motivation on the part of the offender and to facilitate its continuation during the rehabilitative process. To the extent that offenders are amenable to treatment interventions, the domestic violence court thereby can play a special role in motivating offenders, monitoring program compliance, and even participating in a more direct way in the treatment process—heightening the potential that offenders will participate in rehabilitation in a meaningful way and that it will be effective.

Moreover, domestic violence courts can be structured in ways that can allow them to function as instruments of risk management. These courts can use tools like the Spousal Abuse Risk Assessment (SARA) Guide to collect information about the offender, and use this information in ways that facilitate police, prosecutorial, and judicial decision making and supervision and monitoring. These tools can increase the ability of the judicial process accurately to assess the risk of future violence, take appropriate steps to prevent it, and motivate the offender to learn ways of reducing the risk he presents. In addition, proper use of risk assessment tools in this area, as Part III demonstrates, can allow the court to play an important role in the rehabilitation of offenders.

Thus there are many advantages to the use of specialized domestic violence courts. These specialized courts are able to play a more effective role in the rehabilitation of offenders and the healing of their victims. The special role played by the judge in such courts, as well as the court's function in preventing future domestic violence and in dealing directly with the rehabilitation of abusers, makes these courts a more effective vehicle for dealing with the problem in a comprehensive way than would be possible in the criminal court. These courts thus can apply principles of therapeutic jurisprudence to deal more responsively and effectively with the problem of domestic violence.

Although there are many advantages to the use of specialized domestic violence courts rather than generalized criminal courts in the processing of domestic violence cases, there may be one disadvantage. Criminal court judges process a great variety of criminal matters, while domestic violence courts will only see domestic violence offenses. As a result, domestic violence court judges will develop an expertise in the area of domestic violence, reading the literature in this area, understanding the treatment approaches and how they work, and observing similarities in the thousands of victims and batterers that will come before them. Their institutional role also will often make such judges advocates for the plight of domestic violence victims at community meetings, schools, and government and legislative sessions. This expertise and institutional role is likely to produce in many domestic violence court judges an identification with the domestic violence victim that might adversely affect their ability to be fair and impartial adjudicators of cases in which the issue of domestic violence is contested.

While the overwhelming majority of domestic violence perpetrators will plead guilty or seek diversion, some will wish to contest their charges and to demand the fair trial that our Constitution guarantees. In such cases, domestic violence court judges will need to switch modes and remember and respect the presumption of innocence that attaches to all criminal defendants. In adjudicating criminal cases and civil disputes about restraining orders, domestic violence court judges must put aside their rehabilitative and advocacy roles and give fair and impartial consideration to the evidence presented. To the extent that a domestic violence court judge has become jaded and cynical about those accused of domestic violence or has over-identified with the perspective of the domestic violence victim in ways that prevent him or her from being a fair adjudicator, it may be time to request a transfer from domestic violence court to a court of general jurisdiction. Indeed, there may be some wisdom in rotating domestic violence court judges (and judges in other specialized courts) after a period of service in order to avoid these kinds of problems. With this caveat, however, one that most judges will be able to understand and respond to, the advantages of having specialized domestic violence courts rather than generalized criminal courts deal with domestic violence cases are significant.

. . . .

---

As early as November 2004, the Conference of State Court Administrators produced a "White Paper"—"Position Paper on Safety and Accountability: State Courts and Domestic Violence"—to study the challenges posed to the justice system by domestic violence cases. The authors lauded those courts that, together with outside agencies, developed models to meet the needs of domestic violence victims and children, offered easy court access to litigants, maintained comprehensive records and practiced careful judicial monitoring. They wrote:

> Any meaningful effort to address domestic violence will require courts to rethink their traditional emphasis on a purely reactive legal process. The

challenge is how to fashion an assertive judicial role or presence in combating domestic violence that simultaneously preserves the courts' neutrality and incorruptibility as objective assessors of facts whose decisions are morally and legally legitimate.[5]

## Hon. Janice Rosa (ret.), *The Judge as Community First Responder: Because ACE's High is a Losing Hand*
NCJFCJ, 19(2) SYNERGY 16 (Spring 2016)

Juvenile and family courts judges deal with the most troubled of the community's families. Judges have long known that finding effective bench interventions requires working with community stakeholders to find resources, funding, and alternatives. Judges see families in crisis and are in a unique position to serve as leaders who can find and implement solutions. In every sense of the term, we are first responders for families.

. . . .

Increasing respect for vulnerable litigants, both juvenile and adult, along with the knowledge yielded from other professions, had fueled a national movement for trauma-informed decision-making and practices. It has similarly shifted the focus inside the courtroom to one that is increasingly trauma-informed.

The Adverse Childhood Experiences (ACE) Study

The medical and scientific underpinnings for this change in our focus began in several areas. Most notably, it is the result of a large ongoing study by Drs. Felitti and Anda, known as the Adverse Childhood Experiences (ACE) Study.[6] The study, which involved more than 17,000 subjects spanning a period of year, resulted from unsuccessful attempts by Drs. Felitti and Anda to treat long-term obesity and addiction issues. . . .

The study population represented a mainstream, middle to upper-middle class demographic, of fifty-seven years average age, enrolled with California's Kaiser Permanente health care plan. Nearly three-quarters were college-educated and nearly 70% Caucasian. The study relied on a rather succinct health history questionnaire completed by the patients. It asked whether the patients experienced childhood maltreatement (physical, emotional, or sexual) or lived in a household with drug or alcohol abuse, incarceration, domestic violence, divorce, adult mental illness, or depression. Patients were asked to score the number, frequency, and intensity of their reported negative childhood experiences. . . . For example, one incident of child sexual abuse received the same score of "1" as repeated sexual abuse over years.

. . . .

---

5. POSITION PAPER, *supra*, at 15.

6. [n2] Felitti, V.J. et al, *Relationships of Childhood Abuse and Household Dysfunction to Many of the Leading Causes of Death in Adults: The Adverse Childhood Experiences (ACE) Study,* 14 AM. J. PREV. MED. 245 (1998).

The most surprising finding in the ACE study was the incredible prevalence of adverse childhood experiences in this otherwise low-risk middle-class educated white populations. An astonishing two-thirds of the patient group had one or more indicators, many of which tended to occur in clusters—that is, a child with an incarcerated or mentally ill parent often also lived with the chaos of divorce, domestic violence, or child maltreatment. More than 20% of the study group had experiences three ACE's. One out of every eight had experienced four or more.

A decade into the study, researchers began to link the patients' childhood traumatic experiences to early disease onset and resulting death. They found that individuals with a score of four or higher had two to four times the rates of depression, and two to four times the rates of diabetes and hypertension. They were twice as likely to smoke, seven times as likely to be alcoholics, and four times as likely to suffer from breathing problems. They were 12 or more times as likely to have attempted suicide than those with a zero ACE score.

. . . .

The ACE study group doesn't look very much like the families who come before the court. The population we see often includes families living in dangerous neighborhoods, beset with poverty, without the privileges of quality education or healthcare. As a result, some come from decidedly more traumatic environments than the ACE cohort of educated middle class patients. Researchers have replicated the ACE findings in more problematic populations such as these, considering the additional effects of peer violence, community violence, death or forced separation of a caretaker, and exposure to war. And, it comes as no great surprise that the typical courtroom litigant is more challenged, with resulting deeper and much more serious trauma needs.

. . . .

The simultaneously exciting and frustrating fact is that we are right now at the frontier of the subject. Researchers are finding they might reverse the effects of childhood trauma by psychopharmacology in the lab—i.e., fighting toxic neurochemicals with drugs. Even more importantly, they believe they can mend children's responses by changing the behavior of their parents and caregivers. Not surprisingly, timing matters, including how swiftly we intervene with families in crisis to cut off toxic stress messages and replace them with healing measures. Put simply, domestic violence victims and their children need judges who know the resources in their communities, and who lead these communities in collaboration.

We now have the answer as to why so many life issues seem difficult or impossible to ameliorate. And, we are now just discovering promising practices that can shift those outcomes for families to a better, more hopeful, and health future for themselves and their children. As judges, we are in an undeniable position of trust and responsibility, with the ability to convene community stakeholders and order treatment and interventions we now know are critical to child and adult health and well-being. As judges on the frontline of this public health challenge, we have not only the authority to direct services, but also the moral imperative to do so for the communities we serve. We are truly the first responders in this emerging public health field.

## II. Representing Clients in a Domestic Violence Court

### A. Victims

The danger of being a strong victim's advocate is that a lawyer risks identifying too closely with the domestic violence victim. An attorney representing an abused spouse must also recognize that her client may be unwilling to act in a manner that the lawyer thinks is in her best interest. This can be frustrating and lead to counsel/client conflicts. The following excerpt written by two experienced New York advocates describes the challenges.

### B.J. Cling & Dorchen A. Leidholdt, *Interviewing and Assisting Domestic Violence Survivors*

*in* Lawyer's Manual on Domestic Violence; Representing the Victim 43-44 (6th ed. 2015)

. . . .

Some victims of domestic violence also experience "trauma-coerced bonding." Some victims of abuse remain very attached to an abuser, even though he has harmed her significantly. A victim who is traumatically bonded will have very mixed feelings about leaving her abuser, or prosecuting him for his wrongs against her. This phenomenon, originally called "Stockholm Syndrome," occurs when there are two factors present. One, the abuser has to have significant power over the victim. This is the case in domestic violence. Second, the abuser has to be at times punishing, but also at times loving and caring towards the victim. The victim is weakened psychologically by the abuse, and comes to see the abuser more and more as the only person who can help or harm her. Working with this client may seem challenging. She may be very conflicted about leaving, and may backtrack at times. This client needs a great deal of emotional support, and gentle reminders of the negatives of her relationship with the abuser when she is feeling that she must return.

Like PTSD, trauma-coerced bonding is the natural outcome of the way in which your client has been mistreated—it is not reflective of her character or underlying mental fortitude. . . .

Although your client is the one who has been traumatized by her experiences with the abuser, hearing about it in detail, and identifying with your client whom you are trying to help, leads to a certain amount of vicarious trauma. In other words, the experience of hearing about your client's trauma has the effect of causing you secondary trauma.

You should anticipate that it will be upsetting to hear about your client's experiences. It is important to be aware of this phenomenon, so that you do not unconsciously keep your client from talking to avoid upsetting yourself. The best way to counteract this tendency is to maintain awareness that you are likely to get upset. It is important to allow yourself to experience whatever upset you feel, and to seek support for yourself when you do. If you shut this out, you are more likely to let your client avoid important details, and you are also more likely to engage in victim blaming.

It is a natural tendency to distance yourself from the traumatic circumstances of your client's situation. This is because most of us like to feel that these horrible events would never happen to us. We like to feel that we would have acted differently, protected ourselves better. Because of this tendency, you may find yourself blaming your client for not defending herself or for not leaving sooner.

To avoid acting on these self-protective, but ultimately destructive impulses in ourselves, it is important to seek support from other lawyers and from professionals who are qualified to handle these issues. . . .

## B. Perpetrators

Representing batterers in domestic violence courts can be daunting. Given the resources provided to fighting intimate partner abuse in recent years and the seriousness with which many judges and prosecutors now take these cases, a defense lawyer may feel defending an alleged domestic abuser is a hopeless task.

### Lisa Angel & Lee Rosen, *Zealous and Ethical Representation of Batterers*

in THE IMPACT OF DOMESTIC VIOLENCE ON YOUR LEGAL PRACTICE 83-85
(2d ed. 2004)

. . . Zealous representation of a batterer means more than the use of the court to continue the battle and inflict greater injury on the victim. Zealous representation means helping the client make good constructive decisions based upon the guidance and advice of counsel. For the batterer, the best decision is often to move on, apart from the victim, to obtain treatment, and to formulate a new vision of life that does not involve inflicting harm upon others.

The zealous advocate evaluates the prospects for the batterer to have a positive relationship with his or her children, family, and community after the relationship with the victim of family violence is over. The advocate guides the batterer in a direction that serves the client's ultimate purposes rather than a short term view of the situation. Advocacy for the perpetrator of domestic violence requires building a relationship with the client, protecting the client, thinking about the victim's safety and protecting yourself.

#### Build a relationship with the Batterer

. . . .

Advise batterers that they are likely to be treated as guilty people unless you can prove their innocence. Batterers should understand that you will be fighting an uphill battle to obtain any relief and that they will be treated differently by the system because of the alleged violence.

. . . .

Inform the batterer of the events that are likely to take place as you progress through the case. Clarify goals with the batterer. Make sure the batterer has a realistic understanding of what will happen in the system and help the batterer form realistic expectations. If things are going to go poorly, it is important for you to be the source of the bad news. Help the batterer anticipate the outcome and adjust to the changes that will take place.

## Protect the Batterer

Protect the batterer's job. Batterers are often self-defeating and insist on taking steps that destroy their careers, social lives, or positions in the community. Batterers sometimes feel that without their families they have nothing of significance in their lives. . . .

Get the batterer all of the relief the batterer is entitled to receive. Thoroughly evaluate the facts that are favorable to your client. Use those facts to obtain all visitation possible and as much of the assets as the batterer is reasonably entitled to receive. Assess whether the batterer will attempt to use the visitation to threaten the victim. If so, remind the batterer that the purpose of visitation is to maintain contact with the children, not the former partner, and recommend limited contact with the victim as the visitation exchange.

Keep the visitation exchange safe. Look for ways to limit the interaction with the victim and the batterer at visitation exchanges. Visitation provides an opportunity for the batterer to violate the order. In order to avoid these potentials, set up safe visitation exchanges in advance. Consider using supervised visitation centers in your community. If supervised visitation is necessary, explain why and assist the batterer to find a neutral third party who can effectively maintain safe visitation and transfer of the children.

Advise the batterer to remain silent with respect to the allegations of violence. If the batterer is going to make admissions, which may be helpful at some point, you need to control the admissions. You might allow the batterer to acknowledge the conduct in a visitation trial, for instance, but you must be certain that the admissions in the custody trial do not further compromise the batterer's position in a subsequent criminal trial. Do not allow the batterer to make the criminal case more difficult by talking to others about past conduct without your approval.

Settle the case. Rarely is a batterer better off having the matter resolved by the court. Help the batterer understand the likely outcome of a hearing and the damage the hearing may do to the batterer's reputation and possibly to the children. Negotiate the best arrangement possible and resolve the matter by agreement if at all possible.

Protect Yourself

Be aware that people who are abusive in their most personal relationships are more likely to be abusive in other contexts as well. Do not meet with a batterer without taking adequate precautions to protect yourself from violent outbursts. Do not meet with a batterer alone when the staff members have left the building. Be especially sensitive to the possibility of violence in the courthouse. Have a plan of action for dealing with the violent client.

Know the ethical rules in your jurisdiction pertaining to the compromise of civil and criminal cases. Many jurisdictions prohibit the compromise of a civil claim in exchange for an agreement to drop criminal charges. Be certain that you are clear with respect to your obligations under the rules of professional conduct before entering into such a bargain.

. . . .

Be certain that you are emotionally prepared to represent people who harm others. Before you accept the client, determine whether you can meet your obligation of zealous representation of a person who has beaten a spouse and may pose a risk to children. If you have doubts about your ability to do the job, do not take the case. Once you accept the client, you may not be allowed to withdraw from representation at a later date.

Concern about the batterer's behavior is not a sign of unfitness as counsel. It is better for a batterer to be represented by a lawyer who understands domestic violence and wants to enable the client to end the violence.

## III. Sentencing—Jail, Probation, Batterers' Programs, Judicial Monitoring or Circles of Peace

What constitutes an appropriate sanction for a person convicted of a domestic violence-related offense has long been debated in the justice community. The options include jail or probation, as they would for any other crime. But with crimes involving domestic violence, the court also may issue orders directing the defendant to cease all contact with the victim, known as orders of protection, restraining orders or stay-away orders, depending on the jurisdiction. Federal law and many state statutes also require that courts direct those convicted of domestic violence crimes to surrender firearms. Some judges also require those convicted to attend batterers' education programs.

There is a widespread perception that judges are reluctant to send batterers to jail, opting instead for placement in programs designed to prevent future domestic violence. There is also a national movement afoot to choose alternatives to jail in response to historically high levels of incarceration in the United States, particularly among African American males.

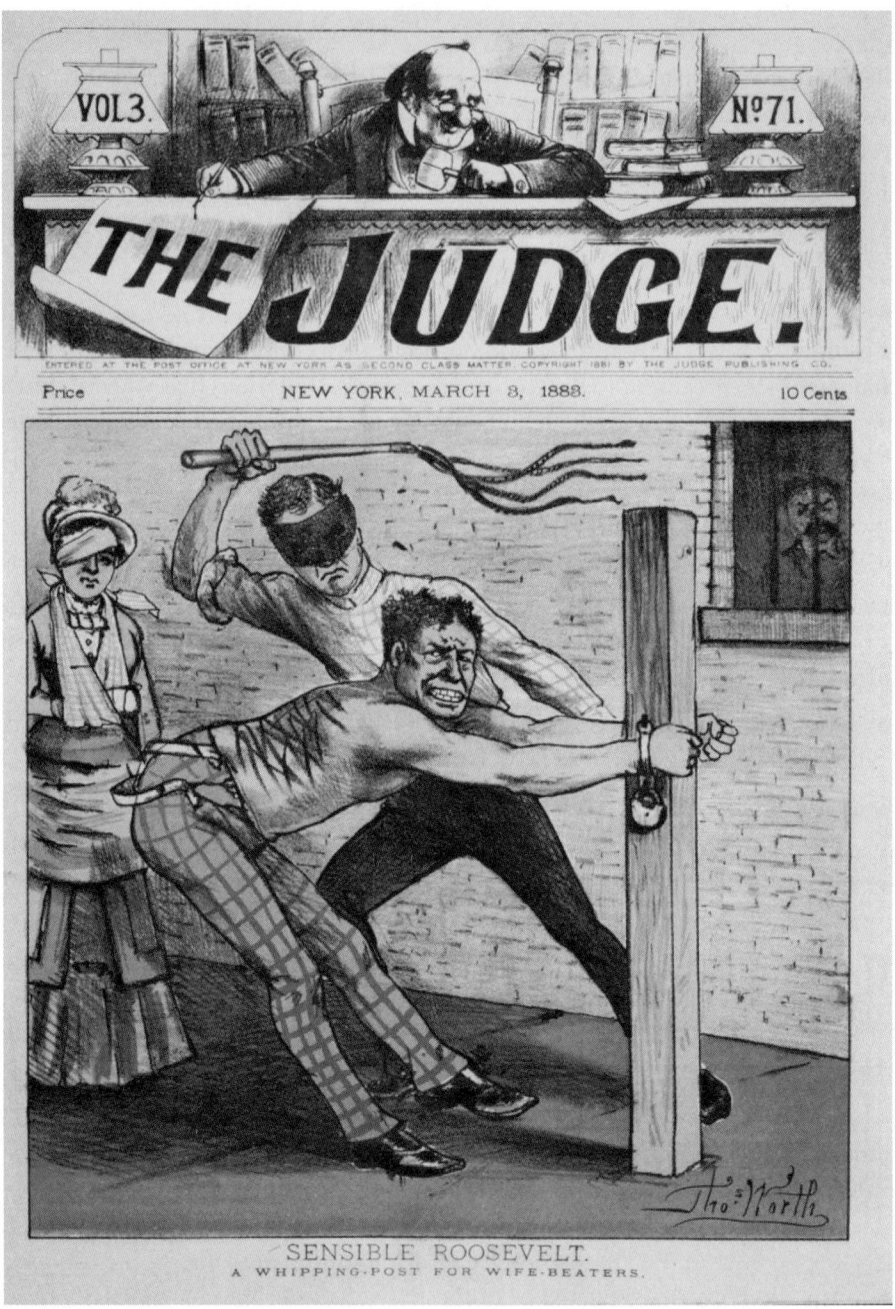

However, recent studies have shown batterers' education programs to be of little or no use in curbing recidivism, therefore causing some judges to have second thoughts about whether these programs remain an appropriate sanction

Unlike stranger-on-stranger crimes, where the only unfortunate contact a victim will have with a criminal is during those few frightening moments of an attack, the victim of domestic violence has had a past intimate relationship with her abuser, and may choose to continue it, despite the violence. Therefore, while jail might seem appropriate to the prosecutor, the judge or the detached observer, it may not be what the victim wants. The convicted batterer may be the household's sole bread winner, and his wife or intimate partner may not want him jailed because the family could end up destitute as a result. A jail sentence could enrage a batterer, and if the term of incarceration is brief, as it often is in D.V. cases, a victim may fear retaliation when he is released.

This following article discusses the competing interests inherent in domestic violence sentencing in criminal cases.

## Cheryl Hanna, *The Paradox of Hope: The Crime and Punishment of Domestic Violence*
39 WM. & MARY L. REV. 1505 (1998)

. . . .

As a former domestic violence prosecutor, I was continually frustrated with the unwillingness of judges to sentence domestic violence offenders to incarceration, opting most often for batterer treatment as a condition of probation. A commitment to gender equality originally brought me to work on women abuse. To me, the emphasis on treatment over punishment reflected a historically sexist system that treated domestic violence as a private family matter. Low sentences equated to gender bias. I blamed the judge.

Yet, at the same time, I found myself recommending probation with a condition of attending a batterer treatment program in cases that, had they involved a stranger, I would have recommended a prison term without hesitation. I justified my sentencing recommendations on the wishes of the victim or the likelihood of obtaining a plea if I recommended jail. My commitment to holding abusive men criminally responsible for their behavior often faltered, particularly at sentencing.

. . . .

### I. A Critical Look at Sentencing Practices: The Disconnection Between Perception and Reality

#### A. The Criminalization of Domestic Violence

The criminalization of domestic violence has made for some strange bedfellows, albeit with different long-term expectations. Feminists argue that criminalization of domestic violence is one way to correct the historical, legal, and moral disparities in legal protections afforded to women, making public what traditionally has been thought of as a private crime. Victims' advocates focus primarily on individual victim safety, supporting criminalization generally but arguing against any policies that might increase danger to the victim or "disempower" her. Criminologists and some legal scholars evaluate current polices almost exclusively on their specific deterrent effects, often ignoring changes in social and legal institutions that feminists have sought to achieve. Finally, social conservatives, not normally supportive of feminist legal reform, advocate using the law to enforce public morality and further the goals of retribution. They too have been supportive of criminal justice reforms in this area.

The federal government also endorses the criminalization of domestic violence. The Violence Against Women Act (VAWA) advocates mandatory arrest and pro-prosecution policies, training for court personnel and judges, better record keeping of statistics, and an increased commitment to victims' services and rehabilitation. VAWA also makes certain domestic violence offenses federal crimes, such as interstate stalking and violation of a protection order.

. . . .

Prosecutors and judges have numerous disposition options once a domestic violence case enters the system: outright dismissal; pretrial diversion; postconviction probation with conditions, including fines; batterer treatment and/or substance abuse counseling; or incarceration. Prosecution policies nationwide are becoming more rigorous, with many jurisdictions forming specialized prosecution units and implementing "no-drop" policies. The available data, however, suggests that most of these cases still end with arrest. The reasons for lack of prosecution are many: victim reluctance or refusal to cooperate; lack of proper police investigation; prosecutors untrained in how to proceed without the victim's testimony; and the belief that these cases are a private family matter. Of those cases that are prosecuted, many are charged or pled down to misdemeanors despite facts that suggest the conduct constituted a felony.

When prosecutors decide to go forward, the final disposition is often a period of probation, either pre-or postconviction, contingent upon completion of a batterer treatment program. For example, in Sussex County, New Jersey, counseling and other social services for both the victim and the abuser, rather than jail time, is the preferred sentence as a matter of jurisdictional policy. There is little evidence, however, that probation departments follow up on these orders, allowing many abusers to slip through the cracks.

In addition, few batterers ever see the inside of a jail cell, even when convicted of a serious offense. A recent American Lawyer story followed all domestic violence arrests in eleven jurisdictions on June 18, 1995. Of the 140 arrests made in the eleven communities, 95 never made it to conviction, plea, or acquittal. Cases were dismissed even in jurisdictions with avowed no-drop policies. Only sixteen of the forty-four defendants who were convicted or pled no contest served any time; the vast majority received probation or a suspended sentence, including one man who sent his wife to the hospital with a broken nose and a broken rib. He received six months' probation. A man who slapped his wife in the face and tried to stab her with a kitchen knife received one year, the longest sentence given on this day. The court found that two prior felony drug convictions, not the severity of the crime, justified the length of the sentence. . . .

### B. The Practice of Punishment

In 1984, the Attorney General's Task Force on Family Violence wrote that "the most successful treatment occurs when mandated by the criminal justice system." Although the report recommended incarceration for serious offenses, it encouraged the use of batterer treatment programs in cases where the injury to the victim was not serious. . . .

Some jurisdictions are moving away from pretrial diversion and instead require a conviction before treatment can be ordered. The rationale for disallowing diversion programs is that they fail to demand that the batterer acknowledge any wrongdoing. Drop-out rates are high; once an abuser stops attending, the prosecution rarely obtains a conviction.

### C. A Review of Treatment Programs

Controversy surrounding who should receive treatment and how it is structured reflects the larger debate between feminists and social scientists as to the root causes of domestic violence. The first major dispute centers around whether clinical intervention should be aimed at both members of the couple or only the male. Couples therapy relies on the underlying premise that poor conflict management skills and anger control cause domestic violence. Both partners are expected to take some responsibility for their behavior to reduce conflict and avoid violence. Treatment programs in which the male and female participate report reducing violence between spouses who wish to stay together.

Many have discredited couples therapy because the dominant paradigm for explaining domestic violence shifted from one of conflict theory to one of feminist theory; most court-ordered treatment programs today treat only men. Feminist-informed treatment resocializes men to be less controlling of women. Women need not participate because men are entirely responsible for their own violent behavior. The reported success rates of male-only treatment programs have not, however, been vastly different from programs that treat both spouses.

Furthermore, many states mandate the length of programs through legislation; treatment programs of six months to a year are becoming commonplace. Yet, there is no convincing evidence that the length of a program determines its effectiveness. . . .

The Duluth, Minnesota model is the prevailing approach utilized by a growing number of jurisdictions. The Duluth model philosophy is: "Batterers, like those who intervene to help them, have been immersed in a culture that supports relationships of dominance. This cultural acceptance of dominance is rooted in the assumption that, based on differences, some people have the legitimate right to master others." The curriculum uses an educational and counseling approach, as opposed to anger-control intervention. It focuses on the use of violence by the batterer to establish power and control over his partner. Men meet in weekly groups run by a facilitator. The facilitator is not necessarily a mental health professional but is a trained lay person.

Participants engage in exercises geared towards confronting their violent behavior. For example, each participant maintains a "control log" or diary that identifies their abusive behavior. Role plays based on individual experiences are used to build non-violent skills. Videotapes, such as Profile of an Assailant, are shown to prompt discussion. Skills such as taking time-outs and recognizing women's anger are also taught. Most of these exercises preclude discussion of the particular relationship, instead focusing on the underlying issues of power and control.

. . . .

### D. The Effectiveness of Batterer Treatment Programs

Empirical research on treatment programs suggests that the preference for treatment as a disposition to a criminal domestic violence case is misinformed public policy. . . .

Some available data suggests that court-ordered treatment correlates to a reduction in physical violence, although treatment neither terminates violence in many cases nor curbs the more subtle psychological forms of abuse. Whether treatment itself, or simply individual "motivation" brought on by legal intervention causes the reduction of violence, is unclear. In fact, some studies have found that men arrested and treated resume their violent behavior as frequently as do men arrested and not referred to treatment. Other studies have found no significant difference in recidivism rates between men who complete batterer treatment and men who drop-out. Holding someone criminally responsible for their actions may be as effective as any treatment modality.

Additionally, treatment does not work for everybody. For men ordered by the court to attend treatment, recidivism rates have been reported as high as fifty-four percent within six months of completing a treatment program. This data might suggest treatment causes at least some men to change their behavior, but it is just as likely that men who complete court-ordered treatment and do not recidivate are the most motivated and amenable to treatment.

. . . .

This research raises ethical and legal dilemmas for those who continue to put their punishment eggs in the treatment basket. Court-mandated treatment in criminal cases may offer a woman "false hope" that her partner will be permanently rehabilitated, when in fact, he may only be deterred in the short term, and perhaps not at all. This is troubling if, as one researcher suggests, a woman is most likely to remain with her abuser if he attends treatment. Violent offenders often are released without evidence that they are "cured," putting some women at an increased risk of further injury or death.

Furthermore, punishment that differs based on the gender and relationship of the victim to the offender implicates issues of equal treatment. As we have seen in the arrest context, courts may soon look at the preference for probation and treatment for these, but not other violent crimes, as violating state and federal equal protection and due process laws.

Finally, these programs have received substantial support from the criminal justice community, states, and the federal government. The more entrenched these programs become, the harder they are to change or eliminate. Policy-makers must examine whether scarce resources are being well-spent. Simply exploring the causal relationship between court-ordered treatment and recidivism rates will likely fuel the battle for ownership. Nevertheless, we cannot be afraid to make the connection between perception and reality.

II. Who's to Blame?: The Complex Motivations that Drive Sentencing Decisions

A. Theories of Punishment and The Privacy of Rehabilitation

. . . .

1. Rehabilitation

. . . .

One of the most frustrating cases that I handled involved a woman whose boyfriend beat her and then intentionally burned her with a curling iron. Prosecutors dropped at least three other cases because the woman was too scared to go forward and no other evidence had been produced to sustain a conviction. In this case, however, the police did an excellent job documenting the battery, including photographing the burns. The defendant pled guilty to battery. I recommended a six-month period of incarceration, which was still disproportionately low to the resulting harm. The victim was too afraid to appear at the sentencing hearing; she just wanted the defendant out of her life. The defense attorney opposed the sentence recommendation, arguing that the defendant should be allowed to enroll in a treatment program in lieu of jail, otherwise he would lose his job. The judge agreed with defense counsel.

A few weeks later the police found cocaine on the defendant during a traffic stop. Because it was the defendant's second offense for possession with intent to distribute, he received a one-year sentence. Neither the judge nor the prosecutor mentioned that he was currently on probation for a battery charge. It struck me as unfair that the justice system would sentence these two cases with such disparity. I blamed the judge in the battery case for "not getting it."

. . . .

2. Deterrence

. . . .

Specific deterrence theory—imposing a sentence on a defendant that will prevent him from repeating the same behavior-avoids the privacy trap by emphasizing the individual costs of wrongdoing. It assumes that people are rational actors; they choose to abuse and thus are less likely to engage in the behavior again if the sentence is high enough. Opponents of specific deterrence cite high recidivism rates for those punished. It is just as likely, however, that the costs associated with beating one's partner have been too low to motivate a change in behavior. . . .

### 3. Therapeutic Jurisprudence

Therapeutic jurisprudence, growing largely from a merger of rehabilitation and specific deterrence theories, focuses on the psychological and behavioral aspects of the offender to prevent future criminal behavior. The goal of punishment is to promote behavioral changes through an understanding of the psychology of the offender. "The schema of therapeutic jurisprudence suggests that the law can act as a therapeutic agent, whereby legal rules, legal procedures, and the roles of legal actors (such as police, lawyers, and judges) can constitute social forces that often produce therapeutic or antitherapeutic results."

. . . .

### 4. Incapacitation

Incapacitation theory provides that for the good of those who abide by the law, offenders who violate social norms ought to be prevented from reoffending in the future. Incapacitation has grown in popularity with the public and lawmakers who are increasingly anxious about stranger-danger in particular. For example, skepticism about treatment has led to statutes intended to remove sex offenders from society indefinitely. . . .

Long-term incapacitation certainly is warranted in many sex offender cases. . . . A time could come, however, when courts classify some offenders as "serial batterers." . . . Advocates of aggressive criminalization of domestic violence are cautioned: We must be careful what we wish for. Taken to its extreme, incapacitation theory signals that we have given up hope entirely. . . .

### 5. Retribution

Finally, retribution theory argues that persons who choose to do wrong deserve punishment. Failure to impose punishment undermines the idea that the offender is a moral agent acting of his own free will. Critics of retribution theory argue that it validates hatred and encourages vengeance. . . . . . .

Retribution theory further adds an air of moral condemnation to domestic violence-a sentiment that the advocacy community has sought to promote. Its emphasis on accountability as opposed to self-improvement is thus consistent with both feminist and conservative rationales for the criminalization of domestic violence.

There are both benefits and drawbacks to any theory of punishment one chooses to justify domestic violence sentencing decisions. Clearly, however, justifying punishment solely on rehabilitation is far more costly than might first appear. Despite notions to the contrary, when judges make sentencing decisions with the sole purpose of rehabilitating the offender, they are often reinforcing the private nature of violence and putting women and the community at great risk. Seemingly well-intentioned sentences often have unintended consequences. Furthermore, criminalizing domestic violence must serve both general and specific objectives; none of the traditional theories of punishment discussed provides an adequate foundation for balancing those often competing goals. Therefore, rather than search for a perfect justification of punishment in this context, we should be pragmatic by distinguishing those men who are genuinely deserving and capable of rehabilitation from those who are not.

B. Feminist Approaches to Punishment

One might assume that incarceration, which ultimately removes male control over women, would drive feminist punishment agendas. But we ought to be careful not to stereotype feminists as wanting all bad men behind bars. A complicated dynamic keeps advocates for battered women from rejecting outright faith in treatment despite the lack of empirical evidence that mandated counseling works. Feminist advocates have not only accepted treatment but have embraced it. Despite feminist criticism of low sentences in particular cases and calls for increased probation supervision, the preference for treatment over incarceration has largely gone unchallenged.

There are many reasons why feminists might prefer treatment over more, arguably male, modes of punishment. The first is largely pragmatic. The domestic violence advocacy community is painfully aware of the reluctance of judges and prosecutors to take these cases seriously, let alone incarcerate offenders. Treatment programs offer at least some state supervision over the offender. Because most of these offenses are misdemeanors, the length of any jail stay would be short; unless some treatment option is available, the offender never learns the skills to change his behavior. Treatment is not perfect, but something is better than nothing.

Treatment also caters to the "upside" of privacy for women. Many in the feminist community argue that autonomous aspects of privacy can further women's equality and freedom. Privacy need not be confined to its historical meaning-as a separate domestic sphere where men are left alone to oppress women-but rather can refer to a preservation of autonomy over important life decisions. Because many women want their partners to change their behavior but do not want to end the relationship with incarceration, treatment is entirely consistent with the feminist notion that the law ought to protect "basic decisions of one's life respecting marriage, divorce, procreation, contraception, and the education and upbringing of children." The availability of treatment thus empowers women to shape their intimate relationships.

. . . .

C. The Realities of Practice

. . . .

1. Not All Cases Are Created Equally

Prosecutors face growing pressure to go forward with as many domestic violence cases as possible, regardless of the sufficiency of the evidence or the seriousness of the offense, particularly in jurisdictions that have policies limiting prosecutorial discretion. At the same time, advocates argue that if the victim will be "revictimized" or "disempowered" as a result of prosecution, the case should not be prosecuted. The advocacy community keeps sending out mixed messages. On one hand, they want the criminal justice system to take these cases seriously; on the other, they are unwilling to acknowledge the practical dilemmas posed when a jurisdiction pursues an aggressive strategy. . . .

Furthermore, prosecutors receive the mixed message that they are both therapist and trial attorney. . . . Yet, supporting the victim emotionally and holding the batterer criminally responsible are often conflicting goals. . . . I find that many well-intentioned district attorneys end up resenting these cases, feeling as if they spend too much time "hand-holding" and not enough time investigating cases, preparing witnesses, and perfecting trial strategies that can increase the likelihood of conviction.

Many jurisdictions handle a staggering number of cases, and most jurisdictions do not have the investigative resources to distinguish and prioritize. Defendants usually refuse to plea bargain unless incarceration is off the table. En masse guilty pleas with treatment recommendations, in lieu of jail, help expedite overcrowded dockets. Everyone ends up with treatment even though offenses and offenders vary greatly.

Experience tells us that these cases are as much differences of kind as differences of degree. Some cases are serious, evincing a pattern of ongoing abuse, while others are isolated incidents, often complicated by alcohol or drug use. For example, while practicing, I often had cases where someone called the police to report noisy neighbors. When the police arrived, both parties were intoxicated and sometimes violent, but no injuries were apparent. Often the male would be arrested under our preferred arrest policy. Upon investigating those cases, it was simply unclear what happened. The woman would tell me that they were both drinking and "things got out of hand" but denied that her partner struck her. She would sometimes claim, "I started it and he was just trying to calm me down." Many times there were no prior arrests for any criminal violation for either the defendant or the alleged victim. Although troubling, cases like these are not as serious as others, and often the evidence supporting the charge is minimal, at best. Nevertheless, with forty to one hundred cases to screen a week, pressure not to drop, and fear about what would happen if my instinct was wrong, I often kept these cases in the system longer than necessary, trying to get some guilty plea with a condition of treatment—just in case.

. . . .

One of the worst cases I handled involved a woman who had been beaten severely by her boyfriend. He once hit her with a belt and strangled her with pantyhose ripped from her legs. She always failed to appear for court despite supportive efforts from my staff and a criminal subpoena. On the day scheduled for trial, I sent a police officer to her home to remind her to attend court, something I did only if the victim had a history of nonappearance. When the officer arrived at her home, he found her handcuffed to the bed, allegedly by the defendant.

The woman was willing to cooperate with the criminal case, but she threatened to disappear unless I recommended probation and counseling. She feared her boyfriend would retaliate if sentenced to jail. There was not enough evidence to proceed without the victim's cooperation, and I did not have the time or the resources to devote the attention this case deserved. I choked on my words as I told the judge that I would be willing to accept probation with attendance in treatment. The victim disappeared soon after the guilty plea. . . .

This story illustrates the frustration that results when there is too much pressure to proceed in every case, too few resources to document the serious ones, and little time to do the job right. Court-mandated treatment programs allow everyone to save face. The prosecutor checks-off "conviction" on his stat sheet; the defense attorney feels like she did some good for her client; the victim has a sense of hope, however false, that the criminal justice system will help her partner change his ways; the offender avoids jail; the judge is not accused of taking these cases too lightly; the treatment program gets yet another client to support its existence; and we all go home happy . . . until the next time.

2. Autonomy and the Rubric of Empowerment

Court-mandated treatment not only facilitates the "administration of justice" in these cases, but it also promotes notions of victim empowerment and decision making. Whether autonomy and the right to make one's own decisions offer more liberation for women, or are false notions masking subordination, continues to be debated in feminist legal scholarship. In practice, most victims want the violence in their relationships to stop and to that extent will cooperate with the state. Many women, however, will resist outcomes that involve criminal records, jail, fines, or other punitive measures. When a woman wants her partner to receive treatment despite a serious offense or his long-term dangerousness, the prosecutor and judge must navigate the tricky waters between a victim's personal autonomy and concerns for public safety and justice.

This dilemma is particularly painful in cases where incarceration could result in financial hardship. In Baltimore City, for example, one of the best defenses to incarceration was employment, or what was often facetiously referred to as "punch and pay." . . . This dynamic is complicated further when judges fear that the stress of unemployment might exacerbate the violence upon the offender's release.

Furthermore, strong emotional ties exist between women and their abusers. Women often feel responsible for breaking this bond; the experience of separation can be traumatic. Defendants may pressure victims to drop charges or to request counseling so the couple can reunite. No evidence suggests that harsher sanctions place victims at greater risk of new violence, but in individual cases, the defendant may escalate violence to coerce his partner into reconciliation.

Finally, there is a deep ambivalence as to whether children who live in violent homes are better served by sending the abuser to treatment or to jail. Children who grow up in violent homes are more likely to be abused themselves and abuse as adults. At the same time, parent absenteeism correlates to a child's future involvement in the criminal justice system. Court-mandated treatment offers at least some compromise as to what might be in the best interest of children.

D. The Paradox of Hope

"Evil" motivations alone cannot account for bad sentencing decisions. All of us who work in this field experience the paradox of hope-the optimistic but unrealistic belief that abusers can unlearn their violence through treatment. . . .

Ironically, the most often asked question in these cases is why the woman does not leave. Women "stay" for many reasons: financial dependence; fear of separation assaults; concern for the children; low self-esteem; a perception that there is no place to go; and hope. Many women believe that the violence will stop and the relationship will improve if only . . . (fill in the blank). The wish list can include: he gets a job; he stops drinking; I keep the kids from crying; I pay more attention to him; I clean the house; or I love him more. Occasionally, women stay until it is too late. This hope masks a deeper sense of powerlessness. Nothing a woman does can stop the violence unless her partner wants and is able to change. . . .

### III. Understanding Differences and Devising Solutions

. . . .

A. The Dangers of Essentialism in Domestic Violence Work

. . . .

Ironically, legal academics, including myself, are guilty of writing about "batterers" as if they constitute a single, homogeneous group. . . . This tendency to essentialize men who abuse as gender-motivated obscures a far more complex phenomenon.

What these men do have in common is their criminal behavior; they assault and batter their intimate partners without legal justification. No evidence yet supports the proposition that there is a "profile of a batterer."

. . . .

1. Batterer Typologies

Some of the most promising domestic violence research attempts to differentiate among batterers. Different "types" of batterers emerge from a synthesis of this research. Amy Holtzworth-Munroe and Gregory Stuart recently reviewed nineteen studies on typologies and identified three subtypes of abusive men: family-only batterers; borderline batterers; and generally violent/antisocial batterers. I rely primary on the categories hypothesized by Holtzworth-Munroe and Stuart, but also integrate the research of Edward Gondolf, Donald Dutton, and others. Emerging typologies among different researchers are surprisingly similar: differences lie more in terminology than in concept. Family-only batterers constitute approximately fifty percent of all batterer samples. These men tend to engage in the least severe marital violence, psychological and sexual abuse. Family-only batterers are less impulsive, less likely to use weapons, and more likely to be apologetic after abusive incidents. These men may be the most deterred by the threat of criminal sanctions and the most treatable because of their ability to function normally outside of their relationships.

Borderline batterers constitute approximately twenty-five percent of batterer samples. These men tend to "engage in moderate to severe abuse, including psychological and sexual abuse." Their violence generally is confined to the family, but not always. They may evince borderline personality characteristics and may have problems associated with drugs and alcohol. Batterer treatment, as it is currently structured, is likely to be insufficient to change their behavior because many men in this group may need more intensive treatment.

Generally violent or antisocial batterers engage in moderate to severe violence, including psychological and sexual abuse. Edward Gondolf terms these batterers sociopathic. It is estimated that this group constitutes twenty-five percent of batterer samples. Uniformly, studies have found that generally violent men engage in more severe family violence than family-only men. This finding challenges the myth that abusers are only violent against family members. Generally violent batterers often have extensive criminal histories, including property, drug or alcohol offenses, and violence crimes against nonfamily victims. These men are the most impulsive, the most likely to use weapons, and feel the least amount of empathy towards their victims. Batterer treatment programs for this group are inappropriate given the high degree of danger they pose. Arguably, sociopathic batterers may be untreatable, and, in many cases, ought to be incarcerated if only to protect their potential victims.

All abusive men are not equally dangerous. Some men are frequent and severe batterers; others are not. Dr. Donald Dutton, a psychology professor at the University of British Columbia and director of the Assaultive Husband's Program in Vancouver, focuses his research on personality traits of abusive men. He distinguishes "cyclical" batterers from men who may occasionally be aggressive in their relationships, "like the distinction between a single fender bender and continual head-on collisions." Cyclical batterers constitute a subgroup of men who are violent only in their intimate relationships. They are repeat offenders who injure their partners, both psychologically and physically, until courts intervene, but appear "normal" to the outside world because they direct their violence primarily at their mates. Dutton theorizes that these characteristics are a product of being abandoned by a loved one earlier in life. These men attribute their negative feelings to real or perceived misdeeds by their partners and retaliate. Violence diminishes anxiety about attachment by maintaining control over a partner.

Dutton's distinction between men who are chronically abusive and those who are not has important implications for prosecutorial and sentencing decisions. "If once in his marriage a man happens to push his wife in reaction to situational stresses, he would still be considered abusive.... But, psychologically, that is a very different type of individual than one who repeatedly abuses or beats up his wife or engages in more serious assaults." According to Dutton, only two percent of the total male population are "repeatedly severely assaultive" to women in any given year. Thus, the criminal justice system ought to be cautious before treating every man who engages in intimate violence as a high-risk offender....

### 2. Biomedical Factors

Some researchers have suggested that some violent behavior may correlate to biomedical conditions. For example, one study found that men with previous head injuries were six times as likely to display marital aggression as other men. This research is consistent with findings that there may be a link between head trauma and violent behavior.

Other research has linked aggressive, dominant and antisocial behavior to high testosterone levels and impulsive aggression to low serotonin levels. To date, however, whether testosterone and/or serotonin are potential correlates of family violence remains unclear.

Sociobiologists and evolutionary psychologists might also add to our understanding of violent behavior by men against women, although the application of evolutionary theories is still too new for any valid conclusions to be drawn. From a biologist's perspective, men have an inherited tendency to secrete adrenalin when they believe themselves to be sexually threatened by other males. The label applied to this arousal, however, will be socially determined. Thus, male aggression against females is part of male reproductive strategies geared toward reproducing offspring and ensuring paternity; this sexual aggression is well-documented throughout the primate world and cross-culturally.

Biomedical factors alone cannot account for all abusive behavior. At best, a more complex interaction of social and neurological factors trigger violence in some. Nor is there any evidence suggesting that biological factors should be a legal excuse to violent behavior. Nevertheless, the emerging research on biology and human behavior may provide valuable future insights. Additionally, screening abusers for medical as well as psychological factors might be prudent. Some men might benefit from medical as well as psychological interventions, especially in cases involving substance addictions or patterns of antisocial behavior. At the very least, this research suggests that we need to take a broader view of what "treatment" or other interventions might entail apart from the current feminist-based group therapy models currently in vogue.

### 3. External Factors

Although domestic violence occurs across all socioeconomic, ethnic, and age groups, some groups may be at higher risk of violence. For example, children exposed to violence are more likely to become violent or to be victims of violence. Couples in their twenties and thirties and those who cohabitate experience more violence than those who are older and married.

The most severely abusive men are not composed of mere low-income or minority cases, as some batterer stereotypes might suggest. Empirical evidence, however, points to a connection between domestic violence and low family income. Other studies have found that abused women are more likely to live in communities with the highest rates of stranger violence, suggesting a link between domestic violence, general violence, and neighborhoods with fewer economic and social resources.

Multiple interpretations can be made from these findings. First, people in lower socioeconomic groups are more likely to report violence to police, police are more likely to arrest people in poor and middle-class neighborhoods than upper-class ones, and women without economic resources are more likely to seek shelter than those with higher incomes. Those with a lower socioeconomic status are likely to be over-represented in batterer samples.

Second, some have theorized that the relationship between lower socioeconomic status and domestic violence is due, in part, to the existence of a "subculture of violence" that condones violence in general and assaultive behavior towards women in particular. This explanation emerges from theories linking domestic violence to deep-seated cultural acceptance of violence more generally. . . .

Those in lower socioeconomic groups might be more susceptible to this "cult of violence" because they have more to gain and less to lose by engaging in violent behavior; in other words, they have no stake in conforming to cultural norms that dictate against violence. "Culture of violence" theories remain highly controversial as they have a tendency to essentialize poor and minority communities as inherently violent. Such theories suggest, however, that violence may be a rational response given certain environmental and social conditions, not pathological or determined behavior.

Just as likely is that those with fewer resources face more stressors. "Indeed, it is generally believed—and certainly makes good clinical sense—that stress in itself does not lead directly to violence, but rather that various other factors exacerbate or buffer the relationship between stress and [domestic] violence." Living in a stressful environment may place some men at higher risk for the use of aggression.

. . . .

C. Recommendations for the Future

. . . .

### 1. Improve Case Screening

Prosecutors and probation departments should screen cases prior to making decisions about case disposition, distinguishing between high-risk offenders and others who pose less danger. . . .

. . . .

Undertaking risk assessments is difficult, particularly for prosecutors untrained in social service skills. One way to ease this burden is for prosecutors' offices to hire social workers to assist in risk assessments and to aid the victim in preparing for the prosecution and sentencing outcomes. This can include preparing a safety plan for the victim, relocating her, or helping her find alternative financial resources if she is economically dependent on the defendant. If jurisdictions employ social workers, then they are likely to find less resentment and frustration among prosecutors.

Furthermore, the victim's wishes should not dictate a sentence, particularly in serious cases that warrant incarceration. Exploring the victim's concerns about the outcome of the case is vital, but prosecutors must recommend sentences that are appropriate to the crime and to the history of the defendant, and judges must order the same. Extreme caution should be used before allowing a victim to state her sentencing preference in front of the abuser. Women may face retaliation for requesting more severe sanctions. In my experience, many women will ask publicly that the case be dismissed or referred to treatment and in private beg that everything be done to keep her partner in jail. Finally, even if the victim believes she would be better off if the defendant goes to treatment and not jail, such an outcome undermines the broader social goals of criminalization. The criminal justice system ought to be sensitive to the victim's needs and wishes, but it cannot, nor should it, serve the victim's personal preferences at the expense of broader community safety.

2. Provide for an Array of Treatment Programs

. . . .

There is not enough evidence to yet suggest whether pretrial diversion programs should be abandoned. Although pretrial diversion can undermine accountability, in some cases pretrial diversion may be appropriate. The issue is not the concept, but rather who may participate. For example, young men in their first relationship who "experiment" with violence may benefit from a pretrial diversion program and avoid the stigma of a criminal record early in their adult life. In addition, others have argued that pretrial diversion can be beneficial to women who get arrested for defending themselves in the midst of a violent argument.

Only those people without any criminal record whatsoever ought to be eligible for such a program. For example, the Connecticut program that allows for pretrial diversion if one has other criminal convictions, though barring those with domestic violence convictions, is clearly inappropriate. Not only does this undermine individual accountability, but it also sends a dangerous message that these cases are not as serious as other offenses. Furthermore, the most dangerous offenders are likely to have criminal records that do not involve family violence offenses. Any criminal conviction ought to make one ineligible for a pretrial diversion program.

Judges should be creative with sentencing options and not fear political backlash if they opt for unconventional alternatives. For example, judges could sentence offenders to weekend incarceration, allowing them to keep their jobs, but impressing upon them the costs associated with engaging in violent behavior toward their family members. Short-term incarceration, with the threat of longer stays, may be enough incentive to motivate some abusers to change their behavior. . . .

Another promising alternative is the use of electronic monitoring devices that monitor the movements of offenders, notifying probation departments if the offender is not within a certain radius. This can help ensure that the defendant obey any stay-away orders forbidding contact with the victim.

### 3. Incarcerate When Appropriate

Too few, not too many, men are incarcerated for severe and chronic violence against their intimate partners.

Their abuse is part of an ingrained pattern of extensive violence and antisocial behavior that is unlikely to yield to either anger-management or feminist-based models of treatment....

Borderline and sociopathic abusers can present the greatest threat to victims during the criminal process because they are impulsive, unpredictable, and may have problems with drugs or alcohol as well as violence. It is incumbent upon prosecutors and victim advocates to help keep these offenders' victims safe during the criminal process. Furthermore, these offenders likely will continue to be violent with new partners given the serial nature of their battering. Thus, incarceration can also protect potential future victims.

Legislators should develop sentencing guidelines that mandate incarceration when certain factors exist. Judges should not have the discretion to allow men who inflict serious injury on their partners, use a deadly weapon, or continue to stalk or harass their victims to remain at large....

Abused women face many hurdles in putting their lives back together. Yet, well-intentioned arguments that incarceration against a woman's wishes "disempowers" her are overstated. These arguments essentialize women as victims, failing to recognize the resilience and strength that many women find after they are safely away from their abusers. A woman often needs the peace of mind that the defendant will be in jail so that she can start her life anew. Incarceration provides both physical and mental security. Although most offenders will be released after only a brief stay in prison, even short-term reprieve from an abuser can provide the victim with some opportunity to make what changes she needs to make without fear.

Those who see economic loss as equally "victimizing" as physical abuse trivialize and obscure the actual harm and risk of death that result when the most dangerous offenders remain at large. A woman may face short-term financial hardship if her partner goes to jail, but this is no different than if her partner was incarcerated for a drug or property offense. Furthermore, incarceration of a spouse may motivate a woman to be more financially independent, reducing the likelihood that she will stay with an abusive partner for financial reasons. In the long term, hopefully she can gain more confidence in herself and the system.

Jurisdictions should automatically notify victims whose abusers are in jail of parole hearings, furloughs, transfers to community facilities, and discharges from incarceration. Women should have the right to participate in parole hearings. When domestic violence victims believe that early parole will jeopardize their safety, prosecutors and advocates can work together to provide the parole board with information before making an early release decision.

....

### 4. Establish Specialized Probation Departments

Many police departments and prosecutor's offices have specialized domestic violence units. This trend can be expanded to probation departments. Specialized probation units give higher priority and follow-up in domestic violence cases that normally slip through the cracks. Probation officers in these units can continue to work with victims as well as offenders, ensuring that if the defendant recidivates, consequences will follow. They can also assist prosecutors in filing violations of probation charges, thus providing more information through intensified supervision of offenders. Finally, it takes experience to develop the skills necessary to monitor these cases; staffing units with dedicated people facilitates long-term success.

### 5. Educate Criminal Justice Personnel

Prosecutors, judges, and other court personnel need education about domestic violence. Some states mandate judicial education. But the education rarely includes issues such as batterer typologies, treatment programs, and the different theories that might be used to better understand this phenomenon. Court personnel need more complete information to make better sentencing decisions.

Furthermore, defense counsel should be included in domestic violence education programs. We often overlook the difficult position many private and public defenders are placed in when having to advise clients on guilty pleas and sentence recommendations. Many defense attorneys are concerned with their clients' long-term well-being as well as their short-term acquittal. Bringing defense counsel into the fold is likely to improve coordinated community responses to domestic violence.

### 6. Undertake More Collaborative Research Efforts

Bridging the gap between lawmakers, activists, and the social sciences holds enormous potential for further understanding and ultimately better policies. Interdisciplinary teams can develop and evaluate creative programs. Funding for research on intervention programs must be adequate. Studies of treatment programs should be longer and broader in scope; random assignments with control and comparison groups are vital to meaningful research in this area.

One reason for the inadequate knowledge base about violence or its interventions has been the traditionally low level of funding for violence research. Reductions in violence, like progress in the fight of disease and technological advancement, will begin when there are investments in knowledge development commensurate with the urgency of the problem.

. . . .

## A. Jail Sentences for Federal Crimes of Domestic Violence

Federal prosecutors have wide discretion in determining which crimes to prosecute in the federal courts and generally focus on the most serious. Federal crimes of domestic violence call for lengthy prison terms upon conviction. Between 1985 and 2005 federal judges had little leeway under mandatory post-conviction sentencing guidelines to deviate from a proscribed sentencing formula, often resulting in lengthy sentences. But in 2005, in *United States v. Booker*, 543 U.S. 220 (2005), the Supreme Court determined mandatory sentencing guidelines were unconstitutional, effectively rendering them advisory.

What follows is the statute outlining the permissible sentencing following a conviction for one of the crimes created under VAWA; interstate travel to violate an order of protection. It is followed by two cases discussing the factors courts consider when imposing sentence.

### 18 U.S.C. § 2262 Interstate violation of protection order

(a) Offenses.

(1) Travel or conduct of offender. A person who travels in interstate or foreign commerce, or enters or leaves Indian country or is present within the special maritime and territorial jurisdiction of the United States, with the intent to engage in conduct that violates the portion of a protection order that prohibits or provides protection against violence, threats, or harassment against, contact or communication with, or physical proximity to, another person, or that would violate such a portion of a protection order in the jurisdiction in which the order was issued, and subsequently engages in such conduct, shall be punished as provided in subsection (b).

(2) Causing travel of victim. A person who causes another person to travel in interstate or foreign commerce or to enter or leave Indian country by force, coercion, duress, or fraud, and in the course of, as a result of, or to facilitate such conduct or travel engages in conduct that violates the portion of a protection order that prohibits or provides protection against violence, threats, or harassment against, contact or communication with, or physical proximity to, another person, or that would violate such a portion of a protection order in the jurisdiction in which the order was issued, shall be punished as provided in subsection (b).

(b) Penalties. A person who violates this section shall be fined under this title, imprisoned—

(1) for life or any term of years, if death of the victim results;

(2) for not more than 20 years if permanent disfigurement or life threatening bodily injury to the victim results;

(3) for not more than 10 years, if serious bodily injury to the victim results or if the offender uses a dangerous weapon during the offense;

(4) as provided for the applicable conduct under chapter 109A [18 U.S.C. §§ 2241 et seq.] if the offense would constitute an offense under chapter 109A (without regard to whether the offense was committed in the special maritime and territorial jurisdiction of the United States or in a Federal prison); and

(5) for not more than 5 years, in any other case,

or both fined and imprisoned.

## United States v. Robinson
### United States Court of Appeals, First Circuit
### 433 F.3d 31 (2005)

STAHL, SENIOR CIRCUIT JUDGE.

Anthony Robinson pled guilty to a charge under the Violence Against Women Act, 18 U.S.C. § 2262, for the interstate violation of a protective order. The district court concluded that the federal Sentencing Guidelines recommended application of the maximum sentence authorized by the statute, a term of 5 years, and sentenced Robinson accordingly. Robinson now contests the court's application of a sentencing enhancement for prior threatening and abusive behavior and challenges the court's failure to reduce his sentence for acceptance of responsibility. Finding that the sentence imposed was reasonable, we reject Robinson's challenges.

### I. Background

Until 2004, Anthony Robinson lived in the state of Washington. In 2003, he began a short prison term for assaulting his wife, Rebecca. Upon his release in 2004, a protective order issued by the state court in Washington came into effect. The order barred Robinson from having any contact with his wife.

In the summer of 2004, Robinson fled Washington and headed for Maine with his wife and two children in tow. In June, a man identifying himself as Rebecca's father called the county sheriff's office in Hancock County, Maine, to inform that office that he had reason to believe that Robinson and his wife had settled in the county after leaving the state of Washington. Soon afterwards, the Washington Department of Human Services contacted its Maine counterpart to ask it to locate the Robinsons' children and investigate their well-being. The Maine agency in turn supplied the sheriff's department with information that enabled the investigating detective from that office to locate the Robinson family. Robinson and his wife were found living together at a campground and working at a local cannery. Robinson was arrested and charged with violating the federal statute that prohibits the interstate violation of a protective order, 18 U.S.C. § 2262.

Robinson pled guilty to the charge without a plea agreement. . . . The U.S. Probation Office prepared and submitted to the parties a proposed presentence investigation report that concluded that the applicable Guidelines sentencing range was 46 to 57 months. After Robinson objected to some portions of the report, the Probation

Office submitted to the court a final, revised report that recommended a sentence of between 37 and 46 months.

The court, sentencing Robinson in April 2005, after the Supreme Court decided *United States v. Booker*, 543 U.S. 220, 125 S. Ct. 738, 160 L. Ed. 2d 621 (2005), appropriately understood the Guidelines to be merely advisory but nevertheless an important consideration in sentencing, and applied the Guidelines to Robinson's case to determine an appropriate sentence. Having done so, the court found the applicable range to be substantially higher than the range suggested by the final presentence report.

. . . .

Although he pled guilty to the offense, which went some way towards demonstrating contrition, the judge was unconvinced. The judge found that three facts strongly suggested that Robinson had not fully accepted responsibility for his crime. First, Robinson attempted to justify his flight from Washington, which he explained was motivated in part by his desire to put some distance between the Robinson family and Rebecca's father, who was constantly "trying to get [Robinson] locked up." Second, Robinson tried to excuse his conduct: he told the court that he been advised by an attorney that the order had no effect outside of the state of Washington, and so had believed that by moving to Maine he could evade the restrictions the protective order had imposed. Third, and most important, Robinson persisted in making illegal contact with Rebecca: while he was incarcerated pending sentencing, Robinson had written a number of letters to his wife. Some of these letters were gentle, some threatening, but all were written in violation of the still-active protective order, which prohibited communication between Robinson and his wife. . . .

The court next considered the applicability of USSG § 2A6.2(b)(1)(D), which provides for a two-level enhancement of a defendant's offense level where the criminal activity under 18 U.S.C. § 2262 "involves . . . a pattern of activity involving stalking, threatening, harassing, or assaulting the same victim." The judge noted three past incidents in which it was demonstrated by a preponderance of the evidence that Robinson had harassed, threatened, or assaulted Rebecca. These included: an attempt by Robinson to choke his wife on April 20, 2003, in Lakewood, Washington, which resulted in an assault conviction; a second incident of abuse in Pierce County, Washington, on March 31, 2004, which resulted in a second assault conviction; and the series of letters to Rebecca that Robinson had written while incarcerated and awaiting sentencing on the instant charge, which were prohibited by the protective order and in some of which Robinson threatened Rebecca with harm. . . .

The court determined that Robinson merited a criminal history level of V, a determination that is not challenged here. With the two-step enhancement to his base offense level in place, Robinson's offense level was 20. The criminal history level and offense level taken together yielded a recommended sentence of 63 to 78 months. The maximum sentence Robinson could receive under § 2262 was 60 months, and the court therefore imposed the full maximum sentence. Robinson timely appealed his sentence.

II. Analysis

. . . .

A. Enhancement for Pattern of Activity

1. Standard of Review

Robinson was sentenced in April 2005, after the Supreme Court decided *United States v. Booker*, 543 U.S. 220, 125 S. Ct. 738, 160 L. Ed. 2d 621 (2005). In *Booker*, the Supreme Court excised the portions of the U.S. Code that purported to make the United States Sentencing Guidelines binding upon the district courts during sentencing. After *Booker*, the Guidelines are merely advisory, which means that a district court has considerable leeway to impose a sentence that falls outside of the range suggested by the Guidelines.

. . . .

Despite *Booker*'s excision of certain portions of the statute, the Sentencing Act still imposes certain requirements on a sentencing court. It prescribes a set of factors, set forth at 18 U.S.C. § 3553(a), that a sentencing court must take into account in imposing a sentence. . . .

Among the factors that a district court must consider is the sentencing range recommended by the Guidelines. 18 U.S.C. § 3553(a)(4)(A). A sentencing court is still required to "consult [the] Guidelines and take them into account when sentencing." *Booker*, 125 S. Ct. at 767. The court is not bound to impose a sentence within the range the Guidelines recommend, of course, and may depart from it if it reasonably concludes that the other § 3553 factors warrant such a departure. However, so far as the Guidelines bear upon the sentence imposed, the court's calculation must be correct, subject of course to the limitations of plain error or harmless error review. . . .

2. Government Waiver

The U.S. Probation Office prepared and submitted to the parties a proposed presentence investigation report, which did not recommend application of § 2A6.2(b)(1)(D). The government stated that it had no objections to the recommendations made in the report. Robinson, however, registered a number of objections. The probation office revised the report in response to Robinson's objections, and submitted the revised version to the district court. In a memorandum submitted to the court only in response to the revised presentence report, the government for the first time asked the court to apply § 2A6.2(b)(1)(D).

Robinson argues that, because the government had an opportunity to ask the court to apply § 2A6.2(b)(1)(D) before submission of the revised report, and did not avail itself of that opportunity, the government waived any possible application of that guideline, and that the court was therefore wrong to apply it. The application of a particular guideline and imposition of a sentence are not, however, the government's to waive in a case, such as this one, where the defendant has pled guilty without the benefit of a plea agreement as to sentencing. . . . The court was therefore free to impose a sentence under the Guidelines regardless of the recommendations in the presentence report or whether any objections to that report were raised by the government.

. . . .

4. Applicability of USSG § 2A6.2(b)(1)(D)

Robinson contests the application of USSG § 2A6.2(b)(1)(D) to raise his offense level from 18 to 20. Section 2A6.2(a) provides a base offense level of 18 for a violation of 18 U.S.C. § 2262. Section 2A6.2(b)(1)(D) then provides: "If the offense involved . . . a pattern of activity involving stalking, threatening, harassing, or assaulting the same victim, increase [the offense level] by 2 levels." Robinson argues that the provision is inapplicable for two reasons.

First, Robinson contends that § 2A6.2(b)(1)(D) was inapplicable because the conduct that resulted in the conviction, which is to say, Robinson's journey to Maine with Rebecca, was not an act of stalking, threatening, harassment, or assault. . . . Robinson's persistent abuse of his wife, consisting of at least the two incidents of assault and the sending of multiple threatening letters, constitutes the proscribed pattern of activity. The offense involved that pattern, because it consisted of the violation of a protective order whose only purpose was to protect Rebecca from that abusive behavior.

Robinson also argues that the guideline is inapplicable because it contemplates a "victim," and Robinson's wife cannot be considered a victim because, he alleges, she gave her consent to travel with him to Maine. The district court rightly concluded that this argument is frivolous. The guideline calls for an enhancement when the charged crime "involved . . . a pattern of activity involving stalking, threatening, harassing, or assaulting the same victim." USSG § 2A6.2. As we have just noted, the pattern of activity in question consisted of two incidents in which Robinson assaulted his wife, and more than one instance in which he threatened her. The question is whether she was the "victim" of the activity which constituted the requisite pattern, and this she plainly was. . . .

B. Acceptance of Responsibility

. . . .

Here, we find no error. While a guilty plea and a truthful account of the conduct constituting an offense are significant evidence of a defendant's acceptance of responsibility, they are not conclusive. See *United States v. Hardy*, 99 F.3d 1242, 1246 (1st Cir. 1996); USSG § 3E1.1, cmt. n. 3. While the defendant's statement to the court suggested some degree of acceptance of responsibility for the crime he had committed, it also contained assertions inconsistent with such an acceptance. Even more important to the district court's determination, however, was the fact that, while in prison pending sentencing, Robinson wrote a series of threatening letters to his wife, a form of communication that the protective order then in force expressly, and by Robinson's own acknowledgment, forbade. The district court thought that Robinson's ongoing violation of the very protective order for whose violation he was then incarcerated was flatly inconsistent with an acceptance of responsibility for the prior violation of that protective order. That determination appears to us to be utterly supportable, and we therefore find no error in the district court's decision not to reduce Robinson's sentence under USSG § 3E1.1.

. . . .

## United States v. Fiume
United States Court of Appeals for the First Circuit

708 F. 3d 59 (2013)

Selya, Circuit Judge.

The principal issue in this sentencing appeal is one of first impression at the federal appellate level. The appeal is premised on the notion that a two-level enhancement to the defendant's guideline sentencing range (GSR) under USSG § 2A6.2(b)(1)(A), when superimposed upon a base offense level dictated by USSG § 2A6.2(a), constitutes an impermissible exercise in double counting. . . .

In June of 2010, defendant-appellant Jason P. Fiume was found guilty in a New York court of assaulting his wife Megan and sentenced to time served. At around the same time, the court entered a protection order, which was to be effective through June 22, 2015. Pertinently, the protection order prohibited the defendant from either approaching or communicating with Megan, and put him on notice that it would be a federal offense to cross state lines in order to violate these conditions.

Unfazed by the protection order, the defendant undertook a course of conduct that flouted its terms. This conduct included attempts to communicate with Megan by telephone, mail, e-mail, text message, and Facebook. His campaign was not limited to remote communicative efforts; on July 2, 2010, he traveled to his in-laws' home in Maine (where Megan was staying) and left a message for Megan on a tree in the yard.

In due season, a federal grand jury returned an indictment that charged the defendant with violating 18 U.S.C. § 2262(a)(1), (b)(5), a statute that, with some conditions, criminalizes interstate travel with the intent to engage in conduct that transgresses a court-imposed protection order. After the defendant entered a guilty plea to this charge, the probation department prepared a presentence investigation report (PSI Report). The PSI Report recommended that the court start with a base offense level of 18, derived from USSG § 2A6.2(a)—a guideline applicable to an array of crimes involving stalking or domestic violence. It further recommended that the court add a two-level enhancement because the offense of conviction involved the violation of a court protection order, *see id.* § 2A6.2(b)(1)(A); another two-level enhancement for a pattern of activity involving stalking, threatening, harassing, or assaulting the same victim, see *id.* § 2A6.2(b)(1)(D); and applied a three-level reduction for acceptance of responsibility, see *id.* § 3E1.1. These calculations, in concert with the defendant's criminal history category (II), yielded a GSR of 33-41 months in prison.

At the disposition hearing, the district court, over the defendant's objections, accepted the guideline calculations limned in the PSI Report and imposed a top-of-the-range sentence of 41 months. This timely appeal ensued. . . .

In the world of criminal sentencing, "double counting is a phenomenon that is less sinister than the name implies." *United States v. Zapata*, 1 F.3d 46, 47 (1st Cir. 1993). Such arithmetic "is often perfectly proper." *Id*. After all, sentencing facts are not found "in hermetically sealed packages, neatly wrapped and segregated one from another." *United States v. Lilly*, 13 F.3d 15, 19 (1st Cir. 1994). Multiple sentencing adjustments may derive from "the same nucleus of operative facts while nonetheless responding to discrete concerns." *Id*. Thus, in the absence of an express prohibition, this court routinely has permitted a single underlying fact to be used more than once when that fact bears upon two separate sentencing considerations. See, e.g., *United States v. Chiaradio*, 684 F.3d 265, 283 (1st Cir. 2012); *United States v. McCarty*, 475 F.3d 39, 46-47 (1st Cir. 2007); *United States v. Wallace*, 461 F.3d 15, 36 (1st Cir. 2006); *United States v. Rivera-Maldonado*, 194 F.3d 224, 235 (1st Cir. 1999); *Lilly*, 13 F.3d at 17-20; *Zapata*, 1 F.3d at 49-50.

These principles are dispositive here. Neither the guideline provision about which the defendant complains, USSG § 2A6.2, nor its associated commentary contains any textual proscription against the use of a two-level upward adjustment under § 2A6.2(b)(1)(A). . . .

The sentencing guideline under which the defendant's base offense level was set targets three separate types of crimes and lumps them within the rubric of "Stalking or Domestic Violence" offenses. Only one of this trio contains as an element the violation of a court protection order. See 18 U.S.C. § 2261 (interstate domestic violence); *id*. § 2261A (interstate stalking); *id*. § 2262 (interstate violation of a protection order). The most logical conclusion, therefore, is that the defendant's base offense level accounts for the general nature of the offense of conviction as one of stalking or domestic violence, but does not account specifically for the violation of a court protection order; the two-level upward adjustment under USSG § 2A6.2(b)(1)(A) bridges the gap and accounts for this feature of the defendant's crime. . . . That is single counting, not double counting.

The able district judge appreciated this distinction. He specifically noted, at the disposition hearing, that the Sentencing Commission may have rationally intended to punish a stalking-type offense more seriously where it simultaneously involved the violation of a court order. He therefore applied the guidelines as written and enhanced the defendant's offense level accordingly. . . .

If more were needed—and we doubt that it is—this result is fortified by the penalty provisions of 18 U.S.C. §§ 2261 and 2261A. These statutes prescribe a special minimum punishment for cases involving violations of court orders. See *id*. § 2261(b)(6) ("Whoever commits the crime of stalking in violation of a temporary or permanent civil or criminal injunction, restraining order, no-contact order, or other order described in [18 U.S.C. § 2266] . . . shall be punished by imprisonment for not less than 1 year."); *id.* § 2261A (incorporating by reference the penalty provisions of § 2261(b)).

The defendant advances yet another argument against the sentence imposed. He claims for the first time on appeal that the purported double-counting scheme subjects him to "punish[ment] twice for the exact same crime" in violation of the Double Jeopardy Clause. We review this new argument only for plain error. *United States v. Olano*, 507 U.S. 725, 731-32, 113 S. Ct. 1770, 123 L. Ed. 2d 508 (1993); *United States v. Duarte*, 246 F.3d 56, 60 (1st Cir. 2001).

The Double Jeopardy Clause, U.S. Const. amend. V, cl. 2, "forbids successive prosecution and cumulative punishment for a greater and lesser included offense," *Brown v. Ohio*, 432 U.S. 161, 169, 97 S. Ct. 2221, 53 L. Ed. 2d 187 (1977), such that a court may not impose multiple punishments for what is essentially the same offense, *id.* at 165. Here, however, the defendant stands convicted of only a single offense and received only a single sentence. By no stretch of even the most active imagination is the Double Jeopardy Clause implicated. . . .

We need go no further. For the reasons elucidated above, we uphold the defendant's sentence.

## B. Sentences in State Courts

The trend in state legislatures has been to increase the severity of sanctions for crimes of domestic violence. Nonetheless, discretion is factored into every sentencing determination. Most state sentencing statutes provide a range of minimum and maximum prison terms, depending on the severity of the crime. Where the judges fall on that grid depends on the seriousness of the crime, the strength of the evidence, the vigor with which the prosecutor pursues the matter and the mitigating factors the defense is able to put forward. Many states have enacted statutes that specifically require graduated sentences for repeat domestic violence offenders. Courts also mandate offenders to batterers' programs.

### S.C. Code Ann. § 16-25-20 (2016) Acts prohibited; penalties.

(A) It is unlawful to:

(1) cause physical harm or injury to a person's own household member; or

(2) offer or attempt to cause physical harm or injury to a person's own household member with apparent present ability under circumstances reasonably creating fear of imminent peril.

(B) Except as otherwise provided in this section, a person commits the offense of domestic violence in the first degree if the person violates the provisions of subsection (A) and:

(1) great bodily injury to the person's own household member results or the act is accomplished by means likely to result in great bodily injury to the person's own household member;

(2) the person violates a protection order and in the process of violating the order commits domestic violence in the second degree;

(3) has two or more prior convictions of domestic violence within ten years of the current offense;

(4) the person uses a firearm in any manner while violating the provisions of subsection (A); or

(5) in the process of committing domestic violence in the second degree one of the following also results:

    (a) the offense is committed in the presence of, or while being perceived by a minor;

    (b) the offense is committed against a person known, or who reasonably should have been known, by the offender to be pregnant;

    (c) the offense is committed during the commission of a robbery, burglary, kidnapping, or theft;

    (d) the offense is committed by impeding the victim's breathing or air flow; or

    (e) the offense is committed using physical force or the threatened use of force against another to block that person's access to any cell phone, telephone, or electronic communication device with the purpose of preventing, obstructing, or interfering with:

        (i) the report of any criminal offense, bodily injury, or property damage to a law enforcement agency; or

        (ii) a request for an ambulance or emergency medical assistance to any law enforcement agency or emergency medical provider.

A person who violates this subsection is guilty of a felony and, upon conviction, must be imprisoned for not more than ten years.

Domestic violence in the first degree is a lesser included offense of domestic violence of a high and aggravated nature, as defined in Section 16-25-65.

(C) A person commits the offense of domestic violence in the second degree if the person violates subsection (A) and:

(1) moderate bodily injury to the person's own household member results or the act is accomplished by means likely to result in moderate bodily injury to the person's own household member;

(2) the person violates a protection order and in the process of violating the order commits domestic violence in the third degree;

(3) the person has one prior conviction for domestic violence in the past ten years from the current offense; or

(4) in the process of committing domestic violence in the third degree one of the following also results:

    (a) the offense is committed in the presence of, or while being perceived by, a minor;

    (b) the offense is committed against a person known, or who reasonably should have been known, by the offender to be pregnant;

    (c) the offense is committed during the commission of a robbery, burglary, kidnapping, or theft;

    (d) the offense is committed by impeding the victim's breathing or air flow; or

    (e) the offense is committed using physical force or the threatened use of force against another to block that person's access to any cell phone, telephone, or electronic communication device with the purpose of preventing, obstructing, or interfering with:

        (i) the report of any criminal offense, bodily injury, or property damage to a law enforcement agency; or

        (ii) a request for an ambulance or emergency medical assistance to any law enforcement agency or emergency medical provider.

A person who violates this subsection is guilty of a misdemeanor and, upon conviction, must be fined not less than two thousand five hundred dollars nor more than five thousand dollars or imprisoned for not more than three years, or both.

Domestic violence in the second degree is a lesser-included offense of domestic violence in the first degree, as defined in subsection (B), and domestic violence of a high and aggravated nature, as defined in Section 16-25-65.

Assault and battery in the second degree pursuant to Section 16-3-600(D) is a lesser-included offense of domestic violence in the second degree as defined in this subsection.

(D) A person commits the offense of domestic violence in the third degree if the person violates subsection (A).

(1) A person who violates this subsection is guilty of a misdemeanor and, upon conviction, must be fined not less than one thousand dollars nor more than two thousand five hundred dollars or imprisoned not more than ninety days, or both. . . .

(2) Domestic violence in the third degree is a lesser-included offense of domestic violence in the second degree, as defined in subsection (C), domestic violence in the first degree, as defined in subsection (B), and domestic violence of a high and aggravated nature, as defined in Section 16-25-65.

(3) Assault and battery in the third degree pursuant to Section 16-3-600(E) is a lesser-included offense of domestic violence in the third degree as defined in this subsection.

(4) A person who violates this subsection is eligible for pretrial intervention pursuant to Chapter 22, Title 17.

(E) When a person is convicted of a violation of Section 16-25-20(B) or (C) or Section 16-25-65, the circuit court may suspend execution of all or part of the sentence and place the offender on probation, or if a person is convicted of a violation of Section 16-25-20(D), the court may suspend execution of all or part of the sentence, conditioned upon:

(1) the offender's mandatory completion, to the satisfaction of the court, of a domestic violence intervention program designed to treat batterers in accordance with the provisions of subsection (G);

(2) fulfillment of all the obligations arising under court order pursuant to this section and Section 16-25-65;

(3) other reasonable terms and conditions of probation as the court may determine necessary to ensure the protection of the victim; and

(4) making restitution as the court deems appropriate.

(F) In determining whether or not to suspend the imposition or execution of all or part of a sentence as provided in this section, the court must consider the nature and severity of the offense, the number of times the offender has repeated the offense, and the best interests and safety of the victim.

(G) An offender who participates in a domestic violence intervention program pursuant to this section, shall participate in a program offered through a government agency, nonprofit organization, or private provider selected and approved by the Circuit Solicitor with jurisdiction over the offense or the Attorney General if the offense is prosecuted by the Attorney General's Office. If the offender moves to a different circuit after entering a treatment program selected by the Circuit Solicitor, the Circuit Solicitor for the county in which the offender resides shall have the authority to select and approve the batterers' treatment program. The offender shall pay a reasonable fee, if required, for participation in the program but no person may be denied participation due to inability to pay. If the offender suffers from a substance abuse problem or mental health concern, the judge may order, or the program may refer, the offender to supplemental treatment coordinated through the Department of Alcohol and Other Drug Abuse Services with the local alcohol and drug treatment authorities pursuant to Section 61-12-20 or the Department of Mental Health or Veterans' Hospital, respectively. The offender must pay a reasonable fee for participation in the substance abuse treatment or mental health program, if required, but no person may be denied participation due to inability to pay.

(H) A person who violates the terms and conditions of an order of protection issued in this State pursuant to Chapter 4, Title 20, the "Protection from Domestic Abuse

Act", or a valid protection order related to domestic or family violence issued by a court of another state, tribe, or territory is guilty of a misdemeanor and, upon conviction, must be imprisoned not more than thirty days and fined not more than five hundred dollars.

(I) Unless the complaint is voluntarily dismissed or the charge is dropped prior to the scheduled trial date, a person charged with a violation provided in this chapter must appear before a judge for disposition of the case or be tried in the person's absence.

---

In New York, a defendant's status as a *victim* of domestic violence may lead to the imposition of a somewhat lesser sentence upon conviction for a violent felony offense, provided that the prior abuse "was a factor" in the commission of the crime.

## N.Y. C.L.S. Penal § 60.12 (2015) Authorized disposition; alternative indeterminate sentence of imprisonment; domestic violence cases

1. Notwithstanding any other provision of law, where a court is imposing sentence pursuant to section 70.02 upon a conviction for an offense enumerated in subdivision one of such section, other than an offense defined in article one hundred thirty of this chapter, and is authorized or required pursuant to such section to impose a determinate sentence of imprisonment for such offense, the court, upon a determination following a hearing that (a) the defendant was the victim of physical, sexual or psychological abuse by the victim or intended victim of such offense, (b) such abuse was a factor in causing the defendant to commit such offense and (c) the victim or intended victim of such offense was a member of the same family or household as the defendant as such term is defined in subdivision one of section 530.11 of the criminal procedure law, may, in lieu of imposing such determinate sentence of imprisonment, impose an indeterminate sentence of imprisonment in accordance with subdivisions two and three of this section.

2. The maximum term of an indeterminate sentence imposed pursuant to subdivision one of this section must be fixed by the court as follows:

(a) For a class B felony, the term must be at least six years and must not exceed twenty-five years;

(b) For a class C felony, the term must be at least four and one-half years and must not exceed fifteen years;

(c) For a class D felony, the term must be at least three years and must not exceed seven years; and

(d) For a class E felony, the term must be at least three years and must not exceed four years.

3. The minimum period of imprisonment under an indeterminate sentence imposed pursuant to subdivision one of this section must be fixed by the court at one-half of the maximum term imposed and must be specified in the sentence.

---

Despite the authorization to impose jail terms, many judges impose non-incarceratory sentences. In 2014, there were approximately 3.9 million adult men and women on probation in the United States. Of that number, about four percent were placed on probation for offenses relating to domestic violence.[7] The levels of supervision vary depending on the severity of the crime for which the probationer was convicted and the size of the community's probation population as compared to the number of probation officials available to supervise them. The extent to which probation acts as a deterrent also depends on the likelihood probation officials will violate non-compliant offenders and the willingness of courts to hold uncooperative probationers accountable.

## C. Electronic Monitoring and Batterers' Programs

Using a Global Positioning System (GPS) device to keep tabs on domestic violence offenders either awaiting trial or after conviction to determine if they are violating protective orders has been an increasingly popular judicial tool. It takes the form of an ankle bracelet. In 2009, only 12 states relied on GPS monitoring; five years later, the number jumped to 23. Another 11 more states were considering implementing GPS monitoring by mid-2015. The biggest obstacle has been expense; it is estimated to cost jurisdictions that rely on GPS monitoring as much as $36-a-day for the service. But it can work. Officials in Connecticut, a pioneer in defendant GPS monitoring since 2004, report that in 11 years in areas that have used it, there have been no domestic violence homicides. In a California study of 516 parolees under GPS monitoring it was shown that those offenders who were not monitored were 38 percent more likely to return to jail.[8]

With the adoption of mandatory arrest laws around the country, domestic violence dockets in state courts grew. District attorney's offices sought to prosecute these cases even in the absence of cooperation from victims. As a result, the justice system sought new ways to end the dangerous cycle of violence underlying these cases. Batterers' programs appeared to be a possible panacea. Courts began mandating offenders to attend in addition to, or in lieu of, jail. Over time, some states passed legislation *requiring* courts to mandate attendance in a batterers' program upon conviction. And, in

---

7. Danielle Kaeble, et. al, U.S. Dep't of Justice, Bureau of Justice Statistics, Probation and Parole in the United States 2014, NCJ 249057 (2015).

8. *At Least 23 States Are Using GPS to Keep Track of High-Risk Domestic Violence Offenders,* July 15, 2015, https://www.domesticshelters.org/domestic-violence-articles-information/using-gps-to-track-batterers#.WDdSo6lrJ3k, accessed November 24, 2016.

some jurisdictions, assignment to a batterers' program has been used as a monitoring technique while a defendant is out on bail.

In 1998, the National Institute of Justice determined that 80 percent of all participants in batterers' programs were mandated to attend by courts or probation officers and conducted a massive nationwide study of the programs to "help criminal justice personnel ... better understand the issues surrounding batterer intervention and enable them to make appropriate referrals to programs and to communicate effectively with program providers."[9]

The NIJ study examined every aspect of batterers' programs, including what they were called. The study quoted Red Crowley of Atlanta's Men Stopping Violence program:

> Let's start with the word *treatment*. We do not see our work as therapy. Battering is the natural outgrowth of patriarchal values. We want to change those values. Batterers' intervention classes serve a number of purposes: they, like shelters, make visible what has been systematically concealed, that is, the horrendous problem of violence against women; create an opportunity to engage the community and the criminal justice system in the effort to stop the violence; and contribute to research. Giving men who want to change the opportunity to do so is just one purpose of the intervention.[10]

Because batterers' intervention programs were an outgrowth of the feminist movement that first helped shape modern public policy about domestic violence, many of the earliest and most widely used programs are based on a feminist model. This perspective is based on a belief that "battering is a gender analysis of power ... [and] violence is a means of maintaining male power in the family when men feel their dominance is being threatened."[11]

The feminist-based educational approach to batterers' programs is the one considered most compatible with the goals of the criminal justice system: batterer behavior is considered criminal; negative consequences for that behavior are considered appropriate; batterers must be accountable for their actions and abusive behavior must be stopped, as opposed to the batterer being healed.[12]

---

9. Kerry Healey, Christine Smith & Chris O'Sullivan, Batterer Intervention: Program Approaches And Criminal Justice Strategies xi, 1 (1998).

10. *Id.* at 17.

11. *Id.* at 18.

12. *Id.* at 26. Some programs are considered highly controversial by the proponents of the feminist model. For example, anger management programs are regarded as short-term programs that address only one aspect of battering—rage—and send the signal that batterers are out of control and cannot help acting violently. The feminist model, in contrast, teaches that batterers are very much *in* control. Couples counseling programs have been criticized because victims can be intimidated and possibly injured for being truthful about the batterer's violence in the sessions and because batterers need to be in group sessions to overcome their denial. Finally, self-help groups run by former batterers have been criticized because the approach is unstructured and there is no indication former batterers are qualified to lead such sessions. *Id.* at 24–25.

One of the highly regarded batterers' intervention programs, developed in 1980 by the Domestic Violence Intervention Project, located in Duluth, Minnesota, is based in part on this approach. It also strongly emphasizes the need for a coordinated community response to the violence. The Duluth Model was part of a community-based project, which was an outgrowth of the battered women's movement, strong feminist activism, and local financial support. The goal of the Duluth strategy is to protect women, engage the criminal justice system by treating domestic violence as a crime, provide victims with legal assistance and assist with law enforcement training.[13]

Part of the Duluth Model includes a 28-session batterers' education program that also offers services to victims. The goal of the program is simple: to stop the violence. If a defendant is sentenced to participate in a batterers' education program, the Duluth Model calls for him to attend an initial intake/orientation session for evaluation and assignment to a group. After the intake session, the victim is contacted for information about the history of the abuse. She is offered information about how to obtain help or shelter in the event the batterer strikes again. If the offender fails to attend the program or commits another act of violence while attending, the staff will ask the court to calendar the case for a hearing to determine whether a further sanction is warranted.[14]

Despite the widespread reliance on batterers' programs by the courts, there is no conclusive evidence they have any impact on stopping or reducing domestic violence.

There have been a number of random studies of the effectiveness of batterer treatment programs.[15] The results have been mixed. One examined the impact of a 10-week batterers' program versus straight probation on 59 men convicted of domestic violence in 1992 in Hamilton, Ontario. Although the results showed only 3 of the 30 men (10 percent) assigned to the batterers' program re-offended over a one-year period, as opposed to 8 of the 26 men (31 percent) assigned to probation, the small number of participants has raised criticism.

Another trial in 2000 involved 861 men at the San Diego Naval Base who were convicted of assaulting their intimate partners. The offenders were randomly assigned to four different sanctions: (1) six months of weekly cognitive-behavior treatment followed by another six months of weekly group sessions; (2) six months of couples' therapy, followed by six months of group sessions; (3) close monitoring and case management and (4) safety planning for victims. There were no significant

---

13. *See* R. EMERSON DOBASH ET AL., CHANGING VIOLENT MEN 47–50 (2000).

14. Domestic Abuse Intervention Project: Community-Based Intervention and Domestic Abuse Intervention Project: An Overview, both available at www.duluth-model.org, accessed March 6, 2017. The Power and Control Wheel, reprinted in the Chapter 1, was created for the Duluth Model and is used as part of the curriculum there.

15. MELISSA LABRIOLA, MICHAEL REMPEL & ROBERT C. DAVIS, CENTER FOR COURT INNOVATION, TESTING THE EFFECTIVENESS OF BATTERER PROGRAMS AND JUDICIAL MONITORING: RESULTS FROM A RANDOMIZED TRIAL AT THE BRONX MISDEMEANOR DOMESTIC VIOLENCE COURT *v* (2005) (Final Report submitted to the National Institute of Justice) [hereinafter CCI Study].

reductions in recidivism, regardless of the group to which the offender was assigned. This study may be of limited utility, however, because it involved only a very low-risk population—they had military jobs, were married, and had no mental health or substance abuse problems or prior criminal records.

In 2002, a third trial was completed involving 404 offenders from the Broward County, Florida misdemeanor domestic violence court. These offenders were randomly assigned to a standard 26-week batterers' program or straight probation. This random trial revealed no correlation between recidivism and attendance in a batterers' program.

Another study in 2000, this one in Brooklyn, New York, randomly assigned 376 misdemeanor domestic violence offenders to either a batterers' program or 40 hours of community service. The results of this trial appeared to indicate a strong connection between reduced recidivism and attendance in a batterers' program, but what the results actually showed was that there was "a strong effect to *assignment* to a batterer program, [but] there was no effect of actually attending it." Indeed, the study showed that "those who completed their batterer program were no less violent than those who attended only some group sessions or who never attended a single session."[16]

In New York City, the Center for Court Innovation, through a grant from the National Institute of Justice, conducted a two-year comprehensive study of the effectiveness of court-ordered batterers' programs and was surprised by the results. The purpose of the study was to determine the effectiveness of batterer programs and varying intensities of judicial monitoring. The study ran from July 23, 2002 through February 27, 2004 at the Bronx, New York, Misdemeanor Domestic Violence Court.[17] It involved offenders who were arraigned for domestic violence misdemeanors but who pled to the minor offense of harassment, known under New York law as a violation. Those who pled to harassment were sentenced to a conditional discharge with the instruction to lead a law-abiding life for one year and obey a one-year order of protection in favor of the victim. This is a very common resolution of misdemeanor cases in the state's domestic violence courts. Offenders were followed for one year after having been sentenced to either a straight conditional discharge, with no further sanction. Others were sentenced to a batterers' program with some level of judicial monitoring to see whether they were doing it, and others were sentenced to just judicial monitoring whereby they had to appear in court periodically and inform the judge they were obeying all directives. All had orders of protection issued against them. It determined that batterer programs had no positive impact on recidivism. It also

---

16. *Id.* at 9. All of the discussion in this section about the results of the Hamilton, Ontario; San Diego, California; Broward Co., Florida; and Brooklyn, New York trials is taken from CCI Study at 8-9

17. The Bronx Misdemeanor Domestic Violence Court was established in 1998 to create a coordinated community response to domestic violence. The Bronx is a borough of New York City with 1.3 million inhabitants. It has the city's highest poverty rate (31 percent) and the lowest per capita income ($13,959) as well as the lowest percentage of city residents with high school diplomas (62 percent). According to the 2000 U.S. Census, it is racially and ethnically diverse, with black, white and Hispanic residents. *See id.* at 13.

found—much to the surprise of the authors of the study—that regular monitoring of convicted defendants by a court had no positive impact on future reoffending.[18]

## Rev. Code Wash. § 26.50.150 (2016) Domestic violence perpetrator programs

Any program that provides domestic violence treatment to perpetrators of domestic violence must be certified by the department of social and health services and meet minimum standards for domestic violence treatment purposes. The department of social and health services shall adopt rules for standards of approval of domestic violence perpetrator programs. The treatment must meet the following minimum qualifications:

(1) All treatment must be based upon a full, complete clinical intake including but not limited to: Current and past violence history; a lethality risk assessment; history of treatment from past domestic violence perpetrator treatment programs; a complete diagnostic evaluation; a substance abuse assessment; criminal history; assessment of cultural issues, learning disabilities, literacy, and special language needs; and a treatment plan that adequately and appropriately addresses the treatment needs of the individual.

(2) To facilitate communication necessary for periodic safety checks and case monitoring, the program must require the perpetrator to sign the following releases:

(a) A release for the program to inform the victim and victim's community and legal advocates that the perpetrator is in treatment with the program, and to provide information, for safety purposes, to the victim and victim's community and legal advocates;

(b) A release to prior and current treatment agencies to provide information on the perpetrator to the program; and

(c) A release for the program to provide information on the perpetrator to relevant legal entities including: Lawyers, courts, parole, probation, child protective services, and child welfare services.

(3) Treatment must be for a minimum treatment period defined by the secretary of the department by rule. The weekly treatment sessions must be in a group unless there is a documented, clinical reason for another modality. Any other therapies, such as individual, marital, or family therapy, substance abuse evaluations or therapy, medication reviews, or psychiatric interviews, may be concomitant with the weekly group treatment sessions described in this section but not a substitute for it.

(4) The treatment must focus primarily on ending the violence, holding the perpetrator accountable for his or her violence, and changing his or her behavior. The treatment must be based on nonvictim-blaming strategies and philosophies and shall include education about the individual, family, and cultural dynamics of domestic

---

18. CCI Study.

violence. If the perpetrator or the victim has a minor child, treatment must specifically include education regarding the effects of domestic violence on children, such as the emotional impacts of domestic violence on children and the long-term consequences that exposure to incidents of domestic violence may have on children.

(5) Satisfactory completion of treatment must be contingent upon the perpetrator meeting specific criteria, defined by rule by the secretary of the department, and not just upon the end of a certain period of time or a certain number of sessions.

(6) The program must have policies and procedures for dealing with reoffenses and noncompliance.

(7) All evaluation and treatment services must be provided by, or under the supervision of, qualified personnel.

(8) The secretary of the department may adopt rules and establish fees as necessary to implement this section.

(9) The department may conduct on-site monitoring visits as part of its plan for certifying domestic violence perpetrator programs and monitoring implementation of the rules adopted by the secretary of the department to determine compliance with the minimum qualifications for domestic violence perpetrator programs. The applicant or certified domestic violence perpetrator program shall cooperate fully with the department in the monitoring visit and provide all program and management records requested by the department to determine the program's compliance with the minimum certification qualifications and rules adopted by the department.

## D. Alternative Solutions

While it might be tempting to suggest domestic violence should be handled by the courts in the same manner as adult stranger-on-stranger violence, this construct ignores the reality that domestic violence is *not* random violence. Instead, it is part of a deliberate pattern of assaultive behavior—physical and psychological—that is focused on a particular victim. No sanction is considered appropriate for batterers that does not take into account the safety of the victim and other household members. The question of whether the criminal justice system needs to look to other disciplines, such as tort litigation and mediation, to craft more relevant, effective sanctions against batterers is a controversial one—without a definitive answer. The idea that the community can band together to impose a meaningful sanction against a domestic abuser, without necessarily involving the criminal justice system, is one that is discussed below.

## C. Quince Hopkins, Mary P. Koss & Karen J. Bachar, *Responding: Two New Solutions: Applying Restorative Justice to Ongoing Intimate Violence: Problems and Possibilities*

23 St. Louis U. Pub. L. Rev. 289 (2004)

. . . .

### II. What is Restorative Justice?

Restorative justice is a philosophy that places emphasis on repairing harm, empowering a victim-driven process, and transforming the community's role in addressing crime. It approaches offender accountability through making reparations and undergoing rehabilitation rather than by punishment. Recent literature reveals numerous thoughtful considerations of the application of restorative justice to crimes against women. Restorative justice models include (a) civil proceedings, (b) victim-offender reparation through mediation, and (c) community conference approaches.

Civil justice for intimate violence is pursued only with responsible parties with substantial financial assets, which limits its applicability as a prevention tool. Furthermore, civil justice is an adversarial process that shares the traumatizing features of retributive justice. It also often involves comparative fault doctrine, a new way to promote victim blame that is not part of criminal trials. On a more theoretical level, a tort action expresses a fundamentally different notion than does a criminal action. That is, a tort claim is entirely private, personal, and individual in nature and aims to adjust rights as between private persons rather than vindicate larger public or community interests.

With respect to the second major form of restorative justice, mediation's conceptual foundation is inappropriate for application to crimes against women because it fails to acknowledge the structural inequalities between the victim and offender and wrongly presumes that there is "voice parity" between the parties such that they have the same "truth-telling capacity." That is, most feminists subscribe to the theory that a batterer uses violence as a tool to maintain power and control over his victim and that the physical violence can be understood as a method of maintaining and reinforcing patriarchal gender roles in particular. Mediation theory, however, rests on the assumption of equal or near-equal bargaining power between the parties. The underlying power dynamic in domestic violence cases thus makes it inappropriate for mediation.

By contrast, many experts believe community conferencing comes the closest to achieving restorative justice ideals, addressing the power disparities often present in crimes of violence against women, and avoiding the trauma and other problems of traditional civil justice. Community conferencing is a coming together of identified family and other supporters for the victim and offender in a professionally facilitated meeting to address the wrong done and the harm that resulted from that wrong—to all parties and their relationships with others—and to identify what the offender is going to do to make right the wrong. Proper and complete preparation is key to a successful outcome of community conferencing, and this is even truer in the case of conferencing applied to violence against women, where underlying belief systems need to be challenged.

. . . .

### IV. Particular Feminist Concerns About Restorative Justice Responses to Violence Against Women

Although restorative justice is now used widely and with some success with juveniles, including juvenile sex offenders, experience with restorative justice in response to violence against adult women is limited. As when moving into any new area of research where lives may be at stake, it is important to maintain a balance between the hope of success and prudence in applying restorative justice to new areas. One must at all times be mindful of the potential risk of harm to participants. Some feminist scholars have raised important questions about the wisdom of using restorative justice in response to gendered violence. The majority of these concerns center on whether restorative justice is an effective and safe response to violence against women. Whether it is in fact safe or effective is, of course, an empirical question. In her careful study of Navajo Peacemaker courts' handling of domestic violence cases, Donna Coker identifies the coerced attendance of battered women coupled with the lack of safety screening as problematic aspects of that program. After arguing that a peacemaking program could be modified to correct these problems, Coker then rightly notes that with such a modified program we may still ultimately find that the potential benefits of restorative justice exist only in theory, but not in practice. The same is true for the potential detriments of restorative justice for intimate violence: whether the detriments will be borne out in practice must be evaluated empirically, something Coker does not purport to undertake. Cognizant of Coker's caution, however, in undertaking such a project, it is critical that restorative justice's foray into the new territory of violence against women takes these concerns seriously. Such a foray must be guided by these caveats in choosing those types of cases that pose the lowest potential risks to participants and the format for responding to them.

In developing our own research on restorative justice for sex offenses between acquaintances, funded by a $1.5 million dollar grant from the Centers for Disease Control, we placed these concerns front and center. In developing our pilot research demonstration project, entitled RESTORE, we specifically chose to focus on a very narrow class of cases which posed the least risk of harm to participants and the highest possible success rate. We have explained the structure of this program and its theoretical grounding at length elsewhere. In brief, we specifically chose to address sexual assaults between acquaintances, rather than cases of physical violence between intimates. We chose to do so precisely because many of the concerns about restorative justice for violence against women, discussed at length below, are less applicable to acquaintance sexual assault. We discuss these distinctions at length in another article but note here just one illustrative distinction. Two of the feminist concerns, discussed below, are that restorative justice will give an offender an opportunity to engage in further violence and to psychologically abuse and manipulate the survivor. In the narrow class of cases eligible for RESTORE—most notably, only cases where the offense was not part of an ongoing pattern of ongoing domestic violence—there is a reduced likelihood of deep emotional, economic, and psychological enmeshment between the parties. Where the parties' interaction with each other is thus less intertwined, the opportunity for the offender to engage in further physical violence or psychological control of the survivor is significantly reduced. It was our conclusion, therefore, that in moving forward with an as yet untested application of restorative justice—that is, its application to gendered violence generally—sexual assault between acquaintances was a "safer" test venue than was ongoing physical violence between intimates.

Joan Pennel and Gale Burford's work . . . by contrast, applies restorative justice to cases of family violence. Similarly, however, their approach also takes seriously the feminist concerns about using restorative justice for violence against women and proceeds cautiously in implementing such a program for domestic violence. Pennel and Burford's research is yielding preliminary evidence of being more effective than traditional justice for intimate violence.

The specific feminist concerns raised about restorative justice in connection with family violence are the following. First, and primarily, if one chooses to address cases of intimate violence where the violence has occurred on more than one occasion already, the face-to-face concept of community conferencing simply creates an opportunity for further acts of violence against the victim. Second, even if the violence has occurred just one time, the face-to-face approach may either intentionally or unintentionally pressure the victim into returning to a potentially dangerous relationship. Third, the psychological impact on victims from ongoing domestic violence may negatively affect her ability to present and protect her interests and wishes during the course of the community conference. Fourth, the power and control dynamics in many domestic violence cases mean that the process of conferencing will yield poor results for victims unable to hold their own in the face-to-face meeting. In addition, not only might fear constrain a victim's full agency, her connection to her children may compromise her otherwise more free choice, as might economic and other enmeshment between the victim and perpetrator. Fifth, to the extent that restorative justice relies on a component of therapeutic intervention with perpetrators, there is only moderate evidence that batterers' treatment is at all effective: this evidence can be found in very high quality programs and only where an offender actually completes the program—a mere 10% of all program participants. Assessment of these programs reveals that treated and non-treated abusers were not significantly different in their future rates of re-offending nor were there differences in the frequency of severe violence or threats of violence. If such treatment is only moderately effective, the argument goes, why should we embrace an approach to intimate violence that relies upon what is only a moderately effective intervention? Sixth, to the extent apology might be important to restorative justice concepts, a debatable question, the use of apology in cases of domestic violence is often coercive rather than healing. An approach to intimate violence that facilitates or encourages apology as an element of restitution (in the colloquial, rather than legal sense of that term) may be ineffective or harmful at worst. Seventh and finally, a restorative justice response to intimate violence against women violates the central tenet of liberal feminism that crimes of interpersonal violence against women receive the same treatment as crimes of interpersonal violence against men. That is, if incarceration and fines are the norm for male on male violence, then taking incarceration and fines off the table constitutes justice "lite" for female victims of male violence.

. . . .

## V. Evidence that Restorative Justice Is Succeeding Where Traditional Pro-Prosecution Approaches Have Not

Given the foregoing criticisms and concerns about applying restorative justice to adult-to-adult family violence, and particularly the concern that victimized women may be pressured into forgiving and reconciling with their violent partners, it is not surprising that researchers have shied away from testing those concerns. As a result, there is little empirical evidence either supporting or rebutting them. In addition to Donna Coker's study of Navajo Peacemaking discussed above, Joan Pennell and Gale Burford's innovative work in Canada and Pennell's continuing work in the United States provides a notable exception to this dearth of hard data on using restorative justice methods for adult domestic violence.

. . . .

### A. Canadian Family Group Decision Making Project

In the early-1990s Pennell and Burford developed and implemented the Family Group Decision Making Project in Canada ("FGDMP" or the "Canadian Project"), a quasi-experimental program that employed the form of restorative justice known as family group conferencing ("FGC") initially directed at cases of child abuse, neglect, and dependency. In the early stages of the Project, however, it quickly became apparent that adult domestic violence was a prevalent co-occurring event in the cases referred to the Project, occurring in twenty-one of the thirty-two families referred. Pennell and Burford embraced this development and incorporated into the FGDMP the adult family violence they uncovered. They ultimately concluded that failure to address the cooccurrence of child and spouse abuse shortchanged families. Pennell and Burford's holistic intervention yielded marked reductions in both child and spouse abuse.

The Canadian Project conducted family group conferences with thirty-two families over the course of a one year implementation period, coupled with a one to two-year follow-up period. The Project requested that the most difficult cases be referred to the FGDMP. Pennell and Burford also established a comparison group, consisting of another set of families who did not go through FGCs. The families were distributed roughly evenly between three different implementation locales.

Upon referral to the Canadian Project, family members engaged in extensive pre-conferencing work with conference coordinators, continuing over a period of weeks, to guarantee that all participants were prepared and that safety of participants was ensured. The conference consisted of three basic phases. First, the coordinator and other professionals outlined the ground rules and the factual basis for referring the family to the Project in the first place. Second, professional outlines provided background material on the problems identified and social and therapeutic services available to address them. Third, the family group was left alone to deliberate and develop a plan to address the identified problems. Fourth, the professionals reviewed the plan developed by the family to ensure that it addressed all issues of concern and, further, that it included adequate monitoring provisions. Once approved, the plan was then implemented. Plans typically included expected components such as mental health and substance abuse services and material assistance from government agencies, but often also included plans for recreation and leisure events with family members. This latter component, when it was included, may have helped in promoting family unity, which Pennell and Burford identified as important to the reduction of family violence.

The results of the Canadian Project were encouraging and provide some evidence of an intervention program that is effective in reducing family violence. The results of the Project also provided welcome answers to some of the concerns posed by feminists and victim advocates about the application of restorative justice to family violence. First, the concern that batterers would use the conference as an opportunity to further abuse their partners was not borne out: in none of the conferences was any violence reported. This is particularly striking given that the families were left alone to work on the issues presented without the oversight of service providers or the conference coordinator.

Second, and more importantly, significant actual reductions in post-conference partner and child abuse were demonstrated. These reductions in family violence were in direct contrast with the comparison group, in which increased incidents of violence during the study period were noted. The families referred for FGC presented more incidents of violence (233 events) prior to entering the Canadian Project than did the comparison families (129 events). By the conclusion of the Canadian Project, violent events within the study families were not eliminated, but were cut almost in half (117 events); by contrast, violent events in the comparison group families rose (165 events). This finding provides important evidence of the effectiveness of restorative justice in reducing the prevalence of family violence.

Third, the study measured some of the controlling behaviors by batterers that feminist advocates are concerned would not be accounted for, much less reduced by restorative justice methods, and found marked reductions in all behaviors studied. For instance, the study measured family functioning including offender's domination of conversation, resistance to her meeting with program personnel without his being present, and control of economic resources. In each of these categories, interviews with the participants in the study group revealed significant improvement: during the average one-year follow up period, domination of the conversation reduced from four to two incidents pre-versus post-conferencing, and control of economic resources reduced from four to zero incidents. By contrast, the comparison group saw little to no improvement, and, in some instances, evidenced a worsening: control of discussion stayed constant at two incidents pre-and post-study, whereas control of economic resources increased from three to four incidents pre-versus post-study. Emotional abuse—unrecognized by traditional criminal justice response—saw similar reductions in the study families and increases in the comparison families. Men in the study families belittled their partner (describing her as stupid, crazy, incompetent, and so on) in five incidents pre-study versus three times post-study and were otherwise overly solicitous and condescending to them in four incidents pre-versus two incidents post-study. The comparison group numbers again demonstrate the reverse trend: no incidents of belittling were indicated pre-study; whereas one incident was noted post-study period, and rates of condescension stayed level at three incidents throughout. The study also measured batterer's minimization of his violence, transference of responsibility for the violence to the victim, and/or refusal to accept responsibility for it. As with the prior non-physical abuse measures, study families saw a reduction from eight to three incidents, pre-versus post-study, whereas the comparison group saw an increase from four to six incidents. Finally, feminist concerns that restorative justice would fail to account for, respond to, or change underlying patriarchal belief systems proved unfounded. The Project tested for offenders' "rigid" adherence to traditional sex roles, including "expecting or demanding that [his partner] serve him." While these beliefs reduced from three to one in the study families pre-versus post-study, these sexist and gendered notions of male/female relationships remained constant at five in the control group. . . .

B. Applicability of Family Group Conferencing with Culturally and Regionally Diverse Populations

In addition to the foregoing concerns about applying restorative justice to gendered violence, at least one commentator has questioned whether restorative justice methods, originally the province of indigenous peoples, would ultimately prove feasible or effective in non-indigenous contexts. Pennell and Burford's Canadian study provides at least a preliminary answer to that question. In the Canadian Family Group Decision Making Project, Pennell and Burford deployed the Project in three culturally and regionally diverse locales in the Canadian province of Newfoundland & Labrador: an Inuit community located on the coast of Labrador, a rural area consisting of a mix of British, French, and Micmac populations, and an urban setting, the capital of the province consisting primarily of residents of Irish and British derivation. Upon completion of the Canadian Project, Pennell joined forces with Marie Weil in developing a United States-based family group conferencing program, the North Carolina Family Group Conferencing Project ("NCFGCP"). The NCFGCP sought to mainstream the Canadian Projects' approach but again included diverse groups within its purview. Early analysis of the North Carolina program indicates that it yields similarly positive outcomes. The diversity of populations included in the Canadian and U.S. studies suggests that FGC can be used with good effect in various cultural and regional milieus.

## VI. Conclusion

The foregoing discussion proposes that we listen to the voices of victims of domestic violence and that we honor those voices in true feminist fashion, by crafting responses to the violence they suffer that mirror the remedies victims request. Further, the failure of three decades of legal reform to change prevalence rates in any significant way suggests that we need to explore alternative, even risky, approaches to the problem of intimate violence. The preliminary evidence from restorative justice programs that address family violence demonstrate that it may be more effective than all of the heavier handed pro-incarceration efforts to which feminists in the United States have been directing their efforts.

But what might we sacrifice if we focus on an individualized response tailored to the needs of particular victims? We are faced with the question of whether the infliction and/or resultant harm of intimate assault is merely the expression and result of local rage of an individual towards a particular victim for a set of relationship-specific reasons, or whether it is group-based with some broader cause or effect. We risk reverting to a focus on the relationship rather than the violence. We miss the impact of intimate violence on women as a group, not just in terms of its disparate impact on women, but also how it more subtly serves to perpetuate patriarchal notions of men's dominance over women. We risk losing the expressive function of law in combating domestic violence and thereby potentially neglect the transformative power of law to change social norms rather than individual behavior. Thus, any restorative justice process must be sensitive to addressing the transformative power of a justice process on changing social norms and must create a process by which the sufferings of the individual are generalized to the treatment of women as a group. In our own work on sexual assault, for example, we decided to issue quarterly press releases in which the functioning of the program, general types of cases received, and actions taken are communicated to the citizenry. In addition, we aim to emphasize empowering the program's community oversight board, not just to respond to individuals, but to take a lead in energizing the community's social change agenda when they see certain patterns of rape that are re-occurring such as alcohol related rape. We continue to seek out new and better ways to expand the transformative potential of RESTORE to alter prevailing social norms that undergird violence against women.

These are not small concerns, however, and not subject to an easy fix. They also are not as subject to empirical test as is effectiveness in individual cases, or even effectiveness in reducing overall prevalence rates. On the other hand, to the extent that the harm at issue affects women as a group rather than individually, intimate violence differs from stranger assault, which requires that women be careful about where they walk, and when, and how, and with whom. In this way, the sexual assault or rape of one woman serves to put all women in fear of a similar assault. This same systemic or political concern is not so clear in the case of intimate violence, but it is nonetheless present. Because of that, we need to move slowly and cautiously in applying new methods like restorative justice to intimate violence against women, despite its great promise. We have to cautiously apply new methods and carefully evaluate them so that we are aware of the impacts of our work both positive and negative. The scholarly debate cannot move much further forward without implementation and empirical evaluation to provide new evidence to move the dialogue forward. Our research in the RESTORE program, where we are using restorative justice for a narrow class of sexual crimes, employs just such an incremental approach to developing empirical data to guide future theorizing and practice.

## IV. Ethical Considerations in Domestic Violence Cases

*. . . I will decide every case based on the record, according to the rule of law, without fear or favor, to the best of my ability. And I will remember that it's my job to call balls and strikes, and not to pitch or bat.*

Chief Justice John G. Roberts Jr. at his confirmation hearing before the Senate Judiciary Committee, September 12, 2005

John G. Roberts, Jr., *Judges Need Humility and Modesty*, N.Y.L.J., Sept. 14, 2005.

*Justice consists not in being neutral between right and wrong, but in finding out the right and upholding it, wherever found, against the wrong.*

Theodore Roosevelt

The establishment of specialized domestic violence courts presents a unique ethical challenge and calls for judges to reconcile the philosophies of Chief Justice Roberts and former President Theodore Roosevelt. Judges presiding in these courts are trained to recognize the cycles of violence that characterize relationships plagued by domestic abuse. A domestic violence judge may be less likely to dismiss a case where a victim is vacillating or recanting her testimony. While an untrained judge might lose patience with a woman who is undecided about whether to cooperate in a prosecution of her abuser, a judge familiar with the dynamic of domestic violence might well view the same vacillating woman as presenting like a battered wife or girlfriend. While specialized training allows judges to gain insight into the dynamic of domestic violence, does it threaten the ability to function fairly and impartially?

### A. The Role of the Judge: Neutral Umpire or Societal Problem Solver?

Problem-solving courts have two goals; "to respond more effectively to social and legal problems . . . . And the second is to shape case resolutions that respond to the concerns of a variety of stakeholders—victims, community residents, defendants, and others—about the criminal justice process."[19]

This new paradigm for judges and courts as problem solvers, championed by the late, well-respected Chief Justice Judith Kaye of the New York Court of Appeals, and others, has generated some concerns. The following is fairly representative:

> Outside the courthouse walls, problem-solving courts have asked judges to establish relationships with community groups, to broaden relationships with government and non-profit agencies, and to think through the real-life impacts of their decisions. As judges have performed this work, they have called into question the independence and neutrality of the judiciary and even the separation-of-powers doctrine.[20]

The development of specialized courts and the intensive, focused training that goes along with them has sparked criticism. Bruce J. Winick, a University of Miami law professor, asserted in his article *Applying the Law Therapeutically in Domestic Violence Cases,* 69 UMKC L. REV. 33, 44 (2000), that specialized judicial training, "is likely to produce in many domestic violence court judges an identification with the domestic violence victim that might adversely affect their ability to be fair and impartial adjudicators of cases in which the issue of domestic violence is contested."

As of 2009 there were 208 domestic violence courts around the country, all created within the prior 30 years.[21] By 2016, there were 3,000 drug courts in the United States.[22] The philosophies behind these courts are very different. Drug courts are defendant-focused with the goal to end addiction. The method for doing so is to foster drug treatment and social services as alternatives to incarceration. In the domestic violence courts, treatment of the batterer is not the primary purpose; in fact, most professionals are skeptical batterers can be "treated." Instead, the goal is to promote victim safety and to demand offender accountability. Whereas the defense bar has been enthusiastic in its support of drug courts, it can be hostile towards the domestic violence courts. Lawsuits have been filed around the country challenging the authority of judicial administrators to create domestic violence courts.

Miami public defender Bennett H. Brummer, in a 1998 speech at the St. Thomas University School of Law, and in a subsequent law review article, criticized the creation of the Dade County Domestic Violence Court, which he claimed, "made it

---

19. Greg Berman, Derek Denckla & John Feinblatt, *Judicial Innovation at the Crossroads: The Future of Problem-Solving Courts,* 13 THE COURT MANAGER 28, 30 (2000).

20. GREG BERMAN & JOHN FEINBLATT, GOOD COURTS: THE CASE FOR PROBLEM-SOLVING JUSTICE 10 (2005).

21. Melissa Labriola, et. al, *A National Portrait of Domestic Violence Courts, Rep. No. 229659,* Center For Court Innovation, *iv* (February 2010), https://www.ncjrs.gov/pdffiles1/nij/grants/229659.pdf, accessed November 10, 2016.

22. U.S. Dept. of Justice, Office of Justice Programs, *Drug Courts* (May 2016), https://www.ncjrs.gov/pdffiles1/nij/238527.pdf, accessed November 10, 2016.

particularly difficult for the judges hearing cases of alleged domestic violence to operate as impartial, disinterested adjudicators."[23] He further wrote:

> [L]oss of judicial independence commonly occurs [with] the establishment of specialized courts with narrow purposes at the behest of special interest groups, allowing those groups undue influence.
>
> Professionalism means working to maintain the courts as impartial, disinterested adjudicators of fact and law in the service of justice, not as enforcement agencies to . . . stop domestic violence, or achieve other social or political goals.[24]

An alternate view was espoused in a thoughtful article, *Morality, Decision-making and Judicial Ethics,* written by Jennifer Juhler, Domestic Abuse Coordinator for the Iowa State Courts, and Justice Mark Cady of the Iowa Supreme Court, an excerpt of which follows.

> . . . .
>
> Philosophers and legal scholars have explored the topic of bias for centuries and have developed procedures to reduce the impact of bias in legal proceedings. One mechanism to reduce bias is creation of and adherence to judicial ethics that seek to reduce the impact of social relationships on judges and also to seek to manage the public's perceptions of the impact of social relationships on judges. With respect to complex and controversial societal issues, avoidance and isolation may inadvertently create or reinforce bias. . . .
>
> People tend to seek evidence, seek goals and make inferences in a way that favors possibilities that already appeal to them. The legal system teaches students the ability to look at both sides of an argument, which has been scientifically proven to reduce bias. The legal system generally requires that judges put decisions into writing, which increases accountability for the decision and thus reduces bias. Also, the legal process anticipates that an individual judge can make mistakes and so provides a process to appeal. . . .
>
> Judgments regarding the credibility of witnesses have a unique bearing in cases involving domestic violence. Since domestic violence involves a complex emotional and psychological dynamic that can be displayed to differing degrees based upon the unique life experience of the person involved, judges need multiple models of victims, non-victims, abusers and non-abusers to correctly inform the decision-making process. If a judge has no previous personal experience with domestic violence, the judge will base decisions about a situation involving domestic violence upon what the judge has learned previously about domestic violence or will search personal memories to look for an analog to use for the purpose of inference. . . .

---

23. Bennett H. Brummer, *Criminal Law Symposium: Independent, Professional Judgment: The Essence of Freedom,* 10 St. Thomas L. Rev. 607, 611 (Spring 1998).

24. *Id.* at 622-23.

The potential for bias from limited life experience has a good chance of influencing judicial decisions that cannot be appealed. Therefore, the legal system should understand the importance of providing not only formal CLE programs, but involvement in community groups to increase the number of exposures of all judges to multiple analogs in order to better understand and make decisions in complex issues such as domestic violence.

. . . .

Research has documented a desire by people to believe the world is fair. Experiments of the "just world" hypothesis have found that when we perceive unfairness, we attempt to restore a sense of justice. However, when our attempts fail "we become less concerned with victims of all sorts . . . [and] will try to deceive [ourselves] into thinking that things are fair."

Without an appreciation of the tremendous complexity of domestic violence, judges will fall into the trap of reinforcing the "just world" hypothesis and will tend to blame victims. With limited time due to the tremendous pressure of the court docket, a judge may not have time to do a fair search to consider all the factors that could contribute to behavior they see in the courtroom. After time, the initial perceptions can be held more strongly. All people share a natural inclination to avoid searching for information that contradicts a favored belief or to dismiss evidence that contradicts a favored belief.

Recently a judge seeking information regarding a potential action asked why he could not sanction plaintiffs in domestic abuse cases for frivolous filings under the rules of civil procedure. He stated that he was aware that the Code of Iowa does not permit taxing costs to a plaintiff in such a proceeding. The reply reminded the judge of the legislative intent that values having an accessible legal system over collecting fees. The judge replied that he believed the practice of sanctioning plaintiffs would also meet with the legislative intent that the system should be used by "plaintiffs who really need protection." The judge's response seems to typify a decision maker dismissing evidence—intent of the Code—to support a favored belief—the importance of sanctioning victims who do not follow through with legal proceedings. Further, the belief seems to stem from a frustration with domestic violence cases and the actions of plaintiffs in domestic abuse actions. [citations omitted][25]

---

25. Jennifer Juhler & Justice Mark Cady, *Morality, Decision-making, and Judicial Ethics,* www.americanbar.org/content/dam/aba/migrated/judicialethics/resources/comm_code_cady_undated.authcheckdam.pdf, accessed November 10, 2016.

## B. The Domestic Violence Judge in the Courtroom

Judges presiding over domestic violence cases must take particular care to demonstrate appropriate sensitivity and concern to the seriousness of the subject matter.

### In re Greene
North Carolina Supreme Court
328 N.C. 639 (1991)

This matter is before the Court upon a recommendation of the Judicial Standards Commission that respondent, George R. Greene, a judge of the General Court of Justice, Superior Court Division, be censured for conduct prejudicial to the administration of justice that brings the judicial office into disrepute in violation of N.C.G.S. §7A-376 and which violates Canons 2A, 3A(2) and 3A(3) of the North Carolina Code of Judicial Conduct.

PER CURIAM

. . . .

The complaint alleged that respondent, while presiding over a criminal session of Wake County District Court on 16 October 1987, heard a case which involved a charge of assault on a female.

The complaint alleged:

> The respondent criticized the victim's decision not to reconcile with the defendant and implied that the assault was justified and deserved. The respondent also made derogatory remarks about Interact, the battered women's assistance group whose representative was present in court in support of the victim, including the comment that they were "a one-sided man-hating bunch of females." Following the trial, the respondent approached where the victim and the Interact representative were standing in the hall. The respondent grinned at . . . the victim in the case, and asked if she forgave him. He then told [the victim] in the presence of the Interact representative that once his wife had slapped him and that he had "laid her on the floor and did not have any more problems from her."

Respondent answered these allegations by denying his conduct was prejudicial to the administration of justice because:

A. The attempted counseling to the prosecuting witness was given after hearing the evidence and finding the defendant "guilty." That his opinion remains that in light of the evidence, the two children of the parties and the obvious pregnancy of the prosecuting witness, a joint working out of their difficulties was the best course for all of the involved parties.

B. The remarks about "Interact" persons were made outside Court and as a result of and in response to their previous disruption in the Courtroom and the proceedings before Respondent by representatives of that group. Further, to the attempts by those same representatives to influence Respondent's decision and invade his impartiality by improper pressure tactics. Finally, to the interference, after Court, in his attempt to mitigate any personally perceived prejudice by the prosecuting witness.

C. Respondent made a good faith and sincere attempt to ameliorate any hostility with the prosecuting witness Myra Sheffield by asking her if she forgave him for any misunderstanding which may have occurred in the Courtroom.

. . . .

Formal hearing after notice before the Commission was conducted on 2 June 1989. Evidence for the Commission tended to show as follows:

On 16 October 1987 respondent presided over a trial involving a charge of assault on a female against the husband of the prosecuting witness. A representative of Interact, a counseling service for persons in violent marriages or domestic situations, was present in court with the victim. Respondent made certain remarks concerning Interact. One witness recalled these remarks as accusing Interact of being "anti-man or man-hater or something like that . . . ." Another witness, the representative from Interact, testified that respondent "lectured the victim." This witness made contemporaneous handwritten notes of respondent's remarks made, she said, in the courtroom. She later used these contemporaneous notes to draft a letter of complaint to the Judicial Standards Commission after which she destroyed the handwritten notes.

Using her letter to the Commission to refresh her recollection, this witness testified that respondent told the prosecuting witness that she shouldn't have anything to do with Interact and "Interact was a one-sided, man-hating bunch of females, a pack of she-dogs." The witness said respondent told the prosecuting witness that "she was being selfish not to go back [to her husband] and that she would ruin her children's lives." Respondent said, "You really haven't been hit that much. You deserve to be hit. How is a man supposed to react?"

There was other testimony that respondent polled the persons in the courtroom to see how many had "had little spats in their marriages."

After the proceeding in court was completed, the Interact witness and the prosecuting witness came into contact with respondent outside the courtroom. According to these witnesses respondent told them that his wife had once slapped him and "he had laid her on the floor and had never had any problems from her since." Respondent then asked the assault victim to forgive him, and she replied negatively.

. . . .

Respondent testified in his own behalf and offered corroborative witnesses. His testimony tended to show as follows:

In the assault case respondent was concerned because he thought there were persons in the courtroom supporting the prosecuting witness who were trying to influence his decision and judgment in the matter. Respondent "got mad." He admitted making the remark about having slapped his wife down, but said that this was an exaggerated version of what actually happened. Respondent said, "And if I lost it, I lost it. But I did the best that I could under the circumstances sitting as judge and jury." Respondent recalled that he was not directing his "she-dogs" remark to Interact or any other particular group. He had no knowledge of Interact at the time and did not know there were Interact representatives in the courtroom. He said, "My recollection is that I said if men got into an argument they would argue, might even sometimes fight, but sooner or later they would forget about it, go on and be friends. Women are just the opposite. They get in an argument, they act like a bunch of she-dogs, something of that effect. I never referred to any particular group as being she-dogs. I said women in general. It was a general comment. It might not have been in good taste, but that's what I recall saying."

. . . .

The Commission recommends to the Court that respondent be censured. In support of this recommendation the Commission advised the Court that it found the following facts on clear and convincing evidence:

(a) The respondent demeaned the dignity and integrity of the proceedings before him and his judicial office when during proceedings in open court in an assault on a female case, *State v. Sheffield*, Wake County file number 87CR50908, over which he presided on 16 October 1987, he embarassed [sic] and humiliated the seven-months' pregnant victim of the assault by telling her she would ruin her children's lives if she did not reconcile with her estranged husband, she deserved to be hit, and she had not been hit that much; he referred in a derogatory manner to the representative of the support group who was with the victim and the support group itself, which he later came to know was Interact, as a one-sided, man-hating bunch of females and a pack of she-dogs; and he polled the courtroom spectators as to how many of them had little spats during their marriages.

. . . .

The Commission concluded respondent's actions constitute conduct prejudicial to the administration of justice that brings the judicial office into disrepute in violation of N.C.G.S. § 7A-376 and which violates Canons 2A, 3A(2), and 3A(3) of the North Carolina Code of Judicial Conduct.

. . . .

Now, therefore, it is ordered by the SUPREME COURT OF NORTH CAROLINA, in conference, that respondent, Judge George R. Greene, be, and he is hereby, censured by this Court for the conduct determined by the Court to be conduct prejudicial to the administration of justice that brings the judicial office into disrepute.

## C. The Lawyer as Advocate in the Domestic Violence Case

### *1. Defense Dilemma: Where to Draw the Line*

Effective, vigorous representation is the right of every client in a criminal case, guilty or not. If a lawyer is representing a client he or she knows to be guilty, the task is not an easy one, particularly in a domestic violence case where a client might make it clear he has been and will continue to be dangerous to his victim. The defense lawyer has more than a duty to his or her client. Lawyers have an ethical duty to reveal a client's intentions to commit a future crime. And, even if the client does not intend to commit future crimes, a lawyer cannot let him lie in court about any material fact. Rule 3.3 of the ABA Model Rules of Professional Conduct states "A lawyer shall not knowingly make a false statement of fact or law to a tribunal or fail to correct a false statement of material fact. . . ." In addition, an attorney shall not knowingly "offer evidence that the lawyer knows to be false." In the official commentary to the rule, it states:

> If a lawyer knows that the client intends to testify falsely or wants the lawyer to introduce false evidence, the lawyer should seek to persuade the client that the evidence should not be offered. If the persuasion is ineffective and the lawyer continues to represent the client, the lawyer must refuse to offer the false evidence . . .

In addition to being mindful of ethical rules involving interactions with a client, a defense lawyer must also pay attention to the ethical rules when having contact with a witness in a criminal case, particularly in one where delicate issues of domestic violence are raised.

Of particular relevance in domestic violence cases is Model Rule 4.3, Dealing With Unrepresented Person, which states in relevant part:

> The lawyer shall not give legal advice to an unrepresented person, other than advice to secure counsel, if the lawyer knows or reasonably should know that the interests of such a person are or have a reasonable possibility of being in conflict with the interests of the client.

This rule is particularly troublesome in a situation that is common in domestic violence litigation—where the victim is unwilling to cooperate in the prosecution of the man who allegedly assaulted her. The scenario goes something like this: the victim is initially fearful enough of her abuser to call the police and have him arrested. Her goal at that time, of course, is to stop the violence and possibly save her own life. After some weeks, she changes her mind and does not want to see him face criminal consequences for the violence. (The reasons for this have been discussed throughout this book and are not relevant for the purpose of this discussion.) The now uncooperative victim first attempts to convince the prosecutor to drop all charges against her alleged abuser. If the prosecutor is not receptive, the victim makes excuses as to why she cannot visit the prosecutor to discuss trial preparation and then may just start failing to show up at scheduled appointments. At some point, she may stop taking the prosecutor's telephone calls. This is particularly true if she and the accused have reconciled and he is at home to hear her phone conversations with the prosecutor.

The victim who has all but vanished from the prosecutor's radar screen becomes a routine visitor to the office of the lawyer defending her abuser. This creates an ethical issue for the defense lawyer. The lawyer's first duty is to her own client. In an effort to help the client, the defense lawyer listens to the victim who figures the best way to get out from under the entire criminal justice situation is to claim the abuse never happened. If the defense lawyer gets involved to the extent of notarizing a recantation statement or providing legal advice on how to respond to a subpoena, the defense lawyer enters a large ethical grey area. What if the alleged victim of abuse has signed a sworn complaint against the lawyer's client at the district attorney's office in which she alleged specified acts of violence? Does the defense lawyer need to insure that the victim understands she could be prosecuted for perjury for signing the initial complaint in which she alleged she was assaulted by the defendant if she now signs a sworn statement the incident never happened? What if that warning results in no recantation letter to help her client? Has the defense lawyer failed in her duties to her own client? Putting aside the issue of whether independent counsel needs to be obtained for the victim, if the recantation letter is signed, does the alleged abuser's lawyer now run the risk of being removed from the case because she is a witness to the circumstances behind the recantation letter?

The following ethics opinion addresses this issue—at least in the context of having an alleged victim talk to the defense lawyer's investigator.

## District of Columbia Bar Ethics Opinion 321
### Communications Between Domestic Violence Petitioner and Counsel for Respondent in a Privately Litigated Proceeding for Criminal Contempt

(June 2003) *available at* www.dcbar.org/bar-resources/legal-ethics/opinions /opinion321.cfm

We have received an inquiry from counsel representing domestic violence petitioners in the District of Columbia, who raises questions related to interviews of domestic violence petitioners by investigators working for defense counsel.

. . . .

[W]e conclude that, as a general matter, counsel for a respondent may direct an investigator to seek an interview with an unrepresented petitioner, but must make reasonable efforts to ensure that the investigator does not mislead the petitioner about the investigator's role. In addition, respondent's counsel must instruct the investigator that, if it appears that the petitioner misunderstands the investigator's role, the investigator should take "whatever reasonable, affirmative steps are necessary to correct the misunderstanding." D.C. Rule 4.3 comment [2]. Finally, an investigator may ask an unrepresented petitioner to sign substantive documents, but must take "great care" that the unrepresented person understands that neither the lawyer nor the investigator is giving legal advice in connection with the preparation or execution of such documents. D.C. Rule 4.3, comment [1]. . . .

### 2. Ethical Problems of the Prosecutor

The question of how to handle the recanting witness is just as problematic for prosecutors as it is for defense lawyers. If the victim tells a story that negates whether a crime ever happened and the prosecutor cannot show that she has been unduly influenced or threatened by the defendant or that the case can be proven with evidence beyond her testimony, ethical problems may ensue. A victim might also take the blame for any violent incident and claim that the defendant acted in self-defense.

Model Rules of Prof'l Conduct R. 3.8 states in relevant part: "The prosecutor in a criminal case shall: (a) refrain from prosecuting a charge that the prosecutor knows is not supported by probable cause; . . . and (d) make timely disclosure to the defense of all evidence or information known to the prosecutor that tends to negate the guilt of the accused or mitigate the offense . . . ."

This is not merely an ethical obligation but a legal one as well. In *Brady v. Maryland,* 373 U.S. 83 (1963), the United States Supreme Court held that upon the request of the defendant, the prosecution has a duty to reveal evidence favorable to the defense that is material to the issue of guilt or punishment. Similarly, material evidence affecting the credibility of a prosecution witness must also be turned over to the defense. *Giglio v. United States,* 405 U.S. 150 (1972).

## V. When Domestic Violence Hits Close to Home

Given the data showing that domestic violence occurs in all social, ethnic, racial and economic groups, it should come as no surprise that members of the legal profession experience it in their personal lives. In the past, domestic violence among the economically privileged segments of society could remain buried in divorce complaints, which remain under seal in most jurisdictions. Women injured by their wealthy or well-connected attorney or judicial spouses could make discreet visits to private doctors, many of whom may have been either unable to recognize the signs of domestic violence, or unwilling to believe it happened in the homes of high status patients. A well-established professional often had a network of loyal friends and family supporters to protect him and his family.

Because of mandatory arrest laws and increased awareness of domestic violence, attorneys may find themselves facing both criminal prosecution and ethical sanctions if they engage in acts of domestic violence in their own homes. Lawyers who handle disciplinary cases for other lawyers and judges say that professional sanctions for incidents of domestic violence are on the rise.[26] The Model Rules of Professional

---

26. David L. Hudson, Jr., *Seeking Cures for an Epidemic: Disciplinary Actions Against Lawyers Who Commit Acts of Domestic Violence Appear to be on the Rise,* ABA Journal 22-23 (November 2015).

Conduct, which govern lawyers in all 50 states and the District of Columbia mandate that an attorney not "engage in illegal conduct that adversely reflects on the lawyer's honesty, trustworthiness or fitness as a lawyer."[27]

## In re Nevill

### California Supreme Court

### 39 Cal. 3d 729 (1985)

This is a proceeding to review a recommendation of the Disciplinary Board of the State Bar that Robert Lee Nevill be suspended from the practice of law for five years on conditions of probation, including actual suspension for thirty months after his release from prison. Petitioner was convicted of voluntary manslaughter (Pen. Code, § 192, subd. (a)) in the shooting death of his wife of 13 years. Upon review, we conclude that disbarment is the more appropriate discipline.

In the disciplinary proceedings below, petitioner and respondent State Bar entered into a "Stipulation as to Facts and Discipline." (See Rules Proc. of State Bar, rules 401-408.) The stipulation contains the following recital of the relevant facts leading up to and including the killing: "[Petitioner] and his wife, Marcie Nevill, began having marital difficulties in approximately August 1981. Some of these difficulties involved Mrs. Nevill's relationship with a male co-worker in her office. On November 20, 1981, [petitioner] picked up the couple's sixteen-month-old daughter from her nursery school and took her to Mrs. Nevill's office. He advised Mrs. Nevill that he and the child were leaving, then took the child home. Shortly thereafter, Mrs. Nevill left her office and also went home. When Mrs. Nevill arrived home, an argument ensued and [petitioner] shot his wife approximately ten times with a rifle in the bedroom of their house. Death was immediate. [Petitioner] telephoned the police, his mother, and his wife's office shortly after the shooting and advised them all that he had just killed his wife. Police officers arriving on the scene found Mrs. Nevill's body in the couple's bedroom. [Petitioner] was outside of the house holding his daughter. He appeared very upset and made numerous unsolicited and emotional statements such as 'I killed her,' 'I did it,' 'I was supposed to kill myself.' [Petitioner] was taken into custody immediately."

This rather abbreviated factual summary may be supplemented by reference to the trial transcript. The transcript reveals the following facts: The Nevills' marital discord was compounded by each spouse's admitted infidelity, Mrs. Nevill's accelerated professional advancement, petitioner's lack of success as a lawyer and his recent loss of a local election. Petitioner wanted his wife to quit work and stay home with their child. The couple argued, reconciled and argued again. After at least one such episode, petitioner became physically violent, throwing his wife down on a couch and striking her repeatedly.

---

27. Model Rules of Prof'l Conduct R. 8.4(b).

On the morning of the killing, Mrs. Nevill declined petitioner's invitation to meet for lunch, telling him that her coworkers were taking her out to celebrate the start of her planned 30-day leave of absence. After she left for work, petitioner visited a friend who "knew a lot of people" to discuss locating someone to beat up Mrs. Nevill's lover and teach him to stay away from her. Petitioner and his friend smoked marijuana and used cocaine.

Petitioner next called his "paramour" to break a lunch date for that afternoon, falsely stating that he was waiting for a phone call "on a verdict." He then called Mrs. Nevill and renewed his invitation to meet for lunch. She declined.

Suspicious, petitioner drove to his wife's office, hid behind a bush and, using binoculars, observed her leaving with a man. Petitioner tried to follow the car but eventually lost track of it. He then had three drinks, returned to Mrs. Nevill's office and used more cocaine. After waiting some time, he drove to his daughter's nursery school, ostensibly to make sure that his wife had not taken her. Finding the child at the school he then took her with him and returned to Mrs. Nevill's office where he confronted her about her lunch date. Mrs. Nevill admitted that she had lied.

Petitioner then announced that he was leaving Mrs. Nevill and taking the child with him. Mrs. Nevill expressed concern that the child was becoming a pawn in their dispute but agreed to move with him for a trial period.

Petitioner put the child in the car and sped home, hoping that Mrs. Nevill would follow. While waiting for her to arrive, he placed a rifle on top of the bed concealing it with a sheet. He began packing and used more cocaine.

When Mrs. Nevill arrived, alone, the couple argued. Petitioner accused her of being seen going into a hotel with the other man. She allegedly responded that she had not slept with the man "this week." Petitioner then told her to call the other man, which she attempted to do without success. Finally, petitioner grabbed the rifle and fired three shots into the bedroom floor. Mrs. Nevill, seated on the bed, called out, "you really are crazy aren't you?" Petitioner immediately turned the gun on her, shooting her 10 or 11 times. He then called the police and Mrs. Nevill's parents, and was subsequently taken into custody.

Petitioner was charged with murder (Pen. Code, § 187). At trial, Dr. Randolph Reed, a forensic psychiatrist who had examined petitioner and conducted a sodium amytal interview with him, testified for the defense that petitioner had a "mixed personality disorder," which meant he was a "psychologically weak, immature, and fragile individual" who dealt with problems in a childlike fashion. Reed opined that this disorder did not cause the shooting, but it contributed to petitioner's inability to handle significant stress. Reed concluded that petitioner was coming apart psychologically before the killing and, therefore, did not have the capacity to intend to kill.

After the jury returned a verdict of voluntary manslaughter, the trial court sentenced petitioner to the upper term of six years plus an additional two years for using a firearm. Upon notice of conviction, this court referred the matter to the State Bar for a report and recommendation as to whether the facts and circumstances surrounding the commission of the crime involved moral turpitude or other misconduct warranting discipline. (Bus. & Prof. Code, § 6102, subds. (a) and (c); *In re Rothrock* (1940) 16 Cal.2d 449, 455 [106 P.2d 907, 131 A.L.R. 226].)

Petitioner and the principal referee for the State Bar entered into the "Stipulation as to Facts and Discipline" referenced above. In addition to the factual statement, the stipulation contains a "Statement of Mitigating Circumstances," which recites what petitioner would have testified to had he been called as a witness in the disciplinary proceedings. In summary, petitioner would have testified that: a confluence of factors contributed to the marital disharmony; Mrs. Nevill had asked for a separation and then changed her mind, promising to stay home and forget the other man; petitioner feared losing his child and had made efforts to obtain marriage counseling; petitioner only took his daughter from the nursery school because she cried to go with him; he secreted the rifle under the sheet to scare Mrs. Nevill's boyfriend in case the couple tried to take the child from him; immediately after killing Mrs. Nevill he was "an emotional basket case" and planned to kill himself; and, Dr. Reed diagnosed petitioner as having a "mixed personality disorder" which prevented him from being "able to deal with relationships or stress in a realistic fashion."

The stipulation does not include an explicit finding regarding moral turpitude; rather, it contains a simple statement that the killing "does involve misconduct warranting discipline." The stipulation includes the following recommended discipline: five-year suspension stayed; probation for five years including thirty months actual suspension following petitioner's release from prison; quarterly reports to the State Bar as to his familiarity and compliance with the provisions of the State Bar Act and the Rules of Professional Conduct; abstinence from the "excessive use of intoxicants and mind-or mood-altering drugs" unless medically prescribed; and psychiatric counseling.

Upon the hearing panel's recommendation, the review department voted to approve the stipulation. Three of the review department referees voted against the stipulation on the ground that the recommended discipline appeared insufficient in view of the stipulated facts.

In reviewing cases of attorney misconduct, this court attributes substantial weight to the State Bar's recommendations as to discipline. (*Olguin v. State Bar* (1980) 28 Cal.3d 195, 199 [167 Cal. Rptr. 876, 616 P.2d 858]; *Inniss, supra*, 20 Cal.3d at p. 558.) The court is duty bound, however, to exercise its independent judgment in determining the appropriate discipline in any given case. (*Garlow v. State Bar* (1982) 30 Cal.3d 912, 916 [180 Cal. Rptr. 831, 640 P.2d 1106]; *Weir v. State Bar* (1979) 23 Cal.3d 564, 576 [152 Cal. Rptr. 921, 591 P.2d 19]; *Jackson v. State Bar* (1979) 23 Cal.3d 509, 513-514 [153 Cal. Rptr. 24, 591 P.2d 47].) . . . .

The discipline ultimately imposed must be consistent with its purpose, that of protecting the public, the courts, and the legal profession from unfit practitioners. (*In re Possino* (1984) 37 Cal.3d 163, 168 [207 Cal. Rptr. 543, 689 P.2d 115].) In determining the extent of discipline to be imposed we must consider each case on its own facts (*Toll v. State Bar* (1974) 12 Cal.3d 824, 831 [117 Cal. Rptr. 427, 528 P.2d 35]), taking into account not only the offense itself, but also any aggravating or mitigating factors. (*Tarver v. State Bar* (1984) 37 Cal.3d 122, 133 [207 Cal. Rptr. 302, 688 P.2d 911].) "There are no fixed standards as to the appropriate penalty" in disciplinary actions. (*Alberton v. State Bar* (1984) 37 Cal.3d 1, 14 [206 Cal. Rptr. 373, 686 P.2d 1177].)

In the instant case, the need to protect the public and the profession is great. The facts indicate that petitioner used his 16-month-old daughter as a pawn to lure his wife into what would be their final confrontation, secreted the rifle under a sheet to insure that he would maintain the upper hand in the anticipated hostilities over the child, and finally killed his wife in an extremely violent and frightening manner. By his actions, petitioner displayed a dangerous volatility which might well prejudice his ability to effectively represent his clients' interests given the pressures associated with the practice of law. Petitioner's professionally diagnosed childlike responses to the stresses of life heighten our concern. While "'we are not insensitive to the personal and professional problems that frequently besiege the practitioner'" (*Tarver, supra,* 37 Cal.3d at p. 134), it is our duty to protect the public from those attorneys who, for whatever reason, are unable to cope with pressure and adversity. The safety of the public, and the integrity of the profession require no less.

For these reasons, we find the State Bar's proposed discipline inadequate. The degree of discipline ultimately imposed must, of necessity, correspond to some reasonable degree with the gravity of the misconduct at issue. Petitioner has committed the ultimate offense: the taking of a life. Two and one-half years actual suspension simply fails to attest to that fact. The circumstances surrounding petitioner's misconduct compel the conclusion that disbarment is the more appropriate discipline.

The factors offered in mitigation do not dissuade us from concluding that petitioner should be disbarred. Where an attorney's criminal act involves actual physical harm to a particular individual, the necessary showing of mitigating circumstances increases accordingly. (Cf. *In re Higbie* (1972) 6 Cal.3d 562, 574 [99 Cal. Rptr. 865, 493 P.2d 97]; *Sullivan v. State Bar* (1955) 45 Cal.2d 112, 119-120 [287 P.2d 778].) Any greater physical harm than that perpetrated in the instant case is inconceivable. In turn, the proffered mitigating circumstances are simply inadequate in the face of this harm.

In formulating the discipline recommendation, the principal referee appears to have considered as mitigating the fact that petitioner: (1) was having marital problems caused in part by his wife's involvement with someone else; (2) used alcohol and cocaine on the day of the killing; (3) argued vehemently with his wife shortly before killing her; (4) admitted his guilt immediately after the crime; (5) was diagnosed as having a personality disorder; and (6) is serving an eight-year sentence for the crime. Additionally, the State Bar asks us to consider as mitigating the fact that petitioner has never before been disciplined for unethical conduct, that he has been cooperative in this matter and that the killing is unrelated to the practice of law.

Bearing in mind that present fitness to practice law is our primary concern (*Possino, supra*, 37 Cal.3d at p. 172; *In re Petty* (1981) 29 Cal.3d 356, 362 [173 Cal. Rptr. 461, 627 P.2d 191]), we cannot indulge the suggestion that these factors constitute adequate mitigation to preclude disbarment....

Our responsibility to protect the public and the profession also prevents us, in the instant case, from looking to the lack of prior discipline and the fact that the offense is unrelated to legal practice as mitigating circumstances. While a "clean record" may be taken into account where an attorney's indiscretion is not great, where restitution has been made or where the attorney has been rehabilitated, "disbarment is not reserved for those possessing prior records." (*In re Weber* (1976) 16 Cal.3d 578, 582 [128 Cal. Rptr. 434, 546 P.2d 1378].) Where, as here, an attorney's misconduct is egregious and is not substantially mitigated by other circumstances, once is one time too many. (See *Benson v. State Bar* (1971) 5 Cal.3d 382, 388 [96 Cal. Rptr. 30, 486 P.2d 1230].) Likewise, that the crime is not directly related to the practice of law does not insulate petitioner from the appropriate discipline. (See *In re Rohan* (1978) 21 Cal.3d 195 [145 Cal. Rptr. 855, 578 P.2d 102].)

....

Beyond the absence of adequate mitigation, disbarment is also appropriate as a cautionary measure. Given petitioner's uncontested volatility, his lengthy incarceration and his extended absence from practice, we can best achieve the goal of protecting the public by imposing discipline which incorporates some mechanism for future reevaluation of petitioner's fitness to practice law and attendant ability to cope with the stresses of everyday life. Disbarment provides such an opportunity for thorough reappraisal; the recommended discipline does not.

....

Disbarment will better protect the public, the profession and the courts. Disbarment guards against the unfit practitioner until such time as he or she affirmatively demonstrates that the disability has been overcome. Requiring petitioner to make such a showing prior to readmission will assure that the discipline imposed has served its recognized purpose....

Petitioner is hereby disbarred on the effective date of this order. Petitioner is further ordered to comply with rule 955 of the California Rules of Court and to comply with subdivisions (a) and (c) of that rule within 30 and 40 days respectively after the effective date of this order.

---

The Supreme Court of New Jersey announced more than 20 years ago it intended to deal harshly with members of the bar who engage in acts of domestic violence.

## In the Matter of Magid

New Jersey Supreme Court

139 N.J. 449 (1995)

PER CURIAM

This disciplinary proceeding arose from a Motion for Final Discipline Based Upon a Criminal Conviction filed by the Office of Attorney Ethics (OAE) before the Disciplinary Review Board (DRB), seeking final discipline of Lawrence Magid, pursuant to Rule 1:20-6(c)(2)(I). That motion was based on respondent's conviction of simple assault, in violation of N.J.S.A. 2:12-1a(1).

The DRB found that respondent had engaged in unethical conduct. Four members recommended that respondent be publicly reprimanded. Two members would have imposed a private reprimand. Our independent review of the record leads us to accept the DRB's recommendation.

I

Respondent was admitted to the bar in 1969. At the time of the assault he had been an attorney with the Prosecutor's Office of Gloucester County for more than sixteen years. The DRB accurately sets forth the relevant facts in its Decision and Recommendation:

> On September 28, 1993, a complaint was filed in Woodbury Heights Municipal Court charging respondent with the disorderly persons offense of assault, in violation of N.J.S.A. 2C:12-1a(1). The complaint charged respondent with attempting "to cause bodily injury to [K.P.], specifically by punching her in the head and face area causing a black eye, knocking her to the ground and kicking her in the neck, head, and lower back, causing other bruising". The incident in question occurred on the evening of September 25, 1993, at Badges, a private club in Woodbury Heights, frequented by law enforcement personnel. At the time of the incident, respondent was the First Assistant Prosecutor of Gloucester County. The victim, [K.P.] was also employed by the Gloucester County Prosecutor's Office and had been dating respondent for several months. As a result of this incident, respondent was discharged from his position in the prosecutor's office.
>
> On December 7, 1993, respondent pleaded guilty to assaulting [K.P.]. The plea was taken by Superior Court Judge Robert W. Page, sitting as Municipal Court Judge for the Woodbury Heights Municipal Court.
>
> At sentencing on February 7, 1993, Judge Page placed respondent on probation for a period of one year, fined him $250, and administered a $50 violent crime penalty. As conditions of probation, Judge Page required that respondent have no contact with [K.P.] and be responsible for any medical expenses incurred by her. He also directed respondent to continue treatment with his psychiatrist and remain drug- and alcohol-free during the course of his probation.

## II

A criminal conviction is conclusive evidence of guilt in a disciplinary proceeding. R. 1:20-6(c)(1). The sole issue to be determined is the extent of discipline to be imposed. R. 1:20-6(c)(2)(ii); *In re Lunetta,* 118 N.J. 443, 445, 572 A.2d 586 (1989); *In re Goldberg,* 105 N.J. 278, 280, 520 A.2d 1147 (1987); *In re Tuso,* 104 N.J. 59, 61, 514 A.2d 1311 (1986). In determining appropriate discipline, we consider the interests of the public, the bar, and the respondent. *In re Litwin,* 104 N.J. 362, 365, 517 A.2d 378 (1986); *In re Mischlich,* 60 N.J. 590, 593, 292 A.2d 23 (1977). The appropriate discipline depends on many factors, including the "nature and severity of the crime, whether the crime is related to the practice of law, and any mitigating factors such as respondent's reputation, his prior trustworthy conduct, and general good conduct." *In re Lunetta, supra,* 118 N.J. at 445, 446, 572 A.2d 586; *In re Kushner,* 101 N.J. 397, 400-01, 502 A.2d 32 (1986). Although we do not make an independent examination of the underlying facts to ascertain guilt, we do consider them relevant to the nature and extent of discipline to be imposed. *In re Goldberg, supra,* 105 N.J. at 280, 520 A.2d 1147; *In re Rosen,* 88 N.J. 1, 438 A.2d 316 (1981).

## III

Respondent's conviction of the disorderly persons offense of simple assault is clear and convincing evidence that he has violated RPC 8.4(b) (by committing a criminal act that reflects adversely on his honesty, trustworthiness, or fitness as a lawyer). The primary purpose of discipline is not to punish the attorney but to preserve the confidence of the public in the bar. We judge each case on its own facts. *In re Kushner, supra,* 101 N.J. at 400.

That respondent's misconduct did not directly involve the practice of law or a client is of little moment. It is well-established that the private conduct of attorneys may be the subject of public discipline. *In re Bock,* 128 N.J. 270, 274, 607 A.2d 1307 (1992)....

## IV

Both this case and *In re Principato,* 139 N.J. 456, 655 A.2d 920 (1995), also decided today, involve acts of domestic violence. The national spotlight is focused on domestic violence. Between three and four million women each year are battered by husbands, partners, and boyfriends. *Domestic Violence: Not Just A Family Matter: Hearing Before the Subcomm. on Crime and Criminal Justice of the House Comm. on the Judiciary,* 103rd Cong., 2nd Sess. (June 30, 1994) (statement of Senator Joseph Biden, Jr.). The New Jersey Legislature has found that

> domestic violence is a serious crime against society; that there are thousands of persons in this State who are regularly beaten, tortured and in some cases even killed by their spouses or cohabitants; that a significant number of women who are assaulted are pregnant; that victims of domestic violence come from all social and economic backgrounds and ethnic groups; that there is a positive correlation between spousal abuse and child abuse; and

that children, even when they are not themselves physically assaulted, suffer deep and lasting emotional effects from exposure to domestic violence. It is therefore, the intent of the Legislature to assure the victims of domestic violence the maximum protection from abuse the law can provide.

[N.J.S.A. 2C:25-18].

Based on those findings, the Legislature enacted one of the toughest domestic violence laws in the nation. N.J.S.A. 2C:25-17 to -33. During the last decade the number of complaints filed in New Jersey courts has increased from 13,842 in fiscal year 1984 to 55,639 in 1994, an increase of 302 percent. Dana Coleman, *Domestic violence charges explode by 302% in decade,* New Jersey Lawyer, Feb. 13, 1995, at 1 (citing the Administrative Office of the Courts).

V

We have not yet addressed the appropriate discipline to be imposed on an attorney convicted of an act of domestic violence. There are few reported attorney ethics cases that involve acts of domestic violence. *In re Nevill,* 39 Cal. 3d 729, 217 Cal. Rptr. 841, 704 P.2d 1332 (Cal. 1985) (disbarring attorney who was convicted of voluntary manslaughter of his wife whom he shot ten times); *In re Knight,* 883 P.2d 1055 (Colo. 1994) (holding that attorney's conviction of third-degree assault of his wife that arose from three days of severe beatings warranted six-month suspension); *In re Wallace,* 837 P.2d 1223 (Colo. 1992) (imposing three-month suspension from practice of law on attorney who assaulted his girlfriend more than once and who on one occasion entered plea of guilty to assault); *In re Walker,* 597 N.E.2d 1271 (Ind. 1992) (imposing six-month suspension on part-time prosecutor for physically assaulting his female companion and her daughter); *In re Runyon,* 491 N.E.2d 189 (Ind. 1986) (disbarring attorney who forced entry into former wife's apartment, struck former wife with club, held her at gunpoint and who additionally was convicted of three felony counts of possession of unregistered firearms); *Committee on Professional Ethics and Conduct of the Iowa State Bar Association v. Patterson,* 369 N.W.2d 798 (Iowa 1985) (imposing three-month suspension from practice of law on attorney convicted of assault for severely beating his girlfriend for two hours while her four-year-old son was at home and aware of the assault).

Respondent's assault was an isolated incident on an otherwise unblemished professional record. Unlike *Nevill, Knight* and *Wallace,* there is no pattern of abusive behavior. And unlike *Wallace, Runyon* and *Patterson,* the actual assault lasted for a very short period of time. Moreover, the intense negative publicity has drastically affected respondent's career. As a result of this incident, respondent lost his long-term position in the Prosecutor's Office. Other mitigating factors also existed at the time of the assault, such as respondent's son's critical illness and his troubled relationship with K.P. However, those mitigating factors neither excuse the attack nor obviate the necessity for public discipline.

Acts of violence are condemned in our society. As we stated in *In re Principato, supra,* 139 N.J. 456, 461, 655 A.2d 920, 922, "Unlike many other 'victimless' disorderly persons offenses, domestic violence offenses always involve victims, often-times vulnerable and defenseless." The Legislature was particularly concerned that police and judicial personnel be trained "in the procedures and enforcement of this act, and about the social and psychological context in which domestic violence occurs." N.J.S.A. 2C:25-18. It is therefore important that victims of domestic violence understand that prosecutors, as members of law enforcement, are sensitive to their problems. As a prosecutor respondent must combat acts of domestic violence, not commit them. This "incident calls into question his ability to zealously prosecute or effectively work with the victims of such crimes." *In re Walker, supra,* 597 N.E.2d at 1271 (Ind. 1992).

Attorneys who hold public office are invested with a public trust and are thereby more visible to the public. Such attorneys are held to the highest of standards. "Respondent's conduct must be viewed from the perspective of an informed and concerned private citizen and be judged in the context of whether the image of the bar would be diminished if such conduct were not publicly disapproved." *In re McLaughlin,* 105 N.J. 457, 461, 522 A.2d 999 (1987) (citation omitted).

Respondent's conduct was a serious violation of RPC 8.4(b). But for the fact that we have not previously addressed the appropriate discipline to be imposed on an attorney who is convicted of an act of domestic violence, and that respondent did not engage in a pattern of abusive behavior, respondent's discipline would be greater than the public reprimand we hereby impose. We caution members of the bar, however, that the Court in the future will ordinarily suspend an attorney who is convicted of an act of domestic violence.

Respondent shall reimburse the Disciplinary Oversight Committee for appropriate administrative costs.

---

An attorney-victim of domestic violence paid the price of professional sanctions when she chose to lie under oath to protect her abuser.

## In The Matter of Fawn Balliro

Supreme Judicial Court of Massachusetts

453 Mass. 75 (2009)

SPINA, J.

The present bar discipline matter is before us on a reservation and report, without decision, from a single justice of this court. The respondent, Fawn Balliro, is an assistant district attorney in Massachusetts and was the victim of a domestic assault in Tennessee, in 2005. The Board of Bar Overseers (board) has recommended that she be given a public reprimand, with conditions, for testifying falsely under oath at the criminal trial of her assailant. At issue is the appropriateness of that sanction given the unique factual circumstances underlying the respondent's misconduct. For the reasons that follow, we conclude that a six-month suspension from the practice of law is the appropriate disciplinary sanction.

1. Background.

The following facts are drawn from the findings of a majority of a hearing committee, which were adopted unanimously by the full board. See *Matter of Brauer*, 452 Mass. 56, 57, 890 N.E.2d 847 (2008). We have supplemented the hearing committee's findings with undisputed facts contained in the record on appeal. See *id.*

The respondent was admitted to the practice of law in this Commonwealth on April 7, 2004. In March, 2004, while working as a law clerk for a Federal judge in Nashville, Tennessee, she began a romantic relationship with Greg Knox. In August, 2004, the respondent moved to Massachusetts to start a new job as an assistant district attorney.

The respondent returned to Tennessee in January, 2005, to spend a long weekend with Knox. On a Saturday evening, they went out for dinner and drinks with another couple. While at a bar, the respondent had a brief conversation with another man, causing Knox to leave the bar. The respondent could tell that he was angry, she followed him outside, they exchanged words, and he knocked her to the ground. Knox then walked back to his apartment. Very upset, but with no visible injuries, the respondent was given a ride to Knox's apartment by a passing police officer. When she arrived, the respondent found the door unlocked and Knox in the shower, fully clothed. A "screaming match" ensued, and the respondent knocked some items off a dresser. Knox pinned her to the bed and repeatedly punched her while she yelled for help. She thought that she was going to die. The respondent suffered injuries to her head and face, including a black eye and cuts to her lips.

Two police officers were dispatched to Knox's apartment in response to a report of a woman screaming for help. When they entered, they saw that the apartment was in disarray. According to the police, the respondent appeared intoxicated, had visible injuries to her eye and mouth, and was crying. She told the officers that she did not want to press charges and did not want to make a statement. The respondent told Knox not to talk with the police, and she asked the officers to leave. They handcuffed the respondent and told her that she was under arrest for disorderly conduct and obstruction of justice. The officers then removed both parties from the apartment and separated them. The respondent began to cry again. She denied that Knox had hit her and said that she had been assaulted while walking home, whereupon the officers removed the handcuffs.

The police officer who had driven the respondent to Knox's apartment arrived on the scene and informed the other officers that the respondent had been uninjured when he saw her. The respondent did not allow herself to be photographed, and she refused to sign the police report of the incident. She also told the officers that she did not want to press charges against the person who, she said, had assaulted her on her way home from the bar. Knox was arrested, taken to jail, and charged with two counts of misdemeanor domestic assault. The next morning, the respondent secured Knox's release on bail, and the two reconciled. Knox had never been violent with the respondent before this incident, and he was not violent after it.

At the end of the long weekend, the respondent returned to Massachusetts. She told only her younger sister about the incident, and, when asked at work about her injuries, she said that she had hit her head on the dashboard of her car.

Two or three weeks later, Knox visited the respondent. He informed her for the first time that he was on probation for drug charges, and that if he violated his probation he would go to jail. Knox further told the respondent that he did not know who would support his two minor daughters if he went to jail because his former wife was not employed. At some point after this visit, Knox's attorney telephoned the respondent and told her that, unlike a number of other defendants charged with domestic violence, Knox was not being offered the option of pretrial probation and counselling in exchange for the eventual dismissal of the charges. The respondent concluded that, if convicted, Knox would be incarcerated. She then created a story about falling and injuring herself, which she told to Knox's attorney.

After this conversation, the respondent received a telephone call from a victim witness advocate in Nashville. The respondent asked the advocate to tell the assistant district attorney that she did not want to press charges against Knox. The advocate did not advise the respondent to seek independent counsel.

In March, 2005, the respondent received in the mail a summons to testify at Knox's trial, and, although she did not want to do so, the respondent believed that the summons obligated her to appear. The respondent did not consult an attorney (or anyone else) because she was embarrassed about the whole incident. Moreover, she did not expect that she actually would have to testify.

The trial was held on April 21, 2005, in a Court of General Sessions in Nashville. The assistant district attorney on the case had not yet been admitted to the Tennessee bar, but was prosecuting cases under special supervision, and he had received no formal training in handling victims of domestic violence. The respondent told him that she did not want to press charges or testify against Knox. When the prosecutor told her that it was not possible to drop the charges, the respondent told him that she had fallen and hurt her face. The prosecutor told her that he thought she was lying, that she had been beaten, and that she would have to testify. He did not advise her to obtain counsel. The prosecutor proceeded to call as witnesses the respondent and at least one of the police officers who had gone to Knox's apartment in the aftermath of the January incident. At the time of her testimony, the respondent felt responsible for triggering Knox's assault, felt guilty over the possibility that Knox's children would be left without support, and wanted the entire matter to go away. Consequently, the respondent testified under oath that she had injured herself by falling on a piece of furniture in Knox's apartment.

At the conclusion of the trial, the charges against Knox were dismissed, and the respondent returned to Massachusetts. In December, 2005, a Tennessee district attorney wrote to the Massachusetts district attorney in whose office the respondent worked and informed her about the respondent's false testimony. Shortly thereafter, two of the respondent's supervisors met with her, informed her that they were concerned her conduct could be an ethical violation, suspended her from her job, and advised her to obtain legal counsel, which she did. In February, 2006, the district attorney placed the respondent on an indefinite leave of absence, and the respondent agreed to report her conduct to the board, to participate in counselling to address issues relating to domestic violence and substance abuse, and to provide monthly documentation of her compliance with these terms. During her leave of absence, the respondent voluntarily refrained from the practice of law. She also went to a psychiatrist for an examination and evaluation. He recommended counselling for six months and referred her to a psychologist, whom the respondent saw weekly for at least ten months. In June, 2006, based on the respondent's full compliance with the conditions of her leave, the district attorney assigned her to the appellate division of her office. The respondent's immediate supervisor described the respondent's work there as "stellar."

On June 2, 2006, bar counsel commenced formal proceedings against the respondent by filing with the board a petition for discipline, alleging that the respondent had engaged in misconduct by knowingly making false statements to the Nashville police in January, 2005, and by knowingly giving false testimony under oath at Knox's criminal trial in April, 2005. In her amended answer to the petition, the respondent admitted to the substantive allegations of misconduct, but she stated that her intoxication on the night of the incident, her physical abuse at the hands of Knox, and her precarious psychological state at the time she testified constituted special factors that rendered her false statements not of her own volition.

Disciplinary hearings were held before a hearing committee of the board. On May 21, 2007, it issued a report setting forth its findings of fact, conclusions of law, and recommendation for discipline. A majority of the hearing committee (the hearing committee) found that the respondent knowingly gave false testimony at Knox's trial. It stated that the respondent had admitted in her amended answer that she knew her testimony was false, and she "freely admit[ted]" to her evaluating psychiatrist, Dr. David Rosmarin, that she "perjured" herself and that she had "concocted" the story to which she testified. The hearing committee did not credit the respondent's testimony that when she testified falsely, she had "pretty much convinced [herself] of [her] own story."

The hearing committee credited the following testimony from Dr. Rosmarin: (1) at the time of Knox's arrest, the respondent was impaired by intoxication, pain, and her injuries; (2) the respondent's actions were motivated by a desire to protect Knox and, to a lesser extent, an irrational fear of prosecution for damaging his property; (3) although the respondent did not suffer from battered woman syndrome, she did have "symptoms and impairments" when she gave false testimony, and she "had a cognitive blind spot for her own ethical and legal jeopardy and focused predominantly on protecting [Mr. Knox] and his children," a reaction "typical" of abused women; (4) the respondent's trial testimony was not self-serving, and her behavior was a one-time exception to a life of hard work, integrity, devotion to the law, and public service; (5) the respondent was not "psychologically prepared" to tolerate the beating by Knox, and she lacked insight into her reaction to the beating when she made her false statements; and (6) the respondent has accepted responsibility for her actions and is highly unlikely to breach her ethical duties in the future. The hearing committee also credited the following testimony from Dr. Patricia Harney, the respondent's treating psychologist: (1) by blaming herself for her beating and Knox's arrest, and by testifying falsely, the respondent followed the pattern of victims of domestic violence; and (2) it is very unlikely that the respondent would engage in the same type of behavior again.

The hearing committee concluded that the respondent's false statements to the Tennessee prosecutor and her false testimony under oath at Knox's trial violated Mass. R. Prof. C. 3.3(a)(1), 426 Mass. 1383 (1998) (lawyer shall not knowingly make false statement of material fact or law to tribunal); Mass. R. Prof. C. 3.3(a)(4), 426 Mas. 1383 (1998) (lawyer shall not knowingly offer evidence that lawyer knows to be false [with exceptions not relevant here]); Mass. R. Prof. C. 8.4(c), 426 Mass. 1429 (1998) (professional misconduct for lawyer to engage in conduct involving dishonesty, fraud, deceit, or misrepresentation); Mass. R. Prof. C. 8.4(d), 426 Mass. 1429 (1998) (professional misconduct for lawyer to engage in conduct prejudicial to administration of justice); and Mass. R. Prof. C. 8.4(h), 426 Mass. 1429 (1998) (professional misconduct for lawyer to engage in any other conduct that adversely reflects on fitness to practice law)....

The hearing committee then considered whether there were any aggravating or mitigating factors that should be evaluated with respect to the imposition of a disciplinary sanction. The committee did not find that the respondent suffered from battered woman syndrome as it has come to be recognized under Massachusetts law, see *Commonwealth v. Pike*, 431 Mass. 212, 221-222, 726 N.E.2d 940 (2000), and neither of the respondent's expert witnesses made that diagnosis. However, the hearing committee found that, at the time of her false testimony, the respondent's dysfunctional psychological state was a significant contributing cause of such testimony. Because the respondent has received treatment, the committee continued, she was not likely to repeat her ethical misconduct, and, therefore, her dysfunctional psychological state at the time of Knox's trial could be considered in mitigation. The hearing committee found no factors in aggravation. It concluded that, in light of the unique and compelling mitigating circumstances of this case, it would deviate substantially downward from the presumptive sanction of a one-year or two-year suspension, and it recommended that the respondent receive a public reprimand, with conditions.

. . . .

On March 10, 2008, the board issued its decision, unanimously adopting the findings of fact, the conclusions of law, and the recommended sanction of the hearing committee. With respect to the respondent's appeal, it concluded that there was no basis for overturning the committee's credibility findings as to the respondent's knowledge regarding her false testimony. With respect to bar counsel's appeal, the board stated that district attorneys are not held to a higher standard of ethical behavior than other lawyers when all attorneys are expected to know and understand their professional obligation to be truthful in court. Moreover, the board pointed out that the respondent's misconduct arose from personal aspects of her private life, not from any connection with her work as an assistant district attorney. Given the serious and substantial mitigating circumstances presented, and noting that a more experienced prosecutor would not have forced the respondent to testify at Knox's trial in the absence of her consultation with independent counsel, the board agreed with the hearing committee that a public reprimand was the appropriate disciplinary sanction.

At bar counsel's request, the board filed an information with the county court pursuant to S.J.C. Rule 4:01, § 8(4), as appearing in 425 Mass. 1309 (1997). After a hearing, a single justice reserved and reported the case, without decision, to the full court. The thrust of bar counsel's argument is that the respondent's misconduct warrants a disciplinary sanction of suspension from the practice of law for one year and one day. In bar counsel's view, given that the minimum sanction for false statements by an attorney under oath is a term suspension of at least two years, her recommendation properly weighs, as factors in mitigation, the stress and emotional upheaval that contributed to the respondent's decision to testify falsely at Knox's criminal trial.

. . . .

### 3. Respondent's knowledge of false testimony.

As a preliminary matter, the respondent contends that bar counsel failed to satisfy her burden of proving that the respondent acted knowingly when she testified falsely about her injuries at Knox's trial. We disagree.

The burden of proof in a disciplinary proceeding is always on bar counsel. See Rule 3.28 of the Rules of the Board of Bar Overseers (2008). See also *Matter of Driscoll*, 447 Mass. 678, 685, 856 N.E.2d 840 (2006). Based on the respondent's answer to an allegation in the petition for discipline and on her testimony at the disciplinary proceedings, the hearing committee found that the respondent had admitted that she knew her testimony was false. Further, it found that when the respondent was evaluated by Dr. Rosmarin, she told him that she "perjured" herself and that she "concocted" the story about how she had been injured. The hearing committee did not credit the respondent's testimony that she had convinced herself of her own (false) story. Moreover, the respondent did not tell Dr. Rosmarin that she had convinced herself that her testimony was true. The hearing committee credited the testimony of Dr. Rosmarin that the respondent had a "cognitive blind spot" for her own ethical and legal jeopardy, but it concluded that such blind spot "did not prevent her from recognizing that her testimony was false." While the hearing committee credited the testimony of Dr. Harney that the respondent was not cognizant of engaging in unethical behavior during her false testimony, it still found that she knew that she was giving false testimony.

There is no basis for overturning the credibility determinations made by the hearing committee. Based on the unambiguous evidence presented by bar counsel, the hearing committee, and then the board, properly could infer that the respondent knew, when she testified at Knox's trial, that she was giving false testimony with respect to how she sustained her injuries. See *Matter of Driscoll*, supra at 685 ("we will not draw an independent inference as to the respondent's knowledge when the facts are subject to several interpretations, particularly where the board declined to accept bar counsel's version of events"). We conclude that bar counsel satisfied her burden of proof as to the respondent's knowledge of the falsity of her testimony.

### 4. Appropriateness of sanction.

When considering a disciplinary sanction, we examine whether the sanction "is markedly disparate from judgments in comparable cases." *Matter of Finn*, 433 Mass. 418, 423, 742 N.E.2d 1075 (2001). See *Matter of Kerlinsky*, 428 Mass. 656, 664, 704 N.E.2d 503, cert. denied, 526 U.S. 1160, 119 S. Ct. 2052, 144 L. Ed. 2d 218 (1999). "While this standard is relatively simple to state, it is one which is not always easy to apply because of factual nuances that distinguish cases from each other." *Matter of Shaw*, 427 Mass. 764, 768, 696 N.E.2d 126 (1998). Ultimately, we decide each bar discipline case "on its own merits and every offending attorney must receive the disposition most appropriate in the circumstances." *Matter of the Discipline of an Attorney*, 392 Mass. 827, 837, 468 N.E.2d 256 (1984). The overriding consideration in bar discipline is "the effect upon, and perception of, the public and the bar." *Matter of Kerlinsky, supra* quoting *Matter of Finnerty*, 418 Mass. 821, 829, 641 N.E.2d 1323 (1994). "We must consider what measure of discipline is necessary to protect the public and deter other attorneys from the same behavior." *Matter of Concemi*, 422 Mass. 326, 329, 662 N.E.2d 1030 (1996).

... The disciplinary sanction for an attorney who gives false testimony, under oath, at a criminal trial in which she was the victim has not been addressed in Massachusetts.

We have stated that "an attorney who lies under oath engages in 'qualitatively different' misconduct from an attorney who makes false statements and presents false evidence." *Matter of Shaw*, 427 Mass. 764, 769, 696 N.E.2d 126 (1998), quoting *Matter of Budnitz*, 425 Mass. 1018, 1019, 681 N.E.2d 813 (1997). In *Matter of Shaw, supra* at 767-769, we concluded that the respondent should be suspended for two years where he made false statements under oath in a Federal criminal trial, filed a false affidavit in a Superior Court proceeding, and forged another attorney's name in the affixation of false notarizations, misconduct that was aggravated by two prior instances of discipline. See *Matter of O'Donnell*, 23 Mass. Att'y Discipline Rep. 508, 514 n.3 (2007) ("the presumptive sanction for lying under oath is a two-year suspension"); *Matter of Early*, 21 Mass. Att'y Discipline Rep. 220, 226 (2005) (misrepresentations made by attorney for personal gain, under oath, regarding crucial and material fact in litigation warranted suspension of at least two years, even in absence of other misconduct).

In more egregious circumstances, typically those involving aggravating factors, an attorney's giving false testimony under oath can justify disbarment. See *Matter of Budnitz, supra* at 1018 (attorney disbarred for knowingly lying to grand jury and perpetuating lies in answer to complaint in disciplinary proceeding). See also *Matter of Bailey*, 439 Mass. 134, 151-152, 786 N.E.2d 337 (2003) (attorney disbarred for giving false testimony under oath, misappropriating client's funds, violating court orders, revealing client confidences, commingling funds, and self-dealing); *Matter of Palmer*, 423 Mass. 647, 650, 670 N.E.2d 389 (1996) (attorney disbarred for fabricating documents and committing perjury during deposition); *Matter of Sleeper*, 251 Mass. 6, 20, 146 N.E. 269 (1925) (attorney disbarred for committing perjury). The ABA Standards for Imposing Lawyer Sanctions § 6.11 (1991), states that, absent aggravating or mitigating circumstances, "[d]isbarment is generally appropriate when a lawyer, with the intent to deceive the court, makes a false statement . . . and . . . causes a significant or potentially significant adverse effect on the legal proceeding."

The present case is not one of egregious circumstances that would justify a sanction of disbarment because there were no findings of matters in aggravation. To the contrary, the board found that the respondent's ethical violation was an aberration in an otherwise promising and exemplary career. In addition, the hearing committee determined that bar counsel did not establish that the respondent had committed the crime of perjury in Tennessee. . . . We conclude that this case is most like those in which a two-year suspension from the practice of law was imposed.

We now turn to the issue of mitigating factors. From the immediate aftermath of the January, 2005, incident until the day of Knox's trial, the respondent was clear and unequivocal that she neither wanted to press charges against Knox nor wanted to testify at trial. Yet, her wishes were ignored, and she was called as a witness against Knox. The hearing committee found credible the opinions of Dr. Rosmarin that the respondent's false testimony was "genuinely but superficially motivated by a moral decision to protect Mr. Knox," that she had a "cognitive blind spot" for her own ethical and legal jeopardy, and that her focus was on protecting Knox and his children. The committee also credited the testimony of Dr. Harney that the respondent "was not cognizant of engaging in unethical behavior during her false testimony." In all, the respondent's dysfunctional psychological state, brought about by the domestic abuse, was a substantial contributing cause of her misconduct. Bar counsel accepts that the respondent did not act for a selfish motive. In addition, the hearing committee credited the testimony of Dr. Rosmarin that, because the respondent has accepted responsibility for her actions and has received psychological treatment, she is highly unlikely to breach her ethical duties again and is "more likely to be hyper alert to even gray zone improprieties." These unique and compelling mitigating circumstances warrant a downward departure from the sanction of a two-year suspension.

By the same token, we cannot overlook or minimize the fact that the respondent knowingly gave false testimony, under oath, at a criminal trial, the result of which was that the charges against Knox were dismissed. As Drs. Rosmarin and Harney testified, the physical and emotional trauma suffered by the respondent was considerable, and it served to explain and put into perspective the underlying reasons for her false testimony. However, those reasons did not negate the fact of the respondent's misconduct. Contrary to the respondent's contention, even though she may not have made her false statement while she, herself, was engaged in the practice of law, the respondent made such statement while participating in a formal legal proceeding at which she was obligated to give truthful testimony. Moreover, the seriousness of that misconduct cannot be downplayed simply by saying that the matter about which she testified falsely was a private one that arose in the context of a purely personal relationship. When the respondent was admitted as an attorney in this Commonwealth, she took an oath of office pursuant to G. L. c. 221, § 38, in which she solemnly swore, among other things, that she would "do no falsehood, nor consent to the doing of any in court." All attorneys, whether those of long standing or those recently admitted to the Massachusetts bar, are expected to know and understand their professional obligation to be truthful in court. It is a simple and unambiguous standard of ethical conduct, and the respondent violated it. Notwithstanding the substantial mitigating factors in this case, we cannot condone the actions of an attorney in giving false testimony under oath, irrespective of the circumstances. We conclude that the appropriate disciplinary sanction for the respondent's misconduct is a six-month suspension from the practice of law.

We recognize and share the board's concern about the perceived inequity of sanctioning the respondent more severely than attorneys who have been convicted of domestic assault. See *Matter of Grella*, 438 Mass. 47, 51, 777 N.E.2d 167 (2002) (attorney suspended for two months after conviction of misdemeanor arising from violent assault on estranged wife). As we have stated, "[e]ngaging in violent conduct is antithetical to the privilege of practicing law." *Id*. at 52. The distinction with respect to the circumstances of the present case is that the respondent's misconduct occurred in the context of testifying under oath in a criminal trial. Such misconduct was a violation of the fundamental tenets of her oath of office and of her ethical obligations, matters at the very heart of the legal profession.

### 5. *Conclusion*.

This case is remanded to the single justice for the entry of an order suspending the respondent from the practice of law for six months.

*So ordered*.

---

And, sometimes the domestic violence perpetrators are the very judges who are sworn to uphold the law. In forgetting their oath to uphold the law, these judges engage in conduct demonstrating they are unfit to sit on the bench.

## In the Matter of Williams
### New Jersey Supreme Court
### 169 N.J. 264 (2001)

PORITZ, C.J.

. . . .

### I

This matter arose when the ACJC issued a formal complaint against respondent alleging, in two separate counts, violations of Canons 1 (requiring that judges personally observe high standards of conduct so that the integrity and independence of the judiciary may be preserved), and 2A (requiring judges to act at all times in a manner that promotes public confidence in the integrity and impartiality of the judiciary) of the Code of Judicial Conduct and Rule 2:15-8(a)(6) (prohibiting conduct prejudicial to the administration of justice that brings the judicial office into disrepute). The first count asserts that respondent engaged in judicial misconduct when, on April 14, 2000, she confronted Alfred Wesley Bridges, with whom she previously had a romantic relationship, and Tami DeVitis, his companion that evening, at the Revere Restaurant in Ewing Township and, later, at Joe's Mill Hill Saloon in Trenton. The second count asserts that respondent engaged in judicial misconduct when she gave false and misleading information to the Trenton police and when she "identified herself as a representative of the Hopewell Police Department" in a telephone call to the Mill Hill Saloon. Respondent denies any judicial misconduct and, more specifically, that she lied to the police or pretended to be a police officer. She maintains that her behavior on April 14, 2000, "should properly be evaluated in the context of what had been a longstanding abusive relationship" with Bridges.

. . . .

## II

From the time of her appointment to the bench on March 5, 1993, up to March 5, 2000, respondent served as a Superior Court Judge in the Mercer Vicinage. She sat in the Mercer County Courthouse, where Bridges, an investigator with the Mercer County Sheriff's Department, also worked. Starting around April 1998, respondent and Bridges became romantically involved, but by April 14, 2000, that relationship had apparently ended. For at least a year prior to that date, respondent and Bridges had been abusive and confrontational toward one another.

On the night of April 14, respondent was having dinner with Assistant Deputy Public Defender Joan Austin at the Revere Restaurant. She noticed Bridges enter the restaurant accompanied by Tami DeVitis, a woman respondent did not know. Respondent was upset by their presence because she believed that Bridges had entered the restaurant knowing that she was inside and that she would be upset. Her car, a blue Land Rover with a bicycle rack, was parked directly in front of the Revere and would have been recognized by Bridges since he had driven it on a number of occasions. Bridges' knowledge of respondent's presence was later confirmed by Tami DeVitis who stated that on their way in to the Revere, Bridges commented that there might be "drama" inside.

After Bridges and DeVitis entered, respondent left her dinner table and confronted Bridges in the back of the restaurant. She told him that it was not appropriate for both of them to be there and that he should be the one to leave because she was in the middle of her meal. Respondent was emotional and acknowledged pulling Bridges' shirt although she claimed that happened when Bridges "shoved [her] away from him." At some point during the evening, Bridges' shirt was torn. Although DeVitis claims that respondent spoke to her using sexually explicit language, respondent denies any confrontation with DeVitis and there were no witnesses to the alleged encounter.

Both Bridges and DeVitis left and respondent followed them out to the parking lot. Another confrontation took place, in which respondent asked whether DeVitis was "with [Bridges]" and Bridges told respondent that he was taking DeVitis to Lorenzo's Restaurant and would return in five minutes. Bridges later testified that he lied to respondent in order to end the confrontation. Bridges and DeVitis then left and respondent returned to the Revere. She indicated to Austin that she would go home rather than wait for Bridges, and the women then paid their bill and also left.

Instead of going home, however, respondent drove in the opposite direction toward Lorenzo's Restaurant. On her way, she saw Bridges and DeVitis entering the Mill Hill Saloon and stopped her car. Respondent testified that when Bridges saw her approach, he yelled at her, threatening to have her arrested and to see to it that she lost her job. Pam Fruscione, respondent's former secretary, corroborated respondent's testimony in respect of Bridges' behavior. Respondent had called Fruscione from the car on a cell phone and Fruscione could overhear Bridges' threats.

Bridges and DeVitis entered the Mill Hill Saloon where Bridges asked the owner to call the police. Respondent left her car at the curb and followed them inside. She heard Bridges' request and knew that Dennis Clark, the proprietor, was on the phone, presumably with the police. A heated exchange then developed between respondent and Bridges. Although no witness heard what was said, respondent was observed gesturing and pulling on Bridges' arm or shirt sleeve. When respondent turned to leave, she and DeVitis screamed at each other, but their testimony as to who started that encounter differs. DeVitis testified that respondent called her a vulgar name after shouting obscenities at her and eliciting a similar response from DeVitis. Respondent testified that DeVitis shouted at her and that she said something "not pleasant" to herself without intending to be heard. No witnesses heard respondent or DeVitis, nor did DeVitis mention the encounter to the police when they questioned her.

Respondent then left the Mill Hill Saloon and drove two blocks to the front entrance of the Richard J. Hughes Justice Complex. From there she called 911 on her cell phone. She gave the operator her name and location and said that there had been a confrontation at the Mill Hill Saloon after Bridges had followed her there. The 911 tape does not indicate, as the ACJC complaint alleges, that she misidentified herself as the person who had made the initial 911 call from the Mill Hill Saloon. Respondent did not at that time state that she was a Superior Court judge.

The police officers, who were already on their way to the Mill Hill Saloon, were rerouted to the Justice Complex. When the police arrived, respondent again represented that Bridges had followed her to the Mill Hill Saloon. She waited at the Justice Complex while the police went to the Saloon where Bridges and DeVitis each gave a statement.

Both declined to file a complaint against respondent. When the police returned to the Justice Complex, respondent similarly declined to file a complaint.

Thomas Keefe, the bartender at the Mill Hill Saloon, testified that at some point after the police officers left there, he answered a call from a woman who identified herself as a police officer from the Hopewell Police Department and asked to speak to Bridges. When Bridges took the phone from Keefe, however, he immediately recognized the voice as respondent's and hung up. According to respondent's testimony, she told the bartender that she was calling from the Hopewell Police Department because she was near there. A tape-recorded telephone message indicates that after her call to the Mill Hill Saloon, respondent called Bridges' home and said she was on route to the Hopewell Police Department. She then called the Mill Hill Saloon a second time and apologized to the owner. At some point thereafter she arrived at the Hopewell Police Department and gave a statement to the police. She informed them that Bridges had a gun, but again declined to file a complaint.

. . . .

## C

On the night of April 14, 2000, Judge Williams acted in such manner as to bring disrepute on herself and on the judiciary. Despite the differences in the testimony about the events of that night, certain core facts stand out and are accepted by us as having been proved by clear and convincing evidence. Respondent accosted Alfred Wesley Bridges and Tammy DeVitis at the Revere Restaurant and in the parking lot in a confrontational and angry manner. She wanted them to leave because she was not yet finished with her dinner and apparently because she believed they could not all dine in the same restaurant. But the Revere is a public place open equally to respondent and to Bridges and his companion. Whether Bridges knew she was there because of the location of her car is irrelevant, even if true, since there was no order restraining him from any contact with respondent.

Respondent admits that she attempted to follow Bridges into Trenton. Provoked by Bridges outside the Mill Hill Saloon, she chose to follow him inside and confront him a third time. Although the witnesses' accounts of what happened there diverge to some extent, we find that respondent again acted with hostility towards Bridges, and then DeVitis, in a public place where others could observe her, and that she pulled on Bridges' arm in her vehemence. She also admits that she knew the owner of the Mill Hill Saloon called the police at the request of Bridges and chose, by calling 911 herself, to divert the officers to the Justice Complex where she could tell her own story. She twice gave false and misleading information, first, when she stated to the police operator that Bridges had followed her, and subsequently, when she repeated that statement to the police. We agree with the ACJC that her explanation is incredible. She knew that she had followed Bridges into Trenton and not the other way around.

Later, when she called the Mill Hill Saloon from her car, she again reshaped the truth to her own ends. We agree with dissenting Committee members Teresa Kluck and Robert McAllister that respondent "pretended to be a [Hopewell] police officer in order to ensure that Bridges would take her call...." She could accomplish that deception, however, by simply stating she was calling from the Hopewell Police Department. Once again, the record demonstrates that, at best, she created a fiction related to her location, and therefore her status, so that she could continue her destructive contact with Bridges.

Respondent's conduct was irresponsible. She did not conform her behavior to the social norms expected of ordinary citizens in our society and certainly not to the heightened standard we expect of judges. Although her actions were related only to her private life, they took place in public where others, knowing of her status as a judge, could lose confidence in the integrity and impartiality of the judiciary. Moreover, as the ACJC found, when respondent misled the police, she subordinated her responsibility to act in conformance with the law to her own personal concerns and needs. She demonstrated a lack of respect for the law that as a judge she has sworn to uphold. Likewise, when she called the Mill Hill Saloon and misrepresented her status, she came dangerously close to impersonating a police officer. Those actions suggest a lack of judgment that is both "prejudicial to the administration of justice [and] brings the judicial office into disrepute." R. 2:15-8(a)(6)....

Four members of the ACJC have recommended that respondent be censured; two members have recommended that she be removed; and one member has recommended that she be subject to a six-month suspension. Removal, as the most severe sanction, requires misconduct flagrant and severe. That sanction is imposed rarely. Willful misconduct in office and willful misuse of office are examples of transgressions that warrant removal of a sitting judge....

Respondent's conduct in the instant matter does not involve the misuse of judicial office such that it "poisons the well of justice".... Neither does her conduct include criminal acts that corrupt the judicial decision-making power as in *In re Corruzi*, or that are "totally incompatible with continued judicial service".... Respondent has committed serious violations but she has not directly and willfully misused her judicial office.

Although we deem removal to be too harsh in this case, we likewise deem censure, as proposed by the ACJC majority, to be too lenient. Censure does not reassure the public that judges will be deterred from "acting out" in public and that such behavior will not reoccur. The gravity of respondent's violations requires a strong response....

We agree with the ACJC that respondent has not established that "she suffers from a condition known as the battered woman's syndrome." The expert reports she submitted from the two psychologists and the therapist who have had contact with her in the last eighteen months do not make a sufficient connection between battered woman's syndrome and her behavior. Cf. *State v. Kelly*, 97 N.J. 178, 193, 478 A.2d 364 (1984) (describing "common characteristics that appear in women who are abused physically and psychologically over an extended period of time by the dominant male figure in their lives"). We find, based on both the expert reports and testimony at the hearing, that respondent lacked control over her behavior in her personal relationship with Bridges. Respondent has herself testified that she exercised "bad judgment."

Respondent's participation in that abusive and damaging relationship suggests that psychological counseling would be helpful to her. Indeed, she has been and continues in therapy to better understand her behavior.

Despite her personal problems, respondent performs well on the bench and has a reputation as a solid and fair judge. Her work with the Inns of Court and her conscientious attention to her judicial duties are commendable. She has served in three divisions of our court system—Criminal, Family, and Civil—in the eight years she has been a judge. Her transgressions are related to her personal life and her dysfunctional relationship with Bridges. Indeed, the picture that emerges from the record is of a person driven by strong emotions, who behaved inappropriately as a result of a flawed personal association.

Notwithstanding those mitigating factors, she has failed to adhere to the high standards we expect and demand of our judges. Her actions affected persons removed from the immediate controversy and her disregard for social norms negatively affects public confidence and brings discredit to the judiciary. Of greatest concern, she misled the Trenton police and, later, implied she was an official from the Hopewell Police Department. Moreover, the events of that night were not isolated. Prior incidents relating to respondent's relationship with Bridges are not before us except insofar as they bear on the quantum of discipline that should be imposed. In one such incident a year earlier, respondent was physically injured during another confrontation with Bridges. Neighbors called the police and respondent filed and then withdrew a complaint against him. She was asked to seek therapy at that time and did so. Although she was reappointed, her reappointment was without tenure due to a break in service. See N.J. Const., art. VI,' 6, P 3 (stating that "the Justices of the Supreme Court and the Judges of the Superior Court shall hold their offices for initial terms of [seven] years and upon reappointment shall hold their offices during good behavior"). Respondent has already paid a heavy price for her intemperate behavior.

## C

Having weighed the aggravating and mitigating factors, and because our primary concern must be to ensure the continued confidence of the public in the judiciary, the Court has determined that a three-month suspension is the proper discipline in this case . . .

So Ordered.

## Notes and Questions

- **MORE ETHICAL ISSUES**

An attorney may NEVER encourage a witness to ignore a lawfully issued subpoena. The case of *In re Douglas E. Rowe, A Suspended Attorney,* 12 A.D.3d 133 (N.Y. Appellate Division, 4th Dept. 2004), involved a defense attorney who was suspended from the practice of law for three years for instructing a complaining witness in a domestic violence case that she was not required to appear before the Grand Jury in response to a subpoena, "and that he in fact, encouraged her not to appear." As a result, he was convicted of a misdemeanor, sentenced to 50 hours of community service and a $1,000 fine, in addition to the suspension.

In the cases of Judge Williams in New Jersey in 2000 and attorney Balliro in Massachusetts in 2009, the courts rejected the idea that they were suffering from Battered Women's Syndrome. Based on your understanding of the syndrome, would you agree? What other information about the women's relationships to their accusers would you want to know before you made a decision whether to reject a BWS defense to those ethical charges?

- **MORE ON DOMESTIC VIOLENCE COURTS**

In their article, *Addressing the Co-Occurrence of Domestic Violence and Substance Abuse,* 6 J. CENTER FOR FAMS., CHILD. & CTS. 53, 54 (2005), authors Lisa Lightman and Francine Byrne wrote that 92 percent of domestic abusers used alcohol or drugs the same day they perpetrated an assault and 72 percent had criminal records or arrests related to the abuse of drugs or alcohol. Does addressing substance abuse in a domestic violence court suggest that violence is either caused by or excused by the use of drugs or alcohol? Would doing so be at odds with current theories that domestic violence is a choice made by the abuser and not a result of poor impulse control or addiction?

In 2013, the New York Center for Court Innovation conducted a two-year study with federal funds on the effectiveness of specialized domestic violence courts on stopping intimate partner abuse as compared to conventional courts. New York with 64 such courts has 31 percent of the nation's domestic violence courts, the highest percentage in the country. The findings showed these courts had only a modest impact on stemming domestic violence. They reduced the rate of rearrests among convicted offenders by three percent; reduced case processing from 260 days to 197 days and increased the conviction rate by four percent. *See* Amanda B. Cissner, et al., *Testing the Effects of New York's Domestic Violence Courts: A Statewide Impact Evaluation,* https://www.ncjrs.gov/pdffiles1/nij/grants/242583.pdf, accessed November 11, 2016. If you were the budget planner for a state court system with limited funds, would you authorize funding for new specialized domestic violence courts relying on these statistics? Why or why not?

- **SANCTIONS**

Professor Linda Mills of New York University has written extensively about what she considers "the flaws in the mainstream feminist approach to intimate violence.

One glove does not fit all hands; mandatory policies do not suit all relationships or all incidents of intimate abuse." She asserts: "Violence that occurs in an intimate relationship is not conducive to a paradigm that assigns all the blame to one party while wholly exonerating the other." LINDA G. MILLS, INSULT TO INJURY: RETHINKING OUR RESPONSES TO INTIMATE ABUSE 27, 31 (2003).

As noted in this chapter, New York Penal Law § 60.12 authorizes a reduced sentence for certain crimes committed by a victim of domestic violence against an abuser. The National Coalition Against Domestic Violence reports that men who kill their female intimate partners serve, on average, two to six years in prison, whereas women who kill their partners serve an average of 15 years in prison.

In 2001, California enacted a law requiring parole boards to take domestic violence histories into account during hearings. Notwithstanding, then-Gov. Gray Davis overturned the board's recommendation that Maria Suarez, a domestic violence victim, be paroled. She was serving a life sentence for murder. Ms. Suarez, as a Mexican teenager, was sold in 1976 for $200 to a 68-year-old California man, who for five years perpetuated physical, emotional and sexual abuse on the girl, until she bludgeoned him to death with the help of two of his tenants. Davis was criticized by the California Coalition for Battered Women in Prison for not permitting Suarez to be released. Some said he feared looking soft on crime during a tough recall election that he ultimately lost. Silja J.A. Talvi, *Cycle of Violence: Battered Women Who Kill Their Abusers Are Being Jailed,* IN THESE TIMES, Oct. 11, 2002, *available at* www.inthesetimes.com/site/main/article/386.

A decade earlier, however, in 1990, Ohio Gov. Richard F. Celeste granted clemency to 25 women who had been convicted of killing or assaulting their husbands or intimate partners who had abused them. The governor explained he did so because the Ohio Supreme Court had for the first time that year ruled that women could present evidence of Battered Woman's Syndrome at trial as a defense to those charges. Therefore, he had reviewed the cases of women convicted prior to the court's ruling for evidence they had been battered by their victims. *See* Isabel Wilkerson, *Clemency Granted to 25 Women Convicted for Assault or Murder: Ohio Governor Says They Were Battered by Men,* N.Y. TIMES, Dec. 22, 1990.

Large numbers of women in prison have been victims of domestic violence according to some studies. In 2000, there were approximately 70,000 women in local jails in the United States and approximately another 92,000 in state and federal prisons. About one-quarter of them report having been physically or sexually abused by a family member. It is believed this is part of the reason why some of these women are incarcerated in the first place. "The salient features that propel women into crime include family violence and battering, substance abuse, and their struggle to support themselves and their children." BARBARA BLOOM, BARBARA OWEN & STEPHANIE COVINGTON, NAT'L INSTITUTE OF CORRECTIONS, GENDER-RESPONSIVE STRATEGIES: RESEARCH, PRACTICE, AND GUIDING PRINCIPLES FOR WOMEN OFFENDERS 5, 20 (2003), *available at* www.nicic.org/library/018017.

Another issue that arises in the context of probation are female probationers who are victims of domestic violence. Abusers of women on probation may threaten to report bogus violations to their probation officers as a method of keeping them under their control. In addition, a probationer who is the victim of domestic violence may need to go into hiding to maintain her safety. Probation officers must be sensitive, therefore, in choosing who to use as the probationer's collateral contacts so as to be able to assist her in remaining safe. For a discussion of these issues, see Sherry Frohman and Connie Neal, both of the New York State Coalition Against Domestic Violence, *The Probation Response to Supervision of Women Who Are Abused*, Violence Against Women Online Resources (2005), *available at* www.mincava.umn.edu/documents/commissioned/probationanddv/probationanddv.html.

# Index

## A

**Abduction of Child**
International child abduction, 513

**Advocates**
Lawyer as advocate in domestic violence cases, 833

**African American Women**
Generally, 42

**Asylum**
Domestic violence as basis for, 738

**Attorneys**
Acts of domestic violence by, 835
Advocate in domestic violence cases, 833
Clients
   Perpetrators, 781
   Victims, 780

## B

**Bail Considerations**
Court cases and, 196

**Battered Child Syndrome** (See Child Abuse)

**Battered Women Syndrome**
Expert testimony (See Expert Testimony)
Redefinition of, 10
Tort liability, 601
Used by Defense, 324
Used by Prosecution, 335
Why abuse victims stay, 19

## C

**Child Abduction**
International child abduction, 513

**Child Abuse**
Battered child syndrome, expert testimony, 349
Duties to protect children, 466
Family violence as form of, 485
History of abuse against children, 436
Modern child protective measures, 439
Reporting, mandatory, 443
Sexual abuse accommodation syndrome, 365
Shaken baby syndrome, 470
Teen dating violence, 481

**Child Custody**
Family violence and, 488
Inter-jurisdictional custody disputes, 501
International child abduction, 513
Uniform Child Custody and Jurisdiction Enforcement Act, 501

**Children**
Child abuse (See Child Abuse)
Child custody (See Child Custody)
Child witnesses in family violence or sexual abuse cases (See Evidentiary Issues)
Failure to protect children from witnessing violence, 499

**Civil Actions** (See Tort Litigation)

**Competency**
Battered women syndrome evidence, 346

**Counselor/Social Worker Privilege**
Domestic violence cases, 318

**Courthouse Dogs**
Generally, 306

**Courts**
Domestic violence courts (See Domestic Violence, subhead: Specialized domestic violence courts)

**Criminal Justice System**
Assault (See Assault)
Attorneys (See Attorneys)
Bail considerations, 196
Criminalization, 193
Domestic violence as crime, 31, 121
Fighting back, 188
Homicide (See Homicide)
Immigration consequences of criminal convictions, 730
Rape (See Rape)
Response to battering, 12
Sentencing in domestic violence cases (See Sentencing)
Stalking, 167
Strangulation, 166
Technology and victims' rights, 177
Victimless prosecutions, fate of, 218

**Custody of Child** (See Child Custody)

# D

**Disabled Women**
Domestic violence in the lives of, 75

**Divorce**
California divorce law, 540
Child custody (See Child Custody)
Distribution of marital assets, domestic violence and, 540
Ground for divorce, domestic violence as, 535
History of divorce, 533
Mediation and domestic violence, 555
Tort actions in, 614

**Domestic Violence**
African American Women, 42
Assault (See Assault)
Asylum, basis for, 738
Attorneys, acts of domestic violence by, 835
Counselor/social worker privilege, 318
Courts (See subhead: Specialized domestic violence courts)
Criminal justice system (See Criminal Justice System)
Disabled women, 75
Divorce and (See Divorce)
Dynamic of, 9
Economic issues, 554
Elderly victims, 520
Evidentiary issues (See Evidentiary Issues)
Family violence (See Family Violence)
Homicide (See Homicide)
Immigration law (See Immigration Law)
International human rights, violation of, 738
Judges (See Judges)
Judges, acts of domestic violence by, 835
Latinas, 45
Lesbians and gay men, battering of, 100
Marital privilege, 317
Muslim women, 49
Native American women, 63
Pacific Asian women, 78
Protective orders (See Protective Orders)

Sentencing (See Sentencing)
Specialized domestic violence courts, 774
Specific crime, as, 143
Tort litigation (See Tort Litigation)
Third World Women, 117
Transgender community and, 100
Violence against Women Act (See Violence Against Women Act)

**Duress**
Battered women syndrome evidence, 340

**Dynamic of Domestic Violence**
Generally, 9

## E

**Economic Issues**
Domestic violence survivors, 554
Patient Protection and Affordable Care Act, 622

**Elderly**
Domestic violence and, 520

**Electronic Monitoring**
Domestic violence cases and, 813

**Emotional Distress, Infliction of**
Tort liability, 604

**Employers**
Domestic violence torts at workplace, 1639

**Evidentiary Issues**
Generally, 217
Child witnesses in family violence or sexual abuse cases
Ability to testify under oath, 289
Accommodations for, 290
Courthouse dogs, 306
Expert testimony (See Expert Testimony)
Medical record evidence, 283
Prior acts of domestic violence in homicide cases, evidence of, 256
Privileges (See Privileges)
Propensity for intimate partner abuse, 279

**Expert Testimony**
Generally, 323
Battered child syndrome, 349
Battered women syndrome
Competency, 346
Duress cases, 340
Use of syndrome evidence by defendants in self-defense cases, 324
Child sexual abuse accommodation syndrome, 365
Competency cases, use of battered women syndrome evidence in, 346
Duress cases, use of battered women syndrome evidence in, 340
Prosecutors, use of expert testimony by, 335
Jurors as experts, 369

## F

**False Arrest**
Claims of, 649

**Family Violence**
Child abuse, as form of, 485
Child custody decisions, 488, 489
Duty to protect children, 466
Elderly victims, 520
Failure to protect children from witnessing violence, 499

**Fighting Back**
Generally, 188

**Firearms Restrictions**
Domestic violence and, 393

## G

**Gay Men**
Battering of, 100

## H

**Homicide**
  Crime of, 124
  Evidence of prior acts of domestic violence in homicide cases, 256
  Fatality review, 128
  Risk factors for intimate partner homicides, 131

**Homosexuals**
  Battering of, 100

## I

**Immigration Law**
  Criminal conviction on removal, impact of, 730
  History of women and immigration law, 704
  In context, 711
  U visa, 728
  Violence against Women Act, 708

**Insurance Issues**
  Patient Protection and Affordable Care Act, 622
  Tort litigation (See Tort Litigation)

**International Human Rights**
  Domestic violence as violation of, 738

**Interspousal Tort Immunity**
  Generally, 584

## J

**Jewish Communities**
  Acknowledging domestic abuse in, 59

**Judges**
  Acts of domestic violence by, 835
  Attitude and demeanor in domestic violence cases, 770
  Role of domestic violence judge, 826

## L

**Latinas**
  Generally, 45

**Law Enforcement "Culture"**
  Domestic violence and, 83

**Lawyers** (See Attorneys)

**Lesbians and Gay Men**
  Battering of, 100

## M

**"Man's Home Is his Castle" Belief**
  Generally, 25

**Marital Privilege**
  Domestic violence cases, 317

**Marital Rape**
  Generally, 161

**Mediation**
  Divorce mediation and domestic violence, 555

**Medical Records**
  Evidentiary issues, 283

**Military "Culture"**
  Domestic violence and, 83

**Muslim Societies**
  Generally, 49

## N

**Native American Women**
  Liability of non-Indian batterers in Indian country, 63

## P

**Pacific Asian Community**
  Cultural defenses, 78

**Police**
  Domestic violence and, 83
  Tort actions against, 629

**Privileges**
    Counselor/social worker privilege, 318
    Marital privilege, 317

**Prosecutors**
    Ethical problems in domestic violence cases, 835
    Expert testimony used by, 335

**Protective Orders**
    Civil protection orders, 660
    Effectiveness of, 685
    Family members, 663
    Relief provided under, 672
    Sanctions for violations, 689
    Violation of, 151

**Public Agencies**
    Mandated reporting of abuse, 443
    Tort actions against, 629

## R

**Race**
    African American women, 42
    Latinas, 45
    Native American women, 63

**Rape**
    Marital rape, 161

**Recidivism**
    Domestic violence court cases, 194

**Relief**
    Protective orders, relief provided under, 672

## S

**Sanctions** (See also, Sentencing)
    Protective orders, violation of, 689

**Sentencing**
    Generally, 783
    Alternative solutions, 818
    Batterers' programs, 813
    Electronic monitoring of domestic violence cases, 813
    Federal crimes of domestic violence, 801
    State courts, sentences in, 808

**Shaken Baby Syndrome**
    Generally, 470

**Social Worker Privilege**
    Domestic violence cases, 318

**Socioeconomic Status**
    Generally, 47

**Specialized Domestic Violence Courts**
    (See Domestic Violence)

**Stalking**
    Generally, 167

**Statute of Limitations**
    Tort litigation against domestic violence offenders, 593

**Strangulation**
    Generally, 166

## T

**Technology**
    Victims' rights and, 177

**Teen Dating Violence**
    Generally, 481

**Tort Litigation**
    Domestic violence offenders
        Battered women syndrome and, 601
        Divorce, tort actions in, 614
        Domestic violence, tort of, 603
        Emotional distress, infliction of, 604
        Statute of limitations, 593
        Workplace, domestic violence torts at, 639
    Insurance issues
        Lack of coverage for acts of domestic violence, 620

Patient Protection and Affordable Care Act, 622
Interspousal tort immunity, 584
Perpetrators, representing, 781
Police and public agencies, 629
Victims, representing, 780
Workplace, domestic violence torts at, 639

**Transgender Community**
Battering and, 100

## U

**Uniform Child Custody and Jurisdiction Enforcement Act**
Effects on battered women, 501

## V

**Victimless Prosecutions**
Fate of, 218

**Violence Against Women Act**
Generally, 377
Act becomes law, 379
Civil provisions struck down, 380
Federal crimes of domestic violence, 387
Federal firearms restrictions, 393
Immigration reform, 708
Setting the stage for VAWA, 378
2005 improvements, 710

## W

**Witness Tampering**
Generally, 147

**Workplace**
Domestic violence torts at, 639